RON SHANDLER's
Baseball
Forecaster
2010
Slugger On Deck Edition

TRIUMPH
BOOKS

Triumph Books
542 South Dearborn Street
Suite 750
Chicago, Illinois 60605
(312) 939-3330
Fax (312) 663-3557

Printed in U.S.A.
ISBN: 978-1-60078-222-0

Statistics provided by Baseball Info Solutions

Cover design by Jon Resh@Go-Undaunted.com
Front cover photograph by Bob Levey/Icon Sports Media, Inc.
Author photograph by Kevin Hurley

Acknowledgments

Ron Shandler's BASEBALL FORECASTER

Editors
Ray Murphy
Rod Truesdell

Data and Charts
Paul Petera
Brent Hershey
Joshua Randall

Player commentaries
Brent Hershey
Brandon Kruse
Bill Macey
Ray Murphy
Stephen Nickrand
Joshua Randall
Brian Rudd
Jock Thompson
Rod Truesdell
Michael Weddell

Research and Articles
Patrick Davitt
Ed DeCaria
Peter Kreutzer
Brandon Kruse
Bill Macey
Tom Mulhall
Ray Murphy
Craig Neuman
Paul Petera
Joshua Randall
Michael Weddell

Minor Leagues
Rob Gordon
Jeremy Deloney

Injuries
Rick Wilton

It is inconceivable to think that I used to put together this entire book by myself. Now it is inconceivable to think what I'd do without the amazing contributors I have. Cast your gaze to the left; these are the people who bring you this year's *Baseball Forecaster*. All of them are smarter than me. Memorize their names; you will be quizzed later.

Those contributors are part of the larger Baseball HQ family. The other fanalytic superstars are Dave Adler, Andy Andres, Matt Baic, Matt Beagle, Doug Dennis, Matt Dodge, Jim Driscoll, Scott Gellman, Dylan Hedges, Phil Hertz, Joe Hoffer, Gerald Holmes, Tom Kephart, Troy Martell, Scott Monroe, Harold Nichols, Frank Noto, Kris Olson, Josh Paley, Greg Pyron, Nick Richards, Mike Shears, Peter Sheridan, Skip Snow, Tom Todaro and Jeffrey Tomich. This group writes more than 1,000 articles each year, not including stats, charts and forum posts. Their dedication is what makes Baseball HQ an industry leader.

Thanks to Mike Krebs, Rob Rosenfeld and Uri Foox, our tech team.

Lynda Knezovich has been making sure you get your books and subscriptions, and has been handling all your issues for more than eight years now. I've given her permission to sic her new Great Dane on anyone who complains. Fair warning.

Greg Ambrosius, Jeff Barton, Matthew Berry, Jim Callis, Tristan Cockcroft, Glen Colton, Don Drooker, Jeff Erickson, Brian Feldman, Steve Gardner, Jason Grey, Eric Karabell, Peter Kreutzer, Gene McCaffrey, Lenny Melnick, John Menna, Lawr Michaels, Steve Moyer, Rob Neyer, Alex Patton, Peter Schoenke, Joe Sheehan, John Sickels, Perry Van Hook, Sam Walker, Brian Walton, Jeff Winick, Rick Wolf, Trace Wood, Todd Zola and probably about 397 others who I've forgotten... these gentlemen represent the intelligentsia of the baseball industry, tough competitors and colleagues. If I have any hope against them in expert league competition, this book *has* to be good.

Thank you to the folks at Fantasy Sports Ventures and Triumph Books for allowing me to do less heavy-lifting.

Thank you to the folks at USA Today, and now the Huffington Post, for giving me new venues for my odd thoughts and occasional soapboxes.

Thank you to my ladies, who shape my world and who have grown up before your eyes in these acknowledgments. Darielle is pursuing her dream of life in the theater at Drew University. After less than one semester, she has already been an actor, sound designer, costume designer and prop master, which means we don't hear from her much any more. I only hope she'll remember us little people once she becomes famous. Thank goodness for Skype and a good webcam.

Justina auditioned and received a scholarship to attend a summer program at Berklee College of Music. She's become an amazing songwriter and performer, but this only means that I now have two kids pursuing the arts. Looks like I am going to be supporting them for a long, long time.

Sue just hit a milestone birthday and I am taking her to Hawaii. I can not imagine anyone in the world who more deserves to go to Hawaii after all she's done for me. Odds are, by time you read this we will have already returned. Just so you know; we had a great time.

Back in November, I began a book tour for this edition (yes, I do book tours now). On my first stop, one of the attendees was a gentleman who has been a regular reader of mine since the Reagan administration. You have no idea what a thrill it is for me to meet the people who have allowed me to live this dream. If you are reading this now, you are one of them. Thank you!

Next year — 25th anniversary edition. BIIIIIIG PARTY!

CONTENTS

Billboards

We are so damn smart.

We observe. We scout. We analyze. We calculate. We create elaborate, sophisticated computer models to predict how a few thousand human beings are going to behave over the course of six months. We use this intelligence to compete against each other in a game derived from another game and declare ultimate superiority based on a sample size of one.

We have been on this journey for more than two decades. Along the way, we've learned many things and have become knowledgeable, competent and possibly even enlightened. A bit.

But, several years ago we passed the point of diminishing returns. In our self-righteous quest for the Holy Grail, we drove right by it. It didn't even register in our peripheral vision.

True, there was no landmark to warn us, no huge billboard shouting, "STOP! You are about to pass the point of diminishing returns!" But we should have thought to slow down, step back and consider, "hey, why am I beating my head against a wall and still coming out in the same place, year after year after year? Why haven't I figured this thing out by now? If I'm so damn smart, *why am I not winning, or not winning more often?*"

Despite all the expert assertions, we are only slightly closer to the Holy Grail than we were 10 years ago. In fact, we were probably in a much better place 20 years ago. Yes, we weren't so damn smart back then, but that might have been a good thing.

So I decided to stop. I decided it was time to turn around, look back, and consider the signs that we might have missed. In doing so, I realized that, although there were no landmarks speaking specifically to us, there were *huge billboards*. We just chose to shrug them off as isolated, unrelated data points.

And I began to realize, we're not so damn smart. We've been so hellbent on speeding towards some unknown Grail that we lost sight of what was happening along the way. We sped right past the City of the Sophisticated into the Kingdom of the Arcane.

Because we missed all the billboards.

Daisuke Matsuzaka

At our local First Pitch Forum events each spring, we conduct an interactive activity where I auction off a few interesting players as if it were a fantasy draft. Attendees participate in open bidding based on a standard $260 budget. Aside from just being fun, the exercise provides a general market value for each player. In addition, comparing the bid results at our sites across the country provides a rough read on possible geographic bias.

Last spring, I opened the forums with Daisuke Matsuzaka, posting the following stats on the screen:

Year	W	IP	K	ERA	WHIP	R$
2007	15	205	201	4.40	1.32	$20
2008	18	168	154	2.90	1.32	$23

Bidding on his projected 2009 value was enthusiastic and animated. In the end, Dice-K's final purchase price was about on par with his 2008 performance, though there was a slight hometown (and apparently, Yankee) bias:

San Francisco	$24
Los Angeles	$23
Cleveland	$25
Chicago	$23
Washington	$24
New York	$22
Boston	$26

During the sessions, we bid on many other players, including C.C. Sabathia (whose prices ranged from $33 in Cleveland to $40 in New York), Aaron Hill and J.J. Putz.

As we came to each successive mock auction in the program, the slides started displaying fewer fantasy-specific stats and more skills-based gauges. Nearing the end of the program, I even stopped revealing the names of the players in advance.

The purpose was to have attendees start thinking more in terms of skills than stats and to conduct their analysis without preconceived notions about any particular player. The last player presented for bid was just a series of base performance indicators, and no name:

Year	bb/9	k/9	k/bb	H%	S%	G/L/F	xERA
2007	3.5	8.8	2.5	31%	70%	38/18/44	4.01
2008	5.0	8.3	1.6	27%	80%	39/18/43	4.50

Attendees familiar with our mode of analysis were able to key in on the fact that this was a pitcher with questionable and declining skills. I opened the mystery pitcher at $1. Bidding was understandably sluggish:

San Francisco	$12
Los Angeles	$12
Cleveland	$11
Chicago	$13
Washington	$11
New York	$15
Boston	$12

While things in general are typically more expensive in New York, those attendees might be perturbed to know that they were now the geographic high bidders for...

Daisuke Matsuzaka.

The takeaway intelligence from this exercise was not that Dice-K could, or would repeat his 2008 performance. If he was lucky once, he could be lucky again, though the percentage play would be to bet against. The real takeaway was that there was a huge $10-$15 gap between his market value and his "real," or projected value. Since this is a game about leveraging market value to assemble the best roster, it meant you should stay far away from Dice-K.

Now, nobody could know that he would implode as badly as he did in 2009, but in many ways his BPIs looked remarkably similar to 2008...

Year	bb/9	k/9	k/bb	H%	S%	G/L/F	xERA
2008	5.0	8.3	1.6	27%	80%	39/18/43	4.50
2009	4.6	8.2	1.8	39%	72%	34/23/43	5.29

...with two key differences. His hit rate, or "batting average on balls in play" was a high 39%, which artificially inflated his ERA. His line drive rate – another indicator mostly out of a pitcher's control – was also high, further inflating his ERA. This was not a 5.00 ERA pitcher; he was more likely a 4.50 ERA pitcher.

But the marketplace will treat him like damaged goods in 2010. So he might be a bargain.

Except that he had a terrific September and October, which could push up his purchase price...

Year	W	IP	K	ERA	WHIP
2009	4	59	54	5.76	1.87
Sept-Oct	3	24	20	2.22	1.40

...unless someone notices the skills behind those stats:

Year	bb/9	k/9	k/bb	H%	S%	G/L/F	xERA
Sept-Oct	4.4	7.4	1.7	29%	88%	40/18/42	4.94

Then there is the issue of sample size. Is there anything you can trust in only 24 innings?

As smart as we'd like to think we are, each step in this analytical process is digging us into a deeper hole. What can you believe in? What slices of data are real? What will Dice-K do in 2010?

True Fact #1

Research has proven that, with the current tools available to us, the maximum projective accuracy we can hope to attain is 70%. That means the *best* we can hope for is to be 30% wrong.

Aaron Hill

As I was doing some research last February, I noticed this fascinating tidbit... In the Average Draft Position rankings at MockDraftCentral.com, Aaron Hill was falling outside the top 300 (#316 to be exact) and was being selected by only 18% of all drafters.

In this short-attention-span, what-have-you-done-for-me-lately world, the sixth best second-baseman in the American League in 2007 was being completely forgotten just two years later. Yes, he missed a good portion of 2008 with a concussion, but he was still at the top of the Blue Jays' depth chart at 2B.

What I was seeing was a player coming off an $18 season in 2007, who was trending north. The *2008 Forecaster* stated, "PX, FB and hr/f trends show that he's developed an effective power stroke. Strong LD rate helps too. It means there's room for even more growth. UP: 25 HR, .300 BA."

I decided to put him up for bid at the forums:

San Francisco	$15
Los Angeles	$8
Cleveland	$9
Chicago	$13
Washington	$15
New York	$16
Boston	$17

Note that these forum sites are listed in the order that we visited them. The California forums were in late February; we wrapped up in Boston on March 15. During the latter part of that period, spring training games were showing off Aaron Hill, looking all healthy and productive. Aside from the San Francisco outlier, the bidding seems to reflect that.

But nobody would venture that Hill could return to, or improve upon, his $18 value in 2007.

More interesting was that MDC drafters weren't moving him up their rankings. By Opening Day, Hill had risen a grand total of five spots – to #311 – and had actually dropped to 17% penetration.

A scan of his stat line is interesting. It doesn't take much to imagine that a healthy 2008 might have yielded the exact stepping stone such that 2009 would have been less of a surprise.

Year	AB	HR	RBI	AVG	R$
2006	546	6	50	.291	$12
2007	608	17	78	.291	$18
*2008	620	25	90	.289	$22
2009	682	36	108	.286	$27
	* Convenient guess				

But that's all speculation. In fact, the marketplace now seems to be classifying 2009 as a fluke, mostly because the leap from 2007 was so great. However, we polled attendees at First Pitch Arizona to classify Hill's 2009 as a "fact" or "fluke," and 75% voted "fact." Our analysis later in this book calls him a "fluke." We are all so damn smart.

True Fact #2

We polled the readers at BaseballHQ.com the past two Septembers to find out the impact of owning that season's surprise players. In essence, we asked "how important was it to have been the lucky sonafabitch to draft Chris Carpenter in the 20th round?" We asked about Cliff Lee and Edinson Volquez in 2008; Carpenter, Kendry Morales, Mark Reynolds and Justin Verlander this past year.

> 25% of the teams owning one or more of those players were in first place.
> 51% of the teams were no lower than third place
> 70% of the teams were no lower than fifth place

We then asked about the impact of drafting major busts like Jose Reyes, Brandon Webb, Grady Sizemore or Francisco Liriano.

**47% were in the lower third of the standings,
with 15% in dead last
Only 25% were still managing to contend**

Yes, drafting those out-of-the-blue surprises is a good thing to do. Avoiding the major busts is also a good thing to do. It would have been nice if any of those performances could have been predicted on Draft Day.

Matt Wieters

Matt Wieters is a member of an illustrious group of players who are highly coveted by fantasy leaguers before they even face a single major league pitch. We all crave to be the one fantasy owner who tucks away an unknown Single-A prospect that emerges as the next Albert Pujols.

But the percentage play for success – particularly *immediate* success, which is the only kind us fantasy leaguers have the patience for – is meager.

Impatience for success, and short memories.

The following players were all Top 10 prospects this past decade: Austin Kearns, Wilson Betemit, Nick Neugebauer, Hee Seop Choi, Joe Borchard, Jesse Foppert, Sean Burroughs, Ryan Anderson, Adam Miller, Dallas McPherson, Jeremy Hermida, Brandon Wood, Alex Gordon, Homer Bailey and Andy Marte.

One player was deemed so talented that he was the #1 prospect for three straight years (2005, 2006 and 2007). Heading into 2010, there will likely be fewer bidding wars for Delmon Young.

In March, Wieters was *guaranteed*. We put him up for bid.

San Francisco	$16
Los Angeles	$14
Cleveland	$16
Chicago	$21
Washington	$25
New York	$22
Boston	$21

After each auction was completed, I turned to the attendees and asked, "what other catchers with more experience could you have gotten for this price?"

The answer: "All of them."

Wieters' actual MLB value in 2009? $7.

True Fact #3

Question: During the 10-year period of 1996-2005, what percentage of players selected in the first round of the Major League Baseball First Year Player Draft went on to become stars?

Answer: 8%

The Most Bankable Player

If I give you $5, I know exactly what that will buy me. Five dollars gets me a venti latte at Starbucks. It's possible that the quality of that latte will vary slightly depending upon the barista, but all in all, a $5 latte is a $5 latte.

Not so in our game. On this past draft day, the following players were projected to earn $5 (15-team mixed league): Bronson Arroyo, Casey Blake, Jeff Francoeur, Chris Iannetta, Jesse Litsch, Paul Maholm, Daniel Murphy, Oliver Perez, J.J. Putz and Jorge Posada. Boy, does that represent a wide range of talent. How many of them do you think ended up earning exactly $5 come October?

One (Iannetta). The others ranged in value from -$11 (Perez) to $17 (Blake). Of the 10 players, only two finished even within $5 of $5.

But that's okay. I think we all know that part of the reason that these players were valued at $5 is that we *expect* there to be variability in their projections. All of the above were essentially full-time players or held firm rotation spots, but their low $5 draft day price tags meant that we just didn't know how they were going to perform.

But what about more expensive players? What about those $30 first-rounders? We should be more confident in their projections, right?

Confident? Perhaps. Accurate? No. Not even for six lattes.

So last spring, I held a contest.

I offered up a player that everyone coveted. He'd be a first round pick and $30-plus commodity in most leagues. A reliability grade of "AAA" meant he was healthy, experienced and consistent. Everyone loved him. Mid-seeded snake drafters were drooling in hopes he'd drop to them in the first round.

I challenged all my readers that nobody could project where his numbers would finish. One of the top players in the league should be easy, right? After all, you wouldn't pay top dollar or use a first round pick unless you were confident he'd produce at a high level. I even told them their projection could finish within +/- 5% of actual. I offered up some free books and free subscriptions, and 173 people took me up on it.

The contest was called the Grady Sizemore Challenge. There were no winners. In fact, even the most pessimistic projection was off by more than 20%.

True Fact #4

There is a 65% chance that a player projected for a certain dollar value will finish the season with a final value within plus-or-minus $5 of that projection. That means, if you value a player at $25, you only have about a 2-in-3 shot of him finishing between $20 and $30.

If you want to get your odds up to 80%, the range now becomes +/- $9. You have an 80% shot that your $25 player will finish somewhere between $16 and $34.

The First Round

Okay, Grady Sizemore was just one player. But as a group, those early rounders must be more projectable, right? We know that those cornerstone players can make or break our season and we spend a good amount of effort analyzing who should be seeded there. So one would think we'd have a pretty good handle on which commodities to be chasing in those early rounds. Right?

Our friends at MockDraftCentral.com provided us with the final ADP Top 15 rankings for the past six years. We matched them up with the actual final player rankings at the conclusion of each season.

YEAR	No. of correct picks of 15
2004	6
2005	7
2006	4
2007	5
2008	7
2009	5

Year	#DL Players	3yr Avg	DL Days	3yr Avg
2002	337		23,724	
2003	351		22,118	
2004	382	357	25,423	23,755
2005	356	363	24,016	23,852
2006	347	362	22,472	23,970
2007	404	369	28,524	25,004
2008	422	391	28,187	26,394
2009	408	411	26,252	27,654

In this analysis, we were not measuring our ability to nail a player's ranking perfectly. No, these results showed our ability to project that a player ranked in the Top 15 in March would finish the season *anywhere* in the top 15. Of these 90 picks, only 34 — 38% -- finished anywhere in the Top 15.

You'd think if we projected a player to finish 3rd, or 7th, or 10th that he'd finish at least a reasonable distance from that rank. But that hasn't been the case, at least not in the past six years.

Here is what the 2009 list looked like:

	ADP		ACTUAL = 5
1	Hanley Ramirez	1	Albert Pujols (2)
2	Albert Pujols	2	Hanley Ramirez (1)
3	Jose Reyes	3	Tim Lincecum
4	David Wright	4	Dan Haren
5	Grady Sizemore	5	Carl Crawford
6	Miguel Cabrera	6	Matt Kemp
7	Ryan Braun	7	Joe Mauer
8	Jimmy Rollins	8	Derek Jeter
9	Ian Kinsler	9	Zack Greinke
10	Josh Hamilton	10	Ryan Braun (7)
11	Ryan Howard	11	Jacoby Ellsbury
12	Mark Teixeira	12	Mark Reynolds
13	Alex Rodriguez	13	Prince Fielder
14	Matt Holliday	14	Chase Utley (15)
15	Chase Utley	15	Miguel Cabrera (6)

For that six-year stretch of top 15 players, only three of those 90 players (3%) finished exactly where we projected them. Only 18 (20%) finished within three spots of where we projected them. Only 22 (24%) even finished within 5 spots of where we projected them.

If a player was projected to finish in the top 5, he actually finished there only 37% of the time.

A Bigger Billboard

After all the time and effort we put into the process of projecting performance and planning our drafts, how can we still be so far off? Are our analytical abilities really that horrible?

Well, we're pretty good, but not nearly as good as we'd like to think we are. However, it's not our fault. The impact of external variables has grown to the point where it is beginning to obscure all the good analysis we've been doing.

In short, "luck" is winning.

And this recent rise in the influence of apparently random variance may be traced to one thing:

The disabled list.

It is no secret that the number of days lost to the disabled list is exorbitant. We can all speculate as to the cause – better diagnoses, teams' need to protect their investments, PED withdrawal – but the numbers are what fantasy leaguers need to be concerned with:

While these numbers seem ridiculously huge and the trends scary, the real impact is not felt as we plod along over a six-month season. A player goes on the DL, we grumble, we replace him and we move on. We might whine about our injury woes at various times during the season, but our discomfort tends to ebb and flow over the 180 days.

That's why we missed this billboard.

It is not until we take more of a macro-look at the phenomenon that the real impact can be seen.

On the opposite page is a list of the top ranked 276 players coming into 2009. In a deep 12-team American League- or National League-only competition, this list constitutes the top half of the player pool, the high-priced foundation players for the league. In a 12-team mixed league, this list is the *entire player population*.

In 2009, 140 of these 276 players lost time to the disabled list, demotion, suspension or release. That's more than half (50.7% to be exact) of the player pool.

When it comes to the issue of projective accuracy, those are 140 players whose projections were immediately wrong.

Remember - these were the commodities that we expected to be the *276 best players* for our teams. These were the 276 players who were going to display the best skills and get the most playing time. And more than half of them fell short of expectation due to playing time losses alone. (And this doesn't include players who lost time but did not go on the DL, or underperformers.)

The Fallout

Playing time is essentially a zero sum proposition. So if 50% of the top players in baseball lost playing time last year, where did those at-bats and innings-pitched go?

If we take a look at last year's most profitable players, that's where we find them. And remember "True Fact #2," the most profitable players have a disproportionately large impact on who is going to win your league.

In 2009, there were 44 batters who earned at least $10 profit on their projected draft purchase price.

64% of them amassed at least 20% more playing time than projected. In real terms, that's 100 more at bats over a full season of play. Among this group were Russ Branyan, Marlon Byrd and Michael Bourn.

59% were deemed undraftable back in March (zero or negative projected value). This group included players like Adam Kennedy, Brendan Ryan and Andrew McCutchen.

It is astounding how many of these surprises were due solely to their role or playing time. Of course, we can't completely ignore skill when evaluating these profits, but the precursor was almost exclusively the unexpected availability of AB, either due to an in-season fine-tuning of

A BIG BILLBOARD — Opening Day 2009 ADPs: The Top Ranked 276 Players

ADP	Player	Pos	Time Lost	
1	Hanley Ramirez	SS		
2	Albert Pujols	1B		
3	Jose Reyes	SS	15DL	
4	David Wright	3B		
5	Grady Sizemore	OF	15DL	15DL
6	Miguel Cabrera	1B		
7	Ryan Braun	OF		
8	Jimmy Rollins	SS		
9	Ian Kinsler	2B	15DL	
10	Josh Hamilton	OF	15DL	
11	Ryan Howard	1B		
12	Matt Holliday	OF		
13	Mark Teixeira	1B		
14	Lance Berkman	1B	15DL	
15	Chase Utley	2B		
16	Alex Rodriguez	3B	15DL	
17	B.J. Upton	OF	15DL	
18	Johan Santana	SP	15DL	
19	Justin Morneau	1B	Sept	
20	Manny Ramirez	OF	Susp	
21	Evan Longoria	3B		
22	Carlos Beltran	OF	15DL	
23	Alfonso Soriano	OF	15DL	
24	Ichiro Suzuki	OF	15DL	
25	Tim Lincecum	SP		
26	Prince Fielder	1B		
27	Carl Crawford	OF		
28	Dustin Pedroia	2B		
29	Carlos Lee	OF		
30	Brandon Phillips	2B		
31	Aramis Ramirez	3B	15DL	
32	Nick Markakis	OF		
33	Jason Bay	OF		
34	CC Sabathia	SP		
35	Adrian Gonzalez	1B		
36	Brian Roberts	2B		
37	Alex Rios	OF		
38	Kevin Youkilis	1B	15DL	
39	Matt Kemp	OF		
40	Vladimir Guerrero	OF	15DL	15DL
41	Carlos Quentin	OF	15DL	
42	Russell Martin	C		
43	Cole Hamels	SP		
44	Jake Peavy	SP	15DL	
45	Brandon Webb	SP	60DL	
46	Alexei Ramirez	2B		
47	Roy Halladay	SP	15DL	
48	Brian McCann	C	15DL	
49	Shane Victorino	OF		
50	Curtis Granderson	OF		
51	Chipper Jones	3B		
52	David Ortiz	DH		
53	Corey Hart	OF	15DL	
54	Jonathan Papelbon	RP		
55	Dan Haren	SP		
56	Nate McLouth	OF	15DL	
57	Jacoby Ellsbury	OF		
58	Brad Lidge	RP	15DL	
59	Bobby Abreu	OF		
60	Rafael Furcal	SS		
61	Adam Dunn	OF		
62	Carlos Pena	1B	60DL	
63	Dan Uggla	2B		
64	Magglio Ordonez	OF		
65	Chris Davis	1B	AAA	
66	Cliff Lee	SP		
67	Francisco Liriano	SP	15DL	
68	Geovany Soto	C	15DL	
69	Josh Beckett	SP		
70	Chone Figgins	3B		
71	Derrek Lee	1B		
72	Garrett Atkins	3B		
73	Roy Oswalt	SP	Sept	
74	Michael Young	SS	Sept	
75	Francisco Rodriguez	RP		
76	Joe Nathan	RP		
77	Robinson Cano	2B		
78	Victor Martinez	C		
79	Hunter Pence	OF		
80	James Shields	SP		
81	Joey Votto	1B	15DL	
82	Mariano Rivera	RP		
83	Aubrey Huff	3B		
84	Scott Kazmir	SP	15DL	
85	Jermaine Dye	OF		
86	Felix Hernandez	SP		
87	Ryan Zimmerman	3B		
88	James Loney	1B		
89	Stephen Drew	SS	15DL	
90	A.J. Burnett	SP		
91	Chad Billingsley	SP		
92	Ryan Ludwick	OF	15DL	

ADP	Player	Pos	Time Lost	
93	Carlos Delgado	1B	15DL	
94	Bobby Jenks	RP	Sept	
95	Joe Mauer	C		
96	John Lackey	SP	15DL	
97	Joba Chamberlain	RP		
98	Joakim Soria	RP	15DL	
99	Jon Lester	SP		
100	Derek Jeter	SS		
101	Chris Young	OF	15DL	AAA
102	Jay Bruce	OF	15DL	
103	Jhonny Peralta	SS		
104	Vernon Wells	OF		
105	Daisuke Matsuzaka	SP	60DL	
106	Troy Tulowitzki	SS		
107	Torii Hunter	OF	15DL	
108	Edinson Volquez	SP	60DL	
109	Carlos Zambrano	SP	15DL	
110	Jose Valverde	RP	15DL	
111	Ervin Santana	SP	15DL	
112	Edwin Encarnacion	3B	60DL	
113	J.J. Hardy	SS	AAA	
114	Andre Ethier	OF		
115	Johnny Damon	OF		
116	Raul Ibanez	OF	15DL	
117	Justin Verlander	SP		
118	Yovani Gallardo	SP		
119	Jonathan Broxton	RP		
120	Nelson Cruz	OF	15DL	
121	Ricky Nolasco	SP	AAA	
122	Brian Fuentes	RP		
123	B.J. Ryan	RP	15DL	
124	Howie Kendrick	2B	AAA	
125	Rich Harden	SP		
126	Ryan Doumit	C	15DL	
127	Matt Cain	SP		
128	Matt Wieters	C	AAA	
129	Adam Wainwright	SP		
130	Brad Hawpe	OF		
131	Chris Iannetta	C	15DL	
132	Brett Myers	SP	15DL	
133	Lastings Milledge	OF	AAA	
134	Javier Vazquez	SP		
135	David Price	RP	AAA	
136	Carlos Marmol	RP		
137	Chris Young	SP	60DL	
138	Jayson Werth	OF		
139	Milton Bradley	OF	Susp	
140	Randy Johnson	SP	60DL	
141	Josh Johnson	SP		
142	Matt Capps	RP		
143	Orlando Cabrera	SS		
144	Zack Greinke	SP		
145	John Danks	SP		
146	Francisco Cordero	RP		
147	Willy Taveras	OF	15DL	
148	Jorge Cantu	3B		
149	Pat Burrell	OF	15DL	
150	Jim Thome	DH		
151	Aaron Harang	SP	15DL	
152	Miguel Tejada	SS		
153	Derek Lowe	SP		
154	Kerry Wood	RP		
155	Jose Lopez	2B		
156	Mike Napoli	C		
157	Xavier Nady	OF	60DL	
158	Paul Konerko	1B		
159	Brian Wilson	RP		
160	Alex Gordon	3B	15DL	AAA
161	Ryan Dempster	SP	15DL	
162	Mike Gonzalez	RP		
163	Kaz Matsui	2B	15DL	
164	Mike Aviles	SS	60DL	
165	Joe Saunders	SP	15DL	
166	Heath Bell	RP		
167	Matt Garza	SP		
168	Matt Lindstrom	RP	15DL	
169	Adam Jones	OF	60DL	
170	Yunel Escobar	SS		
171	Jeremy Hermida	OF		
172	Hank Blalock	1B		
173	Kevin Slowey	SP	60DL	
174	Bengie Molina	C		
175	Ryan Theriot	SS		
176	Gavin Floyd	SP		
177	Eric Byrnes	OF	15DL	
178	Hideki Matsui	OF		
179	Jair Jurrjens	SP		
180	Khalil Greene	SS	15DL	15DL
181	Ty Wigginton	3B		
182	Huston Street	RP	Sept	
183	Max Scherzer	RP	15DL	
184	Trevor Hoffman	RP	15DL	

ADP	Player	Pos	Time Lost	
185	Erik Bedard	SP	60DL	
186	Mark DeRosa	2B	15DL	
187	Joey Devine	RP	60DL	
188	Jason Giambi	1B	Rel	
189	Adrian Beltre	3B	15DL	
190	Melvin Mora	3B	15DL	
191	Johnny Cueto	SP	15DL	
192	Joel Hanrahan	RP		
193	Clayton Kershaw	SP		
194	Ted Lilly	SP	15DL	
195	Casey Kotchman	1B	15DL	
196	Jason Bartlett	SS	15DL	
197	Justin Duchscherer	SP	60DL	
198	Jorge Posada	C	15DL	
199	Nick Swisher	OF		
200	Andy Pettitte	SP		
201	Brad Ziegler	RP		
202	Denard Span	OF	15DL	
203	Brandon Morrow	RP	AAA	
204	Kelly Johnson	2B	15DL	
205	Jesse Litsch	SP	15DL	
206	Chad Qualls	RP	60DL	
207	Justin Upton	OF	15DL	
208	Rick Ankiel	OF	15DL	
209	Jonathan Sanchez	SP		
210	Luke Scott	OF	15DL	
211	Conor Jackson	OF	60DL	
212	Mike Pelfrey	SP		
213	Rickie Weeks	2B	60DL	
214	Jed Lowrie	SS	15DL	15DL
215	Chien-Ming Wang	SP	60DL	
216	Brandon Lyon	RP		
217	Pablo Sandoval	1B		
218	J.J. Putz	RP	60DL	
219	Carlos Guillen	3B	15DL	
220	Fred Lewis	OF		
221	Jeff Clement	C	AAA	
222	Ryan Church	OF	15DL	
223	Adam Lind	OF		
224	Aaron Cook	SP	15DL	
225	Jered Weaver	SP		
226	Edgar Renteria	SS	Sept	
227	Placido Polanco	2B		
228	Gil Meche	SP	15DL	
229	Mark Ellis	2B	60DL	
230	Troy Percival	RP	15DL	
231	Frank Francisco	RP	15DL	15DL
232	Scott Baker	SP	15DL	
233	Chris Volstad	RP	AAA	
234	Juan Pierre	OF		
235	Wandy Rodriguez	SP		
236	Elijah Dukes	OF	15DL	
237	Jeff Francoeur	OF		
238	Dioner Navarro	C		
239	Ramon Hernandez	C	15DL	
240	A.J. Pierzynski	C		
241	Kurt Suzuki	C		
242	Coco Crisp	OF	60DL	
243	Scott Olsen	SP	60DL	
244	Hiroki Kuroda	SP	15DL	
245	Todd Helton	1B		
246	John Maine	SP	15DL	
247	Chris Carpenter	SP	15DL	
248	Jeremy Guthrie	SP		
249	Akinori Iwamura	2B	60DL	
250	Delmon Young	OF	15DL	
251	Casey Blake	3B	Sept	
252	Mark Reynolds	3B		
253	Ivan Rodriguez	C		
254	Armando Galarraga	SP	AAA	
255	John Smoltz	SP	15DL	Rel
256	Koji Uehara	SP	15DL	
257	Mike Jacobs	1B		
258	Gerald Laird	C		
259	Cameron Maybin	OF	AAA	
260	Kelly Shoppach	C		
261	Brandon Inge	C		
262	Orlando Hudson	2B		
263	Kenji Johjima	C	15DL	
264	Cristian Guzman	SS	15DL	
265	Travis Hafner	DH	15DL	
266	Philip Hughes	SP	AAA	
267	George Sherrill	RP		
268	Jason Motte	RP		
269	Paul Maholm	SP		
270	Manny Corpas	RP	60DL	
271	Jose Arredondo	RP	AAA	
272	Jason Varitek	C		
273	Rafael Perez	RP	AAA	
274	Kelvim Escobar	SP	15DL	
275	Adam LaRoche	1B		
276	Shin-Soo Choo	OF		

Legend

15DL	Spent time on 15-day DL, May have lost more than 15 days
60DL	Spent time on 60-day DL, Lost at least 2 months
AAA	Spent time in the minors
Susp	Was suspended
Rel	Was released
Sept	Lost at least two weeks in Sept. when DL moves are not made

276	**TOTAL PLAYERS**
140	No. lost time
51%	Pct.
167	**BATTERS**
81	No. lost time
49%	Pct.
109	**PITCHERS**
59	No. lost time
54%	Pct.

ADP ranking courtesy of MockDraftCentral.com

roles, or another teammate's injury or underperformance.

Ben Zobrist would not likely have exploded without the injuries to B.J. Upton and Akinori Iwamura. Nick Swisher likely would not have gotten a chance without the injury to Xavier Nady. Juan Pierre benefitted from Manny Ramirez's suspension. Gary Sheffield was salvaged from the scrap heap by the Mets. Nyjer Morgan won at bats in Pittsburgh because Eric Hinske and Brandon Moss struggled, then nailed his playing time after getting dealt to Washington. Miguel Montero saw a spike in playing time when A.J. Hinch became the Diamondbacks manager. Martin Prado benefited from Kelly Johnson's failings. Rajai Davis became a regular when Matt Holliday was traded.

For nearly all 44 players, you can track their increase in playing time back to some series of events affecting others.

For pitchers, it's a little bit different. Eight of them generated significant profit by backing into a bunch of saves. From Andrew Bailey, to Ryan Franklin, to Jim Johnson, most of these pitchers had the skills to close, but no clear path to ninth inning work. Injuries, incumbent ineffectiveness and trades opened up the opportunities for nearly everyone on the list.

There were 22 starters that earned at least $10 more than projected.

45% of them amassed at least 20% more playing time than projected. In real terms, that's about 40 innings over a full season of play. These included Josh Johnson, Ubaldo Jimenez and Zach Duke.

68% were deemed undraftable back in March, including Scott Feldman, Jason Marquis and Jarrod Washburn.

Aside from the few that benefited from unexpected good health (like Chris Carpenter), most of the rest demonstrated skill levels beyond what we projected. But for many, rotation spots still needed to open up.

41% of the pitchers were either deemed not good enough to be a part of their respective team's starting rotation on Opening Day, or slotted no higher than a #4 starter. These were pitchers like Ricky Romero, J.A. Happ and Ross Ohlendorf. The fact that they all accumulated significant innings means that they either benefited from someone else's injury/ineffectiveness and/or pitched well enough to move up the depth chart. Still, innings remain the great separator here.

But I selected 20% as an arbitrary delineator for playing time increases. Beyond the 74 batters and pitchers above, when considering *all* playing time increases, and filtering out those players who experienced a clear skills improvement, the results are even more noteworthy:

1. More than 70% of the most profitable players this year were driven in large part by an increase in playing time.

2. The opportunity for those playing time increases was largely dependent on external events, virtually none of which were predictable on Draft Day.

3. And so, more than 70% of this season's most profitable players could not have been predicted on draft day.

Recap

· At best, our player projections are going to be at least 30% wrong.

· We have only a 2 in 3 chance of getting within +/- $5 of our dollar value projections.

· We have only a 38% chance of picking the correct Top 15 players.

· We will incorrectly project playing time for half of the top 276 players.

· We will miss 70% of the most profitable commodities due to unexpected playing time increases.

One would think it's a pointless exercise to even try to project player performance. Are we deluding ourselves into thinking we're smarter than we really are?

Maybe it's time for me to find a new line of work.

Yes, that's exactly what I am going to do.

Meteorology

There was an essay in the *1990 Baseball Forecaster* entitled, "Mostly sunny, increasing darkness towards evening." Twenty years ago, we did not know nearly as much as we do now, so our forecasting efforts were far more rudimentary. We were in no position to make grandiose claims about projective accuracy (though some early touts did anyway). The "experts" at the end of the last century lived in a world of imprecision.

Often, the best we could do was make projections with a broad brush. My player commentaries in that 1990 book were about as broad as you can get. Ben McDonald "has a bright future ahead." Billy Swift "should tail off." Jesse Barfield "has plateaued."

It was a simpler time.

Tonight, the friendly weather forecaster on my local television station has told me that it is going to be partly cloudy tomorrow with a high of 48 degrees.

I suspect that the meteorologist's advanced modeling system spit out that fancy number — 48. I often think, why not 47? Or 49? The truth is, if I were to walk outside right now, I'd feel no difference if it was 47, or 48, or 49.

In fact, it probably requires a good five degrees for me to feel any noticeable difference, and even then, it would be slight. 49 versus 44? 76 versus 71? 97 versus 92? More important, a five degree difference wouldn't likely make me change my behavior. If I'm not wearing a scarf and gloves at 49, I'm not likely going to do so at 44.

The 10-day forecast is an even more interesting exercise. Besides the fact that I don't believe they can accurately tell me that it is going to rain a week from next Sunday, the list of daily high temperatures seem to be an exercise in excessive precision: 50, 52, 51, 52, 50, 47, 47, 47, 44, 46.

What does this tell me? The first half of the week is going to be cold. The second half of the week is going to be marginally colder.

In fact, they could just say that the temp will be in the low 50's and I would be perfectly okay with that. High 40's, low 50's, high 50's, low 60's... that's all I need. They wouldn't even have to bother with mid-40's or mid-50's because that won't change what I am going to wear anyway.

What's more, that extra precision is not buying us anything. We delude ourselves into believing we are gaining accuracy when in fact we are gaining an increased probability of being wrong. We're just not good enough to predict the temperature to the exact degree on a daily basis. We need to come to terms with that. And most important... there's no great need to be so perfect.

Take Miguel Cabrera, for instance.

Coming into the 2009 season, we had projected that he'd hit 39 home runs. That's his M.O. — he hits home runs in the 30's. The fact that "39" would have been a career high for him is almost irrelevant. The 37 he hit in 2008 was his previous career high and the difference between that and 39 would have been, as we say, "two errant gusts of wind."

Cabrera finished 2009 with 34 HR. The difference between 34 and 39 is a bit more noticeable but does not substantively change who Cabrera is. Nor would it have changed the way fantasy leaguers approached him at their 2009 drafts. It won't likely change draft behavior in 2010 either.

What's more, we already know that there will be a minimum 30% error bar around whatever number we attach to his projected home run output. For a 30ish home run hitter, that could be a variance of *ten home runs!* Suddenly, my 39 HR projection doesn't look so bad.

So I have to ask, why do we need to attach a "39" to his projected home run output? Like the weather, we can't predict with that level of precision and the results won't (or shouldn't) change our behavior anyway.

Perhaps we should just project that Cabrera will hit HRs "in the 30s." It's a wide enough range that not only covers our error bar but, oddly, also increases our accuracy. If we design a forecasting model for our drafts that can accommodate the imprecision of performance with the volatility of playing time, we might actually have something useful.

We've spent the past two decades designing all these wonderfully intricate forecasting systems, but maybe we've just been spinning our wheels. I'm not sure we want to go back to the place where I tell you Clay Buchholz "has a bright future ahead," Mark Reynolds "should tail off" and Brad Hawpe "has plateaued." But I believe that obsessing over "I projected he'd hit 33 HRs, you projected he'd hit 30 HRs and he hit 32 HRs, so I win" is a complete waste of brain cells.

He hits home runs in the low 30's. Today's high temperature is going to be in the low 50's. Leave your scarf and gloves at home.

The Mayberry Method

When you exit off of I-77 and head east towards Mt. Airy, NC, there are a few billboards for local fast food restaurants and hotel chains. I estimate that it's a good 5-6 mile ride up Route 89 until you reach town, but once you arrive, you know it.

You've been there before. For those like me who are becoming older than dirt, we grew up with that town in the 1960's. The rest of you young whippersnappers have been watching Mayberry in reruns.

Andy and Opie have moved on to national courtrooms and major motion pictures. The only obvious connection to baseball might be Floyd (if we gave Gavin some scissors, I suppose). But aside from an atypical quadruple murder outside an appliance store this past fall, Mayberry – now Mount Airy – is still how we perceive it.

It is a place where life is simpler.

For us, RFD might well mean, "Rotisserie For Dummies."

Now, those "Dummies" books are not at all for the dim-witted. They are fine works that allow readers to learn the basics for dozens of activities. They bring complicated concepts down to more rudimentary levels.

And the Mayberry Method does likewise, designed to simplify the player evaluation process to a level that will at first seem fuzzy, flawed and imprecise, but you'll actually find to be fuzzy, warm and comfortable.

Like Aunt Bea's apple cobbler.

Sort of.

One of the more popular pre-Rotisserie pastimes of the 1960's was games like Strat-O-Matic and APBA. These games attempted to re-create the statistical records of players using dice-roll probabilities. While the underlying intent might have been to match Harmon Killebrew's 49 home runs in 1964, we all knew that the best we could expect was something relatively close to 49.

And that was perfectly fine.

The Mayberry Method attempts to do likewise. The billboards have already shown us the folly of excess precision. It's time to take a step back and embrace the error bar that we've been so doggedly trying to erase.

The Mayberry Method reduces every player to a 7-character code. You are already familiar with three of those characters; they are our reliability grades. No player evaluation is complete without them so the Mayberry Method makes reliability a part of the system.

The other four characters describe individual elements of the player's skill set, each on a simple scale of 0 to 5.

Jason Bay's MM code is "5225 AAC." His overall MM score for ranking purposes is 70.

Adam Wainwright's MM code is "3405 CAB." His overall MM score for ranking purposes is 80.

Let's start with the batters.

MM Power

The first character in the MM code refers to the batter's power skills. It is assigned using the following table:

PX	MM	Prj 2010 %	Rough HR Approx
0 - 49	0	6%	0
50 - 79	1	24%	up to 10
80 - 99	2	20%	up to 20
100 - 119	3	25%	up to 30
120 - 159	4	22%	up to 40
160+	5	4%	up to 50+

Power skill is assessed without regard to actual home run output. That number will fluctuate; we are more interested in pure skill. It also does not consider playing time, at least not yet. You'll note that there is a reasonable spread of skill across the player pool.

I provide a rough approximation of what these codes equate to for a full-time player in order to get you comfortable with the code. Knowing that a player with a "3" means he has up to 30-HR power makes it easier to understand and connect with the system.

MM Speed

The second character in the MM code refers to the batter's speed skills. It is assigned using the following table:

SX	MM	Prj 2010 %	Rough SB Approx
0 - 49	0	23%	0
50 - 79	1	31%	up to 10
80 - 99	2	21%	up to 20
100 - 119	3	13%	up to 30
120 - 139	4	8%	up to 40
140+	5	5%	up to 50+

Again, actual stolen bases become secondary (though SX does use them). The skills spread reflects the scarcity of SB as compared to HR. The rough SB approximation is probably a little bit rougher here, but it still instills some familiarity into the system.

MM Batting Average

The third character in the MM code refers to batting average, and uses Expected Batting Average to measure it. It is assigned using the following table:

xBA	MM	Prj 2010 %
.000 - .239	0	17%
.240 - .254	1	24%
.255 - .269	2	29%
.270 - .284	3	19%
.285 - .299	4	9%
.300+	5	1%

Same general concept here.

MM Playing Time

This is perhaps the most important part of the code.

Each draft day, we come to the table with a ranked list of players. Each player is defined by a statistical projection. While it is nice to see that stat line, it is a combination of two very separate elements — skill and opportunity. When we combine those elements to create the projection, we impede our ability to evaluate the elements independently.

That ability is more important than ever before. Skill and playing time each requires separate analysis. So we will keep at-bats and innings-pitched separate in the MM code, though we will combine them with skill at the proper time.

At-bats is the fourth character in the MM code.

AB	MM	Prj 2010 %
0 - 99	0	7%
100 - 199	1	19%
200 - 299	2	13%
300 - 399	3	13%
400 - 499	4	20%
500+	5	28%

Still, MM includes at-bats as a part of this skill-based system. Here's why:

1. If we believe that staying healthy is a skill, then there should be some measure rewarding that. However, by gauging this "skill" in 100-AB increments, we are also accepting the fact that players will get hurt. Note that a "5" only requires 500 AB; that essentially builds in the probability of at least one or two disabled list stays during the season.

2. Since Mayberry is strictly skills-based, there is no accommodation for Runs and RBIs. Playing time will drive those stats so including AB in the code is important.

3. The AB character does double-duty; it is also the multiplier we will use to create an overall score for ranking purposes. Simply:

MM Score =
(PX score + SX score + xBA score + AB score) x AB score

The highest score you can get is 100, so this becomes an easy scale to evaluate as well.

Note that the AB variable is both a part of the skills profile as well as the multiplier. That's how important it is. It also becomes an easy "lever" for manipulating a player's score. If a DL stay will significantly impact a player's future playing time, you can just adjust that digit downward and the overall score easily recalculates. If a part-time player backs into more AB's, you can adjust upward for similar effect. And that effect could be quite large.

For instance, let's go back to Jason Bay's 5225 MM, for a score of 70. If he has an extended DL stay, you could downgrade him to 5224, which recalculates out to 52.

Now the pitchers…

MM Overall Skill

The first character in the pitching MM refers to xERA, which captures a pitcher's overall ability and is an easy proxy for ERA, and even WHIP. It is assigned using the following table:

xERA	MM	Prj 2010 %
4.81+	0	13%
4.41 - 4.80	1	22%
4.01 - 4.40	2	28%
3.61 - 4.00	3	18%
3.21 - 3.60	4	13%
3.20-	5	5%

Given how important this measure of overall skill is, we give the xERA value double the weight in the calculation of the overall MM score.

MM Dominance

The second character refers to strikeout ability. It is assigned using the following table:

K/9	MM	Prj 2010 %
0.0 - 4.9	0	8%
5.0 - 5.9	1	18%
6.0 - 6.9	2	22%
7.0 - 7.9	3	25%
8.0 - 8.9	4	13%
9.0+	5	14%

MM Saves

The third character refers to saves. This is the only part of the Mayberry Method that is purely subjective. Saves are tough to project so the best we can do is position ourselves to grab them when we can.

MM	Description
0	No hope for saves; starting pitchers
1	Speculative closer
2	Frontline/shared closer in a pen with alternatives
3	Frontline closer in a firm bullpen role

This code only goes to "3" in order to soften the overall impact that relief pitchers have.

MM Playing Time

Like batters, the playing time code for pitchers — innings pitched — serves multiple purposes

IP	MM	Prj 2010 %
0 - 69	0	43%
70 - 99	1	18%
100 - 129	2	9%
130 - 159	3	7%
160 - 189	4	13%
190+	5	11%

This system penalizes relievers for amassing fewer innings. We've taken that into account in the calculation for the overall score by including the saves variable as a part of the multiplier.:

MM Score
= ((xERA score x 2) + K/9 score + Saves score + IP score) x (IP score + Saves score)

Except in exceedingly rare cases, that multiplier should never add up to more than 5.

Here, as in the batting formula, IP does double duty and greatly affects the MM score. Saves also do the same, so if a reliever moves into a closing role, that too can have an immediate and dramatic impact on the score.

And that's it.

While this description of the Mayberry Method may seem a little complicated, the system is ridiculously simple. (When we first introduced PQS scores, many folks balked at the process, but it became second nature after very little use. I expect the Mayberry Method will do likewise.) In fact, I guarantee that many of you will look at this after awhile and wonder if I'm trying to take everyone back to kindergarten.

We have become so obsessed with increased intricacy that it's tough to see that there are often more simple solutions (see: Occam's Razor). Admittedly, MM might fall a bit short in absolute accuracy, but it will find much greater usability as a player ranking tool, and ultimately draft planning tool.

In the end, the ratings may actually be *more* accurate. There is a higher probability of me being on target if I tell you that Miguel Cabrera is going to hit "up to 40" HRs than if I tell you he is going to hit exactly 37.

A player ranking list for the Mayberry Method appears in the "Ratings and Rankings" section of this book. It is the first step for you to evaluate the system and take it out for a test run. Here's a look at the top batters and pitchers:

BATTERS		REL	MM
Braun,Ryan	5445	AAC	90
Rollins,Jimmy	3545	AAB	85
Pujols,Albert	5155	AAB	80
Utley,Chase	4435	AAA	80
Kemp,Matt	4435	AAB	80
Votto,Joey	5155	ABC	80
Gonzalez,Carlos	4435	ADF	80
Crawford,Carl	2545	BAC	80
Kinsler,Ian	4435	CAC	80
PITCHERS		**REL**	**MM**
Lincecum,Tim	5505	AAA	100
Haren,Dan	5405	AAA	95
Hernandez,Felix	5405	AAA	95
Halladay,Roy	5305	BAA	90
Greinke,Zack	4505	AAA	90
Verlander,J	4505	AAB	90
Vazquez,Javier	4505	AAB	90
Scherzer,Max	4505	ACC	90
Lester,Jon	4505	CAC	90
Nolasco,Ricky	4505	CBC	90

Players in each section are essentially interchangeable commodities, separated only by their risk profile. So, while Max Scherzer and Ricky Nolasco look painfully out of place, for instance, know that their overall skills match up well with the others. What separates them are their ACC and CBC Reliability scores, respectively (which would drop them out of Tier 1 of the Portfolio3 Plan) and any playing time downside, which is something you can easily adjust and recalculate.

The next step is to set up Mayberry benchmarks for Portfolio3. That's coming.

Welcome to the *Baseball Forecaster*, Edition #24.

This is a book about using numbers as a tool to compete successfully in any of the many flavors of fantasy baseball. It is a reference volume containing ideas and concepts that have been compiled over the course of nearly 2.5 decades. But, again, it is just a tool. There is no magic.

This book was conceived as a well-timed collision of sabermetrics and fantasy. The unique, hybrid brand of analysis that we perpetrate here is what we call **fanalytics,** which is a measured, deliberate approach to evaluating and projecting player performance within the context of fantasy baseball. It takes from both schools and provides deeper insight than any other analytical process. Sabermetrics becomes more than just a bunch of incomprehensible formulas, and fantasy becomes more than just blindly picking a bunch of players and praying.

New Readers – Welcome!

The *Baseball Forecaster* was the first book to approach prognostication by breaking performance down into its component parts. Rather than predicting batting average, for instance, we look at the elements of skill that make up that stat and reverse-engineer those skills back into batting average. In all, we call this "component skills analysis."

You should know that there is some rudimentary math involved and there is a bit of a learning curve. The nice thing about the math, though, is that most of it is logical and intuitive. For instance, when we talk about "contact rate," that's just the percentage of time a batter makes contact with the ball. It is calculated simply as ((AB - K) / AB). As you would expect, the more contact a batter makes, the higher his batting average tends to be. We have benchmarks at the upper and lower ends of the scale and we can project a player's batting average off of that.

And the pieces all fit together very neatly in the end.

Naturally, I think this approach is the best way to evaluate and project performance — and 24 years of publication attest to at least some level of public acceptance — but I'll let you decide for yourself. I do ask, however, that you keep an open mind. These tools do work, but you may have to toss away some of your preconceptions in order to embrace the possibilities.

There's a ton of information here. At first glance, it will seem overwhelming. But you don't have to take it in all at once. Start slow; take as much time as you need.

What's New in 2009?

1. *More years of data:* As we accumulate historical data on each player for some of our charts, we provide a more robust look at the trends.

2. *Batter base performance values:* We tossed aside batting BPV several years ago because it just didn't work very well. The formula was overhauled this past summer and we've managed to squeeze it back in to the player boxes. Unfortunately, we had to cut Hits to make room. But you can find that anywhere.

3. *New writers:* We have some terrific new writers who are adding color to the fanalytic landscape. We've also started to update many of the studies in the Forecaster's Toolbox.

4. *Hidden contests and surveys:* There are two players in the book with commentaries that describe opportunities for you to win a free copy of the *2011 Baseball Forecaster*. There is also one commentary that is a survey question that will help us plan out future editions. To participate, send an email to **bf10@ronshandler.com** with the player's name in the subject line and your entry or response in the body of the email. Deadline 4/15/10. Happy hunting, and good luck!

5. *The Mayberry Method!* 'Nuff said.

Updates

Content Update page: If there are any corrections or clarifications on the information in this book, go to:

http://www.baseballhq.com/books/bfupdates.shtml

Free Projections Update: As a buyer of this book, you get one free 2010 projections update, available online at

http://www.baseballhq.com/books/freeupdate/index.shtml

These are spreadsheet data files, to be posted on or about March 1, 2010.

Electronic book: The complete PDF version of the *Forecaster* – plus MS Excel versions of most key charts – is available free to those who bought the book directly through the BaseballHQ.com website. These files will be available in January 2010; contact us if you do not receive information via e-mail about accessing them. If you purchased the *Forecaster* through an online vendor or bookstore, you can purchase these files from us for $9.95. Call 1-800-422-7820 for more information.

Beyond the *Forecaster*

The *Forecaster* is just the beginning. The following companion products and services are described in more detail in the back of the book.

BaseballHQ.com is our home website. It provides regular updates to everything in this book, including daily updated projections, plus a ton more.

First Pitch Forums are a series of conferences we run all over the country, where you can meet some of the top industry analysts and network with fellow fantasy leaguers. We're adding several more cities to the tour in 2010!

RotoHQ.com is a very, very large online library of fantasy strategy essays and tools.

Minor League Baseball Analyst, the fifth edition, is now under the helm of Rob Gordon and Jeremy Deloney. It is a minor league version of the *Forecaster*, with stat boxes for more than 1000 prospects, and more. *Available in January.*

We still have copies available of *How to Value Players for Rotisserie Baseball*, Art McGee's ground-breaking book on valuation theory.

RotoLab is the best draft software on the market, period.

That's it. Get started. Jump in. Have fun. Good luck!

— Ron

II.

FANALYTICS

Forecasting Principles

Forecasts. Projections. Predictions. Prognostications. The crystal ball aura of this process conceals the fact it *is* a process. No voodoo here. We might define it as "the systematic process of determining likely end results." It's scientific and it works.

However, baseball performance forecasting is inherently a high-risk exercise with a very modest accuracy rate. This is because the process involves not only statistics, but also unscientific elements, from random chance to human volatility. And even from within the statistical aspect there are multiple elements that need to be evaluated, from skill to playing time to a host of external variables.

Every system is comprised of the same core elements:
* Players will tend to perform within the framework of past history and/or trends.
* Skills will develop and decline according to age.
* Statistics will be shaped by a player's health, expected role and home ballpark.

While all systems are built from these same elements, they also are constrained by the same limitations. We are all still trying to project a bunch of human beings, each one...
* with his own individual skill set
* with his own rate of growth and decline
* with his own ability to resist and recover from injury
* limited to opportunities determined by other people
* generating a group of statistics largely affected by tons of external noise. For instance, a pitcher's wins requires the analysis of not only skill, but the skills of his team's offense, defense, bullpen and the manager's tendencies. *All* these variables must be analyzed.

Based on the research of multiple sources, the best accuracy rate that can be attained by any system is about 70%. In fact, a simple system that uses three-year averages adjusted for age ("Marcel the Monkey") can attain a success rate of 65%. This means all the advanced systems are fighting for occupation of the remaining 5%.

Other Considerations

Perpetuity: Forecasting is not an exercise that produces a single set of numbers. It is dynamic, cyclical and ongoing. Conditions are constantly changing and we must react to those changes by adjusting our expectations. A pre-season projection is just a snapshot in time. Once the first batter steps to the plate on Opening Day, that projection has become obsolete. Its value is merely to provide a starting point, a baseline for what is about to occur.

During the season, if a projection appears to have been invalidated by current performance, the process continues. It is then that we need to ask... What went wrong? What conditions have changed? In fact, has *anything* changed? We need to analyze the situation and revise our expectation, if necessary. This process must be ongoing.

Process and outcomes: The outcomes of forecasted events should not be confused with the process itself. Outcomes may be the components that are the most closely scrutinized, but as long as the process is sound, the forecast has done the best job it can do. *In the end, forecasting is about analysis, not prophecy.*

Component Skills Analysis

Our brand of forecasting is more about finding logical journeys than blind destinations.

Familiar gauges like HR and ERA have long been used to measure skill. In fact, these gauges only measure the outcome of an individual event, or series of events. They represent statistical output. They are "surface stats."

Raw skill is the talent beneath the stats, the individual elements of a player's makeup. Players use these skills to create the individual events, or components, that we record using measures like HR and ERA. Our approach:

1. It's not about batting average, it's about seeing the ball and making contact. We target hitters based on elements such as their batting eye (walks to strikeouts ratio), how often they make contact and the type of contact they make. We then combine these components into an "expected batting average." By comparing each hitter's actual BA to how he *should* be performing, we can draw conclusions about the future.

2. It's not about home runs, it's about power. From the perspective of a round bat meeting a round ball, it may be only a fraction of an inch at the point of contact that makes the difference between a HR or a long foul ball. When a ball is hit safely, often it is only a few inches that separate a HR from a double. We tend to neglect these facts in our analyses, although the outcomes — the doubles, triples, long fly balls — may be no less a measure of that batter's raw power skill. We must incorporate all these components to paint a complete picture.

3. It's not about ERA, it's about getting the ball over the plate and keeping it in the park. Forget ERA. You want to draft pitchers who walk few batters (control), strike out many (dominance) and succeed at both in tandem (command). You also want pitchers who keep the ball on the ground (because home runs are bad). All of this translates into an "expected ERA" that you can use to compare to a pitcher's actual performance.

4. It's never about wins. For pitchers, winning ballgames is less about skill and more about offensive support. As such, projecting wins is futile and valuing hurlers based on their win history is dangerous. Target skill; wins will come.

5. It's not about saves, it's about opportunity first and skills second. While the highest skilled pitchers have the best potential to succeed as closers, they still have to be given the ball with the game on the line in the 9th inning, and that is a decision left to others. Over the past 10 years, about 40% of relievers drafted for saves failed to hold the role for the entire season. The lesson: Don't take chances on draft day. There will always be saves in the free agent pool.

Luck

Luck has been used as a catch-all term to describe random chance. When we use the term here, we're talking about unexplained variances that shape the statistics. Yes, these variances are random, but they are also often measurable and projectable. In order to get a better read on "luck," we use formulas that capture the external variability of the data.

Through our research and the work of others, we have learned that when raw skill is separated from statistical output, what's remaining is often unexplained variance. The aggregate totals of many of these variances, for all players, is often a constant. For instance, while a pitcher's ERA might fluctuate, the rate at which his opposition's batted balls fall for hits will always tend to be about 30%. Large variances in this rate can be expected to regress to 30%.

Why is all this important? Analysts complain about the lack of predictability of many traditional statistical gauges. The reason they find it difficult is that they are trying to project performance using gauges that are loaded with external noise. Raw skills gauges are more pure and follow better defined trends during a player's career. Then, as we get a better handle on the variances — explained and unexplained — we can construct a complete picture of what a player's statistics really mean.

The Process

The next step is to assemble these evaluators in such a way that they can be used to validate our observations, analyze their relevance and project a likely future direction.

In a perfect world, if a player's raw skills improve, then so should his surface stats. If his skills decline, then his stats should follow as well. But, sometimes a player's skill may increase while his surface stats may decline. These variances may be due to a variety of factors.

Component skills analysis is based on the expectation that events tend to move towards universal order. Surface stats will eventually approach their raw skill levels. Unexplained variances will regress to a mean. And from this, we can identify players whose performance may potentially change.

This process provides an important starting point for any forecasting analysis. For most of us, that analysis begins with the previous season's numbers. Last season provides us with a point of reference, so it's a natural way to begin the process of looking at the future.

Component skills analysis allows us to validate last year's numbers. A batter with few HRs but a high linear weighted power level has a good probability of improving his future HR output. A pitcher whose ERA was solid while his command ratio was poor is a good bet for an ERA spike.

Of course, these leading indicators do not always follow the rules. There are more shades of greys than blacks and whites. When indicators are in conflict – for instance, a pitcher who is displaying both a rising strikeout rate and a rising walk rate – then we have to find ways to sort out what these indicators might be saying.

It is often helpful to look at leading indicators in a hierarchy, of sorts. In fact, a hierarchy of the most important pitching base performance indicators might look like this: command (k/bb), control (bb/9), dominance (k/9) and GB/FB rate. For batters, contact rate might top the list, followed by power, walk rate and speed.

Assimilating Additional Research

Once we've painted the statistical picture of a player's potential, we then use additional criteria and research results to help us add some more color. These other criteria include the player's health, age, changes in role, ballpark, and a variety of other factors. We also use our *Forecaster's Toolbox* research results, which are described in the next section. These analyses look at things like traditional periods of peak performance and breakout profiles.

The final element of the process is assimilating the news into the forecast. This is the element that many fantasy leaguers tend to rely on most since it is the most accessible. However, it is also the element that provides the most noise.

Players, management and the media have absolute control over what we are allowed to know. Factors such as hidden injuries, messy divorces and clubhouse unrest are routinely kept from us, while we are fed red herrings and media spam. *We will never know the entire truth.*

And so... as long as we do not know all the facts, we cannot dismiss the possibility that any one fact is true, no matter how often the media assures it, deplores it, or ignores it. Don't believe everything you read; use your own judgment. If your observations conflict with what is being reported, that's powerful insight that should not be ignored.

Quite often, all you are reading is just other people's opinions... a manager who believes that a player has what it takes to be a regular, a team physician whose diagnosis is that a player is healthy enough to play. These words from experts have some element of truth, but cannot be wholly relied upon to provide an accurate expectation of future events. As such, it is often helpful to develop an appropriate cynicism for what you read.

For instance, if a player is struggling for no apparent reason, and there are denials about health issues, don't dismiss the possibility that an injury does exist. There are often motives for such news to be withheld from the public.

Also remember that nothing lasts forever in major league baseball. *Reality is fluid.* One decision begets a series of events that lead to other decisions. Any reported action can easily be reversed based on subsequent events. My favorite examples are announcements of a team's new bullpen closer. Those are about the shortest realities known to man.

We need the media to provide us with context for our analyses, and the *real* news they provide is valuable intelligence. But separating the news from the noise is difficult. In most cases, the only thing you can trust is how that player actually performs.

Embracing Imprecision

Precision and accuracy in baseball prognosticating is a fool's quest. There are far too many unexpected variables and noise that can render our projections useless. The truth is, the best we can ever hope for is to accurately forecast general tendencies and percentage plays.

However, even when you follow an 80% percentage play, for instance, you will still lose 20% of the time. Those 20% worth of outlying players are what skeptics like to use as justification to dismiss prognosticators. The paradox, of course, is that fantasy league titles are often won or lost by those exceptions. Still, long-term success dictates that you always chase the 80% and accept the fact that you will be wrong 20% of the time. Or, whatever that percentage play happens to be.

For fantasy league purposes, playing the percentages can take on an even less precise spin. The best projections are often the ones that are just far enough away from the field of expectation to alter decision-making. In other words, it doesn't matter if I project Player X to bat .320 and he only bats .295; it matters that I projected .320 and everyone else projected .280.

Or, perhaps we should evaluate projections based upon their intrinsic value. For instance, coming into 2009, would it have been more important for me to tell you that Adam Dunn was going to hit 40 HRs or that Aaron Hill would hit 25 home runs? By season's end, the Dunn projection would have been more accurate, but the Hill projection — even though it was off by 11 HR — would have been far more *valuable*.

And that should be enough. Actually, it *has* to be enough. Any tout who exactly projects any player's statistics dead-on will have just been lucky with his dart throws that day.

About Us Touts

As a group, there is a strong tendency for all pundits to provide numbers that are more palatable than realistic. That's because committing to either end of the range of expectation poses a high risk. Few touts possess the courage to put their credibility on the line like that, even though we all know that those outliers are inevitable. So they take the easy road and just split the difference. I am a member of that group and I can say that we are cowards, all of us.

In the world of prognosticating, this is called the *comfort zone*. This represents the outer tolerances for the public acceptability of a set of numbers. In most circumstances, even if the evidence is outstanding, prognosticators will not stray from within the comfort zone.

As for me, occasionally I do commit to outlying numbers when I feel the data supports it. But on the whole, most of my numbers can be nearly as cowardly as everyone else's. I get around this by providing "color" to the projections in the capsule commentaries. That is where you will find the players whose projection has the best potential to stray beyond the limits of the comfort zone.

As analyst John Burnson once wrote: "The issue is not the success rate for one player, but the success rate for all players. No system is 100% reliable, and in trying to capture the outliers, you weaken the middle and thereby lose more predictive pull than you gain. At some level, everyone is an exception!"

And Just So You Know

We began the conversation about component skills analysis right here in 1993, in the sixth edition of the *Baseball Forecaster*. The LIMA Plan in 1998 pioneered the application of these concepts for fantasy baseball. Since then, we continue to further the discussion, enhancing and refining the process of winning with such tools as Pure Quality Starts and strategies such as the Portfolio3 Plan and now the Mayberry Method.

Thanks to the internet, its community of sharing and the easy dissemination of information, other sources have picked up on the power of these tools. When you see things like contact rate and strand rate cited elsewhere, know that the research and application of these gauges originated *here*, whether these other services provide fair attribution or have adopted the concepts as their own. But the source of the original thought, and the place that continues to pioneer innovative new ideas, is the *Baseball Forecaster* and BaseballHQ.com. This is where you stay ahead of the curve.

For a deeper discussion about my take on baseball forecasting, read "The Great Myths of Projective Accuracy" online at
http://www.baseballhq.com/books/myths.shtml

Forecaster's Toolbox

The following tools, rules and research findings represent the work of many authors, from industry icons like Bill James to the analysts at Baseball HQ.

There are two types of information here. There are analytical tools, which are methods to put events and performances into context. And there are actual research results. Generally, we only include the results of each particular piece of research, rather than take up space with all the methodologies and minutia. The back-up data have appeared in our other publications and on Baseball HQ in the past, and are now being updated regularly. Our purpose here is to give you the tools you need to make evaluations, and quickly. So pardon the lack of support data. Rest assured we're not making this stuff up.

Be aware that these research findings represent tendencies, not absolutes. If we tell you that 96% of batters with eye ratios greater than 1.50 will hit over .250, don't send us hate mail if the former batting champion you drafted in the second round falls into the other 4%. It happens. It's not our fault. Consider this a universal disclaimer.

Beyond that, there is great value here. Consider this your own fanalytic arsenal.

Validating Overall Performance

Performance Validation Criteria

The following is a set of support variables that helps determine whether a player's statistical output is an accurate reflection of his skills. From this we can validate or refute stats that vary from expectation, essentially asking, is this performance "fact or fluke?"

1. Age... Is the player at the stage of development when we might expect a change in performance?

2. Health status... Is he coming off an injury, reconditioned and healthy for the first time in years, or a habitual resident of the disabled list?

3. Minor league performance... Has he ever shown the potential for greater things at some level of the minors? Or does his minor league history show a poor skill set that might indicate a lower skills ceiling?

4. Historical trends... Have his skill levels over time been on an upswing or downswing?

5. Hidden indicators behind traditional stats... Looking beyond batting averages and ERAs, what do his support ratios look like?

6. Ballpark, team, league... Pitchers going to Texas will see their ERA spike. Pitchers going to Petco Park will see their ERA improve.

7. Team performance... Has a player's performance been affected by overall team chemistry or the environment fostered by a winning or losing club?

8. Batting stance, pitching style... Has a change in performance been due to an adjustment made during the off-season?

9. Usage pattern, lineup position, role.... Has a change in RBI opportunities been a result of moving further up or down in the batting order? Has pitching effectiveness been impacted by moving from the bullpen to the rotation? Does he have an undefined role?

10. Coaching effects... Has the coaching staff changed the way a player approaches his conditioning, or how he approaches the game itself?

11. Off-season activity... Has a player spent the winter frequenting workout rooms or banquet tables?

12. Personal factors... Has the player undergone a family crisis? Experienced spiritual rebirth? Given up red meat? Taken up testosterone?

Skills Ownership

Once a player displays a skill, he owns it. That display could occur at any time – earlier in his career, back in the minors, or even in winter ball play. And while that skill may lie dormant after its initial display, the potential is always there for him to tap back into that skill at some point, barring injury or age. That dormant skill can reappear at any time given the right set of circumstances.

Caveat... The initial display of skill must have occurred over an extended period of time. An isolated 1-hit shut-out in Single-A ball amidst a 5.00 ERA season is not enough. The shorter the display of skill in the past, the more likely it can be attributed to random chance. The longer the display, the more likely that any re-emergence is for real.

Corollaries:

1. Once a player displays a vulnerability or skills deficiency, he owns that as well. That vulnerability could be an old injury problem, an inability to hit breaking pitches, or just a tendency to go into prolonged slumps.

2. The probability of a player addressing and correcting a skills deficiency declines with each year he allows that deficiency to continue to exist.

Categories of Surprises

When a player has an uncharacteristically good or bad season, the likelihood of a repeat can be assessed by categorizing the performance.

Career year: Players who have established a certain level of performance over several years, then suddenly put up exceptional numbers. Career years may be explained from the list of validation criteria, but are usually one-shot deals.

Maturation: Players who have also established a certain level of performance over time, but the performance spike is truly indicative of a positive change in skills and will likely be maintained.

Off year: Players who have an established performance level, then suddenly drop off. This could be an anomaly, an adjustment period or caused by an injury. These players have the potential to bounce back.

Comedown: Players with an established performance level whose drop is indicative of a new level at which they will likely plateau.

Opportunity: Players whose rise or decline is not related to skill but to a change in playing time. Often, a role player moves into a full-time job and experiences a marked change in productivity. This can work both ways — he may rise to the occasion, or find that the regular day-to-day grind has an adverse effect on his numbers. Opportunity surprises are created by events like injuries or changes in managerial strategy and can last as long as the opportunity lasts.

No surprise: Players whose rise or decline might have been anticipated. We often form unrealistic expectations about players due to media hype or small samples of past performance, such as with rookies and injured players. The success or failure of unknown, untested or unproven commodities should not be unexpected.

Aberration: Players whose performances cannot be adequately explained by the validation criteria. Chance occurrences do happen. There are stretches in a player's career when a spray hitter might see a few week's worth of fat, juicy homer balls, or a pitcher might face a string of wiffle bats. It just happens, then it stops. Most times, it will never happen again.

Contract Year Performance *(Tom Mullooly)*

There is a contention that players step up their game when they are playing for a contract. Research looked at contract year players and their performance during that year as compared to career levels. Of the batters and pitchers studied, 53% of the batters performed as if they were on a salary drive, while only 15% of the pitchers exhibited some level of contract year behavior.

How do players fare *after* signing a large contract (minimum $4 million per year)? Research from 2005-2008 revealed that only 30% of pitchers and 22% of hitters exhibited an increase of more than 15% in base performance values after signing a large deal either with their new team, or re-signing with the previous team. But nearly half of the pitchers (49%) and nearly half of the hitters (47%) saw a drop in BPV of more than 15% in the year after signing.

Risk Management and Reliability Grades

Forecasts are constructed with the best data available, but there are factors that can impact the variability around that projection. One way we manage this risk is to assign each player Reliability Grades. The more certainty we see in a data set, the higher the reliability grades assigned to that player. The following variables are evaluated:

Health: Players with a history of staying healthy and off the disabled list are valuable to own. Unfortunately, while the ability to stay healthy can be considered skill, it is not very projectable. We can track the number of days spent on the disabled list and draw only rough conclusions. The grades in the player boxes also include an adjustment for older players, who have a higher likelihood of getting hurt. That is the only forward-looking element of the grade.

"A" level players would have accumulated fewer than 30 days on the Major League DL over the past five years. "F" grades go to those who've spent more than 120 days on the DL. Recent DL stays are given a heavier weight in the calculation.

Playing Time and Experience (PT/Exp): The greater the pool of Major League history to draw from, the greater our ability to construct a viable forecast. Length of service is important, as is length of consistent service. So players who bounce up and down from the Majors to the minors are higher risk players. And rookies are all high risk.

For batters, we simply track plate appearances. Major league PAs have greater weight than minor league PAs. "A" level players would have averaged at least 550 major league PA per year over the past three years. "F" graded players averaged fewer than 250 major league PA per year.

For pitchers, workload can be a double-edged sword. On one hand, small IP samples are deceptive in providing a read on a pitcher's true potential. Even a consistent 65-inning reliever can be considered higher risk; just one bad outing can skew an entire year's work.

On the flipside, high workload levels also need to be monitored, especially in the formative years of a pitcher's career. Exceeding those levels elevates the risk of injury, burnout, or breakdown. So, tracking workload must be done within a range of innings. The grades capture this.

Consistency: Consistent performers are easier to project and garner higher reliability grades. Players that mix mediocrity with occasional flashes of brilliance or badness generate higher risk projections. Even those who exhibit a consistent upward or downward trend cannot be considered truly consistent as we do not know whether those trends will continue.

"A" level players are those whose runs created per game level (xERA for pitchers) has fluctuated by less than half a run during each of the past three years. "F" grades go to those whose RC/G has fluctuated by two runs or more.

Remember that these grades have nothing to do with *quality* of performance; they strictly refer to confidence in our expectations. So a grade of **AAA** for Livan Hernandez, for instance, only means that there is a high probability he will perform as poorly as we've projected.

Reliability and Experience

Peak batting reliability occurs at ages 29 and 30, followed by a minor decline for four years. So, to draft the most reliable batters, and maximize the odds of returning at least par value on your investments, you should target the age range of 28-34.

The most reliable age range for pitchers is 29-34. While we are forever looking for "sleepers" and hot prospects, it is very risky to draft any pitcher under 27 or over 35.

Spring Training Spin *(Dave Adler)*

Spring training sound bites raise expectations among fantasy leaguers, but how much of that "news" is really "noise?" Thanks to a summary listed at RotoAuthority.com, we were able to compile the stats for 2009. Verdict: Noise.

BATTERS	No.	IMPROVED	DECLINED
Weight change	30	33%	30%
Fitness program	3	0%	67%
Eye surgery	6	50%	33%
Plans more SB	6	17%	33%

PITCHERS	No.	IMPROVED	DECLINED
Weight change	18	44%	44%
Fitness program	4	50%	50%
Eye surgery	2	0%	50%
New pitch	5	60%	40%

IN-SEASON ANALYSIS

April Performance as a Leading Indicator

We isolated all players who earned at least $10 more or $10 less than we had projected in March. Then we looked at the April stats of these players to see if we could have picked out the $10 outliers after just one month.

	Identifiable in April
Earned $10+ more than projected	
BATTERS	39%
PITCHERS	44%
Earned -$10 less than projected	
BATTERS	56%
PITCHERS	74%

Nearly three out of every four pitchers who earned at least $10 less than projected also struggled in April. For all the other surprises — batters or pitchers — April was not a strong leading indicator. Another look:

	Pct.
Batters who finished +$25	45%
Pitchers who finished +$20	44%
Batters who finished under $0	60%
Pitchers who finished under -$5	78%

April surgers are less than a 50/50 proposition to maintain that level all season. Those who finished April at the bottom of the roto rankings were more likely to continue struggling, especially pitchers. In fact, of those pitchers who finished April with a value *under -$10*, 91% finished the season in the red. Holes are tough to dig out of.

Courtship Period

Any time a player is put into a new situation, he enters into what we might call a *courtship period*. This period might occur when a player switches leagues, or switches teams. It could be the first few games when a minor leaguer is called up. It could occur when a reliever moves into the rotation, or when a lead-off hitter is moved to another spot in the lineup. There is a team-wide courtship period when a manager is replaced. Any external situation that could affect a player's performance sets off a new decision point in evaluating that performance.

During this period, it is difficult to get a true read on how a player is going to ultimately perform. He is adjusting to the new situation. Things could be volatile during this time. For instance, a role change that doesn't work could spur other moves. A rookie hurler might buy himself a few extra starts with a solid debut, even if he has questionable skills.

It is best not to make a decision on a player who is going through a courtship period. Wait until his stats stabilize. Don't cut a struggling pitcher in his first few starts after a managerial change. Don't pick up a hitter who smacks a pair of HRs in his first game after having been traded. Unless, of course, talent and track record say otherwise.

Half-Season Fallacies

A popular exercise at the midpoint of each season is to analyze those players who are *consistent* first half to second half surgers or faders. There are several fallacies with this analytical approach.

1. Half-season consistency is rare. There are very few players who show consistent changes in performance from one half of the season to the other.

Research results from a three-year study conducted in the late-1990s: The test groups... batters with min. 300 AB full season, 150 AB first half, and pitchers with min. 100 IP full season, 50 IP first half. Of those groups (size noted):

3-year consistency in	BATTERS (98)	PITCHERS (42)
1 stat category	40%	57%
2 stat categories	18%	21%
3 stat categories	3%	5%

When the analysis was stretched to a fourth year, only 1% of all players showed consistency in even one category.

2. Analysts often use false indicators. Situational statistics provide us with tools that can be misused. Several sources offer up three and 5-year stats intended to paint a picture of a long-term performance. Some analysts look at a player's half-season swing over that multi-year period and conclude that he is demonstrating consistent performance.

The fallacy is that those multi-year scans may not show any consistency at all. They are not individual season performances but *aggregate* performances. A player whose 5-year batting average shows a 15-point rise in the 2nd half, for instance, may actually have experienced a BA *decline* in several of those years, a fact that might have been offset by a huge BA rise in one of the years.

3. It's arbitrary. The season's midpoint is an arbitrary delineator of performance swings. Some players are slow starters and might be more appropriately evaluated as pre-May 1 and post-May 1. Others bring their game up a notch with a pennant chase and might see a performance swing with August 15 as the cut-off. Each player has his own individual tendency, if, in fact, one exists at all. There's nothing magical about mid-season as the break point, and certainly not over a multi-year period.

Batting Toolbox

Batting Eye as a Leading Indicator

There is a strong correlation between strike zone judgment and batting average. However, research shows that this is more descriptive than predictive:

	Batting Average				
Batting Eye	**2005**	**2006**	**2007**	**2008**	**2009**
0.00 - 0.25	.244	.251	.250	.242	.239
0.26 - 0.50	.261	.267	.265	.261	.259
0.51 - 0.75	.274	.279	.276	.273	.272
0.76 - 1.00	.279	.286	.280	.280	.274
1.01 and over	.290	.287	.305	.285	.292

We can create percentage plays for the different levels:

For Eye	Pct who bat	
Levels of	**.300+**	**.250-**
0.00 - 0.25	7%	39%
0.26 - 0.50	14%	26%
0.51 - 0.75	18%	17%
0.76 - 1.00	32%	14%
1.01 - 1.50	51%	9%
1.51 +	59%	4%

Any batter with an eye ratio more than 1.50 has about a 4% chance of hitting less than .250 over 500 at bats.

Of all .300 hitters, those with ratios of at least 1.00 have a 65% chance of repeating as .300 hitters. Those with ratios less than 1.00 have less than a 50% chance of repeating.

Only 4% of sub-.250 hitters with ratios less than 0.50 will mature into .300 hitters the following year.

In a 1995-2000 study, only 37 batters hit .300-plus with a sub-0.50 eye ratio over at least 300 AB in a season. Of this group, 30% were able to accomplish this feat on a consistent basis. For the other 70%, this was a short-term aberration.

Contact Rate as a Leading Indicator

The more often a batter makes contact with the ball, the higher the likelihood that he will hit safely.

	Batting Average				
Contact Rate	**2005**	**2006**	**2007**	**2008**	**2009**
0% - 60%	.207	.181	.204	.210	.189
61% - 65%	.221	.220	.228	.226	.229
66% - 70%	.244	.251	.237	.235	.241
71% - 75%	.252	.256	.250	.250	.247
76% - 80%	.266	.270	.269	.262	.263
81% - 85%	.270	.274	.277	.273	.275
86% - 90%	.279	.287	.284	.284	.281
Over 90%	.282	.295	.289	.285	.287

Contact Rate & Walk Rate as Leading Indicators

A matrix of contact rates and walk rates can provide expectation benchmarks for a player's batting average:

		bb%			
		0-5	**6-10**	**11-15**	**16+**
ct%	**65-**	.179	.195	.229	.237
	66-75	.190	.248	.254	.272
	76-85	.265	.267	.276	.283
	86+	.269	.279	.301	.309

A contact rate of 65% or lower offers virtually no chance for a player to hit even .250, no matter how high a walk rate he has. The .300 hitters most often come from the group with a minimum 86% contact and 11% walk rate.

Hit Rate (BABIP) as a Leading Indicator

(Patrick Davitt)

Every hitter establishes his own individual hit rate (batting average on balls-in-play) that stabilizes over time. A batter whose seasonal hit rate (H%) varies significantly from the H% he has established over the preceding three seasons is likely to improve or regress to his individual H% mean (with over-performer declines more likely and sharper than under-performer recoveries). Three-year H% levels strongly predict a player's H% the following year.

Power Breakouts

It is not easy to predict which batters will experience a power spike. We can categorize power breakouts to determine the likelihood of a player taking a step up or of a surprise performer repeating his feat. Possibilities:

- Increase in playing time
- History of power skills at some time in the past
- Redistribution of already demonstrated extra base hit power
- Normal skills growth
- Situational breakouts, particularly in hitter-friendly venues
- Increased fly ball tendency
- Use of illegal performance-enhancing substances
- Miscellaneous unexplained variables

Fly Ball Tendency and Power *(Mat Olkin)*

There is a proven connection between a hitter's ground ball-fly ball tendencies and his power production.

1. Extreme ground ball hitters generally do not hit for much power. It's almost impossible for a hitter with a ground/fly ratio over 1.80 to hit enough fly balls to produce even 25 HRs in a season. However, this does not mean that a low G/F ratio necessarily guarantees power production. Some players have no problem getting the ball into the air, but lack the strength to reach the fences consistently.

2. Most batters' ground/fly ratios stay pretty steady over time. Most year-to-year changes are small and random, as they are in any other statistical category. A large, sudden change in G/F, on the other hand, can signal a conscious change in plate approach. And so...

3. If a player posts high G/F ratios in his first few years, he probably isn't ever going to hit for all that much power.

4. When a batter's power suddenly jumps, his G/F ratio often drops at the same time.

5. Every so often, a hitter's ratio will drop significantly even as his power production remains level. In these rare cases, impending power development is likely, since the two factors almost always follow each other.

HR/F Rate as a Leading Indicator *(Joshua Randall)*

Each batter establishes an individual home run to fly ball rate that stabilizes over rolling three-year periods; those levels strongly predict the HR/F in the subsequent year. A batter who varies significantly from his HR/F is likely to regress toward his individual HR/F mean, with over-performance decline more likely and more severe than under-performance recovery.

Handedness Notes

1. While pure southpaws account for about 27% of total ABs (RHers about 55% and switch-hitters about 18%), they hit 31% of the triples and take 30% of the walks.

2. The average lefty posts a batting average about 10 points higher than the average RHer. The on base averages of pure LHers are nearly 20 points higher than RHers, but only 10 points higher than switch-hitters.

3. LHers tend to have a better batting eye ratio than RHers, but about the same as switch-hitters.

4. Pure righties and lefties have virtually identical power skills. Switch-hitters tend to have less power, on average.

5. Switch-hitters tend to have the best speed, followed by LHers, and then RHers.

6. On an overall production basis, LHers have an 8% advantage over RHers and a 14% edge over switch-hitters.

Batting Average Perception

Early season batting average strugglers who surge later in the year get no respect because they have to live with the weight of their early numbers all season long. Conversely, quick starters who fade late get far more accolades than they deserve.

For instance, take Raul Ibanez's 2009 month-by-month batting averages. Perception, which is typically based solely on a player's cumulative season stat line, was that he batted more than .300 for most of the year. Reality is different. He had one truly outstanding month, and it happened to occur in April. How many people knew he batted .256 from May 1 on and .232 in the second half?

Month	BA	Cum BA
April	.359	.359
May	.312	.332
June	.254	.312
July	.258	.301
August	.193	.278
Sept-October	.250	.272

Wasted Talent on the Basepaths

We refer to some players as having "wasted talent," a high level skill that is negated by a deficiency in another skill. Among these types are players who have blazing speed that is negated by a sub-.300 on base average.

These players can have short-term value. However, their stolen base totals are tied so tightly to their "green light" that any change in managerial strategy could completely erase that value. A higher OB mitigates that downside; the good news is that plate patience *can* be taught.

Players in 2009 who had at least 20 SBs with an OB less than .300, and whose SB output could be at risk, are Jimmy Rollins (31 SB, .296), Alex Rios (24, .292), Josh Anderson (25, .274) and Wily Tavares (25, .273).

Spring Training Leading Indicator *(John Dewan)*

A positive difference between a hitter's spring training slugging pct. and his lifetime slugging pct. of .200 or more is a leading indicator for a better than normal season.

Optimal Ages

Players develop at different paces, but in general terms, age can be helpful to determine where they should be along the developmental curve. Bill James' original research showed that batters tended to peak at about age 27. More recent research suggests that a variety of factors have pushed that average up closer to 30. More tendencies:

"26 With Experience" *(John Benson):* While batters may peak at about age 27, the players most likely to exhibit the most dramatic spike in performance are those aged 26 who have several years of major league experience.

Power: Batting power tends to grow consistently between 24 and 29. Many batters experience a power peak at about 30-31. Catchers often see a power spike in the mid-30's.

Speed: Base-running and speed are skills of the young. When given the choice of two speedsters of equivalent abilities and opportunity, always go after the younger one. A sharp drop-off in speed skills typically occurs at age 34.

Batting eye: For batters who continue to play into their 30's, this is a skill that can develop and grow throughout their career. A decline in this level, which can occur at any age, often indicates a decline in overall skills.

Thirtysomethings *(Ed Spaulding):* Batters tend to lose points on their BA but draw more walks. While players on the outside of the defensive spectrum (1B, 3B, LF, RF, DH) often have their best seasons in their 30's, players in the middle (2B, SS, CF) tend to fade. Many former stars move to new positions (Ripken, Molitor, Banks, etc.).

Catchers *(Ed Spaulding):* Many catchers — particularly second line catchers — have their best seasons late in their careers. Some possible reasons why:

1. Catchers, like shortstops, often get to the big leagues for defensive reasons and not their offensive skills. These skills take longer to develop.

2. The heavy emphasis on learning the catching/defense/pitching side of the game detracts from their time to learn about, and practice, hitting.

3. Injuries often curtail their ability to show offensive skills, though these injuries (typically jammed fingers, bruises on the arms, rib injuries from collisions) often don't lead to time on the disabled list.

4. The time spent behind the plate has to impact the ability to recognize, and eventually hit, all kinds of pitches.

Projecting Batting Breakout Performances
(Brandon Kruse)

A breakout performance is defined here as one where a player posts a Rotisserie value of $20 or higher after having never posted a value of $10 previously. These criteria are primarily used to validate an apparent breakout in the current season but may also be used carefully to project a potential breakout for an upcoming season.

- Age 27 or younger.
- An increase in at least two of: H%, PX or SX.
- Minimum league average PX or SX (100)
- Minimum contact rate of 75%
- Minimum xBA of .270

Projecting Runs Batted In (*Patrick Davitt*)

Evaluating players in-season for RBI potential is a function of the interplay among four factors:

- Teammates' ability to reach base ahead of him and to run the bases efficiently
- His own ability to drive them in by hitting, especially XBH
- Number of Games Played
- Place in the batting order

3-4-5 Hitters:
(0.69 x GP x TOB) + (0.30 x ITB) + (0.275 x HR) − (.191 x GP)

6-7-8 Hitters:
(0.63 x GP x TOB) + (0.27 x ITB) + (0.250 x HR) − (.191 x GP)

9-1-2 Hitters:
(0.57 x GP x TOB) + (0.24 x ITB) + (0.225 x HR) − (.191 x GP)

...where GP = games played, TOB = team on-base pct. and ITB = individual total bases (ITB).

Apply this pRBI formula after 70 games played or so (to reduce the variation from small sample size) to find players more than 9 RBI's over or under their projected RBI. There could be a correction coming.

You should also consider other factors, like injury or trade (involving the player or a top-of-the-order speedster) or team SB philosophy and success rate.

Remember: the player himself has an impact on his TOB. When we first did this study, we excluded the player from his TOB and got better results. The formula overestimates projected RBI for players with high OBP who skew his teams' OBP but can't benefit in RBI from that effect.

Dollar Values by Lineup Position (*Michael Roy*)

How much value is derived from batting order position?

Pos	PA	R	RBI	R$
#1	747	107	72	$18.75
#2	728	102	84	$19.00
#3	715	95	100	$19.45
#4	698	93	104	$19.36
#5	682	86	94	$18.18
#6	665	85	82	$17.19
#7	645	81	80	$16.60
#8	623	78	80	$16.19
#9	600	78	73	$15.50

So, a batter moving from the bottom of the order to the clean-up spot, with no change in performance, would gain nearly $4 in value from runs and RBIs alone.

Starting Pitcher Toolbox
Fundamental Skills

Unreliable pitching performance is a fallacy driven by the practice of attempting to project pitching stats using gauges that are poor evaluators of skill.

How can we better evaluate pitching skill? We can start with the three statistical categories that are generally unaffected by external factors. These three stats capture the outcome of an individual pitcher versus batter match-up without regard to supporting offense, defense or bullpen:

Walks Allowed, Strikeouts and Ground Balls

Even with only these stats to observe, there is a wealth of insight that these measures can provide.

Command Ratio as a Leading Indicator

The ability to get the ball over the plate — command of the strike zone — is one of the best leading indicators for future performance. Command ratio (K/BB) can be used to project potential in ERA as well as other skills gauges.

1. Research indicates that there is a high correlation between a pitcher's Cmd ratio and his ERA.

	Earned Run Average				
Command	**2005**	**2006**	**2007**	**2008**	**2009**
0.0 - 1.0	6.22	6.42	6.48	7.00	6.43
1.1 - 1.5	4.93	5.06	5.12	5.07	5.10
1.6 - 2.0	4.41	4.65	4.58	4.60	4.41
2.1 - 2.5	4.28	4.48	4.28	3.96	4.19
2.6 - 3.0	3.60	4.15	3.89	3.89	3.70
3.1 and over	3.45	3.49	3.49	3.35	3.40

We can create percentage plays for the different levels:

For Cmd	Pct who post	
Levels of	**3.50-**	**4.50+**
0.0 - 1.0	0%	87%
1.1 - 1.5	7%	67%
1.6 - 2.0	7%	57%
2.1 - 2.5	19%	35%
2.6 - 3.0	26%	25%
3.1 +	53%	5%

Pitchers who maintain a Command of more than 2.5 have a high probability of long-term success. For fantasy drafting purposes, it is best to avoid pitchers with sub-2.0 ratios. Bullpen closers should be avoided if they have a ratio less than 2.5.

2. A pitcher's command in tandem with dominance (strikeout rate) provides even greater predictive abilities.

	Earned Run Average	
Command	**-5.6 Dom**	**5.6+ Dom**
0.0-0.9	5.36	5.99
1.0-1.4	4.94	5.03
1.5-1.9	4.67	4.47
2.0-2.4	4.32	4.08
2.5-2.9	4.21	3.88
3.0-3.9	4.04	3.46
4.0+	4.12	2.96

This helps to highlight the limited upside potential of soft-tossers with pinpoint control. The extra dominance makes a huge difference.

3. Research also suggests that there is a strong correlation between a pitcher's command ratio and his propensity to win ballgames. Over three quarters of those with ratios over 3.0 post winning records, and the collective W/L record of those command artists is nearly .600.

The command/winning correlation holds up in both leagues, although the effect was much more pronounced in the NL. Over four times more NL hurlers than AL hurlers have command ratios over 3.0, and it appears that higher command ratios are required in the NL to maintain good winning percentages. While a ratio between 2.0 and 2.9 might be good enough for a winning record for over 70% of AL pitchers, that level in the NL will generate an above-.500 mark only slightly more than half the time.

In short, in order to have at least a 70% chance of drafting a pitcher with a winning record, you must target NL pitchers with at least a 3.0 command ratio. To achieve the same odds in the AL, a 2.0 command ratio will suffice.

Strand Rate as a Leading Indicator (*Ed DeCaria*)

Strand Rate finds great utility in explaining variances between a pitcher's ERA and his performance indicators.

S% REGRESSION in YEAR 2

Y1 S%	RP	SP	LR
<60%	100%	94%	94%
65	81%	74%	88%
70	53%	48%	65%
75	55%	85%	100%
80	80%	100%	100%
85	100%	100%	100%

ERA REGRESSION in YEAR 2

Y1 S%	RP	SP	LR
<60%	-2.54	-2.03	-2.79
65	-1.00	-0.64	-0.93
70	-0.10	-0.05	-0.44
75	0.24	0.54	0.75
80	1.15	1.36	2.29
85	1.71	2.21	n/a

Starting pitchers (SP) have a narrower range of strand rate outcomes than do relievers (RP) or swingmen/long relievers (LR). **Relief pitchers** with Y1 strand rates of <=67% or >=78% are likely to experience a +/- ERA regression in Y2. **Starters and swingmen/long relievers** with Y1 strand rates of <=65% or >=75% are likely to experience a +/- ERA regression in Y2. Pitchers with strand rates that deviate more than a few points off of their individual expected strand rates are likely to experience some degree of ERA regression in Y2. Overperforming (or "lucky") pitchers are more likely than underperforming (or "unlucky") pitchers to see such a correction.

Hit Rate as a Leading Indicator (*Voros McCracken*)

In 2000, Voros McCracken published a study that concluded that "there is little if any difference among major league pitchers in their ability to prevent hits on balls hit in the field of play." His assertion was that, while a Johan Santana would have a better ability to prevent a batter from getting wood on a ball, or perhaps keeping the ball in the park, once that ball was hit in the field of play, the probability of it falling for a hit was virtually no different than for any other pitcher.

Among the findings in his study were:

- There is little correlation between what a pitcher does one year in the stat and what he will do the next. This is not true with other significant stats (BB, K, HR).
- You can better predict a pitcher's hits per balls in play from the rate of the rest of the pitcher's team than from the pitcher's own rate.

This last point brings a team's defense into the picture. It begs the question, when a batter gets a hit, is it because the pitcher made a bad pitch, the batter took a good swing, or the defense was not positioned correctly?

Pitchers will often post hit rates per balls-in-play that are far off from the league average, but then revert to the mean the following year. As such, we can use that mean – approximately 30% – in much the same way we use strand rate to project the direction of a pitcher's ERA.

Subsequent research has shown that ground ball or fly ball propensity may have a small impact on hit rate.

HR/FB Rate as a Leading Indicator (*John Burnson*)

McCracken's work focused on "balls in play," omitting home runs from the study. However, pitchers also do not have much control over the percentage of fly balls that turn into HR. Research shows that there is an underlying rate of HR as a percentage of fly balls of about 10%. A pitcher's HR/FB rate will vary each year but always tends to regress to that 10%. The element that pitchers *do* have control over is the number of fly balls they allow. That is the underlying skill or deficiency that controls their HR rate.

Pitchers who keep the ball out of the air more often correlate well with Roto value. The formula *(K + 0.3GB) / Batters Faced* provides a strong gauge for "air superiority."

Line Drive Pct. as a Leading Indicator (*Seth Samuels*)

Also beyond a pitcher's control is the percentage of balls-in-play that are line drives. Line drives do the most damage; from 1994-2003, here are the expected hit rates and number of total bases per type of BIP.

	Type of BIP		
	GB	FB	LD
H%	26%	23%	56%
Total bases	0.29	0.57	0.80

Despite the damage done by LDs, pitchers do not have any innate skill to avoid them. There is little relationship between a pitcher's LD% one year and his rate the next year. All rates tend to regress towards a mean of 22.6%.

However, ground ball pitchers do have a slight ability to prevent line drives (21.7%) and extreme ground ball hurlers even moreso (18.5%). Extreme fly ball pitchers have a slight ability to prevent LDs (21.1%) as well.

Ground Ball Tendency as a Leading Indicator
(*John Burnson*)

Ground ball pitchers tend to give up fewer HRs than do fly ball pitchers. There is also evidence that GB pitchers have higher hit rates. In other words, a ground ball has a higher chance of being a hit than does a fly ball that is not out of the park.

GB pitchers have lower strikeout rates. We should be more forgiving of a low strikeout rate (under 5.5 K/9) if it belongs to an extreme ground ball pitcher.

GB pitchers have a lower ERA than do fly ball pitchers but a higher WHIP. On balance, GB pitchers come out ahead, even when considering strikeouts, because a lower ERA also leads to more wins.

Groundball, Strikeout Tendencies as Indicators
(*Mike Dranchak*)

Pitchers were assembled into 9 groups based on the following profiles (minimum 23 starts in 2005):

Profile	Ground Ball Rate
Ground Ball	higher than 47%
Neutral	42% to 47%
Fly Ball	less than 42%

Profile	Strikeout Rate (k/9)
Strikeout	higher than 6.6 k/9
Average	5.4 to 6.6 k/9
Soft-Tosser	less than 5.4 k/9

Findings: Pitchers with higher strikeout rates had better ERA's and WHIPs than pitchers with lower strikeout rates, regardless of ground ball profile. However, for pitchers with similar strikeout rates, those with higher ground ball rates had better ERA's and WHIPs than those with lower ground ball rates.

Pitchers with higher strikeout rates tended to strand more baserunners than those with lower K rates. Fly ball pitchers tended to strand fewer runners than their GB or neutral counterparts within their strikeout profile.

Ground ball pitchers (especially those who lacked high-dominance) yielded more home runs per fly ball than did fly ball pitchers. However, the ERA risk was mitigated by the fact that ground ball pitchers (by definition) gave up fewer fly balls to begin with.

Skill versus Consistency

Two pitchers have identical 4.50 ERAs and identical 3.0 PQS averages. Their PQS logs look like this:

PITCHER A:	3	3	3	3	3
PITCHER B:	5	0	5	0	5

Which pitcher would you rather have on your team? The risk-averse manager would choose Pitcher A as he represents the perfectly known commodity. Many fantasy leaguers might opt for Pitcher B because his occasional dominating starts show that there is an upside. His Achilles Heel is inconsistency. Is there any hope for Pitcher B?

* If a pitcher's inconsistency is characterized by more poor starts than good starts, his upside is limited.
* Pitchers with extreme inconsistency rarely get a full season of starts.
* However, inconsistency is neither chronic nor fatal.

The outlook for Pitcher A is actually worse. Disaster avoidance might buy these pitchers more starts, but history shows that the lack of dominating outings is more telling of future potential. In short, consistent mediocrity is bad.

Usage Warning Flags

Research suggests that there is a finite number of innings in a pitcher's arm. This number varies by pitcher, by development cycle, and by pitching style and repertoire. We can measure a pitcher's potential for future arm problems and/or reduced effectiveness:

Sharp increases in usage from one year to the next... Any pitcher who increases his workload by 50 IP or more from year #1 to year #2 is a candidate for burnout symptoms in year #3. Increases of 100 IP or more are even more notable. Consider this list of 17 pitchers whose workloads increased by at least 100 IP from 2007 to 2008, and their performance in 2009. Nearly 90% fared poorly in '09.

Starters' overuse... Consistent "batters faced per game" (BF/G) levels of 28.0 or higher, combined with consistent seasonal IP totals of

PITCHER	IP incr	2009
Francisco Liriano	199	137 IP, 5.80 ERA
Dana Eveland	184	44 IP, 7.16 ERA
Ricky Nolasco	173	185 IP, 5.06 ERA
Glen Perkins	155	96 IP, 5.89 ERA
Brett Myers	141	71 IP, 4.84 ERA
Ryan Dempster	140	200 IP, 3.65 ERA
Brandon Backe	138	13 IP, 10.38 ERA
Randy Johnson	137	96 IP, 4.88 ERA
Rich Harden	132	141 IP, 4.09 ERA
Justin Duchscherer	128	0 IP
Glendon Rusch	125	19 IP, 6.75 ERA
Sidney Ponson	124	59 IP, 7.36 ERA
David Purcey	120	48 IP, 6.19 ERA
Darrell Rasner	119	0 IP
Todd Wellemeyer	113	122 IP, 5.89 ERA
Jonathan Sanchez	106	163 IP, 4.24 ERA
Brian Stokes	102	70 IP, 3.97 ERA

200 or more may indicate burnout potential. Within a season, a BF/G of more than 30.0 with a projected IP total of 200 may indicate a late season fade.

Relievers' overuse... Warning flags should be up for relievers who post in excess of 100 IP in a season, while averaging fewer than 2 IP per outing.

When focusing solely on minor league pitchers, research results are striking:

Stamina: Virtually every minor league pitcher who had a BF/G of 28.5 or more in one season experienced a drop-off in BF/G the following year. Many were unable to ever duplicate that previous level of durability.

Performance: Most pitchers experienced an associated drop-off in their BPVs in the years following the 28.5 BF/G season. Some were able to salvage their effectiveness later on by moving to the bullpen.

Optimal Ages

As with batters, pitchers develop at different rates, but a look at their age can help determine where they should be along the developmental curve. Here are some tendencies...

While peaks vary, most all pitchers (who are still around) tend to experience a sharp drop-off in their skills at age 38.

Thirtysomethings *(Ed Spaulding)*: Older pitchers, as they lose velocity and movement on the ball, must rely on more variety and better location. Thus, if strikeouts are a priority, you don't want many pitchers over 30. The over-30 set that tends to be surprising includes finesse types, career minor leaguers who break through for 2-3 seasons often in relief, and knuckleballers (a young knuckleballer is 31).

First Productive Season

(Michael Weddell)

To find those starting pitchers who are about to post their first productive season in the majors (10 wins, 150 IP, ERA of 4.00 or less), look for:

* Pitchers entering their ages 23-26 seasons, especially those about to pitch their age 25 season.
* Pitchers who already have good skills, shown by an xERA in the prior year of 4.25 or less.
* Pitchers coming off of at least a partial season in the majors without a major health problem.
* To the extent that one speculates on pitchers who are one skill away, look for pitchers who only need to improve their control (bb/9).

Projecting Pitching Breakout Performances *(Brandon Kruse)*

A breakout performance is defined here as one where a player posts a Rotisserie value of $20 or higher after having never posted a value of $10 previously. These criteria are primarily used to validate an apparent breakout in the current season but may also be used carefully to project a potential breakout for an upcoming season.

- Age 27 or younger
- Minimum 5.6 Dom, 2.0 Cmd, 1.1 hr/9 and 50 BPV
- Maximum 30% hit rate
- Minimum 71% strand rate
- Starters should have a hit rate no greater than the previous year's hit rate. Relievers should show improved command
- Maximum xERA of 4.00

Career Year Drop-off *(Rick Wilton)*

Research shows that a pitcher's post-career year drop-off, on average, looks like this...

- ERA increases by 1.00
- WHIP increases by 0.14.
- Nearly 6 fewer wins

Protecting Young Pitchers *(Craig Wright)*

There is a link between some degree of eventual arm trouble and a history of heavy workloads in a pitcher's formative years. Some recommendations from this research:

Teenagers (A-ball): No 200 IP seasons and no BF/G over 28.5 in any 150 IP span. No starts on three days rest.

Ages 20-22: Average no more than 105 pitches per start with a single game ceiling of 130 pitches.

Ages 23-24: Average no more than 110 pitches per start with a single game ceiling of 140 pitches.

When possible, a young starter should be introduced to the majors in long relief before he goes into the rotation.

Catchers' Effect on Pitching *(Thomas Hanrahan)*

A typical catcher handles a pitching staff better after having been with a club for a few years. Research has shown that there is an improvement in team ERA of approximately 0.37 runs from a catcher's rookie season to his prime years with a club. Expect a pitcher's ERA to be higher than expected if he is throwing to a rookie backstop.

Handedness Notes

1. LHers tend to peak about a year after RHers.
2. LHers post only 15% of the total saves. Typically, LHers are reserved for specialist roles so few are frontline closers.
3. RHers have slightly better command and HR rate.
4. There is no significant variance in ERA.
5. On an overall basis, RHers have about a 6% advantage.

IN-SEASON ANALYSIS
Pitching Streaks

It is possible to find predictive value in strings of DOMinating (PQS 4/5) or DISaster (PQS 0/1) starts:

Once a pitcher enters into a DOM streak of any length, the probability is that his subsequent start is going to be a better-than-average outing. The further a player is into a DOM streak, the *higher the likelihood* that the subsequent performance will be of high quality. In fact, once a pitcher has posted six DOM starts in a row, there is greater than a 70% probability that the streak will continue. When it does end, there is less than a 10% probability that the streak-breaker is going to be a DISaster.

Once a pitcher enters into a DIS streak of any length, the probability is that his next start is going to be below average, even if it breaks the streak. However, DIS streaks end quickly. Once a pitcher hits the skids, odds are low for him to start posting good numbers in the short term, though the duration of the plummet itself should be brief.

Pitch Counts as a Leading Indicator

Long-term analysis of workload is an ongoing science. However, there have also been questions whether we can draw any conclusions from short-term trends. For this analysis, all pitching starts from 2005-2006 were isolated — looking at pitch counts and PQS scores — and compared side-by-side with each pitcher's subsequent outing. We examined two-start trends, the immediate impact that the length of one performance would have on the next start.

| | | NEXT | START | | |
Pitch Ct	Pct.	PQS	DOM	DIS	qERA
< 80	13%	2.5	33%	28%	4.90
80-89	14%	2.6	35%	29%	4.82
90-99	28%	2.7	37%	26%	4.82
100-109	30%	2.9	41%	23%	4.56
110-119	13%	3.1	46%	18%	4.40
120+	3%	3.0	43%	20%	4.56

There does appear to be merit to the concern over limiting hurlers to 120 pitches per start. The research shows a slight drop-off in performance in those starts following a 120+ pitch outing. However, the impact does not appear to be all that great and the fallout might just affect those pitchers who have no business going that deep into games anyway. Additional detail to this research (not displayed) showed that higher-skilled pitchers were more successful throwing over 120 pitches but less-skilled pitchers were not.

Days of Rest as a Leading Indicator

Workload is only part of the equation. The other part is how often a pitcher is sent out to the mound. For instance, it's possible that a hurler might see no erosion in skill after a 120+ pitch outing if he had enough rest between starts.

| PITCH COUNTS | | NEXT | START | | |
Three days rest	Pct.	PQS	DOM	DIS	qERA
< 100	72%	2.8	35%	17%	4.60
100-119	28%	2.3	44%	44%	5.21
Four Days rest					
< 100	52%	2.7	36%	27%	4.82
100-119	45%	2.9	42%	22%	4.56
120+	3%	3.0	42%	20%	4.44
Five Days rest					
< 100	54%	2.7	38%	25%	4.79
100-119	43%	3.0	44%	19%	4.44
120+	3%	3.2	48%	14%	4.28
Six Days rest					
< 100	58%	2.7	39%	30%	5.00
100-119	40%	2.8	40%	26%	4.82
120+	3%	1.8	20%	60%	7.98
20+ Days rest					
< 100	85%	1.8	20%	46%	6.12
100-119	15%	2.3	33%	33%	5.08

Managers are reluctant to put a starter on the mound with any fewer than four days rest, and the results for those who pitched deeper into games shows why. Four days rest is the most common usage pattern and even appears to mitigate the drop-off at 120+ pitches.

Perhaps most surprising is that an extra day of rest improves performance across the board and squeezes even more productivity out of the 120+ pitch outings.

Performance begins to erode at six days (and continues at 7-20 days, though those are not displayed). The 20+ Days chart represents pitchers who were primarily injury rehabs and failed call-ups, and the length of the "days rest" was occasionally well over 100 days. This chart shows the result of their performance in their first start back. The good news is that the workload was limited for 85% of these returnees. The bad news is that these are not pitchers you want active. So for those who obsess over getting your DL returnees activated in time to catch every start, the better percentage play is to avoid that first outing.

Relief Pitcher Toolbox
Origin of Closers

History has long maintained that ace closers are not easily recognizable early on in their careers, so that every season does see its share of the unexpected. David Aardsma, Andrew Bailey, J.P. Howell, Mike MacDougal, Leo Nunez... who would have thought it a year ago?

Accepted facts, all of which have some element of truth:

* You cannot find major league closers from pitchers who were closers in the minors.
* Closers begin their careers as starters.
* Closers are converted set-up men.
* Closers are pitchers who were unable to develop a third effective pitch.

More simply, closers are a product of circumstance.

Are the minor leagues a place to look at all?

From 1990-2004, there were 280 twenty-save seasons in Double-A and Triple-A, accomplished by 254 pitchers.

Of those 254, only 46 ever made it to the majors at all.

Of those 46, only 13 ever saved 20 games in a season.

Of those 13, only 5 ever posted more than one 20-save season in the majors: John Wetteland, Mark Wohlers, Ricky Bottalico, Braden Looper and Francisco Cordero.

Five out of 254 pitchers, over 15 years, a rate of 2%.

One of the reasons that minor league closers rarely become major league closers is because, in general, they do not get enough innings in the minors to sufficiently develop their arms into big-league caliber.

In fact, organizations do not look at minor league closing performance seriously, assigning that role to pitchers who they do not see as legitimate prospects.

Year	Avg age of all AA and AAA pitchers who posted 20-plus saves
2005	28
2006	27
2007	28
2008	27
2009	27

Elements of Saves Success

The task of finding future closing potential comes down to looking at two elements:

Talent: The raw skills to mow down hitters for short periods of time. Optimal BPVs over 100, but not under 75.

Opportunity: The more important element, yet the one that pitchers have no control over.

There are pitchers that have *Talent, but not Opportunity.* These pitchers are not given a chance to close for a variety of reasons (e.g. being blocked by a solid front-liner in the pen, being left-handed, etc.), but are good to own because they will not likely hurt your pitching staff. You just can't count on them for saves, at least not in the near term.

There are pitchers that have *Opportunity, but not Talent.* MLB managers decide who to give the ball to in the 9th inning based on their own perceptions about what skills are required to succeed, even if those perceived "skills" don't translate into acceptable BPI levels. Those pitchers without the BPIs may have some initial short-term success, but their long-term prognosis is poor and they are high risks to your roster. Classic examples of the short life span of these types of pitchers include Matt Karchner, Heath Slocumb, Ryan Kohlmeier, Dan Miceli and Danny Kolb.

BPV as a Leading Indicator *(Doug Dennis)*

Research has shown that base performance value (BPV) is an excellent indicator of long-term success as a closer. Here are 20-plus saves seasons, by year:

Year	No.	B P V (Pct.) 100+	75+	<75
1999	26	27%	54%	46%
2000	24	25	54	46
2001	25	56	80	20
2002	25	60	72	28
2003	25	36	64	36
2004	23	61	61	39
2005	25	36	64	36
2006	25	52	72	28
2007	23	52	74	26
MEAN	**25**	**45**	**66**	**34**

Though 20-saves success with a 75+ BPV is only a 66% percentage play in any given year, the below-75 group is composed of closers who are rarely able to repeat the feat in the following season:

Year	No. with BPV < 75	No. who followed up 20+ saves <75 BPV
1999	12	2
2000	11	2
2001	5	2
2002	7	3
2003	9	3
2004	9	2
2005	9	1
2006	7	3
2007	6	0

Projecting Holds *(Doug Dennis)*

Here are some general rules of thumb for identifying pitchers who might be in line to accumulate Holds. The percentages represent the portion of 2003's top Holds leaders who fell into the category noted.

1. Left-handed set-up men with excellent BPIs. (43%)

2. A "go-to" right-handed set-up man with excellent BPIs. This is the one set-up RHer that a manager turns to with a small lead in the 7th or 8th innings. These pitchers also tend to vulture wins. (43%, but 6 of the top 9)

3. Excellent BPIs, but not a firm role as the main LHed or RHed set-up man. Roles change during the season; cream rises to the top. Relievers projected to post great BPIs often overtake lesser set-up men during the season. (14%)

Optimal Ages *(Rick Wilton)*

The first 20-save season for a relief ace arrives at about age 26. About three of every four relievers who begin a run of 20-save seasons in their 20's will likely sustain that level for about four years, with their value beginning to decline at the beginning of the third year.

Many aces achieve a certain level of maturity in their 30's and can experience a run of 20-save seasons between ages 33 and 36. For some, this may be their first time in the role of bullpen closer. However, those who achieve their first 20-save season after age 34 are unlikely to repeat.

Minor League Toolbox

Minor League Prospecting in Perspective

In our perpetual quest to be the genius who uncovers the next Albert Pujols when he is in A-ball, there is often an obsessive fascination with minor league prospects. That's not to say that prospecting is not important. The issue is one of perspective. Some rules:

1. Some prospects are going to hit the ground running (Ryan Braun) and some are going to immediately struggle (Alex Gordon), no matter what level of hype follows them.

2. Some prospects are going to start fast (since the league is unfamiliar with them) and then fade (as the league figures them out). Others will start slow (since they are unfamiliar with the opposition) and then improve (as they adjust to the competition). So if you make your free agent and roster decisions based on small early samples sizes, you are just as likely to be an idiot as a genius.

3. How any individual player will perform relative to his talent is largely unknown because there is a psychological element that is vastly unexplored. Some make the transition to the majors seamlessly, some not, completely regardless of how talented they are.

4. Still, talent is the best predictor of future success, so major league equivalent base performance indicators still have a valuable role in the process. As do scouting reports, carefully filtered.

5. Follow the player's path to the majors. Did he have to repeat certain levels? Was he allowed to stay at a level long enough to learn how to adjust to the level of competition? A player with only two great months at Double-A is a good

bet to struggle if promoted directly to the majors because he was never fully tested at Double-A, let alone Triple-A.

6. Younger players holding their own against older competition is a good thing. Older players reaching their physical peak, regardless of their current address, can be a good thing too. The Jorge Campillos and Ryan Ludwicks can have some very profitable years.

7. Remember team context. A prospect with superior potential often will not unseat a steady but unspectacular incumbent, especially one with a large contract.

8. Don't try to anticipate how a team is going to manage their talent, both at the major and minor league level. You might think it's time to promote Justin Smoak and give him an everyday role. You are not running the Rangers.

9. Those who play in shallow, one-year leagues should have little cause to be looking at the minors at all. The risk versus reward is so skewed against you, and there is so much talent available with a track record, that taking a chance on an unproven commodity makes no sense.

10. Decide where your priorities really are. If your goal is to win, prospect analysis is just a *part* of the process, not the entire process.

Factors Affecting Minor League Stats *(Terry Linhart)*

1. Often, there is an exaggerated emphasis on short-term performance in an environment that is supposed to focus on the long-term. Two poor outings don't mean a 21-year-old pitcher is washed up.

2. Ballpark dimensions and altitude create hitters parks and pitchers parks, but a factor rarely mentioned is that many parks in the lower minors are inconsistent in their field quality. Minor league clubs have limited resources to maintain field conditions, and this can artificially depress defensive statistics while inflating stats like batting average.

3. Some players' skills are so superior to the competition at their level that you can't get a true picture of what they're going to do from their stats alone.

4. Many pitchers are told to work on secondary pitches in unorthodox situations just to gain confidence in the pitch. The result is an artificially increased number of walks.

5. The #3, #4, and #5 pitchers in the lower minors are truly longshots to make the majors. They often possess only two pitches and are unable to disguise the off-speed offerings. Hitters can see inflated statistics in these leagues.

Minor League Level versus Age

When evaluating minor leaguers, look at the age of the prospect in relation to the median age of the league he is in:

Low level A	Between 19-20
Upper level A	Around 20
Double-A	21
Triple-A	22

These are the ideal ages for prospects at the particular level. If a prospect is younger than most and holds his own against older and more experienced players, elevate his status. If he is older than the median, reduce his status.

Triple-A Experience as a Leading Indicator

The probability that a minor leaguer will immediately succeed in the Majors can vary depending upon the level of Triple-A experience he has amassed at the time of call-up.

	BATTERS		PITCHERS	
	≤1 Yr	Full	≤1 Yr	Full
Performed well	57%	56%	16%	56%
Performed poorly	21%	38%	77%	33%
2nd half drop-off	21%	7%	6%	10%

The odds of a batter achieving immediate MLB success was slightly more than 50-50. More than 80% of all pitchers promoted with less than a full year at Triple-A struggled in their first year in the majors. Those pitchers with a year in Triple-A succeeded at a level equal to that of batters.

BPIs as a Leading Indicator for Pitching Success

The percentage of hurlers that were good investments in the year that they were called up varied by the level of their historical minor league BPIs *prior* to that year.

Pitchers who had:	Fared well	Fared poorly
Good indicators	79%	21%
Marginal or poor indicators	18%	82%

The data used here were MLE levels from the previous two years, not the season in which they were called up. The significance? Solid current performance is what merits a call-up, but this is not a good indicator of short-term MLB success, because a) the performance data set is too small, typically just a few month's worth of statistics, and b) for those putting up good numbers at a new minor league level, there has typically not been enough time for the scouting reports to make their rounds.

Minor League BPV as a Leading Indicator
(Al Melchior)

There is a link between minor league skill and how a pitching prospect will fare in his first 5 starts upon call-up.

	MLE BPV		
PQS Avg	≤ 50	50-99	100+
0.0-1.9	60%	28%	19%
2.0-2.9	32%	40%	29%
3.0-5.0	8%	33%	52%

Pitchers who demonstrate sub-par skills in the minors (sub-50 BPV) tend to fare poorly in their first big league starts. Three-fifths of these pitchers register a PQS average below 2.0, while only 8% average over 3.0.

Fewer than 1 out of 5 minor leaguers with a 100+ MLE BPV go on to post a sub-2.0 PQS average in their initial major league starts, but more than half average 3.0 or better.

Adjusting to the Competition

All players must "adjust to the competition" at every level of professional play. Players often get off to fast or slow starts. During their second tour at that level is when we get to see whether the slow starters have caught up or whether the league has figured out the fast starters. That second half "adjustment" period is a good baseline for projecting the subsequent season, in the majors or minors.

Premature major league call-ups often negate the ability for us to accurately evaluate a player due to the lack of this adjustment period. For instance, a hotshot Double-A player might open the season in Triple-A. After putting up solid numbers for a month, he gets a call to the bigs, and struggles. The fact is, we do not have enough evidence that the player has mastered the Triple-A level. We don't know whether the rest of the league would have caught up to him during his second tour of the league. But now he's labeled as an underperformer in the bigs when in fact he has never truly proven his skills at the lower levels.

Late Season Performance of Rookie SP *(Ray Murphy)*

Given that a rookie's second tour of the league provides insight as to future success, do rookie pitchers typically run out of gas? We studied 2002-2005, identified 56 rookies who threw at least 75 IP and analyzed their PQS logs. The group:

All rookies	#	#GS/P	DOM%	DIS%	qERA
before 7/31	56	13.3	42%	21%	4.56
after 7/31	56	9.3	37%	29%	4.82

There is some erosion, but a 0.26 run rise in qERA is hardly cause for panic. If we re-focus our study class, the qERA variance increased to 4.44-5.08 for those who made at least 16 starts before July 31. The variance also was larger (3.97-4.56) for those who had a PQS-3 average prior to July 31. The pitchers who intersected these two sub-groups:

PQS>3+GS>15	#	#GS/P	DOM%	DIS%	qERA
before 7/31	8	19.1	51%	12%	4.23
after 7/31	8	9.6	34%	30%	5.08

While the sample size is small, the degree of flameout by these guys (0.85 runs) is more significant.

Bull Durham Prospects

There is some potential talent in older players — age 26, 27 or higher — who, for many reasons (untimely injury, circumstance, bad luck, etc.), don't reach the majors until they have already been downgraded from prospect to suspect. Equating potential with age is an economic reality for Major League clubs, but not necessarily a skills reality.

Skills growth and decline is universal, whether it occurs at the major league level or in the minors. So a high skills journeyman in Triple-A is just as likely to peak at age 27 as a major leaguer of the same age. The question becomes one of opportunity — will the parent club see fit to reap the benefits of that peak performance?

Prospecting these players for your fantasy team is, admittedly, a high risk endeavor, though there are some criteria you can use. Look for a player who is/has:

- Optimally, age 27-28 for overall peak skills, age 30-31 for power skills, or age 28-31 for pitchers.
- At least two seasons of experience at Triple-A. Career Double-A players are generally not good picks.
- Solid base skills levels.
- Shallow organizational depth at their position.
- Notable winter league or spring training performance.

Players who meet these conditions are not typically draftable players, but worthwhile reserve or FAAB picks.

Japanese Baseball Toolbox *(Tom Mulhall)*
Comparing MLB and Japanese *Besuboru*

The Japanese major leagues are generally considered to be equivalent to very good Triple-A ball and the pitching may be even better. However, statistics are difficult to convert due to differences in the way the game is played in Japan.

1. While strong on fundamentals, Japanese baseball's guiding philosophy is risk avoidance. Mistakes are not tolerated. Runners rarely take extra bases, batters focus on making contact rather than driving the ball, and managers play for one run at a time. As a result, offenses score fewer runs than they should given the number of hits. Pitching stats tend to look better than the talent behind them.

2. Stadiums in Japan usually have shorter fences. Normally this would mean more HRs, but given #1 above, it is the American players who make up the majority of Japan's power elite. Power hitters do not make an equivalent transition to the MLB.

3. There are more artificial turf fields, which increases the number of ground ball singles. Only a few stadiums have infield grass and some still use dirt infields.

4. The quality of umpiring is questionable; there are no sanctioned umpiring schools in Japan. Fewer errors are called, reflecting the cultural philosophy of low tolerance for mistakes and the desire to avoid publicly embarrassing a player. Moreover, umpires are routinely intimidated.

5. Teams have smaller pitching staffs, sometimes no more than about seven deep. Three-man pitching rotations are not uncommon and the best starters often work out of the pen between starts. Despite superior conditioning, Japanese pitchers tend to burn out early due to overuse.

6. Japanese leagues use a slightly smaller baseball, making it easier for pitchers to grip and control.

7. Tie games are allowed. If the score remains even after 12 innings, the game goes into the books as a tie.

Japanese Players as Fantasy Farm Selections

Many fantasy leagues have large reserve or farm teams with rules allowing them to draft foreign players before they sign with a MLB team. With increased coverage by fantasy experts, the internet, and exposure from the World Baseball Classic, anyone willing to do a minimum of research can compile an adequate list of good players.

However, the key is not to identify the *best* Japanese players – the key is to identify impact players who have the desire and opportunity to sign with a MLB team. It is easy to overestimate the value of drafting these players. Since 1995, only about three dozen Japanese players have made a big league roster, and about half of them were middle relievers. But for owners who are allowed to carry a large reserve or farm team at reduced salaries, these players could be a real windfall, especially if your competitors do not do their homework.

A list of Japanese League players who could jump to the Majors appears in the Prospects section.

Team Toolbox

Johnson Effect *(Bryan Johnson)*: Teams whose actual won/loss record exceeds or falls short of their statistically projected record in one season will tend to revert to the level of their projection in the following season.

Law of Competitive Balance *(Bill James)*: The level at which a team (or player) will address its problems is inversely related to its current level of success. Low performers will tend to make changes to improve; high performers will not. This law explains the existence of the Plexiglass and Whirlpool Principles.

Plexiglass Principle *(Bill James)*: If a player or team improves markedly in one season, it will likely decline in the next. The opposite is true but not as often (because a poor performer gets fewer opportunities to rebound).

Whirlpool Principle *(Bill James)*: All team and player performances are forcefully drawn to the center. For teams, that center is a .500 record. For players, it represents their career average level of performance.

Other Diamonds

The Fanalytic Fundamentals

1. This is not a game of accuracy or precision. It is a game of human beings and tendencies.

2. This is not a game of projections. It is a game of market value versus real value.

3. Draft skills, not stats.

4. A player's ability to post acceptable stats despite lousy BPIs will eventually run out.

5. Once you display a skill, you own it.

6. Virtually every player is vulnerable to a month of aberrant performance. Or a year.

7. Exercise excruciating patience.

Aging Axioms

1. Age is the only variable for which we can project a rising trend with 100% accuracy. (Or, age never regresses.)

2. The aging process slows down for those who maintain a firm grasp on the strike zone. Plate patience and pitching command can preserve any waning skill they have left.

3. Negatives tend to snowball as you age.

Age 26 Paradox: 26 is when a player begins to reach his peak skill, no matter what his address is. If circumstances have him celebrating that birthday in the majors, he is a breakout candidate. If circumstances have him celebrating that birthday in the minors, he is washed up.

A-Rod 10-Step Path to Stardom: Not all well-hyped prospects hit the ground running. More often they follow an alternative path...

1. Prospect puts up phenomenal minor league numbers.
2. The media machine gets oiled up.
3. Prospect gets called up, but struggles, Year 1.
4. Prospect gets demoted.
5. Prospect tears it up in the minors, Year 2.
6. Prospect gets called up, but struggles, Year 2.
7. Prospect gets demoted.
8. The media turns their backs. Fantasy leaguers reduce their expectations.
9. Prospect tears it up in the minors, Year 3. The public shrugs its collective shoulders.
10. Prospect is promoted in Year 3 and explodes. Some lucky fantasy leaguer lands a franchise player for under $5.

Some players that are currently stuck at one of the interim steps, and may or may not ever reach Step 10, include Matt Gamel, Max Ramirez and Travis Snider.

Steve Avery List: Players who hang onto MLB rosters for six years searching for a skill level they only had for three.

Bylaws of Badness

1. Some players are better than an open roster spot, but not by much.

2. Some players have bad years because they are unlucky. Others have *many* bad years because they are bad... and lucky.

Rickey Bones List: Pitchers with BPIs so incredibly horrible that you have to wonder how they can possibly draw a major league paycheck year after year.

George Brett Path to Retirement: Get out while you're still putting up good numbers and the public perception of you is favorable. (*See Steve Carlton Path to Retirement.*)

Steve Carlton Path to Retirement: Hang around the major leagues long enough for your numbers to become so wretched that people begin to forget your past successes. (*See George Brett Path to Retirement.*)

Among the many players who have taken this path include Jose Mesa, Doc Gooden, Matt Morris, Hideo Nomo and of course, Steve Carlton. Current players who look to be on the same course include Andruw Jones, Nomar Garciaparra and Jason Isringhausen. We'll give John Smoltz a pass on 2009 but he could end up on this list next year.

Chaconian: Having the ability to post many saves despite sub-Mendoza BPIs and an ERA in the stratosphere.

Christie Brinkley Law of Statistical Analysis: Never get married to the model.

Chicken and Egg Problem: Did irregular playing time take its toll on the player's performance or did poor performance force a reduction in his playing time?

Chronology of the Classic Free-Swinger with Pop

1. Gets off to a good start.
2. Thinks he's in a groove.
3. Gets lax, careless.
4. Pitchers begin to catch on.
5. Fades down the stretch.

Crickets: The sound heard when someone's opening draft bid on a player is also the only bid.

Developmental Dogmata

1. Defense is what gets a minor league prospect to the majors; offense is what keeps him there. (*Deric McKamey*)

2. The reason why rapidly promoted minor leaguers often fail is that they are never given the opportunity to master the skill of "adjusting to the competition."

3. Rookies who are promoted in-season often perform better than those that make the club out of spring training. Inferior March competition can inflate the latter group's perceived talent level.

4. Young players rarely lose their inherent skills. Pitchers may uncover weaknesses and the players may have difficulty adjusting. These are bumps along the growth curve, but they do not reflect a loss of skill.

5. Late bloomers have smaller windows of opportunity and much less chance for forgiveness.

6. The greatest risk in this game is to pay for performance that a player has never achieved.

7. Some outwardly talented prospects simply have a ceiling that's spelled AAA.

Bull Durham List: Older minor leaguers who sneak onto major league rosters and shine for brief periods, showing what a mistake it is to pigeon-hole talented players just because they are not 24 and beautiful.

Edwhitsonitis: A dreaded malady marked by the sudden and unexplained loss of pitching ability upon a trade to the New York Yankees.

Scott Elarton List: Players you drop out on when the bidding reaches $1.

Employment Standards

1. If you are right-brain dominant, own a catcher's mitt and are under 40, you will always be gainfully employed.

2. Some teams believe that it is better to employ a pitcher with *any* experience because it has to be better than the devil they don't know.

3. It's not so good to go pffft in a contract year.

Errant Gust of Wind: A unit of measure used to describe the difference between your home run projection and mine.

FAAB Forewarnings

1. Spend early and often.

2. Emptying your budget for one prime league-crosser is a tactic that should be reserved for the desperate.

3. If you chase two rabbits, you will lose them both.

Fantasy Economics 101: The market value for a player is generally based on the aura of past performance, not the promise of future potential. Your greatest advantage is to leverage the variance between market value and real value.

Fantasy Economics 102: The variance between market value and real value is far more important than the absolute accuracy of any individual player projection.

Brad Fullmer List: Players whose leading indicators indicate upside potential, year after year, but consistently fail to reach that full potential.

Good Luck Truism: Good luck is rare and everyone has more of it than you do. That's the law.

The Gravity Principles

1. It is easier to be crappy than it is to be good.

2. All performance starts at zero, ends at zero and can drop to zero at any time.

3. The odds of a good performer slumping are far greater than the odds of a poor performer surging.

4. Once a player is in a slump, it takes several 3-for-5 days to get out of it. Once he is on a streak, it takes a single 0-for-4 day to begin the downward spiral.

Corollary: Once a player is in a slump, not only does it take several 3-for-5 days to get out of it, but he also has to get his name back on the lineup card.

5. Eventually all performance comes down to earth. It may take a week, or a month, or may not happen until he's 45, but eventually it's going to happen.

Health Homilies

1. Staying healthy is a skill.

2. A $40 player can get hurt just as easily as a $5 player but is eight times tougher to replace.

3. Chronically injured players never suddenly get healthy.

4. There are two kinds of pitchers: those that are hurt and those that are not hurt... yet.

5. Players with back problems are always worth $10 less.

6. "Opting out of surgery" usually means it's coming anyway, just later.

7. If staying healthy is a skill, shouldn't "DL Days" be a roto category?

The Health Hush: Players get hurt. Hurt players potentially have a lot to lose. Therefore, there is an incentive for players to hide injuries. HIPAA laws restrict the disclosure of health information. Team doctors and trainers have been instructed not to talk with the media. So, when it comes to information on players' health status, we're all pretty much in the dark.

Hope: A commodity that routinely goes for $5 over value at the draft table.

JA$G: Just Another Dollar Guy.

Jason Jennings Rationalization: Occasional nightmares (2/3 inning, 11 ER) are just a part of the game.

The Knuckleballers Rule: Knuckleballers don't follow any of the rules.

Brad Lidge Lament: When a closer posts a 62% strand rate, he has nobody to blame but himself.

Monocarp: A player whose career consists of only one productive season.

Lance Painter Lesson: Six months of solid performance can be screwed up by one bad outing. (In 2000, Painter finished with an ERA of 4.76. However, prior to his final appearance of the year — in which he pitched 1 inning and gave up 8 earned runs — his ERA was 3.70.)

The Pitching Postulates

1. Never sign a soft-tosser to a long-term contract.

2. Right-brain dominance has a very long shelf life.

3. A fly ball pitcher who gives up many HRs is expected. A ground ball pitcher who gives up many HRs is making mistakes.

4. Never draft a contact fly ball pitcher who plays in a hitter's park.

5. Only bad teams ever have a need for an inning-eater.

6. Never chase wins.

Quack!: An exclamation in response to the educated speculation that a player has used performance enhancing drugs. While it is rare to have absolute proof, there is often enough information to suggest that, "if it looks like a duck and quacks like a duck, then odds are it's a duck."

Reclamation Conundrum: The problem with stockpiling bench players in the hope that one pans out is that you end up evaluating performance using data sets that are far too small to be reliable.

Rule 5 Reminder: Don't ignore the Rule 5 draft lest you ignore the 1% possibility of a Johan Santana.

The Five Saves Certainties:

1. On every team, there *will* be save opportunities and *someone* will get them. At a bare minimum, there will be at least 30 saves to go around, and not unlikely more than 45.

2. *Any* pitcher could end up being the chief beneficiary. Bullpen management is a fickle endeavor.

3. Relief pitchers are often the ones that require the most time at the start of the season to find a groove. The weather is cold, the schedule is sparse and their usage is erratic.

4. Despite the talk about "bullpens by committee," managers prefer a go-to guy. It makes their job easier.

5. As many as 50% of the saves in any year will come from pitchers who are unselected at the end of Draft Day.

Small Sample Certitude: If players' careers were judged based what they did in a single game performance, then Tuffy Rhodes and Mark Whiten would be in the Hall of Fame.

Esix Snead List: Players with excellent speed and sub-.300 on base averages who get a lot of practice running down the line to first base, and then back to the dugout. Also used as an adjective, as in "Esix-Sneadian."

Standings Vantage Points

First Place: It's lonely at the top, but it's comforting to look down upon everyone else.

Sixth Place: The toughest position to be in is mid-pack at dump time.

Last Place in April: The sooner you fall behind, the more time you will have to catch up.

Last Place, Yet Again: If you can't learn to do something well, learn to enjoy doing it badly.

Tenets of Optimal Timing

1. If a second half fader had put up his second half stats in the first half and his first half stats in the second half, then he probably wouldn't even have had a second half.

2. Fast starters can often buy six months of playing time out of one month of productivity.

3. Poor 2nd halves don't get recognized until it's too late.

4. "Baseball is like this. Have one good year and you can fool them for five more, because for five more years they expect you to have another good one." — Frankie Frisch

The Three True Outcomes

1. Strikeouts 2. Walks   3. Home runs

The Three True Handicaps

1. Has power but can't make contact.

2. Has speed but can't hit safely.

3. Has potential but is too old.

Mike Timlin List: Players who you are unable to resist drafting even though they have burned you multiple times in the past.

UGLY (Unreasonable Good Luck Year): The driving force behind every winning team. It's what they really mean when they say "winning ugly."

Walbeckian: Possessing below replacement level stats, as in "Guzman's season was downright Walbeckian." *Alternate usage:* "Guzman's stats were so bad that I might as well have had Walbeck in there."

Zombie: A player who is indestructible, continuing to get work, year-after-year, no matter how dead his BPIs are. Like Seth McClung.

Seasonal Assessment Standard: If you still have reason to be reading the boxscores during the last weekend of the season, then your year has to be considered a success.

The Three Cardinal Rules for Winners: If you cherish this hobby, you will live by them or die by them...

1. Revel in your success; fame is fleeting.

2. Exercise excruciating humility.

3. 100% of winnings must be spent on significant others.

Research Abstracts

Half-season tendencies

Adrian Beltre is a rare breed. While we advise against considering any player as possessing consistent half-season tendencies, Beltre defied us from 2000-2007:

	1st Half		2nd Half	
Year	HR	BAvg	HR	BAvg
2000	7	.259	13	.317
2001	6	.255	7	.271
2002	7	.236	14	.278
2003	6	.220	17	.258
2004	19	.328	29	.341
2005	6	.257	13	.254
2006	7	.258	18	.277
2007	10	.258	16	.288

You will not find another player in all of baseball with as consistent and as long of a track record. So stop looking.

That said, it stands to reason *logically* that there might be some underlying tendencies on a more global scale, first half to second half. In fact, one would think that the player population as a whole might *decline in performance* as the season drones on. There are many variables that might contribute to a player wearing down — workload, weather, boredom — and the longer a player is on the field, the higher the likelihood that he is going to get hurt.

If this supposition is true, it is important information for those fantasy teams near the top of the standings at mid-season. It means that you'd have to expect some level of erosion in the second half, even if you made no further player moves from that point forward and froze every other roster in your league.

I isolated all pitchers over the past five years who threw at least 75 innings in the first half of the season. Those who tossed some minor league innings were screened out. The sample size was 509. Note that half seasons are defined by 81 games, not the All-Star break.

	W	L	IP	ERA	WHIP	Ctl	Dom	Cmd	hr/9
1H	6	5	97	4.13	1.34	2.9	6.2	2.1	1.0
2H	6	5	89	4.34	1.35	2.8	6.5	2.3	1.1

There is some slight erosion in innings and ERA despite marginal improvement in some peripherals. It is interesting that the halves are as close as they are. But let's up the ante. For those who pitched at least 100 innings in the first half:

	W	L	IP	ERA	WHIP	Ctl	Dom	Cmd	hr/9
1H	7	5	107	3.70	1.25	2.6	6.5	2.6	0.9
2H	6	5	97	4.10	1.31	2.6	6.8	2.6	1.0

The ERA regression is more notable as we push the envelope though the other peripherals maintain. So, if your team is riding on the backs of a few workhorse studs, odds are that their ERA is going to get worse in the second half.

Let's see how other performances could regress. For all those pitchers who won at least 10 games in the first half:

	W	L	IP	ERA	WHIP	Ctl	Dom	Cmd	hr/9
1H	10	3	108	3.13	1.18	2.3	6.6	2.8	0.8
2H	7	4	105	3.98	1.29	2.4	6.7	2.7	0.9

There's a fairly significant regression on the 10-plus game winners. Note that only 6% of all pitchers with at least 75 first half innings managed to win 10 games. Of those, only 1 in 4 were able to repeat the feat and win another 10 games in the second half. Overall, 9% of second half pitchers won 10 or more games.

We all know it's a fool's quest to chase wins. Still, what level of first half performance does it take to win 18 or more games over a full season? Here are the first half performances of those pitchers who managed to win at least 18 games during the period studied (2004-2008):

18-GAME WINNERS

	W	L	IP	ERA	WHIP	Ctl	Dom	Cmd	hr/9
1H	9	4	104	3.52	1.25	3.0	7.2	2.4	0.9
2H	9	5	112	3.87	1.28	2.8	7.5	2.6	0.8

19-GAME WINNERS

	W	L	IP	ERA	WHIP	Ctl	Dom	Cmd	hr/9
1H	9	3	106	3.18	1.16	2.0	6.7	3.4	0.7
2H	10	4	116	3.06	1.18	2.3	7.1	3.0	0.6

20+ GAME WINNERS

	W	L	IP	ERA	WHIP	Ctl	Dom	Cmd	hr/9
1H	10	4	109	3.06	1.13	1.8	7.4	4.1	0.7
2H	11	4	118	3.01	1.12	1.9	7.7	4.2	0.7

Some takeaways from this...

There is a solid correlation between skills and wins. This is good news for those of us who chase skills.

Despite the half-season cut at exactly 81 games, the big winners manage to compile *more innings* in the second half.

Not shown above, but only 18% of all these pitchers finished the first half with fewer than 8 victories.

For those who struck out 100 batters in the first half:

	W	L	IP	ERA	WHIP	Ctl	Dom	Cmd	hr/9
1H	8	4	108	3.31	1.15	2.6	9.0	3.5	0.9
2H	7	5	103	3.37	1.15	2.5	8.8	3.5	0.9

While only 52% of these pitchers managed to strike out another 100 in the second half, the overall performances were nearly identical, half-to-half.

How about those with first half ERAs less than 4.00?

	W	L	IP	ERA	WHIP	Ctl	Dom	Cmd	hr/9
1H	7	4	102	3.30	1.21	2.7	6.7	2.5	0.8
2H	6	5	96	4.09	1.31	2.7	6.9	2.6	1.0

The Gravity Principle is alive and well for these high achievers. Only 49% were able to maintain a sub-4.00 ERA in the second half.

We like to use our BPIs to identify disconnects with traditional stats like ERA, and make judgments about the future. Some analysts question whether that can be done in-season. So I filtered out those pitchers with ERAs of 4.50 or greater who also had LIMA-caliber skills.

	W	L	IP	ERA	WHIP	Ctl	Dom	Cmd	hr/9
1H	6	6	94	4.91	1.41	2.6	6.8	2.6	1.0
2H	5	4	87	4.29	1.34	2.8	7.3	2.6	1.2

While the improvement wasn't extraordinary, it still was enough to convert a non-roster-worthy player into someone you'd consider keeping on your pitching staff. So yes, you should hang on to poor performers if they are posting LIMA-caliber skills.

Closers are important too. I looked at 131 relievers with at least 10 saves in the first half during 2004-2008.

	W	Sv	IP	ERA	WHIP	Ctl	Dom	Cmd	hr/9
1H	2	17	33	3.10	1.18	3.2	8.8	2.7	0.8
2H	2	15	31	3.42	1.23	3.1	8.7	2.8	0.9

There is some erosion among closers as well, both in ERA, WHIP and saves. As expected, as we raise the stakes, the drop-off increases. For those who saved at least 15 games in the first half…

	W	Sv	IP	ERA	WHIP	Ctl	Dom	Cmd	hr/9
1H	1	20	34	2.73	1.11	3.0	9.0	3.0	0.8
2H	2	16	31	3.41	1.22	3.1	8.8	2.9	0.9

And finally, those frontline aces who finished the first half with 20 or more saves…

	W	Sv	IP	ERA	WHIP	Ctl	Dom	Cmd	hr/9
1H	1	23	34	2.45	1.07	2.9	9.0	3.1	0.7
2H	2	17	31	3.17	1.18	2.9	9.0	3.1	0.8

Of those closers who saved 20 or more games in the first half, only 39% were able to post 20 or more saves in the second half. In fact, 26% posted fewer than 15 saves, yet another sign of the volatility of the closer role.

In short, if you're riding high as you approach the season's mid-point, you can't stand pat. There is going to be at least some second half regression. Or, using one of my favorite tenets… *to stand still is to move backwards.*

What does it look like on the batting side? I isolated all batters over the past five years who posted at least 250 at-bats in the first half of the season. Those with minor league at-bats were screened out. The sample size was 649.

	AB	HR	RBI	SB	BA	bb%	ct%	Pwr	Sp
1H	283	10	40	6	.281	9%	83%	11.9	4.5
2H	268	10	38	6	.284	9%	83%	12.4	4.6

Overall, batting skills held up pretty well, half to half. There was a 5% erosion of playing time, perhaps thanks to September roster expansion. There was a 4% increase in power. (Note that the last two columns are Linear Weighted Power and Speed Score, the raw data we use to calculate PX and SX.)

Let's isolate some first half statistical milestones. First, those who amassed 300 AB in the first half:

	AB	HR	RBI	SB	BA	bb%	ct%	Pwr	Sp
1H	314	10	42	9	.287	8%	84%	11.5	5.4
2H	301	10	41	9	.292	8%	84%	11.7	5.4

The results were similar. This group had slightly lower power skills overall, and less of a second half improvement. These are more contact hitters with higher batting averages.

15 HR IN FIRST HALF

	AB	HR	RBI	SB	BA	bb%	ct%	Pwr	Sp
1H	285	18	54	4	.290	11%	80%	17.7	3.8
2H	277	16	50	4	.285	12%	79%	16.5	3.9

20 HR IN FIRST HALF

	AB	HR	RBI	SB	BA	bb%	ct%	Pwr	Sp
1H	284	22	60	4	.290	12%	78%	20.2	3.7
2H	287	19	56	4	.282	13%	77%	18.4	3.7

First half power studs did see a regression in the second half, up to 10% for the top HR hitters. Even on the low end, nearly a third of those that hit exactly 15 first half HRs failed to hit even 10 in the second half. Only 2% of the 15-HR hitters managed 20 or more in the second half.

On the high end, 34% of first half 20+ HR hitters hit 15 or fewer in the second half and only 27% were able to improve on their first half output.

10 SB IN FIRST HALF

	AB	HR	RBI	SB	BA	bb%	ct%	Pwr	Sp
1H	294	7	33	18	.282	9%	84%	9.9	6.6
2H	282	7	32	16	.291	9%	84%	10.4	6.5

20 SB IN FIRST HALF

	AB	HR	RBI	SB	BA	bb%	ct%	Pwr	Sp
1H	303	5	29	26	.281	8%	85%	8.4	7.8
2H	292	5	27	21	.294	8%	85%	8.9	7.1

Second half speed waned as well, though moreso at the high end. About 26% of the 20+ SB speedsters stole *at least 10 fewer bases* in the second half. Only 26% increased their second half SB output at all.

Interesting to note the half-to-half batting average spikes; they got on base more but stole less. Perhaps teams are less apt to take risks as the games get more meaningful.

How well do .300 hitters hold up?

	AB	HR	RBI	SB	BA	bb%	ct%	Pwr	Sp
1H	286	11	45	6	.320	9%	86%	12.7	4.5
2H	284	11	42	6	.294	10%	84%	12.5	4.6

These are still valuable hitters in the second half, but not nearly at the level of the first half. In all, 60% of first half .300 hitters fail to hit .300 in the second half. Even among those that hit .325 in the first half, 45% hit less than .300 in the second half. Only 20% showed any second half improvement at all. The regression in batting average is fair warning that even the seemingly safest lead in that category can evaporate.

Of course, most folks expect this. They also expect, or hope, that their first half strugglers will rebound to even things out. Do they?

LESS THAN .250 IN FIRST HALF

	AB	HR	RBI	SB	BA	bb%	ct%	Pwr	Sp
1H	274	9	34	5	.235	9%	80%	11.0	4.3
2H	235	9	33	4	.270	9%	80%	12.5	4.1

LESS THAN .230 IN FIRST HALF

	AB	HR	RBI	SB	BA	bb%	ct%	Pwr	Sp
1H	271	11	37	4	.217	9%	77%	12.3	4.0
2H	250	12	40	4	.270	9%	78%	14.4	3.7

Yes, regression works both ways, and these second half batting averages were amazingly resilient. Given that we've screened for players with at last 250 first half at-bats, this shows that managers stuck it out with their full-timers despite their poor starts, and these players responded in kind. In fact, nearly one in five of the sub-.250 hitters managed to hit *more than .300* in the second half.

At the end of the day, there is a good 25-30 point gap between where the .300 hitters end up and where the .250 hitters end up. These results are good news for your struggling hitters, but you still need to find a balance.

And again, even if you have a comfortable lead in first place at the mid-point, you can't sit still.

Opposite field home runs

by Ed DeCaria

Only about 50 hitters across both leagues possess the power and approach needed to consistently hit even two opposite field home runs (OppHR) each season. Most players who manage this subtle feat are among the best hitters in baseball.

From 2001-2008, nearly 75% of all HRs were hit to the batter's pull field, with the remaining 25% distributed roughly evenly between straight away and opposite field. Left-handers accomplish the feat slightly more often than right-handers (including switch-hitters hitting each way), and younger hitters do it significantly more often than older hitters. The trend toward pulled home runs is especially strong after age 36.

OppHR correlates mildly from one individual hitter season to the next (R=0.6). However, while its relative rarity limits individual hitter year-to-year consistency, opposite field home runs may still serve as a strong indicator of overall home run power (AB/HR), total offensive quality (RC/G), and combined rotisserie value (R$) similarly to how triples (another rare event) indicate speed.

Power Quartile	AB/HR	Opposite Field	Straight Away	Pull Field
Top 25%	17.2	15.8%	16.0%	68.2%
2nd 25%	28.0	10.7%	12.2%	77.0%
3rd 25%	44.1	8.9%	10.0%	81.1%
Bot 25%	94.7	5.4%	5.9%	88.7%

Here we see that power hitters (smaller AB/HR rates) hit a far higher percentage of their HR to the opposite field or straight away (over 30%). Conversely, non-power hitters hit almost 90% of their home runs to their pull field. Indeed, non-power hitters who hit OppHR with any frequency are the exception, not the rule. However, the exceptions in this case may turn out to be exceptional breakout candidates.

We analyzed the performance of over 4,000 MLB batter-seasons with at least one home run from 2001-2008 to understand if any aspect of home run direction in a given year suggested sustained breakout potential for the following three years combined. After pursuing numerous angles, one "trigger" emerged as both the most instructive and the most practical for fantasy implementation:

Performance in Y2-Y4 (% of Group)

Y1 Trigger	<=30 AB/HR	5.5+ RC/G	$16+ R$
2+ OppHR	69%	46%	33%
<2 OppHR	29%	13%	12%

Players who hit just two or more OppHR in the lead season were two to three times as likely as those who hit zero or one OppHR to sustain strong AB/HR rates, RC/G levels, and R$ values over the following three seasons. However, because OppHR also correlates highly with *current* performance, its ability to help generate PROFIT is less than its ability to generate VALUE for fantasy owners.

If we normalize Y1 performance for both groups of hitters by setting a maximum Y1 performance level in each target statistic, the stark differences in Y2-Y4 performance observed previously are minimized to the point that using OppHR as an indicator would be speculative at best.

To improve this, we also applied an age threshold (<=26 years) to see if OppHR can better predict the sustained breakouts of less established players than those of older players with more reliably mediocre performance records:

Y2-Y4 Breakout Performance
(% Breakout by Group, Age <=26 Only)

Y1 Trigger	AB/HR >35 to <=30	RC/G <4.5 to 5.5+	R$ <$8 to $16+
2+ OppHR	32%	21%	30%
<2 OppHR	23%	12%	10%

It can. Roughly one of every 3-4 batters age 26 or younger experiences a *sustained three-year breakout* in AB/HR, RC/G, and/or R$ after a season in which they hit 2+ OppHR. This is a marked improvement in our odds of turning a significant profit compared to the one in 8-10 batters who experience a breakout without the 2+ OppHR trigger.

Every season, about 30 new players (of all ages) hit 2+ OppHR for the first time. In many cases, this coincides with a breakout performance on which fantasy owners cannot subsequently profit. Sometimes, however, it occurs absent the strong surface stats that would otherwise drive market value outside the profitable range.

Using OppHR as a leading indicator would have yielded fantasy owners some very profitable sustained breakouts over the years, including Garrett Atkins ('06-'08), Jason Bay ('04-'06), Travis Hafner ('04-'06), Brad Hawpe ('06-'08), Aubrey Huff ('02-'04), Alex Rios ('06-'08), and Michael Young ('03-'05), as well as some very profitable 2009 acquisitions like Matt Kemp, Jason Kubel, Adam Lind, Joe Mauer, Mark Reynolds, and Ryan Zimmerman following relatively modest 2008 seasons.

These are obviously cherry-picked lists, but they hint at the value of using an indicator like OppHR to help identify players that may not have been considered breakout candidates or to validate unconvincing performances of known entities that were expected to do more.

So who should be on our radar for 2010? Savvy fantasy owners should give extra consideration to any hitter who reached 2+ OppHR for the first time in 2009, especially those aged 26 or under:

Player	OppHR	Player	OppHR
Morales,Kendry	9	Pie,Felix	2
Sandoval,Pablo	7	Young,Chris	2
Wieters,Matt	6	Valbuena,Luis	2
Venable,Will	5	Saltalamacchia,J	2
Snider,Travis	5	Stewart,Ian	2
Thomas,Clete	5	Maxwell,Justin	2
Kendrick,Howie	4	Coghlan,Chris	2
Butler,Billy	4	Pedroia,Dustin	2
Gonzalez,Carlos	3	Stubbs,Drew	2
Longoria,Evan	3		

Some of these hitters are already top performers. Others, along with 2+ OppHR repeaters from 2008 such as Jay Bruce, are well-known breakout candidates. As for the rest of this subtly-defined group, history gives us confidence that several may emerge as 2010's big surprises.

The hit direction information used in this analysis was obtained free of charge from and is copyrighted by Retrosheet. Interested parties may contact Retrosheet at www.retrosheet.org.

P/PA as a leading indicator

by Paul Petera

The art of working the count has long been considered one of the more crucial aspects of good hitting. It is common knowledge that the more pitches a hitter sees, the greater opportunity he has to reach base safely. We decided to study this further, looking at batters who logged at least 100 plate appearances per season, 2002-2008.

Since it's impossible to walk on fewer than four pitches, it's no surprise that on base average improves as P/PA approaches and exceeds 4.00.

ON BASE AVERAGE

P/PA	2002	2003	2004	2005	2006	2007	2008
4.00+	.356	.358	.362	.362	.362	.362	.359
3.75-3.99	.346	.344	.348	.344	.352	.345	.350
3.50-3.74	.332	.337	.334	.328	.337	.334	.337
Under 3.50	.318	.316	.325	.317	.315	.328	.327

With batting average, one would think that hitters have more success the more pitches they see. But getting deeper into the count means drawing more strikes too, and yields an opposite trend.

BATTING AVERAGE

P/PA	2002	2003	2004	2005	2006	2007	2008
4.00+	.260	.263	.267	.268	.269	.266	.258
3.75-3.99	.267	.267	.271	.270	.277	.271	.271
3.50-3.74	.267	.275	.275	.271	.278	.276	.275
Under 3.50	.272	.274	.277	.273	.275	.285	.274

547 players over the seven year study posted 4.00 or better P/PA. Only 46 of them batted better than .300.

% WHO BATTED MORE THAN .300

P/PA	2002	2003	2004	2005	2006	2007	2008
4.00+	9%	6%	12%	8%	8%	9%	7%
3.75-3.99	10%	11%	10%	12%	13%	12%	14%
3.50-3.74	11%	13%	16%	13%	19%	16%	12%
Under 3.50	13%	18%	16%	13%	21%	28%	14%

There was a reverse trend for those with the poorest BA.

% WHO BATTED LESS THAN .250

P/PA	2002	2003	2004	2005	2006	2007	2008
4.00+	42%	40%	37%	34%	28%	41%	49%
3.75-3.99	40%	38%	30%	35%	28%	35%	34%
3.50-3.74	39%	29%	32%	30%	24%	32%	29%
Under 3.50	31%	29%	30%	16%	31%	12%	26%

While a greater percentage of sub-3.50 P/PA hitters batted less than .250 than their 4.00/.300 counterparts, there was a noticeable collection of weak hitters in this group. In other words, many of these players were going to battle the Mendoza Line regardless of how many pitches they saw.

It appears that the days of choking up and shortening the swing with two strikes are gone. Striking out used to be an embarrassment, but it's less so today, and it seems more batters are swinging for the fences regardless of the count. The PX trend bears this out:

POWER INDEX (PX)

P/PA	2002	2003	2004	2005	2006	2007	2008
4.00+	125	119	120	128	131	121	114
3.75-3.99	109	106	108	109	104	108	109
3.50-3.74	99	102	97	93	95	95	89
Under 3.50	83	83	87	92	86	83	75

As a general rule, the more pitches batters see, the greater their power prowess.

% WITH PX MORE THAN 120

P/PA	2002	2003	2004	2005	2006	2007	2008
4.00+	54%	39%	51%	52%	53%	43%	35%
3.75-3.99	33%	31%	34%	31%	30%	30%	32%
3.50-3.74	19%	24%	20%	15%	17%	21%	16%
Under 3.50	15%	13%	11%	16%	10%	5%	5%

Likewise, the reverse is true for "patient" hitters. The 4.00+ group sports the fewest players with a sub-80 PX.

% WITH PX LESS THAN 80

P/PA	2002	2003	2004	2005	2006	2007	2008
4.00+	16%	22%	23%	23%	13%	18%	24%
3.75-3.99	24%	28%	28%	27%	26%	25%	29%
3.50-3.74	33%	29%	38%	40%	33%	40%	47%
Under 3.50	56%	56%	48%	39%	46%	42%	63%

Generally speaking, the more pitches seen, the lower the BA, but the higher the OBA and PX. But what about the outliers, those players that bucked the trend in year #1? Did their performance normalize in year #2? For these "Year #2" trends, we examined all outliers between 2002 and 2007 that had at least 100 PA the year after the anomaly.

There were 69 instances where batters posted a P/PA lower than 3.50 and batted below .250. The following year:

LOW P/PA & LOW BA	#	%
BA Improved	53	77%
BA Did Not	16	23%

The average improvement was 19%. You can expect several from the following list of outliers to see an improvement in batting average in 2010 based on these criteria: Jose Guillen, Manny Burriss, Eric Byrnes, Nick Green, Josh Anderson, Jason LaRue, Yuniesky Betancourt and Humberto Quintero.

HIGH P/PA & HIGH BA	#	%
BA Declined	30	79%
BA Did Not	8	21%

In this example, the average drop was 13%. Players that fit this description in 2009 were Kevin Youkilis, Todd Helton, Luis Castillo, Joe Mauer, David Wright, Joey Votto, Jose Morales, Victor Martinez, Michael Brantley, Adam Lind and Kendry Morales.

For the power outliers, 47 batters had a P/PA lower than 3.50 and posted a PX above 120 in year #1.

LOW P/PA & HIGH PX	#	%
PX Declined	42	89%
PX Did Not	5	11%

The PX declined 20% on average. There were three such power outliers in 2009, Aaron Hill, Pablo Sandoval and Randy Ruiz. The odds of a power repeat are not favorable.

Lastly, there were 63 batters with a 4.00+ P/PA and a PX lower than 80.

HIGH P/PA & LOW PX	#	%
PX Improved	44	70%
PX Did Not	19	30%

The mean power increase was 44%. The following players are examples of those who could see an uptick in power in 2010: Nick Johnson, Chone Figgins, Nick Punto, Akinori Iwamura, Ryan Hanigan, Everth Cabrera and Wes Helms.

Projecting starting pitcher wins

by Ed DeCaria

Projecting wins is a frustrating endeavor. While the typical starting pitcher win% is 35%, we can help ourselves by analyzing the nearly 20,000 SP appearances from 2005-2008 to determine why some pitchers win and others don't.

On the radar chart below, we deconstruct wins into distinct drivers grouped together clockwise from the top by team support, luck, skill, performance, and endurance. The shaded area shows how closely each variable is associated with Win%, while the thick black line shows how stable each metric is on its own from year to year. As either of these moves toward the outer ring, it means that that variable alone explains 50% or more of its target.

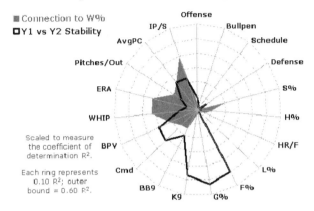

The top Win% drivers include IP/Start, WHIP, ERA, Pitches/Out, Strand Rate, and Hit Rate. Though useful in hindsight, these metrics are quite unstable from year-to-year, which makes it very difficult to *project* wins from them. What we need is a framework for projecting wins that relies as much as possible on drivers that we can better estimate (at least roughly) in advance.

The win projection model that we created includes seven key drivers (explained below). The following chart lists these drivers in descending order of impact that they have on *expected* win percentage (xWin%). The thick 0% line represents the xWin% of a theoretical replacement-level pitcher (about 24%). As pitchers/teams improve from replacement-level to average in a given factor, xWin% increases according to the length of that segment on the horizontal bar. As progress continues or deteriorates, we add to or subtract from the pitcher's xWin% accordingly.

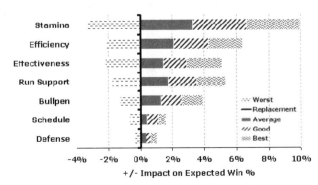

Stamina: Average pitch count (AvgPC) admittedly represents more than just stamina, as efficiency, effectiveness, and bullpen quality/availability also come into play. But since these other factors are already strongly represented in the xWin% model, we prefer AvgPC as our measure of stamina because we can combine it directly with pitch efficiency to calculate expected IP/Start.

Efficiency: For pitchers of a given stamina level, efficiency tells us how many outs a pitcher will record before reaching his point of exit. Actual pitch efficiency (pitches per out) is driven largely by BB and K rates, where walks consume ~5.5 pitches, strikeouts ~4.8 pitches, and batted balls ~3.3 pitches each. To determine a pitcher's *expected* efficiency (xEff), we need to know his BB/9, his K/9, and his expected percentage of outs after contact, which we can estimate using the pitcher's G/L/F profile.

Combining expected efficiency with stamina, we can then determine expected IP/Start. Efficient pitchers (<5.0 xEff) with high stamina (105+ AvgPC) often pitch deep into games. Inefficient pitchers (>6.0 xEff) with low stamina (<90 AvgPC) often struggle to reach the sixth inning. Because actual SP Win% increases sharply as IP/Start rises, xEff and AvgPC combined cover about half of the variability in xWin% that we can comfortably predict, from +16% above replacement-level for the best starters to -6% for the worst.

Effectiveness: Expected ERA (xERA) reflects three simple pitching truths: walks are bad, strikeouts are good, and groundballs are less dangerous than flyballs. xERA can impact xWin% by +5% for top starters (3.00 xERA) and -3% for bottom starters (5.50 xERA).

Run Support: At the high and low ends (roughly 5.3 Runs/Game vs. 4.1 Runs/Game), run support can impact seasonal xWin% by almost as much as the pitcher's effectiveness. This is fairly intuitive, as at the actual game level it is simply a race to see which team can score more runs before the starting pitcher walks off the mound. This brings us to …

Bullpen Support: Whether or not a starter is awarded a win after he exits with a lead is determined almost entirely by his bullpen. Accounting for all other factors, bullpen quality can still impact xWin% by over 5%, a swing of two wins between the best and worst pens in a 32-start season.

Schedule Strength and Team Defense: The final two statistically significant win drivers are of far less practical importance. Accounting for all other factors, schedule strength and team defense combined yield a variance in seasonal xWin% of about 3% (about one win in a 32-start season). Think of them as good tie breakers when choosing between two otherwise equally attractive (or equally gruesome) SP options.

Even a full season is not long enough to completely remove luck from an all-or-nothing statistic with a baseline of less than 35 starts, so some starting pitchers will continue to defy our projected win estimates. Still, revealing the core drivers of win percentage and focusing on the most stable year-over-year components should help to ease the frustration associated with this fickle fantasy stat.

PQS and quality starts

by Paul Petera

It's been well over a decade since we introduced Pure Quality Starts (PQS) to the world of fanalytics. PQS rates starting pitchers based upon their exhibited skills each time they take the mound. It is less rudimentary than the old school Quality Start calculation (6 innings, three earned runs), yet something that can be more easily calculated than Bill James' game score.

Still, the Quality Start remains pervasive in the baseball world with many fantasy leagues using it as a scoring category. Can using the concepts of PQS allow us to make valid assumptions about the ability to throw quality starts?

We reviewed every major league start for the years 2007 and 2008. We were able to determine how many starts for each PQS score resulted in an official Quality Start:

2007 - 2008

PQS	# Starts	# QS	QS%
0	1888	0	0%
1	492	16	3%
2	1241	260	21%
3	2195	1110	51%
4	2155	1616	75%
5	1747	1661	95%

At the low end, failing to go six innings results is neither a Quality Start nor a PQS higher than 0. Very few of the remaining PQS "Disasters" resulted in a Quality Starts either. From there, we see distinct jumps in QS% for each PQS range. A pitcher tossing a PQS-3 has about a coin-flip probability of logging a Quality Start. A similar jump occurs once we move into PQS "Domination" territory, with PQS-5's virtually guaranteeing a Quality Start.

Put another way, only 0.6% of PQS Disasters turned into Quality Starts, while 84% of PQS Dominant outings were Quality Starts.

No surprise that the higher the PQS, the greater probability for a Quality Start. Let's look a little closer. For each season, we looked at every pitcher that made at least fifteen starts to determine how PQS and DOM/DIS looked with regard to Quality Starts.

First, we grouped each pitcher by their Quality Starts as a percentage of their total starts, and reviewed each group's PQS and DOM/DIS trends:

QS%	----------2007----------			----------2008----------		
	#	**PQS**	**DOM/DIS**	**#**	**PQS**	**DOM/DIS**
61-100%	1115	3.5	57/10%	1153	3.5	59/20%
50-60%	1186	3.0	47/18%	1095	3.0	45/31%
40-49%	965	2.6	34/25%	976	2.6	35/41%
<40%	734	2.2	25/36%	761	2.4	34/46%

The average PQS scores for each population are strikingly similar from year to year, and there is an unmistakable drop as you move down. And while the DOM/DIS splits for the lower-percentage QS groups are a bit more variable, the trend is clear here as well. As the percentage of Quality Starts rises, the percent of PQS Dominant scores does as well, while PQS Disasters similarly drop.

Next, in order to understand the characteristics of those who threw the most Quality Starts, we grouped all of the pitchers with at least fifteen starts by their total number of Quality Starts in a given season. The results were pretty similar:

# QS	----------2007----------			
	Starts	**QS%**	**PQS**	**DOM/DIS**
20+	1038	68%	3.5	57/9%
15-19	1278	55%	3.1	48/18%
10-14	821	47%	2.7	36/25%
0-9	863	34%	2.3	26/35%

# QS	----------2008----------			
	Starts	**QS%**	**PQS**	**DOM/DIS**
20+	821	67%	3.6	63/18%
15-19	1281	57%	3.1	46/29%
10-14	1243	44%	2.7	39/40%
0-9	640	33%	2.3	29/48%

2008's DOM/DIS discrepancies from top to bottom were a bit more pronounced, but the story is essentially the same. Pitchers that post many Quality Starts have average PQS scores of about 3.5. They typically put up PQS Dominant starts two-thirds of the time, while limiting their PQS Disasters to less than one in five starts.

They also toe the rubber with great regularity. A total of 57 pitchers logged at least 20 Quality Starts in our sample (32 in 2007, 25 in 2008). Only one of the 57 had fewer than 30 starts (28).

We can also learn something about the outliers. Among the 57 instances of 20+ Quality Starts in 2007 and 2008, there were twelve cases where the pitcher failed to have a DOM% of greater than 50%. The difference? Middle-of-the road PQS Starts. On average, 40% of all PQS 2's and 3's resulted in Quality Starts. But these twelve averaged 65%.

What nearly all of these pitchers shared were high ground ball rates and/or low strikeout Rates. Lower strikeout totals can impact two of the five scoring categories for PQS (K's versus IP and K's versus walks). As a result, many low-dominance guys are more susceptible to middling PQS scores. High GB rates are always a good thing, but they are particularly important to pitchers that don't hurl a ton of strikeouts.

Most of the results here are pretty intuitive. Pitchers who put up many Quality Starts are predominantly the same ones who take the mound with regularity and routinely post high PQS scores. They're also not-so-coincidentally the pitchers we find most fanalytically appealing.

Saves chances and wins

by Craig Neuman

Every Rotisserie team needs a closer (unless you're punting saves). Certainly, the first thing to look for is a pitcher with the talent and opportunity to do the job. But, should the quality of a pitcher's MLB team be a consideration?

There are two schools of thought on this subject. There's one notion that good teams get lots of saves for their closer so you're better off taking a player from a winning team. The flip side is that poor teams, when they win games, do so by a small margin. Therefore, while a bad team may not have as many wins, the likelihood of a save chance in those wins is greater than on a good team.

We looked at the results from the 2003-2008 Major League Baseball seasons while focusing on saves, save opportunities, save percentage, wins, quality starts and run differential. We ran a correlation equation on all of these statistics and the results are below. Note that anything above .50 suggests at least a moderate correlation.

	SV	SVO	W	S%	RD	QS
SV	1					
SVO	.78	1				
W	.66	.41	1			
S%	.66	.05	.56	1		
RD	.48	.26	.92	.44	1	
QS	.41	.24	.58	.34	.60	1

We can see from this data that saves do, in fact, correlate with wins. The more wins a team has, the more saves a team will have. And, what about the theory that teams who play in close games would accumulate more saves than really good teams or really bad teams? Well, the lack of correlation between saves and run differential would seem to dispel that theory a bit.

However, we did find an interesting relationship between wins and the number of saves per win a team achieves. On average, teams registered one save for every two wins. However, when we break down the results into smaller groupings, we find that a trend does exist.

Win Total	Saves/Win
>90	.494
80-89	.492
70-79	.505
<69	.525

Note that teams with fewer wins end up with more saves per win. So, really bad teams, when the do win games, are more likely to get a save in their wins. Of course, there are never any certainties in this game which explains why, in 2009, Heath Bell got 42 saves for a 75-win Padres team while Fernando Rodney got only 37 for the 86-win Tigers.

Which closers will keep their jobs?

by Michael Weddell

This study looked at pitchers during 1988-2008 with 20 or more saves and who led their teams in saves during September. In the following year, only 67.5% of these closers earned 20 or more saves. The high attrition rate is consistent with prior BaseballHQ research.

Next, we ran a multiple regression analysis to determine what best predicted whether a closer would earn 20+ saves in the following year.

Saves history: Career save totals was the most important factor in predicting which closers would earn at least 20 saves in the next season. Saves during the past two seasons were also moderately important.

Age: Closers are most likely to keep their jobs at age 27. For long-time closers, their growing career saves totals more than offset the negative impact of their advanced ages. Older closers without a long history of racking up saves tend to be bad candidates for retaining their roles.

Performance: Surprisingly, actual performance, measured by ERA+, was of only minor importance. Strikeouts per inning pitched in both the current and prior years was important for keeping a closer's role beyond its impact on ERA. Other underlying skills, measured by xERA and then normalized for each season, were not statistically relevant.

Being Right-Handed: Righthanders' odds of retaining the closer's role were 9% higher than lefthanders' odds.

How well can we predict which closers will keep their jobs? Of the 10 best closers during 1989-2007, 90% saved at least 20 games during the following season. Of the 10 worst bets, only 20% saved at least 20 games the next year.

Let's look at the closer odds for 2010:

- Very skeptical (37% - 50%): Mike MacDougal, Ryan Franklin, Fernando Rodney, Heath Bell and Leo Nunez
- Skeptical (54% - 62%): Frank Francisco, Brian Fuentes, Kerry Wood, Rafael Soriano, Matt Capps, Andrew Bailey and David Aardsma
- Confident (76% - 87%): Jonathan Broxton, Francisco Cordero, Brian Wilson, Jose Valverde and Joe Nathan
- Very confident (90%+): Joakim Soria, Trevor Hoffman, Jonathan Papelbon, Mariano Rivera and Francisco Rodriguez

Computing the odds of becoming a closer was a less fruitful exercise. On average, only 3% of non-closing relievers (those who relieved in two-thirds of their games, did not save 20 games, and did not lead or tie for their team's September saves) saved 20+ games in the next season. Other findings for non-closers:

Skills alone are not enough to identify closers-in-waiting. We need to strike when talent and opportunity converge.

The best odds are given to former closers who lost their roles for just the past year.

When a new closer is needed, managers prefer to elevate right-handed relievers with at least a two-year history of high strikeout rates into the closer's role.

A past history of saves is helpful, but once a reliever has gone two consecutive years without being a closer, he likely will need to show strong skills to reclaim the role.

MLEs as a leading indicator

by Bill Macey

The use of major league equivalencies to benchmark the performance of minor league players was introduced by Bill James in the *1985 Baseball Abstract*. MLEs adjust a player's minor league performance for the quality of the competition and suggest how that player would have performed in the major leagues.

MLEs, like any performance metric, can vary year to year and only translate what has already happened. Because fantasy baseball is a forward-looking endeavor, we wish to see if MLEs have any predictive value. This article focuses on linear weighted power (PX) and contact rate (ct%).

The relationship between the minors and Majors

We looked at the MLEs for batters from 2003 to 2007 and their corresponding performance at the MLB level in the subsequent years 2004-2008. The analysis was limited to batters with at least 100 AB at each of the minor and major league levels.

	Year 1 MLE	Year 2 MLB
Observations	496	496
Median PX	95	96
Percent PX > 100	43%	46%

There is a strong relationship between a player's MLE PX in year 1 and their MLB PX in year 2. Further, 53% of the players had a MLB PX in year 2 that exceeded their MLE PX in year 1. The relatively small median increase coupled with a nearly even distribution split between an increase and decrease in performance confirms the projective relevancy of MLEs.

We shouldn't be surprised that there is a slight bias towards improved performance in year 2. Given that the median age of the minor leaguers in the sample was 25.6, a small year-over-year improvement is consistent with general career trajectories.

Slicing the numbers by performance level, we can see a good amount of regression to the mean. The following table segments the sample of players by MLE PX level and presents for each cohort: their subsequent average MLB PX; the percentage of those players whose MLB PX exceeded their MLE PX; and the percentage of players whose subsequent MLB PX was greater than 100 (the league average).

Year 1 MLE PX	Year 2 MLB PX	Percent Increase	Percent MLB PX > 100
<= 50	61	70.3%	5.4%
51-75	85	69.6%	29.4%
76-100	93	55.2%	39.9%
101-125	111	47.4%	62.0%
126-150	119	32.1%	66.1%
> 150	142	28.6%	76.2%

Looking at the numbers in this manner presents an interesting dichotomy. As expected, players with a high MLE PX have a greater MLB PX than do players with a low MLE PX. However, most "low PX" players improve and post a higher MLB PX in year 2, whereas most "high PX" players suffer a decreased PX in year 2.

We considered whether age played a role in the predictive ability of MLE PXs. However, at each of the above segments of performance, age does not appear to be a factor; the difference in PX between year 1 and year 2 was substantially similar across age groups. Thus, putting up a high MLE PX at a young age does not strongly affect the likelihood of repeating that performance the following year at the MLB level.

It is important to note that the above analysis only looks at two consecutive years – it is certainly plausible that players that have a high PX at a young age are good bets for future performance, regardless of whether the initial high PX came at either the minor or major league level.

Where do power hitters come from?

We also looked at the numbers from the opposite direction to see if there was any pattern to those players that achieved a high sustained PX at the MLB level. We filtered for players that had established levels of success at the MLB level according to the following criteria:

- at least two consecutive seasons of MLB PX > 100
- an average MLB PX > 100.

There were 101 players that met these criteria; the median MLB PX for the group over the 2004-2008 period was 125 and the average MLE PX over the 2003-2007 period was 110. Of those 101 players, only 17 did not post a 100 MLE PX at least once between 2003 and before reaching the majors. And even that low number may be misleading as it does not account for any performance prior to 2003. (For example, Travis Hafner posted a MLE PX of 64 in 2003 and subsequent MLB PXs of 159, 176, 201, 216, 117, and 94 from 2003-2008. However, he did post a MLE PX of 112 in 2002.)

In other words, players rarely suddenly develop power at the MLB level if they didn't previously display that skill at the minor league level. However, the relatively large gap between the median MLE PX and MLB PX for these players, 125 to 110, confirms the notion that the best players continue to improve once they reach the major leagues.

If you're looking to roster a player with power, target players with high MLE PXs with the understanding that there could be a small decrease in power from the level established at the minor leagues during the previous year. More importantly, don't roster a player hoping that the power will develop – if it wasn't there at the minor league level, it's unlikely to appear in the majors.

Contact rate and batting average

There is a strong positive correlation (0.63) between a player's MLE ct% in Year 1 and his actual ct% at the MLB level in Year 2.

Despite this close relationship, there does appear to be a sizable drop-off from the MLE ct% in Year 1 to the MLB ct% in Year 2. For the entire sample, the median ct% falls from 84% to 79%. This does not appear to be noise as only 17% of players post a higher ct% in Year 2. This drop-off occurs at all levels of ct%, but is more pronounced for the players with higher ct% rates at the minor league level.

MLE ct%	Count	Year 1 MLE ct%	Year 2 MLB ct%
< 70%	4	69%	68%
70% - 74%	17	73%	72%
75% - 79%	70	77%	75%
80% - 84%	158	82%	77%
85% - 89%	178	87%	82%
90% +	69	91%	86%
TOTAL	**496**	**84%**	**79%**

Looking at the yearly results does not reveal any trends or anomalies. Instead, it's clear that these rates are consistent year after year. The table below presents the median Year 1 MLE ct% and Year 2 MLB ct% for each pair of years used in this analysis:

Years	Count	Year 1 MLE ct%	Year 2 MLB ct%
2003/2004	96	86%	79%
2004/2005	89	85%	79%
2005/2006	96	85%	80%
2006/2007	105	84%	80%
2007/2008	110	84%	78%

So what is the reason for this drop? Is this a short term, single year result of batters adjusting to the major leagues? To answer this question, we considered player performance in Year 3 – the second year at the MLB level. Of the 496 players in the sample, there was Year 3 data for 277 players. The median ct% for the MLB player in Year 3 for this subset of players was nearly identical to Year 1 at 80%.

Turning our attention to batting average, we found very little difference between the median MLE BA in Year 1 and the median MLB BA in Year 2 - the median increases from .261 in Year 1 to .262 in Year 2. Additionally, 49% of players post a greater BA in Year 2, meaning batting average is just as likely to go up as it is to go down.

This helps confirm that the MLE accurately translates BA performance. Again, we present the MLE BA and MLB BA results by MLE ct% cohort to see if there are any trends in the data:

MLE ct%	Count	Year 1 MLE BA	Year 2 MLB BA
< 70%	4	.230	.270
70% - 74%	17	.257	.248
75% - 79%	70	.248	.255
80% - 84%	158	.257	.255
85% - 89%	178	.266	.270
90% +	69	.282	.273
TOTAL	**496**	**.261**	**.262**

Excluding the <70% cohort (which has a tiny sample size), there does appear to be a positive relationship between MLE ct% and MLB BA, although the relationship isn't as pronounced as the one between MLE ct% and MLB ct%. Indeed, batting average tends to jump around regardless of ct%, as the correlation between the two statistics is just 0.17.

Regardless of MLE ct%, there is little difference between MLE BA in Year 1 and MLB BA in Year 2 in the aggregate; the correlation between the two is also low at 0.18. So while there is consistency over larger sample sizes of 50-100 players, any individual player's BA may vary significantly year to year.

Therefore, this doesn't validate MLE BA as an accurate predictor of future MLB BA in so much as it validates MLE BA as an accurate translation of expected current performance at the MLB level.

But where, then, do .300 hitters come from? Of the 496 seasons and 360 distinct players in our sample, only 92 posted a BA of .300 or greater at the MLB level between 2004-2008. Among them, these 92 players had 215 seasons at the minor league level during 2003-2007 with an average MLE ct% of 86%. Only 26 of the 215 (12.1%) observations had a MLE ct% less than 80% and only 1 was less than 70% (Ryan Howard in 2004, who subsequently batted .313 in 2006 but has not come close since).

If we further restrict the data set to players with a BA of .300 or greater in Year 2, the median MLE ct% in Year 1 was 87%. Of those 58 observations, only 8 (13.8%) had a MLE ct% less than 80%. The lowest observed MLE ct% belonged to Josh Phelps with 74% in 2006 and a MLB BA of .306 for the New York Yankees and Pittsburgh Pirates in 2007 (along with a hit rate of 38%).

The key takeaways of this are:

- There is a strong correlation between MLE ct% in Year 1 and MLB ct% in Year 2;
- A batter's MLB ct% tends to drop about five points from his MLE ct%, but this is just a one year drop;
- While a high contact rate alone is not sufficient to post a .300 BA, it certainly seems to be an important part of the equation.

Speculating on Breakouts

by Brandon Kruse

In the *2009 Forecaster*, we conducted an experiment, taking a breakout player profile we had developed and refined for in-season use and applying it to identify breakout candidates before the season started. We defined a breakout season as one where a player posts a Rotisserie value of at least $20 after previously never posting a value higher than $10 at the major league level. We also required that the player had at least one season of MLE (Double-A or higher) or MLB skill stats prior to their $20 season. The criteria we used to identify candidates was:

- Age 27 or younger.
- An increase in at least two of the following categories: H%, PX or SX.
- Minimum league average PX or SX (100)
- Minimum contact rate of 75%
- Minimum xBA of .270

The results were somewhat encouraging, as out of nine candidates, we had two legitimate successes (Erick Aybar and Ben Zobrist) and two moderate successes (Martin Prado and Seth Smith). Of course, we also suggested Brian Anderson and Joe Mather, and no one's going to be thanking us for that anytime soon.

Undeterred, we're giving it another go for 2010. This time around the filters have given us a group of players that, for the most part, leans less toward the sleeper end of the spectrum. In fact, some of you may consider them downright no-brainers. Nonetheless, the reality is that none of these players has earned more than $10 in a single season, and jumping to the $20 level in 2010 would still represent a big leap in value and performance:

Back in 2003, **Michael Aubrey** (1B, BAL) was a first-round draft pick and top hitting prospect, but injuries (including a chronic back problem) have dimmed his star in the years since. However, he responded quite well to a late season call-up with the Orioles in 2009, batting .289 with an 89% contact rate and a 123 PX. It was only 90 AB, so the sample size is extremely small, but it helps paint Aubrey as a Bull Durham Prospect who may finally be ready to deliver at age 27. A playing time opportunity could make him worth a speculative flyer.

Ronald Belisario (RHP, LA) came out of nowhere to win a spot in the Dodgers bullpen, and then proceeded to become one of their best relievers, posting a 2.04 ERA, 8.2 Dom, 56% ground ball rate, and 78 BPV. His skills faltered a bit in the second half (4.23 xERA), as he struggled with elbow stiffness that was likely brought on by being overworked by Joe Torre. One good half-season after many years of unimpressive work in the minors makes him a little risky, but he clearly earned his manager's trust last year. If he can repeat the skills, he could emerge as a secondary saves source.

Neftali Feliz's (RHP, TEX) role may be uncertain, but his talent is not: an 11.3 Dom, 4.9 Cmd, 152 BV, and 3.01 xERA, impressive skills at any age, let alone 21. The Rangers have hinted that he may join their starting rotation in 2010, but he could just as easily become their closer. For now, draft the skills, not the role.

It may seem odd to find **Yovani Gallardo** (RHP, MIL) on this list, but the reality is that despite some good performances, he has yet to hit the $10 Rotisserie value mark in his career. In 2009, that was at least partly due to a lack of run support — Gallardo ranked 45th out of 80 qualifying MLB starters in run support last year, while teammate Braden Looper (who went 14-7 despite a 5.22 ERA) ranked 3rd. Gallardo had walk issues (4.6 Ctl) in 2009 that only got worse as the season went on, so he merits some caution, but he also now has a 3.57 ERA in 320 career IP. At 24, he may finally be ready to become a $20 pitcher.

Matt LaPorta (LF/1B, CLE) brought his power skills (123 PX, 42% FB) to a 181 AB stint in the majors in 2009. An 11% MLE walk rate from 2008 and a career .291 BA in the minors suggest that patience and batting average could be his next step up — and his path to increased value. Arthroscopic surgery on his hip may cause him to miss part of spring training and get a late start on 2010, but there's every indication he'll be in line for a full-time role once he's healthy.

LaPorta's teammate **Joe Smith** (RHP, CLE) also had arthroscopic surgery (in his case, his knee), but is expected to be ready for spring training. Smith improved his Ctl (3.4) and Cmd (2.3) in 2009, while still maintaining a stellar 55% ground ball rate. His 81 BPV and 3.73 xERA suggest he has the skills to become a closer, and with the perennially injured Kerry Wood in front of him, the opportunity could come his way. He's a solid LIMA candidate.

Luis Valbuena (2B, CLE) followed up a promising Double-A campaign in 2008 (MLEs: .270 BA, 87% ct, 0.83 Eye, 15 SB) by adding a line drive swing (22%) and a little bit of power (112 PX) during his time in the majors in 2009. His 77% contact rate and 0.31 Eye with the Indians suggest he's still a work in progress, but frankly, that's what you'd expect from a 24-year-old with just 275 AB of Triple-A experience. If he can consolidate his skills, a patient investment could pay big dividends in 2010.

III.
GAMING

Gaming Research

The changing face of fantasy

Each year at BaseballHQ.com, we keep tabs on ongoing fantasy baseball industry trends by means of our weekly HQ Poll, which we've been running since December 1998. In each edition of the *Forecaster*, we look back at some of these questions and share the results. There are dozens of trends that we track so we rotate the topics each year.

Since these questions are asked at Baseball HQ, they only represent the opinions of folks who a) visit Baseball HQ, and b) respond to online polls. So these are clearly not scientific representations of the industry as a whole. However, even from among our smaller group (note that all poll results had at least 500 responses) we can glean some interesting tidbits about where our hobby may be headed and how fantasy leaguers play the game.

NEWS or NOISE? In general, what percentage of information reported by major league teams probably represents partial truths or outright lies?

	2003	2006	2009
Less than 10%	5%	7%	5%
25%	31%	29%	27%
50%	43%	43%	47%
75%	18%	18%	19%
More than 90%	2%	3%	3%
MEAN	45%	45%	48%

Running these polls three years apart, I was trying to get a read on the trends in our cynicism. I suppose the fact that we think about half of news is noise is damning enough, even if the trend only shows a minor increase in our suspicions.

Are there rivalries in your leagues?

	2006	2008	2009
NO, I try to beat everyone.	23%	28%	26%
YES...			
Friendly rivalries with several owners	29%	30%	33%
I work hard to beat some owners	30%	27%	24%
There are owners I dislike and work harder to beat	17%	14%	17%

This is an interesting question given the skyrocketing rise in online leagues. It would seem that faceless competitors would lead to fewer rivalries, but we can't know for sure from these results.

What this poll does show us is a slight softening in the incidences of individual owner vitriol. Does that mean a decline in trash talk? Is this hobby becoming more civil? Probably not, as nearly three quarters of respondents still do have some type of rivalry.

Does your primary league allow trades?

	2005	2007	2009
Yes	96%	97%	97%
We used to but now we don't	1%	1%	1%
No	3%	2%	2%

This seems like a silly question to ask (and given the results, probably was), but there has always been a tendency of some leagues to reduce disharmony and instill peace by outlawing trading. This was especially prevalent in high stakes competitions (see, National Fantasy Baseball Championship).

Back in the mid-1990's one fantasy expert declared that the future of the hobby would be to eliminate trading because bad deals disrupted the chemistry of leagues. Fifteen years later, that is not the case.

Does your keeper league have any restrictions to roster protection?

	2007	2008	2009
No. We can protect any type of player	34%	33%	30%
Limits to number of farm players	20%	19%	18%
Limits to pitchers vs position players	3%	5%	3%
Limits to both farm and positions	23%	22%	27%
Other types of restrictions	20%	21%	22%

Back in 2007, a reader asked that we run this poll because his league was facing some decisions. After three years, there is now a clear trend towards increasing restrictions on the types of players that can be protected.

In my experience, leagues tend to add restrictions to rules as a means to correct perceived injustices or to prevent wily owners from finding loopholes. After many years, these restrictions tend to snowball until the league constitution becomes a series of band-aids and addendums. Often, the source of the original problem is long gone and intent of the restriction is no longer valid, but the rule sticks. Be careful.

It's Draft Day in a keeper league with standard contract terms. If you project that a prospect will earn $0 this year but $20 next year, what would be your highest bid now?

	2000	2008	2009
$0	4%	3%	2%
$1	21%	12%	12%
$5	38%	40%	42%
$8	20%	24%	26%
$10	6%	11%	9%
$12	4%	6%	7%
$15	3%	2%	2%
More than $15	1%	2%	1%
MEAN	$5.42	$6.52	$6.52

If you follow each of the dollar options across, there is a clear trend towards more people finding present value in the future speculation. Fewer respondents would only pay $1 or less, and more would risk $5, $8 or even $12.

Of course, context is important. A team playing for this year might not take the $5 or $8 hit if it impedes their title push. But for a team playing for the future, investing $8 now on a $20 player next year is nearly a no-brainer.

What is your approach going to be towards this year's #1 amateur draft pick)?

	2007	2008	2009
He's already rostered in my league	10%	11%	37%
Going to make every effort to get him	9%	3%	12%
Take a shot but just as happy with other first-rounders	15%	8%	9%
Passing interest; little relevance to my fantasy team.	39%	44%	25%
Completely uninterested	27%	31%	17%

My quest to find a trend in how deep into the player pool our passion runs slammed up against Stephen Strasburg. David Price in 2007 (somewhat surprisingly) and Tim Beckham in 2008 did not generate nearly as much advance hype. It will be interesting to see whether 2009 was an anomaly or the beginnings of a newfound interest in the First Year Player Draft. We'll have to revisit this one.

Leagues with FAAB... Do your owners tend to hoard or spend freely? What percentage of the teams in your league have at least 75% of their FAAB still remaining at the MLB trading deadline?

	2005	2008	2009
Fewer than 25%	28%	47%	43%
26-50%.	26%	26%	24%
51-75%	23%	15%	17%
More than 75%	24%	11%	16%

One of our rules of FAAB is to "spend early and often." Those who wait for the big league-crossers at the Major League trading deadline are frequently disappointed. The number of those following that advice took a huge jump between 2005 and 2008; it has settled at a level where nearly half the respondents are in leagues where $75 of the $100 FAAB budgets are already spent by July 31. That is a good thing. It could still get better.

How many teams in your league still have a legitimate shot at first place?

	2007	2008	2009
Only one	16%	19%	16%
2	29%	26%	25%
3	29%	27%	29%
4	16%	16%	17%
5	6%	8%	9%
More than 5	4%	4%	4%

This question looks at competitive balance and was asked in August of each year. During these three years, there was a slight increase in parity. Those leagues with only three August contenders dropped from 74% to 72% to 70%. That meant leagues with more than three contenders trended up, from 26% to 28% to 30%.

Of course, the movement is small and could just be statistical noise. But the trend bears watching. Parity increases owner satisfaction and likely builds league longevity.

What is your opinion about fantasy competitions based on the MLB post-season?

	2007	2008	2009
INTERESTED			
I already play in one	3%	4%	4%
I'm ready. Where do I sign up?	6%	6%	5%
I'd be interested if there was a format I could buy into	19%	13%	12%
NOT INTERESTED			
I want to watch the playoffs as a fan	43%	50%	51%
I am burned out by October	12%	17%	17%
It's fantasy football season	17%	10%	11%

It's a long, six-month Major League Baseball season but the most exciting part of it is arguably what happens after the last regular-season pitch is thrown. Apparently not so in the fantasy world.

I've always been a proponent of a post-season format where the regular season stats are entered into a simulation program and the top two, or four, or six teams compete head-to-head in a real play-off series. That idea has never taken off, for the reasons noted above. And the trend looks like that's not going to change any time soon.

Hypothetically, what type of pitcher deserves the Cy Young Award?

	2003	2008	2009
22-game winner, 3.75 ERA	20%	28%	22%
16-game winner, 2.50 ERA	72%	58%	66%
55-save reliever,. 2.00 ERA	8%	13%	12%

Where does the most value lie? What are the qualifications for the award? These are two questions that don't necessarily have the same answers. Those who vote for the award probably could not agree either.

But poll responders clearly discount wins and saves, stats that are more dependent on situation than skill. Baseball HQ subscribers would naturally gravitate toward skill over results. But you have to take a step back, and possibly reconsider.

If the value of any individual player is to help his team win, none of the options above gives us a complete picture of that pitcher's contribution. We can assume that the 16-game winner had perhaps 34 starts and likely kept his team in most games, despite only winning 16.

But the 22-game winner was involved in at least six more actual victories and might have kept his team in just as many games as the 16-game winner. We'd have to examine every start to determine that.

And the closer, heck, he contributed to *39 more victories* than the poll selection! True, many of those saves might have been no-threat, clean 9th inning outings, but the sheer number of "W"s he was a part of must have made him more valuable than the 8-13% of the respondents believe.

Personally, I had hoped the split would have been more like 35%, 45%, 20%.

Making better use of ADP data

by Bill Macey

Baseball HQ's weekly Market Pulse column highlights likely bargains using mock drafts held on popular websites. These results include average draft position (ADP) data as well as the earliest and latest selections for each player.

Although this gives one a good idea of where in the draft each player is selected, it can be misleading when trying to determine how early to target a player. If you wait until your pick closest to the ADP value, you risk that player not being available. But if you draft that player near the point of his earliest selection, you're likely drafting him too soon.

In order to dig deeper, HQ obtained the complete results for 453 drafts conducted on Mock Draft Central in 2008. We examined the draft results for each player to evaluate the distribution of draft picks and to find common trends.

General Findings

Although each player has a unique distribution of picks, the distributions follow a consistent trend - the picks tend to be clustered around the average value and players are no more likely to go earlier than their average position than after it. The chart below summarizes the percentage of players drafted within 15 picks of his ADP as well as the average standard deviation by grouping of players.

ADP Rank	% within 15 picks	Standard Deviation
1-25	100%	2.5
26-50	97%	6.1
51-100	87%	9.6
100-150	72%	14.0
150-200	61%	17.4
200-250	53%	20.9

As the draft progresses, the picks for each player become more widely dispersed and less clustered around the average. Most top 100 players will go within one round of their ADP-converted round. However, as you reach the mid-to-late rounds, there is much more uncertainty as to when a player will be selected. Pitchers have slightly smaller standard deviations than do batters (i.e. they tend to be drafted in a narrower range). This suggests that drafters may be more likely to reach for a batter than for a pitcher.

Mathematical Analysis

We can use the results from all 453 drafts to calculate the standard deviation of each player's picks. A greater standard deviation means that the picks are more dispersed over the range of observed values. We can use the ADP and corresponding standard deviation for each player to estimate the likelihood that a given player will be available at a certain draft pick.

One limitation of historical data is that it doesn't have much predictive value - just as a player's ADP varies from year to year, the standard deviation will likewise vary. Instead, we can use the historical data to predict future standard deviations as a function of the difference between a players average draft position and the earliest pick with which he's selected. Using a statistical technique called ordinary least squares regression, we estimate the predicted standard deviation for each player as follows:

$$Stdev = -0.42 + 0.42*(ADP - Earliest\ Pick)$$

(That the figure 0.42 appears twice is pure coincidence; the numbers are not equal past two decimal points.)

To pick an example, Ted Lilly had a 2008 ADP of 132.5 and his earliest selection was with the 103rd pick. This corresponds to an estimated standard deviation of 12.0 (by comparison, the actual standard deviation was 10.6).

If we assume that the picks are normally distributed, we can use a player's ADP and estimated standard deviation with the cumulative distribution function to estimate the likelihood that the player is available with a certain pick. This function is built into spreadsheet programs like Microsoft Excel and Google Spreadsheets. Specifically, the likelihood that a player is available is given by the formula:

=1-normdist(x,ADP,Standard Deviation,True)

where «x» represents the pick number to be evaluated.

Implementation

We can use this information to prepare for a snake draft by determining how early we may need to reach in order to roster a player. Suppose you have the 8th pick in a 15-team league draft and your target is 2009 sleeper candidate Nelson Cruz. According to the March 10, 2009 Mock Draft Central data, his 2009 ADP is 128.9 and his earliest selection was with the 94th pick. This yields an estimated standard deviation of 14.2. You can then enter these values into the formula above to estimate the likelihood that he is still available at each of the following picks:

Pick	Likelihood Available
83	100%
98	99%
113	87%
128	53%
143	16%
158	2%

It's important to note that these ADP results are specific to Mock Draft Central and that any provider's ADP results are likely influenced by the default rankings of the host. In most online drafts, if a computer is selecting for the owner (either because the human owner didn't select in time or because there weren't enough human owners to fill the draft) it will select the highest ranked player still available. This prevents highly ranked players from falling too low. Also, even if the draft is computer-free, players ranked highest by the host site will remain on top of the draft board as a subtle reminder to the drafters, which almost certainly influences their ADP. Therefore, if your draft is held online, you should also review the default rankings and ADPs provided by your host site.

Conclusions

Most draft picks for each player are clustered around the average value, especially during the early draft rounds.

For those players whom you target as sleepers and absolutely must have, you generally don't need to reach more than a round or two to have a high probability of successfully rostering them.

Online draft results can be heavily influenced by default rankings. Become familiar with the ADP values for your host provider if you are drafting online.

Mapping draft position to auction value

by Bill Macey

In preparing for your league auction, having accurate predicted values for each player is only half the battle. Whether trying to identify draft day bargains or deciding on which keepers to freeze, having a good sense of what price each player will go for is very important.

Unfortunately, reliable average auction values (AAV) are much tougher to come by than average draft position (ADP) data for snake drafts. Therefore, we used historical 2008 AAV's and ADP's to estimate predicted auction prices as a function of ADP, arriving at the following equation:

$$y = -9.8\ln(x) + 57.8$$

where ln(x) is the natural log function, x represents the actual ADP, and y represents the predicted AAV.

We can use this equation and publicly available ADP data to estimate the auction price for each player in the upcoming season. This equation seems to do an admirable job of capturing predicted auction prices. The statistical measure R-squared, which gauges a model's goodness of fit on a scale from 0 to 1, equals 0.93. Regardless, deviations from the trend line are unavoidable. Because of the asymptotic nature of the logarithmic function, the model seems to predict overly high prices for the top players.

Using Predicted Auction Prices to Identify Bargains

One of the advantages of having more accurate projected stats/prices is that it's easier to identify and roster bargains later in the auction, and you can better plan for your auction by building from the bottom-up. Knowing at which positions you can likely roster such substantial profits later in your auction should give you the confidence to go the extra buck and bid full value on your top targets.

Using Predicted Auction Prices to Select Keepers

Typically, when selecting keepers, owners pay the greatest attention to a player's predicted value vs. the cost to keep him. But this ignores an important consideration - how much it would cost to reacquire him at the draft. For example, it does not make sense to freeze a player at $15 if you are confident you can purchase him for $5, even if his predicted value is $20! Remember that your goal should be to come out of the auction with the greatest possible profit, and that may mean leaving some profit on the table pre-auction. Consider these two hypothetical players:

	Keeper Cost	Predicted Value	Predicted Cost
Player A	$10	$15	$11
Player B	$10	$11	$12

Suppose you could freeze only one. In this example, it may make sense to forgo freezing Player A, even though he has a greater pre-auction predicted profit ($5 vs $1). If you freeze Player A, you lock in $5 of profit before the auction, but then have to pay $1 over full value to roster Player B, for a net profit of $4. However, if you freeze Player B, you only lock in $1 of profit before the auction, but after purchasing Player A for $11 at auction, your total profit is $5.

Profiling the End Game

The end game can be a fertile pool of profitability or a vast wasteland. It can be a carefully crafted tactical play or a dart-throwing exercise after the beer is gone. It is often where leagues are won and lost. But it is an accepted fact that the end game is what you make of it.

Those last few rounds of a snake draft, or auction dollar days, typically contain a wide variety of player types. It can be where we fill out the back end of our pitching staff. It can be where we take a chance on rookies or injury rehabs. It can be where we speculate.

But what is the most profitable approach? For most of us, the end of the draft is just about holes in our roster. These holes are driven by the dynamics of what has transpired up to that point. Sometimes you end up with an open catcher spot and three open pitching spots by default. Sometimes it's by design, but is it for the right reasons? Is it possible that a more strategic approach to roster construction might leave you with end-game holes that could provide better profitability?

We already know the LIMA Plan can identify cheap pitchers with upside that can be rostered in the end game. That's an advantage we have here. But what do marketplace tendencies tell us? What is everyone else doing? How well are they doing it? And how can we use that information to our advantage?

I took a look at the 2008 season as a starting point. I assembled dozens of mock draft results, magazine rankings, and player projections. I looked only at 12-team mixed leagues, since these provided the largest sample of data. I pulled out all the players that were drafted, or ranked in the last two rounds, or were purchased for $1.

The pool of players was extraordinarily large, many hundreds deep. Everyone views end-game value differently, and in a 12-team league, there are that many more players to choose from. It was no surprise only a handful of players appeared with any regularity on multiple lists: Jeremy Accardo, Scott Baker, Mark Buehrle, Jason Giambi, Zach Greinke, Mike Napoli, Ryan Theriot and Kerry Wood. A tip of the hat to all the sources that managed to draft or rank these eight players at the end. With the exception of Accardo, all turned a profit in 2008.

But what types of players were the *most* profitable? I began crunching the numbers. The first cut surprised me:

	Avg Value	%Profitable	Avg Prof	Avg Loss
TOTAL	$1.89	51%	$10.37	($7.17)

On aggregate, the hundreds of players drafted in the end-game earned $1.89 on our $1 investments. While they were profitable overall, only 51% of them actually turned a profit. Those that did cleared more than $10 on average. Those that didn't — the other 49% — lost about $7 apiece.

	Avg Val	% Profitable	Avg Prof	Loss
Batters (52%)	$2.42	51%	$10.41	($5.77)
Pitchers (48%)	$1.32	51%	$9.43	($8.26)

The number of batters and pitchers selected was nearly even and far closer than the typical 23-man roster split

(61%/39%). The percentage of each that was profitable was dead-on at 51%, but batters returned about $1 more in profit. Perhaps more important, the end-game pitching losers lost about $2.50 more money than the batting losers.

Now, remember that this data represents the marketplace. I'd expect that our tools would allow us to close this gap, if not provide a better return overall. But these results, and the ones following, might allow us to leverage our tools even more.

Pos	Pct.of tot	Avg Val	%Profit	Avg Prof	Avg Loss
CA	12%	($1.68)	41%	$7.11	($7.77)
CO	9%	$6.12	71%	$10.97	($3.80)
MI	9%	$3.59	53%	$10.33	($4.84)
OF	22%	$2.61	46%	$12.06	($5.90)
SP	29%	$1.96	52%	$8.19	($7.06)
RP	19%	$0.35	50%	$11.33	($10.10)

These results bear out the danger of leaving catchers to the end game. They were the only position that returned negative value.

It is interesting that corner infielders yielded the best return, by far, both on aggregate profitability as well as the per cent of players turning a profit. However, these first and thirdbasemen represented only 9% of all end-game picks. Perhaps this is an opportunity for us; it almost begs the tactic of leaving open a corner spot for the end.

Besides catcher, outfield was the only other position where fewer than 50% of $1 players turned a profit. However, those players who *were* profitable yielded the biggest return ($12.06) of any position. Even the losers were not horrible; their net $5.90 loss was still better than the average $7.17 loss for the entire pool.

The largest representation of any position in this study was by starting pitchers (29%). It is no surprise that the market leaves a few open pitching slots to the end. However, these were wholly poor investments, particularly in comparison to any of the batter groups. And backfilling your staff with relievers? High risk, high reward, but on net, a meager 35 cent return on those $1 investments.

Age	Pct.of tot	Avg Val	%Profit	Avg Prof	Avg Loss
< 25	15%	($0.88)	33%	$8.25	($8.71)
25-29	48%	$2.59	56%	$11.10	($8.38)
30-35	28%	$2.06	44%	$10.39	($5.04)
35+	9%	$2.15	41%	$8.86	($5.67)

The practice of speculating on younger players – mostly rookies – in the end game was a washout. Part of the reason was that those that even made it to the end game were often of the long-term type. The better prospects were typically drafted earlier.

None of the other age groups offered an appreciable advantage, though the older the player the worse the odds of returning a profit.

	Pct.of tot	Avg Val	%Profit	Avg Prof	Avg Loss
Injury rehabs	20%	$3.63	36%	$15.07	($5.65)
Post-hype prospect	6%	$9.70	70%	$18.71	($11.33)
Has-beens	11%	($0.40)	25%	$7.67	($5.30)

One in five end-gamers were players coming back from injury. While only 36% of them were profitable, the healthy ones returned a healthy profit. The group's losses were small, likely because they weren't healthy enough to play.

The very small percentage of post-hype prospects included players like Carlos Quentin, Lastings Milledge and Conor Jackson. These did *very* well.

Among the "has-beens" in the $1 bin were Jacques Jones, Corey Patterson and Curt Schilling.

We can cross-tab these results even further, but the deeper we dig, the smaller the sample sizes and the less projectable they become. Still, these cuts were interesting:

	Pct.of tot	Avg Val	%Profit	Avg Prof	Avg Loss
Starting pitchers under 25 years old	5%	($3.75)	44%	$8.00	($15.50)
Injury rehab starting pitchers	7%	$0.85	31%	$18.25	($5.83)

We already saw that the youngsters lasting into the end-game were poor investments. The rookie starting pitchers were far worse. While only 31% of the injury rehab starters were profitable, those that finished in the black were incredibly profitable, thanks to arms like Rich Harden and Justin Duchscherer.

As always, there are several caveats with this data.

First, it only represents 2008 and so the anomalies of that year are magnified. The most profitable players in this data pool all returned more than $20 — players like Nate McLouth, Carlos Quentin and Ryan Dempster — and appeared in multiple lists. While there are always surprise breakouts each year, I don't know that we can count on them falling neatly into the same positional, age and contextual categories as displayed above.

Second, the results in deeper leagues are going to vary. The sheer number of eligible end-gamers will be far fewer, particularly if a player needs to be on a 25-man roster to be drafted. That is going to bring down these percentages, perhaps significantly. However, you still might be able to project the relative value of one type of player over another.

Drafting catchers

Joe Mauer had a terrific season in 2009. A top-ranked prospect long heralded as a future star, he finished among the top 15 of all players, the first time he's pulled off that feat in his 5-year career.

The road to this point has not been smooth. He has not gone a year without a stint on the disabled list, including 2009. Despite that, he has returned a profit in every season except 2007. As such, Mauer tends to go relatively early in snake drafts, particularly in those leagues where owners are keyed into position scarcity. But perhaps he shouldn't.

Fantasy owners took a huge bath this year on other high-ranked backstops Russell Martin and Geovany Soto. It begs the question: Are top-ranked catchers good investments? Is this particular commodity — no matter how scarce — too risky to chase?

I looked back over the past seven years to see how profitable these investments had been at the top end.

I started with pre-season Top 200 lists from several sources, using those as my baseline for market value. I then pulled out all the catchers that made it into those top 200's each year, and charted their success.

Year	No.	Profitable	$20+	Profitable
2002	8	0	2	0
2003	9	3	2	0
2004	7	3	3	1
2005	11	2	2	1
2006	14	8	1	0
2007	11	2	2	0
2008	7	4	1	0

The two profitable $20+ catcher investments were Ivan Rodriguez (2004) and Victor Martinez 2005).

It is interesting to note — and this is typical of all players, not just catchers — that profits are usually small while losses are often huge. Aside from Brian McCann in 2006, nobody earned big profit at this position. Conversely, 14 of these 67 catchers (21%) returned less than half their draft value. It's just the Gravity Principle at work.

If positional talent was evenly distributed among the top 200, we'd expect at least 17 catchers on each of these lists. But it's not — with a range of talent from 7 (2004, 2008) to 14 (2006) — which is why we have scarcity. And while "position scarcity" rules teach us to reach a bit at the top end in order to avoid the poor value at the bottom, I'm not sure that makes sense here. To wit...

Range	No.	Average		Profitable		Pool
		Proj	Act	No.	Pct	Pct
$20+	11	$23	$16	1	9%	38%
$15-19	18	$17	$14	7	39%	38%
$10-14	32	$12	$10	11	34%	29%
-$10	6	$8	$11	3	50%	27%

These are small sample sizes. Still, if we compare this to the player pool as a whole, we can see where catchers might follow a different set of rules. Only one of 11 (9%) projected for $20-plus value returned profit. That compares to 38% for the $20+ commodities in the entire player pool.

We already know catchers are riskier investments by virtue of the demands on the position they play. It seems that they may also be risky based on even cautious value expectations. Again, small sample, but interesting.

Note that the small bottom range is the only one to show an aggregate dollar profit. We have to remember that this range only includes those catchers who made the Top 200. There are many below that threshold who potentially pull the numbers down. But these catchers who project to have some positive value are important.

If you ran a ranking of players based on their projected stats without positional adjustments, you will end up with fewer catchers than need to be drafted in your league. The only catchers who appear are the ones whose stats project to have positive value. Still, many fantasy leaguers decide to pass on catchers until the end-game, but by then, the only ones remaining have sub-$1 values. *Someone* is going to get stuck with them, though.

What the charts above tell us is that we should probably pass on the more expensive commodities since the odds of profit are low. But we also have to make sure we don't get stuck with catchers that fall below $1 in value. That leaves a target pool of low-to-mid level catchers.

Note that 37% of those projected between $1 and $14 (14 of 38, the bottom two tiers) turned a profit, as compared to 28% of the player pool as a whole. That should be your target group.

This is the strategy of letting someone else go deep on the Mauers and McCanns, and focusing more on the Suzukis and Bakers. It's a strategy of targeting the middle; it's your best chance of returning par value on your investments.

Now, if all the members of your league read this article and decide to pass on the top catchers, the prices may come down to where projected value meets market value. The odds of that happening are slim. But at least this gives you a better sense of where the value and profitability lies.

Sitting stars and starting scrubs *by Ed DeCaria*

"Who should I start this week?" This simple question drives fantasy owners to madness more than any other. Conventional wisdom suggests sticking with trusted stars despite difficult matchups, but the temptation to start inferior pitchers against weaker opponents can be torturous. It is time to put an end to these mental tug-of-war matches and discover the truth about starting pitcher matchups.

In the following analysis, we will look back at the nearly 30,000 starting pitcher appearances in the majors from 2003-2008 to determine when, if ever, we should consider sitting a superior starter with a tough matchup and instead use an inferior starter with an easy matchup.

Let's first establish the baseline starting pitcher performance expectations for each group of SPs and each group of opposing offenses (SPs are grouped by year-end 5x5 roto value; opposing offenses are grouped by year-end runs per game, park-adjusted for each SP appearance):

Group	$	WHIP	ERA	Win%
Elites	$24+	1.10	2.95	52%
Stars	$16+	1.23	3.48	45%
Reg	$8+	1.31	4.03	41%
Scrub	$0+	1.42	4.55	35%
Repl	($4)+	1.54	5.24	28%

Opp	RC/G	WHIP	ERA	Win%
Dom	5.25+	1.52	5.40	32%
Strong	5.00+	1.48	5.11	33%
Neutral	4.25+	1.41	4.53	35%
Weak	4.00+	1.35	4.15	37%
Dormnt	<4.00	1.28	3.62	41%

Here we have a conflict. Better SPs clearly post better results, but better offenses pose a threat to all SPs. We will resolve this conflict by pitting each type of pitcher against each type of opponent to see at which levels, and in which stats, playing the matchups can be more beneficial than blindly riding our better hurlers each week.

Before considering the impact on surface-level results, let's quickly summarize how matchups affect underlying pitching indicators,

notably those that make up BaseballHQ's Pure Quality Start (PQS) scores:

IP/Start: More difficult matchups cost pitchers one to two outs per start on average.

K/9: Quality of opposition has a small effect on strikeouts in some pitcher bands.

K/BB: Tougher opponents inflate walk rates and erode K/BB rates slightly. However, at no point would we prefer an inferior starter with an easy matchup to a superior starter with a tough matchup based on K/BB alone (the same can be said for IP/Start and K/9).

Hit Rate (H%): Dominant offenses generate 2-4% more hits on balls-in-play than dormant ones, which translates to almost one extra base hit allowed per start. For this indicator, we also see a shift in control of the matchup from pitcher toward opponent, so much so that a $19 Star will see a higher H% in a tough matchup than a $4 Scrub will see in an easy matchup.

Home Run Rate: Dominant offenses generate 0.3-0.5 more HR/9 than dormant ones, a strong enough difference that Stars yield significantly more home runs to top-tier offenses than Scrubs do to bottom-tier ones.

Individually, the effect of the opposing offense on each of these five pitching factors seems small: a third of an inning, a quarter of a strikeout, a half of a walk, most of a hit, and a third of a HR. But what happens when we put them all together to estimate their combined impact on key roto categories like WHIP, ERA, and Wins?

Baserunners Allowed (WHIP)		Opponent Group				
Pitcher Group		Dominant	Strong	Neutral	Weak	Dormant
		5.25+	5.00-5.24	4.25-4.99	4.00-4.24	<4.00
Elites	$24.00+	1.19	1.08	1.11	1.06	1.02
Stars	$16.00-23.99	1.31	1.30	1.23	1.16	1.13
Regulars	$8.00-15.99	1.40	1.37	1.30	1.25	1.20
Scrubs	$0.00-7.99	1.52	1.49	1.41	1.34	1.31
Replacements	($4.00)-($0.01)	1.64	1.55	1.53	1.52	1.42

There is a WHIP difference of about 20% between dormant and dominant offenses. At the extremes, Scrubs deliver WHIPs on par with Stars, and Replacements on par with Regulars.

Runs Allowed (ERA)		Opponent Group				
Pitcher Group		Dominant	Strong	Neutral	Weak	Dormant
		5.25+	5.00-5.24	4.25-4.99	4.00-4.24	<4.00
Elites	$24.00+	3.46	3.04	3.04	2.50	2.20
Stars	$16.00-23.99	3.98	3.94	3.44	3.17	2.87
Regulars	$8.00-15.99	4.72	4.57	3.96	3.66	3.24
Scrubs	$0.00-7.99	5.37	4.92	4.47	4.07	3.66
Replacements	($4.00)-($0.01)	6.02	5.41	5.15	4.94	4.42

ERA varies by almost 50% between dormant and dominant offenses. As emphasized by the stair-step pattern of the chart, when the difference in matchup is severe, we are better off with a pitcher one or two "steps" below our default starter.

Game Outcome (Winning %)		Opponent Group				
Pitcher Group		Dominant	Strong	Neutral	Weak	Dormant
		5.25+	5.00-5.24	4.25-4.99	4.00-4.24	<4.00
Elites	$24.00+	48%	51%	51%	57%	58%
Stars	$16.00-23.99	40%	46%	46%	46%	48%
Regulars	$8.00-15.99	40%	39%	40%	44%	45%
Scrubs	$0.00-7.99	31%	33%	35%	37%	42%
Replacements	($4.00)-($0.01)	27%	28%	28%	28%	32%

The pattern holds for wins as well, though wins are unpredictable enough on a single game basis that playing the matchups here would be quite speculative.

So what do we recommend for 2010?

1. Never start below replacement-level pitchers.

2. Always start elite pitchers.

3. Other than that, never say never or always.

Playing matchups can pay off when the difference in opposing offense is severe.

Two-start pitcher weeks

by Ed DeCaria

Most fantasy leaguers drool at the prospect of a two-start week from one of their pitchers. More innings! More wins! More strikeouts! Maybe so. But maybe more isn't always such a good thing. Two-start pitchers can hurl two DOMinant outings, two DISasters, or anything else in between, as shown by these results from 2003-2008:

PQS Pair	% Weeks	ERA	WHIP	Win/Wk	K/Wk
DOM-DOM	20%	2.53	1.02	1.1	12.0
DOM-AVG	28%	3.60	1.25	0.8	9.2
AVG-AVG	14%	4.44	1.45	0.7	6.8
DOM-DIS	15%	5.24	1.48	0.6	7.9
AVG-DIS	17%	6.58	1.74	0.5	5.7
DIS-DIS	6%	8.85	2.07	0.3	5.0

Weeks that include a DISaster start clearly produce terrible fantasy results. Unfortunately, avoiding such disasters is much easier in hindsight than it is when we select our lineups each week. Should we avoid certain pitchers? Should we avoid certain matchups? Or should we just stop giving our pitchers two chances to screw up instead of one?

To find out, we first analyzed the category contributions of one- and two-start weeks for each combination of pitcher quality and matchup difficulty. To do so, we grouped pitchers by year-end 5x5 R$ (as described in the previous essay), and classified opposing offenses as Easy (Runs/Game <4.25), Neutral (R/G 4.25-5.00), or Tough (R/G 5.00+). Here are the category highlights:

ERA and WHIP: When the difference between opponents is severe, inferior pitchers can actually be a better percentage play for managing ERA and WHIP. This is true both for one-start pitchers and two-start pitchers, and for choosing inferior one-start pitchers over superior two-start pitchers.

Strikeouts per Week: Unlike the two rate stats, there is a massive shift in the balance of power between one-start and two-start pitchers in the strikeout category. Even Elites ($24+) and Stars ($16-$23) with easy one-start matchups can only barely keep pace with two-start Replacements (<$0) in strikeouts per week.

Wins per week: Like strikeouts, wins per week are completely dominated by the two-start pitchers. Even the very worst two-start pitchers will earn a half of a win on average, which is the same rate as the very best one-start pitchers.

Based on their potential to accumulate counting stats, it is clear that two-start pitchers are an asset. To find out how these extra counting stats *directly* compare to the potential ERA and WHIP damage caused by DISaster outings, we can use the common valuation language of Standings Gain Points (SGP) to estimate in clear terms the impact of each one-start vs. two-start decision on winning fantasy leagues.

Using an average of standard 12-team AL/NL-only SGP denominators, we quantified the impact (+/– vs. replacement-level) of SP performance on year-end standings using three new facts: Total SGP per Week, Rate SGP per Week (ERA and WHIP only), and Count SGP per Week (Strikeouts and Wins only).

The following chart plots the median Total SGP per Week for each type of matchup along with the 10th, 25th, 75th and 90th percentiles of performance:

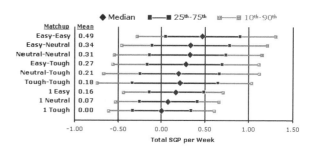

Two-start pitchers have higher mean and median Total SGP per Week values across the board. But while one-start pitchers cannot match the expected impact or upside of the two-start options, they clearly do help to mitigate the downside risk of disaster starts.

The final chart explores this risk versus reward element further by breaking out Rate SGP per Week and Counting SGP per Week separately. The two contoured rings effectively plot all 23,000+ starting pitcher weeks from 2003-2008, marking the outer bounds of performance as measured by SGP:

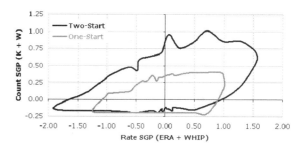

The vertical axis shows the +/- impact of each week's counting stats while the horizontal axis shows the +/- impact of each week's rate stats. The parts of each contour that extend further up/right delivered better SGP results, and the parts that extend further down/left delivered worse SGP results.

This illustrates very clearly that two-start pitchers leave us more vulnerable to significant downside losses as measured by Rate SGP, but offer more upside in both Rate SGP and Count SGP than one-start options.

With these findings, we no longer have to rely on intuition to guide our decision-making. If strikeouts and wins are our strategic priority, we should use as many two-start weeks as the rules allow, even if it means using a Replacement-level pitcher with two tough starts instead of a Regular or Scrub with a single easy start. But if ERA and/or WHIP management are our priority, we must recognize just how powerful two-start pitchers can be, as a single week might impact the standings by over 1.5 points in ERA/WHIP, positively or negatively. Choose wisely.

Fanalytic Rules

The cluelessness of WHIP

by Peter Kreutzer, AskRotoman.com

For years, in the *Fantasy Baseball Guide* (which I edit), we ran the pitching stat called "Ratio." Every year, people would complain and tell me that their league used the pitching stat called WHIP, and ask why we didn't publish that instead.

For years, I replied that:

1. Ratio (((Hits+Walks)*9)/IP)) is much more descriptive and granular than WHIP ((Hits+Walks)/IP), and that,

2. Ratio looks better, since it's on the same scale as ERA.

I then usually also note that I used Ratio in the leagues I played in, and if they had a problem they should do the same.

I didn't win this argument. Many readers said they saw my point, but even if they agreed with me, the other people in their league did not, and so weren't inclined to change. After a lengthy discussion with such readers a few years ago, I changed the magazine. We now publish WHIP instead of Ratio.

To ease the transition, the first year I included a handy WHIP to Ratio converter to cut out of the magazine, which I assume some people are still using. It featured a bodacious picture of WHIP kitten Anna Benson. Unfortunately, I've lost mine.

I bring this up now because I was looking at the Tout Wars AL standings and was struck by the WHIP category:

Team	WHIP	Pts
Siano – MLB.com	1.32	12
Colton/Wolf – RotoWorld	1.34	11
Sam Walker – FantasyLand	1.34	10
Moyer – Baseball Info Solutions	1.37	9
Erickson – Rotowire.com	1.37	8
Michaels – Creative Sports.com	1.37	7
Berry – ESPN.com	1.37	6
Shandler – Baseball HQ	1.37	5
Peterson – STATS LLC	1.38	4
Collette – OwnersEdge.com	1.38	3
Grey – ESPN	1.41	2
Sheehan – Baseball Prospectus	1.42	1

My first reaction, assessing the three-way race for the league title between Mike Siano, Lawr Michaels, and Ron Shandler, is that this is unbearably close. After all, there are five teams at 1.37 and two more at 1.38. Siano is safely atop the category, but couldn't Michaels easily gain two points? Couldn't Shandler easily gain four?

In both cases, such gains would erase Siano's lead in the overall standings. And certainly the numbers say it's that close. It's a virtual tie, for pete's sake.

In fact, it's not, but WHIP isn't granular enough to tell you that. Here are the same rankings using Ratio.

Team	WHIP	Pts
Siano – MLB.com	11.84	12
Colton/Wolf – RotoWorld	12.02	11
Sam Walker – FantasyLand	12.10	10
Moyer – Baseball Info Solutions	12.29	9
Erickson – Rotowire.com	12.29	8
Michaels – Creative Sports.com	12.31	7
Berry – ESPN.com	12.33	6
Shandler – Baseball HQ	12.37	5
Peterson – STATS LLC	12.39	4
Collette – OwnersEdge.com	12.45	3
Grey – ESPN	12.65	2
Sheehan – Baseball Prospectus	12.75	1

To show how much distance there is between these tied teams, here are few facts, looking at Shandler since he's the last of the teams with a 1.37 WHIP:

If Shandler gets 10 innings with no hits or walks his Ratio drops to 12.26, enough to pass everyone, and his WHIP drops to 1.36.

If Shandler gets 10 innings with 10 hits + walks, still a pretty good performance, his ratio drops to 12.34, and he gains no points.

What if Shandler pitches 25 innings the rest of the way, with an excellent Ratio of 9.00 (a WHIP of 1.00) which would be way good, his Ratio would end up at 1.366, which would gain him two points but would still look like 1.37 on these reports. His Ratio would drop to 12.30.

The point is that by using WHIP, especially displayed to the second place, it looks like there's a virtual tie, when the reality is that the standings are close, but it would take an extraordinarily good effort for one team to break ahead of the others. Ratio better illustrates this and it provides better and more information, which is why I still think it is a vastly superior stat.

CONVERTER

RATIO	to	WHIP	WHIP	to	RATIO
8.00	-	0.89	0.90	-	8.10
8.50	-	0.94	0.95	-	8.55
9.00	-	1.00	1.00	-	9.00
9.50	-	1.06	1.05	-	9.45
10.00	-	1.11	1.10	-	9.90
10.50	-	1.17	1.15	-	10.35
11.00	-	1.22	1.20	-	10.80
11.50	-	1.28	1.25	-	11.25
12.00	-	1.33	1.30	-	11.70
12.50	-	1.39	1.35	-	12.15
13.00	-	1.44	1.40	-	12.60
13.50	-	1.50	1.45	-	13.05
14.00	-	1.56	1.50	-	13.50
14.50	-	1.61	1.55	-	13.95
15.00	-	1.67	1.60	-	14.40

ED NOTE (from my conversation with Peter): You should start a grassroots movement to get us back to Ratio. But the term "Ratio" is just not going to cut it. Too vague and vanilla. Needs a better moniker, like Walks plus Hits per Game, or "WHIG." All sorts of literary and political implications transitioning from WHIP to WHIG.

PETER's RESPONSE: Good point about Ratio. How about WH/9, pronounced Whine?

New rules for a new decade

It is always good to take an objective look at your constitution every so often to make sure there are valid reasons behind the rules your league uses. After 11 years with a constitution that was born when the internet was still a novelty, the Tout Wars caretakers recently revisited some rules that did not make sense. If nothing else, it was just a matter of instilling a bit more logic into the process. Here are the changes we made in 2009:

Position eligibility

The original Rotisserie rules state that a player must have appeared in the Majors at a position at least 20 times during the previous season, or failing that, the position at which he appeared the most, to be draft eligible at that spot.

This works fine for most players, but there is an illogical hole for a few. Late season call-ups who only play a few games might not earn enough eligibility at their natural position. For instance, catcher Jeff Clement was only DH-eligible last year.

The new Tout rule states that any player whose 20-game eligibility cannot be determined from Major League games will default to the 20-game eligibility in whatever league he last played in.

Draft eligibility

The original Roto constitution stated that the only players eligible to be drafted are those who are on a MLB team's 25-man roster. Many leagues today spend inordinate effort to even *find* final 25-man rosters.

This is a game of supply and demand where everyone values commodities differently. Why limit the available commodities upon which to bid?

Tout Wars' new rule states that you can draft *anyone*. That includes minor leaguers, those who have been cut, who are on the DL or who are in a foreign league. Nearly everyone is fair game. The only exceptions are players in the opposite league (for AL-Only and NL-Only leagues).

If an owner wishes to spend his precious and scarce draft dollars or draft picks on a speculative player, why prevent him from doing so? He is choosing to incur the risk of rostering a player who may not have a job. He is filling a valuable slot that might otherwise be taken up with a more productive player. This adds another level of strategy to the game. And one person's speculation means there will be one more player with positive value available to bid on.

Previously, if Jason Heyward opens the season in the minors, he would be ineligible to be drafted. You would have to budget your FAAB if you had hopes of getting him, and his fates would rest on the results of a blind auction. Now, you could bring him out in open auction and get a shot at him up front. His true market value would be revealed, albeit framed by the risk that he might not get a call-up, or that he might struggle. What is that risk worth? You'd know on draft day.

An objection to this rule might be that it prevents us from defining a finite player pool from which to calculate projected dollar values. This is *exactly* why this rule is so

good. It forces us to deal with the reality that *there is no such thing as a finite player pool.*

Free agent FAAB eligibility

Here, as on draft day, one has to wonder why our choices have to be limited. In the new rules, there is no restriction on the types of players who may be bid on. (See next essay, *"FAABing the future"*)

Salary reclaims

We have always allowed a team to reclaim the salary of a player who was out for the year due to injury and add it to his FAAB. But "out for the year" is not an official declaration; different sources report varying takes on a player's odds of returning. "60-day DL" does not necessarily mean a player is out for the year either.

In the end, we decided that all we needed to do was take a stand and deal with the exceptions. The 60-day DL became the official declaration and those few DLed players who returned got put back in the free agent pool. The owner has to decide how to handle it and incur the risk of a player returning. With an unlimited DL list, it is not necessary to cut anyone; the decision comes down to how much the owner needs the additional FAAB.

Transaction frequency

Our Founding Fathers created a game with weekly player moves. This was a decision made out of necessity; today we have the capability of managing our roster at least daily.

The good news is that this reflects real-life baseball management. The bad news is that not everyone has the time to be running a daily operation for six months in addition to our own lives. But it doesn't have to be all or nothing.

With the new rule, we retain the weekly deadline for free agent acquisition and trade transactions. We added daily deadlines for intra-roster moves (activations and reserves) but only for replacement of players who are placed on the disabled list, demoted, suspended, or deceased — natural openings. Replacing poor performers and streaming players daily is prohibited.

Incentive to Stay Active

Many leagues are faced with the prospect of owners losing interest if their team falls out of contention. This is a problem even in the experts leagues. So, to ensure that the very best and most involved owners compete in these leagues, any owner who finishes with fewer than a predetermined number of standings points during the preceding two years (that number based on league size) will risk losing his spot. No more than two owners per league can be booted in any season.

Any resulting openings will be filled by high performing owners in the other leagues or by new candidates.

Obviously, most of you would be unable to enact such a rule exactly as written. However, I imagine there are other disincentives that could be implemented, from cash fees to smaller draft budgets. You probably know your league's hot buttons. Perhaps all it would take to keep all owners playing until the end is knowing that they'd avoid having to fund next draft-day's snacks and beer.

FAABing the future

The world of 12-team AL leagues and 13-team NL leagues is facing new obstacles in recent years thanks to changes in the real game. The 14/9 split between batters and pitchers is no longer an accurate reflection of how rosters are structured in the majors anymore. Of the 30 teams, each with 25-man rosters, not one had 14 batters for any length of time in 2009. In fact, nine of the teams spent most of the season with only 12 batters (seven of the nine in the NL, naturally), which meant teams often had *more pitchers than hitters*.

For fantasy purposes in AL- and NL-only leagues, that leaves a disproportionate draft penetration into the batter and pitcher pools:

	BATTERS	PITCHERS
On AL rosters	180	170
Drafted, AL	168	108
Pct.	93%	64%
On NL rosters	201	199
Drafted, NL	182	117
Pct.	91%	59%

These drafts are now depleting about 30% more batters out of the pool than pitchers. Add in those leagues with reserve lists — perhaps an additional 6 players per team removing another 72-78 players — and you can see that the post-draft free agent pools are ridiculously thin, especially on the batting side.

The typical free agent batting pool has become a wasteland of backup catchers, fifth outfielders, and bench infielders, their value blocked by productive front-liners awaiting DL stints. FAAB bidding wars are for players like Jeremy Reed and Brent Lillibridge.

The strategic fallout is that in order to win these leagues, particularly redraft leagues, *you have to ace your draft* and *stay healthy*.

Acing the draft is an admirable goal. However, we often say that you can't win your league on draft day (though you can certainly lose it). With all the uncertainty of six months of play, it is unreasonable to expect any more than just positioning yourself to contend.

Staying healthy is almost laughable.

In order for any team to have a reasonable shot at contending, there needs to be at least some influx of new talent during the season. Otherwise, all these AL-only and NL-only leagues are crowning their champions based strictly on the winner of the attrition sweepstakes. The title goes to the last team standing.

Injuries do provide a steady stream of minor league call-ups, and that is good. However, the sheer number and frequency of DL placements precludes us from adequately evaluating that new talent. Any warm body is going to draw some immediate FAAB activity. We are never afforded the time to assess that maybe Kris Medlen isn't ready for the Show. Too late; he was already FAABed.

The problem is that standard rules prohibit us from bidding on a free agent until he's actually on a major league roster. But why is that?

In a game that contains a finite number of roster spots and a finite FAAB allowance, it would seem that sufficient limitations are already in place to prohibit us from "tossing spaghetti at a wall to see what sticks." Of course, that practice is not so much "prospecting" as "guessing," and not something that a true game of skill would encourage.

So, why not allow us to FAAB anyone?

Tout Wars enacted this as a new rule in 2009, and it has added a completely new strategic layer to the game.

There is no restriction on the types of players who may be bid on — Majors, minors, foreign leagues are all okay. Tout rules allow $0 FAAB bids, but if a player is not on an active Major League roster, the minimum bid has to be $1.

For a team battling to move up in the standings, this rule provides **hope.** For leagues that struggle to keep their owners engaged all season, hope is the cure. To wit...

When I first wrote this essay on May 29, my team was in seventh place, about 20 points out of first. I had the second best offense in the league but my pitchers were struggling.

Prior to this year, I'd spend the summer rotating a stream of LIMA-worthy middle relievers onto and off of my active roster, waiting for a decent starting pitcher prospect to get called up. Then I'd toss a bunch of FAAB at him and pray that I was the high bidder. Hope was driven by a series of random variables.

This year, I was able to speculate on upwardly-mobile talent in advance. Between original reserve picks and FAAB acquisitions, I went through the spring and early summer with pitchers like Clay Buchholz, Wade Miller, Michael Bowden and Chris Tillman on reserve, awaiting call-up. Back in May, I figured that, if even two of this quartet got the call and were productive, I'd have a reasonable shot to close the 20-point gap.

Some might see this "stockpiling" as a bad thing, however, there is a good balance here, for two reasons:

1. It enhances involvement at all levels. Before, FAAB bidding was a reactive process. You'd wait for a player to get called up, then react by having to figure out what to bid on him. Now, you have to keep a pulse on each organization and anticipate moves. It's pro-active.

2. There is always a cost. I had to spend precious FAAB dollars and fill up all four reserve roster slots in order to hold onto my four speculative pitchers. These are finite resources that might have been spent on other commodities. In fact, when David Purcey was demoted, I had to choose to play with his dead roster spot or give up one of my pitching futures. I opted to run short-handed so I could follow Purcey's progress in the minors before having to make a decision. I was able to speculate in advance on pitchers like Vince Mazzaro, Aaron Poreda and Carlos Carrasco similarly. Some panned out, some didn't.

So there are always limits to what you can do. Opening up the pool of available FAAB commodities provides a wider range of options, but you still have to pay, either in FAAB dollars or a roster slot.

But "hope" is worth the cost. For me, it helped close the gap to six points and a third place finish.

Fanalytic Gaming Strategies

The LIMA Plan

The LIMA Plan is a strategy for Rotisserie leagues (though the underlying concept can be used in other formats) that allows you to target high skills pitchers at very low cost, thereby freeing up dollars for offense. LIMA is an acronym for Low Investment Mound Aces, and also pays tribute to Jose Lima, a $1 pitcher in 1998 who exemplified the power of the strategy. In a $260 league:

1. *Budget a maximum of $60 for your pitching staff.*

2. *Allot no more than $30 of that budget for acquiring saves.* In 5x5 leagues, it is reasonable to forego saves at the draft (and acquire them during the season) and re-allocate this $30 to starters ($20) and offense ($10).

3. *Draft only pitchers with:*
- Command ratio (K/BB) of 2.0 or better.
- Strikeout rate of 5.6 or better.
- Expected home run rate of 1.0 or less.

4. *Draft as few innings as your league rules will allow.* This is intended to manage risk. For some game formats, this should be a secondary consideration.

5. *Maximize your batting slots.* Target batters with:
- Contact rate of at least 80%
- Walk rate of at least 10%
- PX or SX level of at least 100

Spend no more than $29 for any player and try to keep the $1 picks to a minimum.

The goal is to ace the batting categories and carefully pick your pitching staff so that it will finish in the upper third in ERA, WHIP and saves (and IP or K's in 5x5), and an upside of perhaps 9th in wins. In a competitive league, that should be enough to win, and definitely enough to finish in the money. Worst case, you should have an excess of offense available that you can deal for pitching.

The strategy works because it better allocates resources. Fantasy leaguers who spend a lot for pitching are not only paying for expected performance, they are also paying for better defined roles – #1 and #2 rotation starters, ace closers, etc. – which are expected to translate into more IP, wins and saves. But roles are highly variable. A pitcher's role will usually come down to his skill and performance; if he doesn't perform, he'll lose the role.

The LIMA Plan says, let's invest in skill and let the roles fall where they may. In the long run, better skills should translate into more innings, wins and saves. And as it turns out, pitching skill costs less than pitching roles do.

In *snake draft leagues*, don't start drafting starting pitchers until Round 10. In *shallow mixed leagues*, the LIMA Plan may not be necessary; just focus on the BPI benchmarks. In *simulation leagues*, also build your staff around BPI benchmarks.

Variations on the LIMA Plan

LIMA Extrema: Limit your total pitching budget to only $30, or less. This can be particularly effective in shallow leagues where LIMA-caliber starting pitcher free agents are plentiful during the season.

SANTANA Plan: Instead of spending $30 on saves, you spend it on a starting pitcher anchor. In 5x5 leagues where you can reasonably punt saves at the draft table, allocating those dollars to a high-end LIMA-caliber starting pitcher can work well as long as you pick the right anchor.

One way to approach that selection is...

The RIMA Plan

LIMA is based on optimal resource allocation. These days, however, no matter how good of a team you draft, player inconsistency, injuries and unexpected *risk factors* can wreak havoc with your season. The RIMA Plan adds the element of **RI**sk **MA**nagement.

Players are not risks by virtue of their price tags alone. A $30 Dan Haren, for example, might be a very good buy since he is a healthy, stable commodity. But most LIMA drafters would not consider him because of the price.

The RIMA Plan involves setting up two pools of players. The first pool consists of those who meet the LIMA criteria. The second pool includes players with high Reliability grades. The set of players who appear in both pools are our prime draft targets. We then evaluate the two pools further, integrating different levels of skill and risk, and creating six hierarchical tiers of players to draft from:

TIER A: LIMA-caliber with high Reliability grades
TIER B: LIMA-caliber with moderate Reliability grades
TIER C: Non-LIMA with high Reliability grades
TIER D: LIMA-caliber with low Reliability grades
TIER E: Non-LIMA with moderate Reliability grades
TIER F: Non-LIMA with low Reliability grades

Tier C is where RIMA opens up more opportunities. While we'd typically stay away from low-skilled players, carefully-chosen "C" bodies can provide valuable support if you are careful. In this group you might find inning-eater hurlers who could help boost your strikeout totals, though might have elevated ERAs. If the rest of your staff has a solid skills foundation, you can often weather the mediocre numbers that come along with these arms. The fact that they are low risk means that you know exactly what you will be getting and so you can better plan for it.

The goal for your roster is to assemble a balanced portfolio of solid performers and steady AB and IP-eaters that provide good return on your investment.

The RIMA concept is also applicable in non-Rotisserie formats. The process of integrating skill and risk management is universal for all types of league formats.

A new look at LIMA

by Ed DeCaria

The LIMA Plan urges fantasy owners to look for beneath-the-surface skills to acquire low-cost pitchers on auction day. First introduced here more than 10 years ago, LIMA predates many now well-known baseball revelations, including:

- Fielding-independent pitching discovery that pitchers exhibit very little control over hits on balls-in-play
- Batted ball segmentation into groundballs, flyballs, line drives, pop-ups, and now even "fliners"
- Home run rate normalization as a function of fly ball rate, park factors, and luck
- Pitch outcome measurements including ball vs. strike ratios, swinging strike rates, and first pitch strikes
- PITCHf/x electronic scouting of pitch types, release points, velocity, movement, and location

Yet as such breakthroughs continue to reveal new insights and breed new strategies, LIMA has proven unusually durable as a straightforward way to capture value and profit on fantasy baseball rosters.

To provide a sense of LIMA's enduring relevance, we analyzed all pitcher-seasons of greater than 50+ IP from 2000 to 2007 ("Y1") who pitched any number of innings in the following season ("Y2"). The following grid shows the migration pattern of pitchers as a comparison of their Y1 LIMA skills vs. Y2 LIMA skills (using the filters of >=6.0 K/9, >=2.0 K/BB, and <=1.0 HR/9). You read this chart from side-to-side in each row:

LIMA SKILL MIGRATION* FROM Y1 to Y2				
# Filters Met by Year:	Y2 = 3	Y2 = 2	Y2 = 1	Y2 = 0
Y1 = 3	45%	33%	17%	5%
Y1 = 2	22%	38%	28%	13%
Y1 = 1	11%	29%	35%	25%
Y1 = 0	6%	15%	33%	46%
*Follow left to right by row; shaded cells indicate no skill change.				

This shows that of all full LIMA qualifiers in Y1, 45% of them also met all three LIMA requirements in Y2. 33% of them still exhibited two of the three LIMA skills, for a cumulative total of almost 80%. Though there is some skill regression from year-to-year (most often in the HR/9 filter that we now more accurately gauge using G/L/F and HR/FB rates), it is unlikely that a LIMA-qualified pitcher in Y1 will suddenly lose all remnants of skill in Y2. The Y2 story is much worse for non-LIMA qualifiers from Y1, as very few of them suddenly turn into full LIMA qualifiers in Y2.

Why is this understanding of migration important? Because Y2 LIMA skills (and by extension Y1 LIMA skills) yield better Y2 results:

Y2 ERA BY LIMA SKILL MIGRATION* FROM Y1 to Y2				
# Filters Met by Year:	Y2 = 3	Y2 = 2	Y2 = 1	Y2 = 0
Y1 = 3	3.12	4.02	4.69	5.34
Y1 = 2	3.35	4.19	4.71	5.33
Y1 = 1	3.48	4.32	4.55	5.37
Y1 = 0	3.67	4.35	4.60	5.28
*Follow left to right by row; shaded cells indicate no skill change.				

The strong ERAs in the upper left quadrant alone suggest that Y1 LIMA-caliber performers should continue to be a high draft priority for Y2. And because Y1 LIMA-caliber performers are much more likely to re-exhibit at least two of the three LIMA skills in Y2, they also help to protect against the disaster ERAs generated by the non-LIMA Y2 performers shown on the right side of the chart above.

Now that we know that LIMA can still help us to capture value, we also want to determine if LIMA can still help us to capture profit. To find out, we analyzed all Y1 pitcher-seasons in the sample with an ERA >=4.00 to determine what percent of them crossed below the 4.00 ERA threshold in Y2, a change that would typically generate a profit for fantasy owners. Of these pitchers, those who met two or three LIMA filters in Y1 were 1.5 to 2.0 times as likely to see a Y2 ERA in the 3.00's (a robust 35-40% breakout success rate) as those pitchers who met only one or zero of the LIMA filters in Y1 (only a 15-25% breakout success rate).

Since 2000, there have been nearly 100 pitchers per season who met two or three LIMA criteria in 50+IP in Y1 who also went on to meet at least two in Y2. These are the pitchers that fantasy leaguers can buy at auction expecting LIMA-caliber skills and good-to-excellent ERAs in Y2.

Our final question is: "Can an owner acquire nine of these pitchers cheaply?" To answer this, we looked at all positive value pitchers from 2008 ("Y2") for a 15-team standard 5x5 mixed league. In such a league, by definition, 135 pitchers (9 pitchers x 15 teams) would have earned positive value as calculated at the *end* of the season. Of these, more than 80% had exhibited two or three LIMA skills in 2007 ("Y1"). As expected, many of these pitchers were already among the game's elite and thus would have commanded a high salary or draft pick.

However, according to late March Average Draft Position (ADP) reports covering 453 drafts, nearly 50% of all 135 positive-value pitchers were likely available for next to nothing, including nearly 50 pitchers that had met two or three LIMA filters he prior year.

Indeed, LIMA continues to serve us well. Should we blindly cling to the original filters in the face of so many new innovations? Of course not. But a strategy aimed at acquiring lower-cost pitchers based on projected skill so that we can spend a disproportionate part of our budget on hitting is still a sound approach.

Revisiting the Santana Plan

by Michael Weddell

The Santana Plan asks, "do elite pitchers tend to be better investments than other pitchers?" If so, how might we identify those elite pitchers?

We compiled seasonal data on all major league pitchers during the period 1988-2008, 21 years, or 42 league-seasons worth of data. Let's assume a consistent format of 12-team leagues. Each team spends $260, and fantasy leagues spend an average of 31% of their dollars on pitchers.

We'd like to focus on a pitcher's skills more than the standard 5x5 R$ does. Let's discard wins and saves because we know those are very noisy categories whose outcomes depend on variables beyond each pitcher's performance. Instead, let's add innings pitched into our R$ calculation. Innings pitched indirectly lead to wins, which are valuable. Also, most leagues value innings pitched indirectly by imposing minimum IP threshold for the season.

Our elite starter filters are:

$24 dollars (when rounded to the nearest whole dollar) or more earned in year 1 when we compute earnings based on K, IP, xERA, and xWHIP.

$24 dollars or more earned in year 0. Consistency significantly improved our results.

No filter based on age. If a pitcher is already at an elite level, we can expect that performance to continue.

$28 dollars or more earned in at least one of year 0 and year 1 when we use the more results-based method of R$, with K, IP, actual ERA, and actual WHIP.

That last filter may surprise us, given that we usually focus on just base performance indicators when possible. We are willing to overlook one less than stellar recent year when the more skills-based indicators are strong, but we do want to see a starter post strong actual results in at least one of the two prior years. Adding this filter did not make a huge difference, but it did improve the results. We'll consider pitchers who would have been elite starters except for this last filter to be on our "honorable mentions" list.

Results of our Elite Starter Analysis

Historically, an elite pitcher meeting those filters on average has kept 80% of his R$ value from year 1 to year 2. This is a terrific result because the baseline case is only 52%. That's the percentage of year 1 R$ earnings that pitchers earn in year 2, considering just pitchers with $1 or more of R$ earnings in year 1 and who had some nonzero number of innings pitched in year 2.

In sum, the filters for the elite pitchers seem to work: they retain much more of their R$ value from year 1 to year 2 than the average pitcher does.

We have 87 elite starters during the 19 years of 1989-2007, an average of about 4.5 each year for mixed leagues.

Historically, 36% of elite pitchers improved, returning a greater R$ in the second year than they did the first year. That is an impressive performance considering they already were at an elite level. 17% collapsed, returning less than a third of their R$ in the second year. The remaining 47% experienced a middling outcome, keeping more than a third but less than all of their R$ from one year to the next.

For 2010, we have eight sound investments::

Zach Greinke (RHP, KC)
Roy Halladay (RHP, TOR)
Cole Hamels (LHP, PHI) .
Danny Haren (RHP, ARI)
Cliff Lee (LHP, CLE/PHI)
Tim Lincecum (RHP, SF)
C.C. Sabathia (RHP, NYY)
Javier Vazquez (RHP, ATL)

Honorable mentions: **Josh Beckett** (RHP, BOS) and **Ricky Nolasco** (RHP, FLA).

The Santana Plan Strategy Tips

There is still downside, undiversified risk. You'll invest heavily in an elite starter knowing that historically 1 out of 6 has been a disaster, returning less than a third of his previous year's R$. If you already have the best team in a keeper format entering this season, the Santana plan still may present too much risk.

Have a back-up plan. There are so few elite pitchers, especially for AL- or NL-only leagues, that you can't count on being able to purchase one anywhere near your price point. Be prepared to shift to a more conventional Portfolio3 or LIMA strategy.

Nominate the elite starters early. Especially in keeper leagues, the first few players often are not bid up to their fully inflated prices. Early in the auction, your competition may believe there are plenty of alternatives in the pool, but you know better. Furthermore, if you aren't going to buy one of the elite starters, you will need to know this early enough to be able to shift to a different strategy.

Individually research the elite starters before the draft. If you are going to bank on one of these guys to lead your pitching staff, make sure you are comfortable with that risk. In particular, consider whether there are any injury risks that you should know about: most of the disasters among elite starters are due to injury-riddled seasons, some of which could have been detected in advance.

Remember that an elite starter's impact on your team's ERA and WHIP will be magnified if your staff has fewer innings. A budget of one elite starter, three lower-priced but fairly high-skilled starters, one closer and the rest LIMA plan relievers should still let you spend the typical 69% of your budget on hitting. Buying more than one elite starter provides diminishing returns and doesn't leave enough money left for your other needs.

Total Control Drafting

Part of the reason we play this game is the aura of "control," our ability to create a team of players we want and manage them to a championship. We make every effort to control as many elements as possible. But in reality, the players that end up on our teams are largely controlled by the other owners. *Their* bidding affects your ability to roster the players you want. In a snake draft, the other owners control your roster to an even greater extent. We are really only able to get the players we want within the limitations set by others.

However, an optimal roster can be constructed from a fanalytic assessment of skill and risk. We can create our teams from that "perfect player pool" and not be forced to roster players that don't fit our criteria. It's now possible. It's just a matter of taking *Total Control*.

Why this makes sense

1. Our obsession with projected player values is holding us back. Fact: Only about 65% of players drafted provide a return within +/-$5 of projection. To get that percentage up to about 85%, you'd have to open the range to +/- $9. This is not indicative of poor forecasting; it's the nature of the beast. So, if a player on your draft list is valued at $20 and you agonize when the bidding hits $23, odds are about two chances in three that he could really earn anywhere from $15 to $25. What this means is, in some cases, and within reason, you should just pay what it takes to get the players you want.

2. There are no such things as bargains. Most of us *don't* just pay what it takes because we are always on the lookout for players who go under value. But we really don't know which players will cost less than they will earn because prices are still driven by the draft table. The concept of "bargain" assumes that we even know what a player's true value is. To wit:

If we target a player at $23 and land him for $20, we might *think* we got a bargain. In reality, this player might earn anywhere from $19 to $26, making that $3 in perceived savings virtually irrelevant.

The point is, a "bargain" is defined by your particular marketplace at the time of your particular draft, not by any list of canned values, or an "expectation" of what the market value of any player might be. So any contention that TCD forces you to overpay for your players is false.

3. "Control" is there for the taking. Most owners are so focused on their own team that they really don't pay much attention to what you're doing. There are some exceptions, and bidding wars do happen, but in general, other owners will not provide that much resistance.

How it's done

1. Create your optimal draft pool.

2. Get those players.

Start by identifying which players will be draftable based on the RIMA criteria. Then, at the draft:

Early Game: Your focus has to be on your roster only. When it's your bid opener, toss a player you need at about 50%-75% of your projected value. Bid aggressively. Forget about bargain-hunting; just pay what you need to pay. Of course, don't spend $40 for a $25 player, but it's okay to exceed your projected value within reason.

Mix up the caliber of openers. Instead of tossing out an Albert Pujols at $35 in the first round, toss out a Denard Span at $11. *Wise Guy Baseball's* Gene McCaffrey suggests tossing all lower-end players early, which makes sense. It helps you bottom-fill your roster with players most others won't chase early, and you can always build the top end of your roster with players others toss out.

Another good early tactic is to gauge the market value of scarce commodities with a $19 opener for Joe Nathan or a $29 opener for Jacoby Ellsbury.

Other owners may pick up on the fact that you are only throwing out names of players you want, so mix in a few non-targets to throw them off. Also, bid aggressively on *every player*; it will obscure which ones you really want.

Mid-Game: If you've successfully rostered 10-12 players with high skills and Reliability grades, you will have likely built a solid foundation for your team. At that point, you can relax some of the reliability constraints and take a few chances on players with high upside, but higher risk, like upwardly mobile rookies.

End game: You will need to relax the reliability targets for your last picks, so it might be a good idea to make sure those last buys are all pitchers (who are inherently more risky). You'll note that most high-skilled end-game LIMA pitchers have low reliability grades by nature.

At the end of the draft, you may have rostered 23 players who could have been purchased at somewhat lower cost. It's tough to say. Those extra dollars likely won't mean much anyway; in fact, you might have just left them on the table. TCD almost ensures that you spend all your money.

In the end, it's okay to pay a slight premium to make sure you get the players with the highest potential to provide a good return on your investment. It's no different than the premium you'd pay to get the last valuable shortstop, or for the position flexibility a player like Jerry Hairston provides. With TCD, you're just spending those extra dollars up front on players with high skill and low risk.

The best part is that you take more control of your destiny. You build your roster with what you consider are the best assemblage of players. You keep the focus on your team. And you don't just roster whatever bargains the rest of the table leaves for you, because a bargain is just a fleeting perception of value we have in March.

The Portfolio3 Plan

The previously discussed strategies have had important roles in furthering our potential for success. The problem is that they all take a broad-stroke approach to the draft. The $35 first round player is evaluated and integrated into the plan in the same way that the end-gamer is. But each player has a different role on your team by virtue of his skill set, dollar value, position and risk profile. When it comes to a strategy for how to approach a specific player, one size does not fit all...

We need some players to return fair value more than others. When you spend $40 on a player, you are buying the promise of putting more than 15% of your budget in the hands of 4% of your roster. By contrast, the $1 players are easily replaceable. If you're in a snake draft league, you know that a first-rounder going belly-up is going to hurt you far more than a 23rd round bust.

We rely on some players for profit more than others. Those first-rounders are not where we are likely going to see the most profit potential. The $10-$20 players are likely to return more pure dollar profit; the end-gamers are most likely to return the highest profit percentage.

We can afford to weather more risk with some players than with others. Since those high-priced early-rounders need to return at least fair value, we cannot afford to take on excessive risk. Since we need more profit potential from the lower priced, later-round picks, that means opening up our tolerance for risk more with those players.

Players have different risk profiles based solely on what roster spot they are going to fill. Catchers are more injury prone. A closer's value is highly dependent on fickle managerial whim. These types of players are high risk even if they have the best skills on the planet. That needs to affect their draft price or draft round.

For some players, the promise of providing a scarce skill, or productivity at a scarce position, may trump risk. Not always, but sometimes. At minimum, we need to be open to the possibility. The determining factor is usually price. A $12, 10th round Fernando Rodney is not something you pass up, even with a Reliability Grade of FCA.

In the end, we need a way to integrate all these different types of players, roles and needs. We need to put some form to the concept of a diversified draft approach. Thus:

The **Portfolio3 Plan** provides a three-tiered approach to the draft. Just like most folks prefer to diversify their stock portfolio, P3 advises to diversify your roster with three different types of players. Depending upon the stage of the draft (and budget constraints in auction leagues), P3 uses a different set of rules for each tier that you'll draft from. The three tiers are:

1. Core Players
2. Mid-Game Players
3. End-Game Players

TIER 1: CORE PLAYERS

Roster Slots	Budget	BATTERS Rel	Ct%	PITCHERS PX or SX	Rel	BPV
5-8	Up to $160	BBB	80%	100 100	BBB	75

These are the players who will provide the foundation to your roster. These are your prime stat contributors and where you will invest the largest percentage of your budget. In snake drafts, these are the names you pick in the early rounds. There is no room for risk here. Given their price tags, there is usually little potential for profit. The majority of your core players should be batters.

The above chart shows general roster goals. In a snake draft, you need to select core-caliber players in the first 5-8 rounds. In an auction, any player purchased for $20 or more should meet the Tier 1 filters.

The filters are not terribly strict, but they are important, so you should stick to them as best as possible. An 80% contact rate ensures that your batting average category is covered. PX and SX ensure that you draft players with a minimum league average power or speed. On the pitching side, a BPV of 75 ensures that, if you must draft a pitcher in your core, it will be one with high-level skill. For both batters and pitchers, minimum reliability grades of BBB should cover your risk.

Since these are going to be the most important players on your roster, the above guidelines help provide a report card, of sorts, for your draft. For instance, if you leave the table with only three Tier 1 players, then you know you have likely rostered too much risk or not enough skill. If you manage to draft nine Tier 1 players, that doesn't necessarily mean you've got a better roster, just a better core. There still may be more work to do in the other tiers.

Tier 1 remains the most important group of players as they are the blue chips that allow you to take chances elsewhere. However, there can be some play within this group on the batting side.

The 80% contact rate is important to help protect the batting average category. However, with some care, you can roster a few BA Suzuki-esque studs to allow you the flexibility to take on some low-contact hitters who excel in other areas (typically power). The tactic would work like this... If you are short on Tier 1 players and have exhausted the pool of those who meet all the filters, you can work your way down the following list...

TIER 1 BATTERS

	Rel	Ct%	PX	or SX
Primary group	BBB	80%	100	100
Secondary	BBB	75%	110	110
Tertiary	BBB	70%	120	120

...knowing full well that, for every player you roster from these lower groups, you are putting your batting average at greater risk. You should only do this if you think the power/speed gains will sufficiently offset any BA shortfalls.

These two sub-groups are not fixed filters; they form a continuum. So if you have a player with a 78% contact rate, your PX/SX requirement would probably be somewhere around 105. I would not go anywhere near a player with a contact rate less than 70%.

TIER 2: MID-GAME PLAYERS

Roster		BATTERS				PITCHERS	
Slots	Budget	Rel	Ct% or	PX or	SX	Rel	BPV
7-13	$50-$100	BBB	80%	100	100	BBB	50

All players must be less than $20
Batters must be projected for at least 500 AB

In previous incarnations of P3, Tier 2 was essentially "everyone else." However, after several failed experiments, we realized that Tier 2 matters. There needs to be a middle tier of players that have a specific function. And at minimum, that function has to minimize risk.

A logical configuration might just do the opposite of Tier 3. That lower tier maintains skill while sacrificing reliability. Could Tier 2 just maintain reliability while sacrificing skill? Yes, almost.

In an early 2008 column, I noted how fellow Tout combatant, Jason Grey, was consistently able to assemble offensive juggernauts by the singular tactic of accumulating massive amounts of often-cheap playing time. Intrinsic skill was irrelevant. On the offensive side, this makes sense.

Runs and RBIs are only tangentially related to skill. If a player is getting 500 AB, he is likely going to provide positive value in those categories just from opportunity alone. And given that his team is seeing fit to give him those AB, he is probably also contributing somewhere else.

These players have value to us. And we can further filter this pool of full-timers who miss the P3 skills criteria by skimming off those with high REL grades.

There are two dangers in this line of thinking. First, it potentially puts the batting average category at risk. You don't want to accumulate bad AB; when you dig yourself into a hole in BA, it is the one category that is nearly impossible to dig out of. However, this just means we need to approach it tactically; if we decide to roster a Mark Reynolds, we must also roster an Ichiro Suzuki.

Second, this line of thinking assumes we can accurately project playing time. But if we focus on those players who are locked into firm roles, there is still a decent-sized pool to draw from.

Tier 2 is often where the biggest auction bargains tend to be found as the blue-chippers are already gone and owners are reassessing their finances. It is in that mid-draft lull where you can scoop up tons of profit. In a snake draft, these players should take you down to about round 16-18.

TIER 3: END-GAME PLAYERS

Roster		BATTERS			PITCHERS	
Slots	Budget	Rel	Ct%	PX or SX	Rel	BPV
5-10	Up to $50	n/a	80%	100 100	n/a	75

All players must be less than $10

For some fantasy leaguers, the end game is when the beer is gone and you have to complete your roster with any warm body. In the Portfolio3 Plan, these are your gambling chips, but every end-gamer must provide the promise of upside. For that reason, the focus must remain on skill and conditional opportunity. P3 drafters should fill the majority of their pitching slots from this group.

By definition, end-gamers are typically high risk players, but risk is something you'll want to embrace here. You

probably don't want a Randy Winn-type player at the end of the draft. His AAB reliability grade would provide stability, but there is no upside, so there is little profit potential. This is where you need to look for profit so it is better here to ignore reliability; instead, take a few chances in your quest for those pockets of possible profit. If the player does not pan out, he can be easily replaced.

As such, a Tier 3 end-gamer should possess the BPI skill levels noted above, and...

- playing time upside as a back-up to a risky front-liner
- an injury history that has depressed his value
- solid skills demonstrated at some point in the past
- minor league potential even if he has been more recently a major league bust

Notes on draft implementation...

Auction leagues: Tier 1 player acquisition should be via the Total Control Drafting method. Simply, pay whatever it takes, within reason. Be willing to pay a small premium for the low risk and high skills combination.

Snake drafters will have choices in the first six rounds or so. There are no guarantees — a swing-pick seed might negate any chance you have for rostering some players — but at least there are some options. If you miss out on the cream, you can either drop down and select a lower round player early, or relax the filters a bit to grab someone who might have higher value but perhaps greater risk.

Position scarcity: While we still promote the use of position scarcity in snake drafts, it may be more important to have solid foundation players in the early rounds.

Drafting pitchers early is still something we advise against. However, if you are going to grab a pitcher in the first six rounds, at least make sure it's a Tier 1 name. It is still a viable strategy to hold off on starting pitchers until as late as Round 10 or 11; however, if it's Round 7 and Dan Haren is still sitting out there, by all means jump.

LIMA Plan: Although LIMA says no starting pitchers over $20, Tier 1 provides a few options where it would be okay to break the rules. You can adjust your $60 pitching budget up to accommodate, or downgrade saves targets.

Punting saves: Still viable, unless a Tier 1 closer falls into your lap. These are extremely rare commodities anyway.

Keeper leagues: When you decide upon your freeze list, you should be looking for two types of keepers — the best values *and* the most valuable players. Freezing a $6 Tim Lincecum is a no-brainer; where some drafters struggle is with the $25 Aramis Ramirez. Given that TCD says that we should be willing to pay a premium for Tier 1 players, any name on that list should be a freeze consideration.

Adding in the variable of potential draft inflation, you should be more flexible with the prices you'd be willing to freeze players at. For instance, if you currently own a $45 Hanley Ramirez, you might be tempted to throw him back. However, between draft inflation and the premium you should be willing to pay for a Tier 1 commodity, his real value is probably well more than $50.

The 2010 lists of Tier 1,2 and 3 players appear in the Ratings & Rankings section.

"Portfolio4:" A Plan for Rebuilders

by Patrick Davitt

Almost all fantasy research and discussion starts from the premise that every owner is playing to win this year. The reality, however, is that most leagues are keeper, and therefore many owners, perhaps half or more, are going to be rebuilding.

Portfolio3 is an example of a tool that focuses on win-now thinking. But with a few tweaks and adjustments, rebuilders can use it as well.

Portfolio 3

Portfolio 3 separates players into three tiers: low-risk foundational studs in Tier 1; cheaper, reliable guys with guaranteed PT in Tier 2; and low-cost, high-skilled, riskier speculations in Tier 3.

But rebuilders need a player mix that meets three different goals:
* Getting potential keepers
* Providing valuable trade fodder
* Competing well enough to maintain interest in the current year.

It's no fun languishing with 32 points, looking up at teams with 70-plus. And in many leagues, it's a rebuilding drawback because draft positions and other benefits go to teams finishing higher.

With that in mind, let's have a cut at a plan for rebuilders.

Rebuilders should value players differently — not just as contributors but as trade chips — so they should be willing to spend outrageous amounts on the top players. But what *kinds* of players? The ones with particular value to the team while they're on its roster *and* big-time trade value.

Tier 1

In Tier 1, we want SB studs, established closers and skilled "name" starting pitchers, preferably on good teams. Roughly 70% of the budget should get four or five such studly players through relentless overbidding. Strike early, before the other owners (especially the other rebuilders) realize what you're doing.

There are two reasons for targeting these studs. First, SBs and Saves (and Wins, to a lesser extent) often offer the quickest path to standings gains, and individual players can have a disproportionate impact on those categories, magnifying their value as trade commodities.

Second, while the rebuilder waits for the race and its trade opportunities to develop, he also compiles good positions in SBs, BA and runs (most SB guys help in these), Saves, Wins, and ERA/WHIP.

The rebuilder ultimately ends up punting power. He has limited resources, otherwise he'd be playing to win. So he targets his limited resources to compete in six categories rather than spreading them around and languishing in eight or 10.

Tier 2 and Tier 3

In Tier Two, the rebuilder spends 20% of his budget on five or six $8-$12 hitters with speed and BA skills – players who buttress this year's BA/SB foundation, and who might grow into decent keepers.

Tier 3 is even more speculative than in P3: 13 or 14 rookies, prospects, fifth outfielders, backup-to-the-backup catchers and the like, and young LIMA fifth starters and setup pitchers with good skills. Regular P3 describes a key aspect of this tier as "fungibility," and the rebuilder needs to be prepared to churn these spots as better options come available in the free agent pool.

One corollary to the Tier 3 guideline: Owners in very shallow leagues (less than 50% penetration) should look to this tier as a chance to load up with relatively good, established SPs and OFs, because there are a lot of them available. In 12-team mixed, if the other 11 teams take five OFs each, plus another each as UT, they'd soak up 66 OFs. That still leaves 24 starting MLB OFs!

Testing

We back-tested P4 using final 2007 pre-season projections and final results. To simulate availability, we randomized players within the tier parameters. We simulated Tier 1 overpayment by going 35% over projected value. And to simulate inflation, we bumped all the Tier 2 guys 10%.

The 4-stud outfit rang up a 4x4 offensive line of 101-478-215-.274. Cellar lows for HR and RBI but good for 9-10 points in BA and a clean win in SB. That's 23-24 offensive points, or the equivalent of six points per category.

The pitching fared similarly: 68-36-3.72-1.31 meant 25-29 pitching points. A shrewd, active owner should be able to upgrade through the FA pool, especially by dropping poor pitchers, which could easily help the ERA/WHIP for a couple of points.

The 48-53 total would compete for seventh or eighth place most years – a big gain over the usual 11th or 12th that is the fate of most rebuilders.

The team ended up with eight useful keepers before any trades, so capturing just one keeper apiece from trading each of its four studs would mean a solid core of 12 keepers for the next year.

Conclusion

This analysis has weaknesses. The simulation didn't account for positions. Inflation adjustments and "the overbidding premium" were guesstimates. The Tier 3 SPs thinned out so fast, we had to "reach" once.

But the idea is sound. P4 would provide an owner a modestly competitive team, with real potential to build quickly for a subsequent year.

This approach is not for the faint of heart, nor for the casual owner. It requires research and preparation going in, and a willingness to work the waiver wire, free-agent pool and trade market all season.

Fanalytic Gaming Formats

It's a game we love, but nobody says we need to be married to any specific set of rules.
The following alternative game formats provide different fanalytic challenges and experiences...

Rotisserie7

Rules

1. Mixed league. Any number of teams.

2. 25-man roster, stocked any way you like so long as all your positions are covered. Each week, 16 of those players will be designated as "active:" 9 position players (1B, 2B, 3B, SS, CA, OF, OF, OF, DH), 5 man starting rotation and 2 relief pitchers. Nine reserves at any position.

3. 4x4 game with the following categories:

   BATTERS: HR, (Runs scored + RBIs - HR), SB, BatAvg
   PITCHERS: Wins, Saves, Strikeouts, ERA

4. Snake draft or auction is fine. For auctions, budget for the 16 active players only, followed by a snake draft for the remaining 9 players.

5. Rotisserie's category ranking system is converted into a weekly won-loss record. Depending upon where your team finishes for that week's isolated statistics determines how many games you win for that week. Each week, your team will play seven games, hence Rotisserie7.

*Place	Record	*Place	Record
1st	7-0	7th	3-4
2nd	6-1	8th	2-5
3rd	6-1	9th	2-5
4th	5-2	10th	1-6
5th	5-2	11th	1-6
6th	4-3	12th	0-7

* Based on overall Rotisserie category ranking for the week.

At the end of each week, all the roto stats revert to zero and you start over. You never dig a hole in any category that you can't climb out of, because all categories themselves are incidental to the standings.

6. There is unlimited once-weekly movement allowed between the active and reserve rosters during the season. Access to the free agent pool is limited to one player per week per team. Free agents are acquired via a snake draft in reverse order of the standings.

7. The regular season lasts for 23 weeks, which is 161 games. Weeks 24, 25 and 26 are for play-offs. The top six teams make the play-offs. In larger leagues (minimum 15 teams), the top eight teams can make the play-offs. Here it becomes a head-to-head game, but Rotisserie standings again determine the victors.

Week 24: Teams 1 and 2 get byes. Team 3 meets Team 6, Team 4 meets Team 5. In larger leagues, Teams 1 and 2 would meet teams 8 and 7, respectively.
Week 25: Team 1 versus Team 4 or Team 5; Team 2 versus Team 3 or Team 6
Week 26: Two winners meet for the championship

The pot is divided 70% for regular season standing and 30% for play-off results.

Stratified Rotisserie

Rules

1. Start with the same basic rules as a standard Rotisserie competition, but this is a pick-a-player contest.

2. A league may include any number of owners. You will be drafting from both American and National leagues.

3. Each team will have a 25-man roster and a 15-man reserve squad. Each active roster will have 15 batters and 10 pitchers. Standard roto positional structure applies, with two DH/utility slots on the offense side. Reserve rosters have no positional restrictions.

4. *The only players available are those who posted a dollar value of $5 or less in the previous season.*

5. Each team stocks its roster individually. There is no draft or auction. While players may end up on more than one team, the spread of talent will likely ensure that no two teams look exactly alike.

6. There is unlimited once-weekly movement allowed between the active and reserve rosters during the season. There is no trading in this league.

7. On June 1 and August 1, you may select up to five new players to add to your team. For each player who is added, an active or reserve player must be dropped. New players must come from the original list of eligibles (less than $5).

Strategic considerations

The players with the best upside value are last year's injury rehabs and minor leaguers looking at significant playing time.

In drafting for your active roster, your key goal is to accumulate quality playing time.

Since you will be playing most of the season from the roster you draft, your reserve squad becomes very important. Naturally, you'll want to grab as many positional backups as possible to protect against injury and excessive bench-sitting of your active players. Your reserve also is a good place to stash upwardly mobile minor leaguers who could get promoted mid-season and have an impact.

Rule modification options for the truly masochistic

1. Draft from only one league, rather than both.
2. Reduce the strata threshold to $3 instead of $5.
3. Make all injury rehabs ineligible if they posted a roto value more than $5 in their last healthy season.
4. Limit the number of players with less than 20 games of major league experience to 5 per roster.
5. No more than 3 players with less than 20 games of major league experience can be active at any time.

Quint-Inning

Object: To assemble a group of players that will amass the most points during a single baseball game.

Auction draft: A player auction is conducted among five "owners" before the ballgame and must be completed prior to the start of the game. Each owner must acquire 5 players from the current 25-man rosters of the two major league teams playing in that game, at a cost not to exceed $55. There are no positional requirements for the 5 players other than one must be a pitcher. All 5 roster spots must be filled.

An owner need not spend his entire auction dollar allotment. Any unspent dollars may be added to an owner's Free Agent Acquisition Budget (FAAB).

The "salaries" paid for the five players have no further relevance once the draft is over. They are essentially acquisition costs only.

Points and standings: Team standings are calculated based on a ranking of points accumulated by players at the time they are on an owner's roster.

BATTERS accumulate points for bases gained or lost:

Single = +1	Double = +2
BB = +1	Triple = +3
HBP = +1	Home run = +4
SB = +1	Error = -2
CS = -1	

PITCHERS accumulate points for IP minus ER:

IP = +1	Earned Run allowed = -1

The IP point is awarded to the pitcher who is on the mound when the third out of the inning is registered.

Win = +5	Save = +3

These points are awarded to the owner who has the pitcher of record on his team at the end of the game, even if the owner did not draft that pitcher. If an unrostered pitcher gets a win or save, these points are not awarded.

"The Quint:" At the beginning of the 5th inning, any owner has the option of doubling the points (positive and negative) for one player on his roster for the remainder of the game. Should that player be traded, or dropped and then re-acquired, his "Quint" status remains for the game.

Ninth Inning: Beginning in the 9th inning, all batting points (positive and negative) are doubled.

FAAB points: Unused FAAB units can be converted to scoring points at the end of the game. The conversion rate is 10 FAAB = 1 point.

In-game roster management: The five drafted players must remain on each owner's roster for at least the first inning. Then, players may be dropped, added or traded, and all roster size restrictions are then lifted, except:

- Rosters must contain at least one player at all times.
- Rosters must contain at least one pitcher at all times.

All player moves take effect at the beginning of each half inning. All player moves must be announced prior to the first pitch of that half inning; otherwise, the move will not take effect until the following half inning.

Dropping players: Any player can be cut from an owner's roster at any time after the first inning. Players who are cut may not be re-acquired by the original owner.

Adding players: Each owner is allotted a free agent acquisition budget (FAAB) of $50 per game for the purpose of acquiring players. Available for FAABing are...

- undrafted players on one of the 25-man rosters
- players that had been cut by other owners
- players of those owners who drop out of the game

An owner can announce that he is placing a bid on a free agent at any time after the first inning. Other owners can then bid until a winner is determined. No other player needs to be dropped. All players accumulate points from the half inning after which they were acquired. Owners are limited to one player per half inning acquired via FAAB.

Trading: A trade can be consummated at any time after the first inning, between any two or more owners. The only commodities that may be traded are rostered players and FAAB dollars. Uneven trades are allowed and roster sizes do not have to be squared up at any time. However, should a team's only pitcher be traded to another owner, a pitcher must be received in return or a free agent pitcher acquired immediately. If a pitcher is not added to a roster before the first pitch of the next half-inning, the trade is nullified.

Stakes: Quint-Inning can be played as a no-stakes, low stakes, moderate or higher stakes competition.

- It costs ($1/$5/$55) to get in the game.
- It costs (25 cents/$1/$5) per inning to stay in the game for the first four innings.
- Beginning with the 5th inning, the stakes go up to (50 cents/$2/$10) per inning to stay in the game.
- Should the game go into extra innings, the stakes rise to ($1/$5/$25) to stay in the game until its conclusion.

Each owner has to decide whether he is still in the game at the end of each full inning. Owners can drop out at the end of any inning, thus forfeiting any monies they've already contributed to the pot. When an owner drops, his players go back into the pool and can be FAABed by the other owners.

Determining the winner: The winner is the owner who finishes the game with the most points. Tie-breakers:

- æ Team with the most number of players contributing positive scoring points.
- æ Team with the most pitching points.
- æ Team with the most FAAB remaining.

Scorekeeping: A Quint-Inning scoresheet, along with more detailed rules and strategies, can be downloaded from http://www.baseballhq.com/free/free050819.shtml

---

The anti-Internet gambling bill that was signed into law in 2006 has carve-out language that defines the legality of fantasy sports. It states that fantasy games are exempt as long as they follow several stipulations. The second stipulation:

2. Winning outcomes are determined by skill for contests that use results from multiple real-life games.

Quint-Inning fails at this, which means we won't be setting up QI games on the internet. But feel free to play at home.

IV.

MAJOR

LEAGUES

The Teams

The following four pages contain stat boxes for all 30 major league teams plus summary boxes for both leagues. The stats themselves will be mostly familiar to you from the player boxes, however, we have included both batter and pitcher BPIs on each line.

Each team box is divided into three sections.

At Home represents all batting and pitching statistics accumulated by that team in its home ballpark.

Away represents all batting and pitching statistics accumulated by that team in its games on the road.

Opp@ represents all batting and pitching statistics accumulated by all visiting teams when they played at the home ballpark.

Within each section are BPIs from the past three years, 2007-2009. Teams that have changed ballparks during that time may cause some inconsistent data.

To get a sense of ballpark effects, look at both the At Home and Opp@ sections in tandem. If the levels are similar, then it may indicate a particular ballpark tendency. If the levels are not similar, then it may be team dependent. You can compare this data from one team's box to another for additional insight.

As an example, the Dodgers' batters have a contact rate at home in the low to mid-80%'s but the opposition at Dodger Stadium has posted levels consistently 5%-7% lower. This could indicate the success of the Dodgers pitching staff as opposed to any park effects. In contrast, Florida's At Home and Opp@ contact rates are both in the high 70%'s, which might be more telling of Land Shark park effects.

In the pitching section of each chart, we also show the number of wins (W) each team had, the Pythagorean projected wins (Py) they should have had based on their runs scored and runs allowed, and the percentage of save opportunities successfully converted. The Braves underperformed in road games in 2008 by a massive 11 games, winning only 29 while they should have won 40. As Bill James' Plexiglass Principle tells us, phenomena like that tend to correct quickly. And it did in 2009.

The save opportunities data are interesting. We don't typically consider that a closer's success might hinge on the friendliness of his environment. However, one of the reasons the Yankees did so well this year might have been their offense's ability to get to opposition bullpens. Visiting teams in Yankee Stadium were only able to close out 38% of their save opportunities, the lowest percentage of any team in either league over the past six years! The Cincinnati bullpen has been showing some improvement over the past three years, closing out their opposition at home by the rates of 48%, 69% and 80% this past year.

Other things to look at include a team's SX and SBO rates, which provide insight into which teams are easier or more difficult to run on. The opposition has been running more and more on the White Sox at home, with SBO rates increasing from 8% in 2007 to 12% in 2008 and 13% in 2009. Compare that to the Cardinals, where opposing runners test Yadier Molina only 5% of the time.

Some other interesting tidbits…

Opposing pitchers have a horrible time in Fenway Park, posting a 5.76 ERA there over the past three years. No other team's home offense brutalized opposing pitchers more than the Red Sox' 5.90 ERA did in 2009.

Home runs per fly ball tend to regress to 10%, but there are a few ballparks where the base rate has been consistently higher over the past three years, including U.S. Cellular Field in Chicago, Cincy, Colorado, Houston, Milwaukee, Philadelphia, Tampa and Texas. As you'd expect, consistent sub-10% rates can be found in places like KC, Dodger Stadium, Oakland, Pittsburgh, San Diego and San Francisco.

The Mets can't blame Citi Field for their woeful season. Park effect differences from Shea were negligible, and if anything, affected the opposition more negatively than it did the Mets. More telling was the Met pitchers' 5.02 xERA on the road, along with a BPV of 17.

And in the new Yankee Stadium, 14% of fly balls went yard overall in 2009, but for the opposition, 16% (and a whopping 1.7 hr/9, highest in either league).

BATTING / PITCHING

ARI	Yr	Avg	OB	Slg	OPS	bb%	ct%	h%	Eye	G	L	F	PX	SX	SBO	xBA	RC/G	W	Py	Sv%	ERA	WHIP	H%	S%	xERA	Ctl	Dom	Cmd	hr/f	hr/9	BPV
At Home	07	260	331	445	776	10	81	29	0.56	41	18	41	110	112	10%	262	5.15	50	42	70%	4.11	1.39	30%	73%	4.18	3.4	6.5	1.9	10%	1.1	47
	08	268	341	446	786	10	78	32	0.49	40	21	39	118	108	6%	262	5.36	48	43	74%	4.10	1.27	31%	70%	4.04	2.6	7.8	2.9	11%	1.0	92
	09	270	340	451	791	10	78	32	0.49	42	19	39	121	107	8%	264	5.38	36	36	62%	4.78	1.38	31%	67%	4.71	3.1	7.3	2.3	10%	1.1	69
Away	07	241	305	382	687	8	78	28	0.41	41	17	42	91	101	9%	234	3.95	40	37	88%	4.17	1.38	30%	72%	4.17	3.4	7.1	2.1	10%	1.0	57
	08	234	308	385	693	10	75	28	0.43	39	21	40	104	87	5%	241	4.09	34	39	52%	3.88	1.32	31%	72%	3.94	3.0	7.7	2.5	9%	0.8	79
	09	237	306	385	691	9	75	29	0.40	44	17	39	100	100	11%	237	4.02	34	39	68%	4.09	1.37	30%	73%	4.13	3.4	7.1	2.1	10%	1.0	56
Opp @ ARI	07	265	332	427	759	9	81	30	0.52	43	19	38	98	85	8%	256	4.90	31	39	67%	4.75	1.38	29%	68%	4.91	3.6	6.4	1.8	10%	1.2	38
	08	254	307	404	712	7	78	30	0.34	46	19	35	101	95	9%	251	4.21	33	38	62%	4.78	1.46	32%	69%	4.77	3.8	7.8	2.0	10%	1.0	55
	09	266	326	428	755	8	79	31	0.43	44	19	37	106	121	10%	261	4.82	45	45	72%	4.64	1.46	32%	71%	4.56	3.7	7.6	2.1	10%	1.1	57

ATL	Yr	Avg	OB	Slg	OPS	bb%	ct%	h%	Eye	G	L	F	PX	SX	SBO	xBA	RC/G	W	Py	Sv%	ERA	WHIP	H%	S%	xERA	Ctl	Dom	Cmd	hr/f	hr/9	BPV
At Home	07	266	335	416	751	9	79	31	0.50	45	19	36	93	88	6%	251	4.80	44	42	75%	3.96	1.34	29%	74%	4.03	3.4	7.0	2.0	11%	1.1	55
	08	278	353	411	764	10	82	32	0.65	46	22	32	85	92	5%	265	5.09	43	39	58%	4.44	1.41	30%	70%	4.38	3.7	6.8	1.8	11%	1.0	48
	09	257	333	392	725	10	80	30	0.58	43	21	36	89	81	7%	254	4.55	40	42	68%	3.43	1.28	30%	74%	3.70	3.3	7.8	2.4	7%	0.7	75
Away	07	282	339	452	790	8	80	33	0.43	43	19	38	108	85	6%	260	5.24	40	46	67%	4.27	1.38	30%	72%	4.21	3.2	6.7	2.1	11%	1.1	58
	08	263	332	405	737	9	81	30	0.56	44	22	34	93	80	5%	266	4.70	29	40	60%	4.50	1.40	30%	70%	4.39	3.6	6.7	1.8	12%	1.0	49
	09	269	338	418	756	9	81	31	0.56	44	19	37	98	84	3%	259	4.91	46	49	62%	3.73	1.36	31%	74%	3.81	3.2	7.3	2.3	9%	0.8	70
Opp @ ATL	07	254	323	407	730	9	79	29	0.49	44	19	37	93	102	9%	250	4.54	37	39	61%	4.41	1.43	31%	72%	4.34	3.6	7.1	2.0	11%	1.1	55
	08	263	334	426	761	10	80	30	0.54	47	21	32	106	110	9%	275	4.99	38	42	57%	4.58	1.55	32%	71%	4.60	4.1	6.4	1.5	8%	0.8	27
	09	245	313	370	683	9	77	30	0.42	46	19	34	87	97	9%	241	3.99	41	39	66%	3.63	1.39	29%	76%	3.86	3.8	6.6	1.7	9%	0.9	37

BAL	Yr	Avg	OB	Slg	OPS	bb%	ct%	h%	Eye	G	L	F	PX	SX	SBO	xBA	RC/G	W	Py	Sv%	ERA	WHIP	H%	S%	xERA	Ctl	Dom	Cmd	hr/f	hr/9	BPV
At Home	07	280	338	430	768	8	84	31	0.57	44	17	38	89	104	12%	258	4.97	35	33	48%	5.38	1.54	31%	66%	5.40	4.2	6.5	1.5	9%	1.0	25
	08	275	338	444	782	9	83	30	0.56	42	19	38	107	92	7%	271	5.15	37	36	63%	5.14	1.54	30%	70%	4.96	4.1	5.9	1.4	12%	1.3	17
	09	288	348	455	804	8	83	32	0.54	44	18	38	106	83	7%	264	5.40	39	40	59%	4.71	1.49	32%	72%	4.54	3.1	5.8	1.9	11%	1.3	42
Away	07	264	324	395	719	8	82	30	0.50	44	18	38	86	106	12%	251	4.42	34	38	61%	4.99	1.50	30%	68%	5.03	4.5	7.2	1.6	10%	1.0	30
	08	260	325	414	739	9	81	30	0.52	43	19	38	102	92	8%	262	4.68	31	37	55%	5.17	1.60	31%	69%	5.29	4.6	5.8	1.3	9%	1.0	3
	09	249	312	376	688	8	81	29	0.48	44	19	38	86	79	8%	246	4.02	25	28	58%	5.66	1.56	31%	66%	5.43	3.8	5.9	1.5	12%	1.4	23
Opp @ BAL	07	276	354	423	777	11	82	31	0.65	45	17	38	92	96	7%	251	5.22	46	48	72%	4.64	1.44	31%	70%	4.78	3.1	5.5	1.8	9%	1.0	37
	08	277	352	448	801	10	83	30	0.70	45	18	37	106	99	10%	272	5.46	43	44	65%	4.91	1.46	31%	69%	4.84	3.4	6.0	1.8	11%	1.2	38
	09	289	345	467	812	8	84	32	0.53	42	19	40	111	96	10%	273	5.46	42	41	78%	5.08	1.51	32%	69%	4.90	3.3	6.1	1.8	11%	1.2	43

BOS	Yr	Avg	OB	Slg	OPS	bb%	ct%	h%	Eye	G	L	F	PX	SX	SBO	xBA	RC/G	W	Py	Sv%	ERA	WHIP	H%	S%	xERA	Ctl	Dom	Cmd	hr/f	hr/9	BPV
At Home	07	297	376	465	841	11	82	34	0.71	41	18	40	107	113	7%	264	6.08	51	51	79%	4.13	1.30	31%	70%	4.40	2.7	7.0	2.6	8%	0.9	74
	08	292	371	468	839	11	82	33	0.70	43	20	38	120	112	9%	280	6.06	56	52	70%	3.78	1.34	30%	74%	4.04	3.4	7.2	2.1	8%	0.8	60
	09	284	360	498	858	11	80	32	0.59	38	19	43	142	106	12%	275	6.22	56	52	66%	4.07	1.35	32%	72%	4.29	3.0	7.4	2.5	8%	0.9	71
Away	07	262	341	424	764	11	81	30	0.62	42	18	40	102	99	7%	254	5.07	45	50	81%	3.60	1.24	28%	75%	3.85	3.3	7.4	2.2	10%	1.0	64
	08	268	338	428	766	10	80	31	0.52	40	20	39	103	92	10%	259	5.00	39	43	66%	4.26	1.31	29%	70%	4.35	3.4	7.5	2.2	10%	1.0	65
	09	257	335	414	749	11	80	29	0.59	40	19	42	101	99	9%	250	4.83	39	41	74%	4.64	1.47	32%	71%	4.43	3.6	8.0	2.2	11%	1.2	65
Opp @ BOS	07	261	315	407	721	7	80	31	0.39	43	17	40	98	95	8%	247	4.38	30	30	63%	5.86	1.72	34%	67%	5.75	4.6	6.5	1.4	9%	1.0	11
	08	253	321	398	719	9	79	30	0.47	44	19	37	103	84	8%	253	4.45	25	29	57%	5.53	1.65	33%	68%	5.44	4.5	6.4	1.4	9%	1.0	15
	09	262	321	412	732	8	79	31	0.40	40	18	41	104	107	9%	249	4.54	25	29	60%	5.90	1.60	32%	66%	5.52	4.3	7.3	1.7	12%	1.5	32

CHW	Yr	Avg	OB	Slg	OPS	bb%	ct%	h%	Eye	G	L	F	PX	SX	SBO	xBA	RC/G	W	Py	Sv%	ERA	WHIP	H%	S%	xERA	Ctl	Dom	Cmd	hr/f	hr/9	BPV
At Home	07	247	316	419	735	9	80	27	0.51	43	18	40	103	78	10%	251	4.55	38	32	70%	4.94	1.43	32%	67%	4.83	2.9	6.4	2.2	10%	1.1	60
	08	272	340	481	821	9	82	29	0.57	38	20	42	128	75	7%	277	5.57	54	52	57%	3.75	1.23	29%	73%	3.81	2.8	7.5	2.7	11%	1.0	83
	09	252	322	415	737	9	82	27	0.56	42	17	41	100	87	10%	252	4.59	43	39	68%	4.22	1.36	30%	72%	4.21	3.4	7.5	2.2	11%	1.1	64
Away	07	246	311	390	701	9	78	29	0.42	45	17	37	94	85	7%	239	4.14	34	35	60%	4.60	1.42	30%	70%	4.73	3.3	6.2	1.9	9%	1.1	42
	08	253	316	414	730	8	81	28	0.49	42	19	39	104	81	7%	260	4.50	35	36	72%	4.50	1.43	32%	70%	4.42	2.9	6.6	2.3	9%	0.9	65
	09	264	327	408	735	8	81	30	0.49	45	18	38	93	88	11%	250	4.57	36	41	66%	4.09	1.34	30%	72%	4.18	2.9	6.5	2.2	10%	1.0	61
Opp @ CHW	07	282	337	437	774	8	82	32	0.45	44	19	37	97	100	8%	260	4.99	43	49	60%	4.26	1.32	27%	73%	4.21	3.5	6.8	2.0	13%	1.4	49
	08	242	300	388	688	8	78	28	0.38	46	19	35	99	106	12%	255	3.93	28	30	60%	5.63	1.46	29%	66%	5.26	3.6	6.3	1.8	15%	1.8	33
	09	258	325	413	738	9	78	30	0.46	44	18	38	105	98	13%	252	4.63	38	42	67%	4.46	1.35	28%	71%	4.56	3.5	6.3	1.8	12%	1.3	38

CHC	Yr	Avg	OB	Slg	OPS	bb%	ct%	h%	Eye	G	L	F	PX	SX	SBO	xBA	RC/G	W	Py	Sv%	ERA	WHIP	H%	S%	xERA	Ctl	Dom	Cmd	hr/f	hr/9	BPV
At Home	07	278	340	439	779	9	81	32	0.49	45	19	36	102	99	8%	262	5.15	44	44	75%	4.19	1.35	30%	72%	4.38	3.6	7.7	2.1	9%	1.0	60
	08	290	365	471	836	11	79	33	0.57	44	20	36	115	88	6%	268	5.92	55	51	76%	3.77	1.26	30%	73%	3.87	3.1	8.2	2.6	10%	1.0	83
	09	265	340	423	763	10	80	30	0.57	42	19	39	103	86	6%	257	5.02	46	44	75%	3.94	1.32	29%	73%	4.12	3.6	7.9	2.2	10%	1.0	65
Away	07	265	321	404	725	8	82	30	0.46	45	19	36	88	84	8%	255	4.45	41	43	72%	3.89	1.29	28%	73%	4.10	3.5	7.4	2.1	10%	1.0	57
	08	267	340	417	757	10	78	32	0.51	42	23	35	102	90	8%	263	4.96	40	45	53%	4.07	1.35	29%	73%	4.22	3.8	7.4	2.0	10%	1.0	51
	09	245	315	392	707	9	77	29	0.44	44	20	36	99	78	6%	248	4.27	37	39	65%	3.74	1.33	29%	75%	3.82	3.7	7.9	2.2	10%	1.0	64
Opp @ CHC	07	251	322	408	730	10	77	30	0.47	41	18	42	102	103	11%	242	4.57	37	37	61%	4.61	1.47	32%	71%	4.46	3.4	6.9	2.0	10%	1.1	56
	08	242	305	391	696	8	76	29	0.38	42	20	38	101	89	8%	245	4.08	26	30	57%	5.51	1.61	33%	68%	4.97	4.2	7.4	1.8	14%	1.4	41
	09	245	318	387	706	10	76	29	0.46	42	18	39	95	96	8%	238	4.26	34	36	73%	4.81	1.46	31%	69%	4.86	4.0	7.0	1.8	10%	1.1	38

CIN	Yr	Avg	OB	Slg	OPS	bb%	ct%	h%	Eye	G	L	F	PX	SX	SBO	xBA	RC/G	W	Py	Sv%	ERA	WHIP	H%	S%	xERA	Ctl	Dom	Cmd	hr/f	hr/9	BPV
At Home	07	265	333	456	789	9	80	29	0.51	40	19	41	115	95	7%	263	5.24	39	39	48%	4.94	1.37	30%	67%	4.83	2.8	6.7	2.4	12%	1.4	63
	08	253	327	428	755	10	80	28	0.54	45	19	36	109	86	8%	264	4.85	43	38	69%	4.51	1.41	31%	72%	4.15	3.3	7.7	2.3	13%	1.3	70
	09	252	323	418	741	10	79	29	0.50	42	19	39	107	90	10%	255	4.68	40	37	80%	4.06	1.33	29%	73%	4.15	3.4	7.0	2.0	11%	1.1	54
Away	07	269	328	418	746	8	80	31	0.45	44	19	37	91	87	10%	250	4.68	33	36	61%	4.98	1.51	33%	69%	4.85	3.2	6.6	2.1	10%	1.1	50
	08	241	308	388	696	9	79	28	0.46	45	20	36	95	81	10%	252	4.09	31	33	55%	4.59	1.50	33%	72%	4.27	3.7	7.6	2.1	12%	1.2	59
	09	242	305	371	676	8	80	28	0.44	45	18	37	87	95	9%	244	3.84	38	39	75%	4.30	1.41	29%	73%	4.38	3.7	6.2	1.7	11%	1.2	31
Opp @ CIN	07	272	326	455	781	7	81	30	0.42	40	18	42	111	88	8%	259	5.05	42	42	67%	4.90	1.42	30%	70%	4.69	3.6	7.0	2.0	13%	1.5	48
	08	272	335	456	791	9	78	32	0.43	42	21	37	119	92	8%	267	5.27	38	43	56%	4.40	1.38	28%	72%	4.23	3.7	6.9	1.9	14%	1.3	46
	09	254	323	414	736	9	79	29	0.49	43	19	38	104	84	10%	254	4.61	41	44	75%	3.76	1.34	29%	76%	3.76	3.6	7.1	2.0	12%	1.2	52

CLE	Yr	Avg	OB	Slg	OPS	bb%	ct%	h%	Eye	G	L	F	PX	SX	SBO	xBA	RC/G	W	Py	Sv%	ERA	WHIP	H%	S%	xERA	Ctl	Dom	Cmd	hr/f	hr/9	BPV
At Home	07	277	348	444	792	10	79	32	0.53	42	19	40	105	91	7%	252	5.33	49	44	74%	4.25	1.35	33%	70%	4.22	2.5	7.3	2.8	9%	0.9	86
	08	272	346	439	785	10	79	32	0.55	40	20	40	113	95	7%	260	5.31	45	47	58%	4.03	1.34	31%	71%	4.17	2.8	6.4	2.3	8%	0.8	63
	09	255	326	388	713	9	79	30	0.49	45	20	36	93	88	7%	249	4.37	35	37	67%	4.40	1.47	32%	71%	4.51	3.5	6.3	1.8	9%	0.9	42
Away	07	260	327	411	737	9	78	31	0.45	40	19	41	101	84	7%	243	4.66	44	45	79%	3.92	1.29	29%	72%	4.21	2.5	5.6	2.3	9%	0.9	56
	08	254	314	410	724	8	77	30	0.39	40	21	39	110	86	7%	255	4.42	36	38	64%	4.92	1.41	31%	69%	4.69	2.7	5.9	2.2	12%	1.4	54
	09	272	341	445	785	9	78	32	0.47	43	20	37	116	98	8%	264	5.27	30	35	54%	5.80	1.56	31%	66%	5.60	4.0	6.0	1.5	12%	1.4	20
Opp @ CLE	07	274	323	409	731	7	79	32	0.35	46	19	35	89	81	9%	246	4.44	28	33	60%	5.08	1.52	32%	69%	4.83	3.9	7.4	1.9	12%	1.3	48
	08	268	324	394	717	8	81	31	0.44	46	21	33	85	77	6%	257	4.33	36	34	65%	5.13	1.50	32%	68%	5.07	4.0	7.4	1.8	10%	1.1	42
	09	277	343	418	761	9	82	32	0.56	45	19	36	94	90	9%	259	4.96	46	44	69%	4.15	1.37	31%	71%	4.30	3.6	7.4	2.0	9%	0.8	58

BATTING / PITCHING

COL	Yr	Avg	OB	Slg	OPS	bb%	ct%	h%	Eye	G	L	F	PX	SX	SBO	xBA	RC/G	W	Py	Sv%	ERA	WHIP	H%	S%	xERA	Ctl	Dom	Cmd	hr/f	hr/9	BPV
At Home	07	298	369	480	849	10	82	34	0.61	43	22	35	109	99	7%	279	6.06	51	48	64%	4.34	1.36	30%	70%	4.43	2.8	5.6	2.0	10%	1.0	51
	08	278	346	454	801	10	80	32	0.52	42	23	35	113	113	11%	278	5.46	43	40	61%	4.83	1.43	32%	68%	4.64	3.1	6.3	2.1	11%	1.0	56
	09	287	367	483	849	11	80	33	0.62	42	20	38	125	116	11%	276	6.17	51	48	65%	4.41	1.40	31%	70%	4.30	3.4	7.2	2.1	10%	0.9	66
Away	07	261	332	395	727	10	78	31	0.48	44	20	37	87	100	8%	243	4.55	39	42	53%	4.29	1.36	29%	71%	4.44	3.4	6.2	1.8	10%	1.0	44
	08	249	317	377	694	9	77	30	0.43	45	20	35	89	89	12%	241	4.09	31	34	61%	4.70	1.49	31%	69%	4.75	4.0	6.7	1.7	9%	0.8	37
	09	235	316	399	715	11	73	29	0.44	41	19	40	114	94	10%	238	4.43	41	41	83%	4.06	1.32	30%	71%	4.19	3.2	7.2	2.2	9%	0.9	66
Opp @ COL	07	274	327	438	765	7	84	30	0.49	46	19	35	98	105	7%	274	4.92	31	34	52%	5.68	1.65	34%	68%	5.18	4.1	6.6	1.6	13%	1.3	30
	08	280	337	435	772	8	82	32	0.48	47	21	31	98	99	7%	276	5.03	38	41	51%	4.96	1.49	32%	69%	4.69	3.7	7.1	1.9	12%	1.2	48
	09	266	331	419	750	9	79	31	0.47	49	20	32	101	125	10%	267	4.82	30	33	62%	5.54	1.60	32%	68%	5.26	4.4	7.1	1.6	12%	1.3	28

DET	Yr	Avg	OB	Slg	OPS	bb%	ct%	h%	Eye	G	L	F	PX	SX	SBO	xBA	RC/G	W	Py	Sv%	ERA	WHIP	H%	S%	xERA	Ctl	Dom	Cmd	hr/f	hr/9	BPV
At Home	07	287	345	475	819	8	82	32	0.50	40	21	39	112	124	9%	276	5.59	45	43	64%	4.65	1.43	30%	70%	4.72	3.5	6.4	1.8	10%	1.1	43
	08	287	349	478	827	9	83	31	0.56	42	19	38	117	100	6%	277	5.68	40	41	63%	4.84	1.48	31%	70%	4.82	3.7	6.4	1.7	10%	1.1	37
	09	270	339	432	771	10	81	31	0.54	41	18	40	101	92	6%	254	5.05	51	46	73%	4.05	1.33	28%	73%	4.30	3.6	6.9	1.9	10%	1.1	49
Away	07	286	338	442	779	7	81	33	0.41	43	19	38	101	106	8%	260	5.08	43	46	72%	4.51	1.43	30%	71%	4.49	3.6	6.6	1.9	11%	1.1	46
	08	256	327	411	738	10	79	30	0.51	44	18	38	102	88	6%	253	4.67	34	37	47%	4.98	1.54	30%	69%	5.18	4.4	5.9	1.4	9%	1.0	8
	09	252	314	402	716	8	79	29	0.44	43	18	39	97	90	7%	246	4.30	35	35	55%	4.64	1.50	31%	72%	4.47	3.8	6.8	1.8	12%	1.2	40
Opp @ DET	07	268	334	431	765	9	82	30	0.54	44	18	38	99	100	7%	259	4.99	36	38	74%	5.36	1.50	32%	66%	5.15	3.1	6.3	2.0	11%	1.3	46
	08	276	344	437	781	9	82	31	0.58	44	19	38	104	92	6%	264	5.20	41	40	57%	5.23	1.52	31%	69%	4.90	3.4	6.2	1.8	13%	1.4	39
	09	249	320	402	722	10	80	28	0.51	42	17	41	99	86	9%	243	4.45	30	35	61%	4.75	1.47	31%	71%	4.69	3.7	6.9	1.9	11%	1.2	43

FLA	Yr	Avg	OB	Slg	OPS	bb%	ct%	h%	Eye	G	L	F	PX	SX	SBO	xBA	RC/G	W	Py	Sv%	ERA	WHIP	H%	S%	xERA	Ctl	Dom	Cmd	hr/f	hr/9	BPV
At Home	07	271	333	466	800	9	76	32	0.40	40	20	40	124	104	9%	258	5.41	36	36	58%	4.80	1.58	34%	71%	4.72	4.4	7.9	1.8	9%	0.9	42
	08	247	319	419	738	10	73	30	0.39	42	19	39	117	104	8%	244	4.69	45	39	63%	4.31	1.39	31%	71%	4.46	3.6	7.6	2.1	9%	0.9	57
	09	273	344	428	772	10	78	32	0.49	41	20	40	102	91	7%	249	5.11	43	38	58%	4.51	1.44	32%	71%	4.42	3.9	8.2	2.1	10%	1.0	64
Away	07	263	326	431	756	8	76	32	0.39	40	19	41	110	99	10%	246	4.86	35	36	67%	5.13	1.58	32%	70%	4.90	3.8	6.3	1.7	11%	1.3	31
	08	261	323	446	769	8	77	30	0.40	42	20	38	122	83	7%	261	4.97	39	42	58%	4.58	1.41	29%	70%	4.63	3.7	6.5	1.7	11%	1.1	37
	09	263	327	403	731	9	78	31	0.44	43	20	37	97	88	7%	249	4.55	44	44	73%	4.12	1.35	30%	72%	4.27	3.6	7.3	2.1	10%	1.0	56
Opp @ FLA	07	280	361	431	792	11	78	34	0.56	41	21	38	99	101	9%	251	5.48	45	45	71%	4.70	1.41	32%	71%	4.37	3.2	8.2	2.5	13%	1.4	78
	08	257	328	400	727	9	78	31	0.47	40	21	39	96	96	9%	248	4.53	36	42	62%	4.47	1.35	31%	70%	4.21	3.7	9.4	2.6	13%	1.2	90
	09	261	336	409	745	10	77	32	0.48	44	19	37	101	105	10%	247	4.80	38	43	59%	4.61	1.48	32%	71%	4.51	3.8	7.7	2.0	10%	1.1	56

HOU	Yr	Avg	OB	Slg	OPS	bb%	ct%	h%	Eye	G	L	F	PX	SX	SBO	xBA	RC/G	W	Py	Sv%	ERA	WHIP	H%	S%	xERA	Ctl	Dom	Cmd	hr/f	hr/9	BPV
At Home	07	266	333	422	755	9	82	30	0.56	43	18	39	93	92	6%	253	4.86	42	40	48%	4.05	1.33	31%	74%	3.88	2.9	7.7	2.6	12%	1.3	81
	08	277	332	451	783	8	82	31	0.44	46	19	36	108	101	13%	270	5.10	47	40	78%	4.28	1.36	30%	72%	4.11	3.2	7.3	2.3	12%	1.2	67
	09	269	330	418	748	8	82	30	0.50	48	17	34	93	102	11%	259	4.73	44	39	67%	4.01	1.38	32%	74%	3.84	3.0	7.4	2.5	11%	1.0	77
Away	07	254	319	403	722	9	81	29	0.49	44	17	39	93	69	7%	244	4.42	31	33	72%	5.42	1.51	31%	66%	5.25	3.4	5.9	1.8	11%	1.3	37
	08	254	311	389	700	8	80	29	0.42	45	20	34	87	84	11%	253	4.09	39	38	70%	4.48	1.38	30%	71%	4.34	3.1	6.6	2.1	12%	1.2	56
	09	252	304	383	687	7	82	29	0.41	48	18	34	86	97	11%	254	3.93	30	29	50%	5.12	1.51	32%	68%	4.88	3.9	6.9	1.8	12%	1.2	43
Opp @ HOU	07	262	319	439	758	8	78	30	0.38	44	16	40	112	89	8%	248	4.81	39	41	63%	4.26	1.40	30%	72%	4.48	3.4	6.1	1.8	9%	1.0	38
	08	261	323	438	761	8	79	30	0.44	44	19	37	114	84	6%	264	4.88	31	38	55%	4.60	1.40	31%	70%	4.36	2.9	6.5	2.3	12%	1.2	63
	09	273	331	424	755	8	79	32	0.41	46	19	35	100	76	5%	253	4.79	37	42	61%	3.99	1.37	30%	74%	4.02	3.1	6.2	2.0	10%	1.0	54

KC	Yr	Avg	OB	Slg	OPS	bb%	ct%	h%	Eye	G	L	F	PX	SX	SBO	xBA	RC/G	W	Py	Sv%	ERA	WHIP	H%	S%	xERA	Ctl	Dom	Cmd	hr/f	hr/9	BPV
At Home	07	267	321	403	724	7	82	31	0.44	46	20	34	88	102	7%	260	4.46	35	36	76%	4.61	1.47	32%	70%	4.72	3.3	6.1	1.9	9%	1.0	42
	08	275	323	396	719	7	83	32	0.42	46	21	33	83	85	7%	262	4.34	38	37	76%	4.13	1.33	30%	71%	4.43	3.1	6.2	2.0	8%	0.9	51
	09	276	338	421	760	9	83	31	0.55	46	17	36	92	111	7%	260	4.94	33	34	58%	4.86	1.49	33%	68%	4.87	3.5	7.2	2.0	8%	0.8	56
Away	07	256	309	373	682	7	79	31	0.37	48	18	33	77	100	10%	240	3.87	34	38	59%	4.39	1.41	30%	72%	4.46	3.3	6.3	1.9	10%	1.1	44
	08	263	310	398	708	6	81	30	0.36	47	19	34	89	90	9%	255	4.15	37	35	71%	4.89	1.42	32%	68%	4.85	3.4	7.3	2.2	10%	1.1	59
	09	242	292	390	682	7	78	28	0.32	45	19	37	98	102	10%	249	3.81	32	32	63%	4.80	1.43	30%	70%	4.71	4.1	7.4	1.8	12%	1.3	45
Opp @ KC	07	283	343	450	794	8	83	32	0.53	41	20	39	110	89	6%	272	5.34	46	45	93%	4.29	1.32	31%	68%	4.62	2.7	6.2	2.3	7%	0.6	63
	08	260	320	402	722	8	82	30	0.49	43	19	38	93	92	7%	256	4.43	43	44	70%	3.92	1.35	32%	72%	4.14	2.5	6.0	2.4	7%	0.6	64
	09	280	346	423	769	9	80	33	0.49	44	18	37	96	108	8%	252	5.06	48	47	74%	4.40	1.44	31%	71%	4.57	3.3	6.1	1.8	8%	0.8	44

LA	Yr	Avg	OB	Slg	OPS	bb%	ct%	h%	Eye	G	L	F	PX	SX	SBO	xBA	RC/G	W	Py	Sv%	ERA	WHIP	H%	S%	xERA	Ctl	Dom	Cmd	hr/f	hr/9	BPV
At Home	07	277	344	407	750	9	84	31	0.65	48	18	34	76	99	13%	253	4.83	43	41	72%	4.24	1.34	32%	70%	4.28	3.0	7.8	2.5	9%	0.9	80
	08	266	332	397	729	9	81	31	0.52	46	21	33	83	96	12%	257	4.53	48	51	72%	3.01	1.13	29%	75%	3.31	2.6	8.0	3.1	7%	0.6	103
	09	265	330	407	737	9	81	31	0.51	45	21	34	91	103	11%	262	4.63	50	51	66%	3.10	1.19	28%	76%	3.53	3.1	7.9	2.5	7%	0.7	80
Away	07	273	328	405	732	8	85	30	0.54	44	19	37	80	93	10%	257	4.57	39	41	71%	4.16	1.37	30%	72%	4.20	3.4	6.9	2.0	10%	0.9	57
	08	263	328	400	729	9	82	30	0.53	47	21	32	88	98	10%	265	4.56	36	37	57%	4.40	1.45	32%	72%	4.16	3.4	6.9	2.0	11%	0.9	60
	09	275	352	416	769	11	81	32	0.62	46	21	33	91	105	9%	264	5.14	45	48	61%	3.74	1.32	28%	74%	4.04	4.0	7.7	1.9	9%	0.9	49
Opp @ LA	07	263	323	394	717	8	77	32	0.39	45	19	36	86	84	10%	238	4.33	38	40	71%	4.50	1.48	31%	71%	4.61	3.5	5.5	1.5	9%	0.9	29
	08	228	284	333	617	7	76	28	0.32	50	18	32	75	91	8%	227	3.01	33	30	73%	4.09	1.40	30%	73%	4.13	3.4	6.5	1.9	10%	0.9	49
	09	229	295	343	638	9	76	28	0.40	45	18	38	80	86	10%	226	3.34	31	30	58%	4.23	1.39	30%	71%	4.34	3.3	6.5	2.0	9%	0.9	50

LAA	Yr	Avg	OB	Slg	OPS	bb%	ct%	h%	Eye	G	L	F	PX	SX	SBO	xBA	RC/G	W	Py	Sv%	ERA	WHIP	H%	S%	xERA	Ctl	Dom	Cmd	hr/f	hr/9	BPV
At Home	07	305	368	445	813	9	85	34	0.66	47	17	36	88	107	12%	261	5.61	54	51	68%	3.85	1.32	31%	73%	4.18	2.9	7.1	2.5	7%	0.8	69
	08	277	329	414	744	7	83	31	0.45	46	18	36	89	96	11%	256	4.62	50	43	76%	4.07	1.28	30%	71%	4.21	2.5	6.6	2.6	10%	1.0	73
	09	288	353	450	803	9	83	32	0.57	44	18	38	102	104	11%	264	5.43	49	46	70%	4.44	1.40	31%	72%	4.39	3.1	6.7	2.1	11%	1.3	54
Away	07	263	319	393	712	8	83	30	0.50	47	18	35	82	94	13%	253	4.29	39	37	88%	4.64	1.41	32%	69%	4.53	3.0	7.5	2.5	10%	1.0	73
	08	260	324	411	736	9	82	29	0.52	47	18	35	97	101	12%	261	4.59	50	44	73%	3.92	1.36	31%	74%	3.92	3.2	7.2	2.3	10%	1.0	65
	09	283	345	434	778	9	80	33	0.48	45	20	36	99	109	15%	261	5.13	48	46	76%	4.47	1.41	31%	70%	4.60	3.4	6.5	1.9	9%	1.0	48
Opp @ LAA	07	260	316	397	713	8	80	31	0.41	42	17	41	91	98	10%	240	4.28	27	30	64%	5.43	1.62	34%	66%	5.46	3.6	5.4	1.5	7%	0.8	26
	08	260	310	404	714	7	81	30	0.38	45	18	37	93	97	10%	252	4.21	31	38	54%	4.47	1.39	31%	69%	4.54	2.8	6.1	2.2	9%	0.9	59
	09	273	333	439	772	8	81	31	0.47	40	19	41	106	91	10%	257	4.98	32	35	66%	5.29	1.53	32%	67%	5.16	3.5	6.2	1.7	11%	1.2	37

MIL	Yr	Avg	OB	Slg	OPS	bb%	ct%	h%	Eye	G	L	F	PX	SX	SBO	xBA	RC/G	W	Py	Sv%	ERA	WHIP	H%	S%	xERA	Ctl	Dom	Cmd	hr/f	hr/9	BPV
At Home	07	268	333	476	809	9	80	30	0.48	41	17	41	127	102	10%	266	5.48	51	47	81%	4.06	1.32	30%	72%	4.16	3.2	7.6	2.3	10%	1.0	69
	08	251	324	433	756	10	77	29	0.47	42	18	40	118	96	10%	256	4.89	49	45	63%	3.51	1.32	29%	76%	3.56	3.4	7.1	2.1	11%	0.9	59
	09	257	334	437	772	10	77	30	0.51	43	18	39	117	92	6%	255	5.12	40	38	64%	4.43	1.39	30%	72%	4.38	3.6	7.6	2.1	11%	1.2	59
Away	07	256	314	437	750	8	79	29	0.41	41	19	40	108	96	8%	255	4.69	32	37	61%	4.85	1.48	34%	69%	4.80	3.1	7.0	2.3	9%	1.0	62
	08	254	317	429	746	8	79	29	0.44	42	19	39	114	104	11%	262	4.71	41	42	64%	4.26	1.35	29%	73%	4.10	3.1	6.6	2.1	13%	1.3	58
	09	268	338	415	753	10	78	32	0.48	43	19	38	98	94	8%	247	4.87	40	39	70%	5.28	1.54	31%	69%	4.99	4.0	6.2	1.6	13%	1.4	25
Opp @ MIL	07	252	316	401	717	9	78	30	0.43	42	18	40	96	86	8%	242	4.33	30	34	74%	5.23	1.43	30%	68%	4.91	3.4	7.2	2.1	14%	1.6	56
	08	252	321	386	706	9	79	29	0.48	46	21	33	85	77	9%	252	4.24	32	36	52%	4.33	1.36	29%	72%	4.25	3.7	7.7	2.1	12%	1.3	60
	09	258	328	437	766	9	78	30	0.48	42	17	41	120	101	7%	257	5.01	41	43	64%	4.51	1.42	30%	72%	4.34	4.0	7.8	2.0	12%	1.3	54

BATTING / PITCHING

MIN	Yr	Avg	OB	Slg	OPS	bb%	ct%	h%	Eye	G	L	F	PX	SX	SBO	xBA	RC/G	W	Py	Sv%	ERA	WHIP	H%	S%	xERA	Ctl	Dom	Cmd	hr/f	hr/9	BPV
At Home	07	263	326	376	702	9	85	29	0.64	50	18	33	70	108	10%	252	4.29	41	39	70%	3.84	1.27	30%	73%	4.02	2.6	7.1	2.8	9%	1.0	79
	08	289	348	429	777	8	84	33	0.55	46	21	33	91	112	9%	273	5.15	53	53	83%	3.27	1.22	29%	77%	3.45	2.2	6.3	2.9	9%	1.0	75
	09	278	348	448	795	10	82	31	0.60	47	17	36	105	113	9%	269	5.37	49	44	69%	4.49	1.35	31%	69%	4.55	2.6	6.6	2.6	9%	1.1	69
Away	07	266	328	405	733	8	84	29	0.58	50	17	33	85	106	9%	259	4.60	38	41	76%	4.54	1.42	32%	72%	4.24	2.7	6.5	2.4	12%	1.3	67
	08	269	333	388	722	9	82	31	0.53	47	19	34	80	100	9%	250	4.48	35	37	50%	5.12	1.50	32%	68%	4.89	2.9	6.0	2.1	11%	1.3	50
	09	271	338	411	749	9	81	31	0.55	45	19	36	90	86	6%	253	4.81	38	42	82%	4.51	1.41	30%	71%	4.58	3.2	6.4	2.0	10%	1.2	47
Opp @ MIN	07	255	307	403	711	7	79	30	0.36	42	18	40	95	83	7%	244	4.18	40	42	76%	3.82	1.36	29%	72%	4.26	3.2	5.0	1.6	6%	0.6	31
	08	255	299	396	694	6	82	29	0.35	43	20	37	91	80	9%	256	3.93	28	28	66%	5.19	1.49	33%	65%	5.24	3.2	5.8	1.8	8%	0.7	42
	09	273	322	426	749	7	81	31	0.39	41	19	41	99	108	11%	254	4.63	33	38	52%	5.10	1.49	31%	68%	4.94	3.7	6.2	1.7	12%	1.2	36

NYM	Yr	Avg	OB	Slg	OPS	bb%	ct%	h%	Eye	G	L	F	PX	SX	SBO	xBA	RC/G	W	Py	Sv%	ERA	WHIP	H%	S%	xERA	Ctl	Dom	Cmd	hr/f	hr/9	BPV
At Home	07	270	335	425	760	9	83	30	0.58	44	19	37	92	106	16%	262	4.92	41	40	65%	4.20	1.33	29%	70%	4.50	3.5	7.1	2.0	9%	1.0	53
	08	267	348	430	778	11	82	30	0.68	46	22	32	99	99	9%	276	5.23	48	45	57%	3.78	1.27	28%	73%	3.96	3.5	7.4	2.1	10%	0.9	62
	09	274	339	408	747	9	83	32	0.57	46	19	35	86	113	11%	260	4.83	41	40	70%	3.98	1.34	29%	73%	4.27	3.6	6.9	1.9	9%	1.0	47
Away	07	280	344	439	783	9	82	31	0.55	45	20	35	96	108	15%	266	5.18	47	46	73%	4.34	1.41	30%	72%	4.45	3.6	6.9	1.9	10%	1.1	47
	08	265	330	411	741	9	82	30	0.54	46	24	30	91	114	12%	277	4.70	41	45	62%	4.39	1.48	32%	73%	4.25	3.8	7.1	1.9	11%	1.1	45
	09	266	330	381	711	9	83	31	0.57	47	21	32	77	101	10%	261	4.38	29	33	60%	4.99	1.57	32%	70%	5.02	4.2	6.1	1.5	9%	1.0	17
Opp @ NYM	07	247	316	393	709	9	79	29	0.49	41	18	41	92	99	9%	243	4.29	40	41	63%	4.40	1.42	30%	71%	4.48	3.4	5.9	1.7	10%	1.1	37
	08	236	307	369	676	9	78	28	0.47	44	21	36	88	67	5%	245	3.85	33	36	62%	4.47	1.51	30%	74%	4.23	4.3	6.4	1.5	13%	1.2	23
	09	248	319	396	715	9	80	28	0.52	42	17	41	98	83	7%	245	4.39	40	41	80%	4.08	1.41	31%	71%	4.43	3.3	5.9	1.8	6%	0.6	40

NYY	Yr	Avg	OB	Slg	OPS	bb%	ct%	h%	Eye	G	L	F	PX	SX	SBO	xBA	RC/G	W	Py	Sv%	ERA	WHIP	H%	S%	xERA	Ctl	Dom	Cmd	hr/f	hr/9	BPV
At Home	07	300	374	474	848	11	84	33	0.72	45	19	36	104	111	10%	275	6.05	52	52	65%	4.32	1.37	30%	71%	4.51	3.3	6.7	2.1	9%	1.0	53
	08	281	342	440	783	9	82	31	0.53	45	19	36	102	101	10%	268	5.15	48	45	82%	4.11	1.30	30%	70%	4.26	3.1	7.4	2.4	9%	0.8	73
	09	284	364	490	854	11	83	30	0.72	44	20	37	126	89	9%	287	6.10	57	50	76%	4.03	1.34	29%	74%	3.94	3.6	7.8	2.2	12%	1.2	64
Away	07	280	348	453	801	9	82	31	0.58	46	19	35	107	103	9%	273	5.45	42	45	59%	4.69	1.50	31%	70%	4.95	3.9	5.8	1.5	8%	0.9	19
	08	262	328	414	743	9	81	30	0.52	47	20	33	99	90	11%	267	4.69	41	42	83%	4.47	1.43	33%	71%	4.36	3.0	6.9	2.3	10%	1.0	66
	09	283	353	466	819	10	82	32	0.59	43	19	38	117	110	8%	276	5.67	46	46	79%	4.54	1.37	31%	69%	4.58	3.5	7.9	2.2	10%	1.0	66
Opp @ NYY	07	263	326	412	738	9	81	30	0.49	42	18	39	96	95	10%	251	4.63	29	29	60%	6.32	1.70	33%	65%	5.79	4.3	6.0	1.4	13%	1.4	15
	08	253	315	387	702	8	78	30	0.42	46	19	35	92	87	11%	249	4.16	33	36	55%	4.83	1.48	32%	70%	4.64	3.3	6.3	1.9	11%	1.2	46
	09	249	321	404	725	10	77	29	0.46	43	19	38	102	95	12%	248	4.46	24	31	38%	5.60	1.62	30%	70%	4.99	4.5	6.2	1.4	16%	1.7	13

OAK	Yr	Avg	OB	Slg	OPS	bb%	ct%	h%	Eye	G	L	F	PX	SX	SBO	xBA	RC/G	W	Py	Sv%	ERA	WHIP	H%	S%	xERA	Ctl	Dom	Cmd	hr/f	hr/9	BPV
At Home	07	240	325	385	709	11	82	27	0.71	41	19	40	88	88	4%	250	4.42	40	38	55%	3.79	1.31	29%	72%	4.24	3.4	6.2	1.8	7%	0.7	45
	08	243	314	368	682	9	78	29	0.47	40	19	41	89	91	7%	237	3.97	42	40	67%	3.53	1.27	28%	75%	4.03	3.5	6.5	1.9	8%	0.8	44
	09	259	329	403	732	9	81	30	0.55	41	20	39	95	103	10%	256	4.61	40	46	77%	3.88	1.32	31%	72%	4.06	2.9	7.1	2.4	8%	0.8	71
Away	07	271	346	427	773	10	78	32	0.51	40	19	41	104	65	4%	246	5.13	36	41	63%	4.85	1.45	32%	68%	4.80	3.2	6.7	2.1	9%	1.0	55
	08	241	313	367	681	10	77	29	0.46	43	18	38	88	98	8%	236	3.95	32	34	63%	4.55	1.44	31%	70%	4.78	3.8	6.7	1.8	8%	0.9	36
	09	265	323	392	715	8	81	31	0.46	42	19	39	87	93	14%	248	4.32	35	35	75%	4.71	1.46	31%	70%	4.69	3.6	6.9	1.9	10%	1.1	49
Opp @ OAK	07	249	317	372	689	9	82	29	0.54	46	18	36	76	111	10%	245	4.08	41	43	69%	3.85	1.37	27%	75%	4.30	4.2	6.0	1.4	9%	1.0	12
	08	240	311	368	679	9	80	28	0.53	42	18	40	85	79	8%	241	3.94	37	39	64%	3.77	1.32	30%	73%	4.21	3.6	7.5	2.1	7%	0.8	57
	09	260	318	393	711	8	79	31	0.41	44	20	37	90	91	9%	249	4.25	41	35	88%	4.76	1.40	30%	67%	5.06	3.6	6.5	1.8	8%	0.9	39

PHI	Yr	Avg	OB	Slg	OPS	bb%	ct%	h%	Eye	G	L	F	PX	SX	SBO	xBA	RC/G	W	Py	Sv%	ERA	WHIP	H%	S%	xERA	Ctl	Dom	Cmd	hr/f	hr/9	BPV
At Home	07	280	350	475	825	10	79	32	0.52	43	19	38	117	120	10%	268	5.73	47	43	60%	4.79	1.43	30%	71%	4.31	3.4	6.8	2.0	16%	1.5	54
	08	262	336	447	784	10	80	29	0.57	41	23	36	114	118	13%	278	5.23	48	48	68%	3.67	1.33	30%	75%	3.67	3.0	6.7	2.2	11%	1.0	61
	09	263	336	455	791	10	79	30	0.53	41	21	38	123	114	10%	275	5.32	45	44	75%	4.29	1.36	31%	72%	4.15	3.0	7.4	2.5	12%	1.2	71
Away	07	268	345	442	787	10	78	31	0.54	40	19	41	111	111	10%	254	5.35	42	44	73%	4.74	1.47	31%	69%	4.89	3.5	6.1	1.7	8%	0.9	36
	08	249	318	429	747	9	79	28	0.49	44	19	37	113	110	9%	267	4.73	44	45	81%	4.13	1.40	30%	73%	4.12	3.6	6.7	1.9	11%	1.0	48
	09	253	322	439	762	9	79	28	0.49	40	19	41	118	108	10%	261	4.91	48	47	61%	4.03	1.35	30%	74%	4.08	3.1	6.9	2.2	10%	1.1	59
Opp @ PHI	07	273	338	474	811	9	80	30	0.49	44	21	35	122	76	7%	280	5.49	34	38	63%	5.34	1.54	32%	69%	4.84	3.9	7.4	1.9	14%	1.5	49
	08	258	318	400	718	8	81	30	0.45	44	23	33	92	87	10%	268	4.35	33	33	64%	4.91	1.44	29%	70%	4.65	3.9	6.9	1.8	14%	1.4	38
	09	267	325	430	755	8	79	31	0.40	41	21	38	108	87	8%	261	4.77	36	37	58%	4.95	1.45	30%	70%	4.67	3.8	7.3	1.9	13%	1.4	46

PIT	Yr	Avg	OB	Slg	OPS	bb%	ct%	h%	Eye	G	L	F	PX	SX	SBO	xBA	RC/G	W	Py	Sv%	ERA	WHIP	H%	S%	xERA	Ctl	Dom	Cmd	hr/f	hr/9	BPV
At Home	07	272	327	415	742	8	80	32	0.41	42	20	38	93	80	6%	252	4.65	37	39	54%	4.55	1.39	31%	69%	4.64	2.9	6.0	2.1	9%	0.9	53
	08	263	318	410	728	8	83	30	0.47	42	21	36	94	88	5%	266	4.47	39	36	75%	4.52	1.53	31%	72%	4.58	3.9	5.6	1.4	9%	0.9	16
	09	270	332	420	752	8	81	31	0.50	45	19	36	96	103	8%	261	4.80	40	41	63%	4.03	1.37	29%	72%	4.36	3.3	5.8	1.7	8%	0.8	36
Away	07	254	312	408	720	8	79	29	0.41	42	17	41	97	95	7%	242	4.35	31	31	74%	5.36	1.58	33%	68%	5.10	3.6	6.4	1.8	11%	1.3	40
	08	254	314	396	710	8	80	29	0.44	43	20	38	93	85	5%	253	4.24	28	31	46%	5.73	1.61	32%	66%	5.38	4.2	6.3	1.5	12%	1.3	23
	09	234	298	354	652	8	76	29	0.39	45	18	37	87	93	9%	232	3.54	22	26	61%	5.22	1.54	31%	68%	5.21	3.8	5.9	1.5	10%	1.1	25
Opp @ PIT	07	280	335	425	760	8	83	32	0.48	45	20	36	91	80	8%	260	4.86	44	42	79%	4.42	1.36	32%	68%	4.62	2.8	6.8	2.4	8%	0.8	67
	08	282	355	434	789	10	84	31	0.70	44	22	34	97	79	8%	278	5.38	42	45	64%	4.26	1.32	30%	70%	4.49	2.8	6.0	2.1	9%	0.9	52
	09	265	330	407	738	9	83	30	0.58	44	20	36	93	95	8%	264	4.69	41	40	74%	4.26	1.40	31%	72%	4.33	3.2	6.4	2.0	9%	1.0	52

SD	Yr	Avg	OB	Slg	OPS	bb%	ct%	h%	Eye	G	L	F	PX	SX	SBO	xBA	RC/G	W	Py	Sv%	ERA	WHIP	H%	S%	xERA	Ctl	Dom	Cmd	hr/f	hr/9	BPV
At Home	07	235	305	378	684	9	76	28	0.42	41	18	41	92	96	6%	231	3.96	47	46	86%	3.02	1.16	29%	75%	3.60	2.6	7.1	2.7	6%	0.5	81
	08	239	311	366	677	9	77	29	0.46	43	19	38	84	75	4%	234	3.88	35	35	53%	3.65	1.27	29%	73%	3.95	3.1	7.0	2.2	9%	0.8	63
	09	219	307	342	649	11	77	26	0.55	44	17	39	83	90	6%	228	3.61	42	35	71%	3.44	1.26	28%	75%	3.77	3.6	7.7	2.1	8%	0.8	63
Away	07	265	330	440	770	9	80	30	0.49	40	19	42	111	74	5%	256	5.04	42	44	53%	4.46	1.37	31%	69%	4.54	3.2	6.7	2.1	9%	0.9	59
	08	260	316	412	729	8	78	31	0.37	43	20	37	100	71	3%	250	4.44	28	33	54%	5.24	1.53	32%	68%	5.03	3.9	6.6	1.7	12%	1.2	34
	09	264	325	416	741	8	79	31	0.44	44	20	36	101	99	9%	258	4.64	33	33	62%	5.40	1.54	32%	67%	5.13	3.9	7.0	1.8	12%	1.3	42
Opp @ SD	07	235	290	336	626	7	79	28	0.37	45	18	37	66	107	14%	227	3.17	34	35	72%	3.87	1.25	29%	71%	4.20	3.4	8.0	2.4	9%	0.9	72
	08	246	310	368	677	8	79	29	0.45	43	20	37	78	100	14%	242	3.84	46	46	73%	3.38	1.28	29%	76%	3.69	3.5	7.7	2.2	8%	0.8	64
	09	233	308	353	662	10	77	28	0.47	44	18	38	80	88	9%	229	3.68	39	46	56%	3.31	1.25	26%	76%	3.83	4.1	7.5	1.8	8%	0.8	44

SEA	Yr	Avg	OB	Slg	OPS	bb%	ct%	h%	Eye	G	L	F	PX	SX	SBO	xBA	RC/G	W	Py	Sv%	ERA	WHIP	H%	S%	xERA	Ctl	Dom	Cmd	hr/f	hr/9	BPV
At Home	07	283	334	417	752	7	84	32	0.47	47	18	35	81	93	9%	252	4.70	49	39	74%	4.50	1.43	32%	70%	4.66	3.3	6.8	2.0	8%	0.9	54
	08	271	320	398	718	7	84	30	0.46	46	19	35	83	90	7%	259	4.33	35	36	69%	4.40	1.47	31%	72%	4.50	4.0	6.8	1.7	9%	0.9	38
	09	255	313	395	708	8	80	30	0.41	44	18	38	92	83	8%	246	4.19	48	38	68%	3.62	1.26	28%	74%	3.94	3.2	6.6	2.1	9%	1.0	52
Away	07	290	331	432	763	6	86	32	0.43	47	19	34	86	95	5%	269	4.80	39	40	75%	4.98	1.52	32%	68%	5.01	3.5	6.0	1.7	9%	0.9	35
	08	260	312	381	692	7	84	29	0.47	47	20	33	78	83	9%	258	4.02	26	31	40%	5.08	1.56	32%	69%	4.94	3.9	5.9	1.5	11%	1.1	25
	09	260	307	409	716	6	81	30	0.36	45	17	39	98	91	10%	250	4.22	37	37	60%	4.15	1.35	28%	73%	4.33	3.4	6.3	1.8	10%	1.2	40
Opp @ SEA	07	272	335	416	751	9	81	32	0.49	44	17	39	95	81	8%	246	4.81	32	42	55%	4.34	1.42	32%	72%	4.34	2.7	5.8	2.1	9%	1.0	55
	08	268	343	409	751	10	80	31	0.58	45	19	37	95	82	9%	253	4.89	46	45	72%	3.85	1.34	31%	73%	4.14	2.6	5.5	2.2	7%	0.7	54
	09	243	308	376	684	9	81	28	0.48	42	20	39	87	73	9%	247	3.93	33	43	67%	3.67	1.30	30%	75%	3.80	2.9	7.0	2.4	9%	1.0	70

BATTING | PITCHING

SF	Yr	Avg	OB	Slg	OPS	bb%	ct%	h%	Eye	G	L	F	PX	SX	SBO	xBA	RC/G	W	Py	Sv%	ERA	WHIP	H%	S%	xERA	Ctl	Dom	Cmd	hr/f	hr/9	BPV
At Home	07	259	325	382	706	9	84	29	0.62	47	17	35	74	99	10%	248	4.33	39	38	62%	4.02	1.41	31%	73%	4.28	3.3	6.4	2.0	7%	0.8	49
	08	264	322	391	712	8	82	31	0.47	50	18	31	85	101	11%	257	4.34	37	32	62%	4.45	1.44	31%	71%	4.62	4.0	7.6	1.9	9%	0.9	45
	09	268	322	412	734	7	79	32	0.39	45	20	35	93	118	8%	257	4.52	52	48	77%	3.27	1.21	29%	75%	3.52	3.0	8.1	2.7	9%	0.8	88
Away	07	249	314	391	706	9	83	28	0.56	44	17	39	85	102	11%	248	4.26	32	39	61%	4.39	1.39	29%	70%	4.81	4.1	6.7	1.6	8%	0.9	29
	08	260	314	374	688	7	81	31	0.40	47	19	34	77	89	10%	245	3.98	35	37	74%	4.30	1.43	31%	72%	4.44	4.1	7.9	1.9	9%	0.9	48
	09	247	292	368	660	6	78	30	0.30	46	18	37	84	91	7%	236	3.54	36	38	63%	3.85	1.36	29%	74%	4.06	4.3	8.1	1.9	10%	1.0	49
Opp @ SF	07	270	333	412	745	9	82	31	0.51	44	19	37	89	104	8%	255	4.76	42	43	68%	3.74	1.36	29%	73%	4.21	3.3	5.3	1.6	7%	0.7	32
	08	259	336	412	749	10	78	31	0.53	39	21	39	102	108	9%	254	4.89	44	49	60%	3.54	1.33	31%	74%	3.82	2.9	6.3	2.1	7%	0.6	62
	09	234	296	361	658	8	76	29	0.37	44	20	36	89	95	11%	238	3.57	29	33	71%	4.39	1.33	31%	68%	4.45	2.7	7.1	2.6	9%	0.9	77

STL	Yr	Avg	OB	Slg	OPS	bb%	ct%	h%	Eye	G	L	F	PX	SX	SBO	xBA	RC/G	W	Py	Sv%	ERA	WHIP	H%	S%	xERA	Ctl	Dom	Cmd	hr/f	hr/9	BPV
At Home	07	283	343	405	749	8	85	31	0.62	43	19	38	74	73	6%	250	4.79	43	39	78%	4.17	1.37	30%	71%	4.52	3.0	5.6	1.9	7%	0.8	41
	08	285	350	430	780	9	83	32	0.58	43	22	35	88	80	6%	267	5.16	46	42	61%	4.06	1.35	29%	72%	4.18	3.1	5.8	1.9	10%	1.0	43
	09	263	330	404	734	9	81	30	0.54	47	18	35	92	94	8%	254	4.64	46	43	79%	3.44	1.28	30%	74%	3.65	2.9	6.7	2.3	8%	0.7	71
Away	07	265	326	405	731	8	82	30	0.51	44	18	37	86	66	6%	248	4.52	35	33	72%	5.21	1.45	30%	67%	5.05	3.4	6.2	1.8	12%	1.3	43
	08	277	346	436	783	10	82	31	0.59	45	21	34	99	87	7%	271	5.21	40	44	54%	4.35	1.42	31%	72%	4.26	3.0	6.1	2.0	11%	1.0	52
	09	263	325	425	751	9	81	30	0.48	43	19	39	104	93	7%	259	4.75	45	47	71%	3.89	1.32	30%	73%	3.99	2.9	6.4	2.2	10%	0.9	65
Opp @ STL	07	269	326	409	735	8	84	30	0.53	43	20	38	85	91	7%	258	4.60	38	42	65%	4.29	1.45	31%	72%	4.64	3.2	5.2	1.6	7%	0.8	27
	08	261	322	416	738	8	83	29	0.54	44	21	34	98	84	5%	274	4.63	35	39	74%	4.47	1.50	32%	72%	4.40	3.5	6.1	1.7	10%	1.0	36
	09	254	313	366	678	8	80	30	0.43	50	19	31	76	75	5%	242	3.86	35	38	73%	4.13	1.39	30%	72%	4.32	3.4	6.4	1.9	9%	0.9	47

TAM	Yr	Avg	OB	Slg	OPS	bb%	ct%	h%	Eye	G	L	F	PX	SX	SBO	xBA	RC/G	W	Py	Sv%	ERA	WHIP	H%	S%	xERA	Ctl	Dom	Cmd	hr/f	hr/9	BPV
At Home	07	256	320	421	741	9	77	30	0.42	42	18	40	103	104	11%	246	4.63	34	32	55%	5.06	1.49	34%	68%	4.86	3.4	7.7	2.3	10%	1.1	67
	08	273	353	440	793	11	78	32	0.57	42	20	38	110	116	13%	260	5.44	54	48	79%	3.33	1.22	27%	75%	3.75	3.2	7.1	2.2	8%	0.9	61
	09	273	349	462	811	10	77	32	0.51	39	21	40	125	127	19%	265	5.64	52	49	71%	3.72	1.28	29%	74%	3.95	3.1	7.3	2.4	9%	1.0	68
Away	07	276	341	442	782	9	75	34	0.40	43	20	38	113	109	12%	251	5.25	29	33	58%	6.09	1.62	34%	64%	5.57	3.8	7.3	2.0	12%	1.4	50
	08	248	319	405	724	9	78	29	0.47	46	19	35	107	93	11%	257	4.48	40	42	72%	4.34	1.37	30%	72%	4.41	3.3	7.1	2.2	10%	1.2	57
	09	252	331	418	749	11	78	29	0.53	42	19	39	110	100	14%	254	4.84	32	37	59%	5.04	1.43	31%	68%	4.85	3.4	6.9	2.0	12%	1.3	51
Opp @ TAM	07	284	347	452	799	9	78	34	0.44	42	18	40	110	102	7%	253	5.41	44	46	62%	4.25	1.33	30%	72%	4.18	3.2	7.7	2.4	12%	1.2	72
	08	231	299	367	665	9	79	27	0.45	41	19	39	92	84	7%	243	3.72	24	30	44%	4.86	1.53	32%	71%	4.67	4.3	7.6	1.8	12%	1.2	41
	09	247	309	395	704	8	79	29	0.42	41	18	41	98	97	9%	244	4.17	29	32	65%	5.19	1.52	32%	69%	4.87	4.1	8.0	2.0	12%	1.3	51

TEX	Yr	Avg	OB	Slg	OPS	bb%	ct%	h%	Eye	G	L	F	PX	SX	SBO	xBA	RC/G	W	Py	Sv%	ERA	WHIP	H%	S%	xERA	Ctl	Dom	Cmd	hr/f	hr/9	BPV
At Home	07	277	338	451	789	8	78	33	0.42	42	20	38	110	116	8%	259	5.25	47	42	76%	4.30	1.45	30%	72%	4.39	3.9	6.4	1.7	9%	0.9	37
	08	297	369	494	863	10	79	34	0.55	42	23	35	131	112	7%	288	6.29	40	39	50%	5.47	1.55	32%	66%	5.28	3.6	6.2	1.7	11%	1.2	33
	09	273	336	479	815	9	78	31	0.43	39	20	42	133	122	14%	268	5.54	48	46	80%	4.27	1.37	29%	72%	4.34	3.2	6.3	2.0	11%	1.1	47
Away	07	249	311	402	712	8	78	29	0.40	42	18	40	100	100	8%	245	4.27	28	36	74%	5.25	1.63	31%	69%	5.18	4.6	5.9	1.3	10%	1.1	5
	08	268	331	431	762	9	79	31	0.44	42	21	37	113	90	6%	265	4.94	39	37	62%	5.26	1.61	32%	68%	5.19	4.2	5.8	1.4	10%	1.0	14
	09	248	301	412	714	7	77	29	0.33	41	19	40	111	100	13%	250	4.19	39	39	75%	4.51	1.37	29%	69%	4.70	3.4	6.4	1.9	9%	1.0	44
Opp @ TEX	07	263	336	402	738	10	82	30	0.60	47	19	34	88	86	8%	256	4.72	34	39	67%	5.00	1.45	33%	68%	4.70	3.3	7.8	2.4	12%	1.2	72
	08	289	354	468	822	9	83	32	0.59	42	21	37	115	117	10%	281	5.70	41	42	61%	5.77	1.66	35%	68%	5.09	4.1	7.6	1.8	14%	1.4	44
	09	262	325	425	750	9	82	29	0.51	42	20	38	104	96	10%	266	4.75	33	35	68%	5.17	1.44	31%	68%	4.75	3.3	7.7	2.3	14%	1.6	65

TOR	Yr	Avg	OB	Slg	OPS	bb%	ct%	h%	Eye	G	L	F	PX	SX	SBO	xBA	RC/G	W	Py	Sv%	ERA	WHIP	H%	S%	xERA	Ctl	Dom	Cmd	hr/f	hr/9	BPV
At Home	07	260	328	433	761	9	80	30	0.50	40	20	40	112	93	5%	261	4.94	49	46	71%	3.67	1.18	27%	72%	3.70	2.7	7.1	2.6	12%	1.0	82
	08	264	329	413	742	9	83	30	0.55	44	21	36	97	107	6%	269	4.73	47	48	83%	3.12	1.21	29%	76%	3.39	3.0	7.7	2.5	8%	0.7	84
	09	259	328	439	767	9	81	29	0.54	40	19	41	117	93	7%	266	4.99	44	42	57%	4.11	1.32	30%	72%	4.05	3.2	7.4	2.3	11%	1.1	70
Away	07	258	321	406	727	8	82	29	0.52	40	20	40	95	87	6%	256	4.51	34	40	58%	4.35	1.39	30%	71%	4.43	3.2	6.1	1.9	9%	0.9	49
	08	264	326	386	712	8	83	30	0.56	44	20	36	82	88	8%	255	4.36	39	44	74%	3.89	1.28	30%	73%	3.92	2.8	7.0	2.5	11%	1.0	74
	09	273	333	441	774	8	83	30	0.52	38	18	44	108	77	6%	256	5.03	31	41	65%	4.85	1.52	33%	71%	4.51	3.6	7.3	2.0	12%	1.2	55
Opp @ TOR	07	235	292	385	677	7	79	27	0.38	49	19	32	96	108	12%	259	3.78	32	35	73%	4.61	1.39	30%	70%	4.64	3.5	7.0	2.0	11%	1.2	50
	08	234	298	361	659	8	77	29	0.39	48	19	33	91	88	9%	244	3.64	34	33	53%	4.20	1.39	30%	71%	4.42	3.4	6.1	1.8	9%	0.9	40
	09	255	319	417	736	9	78	30	0.43	46	19	35	109	89	9%	261	4.59	37	39	66%	4.68	1.40	29%	70%	4.68	3.6	6.6	1.8	11%	1.3	41

WAS	Yr	Avg	OB	Slg	OPS	bb%	ct%	h%	Eye	G	L	F	PX	SX	SBO	xBA	RC/G	W	Py	Sv%	ERA	WHIP	H%	S%	xERA	Ctl	Dom	Cmd	hr/f	hr/9	BPV
At Home	07	259	323	383	706	9	81	31	0.49	47	18	35	83	87	5%	245	4.29	40	37	65%	4.08	1.36	29%	72%	4.58	3.3	6.0	1.8	8%	0.9	35
	08	251	323	368	691	10	81	30	0.54	49	21	29	77	83	9%	252	4.12	34	29	55%	4.57	1.42	30%	71%	4.49	3.4	6.3	1.9	12%	1.2	44
	09	257	334	408	742	10	79	30	0.54	44	19	37	97	103	8%	251	4.78	33	35	57%	4.69	1.42	29%	69%	4.91	3.6	5.5	1.5	10%	1.0	23
Away	07	254	319	397	716	9	79	30	0.44	45	20	35	91	91	7%	249	4.36	33	33	62%	5.11	1.53	30%	70%	5.02	3.9	5.6	1.4	12%	1.4	14
	08	250	311	378	689	8	80	29	0.44	46	21	33	85	81	7%	252	4.00	25	33	47%	4.76	1.49	31%	71%	4.61	4.0	7.0	1.8	12%	1.2	38
	09	258	331	404	736	10	77	31	0.48	45	19	36	99	73	7%	246	4.65	26	31	57%	5.37	1.62	32%	69%	5.17	4.3	6.0	1.4	11%	1.1	14
Opp @ WAS	07	259	325	402	726	9	83	29	0.56	39	17	43	88	93	8%	243	4.52	41	44	74%	3.81	1.34	31%	72%	4.18	3.2	6.6	2.0	6%	0.6	57
	08	269	334	434	768	9	82	30	0.54	43	21	36	104	96	9%	272	5.00	46	51	72%	3.71	1.33	29%	73%	3.93	3.5	6.5	1.8	8%	0.6	50
	09	263	333	431	764	9	84	29	0.66	44	19	37	107	85	6%	274	5.03	48	46	61%	4.31	1.42	30%	72%	4.40	4.0	7.3	1.8	10%	1.0	47

AL	Yr	Avg	OB	Slg	OPS	bb%	ct%	h%	Eye	G	L	F	PX	SX	SBO	xBA	RC/G	W	Py	Sv%	ERA	WHIP	H%	S%	xERA	Ctl	Dom	Cmd	hr/f	hr/9	BPV
At Home	07	275	341	431	772	9	82	31	0.56	44	19	37	100	100	8%	263	5.07	45	43	66%	4.28	1.37	30%	71%	4.41	3.2	6.7	2.1	9%	1.0	55
	08	273	335	424	759	9	82	31	0.51	44	20	36	100	100	9%	266	4.89	44	43	72%	4.00	1.34	30%	72%	4.19	3.2	6.8	2.1	9%	0.9	56
	09	270	339	440	779	9	81	30	0.54	43	19	38	100	100	10%	258	5.15	47	44	71%	4.09	1.34	30%	72%	4.18	3.2	7.1	2.2	10%	1.1	61
Away	07	272	333	424	757	8	81	31	0.48	44	19	37	100	100	8%	260	4.85	37	41	67%	4.82	1.48	32%	69%	4.81	3.5	6.4	1.8	10%	1.0	42
	08	258	321	399	720	9	81	30	0.48	45	19	35	100	100	9%	262	4.41	37	38	64%	4.62	1.45	31%	70%	4.62	3.5	6.6	1.9	10%	1.0	45
	09	264	325	420	745	8	80	30	0.46	43	19	39	100	100	10%	254	4.68	39	40	68%	4.55	1.41	30%	71%	4.55	3.5	6.9	2.0	10%	1.1	50

NL	Yr	Avg	OB	Slg	OPS	bb%	ct%	h%	Eye	G	L	F	PX	SX	SBO	xBA	RC/G	W	Py	Sv%	ERA	WHIP	H%	S%	xERA	Ctl	Dom	Cmd	hr/f	hr/9	BPV
At Home	07	268	332	420	752	9	81	31	0.51	44	19	37	100	100	9%	260	4.82	43	41	67%	4.12	1.35	30%	72%	4.29	3.1	6.8	2.2	9%	0.9	60
	08	263	330	414	745	9	80	30	0.51	44	21	35	100	100	9%	265	4.74	43	41	65%	3.99	1.34	30%	73%	4.10	3.3	6.8	2.1	10%	0.9	56
	09	263	333	415	749	10	80	30	0.53	45	19	37	100	100	9%	258	4.82	44	41	68%	3.97	1.34	30%	73%	4.13	3.3	7.1	2.1	9%	0.9	60
Away	07	263	327	418	745	9	80	30	0.48	43	19	38	100	100	9%	256	4.71	37	39	65%	4.76	1.45	31%	70%	4.74	3.5	6.5	1.9	10%	1.1	44
	08	259	321	405	727	8	80	30	0.46	45	20	35	100	100	8%	263	4.47	35	38	59%	4.73	1.47	31%	70%	4.60	3.7	6.7	1.8	11%	1.1	43
	09	257	322	398	721	9	79	30	0.46	44	19	36	100	100	9%	256	4.42	35	37	65%	4.69	1.46	31%	70%	4.69	3.8	6.7	1.8	10%	1.1	40

The Batters

QUALIFICATION: All batters who had at least 100 at bats in the majors in 2009, nearly all who accumulated 50-99 AB and a handful with fewer than 50 AB have been included. The decision often comes down to whether they will have an impact in 2010. Those who may have a role but have battled injuries for several years are often not included, though an injury status update appears on page 194. All of these players will appear at Baseball HQ as roles become clearer.

POSITIONS: Up to three positions are listed for each batter and represent those for which he appeared a minimum of 20 games in 2009. Positions are shown with their numeric designation (2=CA, 3=1B, 7=LF, 0=DH, etc.)

AGE: Each batter's age as of Opening Day 2010 is shown.

BATS: Shows which side of the plate he bats from — right (R), left (L) or switch-hitter (S).

RELIABILITY GRADES: An analysis of each player's forecast risk, on an A-F scale. High grades go to those batters who have accumulated few disabled list days (Health), have a history of substantial and regular major league playing time (PT/Exp) and have displayed consistent performance over the past three years, using RC/G (Consist).

LIMA PLAN GRADE: Rating that evaluates how well a batter would fit into a team using the LIMA Plan. Best grades go to batters who have excellent base skills, are expected to see a good amount of playing time, and are in the $10-$30 Rotisserie value range. Lowest grades will go to poor skills, few AB and values less than $5 or more than $30.

RAND VAR: A score that measures the impact random variance had on the batter's 2009 stats and the probability that his 2010 performance will exceed or fall short of 2009. The variables tracked are levels for h%, hr/f and xBA that would be prone to regression. Players are rated on a scale of –5 to +5 with positive scores indicating rebounds and negative scores indicating corrections.

PLAYER STAT LINES: The past five years' statistics represent the total accumulated in the majors as well as in Triple-A, Double-A ball and various foreign leagues during each year. All non-major league stats used have been converted to a major league equivalent (MLE) performance level. Minor league levels below AA are not included.

Nearly all baseball publications separate a player's statistical experiences in the major leagues from the minor leagues and outside leagues. While this may be appropriate for the sake of official record-keeping, it is not an accurate snapshot of a player's complete performance for the year.

Bill James has proven that minor league statistics (converted to MLEs), at Double-A level or above, provide as accurate a record of a player's performance as Major League statistics. Other researchers have also devised conversion factors for foreign leagues. Since these are accurate barometers, we include them in the pool of historical data.

TEAM DESIGNATIONS: An asterisk (*) appearing with a team name means that major league equivalent Triple-A and/or Double-A numbers are included in that year's stat line. A designation of "a/a" means the stats were accumulated at both levels that year. Other designations: JPN (Japan), MEX (Mexico), KOR (Korea), CUB (Cuba), VNZ (Venezuela) and ind (independent league). All these stats are converted to major league equivalents.

The designation "2TM" appears whenever a player was on more than one major league team, crossing leagues, in a season. "2AL" and "2NL" represent more than one team in the same league. Complete season stats are presented for players who crossed leagues during the season.

SABERMETRIC CATEGORIES: Descriptions of all the categories appear in the glossary. The decimal point has been suppressed on some categories to conserve space.
- Platoon data (vL, vR) and Ball-in-play data (G/L/F) are for major league performance only.
- xBA only appears for years in which G/L/F data is available.

2010 FORECASTS: It is far too early to be making definitive projections for 2010, especially on playing time. Focus on the skill levels and trends, then consult Baseball HQ for playing time revisions as players change teams and roles become finalized. A free projections update will also be available online in March.

Forecasts are computed from a player's trends over the past five years. Adjustments were made for leading indicators and variances between skill and statistical output. After reviewing the leading indicators, you might opt to make further adjustments.

Although each year's numbers include all playing time at the Double-A level or above, the 2010 forecast only represents potential playing time at the major league level, and again is highly preliminary.

CAPSULE COMMENTARIES: For each player, a brief analysis of their BPI's and the potential impact on performance in 2010 is provided. For those who played only a portion of 2009 at the major league level, and whose isolated MLB stats are significantly different from their full-season total, their MLB stats are listed here. Note that these commentaries generally look at performance related issues only. Playing time expectations may impact these analyses, so you will have to adjust accordingly. Upside (UP) and downside (DN) statistical potential appears for some players. These are less grounded in hard data and more speculative of skills potential.

DO-IT-YOURSELF ANALYSIS: Here are some data points you can look at in doing your own player analysis:
- Variance between vLH and vRH batting averages
- Growth or decline in walk rate (bb%)
- Growth or decline in contact rate (ct%)
- Variance in 2009 hit rate (h%) to 2006-2008 three-year avg
- Variance between Avg and xBA each year
- Growth or decline in power index (PX) rate
- Variance in 2009 hr/f rate to 2006-2008 three-year average
- Growth or decline in speed index (SX) rate
- Concurrent growth/decline of gauges like ct%, PX, F
- Concurrent growth/decline of gauges like SX, SBO, OB

Abreu,Bobby

		Year	AB	R	HR	RBI	SB	Avg	vL	vR	OB	Slg	OPS	bb%	ct%	h%	Eye	xBA	G	L	F	PX	hr/f	SX	SBO	RC/G	RAR	BPV	R$
Pos	9	05 PHI	588	104	24	102	31	286	275	292	404	474	879	17	77	33	0.87	289	47	24	29	129	18%	101	18%	6.84	26.7	78	$32
Age	36	06 2TM	548	98	15	107	30	297	293	299	427	462	889	18	75	37	0.90	271	45	26	29	117	13%	105	16%	7.23	30.8	64	$27
Bats	Left	07 NYY	605	123	16	101	25	283	262	289	370	445	815	12	81	33	0.73	281	46	20	34	109	9%	129	17%	5.83	5.6	76	$26
Health	A	08 NYY	609	100	20	100	22	296	315	287	371	471	842	11	82	33	0.67	291	48	23	30	114	13%	106	17%	6.03	11.6	75	$27
PT/Exp	A	09 LAA	563	96	15	103	30	293	267	305	394	435	829	14	80	34	0.83	262	48	19	33	90	10%	108	18%	6.11	12.4	55	$27
Consist	A	1st Half	257	37	4	44	17	296			401	416	817	15	81	35	0.94	257	51	17	32	80	6%	109	20%	6.05	5.2	54	$12
LIMA Plan	B	2nd Half	306	59	11	59	13	291			389	451	840	14	79	34	0.75	266	45	22	33	99	14%	98	16%	6.16	7.2	53	$15
Rand Var	-2	10 Proj	**567**	**100**	**17**	**90**	**26**	**282**			**378**	**439**	**818**	**13**	**80**	**33**	**0.78**	**274**	**47**	**21**	**32**	**102**	**12%**	**109**	**18%**	**5.90**	**9.0**	**64**	**$25**

Gotta love the consistent value and record of health. That said, there are signs of underlying skill decline, and a sizable gap between BA and xBA. Good chance he reaches $25+ again, but you can't ignore the risk.

Abreu,Tony

		Year	AB	R	HR	RBI	SB	Avg	vL	vR	OB	Slg	OPS	bb%	ct%	h%	Eye	xBA	G	L	F	PX	hr/f	SX	SBO	RC/G	RAR	BPV	R$
Pos	4	05	0	0	0	0	0	0							0			0						0					
Age	25	06 aa	457	64	6	53	8	269			316	365	681	6	85	31	0.45	0				62		91	10%	3.90	-6.0	31	$11
Bats	Both	07 LA	* 400	60	4	32	4	300	214	290	332	435	767	5	88	34	0.38	285	52	15	32	91	4%	104	4%	4.89	2.1	65	$11
Health	F	08 LA	0	0	0	0	0	0							0			0						0					
PT/Exp	F	09 a/a	307	38	10	44	3	294			319	463	782	4	85	32	0.25	0				104		72	8%	4.87	1.2	54	$11
Consist	A	1st Half	119	11	1	5	0	226			238	307	545	2	89	25	0.14	0				50		71	13%	2.20	-9.4	21	$0
LIMA Plan	F	2nd Half	188	28	9	39	3	337			369	562	931	5	83	37	0.30	0				140		81	6%	6.67	9.5	79	$11
Rand Var	-4	10 Proj	**134**	**18**	**3**	**16**	**1**	**284**			**314**	**428**	**743**	**4**	**86**	**31**	**0.32**	**280**	**49**	**18**	**33**	**93**	**7%**	**85**	**7%**	**4.52**	**-0.6**	**54**	**$4**

Impressive 2nd half performance at Triple-A and talk of a move to second base makes him one to put on your watchlist. Eroding Eye is a concern, but one we can live with if it means double digit HRs in a full-time role.

Alfonzo,Eliezer

		Year	AB	R	HR	RBI	SB	Avg	vL	vR	OB	Slg	OPS	bb%	ct%	h%	Eye	xBA	G	L	F	PX	hr/f	SX	SBO	RC/G	RAR	BPV	R$
Pos	2	05 a/a	186	23	5	23	1	242			263	373	636	3	81	27	0.16	0				85		56	2%	3.03	-4.9	18	$4
Age	31	06 SF	* 425	37	14	49	2	240	246	271	269	397	666	4	75	29	0.16	236	41	19	40	101	11%	62	2%	3.44	-11.4	8	$7
Bats	Right	07 SF	* 128	13	4	16	0	266			282	438	720	2	76	32	0.10	0				117		61	4%	4.09	-1.3	22	$3
Health	A	08 aa	196	19	5	30	1	268			292	426	718	3	75	33	0.14	0				117		58	2%	4.15	-0.3	20	$5
PT/Exp	F	09 SD	* 318	25	11	33	1	204	208	167	224	343	567	2	73	24	0.09	220	43	18	40	95	12%	35	2%	2.01	-22.3	-14	$3
Consist	C	1st Half	174	14	7	18	0	224			237	385	622	2	75	26	0.07	219	52	13	35	108	15%	15	0%	2.70	-8.2	-3	$2
LIMA Plan	F	2nd Half	144	11	4	15	1	181			208	292	500	3	70	23	0.12	204	39	19	42	80	9%	44	4%	1.13	-14.5	-34	$0
Rand Var	+2	10 Proj	**102**	**9**	**3**	**12**	**0**	**225**			**248**	**367**	**614**	**3**	**74**	**27**	**0.11**	**229**	**41**	**18**	**41**	**100**	**10%**	**37**	**3%**	**2.71**	**-4.8**	**-5**	**$1**

2-8-.175 in 114 AB at SD. Power history looks intriguing, but his MLB PX last year was 59, and a lack of secondary skills keeps his BA unrosterable. Backups who flirt with Mendoza aren't long for this game.

Allen,Brandon

		Year	AB	R	HR	RBI	SB	Avg	vL	vR	OB	Slg	OPS	bb%	ct%	h%	Eye	xBA	G	L	F	PX	hr/f	SX	SBO	RC/G	RAR	BPV	R$
Pos	3	05	0	0	0	0	0	0							0			0						0					
Age	24	06	0	0	0	0	0	0							0			0						0					
Bats	Left	07	0	0	0	0	0	0							0			0						0					
Health	A	08 aa	153	27	15	29	3	268			345	614	959	11	76	26	0.49	0				208		84	11%	7.32	8.1	118	$8
PT/Exp	F	09 ARI	* 551	70	20	69	5	255	91	232	316	430	746	8	81	28	0.48	262	44	17	39	111	11%	80	5%	4.69	-29.5	57	$15
Consist	F	1st Half	298	33	7	31	1	253			306	391	697	7	86	28	0.53	0				85		67	4%	4.14	-20.9	47	$6
LIMA Plan	D	2nd Half	253	37	13	38	4	257			328	476	804	10	77	29	0.45	270	44	17	39	145	17%	79	6%	5.45	-7.8	67	$9
Rand Var	0	10 Proj	**127**	**19**	**6**	**20**	**2**	**260**			**329**	**464**	**792**	**9**	**79**	**29**	**0.48**	**266**	**44**	**17**	**39**	**127**	**15%**	**89**	**7%**	**5.27**	**-3.4**	**63**	**$5**

4-14-.202 in 104 AB at AZ. Things to like about his short stint in the majors: 159 PX, 17% hr/f, 10% bb rate. Things not to like: 62% ct rate, 17% LD, .225 xBA. He's still a work in progress.

Anderson,Brian

		Year	AB	R	HR	RBI	SB	Avg	vL	vR	OB	Slg	OPS	bb%	ct%	h%	Eye	xBA	G	L	F	PX	hr/f	SX	SBO	RC/G	RAR	BPV	R$
Pos	8	05 CHW	* 474	61	17	48	4	262	83	227	314	424	738	7	78	30	0.34	264	36	27	36	107	13%	71	5%	4.49	2.9	34	$12
Age	28	06 CHW	365	46	8	33	4	225	226	223	284	359	642	8	75	28	0.33	243	44	21	35	97	8%	68	14%	3.37	-14.6	17	$4
Bats	Right	07 aaa	200	26	9	28	3	243			305	421	725	8	78	27	0.41	0				108		74	10%	4.34	-1.2	40	$5
Health	A	08 CHW	181	24	8	26	5	232	225	238	272	436	709	5	75	27	0.22	269	45	17	38	145	15%	84	19%	4.05	-7.1	54	$5
PT/Exp	F	09 2AL	* 325	46	9	30	3	228	194	264	296	357	652	9	71	30	0.33	213	47	14	39	91	9%	67	14%	3.51	-11.5	-4	$5
Consist	A	1st Half	186	26	2	11	2	239			309	318	627	9	71	33	0.35	190	46	13	41	60	4%	74	17%	3.24	-8.2	-25	$2
LIMA Plan	F	2nd Half	139	20	7	19	1	214			278	408	686	8	70	26	0.30	250	52	16	32	134	21%	55	10%	3.87	-3.3	23	$3
Rand Var	-2	10 Proj	**129**	**17**	**5**	**15**	**2**	**233**			**291**	**397**	**688**	**8**	**73**	**28**	**0.31**	**242**	**46**	**16**	**38**	**115**	**13%**	**61**	**13%**	**3.89**	**-3.6**	**21**	**$3**

4-18-.243 in 202 AB at CHW/BOS. Continues to tease us with flashes of plus power, but his growing inability to put the bat on the ball is undermining everything. Peak age keeps him worthy of a speculative bid.

Anderson,Garret

		Year	AB	R	HR	RBI	SB	Avg	vL	vR	OB	Slg	OPS	bb%	ct%	h%	Eye	xBA	G	L	F	PX	hr/f	SX	SBO	RC/G	RAR	BPV	R$
Pos	7	05 ANA	575	68	17	96	1	283	330	259	311	435	746	4	85	31	0.27	268	42	21	38	97	9%	43	1%	4.45	-4.4	42	$17
Age	38	06 LAA	543	63	17	85	1	280	248	294	327	433	760	7	83	31	0.40	263	41	22	37	94	10%	51	1%	4.75	-6.5	35	$14
Bats	Left	07 LAA	417	67	16	80	1	297	288	300	340	492	832	6	87	31	0.50	297	40	19	41	121	11%	60	1%	5.59	6.3	77	$16
Health	B	08 LAA	557	66	15	84	7	293	290	293	328	433	760	5	86	32	0.38	271	42	21	36	86	9%	77	7%	4.70	-2.4	48	$18
PT/Exp	B	09 ATL	496	52	13	61	1	268	283	262	306	401	707	5	85	29	0.37	259	41	20	38	86	8%	36	1%	4.09	-21.0	33	$12
Consist	B	1st Half	194	17	4	27	1	284			319	407	726	5	87	31	0.40	271	39	24	38	82	6%	34	2%	4.34	-6.6	36	$5
LIMA Plan	D+	2nd Half	302	35	9	34	0	258			298	397	695	5	84	28	0.35	250	43	18	38	89	9%	27	0%	3.92	-14.4	28	$7
Rand Var	0	10 Proj	**464**	**55**	**13**	**67**	**2**	**263**			**302**	**409**	**711**	**5**	**86**	**28**	**0.39**	**265**	**42**	**19**	**39**	**91**	**9%**	**60**	**3%**	**4.14**	**-17.8**	**46**	**$12**

xBA is in freefall thanks to fading power and slight ct% erosion. Third straight year that he's had a sub-.700 OPS for half the season. Won't be long before that's the full-season reality. DN: .240 BA, less than 300 AB.

Anderson,Josh

		Year	AB	R	HR	RBI	SB	Avg	vL	vR	OB	Slg	OPS	bb%	ct%	h%	Eye	xBA	G	L	F	PX	hr/f	SX	SBO	RC/G	RAR	BPV	R$
Pos	798	05 aa	524	61	1	23	46	267			300	335	635	5	86	31	0.34	0				42		157	47%	3.33	-26.9	35	$17
Age	28	06 aa	561	67	3	41	35	271			298	339	637	4	88	30	0.33	0				43		123	34%	3.34	-31.2	34	$16
Bats	Left	07 HOU	* 580	58	2	43	31	238	389	347	274	292	566	5	87	27	0.37	277	64	19	17	34	2%	120	28%	2.55	-49.7	22	$10
Health	A	08 ATL	* 630	82	6	43	43	272	200	341	307	356	664	5	86	31	0.37	269	52	22	26	56	4%	134	31%	3.65	-32.4	42	$22
PT/Exp	C	09 2AL	283	42	1	24	25	240	200	248	274	304	578	4	85	28	0.30	257	61	16	23	37	2%	168	43%	2.61	-20.7	30	$9
Consist	C	1st Half	137	18	0	12	12	255			287	321	608	4	88	29	0.38	263	60	16	24	35	0%	162	40%	3.09	-7.8	40	$4
LIMA Plan	F	2nd Half	146	24	1	12	13	226			261	288	549	5	82	27	0.26	251	61	17	22	39	4%	158	47%	2.16	-13.0	16	$4
Rand Var	+2	10 Proj	**134**	**18**	**1**	**10**	**10**	**246**			**280**	**307**	**587**	**5**	**85**	**28**	**0.33**	**258**	**60**	**17**	**23**	**39**	**3%**	**136**	**38%**	**2.73**	**-9.1**	**24**	**$4**

Pure Esix Sneadian skill set. Three teams in three years lets you know that MLB teams see the same mediocrity that you do. An end-gamer if you crave speed, but you're gonna take a hit everywhere else.

Andino,Robert

		Year	AB	R	HR	RBI	SB	Avg	vL	vR	OB	Slg	OPS	bb%	ct%	h%	Eye	xBA	G	L	F	PX	hr/f	SX	SBO	RC/G	RAR	BPV	R$
Pos	6	05 aa	516	56	4	42	19	246			293	324	616	6	80	30	0.33	0				62		88	21%	3.05	-18.8	10	$10
Age	26	06 aaa	498	57	6	38	11	232			273	323	596	5	84	26	0.36	0				53		99	21%	2.84	-24.1	21	$6
Bats	Right	07 aa	598	70	11	42	17	245			287	368	655	6	80	29	0.29	0				77		118	23%	3.48	-16.3	29	$11
Health	A	08 FLA	* 244	28	6	29	7	234			289	376	665	7	79	27	0.37	0				96		96	23%	3.66	-7.3	36	$5
PT/Exp	F	09 BAL	198	31	2	10	3	222	226	221	277	288	565	7	76	28	0.32	220	53	17	30	48	4%	79	12%	2.33	-13.1	-16	$2
Consist	B	1st Half	125	18	1	7	2	248			277	312	589	4	80	30	0.20	224	51	16	33	47	3%	77	13%	2.55	-7.1	-10	$2
LIMA Plan	F	2nd Half	73	13	1	3	1	178			277	247	524	12	70	24	0.45	211	57	18	25	51	8%	79	10%	1.80	-6.3	-30	$0
Rand Var	0	10 Proj	**97**	**14**	**2**	**7**	**2**	**227**			**286**	**315**	**600**	**8**	**77**	**28**	**0.35**	**233**	**54**	**17**	**29**	**63**	**7%**	**73**	**16%**	**2.81**	**-4.8**	**-3**	**$1**

Four years of ct% decline culminated in a nightmare 2H. Speed continues to go to waste because he simply can't get on base.

Andrus,Elvis

		Year	AB	R	HR	RBI	SB	Avg	vL	vR	OB	Slg	OPS	bb%	ct%	h%	Eye	xBA	G	L	F	PX	hr/f	SX	SBO	RC/G	RAR	BPV	R$
Pos	6	05	0	0	0	0	0	0							0			0						0					
Age	22	06	0	0	0	0	0	0							0			0						0					
Bats	Right	07	0	0	0	0	0	0							0			0						0					
Health	A	08 aa	482	66	3	53	43	271			314	335	649	6	86	31	0.44	0				44		125	46%	3.53	-13.8	30	$20
PT/Exp	D	09 TEX	480	72	6	40	33	267	279	262	323	373	696	8	84	31	0.52	279	55	22	23	61	6%	154	28%	4.17	-3.9	48	$17
Consist	B	1st Half	208	30	3	14	15	269			321	380	701	7	87	30	0.59	278	57	19	24	55	7%	155	27%	4.24	-1.2	55	$7
LIMA Plan	C+	2nd Half	272	42	3	26	18	265			324	368	692	8	82	32	0.48	278	53	24	22	67	6%	138	30%	4.12	-2.6	40	$9
Rand Var	0	10 Proj	**502**	**73**	**5**	**47**	**39**	**269**			**327**	**359**	**685**	**8**	**85**	**31**	**0.56**	**275**	**55**	**22**	**23**	**55**	**5%**	**141**	**34%**	**4.06**	**-5.0**	**43**	**$18**

Not bad, considering he couldn't drink a post-game beer 'til 8/26. Hidden in 2H stats is a .342 OB and .289 xBA after Aug 1. If you want to speculate on the next step up in his growth pattern, add 10 points of BA and 5 SB.

BRANDON KRUSE

Ankiel,Rick

			AB	R	HR	RBI	SB	Avg	vL	vR	OB	Slg	OPS	bb%	ct%	h%	Eye	xBA	G	L	F	PX	hr/f	SX	SBO	RC/G	RAR	BPV	R$
Pos	897	05 aa	136	11	6	19	0	179			214	352	566	4	81	17	0.24	0				105		17	0%	2.22	-9.6	25	$1
Age	31	06	0	0	0	0	0	0							0			0						0					
Bats	Left	07 STL	* 559	72	31	97	3	236	391	246	275	445	720	5	77	25	0.23	257	44	15	41	125	18%	68	6%	4.06	-7.9	39	$16
Health	A	08 STL	413	65	25	71	2	264	224	279	332	506	838	9	76	29	0.42	267	36	19	45	154	18%	69	3%	5.84	13.1	68	$16
PT/Exp	C	09 STL	372	50	11	38	4	231	234	230	281	387	669	7	73	29	0.26	228	40	15	45	113	9%	85	9%	3.64	-12.4	25	$7
Consist	D	1st Half	196	29	5	21	1	235			286	398	684	7	76	28	0.30	247	43	15	41	122	8%	81	5%	3.89	-5.0	41	$4
LIMA Plan	D	2nd Half	176	21	6	17	3	227			277	375	652	6	70	29	0.23	206	36	15	49	103	10%	87	13%	3.36	-7.4	5	$3
Rand Var	0	10 Proj	**354**	**47**	**15**	**47**	**3**	**234**			**286**	**424**	**710**	**7**	**75**	**27**	**0.29**	**243**	**38**	**17**	**45**	**125**	**13%**	**83**	**7%**	**4.11**	**-6.1**	**40**	**$9**

Was never the same after running into wall in early May. Dwindling ct% means BA won't return even if power does. And he's made no progress vs. LH, so he won't find full-time AB on a good club. Truly has hit a wall.

Atkins,Garrett

			AB	R	HR	RBI	SB	Avg	vL	vR	OB	Slg	OPS	bb%	ct%	h%	Eye	xBA	G	L	F	PX	hr/f	SX	SBO	RC/G	RAR	BPV	R$
Pos	53	05 COL	519	62	13	89	0	287	291	285	344	426	770	8	86	31	0.63	288	46	24	30	90	10%	34	1%	5.02	3.5	44	$17
Age	30	06 COL	602	117	29	120	4	329	341	327	407	556	963	12	87	34	1.04	302	37	22	41	131	13%	67	2%	7.44	30.9	99	$32
Bats	Right	07 COL	605	83	25	111	3	301	286	307	371	486	856	10	84	32	0.70	284	31	24	44	111	11%	48	2%	6.09	8.0	62	$24
Health	A	08 COL	611	86	21	99	1	286	357	265	330	452	782	6	84	31	0.40	266	37	22	41	101	10%	62	1%	4.99	-6.5	48	$21
PT/Exp	A	09 COL	354	37	9	48	0	226	268	199	306	342	648	10	84	25	0.71	228	42	16	42	71	7%	31	0%	3.65	-16.0	23	$5
Consist	C	1st Half	223	23	6	25	0	224			300	336	636	10	86	24	0.75	228	42	17	41	67	8%	21	0%	3.51	-11.1	24	$3
LIMA Plan	D+	2nd Half	131	14	3	23	0	229			318	351	669	11	80	26	0.65	224	41	16	43	78	7%	46	0%	3.92	-4.8	22	$2
Rand Var	+4	10 Proj	**403**	**50**	**12**	**65**	**1**	**261**			**330**	**410**	**740**	**9**	**83**	**29**	**0.62**	**255**	**39**	**20**	**41**	**92**	**9%**	**55**	**1%**	**4.70**	**-6.7**	**44**	**$11**

Skill declines don't get much more steep than this. PX and xBA tell the story. h% recovery will help BA, but trend vs. RHers will limit a full return. Still horrible on road too. Can't get worse though, so there's profit... at $1.

Aubrey,Michael

			AB	R	HR	RBI	SB	Avg	vL	vR	OB	Slg	OPS	bb%	ct%	h%	Eye	xBA	G	L	F	PX	hr/f	SX	SBO	RC/G	RAR	BPV	R$
Pos	3	05 aa	106	15	3	16	1	247			286	393	680	5	84	27	0.35	0				89		93	4%	3.78	-4.9	50	$3
Age	28	06 aa	26	3	1	2	0	231			286	423	709	7	81	25	0.40	0				124		26	0%	4.17	-1.2	46	$0
Bats	Left	07 aa	207	17	5	27	0	204			238	330	568	4	83	22	0.26	0				81		21	0%	2.37	-21.5	15	$1
Health	A	08 a/a	388	36	7	44	0	242			281	368	649	5	87	26	0.41	0				84		33	0%	3.50	-23.1	35	$5
PT/Exp	F	09 BAL	* 466	46	11	57	2	257	150	329	289	400	689	4	90	27	0.45	244	34	14	53	86	5%	44	4%	3.97	-23.8	53	$9
Consist	B	1st Half	241	25	5	29	1	258			284	396	680	4	88	28	0.31	0				88		57	4%	3.81	-13.4	49	$4
LIMA Plan	F	2nd Half	225	21	7	28	1	256			294	404	698	5	92	25	0.69	247	34	14	53	84	6%	32	4%	4.14	-10.4	58	$4
Rand Var	-1	10 Proj	**233**	**23**	**6**	**29**	**1**	**245**			**280**	**386**	**666**	**5**	**88**	**26**	**0.41**	**238**	**34**	**14**	**53**	**86**	**5%**	**51**	**2%**	**3.68**	**-12.5**	**47**	**$4**

4-14-.289 in 90 AB at BAL. Flashed power w/BAL late in year, but this remains an all-contact, no-pop bat. An oft-injured one too. It's too bad, since he can loft ball well. At age 28, time is running out.

Aurilia,Rich

			AB	R	HR	RBI	SB	Avg	vL	vR	OB	Slg	OPS	bb%	ct%	h%	Eye	xBA	G	L	F	PX	hr/f	SX	SBO	RC/G	RAR	BPV	R$
Pos	3	05 CIN	426	61	14	68	2	282	272	286	339	444	783	8	84	31	0.55	275	41	21	38	101	10%	70	2%	5.13	-5.7	57	$15
Age	39	06 CIN	440	61	23	70	3	300	347	276	350	518	868	7	88	30	0.67	290	38	20	42	117	14%	59	3%	6.00	0.0	82	$18
Bats	Right	07 SF	329	40	5	33	0	252	240	260	299	368	667	6	86	28	0.49	267	39	22	38	74	5%	52	0%	3.79	-22.6	35	$5
Health	C	08 SF	407	33	10	52	1	283	321	263	332	413	745	7	86	31	0.54	248	41	18	41	81	7%	33	2%	4.65	-12.4	35	$10
PT/Exp	D	09 SF	122	10	2	16	0	213	250	186	262	279	540	6	80	25	0.33	184	48	13	40	41	5%	21	0%	2.02	-16.9	-25	$1
Consist	D	1st Half	95	7	1	13	0	211			272	263	535	8	80	25	0.42	185	50	14	36	36	4%	18	0%	2.06	-13.1	-28	$0
LIMA Plan	F	2nd Half	27	3	1	3	0	222			222	333	556	0	81	24	0.00	182	39	9	52	58	9%	39	0%	1.80	-3.9	-14	$0
Rand Var	0	10 Proj	**97**	**10**	**2**	**13**	**0**	**258**			**311**	**368**	**679**	**7**	**85**	**29**	**0.50**	**240**	**43**	**19**	**39**	**70**	**7%**	**31**	**1%**	**3.86**	**-6.6**	**20**	**$2**

Ankle issues kept him on pine for most of year. Even if he were healthy, his '06 levels are a distant memory. h% could bounce back, but w/o power it won't matter. MI eligibility long gone too. Not roster-worthy.

Ausmus,Brad

			AB	R	HR	RBI	SB	Avg	vL	vR	OB	Slg	OPS	bb%	ct%	h%	Eye	xBA	G	L	F	PX	hr/f	SX	SBO	RC/G	RAR	BPV	R$
Pos	2	05 HOU	387	35	3	47	5	258	293	251	345	331	675	12	88	29	1.06	267	54	21	25	52	3%	47	6%	4.25	5.2	32	$7
Age	41	06 HOU	439	37	2	39	3	230	266	220	302	285	586	9	84	27	0.63	233	53	19	28	38	2%	52	3%	2.95	-18.5	2	$2
Bats	Right	07 HOU	349	38	3	25	6	235	239	234	308	324	632	10	79	29	0.50	240	51	17	31	63	3%	95	7%	3.42	-10.6	15	$4
Health	A	08 HOU	216	15	3	24	0	218	277	192	299	296	595	10	81	26	0.61	213	45	18	36	55	5%	15	3%	2.98	-8.3	-5	$1
PT/Exp	F	09 LA	95	9	1	9	1	295	286	299	330	368	698	5	78	37	0.24	234	39	26	35	57	4%	41	4%	3.94	-0.8	-19	$2
Consist	B	1st Half	53	6	0	4	1	283			321	321	642	5	81	35	0.30	250	42	30	28	34	0%	56	6%	3.33	-1.4	-19	$1
LIMA Plan	F	2nd Half	42	3	1	5	0	310			341	429	769	5	74	40	0.18	206	35	19	45	89	7%	1	0%	4.85	0.7	-23	$1
Rand Var	-5	10 Proj	**96**	**9**	**1**	**8**	**1**	**240**			**305**	**300**	**606**	**9**	**82**	**29**	**0.51**	**237**	**48**	**22**	**30**	**47**	**3%**	**48**	**6%**	**3.07**	**-3.4**	**-2**	**$1**

His most productive year in nearly a decade puts him right back on our radars. Oh wait, he's 41 and his xBA says the BA was a complete fluke, given h% spike. Hot flashes in your golden years come and go.

Avila,Alex

			AB	R	HR	RBI	SB	Avg	vL	vR	OB	Slg	OPS	bb%	ct%	h%	Eye	xBA	G	L	F	PX	hr/f	SX	SBO	RC/G	RAR	BPV	R$
Pos	2	05	0	0	0	0	0	0							0			0						0					
Age	23	06	0	0	0	0	0	0							0			0						0					
Bats	Left	07	0	0	0	0	0	0							0			0						0					
Health	A	08	0	0	0	0	0	0							0			0						0					
PT/Exp	F	09 DET	* 390	52	15	60	2	246	400	255	336	431	767	12	79	27	0.66	252	43	14	43	117	11%	52	3%	5.14	10.0	53	$10
Consist	F	1st Half	234	28	6	33	2	269			357	432	789	12	81	31	0.71	0				109		56	4%	5.50	8.3	53	$6
LIMA Plan	D	2nd Half	156	24	9	27	0	212			305	429	735	12	78	21	0.60	252	43	14	43	131	17%	31	0%	4.58	1.5	50	$4
Rand Var	0	10 Proj	**247**	**35**	**11**	**40**	**1**	**235**			**326**	**426**	**752**	**12**	**79**	**26**	**0.64**	**251**	**43**	**14**	**43**	**122**	**13%**	**39**	**2%**	**4.89**	**4.8**	**51**	**$6**

5-14-.279 in 61 AB at DET. Emerged on prospect scene w/ strong year in Double-A. MLB hurlers found a big hole in swing, but he showed good power when bat met ball. Needs more seasoning. Watch him.

Aviles,Mike

			AB	R	HR	RBI	SB	Avg	vL	vR	OB	Slg	OPS	bb%	ct%	h%	Eye	xBA	G	L	F	PX	hr/f	SX	SBO	RC/G	RAR	BPV	R$
Pos	6	05 aa	521	56	9	57	8	228			259	348	607	4	91	24	0.44	0				73		95	15%	3.11	-18.5	59	$8
Age	29	06 aaa	469	46	6	42	12	245			283	340	623	5	91	26	0.60	0				56		94	15%	3.34	-14.7	49	$7
Bats	Right	07 aa	538	58	11	57	3	239			270	362	632	4	90	25	0.40	0				71		73	8%	3.31	-17.2	47	$8
Health	F	08 KC	* 633	100	17	83	11	313	348	313	341	495	836	4	88	34	0.34	301	46	20	33	113	9%	123	9%	5.57	21.4	87	$25
PT/Exp	D	09 KC	120	10	1	8	1	183	195	177	210	250	460	3	78	23	0.15	217	45	19	36	43	3%	85	5%	0.90	-13.6	-19	($1)
Consist	F	1st Half	120	10	1	8	1	183			210	250	460	3	78	23	0.15	217	45	19	36	43	3%	85	5%	0.90	-13.6	-19	($1)
LIMA Plan	D	2nd Half	0	0	0	0	0	0							0			0											
Rand Var	+5	10 Proj	**437**	**48**	**7**	**43**	**6**	**240**			**270**	**355**	**625**	**4**	**86**	**26**	**0.30**	**261**	**46**	**19**	**35**	**70**	**6%**	**95**	**9%**	**3.14**	**-16.5**	**39**	**$6**

Elbow injury resulted in Tommy John, ending season in May. He owns those '08 numbers, but remember that his BA was h%-induced and the power came out of nowhere. There's profit here, but not much.

Aybar,Erick

			AB	R	HR	RBI	SB	Avg	vL	vR	OB	Slg	OPS	bb%	ct%	h%	Eye	xBA	G	L	F	PX	hr/f	SX	SBO	RC/G	RAR	BPV	R$
Pos	6	05 aa	535	78	7	42	38	265			294	376	670	4	93	28	0.55	0				65		144	53%	3.84	-6.9	76	$19
Age	26	06 LAA	* 379	56	5	39	27	259	250	250	291	370	660	4	91	27	0.48	268	70	3	27	66	6%	137	58%	3.70	-8.5	68	$13
Bats	Both	07 LAA	194	18	1	19	4	237	304	216	275	289	563	5	84	28	0.31	214	52	12	36	35	2%	79	16%	2.40	-11.3	-2	$2
Health	B	08 LAA	346	53	3	39	7	277	286	274	306	384	690	4	87	31	0.31	270	52	18	30	69	3%	129	11%	3.94	-3.8	51	$9
PT/Exp	C	09 LAA	504	70	5	58	14	312	325	305	350	423	773	6	89	34	0.56	273	46	21	33	63	3%	120	14%	5.01	7.8	57	$18
Consist	C	1st Half	211	25	2	21	5	275			314	370	684	5	88	31	0.46	254	48	17	35	58	3%	98	13%	3.96	-3.0	40	$5
LIMA Plan	C+	2nd Half	293	45	3	37	9	338			376	461	837	6	90	37	0.64	285	44	24	32	66	4%	123	15%	5.76	10.2	65	$13
Rand Var	-5	10 Proj	**566**	**77**	**5**	**62**	**22**	**288**			**323**	**388**	**711**	**5**	**88**	**32**	**0.44**	**264**	**49**	**19**	**33**	**60**	**3%**	**128**	**20%**	**4.25**	**-2.3**	**51**	**$18**

BA inflated by h% spike, so we have to expect BA erosion. But bb% + ct% gains should keep OB high. With his good wheels, there's more SB upside given the opportunities. Age 26-with-experience too. UP: 30 SB

Aybar,Willy

			AB	R	HR	RBI	SB	Avg	vL	vR	OB	Slg	OPS	bb%	ct%	h%	Eye	xBA	G	L	F	PX	hr/f	SX	SBO	RC/G	RAR	BPV	R$
Pos	340	05 LA	* 487	44	4	51	4	258	250	382	320	350	669	8	91	28	0.96	263	53	16	31	62	3%	50	11%	4.08	-22.2	45	$8
Age	27	06 2NL	* 450	57	11	62	2	278	328	263	346	420	766	9	87	30	0.82	249	44	14	42	86	7%	42	6%	5.10	-11.6	52	$12
Bats	Both	07	0	0	0	0	0	0							0			0						0					
Health	B	08 TAM	324	33	10	33	2	253	266	245	320	410	731	9	86	27	0.73	272	40	21	40	95	9%	55	5%	4.62	-6.2	58	$6
PT/Exp	F	09 TAM	296	38	12	41	1	253	265	247	330	416	746	10	82	27	0.63	266	42	22	36	95	14%	37	1%	4.74	-8.4	37	$7
Consist	A	1st Half	144	27	7	25	0	285			383	479	862	14	84	30	1.00	285	39	23	38	111	15%	33	0%	6.35	2.6	64	$6
LIMA Plan	D	2nd Half	152	11	5	16	1	224			276	355	631	7	80	25	0.35	247	46	21	33	79	12%	27	3%	3.12	-12.0	5	$2
Rand Var	-3	10 Proj	**349**	**39**	**12**	**43**	**2**	**264**			**332**	**422**	**754**	**9**	**84**	**28**	**0.66**	**270**	**42**	**20**	**37**	**95**	**11%**	**44**	**4%**	**4.85**	**-6.5**	**47**	**$8**

His value comes from his versatility. His bat, not so much. Unless you look closely. Had elite skills in June, including 143 PX. Former toolsy types like these can develop quickly given regular AB. Late stash.

STEPHEN NICKRAND

Bailey,Jeff

			AB	R	HR	RBI	SB	Avg	vL	vR	OB	Slg	OPS	bb%	ct%	h%	Eye	xBA	G	L	F	PX	hr/f	SX	SBO	RC/G	RAR	BPV	R$
Pos	3	05 a/a	219	26	9	28	3	218			285	390	676	9	77	24	0.41	0				116		58	7%	3.75	-10.8	36	$4
Age	31	06 aaa	458	57	19	72	1	257			351	448	799	13	76	30	0.60	0				120		56	2%	5.60	-1.5	44	$12
Bats	Right	07 aaa	404	54	12	50	7	221			306	373	679	11	76	26	0.52	0				106		74	13%	3.96	-21.8	36	$7
Health	C	08 aaa	418	64	16	54	3	245			318	434	752	10	79	27	0.52	0				125		76	5%	4.83	-8.4	61	$11
PT/Exp	F	09 BOS	* 306	43	11	32	2	222	400	115	311	371	682	11	74	26	0.51	212	43	11	46	93	10%	75	2%	3.98	-16.2	19	$5
Consist	B	1st Half	213	33	8	20	2	219			316	374	690	12	73	26	0.53	212	43	11	45	93	12%	89	3%	4.10	-10.5	21	$4
LIMA Plan	F	2nd Half	93	10	3	12	0	228			299	366	665	9	77	27	0.44	162	33	0	67	93	5%	23	0%	3.70	-5.7	10	$1
Rand Var	0	10 Proj	63	8	2	8	0	238			317	388	705	10	77	28	0.49	221	43	11	45	100	10%	44	4%	4.23	-2.4	23	$1

3-9-.208 in 77 AB at BOS Career minor leaguer with some pop. Low h% and ct% means his MLB career will be a constant struggle to stay above the Mendoza Line. If he were 21, we'd be patient; at 31, not.

Baker,Jeff

			AB	R	HR	RBI	SB	Avg	vL	vR	OB	Slg	OPS	bb%	ct%	h%	Eye	xBA	G	L	F	PX	hr/f	SX	SBO	RC/G	RAR	BPV	R$
Pos	45	05 aaa	228	25	8	26	2	263			294	439	733	4	89	27	0.38	0				105		66	6%	4.37	0.2	69	$6
Age	29	06 COL	* 539	65	22	101	7	292	438	341	335	497	832	6	83	32	0.38	306	44	28	28	120	17%	89	6%	5.59	14.9	69	$21
Bats	Right	07 COL	144	17	4	12	0	222	246	205	287	347	634	8	72	28	0.33	219	40	20	39	75	10%	72	0%	3.20	-6.6	-11	$1
Health	C	08 COL	299	55	12	48	4	268	290	256	326	468	794	8	72	34	0.31	268	43	24	33	148	17%	100	6%	5.44	5.7	53	$12
PT/Exp	F	09 2NL	226	27	4	24	1	288	279	291	340	425	765	7	77	36	0.34	248	45	19	35	102	7%	71	2%	4.99	2.9	26	$6
Consist	C	1st Half	46	2	1	4	1	161			222	300	522	7	80	18	0.39	244	56	13	31	86	8%	83	14%	1.96	-3.9	29	($0)
LIMA Plan	F	2nd Half	180	25	3	20	0	320			370	457	827	7	76	41	0.33	247	44	20	36	106	6%	49	0%	5.82	6.2	19	$6
Rand Var	-4	10 Proj	227	31	7	29	1	273			326	437	763	7	76	33	0.33	258	44	21	35	112	11%	82	2%	4.90	1.8	36	$7

PRO: Glimmers of hope in ct%, probable hr/f rebound.
CON: BA (especially in 2H) was h%-fueled mirage, climbing GB% bodes ill for power. Admire '08; we're now on the backside of the peak.

Baker,John

			AB	R	HR	RBI	SB	Avg	vL	vR	OB	Slg	OPS	bb%	ct%	h%	Eye	xBA	G	L	F	PX	hr/f	SX	SBO	RC/G	RAR	BPV	R$
Pos	2	05 aaa	346	33	4	32	1	202			252	312	564	6	80	24	0.33	0				82		68	2%	2.43	-15.9	20	$1
Age	29	06 aaa	293	39	3	30	5	240			312	338	650	9	79	29	0.51	0				72		92	6%	3.65	-6.4	23	$4
Bats	Left	07 aaa	270	26	6	30	2	226			283	338	622	7	77	27	0.36	0				79		45	3%	3.07	-10.6	3	$3
Health	A	08 FLA	* 390	58	10	55	1	281	213	327	361	424	785	11	79	33	0.60	274	49	25	26	101	12%	49	2%	5.38	13.0	36	$12
PT/Exp	D	09 FLA	373	59	9	50	0	271	171	281	343	410	753	10	76	33	0.46	249	49	20	31	105	10%	36	0%	4.92	7.1	21	$11
Consist	C	1st Half	183	32	6	20	0	240			315	393	709	10	73	30	0.40	241	55	16	29	113	16%	45	0%	4.30	0.2	16	$4
LIMA Plan	D+	2nd Half	190	27	3	30	0	300			370	426	796	10	79	36	0.54	260	44	23	33	98	6%	30	0%	5.51	6.5	27	$6
Rand Var	-3	10 Proj	411	58	9	54	1	265			336	394	730	10	78	32	0.48	255	48	21	31	95	9%	46	1%	4.61	4.2	22	$10

A decent enough follow-up to his '08 debut. GB% puts drag on league-average power, and xBA warns of substantial downside, but you could do worse for your second catcher slot.

Bako,Paul

			AB	R	HR	RBI	SB	Avg	vL	vR	OB	Slg	OPS	bb%	ct%	h%	Eye	xBA	G	L	F	PX	hr/f	SX	SBO	RC/G	RAR	BPV	R$
Pos	2	05 LA	40	1	0	4	0	250	250	250	362	300	662	15	70	36	0.58	115	67	19	15	52	0%	0	0%	4.02	0.3	-46	$0
Age	38	06 KC	153	7	0	10	0	209	200	210	262	229	491	7	70	30	0.24	171	56	19	24	20	0%	11	0%	1.21	-15.2	-86	($1)
Bats	Left	07 BAL	156	13	1	8	0	205	192	208	275	256	531	9	68	30	0.30	212	56	23	21	40	5%	52	2%	1.83	-12.1	-61	($1)
Health	B	08 CIN	299	30	6	35	0	217	197	224	297	328	625	10	70	29	0.38	220	56	18	26	81	11%	49	3%	3.21	-9.2	-18	$3
PT/Exp	F	09 PHI	* 158	15	3	16	0	240		252	301	328	629	8	75	30	0.34	215	46	20	34	63	8%	27	2%	3.14	-5.3	-25	$2
Consist	B	1st Half	49	3	0	7	0	284			296	301	597	2	77	37	0.08	191	25	25	50	16	0%	19	0%	2.45	-2.5	-68	$1
LIMA Plan	F	2nd Half	109	12	3	9	0	220			303	339	643	11	73	27	0.45	226	47	20	33	85	11%	30	3%	3.42	-2.8	-6	$1
Rand Var	-2	10 Proj	95	8	1	7	0	211			284	286	570	9	70	28	0.35	209	53	21	26	59	8%	29	2%	2.38	-5.5	-42	$0

RAR and BPV say he's getting slightly less crappy as he pushes 40. That's like saying, "a skunk smells less horrible the further you are away from it." But it still smells bad and you still need to be far away from it.

Baldelli,Rocco

			AB	R	HR	RBI	SB	Avg	vL	vR	OB	Slg	OPS	bb%	ct%	h%	Eye	xBA	G	L	F	PX	hr/f	SX	SBO	RC/G	RAR	BPV	R$
Pos	9	05 TAM	0	0	0	0	0	0							0			0						0					
Age	29	06 TAM	* 411	66	16	61	10	311	297	303	340	527	867	4	81	36	0.22	286	51	16	34	134	14%	134	13%	5.96	3.4	79	$18
Bats	Right	07 TAM	137	16	5	12	4	204	156	219	253	358	611	6	74	24	0.26	238	38	18	44	106	11%	78	19%	2.78	-11.7	20	$2
Health	F	08 TAM	80	12	4	13	0	263	292	219	322	475	797	8	69	33	0.28	246	49	15	36	159	20%	31	0%	5.50	0.3	30	$3
PT/Exp	F	09 BOS	150	23	7	23	1	253	290	193	304	433	738	7	75	29	0.30	250	46	18	36	106	17%	79	3%	4.42	-4.0	26	$5
Consist	D	1st Half	76	12	4	13	0	289			349	487	836	8	75	34	0.37	256	44	21	35	110	20%	68	0%	5.78	1.0	27	$3
LIMA Plan	F	2nd Half	74	11	3	10	1	216			256	378	635	5	76	25	0.22	243	47	16	37	103	15%	72	7%	3.03	-5.2	19	$2
Rand Var	0	10 Proj	164	23	6	21	3	256			301	417	718	6	76	31	0.27	245	44	17	39	104	12%	94	9%	4.19	-5.6	29	$5

Simply can't stay healthy. In addition to cellular disorder, battled hamstring, foot, and hip injuries. At some point we have to write him off despite flashes of former potential. Now might be that point.

Balentien,Wladimi

			AB	R	HR	RBI	SB	Avg	vL	vR	OB	Slg	OPS	bb%	ct%	h%	Eye	xBA	G	L	F	PX	hr/f	SX	SBO	RC/G	RAR	BPV	R$
Pos	7	05	0	0	0	0	0	0							0			0						0					
Age	26	06 aa	444	72	21	77	13	216			322	412	734	13	69	26	0.50	0				136		90	17%	4.78	-6.0	40	$13
Bats	Right	07 aaa	477	65	19	71	13	256			324	433	757	9	79	29	0.48	0				111		88	14%	4.82	-5.4	52	$15
Health	A	08 SEA	* 476	61	20	67	2	214	218	194	277	406	684	8	74	24	0.34	250	47	14	39	137	15%	42	8%	3.85	-15.0	37	$9
PT/Exp	D	09 2TM	265	30	7	24	2	234	165	263	307	385	692	10	74	29	0.40	234	45	15	40	111	9%	62	5%	4.11	-9.4	23	$4
Consist	B	1st Half	138	15	3	10	1	225			277	362	639	7	74	28	0.26	225	44	13	42	107	7%	50	4%	3.30	-8.3	12	$1
LIMA Plan	F	2nd Half	127	15	4	14	1	244			338	409	747	12	73	30	0.53	242	45	17	38	115	11%	69	5%	4.97	-1.2	33	$3
Rand Var	-1	10 Proj	189	24	7	23	2	233			308	408	716	10	74	28	0.42	245	45	15	39	122	12%	73	8%	4.40	-4.7	37	$4

Failure to improve ct% means he had to display power to have any worth. He didn't, possibly due to early April wrist injury. With enough AB, could hit 20+ HR, but weigh that against the BA damage he'll do.

Barajas,Rod

			AB	R	HR	RBI	SB	Avg	vL	vR	OB	Slg	OPS	bb%	ct%	h%	Eye	xBA	G	L	F	PX	hr/f	SX	SBO	RC/G	RAR	BPV	R$
Pos	2	05 TEX	410	53	21	60	0	254	272	251	298	466	764	6	83	26	0.37	271	29	20	51	131	12%	27	0%	4.70	8.2	59	$12
Age	35	06 TEX	344	49	11	41	0	256	156	279	291	410	701	5	85	27	0.33	244	32	17	51	94	7%	41	0%	3.97	-4.4	40	$7
Bats	Right	07 PHI	122	16	4	10	0	230	226	231	343	393	736	15	80	26	0.88	240	31	15	54	109	8%	29	3%	4.91	1.8	48	$2
Health	A	08 TOR	349	44	11	49	0	249	204	270	284	410	694	5	83	27	0.28	254	37	17	46	107	8%	34	0%	3.87	-3.3	37	$8
PT/Exp	D	09 TOR	429	43	19	71	1	226	267	213	261	403	664	4	82	23	0.26	233	29	14	57	103	9%	35	1%	3.42	-11.1	33	$9
Consist	B	1st Half	221	24	8	39	1	267			305	434	739	5	83	29	0.32	234	24	15	60	102	7%	38	2%	4.41	0.9	38	$6
LIMA Plan	D	2nd Half	208	19	11	32	0	183			213	370	583	4	81	17	0.21	227	34	13	53	104	12%	18	0%	2.34	-12.8	23	$2
Rand Var	+1	10 Proj	390	44	16	55	0	244			289	415	704	6	82	26	0.36	241	32	15	52	105	9%	31	1%	4.02	-2.7	36	$9

Took the FB hitting to new extremes, which coupled with more AB pumped up HR total. Brutal 2H h% will rebound and give him a little BA improvement, making the power a bit easier to enjoy.

Barden,Brian

			AB	R	HR	RBI	SB	Avg	vL	vR	OB	Slg	OPS	bb%	ct%	h%	Eye	xBA	G	L	F	PX	hr/f	SX	SBO	RC/G	RAR	BPV	R$
Pos	5	05 aaa	514	54	11	59	10	272			310	418	728	5	85	30	0.37	0				96		91	13%	4.40	-3.6	57	$14
Age	29	06 aaa	494	61	13	73	1	271			318	425	743	7	86	29	0.49	0				96		49	4%	4.64	-8.7	49	$12
Bats	Right	07 aaa	352	30	3	26	2	203			258	255	512	7	82	24	0.41	0				35		49	6%	1.84	-37.9	-13	($0)
Health	A	08 aaa	411	42	5	25	2	223			271	315	587	6	85	25	0.44	0				59		63	6%	2.80	-29.4	21	$3
PT/Exp	F	09 STL	* 290	31	7	29	1	216	191	268	250	326	576	4	79	25	0.22	239	51	19	31	74	9%	47	3%	2.36	-24.9	2	$3
Consist	B	1st Half	160	15	5	14	1	211			243	332	575	4	79	24	0.20	240	50	19	31	77	12%	45	3%	2.28	-14.2	1	$2
LIMA Plan	F	2nd Half	130	15	2	16	0	223			259	318	577	5	80	27	0.24	237	100	0	0	71		47	3%	2.45	-10.7	2	$1
Rand Var	+2	10 Proj	66	7	1	6	0	227			269	324	592	5	82	26	0.31	242	51	18	31	66	7%	47	5%	2.70	-5.2	8	$1

4-10-.233 in 103 AB at STL Awesome April (3 HR, .385 BA, 139 PX) on strength of 40% h%, 25% hr/f. Then he woke up and realized he's Brian Barden. There is a reason he's a AAA lifer.

Bard,Josh

			AB	R	HR	RBI	SB	Avg	vL	vR	OB	Slg	OPS	bb%	ct%	h%	Eye	xBA	G	L	F	PX	hr/f	SX	SBO	RC/G	RAR	BPV	R$
Pos	2	05 CLE	83	6	1	9	0	193	148	214	272	277	549	10	87	21	0.82	227	43	18	39	59	4%	16	0%	2.63	-3.6	20	($0)
Age	32	06 2TM	249	30	9	40	1	333	333	333	405	522	927	11	83	37	0.71	289	52	21	27	120	16%	30	1%	7.05	17.4	61	$10
Bats	Both	07 SD	389	42	5	51	0	285	376	250	367	404	770	11	85	33	0.86	268	52	18	30	81	5%	39	1%	5.31	9.6	42	$9
Health	C	08 SD	178	11	1	16	0	202	135	230	276	270	545	9	86	23	0.72	239	47	22	31	51	2%	14	0%	2.55	-9.2	9	($0)
PT/Exp	D	09 WAS	* 314	22	6	32	0	217	240	228	278	334	612	8	81	25	0.45	233	40	19	41	84	6%	15	1%	3.08	-11.5	14	$2
Consist	D	1st Half	133	12	1	15	0	234			305	330	635	9	82	28	0.56	221	36	17	47	78	2%	21	0%	3.52	-3.0	16	$1
LIMA Plan	F	2nd Half	181	10	5	17	0	204			258	337	595	7	81	23	0.37	239	42	20	38	89	9%	11	3%	2.75	-8.6	12	$1
Rand Var	+4	10 Proj	159	12	3	17	0	233			301	346	647	9	83	27	0.58	247	45	20	35	80	6%	20	1%	3.62	-3.0	23	$2

6-31-.230 in 274 AB at WAS When inching your way back from injury, being less patient at the plate isn't the way to do it. Impending FB% correction will sap what little power he has. '06-'07 a distant memory now.

JOSHUA RANDALL

Barmes,Clint

		Yr	AB	R	HR	RBI	SB	Avg	vL	vR	OB	Slg	OPS	bb%	ct%	h%	Eye	xBA	G	L	F	PX	hr/f	SX	SBO	RC/G	RAR	BPV	R$
Pos	4	05 COL	350	55	10	46	6	289	289	283	320	434	754	4	90	30	0.44	280	36	23	41	87	8%	90	11%	4.63	0.7	66	$13
Age	31	06 COL	478	57	7	56	5	220	267	209	254	335	589	4	85	25	0.31	231	34	18	48	72	4%	92	10%	2.75	-27.4	36	$5
Bats	Right	07 COL	* 465	50	8	30	6	229	444	143	255	337	592	3	86	25	0.26	206	21	17	63	64	3%	87	12%	2.73	-28.2	32	$4
Health	B	08 COL	393	47	11	44	13	290	307	283	320	468	788	4	82	33	0.25	254	29	22	49	112	7%	128	19%	5.01	2.7	68	$14
PT/Exp	B	09 COL	550	69	23	76	12	245	245	246	286	440	726	5	78	28	0.26	253	31	20	49	128	11%	90	20%	4.25	-4.6	54	$17
Consist	D	1st Half	263	41	9	38	6	278			317	471	788	5	77	33	0.25	260	34	22	44	133	10%	112	19%	5.13	4.6	60	$10
LIMA Plan	C+	2nd Half	287	28	14	38	6	216			257	411	669	5	79	23	0.27	247	28	18	54	124	12%	57	22%	3.48	-9.5	45	$7
Rand Var	0	10 Proj	501	60	17	59	11	253			288	425	713	5	81	28	0.26	251	31	21	48	108	8%	100	18%	4.10	-7.8	54	$14

PRO:
- still more PX gains
- stayed healthy and active

CON:
- xBA shows '08 Avg is outlier
- ct% trend = no BA help coming

Value solely in HR, SB totals.

Bartlett,Jason

		Yr	AB	R	HR	RBI	SB	Avg	vL	vR	OB	Slg	OPS	bb%	ct%	h%	Eye	xBA	G	L	F	PX	hr/f	SX	SBO	RC/G	RAR	BPV	R$
Pos	6	05 MIN	* 453	68	7	44	6	272	290	226	339	375	714	9	85	31	0.68	249	47	18	35	67	5%	92	6%	4.47	-1.2	42	$11
Age	30	06 MIN	* 568	85	3	51	16	303	314	307	339	407	746	5	87	35	0.42	267	44	22	34	72	2%	112	15%	4.69	4.4	50	$16
Bats	Right	07 MIN	510	75	5	43	23	265	319	245	330	361	691	9	86	30	0.68	256	44	20	36	60	3%	140	17%	4.23	-0.9	52	$14
Health	B	08 TAM	454	48	1	37	20	286	379	248	319	361	681	5	85	34	0.32	257	49	21	30	56	1%	107	21%	3.84	-6.3	28	$12
PT/Exp	B	09 TAM	500	90	14	66	30	320	338	312	386	490	876	10	82	37	0.61	272	35	26	39	102	9%	138	23%	6.42	26.8	74	$26
Consist	C	1st Half	218	43	7	36	17	362			401	560	960	6	84	41	0.40	292	32	29	39	119	10%	151	27%	7.15	14.8	90	$15
LIMA Plan	B	2nd Half	282	47	7	30	13	287			376	436	812	12	81	33	0.74	257	37	23	39	89	8%	120	20%	5.80	11.0	58	$11
Rand Var	-5	10 Proj	519	79	9	56	26	289			347	417	764	8	84	33	0.54	265	41	23	36	81	6%	131	21%	4.99	8.8	57	$19

Superb breakout hides a wart or two, most notably sharp BA/xBA spread. That means Avg will regress, probably SB with it. Now age 30, given big negative Rand Var, it's safe to assume it goes downhill from here.

Barton,Daric

		Yr	AB	R	HR	RBI	SB	Avg	vL	vR	OB	Slg	OPS	bb%	ct%	h%	Eye	xBA	G	L	F	PX	hr/f	SX	SBO	RC/G	RAR	BPV	R$
Pos	3	05 aa	212	32	4	30	1	292			376	451	826	12	89	31	1.24	0				106		60	3%	6.04	4.1	85	$7
Age	25	06 aaa	147	22	2	19	1	247			366	367	732	16	88	27	1.51	0				68		88	2%	5.16	-2.4	65	$3
Bats	Left	07 OAK	* 588	87	11	67	4	279	296	378	360	423	784	11	89	30	1.12	287	32	24	44	96	5%	67	5%	5.50	4.1	76	$15
Health	B	08 OAK	451	59	9	47	2	224	273	208	322	344	665	13	78	27	0.66	222	35	19	46	78	6%	81	2%	3.93	-18.5	26	$6
PT/Exp	B	09 OAK	* 413	65	9	58	1	232	333	257	326	376	702	12	86	25	1.03	259	31	20	48	91	5%	60	3%	4.55	-14.5	63	$8
Consist	C	1st Half	238	31	4	29	1	198			282	323	606	11	87	21	0.90	195	23	8	69	81	3%	66	2%	3.36	-17.6	56	$2
LIMA Plan	D+	2nd Half	175	34	5	29	0	278			383	448	831	15	86	30	1.18	273	32	22	46	105	7%	61	3%	6.17	2.3	75	$6
Rand Var	+3	10 Proj	397	61	11	52	1	259			353	424	777	13	85	28	0.95	263	33	20	47	102	7%	66	3%	5.40	-1.0	67	$10

3-34-.269 in 160 AB at OAK. After more dismal-ness in 1H, one-time prospect showed a bit of a pulse. Eye healthy, FB% trend also gives hope. At 24, it's not like he's ready for the home. Worth a speculative bid.

Bautista,Jose

		Yr	AB	R	HR	RBI	SB	Avg	vL	vR	OB	Slg	OPS	bb%	ct%	h%	Eye	xBA	G	L	F	PX	hr/f	SX	SBO	RC/G	RAR	BPV	R$
Pos	795	05 PIT	* 515	53	16	69	7	238			294	390	684	7	82	26	0.45	0				98		66	10%	3.89	-22.6	45	$12
Age	29	06 PIT	* 501	70	18	60	4	243	283	216	323	420	743	11	74	29	0.46	228	40	13	47	117	10%	71	7%	4.79	-7.0	36	$11
Bats	Right	07 PIT	532	75	15	63	6	254	256	253	338	414	752	11	81	29	0.67	256	40	16	43	106	8%	73	6%	4.97	-6.0	55	$13
Health	A	08 2TM	370	45	15	54	1	238	250	233	312	405	718	10	75	28	0.44	235	46	15	39	113	14%	35	2%	4.34	-8.8	24	$9
PT/Exp	B	09 TOR	336	54	13	40	4	235	293	202	344	408	752	14	75	28	0.66	239	41	17	42	107	12%	93	4%	5.04	0.3	43	$8
Consist	B	1st Half	126	23	2	11	3	254			390	365	755	18	69	35	0.72	220	42	22	36	84	6%	96	6%	5.46	1.7	11	$3
LIMA Plan	D	2nd Half	210	31	11	29	1	224			315	433	748	12	78	24	0.61	250	41	14	45	120	15%	78	2%	4.79	-1.4	57	$5
Rand Var	0	10 Proj	369	53	14	46	4	238			331	405	737	12	76	28	0.58	242	42	16	42	108	12%	76	4%	4.74	-2.5	40	$9

Settling into utility role, which is good for his ML career, but not so much for fanalytic value. That said, 15-ish HR is coming every year, if you can take the certain BA hit. There are sexier picks, but there's value in reliability.

Bay,Jason

		Yr	AB	R	HR	RBI	SB	Avg	vL	vR	OB	Slg	OPS	bb%	ct%	h%	Eye	xBA	G	L	F	PX	hr/f	SX	SBO	RC/G	RAR	BPV	R$
Pos	7	05 PIT	599	110	32	101	21	306	342	292	401	559	960	14	76	36	0.67	293	38	22	40	170	17%	133	11%	7.76	39.6	110	$34
Age	32	06 PIT	570	101	35	109	11	286	304	280	394	532	926	15	73	34	0.65	257	41	15	44	155	19%	87	7%	7.43	35.0	73	$27
Bats	Right	07 PIT	538	78	21	84	4	247	227	254	322	418	740	10	74	30	0.42	237	38	17	45	114	12%	73	3%	4.68	-10.8	30	$14
Health	A	08 2TM	577	111	31	101	10	286	252	296	374	522	896	12	76	33	0.59	266	38	17	46	154	15%	111	6%	6.80	26.9	88	$27
PT/Exp	A	09 BOS	531	103	36	119	13	267	292	257	378	537	914	15	69	32	0.58	260	33	18	49	179	20%	102	10%	7.38	36.4	84	$27
Consist	C	1st Half	282	50	19	69	5	262			368	535	903	14	73	29	0.62	272	37	16	47	173	20%	92	7%	7.03	16.6	89	$14
LIMA Plan	B+	2nd Half	249	53	17	50	8	273			389	538	927	16	65	35	0.55	247	29	20	52	187	20%	99	12%	7.84	20.3	75	$13
Rand Var	-1	10 Proj	574	107	34	112	12	272			371	515	886	14	72	32	0.56	259	35	18	47	163	17%	99	8%	6.85	31.0	77	$26

As with many BOS hitters, more productive overall at home, but more road HR (21). So eventual destination not an issue. Low ct% limits BA; otherwise, an elite contributor, and sim stud. And, uh, 2007? Fuggedaboutit.

Beckham,Gordon

		Yr	AB	R	HR	RBI	SB	Avg	vL	vR	OB	Slg	OPS	bb%	ct%	h%	Eye	xBA	G	L	F	PX	hr/f	SX.	SBO	RC/G	RAR	BPV	R$
Pos	5	05	0	0	0	0	0	0							0			0						0					
Age	24	06	0	0	0	0	0	0							0			0						0					
Bats	Right	07	0	0	0	0	0	0							0			0						0					
Health	A	08	0	0	0	0	0	0							0			0						0					
PT/Exp	F	09 CHW	* 553	83	18	85	9	278	318	250	342	467	809	9	84	30	0.61	277	40	17	43	121	9%	74	9%	5.55	13.7	75	$19
Consist	F	1st Half	254	37	6	36	3	291			347	458	805	8	86	32	0.60	279	40	18	42	112	7%	57	9%	5.48	5.7	67	$8
LIMA Plan	B	2nd Half	299	46	12	49	6	268			338	475	813	10	83	29	0.62	278	41	16	43	130	11%	88	9%	5.60	8.0	82	$11
Rand Var	0	10 Proj	510	77	20	79	9	276			341	485	826	9	84	30	0.61	285	40	16	43	133	11%	80	9%	5.72	13.9	86	$18

14-63-.270 in 378 AB at CHW. So much for seasoning: spent all of 3 months in minors before arriving to stay. Overcame 0-13 start to finish well. Value would be higher at SS, but helps now even at 3B; golden as a keeper.

Belliard,Ronnie

		Yr	AB	R	HR	RBI	SB	Avg	vL	vR	OB	Slg	OPS	bb%	ct%	h%	Eye	xBA	G	L	F	PX	hr/f	SX	SBO	RC/G	RAR	BPV	R$
Pos	4	05 CLE	536	71	17	78	2	284	287	285	327	450	777	6	87	30	0.49	276	45	18	37	105	10%	50	3%	4.98	12.8	60	$17
Age	35	06 2TM	544	63	13	67	2	272	220	295	317	403	720	6	85	30	0.44	256	46	19	35	81	8%	44	4%	4.31	-0.7	33	$15
Bats	Right	07 WAS	511	57	11	58	3	290	329	275	334	427	761	6	86	32	0.47	265	44	17	39	89	6%	59	2%	4.83	1.8	48	$13
Health	B	08 WAS	296	37	11	46	3	287	307	279	366	473	839	11	80	33	0.64	281	42	23	35	125	13%	44	6%	6.01	10.4	59	$11
PT/Exp	C	09 2NL	264	39	10	39	3	277	282	275	327	451	778	7	79	32	0.36	266	42	22	36	114	13%	79	4%	5.00	3.5	46	$10
Consist	C	1st Half	88	5	2	7	0	159			204	261	466	5	74	19	0.22	208	41	20	39	62	8%	51	0%	0.85	-10.7	-27	($1)
LIMA Plan	D+	2nd Half	176	34	8	32	3	335			387	545	933	8	81	38	0.45	294	42	23	35	138	16%	72	6%	6.91	10.9	75	$10
Rand Var	-1	10 Proj	318	41	11	44	3	277			333	443	776	8	81	31	0.44	268	43	21	36	109	11%	70	4%	5.03	3.7	49	$10

Probably earned another contract with late-season push. Late-career power surge looks fluky, but that's two 13% hr/f years in a row, so who knows? Expect similar, modest, part-time, across-the-board help.

Beltran,Carlos

		Yr	AB	R	HR	RBI	SB	Avg	vL	vR	OB	Slg	OPS	bb%	ct%	h%	Eye	xBA	G	L	F	PX	hr/f	SX	SBO	RC/G	RAR	BPV	R$
Pos	8	05 NYM	582	83	16	78	17	266	308	254	331	414	745	9	84	30	0.58	270	44	19	37	96	9%	102	14%	4.75	3.2	61	$20
Age	33	06 NYM	510	127	41	116	18	275	247	288	388	594	983	16	81	27	0.96	305	37	17	47	186	21%	108	14%	7.87	50.2	137	$31
Bats	Both	07 NYM	554	93	33	112	23	276	304	265	356	525	882	11	80	29	0.62	291	38	19	43	150	17%	113	16%	6.44	30.1	98	$28
Health	D	08 NYM	606	116	27	112	25	284	326	266	378	500	878	13	84	30	0.96	300	45	22	33	131	16%	127	15%	6.57	31.4	107	$32
PT/Exp	A	09 NYM	308	50	10	48	11	325	326	324	414	500	914	13	86	35	1.09	289	45	20	35	112	11%	94	11%	7.05	19.0	90	$17
Consist	A	1st Half	241	40	8	40	11	336			424	527	951	13	86	37	1.09	296	44	20	36	124	11%	96	13%	7.51	17.6	100	$14
LIMA Plan	B	2nd Half	67	10	2	8	0	284			377	403	780	13	87	30	1.11	252	50	19	31	69	11%	27	0%	5.40	1.3	38	$2
Rand Var	-4	10 Proj	489	83	20	80	14	292			383	481	864	13	84	31	0.93	286	45	20	35	114	14%	101	10%	6.36	22.9	87	$23

Get used to seeing notes on injured Mets. Before the knee bruise that shelved this one, past trends were continuing: Eye up, PX down. The slow decline is underway; we may not see '08 again, let alone '06.

Beltre,Adrian

		Yr	AB	R	HR	RBI	SB	Avg	vL	vR	OB	Slg	OPS	bb%	ct%	h%	Eye	xBA	G	L	F	PX	hr/f	SX	SBO	RC/G	RAR	BPV	R$
Pos	5	05 SEA	603	69	19	87	3	255	281	249	300	413	712	6	82	28	0.35	264	46	19	35	104	11%	56	3%	4.16	-6.0	42	$15
Age	31	06 SEA	620	88	25	89	11	268	280	264	319	465	784	7	81	30	0.40	270	37	21	42	121	12%	98	11%	5.07	1.1	67	$19
Bats	Right	07 SEA	595	87	26	99	14	276	280	274	319	482	801	6	83	30	0.37	291	44	17	39	132	13%	101	12%	5.21	5.7	80	$23
Health	C	08 SEA	556	74	25	77	8	266	338	240	327	457	784	8	84	28	0.56	283	40	22	39	116	14%	70	7%	5.09	3.4	67	$18
PT/Exp	A	09 SEA	449	54	8	44	13	265	298	253	295	379	673	4	84	30	0.26	249	46	16	38	76	6%	88	15%	3.64	-13.5	32	$11
Consist	B	1st Half	297	36	5	31	9	259			286	374	659	4	84	30	0.23	248	45	16	39	78	5%	87	17%	3.46	-10.6	33	$7
LIMA Plan	C	2nd Half	152	18	3	13	4	276			312	388	701	5	83	32	0.31	249	47	17	36	73	7%	71	10%	3.99	-3.0	23	$4
Rand Var	0	10 Proj	513	66	16	62	11	269			312	423	735	6	83	30	0.37	266	44	18	38	98	10%	90	11%	4.43	-5.0	51	$15

Speaking of declines.... Injuries of various types are starting to plague him -- note AB trends -- and most aren't fluke injuries. Beltre needs large AB totals to amass value, but injury-prone players usually stay that way.

JOSHUA RANDALL

Berkman,Lance

		AB	R	HR	RBI	SB	Avg	vL	vR	OB	Slg	OPS	bb%	ct%	h%	Eye	xBA	G	L	F	PX	hr/f	SX	SBO	RC/G	RAR	BPV	R$
Pos 3	05 HOU	468	76	24	82	4	293	296	295	408	524	931	16	85	30	1.26	319	46	23	32	142	19%	62	3%	7.37	23.0	105	$21
Age 34	06 HOU	536	95	45	136	3	315	266	335	421	621	1042	15	80	32	0.92	301	39	19	42	173	25%	35	3%	8.58	37.4	102	$32
Bats Both	07 HOU	561	95	34	102	7	278	265	282	382	510	891	14	78	30	0.75	280	44	18	38	139	21%	70	5%	6.75	9.9	74	$24
Health B	08 HOU	554	114	29	106	18	312	276	327	417	567	983	15	81	35	0.92	298	43	18	39	163	17%	113	11%	8.03	34.7	119	$33
PT/Exp A	09 HOU	460	73	25	80	7	274	231	291	400	509	909	17	79	30	0.99	283	43	18	39	153	18%	60	7%	7.19	9.0	92	$20
Consist C	1st Half	257	39	17	47	5	261			389	518	907	17	79	27	1.02	284	40	17	42	157	20%	64	8%	7.06	4.1	99	$12
LIMA Plan B+	2nd Half	203	34	8	33	2	291			415	498	912	17	78	34	0.96	281	46	19	35	148	15%	43	5%	7.36	4.9	80	$9
Rand Var +2	10 Proj	**540**	**94**	**29**	**98**	**9**	**289**			**404**	**529**	**933**	**16**	**79**	**32**	**0.94**	**290**	**43**	**19**	**38**	**154**	**18%**	**78**	**7%**	**7.44**	**19.1**	**98**	**$26**

Calf injury caused August HR slump plus SB drop, but Sept. HR surge indicates return to health. Plate discipline, batting eye held up well. At 34, injuries could become more frequent. but expect slight rebound.

Betancourt,Yuniesky

		AB	R	HR	RBI	SB	Avg	vL	vR	OB	Slg	OPS	bb%	ct%	h%	Eye	xBA	G	L	F	PX	hr/f	SX	SBO	RC/G	RAR	BPV	R$
Pos 6	05 SEA *	621	57	7	58	17	253	283	248	282	367	649	4	91	27	0.47	244	38	17	45	66	3%	113	25%	3.60	-18.0	62	$12
Age 28	06 SEA	558	68	8	47	11	289	240	303	310	403	713	3	90	31	0.31	264	46	18	36	67	4%	101	14%	4.16	-3.9	53	$13
Bats Right	07 SEA	536	72	9	67	5	289	333	277	309	418	726	3	91	30	0.31	286	43	19	38	84	5%	78	7%	4.31	0.3	62	$14
Health A	08 SEA	559	66	7	51	4	279	273	281	300	392	692	3	92	29	0.40	272	40	20	40	72	3%	75	6%	4.01	-5.1	58	$12
PT/Exp B	09 2AL	470	40	6	49	3	245	283	231	277	351	628	4	91	26	0.48	251	42	17	41	60	3%	75	6%	3.36	-15.4	43	$6
Consist A	1st Half	224	15	2	22	3	250			282	330	612	4	92	26	0.56	246	41	18	41	49	2%	60	8%	3.22	-8.2	36	$3
LIMA Plan D	2nd Half	246	25	4	27	0	240			272	370	642	4	89	25	0.42	255	43	16	41	70	4%	81	4%	3.49	-7.2	48	$3
Rand Var +2	10 Proj	**443**	**46**	**6**	**46**	**4**	**262**			**289**	**377**	**666**	**4**	**91**	**28**	**0.42**	**262**	**42**	**18**	**40**	**68**	**4%**	**80**	**7%**	**3.74**	**-8.6**	**52**	**$8**

Nine times out of 10 he'll make contact, but with a declining PX now 40% below league avg, those hits do no harm. Ever. Lousy RAR and defense mean his grip on any starting job is tenuous. Not worth the PT risk.

Blake,Casey

		AB	R	HR	RBI	SB	Avg	vL	vR	OB	Slg	OPS	bb%	ct%	h%	Eye	xBA	G	L	F	PX	hr/f	SX	SBO	RC/G	RAR	BPV	R$
Pos 5	05 CLE	523	72	23	58	4	241	241	241	299	438	736	8	78	27	0.37	263	37	20	42	132	13%	63	8%	4.49	-0.1	53	$13
Age 37	06 CLE	401	63	19	68	6	282	272	286	354	479	833	10	77	33	0.48	267	40	23	37	124	17%	82	5%	5.84	9.4	53	$15
Bats Right	07 CLE	588	81	18	78	4	270	256	276	332	437	769	8	79	32	0.44	259	39	18	43	113	9%	71	6%	5.01	2.4	47	$16
Health B	08 2TM	536	71	21	81	3	274	287	270	335	463	798	8	78	32	0.41	268	38	22	40	129	13%	63	2%	5.35	3.4	51	$17
PT/Exp A	09 LA	485	84	18	79	3	280	320	270	363	468	831	11	76	34	0.54	266	42	23	35	124	14%	89	5%	5.99	11.8	55	$19
Consist A	1st Half	255	42	11	48	2	286			352	494	846	9	78	33	0.46	274	40	20	40	141	14%	70	4%	6.01	6.2	66	$11
LIMA Plan C	2nd Half	230	42	7	31	1	274			375	439	814	14	74	34	0.62	258	44	26	30	104	14%	95	5%	5.95	5.4	37	$8
Rand Var -2	10 Proj	**458**	**72**	**17**	**69**	**3**	**275**			**349**	**457**	**807**	**10**	**77**	**33**	**0.49**	**263**	**40**	**22**	**37**	**120**	**13%**	**82**	**4%**	**5.59**	**4.2**	**50**	**$16**

Hamstring problems wore him down in 2nd half. Previously healthy, so a winter's rest should fix that. Doesn't usually outperform xBA this much, so expect some BA correction. Skills are aging gently so far.

Blalock,Hank

		AB	R	HR	RBI	SB	Avg	vL	vR	OB	Slg	OPS	bb%	ct%	h%	Eye	xBA	G	L	F	PX	hr/f	SX	SBO	RC/G	RAR	BPV	R$
Pos 30	05 TEX	647	80	25	92	1	263	196	290	317	431	748	7	80	30	0.39	269	39	24	36	111	13%	38	1%	4.61	-9.0	35	$18
Age 29	06 TEX	591	76	16	89	1	266	216	284	324	401	725	8	83	30	0.52	256	42	21	37	81	9%	62	1%	4.44	-16.7	35	$14
Bats Left	07 TEX	208	32	10	33	4	293	298	292	358	543	901	9	82	32	0.55	300	33	21	46	157	13%	103	9%	6.65	8.1	104	$9
Health F	08 TEX	258	37	12	38	1	287	277	291	336	508	843	7	84	30	0.48	295	36	21	43	137	13%	59	2%	5.75	3.5	81	$9
PT/Exp D	09 TEX	462	62	25	66	2	234	221	239	275	459	733	5	77	25	0.24	263	37	18	44	135	16%	83	2%	4.30	-19.5	52	$12
Consist C	1st Half	220	36	16	35	1	245			284	536	821	5	80	24	0.27	295	32	21	47	166	19%	86	3%	5.30	-2.6	91	$8
LIMA Plan D+	2nd Half	242	26	9	31	1	223			266	388	654	5	74	27	0.22	233	43	16	41	105	12%	71	2%	3.34	-17.5	12	$4
Rand Var +3	10 Proj	**421**	**57**	**19**	**61**	**1**	**259**			**307**	**467**	**774**	**7**	**80**	**28**	**0.34**	**271**	**37**	**20**	**43**	**129**	**13%**	**63**	**1%**	**4.90**	**-7.2**	**55**	**$12**

Now we know what hr/f to expect when healthy, but HRs are all he gives. xBA and h% show some room for rebound but everything needs to fall right. That 2H means no '10 margin for error; another PT risk.

Blanco,Andres

		AB	R	HR	RBI	SB	Avg	vL	vR	OB	Slg	OPS	bb%	ct%	h%	Eye	xBA	G	L	F	PX	hr/f	SX	SBO	RC/G	RAR	BPV	R$
Pos 4	05 KC *	225	21	1	17	2	220	125	269	255	276	531	4	89	24	0.42	230	52	15	32	30	2%	92	6%	2.22	-16.2	18	$1
Age 26	06 aaa	283	28	2	19	5	234			284	312	596	7	88	26	0.60	0				45		92	13%	3.06	-11.5	32	$2
Bats Both	07 aaa	97	8	0	8	0	186			225	206	432	5	87	21	0.38	0				17		33	0%	1.01	-10.4	-18	($1)
Health C	08 aaa	298	22	1	27	7	242			268	283	551	3	92	26	0.42	0				27		72	14%	2.48	-18.1	19	$4
PT/Exp F	09 CHC *	353	39	7	36	5	264	250	253	305	391	696	6	89	28	0.54	284	53	19	28	83	8%	67	9%	4.12	-5.6	55	$8
Consist D	1st Half	233	20	4	28	3	263			301	365	665	5	89	28	0.48	268	56	18	26	67	7%	44	10%	3.72	-6.4	34	$5
LIMA Plan F	2nd Half	120	18	3	8	2	265			314	441	755	7	89	28	0.64	307	47	21	32	114	9%	96	7%	4.88	0.8	90	$3
Rand Var 0	10 Proj	**99**	**10**	**3**	**8**	**2**	**253**			**292**	**422**	**715**	**5**	**89**	**25**	**0.53**	**296**	**51**	**19**	**30**	**96**	**12%**	**84**	**12%**	**4.27**	**-0.9**	**72**	**$2**

1-12-.252 in 123 AB at CHC. Good glove, no bat, no speed. Age, time passed since shoulder woes, and doubles power in both minors and majors all suggest that the BA growth is real and projectable.

Blanco,Henry

		AB	R	HR	RBI	SB	Avg	vL	vR	OB	Slg	OPS	bb%	ct%	h%	Eye	xBA	G	L	F	PX	hr/f	SX	SBO	RC/G	RAR	BPV	R$
Pos 2	05 CHC	161	16	6	25	0	242	194	254	291	391	682	6	85	25	0.46	250	42	17	41	88	11%	19	0%	3.81	0.1	31	$4
Age 39	06 CHC	241	23	6	37	0	266	325	236	306	419	725	5	84	29	0.37	273	38	24	38	93	8%	42	0%	4.35	0.1	37	$5
Bats Right	07 CHC	54	3	0	4	0	167	50	235	196	222	419	4	78	21	0.17	190	29	17	55	51	0%	24	0%	0.44	-7.0	-32	($1)
Health C	08 CHC	120	15	3	12	0	292	316	270	325	392	717	5	82	34	0.27	215	42	17	42	61	7%	30	0%	4.08	-0.4	-4	$3
PT/Exp F	09 SD	204	21	6	16	0	235	322	200	322	382	704	11	75	28	0.52	225	41	16	43	107	9%	18	0%	4.31	0.3	17	$3
Consist D	1st Half	106	14	4	10	0	208			288	358	647	10	78	23	0.52	223	40	14	46	97	11%	31	0%	3.45	-2.7	23	$1
LIMA Plan F	2nd Half	98	7	2	6	0	265			357	408	765	12	72	35	0.52	224	42	18	40	119	7%	7	0%	5.31	3.0	14	$1
Rand Var -1	10 Proj	**174**	**18**	**5**	**18**	**0**	**247**			**311**	**381**	**692**	**8**	**79**	**29**	**0.44**	**233**	**41**	**18**	**41**	**91**	**8%**	**21**	**0%**	**4.01**	**-1.2**	**14**	**$3**

Highest PX since 2000. bb% and ct% show that he used a "wait for your pitch and then swing hard" approach, so HRs may continue, esp. v LHP. Fine xBA growth; he might be draftable by age 57.

Blanks,Kyle

		AB	R	HR	RBI	SB	Avg	vL	vR	OB	Slg	OPS	bb%	ct%	h%	Eye	xBA	G	L	F	PX	hr/f	SX	SBO	RC/G	RAR	BPV	R$
Pos 9	05	0	0	0	0	0	0							0			0						0					
Age 24	06	0	0	0	0	0	0							0			0						0					
Bats Right	07	0	0	0	0	0	0							0			0						0					
Health B	08 aa	492	65	16	92	4	287			344	439	783	8	83	32	0.52	0				90		70	6%	5.11	-2.2	45	$18
PT/Exp F	09 SD *	381	51	19	52	1	241	220	262	328	436	764	11	71	29	0.45	224	37	13	51	134	14%	44	2%	5.07	2.1	31	$11
Consist A	1st Half	260	30	9	33	0	234			324	381	705	12	75	28	0.54	235	29	24	47	98	10%	36	0%	4.29	-4.6	16	$5
LIMA Plan C	2nd Half	121	21	10	19	1	256			338	554	892	11	63	32	0.33	251	38	11	51	226	26%	47	7%	7.25	8.5	71	$5
Rand Var -1	10 Proj	**441**	**63**	**22**	**71**	**3**	**252**			**326**	**455**	**782**	**10**	**74**	**29**	**0.43**	**232**	**38**	**11**	**51**	**133**	**13%**	**66**	**5%**	**5.19**	**2.8**	**44**	**$15**

10-22-.250 in 128 AB at SD. Exciting 207 PX in majors but
- plantar fasciitis ended season
- might not stick as OF
- didn't hit LHP
- low ct% will cause trouble

A promising work in progress.

Bloomquist,Willie

		AB	R	HR	RBI	SB	Avg	vL	vR	OB	Slg	OPS	bb%	ct%	h%	Eye	xBA	G	L	F	PX	hr/f	SX	SBO	RC/G	RAR	BPV	R$
Pos 968	05 SEA	249	27	0	22	14	257	247	262	288	333	622	4	85	30	0.29	256	45	24	32	59	0%	131	26%	3.16	-11.2	36	$6
Age 32	06 SEA	251	36	1	15	16	247	253	243	313	299	612	9	84	29	0.60	218	46	17	37	32	1%	132	25%	3.22	-18.4	21	$6
Bats Right	07 SEA	173	28	2	13	7	277	238	290	317	329	646	5	80	34	0.29	245	61	19	20	35	7%	89	23%	3.28	-11.3	-14	$5
Health B	08 SEA	165	32	0	9	14	279	351	220	374	285	659	13	82	34	0.86	224	56	20	24	5	0%	108	24%	3.97	-6.7	-5	$7
PT/Exp D	09 KC	434	52	4	29	25	265	248	275	308	355	663	6	83	31	0.37	246	46	21	33	50	3%	145	26%	3.65	-21.4	30	$12
Consist A	1st Half	184	24	1	14	14	266			325	353	678	8	84	31	0.53	243	53	17	31	44	2%	148	29%	4.01	-7.1	33	$6
LIMA Plan D	2nd Half	250	28	3	15	11	264			295	356	651	4	83	31	0.26	248	41	24	35	55	4%	118	24%	3.39	-14.3	21	$6
Rand Var -1	10 Proj	**360**	**42**	**2**	**24**	**20**	**269**			**325**	**334**	**659**	**8**	**83**	**32**	**0.47**	**242**	**50**	**20**	**29**	**39**	**3%**	**123**	**23%**	**3.68**	**-17.6**	**16**	**$10**

SBs were driven by playing time spike. Revisit playing time outlook next spring because he's not that good. Believe it or not: 29 RBIs were a career high and 3rd worst among MLB batters with 400+ AB.

Blum,Geoff

		AB	R	HR	RBI	SB	Avg	vL	vR	OB	Slg	OPS	bb%	ct%	h%	Eye	xBA	G	L	F	PX	hr/f	SX	SBO	RC/G	RAR	BPV	R$
Pos 5	05 2TM	319	32	6	25	3	229	213	236	291	345	636	8	87	25	0.65	258	40	21	39	73	6%	69	8%	3.52	-11.0	43	$4
Age 37	06 SD	276	27	4	34	0	254	167	267	297	366	663	6	82	30	0.33	247	36	23	41	77	4%	41	2%	3.62	-15.2	13	$4
Bats Both	07 SD	330	34	5	33	0	252	238	256	318	367	684	9	84	29	0.62	250	36	20	44	79	4%	32	0%	4.10	-14.6	29	$4
Health B	08 HOU	325	36	14	53	1	240	229	242	286	418	705	6	83	25	0.39	261	36	20	44	105	12%	45	4%	4.02	-13.2	45	$8
PT/Exp F	09 HOU	381	34	10	49	0	247	345	239	307	367	674	8	84	27	0.54	232	36	18	46	74	7%	27	1%	3.83	-14.8	21	$7
Consist A	1st Half	165	15	1	20	0	261			330	315	645	9	88	29	0.85	226	36	21	43	39	2%	24	2%	3.75	-6.7	11	$3
LIMA Plan F	2nd Half	216	19	9	29	0	236			289	407	696	7	81	25	0.39	238	35	16	49	104	11%	31	0%	3.94	-7.8	32	$4
Rand Var 0	10 Proj	**291**	**28**	**8**	**38**	**0**	**241**			**297**	**377**	**675**	**7**	**84**	**26**	**0.50**	**246**	**36**	**19**	**45**	**85**	**8%**	**42**	**2%**	**3.82**	**-12.6**	**32**	**$5**

Only 29 AB v LHP, so ignore that platoon split. HRs have been fun the past two years but hr/f looks fluky and xBA shows the end is near. DN: .200 BA, released next July.

MICHAEL WEDDELL

Bonifacio,Emilio

		Year	AB	R	HR	RBI	SB	Avg	vL	vR	OB	Slg	OPS	bb%	ct%	h%	Eye	xBA	G	L	F	PX	hr/f	SX	SBO	RC/G	RAR	BPV	R$
Pos	5	05	0	0	0	0	0	0							0			0						0					
Age	25	06	0	0	0	0	0	0							0			0						0					
Bats	Both	07 aa	574	72	2	36	34	265			308	326	634	6	84	31	0.40	281	63	21	16	42	3%	120	31%	3.34	-32.6	22	$15
Health	A	08 2NL	* 567	76	1	40	24	264	163	270	311	343	653	6	82	32	0.37	258	55	21	23	53	1%	136	25%	3.59	-30.2	25	$14
PT/Exp	C	09 FLA	461	72	1	27	21	252	315	223	303	308	611	7	79	32	0.36	229	53	19	28	37	1%	143	23%	3.02	-29.4	6	$11
Consist	A	1st Half	308	44	1	20	17	250			300	302	602	7	79	31	0.34	223	49	21	31	35	1%	132	26%	2.87	-21.1	-1	$8
LIMA Plan	F	2nd Half	153	28	0	7	4	255			309	320	629	7	80	32	0.40	242	62	16	22	42	0%	141	16%	3.33	-8.3	14	$3
Rand Var	-1	10 Proj	252	38	0	15	11	258			307	327	634	7	81	32	0.38	246	57	18	25	45	1%	143	24%	3.35	-14.5	19	$6

Emilio plays Tuffy: 1 HR, 3 SB on Opening Day followed by a mad dash to mediocrity. Credit MLE for nailing his 1st full year: elite speed; poor approach. Use 2H (supersub) as 2010 base: a few SB, zero BA or power.

Borbon,Julio

		Year	AB	R	HR	RBI	SB	Avg	vL	vR	OB	Slg	OPS	bb%	ct%	h%	Eye	xBA	G	L	F	PX	hr/f	SX	SBO	RC/G	RAR	BPV	R$
Pos	0	05	0	0	0	0	0	0							0			0						0					
Age	24	06	0	0	0	0	0	0							0			0						0					
Bats	Left	07	0	0	0	0	0	0							0			0						0					
Health	A	08 aa	255	31	4	17	13	306			335	412	746	4	90	33	0.44	0				63		103	36%	4.58	-2.6	52	$10
PT/Exp	F	09 TEX	* 564	87	6	48	39	288	125	333	337	367	704	7	89	32	0.67	267	54	19	27	43	4%	134	28%	4.28	-14.4	47	$22
Consist	A	1st Half	307	43	2	24	16	268			312	345	657	6	91	29	0.74	232	67	0	33	43	2%	131	24%	3.81	-12.3	53	$9
LIMA Plan	C	2nd Half	257	44	4	25	23	313			366	394	760	8	86	35	0.62	260	54	19	27	44	7%	129	33%	4.89	-2.0	37	$13
Rand Var	-1	10 Proj	461	66	6	37	30	278			320	368	688	6	89	30	0.58	273	54	19	27	52	6%	123	34%	4.03	-18.4	48	$16

4-20-19-.312 in 157 AB at TEX. PRO: improving bb% (9% MLB), high ct% bodes well for OBP. CON: 2H h% inflated BA and SB. Good speed source with upside, just don't expect 20 SB per 150 AB again.

Bourn,Michael

		Year	AB	R	HR	RBI	SB	Avg	vL	vR	OB	Slg	OPS	bb%	ct%	h%	Eye	xBA	G	L	F	PX	hr/f	SX	SBO	RC/G	RAR	BPV	R$
Pos	8	05 aa	539	68	6	37	32	249			315	334	649	9	81	30	0.50	0				55		132	29%	3.59	-13.6	27	$15
Age	27	06 a/a	470	91	5	39	42	274			345	379	724	10	81	33	0.56	0				56		181	31%	4.61	0.8	43	$20
Bats	Left	07 PHI	119	29	1	6	18	277	154	312	348	378	727	10	82	33	0.62	267	58	18	24	56	4%	198	49%	4.67	0.5	56	$7
Health	B	08 HOU	467	57	5	29	41	229	190	242	286	300	586	7	76	29	0.33	220	54	17	29	46	5%	146	41%	2.61	-30.9	2	$14
PT/Exp	C	09 HOU	606	97	3	35	61	285	287	285	353	384	737	9	77	37	0.45	257	58	21	22	69	3%	168	38%	4.80	1.2	34	$28
Consist	F	1st Half	291	44	2	19	25	289			363	402	765	10	78	36	0.54	265	51	25	25	79	4%	152	34%	5.22	4.1	45	$13
LIMA Plan	C+	2nd Half	315	53	1	16	36	283			343	368	711	8	76	37	0.38	251	64	17	19	61	2%	176	41%	4.41	-2.9	22	$15
Rand Var	-4	10 Proj	588	96	4	35	56	267			332	357	689	9	78	34	0.44	249	57	19	24	59	4%	172	37%	4.11	-9.9	30	$24

Figured out how to hit lefties; the result was a near-$30 year and a verified SB stud. But let xBA and h% serve as your BA warning, and 2H BPV drop a concern. Given his SX and SBO, expect a SB repeat.

Bradley,Milton

		Year	AB	R	HR	RBI	SB	Avg	vL	vR	OB	Slg	OPS	bb%	ct%	h%	Eye	xBA	G	L	F	PX	hr/f	SX	SBO	RC/G	RAR	BPV	R$
Pos	9	05 LA	283	49	13	38	6	290	278	294	347	484	832	8	83	31	0.53	297	45	23	32	117	17%	99	9%	5.65	3.2	75	$13
Age	32	06 OAK	351	53	14	52	10	276	293	270	368	447	815	13	81	31	0.78	263	52	15	33	99	15%	94	10%	5.75	0.9	61	$13
Bats	Both	07 2TM	209	37	13	37	5	306	304	307	396	545	941	13	80	33	0.76	286	39	19	43	141	18%	81	10%	7.25	11.9	86	$11
Health	D	08 TEX	414	78	22	77	5	321	341	312	431	563	994	16	73	40	0.71	290	41	25	34	173	21%	62	5%	8.51	35.0	83	$22
PT/Exp	C	09 CHC	393	61	12	40	2	257	333	231	364	397	761	14	76	31	0.69	243	47	20	33	96	12%	51	4%	5.19	3.6	26	$10
Consist	F	1st Half	184	25	5	17	0	239			346	375	721	14	77	28	0.71	245	48	20	32	91	11%	45	0%	4.67	-1.2	26	$3
LIMA Plan	D+	2nd Half	209	36	7	23	2	273			380	416	796	15	75	34	0.68	239	46	19	34	100	13%	48	6%	5.67	4.8	24	$7
Rand Var	+1	10 Proj	399	67	15	55	5	283			385	453	838	14	76	34	0.70	259	44	21	35	114	14%	67	6%	6.19	13.9	47	$15

Most important trend? See the 2nd column: LA/OAK/2TM/TEX/CHC. Back-to-back .900-OPS seasons showcase his electric skills and buy him chance after chance, but fanalytic risk (AB totals) trumps potential returns.

Brantley,Michael

		Year	AB	R	HR	RBI	SB	Avg	vL	vR	OB	Slg	OPS	bb%	ct%	h%	Eye	xBA	G	L	F	PX	hr/f	SX	SBO	RC/G	RAR	BPV	R$
Pos	8	05	0	0	0	0	0	0							0			0						0					
Age	23	06	0	0	0	0	0	0							0			0						0					
Bats	Left	07 aa	187	25	0	19	15	241			338	286	624	13	88	27	1.25	0				32		115	27%	3.78	-4.3	41	$5
Health	A	08 aa	420	65	3	32	22	284			349	346	696	9	95	29	1.95	0				39		103	23%	4.53	-6.2	62	$14
PT/Exp	D	09 CLE	* 569	76	5	41	42	255	462	267	325	325	650	9	90	28	1.00	280	47	26	27	45	4%	108	30%	3.87	-13.1	47	$17
Consist	B	1st Half	310	46	3	20	26	229			305	300	605	10	89	25	1.03	0				43		126	32%	3.39	-11.9	52	$9
LIMA Plan	C	2nd Half	259	30	2	21	16	286			349	355	704	9	90	31	0.96	282	47	26	27	46	3%	81	27%	4.44	-1.5	41	$9
Rand Var	+2	10 Proj	484	67	3	38	32	267			324	330	654	8	89	29	0.79	277	47	26	27	42	3%	111	29%	3.81	-14.0	42	$15

0-11-.313, 4 SB in 112 AB at CLE. PRO: Elite batting eye; very good ct% and bb% will keep OBP high. CON: 38% MLB h% raises expectations; SX low for a base stealer. Utter lack of PX keeps him one-dimensional.

Branyan,Russell

		Year	AB	R	HR	RBI	SB	Avg	vL	vR	OB	Slg	OPS	bb%	ct%	h%	Eye	xBA	G	L	F	PX	hr/f	SX	SBO	RC/G	RAR	BPV	R$
Pos	3	05 MIL	202	23	12	31	1	257	50	280	378	490	868	16	60	36	0.49	244	29	24	47	192	21%	24	1%	7.36	10.3	37	$7
Age	34	06 2TM	241	37	18	36	2	228	220	230	324	498	822	12	63	28	0.38	241	29	19	52	194	23%	49	3%	6.18	3.4	49	$7
Bats	Left	07 2NL	196	22	10	26	1	196	158	201	314	423	737	15	58	26	0.41	215	29	18	53	178	20%	66	2%	5.25	-4.5	24	$3
Health	C	08 MIL	* 285	40	21	44	4	262		280	345	548	892	11	69	31	0.40	265	22	21	57	206	18%	50	6%	6.92	9.9	79	$12
PT/Exp	D	09 SEA	431	64	31	76	2	251	222	267	339	520	859	12	65	31	0.39	250	33	17	50	188	22%	56	2%	6.63	11.6	55	$16
Consist	B	1st Half	245	46	19	40	2	298			388	596	984	13	68	37	0.46	271	31	20	49	202	24%	69	3%	8.38	18.0	81	$12
LIMA Plan	C	2nd Half	186	18	12	36	0	188			274	419	693	11	62	22	0.31	212	34	14	52	168	20%	7	0%	4.16	-9.2	9	$3
Rand Var	-1	10 Proj	343	46	24	58	2	236			329	498	827	12	64	29	0.39	246	30	18	52	191	21%	55	3%	6.23	7.6	53	$11

Career-high HR a product of career-high AB. 1H hit rate was the gift that made both possible. With FB, hr/f and PX all stable, playing time will determine future production. Beware 2H; aches and pains mounting.

Braun,Ryan

		Year	AB	R	HR	RBI	SB	Avg	vL	vR	OB	Slg	OPS	bb%	ct%	h%	Eye	xBA	G	L	F	PX	hr/f	SX	SBO	RC/G	RAR	BPV	R$
Pos	7	05	0	0	0	0	0	0							0			0						0					
Age	26	06 aa	231	40	15	38	11	294			353	580	933	8	81	31	0.47	0				173		119	20%	6.92	10.9	115	$13
Bats	Right	07 MIL	* 568	116	43	116	19	322	450	282	370	637	1007	7	79	35	0.35	310	39	16	45	190	21%	124	19%	7.78	37.3	119	$37
Health	A	08 MIL	611	92	37	106	14	285	287	284	331	553	884	6	79	31	0.33	286	39	17	44	166	17%	115	14%	6.24	14.3	98	$29
PT/Exp	A	09 MIL	635	113	32	114	20	320	395	302	376	551	927	8	81	35	0.47	296	47	19	34	144	18%	116	14%	6.86	22.4	92	$37
Consist	C	1st Half	288	56	16	57	6	330			402	573	975	11	78	38	0.56	302	45	25	30	156	24%	92	10%	7.69	16.4	89	$18
LIMA Plan	D+	2nd Half	347	57	16	57	14	311			352	533	885	6	83	34	0.38	289	48	15	37	134	15%	126	19%	6.19	6.0	92	$19
Rand Var	-3	10 Proj	583	101	34	105	19	300			352	560	912	7	80	33	0.41	298	43	18	39	160	19%	128	16%	6.63	18.8	104	$32

Another solid season, but BPI trends to keep an eye on:
- 1H h% carried rise in BA
- FB decline led to PX dive
- 2H SBO returned to MLE level
- 2H approach (less bb and k)

Expect a repeat, not a breakout.

Brignac,Reid

		Year	AB	R	HR	RBI	SB	Avg	vL	vR	OB	Slg	OPS	bb%	ct%	h%	Eye	xBA	G	L	F	PX	hr/f	SX	SBO	RC/G	RAR	BPV	R$
Pos	6	05	0	0	0	0	0	0							0			0						0					
Age	24	06 aa	110	20	3	18	3	315			358	496	854	6	71	42	0.23	0				123		134	10%	6.26	5.5	39	$5
Bats	Left	07 aa	527	77	15	69	13	235			299	387	686	8	84	25	0.59	0				93		107	15%	4.04	-5.3	63	$13
Health	A	08 aaa	352	36	7	36	4	222			265	358	623	6	78	27	0.27	0				99		81	9%	3.08	-15.2	28	$4
PT/Exp	D	09 TAM	* 505	54	8	44	6	259	50	343	296	388	684	5	84	30	0.32	258	34	23	43	84	4%	76	12%	3.87	-8.7	37	$9
Consist	B	1st Half	280	35	6	24	3	264			310	415	724	6	86	29	0.47	267	43	17	40	95	6%	76	14%	4.44	-0.1	57	$6
LIMA Plan	F	2nd Half	225	19	2	21	3	253			279	354	633	3	81	31	0.18	251	17	35	48	70	2%	80	10%	3.14	-8.7	13	$3
Rand Var	0	10 Proj	132	15	3	14	2	250			292	383	674	6	81	29	0.31	253	31	26	44	89	5%	84	11%	3.73	-2.6	33	$2

1-6-.278 in 90 AB at TAM. 35% hit rate overshadowed poor plate skills (0.15 Eye) in the majors. MLE shows average pop and speed, but bb% trend and OBP history unconvincing. Safely ignored for now.

Bruce,Jay

		Year	AB	R	HR	RBI	SB	Avg	vL	vR	OB	Slg	OPS	bb%	ct%	h%	Eye	xBA	G	L	F	PX	hr/f	SX	SBO	RC/G	RAR	BPV	R$
Pos	9	05	0	0	0	0	0	0							0			0						0					
Age	23	06	0	0	0	0	0	0							0			0						0					
Bats	Left	07 a/a	253	36	15	39	3	322			376	600	976	8	79	36	0.41	0				177		73	10%	7.51	15.9	97	$12
Health	C	08 CIN	* 597	91	30	82	11	281	190	286	329	487	817	7	75	33	0.29	267	45	21	34	131	20%	95	12%	5.47	4.7	51	$25
PT/Exp	D	09 CIN	345	47	22	58	3	223	210	229	300	470	770	10	78	22	0.51	263	39	13	49	150	17%	71	8%	4.93	0.6	76	$11
Consist	C	1st Half	273	38	18	40	3	212			290	458	748	10	79	20	0.52	263	38	13	49	148	17%	68	9%	4.63	-2.1	76	$8
LIMA Plan	C+	2nd Half	72	9	4	18	0	264			337	514	851	10	76	29	0.47	262	41	11	48	160	15%	72	6%	6.10	2.6	77	$3
Rand Var	+5	10 Proj	480	67	27	84	5	269			331	507	839	9	77	30	0.40	268	41	15	44	150	17%	80	9%	5.81	11.8	71	$19

Five reasons to buy now:
1. 1.078 OPS upon injury return
2. Horrific h% will keep bids low
3. Marked growth in bb%, ct%
4. PX, FB numbers also up
5. Still green at 23 years old

Last big hurdle: solving LHP.

BRENT HERSHEY

Bruntlett,Eric

		Year	AB	R	HR	RBI	SB	Avg	vL	vR	OB	Slg	OPS	bb%	ct%	h%	Eye	xBA	G	L	F	PX	hr/f	SX	SBO	RC/G	RAR	BPV	R$
Pos	4	05 HOU	109	19	4	14	7	220	295	125	286	413	699	8	77	25	0.40	263	31	28	41	122	12%	172	39%	4.11	-1.5	76	$4
Age	32	06 HOU	* 192	21	1	16	5	245	350	241	341	313	653	13	81	30	0.78	225	41	20	38	52	2%	57	13%	3.90	-4.1	11	$3
Bats	Right	07 HOU	* 365	36	1	28	14	210	237	253	286	263	549	10	82	26	0.58	226	46	19	35	37	1%	101	21%	2.46	-25.9	7	$3
Health	A	08 PHI	212	37	2	15	9	217	254	199	288	297	585	9	83	25	0.60	244	47	20	33	55	3%	128	20%	2.90	-12.3	37	$4
PT/Exp	F	09 PHI	105	15	0	7	2	171	229	123	209	238	447	5	75	23	0.19	209	34	22	44	65	0%	107	13%	0.78	-12.8	-4	($0)
Consist	C	1st Half	67	6	0	5	0	134			194	194	388	7	76	18	0.31	206	37	20	43	57	0%	43	0%	0.13	-10.0	-21	($1)
LIMA Plan	F	2nd Half	38	9	0	2	2	237			237	316	553	0	74	32	0.00	209	29	25	46	78	0%	165	33%	1.93	-3.0	9	$1
Rand Var	+5	10 Proj	96	12	1	8	3	208			280	271	550	9	80	25	0.49	220	38	22	40	49	2%	76	15%	2.35	-6.8	1	$1

For most players, a h% this low would represent some bad luck. But given his history, this is just another item in the long list of things that he's not very good at. Avoid.

Buck,John

		Year	AB	R	HR	RBI	SB	Avg	vL	vR	OB	Slg	OPS	bb%	ct%	h%	Eye	xBA	G	L	F	PX	hr/f	SX	SBO	RC/G	RAR	BPV	R$
Pos	2	05 KC	401	40	12	47	2	242	310	214	283	389	672	5	77	29	0.24	235	44	17	40	103	10%	51	5%	3.60	-5.1	16	$7
Age	30	06 KC	371	37	11	50	0	245	246	245	295	396	691	7	77	29	0.31	247	45	20	35	101	11%	32	2%	3.91	-5.5	15	$6
Bats	Right	07 KC	347	41	18	48	0	222	189	231	295	429	724	9	73	25	0.39	246	43	13	44	142	16%	23	1%	4.39	1.1	35	$7
Health	B	08 KC	370	48	9	48	0	224	236	219	297	365	661	9	74	28	0.40	230	43	16	41	106	8%	43	3%	3.69	-5.7	15	$5
PT/Exp	D	09 KC	* 213	18	9	39	1	240	213	259	284	463	747	6	71	30	0.21	253	37	18	45	148	13%	75	5%	4.72	2.9	40	$5
Consist	B	1st Half	111	9	4	22	0	218			288	420	708	9	75	26	0.40	254	41	19	40	122	12%	57	0%	4.31	0.1	35	$2
LIMA Plan	D	2nd Half	102	9	5	17	1	265			279	510	789	2	68	34	0.06	253	33	17	49	179	15%	71	13%	5.27	3.0	41	$3
Rand Var	0	10 Proj	303	31	12	47	1	244			295	439	734	7	73	30	0.26	247	40	17	43	134	12%	65	4%	4.53	2.6	32	$7

8-36-.247 in 186 AB at KC. Herniated disc cut into his playing time. Increased PX in the 2nd half, but at the expense of ct% and bb%. He needs to fix that if he wants to see any good pitches to swing at.

Buck,Travis

		Year	AB	R	HR	RBI	SB	Avg	vL	vR	OB	Slg	OPS	bb%	ct%	h%	Eye	xBA	G	L	F	PX	hr/f	SX	SBO	RC/G	RAR	BPV	R$
Pos	9	05	0	0	0	0	0	0							0			0						0					
Age	26	06 aa	212	27	3	19	8	274			330	425	755	8	85	31	0.56	0				105		102	18%	4.95	-1.6	72	$6
Bats	Left	07 OAK	285	41	7	34	4	288	323	277	373	474	847	12	77	35	0.59	276	44	19	37	131	9%	107	6%	6.34	6.7	71	$9
Health	C	08 OAK	* 324	37	8	37	4	235	196	239	299	370	668	8	80	27	0.46	237	46	14	41	89	8%	79	6%	3.76	-15.6	34	$6
PT/Exp	D	09 OAK	* 337	36	6	30	3	216	143	231	272	319	591	7	84	24	0.49	237	30	23	47	62	4%	73	6%	2.86	-25.7	25	$3
Consist	D	1st Half	148	19	4	15	1	256			315	388	703	8	84	28	0.54	256	32	23	45	82	7%	47	8%	4.19	-5.0	34	$3
LIMA Plan	F	2nd Half	189	17	2	15	2	185			238	264	502	7	84	21	0.45	204	21	21	57	47	2%	85	5%	1.83	-21.2	16	($0)
Rand Var	+5	10 Proj	161	19	3	16	2	236			299	363	662	8	82	27	0.50	247	40	19	42	83	6%	76	7%	3.73	-7.8	37	$2

3-10-.219 in 105 AB at OAK. Other than a rising ct%, his skills are slipping at an age where we'd expect them to improve. High FB% but substandard and declining PX mean lots of harmless fly balls.

Burke,Chris

		Year	AB	R	HR	RBI	SB	Avg	vL	vR	OB	Slg	OPS	bb%	ct%	h%	Eye	xBA	G	L	F	PX	hr/f	SX	SBO	RC/G	RAR	BPV	R$
Pos	6	05 HOU	* 408	60	7	34	18	254	265	239	304	384	688	7	82	29	0.40	250	38	19	42	87	5%	137	24%	3.98	0.3	56	$12
Age	30	06 HOU	366	58	9	40	11	276	327	257	326	418	744	7	79	33	0.35	247	36	23	41	95	8%	102	13%	4.62	2.7	38	$12
Bats	Right	07 HOU	* 385	49	8	33	12	222	292	197	279	344	622	7	85	24	0.51	243	38	17	45	77	5%	107	20%	3.26	-14.2	49	$6
Health	A	08 ARI	165	20	2	12	5	194	209	177	307	273	580	14	80	23	0.82	209	38	18	44	52	3%	96	10%	2.95	-8.7	20	$1
PT/Exp	D	09 2TM	* 394	42	4	32	15	218	91	250	270	304	574	7	81	26	0.38	224	44	16	41	64	3%	104	21%	2.58	-24.1	21	$6
Consist	A	1st Half	178	18	3	13	7	207			260	305	565	7	80	24	0.36	226	44	16	41	71	5%	84	22%	2.41	-12.0	17	$2
LIMA Plan	F	2nd Half	216	24	1	19	9	227			279	303	581	7	82	27	0.39	0				58		107	20%	2.72	-12.1	21	$3
Rand Var	+1	10 Proj	64	8	1	5	5	219			286	303	589	9	81	26	0.50	222	39	18	43	61	4%	98	35%	2.84	-3.2	22	$2

1-5-.207 with 4 SB in 82 AB at SD. He has a low historical h% for a batter of average speed, but that can't take all the blame. xBA history and falling PX tell you to forget memories of 2006.

Burrell,Pat

		Year	AB	R	HR	RBI	SB	Avg	vL	vR	OB	Slg	OPS	bb%	ct%	h%	Eye	xBA	G	L	F	PX	hr/f	SX	SBO	RC/G	RAR	BPV	R$
Pos	0	05 PHI	562	78	32	117	0	281	318	269	389	504	892	15	72	34	0.62	266	31	24	45	153	18%	27	0%	7.00	15.5	48	$24
Age	34	06 PHI	462	80	29	95	0	258	290	244	388	502	890	18	72	30	0.75	257	31	21	48	158	18%	32	0%	7.03	8.1	59	$18
Bats	Right	07 PHI	472	77	30	97	0	256	255	257	401	502	903	19	75	28	0.95	266	31	18	51	158	17%	18	0%	7.21	13.4	71	$18
Health	B	08 PHI	536	74	33	86	0	250	279	238	370	507	877	16	75	28	0.75	275	34	20	45	169	18%	41	0%	6.73	28.5	80	$18
PT/Exp	A	09 TAM	412	45	14	64	2	221	202	229	316	367	682	12	71	28	0.48	215	34	18	48	99	10%	49	2%	4.01	-14.7	4	$7
Consist	D	1st Half	156	17	3	23	2	224			339	314	653	15	75	28	0.69	191	37	14	48	61	5%	45	4%	3.78	-6.6	-6	$2
LIMA Plan	C	2nd Half	256	28	11	41	0	219			301	398	699	10	69	27	0.38	228	32	21	48	124	13%	37	0%	4.19	-7.7	8	$5
Rand Var	+1	10 Proj	448	58	21	76	1	250			360	444	804	15	73	30	0.63	242	33	19	48	130	14%	41	1%	5.75	4.9	38	$13

Went on the DL for neck injury in May and never seemed to recover; even 2H skills were far below career levels. If health was the true culprit, previously stable PX and Eye say he can hit 30 HR again.

Burriss,Emmanuel

		Year	AB	R	HR	RBI	SB	Avg	vL	vR	OB	Slg	OPS	bb%	ct%	h%	Eye	xBA	G	L	F	PX	hr/f	SX	SBO	RC/G	RAR	BPV	R$
Pos	4	05	0	0	0	0	0	0							0			0						0					
Age	25	06	0	0	0	0	0	0							0			0						0					
Bats	Both	07	0	0	0	0	0	0							0			0						0					
Health	B	08 SF	* 302	41	1	23	15	274	292	278	329	320	649	8	90	30	0.86	257	65	14	21	28	2%	110	22%	3.78	-8.8	34	$9
PT/Exp	F	09 SF	* 273	26	1	19	16	239	333	208	283	286	569	6	86	27	0.45	243	56	17	27	33	2%	103	30%	2.63	-15.9	16	$6
Consist	C	1st Half	273	26	1	19	16	239			283	286	569	6	86	27	0.45	243	56	17	27	33	2%	103	30%	2.63	-15.9	16	$6
LIMA Plan	F	2nd Half	0	0	0	0	0	0							0			0											
Rand Var	0	10 Proj	294	33	1	21	16	252			301	296	597	7	88	28	0.58	248	60	16	24	30	2%	102	27%	3.04	-14.1	22	$7

0-13-.238 with 11 SB in 202 AB at SF. Broken toe ended his season in early July. Anemic PX says 2 HR could be his career high, but if high ct% and SBO rates hold...
UP: 30 SB

Buscher,Brian

		Year	AB	R	HR	RBI	SB	Avg	vL	vR	OB	Slg	OPS	bb%	ct%	h%	Eye	xBA	G	L	F	PX	hr/f	SX	SBO	RC/G	RAR	BPV	R$
Pos	5	05 aa	215	15	1	18	4	199			255	252	507	7	85	23	0.51	0				37		70	13%	1.94	-18.5	8	$0
Age	29	06 aa	467	40	6	45	5	233			288	330	618	7	82	27	0.43	0				62		66	7%	3.15	-29.8	15	$4
Bats	Left	07 MIN	* 461	55	13	58	4	256	200	250	320	394	714	9	87	27	0.74	264	43	16	40	85	8%	59	4%	4.43	-6.0	55	$10
Health	A	08 MIN	* 403	50	9	70	1	277	205	316	332	394	727	8	85	31	0.54	272	33	28	39	76	7%	32	4%	4.46	-4.9	26	$11
PT/Exp	D	09 MIN	* 214	18	3	14	0	203	200	240	306	267	573	13	75	26	0.59	214	33	26	40	39	4%	39	1%	2.63	-13.8	-30	($0)
Consist	B	1st Half	91	7	2	9	0	198			336	308	644	17	75	24	0.83	213	36	20	43	67	7%	42	0%	3.75	-2.7	1	$0
LIMA Plan	F	2nd Half	123	11	1	5	0	207			282	236	519	10	75	27	0.41	248	27	39	33	19	3%	31	2%	1.75	-11.3	-56	($0)
Rand Var	+2	10 Proj	126	13	2	13	0	230			309	314	623	10	80	27	0.57	241	34	27	40	55	6%	32	3%	3.26	-5.8	-4	$1

2nd straight year with an incredible LD rate, but BA says they all must have been soft liners. He's one of an elite group of 2009 batters who have a negative BPV. That's not a good thing.

Butler,Billy

		Year	AB	R	HR	RBI	SB	Avg	vL	vR	OB	Slg	OPS	bb%	ct%	h%	Eye	xBA	G	L	F	PX	hr/f	SX	SBO	RC/G	RAR	BPV	R$
Pos	3	05 aa	112	12	3	15	0	295			328	462	789	5	89	31	0.47	0				107		22	0%	5.07	-0.9	61	$3
Age	24	06 aa	477	67	11	79	1	308			354	447	801	7	90	33	0.71	0				84		55	1%	5.34	-4.7	59	$16
Bats	Right	07 KC	* 532	72	18	92	1	282	340	272	360	457	817	11	85	31	0.79	294	47	21	33	110	12%	56	1%	5.73	7.0	67	$17
Health	A	08 KC	* 544	60	15	66	0	283	340	244	338	421	759	8	88	30	0.71	260	49	17	35	84	9%	26	1%	4.89	-5.9	46	$14
PT/Exp	B	09 KC	608	78	21	93	1	301	330	289	362	492	854	9	83	33	0.56	284	47	18	35	122	12%	39	1%	6.05	5.7	61	$21
Consist	C	1st Half	276	34	7	34	0	293			346	449	795	7	83	33	0.46	269	49	19	32	105	10%	25	0%	5.29	-3.2	38	$8
LIMA Plan	C	2nd Half	332	44	14	59	1	307			375	527	902	10	83	33	0.65	293	46	18	37	137	14%	43	1%	6.68	8.7	78	$13
Rand Var	-2	10 Proj	585	73	24	97	1	291			351	488	839	9	85	31	0.63	288	48	18	35	121	14%	35	1%	5.82	5.4	67	$20

Nice growth year as he improved across the board in 2nd half. Skills don't yet support a .300 BA, but the pieces (esp. v. RHP) are coming together. Extending the 2nd half line...
UP: 30 HR

Byrd,Marlon

		Year	AB	R	HR	RBI	SB	Avg	vL	vR	OB	Slg	OPS	bb%	ct%	h%	Eye	xBA	G	L	F	PX	hr/f	SX	SBO	RC/G	RAR	BPV	R$
Pos	87	05 2NL	* 329	38	8	38	8	287	326	228	338	434	772	7	82	33	0.44	267	38	22	40	100	7%	92	11%	5.01	4.2	52	$11
Age	33	06 WAS	* 352	44	10	42	6	223	188	242	293	361	654	9	78	26	0.46	246	45	21	34	87	11%	71	11%	3.54	-9.8	21	$6
Bats	Right	07 TEX	* 590	78	14	89	7	286	327	300	328	432	761	6	79	34	0.30	265	47	20	33	94	9%	105	7%	4.79	4.4	36	$18
Health	B	08 TEX	403	70	10	53	7	298	277	308	370	462	831	10	85	33	0.74	288	46	21	33	106	9%	105	7%	5.92	6.4	77	$15
PT/Exp	B	09 TEX	547	66	20	89	8	283	244	300	323	479	802	6	82	31	0.33	279	41	19	41	124	11%	74	10%	5.23	9.1	63	$19
Consist	B	1st Half	251	30	7	39	3	287			319	478	797	5	84	32	0.29	290	43	19	38	127	9%	71	8%	5.18	3.8	69	$8
LIMA Plan	C+	2nd Half	296	36	13	50	5	280			326	480	806	6	81	31	0.35	269	39	18	43	122	13%	69	11%	5.27	5.3	56	$11
Rand Var	0	10 Proj	507	69	16	76	8	284			335	460	794	7	82	32	0.42	275	43	20	38	112	10%	90	9%	5.25	6.6	61	$17

Increased HR output supported by FB% surge, while maintaining .300 BA v. RHP. Slugged .538 at home (+7% HR to RHB) but just .419 away, so pay close attention to where he lands in free agency.

BILL MACEY

Byrnes,Eric			AB	R	HR	RBI	SB	Avg	vL	vR	OB	Slg	OPS	bb%	ct%	h%	Eye	xBA	G	L	F	PX	hr/f	SX	SBO	RC/G	RAR	BPV	R$
Pos	7	05 2TM	412	49	10	40	7	226	263	205	282	371	653	7	83	25	0.45	246	32	20	48	96	6%	102	10%	3.58	-18.3	55	$7
Age	34	06 ARI	562	82	26	79	25	267	323	244	309	482	791	6	84	28	0.39	276	38	18	44	124	12%	120	24%	5.06	-3.1	86	$23
Bats	Right	07 ARI	626	103	21	83	50	286	248	297	346	460	806	8	84	31	0.58	261	35	19	46	101	9%	148	32%	5.43	1.3	81	$32
Health	F	08 ARI	206	28	6	23	4	209	258	188	266	369	635	7	83	23	0.44	257	39	19	42	104	8%	98	21%	3.34	-13.6	59	$3
PT/Exp	C	09 ARI	*307	36	10	38	10	226	228	225	263	398	660	5	89	23	0.46	269	40	15	45	104	8%	109	24%	3.65	-18.0	84	$8
Consist	C	1st Half	194	22	5	24	7	216			251	361	612	4	88	22	0.38	258	42	15	42	89	7%	109	29%	3.05	-15.2	65	$4
LIMA Plan	D+	2nd Half	113	14	5	14	3	242			282	461	743	5	92	23	0.67	277	28	15	56	127	8%	98	15%	4.65	-3.1	110	$3
Rand Var	+5	10 Proj	300	40	10	36	10	250			296	427	724	6	87	26	0.49	267	37	17	46	107	8%	115	21%	4.38	-9.7	82	$9

Spent most of 2H on DL after fracturing hand on HBP. SBO and 75% SB success say he can still run, but he doesn't get on base enough to add value. via SB. Stable xBA and PX say no late-career rebound coming.

Cabrera,Asdrubal			AB	R	HR	RBI	SB	Avg	vL	vR	OB	Slg	OPS	bb%	ct%	h%	Eye	xBA	G	L	F	PX	hr/f	SX	SBO	RC/G	RAR	BPV	R$
Pos	64	05	0	0	0	0	0	0							0			0						0					
Age	24	06 aaa	393	58	5	39	13	269			332	375	706	9	80	33	0.47	0				76		88	22%	4.31	-0.9	27	$10
Bats	Both	07 CLE	*565	108	9	75	23	295	340	259	365	423	788	10	87	33	0.86	279	44	20	36	84	5%	122	18%	5.44	18.3	75	$23
Health	A	08 CLE	*493	71	10	59	6	274	349	230	344	394	738	10	80	33	0.52	253	46	21	34	85	8%	67	8%	4.71	5.4	27	$13
PT/Exp	B	09 CLE	523	81	6	68	17	308	306	309	362	438	799	8	83	36	0.49	280	48	22	30	91	5%	113	14%	5.44	14.3	56	$20
Consist	B	1st Half	218	39	2	30	7	307			366	417	783	8	81	37	0.49	273	49	24	27	77	4%	118	12%	5.28	4.9	40	$9
LIMA Plan	C+	2nd Half	305	42	4	38	10	308			359	452	811	7	84	36	0.50	286	47	21	32	100	5%	98	15%	5.56	9.3	63	$11
Rand Var	-3	10 Proj	544	85	8	68	19	285			347	409	756	9	82	33	0.54	272	47	22	31	87	6%	108	16%	4.94	8.4	51	$18

A legitimate .300 hitter?
PRO: gains v. RHP and ct%, promising uptick in 2H PX.
CON: hit rate spike likely unsustainable, xBA improving but doesn't support .300. Could hit .300 again, just not in '10.

Cabrera,Everth			AB	R	HR	RBI	SB	Avg	vL	vR	OB	Slg	OPS	bb%	ct%	h%	Eye	xBA	G	L	F	PX	hr/f	SX	SBO	RC/G	RAR	BPV	R$
Pos	6	05	0	0	0	0	0	0							0			0						0					
Age	23	06	0	0	0	0	0	0							0			0						0					
Bats	Both	07	0	0	0	0	0	0							0			0						0					
Health	C	08	0	0	0	0	0	0							0			0						0					
PT/Exp	F	09 SD	*404	63	2	31	26	257	239	261	335	361	696	10	77	33	0.51	253	63	15	23	74	3%	154	28%	4.33	-4.0	36	$13
Consist	F	1st Half	79	15	0	4	4	291			333	405	738	6	81	36	0.33	263	62	13	26	80	0%	156	19%	4.67	0.0	49	$3
LIMA Plan	B+	2nd Half	325	48	2	27	22	249			335	351	686	11	76	32	0.54	250	63	15	22	73	4%	148	30%	4.23	-4.3	31	$10
Rand Var	0	10 Proj	508	84	2	36	36	266			334	373	707	9	78	34	0.46	259	62	14	23	75	2%	170	30%	4.43	-2.1	44	$18

2-31-.255 with 25 SB in 388 AB at SD. Three key elements of an elite speed source: high GB%, plate patience, and good SB%. 75% SB success, and 23 errors st SS are his only blemishes. Fix them, and... UP: 60 SB.

Cabrera,Melky			AB	R	HR	RBI	SB	Avg	vL	vR	OB	Slg	OPS	bb%	ct%	h%	Eye	xBA	G	L	F	PX	hr/f	SX	SBO	RC/G	RAR	BPV	R$
Pos	897	05 a/a	523	63	12	68	12	255			297	371	669	6	86	28	0.44	0				72		100	11%	3.71	-11.0	46	$14
Age	26	06 NYY	*582	93	11	73	15	301	286	278	372	423	795	10	89	33	0.98	267	49	17	33	73	7%	99	11%	5.50	13.7	65	$20
Bats	Both	07 NYY	545	66	8	73	13	273	250	282	327	391	717	7	88	30	0.63	283	51	20	29	71	6%	112	12%	4.46	-1.1	57	$14
Health	A	08 NYY	414	42	8	37	9	249	213	265	298	341	639	7	86	27	0.50	246	46	19	35	55	6%	79	10%	3.39	-24.0	27	$8
PT/Exp	B	09 NYY	485	66	13	68	10	274	268	277	333	416	750	8	88	29	0.73	290	50	21	30	85	10%	85	9%	4.82	2.5	63	$15
Consist	A	1st Half	216	32	8	32	5	287			350	454	804	9	85	31	0.64	289	48	22	30	99	14%	66	11%	5.41	4.7	57	$8
LIMA Plan	C	2nd Half	269	34	5	36	5	264			320	387	706	8	90	28	0.85	290	51	20	29	74	7%	86	7%	4.39	-1.9	63	$7
Rand Var	+1	10 Proj	448	56	10	56	10	272			327	394	722	8	87	29	0.65	275	49	20	31	73	8%	87	10%	4.47	-4.1	52	$12

BA and xBA recovered to 2007 levels, but little reason to project further growth. Even in a launching pad of a home park, 50% ground balls limits power upside, and speed isn't his game, either.

Cabrera,Miguel			AB	R	HR	RBI	SB	Avg	vL	vR	OB	Slg	OPS	bb%	ct%	h%	Eye	xBA	G	L	F	PX	hr/f	SX	SBO	RC/G	RAR	BPV	R$
Pos	3	05 FLA	613	106	33	116	1	323	304	329	387	561	948	9	80	36	0.51	303	38	24	37	154	18%	59	1%	7.22	26.3	80	$32
Age	27	06 FLA	576	112	26	114	9	339	321	344	424	568	992	13	81	38	0.80	300	40	24	35	144	16%	74	7%	8.02	30.6	90	$32
Bats	Right	07 FLA	588	91	34	119	2	320	364	309	400	565	965	12	78	36	0.62	293	40	21	39	153	19%	50	2%	7.59	23.0	77	$29
Health	A	08 DET	616	85	37	127	1	292	311	286	351	537	889	8	80	32	0.44	290	41	20	39	153	19%	47	1%	6.36	18.6	74	$27
PT/Exp	A	09 DET	611	96	34	103	6	324	315	326	392	547	938	10	82	35	0.64	290	43	20	37	129	18%	53	4%	7.02	21.4	71	$30
Consist	B	1st Half	284	48	16	47	1	331			393	556	949	9	84	35	0.64	296	45	20	35	128	19%	36	3%	7.07	10.3	71	$14
LIMA Plan	C	2nd Half	327	48	18	56	5	318			391	538	929	11	81	35	0.63	284	41	20	39	130	18%	57	5%	6.98	11.1	69	$16
Rand Var	-2	10 Proj	598	92	34	111	4	316			385	549	934	10	81	35	0.58	292	42	21	38	141	18%	54	3%	7.01	24.5	75	$29

Skills remain superb, but final-weekend off-field incident raises questions:

OPS	2009	Career
Night	.998	.947
Day	.831	.873

Best years should be here, but...

Cabrera,Orlando			AB	R	HR	RBI	SB	Avg	vL	vR	OB	Slg	OPS	bb%	ct%	h%	Eye	xBA	G	L	F	PX	hr/f	SX	SBO	RC/G	RAR	BPV	R$
Pos	6	05 ANA	540	70	8	57	21	257	242	266	306	365	671	7	91	27	0.76	260	41	19	39	67	4%	123	17%	3.96	-9.5	69	$15
Age	35	06 LAA	607	95	9	72	27	282	243	297	337	404	741	8	90	30	0.88	259	39	17	43	79	4%	114	18%	4.82	7.0	77	$20
Bats	Right	07 LAA	638	101	8	86	20	301	308	299	346	397	743	6	90	33	0.69	263	43	18	39	64	4%	100	13%	4.71	7.4	56	$23
Health	A	08 CHW	661	93	8	57	19	281	273	284	338	371	708	8	89	31	0.79	268	46	21	33	59	4%	90	13%	4.40	1.3	49	$18
PT/Exp	A	09 2AL	656	83	9	77	13	284	271	290	321	389	710	5	89	31	0.51	265	46	19	36	65	4%	91	10%	4.25	-3.8	49	$18
Consist	A	1st Half	308	30	2	25	3	250			296	318	614	6	91	27	0.71	250	44	20	37	46	2%	46	9%	3.32	-10.4	29	$4
LIMA Plan	C	2nd Half	348	53	7	52	10	313			343	451	795	4	88	34	0.37	277	47	18	35	83	7%	116	11%	5.11	6.2	62	$14
Rand Var	-1	10 Proj	558	77	8	64	10	276			321	380	701	6	89	30	0.62	266	45	19	36	66	4%	92	9%	4.22	-2.9	52	$14

Flashed vintage skills in 2H, but trends show that his career has reached the "graceful fade" stage. SB decline is well under way. If not for 2H h% spike, BA might match xBA.
DN: .250, less than 10 SB.

Callaspo,Alberto			AB	R	HR	RBI	SB	Avg	vL	vR	OB	Slg	OPS	bb%	ct%	h%	Eye	xBA	G	L	F	PX	hr/f	SX	SBO	RC/G	RAR	BPV	R$
Pos	4	05 a/a	557	60	8	59	8	264			299	357	656	5	96	26	1.27	0				56		57	17%	3.85	-8.3	58	$12
Age	27	06 ARI	*532	74	6	59	6	305	278	208	362	427	789	8	95	31	1.78	237	46	8	46	63	3%	94	8%	5.50	13.6	77	$16
Bats	Both	07 ARI	*370	48	5	31	2	271	219	214	329	380	709	8	92	28	1.11	286	47	21	32	68	4%	60	5%	4.53	-1.9	59	$7
Health	B	08 KC	213	21	0	16	2	305	333	291	362	371	733	8	93	33	1.36	285	47	26	28	40	0%	77	4%	4.87	-0.1	47	$5
PT/Exp	C	09 KC	576	79	11	73	2	300	361	273	358	457	815	8	91	32	1.02	277	41	17	42	91	5%	79	2%	5.69	12.1	79	$17
Consist	B	1st Half	262	34	5	28	1	298			350	447	796	7	93	31	1.17	285	44	17	39	88	5%	65	3%	5.46	3.8	79	$7
LIMA Plan	B	2nd Half	314	45	6	45	1	303			365	465	830	9	89	32	0.94	270	38	17	44	93	5%	87	1%	5.90	8.3	78	$10
Rand Var	-2	10 Proj	542	73	10	63	2	292			349	431	780	8	92	30	1.13	285	43	20	37	80	5%	77	3%	5.30	9.1	74	$14

Finally translated his long-held control of the strike zone into production. xBA isn't totally convinced, but high ct% sets a nice BA floor. Power and speed are barely average, so this may be as good as it gets.

Cameron,Mike			AB	R	HR	RBI	SB	Avg	vL	vR	OB	Slg	OPS	bb%	ct%	h%	Eye	xBA	G	L	F	PX	hr/f	SX	SBO	RC/G	RAR	BPV	R$
Pos	8	05 NYM	308	47	12	39	13	273	311	261	335	477	813	9	72	34	0.34	270	42	21	38	151	14%	126	18%	5.71	10.1	68	$13
Age	37	06 SD	552	88	22	83	25	268	252	273	352	482	833	11	74	32	0.50	250	38	17	45	137	12%	134	22%	6.08	26.5	72	$23
Bats	Right	07 SD	571	88	21	78	18	242	294	222	321	431	752	11	72	30	0.42	246	37	19	44	131	12%	122	16%	4.96	7.5	52	$17
Health	B	08 MIL	444	69	25	70	17	243	282	231	325	477	803	11	68	30	0.38	248	33	22	46	169	18%	108	20%	5.71	12.9	64	$18
PT/Exp	A	09 MIL	544	78	24	70	7	250	271	244	341	452	793	12	71	31	0.48	240	35	17	48	145	13%	84	7%	5.57	13.5	53	$17
Consist	A	1st Half	254	34	12	33	4	240			352	445	797	15	72	29	0.62	247	39	17	44	144	15%	72	6%	5.69	7.3	56	$8
LIMA Plan	C+	2nd Half	290	44	12	37	3	259			330	459	789	10	71	33	0.36	235	31	17	52	146	11%	82	7%	5.45	6.1	46	$9
Rand Var	0	10 Proj	498	75	23	69	5	249			333	455	788	11	71	31	0.43	244	35	19	47	147	14%	83	7%	5.47	11.7	50	$15

As we see so often, speed is the first skill to fade. How quickly will others follow? Rest of his skill set is rock-solid, so 2009 repeat is likely. But without the wheels, the pop/low-BA tradeoff is far less appealing.

Cano,Robinson			AB	R	HR	RBI	SB	Avg	vL	vR	OB	Slg	OPS	bb%	ct%	h%	Eye	xBA	G	L	F	PX	hr/f	SX	SBO	RC/G	RAR	BPV	R$
Pos	4	05 NYY	*630	95	17	83	1	299	270	305	322	466	788	3	88	32	0.27	295	50	21	29	103	11%	76	3%	4.95	14.3	64	$21
Age	27	06 NYY	482	62	15	78	5	342	287	363	366	525	891	4	89	36	0.33	307	52	20	28	112	12%	66	6%	6.10	24.8	74	$20
Bats	Left	07 NYY	617	93	19	97	4	306	328	296	348	488	835	6	86	33	0.46	301	52	17	31	112	12%	85	6%	5.66	28.2	74	$23
Health	A	08 NYY	597	70	14	72	2	271	292	263	302	410	712	4	89	29	0.40	280	47	19	33	86	8%	55	4%	4.18	-12.1	52	$14
PT/Exp	A	09 NYY	637	103	25	85	5	320	309	322	351	520	870	4	90	33	0.48	310	47	20	33	114	13%	63	8%	5.91	17.0	81	$26
Consist	D	1st Half	310	49	12	42	4	300			332	481	813	5	92	30	0.60	307	49	20	31	98	13%	74	9%	5.30	3.2	79	$12
LIMA Plan	D+	2nd Half	327	54	13	43	1	339			368	557	925	4	88	36	0.39	313	44	20	36	129	13%	52	6%	6.53	13.8	83	$15
Rand Var	-1	10 Proj	621	91	19	84	4	308			339	478	816	5	89	32	0.43	297	48	19	33	102	10%	64	6%	5.35	11.0	68	$22

Bled career-year results from stable skill set. Now a consistent .300 hitter, but can he sustain 20+ HR? Still hits too many GB, PX is pedestrian, new Stadium helped hr/f uptick. Set your expectations against 2007 line.

Cantu,Jorge

Cantu,Jorge			AB	R	HR	RBI	SB	Avg	vL	vR	OB	Slg	OPS	bb%	ct%	h%	Eye	xBA	G	L	F	PX	hr/f	SX	SBO	RC/G	RAR	BPV	R$
Pos	35	05 TAM	598	73	28	117	1	286	256	296	308	497	805	3	86	29	0.23	296	42	21	37	128	15%	44	1%	5.03	-1.0	68	$22
Age	28	06 TAM	413	40	14	62	1	249	233	256	294	404	698	6	78	29	0.29	244	42	20	38	97	11%	50	2%	3.93	-18.1	18	$8
Bats	Right	07 2TM	* 300	33	4	33	0	255	232	283	308	374	682	7	81	31	0.39	264	45	22	34	89	5%	42	0%	3.94	-15.4	22	$4
Health	A	08 FLA	628	92	29	95	6	277	293	272	320	481	801	6	82	30	0.36	274	34	21	45	128	13%	67	6%	5.17	-9.9	66	$24
PT/Exp	B	09 FLA	585	67	16	100	3	289	322	278	342	443	785	7	86	31	0.58	271	36	21	43	102	7%	44	3%	5.16	-22.1	56	$20
Consist	B	1st Half	279	31	9	47	1	287			323	455	778	5	85	31	0.37	266	35	19	46	110	8%	37	2%	4.91	-12.5	53	$10
LIMA Plan	C	2nd Half	306	36	7	53	2	291			358	431	789	9	87	32	0.80	276	37	23	40	94	7%	41	3%	5.38	-9.7	56	$11
Rand Var	-1	10 Proj	587	71	18	92	3	279			329	440	769	7	84	31	0.46	269	37	21	42	105	9%	49	3%	4.91	-21.2	51	$19

PRO: Multi-year trends of rising ct%, OBP. healthy FB rate. .881 OPS vs LH last 2 years. CON: 2008 now looks like PX outlier, leaving only average power. Don't expect a return to 20 HR level.

Carp,Mike

Carp,Mike			AB	R	HR	RBI	SB	Avg	vL	vR	OB	Slg	OPS	bb%	ct%	h%	Eye	xBA	G	L	F	PX	hr/f	SX	SBO	RC/G	RAR	BPV	R$
Pos	3	05	0	0	0	0	0	0							0			0						0					
Age	24	06	0	0	0	0	0	0							0			0						0					
Bats	Left	07 aa	359	46	8	40	2	223			286	331	618	8	83	25	0.52	0				70		54	3%	3.16	-27.8	22	$4
Health	A	08 aa	478	57	14	61	1	270			360	418	778	12	85	29	0.91	0				94		37	2%	5.35	-2.0	51	$12
PT/Exp	D	09 SEA	* 467	65	14	61	0	253	286	319	339	404	743	12	78	30	0.58	252	44	20	36	99	11%	43	1%	4.84	-12.0	27	$10
Consist	C	1st Half	219	36	9	28	0	264			369	456	825	14	78	30	0.76	0				127		32	1%	6.00	1.0	54	$6
LIMA Plan	F	2nd Half	248	29	5	32	0	242			311	358	669	9	77	30	0.43	235	44	20	36	75	7%	55	0%	3.78	-14.2	4	$4
Rand Var	-1	10 Proj	124	16	4	16	0	266			348	422	769	11	81	30	0.65	259	44	20	36	98	12%	30	1%	5.10	-1.4	34	$3

1-5-.315 in 54 AB at SEA. Should hit for high BA some day, but ct% says not quite yet. Won't have much value at 1B unless he can recapture that 1H power spike, which he is still young enough to do.

Carroll,Brett

Carroll,Brett			AB	R	HR	RBI	SB	Avg	vL	vR	OB	Slg	OPS	bb%	ct%	h%	Eye	xBA	G	L	F	PX	hr/f	SX	SBO	RC/G	RAR	BPV	R$
Pos	9	05	0	0	0	0	0	0							0			0						0					
Age	28	06 aa	251	28	8	29	4	208			261	375	636	7	73	26	0.26	0				112		107	10%	3.23	-15.6	28	$3
Bats	Right	07 FLA	* 466	66	17	69	0	255			299	450	749	6	79	29	0.29	0				125		67	7%	4.62	-3.6	49	$12
Health	A	08 FLA	* 84	20	8	22	1	321			387	690	1078	10	68	39	0.33	0				253		112	9%	9.56	9.9	129	$6
PT/Exp	F	09 FLA	* 244	31	7	28	0	218	258	213	270	368	639	7	77	26	0.31	239	39	19	42	99	9%	80	2%	3.27	-12.1	27	$3
Consist	F	1st Half	90	12	2	6	0	231			285	353	638	7	77	28	0.33	232	31	25	44	79	7%	71	0%	3.27	-4.4	10	$1
LIMA Plan	F	2nd Half	154	19	5	22	0	211			262	377	639	6	77	24	0.30	244	45	15	40	110	10%	83	3%	3.27	-7.7	36	$2
Rand Var	+4	10 Proj	112	14	3	14	0	241			290	405	695	6	77	28	0.30	248	38	20	42	110	10%	78	4%	3.97	-3.4	34	$2

3-18-.234 in 141 AB at FLA. Has shown hints of power upside in recent years, but below average ct% means the BA risk outweighs power upside. But he can still cherish his 84-AB peak in 2008.

Carroll,Jamey

Carroll,Jamey			AB	R	HR	RBI	SB	Avg	vL	vR	OB	Slg	OPS	bb%	ct%	h%	Eye	xBA	G	L	F	PX	hr/f	SX	SBO	RC/G	RAR	BPV	R$
Pos	45	05 WAS	303	44	0	22	3	251	293	235	326	284	610	10	82	31	0.62	254	53	26	21	27	0%	76	7%	3.23	-12.1	-6	$4
Age	36	06 COL	463	84	5	36	10	300	359	283	376	404	780	11	86	34	0.85	269	49	23	29	64	4%	95	14%	5.39	10.3	46	$15
Bats	Right	07 COL	227	45	2	22	6	225	262	194	310	300	609	11	85	26	0.82	261	44	25	32	50	3%	113	12%	3.35	-9.4	38	$4
Health	B	08 CLE	347	60	1	36	7	277	261	284	341	346	687	9	81	34	0.52	256	45	27	27	49	1%	117	9%	4.12	-7.7	19	$9
PT/Exp	D	09 CLE	315	53	2	26	4	276	271	278	350	340	690	10	80	34	0.57	240	46	24	30	43	3%	92	6%	4.18	-6.8	4	$7
Consist	A	1st Half	127	25	0	8	0	283			368	354	722	12	82	35	0.74	246	46	23	31	47	0%	96	4%	4.76	-0.6	19	$3
LIMA Plan	F	2nd Half	188	28	2	18	4	271			338	330	668	9	79	34	0.48	236	46	25	29	40	5%	74	6%	3.78	-6.2	-11	$5
Rand Var	-4	10 Proj	252	44	1	23	3	266			340	335	674	10	81	32	0.60	250	46	25	29	47	2%	95	7%	4.01	-5.1	14	$5

Consistently high LD% has helped him maintain elevated h%. xBA, ct% trending in wrong direction, though, and at age 36, SX is likely gone for good. Singles hitters with no legs have no value.

Casilla,Alexi

Casilla,Alexi			AB	R	HR	RBI	SB	Avg	vL	vR	OB	Slg	OPS	bb%	ct%	h%	Eye	xBA	G	L	F	PX	hr/f	SX	SBO	RC/G	RAR	BPV	R$
Pos	4	05	0	0	0	0	0	0							0			0						0					
Age	26	06 aa	170	26	1	12	18	282			348	371	718	9	88	32	0.85	0				59		134	42%	4.63	1.3	61	$7
Bats	Both	07 MIN	* 509	67	3	29	35	248	274	181	302	308	611	7	84	29	0.50	263	62	16	22	43	3%	118	34%	3.13	-13.5	24	$13
Health	A	08 MIN	* 481	67	7	52	10	262	264	289	325	343	668	8	87	29	0.72	241	52	15	34	52	5%	73	10%	3.90	-13.9	32	$12
PT/Exp	C	09 MIN	* 384	42	2	31	19	240	182	205	295	310	606	7	85	28	0.53	225	51	12	36	40	2%	126	24%	3.13	-21.1	27	$7
Consist	B	1st Half	240	23	1	16	9	240			286	300	586	6	85	28	0.42	234	56	14	29	35	2%	104	24%	2.80	-15.8	12	$3
LIMA Plan	D	2nd Half	144	19	1	15	10	239			310	327	638	9	86	27	0.74	221	47	11	42	48	2%	149	24%	3.66	-5.5	48	$4
Rand Var	0	10 Proj	349	45	3	30	19	249			310	324	635	8	86	28	0.63	234	51	13	35	47	3%	120	24%	3.52	-12.4	36	$9

0-17-11-.202 in 228 AB at MIN. Combo of good speed, high ct% and lots of GBs should be yielding better results. High SBO and 90% career SB success rate shows potential if he can get on base more... UP: 35 SB

Castillo,Luis

Castillo,Luis			AB	R	HR	RBI	SB	Avg	vL	vR	OB	Slg	OPS	bb%	ct%	h%	Eye	xBA	G	L	F	PX	hr/f	SX	SBO	RC/G	RAR	BPV	R$
Pos	4	05 FLA	439	72	4	30	10	301	423	259	391	374	764	13	93	32	2.03	304	63	22	15	41	6%	96	10%	5.47	11.2	60	$14
Age	35	06 MIN	584	84	3	49	25	296	256	316	358	370	728	9	90	33	0.97	277	61	18	21	44	3%	117	18%	4.74	10.2	50	$18
Bats	Both	07 2TM	548	91	1	38	19	301	296	303	363	359	722	9	92	33	1.18	284	67	15	18	37	1%	115	13%	4.73	5.8	51	$17
Health	B	08 NYM	298	46	3	28	17	245	211	257	353	305	659	14	88	27	1.43	264	66	16	18	36	6%	108	17%	4.21	-5.0	45	$9
PT/Exp	B	09 NYM	486	77	1	40	20	302	264	319	389	346	735	12	88	34	1.19	270	59	23	19	29	1%	105	13%	5.00	6.4	33	$18
Consist	B	1st Half	222	40	0	16	10	275			374	329	702	14	92	30	2.06	281	62	19	19	36	0%	115	15%	4.88	2.2	62	$7
LIMA Plan	C+	2nd Half	264	37	1	24	10	326			403	360	763	11	84	38	0.83	261	55	26	18	22	2%	87	11%	5.16	4.5	7	$11
Rand Var	-3	10 Proj	461	72	2	38	19	289			375	341	716	12	89	32	1.23	273	62	20	18	33	3%	110	13%	4.78	2.1	41	$15

High OBP driven by bb%, ct%, and GB/speed combo. Note the slow, steady decline in speed skills, which accelerated in 2H. Will soon be a singles hitter without wheels.

Castro,Juan

Castro,Juan			AB	R	HR	RBI	SB	Avg	vL	vR	OB	Slg	OPS	bb%	ct%	h%	Eye	xBA	G	L	F	PX	hr/f	SX	SBO	RC/G	RAR	BPV	R$
Pos	64	05 MIN	272	27	5	33	0	257	247	262	281	386	667	3	86	29	0.23	267	50	19	31	87	7%	47	2%	3.58	-7.8	35	$5
Age	38	06 2TM	251	18	3	28	1	251	268	244	282	351	633	4	86	28	0.31	259	49	21	29	59	5%	65	5%	3.25	-8.4	20	$3
Bats	Right	07 CIN	89	5	0	5	0	180	226	155	215	236	451	4	76	24	0.19	199	39	17	43	52	0%	21	0%	0.83	-10.4	-36	($1)
Health	A	08 2TM	* 213	23	3	18	0	207	185	196	259	286	545	7	84	23	0.44	212	49	13	38	54	4%	35	0%	2.28	-14.6	5	$1
PT/Exp	F	09 LA	112	18	1	9	0	277	240	287	314	339	653	5	78	35	0.24	212	34	23	43	48	3%	48	0%	3.37	-4.1	-24	$3
Consist	C	1st Half	60	14	1	7	0	333			394	417	811	9	75	43	0.40	217	24	28	48	61	5%	54	0%	5.62	1.5	-15	$3
LIMA Plan	F	2nd Half	52	4	0	2	0	212			212	250	462	0	81	26	0.00	202	45	18	38	35	0%	35	0%	0.86	-6.1	-37	($0)
Rand Var	-5	10 Proj	100	12	1	8	0	250			283	321	605	4	82	30	0.25	225	43	20	38	52	3%	44	1%	2.80	-5.2	-8	$1

Inflated h% propped up BA, but xBA tells the true tale. So how exactly has a career .230 hitter with no power or speed racked up 2,500 major league ABs? Most creative answer gets a free copy of the 2011 book. See p.10.

Castro,Ramon

Castro,Ramon			AB	R	HR	RBI	SB	Avg	vL	vR	OB	Slg	OPS	bb%	ct%	h%	Eye	xBA	G	L	F	PX	hr/f	SX	SBO	RC/G	RAR	BPV	R$
Pos	2	05 NYM	* 339	43	13	59	2	223	290	236	293	412	705	9	76	26	0.41	258	36	19	45	133	11%	61	3%	4.19	4.2	48	$8
Age	34	06 NYM	126	13	4	12	0	238	269	230	319	389	708	11	68	32	0.38	222	36	22	42	112	11%	17	0%	4.40	0.2	-9	$2
Bats	Right	07 NYM	144	24	11	31	0	285	276	287	331	556	887	6	73	32	0.26	272	36	18	46	171	23%	30	0%	6.34	7.7	52	$7
Health	D	08 NYM	143	15	7	24	0	245	277	218	308	441	748	8	76	27	0.38	264	36	24	40	128	16%	15	0%	4.64	1.8	30	$4
PT/Exp	F	09 2TM	* 285	28	9	34	0	222	222	218	284	366	650	8	78	26	0.39	247	35	22	42	97	9%	24	1%	3.43	-7.3	14	$4
Consist	C	1st Half	124	13	5	20	0	241			316	430	746	10	82	26	0.61	265	37	19	44	121	11%	17	0%	4.76	1.8	52	$3
LIMA Plan	F	2nd Half	161	14	4	15	0	207			258	317	575	6	74	26	0.27	246	32	30	38	77	8%	29	3%	2.35	-9.6	-17	$1
Rand Var	+5	10 Proj	129	14	5	19	0	240			301	414	714	8	76	28	0.36	251	36	22	42	114	13%	26	1%	4.20	-0.2	20	$3

7-25-.219 in 155 AB with NYM and CHW. Another year of part-time AB's with decent power but BA drag. PX dropped in 2H, but track record says he is still a marginal option for an end-game desperation catcher.

Catalanotto,Frank

Catalanotto,Frank			AB	R	HR	RBI	SB	Avg	vL	vR	OB	Slg	OPS	bb%	ct%	h%	Eye	xBA	G	L	F	PX	hr/f	SX	SBO	RC/G	RAR	BPV	R$
Pos	9	05 TOR	419	56	8	59	0	301	290	302	357	451	809	8	87	33	0.70	280	45	21	35	96	6%	64	2%	5.56	9.9	64	$13
Age	36	06 TOR	437	56	7	56	1	300	237	306	374	439	814	11	92	32	1.41	284	48	19	34	88	5%	46	3%	5.86	2.4	74	$11
Bats	Left	07 TEX	331	52	11	44	2	260	231	261	318	444	762	8	89	27	0.76	312	51	19	30	108	12%	93	4%	4.97	-5.2	87	$9
Health	A	08 TEX	248	28	2	21	1	274	167	280	328	399	728	7	88	30	0.69	284	53	18	30	92	3%	56	3%	4.67	-4.9	60	$4
PT/Exp	D	09 MIL	144	18	1	9	2	278	91	293	342	382	724	9	84	33	0.61	246	52	15	33	65	3%	106	5%	4.62	-1.1	40	$3
Consist	A	1st Half	30	1	0	2	0	267			313	367	679	6	77	35	0.29	232	48	22	30	64	0%	52	0%	3.93	-0.8	-12	$0
LIMA Plan	D	2nd Half	114	17	1	7	2	281			349	386	735	10	86	32	0.75	250	52	14	33	65	3%	109	6%	4.81	-0.2	50	$3
Rand Var	-3	10 Proj	160	22	3	16	1	281			344	426	769	9	88	31	0.80	282	51	17	32	91	6%	89	4%	5.17	0.9	71	$4

Just 36 AB's vs LH in past 3 years. Now that ct% and PX are falling off, he is losing AB's vs RH's as well. Empty BA in a part-time role is all he has left to offer.

BRIAN RUDD

Cedeno,Ronny

			AB	R	HR	RBI	SB	Avg	vL	vR	OB	Slg	OPS	bb%	ct%	h%	Eye	xBA	G	L	F	PX	hr/f	SX	SBO	RC/G	RAR	BPV	R$
Pos	6	05 CHC	* 325	48	8	35	10	323	256	341	365	454	819	6	89	34	0.63	290	61	14	25	79	12%	91	14%	5.48	13.3	62	$15
Age	27	06 CHC	534	51	6	41	8	245	230	251	269	339	608	3	80	30	0.16	222	47	16	37	58	4%	96	14%	2.76	-25.8	1	$7
Bats	Right	07 CHC	* 361	48	13	42	7	294	176	225	343	451	794	7	84	32	0.45	264	33	23	44	92	9%	76	12%	5.16	7.3	47	$13
Health	A	08 CHC	216	36	2	28	4	269	257	282	325	352	677	8	81	32	0.44	243	52	18	30	64	4%	83	8%	3.88	-4.7	18	$6
PT/Exp	D	09 2TM	341	32	10	38	5	208	193	213	250	337	587	5	77	24	0.24	220	51	11	38	78	10%	91	10%	2.48	-22.1	9	$4
Consist	C	1st Half	103	11	3	8	1	136			205	252	458	8	69	16	0.28	179	52	5	44	73	10%	101	17%	0.65	-13.9	-18	($1)
LIMA Plan	F	2nd Half	238	21	7	30	4	239			270	374	644	4	80	27	0.21	238	51	13	36	79	10%	90	8%	3.18	-9.8	22	$5
Rand Var	+3	10 Proj	**291**	**35**	**7**	**33**	**5**	**237**			**285**	**357**	**642**	**6**	**79**	**28**	**0.32**	**233**	**51**	**14**	**36**	**76**	**8%**	**93**	**11%**	**3.28**	**-10.6**	**19**	**$6**

Growth age, pop and speed flashes hint at upside. Sub-par bb%, ct% and GB% expose upside limits. End-game SS flyer who won't help your BA, but at 27, another 2007 is always a possibility. Just don't pay for it.

Cervelli,Francisco

			AB	R	HR	RBI	SB	Avg	vL	vR	OB	Slg	OPS	bb%	ct%	h%	Eye	xBA	G	L	F	PX	hr/f	SX	SBO	RC/G	RAR	BPV	R$
Pos	2	05	0	0	0	0	0	0							0			0						0					
Age	24	06	0	0	0	0	0	0							0			0						0					
Bats	Right	07	0	0	0	0	0	0							0			0						0					
Health	A	08 aa	78	8	0	8	0	282			364	346	710	11	77	37	0.56	0				60		21	0%	4.54	0.7	-13	$1
PT/Exp	F	09 NYY	* 221	27	4	24	0	255	345	277	290	353	644	5	83	29	0.30	248	46	20	34	63	6%	38	9%	3.30	-6.5	7	$4
Consist	C	1st Half	125	17	3	14	0	230			276	325	601	6	81	26	0.32	225	44	18	38	56	8%	47	3%	2.74	-5.8	-4	$2
LIMA Plan	F	2nd Half	96	10	1	10	0	288			309	390	699	3	87	32	0.24	289	50	25	25	72	5%	41	17%	3.97	-0.9	26	$2
Rand Var	0	10 Proj	**115**	**13**	**2**	**12**	**0**	**261**			**292**	**360**	**651**	**4**	**85**	**30**	**0.28**	**260**	**47**	**22**	**32**	**67**	**6%**	**43**	**12%**	**3.40**	**-2.9**	**15**	**$2**

1-11-.298 in 94 AB at NYY.
PRO: Improving ct%, health, age.
CON: Everything else.
Might not hurt you with more PT, which is sometimes all you need from a #2 catcher.

Chavez,Endy

			AB	R	HR	RBI	SB	Avg	vL	vR	OB	Slg	OPS	bb%	ct%	h%	Eye	xBA	G	L	F	PX	hr/f	SX	SBO	RC/G	RAR	BPV	R$
Pos	7	05 2NL	* 203	27	1	14	6	207	381	179	257	285	542	6	91	23	0.71	287	57	21	23	46	2%	137	19%	2.57	-17.8	55	$2
Age	32	06 NYM	353	48	4	42	12	306	333	298	350	431	781	6	88	34	0.55	289	55	20	25	76	5%	120	15%	5.15	-1.0	61	$13
Bats	Left	07 NYM	150	20	1	17	5	287	276	289	327	380	707	6	89	32	0.56	285	60	17	23	57	3%	111	17%	4.29	-4.6	50	$4
Health	F	08 NYM	270	30	1	12	6	267	194	278	310	330	640	6	92	29	0.77	263	53	19	28	40	1%	99	9%	3.63	-14.0	43	$5
PT/Exp	F	09 SEA	161	17	2	13	9	273	258	277	331	342	673	8	86	31	0.64	251	53	19	28	38	5%	99	19%	3.91	-5.1	23	$5
Consist	A	1st Half	161	17	2	13	9	273			331	342	673	8	86	31	0.64	250	54	18	28	38	5%	99	19%	3.91	-5.1	23	$5
LIMA Plan	F	2nd Half	0	0	0	0	0	0																					
Rand Var	-1	10 Proj	**206**	**25**	**2**	**18**	**2**	**272**			**320**	**355**	**675**	**7**	**89**	**30**	**0.63**	**268**	**56**	**18**	**26**	**51**	**4%**	**80**	**6%**	**3.96**	**-6.0**	**35**	**$4**

Serious knee surgery (ACL+ MCL) killed 2009, threatens future. Made marginal living off off ct% and legs; GBs + zero power won't cut it if speed falls off the cliff. Advancing age adds to bleak profile.

Chavez,Eric

			AB	R	HR	RBI	SB	Avg	vL	vR	OB	Slg	OPS	bb%	ct%	h%	Eye	xBA	G	L	F	PX	hr/f	SX	SBO	RC/G	RAR	BPV	R$
Pos	5	05 OAK	625	92	27	101	6	269	260	271	331	466	796	8	79	30	0.45	263	39	18	43	130	13%	77	4%	5.29	14.2	64	$22
Age	32	06 OAK	485	74	22	72	3	241	197	257	353	435	788	15	79	26	0.84	255	39	18	44	118	13%	68	2%	5.50	7.1	64	$12
Bats	Left	07 OAK	341	43	15	46	4	240	234	244	309	446	755	9	78	27	0.45	266	36	17	46	136	12%	78	8%	4.82	-0.5	63	$8
Health	F	08 OAK	89	10	2	14	0	247	333	215	295	393	688	6	80	29	0.33	248	42	17	41	108	7%	28	0%	3.93	-2.5	29	$2
PT/Exp	F	09 OAK	30	0	0	1	0	100	111	83	129	133	262	3	77	13	0.14	107	43	13	43	30	0%	0	0%	-1.63	-6.7	-61	($1)
Consist	F	1st Half	30	0	0	1	0	100			129	133	262	3	77	13	0.14	107	43	13	43	30	0%	-9	0%	-1.63	-6.7	-63	($1)
LIMA Plan	F	2nd Half	0	0	0	0	0	0																					
Rand Var	+5	10 Proj	**94**	**13**	**4**	**14**	**1**	**255**			**332**	**451**	**783**	**10**	**79**	**28**	**0.54**	**261**	**38**	**18**	**45**	**127**	**13%**	**46**	**4%**	**5.22**	**1.2**	**53**	**$3**

AB trend, straight-F reliability tell all. Back surgery aborted 2009, but upper body issues had eroded PT for previous three seasons. Power in doubt even with health; only age makes him remotely watchable.

Chavez,Raul

			AB	R	HR	RBI	SB	Avg	vL	vR	OB	Slg	OPS	bb%	ct%	h%	Eye	xBA	G	L	F	PX	hr/f	SX	SBO	RC/G	RAR	BPV	R$
Pos	2	05 HOU	* 218	12	2	16	1	185	133	188	213	256	468	3	83	22	0.20	203	44	12	43	52	3%	38	3%	1.17	-18.2	-8	($1)
Age	37	06 aa	196	12	1	14	0	171			203	229	431	4	87	19	0.30	0				39		23	0%	0.97	-21.7	-5	($2)
Bats	Right	07 aaa	290	23	4	25	1	186			211	264	474	3	86	20	0.23	0				52		47	2%	1.37	-27.7	8	($1)
Health	A	08 PIT	* 201	19	3	19	0	255	240	264	278	345	623	3	88	28	0.27	255	41	23	36	57	4%	42	0%	3.10	-6.5	17	$3
PT/Exp	F	09 TOR	159	10	2	15	1	258	244	263	285	346	631	4	86	29	0.26	251	46	21	34	59	4%	30	5%	3.16	-5.2	7	$2
Consist	B	1st Half	70	3	2	7	0	271			271	371	643	0	93	27	0.00	ERR	54	13	33	48	9%	-2	0%	3.14	-2.3	11	$1
LIMA Plan	F	2nd Half	89	7	0	8	1	247			295	326	621	6	80	31	0.33	260	38	28	34	69	0%	43	10%	3.18	-2.9	2	$1
Rand Var	-3	10 Proj	**135**	**10**	**2**	**12**	**1**	**237**			**264**	**317**	**580**	**3**	**86**	**27**	**0.26**	**249**	**44**	**22**	**34**	**54**	**4%**	**34**	**3%**	**2.58**	**-6.8**	**6**	**$1**

We've saved the least valuable Chavez for last. If you spend much more time on on this one, either your league depth or CA requirements aren't resonating with us. Or maybe this game isn't for you.

Choo,Shin-Soo

			AB	R	HR	RBI	SB	Avg	vL	vR	OB	Slg	OPS	bb%	ct%	h%	Eye	xBA	G	L	F	PX	hr/f	SX	SBO	RC/G	RAR	BPV	R$
Pos	97	05 aaa	444	61	9	45	16	239		91	332	356	688	12	80	28	0.70	230	57	7	36	78	7%	102	20%	4.22	-10.4	40	$11
Age	28	06 2AL	* 532	84	14	63	27	288	278	281	358	444	801	10	78	35	0.50	287	56	24	20	102	17%	126	22%	5.53	-2.0	54	$21
Bats	Left	07 aaa	208	29	2	23	9	233			297	324	620	8	83	27	0.53	0				64		111	22%	3.29	-12.1	35	$4
Health	B	08 CLE	* 359	69	15	69	5	299	286	317	382	523	905	12	74	37	0.53	284	41	23	36	161	15%	91	10%	7.08	17.4	79	$17
PT/Exp	C	09 CLE	583	87	20	86	21	300	275	312	383	489	872	12	74	38	0.52	264	42	22	36	127	13%	119	12%	6.64	21.0	59	$25
Consist	F	1st Half	284	45	10	46	12	292			395	451	845	14	74	37	0.65	259	46	24	30	104	16%	98	11%	6.36	8.1	40	$13
LIMA Plan	B	2nd Half	299	42	10	40	9	308			371	525	896	9	74	39	0.39	269	39	20	42	149	11%	121	13%	6.88	12.7	73	$13
Rand Var	-5	10 Proj	**592**	**93**	**18**	**88**	**19**	**287**			**365**	**469**	**834**	**11**	**76**	**35**	**0.51**	**267**	**42**	**22**	**36**	**124**	**11%**	**115**	**14%**	**6.05**	**11.8**	**62**	**$23**

Sacrificed patience for power in 2H, but couldn't up HR total even with fortunate h% and more AB. 2009 could be his upside, and the 20-20 profile remains attractive. But ct% says there's no next step coming.

Church,Ryan

			AB	R	HR	RBI	SB	Avg	vL	vR	OB	Slg	OPS	bb%	ct%	h%	Eye	xBA	G	L	F	PX	hr/f	SX	SBO	RC/G	RAR	BPV	R$
Pos	98	05 WAS	268	41	9	42	3	287	367	277	346	466	812	8	74	36	0.34	273	46	24	30	125	15%	102	7%	5.64	3.0	45	$10
Age	31	06 WAS	* 390	47	17	60	10	232	265	279	316	425	741	11	72	28	0.44	241	39	18	43	130	14%	79	12%	4.76	-0.2	39	$11
Bats	Left	07 WAS	470	57	15	70	3	272	229	287	341	464	805	9	77	32	0.46	286	43	22	35	138	12%	53	4%	5.58	9.4	56	$13
Health	C	08 NYM	319	54	12	49	2	276	264	282	344	439	783	9	74	34	0.40	255	45	24	31	110	16%	69	5%	5.23	0.4	25	$12
PT/Exp	C	09 2NL	359	46	4	40	6	273	213	290	334	384	719	8	84	32	0.57	263	46	20	33	85	4%	68	8%	4.50	-3.9	43	$9
Consist	B	1st Half	203	23	2	19	6	286			341	389	730	8	84	33	0.52	262	47	21	32	80	4%	68	14%	4.59	-1.7	37	$6
LIMA Plan	D	2nd Half	156	23	2	21	0	256			326	378	704	9	84	29	0.64	261	45	19	35	92	4%	38	0%	4.39	-2.3	42	$3
Rand Var	0	10 Proj	**305**	**43**	**7**	**41**	**3**	**269**			**335**	**416**	**751**	**9**	**79**	**32**	**0.48**	**265**	**45**	**21**	**33**	**104**	**9%**	**75**	**6%**	**4.85**	**-1.1**	**43**	**$9**

Concussions gone, but power drain continued amid nagging injuries (hamstring, elbow, back). Ct% is up, other skills holding steady, but there's nothing interesting here unless health and power return.

Clement,Jeff

			AB	R	HR	RBI	SB	Avg	vL	vR	OB	Slg	OPS	bb%	ct%	h%	Eye	xBA	G	L	F	PX	hr/f	SX	SBO	RC/G	RAR	BPV	R$
Pos	0	05	0	0	0	0	0	0							0			0						0					
Age	27	06 aaa	304	26	5	36	0	237			284	342	626	6	82	27	0.36	0				69		38	3%	3.18	-29.9	9	$3
Bats	Left	07 aa	455	62	16	66	0	236			315	420	734	10	81	26	0.61	0				120		44	0%	4.67	-21.3	57	$9
Health	A	08 SEA	* 375	48	15	56	0	253	289	209	330	448	778	10	76	29	0.48	261	41	18	40	135	13%	35	1%	5.21	3.1	46	$10
PT/Exp	D	09 aa	470	62	15	69	2	231			292	399	691	8	80	26	0.43	0				112		67	3%	4.02	-16.4	48	$10
Consist	B	1st Half	299	44	9	40	1	240			308	412	720	9	76	29	0.42	0				119		77	1%	4.44	-6.5	44	$7
LIMA Plan	F	2nd Half	171	17	6	29	1	215			263	377	639	6	87	22	0.48	0				100		44	6%	3.40	-9.4	54	$3
Rand Var	0	10 Proj	**128**	**16**	**4**	**19**	**0**	**242**			**306**	**404**	**709**	**8**	**81**	**27**	**0.47**	**256**	**41**	**18**	**40**	**107**	**10%**	**37**	**2%**	**4.24**	**-4.3**	**38**	**$3**

One-time top prospect's poor year puts future at crossroad. Calling card power diminished by push for better ct%, MLB AB limited due to defensive issues. Age is a plus, but we don't see the silver lining here.

Coghlan,Chris

			AB	R	HR	RBI	SB	Avg	vL	vR	OB	Slg	OPS	bb%	ct%	h%	Eye	xBA	G	L	F	PX	hr/f	SX	SBO	RC/G	RAR	BPV	R$
Pos	7	05	0	0	0	0	0	0							0			0						0					
Age	25	06	0	0	0	0	0	0							0			0						0					
Bats	Left	07	0	0	0	0	0	0							0			0						0					
Health	A	08 aa	483	68	6	61	27	264			342	375	718	11	88	29	0.98	0				73		117	27%	4.70	-6.3	68	$17
PT/Exp	D	09 FLA	* 595	103	12	67	15	323	316	323	388	472	860	10	85	36	0.72	287	48	23	30	97	8%	113	11%	6.23	10.8	73	$26
Consist	D	1st Half	268	47	5	31	12	279			368	414	782	12	83	32	0.83	274	49	21	31	93	7%	118	16%	5.46	-0.7	68	$11
LIMA Plan	B+	2nd Half	327	56	7	36	3	359			405	520	925	7	87	40	0.60	296	47	23	30	100	8%	91	8%	6.81	10.5	72	$16
Rand Var	-2	10 Proj	**541**	**86**	**13**	**64**	**10**	**292**			**362**	**450**	**812**	**10**	**86**	**32**	**0.80**	**293**	**48**	**23**	**30**	**98**	**9%**	**103**	**12%**	**5.68**	**3.2**	**76**	**$20**

9-47-.321 in 504 AB at FLA. Unreal 2H fueled by h% unlike any in his past screams regression. Solid-not-special skill set, would play better as a 2B or even 3B - his college and minor league postions.

JOCK THOMPSON

Conrad,Brooks

Conrad,Brooks			AB	R	HR	RBI	SB	Avg	vL	vR	OB	Slg	OPS	bb%	ct%	h%	Eye	xBA	G	L	F	PX	hr/f	SX	SBO	RC/G	RAR	BPV	R$
Pos	4	05 a/a	491	77	17	53	16	224			299	389	688	10	79	25	0.51	0				107		123	16%	4.01	-5.0	60	$13
Age	30	06 aaa	532	81	19	76	12	237			294	458	751	7	78	27	0.37	0				134		136	18%	4.79	6.9	79	$14
Bats	Both	07 aaa	533	58	16	48	8	164			225	308	533	7	73	19	0.29	0				104		95	13%	1.82	-44.4	19	$1
Health	A	08 aaa	465	58	18	62	3	182			233	356	588	6	78	20	0.29	0				113		88	5%	2.56	-33.9	42	$5
PT/Exp	D	09 ATL	* 452	54	11	54	9	209	222	200	276	334	610	8	73	26	0.34	204	29	18	53	91	6%	103	10%	2.93	-22.5	16	$7
Consist	B	1st Half	259	33	6	28	6	203			277	312	589	9	76	24	0.42	0				78		80	11%	2.69	-14.9	10	$4
LIMA Plan	F	2nd Half	193	22	5	26	3	217			274	364	638	7	70	29	0.26	208	29	18	53	111	6%	103	9%	3.31	-7.2	16	$3
Rand Var	-2	10 Proj	65	8	2	8	1	200			260	334	594	8	74	24	0.32	213	29	18	53	95	7%	65	9%	2.65	-4.0	9	$1

2-8-.204 in 54 AB at ATL. Living proof that MLEs provide an accurate warning, especially with so many years of MLEs. Has some pop for a middle infielder, but too many Ks and fly balls wreak havoc on his BA.

Cora,Alex

Cora,Alex			AB	R	HR	RBI	SB	Avg	vL	vR	OB	Slg	OPS	bb%	ct%	h%	Eye	xBA	G	L	F	PX	hr/f	SX	SBO	RC/G	RAR	BPV	R$
Pos	6	05 2AL	250	25	3	24	7	232	281	227	264	332	596	4	88	25	0.37	259	52	17	30	57	4%	121	17%	2.91	-12.5	45	$4
Age	34	06 BOS	235	31	1	18	6	238	333	219	295	298	593	7	88	27	0.66	238	51	16	32	37	2%	108	12%	3.06	-9.6	29	$3
Bats	Left	07 BOS	207	30	3	18	1	246	179	257	271	386	658	3	89	27	0.30	280	43	20	37	81	4%	115	5%	3.60	-4.2	63	$3
Health	D	08 BOS	152	14	0	9	1	270	286	266	339	349	688	10	91	29	1.23	277	42	25	33	53	0%	71	4%	4.44	0.5	50	$2
PT/Exp	F	09 NYM	271	31	1	18	8	251	292	238	314	310	624	8	90	28	0.89	250	47	20	33	41	1%	89	14%	3.55	-9.0	37	$5
Consist	B	1st Half	146	18	0	11	6	253			351	322	673	13	87	29	1.16	239	40	21	40	52	0%	92	16%	4.35	-1.3	45	$3
LIMA Plan	F	2nd Half	125	13	1	7	2	248			266	296	562	2	93	26	0.33	260	54	20	26	30	3%	64	10%	2.54	-7.9	21	$2
Rand Var	0	10 Proj	228	26	1	16	4	254			305	328	633	7	90	28	0.74	260	47	21	32	46	2%	92	10%	3.56	-6.8	41	$4

Hard to tell from erratic Eye history if he's inconsistent, or if pitchers sometimes forget who they're dealing with. 1H showed he can still deliver SB value if walks are there, which makes owning him a leap of faith.

Coste,Chris

Coste,Chris			AB	R	HR	RBI	SB	Avg	vL	vR	OB	Slg	OPS	bb%	ct%	h%	Eye	xBA	G	L	F	PX	hr/f	SX	SBO	RC/G	RAR	BPV	R$
Pos	2	05 aaa	499	50	15	59	2	233			273	368	641	5	86	24	0.39	0				81		40	6%	3.31	-9.0	32	$8
Age	37	06 PHI	* 345	36	9	45	1	256	288	345	293	394	688	5	82	29	0.30	282	40	29	31	89	10%	35	2%	3.82	-5.2	23	$7
Bats	Right	07 PHI	* 327	29	9	49	0	228	405	228	258	341	600	4	85	24	0.28	234	43	17	40	66	8%	22	0%	2.74	-16.8	10	$4
Health	A	08 PHI	274	28	9	36	0	263	296	249	303	423	727	6	81	29	0.31	265	38	23	39	106	10%	24	2%	4.29	0.7	31	$7
PT/Exp	D	09 2NL	205	15	2	18	0	224	222	225	300	317	617	10	73	30	0.40	215	41	21	38	81	3%	15	0%	3.15	-6.9	-17	$1
Consist	C	1st Half	100	12	2	8	0	250			342	390	732	12	75	32	0.56	256	37	25	37	112	7%	24	0%	4.81	1.6	23	$2
LIMA Plan	F	2nd Half	105	3	0	10	0	200			257	248	504	7	71	28	0.27	160	45	16	39	49	0%	3	0%	1.50	-9.1	-58	($1)
Rand Var	0	10 Proj	130	11	2	15	0	231			285	342	627	7	78	28	0.35	234	41	21	39	81	6%	23	1%	3.16	-4.3	-0	$1

Last three seasons...
1H: .267 BA, 84% ct, 103 PX
2H: .203 BA, 77% ct, 64 PX
Not surprising for a catcher, particularly one in the twilight of his career. If you roster him at all, do it early.

Counsell,Craig

Counsell,Craig			AB	R	HR	RBI	SB	Avg	vL	vR	OB	Slg	OPS	bb%	ct%	h%	Eye	xBA	G	L	F	PX	hr/f	SX	SBO	RC/G	RAR	BPV	R$
Pos	456	05 ARI	578	85	9	42	26	256	269	253	345	375	720	12	88	28	1.13	284	49	20	31	77	6%	123	18%	4.79	3.9	77	$17
Age	40	06 ARI	372	56	4	30	15	255	256	255	313	347	659	8	87	28	0.66	258	48	20	31	53	4%	118	22%	3.81	-8.8	45	$9
Bats	Left	07 MIL	282	31	3	24	4	220	157	234	319	309	627	13	83	25	0.87	233	46	15	38	58	3%	77	7%	3.61	-9.5	30	$2
Health	B	08 MIL	248	31	1	14	3	226	190	229	347	302	649	16	83	27	1.10	253	47	23	30	59	2%	69	5%	4.07	-5.3	33	$2
PT/Exp	C	09 MIL	404	61	4	39	3	285	237	290	352	408	760	9	87	32	0.78	267	44	21	35	77	3%	102	6%	5.12	6.8	60	$11
Consist	B	1st Half	188	29	2	14	2	298			365	426	791	10	89	33	1.00	280	43	24	34	76	4%	107	5%	5.52	5.2	72	$6
LIMA Plan	D	2nd Half	216	32	2	25	1	273			340	394	734	9	84	32	0.65	255	45	19	36	78	3%	92	6%	4.77	1.5	48	$5
Rand Var	-3	10 Proj	217	30	2	18	3	258			343	363	706	11	85	30	0.88	258	45	21	34	68	3%	99	7%	4.58	-0.3	50	$4

Skills came back to life with increased ABs, though xBA shows things weren't quite as rosy as they appeared. At his age, a repeat of production or playing time seems unlikely. Back to the endgame for him.

Crawford,Carl

Crawford,Carl			AB	R	HR	RBI	SB	Avg	vL	vR	OB	Slg	OPS	bb%	ct%	h%	Eye	xBA	G	L	F	PX	hr/f	SX	SBO	RC/G	RAR	BPV	R$
Pos	7	05 TAM	644	101	15	81	46	301	244	326	329	469	798	4	87	33	0.32	281	45	20	35	97	8%	172	34%	5.15	7.7	87	$32
Age	29	06 TAM	600	89	18	77	58	305	288	311	345	482	827	6	86	33	0.44	285	52	18	30	92	12%	168	40%	5.55	6.2	81	$33
Bats	Left	07 TAM	584	93	11	80	50	315	318	314	351	466	816	5	81	38	0.29	279	48	20	32	101	7%	160	38%	5.46	6.8	65	$31
Health	B	08 TAM	443	69	8	57	25	273	248	285	319	400	719	6	86	30	0.50	272	49	21	30	69	7%	156	26%	4.38	-6.1	62	$17
PT/Exp	A	09 TAM	606	96	15	68	60	305	269	322	359	452	811	8	84	35	0.52	280	52	19	29	85	10%	149	41%	5.49	8.3	65	$33
Consist	C	1st Half	319	55	8	38	40	320			371	461	832	8	84	36	0.50	275	50	20	30	83	10%	149	46%	5.71	6.1	63	$21
LIMA Plan	D+	2nd Half	287	41	7	30	20	289			346	443	789	8	84	33	0.53	284	55	19	27	88	11%	135	35%	5.26	2.1	63	$12
Rand Var	-2	10 Proj	587	101	18	71	58	302			349	472	821	7	84	33	0.46	288	51	20	30	98	12%	164	43%	5.53	9.4	80	$34

As expected, a healthy season brought him right back to where he left off. Can't act like 2008 never happened, but if you discount it a little, he's a lot more consistent than his "C" grade would lead you to believe.

Crede,Joe

Crede,Joe			AB	R	HR	RBI	SB	Avg	vL	vR	OB	Slg	OPS	bb%	ct%	h%	Eye	xBA	G	L	F	PX	hr/f	SX	SBO	RC/G	RAR	BPV	R$
Pos	5	05 CHW	432	54	22	62	1	252	277	246	293	454	747	5	85	25	0.38	269	36	18	45	119	13%	38	2%	4.47	-0.4	59	$12
Age	32	06 CHW	544	76	30	94	0	283	273	288	318	506	824	5	89	27	0.48	279	31	18	51	121	12%	28	2%	5.34	5.1	74	$19
Bats	Right	07 CHW	167	13	4	22	0	216	206	218	260	317	577	6	86	23	0.42	213	32	15	53	61	5%	23	3%	2.60	-11.7	12	$1
Health	F	08 CHW	335	41	17	55	0	248	122	289	310	460	769	8	87	24	0.67	262	32	14	54	123	11%	32	4%	4.94	0.6	73	$9
PT/Exp	D	09 MIN	333	42	15	48	0	225	202	235	287	414	702	8	83	23	0.52	249	30	16	53	109	10%	37	0%	4.10	-5.9	49	$7
Consist	D	1st Half	219	26	11	35	0	233			303	443	746	9	82	24	0.56	258	31	17	52	121	12%	39	0%	4.67	-0.1	57	$5
LIMA Plan	D	2nd Half	114	16	4	13	0	211			256	360	616	6	85	22	0.41	232	30	15	55	86	8%	44	0%	3.03	-5.8	36	$1
Rand Var	+2	10 Proj	321	39	14	46	0	231			284	410	694	7	85	23	0.51	248	31	16	53	103	9%	40	2%	3.99	-7.5	51	$6

The Crede Conundrum:
- He simply cannot stay healthy.
- Because he can't stay healthy, his power comes and goes.
- And that kills his BA and value.
- Even so, it's hard to ignore '06.
Be strong. Avert your gaze.

Crisp,Coco

Crisp,Coco			AB	R	HR	RBI	SB	Avg	vL	vR	OB	Slg	OPS	bb%	ct%	h%	Eye	xBA	G	L	F	PX	hr/f	SX	SBO	RC/G	RAR	BPV	R$
Pos	8	05 CLE	594	86	16	69	15	300	252	325	348	465	813	7	86	33	0.54	286	46	20	34	106	9%	105	13%	5.47	19.7	77	$22
Age	30	06 BOS	413	58	8	36	22	264	277	259	315	385	700	7	84	30	0.46	251	48	16	36	77	6%	125	24%	4.14	-6.3	50	$12
Bats	Both	07 BOS	526	85	6	60	28	268	270	267	332	382	714	9	84	31	0.60	260	47	17	36	75	4%	146	23%	4.47	-1.0	60	$17
Health	F	08 BOS	361	55	7	41	20	283	295	278	346	407	753	9	84	32	0.59	252	41	20	39	80	6%	119	25%	4.88	-4.9	54	$14
PT/Exp	C	09 KC	180	30	3	14	13	228	222	231	335	378	713	14	87	25	1.26	276	48	18	34	81	6%	152	28%	4.84	1.1	89	$5
Consist	A	1st Half	180	30	3	14	13	228			335	378	713	14	87	25	1.26	276	48	18	34	81	6%	152	28%	4.84	1.1	89	$5
LIMA Plan	C+	2nd Half	0	0	0	0	0	0																					
Rand Var	+5	10 Proj	311	49	5	31	19	270			352	406	758	11	85	30	0.85	265	46	18	36	82	6%	141	23%	5.14	3.3	73	$11

Rotator cuff surgery may delay start of his season. Eye growth was encouraging, and dates back to 2H of 2008, so perhaps he's figuring things out. A cautious investment could net you 30 SB and a solid BA.

Crosby,Bobby

Crosby,Bobby			AB	R	HR	RBI	SB	Avg	vL	vR	OB	Slg	OPS	bb%	ct%	h%	Eye	xBA	G	L	F	PX	hr/f	SX	SBO	RC/G	RAR	BPV	R$
Pos	35	05 OAK	333	66	9	38	0	276	314	260	345	456	802	10	84	31	0.65	293	54	18	28	118	12%	86	0%	5.53	4.1	76	$10
Age	30	06 OAK	358	42	9	40	8	229	185	242	299	338	637	9	79	27	0.47	231	47	18	35	69	9%	75	9%	3.34	-22.6	13	$6
Bats	Right	07 OAK	349	40	8	31	10	226	222	228	274	341	615	6	82	25	0.37	263	48	20	32	77	9%	84	15%	3.01	-24.0	30	$6
Health	D	08 OAK	559	66	7	61	7	238	222	244	299	349	648	8	83	28	0.51	249	48	16	36	82	4%	71	7%	3.61	-27.9	37	$9
PT/Exp	C	09 OAK	238	35	6	29	2	223	265	184	294	357	651	9	82	25	0.55	241	44	15	40	81	8%	91	5%	3.61	-15.3	38	$4
Consist	A	1st Half	153	22	3	19	2	203			295	314	609	12	82	23	0.74	227	41	16	43	62	6%	104	5%	3.25	-11.8	35	$2
LIMA Plan	F	2nd Half	85	13	3	10	0	259			292	435	727	4	80	29	0.24	261	51	13	36	115	12%	54	6%	4.25	-3.7	39	$2
Rand Var	+2	10 Proj	227	31	5	25	3	238			295	375	670	8	82	27	0.44	254	48	16	36	90	8%	78	7%	3.77	-11.7	39	$4

Before you get too excited about that 2H PX, note the sample size, then survey the wasteland that is his last four years. You can toss a buck at him on the off chance there's something here, just don't be foolish.

Crowe,Trevor

Crowe,Trevor			AB	R	HR	RBI	SB	Avg	vL	vR	OB	Slg	OPS	bb%	ct%	h%	Eye	xBA	G	L	F	PX	hr/f	SX	SBO	RC/G	RAR	BPV	R$
Pos	78	05	0	0	0	0	0	0							0			0						0					
Age	26	06 aa	154	18	1	12	15	214			301	292	593	11	86	24	0.86	0				51		123	49%	3.21	-6.7	45	$4
Bats	Both	07 aa	518	74	4	43	24	230			305	309	614	10	87	26	0.84	0				54		111	24%	3.42	-17.8	47	$10
Health	A	08 a/a	344	61	8	36	15	271			344	424	768	10	80	32	0.55	0				109		117	24%	5.15	1.0	63	$13
PT/Exp	D	09 CLE	* 368	43	3	32	17	245	255	228	311	339	650	9	82	29	0.53	256	56	16	27	63	4%	118	25%	3.68	-10.8	33	$8
Consist	D	1st Half	185	21	2	12	8	212			289	284	573	10	80	26	0.54	234	54	17	29	52	4%	80	21%	2.67	-15.7	7	$2
LIMA Plan	D	2nd Half	183	21	1	20	10	278			333	396	729	8	84	33	0.52	273	58	16	26	74	2%	129	29%	4.65	0.0	51	$6
Rand Var	0	10 Proj	254	34	3	23	13	252			322	356	678	9	83	30	0.60	263	57	16	27	71	5%	113	27%	4.04	-5.7	42	$7

1-17-.235 in 183 AB at CLE. Seeds of a potentially good player are scattered throughout his skill history, though '08 PX admittedly looks like an outlier. Target the speed for now, keep an eye on the rest.

BRANDON KRUSE

Cruz,Nelson

			AB	R	HR	RBI	SB	Avg	vL	vR	OB	Slg	OPS	bb%	ct%	h%	Eye	xBA	G	L	F	PX	hr/f	SX	SBO	RC/G	RAR	BPV	R$
Pos	9	05 a/a	455	57	20	60	14	244			313	438	752	9	76	28	0.42	0				134		73	21%	4.77	-2.8	53	$15
Age	30	06 2TM	* 501	75	25	87	16	265	217	226	327	465	792	8	75	31	0.36	244	46	12	42	126	16%	91	18%	5.23	0.3	47	$20
Bats	Right	07 TEX	* 469	57	21	66	3	249	212	245	303	441	743	7	74	29	0.30	248	38	16	46	129	13%	63	8%	4.58	-12.9	35	$12
Health	A	08 TEX	* 498	83	34	95	20	287	419	298	357	551	908	10	79	30	0.52	297	40	22	38	160	23%	98	21%	6.66	18.6	94	$27
PT/Exp	C	09 TEX	462	75	33	76	20	260	235	270	331	524	855	10	74	28	0.42	270	38	16	46	161	21%	99	21%	6.04	9.6	78	$22
Consist	C	1st Half	269	45	19	47	13	264			331	532	863	9	77	28	0.44	280	37	18	45	158	20%	109	22%	6.06	5.7	89	$14
LIMA Plan	B	2nd Half	193	30	14	29	7	254			330	513	843	10	70	29	0.39	255	41	13	46	166	22%	71	20%	6.03	4.1	59	$8
Rand Var	+1	10 Proj	508	83	36	103	18	274			341	540	881	9	75	30	0.41	275	39	16	45	165	21%	94	19%	6.37	15.1	81	$26

Battled through nagging injuries and proved '08 breakout was no fluke. Elite HR + SB combo, and after another 160 PX, power is legit, especially with added FB. Faded in Sept, but this was first full MLB season. UP: 40 HR

Cuddyer,Michael

			AB	R	HR	RBI	SB	Avg	vL	vR	OB	Slg	OPS	bb%	ct%	h%	Eye	xBA	G	L	F	PX	hr/f	SX	SBO	RC/G	RAR	BPV	R$
Pos	93	05 MIN	422	55	12	42	3	263	280	260	328	422	750	9	78	31	0.44	264	53	18	29	109	13%	72	6%	4.81	1.4	40	$10
Age	31	06 MIN	557	102	24	109	6	284	297	276	355	504	860	10	77	33	0.48	280	44	21	35	145	16%	110	4%	6.28	9.7	78	$22
Bats	Right	07 MIN	547	87	16	81	5	276	308	263	352	433	785	10	80	32	0.60	268	45	19	36	102	10%	98	3%	5.32	-2.7	55	$17
Health	D	08 MIN	249	30	3	36	5	249	250	249	318	369	687	9	84	29	0.63	263	46	21	33	78	4%	113	9%	4.18	-8.7	52	$5
PT/Exp	B	09 MIN	588	93	32	94	6	276	307	264	336	520	857	8	80	30	0.46	286	44	16	40	144	17%	105	5%	6.02	11.5	85	$23
Consist	C	1st Half	267	43	12	42	4	277			359	513	872	11	79	31	0.62	293	51	16	33	141	17%	110	7%	6.45	8.6	88	$10
LIMA Plan	C+	2nd Half	321	50	20	52	2	274			317	526	843	6	80	29	0.32	281	38	17	45	146	17%	80	3%	5.63	2.8	76	$13
Rand Var	0	10 Proj	584	87	25	89	7	274			338	481	819	9	81	30	0.50	280	45	18	37	125	14%	102	6%	5.61	4.3	74	$20

A career year at age 30, and it didn't come in peaks. Had a 125+ PX in five of six months. He's never posted consecutive elite power years, so that's the next step. In meantime, bid on 25 HR; anything more is gravy.

Cunningham,Aaro

			AB	R	HR	RBI	SB	Avg	vL	vR	OB	Slg	OPS	bb%	ct%	h%	Eye	xBA	G	L	F	PX	hr/f	SX	SBO	RC/G	RAR	BPV	R$
Pos	9	05	0	0	0	0	0	0							0			0						0					
Age	24	06	0	0	0	0	0	0							0			0						0					
Bats	Right	07 aa	118	21	5	17	1	271			328	517	845	8	81	30	0.45	0				148		112	15%	5.93	2.6	95	$4
Health	A	08 OAK	* 506	75	13	65	15	283	208	268	340	435	775	8	79	34	0.42	227	34	14	52	102	6%	112	15%	5.08	-4.1	50	$18
PT/Exp	D	09 OAK	* 387	51	9	41	8	236	176	139	285	368	653	6	82	27	0.38	247	49	14	38	86	7%	85	15%	3.50	-21.6	36	$8
Consist	C	1st Half	193	28	7	27	4	219			264	392	656	6	80	24	0.30	256	48	13	39	108	12%	100	19%	3.44	-11.4	48	$4
LIMA Plan	F	2nd Half	194	24	2	15	4	253			305	344	649	7	84	29	0.48	248	50	17	33	65	4%	67	12%	3.58	-10.1	25	$3
Rand Var	+2	10 Proj	162	23	4	19	4	259			313	410	723	7	81	30	0.41	244	42	14	45	99	7%	90	15%	4.40	-4.6	47	$4

1-6-.151 in 53 AB at OAK. Solid prospect, but heading in wrong direction. Bad BA was H%-driven, so it should rebound. Declining power is a bigger issue. No signs of light coming on soon, but he's still just 24.

Cust,Jack

			AB	R	HR	RBI	SB	Avg	vL	vR	OB	Slg	OPS	bb%	ct%	h%	Eye	xBA	G	L	F	PX	hr/f	SX	SBO	RC/G	RAR	BPV	R$
Pos	9	05 aaa	476	71	15	56	2	220			353	367	720	17	74	27	0.80	0				105		46	4%	4.76	-3.2	31	$8
Age	31	06 aaa	441	71	19	57	0	233			384	405	789	20	76	26	1.02	0				109		20	2%	5.73	6.9	38	$9
Bats	Left	07 OAK	* 475	73	32	96	0	250	218	273	400	507	906	20	58	35	0.60	254	42	23	35	214	34%	27	1%	8.25	38.6	54	$17
Health	A	08 OAK	485	79	35	80	0	233	235	229	376	489	864	19	59	31	0.56	241	40	21	39	204	31%	19	0%	7.33	28.7	45	$16
PT/Exp	B	09 OAK	513	88	25	70	4	240	221	247	356	417	774	15	64	32	0.50	217	37	20	43	127	18%	57	3%	5.57	3.6	7	$15
Consist	C	1st Half	267	42	14	41	2	225			315	416	730	12	70	27	0.43	227	35	17	48	125	16%	56	3%	4.58	-6.1	21	$7
LIMA Plan	C	2nd Half	246	46	11	29	2	256			398	419	817	19	58	40	0.56	206	40	23	37	129	21%	48	3%	6.82	10.7	-12	$8
Rand Var	0	10 Proj	408	68	23	61	2	235			369	440	809	18	62	32	0.56	230	39	21	40	154	22%	39	2%	6.25	11.1	21	$12

•
Why he'll be a part-timer soon...
- 3 HR in 140 AB vs. LHers
- xBA trend, including 2H
- Eroding eye

hr/f determines his fate. Banking on 1/3 of FB to go out is risky. Use 400 AB, 20 HR as baseline.

Damon,Johnny

			AB	R	HR	RBI	SB	Avg	vL	vR	OB	Slg	OPS	bb%	ct%	h%	Eye	xBA	G	L	F	PX	hr/f	SX	SBO	RC/G	RAR	BPV	R$
Pos	7	05 BOS	624	117	10	75	18	316	327	310	369	439	808	8	89	34	0.77	280	45	23	32	77	6%	136	10%	5.53	13.6	76	$26
Age	36	06 NYY	593	115	24	80	25	285	297	280	358	482	840	10	86	30	0.79	280	41	18	41	113	12%	124	20%	5.93	12.8	83	$26
Bats	Left	07 NYY	533	93	12	63	27	270	281	266	351	396	746	11	85	30	0.84	274	48	18	33	81	8%	121	18%	4.93	-1.6	66	$20
Health	A	08 NYY	555	95	17	71	29	303	258	321	375	461	836	10	85	33	0.78	281	44	22	34	95	11%	125	20%	5.92	16.6	77	$26
PT/Exp	A	09 NYY	550	107	24	82	12	282	269	288	364	489	853	11	82	31	0.72	276	41	16	42	125	13%	113	7%	6.16	17.8	87	$23
Consist	B	1st Half	281	57	15	47	8	292			368	541	909	11	82	31	0.68	290	39	17	44	145	15%	125	10%	6.79	13.9	106	$14
LIMA Plan	B	2nd Half	269	50	9	35	4	271			359	435	794	12	82	30	0.77	259	44	16	41	103	10%	74	5%	5.51	3.8	60	$9
Rand Var	0	10 Proj	530	98	18	72	13	287			365	460	825	11	84	31	0.76	275	43	19	38	106	11%	107	10%	5.82	12.7	76	$21

Hit 17 of 24 HR at home, so new park gets credit for HR surge. SB drop expected in mid-30s, but it actually was driven by lack of green light. Buy him for his consistency. Just know that his 20/20 days probably are over.

Davis,Chris

			AB	R	HR	RBI	SB	Avg	vL	vR	OB	Slg	OPS	bb%	ct%	h%	Eye	xBA	G	L	F	PX	hr/f	SX	SBO	RC/G	RAR	BPV	R$
Pos	3	05	0	0	0	0	0	0							0			0						0					
Age	24	06	0	0	0	0	0	0							0			0						0					
Bats	Left	07 aa	109	18	11	21	0	275			342	642	984	9	80	25	0.50	0				218		19	0%	7.42	6.8	119	$5
Health	A	08 TEX	* 592	104	36	112	6	294	279	287	339	557	896	6	76	34	0.28	295	35	25	40	176	20%	88	7%	6.49	26.5	84	$28
PT/Exp	D	09 TEX	* 556	70	26	84	0	255	189	260	311	449	759	7	67	33	0.24	234	35	21	44	136	16%	39	1%	5.00	5.2	6	$15
Consist	C	1st Half	251	31	15	33	0	203			254	422	676	6	56	29	0.15	211	36	18	46	180	23%	27	0%	4.26	-3.3	-10	$4
LIMA Plan	C	2nd Half	305	39	11	51	0	298			357	470	827	8	77	36	0.38	258	34	24	42	110	11%	48	1%	5.74	8.9	27	$11
Rand Var	-3	10 Proj	473	70	28	81	1	264			318	507	825	7	73	31	0.29	273	35	23	42	162	19%	56	2%	5.69	12.6	53	$17

21-59-.238 in 391 AB at TEX. 1H ct% issues well-documented. Gains after 2H return were real (except perhaps h%-influenced BA). If ct% stays close to 2H and he improves vs. LHers... hey, it's still true -- UP: 40 HR

Davis,Rajai

			AB	R	HR	RBI	SB	Avg	vL	vR	OB	Slg	OPS	bb%	ct%	h%	Eye	xBA	G	L	F	PX	hr/f	SX	SBO	RC/G	RAR	BPV	R$
Pos	8	05 aa	499	62	3	26	34	242			287	310	597	6	88	27	0.52	0				46		133	35%	3.02	-21.3	43	$13
Age	29	06 aaa	385	50	2	20	44	278			323	345	668	6	85	32	0.46	0				47		127	50%	3.77	-8.9	32	$16
Bats	Right	07 2NL	* 401	55	4	32	43	269	299	258	329	372	701	8	87	30	0.69	252	43	17	40	66	3%	144	51%	4.35	-2.2	62	$17
Health	A	08 2TM	218	31	3	20	30	248	232	250	278	358	635	4	82	29	0.23	254	48	22	30	62	6%	191	72%	3.19	-12.4	44	$11
PT/Exp	D	09 OAK	390	65	3	48	41	305	316	299	353	423	776	7	82	37	0.41	261	46	20	34	81	3%	152	47%	5.13	5.4	54	$21
Consist	D	1st Half	105	16	1	4	9	229			289	305	594	8	77	29	0.38	222	44	20	35	49	3%	139	46%	2.79	-6.2	8	$3
LIMA Plan	C+	2nd Half	285	49	2	44	32	333			377	467	844	7	84	39	0.43	275	46	20	34	92	2%	157	47%	5.93	10.0	71	$18
Rand Var	-5	10 Proj	459	69	4	43	46	275			321	379	700	6	83	32	0.39	255	46	20	34	68	3%	158	48%	4.14	-8.8	48	$20

Single-handedly gave owners SB crown with that 2H, and SX history says wheels are legit. But an elevated H% drove OB spike, so we can't expect that again. Without more bb, his wheels are SBO-driven. Don't overbid.

DeJesus,David

			AB	R	HR	RBI	SB	Avg	vL	vR	OB	Slg	OPS	bb%	ct%	h%	Eye	xBA	G	L	F	PX	hr/f	SX	SBO	RC/G	RAR	BPV	R$
Pos	7	05 KC	461	69	9	56	5	293	270	303	352	445	797	8	84	34	0.55	278	45	22	32	100	7%	99	8%	5.41	9.0	63	$14
Age	30	06 KC	491	83	8	56	6	295	307	291	352	446	798	8	86	33	0.61	290	49	22	29	95	7%	113	7%	5.45	3.7	71	$14
Bats	Left	07 KC	605	101	7	58	10	260	240	267	330	372	702	10	86	29	0.77	265	46	19	36	71	4%	120	8%	4.42	-10.9	59	$13
Health	A	08 KC	518	70	12	73	11	307	302	310	363	452	815	8	86	34	0.65	290	46	25	29	87	9%	101	12%	5.58	10.6	63	$19
PT/Exp	A	09 KC	558	74	13	71	4	281	290	277	342	434	775	8	84	31	0.59	271	46	20	34	88	8%	84	8%	5.13	2.0	52	$15
Consist	B	1st Half	282	33	6	34	1	245			295	404	699	7	83	28	0.42	265	45	18	36	94	7%	92	3%	4.15	-7.3	50	$5
LIMA Plan	C+	2nd Half	276	41	7	37	3	319			388	464	851	10	86	35	0.79	277	46	22	32	83	9%	75	11%	6.11	8.5	55	$11
Rand Var	0	10 Proj	576	82	12	72	6	290			351	432	783	9	85	32	0.64	276	46	21	33	85	8%	90	9%	5.25	4.6	55	$17

Rocky 1H, but in the end, his year was more of the same, excluding SB dive. SX trend suggests SB won't come back, especially with lack of green light. Pay for consistency, not upside, for there's none here.

Delgado,Carlos

			AB	R	HR	RBI	SB	Avg	vL	vR	OB	Slg	OPS	bb%	ct%	h%	Eye	xBA	G	L	F	PX	hr/f	SX	SBO	RC/G	RAR	BPV	R$
Pos	3	05 FLA	521	81	33	115	0	301	229	327	386	582	968	12	77	34	0.60	311	40	23	37	186	22%	47	0%	7.71	30.1	97	$27
Age	38	06 NYM	524	89	38	114	0	265	226	282	356	548	904	12	77	28	0.62	286	42	18	40	168	23%	40	0%	6.78	11.8	81	$22
Bats	Left	07 NYM	538	71	24	87	4	258	267	254	324	448	772	9	78	29	0.44	260	39	18	43	122	13%	56	3%	4.98	-18.0	46	$16
Health	F	08 NYM	598	96	38	115	1	271	267	273	349	518	868	11	79	28	0.58	297	42	25	34	152	24%	42	1%	6.21	8.3	74	$26
PT/Exp	B	09 NYM	94	15	4	23	0	298	333	289	377	521	899	11	79	34	0.60	280	39	20	41	148	13%	62	0%	6.81	0.8	77	$5
Consist	B	1st Half	94	15	4	23	0	298			377	521	899	11	79	34	0.60	280	39	20	41	148	13%	62	0%	6.81	0.8	77	$5
LIMA Plan	C	2nd Half	0	0	0	0	0	0																					
Rand Var	-2	10 Proj	464	71	25	96	0	278			356	511	867	11	78	31	0.56	282	40	20	40	149	17%	49	0%	6.29	1.4	70	$20

Hip surgery ended year in May. If healthy, we'll all want to bid on '08. But PX and xBA were in steep decline prior to then, and at age 37, those kind of spikes aren't likely again. Spacious RF in Citi Field will hurt too. Use '07.

STEPHEN NICKRAND

DeRosa,Mark			AB	R	HR	RBI	SB	Avg	vL	vR	OB	Slg	OPS	bb%	ct%	h%	Eye	xBA	G	L	F	PX	hr/f	SX	SBO	RC/G	RAR	BPV	R$
Pos	57	05 TEX	148	26	8	20	1	243	322	188	317	439	756	10	76	27	0.46	259	47	19	35	123	21%	60	3%	4.76	1.2	44	$5
Age	35	06 TEX	520	78	13	74	4	296	342	278	351	456	807	8	80	35	0.43	280	49	23	29	109	11%	70	6%	5.48	6.8	47	$16
Bats	Right	07 CHC	502	64	10	72	1	293	283	297	366	420	786	10	81	34	0.62	261	42	22	36	84	7%	50	2%	5.37	-3.4	31	$14
Health	B	08 CHC	505	103	21	87	6	285	310	275	371	481	852	12	79	33	0.65	272	40	22	38	126	14%	104	4%	6.22	12.0	74	$23
PT/Exp	A	09 2TM	515	78	23	78	3	250	278	242	313	433	746	8	77	29	0.39	250	43	17	40	117	15%	66	4%	4.63	-4.3	38	$16
Consist	C	1st Half	287	47	13	50	1	261			331	443	774	9	78	30	0.47	255	44	18	38	115	15%	49	3%	5.02	0.9	38	$10
LIMA Plan	C	2nd Half	228	31	10	28	2	237			290	421	711	7	75	27	0.30	242	42	15	43	119	14%	78	6%	4.12	-5.4	34	$6
Rand Var	+1	10 Proj	476	76	19	71	3	265			334	442	776	9	78	30	0.47	259	42	19	38	114	13%	76	4%	5.10	1.1	46	$16

Familiar story: player doubles HR total ('08 vs '07); player likes hitting HR and abandons plate patience; HRs stay, other skills nosedive. At 35, needs to pick one path. '07 or '09 worth similar R$, but '08 won't recur.

Desmond,Ian			AB	R	HR	RBI	SB	Avg	vL	vR	OB	Slg	OPS	bb%	ct%	h%	Eye	xBA	G	L	F	PX	hr/f	SX	SBO	RC/G	RAR	BPV	R$
Pos	6	05	0	0	0	0	0	0							0			0						0					
Age	25	06 aa	121	7	0	3	4	165			192	215	407	3	74	22	0.13	0				39		108	26%	0.10	-17.1	-34	($1)
Bats	Right	07	0	0	0	0	0	0							0			0						0					
Health	A	08 aa	323	32	9	34	10	212			266	334	600	7	80	24	0.37	0				79		68	28%	2.78	-17.6	20	$5
PT/Exp	F	09 WAS	* 430	55	10	39	19	295	300	278	349	449	797	8	82	34	0.46	264	54	12	34	104	8%	114	21%	5.35	8.4	63	$17
Consist	F	1st Half	143	21	5	14	11	262			317	430	747	7	77	31	0.36	0				119		102	39%	4.66	-0.0	52	$6
LIMA Plan	D+	2nd Half	287	34	5	24	9	311			365	458	823	8	84	36	0.53	265	54	12	34	97	6%	108	14%	5.69	8.1	64	$11
Rand Var	-5	10 Proj	457	50	10	40	18	256			306	382	687	7	80	30	0.35	242	54	12	34	86	8%	96	23%	3.91	-9.0	32	$12

4-12-.280 in 82 AB at WAS
Wherever that 1H PX came from, it'll disappear with full-time MLB exposure. So will BA when h% reverts. Pay for the SB (especially with elite SBO) while awaiting development.

DeWitt,Blake			AB	R	HR	RBI	SB	Avg	vL	vR	OB	Slg	OPS	bb%	ct%	h%	Eye	xBA	G	L	F	PX	hr/f	SX	SBO	RC/G	RAR	BPV	R$
Pos	5	05	0	0	0	0	0	0							0			0						0					
Age	25	06 aa	104	6	1	6	0	173			225	212	437	6	80	21	0.33	0				23		26	4%	0.75	-12.3	-40	($1)
Bats	Left	07 aa	178	17	5	17	0	253			277	416	693	3	88	26	0.27	0				101		48	3%	3.89	-2.4	54	$3
Health	A	08 LA	* 479	58	12	66	4	264	286	257	337	386	723	10	83	30	0.66	250	47	19	34	74	9%	77	3%	4.54	-3.2	37	$12
PT/Exp	D	09 LA	* 401	57	8	42	2	219	200	205	295	354	649	10	88	23	0.91	237	49	7	44	82	5%	90	4%	3.84	-8.5	67	$6
Consist	B	1st Half	230	30	2	19	2	205			286	318	604	10	89	22	1.04	227	59	0	41	74	2%	94	7%	3.45	-7.8	66	$1
LIMA Plan	F	2nd Half	171	27	6	23	0	237			308	402	710	9	87	24	0.76	245	42	12	46	94	9%	74	0%	4.39	-0.7	65	$4
Rand Var	+2	10 Proj	160	20	4	18	1	256			319	382	701	8	86	28	0.65	250	47	16	37	77	7%	62	3%	4.25	-1.7	42	$3

2-4-.204 in 49 AB at LA
Eye provides strong foundation. What if h% was bad luck (30% in minors career)? Then he deserves a chance to recapture other skills. At age 25, has time to do so.

Diaz,Matt			AB	R	HR	RBI	SB	Avg	vL	vR	OB	Slg	OPS	bb%	ct%	h%	Eye	xBA	G	L	F	PX	hr/f	SX	SBO	RC/G	RAR	BPV	R$
Pos	97	05 KC	* 374	44	10	51	8	276	370	143	303	436	739	4	83	31	0.23	281	51	20	29	101	11%	106	15%	4.40	-3.3	55	$11
Age	32	06 ATL	297	37	7	32	5	327	295	358	351	475	825	4	84	37	0.22	282	50	24	27	87	11%	92	12%	5.39	5.0	40	$11
Bats	Right	07 ATL	358	44	12	45	4	338	356	318	366	497	864	4	82	39	0.25	278	46	21	34	101	12%	55	4%	5.82	8.8	38	$15
Health	D	08 ATL	* 173	13	3	18	4	231	319	159	253	295	548	3	77	28	0.13	233	52	25	24	39	10%	59	15%	1.83	-17.8	-36	$2
PT/Exp	D	09 ATL	371	56	13	58	12	313	412	255	372	488	860	9	76	38	0.39	274	48	25	27	117	17%	109	15%	6.22	13.6	48	$18
Consist	F	1st Half	133	22	4	19	3	286			349	451	800	9	77	34	0.43	272	48	24	28	107	14%	117	8%	5.46	2.2	50	$5
LIMA Plan	D+	2nd Half	238	34	9	39	9	328			385	508	893	8	75	41	0.37	274	48	25	27	122	19%	97	18%	6.66	11.5	45	$13
Rand Var	-5	10 Proj	390	49	14	53	12	295			337	462	799	6	78	35	0.29	274	49	24	28	105	17%	100	15%	5.21	2.6	40	$16

PRO: Drool-inducing LD rate suggests hit rate is legit, huge bb% gain, reclaimed SX.
CON: falling ct%, inflated hr/f, low FB%, stopped hitting RHP.
UP: 15/15, .300
DN: 5/5, .250

Diaz,Robinzon			AB	R	HR	RBI	SB	Avg	vL	vR	OB	Slg	OPS	bb%	ct%	h%	Eye	xBA	G	L	F	PX	hr/f	SX	SBO	RC/G	RAR	BPV	R$
Pos	2	05	0	0	0	0	0	0							0			0						0					
Age	27	06	0	0	0	0	0	0							0			0						0					
Bats	Right	07 a/a	366	30	4	32	4	289			307	376	684	3	95	30	0.50	0				54		62	4%	3.93	-4.4	48	$7
Health	A	08 aaa	145	6	1	13	1	227			246	305	551	3	94	24	0.44	0				49		46	13%	2.57	-7.4	36	$0
PT/Exp	F	09 PIT	* 278	23	3	30	0	249	237	314	273	318	591	3	93	26	0.48	251	56	18	26	44	4%	26	3%	2.93	-11.0	23	$3
Consist	B	1st Half	118	10	1	17	0	275			287	351	637	2	93	29	0.24	260	56	18	26	51	3%	31	4%	3.32	-3.2	28	$2
LIMA Plan	F	2nd Half	160	13	2	13	0	229			264	293	557	4	93	24	0.64	252	56	19	26	39	5%	29	2%	2.63	-7.9	22	$1
Rand Var	0	10 Proj	126	8	1	12	0	270			291	337	628	3	94	28	0.47	256	56	18	26	43	4%	29	6%	3.32	-3.4	25	$2

1-19-.279 in 129 AB at PIT
Your 23rd pick, right here. A #2 catcher with 90%+ contact rates means he won't likely hurt your batting average (he has a .300+ BA in the minors). What else can you ask for from a #2 catcher?

Dickerson,Chris			AB	R	HR	RBI	SB	Avg	vL	vR	OB	Slg	OPS	bb%	ct%	h%	Eye	xBA	G	L	F	PX	hr/f	SX	SBO	RC/G	RAR	BPV	R$
Pos	789	05	0	0	0	0	0	0							0			0						0					
Age	28	06 aa	389	58	11	43	19	217			316	376	692	13	68	29	0.44	0				116		131	23%	4.29	-11.2	29	$9
Bats	Left	07 a/a	468	57	12	46	25	231			304	355	659	9	69	31	0.33	0				87		118	25%	3.64	-22.5	-0	$12
Health	B	08 CIN	* 451	69	15	55	24	254	286	309	339	435	774	11	72	32	0.46	233	37	18	45	125	10%	138	27%	5.32	-1.4	54	$17
PT/Exp	D	09 CIN	255	31	2	15	11	275	243	280	371	373	743	13	74	36	0.59	238	49	22	29	76	4%	113	15%	5.07	-3.6	19	$7
Consist	B	1st Half	159	22	2	11	5	283			384	403	786	14	73	38	0.60	241	45	23	31	91	6%	103	12%	5.71	0.7	26	$5
LIMA Plan	C+	2nd Half	96	9	0	4	6	260			349	323	672	12	76	34	0.57	231	56	19	25	50	0%	107	21%	4.06	-4.2	2	$2
Rand Var	-5	10 Proj	463	59	8	38	24	255			343	375	719	12	72	34	0.49	240	51	21	29	87	9%	124	21%	4.62	-11.7	22	$14

Litany of injuries curtailed his playing time and may explain loss of PX and hr/f. But low FB% ('08 was a fluke) puts damper on power regardless. Took a few more walks overall; that's his real path to success.

Dobbs,Greg			AB	R	HR	RBI	SB	Avg	vL	vR	OB	Slg	OPS	bb%	ct%	h%	Eye	xBA	G	L	F	PX	hr/f	SX	SBO	RC/G	RAR	BPV	R$
Pos	5	05 SEA	* 332	29	3	37	5	260			303	336	639	6	86	29	0.45	241	35	24	42	53	2%	66	8%	3.42	-10.4	21	$6
Age	32	06 SEA	* 406	51	7	47	11	270			321	385	706	7	85	30	0.51	275	52	22	26	70	8%	99	16%	4.23	-9.2	43	$10
Bats	Left	07 PHI	324	45	10	55	3	272	214	277	331	451	782	8	79	32	0.43	255	38	16	46	115	9%	98	4%	5.18	-3.9	57	$10
Health	B	08 PHI	226	30	9	40	3	301	111	309	333	491	824	5	82	33	0.28	272	30	25	45	119	11%	74	7%	5.39	0.2	58	$10
PT/Exp	D	09 PHI	154	15	5	20	1	247	429	238	297	383	680	7	81	28	0.38	233	29	20	51	86	8%	37	3%	3.75	-6.3	20	$3
Consist	B	1st Half	79	10	4	10	1	228			291	418	708	8	80	24	0.44	247	28	20	52	116	12%	49	6%	4.10	-2.5	45	$2
LIMA Plan	F	2nd Half	75	5	1	10	0	267			304	347	650	5	83	31	0.31	219	30	21	49	56	3%	12	0%	3.39	-3.8	-9	$1
Rand Var	0	10 Proj	164	18	5	24	2	268			314	419	733	6	82	30	0.36	246	31	21	48	95	8%	67	5%	4.42	-4.0	38	$5

Of all the types of batted balls, fly balls fall for hits least often. You can see how that effect manifested itself in his batting average volatility the past two years. End of lesson.

Doumit,Ryan			AB	R	HR	RBI	SB	Avg	vL	vR	OB	Slg	OPS	bb%	ct%	h%	Eye	xBA	G	L	F	PX	hr/f	SX	SBO	RC/G	RAR	BPV	R$
Pos	2	05 PIT	* 396	56	15	62	3	278	296	243	317	455	772	5	81	31	0.31	274	51	16	33	114	14%	64	9%	4.82	11.7	49	$14
Age	29	06 PIT	* 171	18	6	24	0	222	208	208	292	397	689	9	73	27	0.37	239	46	17	38	118	13%	44	0%	4.01	-1.7	20	$2
Bats	Both	07 PIT	* 305	44	12	47	4	286	246	296	346	487	833	8	77	34	0.40	278	42	21	38	136	13%	77	9%	5.85	12.4	58	$11
Health	F	08 PIT	431	71	15	69	2	318	330	314	352	501	854	5	87	34	0.42	298	41	23	35	116	11%	55	4%	5.77	18.1	70	$19
PT/Exp	D	09 PIT	280	31	10	38	4	250	266	244	300	414	714	7	83	27	0.41	261	42	18	40	106	11%	60	6%	4.20	-0.5	48	$8
Consist	B	1st Half	45	5	2	9	0	244			277	467	743	4	78	27	0.20	251	47	8	44	157	13%	24	0%	4.45	0.3	54	$1
LIMA Plan	D+	2nd Half	235	26	8	29	4	251			304	404	709	7	83	27	0.46	261	41	20	39	97	10%	61	7%	4.17	-0.6	46	$6
Rand Var	+2	10 Proj	395	52	14	57	4	271			323	446	769	7	81	30	0.40	270	43	20	37	115	12%	67	6%	4.91	7.4	52	$13

Fractured wrist in April; when he returned, power was gone. Year-long low h% was just kicking a man while he's down. He still hasn't shown us a full year of success. Pay for the projections; anything more is gravy.

Drew,J.D.			AB	R	HR	RBI	SB	Avg	vL	vR	OB	Slg	OPS	bb%	ct%	h%	Eye	xBA	G	L	F	PX	hr/f	SX	SBO	RC/G	RAR	BPV	R$
Pos	9	05 LA	252	48	15	36	1	286	235	304	406	520	926	17	80	30	1.02	282	46	15	39	142	19%	57	2%	7.30	14.6	87	$11
Age	34	06 LA	494	84	20	100	2	283	244	296	393	498	891	15	79	33	0.84	276	45	19	36	133	14%	76	3%	6.94	30.4	76	$19
Bats	Left	07 BOS	466	84	11	64	4	270	224	286	376	423	799	14	79	32	0.79	263	46	18	37	107	8%	89	4%	5.77	3.7	57	$13
Health	B	08 BOS	368	79	19	64	4	280	284	279	407	519	926	18	78	31	0.99	285	42	18	40	153	17%	99	4%	7.47	22.0	102	$16
PT/Exp	B	09 BOS	452	84	24	68	2	279	272	281	390	522	912	15	76	32	0.75	279	39	20	41	154	17%	65	5%	7.20	24.4	79	$18
Consist	B	1st Half	230	43	10	35	2	265			383	487	870	16	73	32	0.71	268	41	21	38	147	15%	94	5%	6.82	10.0	72	$8
LIMA Plan	B	2nd Half	222	41	14	33	0	293			396	559	955	15	79	32	0.81	290	38	19	43	161	18%	47	5%	7.59	14.3	90	$10
Rand Var	0	10 Proj	442	85	22	69	3	274			388	502	891	16	78	31	0.84	279	41	19	40	145	16%	75	4%	6.93	20.1	83	$17

Other than 1H/2H ct% variance (note effects on his BA), BPIs virtually identical to 2008. You still can't pay full value due to nagging injuries, but this is a stable skill set. Easier to own the more flexible your trannies.

JOSHUA RANDALL

Drew,Stephen			AB	R	HR	RBI	SB	Avg	vL	vR	OB	Slg	OPS	bb%	ct%	h%	Eye	xBA	G	L	F	PX	hr/f	SX	SBO	RC/G	RAR	BPV	R$
Pos	6	05 aa	101	10	3	10	2	198			277	327	604	10	74	24	0.42	0				90		54	21%	2.85	-4.6	7	$1
Age	27	06 ARI	* 551	69	16	62	4	279	350	308	328	452	780	7	84	31	0.45	270	36	24	40	98	9%	89	6%	5.07	11.2	57	$15
Bats	Left	07 ARI	543	60	12	60	9	238	246	235	313	370	684	10	82	27	0.60	239	38	16	46	85	6%	96	6%	4.07	-6.1	45	$9
Health	A	08 ARI	611	91	21	67	3	291	267	300	336	502	838	6	82	33	0.38	280	35	23	43	132	10%	102	4%	5.76	19.3	79	$20
PT/Exp	A	09 ARI	533	71	12	65	5	261	200	282	323	428	751	8	84	29	0.56	260	39	19	42	102	6%	113	4%	4.88	3.3	69	$14
Consist	C	1st Half	218	30	5	31	2	248			314	399	713	9	80	29	0.49	246	35	19	46	104	6%	87	6%	4.38	-1.8	50	$5
LIMA Plan	B	2nd Half	315	41	7	34	3	270			329	448	777	8	86	30	0.64	270	41	19	40	101	6%	109	4%	5.21	5.0	76	$8
Rand Var	0	10 Proj	611	90	19	71	6	280			338	466	804	8	83	31	0.51	266	38	20	43	114	9%	116	5%	5.45	15.2	74	$19

Off year, but two things to note:
- Hamstring injury likely culprit for .211 BA in Apr/May; hit .274 with 86% ct% after that.
- In 2008-09, hit .309 w/.533 Slg in 518 AB in lead-off role.
Still has big potential. Invest.

Dukes,Elijah			AB	R	HR	RBI	SB	Avg	vL	vR	OB	Slg	OPS	bb%	ct%	h%	Eye	xBA	G	L	F	PX	hr/f	SX	SBO	RC/G	RAR	BPV	R$
Pos	98	05 aa	443	61	14	61	16	257			315	413	728	8	84	28	0.54	0				93		113	24%	4.47	-6.8	63	$15
Age	26	06 aaa	283	57	9	49	8	289			383	471	854	13	85	31	1.00	0				103		122	13%	6.34	9.0	86	$13
Bats	Right	07 TAM	184	27	10	21	2	190	260	164	313	391	705	15	76	19	0.75	238	42	11	48	118	15%	79	11%	4.32	-7.1	55	$3
Health	C	08 WAS	* 323	55	14	49	14	257	231	278	368	455	824	15	70	33	0.58	251	47	18	35	143	18%	107	19%	6.18	9.6	57	$14
PT/Exp	D	09 WAS	* 432	45	10	66	7	250	243	252	333	401	733	11	81	29	0.65	250	44	16	40	102	7%	71	15%	4.76	-1.6	51	$11
Consist	D	1st Half	193	18	6	30	2	244			308	415	723	9	76	29	0.38	248	38	19	43	123	10%	55	20%	4.45	-2.6	36	$5
LIMA Plan	C+	2nd Half	239	27	4	36	5	255			351	389	741	13	85	29	1.00	253	50	13	37	87	5%	85	12%	5.05	1.2	64	$6
Rand Var	+1	10 Proj	459	61	16	68	9	257			351	433	784	13	78	30	0.66	252	45	16	40	114	12%	84	14%	5.41	6.1	56	$15

PRO: Reversed ct% trend, plus power in 1H, strong 2H Eye.
CON: No power in 2H, 3-for-13 in SB attempts, has .242 BA, .421 Slg in 824 career AB.
Prospects have dimmed, but he's still too young to give up on.

Duncan,Chris			AB	R	HR	RBI	SB	Avg	vL	vR	OB	Slg	OPS	bb%	ct%	h%	Eye	xBA	G	L	F	PX	hr/f	SX	SBO	RC/G	RAR	BPV	R$
Pos	7	05 aaa	430	45	16	58	1	233			314	395	709	11	80	25	0.61	0				104		33	4%	4.32	-9.3	38	$8
Age	29	06 STL	* 461	81	28	71	1	277	170	318	351	519	870	10	75	31	0.45	275	44	21	35	148	23%	63	2%	6.34	14.4	59	$18
Bats	Left	07 STL	375	51	21	70	2	259	213	271	353	480	833	13	67	33	0.45	248	40	18	42	160	20%	36	3%	6.25	9.8	35	$13
Health	B	08 STL	222	26	6	27	2	248	147	266	348	365	713	13	77	30	0.65	236	42	23	36	79	10%	42	4%	4.49	-6.1	10	$5
PT/Exp	D	09 2TM	* 345	32	7	41	0	214	231	226	309	338	647	12	74	27	0.53	225	51	15	35	90	8%	45	1%	3.63	-17.6	9	$3
Consist	C	1st Half	236	25	5	31	0	246			341	390	731	13	75	31	0.59	238	49	15	36	103	8%	52	1%	4.80	-3.4	27	$4
LIMA Plan	F	2nd Half	109	7	2	10	0	146			238	227	466	11	72	19	0.43	166	73	7	20	60	11%	14	0%	0.99	-15.7	-36	($1)
Rand Var	+4	10 Proj	123	13	5	16	0	244			335	396	731	12	74	30	0.52	233	46	18	36	103	14%	26	2%	4.65	-2.1	11	$3

159 PX and 46% FB in April, 72 PX and 30% FB after that. Sure seems like he wasn't 100% healthy. xBA, OPS in four-year slide, yet power skills and age give him sleeper potential.
UP: 2006. DN: Chris who?

Dunn,Adam			AB	R	HR	RBI	SB	Avg	vL	vR	OB	Slg	OPS	bb%	ct%	h%	Eye	xBA	G	L	F	PX	hr/f	SX	SBO	RC/G	RAR	BPV	R$
Pos	379	05 CIN	543	107	40	101	4	247	199	273	377	540	917	17	69	28	0.68	280	36	17	47	209	23%	77	4%	7.50	30.6	103	$24
Age	30	06 CIN	561	99	40	92	7	234	270	215	361	490	851	17	65	28	0.58	246	28	24	49	176	22%	66	4%	6.63	10.6	58	$20
Bats	Left	07 CIN	522	101	40	106	9	264	239	278	384	554	937	16	68	31	0.61	274	35	19	47	197	24%	87	6%	7.76	24.7	92	$26
Health	A	08 2NL	517	79	40	100	2	236	195	253	382	513	894	19	68	26	0.74	259	36	18	46	190	25%	31	2%	7.19	22.6	75	$20
PT/Exp	A	09 WAS	546	81	38	105	0	267	268	267	396	529	925	18	68	33	0.66	260	31	20	49	189	21%	14	1%	7.71	18.9	63	$24
Consist	B	1st Half	269	36	20	56	0	260			397	528	925	18	68	31	0.70	257	30	20	50	189	22%	10	1%	7.69	9.3	64	$12
LIMA Plan	B	2nd Half	277	45	18	49	0	274			395	531	925	17	68	34	0.61	262	32	21	47	190	21%	20	0%	7.73	9.6	63	$12
Rand Var	-2	10 Proj	548	88	39	105	2	257			388	520	908	18	68	31	0.66	259	33	20	47	186	22%	38	2%	7.43	19.9	69	$23

Apart from speed, which seems to be gone for good, his skills are remarkably stable. BA remains a game of roulette; value him at the .240 level, and let anything more be a bonus.

Dye,Jermaine			AB	R	HR	RBI	SB	Avg	vL	vR	OB	Slg	OPS	bb%	ct%	h%	Eye	xBA	G	L	F	PX	hr/f	SX	SBO	RC/G	RAR	BPV	R$
Pos	9	05 CHW	529	74	31	86	11	274	252	278	324	512	836	7	81	29	0.39	287	38	21	41	145	18%	86	12%	5.60	13.8	83	$22
Age	36	06 CHW	539	103	44	120	7	315	337	305	383	622	1004	10	78	33	0.50	301	39	20	40	179	26%	84	6%	7.86	32.1	102	$31
Bats	Right	07 CHW	508	68	28	78	2	254	292	241	315	486	801	8	79	27	0.42	285	35	19	46	152	15%	42	3%	5.29	-3.2	68	$15
Health	A	08 CHW	590	96	34	96	3	292	285	294	341	541	881	7	82	31	0.42	300	35	22	43	154	16%	67	4%	6.17	13.3	89	$25
PT/Exp	A	09 CHW	503	78	27	81	0	250	292	236	335	453	788	11	79	27	0.59	253	40	17	44	119	16%	37	1%	5.26	-1.1	45	$15
Consist	B	1st Half	255	46	18	48	0	294			359	565	924	9	78	31	0.46	283	42	16	42	159	21%	48	3%	6.85	10.8	74	$12
LIMA Plan	C+	2nd Half	248	32	9	33	0	206			311	339	650	13	79	22	0.73	224	37	18	45	77	10%	25	0%	3.64	-13.1	14	$3
Rand Var	+2	10 Proj	506	77	28	81	2	261			332	478	810	10	80	28	0.53	271	37	19	44	131	16%	52	3%	5.46	1.6	61	$17

Was it a bad back or a case of Alex Rios envy that caused 2H collapse? Given the strength of his 1H skills and overall history, you gotta figure he was playing hurt. Should rebound, but backs can be tricky (ask Joe Crede).

Eckstein,David			AB	R	HR	RBI	SB	Avg	vL	vR	OB	Slg	OPS	bb%	ct%	h%	Eye	xBA	G	L	F	PX	hr/f	SX	SBO	RC/G	RAR	BPV	R$
Pos	4	05 STL	630	90	8	61	11	294	262	306	353	395	748	8	93	31	1.32	289	46	23	31	59	4%	100	9%	5.00	7.7	68	$19
Age	35	06 STL	500	68	2	23	7	292	280	298	333	344	677	6	92	32	0.76	261	49	22	29	34	1%	67	8%	4.00	-8.4	28	$10
Bats	Right	07 STL	434	58	3	31	10	309	298	314	345	382	727	5	95	32	1.09	275	41	22	37	49	2%	82	8%	4.59	-1.3	56	$13
Health	C	08 2TM	324	32	2	27	2	265	313	246	330	349	678	9	90	29	0.97	269	51	20	28	61	2%	42	3%	4.20	-5.9	41	$5
PT/Exp	B	09 SD	503	64	2	50	3	260	244	268	314	334	648	7	91	28	0.85	257	46	19	34	52	1%	74	3%	3.79	-10.9	44	$9
Consist	A	1st Half	274	29	1	31	2	270			320	343	663	7	93	29	1.00	264	43	22	36	51	1%	63	4%	3.99	-4.3	46	$5
LIMA Plan	D	2nd Half	229	35	1	19	1	249			306	323	630	8	89	28	0.73	248	51	17	33	53	1%	76	2%	3.54	-6.7	37	$4
Rand Var	0	10 Proj	408	51	2	35	4	257			312	333	644	7	91	28	0.89	263	47	20	33	52	2%	75	5%	3.76	-10.3	46	$7

How many more of these lousy seasons will it take for teams to realize the guy who hit .300 ain't coming back? Eye, xBA both in decline, and RC/G and RAR tell the story: he's a drain on offenses, real or fanalytic.

Ellis,Mark			AB	R	HR	RBI	SB	Avg	vL	vR	OB	Slg	OPS	bb%	ct%	h%	Eye	xBA	G	L	F	PX	hr/f	SX	SBO	RC/G	RAR	BPV	R$
Pos	4	05 OAK	434	76	13	52	1	316	313	318	379	477	856	9	88	34	0.86	277	47	18	35	93	10%	78	3%	6.10	23.1	71	$17
Age	33	06 OAK	441	64	11	52	4	249	278	242	312	385	697	8	83	28	0.53	249	39	19	42	87	7%	82	4%	4.15	0.3	44	$9
Bats	Right	07 OAK	583	84	19	76	9	276	313	263	327	441	768	7	84	30	0.47	256	32	18	50	104	8%	89	9%	4.90	15.0	61	$18
Health	C	08 OAK	442	55	12	41	14	233	176	256	315	373	688	11	85	25	0.82	249	34	20	46	85	7%	108	13%	4.22	-9.0	65	$10
PT/Exp	B	09 OAK	377	52	10	61	10	263	260	264	305	403	708	6	86	28	0.43	268	40	20	39	87	8%	83	15%	4.16	-8.5	51	$13
Consist	A	1st Half	77	8	2	13	2	208			256	325	581	6	82	23	0.36	256	48	21	32	72	10%	65	19%	2.56	-5.8	19	$1
LIMA Plan	C	2nd Half	300	44	8	48	8	277			318	423	741	6	87	30	0.45	270	38	20	41	91	7%	84	14%	4.55	-3.3	58	$11
Rand Var	0	10 Proj	462	62	13	63	11	253			309	392	702	8	85	27	0.54	258	38	20	42	86	8%	89	12%	4.17	-7.3	52	$13

Battled a calf injury for most of 1H, so focus on the 2H skills: best ct%, xBA since 2005, and 8-for-10 in SB attempts. His upside is still a 20/20 season, but that may require an AB total he's incapable of reaching.

Ellsbury,Jacoby			AB	R	HR	RBI	SB	Avg	vL	vR	OB	Slg	OPS	bb%	ct%	h%	Eye	xBA	G	L	F	PX	hr/f	SX	SBO	RC/G	RAR	BPV	R$
Pos	8	05	0	0	0	0	0	0							0			0						0					
Age	27	06 aa	198	25	3	16	14	289			358	407	765	10	89	32	0.94	0				70		113	35%	5.17	3.7	66	$7
Bats	Left	07 BOS	* 552	89	5	53	44	312	346	356	358	418	776	7	89	35	0.63	287	52	19	29	70	4%	143	31%	5.12	9.0	68	$25
Health	A	08 BOS	554	98	9	47	50	280	295	275	329	394	723	7	86	31	0.51	274	52	20	28	69	7%	161	39%	4.44	-14.7	61	$25
PT/Exp	A	09 BOS	624	94	8	60	70	301	318	294	352	415	767	7	88	33	0.66	270	50	18	32	65	5%	157	43%	5.03	6.9	68	$33
Consist	B	1st Half	299	41	4	26	33	304			348	405	753	6	90	33	0.69	267	51	17	33	57	5%	140	42%	4.81	1.4	63	$16
LIMA Plan	B	2nd Half	325	53	4	34	37	298			356	425	781	8	86	34	0.64	271	49	19	32	72	4%	168	43%	5.25	5.6	71	$18
Rand Var	-2	10 Proj	616	97	8	57	60	292			345	407	751	7	87	32	0.64	274	51	19	31	68	5%	157	40%	4.85	1.2	68	$30

Keeps increasing SB totals by raising SBO and success rate (85% last year), but he's running out of room to grow. And if BA regresses (see xBA), that could take a bite out of OB, making 2010 a lot more like 2008.

Encarnacion,Edwin			AB	R	HR	RBI	SB	Avg	vL	vR	OB	Slg	OPS	bb%	ct%	h%	Eye	xBA	G	L	F	PX	hr/f	SX	SBO	RC/G	RAR	BPV	R$
Pos	5	05 CIN	* 501	63	23	77	9	268	246	234	331	479	810	9	80	30	0.47	298	41	24	35	142	16%	70	9%	5.47	10.0	73	$18
Age	27	06 CIN	406	60	15	72	6	276	248	287	342	473	815	9	81	31	0.53	280	41	21	37	127	12%	72	9%	5.62	1.5	66	$14
Bats	Right	07 CIN	* 548	77	19	82	9	297	284	291	345	456	801	7	84	33	0.44	261	38	19	43	97	10%	78	6%	5.25	-5.5	50	$21
Health	D	08 CIN	506	75	26	68	1	251	292	235	332	466	798	11	80	27	0.60	257	34	16	50	135	13%	51	1%	5.39	0.3	66	$15
PT/Exp	C	09 2TM	293	35	13	39	2	225	250	219	312	410	722	11	77	25	0.55	243	37	17	46	113	13%	67	4%	4.45	-4.1	43	$6
Consist	B	1st Half	63	2	1	6	1	127			276	190	467	17	70	16	0.68	162	52	11	36	45	6%	21	11%	1.06	-8.5	-42	($1)
LIMA Plan	C	2nd Half	230	33	12	33	1	252			323	470	792	9	79	27	0.50	260	33	19	48	130	14%	74	2%	5.25	2.3	63	$7
Rand Var	+3	10 Proj	499	60	22	67	5	257			337	446	783	11	78	29	0.56	251	38	17	45	118	13%	61	5%	5.23	3.1	50	$14

PRO: Solid 2H, including best hr/f since 2005, sustained bb% growth, still only 27.
CON: Long-term ct%, LD%, and xBA erosion.
After injury-marred year, enough skill here to merit speculation.

BRANDON KRUSE

Erstad,Darin

			AB	R	HR	RBI	SB	Avg	vL	vR	OB	Slg	OPS	bb%	ct%	h%	Eye	xBA	G	L	F	PX	hr/f	SX	SBO	RC/G	RAR	BPV	R$
Pos	7	05 ANA	609	86	7	66	10	273	232	291	325	371	696	7	82	32	0.43	257	48	22	30	71	5%	100	8%	4.10	-10.8	31	$15
Age	36	06 LAA	95	8	0	5	1	221	192	232	267	326	594	6	81	27	0.33	235	51	12	37	82	0%	82	11%	2.91	-6.7	28	($0)
Bats	Left	07 CHW	* 357	36	4	34	7	231	157	282	295	306	601	8	83	27	0.55	246	53	17	30	52	4%	75	9%	3.03	-21.8	16	$4
Health	D	08 HOU	322	49	4	31	2	276	243	286	307	363	670	4	79	34	0.21	257	51	25	24	65	7%	63	6%	3.55	-17.3	-3	$8
PT/Exp	D	09 HOU	134	13	2	11	0	194	154	198	270	328	599	9	77	24	0.45	247	56	15	29	96	7%	79	7%	2.97	-11.2	29	$0
Consist	B	1st Half	80	10	1	5	0	163			239	263	501	9	79	19	0.47	232	60	11	29	67	5%	100	13%	1.72	-10.4	19	($1)
LIMA Plan	F	2nd Half	54	3	1	6	0	241			317	426	743	10	74	31	0.43	271	50	20	30	142	8%	53	0%	4.96	-1.0	48	$1
Rand Var	+5	10 Proj	**129**	**14**	**2**	**12**	**1**	**233**			**293**	**352**	**645**	**8**	**78**	**28**	**0.39**	**254**	**52**	**19**	**29**	**87**	**6%**	**73**	**6%**	**3.49**	**-7.8**	**23**	**$1**

This year's health issues...
- Stress fracture in cheek
- Cortisone shot in shoulder
- Strained hamstring
- Back spasms

The net result?
- Amputated fanalytic interest

Escobar,Alcides

			AB	R	HR	RBI	SB	Avg	vL	vR	OB	Slg	OPS	bb%	ct%	h%	Eye	xBA	G	L	F	PX	hr/f	SX	SBO	RC/G	RAR	BPV	R$
Pos	6	05	0	0	0	0	0	0							0			0						0					
Age	23	06	0	0	0	0	0	0							0			0						0					
Bats	Right	07 aa	226	24	1	25	3	274			306	339	646	4	86	31	0.33	0				38		93	10%	3.42	-6.3	14	$4
Health	A	08 aa	547	77	7	61	28	292			324	384	708	5	88	32	0.39	0				58		120	25%	4.14	-5.3	45	$21
PT/Exp	D	09 MIL	* 555	81	4	38	37	274	480	260	312	359	671	5	87	31	0.43	256	52	17	31	56	3%	134	34%	3.80	-14.1	46	$20
Consist	B	1st Half	327	46	2	22	22	269			309	370	679	5	87	31	0.43	0				71		138	37%	3.93	-7.0	57	$11
LIMA Plan	D+	2nd Half	228	35	2	16	15	281			317	342	659	5	88	31	0.43	241	52	17	31	35	3%	129	31%	3.60	-7.1	29	$9
Rand Var	-1	10 Proj	**366**	**51**	**3**	**33**	**20**	**281**			**316**	**361**	**677**	**5**	**87**	**32**	**0.40**	**252**	**52**	**17**	**31**	**49**	**3%**	**126**	**27%**	**3.81**	**-8.0**	**38**	**$13**

1-11-.304 in 125 AB at MIL. Top prospect didn't show any pop during first extended MLB look, but all is not lost. SX trend, good ct% are solid building blocks. If small bb% gains continue...
UP: 30 SB

Escobar,Yunel

			AB	R	HR	RBI	SB	Avg	vL	vR	OB	Slg	OPS	bb%	ct%	h%	Eye	xBA	G	L	F	PX	hr/f	SX	SBO	RC/G	RAR	BPV	R$
Pos	6	05	0	0	0	0	0	0							0			0						0					
Age	27	06 aa	428	51	2	43	7	249			337	322	658	12	82	30	0.73	0				51		78	11%	3.93	-5.9	17	$6
Bats	Right	07 ATL	* 499	72	7	54	11	323	355	303	373	443	816	7	86	36	0.58	296	56	21	23	81	7%	83	11%	5.58	15.2	52	$18
Health	A	08 ATL	514	71	10	60	2	288	262	299	361	401	762	10	88	31	0.95	267	58	17	25	69	9%	51	4%	5.12	7.1	45	$15
PT/Exp	B	09 ATL	528	89	14	76	5	299	232	327	368	436	803	10	88	32	0.92	281	50	20	30	82	10%	74	5%	5.53	12.8	63	$21
Consist	A	1st Half	259	39	7	40	3	293			337	432	769	6	89	31	0.59	282	52	18	30	87	10%	64	6%	4.91	1.8	58	$10
LIMA Plan	C+	2nd Half	269	50	7	36	2	305			395	439	833	13	88	33	1.21	278	49	21	30	78	10%	75	5%	6.09	10.7	64	$11
Rand Var	-1	10 Proj	**567**	**87**	**12**	**72**	**6**	**296**			**366**	**420**	**786**	**10**	**87**	**32**	**0.86**	**278**	**53**	**19**	**28**	**77**	**9%**	**77**	**6%**	**5.37**	**12.7**	**55**	**$19**

PRO:
- Maintaining solid contact rate
- bb% jump in 2nd half

CON:
- Mediocre PX, SX
- Increasing struggles vs LHers

Speculate on 2H, expect '09.

Ethier,Andre

			AB	R	HR	RBI	SB	Avg	vL	vR	OB	Slg	OPS	bb%	ct%	h%	Eye	xBA	G	L	F	PX	hr/f	SX	SBO	RC/G	RAR	BPV	R$
Pos	9	05 a/a	516	81	14	64	1	281			332	424	756	7	85	31	0.52	0				91		58	4%	4.78	-2.8	48	$16
Age	28	06 LA	* 482	62	12	64	7	307	351	298	366	469	835	9	81	36	0.50	262	41	22	37	95	8%	98	9%	5.87	14.6	50	$17
Bats	Left	07 LA	447	50	13	64	0	284	279	286	351	452	803	9	85	31	0.68	276	46	18	36	106	10%	30	3%	5.50	7.8	54	$12
Health	A	08 LA	525	90	20	77	6	305	243	326	375	510	885	10	83	34	0.67	302	41	27	32	129	14%	95	6%	6.51	19.1	87	$23
PT/Exp	A	09 LA	596	92	31	106	6	272	194	302	350	508	859	11	81	29	0.62	289	38	20	42	151	16%	74	6%	6.18	22.3	89	$25
Consist	B	1st Half	280	40	15	52	4	257			342	482	824	11	79	28	0.62	269	38	17	45	143	15%	66	9%	5.75	7.2	76	$11
LIMA Plan	B	2nd Half	316	52	16	54	2	285			358	532	890	10	82	31	0.62	305	38	23	38	159	16%	75	4%	6.54	14.8	99	$14
Rand Var	+2	10 Proj	**589**	**89**	**30**	**104**	**5**	**285**			**357**	**521**	**878**	**10**	**82**	**30**	**0.63**	**299**	**40**	**22**	**38**	**146**	**16%**	**76**	**6%**	**6.36**	**23.2**	**90**	**$25**

A breakout w/full skill support. And he did it despite deep struggles vs. LHers and on road (.238 BA, .389 Slg). PX trend and FB spike say there's more power on the horizon.
UP: 40 HR, if he masters LHers.

Evans,Nick

			AB	R	HR	RBI	SB	Avg	vL	vR	OB	Slg	OPS	bb%	ct%	h%	Eye	xBA	G	L	F	PX	hr/f	SX	SBO	RC/G	RAR	BPV	R$
Pos	7	05	0	0	0	0	0	0							0			0						0					
Age	24	06	0	0	0	0	0	0							0			0						0					
Bats	Right	07	0	0	0	0	0	0							0			0						0					
Health	A	08 NYM	* 405	62	13	54	2	274	319	135	323	462	784	7	81	31	0.37	282	44	23	33	121	12%	98	3%	5.12	-3.5	65	$13
PT/Exp	F	09 NYM	* 407	38	11	37	2	203	321	162	258	355	614	7	80	23	0.37	246	49	13	38	103	9%	71	3%	3.02	-32.3	38	$3
Consist	F	1st Half	198	19	6	17	2	184			254	343	597	9	78	21	0.43	299	57	29	14	110	27%	70	5%	2.83	-17.3	40	$1
LIMA Plan	F	2nd Half	209	20	5	21	0	221			263	367	630	5	81	25	0.30	216	45	6	48	97	6%	54	0%	3.18	-15.2	31	$2
Rand Var	+3	10 Proj	**163**	**19**	**5**	**18**	**1**	**245**			**296**	**417**	**713**	**7**	**80**	**28**	**0.36**	**266**	**46**	**18**	**36**	**112**	**10%**	**85**	**3%**	**4.25**	**-5.9**	**51**	**$3**

1-7-.231 in 65 AB at NYM. Hit LHers hard in a small data sample for 2nd straight year. h% rebound will help BA, and he does own that '08 PX. But as a GBer with mediocre plate approach, his upside is limited.

Everett,Adam

			AB	R	HR	RBI	SB	Avg	vL	vR	OB	Slg	OPS	bb%	ct%	h%	Eye	xBA	G	L	F	PX	hr/f	SX	SBO	RC/G	RAR	BPV	R$
Pos	6	05 HOU	549	58	11	54	21	248	227	255	282	364	646	5	81	29	0.25	242	39	19	42	79	6%	107	23%	3.30	-10.9	32	$14
Age	33	06 HOU	514	52	6	59	9	239	250	237	286	352	639	6	86	27	0.48	245	37	20	43	69	3%	95	13%	3.48	-13.7	43	$8
Bats	Right	07 HOU	220	18	2	15	4	232	214	238	278	318	596	6	86	26	0.45	243	45	17	38	58	3%	70	12%	2.95	-10.1	25	$2
Health	F	08 MIN	127	19	2	20	0	213	310	184	281	323	603	9	88	23	0.80	236	39	15	46	68	4%	71	0%	3.26	-4.2	48	$2
PT/Exp	F	09 DET	345	43	3	44	5	238	273	218	283	325	608	6	82	28	0.36	235	43	18	40	64	3%	72	9%	3.00	-15.1	16	$6
Consist	A	1st Half	178	26	2	27	3	275			317	371	688	6	86	31	0.44	259	47	19	34	66	4%	72	9%	3.99	-2.4	32	$5
LIMA Plan	F	2nd Half	167	17	1	17	2	198			247	275	523	6	78	25	0.31	209	37	16	47	62	2%	63	9%	1.87	-13.7	-3	$0
Rand Var	-1	10 Proj	**294**	**35**	**3**	**36**	**4**	**228**			**279**	**322**	**601**	**7**	**84**	**26**	**0.44**	**234**	**41**	**17**	**42**	**65**	**3%**	**81**	**8%**	**2.98**	**-12.7**	**28**	**$4**

Took all-glove, no-bat profile to new depths with this 2H. And his h% was actually higher than his previous norms. No power, no speed, no BA, and no signs of either emerging. At least he's consistent.

Everidge,Tommy

			AB	R	HR	RBI	SB	Avg	vL	vR	OB	Slg	OPS	bb%	ct%	h%	Eye	xBA	G	L	F	PX	hr/f	SX	SBO	RC/G	RAR	BPV	R$
Pos	3	05	0	0	0	0	0	0							0			0						0					
Age	27	06	0	0	0	0	0	0							0			0						0					
Bats	Right	07	0	0	0	0	0	0							0			0						0					
Health	A	08 aa	531	65	15	84	0	227			280	365	645	7	81	26	0.38	0				93		33	0%	3.37	-34.3	22	$10
PT/Exp	F	09 OAK	* 515	68	15	71	0	257	333	180	314	410	724	8	86	27	0.61	276	43	20	36	93	9%	37	1%	4.48	-18.6	48	$12
Consist	C	1st Half	329	41	7	48	0	249			302	383	685	7	88	26	0.62	0				82		44	1%	4.04	-16.2	46	$6
LIMA Plan	F	2nd Half	186	27	8	24	0	270			335	458	794	9	84	29	0.60	282	43	20	36	114	13%	29	0%	5.29	-2.3	55	$5
Rand Var	+1	10 Proj	**97**	**13**	**3**	**14**	**0**	**247**			**305**	**402**	**707**	**8**	**84**	**27**	**0.50**	**270**	**43**	**20**	**36**	**99**	**10%**	**34**	**0%**	**4.21**	**-3.6**	**41**	**$2**

2-7-.224 in 85 AB at OAK. Made his MLB debut at age 26 and never was roster-worthy. As a 1Bman, he just doesn't have the power potential worth speculating on. His upside is as a high contact, no pop type.

Feliz,Pedro

			AB	R	HR	RBI	SB	Avg	vL	vR	OB	Slg	OPS	bb%	ct%	h%	Eye	xBA	G	L	F	PX	hr/f	SX	SBO	RC/G	RAR	BPV	R$
Pos	5	05 SF	569	69	20	81	0	250	271	245	297	422	718	6	82	27	0.37	265	44	17	39	108	11%	55	2%	4.24	-9.0	46	$14
Age	35	06 SF	603	75	22	98	1	244	212	253	283	428	711	5	81	27	0.29	256	40	16	43	110	10%	69	2%	4.10	-25.0	47	$14
Bats	Right	07 SF	557	61	20	72	2	253	257	252	290	418	708	5	87	26	0.41	266	43	15	42	95	10%	53	3%	4.10	-24.7	53	$12
Health	B	08 PHI	425	43	14	58	0	249	288	231	303	402	706	7	87	26	0.61	256	47	16	37	89	10%	34	0%	4.22	-14.4	47	$9
PT/Exp	A	09 PHI	580	62	12	82	0	266	208	282	307	386	694	6	88	28	0.51	268	44	21	35	76	7%	40	1%	4.05	-18.2	39	$14
Consist	A	1st Half	264	30	5	39	0	292			342	420	762	7	88	32	0.63	278	40	24	36	84	6%	38	0%	4.93	-1.5	47	$8
LIMA Plan	D+	2nd Half	316	32	7	43	0	244			278	358	636	5	89	26	0.42	259	47	19	34	69	7%	39	1%	3.32	-17.1	32	$6
Rand Var	0	10 Proj	**499**	**53**	**11**	**69**	**0**	**257**			**300**	**380**	**680**	**6**	**87**	**28**	**0.49**	**258**	**44**	**19**	**37**	**76**	**7%**	**46**	**1%**	**3.89**	**-20.2**	**38**	**$10**

Three reasons why his full-time days are numbered...
- Steep PX decline
- Hitting fewer fly balls
- Bottom fell out in 2nd half

3Bman with a .250 BA, 10-15 HR profile can't be hidden for long.

Fielder,Prince

			AB	R	HR	RBI	SB	Avg	vL	vR	OB	Slg	OPS	bb%	ct%	h%	Eye	xBA	G	L	F	PX	hr/f	SX	SBO	RC/G	RAR	BPV	R$
Pos	3	05 MIL	* 437	58	25	80	7	281	500	281	351	510	860	10	81	30	0.58	330	37	35	28	142	25%	49	11%	6.06	5.8	75	$19
Age	26	06 MIL	569	82	28	81	7	271	247	280	339	483	822	9	78	30	0.47	268	42	18	39	132	16%	70	6%	5.66	-5.6	59	$19
Bats	Left	07 MIL	573	109	50	119	2	288	261	301	385	618	1002	14	79	29	0.74	317	35	19	46	196	24%	53	2%	8.01	30.2	117	$31
Health	A	08 MIL	588	86	34	102	3	276	239	295	366	507	873	13	77	30	0.63	271	41	19	40	146	19%	55	3%	6.44	11.9	69	$24
PT/Exp	A	09 MIL	591	103	46	141	2	299	292	303	409	602	1012	16	77	32	0.80	295	41	16	43	191	24%	49	2%	8.39	30.7	108	$35
Consist	D	1st Half	278	47	20	74	0	306			419	604	1023	16	76	34	0.82	291	38	16	46	193	20%	43	2%	8.64	16.3	107	$17
LIMA Plan	B	2nd Half	313	56	26	67	2	294			401	601	1002	15	77	31	0.78	299	43	17	40	190	27%	54	3%	8.16	14.4	108	$18
Rand Var	-2	10 Proj	**585**	**97**	**42**	**122**	**3**	**289**			**388**	**569**	**957**	**14**	**77**	**31**	**0.72**	**290**	**40**	**18**	**42**	**174**	**22%**	**54**	**3%**	**7.55**	**22.4**	**95**	**$30**

Solved LHers, added bb%, and boom: another elite year. Unless ct% drops out, there's no reason to expect anything less. He's still in his pre-peak years too. And he's as durable as they come. Ride him.

STEPHEN NICKRAND

Fields,Josh

			AB	R	HR	RBI	SB	Avg	vL	vR	OB	Slg	OPS	bb%	ct%	h%	Eye	xBA	G	L	F	PX	hr/f	SX	SBO	RC/G	RAR	BPV	R$
Pos	5	05 aa	474	55	14	57	5	207			267	338	605	8	73	25	0.31	0				95		60	12%	2.79	-27.8	4	$7
Age	27	06 aaa	482	82	21	66	26	290	167	143	362	500	862	10	72	36	0.41	261	58	8	33	143	18%	126	22%	6.42	15.9	64	$23
Bats	Right	07 CHW *	578	79	34	100	8	251	321	213	333	481	814	11	69	31	0.39	257	41	17	43	166	20%	60	9%	5.82	16.3	49	$20
Health	A	08 CHW *	308	37	9	31	7	212	273	95	290	361	651	10	65	29	0.32	223	67	7	27	118	18%	95	11%	3.62	-12.1	5	$5
PT/Exp	D	09 CHW *	337	43	11	41	3	228	243	213	305	365	670	10	70	29	0.37	215	41	18	41	89	11%	70	9%	3.75	-9.6	-6	$6
Consist	C	1st Half	205	24	6	25	2	234			311	366	677	10	68	32	0.35	212	41	20	39	88	11%	77	9%	3.93	-4.7	-13	$4
LIMA Plan	F	2nd Half	132	19	5	16	1	220			295	364	658	10	73	26	0.40	197	42	8	50	92	10%	53	9%	3.52	-4.8	4	$2
Rand Var	+1	10 Proj	189	25	7	24	3	228			304	387	691	10	69	29	0.36	223	43	16	41	110	13%	80	10%	4.06	-4.1	12	$4

7-30-.222 in 239 AB at CHW. While injury accounted for 2008 dive, no known excuse exists for 2009. Serious ct% issues (68% at CHW), inability to hit RHP remains. Currently a platoon player at best.

Figgins,Chone

			AB	R	HR	RBI	SB	Avg	vL	vR	OB	Slg	OPS	bb%	ct%	h%	Eye	xBA	G	L	F	PX	hr/f	SX	SBO	RC/G	RAR	BPV	R$
Pos	5	05 ANA	642	113	8	57	62	290	244	313	354	397	751	9	84	33	0.63	247	41	22	37	66	4%	162	38%	4.92	7.7	59	$32
Age	32	06 LAA	604	93	9	62	52	267	233	280	338	376	714	10	83	31	0.65	247	44	21	36	65	5%	151	37%	4.48	-9.6	53	$24
Bats	Both	07 LAA	442	81	3	58	41	330	326	331	400	432	832	10	82	40	0.63	279	47	26	26	72	3%	147	32%	6.00	13.7	51	$25
Health	B	08 LAA	453	72	1	22	34	276	272	277	363	318	681	12	82	33	0.78	238	46	24	30	33	1%	109	27%	4.21	-9.0	14	$15
PT/Exp	A	09 LAA	615	114	5	54	42	298	246	323	397	393	790	14	81	36	0.89	248	41	24	36	64	3%	130	24%	5.70	18.0	46	$26
Consist	D	1st Half	295	56	1	23	24	312			394	407	801	12	84	37	0.85	251	39	24	37	61	1%	148	28%	5.75	8.8	55	$14
LIMA Plan	C+	2nd Half	320	58	4	31	18	284			399	381	780	16	79	35	0.91	245	43	23	34	66	5%	107	21%	5.64	9.0	35	$12
Rand Var	-4	10 Proj	550	97	4	47	36	285			376	369	746	13	82	34	0.80	250	43	24	33	57	3%	126	25%	5.05	4.6	38	$21

His 5-yr bb% trend is just what the speed doctor ordered and ushered in return of elite OBP. A healthy AB total, though, hides a five-year SBO slide. LD history and return of PX should sustain his value to 2010 employer.

Flores,Jesus

			AB	R	HR	RBI	SB	Avg	vL	vR	OB	Slg	OPS	bb%	ct%	h%	Eye	xBA	G	L	F	PX	hr/f	SX	SBO	RC/G	RAR	BPV	R$
Pos	2	05	0	0	0	0	0	0							0			0						0					
Age	25	06	0	0	0	0	0	0							0			0						0					
Bats	Right	07 WAS	180	21	4	25	0	244	270	220	299	361	660	7	73	31	0.29	225	50	17	34	86	9%	34	2%	3.55	-4.7	-11	$3
Health	F	08 WAS *	360	30	9	65	0	236	308	238	279	374	654	6	74	30	0.23	244	37	25	38	103	9%	35	1%	3.41	-8.6	0	$7
PT/Exp	F	09 WAS	93	13	4	15	0	301	276	313	375	505	880	11	72	38	0.42	226	28	18	54	131	11%	71	0%	6.71	6.3	37	$4
Consist	D	1st Half	90	13	4	15	0	311			386	522	908	11	71	40	0.42	229	28	18	54	137	12%	71	0%	7.16	7.1	39	$4
LIMA Plan	D	2nd Half	3	0	0	0	0	0			0	0	0	0	100	0	0.00	0	33	0	67	0	0%	0	0%	0.00	-0.8	0	($0)
Rand Var	-5	10 Proj	354	42	11	56	0	266			325	420	745	8	73	34	0.32	231	39	19	42	107	10%	56	1%	4.74	5.0	11	$10

h% makes these AB look better than they were; shoulder trouble derailed his year. September labrum surgery clouds 2010, though Nats insist he'll be ready. Can't consider PX, bb% gains sustainable in this sample size.

Flowers,Tyler

			AB	R	HR	RBI	SB	Avg	vL	vR	OB	Slg	OPS	bb%	ct%	h%	Eye	xBA	G	L	F	PX	hr/f	SX	SBO	RC/G	RAR	BPV	R$
Pos	2	05	0	0	0	0	0	0							0			0						0					
Age	24	06	0	0	0	0	0	0							0			0						0					
Bats	Right	07	0	0	0	0	0	0							0			0						0					
Health	A	08	0	0	0	0	0	0							0			0						0					
PT/Exp	F	09 CHW *	369	62	15	49	3	271	250	125	377	468	845	15	71	34	0.59	249	50	13	38	141	15%	70	2%	6.46	23.1	49	$12
Consist	F	1st Half	233	43	13	37	2	265			386	501	887	17	73	31	0.74	0				155		71	2%	6.97	18.1	73	$9
LIMA Plan	F	2nd Half	136	19	2	12	1	281			360	411	771	11	67	41	0.37	215	50	13	38	116	6%	46	2%	5.55	4.9	-1	$3
Rand Var	-1	10 Proj	122	19	4	14	1	279			373	444	817	13	70	37	0.50	232	50	13	38	130	12%	46	2%	6.10	6.4	25	$4

0-0-.188 in 16 AB at CHW. Plate patience and power are the reasons CHW envisions him as part of their future; ct%, shaky defense the reasons that it might not happen just yet. Still a year or two away.

Fontenot,Mike

			AB	R	HR	RBI	SB	Avg	vL	vR	OB	Slg	OPS	bb%	ct%	h%	Eye	xBA	G	L	F	PX	hr/f	SX	SBO	RC/G	RAR	BPV	R$
Pos	45	05 aaa	375	45	5	30	2	232			315	348	664	11	84	27	0.74	0				76		87	4%	3.98	-4.2	45	$4
Age	30	06 aaa	362	49	8	32	5	271			348	418	766	11	83	31	0.70	0				96		76	8%	5.15	8.3	56	$8
Bats	Left	07 CHC *	445	64	8	53	7	269	212	297	319	409	728	7	83	31	0.43	271	47	19	34	88	6%	110	11%	4.50	-2.6	51	$12
Health	A	08 CHC	243	42	9	40	2	305	333	302	390	514	904	12	79	36	0.67	287	38	24	38	146	12%	71	3%	6.96	14.5	81	$11
PT/Exp	D	09 CHC	377	38	9	43	4	236	212	240	301	377	678	8	78	28	0.42	244	44	18	38	99	8%	72	5%	3.88	-7.4	32	$7
Consist	F	1st Half	214	19	6	27	2	220			304	355	659	11	77	26	0.52	230	45	16	39	91	9%	57	5%	3.69	-5.5	20	$3
LIMA Plan	D	2nd Half	163	19	3	16	2	258			297	405	701	5	80	31	0.27	259	43	19	38	108	6%	80	6%	4.07	-2.2	42	$4
Rand Var	+2	10 Proj	319	42	8	39	4	263			329	419	748	9	80	31	0.48	262	42	20	38	108	8%	85	6%	4.81	1.8	51	$8

Got more AB filling in at 3B, but struggles vs LHP returned and solidified his platoon role. Easy now to attribute 2009 to h%. BA will rebound some, but replacement level looks like his upside.

Fowler,Dexter

			AB	R	HR	RBI	SB	Avg	vL	vR	OB	Slg	OPS	bb%	ct%	h%	Eye	xBA	G	L	F	PX	hr/f	SX	SBO	RC/G	RAR	BPV	R$
Pos	8	05	0	0	0	0	0	0							0			0						0					
Age	24	06	0	0	0	0	0	0							0			0						0					
Bats	Both	07	0	0	0	0	0	0							0			0						0					
Health	A	08 aa	421	66	7	46	14	304			373	449	822	10	86	34	0.77	0				93		116	18%	5.83	9.3	74	$16
PT/Exp	F	09 COL	433	73	4	34	27	266	321	240	364	406	770	13	73	35	0.58	241	42	21	37	106	3%	147	27%	5.52	10.2	51	$15
Consist	A	1st Half	244	35	3	18	14	250			344	381	725	13	73	33	0.53	235	41	20	38	104	4%	129	26%	4.81	0.6	41	$7
LIMA Plan	B+	2nd Half	189	38	1	16	13	286			389	439	828	14	74	38	0.64	248	44	22	34	109	2%	150	27%	6.43	9.4	57	$8
Rand Var	-2	10 Proj	479	81	8	44	29	282			369	438	807	12	78	35	0.64	260	43	21	36	107	6%	150	27%	5.83	16.0	70	$20

Made club out of spring training and held his own. Speed game ahead of power, and he knows how to get on base. If he can improve ct%, both BA and Slg spikes will follow. At 24, there's time.

Fox,Jake

			AB	R	HR	RBI	SB	Avg	vL	vR	OB	Slg	OPS	bb%	ct%	h%	Eye	xBA	G	L	F	PX	hr/f	SX	SBO	RC/G	RAR	BPV	R$
Pos	57	05	0	0	0	0	0	0							0			0						0					
Age	28	06	0	0	0	0	0	0							0			0						0					
Bats	Right	07	0	0	0	0	0	0							0			0						0					
Health	A	08 aa	505	65	23	74	5	237			284	443	726	6	82	25	0.37	0				130		73	7%	4.30	-12.5	69	$13
PT/Exp	F	09 CHC *	380	56	25	85	2	299	250	263	351	574	924	7	80	32	0.39	291	34	19	47	171	18%	60	3%	6.73	16.7	91	$20
Consist	F	1st Half	221	38	16	52	2	342			395	661	1055	8	82	36	0.49	320	35	20	45	193	20%	75	5%	8.30	18.1	125	$15
LIMA Plan	D+	2nd Half	159	18	9	33	0	239			288	453	741	6	76	26	0.29	252	33	19	48	138	15%	18	0%	4.41	-3.4	35	$5
Rand Var	0	10 Proj	322	43	18	61	2	264			313	502	815	7	80	28	0.36	276	33	19	48	148	15%	62	4%	5.37	1.0	73	$12

11-44-.259 in 216 AB at CHC. PRO: Strong FB/PX profile; sustained ct% upon promotion; multi-positional eligibility. CON: borderline bb%; at 27 his peak has almost arrived. Still, potential pop in the end game.

Francisco,Ben

			AB	R	HR	RBI	SB	Avg	vL	vR	OB	Slg	OPS	bb%	ct%	h%	Eye	xBA	G	L	F	PX	hr/f	SX	SBO	RC/G	RAR	BPV	R$
Pos	7	05 a/a	330	39	5	39	12	276			319	400	719	6	85	31	0.41	0				81		119	20%	4.35	-6.5	52	$10
Age	28	06 aaa	515	76	14	56	24	260			318	416	734	8	86	28	0.63	0				93		123	22%	4.62	-9.0	75	$17
Bats	Right	07 CLE *	439	61	13	56	19	287	286	273	340	452	792	8	82	33	0.45	283	47	19	35	112	10%	91	26%	5.24	2.6	63	$17
Health	A	08 CLE *	539	72	16	60	7	255	269	265	318	411	730	9	79	30	0.45	245	34	18	48	109	8%	70	7%	4.52	-5.3	44	$13
PT/Exp	C	09 2TM	405	58	15	46	14	257	247	260	321	447	767	9	80	29	0.46	265	38	18	44	127	11%	93	22%	4.98	-3.6	67	$14
Consist	B	1st Half	241	31	5	23	11	228			290	361	651	8	79	27	0.41	239	40	18	43	93	6%	115	22%	3.54	-12.8	42	$6
LIMA Plan	F	2nd Half	164	27	10	23	3	299			365	573	938	9	80	32	0.53	303	35	20	46	176	17%	56	22%	7.06	8.4	100	$8
Rand Var	0	10 Proj	174	25	6	21	5	270			331	454	785	8	81	30	0.47	264	36	19	45	123	10%	71	19%	5.18	-0.2	61	$6

Four reasons to be optimistic:
1. Just 164 AB, but something clicked in 2H
2. xBA, PX, hr/f growth from 08
3. Now plays in a hitter's park.
4. Backup for an aging LFer

UP: 350 AB, 20 HR

Francoeur,Jeff

			AB	R	HR	RBI	SB	Avg	vL	vR	OB	Slg	OPS	bb%	ct%	h%	Eye	xBA	G	L	F	PX	hr/f	SX	SBO	RC/G	RAR	BPV	R$
Pos	9	05 ATL *	592	76	25	99	14	272	403	268	306	483	789	5	79	31	0.23	282	40	19	41	144	13%	96	17%	5.02	-3.9	71	$23
Age	26	06 ATL	651	83	29	103	1	260	292	248	285	449	733	3	80	29	0.17	259	45	18	37	107	15%	60	5%	4.20	-11.0	32	$18
Bats	Right	07 ATL	642	84	19	105	5	293	317	281	336	444	780	6	80	34	0.33	262	43	19	37	101	10%	55	4%	4.99	2.0	32	$22
Health	A	08 ATL	599	70	11	71	0	239	210	251	285	359	644	6	81	28	0.35	251	45	21	34	82	7%	54	1%	3.39	-32.2	22	$9
PT/Exp	A	09 2NL	593	72	15	76	6	280	344	256	307	423	730	4	84	31	0.25	258	38	21	41	91	7%	84	7%	4.28	-10.2	45	$18
Consist	C	1st Half	283	30	5	33	5	251			281	350	631	4	86	28	0.29	239	41	20	40	60	5%	93	9%	3.17	-14.3	28	$6
LIMA Plan	D+	2nd Half	310	42	10	43	1	306			330	490	821	3	84	34	0.22	276	35	22	43	120	9%	66	6%	5.31	3.7	59	$12
Rand Var	-1	10 Proj	467	58	12	63	3	272			306	418	724	5	82	31	0.28	260	41	20	39	95	8%	69	5%	4.25	-9.7	38	$13

Why his 2H "resurgence" requires quotation marks:
- Has shown he can't sustain 34% hit rate (see 2007)
- bb%, eye only got worse
- Still easily replaceable (RAR)

Talk up that 2H in March, though.

BRENT HERSHEY

Frandsen,Kevin

			AB	R	HR	RBI	SB	Avg	vL	vR	OB	Slg	OPS	bb%	ct%	h%	Eye	xBA	G	L	F	PX	hr/f	SX	SBO	RC/G	RAR	BPV	R$
Pos	4	05 a/a	218	31	3	26	6	280			296	394	690	2	93	29	0.33	0				77		89	23%	3.95	-2.5	67	$7
Age	28	06 SF	*386	47	4	30	5	256	200	217	279	368	647	3	90	28	0.32	254	48	13	39	71	3%	80	14%	3.49	-12.7	50	$6
Bats	Right	07 SF	*331	36	6	36	7	282	262	274	337	392	729	8	91	30	0.92	291	53	21	26	66	7%	65	12%	4.65	-0.5	53	$9
Health	F	08 SF	1	0	0	0	0	0			0	0	0	0	100	0	0.00	0	100	0	0			0	0%	0.00	-0.3	0	($0)
PT/Exp	F	09 SF	*477	56	9	44	3	237	154	135	269	340	609	4	92	24	0.58	258	55	14	32	59	6%	68	6%	3.16	-19.8	48	$7
Consist	F	1st Half	281	32	5	26	2	238			266	340	607	4	91	24	0.46	258	60	12	28	58	8%	72	7%	3.06	-12.5	43	$4
LIMA Plan	F	2nd Half	196	25	4	18	1	237			274	339	613	5	94	24	0.83	258	47	16	37	62	5%	55	4%	3.30	-7.3	53	$3
Rand Var	0	10 Proj	100	12	2	10	1	260			295	360	656	5	92	27	0.63	277	52	19	29	62	6%	59	10%	3.69	-2.7	48	$2

0-1-.140 in 50 AB at SF. A year off an Achilles injury, nothing he did suggested anything more than future bench player. Very good ct%, but little speed and less power. Potentially useful in real-life, not so much in fantasy.

Freel,Ryan

			AB	R	HR	RBI	SB	Avg	vL	vR	OB	Slg	OPS	bb%	ct%	h%	Eye	xBA	G	L	F	PX	hr/f	SX	SBO	RC/G	RAR	BPV	R$
Pos	9	05 CIN	369	69	4	21	36	271	302	263	360	371	731	12	84	31	0.86	283	53	24	24	68	5%	149	37%	4.86	-4.2	62	$17
Age	34	06 CIN	454	67	8	27	37	271	303	261	352	399	751	11	78	33	0.58	251	44	21	35	89	6%	114	34%	4.99	3.0	43	$17
Bats	Right	07 CIN	277	44	3	16	15	245	143	315	292	347	638	6	83	29	0.38	255	49	18	33	66	4%	141	34%	3.38	-12.8	41	$7
Health	F	08 CIN	131	17	0	10	6	298	339	261	338	359	697	6	86	35	0.44	263	56	20	24	51	0%	82	26%	4.12	-4.0	24	$4
PT/Exp	F	09 2TM	*127	17	0	10	5	214	143	226	290	257	547	10	76	28	0.45	195	46	15	39	40	0%	92	17%	2.27	-11.2	-14	$2
Consist	C	1st Half	43	3	0	2	1	140			260	140	400	14	74	19	0.64	137	47	9	44	0	0%	46	8%	0.32	-6.9	-59	($1)
LIMA Plan	F	2nd Half	84	14	0	8	4	252			306	317	623	7	77	33	0.34	229	45	21	34	59	0%	104	23%	3.20	-4.8	4	$2
Rand Var	0	10 Proj	65	10	0	5	4	262			318	342	661	8	81	32	0.45	243	50	18	32	64	2%	97	30%	3.72	-2.8	23	$2

Injuries and attitude are at the center of this descending spiral. As speed was his main asset back in the day when he was a mid-teens earner, he's not likely to get that back at age 34, health or not.

Freese,David

			AB	R	HR	RBI	SB	Avg	vL	vR	OB	Slg	OPS	bb%	ct%	h%	Eye	xBA	G	L	F	PX	hr/f	SX	SBO	RC/G	RAR	BPV	R$
Pos	5	05	0	0	0	0	0	0							0			0						0					
Age	27	06	0	0	0	0	0	0							0			0						0					
Bats	Right	07	0	0	0	0	0	0							0			0						0					
Health	A	08 aa	464	62	18	68	4	251			295	427	723	6	80	28	0.32	0				112		75	6%	4.24	-12.1	47	$13
PT/Exp	F	09 STL	*247	30	8	37	1	257	176	500	311	418	729	7	79	29	0.38	235	44	12	44	111	10%	41	2%	4.41	-5.2	34	$7
Consist	A	1st Half	98	7	1	7	1	190			235	267	502	5	81	22	0.31	175	41	6	53	58	2%	42	5%	1.64	-10.9	-2	($0)
LIMA Plan	D	2nd Half	149	23	7	31	0	300			359	518	877	8	78	34	0.41	296	50	25	25	146	26%	28	0%	6.32	4.8	55	$7
Rand Var	-1	10 Proj	327	41	12	48	2	254			304	424	727	7	80	29	0.35	241	44	12	44	112	10%	66	3%	4.36	-8.7	43	$9

'1-7-.323 in 31 AB at STL. A woeful April and May ankle surgery derailed his season. 2H return, mostly at AAA, showed some gains in bb% and Eye, but fluky h% and hr/f skewed totals. Needs more seasoning.

Fukudome,Kosuke

			AB	R	HR	RBI	SB	Avg	vL	vR	OB	Slg	OPS	bb%	ct%	h%	Eye	xBA	G	L	F	PX	hr/f	SX	SBO	RC/G	RAR	BPV	R$
Pos	89	05 JPN	612	99	17	100	12	257			338	434	772	11	80	30	0.62	0				115		126	10%	5.23	14.6	75	$20
Age	33	06 JPN	578	114	19	101	10	281			349	485	834	10	85	30	0.69	0				123		133	8%	5.91	22.3	98	$22
Bats	Left	07 JPN	269	62	8	47	5	274			398	441	839	17	77	33	0.89	0				123		74	7%	6.43	14.7	64	$11
Health	B	08 CHC	501	79	10	58	12	257	276	251	361	379	740	14	79	31	0.78	252	51	19	30	83	8%	97	9%	4.97	3.4	42	$14
PT/Exp	B	09 CHC	499	79	11	54	6	259	164	270	375	421	796	16	78	31	0.83	276	46	24	30	118	10%	82	10%	5.83	16.4	62	$13
Consist	C	1st Half	223	34	6	24	6	260			377	426	803	16	77	31	0.82	276	46	25	29	117	12%	91	13%	5.90	7.7	63	$7
LIMA Plan	C+	2nd Half	276	45	5	30	0	257			373	417	790	16	78	31	0.84	275	46	23	30	118	8%	65	7%	5.78	8.7	59	$6
Rand Var	+1	10 Proj	417	72	10	53	7	261			372	415	786	15	78	31	0.81	272	48	22	30	108	10%	89	9%	5.64	11.8	59	$13

Unlike 2008, a consistent 1H to 2H. But final results were a near match to 2008. GB% hampers power potential, though strong bb% a boon for OBP and sim leagues. Worth noting: SB and SX took serious 2H dive.

Fuld,Sam

			AB	R	HR	RBI	SB	Avg	vL	vR	OB	Slg	OPS	bb%	ct%	h%	Eye	xBA	G	L	F	PX	hr/f	SX	SBO	RC/G	RAR	BPV	R$
Pos	78	05	0	0	0	0	0	0							0			0						0					
Age	28	06	0	0	0	0	0	0							0			0						0					
Bats	Left	07	0	0	0	0	0	0							0			0						0					
Health	A	08 aa	402	41	5	37	7	215			287	300	587	9	89	23	0.91	0				54		70	18%	3.12	-25.8	40	$4
PT/Exp	F	09 CHC	*425	65	3	27	19	252	308	296	325	355	680	10	92	27	1.37	290	47	25	28	61	3%	136	21%	4.37	-15.1	80	$11
Consist	C	1st Half	287	42	0	21	15	242			304	333	637	8	92	26	1.14	0				57		147	29%	3.85	-15.0	78	$7
LIMA Plan	D	2nd Half	138	22	3	7	4	274			368	399	766	13	92	28	1.83	293	49	23	28	68	8%	107	8%	5.45	-0.4	82	$4
Rand Var	+3	10 Proj	63	8	1	4	2	238			316	352	668	10	91	25	1.23	290	48	24	28	67	5%	112	17%	4.21	-2.4	73	$1

1-2-.199 in 97 AB in CHC. Young player quandary: Needs to prove that two-season h% trend is an aberration, but how will he get the AB? With his elite approach, SB would follow. But he'd still be one-dimensional.

Furcal,Rafael

			AB	R	HR	RBI	SB	Avg	vL	vR	OB	Slg	OPS	bb%	ct%	h%	Eye	xBA	G	L	F	PX	hr/f	SX	SBO	RC/G	RAR	BPV	R$
Pos	6	05 ATL	616	100	12	58	46	284	288	280	350	429	778	9	87	31	0.79	295	47	24	30	86	8%	163	31%	5.27	23.1	87	$29
Age	32	06 LA	654	113	15	63	37	300	324	293	370	445	815	10	85	33	0.74	279	50	21	29	83	9%	133	23%	5.70	24.8	69	$28
Bats	Both	07 LA	581	87	6	47	25	270	313	254	333	355	688	9	88	30	0.81	264	50	19	32	52	4%	116	17%	4.21	-4.0	49	$16
Health	F	08 LA	143	34	5	16	8	357	365	352	436	573	1009	12	88	38	1.18	315	49	19	32	130	12%	136	21%	8.11	13.0	124	$10
PT/Exp	B	09 LA	613	92	9	47	12	269	296	261	335	375	711	9	85	30	0.69	266	53	19	28	68	6%	100	10%	4.43	-4.1	47	$16
Consist	F	1st Half	275	35	3	17	4	240			313	320	633	10	83	28	0.63	240	53	17	30	58	4%	59	10%	3.48	-9.8	19	$4
LIMA Plan	B	2nd Half	338	57	6	30	8	293			354	420	774	9	87	32	0.74	284	53	21	26	76	8%	122	10%	5.18	4.9	66	$12
Rand Var	+1	10 Proj	582	92	8	52	13	287			357	402	759	10	87	32	0.82	273	51	19	30	74	5%	106	11%	5.09	8.6	59	$18

Easy to see now that small-sample '08 was a fluke. '09 was a repeat of '07, when SX was just average (and SB var. was all in the opps). 2H provides hope that '05-'06 can return but SBO trend points to tired legs.

Gamel,Mat

			AB	R	HR	RBI	SB	Avg	vL	vR	OB	Slg	OPS	bb%	ct%	h%	Eye	xBA	G	L	F	PX	hr/f	SX	SBO	RC/G	RAR	BPV	R$
Pos	5	05	0	0	0	0	0	0							0			0						0					
Age	25	06	0	0	0	0	0	0							0			0						0					
Bats	Left	07	0	0	0	0	0	0							0			0						0					
Health	A	08 a/a	529	76	16	76	5	280			337	443	780	8	81	32	0.46	0				106		75	10%	5.12	-0.0	49	$17
PT/Exp	F	09 MIL	*401	43	14	56	2	238	304	229	320	403	723	11	68	32	0.37	226	23	27	51	127	10%	59	2%	4.66	-5.8	14	$9
Consist	A	1st Half	211	26	9	36	1	268			360	480	840	13	70	34	0.48	251	24	26	50	158	12%	68	2%	6.35	7.3	54	$7
LIMA Plan	F	2nd Half	190	16	5	20	1	204			274	317	592	9	65	29	0.28	205	18	29	53	91	8%	34	2%	2.66	-14.7	-38	$2
Rand Var	0	10 Proj	254	30	8	35	2	252			322	409	731	9	73	32	0.38	236	22	27	51	113	8%	58	5%	4.61	-4.9	19	$6

5-20-.242 in 128 AB at MIL. Despite power numbers, he looked overmatched upon his promotion (.214 xBA, 58% ct%) and his skills fell apart in the 2H. Several adjustments away from reaching his potential.

Garciaparra,Nomar

			AB	R	HR	RBI	SB	Avg	vL	vR	OB	Slg	OPS	bb%	ct%	h%	Eye	xBA	G	L	F	PX	hr/f	SX	SBO	RC/G	RAR	BPV	R$
Pos	0	05 CHC	230	28	9	30	0	283	281	285	318	452	770	5	90	28	0.50	303	40	25	35	99	13%	26	0%	4.80	-7.9	57	$7
Age	37	06 LA	469	82	20	93	3	303	341	294	360	505	865	8	94	29	1.40	300	38	20	42	107	11%	76	2%	6.15	-3.6	101	$21
Bats	Right	07 LA	431	39	7	59	3	283	213	303	331	371	702	7	90	30	0.76	255	43	19	37	53	5%	40	3%	4.26	-24.1	32	$10
Health	F	08 LA	163	24	8	28	1	264	339	224	326	466	792	8	93	24	1.36	290	40	18	43	109	12%	48	5%	5.33	1.9	94	$6
PT/Exp	D	09 OAK	160	17	3	16	2	281	297	267	315	388	703	5	83	33	0.29	247	33	24	43	70	5%	52	5%	3.99	-5.3	13	$4
Consist	C	1st Half	66	8	2	9	0	242			286	364	649	6	83	26	0.36	244	36	21	43	70	8%	31	0%	3.36	-3.6	12	$1
LIMA Plan	F	2nd Half	94	9	1	7	2	309			337	404	741	4	82	37	0.24	250	31	26	43	70	3%	52	8%	4.45	-1.8	9	$3
Rand Var	-4	10 Proj	164	19	5	21	2	268			313	401	714	6	87	28	0.52	264	37	21	42	80	8%	49	4%	4.26	-5.3	42	$4

Don't be fooled by BA spike: Just about every indicator declined, and stats are eroding at a similar pace. Slight rebound possible, but he's in full-blown Steve Carlton Path to Retirement mode.

Gardner,Brett

			AB	R	HR	RBI	SB	Avg	vL	vR	OB	Slg	OPS	bb%	ct%	h%	Eye	xBA	G	L	F	PX	hr/f	SX	SBO	RC/G	RAR	BPV	R$
Pos	8	05	0	0	0	0	0	0							0			0						0					
Age	27	06 aa	217	39	0	13	26	255			330	291	620	10	81	31	0.60	0				23		161	42%	3.34	-7.9	14	$9
Bats	Left	07 a/a	384	75	1	24	36	260			343	341	684	11	80	32	0.64	0				56		169	34%	4.23	-3.4	42	$15
Health	B	08 NYY	*468	75	3	43	44	251	125	252	343	338	681	12	78	32	0.64	226	48	17	35	58	2%	163	35%	4.19	-16.4	34	$18
PT/Exp	D	09 NYY	248	48	3	23	26	270	291	264	339	379	718	9	84	31	0.65	251	49	19	33	58	4%	174	40%	4.55	-0.6	55	$12
Consist	A	1st Half	159	32	3	13	17	289			365	421	787	11	86	32	0.86	269	47	21	32	67	7%	168	35%	5.44	3.6	72	$9
LIMA Plan	C	2nd Half	89	16	0	10	9	236			292	303	595	7	80	30	0.39	219	51	14	34	39	0%	175	50%	2.90	-4.9	20	$3
Rand Var	-1	10 Proj	315	57	2	28	32	257			332	341	673	10	81	31	0.59	234	49	17	34	51	2%	173	39%	4.01	-7.4	38	$13

Broken thumb put a damper on first full MLB season. Ct% growth, GB and plate patience all good signs. Runs often (SBO) and well (85% success rate. Impact depends on AB. UP: 400 AB, 40 SB

BRENT HERSHEY

Garko,Ryan

		Year	AB	R	HR	RBI	SB	Avg	vL	vR	OB	Slg	OPS	bb%	ct%	h%	Eye	xBA	G	L	F	PX	hr/f	SX	SBO	RC/G	RAR	BPV	R$
Pos	3	05 aaa	452	58	13	59	1	263			315	409	724	7	84	29	0.46	0				93		52	4%	4.38	-12.8	40	$11
Age	29	06 CLE *	549	69	20	100	4	250	333	281	321	413	734	9	81	28	0.56	248	42	17	41	102	11%	43	6%	4.58	-13.7	41	$14
Bats	Right	07 CLE	484	62	21	61	0	289	310	281	336	483	819	7	81	32	0.36	272	38	19	44	125	12%	34	1%	5.45	2.5	48	$15
Health	A	08 CLE	495	61	14	90	0	273	315	259	333	404	737	8	83	31	0.52	247	39	20	41	83	8%	35	0%	4.59	-9.7	26	$14
PT/Exp	B	09 2TM	354	39	13	51	0	268	308	249	324	421	745	8	86	28	0.58	252	43	17	40	86	11%	29	0%	4.62	-15.1	39	$10
Consist	A	1st Half	173	20	8	32	0	260			333	439	773	10	84	27	0.68	239	45	13	42	103	13%	17	0%	5.03	-5.4	45	$5
LIMA Plan	F	2nd Half	181	19	5	19	0	276			314	403	717	5	88	29	0.45	261	42	21	37	71	8%	42	0%	4.23	-9.7	33	$4
Rand Var	0	10 Proj	292	34	10	43	0	271			325	425	750	7	84	29	0.51	257	41	18	40	92	10%	42	1%	4.68	-9.7	40	$8

Looking for a breakout season? PRO: Peak age, consistency, increased ct% nudges eye upwards. CON: Power now less than average, slide v. RHP says he's a platoon candidate. With only 115 AB in SF, bet against.

Gerut,Jody

		Year	AB	R	HR	RBI	SB	Avg	vL	vR	OB	Slg	OPS	bb%	ct%	h%	Eye	xBA	G	L	F	PX	hr/f	SX	SBO	RC/G	RAR	BPV	R$
Pos	89	05 2TM *	218	23	3	20	1	278	103	284	352	399	750	10	88	31	0.93	276	50	19	31	83	5%	51	3%	5.04	3.9	55	$4
Age	33	06	0	0	0	0	0	0							0			0						0					
Bats	Left	07	0	0	0	0	0	0							0			0						0					
Health	F	08 SD *	435	62	17	56	9	280	308	293	337	476	813	8	85	29	0.59	281	47	17	36	113	13%	108	12%	5.47	9.1	82	$16
PT/Exp	F	09 2NL	274	40	9	35	6	230	194	235	280	376	656	6	84	24	0.44	268	47	19	34	91	12%	85	13%	3.52	-10.1	50	$7
Consist	D	1st Half	145	20	4	15	4	193			235	317	553	5	81	21	0.30	245	45	18	37	81	9%	97	19%	2.17	-11.9	32	$2
LIMA Plan	D+	2nd Half	129	20	5	20	2	271			329	442	770	8	88	28	0.69	293	50	20	30	102	15%	63	9%	4.98	0.9	69	$5
Rand Var	+3	10 Proj	355	50	12	45	6	265			321	429	750	8	86	28	0.58	280	48	19	34	99	12%	91	10%	4.75	0.7	66	$11

After hit rate returned in 2H, he was a similar player to 2008, but 1H cost him playing time. Enough here (solid ct%, league-average PX) to surprise if given the opportunity. Perfect low-risk end-gamer.

Getz,Chris

		Year	AB	R	HR	RBI	SB	Avg	vL	vR	OB	Slg	OPS	bb%	ct%	h%	Eye	xBA	G	L	F	PX	hr/f	SX	SBO	RC/G	RAR	BPV	R$
Pos	4	05	0	0	0	0	0	0							0			0						0					
Age	27	06 aa	508	63	2	34	17	244			310	304	614	9	91	27	1.02	0				34		117	15%	3.49	-13.3	45	$8
Bats	Left	07 aa	278	35	3	26	11	270			346	338	684	10	89	29	1.10	0				42		82	19%	4.30	-0.4	39	$7
Health	B	08 aaa	404	51	10	43	10	265			323	398	721	8	88	28	0.71	0				81		84	13%	4.48	-4.1	59	$11
PT/Exp	D	09 CHW	375	49	2	31	25	261	246	265	316	347	663	7	86	30	0.56	254	47	19	33	55	2%	137	26%	3.82	-12.1	45	$11
Consist	A	1st Half	215	29	1	18	11	247			299	344	643	7	86	28	0.53	258	45	20	35	63	2%	141	23%	3.61	-8.5	53	$5
LIMA Plan	C	2nd Half	160	20	1	13	14	281			339	350	689	8	85	33	0.58	246	51	18	31	45	2%	120	29%	4.12	-3.7	30	$6
Rand Var	-1	10 Proj	491	62	5	43	28	265			325	353	678	8	87	29	0.70	258	49	19	33	56	4%	118	23%	4.05	-9.4	47	$15

Oblique, sports hernia cut into AB, but in-season growth is notable. 2H SBO points to increased comfort level; plate approach should provide future opps. Count any power a bonus, but w/ health... UP: 35 SB.

Giambi,Jason

		Year	AB	R	HR	RBI	SB	Avg	vL	vR	OB	Slg	OPS	bb%	ct%	h%	Eye	xBA	G	L	F	PX	hr/f	SX	SBO	RC/G	RAR	BPV	R$
Pos	30	05 NYY	417	74	32	87	0	271	261	276	421	535	956	21	74	29	0.99	264	33	19	48	167	22%	18	0%	7.92	33.7	77	$19
Age	39	06 NYY	446	92	37	113	2	253	213	270	401	558	959	20	76	25	1.04	280	30	16	53	185	20%	48	1%	7.84	31.6	109	$21
Bats	Left	07 NYY	254	31	14	39	1	236	239	235	340	433	773	14	74	26	0.61	237	30	16	53	127	14%	29	1%	5.18	-0.6	35	$6
Health	C	08 NYY	458	68	32	96	2	247	231	253	354	502	856	14	76	26	0.68	266	33	17	50	160	18%	46	2%	6.25	13.3	75	$18
PT/Exp	C	09 2TM	293	43	13	51	0	201	213	196	331	382	714	16	73	23	0.71	225	33	15	51	123	12%	27	0%	4.55	-14.4	32	$6
Consist	C	1st Half	241	36	11	40	0	199			328	378	705	16	74	22	0.74	223	35	14	50	117	12%	28	0%	4.40	-12.9	33	$5
LIMA Plan	D	2nd Half	52	7	2	11	0	212			349	404	753	17	65	28	0.61	231	24	21	56	158	11%	21	0%	5.38	-1.2	31	$1
Rand Var	+4	10 Proj	235	34	13	46	0	238			361	453	813	16	72	28	0.68	242	30	17	52	146	14%	29	1%	5.91	0.5	48	$7

First glance: h% responsible for Mr. Mendoza. Second glance: h% is not the outlier it seems. Value is in patience and power, and though past his prime, pop still present. Any further PX or hr/f drop will be value-killer.

Giles,Brian

		Year	AB	R	HR	RBI	SB	Avg	vL	vR	OB	Slg	OPS	bb%	ct%	h%	Eye	xBA	G	L	F	PX	hr/f	SX	SBO	RC/G	RAR	BPV	R$
Pos	9	05 SD	545	92	15	83	13	301	289	306	426	483	909	18	88	32	1.86	298	37	24	39	110	8%	111	8%	7.35	31.8	112	$24
Age	39	06 SD	604	87	14	83	9	263	217	282	371	397	769	15	90	27	1.73	259	40	18	43	79	6%	63	6%	5.53	13.4	74	$16
Bats	Left	07 SD	483	72	13	51	4	271	241	286	356	416	773	12	87	29	1.05	270	40	19	40	87	8%	60	7%	5.31	6.0	63	$12
Health	F	08 SD	559	81	12	63	2	306	301	309	399	456	856	13	91	32	1.67	286	42	21	37	93	6%	63	2%	6.48	19.7	85	$18
PT/Exp	B	09 SD	225	18	2	23	1	191	136	222	275	271	546	10	86	21	0.84	237	44	19	37	55	3%	51	2%	2.63	-16.1	27	($0)
Consist	F	1st Half	225	18	2	23	1	191			275	271	546	10	86	21	0.84	237	44	19	37	55	3%	51	2%	2.63	-16.1	27	($0)
LIMA Plan	D+	2nd Half	0	0	0	0	0	0																					
Rand Var	+5	10 Proj	353	45	7	41	3	255			350	383	733	13	88	27	1.24	264	41	20	39	80	6%	69	5%	4.97	-0.1	65	$8

June knee injury wiped out the rest of 2009. Though bb%, ct% slipped a bit, h% slammed the door. If he returns, skills most suited to OBP leagues. But a creaky knee makes durability -- long an asset -- a risk.

Gimenez,Chris

		Year	AB	R	HR	RBI	SB	Avg	vL	vR	OB	Slg	OPS	bb%	ct%	h%	Eye	xBA	G	L	F	PX	hr/f	SX	SBO	RC/G	RAR	BPV	R$
Pos	7	05	0	0	0	0	0	0							0			0						0					
Age	27	06	0	0	0	0	0	0							0			0						0					
Bats	Right	07 aa	113	17	5	10	1	193			244	370	614	6	74	22	0.26	0				121		73	5%	2.82	-8.5	29	$1
Health	A	08 a/a	372	59	8	39	2	268			379	392	771	15	75	34	0.72	0				93		55	3%	5.45	3.4	24	$9
PT/Exp	F	09 CLE *	247	27	8	18	1	173	143	144	260	299	559	10	71	21	0.40	215	41	19	40	86	11%	41	4%	2.20	-22.6	-12	$0
Consist	F	1st Half	165	20	7	13	0	210			284	375	659	9	75	24	0.41	259	32	27	41	107	13%	26	0%	3.54	-7.5	13	$2
LIMA Plan	F	2nd Half	82	7	1	5	1	98			213	146	359	13	63	14	0.40	159	45	15	40	37	5%	53	11%	-0.92	-17.4	-73	($2)
Rand Var	+5	10 Proj	154	20	4	13	1	208			303	322	624	12	71	27	0.47	210	44	17	40	83	9%	47	4%	3.22	-8.4	-9	$1

3-7-.144 in 111 AB at CLE. Versatility would be a plus (8 G at CA; 18 at OF), but generally you have to hit. Ct% problems swelled with June promotion. With no power or speed, there's not much to wait for. Pass.

Glaus,Troy

		Year	AB	R	HR	RBI	SB	Avg	vL	vR	OB	Slg	OPS	bb%	ct%	h%	Eye	xBA	G	L	F	PX	hr/f	SX	SBO	RC/G	RAR	BPV	R$
Pos	5	05 ARI	538	78	37	97	4	258	244	263	359	522	881	14	73	29	0.58	275	37	17	46	177	20%	54	4%	6.66	29.5	79	$22
Age	34	06 TOR	540	105	38	104	3	252	292	238	355	513	868	14	75	27	0.64	264	34	17	49	162	19%	55	3%	6.40	22.1	76	$21
Bats	Right	07 TOR	385	60	20	62	0	262	361	235	363	473	836	14	74	31	0.60	264	34	21	45	142	16%	35	1%	6.11	13.9	48	$12
Health	F	08 STL	544	69	27	99	0	270	221	290	371	483	854	14	81	29	0.84	269	38	19	43	133	14%	26	1%	6.28	14.1	67	$19
PT/Exp	C	09 STL *	89	10	2	9	1	161		192	270	241	511	13	73	20	0.54	203	19	29	52	56	5%	47	4%	1.67	-10.2	-23	($0)
Consist	F	1st Half	0	0	0	0	0	0																					
LIMA Plan	D+	2nd Half	89	10	2	9	1	161			270	241	511	13	73	20	0.54	203	19	29	52	56	5%	47	4%	1.67	-10.1	-23	($0)
Rand Var	+5	10 Proj	363	51	17	56	2	251			352	433	785	13	75	29	0.62	243	34	20	46	121	13%	40	2%	5.39	1.3	37	$11

Shoulder surgery in January, bulging disk in August, oblique strain in September. After 2008, power indicators strong, but PX, hr/f in decline. Only 33, so some level of production will come if he gets 500 AB. Big, "if," though.

Gload,Ross

		Year	AB	R	HR	RBI	SB	Avg	vL	vR	OB	Slg	OPS	bb%	ct%	h%	Eye	xBA	G	L	F	PX	hr/f	SX	SBO	RC/G	RAR	BPV	R$
Pos	3	05 aaa	236	34	13	34	0	308			353	555	909	6	86	32	0.50	0				149		44	2%	6.45	7.1	92	$10
Age	34	06 CHW	156	22	3	18	6	327	308	333	352	462	813	4	90	35	0.40	293	51	21	27	76	8%	121	14%	5.29	-0.5	68	$6
Bats	Left	07 KC	320	37	7	51	2	288	388	269	321	441	762	5	88	31	0.41	297	50	19	31	97	8%	74	5%	4.79	-4.2	63	$9
Health	B	08 KC	388	46	3	37	3	273	263	277	314	348	662	6	90	30	0.59	266	46	22	32	51	3%	60	7%	3.77	-16.8	32	$7
PT/Exp	D	09 FLA	230	33	6	30	0	261	194	271	328	400	728	9	87	28	0.77	262	40	21	39	82	8%	58	0%	4.62	-12.6	51	$6
Consist	B	1st Half	116	19	3	12	0	284			352	422	774	9	87	31	0.80	268	37	24	39	82	8%	61	0%	5.17	-4.4	53	$4
LIMA Plan	F	2nd Half	114	14	3	18	0	237			304	377	681	9	87	25	0.73	256	43	18	40	83	8%	53	0%	4.06	-8.3	50	$2
Rand Var	+1	10 Proj	130	17	3	17	0	269			321	404	726	7	88	29	0.64	273	44	21	35	82	7%	66	2%	4.52	-6.3	54	$3

Power rebound, spike in bb% likely extends his MLB career. Has always made solid contact, just doesn't do much thereafter. Trends in xBA and against LHP tell the story: at 34, nowhere to go but down.

Gomes,Jonny

		Year	AB	R	HR	RBI	SB	Avg	vL	vR	OB	Slg	OPS	bb%	ct%	h%	Eye	xBA	G	L	F	PX	hr/f	SX	SBO	RC/G	RAR	BPV	R$
Pos	79	05 TAM *	510	86	30	87	14	276	287	280	354	524	877	11	71	33	0.42	255	29	23	48	166	17%	118	14%	6.62	27.9	77	$24
Age	29	06 TAM	385	53	20	59	1	216	297	187	323	431	754	14	70	25	0.53	233	29	17	54	149	14%	44	6%	5.04	-1.6	41	$8
Bats	Right	07 TAM *	391	54	18	56	16	247	313	218	326	451	777	10	64	34	0.32	229	26	21	53	163	14%	105	21%	5.58	6.4	40	$14
Health	A	08 TAM *	261	37	10	32	8	190	182	182	258	364	622	8	71	23	0.32	212	34	10	56	127	9%	112	20%	3.05	-15.1	37	$5
PT/Exp	D	09 CIN *	412	52	28	71	6	257	307	244	315	525	840	8	71	30	0.29	271	34	20	46	187	21%	63	9%	5.93	4.5	70	$17
Consist	F	1st Half	202	22	12	35	4	271			333	526	859	9	73	32	0.34	281	37	23	40	178	20%	67	10%	6.22	3.9	72	$8
LIMA Plan	C+	2nd Half	210	30	16	36	2	243			296	524	820	7	69	27	0.25	267	34	18	48	197	23%	50	8%	5.65	0.5	65	$8
Rand Var	-1	10 Proj	415	57	23	64	9	236			303	466	769	9	70	28	0.31	246	32	18	50	163	16%	84	13%	5.06	-5.1	53	$14

20-51-.267 in 281 AB at CIN. Chalk up park effects to his hr/f leap. Always had the power, but ct%, RHP continue to keep him from a full-time gig. This is his peak -- and a repeat (bunch of HR; limited role) seems likely.

BRENT HERSHEY

Gomez,Carlos

Gomez,Carlos		AB	R	HR	RBI	SB	Avg	vL	vR	OB	Slg	OPS	bb%	ct%	h%	Eye	xBA	G	L	F	PX	hr/f	SX	SBO	RC/G	RAR	BPV	R$
Pos 8	05	0	0	0	0	0	0							0			0						0					
Age 24	06 aa	430	54	6	48	42	283			326	410	736	6	80	34	0.31	0				84		148	46%	4.54	-0.2	44	$19
Bats Right	07 NYM *	265	34	4	23	26	245	254	212	301	336	637	7	83	28	0.46	234	45	16	39	58	5%	124	48%	3.37	-9.5	31	$9
Health B	08 MIN	577	79	7	59	33	258	270	254	289	360	650	4	75	33	0.18	221	44	17	39	73	4%	150	32%	3.32	-34.9	15	$18
PT/Exp C	09 MIN	315	51	3	28	14	229	204	239	279	337	615	7	77	29	0.31	236	45	19	36	72	3%	152	30%	3.06	-15.5	27	$7
Consist A	1st Half	170	24	1	12	7	229			284	335	619	7	77	29	0.33	228	39	20	41	73	2%	142	28%	3.17	-7.8	25	$3
LIMA Plan C	2nd Half	145	27	2	16	7	228			273	338	611	6	77	28	0.27	246	52	18	30	71	6%	158	31%	2.93	-7.7	27	$4
Rand Var +2	10 Proj	428	64	5	42	26	243			296	347	643	7	78	30	0.34	234	46	18	36	71	4%	144	34%	3.40	-18.1	27	$12

Baby steps in approach, but overall a very disappointing season. Speed skills very much intact, but playing time will determine his SB impact. OBP trend not encouraging. Though 24, it's time to pick up the pace.

Gonzalez,Adrian

Gonzalez,Adrian		AB	R	HR	RBI	SB	Avg	vL	vR	OB	Slg	OPS	bb%	ct%	h%	Eye	xBA	G	L	F	PX	hr/f	SX	SBO	RC/G	RAR	BPV	R$
Pos 3	05 TEX *	478	60	20	63	0	278	71	243	325	458	783	6	86	29	0.49	271	39	20	41	105	12%	40	0%	5.00	-1.3	55	$14
Age 28	06 SD	570	83	24	82	0	304	312	301	362	500	862	8	80	34	0.46	281	44	23	33	122	16%	35	1%	6.10	1.5	48	$21
Bats Left	07 SD	646	101	30	100	0	282	263	290	347	502	849	9	78	32	0.46	278	37	19	44	143	14%	49	0%	6.02	-2.1	62	$23
Health A	08 SD	616	103	36	119	0	279	213	320	357	510	866	11	77	31	0.52	275	43	20	37	146	21%	35	0%	6.26	9.2	59	$27
PT/Exp A	09 SD	552	90	40	99	1	277	234	305	405	551	956	18	80	28	1.09	297	39	21	40	164	22%	40	1%	7.67	18.2	101	$26
Consist B	1st Half	265	48	24	48	1	268			410	581	991	19	79	25	1.16	304	40	20	41	181	28%	43	2%	8.12	12.3	116	$14
LIMA Plan C+	2nd Half	287	42	16	51	0	286			401	523	923	16	81	30	1.02	291	38	22	40	148	17%	31	0%	7.25	6.0	86	$12
Rand Var +2	10 Proj	575	91	35	101	0	280			377	524	902	14	79	30	0.76	288	40	21	40	150	19%	44	1%	6.82	10.3	81	$24

Aside from the 40 knocks, BPV says this was his best season yet by far. If he can sustain the huge gains in bb% and PX, it's repeatable. More likely, though, is a return to 2008 -- still excellent by any measure.

Gonzalez,Alberto

Gonzalez,Alberto		AB	R	HR	RBI	SB	Avg	vL	vR	OB	Slg	OPS	bb%	ct%	h%	Eye	xBA	G	L	F	PX	hr/f	SX	SBO	RC/G	RAR	BPV	R$
Pos 46	05	0	0	0	0	0	0							0			0						0					
Age 27	06 a/a	449	58	5	43	4	272			322	363	685	7	92	29	0.94	0				53		84	4%	4.17	-2.4	52	$9
Bats Right	07 a/a	493	58	1	48	12	244			289	338	627	6	87	28	0.49	0				63		119	15%	3.42	-13.9	49	$7
Health A	08 2TM *	322	33	5	34	3	230	219	275	275	328	603	6	86	25	0.44	279	44	28	29	68	6%	52	8%	2.99	-18.1	26	$4
PT/Exp D	09 WAS *	381	36	1	41	2	268	397	228	316	346	663	7	85	31	0.48	251	43	23	34	56	1%	69	4%	3.78	-8.3	22	$7
Consist B	1st Half	183	16	1	18	2	289			319	363	682	4	93	31	0.58	280	39	29	32	45	2%	75	4%	3.98	-2.8	39	$4
LIMA Plan F	2nd Half	198	20	0	23	0	248			314	331	645	9	79	32	0.45	232	45	20	35	67	0%	66	4%	3.61	-5.5	8	$2
Rand Var -3	10 Proj	262	27	2	27	2	252			301	339	640	7	86	29	0.49	259	43	23	34	61	2%	77	6%	3.51	-8.6	30	$4

Decent contact rate is the extent of the good news. Neither the power, speed nor minor league history to warrant a bid. Maybe you take an end-game shot on someone like this who plays for a good team... Nah.

Gonzalez,Alex

Gonzalez,Alex		AB	R	HR	RBI	SB	Avg	vL	vR	OB	Slg	OPS	bb%	ct%	h%	Eye	xBA	G	L	F	PX	hr/f	SX	SBO	RC/G	RAR	BPV	R$
Pos 6	05 FLA	435	45	5	45	5	264	216	277	313	368	681	7	81	32	0.38	234	37	18	45	80	3%	57	7%	3.90	-0.8	22	$9
Age 33	06 BOS	388	48	9	50	1	255	278	244	295	397	692	5	83	29	0.33	250	37	20	43	91	6%	68	1%	3.93	-5.4	37	$7
Bats Right	07 CIN	393	55	16	55	0	272	234	287	314	468	782	6	81	30	0.32	279	34	22	44	125	12%	43	1%	4.97	5.9	50	$11
Health F	08 CIN	0	0	0	0	0	0																					
PT/Exp D	09 2TM	391	42	8	41	2	238	212	247	275	355	630	5	83	27	0.31	231	37	16	47	79	5%	51	4%	3.17	-16.2	24	$6
Consist D	1st Half	182	10	2	20	0	214			251	302	554	5	86	24	0.35	237	36	20	43	62	3%	19	3%	2.37	-12.3	9	$0
LIMA Plan D	2nd Half	209	32	6	21	2	258			295	402	697	5	81	29	0.28	227	37	12	51	95	7%	72	4%	3.91	-3.9	35	$5
Rand Var -3	10 Proj	398	48	10	46	2	254			294	398	692	5	82	29	0.32	248	36	18	46	96	7%	60	3%	3.91	-6.7	37	$8

Provided some SS stability upon arrival in BOS in mid-Aug, and hit a little too (5 HR, 26 R in 148 AB). Likely earned his next paycheck, where double-digit HR could result. Poor eye, injury history are significant downsides.

Gonzalez,Carlos

Gonzalez,Carlos		AB	R	HR	RBI	SB	Avg	vL	vR	OB	Slg	OPS	bb%	ct%	h%	Eye	xBA	G	L	F	PX	hr/f	SX	SBO	RC/G	RAR	BPV	R$
Pos 78	05	0	0	0	0	0	0							0			0						0					
Age 24	06	0	0	0	0	0	0							0			0						0					
Bats Left	07 aa	500	60	16	71	8	272			316	454	770	6	82	30	0.36	0				119		78	13%	4.89	-4.5	62	$15
Health A	08 OAK *	475	49	7	48	5	242	188	263	280	358	638	5	77	30	0.23	246	49	18	33	88	6%	76	7%	3.23	-23.0	15	$7
PT/Exp D	09 COL *	470	87	22	77	21	297	276	286	360	544	904	9	80	33	0.48	288	38	23	39	148	15%	146	22%	6.71	15.2	101	$26
Consist F	1st Half	254	42	10	52	8	290			348	515	863	8	82	32	0.49	312	38	35	28	133	17%	131	16%	6.17	4.4	91	$13
LIMA Plan B	2nd Half	216	45	12	25	13	306			372	579	951	10	77	35	0.47	286	38	20	42	167	17%	152	28%	7.39	11.0	109	$13
Rand Var -2	10 Proj	520	78	18	69	13	275			327	468	795	7	79	32	0.37	272	42	21	37	124	12%	128	15%	5.29	-2.7	70	$19

13-29-16-.284 in 278 AB at COL. Given 2008, he arrived early, but one caveat: he hardly faced LHP (58 AB). So while PX and SX exploded, this is only half the picture. Might become a star, but don't base 2010 on '09 2H.

Gonzalez,Edgar

Gonzalez,Edgar		AB	R	HR	RBI	SB	Avg	vL	vR	OB	Slg	OPS	bb%	ct%	h%	Eye	xBA	G	L	F	PX	hr/f	SX	SBO	RC/G	RAR	BPV	R$
Pos 4	05 a/a	384	35	5	36	3	213			268	322	589	7	81	25	0.38	0				79		61	14%	2.78	-19.0	20	$3
Age 32	06 a/a	353	42	9	54	9	306			378	450	829	10	82	35	0.63	0				89		85	13%	5.87	14.9	46	$13
Bats Right	07 aa	459	40	5	33	9	204			255	289	545	6	84	23	0.42	0				60		83	13%	2.30	-29.7	22	$2
Health B	08 SD *	407	46	10	42	1	263	283	268	319	372	690	8	78	32	0.38	229	47	19	33	74	9%	27	7%	3.94	-10.0	-3	$8
PT/Exp F	09 SD	153	16	4	18	1	216	204	222	268	373	641	7	76	26	0.31	239	39	18	43	106	8%	86	10%	3.32	-5.8	32	$2
Consist C	1st Half	103	12	4	11	0	184			229	379	608	6	73	21	0.21	233	29	21	50	127	11%	102	13%	2.77	-5.9	36	$1
LIMA Plan F	2nd Half	50	4	0	7	1	280			345	360	705	9	84	33	0.63	238	56	14	30	70	0%	41	7%	4.44	-0.1	24	$1
Rand Var +3	10 Proj	97	10	2	11	1	247			304	350	655	8	80	29	0.41	232	46	17	36	74	6%	46	9%	3.55	-3.1	10	$2

Why the last Gonzo on this page is appropriately placed:
- 1st full MLB season at age 30
- ct%, eye ratio in decline
- PX, SX ok, but too few AB
- 2009 BA was bested by his pitching namesake

Gordon,Alex

Gordon,Alex		AB	R	HR	RBI	SB	Avg	vL	vR	OB	Slg	OPS	bb%	ct%	h%	Eye	xBA	G	L	F	PX	hr/f	SX	SBO	RC/G	RAR	BPV	R$
Pos 5	05	0	0	0	0	0	0							0			0						0					
Age 26	06 aa	486	87	20	79	17	286			361	490	851	10	83	31	0.67	0				127		104	15%	6.09	11.6	85	$21
Bats Left	07 KC	543	60	15	60	14	247	217	258	300	411	710	7	75	30	0.30	251	37	19	44	120	8%	100	15%	4.24	-10.2	41	$12
Health D	08 KC	493	72	16	59	9	260	234	273	347	432	779	12	76	31	0.55	248	31	21	48	125	9%	82	8%	5.34	6.7	53	$14
PT/Exp B	09 KC *	261	44	9	37	5	250	163	261	339	407	746	12	77	29	0.58	238	44	14	42	100	10%	92	6%	4.86	1.4	41	$8
Consist B	1st Half	21	2	1	3	1	95			208	238	446	13	62	8	0.38	191	46	15	38	94	20%	62	25%	0.20	-3.3	-32	$0
LIMA Plan C+	2nd Half	240	42	8	34	4	264			350	422	772	12	78	31	0.62	241	43	14	42	101	10%	88	5%	5.21	3.6	46	$8
Rand Var 0	10 Proj	489	72	18	73	11	260			353	442	795	13	77	30	0.63	255	37	19	44	123	11%	89	9%	5.56	11.3	61	$16

Hip injury sidelined him for 3 months; rust evident upon his return. Low LD% extinguished hopes of 2H growth compared to 2008. Pedigree or not, it's soon time to lower expectations. Give him one more year.

Granderson,Curtis

Granderson,Curtis		AB	R	HR	RBI	SB	Avg	vL	vR	OB	Slg	OPS	bb%	ct%	h%	Eye	xBA	G	L	F	PX	hr/f	SX	SBO	RC/G	RAR	BPV	R$
Pos 8	05 DET *	607	87	20	77	20	275	364	257	332	488	820	8	75	34	0.34	265	48	17	35	137	12%	137	19%	5.77	26.2	68	$22
Age 29	06 DET	596	90	19	68	8	260	218	274	334	438	772	10	71	34	0.38	241	39	22	39	122	12%	116	8%	5.28	10.8	37	$15
Bats Left	07 DET	612	122	23	74	26	302	160	337	357	552	909	8	77	36	0.37	281	34	21	45	158	11%	165	18%	6.89	39.6	101	$29
Health A	08 DET	553	112	22	66	12	280	259	288	362	494	856	11	80	32	0.64	272	40	19	41	128	12%	137	10%	6.26	14.3	88	$22
PT/Exp A	09 DET	631	91	30	71	20	249	180	275	326	453	779	10	78	28	0.51	249	30	21	49	119	12%	119	15%	5.15	9.6	64	$20
Consist B	1st Half	304	49	18	43	13	257			339	474	813	11	79	27	0.58	250	30	19	51	121	15%	106	19%	5.53	8.1	67	$13
LIMA Plan B	2nd Half	327	42	12	28	7	242			313	434	747	9	77	28	0.45	248	29	23	48	117	10%	116	11%	4.79	1.5	56	$7
Rand Var +2	10 Proj	599	99	25	68	17	265			339	476	814	10	78	30	0.49	258	34	21	45	127	12%	137	14%	5.66	15.3	75	$21

Why he won't repeat 30 HR:
1. Struggles vs LHP resurfaced
2. hr/f rate stable
3. SLG, PX each a 3-year low
4. FB%, AB each a career high

In addition, speed skills down; could be his last 20/20 season.

Greene,Khalil

Greene,Khalil		AB	R	HR	RBI	SB	Avg	vL	vR	OB	Slg	OPS	bb%	ct%	h%	Eye	xBA	G	L	F	PX	hr/f	SX	SBO	RC/G	RAR	BPV	R$
Pos 6	05 SD	436	51	15	70	5	250	200	267	291	431	722	5	79	29	0.27	266	33	22	44	124	10%	92	6%	4.25	3.7	55	$12
Age 30	06 SD	412	56	15	55	5	245	271	237	310	427	738	9	79	28	0.45	251	35	19	46	115	10%	83	6%	4.60	3.0	52	$10
Bats Right	07 SD	611	89	27	97	4	254	268	249	291	468	759	5	79	28	0.25	271	35	18	47	139	12%	90	4%	4.66	3.7	66	$18
Health F	08 SD	389	30	10	35	5	213	188	222	255	339	595	5	74	26	0.22	215	32	21	48	86	7%	75	8%	2.58	-24.6	1	$4
PT/Exp C	09 STL *	239	28	9	32	2	207	180	211	259	366	624	7	82	21	0.40	238	31	18	51	97	9%	55	6%	3.08	-11.8	39	$4
Consist C	1st Half	130	18	5	19	2	200			273	354	627	9	82	21	0.57	237	29	19	51	94	9%	67	10%	3.24	-5.9	45	$3
LIMA Plan F	2nd Half	109	10	4	13	0	215			241	380	621	3	83	22	0.20	220	39	11	50	100	10%	20	0%	2.86	-6.0	25	$2
Rand Var +5	10 Proj	222	24	7	28	2	239			281	393	675	6	80	27	0.29	238	33	19	49	100	8%	72	5%	3.65	-6.1	33	$5

6-24-.200 in 170 AB at STL. Only 2 years removed from 27 HR, but a closer inspection of that year reveals a soft skill set not far off from any other year. h% bodes for some rebound but not nearly enough to chase.

BRENT HERSHEY

87

Greene,Tyler

	Yr	AB	R	HR	RBI	SB	Avg	vL	vR	OB	Slg	OPS	bb%	ct%	h%	Eye	xBA	G	L	F	PX	hr/f	SX	SBO	RC/G	RAR	BPV	R$
Pos 6	05	0	0	0	0	0	0							0			0						0					
Age 27	06	0	0	0	0	0	0							0			0						0					
Bats Right	07 aa	221	31	6	19	8	202			244	352	597	5	76	24	0.23	0				108		126	26%	2.68	-11.8	41	$3
Health A	08 aa	485	58	10	36	15	205			244	318	561	5	78	24	0.23	0				75		116	23%	2.19	-35.2	17	$6
PT/Exp F	09 STL	* 448	60	12	37	25	232	188	237	283	355	638	7	77	28	0.30	231	44	18	38	79	9%	133	27%	3.21	-19.8	26	$13
Consist B	1st Half	214	25	5	19	11	249			304	357	661	7	78	30	0.35	222	47	15	38	71	8%	103	23%	3.55	-7.0	15	$6
LIMA Plan F	2nd Half	234	35	7	18	14	217			263	354	617	6	76	25	0.26	265	17	50	33	87	12%	148	31%	2.88	-12.9	32	$7
Rand Var -1	10 Proj	99	13	2	8	4	232			276	369	645	6	77	28	0.26	235	47	15	38	89	9%	128	25%	3.29	-3.9	31	$2

2-7-.222 in 108 AB at STL. Ignore the 50% LD in the 2nd half as he just had 7 AB after June. If he could just learn to get on base and earn some AB (stop us if you've heard this one before)... UP: 25 SB

Green,Nick

	Yr	AB	R	HR	RBI	SB	Avg	vL	vR	OB	Slg	OPS	bb%	ct%	h%	Eye	xBA	G	L	F	PX	hr/f	SX	SBO	RC/G	RAR	BPV	R$
Pos 6	05 TAM	318	53	5	29	3	239	290	217	311	346	656	9	73	31	0.38	218	38	21	41	81	5%	100	5%	3.65	-8.7	8	$6
Age 32	06 2AL	* 204	17	3	9	2	190	150	203	250	275	526	8	67	27	0.25	195	37	21	41	71	5%	44	14%	1.69	-18.0	-44	($1)
Bats Right	07 aa	387	40	14	43	3	213			244	372	616	4	70	27	0.13	0				111		79	11%	2.80	-19.1	1	$5
Health A	08 aaa	391	31	9	38	3	185			222	291	513	5	73	23	0.17	0				74		58	6%	1.42	-38.4	-22	$1
PT/Exp F	09 BOS	276	35	6	35	1	236	235	236	287	366	653	7	75	29	0.29	230	38	18	44	96	7%	45	8%	3.47	-8.3	6	$4
Consist B	1st Half	180	24	4	26	1	267			302	411	713	5	78	32	0.23	245	42	16	41	104	7%	52	10%	4.14	-1.6	23	$4
LIMA Plan F	2nd Half	96	11	2	9	0	177			262	281	543	10	69	23	0.37	204	29	23	48	79	6%	42	5%	2.00	-7.7	-27	($0)
Rand Var -2	10 Proj	131	14	3	14	1	206			258	322	581	7	72	26	0.25	218	36	21	44	86	7%	48	7%	2.43	-8.1	-14	$1

In 1st half, finally got opportunity to show what he could do with full time AB: not much. Eye and ct% marginally improving; PX and SX are not. For a 32-year-old, that's not a combination destined to generate value.

Griffey Jr.,Ken

	Yr	AB	R	HR	RBI	SB	Avg	vL	vR	OB	Slg	OPS	bb%	ct%	h%	Eye	xBA	G	L	F	PX	hr/f	SX	SBO	RC/G	RAR	BPV	R$
Pos 0	05 CIN	491	85	35	92	0	301	278	314	371	576	947	10	81	31	0.58	307	34	22	44	168	20%	29	1%	7.09	14.5	89	$26
Age 40	06 CIN	428	62	27	72	0	252	204	278	315	486	801	8	82	25	0.50	262	42	15	43	130	18%	25	0%	5.21	-15.3	58	$14
Bats Left	07 CIN	528	78	30	93	6	277	236	300	377	496	873	14	81	29	0.86	266	35	16	49	128	14%	63	4%	6.46	3.2	76	$21
Health B	08 2TM	486	66	18	71	0	247	202	272	350	422	772	14	82	27	0.87	263	38	20	42	112	11%	34	1%	5.30	5.3	56	$12
PT/Exp B	09 SEA	387	44	19	57	0	214	213	215	324	411	735	14	79	22	0.79	244	37	16	47	118	13%	14	0%	4.75	-5.0	46	$7
Consist B	1st Half	201	23	10	26	0	219			335	418	753	15	82	22	0.97	247	35	15	50	116	12%	13	0%	5.04	-0.8	57	$4
LIMA Plan D	2nd Half	186	21	9	31	0	210			313	403	716	13	76	23	0.64	241	40	16	44	121	15%	16	0%	4.44	-4.2	35	$3
Rand Var +4	10 Proj	303	39	15	47	0	238			339	437	777	13	80	25	0.77	257	37	17	45	123	13%	21	0%	5.25	-1.1	54	$7

Will he retire? xBA and h% suggest low BA due to poor luck. HR/FB says he can still hit 20 HR with regular AB. While 2010 may be in question, the Hall of Fame is not.

Gross,Gabe

	Yr	AB	R	HR	RBI	SB	Avg	vL	vR	OB	Slg	OPS	bb%	ct%	h%	Eye	xBA	G	L	F	PX	hr/f	SX	SBO	RC/G	RAR	BPV	R$
Pos 9	05 TOR	* 482	62	6	44	12	270	91	272	341	391	732	10	82	32	0.59	233	30	21	49	88	3%	104	11%	4.74	0.5	50	$12
Age 30	06 MIL	208	42	9	38	1	274	95	294	381	476	857	15	71	35	0.60	254	34	23	42	143	14%	52	1%	6.61	10.9	46	$8
Bats Left	07 MIL	* 259	39	11	33	5	258	91	244	351	470	822	13	80	28	0.74	280	39	20	41	128	13%	108	8%	5.87	7.5	84	$8
Health A	08 2TM	345	46	13	40	4	238	191	249	334	414	749	13	76	28	0.61	244	41	17	43	115	12%	83	6%	4.93	-3.6	49	$8
PT/Exp D	09 TAM	282	31	6	36	6	227	172	233	327	355	682	13	72	29	0.53	237	40	23	36	94	8%	71	11%	4.13	-10.4	13	$5
Consist B	1st Half	142	24	4	24	6	282			393	437	829	15	77	34	0.79	266	38	28	34	102	11%	95	17%	6.20	3.6	50	$6
LIMA Plan F	2nd Half	140	7	2	12	0	171			256	271	528	10	67	24	0.35	191	43	18	39	85	5%	7	0%	1.83	-15.9	-39	($1)
Rand Var +1	10 Proj	219	27	5	27	3	233			328	368	697	12	74	29	0.55	237	40	20	39	97	8%	74	8%	4.30	-7.0	24	$4

Decent 1H production was a mirage, driven by high h% and unsustainable LD rate. Multi-year declines in PX, SX, xBA indicate that his productive years (such as they were) are over.

Guerrero,Vladimir

	Yr	AB	R	HR	RBI	SB	Avg	vL	vR	OB	Slg	OPS	bb%	ct%	h%	Eye	xBA	G	L	F	PX	hr/f	SX	SBO	RC/G	RAR	BPV	R$
Pos 0	05 ANA	520	95	32	108	13	317	313	319	389	565	954	10	91	30	1.27	313	44	17	39	135	18%	100	9%	7.17	16.0	124	$31
Age 35	06 LAA	607	92	33	116	15	329	401	307	381	552	932	8	89	33	0.74	299	44	19	37	121	16%	76	11%	6.73	4.9	92	$32
Bats Right	07 LAA	574	89	27	125	2	324	321	325	398	547	945	11	89	33	1.15	311	48	16	36	133	15%	38	3%	7.19	14.6	99	$28
Health C	08 LAA	541	85	27	91	5	303	286	309	363	521	884	9	86	31	0.66	296	47	17	36	128	16%	74	5%	6.30	20.4	87	$24
PT/Exp B	09 LAA	383	59	15	50	2	295	250	311	328	460	788	5	85	33	0.34	265	42	18	40	92	11%	64	3%	4.93	-2.6	46	$14
Consist C	1st Half	152	17	2	13	2	289			316	388	705	4	86	33	0.27	237	45	15	40	62	4%	73	8%	4.02	-4.9	23	$4
LIMA Plan C	2nd Half	231	42	13	37	0	299			336	506	843	5	85	30	0.38	283	40	20	40	112	16%	41	0%	5.52	2.2	56	$10
Rand Var -1	10 Proj	488	76	22	78	4	289			339	485	824	7	86	30	0.56	286	44	18	38	112	14%	73	5%	5.51	1.9	73	$19

Missed 6 weeks with a torn pec. Ct% still good, but no longer at elite levels. Also walking less. For such a free swinger, this may mark beginning of the end. Still capable of doubling 2H, but degree of difficulty is increasing.

Guillen,Carlos

	Yr	AB	R	HR	RBI	SB	Avg	vL	vR	OB	Slg	OPS	bb%	ct%	h%	Eye	xBA	G	L	F	PX	hr/f	SX	SBO	RC/G	RAR	BPV	R$
Pos 70	05 DET	334	48	5	23	2	320	368	306	366	434	800	7	87	36	0.53	266	44	23	33	70	5%	82	5%	5.33	5.5	43	$10
Age 35	06 DET	543	100	19	85	20	320	291	332	399	519	918	12	84	35	0.82	285	42	20	38	122	11%	114	16%	7.01	27.2	93	$26
Bats Both	07 DET	564	86	21	102	13	296	302	295	359	502	860	9	84	32	0.59	289	39	20	41	126	11%	112	13%	6.14	17.5	88	$24
Health D	08 DET	420	68	10	54	9	286	287	285	375	436	811	13	84	32	0.90	277	45	20	35	100	8%	92	9%	5.80	11.3	71	$14
PT/Exp B	09 DET	277	36	11	41	1	242	244	245	335	419	754	12	80	27	0.70	252	37	20	43	102	11%	65	5%	4.97	-0.3	47	$7
Consist B	1st Half	90	11	0	6	1	200			265	244	510	8	83	24	0.53	231	42	22	36	37	0%	63	5%	1.98	-8.6	0	$0
LIMA Plan C+	2nd Half	187	25	11	35	0	262			367	503	870	14	78	28	0.76	264	34	19	47	135	16%	61	5%	6.48	8.1	69	$6
Rand Var +3	10 Proj	408	59	13	57	5	267			350	433	783	11	82	30	0.71	265	40	20	40	101	10%	84	8%	5.34	4.4	59	$12

Spent two months on DL due to shoulder injury. Traded contact for power in 2nd half. SX and SBO says won't reach double digit SBs again; 2nd half PX gains likely won't stick either at age 35.

Guillen,Jose

	Yr	AB	R	HR	RBI	SB	Avg	vL	vR	OB	Slg	OPS	bb%	ct%	h%	Eye	xBA	G	L	F	PX	hr/f	SX	SBO	RC/G	RAR	BPV	R$
Pos 9	05 WAS	551	81	24	76	1	283	215	303	321	479	800	5	81	31	0.30	289	44	22	34	124	16%	61	2%	5.14	-1.8	56	$20
Age 34	06 WAS	241	28	9	40	1	216	200	221	262	398	660	6	80	23	0.31	247	41	14	45	113	10%	61	2%	3.50	-9.4	43	$4
Bats Right	07 SEA	593	84	23	99	5	290	362	268	336	460	796	6	80	33	0.35	268	48	16	36	108	14%	75	4%	5.16	-5.6	45	$21
Health D	08 KC	598	66	20	97	2	264	305	248	291	438	730	4	82	29	0.22	275	47	18	35	116	12%	49	3%	4.24	-19.3	46	$16
PT/Exp B	09 KC	281	30	9	40	1	242	181	273	297	367	664	7	82	27	0.44	226	46	14	40	72	10%	37	1%	3.59	-14.6	14	$6
Consist B	1st Half	224	23	8	34	1	254			318	397	716	9	84	27	0.58	236	47	13	39	81	11%	32	2%	4.31	-6.7	30	$5
LIMA Plan D	2nd Half	57	7	1	6	0	193			207	246	453	2	75	24	0.07	185	39	18	43	28	5%	56	0%	0.52	-8.7	-53	$0
Rand Var 0	10 Proj	415	50	13	59	1	243			279	379	657	5	80	28	0.25	240	44	17	39	84	10%	58	2%	3.37	-24.4	16	$8

Season bookended by injuries - torn groin in April and torn knee ligament in July. Huge drop in PX shows he was never really healthy. Return to 2008 levels a best case scenario, but age is not on his side.

Gutierrez,Franklin

	Yr	AB	R	HR	RBI	SB	Avg	vL	vR	OB	Slg	OPS	bb%	ct%	h%	Eye	xBA	G	L	F	PX	hr/f	SX	SBO	RC/G	RAR	BPV	R$
Pos 8	05 a/a	450	65	8	40	13	231			278	358	635	6	83	26	0.38	0				88		114	21%	3.33	-15.0	51	$9
Age 27	06 CLE	* 485	81	9	44	12	266	262	277	336	396	732	10	77	33	0.46	256	43	23	34	97	7%	83	15%	4.66	-0.1	33	$12
Bats Right	07 CLE	* 400	66	16	50	14	283	330	232	329	463	792	7	76	34	0.29	255	43	15	42	120	13%	108	19%	5.17	7.3	49	$16
Health A	08 CLE	399	54	8	41	9	248	252	246	296	383	679	6	78	30	0.31	243	42	17	41	98	6%	103	13%	3.81	-18.2	37	$9
PT/Exp B	09 SEA	565	85	18	70	16	283	335	262	337	425	762	8	78	33	0.38	250	45	19	36	89	11%	92	13%	4.82	2.8	29	$20
Consist B	1st Half	237	33	7	28	5	278			345	409	754	9	78	33	0.45	245	44	21	35	80	11%	74	12%	4.82	1.2	17	$7
LIMA Plan C+	2nd Half	328	52	11	42	11	287			331	436	767	6	79	33	0.32	254	45	18	37	95	12%	92	13%	4.81	1.5	34	$13
Rand Var -3	10 Proj	539	81	16	62	15	267			319	413	732	7	78	32	0.35	250	44	18	38	97	10%	100	15%	4.45	-5.2	36	$17

PRO: Improving Eye, BA vs RH
CON: Declining PX, FB%.
Full-time AB, but skills of a 4th OF. His defense, not his bat, will keep him on the field. xBA says don't expect a repeat of 2009.

Guzman,Cristian

	Yr	AB	R	HR	RBI	SB	Avg	vL	vR	OB	Slg	OPS	bb%	ct%	h%	Eye	xBA	G	L	F	PX	hr/f	SX	SBO	RC/G	RAR	BPV	R$
Pos 6	05 WAS	456	39	4	31	7	219	161	242	260	314	573	5	83	26	0.33	269	56	20	24	62	4%	106	11%	2.58	-19.4	27	$3
Age 32	06 WAS	0	0	0	0	0	0																					
Bats Both	07 WAS	174	31	2	14	2	328	357	318	381	466	846	8	88	36	0.71	294	60	17	23	72	6%	114	3%	6.02	7.2	61	$6
Health F	08 WAS	579	77	9	55	6	316	354	299	342	440	783	4	90	34	0.40	297	53	23	25	77	7%	84	7%	4.98	5.5	57	$19
PT/Exp C	09 WAS	531	74	6	52	4	284	307	277	305	390	695	3	86	32	0.21	261	54	17	29	67	5%	96	7%	3.89	-11.6	33	$14
Consist C	1st Half	277	40	3	18	1	318			335	430	764	2	86	36	0.18	271	59	17	25	71	5%	89	5%	4.65	-0.1	34	$8
LIMA Plan C	2nd Half	254	34	3	34	3	248			274	346	620	3	86	28	0.25	249	50	17	33	61	4%	107	9%	3.06	-12.1	33	$6
Rand Var 0	10 Proj	522	72	6	50	5	278			308	391	699	4	87	31	0.34	275	54	19	27	69	5%	109	7%	4.05	-7.8	46	$13

All he really has to offer is BA, which is driven entirely by his excellent ct%. xBA shows the effect of ct% deterioration. Continued decline in bb% says drop in ct% could continue. DN: .250 BA

BILL MACEY

Gwynn,Tony

Gwynn,Tony		Yr	AB	R	HR	RBI	SB	Avg	vL	vR	OB	Slg	OPS	bb%	ct%	h%	Eye	xBA	G	L	F	PX	hr/f	SX	SBO	RC/G	RAR	BPV	R$
Pos	8	05 aa	505	65	1	32	24	232			313	286	599	10	88	26	0.94	0				38		108	27%	3.32	-17.4	36	$9
Age	28	06 MIL	* 524	71	4	42	30	277	167	268	329	361	690	7	82	33	0.44	257	50	23	27	54	3%	120	28%	4.05	-6.0	25	$16
Bats	Left	07 MIL	* 249	30	0	21	12	261	316	250	316	317	633	7	85	31	0.54	244	53	18	29	34	0%	125	21%	3.47	-7.8	22	$6
Health	A	08 aaa	375	33	2	18	14	218			260	263	523	5	88	25	0.45	0				27		95	22%	2.10	-34.6	13	$3
PT/Exp	D	09 SD	* 545	84	3	27	22	265	215	290	342	339	681	10	85	31	0.76	253	46	24	30	47	2%	126	17%	4.19	-8.7	37	$14
Consist	D	1st Half	281	46	2	13	13	276			350	365	715	10	85	32	0.73	254	40	26	34	58	2%	133	18%	4.58	-1.3	46	$9
LIMA Plan	F	2nd Half	264	38	1	14	9	254			334	311	645	11	85	30	0.80	248	49	23	28	35	2%	114	15%	3.77	-7.5	25	$6
Rand Var	-1	10 Proj	288	37	1	17	12	250			315	311	626	9	86	29	0.65	250	49	22	29	39	2%	118	19%	3.44	-10.8	28	$6

2-21-.270 in 393 AB at SD. He walks, and steals a few bags. That's about it. Fine CF defense keeps him around, otherwise he'd be about out of chances. And would he even get another one if his name was John Doe?

Hafner,Travis

Hafner,Travis		Yr	AB	R	HR	RBI	SB	Avg	vL	vR	OB	Slg	OPS	bb%	ct%	h%	Eye	xBA	G	L	F	PX	hr/f	SX	SBO	RC/G	RAR	BPV	R$
Pos	0	05 CLE	486	94	33	108	0	305	269	319	402	595	996	14	75	35	0.64	301	43	20	37	201	25%	30	0%	8.26	29.6	99	$26
Age	33	06 CLE	454	100	42	117	0	308	321	300	433	659	1092	18	76	33	0.90	316	39	21	40	216	30%	37	0%	9.57	38.7	124	$28
Bats	Left	07 CLE	545	80	24	100	1	266	274	261	382	451	833	16	79	30	0.89	269	48	17	35	118	16%	44	1%	6.14	-1.6	56	$18
Health	D	08 CLE	198	21	5	24	1	197	220	189	293	323	617	12	72	25	0.49	242	42	25	33	96	11%	38	4%	3.14	-11.3	3	$1
PT/Exp	C	09 CLE	338	46	16	49	0	272	210	292	351	470	821	11	80	30	0.61	271	39	21	40	121	15%	22	0%	5.70	5.1	47	$11
Consist	F	1st Half	110	17	8	18	0	282			378	573	951	13	81	28	0.81	294	34	17	49	172	18%	18	0%	7.36	6.8	95	$5
LIMA Plan	D+	2nd Half	228	29	8	31	0	268			337	421	758	10	80	30	0.52	262	42	23	36	96	12%	23	0%	4.87	-1.9	24	$6
Rand Var	0	10 Proj	424	59	20	66	1	269			360	464	824	13	78	31	0.64	268	41	21	38	126	16%	29	1%	5.85	5.8	47	$13

Showed glimmers of the old Pronk, but the shoulder issues gradually wore him down. Really tanked vs. LHP, another warning sign. Remember: others with his "old player skills" have fallen fast. DN: repeat of 2008.

Hairston,Jerry

Hairston,Jerry		Yr	AB	R	HR	RBI	SB	Avg	vL	vR	OB	Slg	OPS	bb%	ct%	h%	Eye	xBA	G	L	F	PX	hr/f	SX	SBO	RC/G	RAR	BPV	R$
Pos	567	05 CHC	380	51	4	30	8	261	255	263	316	368	685	8	88	29	0.67	277	43	22	34	75	4%	92	17%	4.13	-7.4	56	$8
Age	34	06 2TM	170	25	0	10	5	206	153	245	262	253	515	7	80	26	0.38	203	42	17	41	36	0%	119	17%	1.87	-18.2	0	$1
Bats	Right	07 TEX	159	22	3	16	5	189	228	150	241	289	530	6	85	20	0.46	219	35	14	52	66	4%	100	19%	2.13	-14.0	38	$2
Health	C	08 CIN	* 340	55	9	48	16	324	345	316	371	502	873	7	87	35	0.57	288	32	27	41	113	7%	121	21%	6.18	7.4	91	$18
PT/Exp	D	09 2TM	383	62	10	39	7	251	242	255	308	394	703	8	86	27	0.59	266	34	23	43	90	7%	92	12%	4.23	-7.8	61	$10
Consist	F	1st Half	229	39	7	22	7	245			297	389	685	7	84	26	0.47	260	35	24	41	86	9%	114	16%	3.91	-6.9	56	$7
LIMA Plan	D	2nd Half	154	23	3	17	0	260			325	403	728	9	88	28	0.83	274	33	22	45	96	5%	45	5%	4.70	-1.0	63	$3
Rand Var	+1	10 Proj	324	50	7	35	8	259			314	396	710	7	86	28	0.59	262	34	22	44	88	6%	95	15%	4.33	-6.5	61	$9

Quit running even before trade to NYY, and poof went the value. In the right role, SB could return, but recall the Forecaster's Toolbox mantra: speed is a skill of the young. Age 34 is the usual tipping point; he's getting close.

Hairston,Scott

Hairston,Scott		Yr	AB	R	HR	RBI	SB	Avg	vL	vR	OB	Slg	OPS	bb%	ct%	h%	Eye	xBA	G	L	F	PX	hr/f	SX	SBO	RC/G	RAR	BPV	R$
Pos	78	05 ARI	* 229	31	12	28	2	259	182		305	471	776	6	85	26	0.43	233	29	7	64	119	9%	87	4%	4.85	-3.2	76	$7
Age	30	06 aaa	396	64	20	63	2	292	375	429	358	510	868	9	83	31	0.62	325	50	30	20	126	31%	62	2%	6.15	10.3	74	$16
Bats	Right	07 2NL	263	37	11	36	2	243	235	247	311	452	764	9	79	27	0.47	261	34	15	50	134	10%	79	3%	4.95	-3.2	67	$7
Health	D	08 SD	326	42	17	31	3	248	280	224	308	479	786	8	74	28	0.33	251	38	14	48	151	15%	88	6%	5.19	-2.3	62	$9
PT/Exp	C	09 2TM	430	50	17	64	11	265	318	243	305	456	761	5	81	29	0.30	250	34	15	51	121	10%	95	15%	4.70	-7.3	61	$15
Consist	A	1st Half	181	24	9	27	7	309			359	541	900	7	77	36	0.33	275	32	23	45	153	14%	94	17%	6.59	6.5	74	$9
LIMA Plan	C	2nd Half	249	26	8	37	4	233			265	394	659	4	84	25	0.27	229	35	10	54	100	7%	78	13%	3.45	-13.9	48	$6
Rand Var	0	10 Proj	410	52	18	54	7	259			309	466	775	7	79	29	0.35	254	35	15	50	132	11%	92	10%	4.95	-3.2	66	$13

Healthy enough to eek out 400+ AB, but not really healthy. More aches & pains did in a fine start. Power skills remain intriguing, but we've said it 1000 times: injury-prone players rarely get suddenly healthy.

Hall,Bill

Hall,Bill		Yr	AB	R	HR	RBI	SB	Avg	vL	vR	OB	Slg	OPS	bb%	ct%	h%	Eye	xBA	G	L	F	PX	hr/f	SX	SBO	RC/G	RAR	BPV	R$
Pos	57	05 MIL	501	69	17	62	18	291	328	277	343	495	838	7	79	34	0.38	293	43	22	34	138	12%	124	20%	5.83	14.9	81	$21
Age	30	06 MIL	537	101	35	85	8	270	300	261	347	553	900	11	70	32	0.39	268	33	19	48	192	19%	92	13%	7.01	23.9	83	$23
Bats	Right	07 MIL	452	59	14	63	4	254	270	247	315	425	740	8	72	33	0.31	255	36	23	41	131	10%	50	8%	4.72	-11.9	24	$11
Health	A	08 MIL	404	50	15	55	5	225	306	174	290	396	686	8	69	29	0.30	235	39	21	40	127	13%	66	12%	3.96	-17.6	17	$9
PT/Exp	C	09 2TM	334	32	8	36	2	201	223	186	260	338	599	7	64	29	0.23	208	39	18	43	117	9%	60	6%	2.82	-22.0	-15	$2
Consist	B	1st Half	182	18	5	18	1	203			264	341	605	8	68	27	0.26	217	38	19	42	108	10%	44	3%	2.81	-11.9	-11	$1
LIMA Plan	D	2nd Half	152	14	3	18	1	197			256	336	592	7	59	31	0.19	197	41	16	43	129	8%	76	11%	2.92	-9.7	-21	$1
Rand Var	+2	10 Proj	336	38	10	42	3	223			285	383	667	8	67	30	0.26	227	39	20	42	127	11%	67	10%	3.78	-12.9	7	$6

And the spiral continues, as the whiffs pile up. Versatility and long memories will keep getting him AB, but not much longer. One of those guys who you see where he was pre-peak and wonder, "what went wrong?"

Hamilton,Josh

Hamilton,Josh		Yr	AB	R	HR	RBI	SB	Avg	vL	vR	OB	Slg	OPS	bb%	ct%	h%	Eye	xBA	G	L	F	PX	hr/f	SX	SBO	RC/G	RAR	BPV	R$
Pos	89	05	0	0	0	0	0	0							0			0						0					
Age	29	06	0	0	0	0	0	0							0			0						0					
Bats	Left	07 CIN	* 338	60	23	54	6	295	222	314	364	563	927	10	78	32	0.50	308	45	22	33	161	26%	88	10%	6.93	22.7	90	$17
Health	C	08 TEX	624	98	32	130	9	304	288	313	369	530	900	9	80	34	0.51	295	46	21	33	141	20%	100	5%	6.60	21.3	82	$30
PT/Exp	C	09 TEX	336	43	10	54	8	268	327	239	317	426	742	7	76	32	0.30	248	36	22	42	104	9%	95	13%	4.59	-0.5	33	$11
Consist	C	1st Half	125	20	6	24	3	240			291	456	747	7	75	27	0.29	242	34	15	51	130	13%	130	12%	4.60	-0.1	59	$4
LIMA Plan	C+	2nd Half	211	23	4	30	5	284			332	408	739	7	77	35	0.31	255	38	26	37	90	7%	59	14%	4.58	-0.4	14	$6
Rand Var	0	10 Proj	483	71	21	86	9	284			341	482	824	8	78	33	0.40	273	41	22	38	126	15%	95	10%	5.63	11.6	59	$19

Obviously, the litany of injuries did in '09. He's not been injury-prone, but his history is so unique, no one knows if he'll remain at risk. Know this: with health, still owns '07 & '08, and is young enough to do even better.

Hanigan,Ryan

Hanigan,Ryan		Yr	AB	R	HR	RBI	SB	Avg	vL	vR	OB	Slg	OPS	bb%	ct%	h%	Eye	xBA	G	L	F	PX	hr/f	SX	SBO	RC/G	RAR	BPV	R$
Pos	2	05 aa	330	31	3	21	3	254			324	311	635	9	89	28	0.93	0				39		46	3%	3.66	-2.4	21	$4
Age	30	06 a/a	139	16	0	13	0	207			310	220	530	13	81	26	0.78	0				11		31	0%	2.32	-8.9	-31	($0)
Bats	Right	07 a/a	324	35	3	27	0	226			312	311	624	11	86	25	0.91	0				58		36	2%	3.57	-7.8	27	$2
Health	A	08 CIN	* 357	35	6	34	1	264	237	298	318	348	667	7	87	29	0.63	255	51	21	28	54	6%	35	1%	3.82	-4.0	19	$6
PT/Exp	D	09 CIN	251	22	3	11	0	263	291	255	358	331	688	13	88	29	1.19	256	48	24	27	41	5%	28	0%	4.43	1.2	19	$3
Consist	A	1st Half	131	16	1	8	0	321			411	389	800	13	91	35	1.67	270	47	25	28	42	3%	45	0%	5.85	5.5	39	$4
LIMA Plan	F	2nd Half	120	6	2	3	0	200			299	267	566	12	84	22	0.89	224	51	23	26	40	8%	3	0%	2.80	-5.5	-4	($1)
Rand Var	-1	10 Proj	249	23	3	16	0	269			350	334	684	11	87	30	0.93	252	49	24	27	42	5%	22	1%	4.23	-0.2	11	$4

All we ask from a $1 catcher is: First, do no harm. That means high ct% + low AB. It sets a BA floor, and worst case, few AB. It's like the old Yiddish joke: Lady 1: This food is terrible. Lady 2: And such small portions.

Hannahan,Jack

Hannahan,Jack		Yr	AB	R	HR	RBI	SB	Avg	vL	vR	OB	Slg	OPS	bb%	ct%	h%	Eye	xBA	G	L	F	PX	hr/f	SX	SBO	RC/G	RAR	BPV	R$
Pos	5	05 a/a	257	25	3	24	5	218			282	296	578	8	78	27	0.40	0				60		62	12%	2.59	-16.4	-4	$2
Age	30	06 aaa	415	53	8	56	8	257			344	369	714	12	74	33	0.51	0				84		59	10%	4.51	-9.1	6	$10
Bats	Left	07 OAK	* 480	65	13	79	6	267	400	239	380	416	796	15	74	34	0.69	253	37	23	39	111	10%	55	6%	5.79	12.8	33	$14
Health	A	08 OAK	441	49	10	48	2	218	204	223	304	347	651	11	70	29	0.41	225	37	21	42	106	8%	46	2%	3.63	-16.9	2	$5
PT/Exp	C	09 2AL	* 345	35	6	29	1	209	191	225	283	333	617	9	71	28	0.36	221	40	18	42	95	6%	60	4%	3.12	-16.8	-0	$2
Consist	C	1st Half	186	15	2	14	0	175			242	272	514	8	70	24	0.29	196	37	17	46	74	3%	65	2%	1.64	-18.4	-23	($1)
LIMA Plan	F	2nd Half	159	20	4	15	1	249			331	405	736	11	73	32	0.45	245	42	19	39	118	9%	41	5%	4.79	0.5	22	$3
Rand Var	+3	10 Proj	125	14	3	13	1	224			309	352	661	11	72	29	0.44	228	39	20	41	100	7%	42	5%	3.76	-3.9	4	$1

4-19-.213 in 267 AB at OAK/SEA. There it was, his peak flashing by in 2007. I think it's safe to say at this point that he's just not a good hitter. Even 2H "rebound" barely replacement. He's now officially fanalytically irrelevent.

Hardy,J.J.

Hardy,J.J.		Yr	AB	R	HR	RBI	SB	Avg	vL	vR	OB	Slg	OPS	bb%	ct%	h%	Eye	xBA	G	L	F	PX	hr/f	SX	SBO	RC/G	RAR	BPV	R$
Pos	6	05 MIL	372	46	9	50	0	247	245	240	327	384	711	11	87	26	0.92	274	44	20	35	88	8%	38	0%	4.54	6.3	53	$8
Age	28	06 MIL	128	13	5	14	1	242	294	223	297	398	696	7	82	26	0.43	255	47	19	34	90	14%	36	6%	3.96	-1.5	28	$2
Bats	Right	07 MIL	592	89	26	80	2	277	316	264	323	463	786	6	88	28	0.55	279	41	17	42	105	12%	50	3%	5.03	9.8	64	$19
Health	B	08 MIL	569	78	24	74	2	283	304	276	343	478	821	8	83	31	0.53	272	48	15	36	118	14%	68	2%	5.58	15.2	65	$19
PT/Exp	C	09 MIL	* 485	58	14	55	0	226	169	245	292	355	648	9	81	25	0.49	227	46	14	40	82	9%	45	1%	3.48	-17.4	22	$8
Consist	C	1st Half	262	37	8	32	0	233			307	366	673	10	81	26	0.56	231	45	15	40	83	9%	49	0%	3.84	-6.4	26	$5
LIMA Plan	D+	2nd Half	223	21	6	23	0	217			275	342	617	7	81	24	0.41	222	49	12	39	80	8%	42	2%	3.06	-11.0	17	$2
Rand Var	+2	10 Proj	441	55	17	53	0	259			318	429	747	8	83	28	0.51	255	46	15	38	103	12%	45	1%	4.66	1.2	45	$11

11-47-.229 in 414 AB at MIL. Talk about out of nowhere. He's upset about losing a year of free agency due to minors demotion. Now whose fault is that? Minor rebound potential in the BPIs but that may not be enough.

ROD TRUESDELL

Harris,Brendan

			AB	R	HR	RBI	SB	Avg	vL	vR	OB	Slg	OPS	bb%	ct%	h%	Eye	xBA	G	L	F	PX	hr/f	SX	SBO	RC/G	RAR	BPV	R$
Pos	65	05 aaa	470	49	9	58	7	225			270	331	601	6	88	24	0.51	0				64		78	12%	3.01	-18.2	40	$7
Age	30	06 CIN	* 409	55	11	54	4	269			329	421	750	8	80	31	0.44	215	37	9	54	101	6%	65	5%	4.79	5.0	38	$11
Bats	Right	07 TAM	521	72	12	59	4	286	345	264	339	434	773	7	82	33	0.44	276	43	21	35	102	8%	79	4%	5.04	10.9	48	$14
Health	A	08 MIN	434	57	7	49	1	265	265	265	326	394	720	8	77	33	0.40	251	53	16	30	96	7%	68	2%	4.45	1.5	25	$9
PT/Exp	B	09 MIN	414	44	6	37	0	261	302	239	309	362	672	7	81	31	0.37	231	51	15	34	69	5%	35	2%	3.74	-8.5	6	$6
Consist	B	1st Half	235	26	4	21	0	285			331	387	718	6	80	34	0.34	229	55	16	29	70	7%	24	0%	4.26	-1.2	-2	$5
LIMA Plan	D	2nd Half	179	18	2	16	0	229			281	330	611	7	83	27	0.42	231	46	15	40	68	3%	53	5%	3.09	-7.5	17	$1
Rand Var	-1	10 Proj	325	38	5	33	1	258			312	373	684	7	81	31	0.40	243	49	16	34	80	6%	49	3%	3.94	-4.4	18	$6

Nearly every skill is trending downward over the last three seasons; only a high 1H h% kept '09 from being a complete disaster. Playing time will likely be the next domino to fall. DN: .230 BA, 150 AB.

Harris,Willie

			AB	R	HR	RBI	SB	Avg	vL	vR	OB	Slg	OPS	bb%	ct%	h%	Eye	xBA	G	L	F	PX	hr/f	SX	SBO	RC/G	RAR	BPV	R$
Pos	87	05 CHW	* 230	33	2	16	18	242	286	252	317	335	652	10	79	30	0.53	244	52	19	30	68	4%	139	34%	3.70	-4.1	34	$7
Age	32	06 BOS	* 263	45	7	16	15	193			273	307	580	10	75	23	0.44	238	68	9	24	74	14%	133	33%	2.58	-17.8	21	$5
Bats	Left	07 ATL	* 402	70	3	37	22	277	191	283	351	408	760	10	81	34	0.60	260	42	21	37	88	2%	144	30%	5.16	7.6	59	$14
Health	A	08 WAS	367	58	13	43	13	251	240	255	341	417	757	12	82	27	0.76	258	43	18	38	98	11%	123	14%	5.03	3.2	69	$12
PT/Exp	C	09 WAS	323	47	7	27	11	235	121	248	350	393	743	15	81	27	0.92	239	39	15	47	102	6%	125	15%	5.12	3.8	74	$8
Consist	A	1st Half	147	22	4	15	9	245			347	429	776	14	81	28	0.82	279	50	16	34	123	10%	131	24%	5.44	3.1	90	$5
LIMA Plan	D+	2nd Half	176	25	3	12	2	227			352	364	716	16	81	27	1.00	206	28	14	58	84	4%	96	8%	4.84	0.6	53	$2
Rand Var	+1	10 Proj	274	42	7	25	11	245			343	402	746	13	81	28	0.78	247	40	17	43	99	7%	125	18%	5.01	2.7	68	$8

2H FB surge killed his BA, but combined with Eye and PX growth, you have to wonder: is a power breakout coming? Frankly, we'd prefer the speed but there is little SB upside for a 30something player.

Hart,Corey

			AB	R	HR	RBI	SB	Avg	vL	vR	OB	Slg	OPS	bb%	ct%	h%	Eye	xBA	G	L	F	PX	hr/f	SX	SBO	RC/G	RAR	BPV	R$
Pos	9	05 MIL	* 486	73	15	59	25	259	211	184	318	440	759	8	84	28	0.54	311	54	22	24	112	15%	146	29%	4.89	-5.2	87	$19
Age	28	06 MIL	* 337	47	13	50	14	279	304	272	332	474	806	7	75	34	0.32	253	42	17	41	128	12%	105	29%	5.47	6.9	51	$14
Bats	Right	07 MIL	505	86	24	81	23	295	331	278	342	539	881	7	80	33	0.36	283	37	17	46	147	13%	146	25%	6.26	19.6	98	$25
Health	B	08 MIL	612	76	20	91	23	268	281	263	299	459	758	4	82	30	0.25	274	40	19	40	123	10%	124	25%	4.65	-9.6	75	$23
PT/Exp	B	09 MIL	419	64	12	48	11	260	248	264	329	418	747	9	78	31	0.47	245	41	17	42	107	9%	103	15%	4.79	-1.2	49	$14
Consist	B	1st Half	279	46	9	34	5	251			319	427	746	9	76	30	0.42	248	40	18	42	120	10%	109	11%	4.77	-0.9	53	$9
LIMA Plan	C+	2nd Half	140	18	3	14	6	279			348	400	748	10	82	32	0.60	238	42	16	42	84	6%	71	21%	4.84	-0.2	39	$5
Rand Var	0	10 Proj	550	78	17	71	21	273			328	449	777	8	80	31	0.42	260	40	18	42	115	9%	119	21%	5.06	1.5	67	$21

Yikes. This is not what you want to see in a player's peak years. Bruised foot and appendectomy can be blamed for 2H, but 1H xBA and RC/G show he was struggling even when healthy. Buy only at a discount.

Hawpe,Brad

			AB	R	HR	RBI	SB	Avg	vL	vR	OB	Slg	OPS	bb%	ct%	h%	Eye	xBA	G	L	F	PX	hr/f	SX	SBO	RC/G	RAR	BPV	R$
Pos	9	05 COL	305	38	9	47	2	262	250	264	353	403	757	12	77	31	0.61	248	52	17	32	90	12%	76	4%	5.04	-1.9	29	$9
Age	31	06 COL	499	67	22	84	5	293	232	302	384	515	899	13	75	35	0.60	274	42	22	36	142	16%	77	6%	6.98	31.0	66	$19
Bats	Left	07 COL	516	80	29	116	0	291	214	315	387	539	926	14	73	35	0.59	279	36	21	43	165	18%	48	1%	7.37	35.9	69	$23
Health	A	08 COL	488	69	25	85	2	283	282	283	379	498	877	13	73	34	0.57	260	38	23	39	144	18%	58	2%	6.73	21.2	52	$19
PT/Exp	A	09 COL	501	82	23	86	1	285	243	303	383	519	902	14	71	36	0.54	274	43	20	36	175	18%	56	3%	7.23	33.3	71	$21
Consist	B	1st Half	252	46	13	56	0	333			406	603	1010	11	78	39	0.55	303	38	21	41	186	16%	61	3%	8.24	22.4	102	$15
LIMA Plan	C+	2nd Half	249	36	10	30	1	237			360	434	794	16	64	33	0.54	245	50	19	31	162	20%	55	3%	6.04	8.7	38	$6
Rand Var	-1	10 Proj	483	73	23	84	1	280			378	500	878	14	72	35	0.56	266	42	21	37	157	18%	58	3%	6.84	25.7	59	$19

Third straight year with sizable 2H ct% loss (79/68 in 2007, 76/70 in 2008), and this time it cost him a career year. Setback vs. LH may keep him platooned. Upside remains 1H times two, reality may be more of same.

Headley,Chase

			AB	R	HR	RBI	SB	Avg	vL	vR	OB	Slg	OPS	bb%	ct%	h%	Eye	xBA	G	L	F	PX	hr/f	SX	SBO	RC/G	RAR	BPV	R$
Pos	75	05	0	0	0	0	0	0							0			0						0					
Age	26	06	0	0	0	0	0	0							0			0						0					
Bats	Both	07 aa	451	73	17	69	1	288	167	250	382	495	877	13	74	36	0.58	270	36	21	43	145	12%	69	1%	6.75	19.6	62	$16
Health	A	08 SD	* 590	74	19	71	4	263	276	265	326	432	758	9	72	34	0.33	251	38	25	37	125	12%	75	3%	4.98	-7.5	30	$16
PT/Exp	C	09 SD	543	62	12	64	10	262	244	270	337	392	729	10	76	33	0.47	233	45	17	38	96	8%	81	8%	4.64	-14.6	26	$14
Consist	C	1st Half	246	23	7	29	7	236			309	370	679	10	72	30	0.38	224	41	19	40	96	10%	80	14%	3.89	-12.5	10	$6
LIMA Plan	C+	2nd Half	297	39	5	35	3	283			360	411	771	11	78	35	0.56	240	48	14	37	97	6%	71	3%	5.24	-2.7	36	$9
Rand Var	0	10 Proj	566	72	16	70	6	267			341	424	765	10	74	33	0.44	246	44	18	38	114	10%	83	5%	5.11	-5.9	36	$16

PX, OPS, and xBA trends are not good, but daily transaction owners should note the home/away splits: .218 career BA at Petco, .301 BA everywhere else. May take a change of scenery for him to fully develop.

Helms,Wes

			AB	R	HR	RBI	SB	Avg	vL	vR	OB	Slg	OPS	bb%	ct%	h%	Eye	xBA	G	L	F	PX	hr/f	SX	SBO	RC/G	RAR	BPV	R$
Pos	5	05 MIL	168	18	4	24	0	298	305	294	352	458	810	8	82	34	0.47	269	44	18	38	111	8%	46	2%	5.51	3.4	49	$5
Age	34	06 FLA	240	30	10	47	0	329	336	323	383	575	958	8	77	39	0.38	294	38	26	36	155	15%	66	6%	7.48	12.9	70	$11
Bats	Right	07 PHI	280	21	5	39	0	246	282	221	294	368	662	6	78	30	0.31	240	39	20	41	90	6%	14	0%	3.59	-16.7	3	$4
Health	A	08 FLA	251	28	5	31	0	243	258	234	291	347	638	6	74	31	0.26	219	42	20	38	77	7%	30	0%	3.20	-16.1	-19	$4
PT/Exp	D	09 FLA	214	18	3	33	1	271	273	270	313	364	677	6	75	35	0.24	212	43	18	39	74	5%	32	4%	3.73	-8.7	-18	$5
Consist	A	1st Half	100	7	1	15	1	240			290	300	590	7	71	33	0.24	187	45	18	38	49	4%	36	7%	2.57	-7.8	-51	$1
LIMA Plan	F	2nd Half	114	11	2	18	0	298			333	421	754	5	78	37	0.24	232	42	18	40	95	6%	19	0%	4.68	-1.5	6	$3
Rand Var	-4	10 Proj	99	9	2	14	0	253			298	368	666	6	76	32	0.27	229	42	19	39	88	6%	32	2%	3.60	-4.8	-2	$2

2006 PX and hr/f starting to look like typos rather than mere outliers. Minus those skills, he's everything you don't want in a hitter. It takes a massive effort to post a sub-Mendoza BPV but he's done it two years running.

Helton,Todd

			AB	R	HR	RBI	SB	Avg	vL	vR	OB	Slg	OPS	bb%	ct%	h%	Eye	xBA	G	L	F	PX	hr/f	SX	SBO	RC/G	RAR	BPV	R$
Pos	3	05 COL	509	92	20	79	3	320	245	351	437	534	972	17	84	35	1.33	304	33	24	42	140	11%	69	1%	8.01	32.7	106	$24
Age	37	06 COL	546	94	15	81	3	302	326	295	402	476	878	14	88	32	1.42	285	35	24	41	102	8%	76	3%	6.74	11.2	88	$20
Bats	Left	07 COL	557	86	17	91	0	320	285	334	437	494	931	17	87	35	1.57	300	40	24	36	109	10%	34	0%	7.53	20.8	80	$22
Health	C	08 COL	299	39	7	29	0	264	246	270	389	388	777	17	83	30	1.22	256	38	23	38	82	7%	20	0%	5.61	-1.0	41	$6
PT/Exp	A	09 COL	544	79	15	86	0	325	311	332	420	489	909	14	87	36	1.22	291	40	25	36	104	9%	41	0%	7.07	8.1	72	$23
Consist	D	1st Half	266	43	9	53	0	312			398	504	902	13	84	35	0.88	293	43	23	35	124	12%	52	0%	6.88	2.6	77	$12
LIMA Plan	B+	2nd Half	278	36	6	33	0	338			441	475	916	16	89	36	1.70	291	37	26	36	87	7%	33	1%	7.27	5.5	69	$11
Rand Var	-4	10 Proj	545	79	15	76	0	308			416	465	880	16	86	34	1.31	285	39	24	37	100	8%	40	1%	6.82	9.4	69	$20

Back surgery appears to have erased awful taste of 2008, and while he's no longer the force he once was, R$ shows he can still deliver dependable value as a second-tier 1B. Age is all about adjusting expectations.

Hermida,Jeremy

			AB	R	HR	RBI	SB	Avg	vL	vR	OB	Slg	OPS	bb%	ct%	h%	Eye	xBA	G	L	F	PX	hr/f	SX	SBO	RC/G	RAR	BPV	R$
Pos	97	05 FLA	* 427	77	19	67	22	269	200	306	415	480	895	20	78	31	1.12	274	31	24	45	142	13%	114	14%	7.20	24.0	100	$21
Age	26	06 FLA	307	37	5	28	4	251	219	261	324	368	692	10	77	31	0.47	241	45	20	35	84	6%	72	6%	4.15	-5.6	19	$5
Bats	Left	07 FLA	429	54	18	63	3	296	292	297	366	501	867	10	76	36	0.45	278	44	21	35	141	16%	45	6%	6.37	17.9	50	$15
Health	B	08 FLA	502	74	17	61	6	249	240	252	315	406	721	9	73	31	0.35	237	46	18	36	109	13%	99	5%	4.41	-11.5	26	$14
PT/Exp	B	09 FLA	429	48	13	47	5	259	189	282	344	392	736	12	76	31	0.55	233	41	20	39	86	10%	68	5%	4.71	-2.2	20	$11
Consist	C	1st Half	260	27	8	29	4	254			347	385	731	12	77	30	0.62	231	42	19	39	84	10%	59	7%	4.69	-1.5	20	$6
LIMA Plan	C	2nd Half	169	21	5	18	1	266			340	402	743	10	76	33	0.46	235	39	22	40	90	10%	65	2%	4.74	-0.7	17	$4
Rand Var	-1	10 Proj	420	54	14	50	5	264			343	418	760	11	75	32	0.48	244	42	20	38	103	12%	78	5%	5.00	0.4	31	$12

Exactly what you do NOT want to see from your 25-year-old slugger: more FB yet fewer HR, and a declining xBA as a result. Still young enough to turn this around, but there's no reason to believe that's coming in 2010.

Hernandez,Anderson

			AB	R	HR	RBI	SB	Avg	vL	vR	OB	Slg	OPS	bb%	ct%	h%	Eye	xBA	G	L	F	PX	hr/f	SX	SBO	RC/G	RAR	BPV	R$
Pos	46	05 a/a	526	65	7	44	28	287			323	373	696	5	84	33	0.33	0				55		107	32%	3.95	-6.1	24	$19
Age	27	06 NYM	* 480	47	1	25	15	229	211	128	261	277	539	4	84	27	0.27	213	49	15	36	30	1%	107	18%	2.09	-36.9	1	$4
Bats	Both	07 aa	554	67	4	33	12	259			291	334	625	4	87	29	0.35	0				51		94	16%	3.20	-18.9	28	$9
Health	A	08 WAS	* 560	56	4	45	8	193	366	300	247	269	515	7	84	22	0.44	259	39	30	31	51	3%	93	14%	1.97	-50.6	18	$1
PT/Exp	C	09 2NL	366	39	3	37	7	251	273	245	313	339	652	8	83	30	0.52	257	55	20	25	59	4%	94	12%	3.67	-9.4	25	$7
Consist	C	1st Half	195	22	1	21	5	256			322	323	646	9	85	30	0.63	258	54	22	24	48	2%	84	14%	3.66	-5.0	21	$4
LIMA Plan	F	2nd Half	171	17	2	16	2	246			303	357	659	8	81	29	0.42	254	57	17	25	72	6%	92	9%	3.69	-4.3	25	$3
Rand Var	-1	10 Proj	191	20	2	16	4	246			297	333	630	7	83	29	0.44	258	55	20	26	58	4%	94	14%	3.34	-7.4	24	$3

bb% growth is encouraging, but it's lost in a sea of middling skills. If he's going to run less, what's the point of adding walks? (At that comment, fantasy owners nod; sabermetricians cringe. I like making people cringe.)

BRANDON KRUSE

Hernandez,Diory			AB	R	HR	RBI	SB	Avg	vL	vR	OB	Slg	OPS	bb%	ct%	h%	Eye	xBA	G	L	F	PX	hr/f	SX	SBO	RC/G	RAR	BPV	R$
Pos	6	05	0	0	0	0	0	0							0			0						0					
Age	26	06	0	0	0	0	0	0							0			0						0					
Bats	Right	07 aa	433	43	6	50	18	280			318	379	697	5	85	32	0.39	0				67		75	35%	4.03	-4.5	31	$13
Health	A	08 a/a	536	43	6	49	7	253			281	339	619	4	87	28	0.29	0				56		65	13%	3.08	-22.5	21	$8
PT/Exp	F	09 ATL	* 289	20	2	31	7	233	87	161	290	319	609	7	82	28	0.43	234	54	14	32	66	3%	64	20%	3.09	-14.1	16	$4
Consist	A	1st Half	162	13	1	17	4	252			306	347	652	7	87	29	0.58	249	63	10	28	73	3%	56	14%	3.73	-4.5	39	$3
LIMA Plan	F	2nd Half	127	7	1	14	3	210			270	284	554	8	75	27	0.33	213	39	22	39	56	3%	66	28%	2.24	-10.1	-17	$1
Rand Var	0	10 Proj	113	9	1	12	2	230			275	329	604	6	83	27	0.37	244	50	16	34	68	3%	85	23%	2.97	-5.7	26	$1

1-6-.141 in 85 AB at ATL. Often, these fringe types can have hidden upside. This isn't one of them. PX, SX show zero life. His glove has life, and he can play all around infield. Too bad he can't hit ball with glove.

Hernandez,Michel			AB	R	HR	RBI	SB	Avg	vL	vR	OB	Slg	OPS	bb%	ct%	h%	Eye	xBA	G	L	F	PX	hr/f	SX	SBO	RC/G	RAR	BPV	R$
Pos	2	05 aaa	264	14	2	23	0	234			311	291	602	10	89	26	1.04	0				37		23	0%	3.36	-4.3	15	$1
Age	32	06 aaa	285	20	2	23	3	241			297	300	597	7	90	26	0.80	0				36		53	5%	3.17	-10.3	22	$2
Bats	Right	07 a/a	170	19	4	16	0	241			301	327	627	8	92	25	1.02	0				46		31	2%	3.51	-4.3	31	$2
Health	A	08 aaa	252	21	2	13	0	213			248	287	535	5	86	24	0.34	0				53		48	3%	2.17	-16.0	11	($0)
PT/Exp	F	09 TAM	* 145	14	1	16	2	212	200	261	269	268	537	7	87	24	0.59	247	57	17	25	32	3%	78	8%	2.35	-8.7	13	$1
Consist	B	1st Half	68	7	1	11	2	265			286	338	624	3	91	28	0.33	266	61	16	23	42	7%	64	18%	3.15	-2.2	25	$2
LIMA Plan	F	2nd Half	77	7	0	5	0	166			256	205	461	11	83	20	0.71	221	48	20	32	22	0%	61	0%	1.50	-7.0	-9	($1)
Rand Var	+3	10 Proj	65	6	1	6	0	215			270	272	542	7	87	24	0.59	242	57	17	26	37	4%	42	5%	2.40	-3.7	8	$0

1-12-.242 in 99 AB at TAM. When mining for $1 CA gold, dad always told me to look for power. This one has 30 HR pop! ....over the course of a DECADE. Good ct% is only saving's grace, but even that's fading.

Hernandez,Ramon			AB	R	HR	RBI	SB	Avg	vL	vR	OB	Slg	OPS	bb%	ct%	h%	Eye	xBA	G	L	F	PX	hr/f	SX	SBO	RC/G	RAR	BPV	R$
Pos	23	05 SD	369	36	12	58	1	290	238	304	323	450	773	5	89	30	0.45	294	46	21	33	93	11%	53	1%	4.84	10.8	59	$12
Age	34	06 BAL	501	66	23	91	1	275	291	270	333	479	812	8	84	29	0.54	280	44	19	38	119	14%	53	1%	5.42	14.4	65	$16
Bats	Right	07 BAL	364	40	9	62	1	258	250	261	325	382	707	9	84	29	0.61	250	49	16	35	81	8%	29	4%	4.30	0.1	29	$8
Health	D	08 BAL	467	49	15	65	0	257	283	245	305	407	711	6	87	27	0.51	272	47	20	33	91	11%	31	0%	4.22	0.4	43	$10
PT/Exp	C	09 CIN	287	25	5	37	1	258	288	246	334	362	697	10	88	28	0.97	259	49	19	32	66	6%	44	1%	4.39	1.1	41	$6
Consist	A	1st Half	243	21	5	32	1	251			328	370	699	10	88	27	1.00	266	51	18	31	74	8%	44	1%	4.42	1.1	49	$5
LIMA Plan	D	2nd Half	44	4	0	5	0	295			367	318	686	10	86	34	0.83	220	43	23	35	19	0%	18	0%	4.23	-0.0	-11	$1
Rand Var	+1	10 Proj	417	43	10	64	1	261			323	389	712	8	86	28	0.66	261	48	19	34	80	8%	43	2%	4.37	1.4	40	$10

Knee surgery cost him most of 2H. Before that, it was more of the same, with less power. And power will be gone for good if FB trend continues. Good pop in even years though, so decent $10+ pick for the superstitious.

Hill,Aaron			AB	R	HR	RBI	SB	Avg	vL	vR	OB	Slg	OPS	bb%	ct%	h%	Eye	xBA	G	L	F	PX	hr/f	SX	SBO	RC/G	RAR	BPV	R$
Pos	4	05 TOR	* 517	67	7	55	4	277	298	269	325	398	723	7	89	30	0.67	276	43	22	36	81	4%	83	4%	4.54	6.0	63	$12
Age	28	06 TOR	546	70	6	50	5	291	298	288	342	386	728	7	88	32	0.64	255	46	19	35	61	4%	80	4%	4.57	6.9	40	$12
Bats	Right	07 TOR	608	87	17	78	4	291	317	283	336	459	795	6	83	33	0.40	284	40	21	39	114	9%	69	5%	5.21	20.7	59	$18
Health	D	08 TOR	205	19	2	20	4	263	286	258	317	361	678	7	85	30	0.52	233	35	17	47	73	2%	55	11%	3.95	-5.6	31	$4
PT/Exp	B	09 TOR	682	103	36	108	6	286	298	282	327	499	826	6	86	29	0.43	288	39	20	41	119	15%	62	5%	5.40	9.1	70	$27
Consist	C	1st Half	345	48	19	56	3	301			340	504	844	5	85	31	0.39	285	38	22	40	110	16%	49	4%	5.55	5.9	56	$15
LIMA Plan	C	2nd Half	337	55	17	52	3	270			315	493	807	6	86	27	0.47	291	41	17	42	129	14%	66	6%	5.26	3.2	81	$12
Rand Var	0	10 Proj	590	84	23	83	5	280			326	465	790	6	85	30	0.47	278	39	19	42	112	11%	61	5%	5.11	6.8	65	$19

Reasons to expect '07, not '09...
- HR surge driven by hr/f spike
- PX nearly identical to '07.
- bb%, ct% stayed flat

Maintaining 40%+ FB% is key. 2B with good pop are scarce, but this one will be overvalued.

Hill,Koyie			AB	R	HR	RBI	SB	Avg	vL	vR	OB	Slg	OPS	bb%	ct%	h%	Eye	xBA	G	L	F	PX	hr/f	SX	SBO	RC/G	RAR	BPV	R$
Pos	2	05 ARI	* 246	21	4	23	2	211	261	212	290	318	608	10	79	25	0.52	235	51	15	34	78	6%	57	5%	3.10	-5.3	16	$1
Age	31	06 aaa	70	4	1	5	0	129			187	200	387	7	74	16	0.28	0				50		19	0%	-0.11	-10.7	-42	($1)
Bats	Both	07 CHC	* 242	22	4	28	1	211			257	326	583	6	82	24	0.35	0				82		40	3%	2.67	-13.2	20	$1
Health	A	08 aaa	364	37	12	42	2	210			263	366	629	7	81	23	0.37	0				101		52	5%	3.15	-11.9	35	$4
PT/Exp	F	09 CHC	253	26	2	24	0	237	256	233	311	324	635	10	69	34	0.35	219	50	22	28	73	4%	54	0%	3.42	-6.4	-27	$3
Consist	A	1st Half	66	6	2	7	0	212			307	333	640	12	62	31	0.36	204	59	22	20	98	25%	14	0%	3.52	-1.5	-43	$1
LIMA Plan	F	2nd Half	187	20	0	17	0	246			312	321	633	9	72	34	0.34	220	48	22	30	66	0%	63	0%	3.40	-4.7	-23	$2
Rand Var	-5	10 Proj	160	16	3	17	0	231			297	349	646	9	74	29	0.36	245	52	22	27	86	9%	59	2%	3.46	-3.8	3	$2

Handed semi-regular PT in 2H. That was a mistake. Save for 128 PX in Aug and decent bb%, there's no reason for optimism, especially given extreme GB approach and age. Mine for $1 catchers elsewhere.

Hinske,Eric			AB	R	HR	RBI	SB	Avg	vL	vR	OB	Slg	OPS	bb%	ct%	h%	Eye	xBA	G	L	F	PX	hr/f	SX	SBO	RC/G	RAR	BPV	R$
Pos	9	05 TOR	477	79	15	68	8	262	172	281	327	430	757	9	75	32	0.38	250	41	20	39	122	11%	99	10%	4.91	3.0	45	$15
Age	33	06 2AL	277	43	13	34	2	271	167	293	353	487	840	11	71	34	0.44	248	40	16	43	148	15%	77	5%	6.18	4.2	52	$8
Bats	Left	07 BOS	186	25	6	21	3	204	200	205	308	398	706	13	71	25	0.52	246	45	11	44	142	10%	112	7%	4.49	-5.9	59	$3
Health	A	08 TAM	381	59	20	60	10	247	143	262	329	465	794	11	77	27	0.53	272	39	20	41	142	17%	87	13%	5.37	0.1	71	$14
PT/Exp	D	09 2TM	190	31	8	25	1	242	244	242	336	432	768	12	73	29	0.52	245	37	18	45	135	13%	51	2%	5.20	0.5	40	$5
Consist	C	1st Half	106	18	1	11	0	255			358	368	726	14	75	33	0.63	225	45	15	40	97	3%	40	0%	4.86	-0.7	17	$2
LIMA Plan	D	2nd Half	84	13	7	14	1	226			309	512	820	11	70	23	0.40	267	28	21	51	185	23%	48	5%	5.67	1.4	66	$3
Rand Var	0	10 Proj	208	32	10	29	3	236			325	449	774	12	73	27	0.49	255	38	18	44	145	15%	83	6%	5.21	0.3	59	$6

We've come to expect flashes of power from him, and this was no exception. But the 2H surge was fueled by flukey 23% hr/f. Gains vs. LHers stick out as an aberration too. PX confirms power upside, but it needs AB.

Hoffpauir,Micah			AB	R	HR	RBI	SB	Avg	vL	vR	OB	Slg	OPS	bb%	ct%	h%	Eye	xBA	G	L	F	PX	hr/f	SX	SBO	RC/G	RAR	BPV	R$
Pos	39	05 a/a	413	38	4	37	2	219			272	283	555	7	86	25	0.53	0				41		65	2%	2.50	-36.1	12	$2
Age	30	06 a/a	393	55	21	71	1	238			321	451	772	11	75	27	0.49	0				132		55	3%	5.07	-7.5	46	$11
Bats	Left	07 aaa	310	39	12	51	2	246			285	428	713	5	89	24	0.48	0				107		50	4%	4.18	-13.9	68	$8
Health	A	08 CHC	* 363	56	20	76	3	302	273	355	334	575	909	5	82	32	0.27	337	22	41	37	177	19%	73	4%	6.41	6.7	103	$18
PT/Exp	F	09 CHC	* 317	37	13	44	3	223	172	249	278	397	675	7	82	24	0.42	248	28	21	52	109	9%	71	4%	3.73	-26.9	52	$7
Consist	F	1st Half	141	13	7	22	0	248			293	447	740	6	74	29	0.25	251	25	22	53	134	13%	10	0%	4.44	-8.6	22	$4
LIMA Plan	F	2nd Half	176	24	6	22	3	202			266	357	623	8	88	20	0.71	251	31	19	50	91	7%	93	8%	3.36	-17.3	70	$3
Rand Var	+3	10 Proj	197	25	8	32	2	244			292	443	735	6	83	25	0.40	269	28	23	50	123	10%	74	4%	4.43	-10.3	67	$6

10-35-.239 in 234 AB at CHC. First extended MLB look yielded flashes of power, not much else. '08 BA looks like the outlier, since it was driven by h% spike. Now in his 30s, his window of opportunity is closing quick.

Holliday,Matt			AB	R	HR	RBI	SB	Avg	vL	vR	OB	Slg	OPS	bb%	ct%	h%	Eye	xBA	G	L	F	PX	hr/f	SX	SBO	RC/G	RAR	BPV	R$
Pos	7	05 COL	479	68	19	87	14	307	324	302	355	505	861	7	84	34	0.46	298	48	21	31	118	15%	125	13%	5.98	8.4	82	$24
Age	30	06 COL	602	119	34	114	10	326	327	325	374	586	961	7	82	35	0.43	307	45	21	34	153	20%	104	9%	7.19	31.2	97	$33
Bats	Right	07 COL	636	120	36	137	11	340	301	351	399	607	1006	9	80	38	0.50	314	44	20	36	166	20%	101	8%	7.92	42.5	104	$38
Health	A	08 COL	539	107	25	88	28	321	293	329	403	538	941	12	81	36	0.71	295	46	22	33	139	18%	121	16%	7.30	27.1	97	$34
PT/Exp	A	09 2TM	581	94	24	109	14	313	289	322	389	515	904	11	83	35	0.71	279	44	16	39	125	13%	90	11%	6.76	23.5	81	$29
Consist	B	1st Half	280	39	8	40	9	275			362	425	787	12	84	31	0.83	259	47	15	38	95	9%	87	13%	5.43	1.2	62	$10
LIMA Plan	B	2nd Half	301	55	16	69	5	349			415	598	1013	10	82	39	0.62	296	42	18	41	154	16%	83	9%	8.03	21.5	97	$19
Rand Var	-1	10 Proj	564	100	30	107	13	305			378	546	924	11	82	33	0.64	299	45	19	37	148	18%	95	11%	6.94	26.8	97	$29

How much you wanna bet he signs in NL again? 2H BA came from h% jump, but he's still a .300 hitter. FB jump, 2H PX help erase memories of Coors factor, and says there's another 30 HR season on the horizon.

Howard,Ryan			AB	R	HR	RBI	SB	Avg	vL	vR	OB	Slg	OPS	bb%	ct%	h%	Eye	xBA	G	L	F	PX	hr/f	SX	SBO	RC/G	RAR	BPV	R$
Pos	3	05 PHI	* 522	82	36	106	0	307	148	320	381	584	965	11	71	37	0.41	303	44	27	29	193	33%	43	1%	7.84	31.9	74	$27
Age	30	06 PHI	581	104	58	149	0	313	279	331	421	659	1080	16	69	36	0.60	293	42	22	36	220	40%	24	0%	9.69	57.7	92	$36
Bats	Left	07 PHI	529	94	47	136	1	268	225	297	392	584	976	17	62	34	0.54	278	31	24	44	233	32%	31	1%	8.78	40.2	81	$27
Health	A	08 PHI	610	105	48	146	1	251	224	268	339	543	881	12	67	29	0.41	276	41	22	36	200	32%	68	1%	6.80	19.2	76	$29
PT/Exp	A	09 PHI	616	105	45	141	8	279	207	320	357	571	929	11	70	33	0.40	284	36	23	41	204	26%	93	6%	7.38	15.1	94	$34
Consist	C	1st Half	297	47	20	60	3	256			324	535	860	9	69	30	0.32	275	39	19	42	201	23%	90	5%	6.41	-0.9	83	$13
LIMA Plan	B	2nd Half	319	58	25	81	5	301			387	605	992	12	71	35	0.48	294	34	27	39	206	28%	85	6%	8.25	15.3	101	$20
Rand Var	+1	10 Proj	583	101	41	129	3	268			358	541	898	12	68	32	0.44	274	37	23	39	192	26%	79	3%	7.09	15.2	76	$28

On surface, he remains elite. But the power vs LH is in big slide...

	HR	SLG
'07	16	.493
'08	14	.451
'09	6	.356

His hold on 40 HR is at risk now.

STEPHEN NICKRAND

Hudson,Orlando

		Yr	AB	R	HR	RBI	SB	Avg	vL	vR	OB	Slg	OPS	bb%	ct%	h%	Eye	xBA	G	L	F	PX	hr/f	SX	SBO	RC/G	RAR	BPV	R$
Pos	4	05 TOR	461	62	10	63	7	271	227	288	316	412	728	6	86	30	0.46	282	52	20	28	88	9%	108	7%	4.45	4.2	61	$13
Age	32	06 ARI	579	87	15	67	9	287	338	270	355	454	809	10	87	31	0.78	284	49	19	32	95	9%	100	9%	5.62	16.8	73	$18
Bats	Both	07 ARI	517	69	10	63	10	294	281	298	378	441	819	12	83	34	0.80	284	52	20	28	90	8%	110	7%	5.90	17.3	64	$16
Health	B	08 ARI	407	54	8	41	4	305	269	321	367	450	817	9	85	34	0.65	286	48	23	29	96	8%	82	4%	5.68	10.1	61	$13
PT/Exp	B	09 LA	551	74	9	62	8	283	293	280	356	417	773	10	82	33	0.63	276	56	19	26	92	8%	104	5%	5.24	11.0	55	$16
Consist	A	1st Half	313	48	5	41	6	294			365	425	790	10	82	34	0.64	275	52	20	28	93	7%	96	6%	5.44	7.9	55	$11
LIMA Plan	B	2nd Half	238	26	4	21	2	269			343	408	751	10	82	32	0.61	273	61	16	22	91	9%	87	4%	4.97	3.0	47	$5
Rand Var	0	10 Proj	514	67	9	56	7	278			349	419	769	10	83	32	0.65	281	54	20	27	92	8%	102	6%	5.17	8.0	59	$14

Upward trend in GB% (it rose every month but August) would work better if OB weren't in slow decline and if he had higher SX. It's the slow aging process. Get used to it; one day you'll lose your power and speed too.

Huff,Aubrey

		Yr	AB	R	HR	RBI	SB	Avg	vL	vR	OB	Slg	OPS	bb%	ct%	h%	Eye	xBA	G	L	F	PX	hr/f	SX	SBO	RC/G	RAR	BPV	R$
Pos	30	05 TAM	575	70	22	92	8	261	254	262	319	428	747	8	85	28	0.56	262	48	15	37	100	12%	69	10%	4.66	-7.2	57	$18
Age	33	06 2TM	454	57	21	66	0	267	233	278	339	469	808	10	86	27	0.78	281	45	19	36	114	15%	35	0%	5.51	-2.6	67	$13
Bats	Left	07 BAL	550	68	15	72	1	280	305	272	338	442	780	8	84	31	0.55	272	46	16	38	103	9%	64	1%	5.14	-1.8	56	$14
Health	A	08 BAL	598	96	32	108	4	304	270	321	361	552	913	8	85	31	0.60	305	41	17	42	152	15%	76	3%	6.62	22.0	103	$27
PT/Exp	A	09 2AL	536	59	15	85	0	241	232	245	307	384	691	9	84	26	0.59	248	48	15	36	89	9%	28	4%	4.09	-26.2	34	$10
Consist	F	1st Half	285	33	10	52	0	270			340	442	782	10	86	29	0.73	268	48	16	36	101	11%	34	6%	5.22	-4.1	55	$8
LIMA Plan	D+	2nd Half	251	26	5	33	0	207			268	319	587	8	82	23	0.46	230	49	15	37	74	7%	32	2%	2.77	-23.1	13	$2
Rand Var	+2	10 Proj	481	60	17	75	1	270			331	445	776	8	84	29	0.57	269	46	16	38	108	11%	47	3%	5.08	-5.7	55	$14

Along with Wigginton and Scott, they were three identical players trying to fit into one body. Never got into a groove and his hit rate plummeted in July/Aug (.190 BA). He will rebound some, but nobody loves him anymore.

Hundley,Nick

		Yr	AB	R	HR	RBI	SB	Avg	vL	vR	OB	Slg	OPS	bb%	ct%	h%	Eye	xBA	G	L	F	PX	hr/f	SX	SBO	RC/G	RAR	BPV	R$
Pos	2	05	0	0	0	0	0	0							0			0						0					
Age	27	06	0	0	0	0	0	0							0			0						0					
Bats	Right	07 aa	373	47	17	61	0	211			281	402	683	9	80	22	0.48	0				118		39	2%	3.87	-5.7	46	$7
Health	B	08 SD	* 422	47	13	55	0	211			253	348	602	5	77	24	0.25	0				90		43	0%	2.68	-19.9	8	$5
PT/Exp	D	09 SD	256	23	8	30	5	238	159	267	313	406	720	10	70	31	0.37	231	31	22	47	126	9%	82	9%	4.53	2.1	28	$6
Consist	D	1st Half	140	10	3	11	1	236			335	379	714	13	71	31	0.53	224	30	23	47	104	6%	68	5%	4.62	1.5	18	$2
LIMA Plan	D	2nd Half	116	13	5	19	4	241			285	440	724	6	69	31	0.19	241	34	19	47	153	13%	73	18%	4.40	0.5	34	$4
Rand Var	-3	10 Proj	347	37	12	47	4	239			296	401	698	8	74	29	0.31	235	32	21	47	113	10%	71	6%	4.03	-2.3	25	$8

Fractured wrist cost him month-and-a-half in mid-season, and remaining sample pretty small. High FB% and 2H PX are nice, but oh!, that ct%. "Chicks dig the longball" is so yesterday; they dig balls in play more often.

Hunter,Torii

		Yr	AB	R	HR	RBI	SB	Avg	vL	vR	OB	Slg	OPS	bb%	ct%	h%	Eye	xBA	G	L	F	PX	hr/f	SX	SBO	RC/G	RAR	BPV	R$
Pos	8	05 MIN	372	63	14	56	23	269	283	263	330	452	782	8	83	29	0.52	274	49	14	36	118	13%	119	32%	5.13	9.2	79	$17
Age	35	06 MIN	557	86	31	98	12	278	319	262	332	490	822	7	81	30	0.42	271	45	18	37	121	18%	88	12%	5.46	12.7	62	$23
Bats	Right	07 MIN	600	94	28	107	18	287	314	276	331	505	836	6	83	31	0.40	299	49	14	38	140	15%	88	20%	5.62	18.8	85	$27
Health	C	08 LAA	551	85	21	78	19	278	304	268	338	466	804	8	83	31	0.46	281	46	19	35	125	14%	105	17%	5.41	0.9	72	$22
PT/Exp	A	09 LAA	451	74	22	90	18	299	336	287	365	508	873	9	80	34	0.51	277	47	16	36	127	17%	96	17%	6.27	20.5	70	$24
Consist	B	1st Half	259	51	17	59	13	305			381	575	957	11	81	32	0.67	306	46	16	37	158	22%	106	21%	7.32	19.2	108	$17
LIMA Plan	C+	2nd Half	192	23	5	31	5	292			343	417	760	7	77	36	0.34	236	49	16	35	84	10%	64	11%	4.81	0.9	11	$7
Rand Var	-3	10 Proj	510	78	24	93	13	288			346	497	843	8	80	32	0.45	281	47	17	36	130	17%	85	13%	5.83	15.1	69	$23

On pace for career year before injuries destroyed 2H ouput. End result was similar to prior seasons. Assuming he's fully recovered, some of that 1H power could return, so there's upside here even at age 34.

Iannetta,Chris

		Yr	AB	R	HR	RBI	SB	Avg	vL	vR	OB	Slg	OPS	bb%	ct%	h%	Eye	xBA	G	L	F	PX	hr/f	SX	SBO	RC/G	RAR	BPV	R$
Pos	2	05 aa	60	6	1	9	0	200			284	283	567	10	72	26	0.41	0				64		25	0%	2.39	-2.9	-32	$0
Age	27	06 COL	* 384	59	14	47	1	307	231	266	386	495	880	11	85	33	0.88	303	52	23	25	108	17%	59	2%	6.51	22.7	71	$14
Bats	Right	07 COL	* 251	29	5	33	0	228	204	223	322	354	676	12	75	29	0.55	227	41	18	41	85	6%	62	0%	4.03	-3.0	12	$3
Health	A	08 COL	333	50	18	65	0	264	275	261	370	505	875	14	72	31	0.61	270	38	21	41	166	18%	47	0%	6.75	24.4	67	$13
PT/Exp	D	09 COL	289	41	16	52	0	228	296	202	328	460	789	13	74	25	0.57	250	32	16	52	154	14%	51	1%	5.42	10.2	62	$9
Consist	F	1st Half	153	23	10	27	0	229			344	484	828	15	74	24	0.68	266	29	19	52	172	17%	27	2%	5.99	8.1	73	$5
LIMA Plan	C	2nd Half	136	18	6	25	0	228			309	434	743	11	74	26	0.46	233	35	13	52	134	11%	70	0%	4.76	2.1	48	$4
Rand Var	+4	10 Proj	367	51	22	63	0	259			353	510	863	13	75	29	0.58	267	36	17	47	162	17%	53	1%	6.38	22.8	73	$13

Added even more FB% to his mix while maintaining core plate approach, but low h% meant results didn't show that growth. Regression to mean coupled with another chance at full-time AB could net HR breakout.

Ibanez,Raul

		Yr	AB	R	HR	RBI	SB	Avg	vL	vR	OB	Slg	OPS	bb%	ct%	h%	Eye	xBA	G	L	F	PX	hr/f	SX	SBO	RC/G	RAR	BPV	R$
Pos	7	05 SEA	614	92	20	89	9	280	274	283	355	436	791	10	84	31	0.72	273	46	21	34	98	12%	82	7%	5.37	11.3	61	$21
Age	38	06 SEA	626	103	33	123	2	289	243	308	356	516	872	9	82	31	0.57	281	42	19	39	132	17%	65	3%	6.22	18.4	72	$25
Bats	Left	07 SEA	573	80	21	105	0	291	256	305	351	480	831	8	83	32	0.55	279	42	18	40	118	11%	56	0%	5.74	11.2	62	$20
Health	B	08 SEA	635	85	23	110	2	293	305	288	358	479	836	9	83	32	0.58	275	41	19	40	120	11%	52	3%	5.85	17.8	63	$23
PT/Exp	A	09 PHI	500	93	34	93	4	272	285	267	345	552	897	10	76	29	0.47	290	43	15	42	182	21%	93	3%	6.64	15.5	100	$24
Consist	A	1st Half	250	51	22	59	4	312			368	656	1024	8	80	31	0.45	323	42	16	42	206	26%	104	7%	7.91	15.9	135	$17
LIMA Plan	C	2nd Half	250	42	12	34	0	232			324	448	772	12	72	27	0.49	254	44	15	41	154	16%	56	0%	5.23	-2.5	54	$7
Rand Var	+1	10 Proj	537	87	24	94	1	277			348	488	836	10	80	31	0.54	272	42	17	40	134	14%	60	1%	5.85	5.9	67	$21

Just as in Dickens, tale of two halves ended with beheading of most of his BPIs. Groin injury in June partly to blame, but he was bound to return to earth. Lower ct%, higher PX mix could linger, though don't count on it.

Infante,Omar

		Yr	AB	R	HR	RBI	SB	Avg	vL	vR	OB	Slg	OPS	bb%	ct%	h%	Eye	xBA	G	L	F	PX	hr/f	SX	SBO	RC/G	RAR	BPV	R$
Pos	4	05 DET	406	36	9	43	8	222	178	236	251	367	618	4	82	25	0.22	235	33	16	51	101	5%	101	12%	2.98	-14.3	48	$6
Age	28	06 DET	224	35	4	25	3	277	286	273	319	415	735	6	80	33	0.31	236	38	19	43	86	5%	122	9%	4.50	2.5	39	$6
Bats	Right	07 DET	* 204	27	2	21	5	284	281	265	326	362	688	6	85	33	0.42	229	33	21	47	53	2%	94	10%	3.96	-0.2	24	$5
Health	F	08 ATL	317	45	3	40	0	293	325	273	339	416	756	6	86	33	0.50	282	33	30	37	85	3%	70	1%	4.87	0.9	49	$9
PT/Exp	F	09 ATL	203	24	2	27	2	305	323	298	365	389	754	9	86	35	0.68	251	32	27	41	56	3%	64	3%	4.92	2.2	28	$7
Consist	A	1st Half	86	13	1	11	1	349			391	430	822	7	92	37	0.86	254	28	25	47	53	3%	52	3%	5.58	2.3	41	$4
LIMA Plan	D	2nd Half	117	11	1	16	1	274			346	359	705	10	82	33	0.62	250	36	28	36	59	3%	66	3%	4.39	-0.5	17	$3
Rand Var	-5	10 Proj	324	41	3	40	3	284			336	381	717	7	85	32	0.54	253	33	26	41	66	3%	81	4%	4.42	-1.9	35	$9

Small sample, but 75 point drop in BA, 1H to 2H, was stunning. Notice, though, that xBA wasn't fooled, and says there could be much worse to come. He's defied xBA before, but do you you want to take that chance?

Inge,Brandon

		Yr	AB	R	HR	RBI	SB	Avg	vL	vR	OB	Slg	OPS	bb%	ct%	h%	Eye	xBA	G	L	F	PX	hr/f	SX	SBO	RC/G	RAR	BPV	R$
Pos	5	05 DET	616	75	16	72	7	261	288	257	330	419	749	9	77	32	0.45	240	40	18	42	105	8%	98	8%	4.84	6.2	43	$15
Age	33	06 DET	542	83	27	83	7	253	243	256	308	463	771	7	76	28	0.34	249	40	14	46	133	14%	85	9%	4.90	-1.8	54	$17
Bats	Right	07 DET	508	64	14	71	9	236	333	209	301	376	677	8	70	31	0.31	234	37	22	41	105	10%	93	9%	3.85	-15.6	13	$11
Health	A	08 DET	347	41	11	51	4	205	232	196	292	369	661	11	73	25	0.46	228	37	16	46	113	9%	93	8%	3.72	-12.7	34	$5
PT/Exp	B	09 DET	562	71	27	84	2	230	243	225	297	404	701	9	70	28	0.32	217	41	15	44	112	16%	43	5%	4.07	-10.5	1	$13
Consist	A	1st Half	265	46	18	52	2	275			356	521	876	11	73	31	0.46	254	41	14	45	149	21%	58	8%	6.45	13.6	54	$12
LIMA Plan	C	2nd Half	297	25	9	32	0	189			242	300	542	7	67	25	0.21	183	41	15	44	76	10%	23	2%	1.78	-27.5	-50	$1
Rand Var	-1	10 Proj	505	62	19	72	4	224			294	389	683	9	71	28	0.34	225	39	17	44	111	12%	73	7%	3.89	-13.7	15	$10

Notice how similar '09 was to '06. It's all about the hr/f. Without a fifth of his FB going yard in the 1H, he's basically worthless. It's tough to hit 27 HRs, and have a PX of just 112 and a BPV of 1. Take heed.

Inglett,Joe

		Yr	AB	R	HR	RBI	SB	Avg	vL	vR	OB	Slg	OPS	bb%	ct%	h%	Eye	xBA	G	L	F	PX	hr/f	SX	SBO	RC/G	RAR	BPV	R$
Pos	7	05 aaa	322	41	1	29	10	268			295	360	655	4	89	30	0.36	0				60		127	21%	3.62	-13.4	52	$8
Age	32	06 CLE	* 422	59	5	39	13	288	217	292	341	390	731	7	83	34	0.47	264	47	24	29	67	4%	112	14%	4.56	-7.5	37	$12
Bats	Left	07 aaa	392	35	3	45	5	209			270	293	562	8	85	24	0.54	0				52		86	20%	2.63	-32.5	23	$2
Health	A	08 TOR	* 398	54	4	44	10	301	276	298	355	416	771	8	87	34	0.65	287	49	25	26	68	4%	123	11%	5.12	2.9	57	$13
PT/Exp	F	09 TOR	* 250	30	2	22	6	273		291	323	369	692	7	85	32	0.49	247	35	23	42	65	2%	89	13%	4.11	-6.5	35	$5
Consist	D	1st Half	101	10	1	8	2	250			294	326	619	6	85	29	0.41	219	22	22	56	54	2%	54	11%	3.16	-5.6	12	$1
LIMA Plan	F	2nd Half	149	20	1	14	4	289			342	398	740	7	85	34	0.54	262	40	23	38	73	2%	101	15%	4.75	-1.1	46	$4
Rand Var	-2	10 Proj	195	24	1	19	4	272			323	366	689	7	86	31	0.53	266	43	24	32	62	3%	93	14%	4.10	-4.9	36	$4

0-6-.281 in 89 AB at TOR
PRO: 1H to 2H improvements in Eye, xBA, PX, SX, OBP.
CON: Still below replacement level and not getting younger. Stash on reserve; only use in case of emergency.

JOSHUA RANDALL

Ishikawa,Travis			AB	R	HR	RBI	SB	Avg	vL	vR	OB	Slg	OPS	bb%	ct%	h%	Eye	xBA	G	L	F	PX	hr/f	SX	SBO	RC/G	RAR	BPV	R$
Pos	3	05	0	0	0	0	0	0							0			0						0					
Age	27	06 aa	298	33	10	42	0	225			306	391	697	10	70	29	0.38	0				112		67	0%	4.22	-13.5	11	$4
Bats	Left	07 aa	173	13	2	13	1	181			240	242	481	7	76	23	0.32	0				39		60	2%	1.24	-24.8	-30	($1)
Health	A	08 SF	* 500	70	21	94	9	263		280	329	471	800	9	80	29	0.49	294	56	18	26	138	20%	83	13%	5.40	-4.8	74	$19
PT/Exp	D	09 SF	326	49	9	39	2	261	278	259	323	387	710	8	73	33	0.34	222	45	18	37	86	10%	78	4%	4.24	-21.6	2	$9
Consist	F	1st Half	154	22	5	25	1	253			311	403	714	8	69	33	0.28	219	35	20	44	108	11%	76	5%	4.34	-9.9	5	$5
LIMA Plan	F	2nd Half	172	27	4	14	1	267			333	372	705	9	76	33	0.40	225	52	17	31	68	10%	73	4%	4.20	-11.5	-2	$4
Rand Var	-5	10 Proj	256	34	7	33	1	246			311	387	698	9	75	30	0.38	238	47	18	35	94	11%	78	4%	4.10	-15.9	17	$6

Showed isolated power flashes, but '08's 2H Triple-A surge looks more and more like the outlier. xBA shows a bigger downside. A stellar fielder, but that's not enough to hold a 1B job (and likely doesn't help you anyway).

Iwamura,Akinori			AB	R	HR	RBI	SB	Avg	vL	vR	OB	Slg	OPS	bb%	ct%	h%	Eye	xBA	G	L	F	PX	hr/f	SX	SBO	RC/G	RAR	BPV	R$
Pos	4	05 JPN	548	81	18	99	5	298			357	475	832	8	75	37	0.37	0				122		99	5%	5.90	23.7	46	$22
Age	31	06 JPN	546	82	19	75	7	290			357	456	813	9	78	34	0.47	0				104		94	4%	5.59	18.7	43	$19
Bats	Left	07 TAM	491	82	7	34	12	285	323	268	361	411	772	11	77	36	0.51	250	46	20	34	84	6%	123	13%	5.27	17.9	34	$14
Health	F	08 TAM	627	91	6	48	8	274	260	280	347	380	727	10	79	34	0.53	244	47	20	33	73	4%	102	7%	4.66	-4.1	27	$13
PT/Exp	B	09 TAM	231	28	1	22	9	290	386	248	357	390	746	9	81	35	0.55	250	44	21	36	74	2%	108	14%	4.92	-0.1	36	$7
Consist	A	1st Half	155	19	0	16	8	310			378	406	784	10	81	38	0.57	244	43	18	38	78	0%	104	18%	5.45	2.2	38	$6
LIMA Plan	C+	2nd Half	76	9	1	6	1	250			313	355	669	8	82	30	0.50	262	44	25	30	65	5%	89	5%	3.84	-2.4	24	$1
Rand Var	-3	10 Proj	539	73	6	48	12	278			347	392	739	9	80	34	0.51	252	45	21	33	77	4%	114	9%	4.78	1.2	35	$14

Was off to a running start (30 SB pace) before partial ACL tear. Clearly not the same after return, but still. Nobody else will want him now, so watch early SBO numbers; if he's running near 1H level, grab him cheap.

Izturis,Cesar			AB	R	HR	RBI	SB	Avg	vL	vR	OB	Slg	OPS	bb%	ct%	h%	Eye	xBA	G	L	F	PX	hr/f	SX	SBO	RC/G	RAR	BPV	R$
Pos	6	05 LA	444	48	2	31	8	257	303	242	296	322	618	5	89	29	0.49	271	52	22	26	46	2%	81	14%	3.24	-9.5	28	$7
Age	30	06 2NL	252	21	1	20	1	240	206	253	296	308	603	7	94	25	1.23	251	52	16	31	43	1%	44	8%	3.41	-7.3	39	$1
Bats	Both	07 2NL	314	31	0	16	3	258	186	285	300	315	616	6	94	27	1.00	280	49	23	28	39	0%	69	7%	3.46	-9.1	41	$3
Health	D	08 STL	414	50	1	24	24	263	304	237	312	309	621	7	94	28	1.12	259	47	22	31	27	1%	120	24%	3.53	-13.4	48	$11
PT/Exp	C	09 BAL	387	34	2	30	12	256	290	238	289	328	617	4	90	28	0.47	264	49	20	30	43	2%	102	16%	3.23	-13.9	37	$6
Consist	A	1st Half	150	16	1	13	9	260			284	327	611	3	92	28	0.42	270	51	20	29	39	3%	117	24%	3.12	-5.8	43	$4
LIMA Plan	D	2nd Half	237	18	1	17	3	253			292	329	621	5	89	28	0.50	260	48	21	31	45	2%	76	12%	3.30	-8.1	28	$2
Rand Var	0	10 Proj	454	45	2	31	15	258			297	321	619	5	92	28	0.68	267	49	21	30	39	1%	102	17%	3.37	-13.9	42	$8

A model of consistency. Sees the ball, hits the ball, walks back to the dugout 7 out of every 10 plate appearances, like clock-work. Appendicitis cut into his 1st half, but he came right back to mediocrity upon his return.

Izturis,Maicer			AB	R	HR	RBI	SB	Avg	vL	vR	OB	Slg	OPS	bb%	ct%	h%	Eye	xBA	G	L	F	PX	hr/f	SX	SBO	RC/G	RAR	BPV	R$
Pos	46	05 ANA	* 222	25	1	16	12	265	191	268	331	369	700	9	89	29	0.91	264	45	20	35	66	1%	128	28%	4.48	2.3	68	$6
Age	30	06 LAA	352	64	5	44	14	293	247	307	362	412	773	10	90	31	1.09	278	49	19	32	73	5%	119	18%	5.31	11.9	76	$13
Bats	Both	07 LAA	336	47	6	51	7	289	280	291	352	405	757	9	88	31	0.85	266	45	17	38	73	5%	92	8%	5.00	9.4	59	$11
Health	D	08 LAA	290	44	3	37	11	269	258	272	329	362	691	8	91	29	0.96	283	49	23	29	59	4%	114	15%	4.30	-4.9	63	$9
PT/Exp	C	09 LAA	387	74	8	65	13	300	380	288	358	434	792	8	89	32	0.85	272	43	19	38	78	6%	117	15%	5.37	4.7	74	$17
Consist	B	1st Half	168	35	2	25	6	286			337	393	730	7	89	31	0.68	265	45	20	36	63	4%	136	16%	4.62	-1.5	62	$7
LIMA Plan	C	2nd Half	219	39	6	40	7	311			373	466	839	9	90	32	1.00	277	41	18	41	90	7%	94	14%	5.93	6.1	80	$10
Rand Var	-3	10 Proj	357	60	6	53	12	289			349	409	758	9	90	31	0.90	274	45	20	35	72	5%	114	15%	5.02	3.2	70	$13

Again there to pick up AB when others faltered. Stable skills given injury history and always-uncertain role. Of course, injuries happen, and now he's a victim of his own flexibility. Write in 300 AB, don't bet on 400.

Jackson,Conor			AB	R	HR	RBI	SB	Avg	vL	vR	OB	Slg	OPS	bb%	ct%	h%	Eye	xBA	G	L	F	PX	hr/f	SX	SBO	RC/G	RAR	BPV	R$
Pos	7	05 ARI	* 418	54	8	59	2	294	258	157	387	455	841	13	92	31	1.91	276	44	12	44	105	5%	52	4%	6.35	11.8	96	$13
Age	28	06 ARI	485	75	15	79	1	291	296	288	362	441	803	10	85	32	0.74	260	38	21	41	89	9%	52	1%	5.50	3.4	49	$16
Bats	Right	07 ARI	415	56	15	60	2	284	320	270	365	467	833	11	88	29	1.06	288	38	20	43	110	10%	47	3%	5.96	7.1	78	$13
Health	F	08 ARI	540	87	12	75	10	300	315	295	369	446	815	10	89	32	0.97	274	40	22	38	87	7%	109	7%	5.73	4.7	79	$21
PT/Exp	C	09 ARI	99	8	1	14	5	182	172	186	264	253	516	10	84	21	0.69	223	41	18	41	51	3%	76	21%	2.13	-10.9	21	$1
Consist	D	1st Half	99	8	1	14	5	182			264	253	516	10	84	21	0.69	223	41	18	41	51	3%	76	21%	2.13	-10.9	21	$1
LIMA Plan	B	2nd Half	0	0	0	0	0	0																					
Rand Var	+5	10 Proj	510	64	15	74	11	278			355	432	787	11	87	30	0.90	269	39	20	41	95	8%	88	8%	5.39	-1.1	73	$18

Likely the worst case of valley fever (coccidioidomycosis, if you prefer) to strike ML player. Said to be fully recovered; if so, there's no reason to think he can't enter '10 as he did '09, as a sleeper breakout candidate.

Jacobs,Mike			AB	R	HR	RBI	SB	Avg	vL	vR	OB	Slg	OPS	bb%	ct%	h%	Eye	xBA	G	L	F	PX	hr/f	SX	SBO	RC/G	RAR	BPV	R$
Pos	0	05 NYM	* 533	67	30	91	1	277	400	305	322	522	843	6	81	29	0.34	308	41	23	37	156	19%	41	3%	5.68	-5.2	75	$21
Age	29	06 FLA	469	54	20	77	3	262	182	281	327	473	800	9	78	30	0.43	271	40	20	40	138	14%	55	3%	5.41	-13.9	57	$14
Bats	Left	07 FLA	426	57	17	54	1	265	290	257	315	458	773	7	76	31	0.31	256	36	18	46	128	11%	57	3%	4.96	-15.8	41	$11
Health	A	08 FLA	477	67	32	93	1	247	218	257	300	514	814	7	75	26	0.30	272	35	18	47	171	19%	61	1%	5.41	6.7	72	$18
PT/Exp	B	09 KC	434	46	19	61	0	228	178	243	295	401	696	9	70	28	0.31	220	37	17	46	116	14%	27	0%	4.03	-14.9	-2	$8
Consist	B	1st Half	231	24	10	27	0	229			305	416	720	10	69	29	0.35	227	35	18	47	128	13%	35	0%	4.47	-4.9	12	$4
LIMA Plan	D+	2nd Half	203	22	9	34	0	227			283	384	667	7	70	28	0.26	212	40	17	43	102	15%	20	0%	3.54	-10.1	-16	$4
Rand Var	0	10 Proj	452	54	23	71	1	246			303	454	758	8	73	29	0.31	248	37	18	45	138	16%	39	1%	4.77	-8.0	32	$12

While hr/f regression wasn't surprising, the corrollary says his abysmal -- and aberrant -- ct% should also regress to the mean. If so, the disaster of this season could beget a power bargain. UP: .270, 30+ HR

Janish,Paul			AB	R	HR	RBI	SB	Avg	vL	vR	OB	Slg	OPS	bb%	ct%	h%	Eye	xBA	G	L	F	PX	hr/f	SX	SBO	RC/G	RAR	BPV	R$
Pos	6	05	0	0	0	0	0	0							0			0						0					
Age	27	06	0	0	0	0	0	0							0			0						0					
Bats	Right	07 a/a	523	55	4	33	10	210			283	289	572	9	86	24	0.71	0				56		87	10%	2.86	-24.7	34	$2
Health	A	08 CIN	* 398	39	7	38	2	211			261	319	580	6	80	25	0.34	0				75		62	2%	2.58	-25.3	13	$3
PT/Exp	D	09 CIN	256	36	1	16	2	211	230	203	284	305	588	9	84	25	0.65	240	37	19	44	77	1%	70	3%	3.06	-12.7	41	$1
Consist	A	1st Half	68	9	0	3	0	250			292	309	600	6	78	22	0.27	216	38	21	40	55	0%	43	0%	2.82	-3.7	-18	$1
LIMA Plan	D	2nd Half	188	27	1	13	2	197			281	303	584	10	87	22	0.88	249	37	18	45	84	1%	73	5%	3.17	-8.8	59	$1
Rand Var	+2	10 Proj	424	51	4	31	3	226			287	321	609	8	82	27	0.49	233	37	19	43	72	2%	76	4%	3.12	-18.6	28	$4

Is this 2010, or 1970? Where are all the all-hit, no field SS of the good old aughts? A glance at these skills conjures thoughts of a Belanger, or a Brinkman. (Don't worry Reds fans: we won't compare him to Concepcion.)

Jaramillo,Jason			AB	R	HR	RBI	SB	Avg	vL	vR	OB	Slg	OPS	bb%	ct%	h%	Eye	xBA	G	L	F	PX	hr/f	SX	SBO	RC/G	RAR	BPV	R$
Pos	2	05	0	0	0	0	0	0							0			0						0					
Age	28	06 a/a	328	32	6	37	0	234			294	364	658	8	84	26	0.54	0				87		36	1%	3.73	-6.4	34	$3
Bats	Both	07 aaa	435	44	6	48	0	253			319	336	654	9	84	29	0.61	0				52		37	1%	3.70	-8.5	9	$6
Health	A	08 aaa	421	39	7	31	1	229			286	323	609	7	81	27	0.42	0				64		33	2%	2.99	-15.4	4	$3
PT/Exp	F	09 PIT	206	20	3	26	1	252	161	269	309	364	673	8	84	29	0.52	258	49	20	32	81	5%	39	2%	3.89	-2.2	30	$4
Consist	B	1st Half	139	16	3	19	1	273			344	417	761	10	83	31	0.65	287	46	25	29	103	9%	40	3%	5.05	3.1	49	$4
LIMA Plan	F	2nd Half	67	4	0	7	0	209			232	254	486	3	85	25	0.20	181	54	9	37	39	0%	21	0%	1.48	-5.8	-15	($0)
Rand Var	0	10 Proj	131	12	2	14	0	244			295	335	630	7	84	28	0.44	230	51	15	34	65	4%	31	1%	3.31	-3.7	11	$2

Yet another reserve catcher with nearly adequate skills. Okay, he does switch-hit, which is cause for SOME interest. And he's a Jaramillo, so maybe he's related to Rudy, and can score some free hitting coaching.

Jeter,Derek			AB	R	HR	RBI	SB	Avg	vL	vR	OB	Slg	OPS	bb%	ct%	h%	Eye	xBA	G	L	F	PX	hr/f	SX	SBO	RC/G	RAR	BPV	R$
Pos	6	05 NYY	654	122	19	70	14	309	317	305	382	450	831	11	82	35	0.66	281	60	19	21	86	17%	108	8%	5.87	23.4	53	$27
Age	36	06 NYY	623	118	14	97	34	343	390	328	409	483	892	10	84	39	0.68	300	59	22	18	90	15%	125	17%	6.61	35.7	66	$34
Bats	Right	07 NYY	639	102	12	73	15	322	317	324	377	452	829	8	84	37	0.56	293	56	20	24	87	9%	93	11%	5.75	25.2	53	$25
Health	A	08 NYY	596	88	11	69	11	300	302	300	356	408	764	8	86	34	0.61	274	58	18	24	68	9%	91	8%	4.96	10.4	42	$20
PT/Exp	A	09 NYY	634	107	18	66	30	334	395	311	402	465	868	10	86	37	0.80	289	57	20	23	76	15%	96	15%	6.26	30.3	55	$31
Consist	C	1st Half	296	48	9	32	17	307			377	449	826	10	88	33	0.89	296	58	19	23	83	15%	96	18%	5.78	10.7	67	$14
LIMA Plan	C	2nd Half	338	59	9	34	13	358			424	479	904	10	84	41	0.74	282	56	22	22	70	14%	87	12%	6.70	19.5	42	$18
Rand Var	-4	10 Proj	612	101	15	68	16	301			366	425	791	9	85	33	0.70	286	57	20	23	76	12%	96	11%	5.34	15.9	51	$23

New Yankee Stadium boosted HR (13 home, 5 road), but the rest was solid both home and away. 2H h% won't repeat, so BA will regress a bit. Eventually age will strike even Jeter, but this LD stroke is aging well.

ROD TRUESDELL

93

Johjima,Kenji			AB	R	HR	RBI	SB	Avg	vL	vR	OB	Slg	OPS	bb%	ct%	h%	Eye	xBA	G	L	F	PX	hr/f	SX	SBO	RC/G	RAR	BPV	R$
Pos	2	05 JPN	411	68	14	56	3	288			331	477	808	6	93	28	0.88	0				102		100	7%	5.41	17.5	97	$15
Age	34	06 SEA	506	61	18	76	3	291	263	298	317	451	768	4	91	29	0.43	281	45	19	36	88	11%	56	3%	4.73	4.6	60	$15
Bats	Right	07 SEA	485	52	14	61	0	287	327	276	308	433	741	3	92	29	0.37	290	46	20	34	88	9%	24	2%	4.43	1.9	52	$12
Health	B	08 SEA	379	29	7	39	2	227	205	237	264	332	596	5	91	23	0.58	273	45	21	34	66	6%	42	3%	3.02	-13.4	42	$3
PT/Exp	C	09 SEA	239	24	9	22	2	247	244	248	283	406	689	5	88	25	0.43	261	50	13	36	88	12%	42	8%	3.87	-2.9	48	$5
Consist	C	1st Half	100	10	3	11	2	250			272	380	652	3	93	24	0.43	252	58	8	35	69	9%	58	10%	3.49	-2.3	53	$2
LIMA Plan		2nd Half	139	14	6	11	0	245			291	424	715	6	85	25	0.43	268	45	18	37	103	14%	25	7%	4.17	-0.4	44	$2
Rand Var	+1	10 Proj	0	0	0	0	0	0																					

Made two separate trips to DL for injuries to hamstring and toe. Sacrificed ct% for power in 2H. xBA holds out hope for BA recovery, but GB rate tempers any expectations of a return to double digit HRs... in Japan.

Johnson,Chris			AB	R	HR	RBI	SB	Avg	vL	vR	OB	Slg	OPS	bb%	ct%	h%	Eye	xBA	G	L	F	PX	hr/f	SX	SBO	RC/G	RAR	BPV	R$
Pos	5	05	0	0	0	0	0	0							0			0						0					
Age	26	06	0	0	0	0	0	0							0			0						0					
Bats	Right	07	0	0	0	0	0	0							0			0						0					
Health	A	08 aa	431	38	10	48	4	249			280	370	650	4	84	28	0.27	0				78		65	4%	3.35	-22.5	28	$8
PT/Exp	F	09 HOU	* 406	37	11	32	2	232		133	262	371	633	4	81	26	0.21	245	81	0	19	89	17%	72	4%	3.09	-25.2	24	$5
Consist	A	1st Half	177	14	2	11	1	228			244	325	570	2	79	28	0.11	0				67		79	6%	2.26	-15.6	2	$1
LIMA Plan	F	2nd Half	229	22	9	21	1	235			275	407	682	5	81	25	0.29	257	81	0	19	105	25%	65	2%	3.71	-9.8	41	$4
Rand Var	+1	10 Proj	245	22	6	22	2	241			271	377	647	4	82	27	0.23	255	48	18	34	85	9%	70	4%	3.29	-14.5	27	$4

0-1-.091 in 22 AB with HOU. Historically struggled with injuries at minor league level, so beware the "A" Health rating. Poor Eye says that he'll likely struggle during his first exposure to MLB pitching.

Johnson,Kelly			AB	R	HR	RBI	SB	Avg	vL	vR	OB	Slg	OPS	bb%	ct%	h%	Eye	xBA	G	L	F	PX	hr/f	SX	SBO	RC/G	RAR	BPV	R$
Pos	4	05 ATL	* 445	77	16	59	8	256	257	236	357	438	795	14	79	29	0.74	287	44	26	30	117	15%	115	7%	5.61	13.7	73	$15
Age	28	06 aaa	* 39	3	1	7	1	308			400	487	887	13	85	34	1.00	0				121		32	8%	6.81	2.6	74	$2
Bats	Left	07 ATL	521	91	16	68	9	276	272	278	372	457	828	13	78	33	0.68	262	43	19	39	113	10%	116	8%	6.07	20.6	63	$18
Health	D	08 ATL	547	86	12	69	11	287	333	270	349	446	795	9	79	34	0.46	266	39	25	36	110	8%	111	11%	5.42	10.1	58	$19
PT/Exp	B	09 ATL	* 355	54	10	41	8	230	325	188	298	396	694	9	83	25	0.56	258	39	18	43	107	8%	121	12%	4.17	-3.9	72	$9
Consist	B	1st Half	233	33	5	20	4	215			280	361	640	8	83	24	0.53	253	38	19	43	98	6%	107	12%	3.51	-7.4	60	$3
LIMA Plan	B	2nd Half	122	21	5	21	4	258			333	463	796	10	82	28	0.63	266	42	14	44	125	11%	129	12%	5.42	3.2	89	$5
Rand Var	+5	10 Proj	422	69	13	56	9	270			345	447	792	10	81	31	0.58	265	40	20	39	113	9%	124	10%	5.42	9.7	72	$15

8-29-.224 in 303 AB with ATL. Injury and poor h% obscure otherwise solid BPIs. BPV trend tells the real story; +5 Rand Var says to chalk 2009 up to bad luck. Great buy-low candidate. UP: 20 HR and 15 SB.

Johnson,Nick			AB	R	HR	RBI	SB	Avg	vL	vR	OB	Slg	OPS	bb%	ct%	h%	Eye	xBA	G	L	F	PX	hr/f	SX	SBO	RC/G	RAR	BPV	R$
Pos	3	05 WAS	453	66	15	74	3	289	328	277	396	479	875	15	81	33	0.92	288	44	21	35	129	12%	59	7%	6.73	14.6	76	$17
Age	32	06 WAS	500	100	23	77	10	290	303	285	418	520	938	18	80	32	1.11	297	42	22	36	148	16%	69	7%	7.65	23.1	98	$22
Bats	Left	07 WAS	0	0	0	0	0	0							0									0					
Health	F	08 WAS	109	15	5	20	0	220	167	247	401	431	833	23	77	24	1.32	277	38	24	39	144	15%	14	0%	6.49	2.5	76	$3
PT/Exp	F	09 2NL	457	71	8	62	2	291	316	281	417	405	822	18	82	34	1.18	253	43	22	34	78	6%	47	3%	6.26	-3.2	41	$15
Consist	A	1st Half	271	35	5	33	1	295			397	413	811	15	83	34	0.98	263	42	25	33	78	7%	56	2%	5.92	-4.4	41	$8
LIMA Plan	C+	2nd Half	186	36	3	29	1	285			444	392	836	22	80	34	1.43	237	45	18	36	80	6%	38	4%	6.69	0.9	42	$7
Rand Var	-5	10 Proj	378	62	9	59	2	272			415	419	834	20	80	32	1.21	262	42	22	36	102	9%	49	3%	6.47	3.1	57	$12

Stayed relatively healthy (only 1 DL trip). Maintained elite eye, but what happened to his power? Expect a rebound to PX as HR/FB should revert to career average, but reaching 450 AB again unlikely.

Johnson,Reed			AB	R	HR	RBI	SB	Avg	vL	vR	OB	Slg	OPS	bb%	ct%	h%	Eye	xBA	G	L	F	PX	hr/f	SX	SBO	RC/G	RAR	BPV	R$
Pos	8	05 TOR	398	55	8	58	5	269	279	262	307	412	719	5	79	32	0.27	270	51	22	27	95	9%	110	12%	4.27	-0.2	39	$11
Age	33	06 TOR	461	86	12	49	8	319	323	316	364	479	844	7	82	37	0.41	276	47	20	33	105	10%	101	8%	5.83	14.4	60	$18
Bats	Right	07 TOR	275	31	2	14	4	236	325	202	278	320	598	5	80	29	0.29	240	47	19	34	62	3%	91	9%	2.80	-14.4	8	$2
Health	F	08 CHC	333	52	6	50	5	303	333	280	341	420	761	5	80	37	0.28	254	41	24	35	86	7%	67	12%	4.76	0.2	20	$13
PT/Exp	D	09 CHC	165	23	4	22	2	255	324	206	309	412	721	7	84	28	0.48	273	50	17	33	101	9%	97	8%	4.43	-1.5	61	$4
Consist	C	1st Half	112	16	4	16	1	268			317	446	763	7	86	28	0.50	275	53	13	34	107	12%	83	4%	4.83	0.3	69	$4
LIMA Plan	F	2nd Half	53	7	0	6	1	226			293	340	633	9	79	29	0.45	267	44	27	29	87	0%	120	17%	3.51	-2.0	42	$1
Rand Var	+3	10 Proj	163	23	2	20	2	264			313	395	708	7	81	31	0.38	263	46	21	32	89	6%	103	11%	4.24	-2.1	41	$4

PRO: PX, SX and Eye each rebounded.
CON: Still can't hit RH nor can he stay healthy.
Best used in platoon role with .878 OPS in 292 AB vs. LH over 2007-2009.

Johnson,Rob			AB	R	HR	RBI	SB	Avg	vL	vR	OB	Slg	OPS	bb%	ct%	h%	Eye	xBA	G	L	F	PX	hr/f	SX	SBO	RC/G	RAR	BPV	R$
Pos	2	05	0	0	0	0	0	0							0			0						0					
Age	27	06 aaa	337	24	3	28	12	205			230	267	497	3	80	25	0.17	0				39		96	30%	1.41	-32.1	-10	$2
Bats	Right	07 aaa	422	47	5	32	6	230			286	317	603	7	86	26	0.55	0				62		56	13%	3.09	-16.5	26	$4
Health	A	08 aaa	417	42	7	38	6	257			306	365	671	7	86	28	0.52	0				74		51	12%	3.83	-4.6	36	$8
PT/Exp	F	09 SEA	258	21	2	27	1	213	171	233	285	326	611	9	77	27	0.43	248	46	21	33	86	3%	58	3%	3.15	-9.0	14	$1
Consist	B	1st Half	123	7	0	13	0	187			237	293	529	6	72	26	0.23	232	44	22	34	87	0%	76	5%	1.93	-9.3	-7	($1)
LIMA Plan	D	2nd Half	135	14	2	14	1	237			327	356	682	12	81	28	0.72	261	47	21	32	85	6%	39	3%	4.20	-0.3	31	$2
Rand Var	+2	10 Proj	318	29	3	30	4	242			301	344	645	8	81	29	0.45	255	46	21	33	75	4%	61	9%	3.53	-6.8	21	$4

Struggled in his MLB debut in 1H, but 2H more in line with his MLEs. xBA says there's some BA upside, but young catchers are notoriously hard to predict. Multiple off-season surgeries merit attention.

Jones,Adam			AB	R	HR	RBI	SB	Avg	vL	vR	OB	Slg	OPS	bb%	ct%	h%	Eye	xBA	G	L	F	PX	hr/f	SX	SBO	RC/G	RAR	BPV	R$
Pos	8	05 aa	228	32	6	19	8	286			349	428	777	9	81	33	0.51	0				89		107	18%	5.11	4.5	48	$8
Age	25	06 SEA	* 454	71	16	66	15	273	235	211	317	441	758	6	81	31	0.34	284	44	27	29	102	15%	111	19%	4.69	0.3	54	$16
Bats	Right	07 SEA	* 485	81	23	77	9	280	310	194	330	499	829	7	75	33	0.30	284	34	27	39	145	16%	104	15%	5.69	16.3	65	$19
Health	B	08 BAL	480	61	9	57	10	269	256	275	304	398	701	5	77	33	0.22	243	47	18	35	86	7%	124	11%	4.01	-18.6	27	$13
PT/Exp	B	09 BAL	473	83	19	70	10	277	246	295	328	457	785	7	80	31	0.39	280	55	17	28	107	18%	108	11%	5.06	5.7	55	$18
Consist	C	1st Half	279	50	12	44	5	305			353	509	862	7	79	35	0.36	292	51	20	28	126	19%	96	11%	6.04	10.8	62	$13
LIMA Plan	C+	2nd Half	194	33	7	26	5	237			292	381	673	7	82	26	0.43	260	61	11	28	80	16%	110	13%	3.69	-5.5	41	$6
Rand Var	0	10 Proj	528	84	21	72	12	269			317	452	768	7	79	30	0.34	274	53	16	30	111	17%	112	13%	4.84	0.8	54	$19

Knee, ankle injuries hampered him in 2H, but we can't just give him a pass and project 1H x 2. Improving ct% and excellent hr/f are encouraging, but high GB% and lofty 1H h% indicate more skill consolidation needed.

Jones,Andruw			AB	R	HR	RBI	SB	Avg	vL	vR	OB	Slg	OPS	bb%	ct%	h%	Eye	xBA	G	L	F	PX	hr/f	SX	SBO	RC/G	RAR	BPV	R$
Pos	0	05 ATL	586	95	51	128	5	263	254	265	335	575	910	10	81	24	0.57	311	42	16	42	180	26%	73	6%	6.56	9.2	111	$30
Age	33	06 ATL	565	107	41	129	4	262	260	263	355	531	886	13	78	27	0.65	282	39	19	42	158	22%	59	3%	6.54	1.8	82	$26
Bats	Right	07 ATL	572	83	26	94	5	222	225	221	307	413	719	11	76	25	0.51	252	39	17	44	122	14%	74	5%	4.41	-32.1	47	$14
Health	C	08 LA	209	21	3	14	0	158	178	147	254	249	503	11	64	23	0.36	178	48	13	39	77	6%	55	2%	1.42	-24.3	-42	($2)
PT/Exp	C	09 TEX	281	43	17	43	5	214	218	210	322	459	781	14	74	22	0.63	263	34	16	50	159	16%	64	9%	5.32	1.3	74	$8
Consist	F	1st Half	138	23	9	23	3	239			348	507	855	14	74	26	0.64	281	39	17	43	176	20%	63	8%	6.35	4.9	86	$5
LIMA Plan	D+	2nd Half	143	20	8	20	2	189			297	413	710	13	75	19	0.61	244	30	15	56	143	13%	53	9%	4.33	-3.9	59	$3
Rand Var	+4	10 Proj	328	46	19	46	3	235			330	465	795	12	72	27	0.52	254	38	16	46	153	17%	64	6%	5.49	1.2	58	$9

Hamstring injury in Aug ended a nice comeback year. H% says he was unlucky, but has history of BA's less than his xBA's. Return to elite PX makes him worth a speculative play, but beware his inconsistency.

Jones,Chipper			AB	R	HR	RBI	SB	Avg	vL	vR	OB	Slg	OPS	bb%	ct%	h%	Eye	xBA	G	L	F	PX	hr/f	SX	SBO	RC/G	RAR	BPV	R$
Pos	5	05 ATL	358	66	21	72	5	296	254	303	414	556	970	17	84	30	1.29	328	42	23	35	162	20%	62	5%	7.84	30.3	121	$19
Age	38	06 ATL	411	87	26	86	6	324	293	332	411	596	1007	13	82	34	0.84	301	41	19	40	156	19%	93	5%	8.07	28.2	109	$24
Bats	Both	07 ATL	513	108	29	102	5	337	274	378	429	604	1033	14	85	35	1.09	325	44	19	37	157	18%	87	3%	8.42	37.6	123	$30
Health	C	08 ATL	439	82	22	75	4	364	394	349	473	574	1047	17	86	39	1.48	303	43	24	33	121	18%	64	2%	8.78	37.3	97	$27
PT/Exp	A	09 ATL	488	80	18	71	4	264	289	252	390	430	821	17	82	29	1.13	267	45	20	35	104	13%	67	3%	6.09	13.4	66	$17
Consist	D	1st Half	233	38	9	36	1	292			406	481	887	16	84	32	1.22	285	47	20	33	115	14%	66	2%	6.88	11.3	82	$9
LIMA Plan	B+	2nd Half	255	42	9	35	3	239			376	384	761	18	80	27	1.08	251	43	20	36	93	12%	57	3%	5.33	1.5	48	$7
Rand Var	+4	10 Proj	409	74	17	68	3	279			397	466	864	16	83	30	1.18	284	44	21	35	115	14%	75	2%	6.59	15.3	83	$16

Poor 2nd half has this perennial all-star talking about retirement. Bad luck plagued 2H, but even 1H skills were down across the board. Lots of wear and tear on this body. Fading PX says: DN: fewer than 15 HR

BILL MACEY

Jones,Garrett			AB	R	HR	RBI	SB	Avg	vL	vR	OB	Slg	OPS	bb%	ct%	h%	Eye	xBA	G	L	F	PX	hr/f	SX	SBO	RC/G	RAR	BPV	R$
Pos	93	05 aaa	481	59	18	58	4	222			268	387	655	6	80	24	0.32	0				103		82	5%	3.40	-23.2	42	$9
Age	29	06 aaa	525	71	21	91	3	230			294	421	714	8	76	27	0.37	0				125		70	6%	4.28	-14.9	42	$12
Bats	Left	07 MIN	* 477	61	14	72	3	254			305	426	730	7	77	30	0.32	0				120		79	6%	4.47	-14.5	45	$11
Health	A	08 aaa	527	62	16	69	7	225			275	376	651	6	82	25	0.38	0				96		87	8%	3.44	-29.6	45	$10
PT/Exp	C	09 PIT	* 591	78	29	80	21	272	208	333	331	484	815	8	80	30	0.44	275	40	18	41	137	15%	84	18%	5.48	10.2	73	$25
Consist	D	1st Half	281	33	8	36	11	244			276	385	661	4	85	26	0.29	297	100	0	0	91		86	26%	3.49	-11.8	48	$8
LIMA Plan	C+	2nd Half	310	45	21	44	10	297			377	574	951	11	76	33	0.53	291	40	19	42	183	21%	82	13%	7.44	22.1	99	$16
Rand Var	0	10 Proj	517	66	22	72	12	265			321	458	779	8	80	30	0.40	265	40	19	42	125	13%	89	12%	5.04	1.0	62	$18

21-44-.293 with 10 SB in 314 AB at PIT. Can he do this again? PRO: Elite 2H PX, solid xBA and improving Eye. CON: 2H h% above career avg and SX doesn't support SBO. Pay for the HRs, not the SB.

Joyce,Matt			AB	R	HR	RBI	SB	Avg	vL	vR	OB	Slg	OPS	bb%	ct%	h%	Eye	xBA	G	L	F	PX	hr/f	SX	SBO	RC/G	RAR	BPV	R$
Pos	9	05	0	0	0	0	0	0							0			0						0					
Age	26	06	0	0	0	0	0	0							0			0						0					
Bats	Left	07 aa	456	57	15	66	4	236			308	408	717	9	73	29	0.39	0				124		70	9%	4.43	-10.6	34	$9
Health	A	08 DET	* 442	69	23	67	2	244			323	482	805	10	73	28	0.43	0				162		82	7%	5.60	3.2	70	$13
PT/Exp	D	09 TAM	* 449	63	16	62	12	233	250	179	323	419	742	12	78	27	0.60	242	38	12	50	122	9%	88	16%	4.82	-7.0	61	$12
Consist	B	1st Half	254	33	11	37	9	231			315	444	759	11	75	26	0.48	247	38	12	50	143	12%	92	16%	4.99	-2.6	64	$7
LIMA Plan	D	2nd Half	195	30	5	24	4	236			333	386	718	13	82	27	0.80	0				97		81	15%	4.66	-4.0	57	$4
Rand Var	+1	10 Proj	218	32	8	31	3	243			327	442	769	11	76	28	0.52	244	38	12	50	132	10%	87	11%	5.15	-1.3	61	$6

3-7-.188 in 32 AB at TAM. Hasn't earned much playing time at the MLB level, but he's young, and FB% and PX say he can still develop into a good power hitter. Great end-game speculative pick.

Kapler,Gabe			AB	R	HR	RBI	SB	Avg	vL	vR	OB	Slg	OPS	bb%	ct%	h%	Eye	xBA	G	L	F	PX	hr/f	SX	SBO	RC/G	RAR	BPV	R$
Pos	9	05 BOS	97	15	1	9	1	247	314	210	270	351	621	3	85	28	0.20	260	54	16	30	78	4%	81	5%	3.03	-4.8	33	$2
Age	35	06 BOS	* 155	23	2	14	1	244	265	242	313	359	672	9	86	27	0.73	247	47	14	38	76	4%	77	5%	4.04	-7.5	50	$2
Bats	Right	07	0	0	0	0	0	0							0			0						0					
Health	A	08 MIL	229	36	8	38	3	301	354	272	339	498	837	5	83	34	0.33	283	46	18	36	125	12%	98	7%	5.64	2.8	74	$10
PT/Exp	F	09 TAM	205	26	8	32	5	239	276	150	333	439	772	12	81	26	0.74	280	36	22	41	126	12%	79	13%	5.25	-0.5	75	$6
Consist	A	1st Half	103	12	4	19	3	243			333	495	828	12	84	25	0.88	306	34	19	47	160	10%	87	23%	6.01	2.1	118	$3
LIMA Plan	D	2nd Half	102	14	4	13	2	235			333	382	716	13	77	27	0.65	258	39	26	35	88	14%	54	6%	4.44	-2.7	24	$3
Rand Var	0	10 Proj	217	31	7	32	4	263			333	442	775	9	82	29	0.59	277	41	20	39	115	11%	82	9%	5.14	-1.3	66	$7

Skills relatively unchanged from 2008; low BA was driven by h%. Don't read too much into 1H/2H splits as sample size was too small. Capable of a 20 HR season with regular AB, but platoon split makes that unlikely.

Kearns,Austin			AB	R	HR	RBI	SB	Avg	vL	vR	OB	Slg	OPS	bb%	ct%	h%	Eye	xBA	G	L	F	PX	hr/f	SX	SBO	RC/G	RAR	BPV	R$
Pos	9	05 CIN	* 498	81	24	84	0	254	233	240	331	483	813	10	73	30	0.43	292	49	23	29	166	23%	46	0%	5.72	6.8	63	$17
Age	30	06 2NL	537	86	24	86	9	264	336	236	356	467	823	12	75	31	0.56	259	42	19	39	132	15%	78	8%	5.91	17.8	55	$19
Bats	Right	07 WAS	587	84	16	74	2	266	292	258	345	411	756	11	82	30	0.67	268	45	20	35	95	10%	47	2%	4.98	1.7	41	$14
Health	F	08 WAS	313	40	7	32	2	217	153	241	296	316	612	10	80	25	0.56	238	47	21	32	64	9%	51	5%	3.10	-20.2	8	$4
PT/Exp	C	09 WAS	174	20	3	17	1	195	122	224	320	305	625	16	71	26	0.63	214	46	19	36	79	7%	77	4%	3.42	-8.1	2	$1
Consist	C	1st Half	152	17	3	16	1	197			311	322	633	14	71	26	0.57	215	43	18	40	90	7%	85	2%	3.49	-6.6	12	$1
LIMA Plan	D	2nd Half	22	3	0	1	0	182			379	182	561	24	68	27	1.00	208	67	27	7	0	0%	40	9%	2.67	-1.6	-65	($0)
Rand Var	+3	10 Proj	229	31	7	28	2	245			334	392	726	12	76	29	0.57	248	45	20	36	101	11%	68	3%	4.63	-2.3	33	$5

Multi-year decline highlighted by BPV freefall. Injuries sapped power, but Health score shows that this is a chronic concern. No evidence in skill set that he can turn this around. Let somebody else take the risk.

Kemp,Matt			AB	R	HR	RBI	SB	Avg	vL	vR	OB	Slg	OPS	bb%	ct%	h%	Eye	xBA	G	L	F	PX	hr/f	SX	SBO	RC/G	RAR	BPV	R$
Pos	8	05	0	0	0	0	0	0							0			0											
Age	26	06 LA	* 535	93	16	84	28	293	229	264	343	464	806	7	79	34	0.36	267	40	24	36	107	10%	134	24%	5.40	14.5	59	$25
Bats	Right	07 LA	* 453	73	14	58	18	324	390	318	359	505	863	5	80	38	0.28	273	45	17	37	113	10%	132	20%	5.99	17.9	64	$22
Health	A	08 LA	606	93	18	76	35	290	369	260	340	459	799	7	75	36	0.30	262	45	23	32	119	12%	133	29%	5.40	11.4	50	$28
PT/Exp	A	09 LA	606	97	26	101	34	297	362	278	353	490	843	8	77	35	0.37	261	40	21	38	121	15%	138	24%	5.88	19.5	65	$34
Consist	B	1st Half	291	43	10	41	19	302			364	474	838	9	75	37	0.39	247	42	20	38	109	12%	144	24%	5.95	9.9	51	$16
LIMA Plan	D+	2nd Half	315	54	16	60	15	292			342	505	847	7	79	33	0.36	274	39	22	39	133	17%	119	24%	5.81	9.6	73	$18
Rand Var	-3	10 Proj	608	98	29	107	32	299			349	511	860	7	77	35	0.34	275	42	21	36	134	17%	136	25%	6.04	23.3	74	$34

Excellent growth season was fully supported by BPIs. BA has now exceeded xBA 4 years in a row. Power surge supported by rise in FB and HR/FB rates. Extending the 2nd half...
UP: 35 HR, 120 RBI

Kendall,Jason			AB	R	HR	RBI	SB	Avg	vL	vR	OB	Slg	OPS	bb%	ct%	h%	Eye	xBA	G	L	F	PX	hr/f	SX	SBO	RC/G	RAR	BPV	R$
Pos	2	05 OAK	601	70	0	53	8	271	293	264	327	321	648	8	94	29	1.28	269	53	21	26	38	0%	72	6%	3.92	-1.8	43	$11
Age	36	06 OAK	552	76	1	50	11	295	331	285	357	342	699	9	90	33	0.98	267	50	24	26	35	1%	72	8%	4.41	0.1	30	$13
Bats	Right	07 2TM	466	45	3	41	3	242	198	259	290	309	599	6	91	26	0.74	249	44	19	38	45	2%	53	6%	3.17	-16.7	30	$4
Health	A	08 MIL	516	46	2	49	8	246	250	245	313	324	636	9	91	27	1.11	252	46	18	37	54	1%	75	8%	3.80	-6.4	51	$7
PT/Exp	B	09 MIL	452	48	2	43	7	241	218	246	311	305	617	9	87	27	0.79	241	44	20	36	46	1%	79	7%	3.43	-11.3	29	$6
Consist	A	1st Half	220	24	0	21	1	232			316	273	589	11	87	27	0.93	239	45	23	32	31	0%	56	3%	3.20	-7.1	12	$2
LIMA Plan	D	2nd Half	232	24	2	22	6	250			307	336	643	8	88	28	0.66	242	43	18	39	59	3%	85	11%	3.63	-4.3	40	$4
Rand Var	0	10 Proj	403	41	2	38	6	248			311	314	626	8	89	27	0.86	247	45	19	36	47	1%	73	7%	3.55	-8.4	35	$6

Stable skill set offers little hope of higher BA or HR totals, but still a decent source of SB at catcher. At 36, the dip in ct% may be a sign that the end is near.

Kendrick,Howie			AB	R	HR	RBI	SB	Avg	vL	vR	OB	Slg	OPS	bb%	ct%	h%	Eye	xBA	G	L	F	PX	hr/f	SX	SBO	RC/G	RAR	BPV	R$
Pos	4	05 aa	190	27	5	33	9	300			318	484	802	3	92	31	0.31	0				117		118	37%	5.14	4.3	102	$9
Age	27	06 LAA	* 557	70	14	79	15	307	264	295	329	476	804	3	85	34	0.22	283	52	15	33	107	9%	109	15%	5.14	15.6	68	$20
Bats	Right	07 LAA	* 388	63	8	49	6	315	325	322	332	451	783	3	82	37	0.14	275	54	16	30	94	8%	95	10%	4.83	8.8	39	$14
Health	D	08 LAA	340	43	3	37	11	306	300	308	330	421	750	3	83	36	0.21	278	54	20	26	86	4%	103	18%	4.57	-3.0	40	$11
PT/Exp	D	09 LAA	* 452	70	12	70	15	294	313	278	332	449	780	5	82	34	0.31	281	54	19	27	97	12%	117	18%	4.98	0.6	52	$18
Consist	A	1st Half	264	33	6	31	10	253			295	389	684	6	81	29	0.32	262	58	13	29	83	9%	118	22%	3.84	-8.6	41	$7
LIMA Plan	D+	2nd Half	188	37	6	39	5	351			384	532	916	5	82	41	0.29	302	50	24	26	115	15%	101	13%	6.56	7.9	62	$11
Rand Var	-1	10 Proj	489	75	16	72	14	311			339	489	828	4	83	35	0.25	297	53	20	27	113	14%	104	17%	5.45	10.0	63	$21

10-61-.291 in 374 AB at LAA. His torrid 2H was driven by unsustainable LD and h% rates, but Eye, PX, and SX headed in the right direction.
UP: Batting title, 25 SB

Kennedy,Adam			AB	R	HR	RBI	SB	Avg	vL	vR	OB	Slg	OPS	bb%	ct%	h%	Eye	xBA	G	L	F	PX	hr/f	SX	SBO	RC/G	RAR	BPV	R$
Pos	54	05 ANA	416	49	2	37	19	300	296	302	346	370	716	7	85	35	0.45	248	41	24	35	55	2%	90	18%	4.34	-1.8	25	$14
Age	34	06 LAA	451	50	4	55	16	273	193	291	331	384	714	8	84	32	0.54	268	41	27	32	72	3%	113	21%	4.44	-7.5	46	$11
Bats	Left	07 STL	279	27	3	18	6	219	122	235	276	290	566	7	88	24	0.67	237	43	17	40	44	3%	81	11%	2.73	-24.8	29	$2
Health	B	08 STL	339	42	2	36	7	280	270	283	322	372	694	6	87	32	0.49	266	43	25	32	60	2%	114	9%	4.12	-12.0	45	$9
PT/Exp	C	09 OAK	* 611	74	14	70	22	280	241	307	337	402	739	8	84	32	0.53	266	41	24	36	78	7%	83	16%	4.63	-0.8	40	$19
Consist	B	1st Half	278	31	9	32	9	266			328	413	741	8	85	29	0.61	275	40	24	37	87	10%	78	16%	4.67	-0.1	51	$8
LIMA Plan	D+	2nd Half	333	43	5	38	13	291			344	393	738	7	83	34	0.47	258	42	23	35	70	5%	82	16%	4.61	-0.7	29	$11
Rand Var	-2	10 Proj	455	54	7	47	10	273			325	375	700	7	85	31	0.53	263	42	23	35	67	5%	83	11%	4.19	-7.6	36	$11

11-63-.289 with 20 SB in 529 AB at OAK. Career resurgence due to increased playing time and a little good luck. hr/f well above average (in a bad park), and SBO spike at 33 is unusual. Don't pay for a repeat.

Keppinger,Jeff			AB	R	HR	RBI	SB	Avg	vL	vR	OB	Slg	OPS	bb%	ct%	h%	Eye	xBA	G	L	F	PX	hr/f	SX	SBO	RC/G	RAR	BPV	R$
Pos	54	05 aaa	255	34	3	25	4	307			340	412	752	5	96	31	1.16	0				63		94	7%	4.84	1.4	73	$8
Age	30	06 KC	* 510	67	6	50	0	298	222	303	354	378	732	8	93	31	1.25	267	58	19	23	48	5%	31	2%	4.77	-3.4	38	$11
Bats	Right	07 CIN	* 469	66	7	47	3	331	362	320	387	450	837	8	95	34	1.67	298	47	21	32	71	5%	66	3%	5.97	4.5	74	$16
Health	B	08 CIN	459	45	3	43	3	266	360	225	311	346	657	6	95	28	1.25	281	51	21	28	52	2%	65	3%	3.95	-18.9	54	$8
PT/Exp	B	09 HOU	305	35	7	29	0	256	314	227	316	387	703	8	89	27	0.82	275	50	20	30	76	9%	56	3%	4.34	-7.2	53	$6
Consist	C	1st Half	148	17	3	11	0	257			337	385	722	11	89	27	1.13	263	53	15	32	79	7%	48	5%	4.75	-1.7	58	$2
LIMA Plan	D	2nd Half	157	18	4	18	0	255			295	389	684	5	89	26	0.53	284	52	21	26	73	11%	63	0%	3.93	-5.5	47	$3
Rand Var	+2	10 Proj	292	34	5	28	0	267			320	379	699	7	92	28	0.96	280	52	20	29	66	6%	56	2%	4.33	-7.9	54	$6

Elite ct%, but not much else. Won't be a drain on your BA but xBA and decline in ct% says he won't hit .300 again. Recent struggles against RH another reason to not go the extra $1.

BILL MACEY

Kinsler,Ian

		AB	R	HR	RBI	SB	Avg	vL	vR	OB	Slg	OPS	bb%	ct%	h%	Eye	xBA	G	L	F	PX	hr/f	SX	SBO	RC/G	RAR	BPV	R$
Pos 4	05 aaa	526	71	18	64	13	241			291	395	687	7	88	24	0.61	0				91		89	16%	3.98	-5.7	68	$14
Age 28	06 TEX	423	65	14	55	11	286	271	292	348	454	802	9	85	31	0.63	264	35	21	44	103	9%	89	13%	5.40	15.4	68	$15
Bats Right	07 TEX	483	96	20	61	23	263	339	239	347	441	788	11	83	28	0.75	265	35	20	46	108	11%	125	17%	5.34	18.8	80	$20
Health C	08 TEX	518	102	18	71	26	319	281	332	373	517	890	8	87	34	0.67	291	32	24	43	124	9%	138	19%	6.42	21.3	107	$28
PT/Exp A	09 TEX	566	101	31	86	31	253	310	230	323	488	811	9	86	24	0.77	270	30	16	54	129	12%	134	27%	5.49	9.4	110	$26
Consist C	1st Half	312	55	19	51	16	263			339	513	852	10	86	25	0.82	273	30	15	55	136	13%	123	23%	5.99	9.7	112	$15
LIMA Plan B+	2nd Half	254	46	12	35	15	240			303	457	760	8	87	23	0.70	267	30	17	53	120	10%	139	33%	4.88	-0.4	104	$10
Rand Var +3	10 Proj	509	93	23	71	26	269			335	476	811	9	86	27	0.72	273	32	19	49	120	11%	129	22%	5.51	11.9	99	$23

BA dove as FB% fed HR spike. What's sustainable here? H%, xBA point to modest BA gain. Only 5 MLB batters had 50%+ FB in 400+ AB, that should regress. Pay for 25/25, not a 30/30 repeat.

Konerko,Paul

		AB	R	HR	RBI	SB	Avg	vL	vR	OB	Slg	OPS	bb%	ct%	h%	Eye	xBA	G	L	F	PX	hr/f	SX	SBO	RC/G	RAR	BPV	R$
Pos 3	05 CHW	575	98	40	100	0	283	261	289	372	534	906	12	81	29	0.74	294	33	25	42	148	20%	26	0%	6.71	26.1	77	$26
Age 34	06 CHW	566	97	35	113	1	313	318	310	379	551	930	10	82	33	0.58	290	33	25	42	139	18%	41	1%	6.88	22.2	71	$27
Bats Right	07 CHW	549	71	31	90	0	259	296	244	351	490	841	12	81	27	0.76	283	38	17	45	145	16%	17	1%	5.99	11.7	73	$17
Health A	08 CHW	438	59	22	62	2	240	236	241	338	438	776	13	82	25	0.81	279	41	22	38	119	16%	52	2%	5.23	-0.6	66	$12
PT/Exp A	09 CHW	546	75	28	88	1	277	338	253	346	489	835	10	84	29	0.65	275	36	19	46	122	13%	44	1%	5.77	0.9	67	$19
Consist B	1st Half	276	35	13	49	0	290			344	493	837	8	84	31	0.51	282	35	22	43	120	13%	20	0%	5.69	-0.1	54	$10
LIMA Plan C+	2nd Half	270	40	15	39	1	263			348	485	833	11	84	27	0.80	267	36	15	48	124	14%	53	1%	5.83	0.9	75	$9
Rand Var 0	10 Proj	529	74	26	83	1	265			347	469	816	11	83	28	0.72	274	37	19	44	121	14%	46	1%	5.63	2.2	65	$17

Returned to pounding LH (1.006 OPS) after one-year hiatus, driving this rebound season. Stable skill set and late-prime age say he should have a couple more years at this level.

Kotchman,Casey

		AB	R	HR	RBI	SB	Avg	vL	vR	OB	Slg	OPS	bb%	ct%	h%	Eye	xBA	G	L	F	PX	hr/f	SX	SBO	RC/G	RAR	BPV	R$
Pos 3	05 ANA *	489	63	14	66	1	263	250	277	327	408	735	9	91	27	1.02	296	55	21	24	86	13%	43	4%	4.74	-5.0	64	$12
Age 27	06 LAA	79	6	1	6	0	152	214	138	221	215	436	8	84	17	0.54	213	67	11	23	40	7%	37	6%	1.04	-11.7	-4	($1)
Bats Left	07 LAA	443	64	11	68	2	296	315	292	371	467	838	11	90	31	1.23	303	51	16	33	109	8%	58	5%	6.09	10.2	89	$14
Health C	08 2TM	525	65	14	74	2	272	303	261	319	410	729	6	93	27	0.92	286	53	18	30	80	10%	51	2%	4.57	-13.9	64	$14
PT/Exp B	09 2TM	385	37	7	48	1	268	250	275	335	382	717	9	89	29	0.93	270	51	19	29	73	7%	32	1%	4.58	-17.0	45	$8
Consist B	1st Half	226	17	2	28	0	265			322	372	694	8	90	29	0.83	265	48	20	33	76	3%	15	0%	4.31	-11.7	42	$4
LIMA Plan F	2nd Half	159	20	5	20	1	270			352	396	748	11	88	28	1.05	269	57	18	25	70	14%	39	2%	4.94	-5.3	45	$4
Rand Var -1	10 Proj	255	30	6	34	1	275			340	403	743	9	90	29	1.00	276	53	18	29	78	9%	37	2%	4.84	-7.2	54	$7

High GB% continues to strangle any latent power potential. Strong plate patience would give him value if he could muster even league-average PX. but there's no sign of that. Age is only reason for hope.

Kotsay,Mark

		AB	R	HR	RBI	SB	Avg	vL	vR	OB	Slg	OPS	bb%	ct%	h%	Eye	xBA	G	L	F	PX	hr/f	SX	SBO	RC/G	RAR	BPV	R$
Pos 39	05 OAK	582	75	15	82	5	280	324	261	326	421	747	6	91	29	0.78	292	40	25	35	86	8%	58	7%	4.75	-5.6	66	$17
Age 34	06 OAK	502	57	7	59	6	275	265	278	333	386	720	8	89	30	0.80	263	46	19	35	70	4%	77	6%	4.56	-12.3	53	$10
Bats Left	07 OAK *	243	21	1	21	2	207	130	238	276	280	556	9	91	22	1.08	243	45	15	41	54	1%	50	6%	2.90	-17.9	43	$0
Health F	08 2TM	402	45	6	49	2	276	250	288	329	403	732	7	89	30	0.71	276	42	22	36	80	5%	68	6%	4.67	-9.6	57	$9
PT/Exp D	09 2AL	187	16	4	23	3	278	219	290	332	390	722	7	89	30	0.71	263	47	19	34	67	7%	41	9%	4.48	-6.6	38	$5
Consist B	1st Half	45	3	1	2	0	289			319	378	697	4	84	32	0.29	236	42	21	37	50	7%	22	8%	3.85	-2.4	-5	$1
LIMA Plan D	2nd Half	142	13	3	21	3	275			335	394	730	8	90	29	0.93	272	49	18	33	72	7%	48	10%	4.68	-4.2	51	$4
Rand Var -2	10 Proj	225	23	3	28	3	267			326	378	704	8	90	28	0.88	269	45	19	36	70	5%	63	7%	4.40	-7.1	53	$5

Surgery to correct yet another back problem cost him 1H. Skills were intact upon return. Unfortunately for him, that just means he makes a lot of contact but doesn't hit with any authority.

Kottaras,George

		AB	R	HR	RBI	SB	Avg	vL	vR	OB	Slg	OPS	bb%	ct%	h%	Eye	xBA	G	L	F	PX	hr/f	SX	SBO	RC/G	RAR	BPV	R$
Pos 2	05 aa	101	15	2	14	0	257			370	376	746	15	75	32	0.72	0				92		30	0%	5.10	3.5	15	$2
Age 27	06 a/a	376	46	7	43	0	223			321	359	680	13	77	27	0.61	0				97		49	1%	4.14	-2.7	26	$4
Bats Left	07 aaa	294	29	8	35	1	238			304	401	706	9	78	28	0.44	0				119		32	3%	4.26	-0.9	37	$4
Health B	08 aaa	395	50	16	52	0	214			302	383	685	11	75	24	0.51	0				114		26	0%	3.98	-2.7	25	$7
PT/Exp F	09 BOS *	117	16	1	10	0	243	111	267	337	394	731	12	73	32	0.52	253	30	23	48	134	2%	32	0%	4.96	2.4	35	$1
Consist B	1st Half	68	11	0	8	0	221			293	353	646	9	72	31	0.37	242	31	21	48	128	0%	51	0%	3.72	-1.1	26	$1
LIMA Plan F	2nd Half	49	5	1	2	0	274			392	451	844	16	74	35	0.76	289	26	26	47	142	6%	1	0%	6.59	3.2	46	$1
Rand Var -1	10 Proj	139	18	3	17	0	245			325	390	714	11	75	31	0.48	244	31	21	48	114	5%	36	1%	4.51	1.1	27	$2

1-10-.237 in 93 AB at BOS. Designated Wakefield caddy wasn't completely helpless vs. RHP (.769). Rare breed LH CA allows him to earn a living as a #2 CA on a MLB team. But no reason for you to employ him.

Kouzmanoff,Kevin

		AB	R	HR	RBI	SB	Avg	vL	vR	OB	Slg	OPS	bb%	ct%	h%	Eye	xBA	G	L	F	PX	hr/f	SX	SBO	RC/G	RAR	BPV	R$
Pos 5	05	0	0	0	0	0	0							0			0						0					
Age 29	06 CLE *	402	65	20	78	4	321	167	227	376	546	922	8	85	34	0.61	288	59	9	32	132	18%	61	7%	6.71	18.5	84	$19
Bats Right	07 SD	484	57	18	74	1	275	356	240	320	457	776	6	81	31	0.34	268	41	18	41	116	11%	50	1%	4.93	-9.3	44	$14
Health A	08 SD	624	71	23	84	0	260	237	269	286	433	719	4	78	30	0.17	256	40	22	39	112	12%	52	0%	4.07	-23.6	25	$16
PT/Exp A	09 SD	529	50	18	88	1	255	291	241	291	420	711	5	80	29	0.25	261	44	20	36	110	12%	41	1%	4.06	-16.8	32	$14
Consist A	1st Half	285	23	10	40	1	239			264	389	654	3	79	27	0.17	244	46	18	36	96	12%	45	2%	3.23	-16.2	15	$6
LIMA Plan C	2nd Half	244	27	8	48	0	275			322	455	777	7	81	31	0.37	277	42	22	36	126	11%	21	0%	4.99	-1.0	46	$8
Rand Var +1	10 Proj	597	67	22	87	1	260			299	438	737	5	80	29	0.28	268	43	20	37	117	12%	53	1%	4.40	-15.1	43	$16

Off-season shoulder surgery sapped power in 1H. Poor plate control, too many GB, and Petco continued to stifle his power even as PX returned. Too bad none of those problems can be fixed with a scalpel.

Kubel,Jason

		AB	R	HR	RBI	SB	Avg	vL	vR	OB	Slg	OPS	bb%	ct%	h%	Eye	xBA	G	L	F	PX	hr/f	SX	SBO	RC/G	RAR	BPV	R$
Pos 97	05 MIN	0	0	0	0	0	0							0			0						0					
Age 28	06 MIN *	340	41	12	48	4	253	243	240	302	415	717	7	80	29	0.35	265	49	21	31	99	14%	83	5%	4.21	-14.5	38	$8
Bats Left	07 MIN	418	49	13	65	5	273	236	280	338	450	787	9	81	31	0.52	289	43	22	35	121	11%	79	5%	5.28	-2.6	64	$12
Health B	08 MIN	463	74	20	78	0	272	232	283	339	471	810	9	80	30	0.52	269	40	20	41	122	13%	69	1%	5.50	1.9	60	$16
PT/Exp B	09 MIN	514	73	28	103	1	300	245	322	368	539	907	10	79	33	0.53	285	39	20	41	147	17%	44	1%	6.73	19.8	70	$22
Consist B	1st Half	247	36	13	42	0	308			367	543	909	9	79	35	0.44	284	40	20	40	145	17%	37	0%	6.69	9.2	62	$10
LIMA Plan C+	2nd Half	267	37	15	61	1	292			370	536	906	11	80	32	0.61	285	38	19	43	148	17%	45	3%	6.76	10.7	75	$12
Rand Var -3	10 Proj	512	72	24	93	2	283			350	495	845	9	80	31	0.51	279	40	20	40	131	15%	62	2%	5.93	8.4	64	$19

Reasons not to expect another step forward after 2009's long-awaited breakout:
- Mild h% correction likely
- LHPs still own him.

Power repeat likely, but BA repeat improbable.

Laird,Gerald

		AB	R	HR	RBI	SB	Avg	vL	vR	OB	Slg	OPS	bb%	ct%	h%	Eye	xBA	G	L	F	PX	hr/f	SX	SBO	RC/G	RAR	BPV	R$
Pos 2	05 TEX *	321	43	14	42	8	269			315	457	772	6	85	28	0.44	257	39	15	45	108	11%	104	14%	4.86	7.8	71	$11
Age 30	06 TEX	243	46	7	22	3	296	400	241	329	473	803	5	78	36	0.22	251	34	19	46	124	8%	99	7%	5.27	5.8	51	$8
Bats Right	07 TEX	407	48	9	47	6	224	239	218	277	349	626	7	75	28	0.29	202	33	12	55	89	5%	94	9%	3.10	-14.9	14	$6
Health A	08 TEX	344	54	6	41	2	276	245	288	322	398	720	6	82	32	0.37	254	38	22	41	90	5%	57	7%	4.32	1.3	30	$9
PT/Exp C	09 DET	413	49	4	33	5	225	248	222	294	320	613	9	84	26	0.59	225	41	14	45	65	3%	90	5%	3.25	-12.7	32	$4
Consist C	1st Half	199	26	3	20	1	236			312	357	669	10	81	28	0.58	231	42	15	43	79	4%	78	2%	3.93	-2.0	32	$3
LIMA Plan D	2nd Half	214	23	1	13	4	215			276	285	561	8	86	25	0.60	217	40	14	46	52	1%	72	8%	2.67	-10.6	25	$1
Rand Var +3	10 Proj	389	51	6	38	5	239			296	350	646	7	82	28	0.44	231	39	16	45	78	4%	79	7%	3.51	-8.7	30	$6

Ct% gains more than offset by below-average-and-dropping PX. Back problems may have contributed. Handful of SB helps, but you're better off with a 2nd CA who plays less and thus doesn't wreck your BA.

Langerhans,Ryan

		AB	R	HR	RBI	SB	Avg	vL	vR	OB	Slg	OPS	bb%	ct%	h%	Eye	xBA	G	L	F	PX	hr/f	SX	SBO	RC/G	RAR	BPV	R$
Pos 7	05 ATL	326	48	8	42	0	267	298	261	342	426	768	10	77	33	0.49	274	40	26	33	114	10%	66	2%	5.16	-1.7	41	$9
Age 30	06 ATL	315	46	7	28	1	241	308	232	345	378	723	14	71	32	0.55	227	41	21	38	96	8%	72	3%	4.76	-4.6	12	$5
Bats Left	07 2TM *	261	37	7	25	4	181	219	157	275	314	590	11	63	26	0.35	198	44	13	43	105	10%	102	8%	2.74	-20.7	-7	$2
Health A	08 WAS *	324	47	5	36	11	243	217	239	351	367	718	14	73	32	0.62	243	44	25	31	93	6%	121	13%	4.75	-6.5	33	$8
PT/Exp D	09 SEA *	306	37	9	39	5	221	212	221	304	378	681	11	75	27	0.47	232	37	16	47	108	8%	68	16%	3.99	-9.8	30	$5
Consist C	1st Half	205	25	6	29	5	222			299	373	672	10	76	26	0.46	0				104		62	23%	3.83	-7.7	29	$4
LIMA Plan F	2nd Half	101	12	3	10	0	218			313	386	699	12	72	27	0.50	229	37	16	47	117	9%	65	4%	4.33	-2.1	29	$1
Rand Var +2	10 Proj	154	20	4	17	2	227			321	373	694	12	72	29	0.49	231	40	18	42	107	8%	80	10%	4.26	-3.4	24	$3

3-10-.218 in 101 AB at SEA. Nudged PX into triple-digits, but too many other skills remain below average. Good defense may help him hang around a bit longer, but we can close the book on his fantasy relevance.

RAY MURPHY

LaPorta,Matt

LaPorta,Matt		AB	R	HR	RBI	SB	Avg	vL	vR	OB	Slg	OPS	bb%	ct%	h%	Eye	xBA	G	L	F	PX	hr/f	SX	SBO	RC/G	RAR	BPV	R$
Pos 7	05	0	0	0	0	0	0							0			0						0					
Age 25	06	0	0	0	0	0	0							0			0						0					
Bats Right	07	0	0	0	0	0	0							0			0						0					
Health A	08	0	0	0	0	0	0							0			0						0					
PT/Exp F	09 CLE *	519	79	20	68	3	257	211	266	318	443	761	8	83	27	0.54	272	40	18	42	113	11%	61	5%	4.86	-2.3	60	$14
Consist F	1st Half	257	44	9	34	2	255			317	420	737	8	83	28	0.54	279	44	22	34	100	12%	79	5%	4.59	-3.1	55	$7
LIMA Plan C	2nd Half	262	35	12	34	1	259			319	465	784	8	83	27	0.53	275	39	18	44	125	12%	38	6%	5.12	0.9	63	$7
Rand Var +1	10 Proj	441	66	18	58	2	265			326	457	783	8	83	28	0.53	274	39	18	42	119	11%	57	5%	5.12	1.9	63	$13

7-21-.254 in 181 AB at CLE. Fared better in 2H callup (.283 xBA, 139 PX), hinting at near-term upside of a slugger with decent strike zone control. Season ended with hip surgery that may slow him early in 2010.

Larish,Jeff

Larish,Jeff		AB	R	HR	RBI	SB	Avg	vL	vR	OB	Slg	OPS	bb%	ct%	h%	Eye	xBA	G	L	F	PX	hr/f	SX	SBO	RC/G	RAR	BPV	R$
Pos 0	05	0	0	0	0	0	0							0			0						0					
Age 27	06	0	0	0	0	0	0							0			0						0					
Bats Left	07 aa	454	66	25	93	5	241			354	460	815	15	76	26	0.74	0				139		68	5%	5.82	-5.7	69	$15
Health B	08 DET *	488	51	18	67	2	223	250	260	292	388	680	9	74	27	0.37	243	44	19	37	114	13%	48	4%	3.84	-16.4	20	$8
PT/Exp D	09 DET *	285	44	9	28	2	227		235	341	374	715	15	73	28	0.63	224	46	14	40	101	10%	60	5%	4.60	-5.0	21	$5
Consist C	1st Half	181	30	7	20	0	236			346	416	763	14	72	29	0.60	238	46	14	40	124	13%	62	2%	5.26	0.5	36	$4
LIMA Plan F	2nd Half	104	14	2	8	2	212			331	301	631	15	74	27	0.68	0				63		53	11%	3.49	-5.5	-7	$1
Rand Var -1	10 Proj	135	18	6	17	1	230			328	398	726	13	74	27	0.56	235	46	15	39	113	14%	41	6%	4.59	-3.3	25	$3

4-7-.216 in 74 AB at DET. Owns intriguing PX, even if trending in wrong direction of late. Poor and eroding ct% is his undoing, along with too many GBs. Not to old to repeat 2007 in the bigs, but time is now his enemy.

LaRoche,Adam

LaRoche,Adam		AB	R	HR	RBI	SB	Avg	vL	vR	OB	Slg	OPS	bb%	ct%	h%	Eye	xBA	G	L	F	PX	hr/f	SX	SBO	RC/G	RAR	BPV	R$
Pos 3	05 ATL	451	53	20	78	0	259	191	269	318	455	773	8	81	28	0.45	282	44	21	34	127	16%	21	2%	4.95	-8.5	49	$14
Age 30	06 ATL	492	89	32	90	0	285	241	297	356	561	917	10	74	33	0.43	286	38	21	41	180	21%	41	2%	7.02	14.1	74	$21
Bats Left	07 PIT	563	71	21	88	1	272	299	262	344	458	802	10	77	32	0.47	265	36	21	44	130	11%	31	1%	5.51	-9.9	42	$16
Health A	08 PIT	492	66	25	85	1	270	241	282	342	500	842	10	75	31	0.44	269	37	20	43	154	16%	57	2%	6.02	4.1	63	$18
PT/Exp A	09 2TM	555	78	25	83	2	277	243	293	357	488	846	11	74	33	0.49	264	35	22	43	145	14%	52	3%	6.17	0.9	53	$19
Consist A	1st Half	269	43	11	37	2	268			362	480	842	13	77	31	0.63	275	37	22	42	147	13%	63	5%	6.21	0.7	70	$9
LIMA Plan C+	2nd Half	286	35	14	46	0	287			352	497	849	9	72	35	0.37	255	33	22	45	143	15%	32	0%	6.14	0.3	34	$10
Rand Var -1	10 Proj	539	73	26	91	1	275			349	494	843	10	75	32	0.46	270	36	21	43	149	15%	48	2%	6.05	3.3	56	$19

Has a well-earned reputation for streakiness, but '09 halves were near identical, and multi-year skill set is extremely stable (as evidenced by AAA Reliability). If you roster him, just ignore the monthly variance.

LaRoche,Andy

LaRoche,Andy		AB	R	HR	RBI	SB	Avg	vL	vR	OB	Slg	OPS	bb%	ct%	h%	Eye	xBA	G	L	F	PX	hr/f	SX	SBO	RC/G	RAR	BPV	R$
Pos 5	05 aa	223	33	7	34	2	238			312	377	688	10	80	27	0.55	0				91		59	7%	4.03	-4.1	33	$6
Age 27	06 a/a	432	66	17	69	8	282			363	461	824	11	87	29	0.96	0				102		71	10%	5.81	7.0	74	$16
Bats Right	07 LA *	358	60	16	48	4	258	200	235	351	455	806	13	83	27	0.83	280	41	19	40	119	14%	66	6%	5.62	0.1	73	$11
Health A	08 2NL *	368	47	9	40	4	198	143	175	302	293	595	13	85	21	1.00	232	49	16	35	56	8%	61	4%	3.19	-25.4	31	$4
PT/Exp C	09 PIT	524	64	12	64	3	258	285	249	322	401	723	9	84	29	0.60	264	49	17	34	91	8%	80	3%	4.52	-9.4	52	$12
Consist D	1st Half	255	35	3	33	2	278			343	396	739	9	84	32	0.63	273	47	24	29	79	5%	91	3%	4.78	-2.6	48	$7
LIMA Plan C+	2nd Half	269	29	9	31	1	238			303	405	708	9	84	25	0.57	253	50	12	38	103	10%	59	3%	4.27	-7.0	54	$5
Rand Var 0	10 Proj	510	67	15	63	4	261			339	406	744	11	84	29	0.73	259	49	16	35	89	10%	74	4%	4.83	-6.4	52	$13

2H PX finally suggests that there may be more than a noodle bat here, but still much work to do: not enough ct% to make up for barely-average PX, too many GBs. Right age to step up, but little reason to expect it.

LaRue,Jason

LaRue,Jason		AB	R	HR	RBI	SB	Avg	vL	vR	OB	Slg	OPS	bb%	ct%	h%	Eye	xBA	G	L	F	PX	hr/f	SX	SBO	RC/G	RAR	BPV	R$
Pos 2	05 CIN	361	38	14	60	0	260	257	262	336	452	787	10	72	33	0.41	264	42	23	36	145	15%	16	0%	5.42	17.1	31	$10
Age 36	06 CIN	191	22	8	21	1	194	235	179	294	346	639	12	73	22	0.53	230	44	20	36	94	16%	37	2%	3.34	-6.0	6	$2
Bats Right	07 KC	169	14	4	13	1	148	160	143	226	272	498	9	61	21	0.26	205	48	17	35	114	11%	42	3%	1.27	-17.0	-32	($2)
Health A	08 STL	164	17	4	21	0	213	196	220	279	348	627	8	88	22	0.75	252	39	18	43	80	6%	46	0%	3.46	-3.8	48	$2
PT/Exp F	09 STL	104	10	2	6	1	240	259	234	262	327	589	3	79	29	0.14	213	49	15	36	58	7%	50	4%	2.41	-5.7	-16	$1
Consist D	1st Half	53	5	1	3	0	264			278	358	636	2	79	32	0.09	219	60	14	26	65	9%	25	0%	2.96	-2.0	-17	$1
LIMA Plan F	2nd Half	51	5	1	3	1	216			245	294	539	4	78	26	0.18	194	38	15	46	50	5%	59	9%	1.83	-3.8	-19	$0
Rand Var -4	10 Proj	117	11	3	10	1	222			270	335	605	6	78	26	0.29	224	44	17	39	78	8%	45	3%	2.78	-5.2	1	$1

Flip to the back of the book and find the "Cheater's bookmark". Note the "Bad Under" column. Other than a barely-tolerable ct%, he falls below every one of those "Bad Under" thresholds. Need we say more?

Lee,Carlos

Lee,Carlos		AB	R	HR	RBI	SB	Avg	vL	vR	OB	Slg	OPS	bb%	ct%	h%	Eye	xBA	G	L	F	PX	hr/f	SX	SBO	RC/G	RAR	BPV	R$
Pos 7	05 MIL	618	85	32	114	13	265	261	267	327	487	814	8	86	26	0.66	292	34	20	46	134	13%	76	11%	5.47	2.4	92	$26
Age 34	06 2TM	624	102	37	116	19	300	313	296	359	540	899	9	90	29	0.89	305	40	20	40	128	16%	95	12%	6.42	20.8	108	$31
Bats Right	07 HOU	627	93	32	119	10	303	338	292	357	528	885	8	90	30	0.84	298	38	16	46	126	12%	67	9%	6.26	15.6	98	$29
Health B	08 HOU	436	61	28	100	4	314	330	309	368	569	937	8	89	30	0.76	308	35	21	44	142	17%	49	4%	6.77	15.9	101	$24
PT/Exp A	09 HOU	610	65	26	102	5	300	325	293	344	489	833	6	92	29	0.80	288	36	20	44	107	11%	45	5%	5.61	0.8	80	$24
Consist B	1st Half	283	34	12	46	2	300			355	481	836	8	92	29	1.04	281	42	17	41	99	11%	51	5%	5.74	1.4	79	$12
LIMA Plan C	2nd Half	327	31	14	56	3	300			334	495	830	5	91	29	0.61	296	31	22	46	114	10%	38	5%	5.49	-0.7	80	$13
Rand Var 0	10 Proj	595	69	25	107	7	303			351	495	846	7	90	30	0.78	288	36	20	44	110	11%	57	6%	5.80	5.4	83	$25

Only real difference from studly '08 to merely solid '09 was ping-ponging of hr/f level. 1H may have included some lingering issues from '08 broken pinkie, too. Elite ct% preserves value even as PX, SX gently fade.

Lee,Derrek

Lee,Derrek		AB	R	HR	RBI	SB	Avg	vL	vR	OB	Slg	OPS	bb%	ct%	h%	Eye	xBA	G	L	F	PX	hr/f	SX	SBO	RC/G	RAR	BPV	R$
Pos 3	05 CHC	594	120	46	107	15	335	333	339	418	662	1080	13	82	35	0.78	338	39	22	39	202	24%	104	10%	8.91	51.7	146	$41
Age 35	06 CHC	175	30	8	30	8	286	292	283	375	474	849	13	77	33	0.61	257	41	20	38	118	16%	75	21%	6.19	1.0	50	$8
Bats Right	07 CHC	567	91	22	82	6	317	339	312	393	513	907	11	80	37	0.62	283	41	21	38	129	13%	60	6%	6.86	11.3	65	$24
Health B	08 CHC	623	93	20	90	8	291	306	286	363	462	825	10	81	33	0.60	275	45	21	34	113	12%	88	5%	5.81	1.3	63	$23
PT/Exp A	09 CHC	532	91	35	111	1	306	300	308	393	579	972	13	80	33	0.70	293	35	19	46	172	18%	51	1%	7.65	16.6	98	$29
Consist C	1st Half	245	33	12	41	0	282			362	478	840	11	79	31	0.61	249	39	16	45	124	14%	20	0%	5.94	-3.9	47	$9
LIMA Plan C+	2nd Half	287	58	23	70	1	328			419	666	1084	14	80	34	0.78	324	32	22	47	212	22%	66	1%	9.10	19.6	137	$20
Rand Var -1	10 Proj	556	93	28	101	1	297			380	525	904	12	80	33	0.66	285	39	20	41	146	15%	53	2%	6.82	9.8	78	$25

Proof of "once you display a skill", overcomes long-term back/neck issues to reprise monster 2005. Sudden reversal of G/F ratio an obvious key. But back problems in mid-30s don't just disappear. Be skeptical.

Lewis,Fred

Lewis,Fred		AB	R	HR	RBI	SB	Avg	vL	vR	OB	Slg	OPS	bb%	ct%	h%	Eye	xBA	G	L	F	PX	hr/f	SX	SBO	RC/G	RAR	BPV	R$
Pos 7	05 aa	508	62	5	38	24	238			311	340	651	10	78	29	0.49	0				73		128	27%	3.68	-21.3	32	$11
Age 29	06 aaa	439	64	9	43	14	241			320	379	698	10	82	28	0.64	0				80		130	20%	4.31	-12.2	54	$10
Bats Left	07 SF *	328	57	8	42	11	259	276	289	327	413	739	9	80	30	0.50	267	55	15	30	92	10%	145	14%	4.71	-6.2	56	$11
Health A	08 SF	468	81	9	40	21	282	270	285	353	440	793	10	74	37	0.41	256	54	18	28	109	9%	150	20%	5.58	2.1	47	$18
PT/Exp C	09 SF	295	49	4	20	8	258	164	279	338	390	728	11	72	35	0.43	252	52	21	27	108	7%	117	14%	4.79	-6.7	31	$8
Consist B	1st Half	200	37	4	11	5	255			329	395	724	10	70	35	0.37	244	49	22	29	110	10%	118	16%	4.67	-5.3	25	$5
LIMA Plan D	2nd Half	95	12	0	9	3	263			358	379	737	13	75	35	0.58	266	59	20	21	103	0%	101	10%	5.07	-1.4	40	$2
Rand Var -1	10 Proj	250	39	4	22	9	264			342	402	745	11	75	34	0.47	261	55	19	26	101	7%	134	16%	4.96	-3.7	44	$7

Ongoing ct% erosion now at dangerous levels, overshadows the raw elements of a valuable speed source in these skills. Pushing 30, just about too late for the light bulb to go "on" and change his plate approach.

Lillibridge,Brent

Lillibridge,Brent		AB	R	HR	RBI	SB	Avg	vL	vR	OB	Slg	OPS	bb%	ct%	h%	Eye	xBA	G	L	F	PX	hr/f	SX	SBO	RC/G	RAR	BPV	R$
Pos 4	05	0	0	0	0	0	0							0			0						0					
Age 27	06	0	0	0	0	0	0							0			0						0					
Bats Right	07 a/a	525	67	11	50	36	257			302	371	673	6	79	31	0.30	0				75		126	36%	3.68	-10.5	27	$17
Health A	08 ATL *	435	46	4	39	21	190	171	222	241	291	532	6	76	24	0.28	206	45	11	44	73	3%	145	35%	1.96	-39.7	20	$5
PT/Exp D	09 CHW *	341	38	3	23	20	200	214	134	282	263	545	10	76	26	0.47	215	47	19	34	43	3%	115	25%	2.22	-29.4	-5	$5
Consist B	1st Half	208	24	1	10	10	181			253	239	492	9	74	24	0.37	207	41	22	37	41	2%	127	21%	1.44	-23.4	-13	$1
LIMA Plan F	2nd Half	133	14	2	13	10	231			326	300	626	12	78	28	0.65	223	59	14	27	46	6%	81	30%	3.39	-6.4	1	$4
Rand Var +1	10 Proj	174	19	2	15	10	224			291	304	594	9	77	28	0.40	217	49	15	36	55	4%	108	29%	2.81	-10.2	3	$3

0-3-.158 with 6 SB in 95 AB at CHW. Like Lewis above, runs like the wind but can't put the bat on the ball. Tiny 2H sample hints at some improvement there, and keeps him on our end-game radar for one more year.

RAY MURPHY

Lind,Adam

Lind,Adam		Yr	AB	R	HR	RBI	SB	Avg	vL	vR	OB	Slg	OPS	bb%	ct%	h%	Eye	xBA	G	L	F	PX	hr/f	SX	SBO	RC/G	RAR	BPV	R$
Pos	7	05	0	0	0	0	0	0							0			0						0					
Age	27	06 TOR	* 517	66	26	91	3	331	444	353	389	559	948	9	79	38	0.44	272	35	19	46	148	14%	39	3%	7.21	27.6	64	$23
Bats	Left	07 TOR	* 464	51	17	70	1	254	194	251	297	420	717	6	78	29	0.28	261	45	19	37	109	13%	46	3%	4.15	-12.1	27	$11
Health	A	08 TOR	* 515	69	15	83	3	288	253	294	330	458	788	6	82	33	0.34	281	51	19	30	110	12%	88	3%	5.11	3.7	55	$17
PT/Exp	B	09 TOR	587	93	35	114	1	305	275	317	367	562	930	9	81	33	0.53	304	43	20	37	157	20%	35	1%	6.90	30.3	81	$27
Consist	C	1st Half	302	47	16	53	1	315			384	556	940	10	82	34	0.63	310	44	23	33	149	19%	36	2%	7.12	17.2	80	$14
LIMA Plan	C	2nd Half	285	46	19	61	0	295			350	568	918	8	80	31	0.43	296	42	17	40	165	21%	27	0%	6.66	13.0	79	$13
Rand Var	0	10 Proj	592	84	34	107	2	294			347	540	887	8	80	32	0.42	298	45	19	36	152	20%	53	2%	6.31	22.0	76	$24

Breakout season fully supported by indicators: PX finally matched 2006's potential, while improving plate control and solving LHPs. 2H FB/PX combo says that this isn't his power peak, either.
UP: 40 HR

Loney,James

Loney,James		Yr	AB	R	HR	RBI	SB	Avg	vL	vR	OB	Slg	OPS	bb%	ct%	h%	Eye	xBA	G	L	F	PX	hr/f	SX	SBO	RC/G	RAR	BPV	R$
Pos	3	05 aa	500	59	9	51	0	242			306	350	656	8	86	27	0.65	0				71		37	4%	3.74	-24.2	30	$7
Age	26	06 LA	* 468	73	10	74	8	333	350	268	379	503	882	7	92	35	0.96	280	49	12	39	96	6%	96	11%	6.32	4.0	91	$21
Bats	Left	07 LA	* 577	63	16	93	2	295	319	336	350	455	805	8	84	33	0.54	280	42	22	36	98	9%	61	2%	5.41	-11.5	52	$18
Health	A	08 LA	595	66	13	90	7	289	249	305	339	434	773	7	86	32	0.53	275	44	22	34	90	7%	84	7%	5.03	-11.8	56	$19
PT/Exp	A	09 LA	576	73	13	90	7	281	274	283	359	399	758	11	88	30	1.03	268	43	22	35	72	7%	70	5%	5.10	-23.0	55	$19
Consist	A	1st Half	298	35	5	49	5	279			347	389	736	9	88	30	0.89	265	41	22	37	72	5%	70	7%	4.79	-14.6	52	$10
LIMA Plan	C+	2nd Half	278	38	8	41	2	284			372	410	782	12	88	30	1.18	271	45	22	33	72	10%	55	4%	5.43	-8.5	53	$10
Rand Var	0	10 Proj	572	70	16	87	6	290			356	436	792	9	87	31	0.79	278	43	22	35	87	9%	75	5%	5.37	-13.2	61	$19

Carbon-copy production masks some skills growth: a few more BBs, ct% trending upward. With minor recovery in h% and PX, there's a career year lurking:
UP: .325, 20 HR

Longoria,Evan

Longoria,Evan		Yr	AB	R	HR	RBI	SB	Avg	vL	vR	OB	Slg	OPS	bb%	ct%	h%	Eye	xBA	G	L	F	PX	hr/f	SX	SBO	RC/G	RAR	BPV	R$
Pos	5	05	0	0	0	0	0	0							0			0						0					
Age	25	06 aa	105	15	6	20	2	257			264	476	740	1	80	27	0.05	0				128		78	18%	4.08	-3.6	50	$4
Bats	Right	07 a/a	485	91	25	90	4	292			382	507	889	13	80	32	0.73	0				134		65	3%	6.63	18.7	75	$22
Health	A	08 TAM	448	67	27	85	7	272	242	284	340	531	871	9	73	32	0.38	281	39	20	42	180	20%	91	6%	6.42	19.7	83	$19
PT/Exp	B	09 TAM	584	100	33	113	9	281	289	277	360	526	885	11	76	32	0.51	282	39	19	42	160	18%	78	6%	6.59	31.5	79	$26
Consist	A	1st Half	276	45	16	63	2	297			372	558	930	11	74	35	0.45	285	36	20	43	178	18%	49	3%	7.28	19.8	75	$13
LIMA Plan	B	2nd Half	308	55	17	50	7	266			349	497	845	11	78	29	0.58	279	41	18	41	144	17%	82	8%	6.02	11.9	77	$13
Rand Var	0	10 Proj	600	100	35	113	11	288			358	535	893	10	76	33	0.46	284	39	19	42	160	18%	89	7%	6.61	30.9	82	$28

Quietly consolidated skills in sophomore campaign: bb% and ct% trending up (esp. in 2H), all while PX remained elite. 2H SBO hints at double-digit SB for icing on the cake. A worthy foundation-level player.

Lopez,Felipe

Lopez,Felipe		Yr	AB	R	HR	RBI	SB	Avg	vL	vR	OB	Slg	OPS	bb%	ct%	h%	Eye	xBA	G	L	F	PX	hr/f	SX	SBO	RC/G	RAR	BPV	R$
Pos	4	05 CIN	580	97	23	85	15	291	244	312	355	486	841	9	81	33	0.51	300	54	20	27	124	18%	115	13%	5.89	21.8	77	$26
Age	30	06 2NL	617	98	11	52	44	274	246	285	358	381	739	12	80	33	0.64	247	50	19	30	69	7%	118	27%	4.83	4.2	34	$24
Bats	Both	07 WAS	603	70	9	50	24	245	269	235	306	352	658	8	82	29	0.49	260	50	20	30	67	6%	113	20%	3.68	-18.5	33	$13
Health	A	08 2NL	481	64	6	46	8	283	306	270	342	387	728	8	83	33	0.52	254	50	19	31	73	5%	76	11%	4.57	-2.8	32	$13
PT/Exp	A	09 2TM	604	88	9	57	6	310	320	306	382	427	809	11	83	36	0.71	277	52	22	26	80	7%	71	6%	5.69	15.9	43	$19
Consist	C	1st Half	293	38	4	16	6	304			358	413	771	8	81	36	0.45	272	53	23	25	78	7%	82	9%	5.06	2.6	30	$9
LIMA Plan	C	2nd Half	311	50	5	41	0	315			403	441	844	13	86	36	1.02	279	51	22	27	83	7%	48	3%	6.27	13.1	50	$11
Rand Var	-4	10 Proj	537	76	8	53	7	277			348	394	741	10	83	32	0.63	269	51	21	28	79	7%	78	9%	4.81	2.3	40	$14

As Rand Var field shows, nearly everything went right in 2009. Give back the h% spike, hr/f uptick, and a couple of extra BBs, and what you have left is a guy who hits lots of GB but is too slow to beat them out.

Lopez,Jose

Lopez,Jose		Yr	AB	R	HR	RBI	SB	Avg	vL	vR	OB	Slg	OPS	bb%	ct%	h%	Eye	xBA	G	L	F	PX	hr/f	SX	SBO	RC/G	RAR	BPV	R$
Pos	4	05 SEA	* 372	44	6	54	6	277	273	235	303	430	733	4	88	30	0.30	281	41	19	40	110	5%	67	17%	4.43	3.2	69	$10
Age	26	06 SEA	603	78	10	79	5	282	331	265	312	405	716	4	87	31	0.33	263	49	18	33	72	6%	100	5%	4.21	1.5	45	$15
Bats	Right	07 SEA	524	58	11	62	2	252	244	254	279	355	634	4	88	27	0.31	251	46	17	37	61	6%	58	4%	3.22	-12.1	27	$9
Health	A	08 SEA	644	80	17	89	6	297	298	296	325	443	767	4	90	31	0.40	285	44	20	36	91	8%	64	6%	4.77	-2.1	60	$21
PT/Exp	A	09 SEA	613	69	25	96	3	272	286	266	300	463	763	4	89	27	0.35	287	41	19	41	110	11%	41	5%	4.66	-4.8	65	$18
Consist	B	1st Half	267	30	10	46	2	258			290	423	714	4	89	26	0.41	272	39	19	42	92	10%	45	7%	4.14	-6.2	54	$7
LIMA Plan	D+	2nd Half	346	39	15	50	1	283			307	494	801	3	88	29	0.30	297	42	19	40	123	12%	34	3%	5.06	1.3	72	$11
Rand Var	+1	10 Proj	640	74	26	92	4	284			312	474	786	4	89	29	0.35	290	43	19	38	110	12%	50	5%	4.90	3.5	67	$21

Turned 2008's breakout into a stepping stone, and still may not have peaked. xBA and h% ping-pong say he can recapture 2008 BA. Improved FB/PX and strong 2H say power is legit. Add it up, and... UP: 300, 30 HR.

Loretta,Mark

Loretta,Mark		Yr	AB	R	HR	RBI	SB	Avg	vL	vR	OB	Slg	OPS	bb%	ct%	h%	Eye	xBA	G	L	F	PX	hr/f	SX	SBO	RC/G	RAR	BPV	R$
Pos	5	05 SD	404	54	3	38	8	280	309	269	352	347	698	10	92	30	1.32	280	40	28	32	44	3%	80	9%	4.52	-3.0	48	$11
Age	39	06 BOS	635	75	5	59	4	285	274	290	336	361	697	7	90	31	0.78	266	35	27	38	51	2%	56	3%	4.27	-13.3	34	$12
Bats	Right	07 HOU	460	52	4	41	1	287	317	278	349	372	721	9	91	31	1.07	268	41	22	36	54	3%	46	2%	4.67	-12.1	41	$9
Health	A	08 HOU	261	27	4	38	0	280	330	250	352	383	735	10	89	30	0.97	278	37	27	36	69	5%	20	0%	4.83	-4.0	37	$6
PT/Exp	D	09 LA	181	19	0	25	1	232	273	214	308	276	585	10	88	26	0.95	229	41	20	39	37	0%	43	4%	3.16	-10.9	18	$2
Consist	B	1st Half	96	14	0	14	0	250			345	302	648	13	86	29	1.08	234	43	20	36	44	0%	36	0%	3.99	-3.2	19	$2
LIMA Plan	F	2nd Half	85	5	0	11	1	212			264	247	511	7	91	23	0.75	221	39	19	42	29	0%	39	10%	2.22	-7.8	12	$0
Rand Var	+2	10 Proj	127	13	1	16	1	252			321	317	638	9	89	28	0.95	250	40	23	38	47	2%	40	3%	3.73	-5.8	27	$2

When all you hit are singles, your value is completely dependent on h%. A few balls don't find holes, and poof! 50 pts of BA disappear. Still, the plunge in LD% suggests that this wasn't all luck.

Lowell,Mike

Lowell,Mike		Yr	AB	R	HR	RBI	SB	Avg	vL	vR	OB	Slg	OPS	bb%	ct%	h%	Eye	xBA	G	L	F	PX	hr/f	SX	SBO	RC/G	RAR	BPV	R$
Pos	5	05 FLA	500	56	8	58	4	236	308	222	300	360	660	8	88	25	0.79	261	32	21	47	84	4%	75	3%	3.91	-13.0	62	$8
Age	36	06 BOS	573	79	20	80	2	284	241	302	339	475	813	8	89	29	0.77	295	38	22	41	114	10%	48	3%	5.53	8.4	80	$17
Bats	Right	07 BOS	589	79	21	120	3	324	323	325	380	501	881	8	88	34	0.75	279	36	18	46	107	9%	55	3%	6.29	22.2	73	$25
Health	C	08 BOS	419	58	17	73	2	274	318	263	335	461	795	8	85	29	0.62	275	32	21	47	116	10%	43	4%	5.28	4.8	66	$14
PT/Exp	B	09 BOS	445	54	17	75	2	290	301	285	339	474	813	7	86	31	0.54	284	39	21	41	108	11%	49	3%	5.41	9.1	62	$15
Consist	B	1st Half	266	30	10	41	0	282			318	470	788	5	88	29	0.42	291	39	21	40	109	11%	39	2%	5.02	2.6	61	$8
LIMA Plan	C	2nd Half	179	24	7	34	2	302			369	480	849	10	84	33	0.68	273	38	20	42	107	11%	47	4%	5.99	6.4	58	$7
Rand Var	0	10 Proj	483	63	18	84	3	290			347	470	817	8	86	31	0.63	278	36	20	44	109	10%	55	3%	5.53	10.3	66	$17

Slow start following off-season hip surgery, but rebounded in 2H after brief DL stint. Skills held up well over full season, another year removed from surgery should help durability and counting stats.

Lowrie,Jed

Lowrie,Jed		Yr	AB	R	HR	RBI	SB	Avg	vL	vR	OB	Slg	OPS	bb%	ct%	h%	Eye	xBA	G	L	F	PX	hr/f	SX	SBO	RC/G	RAR	BPV	R$
Pos	6	05	0	0	0	0	0	0							0			0						0					
Age	26	06	0	0	0	0	0	0							0			0						0					
Bats	Both	07 a/a	497	71	10	60	4	288			371	471	842	12	84	33	0.85	0				126		77	6%	6.22	25.9	87	$14
Health	D	08 BOS	* 458	62	6	72	2	253	338	222	340	395	734	12	77	32	0.57	255	32	25	43	111	4%	81	2%	4.88	7.3	47	$10
PT/Exp	D	09 BOS	* 136	13	5	19	0	156	211	122	256	305	561	12	75	17	0.54	188	24	10	66	97	7%	21	0%	2.36	-9.4	10	($0)
Consist	D	1st Half	18	0	0	0	0	56			150	56	206	10	56	10	0.25		20	0	80	0	0%	-9	0%	-3.89	-5.6	-159	($1)
LIMA Plan	D	2nd Half	118	13	5	19	0	172			272	343	615	12	78	18	0.63	214	25	13	63	107	8%	23	0%	3.13	-5.0	31	$1
Rand Var	+5	10 Proj	353	46	10	50	2	258			345	434	779	12	80	30	0.68	251	28	19	53	119	7%	59	3%	5.36	9.9	60	$8

2-11-.147 in 68 AB at BOS. Lost season to April wrist surgery. Still waiting to see if he can carry that 2007 power/patience profile to MLB. Despite low BA, small 2H sample hints that he can. Excellent speculative play.

Ludwick,Ryan

Ludwick,Ryan		Yr	AB	R	HR	RBI	SB	Avg	vL	vR	OB	Slg	OPS	bb%	ct%	h%	Eye	xBA	G	L	F	PX	hr/f	SX	SBO	RC/G	RAR	BPV	R$
Pos	9	05 CLE	* 229	27	7	16	0	168			233	303	536	8	77	19	0.37	185	32	7	61	89	6%	61	5%	1.95	-20.8	15	($0)
Age	32	06 aaa	508	71	23	70	2	233			291	434	725	8	68	30	0.25	0				145		63	7%	4.51	-10.9	22	$11
Bats	Right	07 STL	* 409	59	19	75	5	257	221	298	311	459	770	7	77	29	0.34	260	37	16	47	134	13%	57	10%	4.90	0.2	50	$14
Health	A	08 STL	538	104	37	113	4	299	266	316	372	591	963	10	73	35	0.42	288	27	26	47	198	20%	81	6%	7.69	37.4	97	$30
PT/Exp	B	09 STL	486	63	22	97	4	265	269	264	323	447	769	8	78	30	0.39	243	33	18	49	115	12%	60	5%	4.87	-0.2	40	$18
Consist	F	1st Half	205	25	11	39	3	234			299	434	733	8	80	24	0.46	237	27	17	57	117	12%	75	6%	4.41	-2.9	55	$7
LIMA Plan	C	2nd Half	281	38	11	58	1	288			340	456	795	7	77	34	0.34	246	38	20	43	113	12%	37	4%	5.22	2.7	25	$12
Rand Var	0	10 Proj	513	76	23	98	4	267			328	459	787	8	76	31	0.38	250	32	20	48	128	12%	65	6%	5.18	3.1	44	$19

Follow-up to career year looks a lot like the years preceding, just that those years were spent in the minors. Likely that neither the power nor the BA from 2008 will ever be seen again. 2009 is his new reality.

RAY MURPHY

Lugo,Julio			AB	R	HR	RBI	SB	Avg	vL	vR	OB	Slg	OPS	bb%	ct%	h%	Eye	xBA	G	L	F	PX	hr/f	SX	SBO	RC/G	RAR	BPV	R$
Pos	46	05 TAM	616	89	6	57	39	295	306	291	359	403	762	9	88	33	0.85	274	49	20	31	71	4%	131	26%	5.11	17.1	69	$24
Age	34	06 2TM	435	69	12	37	24	278	263	284	338	421	758	8	83	31	0.51	263	47	20	34	87	10%	114	27%	4.86	6.3	53	$16
Bats	Right	07 BOS	570	71	8	73	33	237	226	241	296	349	645	8	86	26	0.59	264	46	17	37	78	4%	120	28%	3.62	-6.6	58	$15
Health	D	08 BOS	261	27	1	22	12	268	283	264	353	330	682	12	80	33	0.67	243	60	18	23	51	2%	73	18%	4.18	-5.5	10	$6
PT/Exp	C	09 2TM	257	40	3	21	9	280	278	281	353	405	758	10	82	33	0.64	251	40	21	38	78	4%	143	11%	5.08	2.6	58	$8
Consist	B	1st Half	103	16	1	8	2	301			368	388	757	10	84	35	0.69	246	37	24	38	55	3%	95	6%	5.01	0.8	32	$3
LIMA Plan	D	2nd Half	154	24	2	13	7	266			343	416	759	10	81	32	0.62	257	43	19	38	94	4%	145	16%	5.13	1.8	66	$5
Rand Var	-3	10 Proj	378	52	4	34	9	272			345	379	724	10	83	32	0.64	254	47	20	34	71	4%	107	10%	4.64	-0.2	42	$10

Are even more SB in the cards? Huge SX gain at STL says yes, but look closer: 4 fluky 2H triples caused that. Bad defense limits PT, and injury prone players don't become healthy. Don't bid on 2nd half times two.

Macias,Drew			AB	R	HR	RBI	SB	Avg	vL	vR	OB	Slg	OPS	bb%	ct%	h%	Eye	xBA	G	L	F	PX	hr/f	SX	SBO	RC/G	RAR	BPV	R$
Pos	7	05	0	0	0	0	0	0							0			0						0					
Age	27	06 aa	430	41	6	44	4	232			302	329	631	9	77	29	0.43	0				66		60	14%	3.32	-25.5	-1	$4
Bats	Left	07 a/a	441	48	9	52	7	222			317	340	658	12	82	25	0.79	0				73		80	13%	3.90	-18.0	38	$6
Health	A	08 aa	504	74	8	53	14	237			325	341	666	12	85	27	0.85	0				67		101	14%	4.02	-17.1	47	$11
PT/Exp	D	09 SD	* 373	39	5	27	4	183	222	190	265	274	539	10	82	21	0.63	224	45	15	40	67	4%	53	10%	2.35	-38.9	21	$0
Consist	B	1st Half	212	20	2	17	0	184			248	274	521	8	87	20	0.64	161	36	0	64	66	2%	36	4%	2.24	-22.7	28	($1)
LIMA Plan	F	2nd Half	161	20	3	10	4	182			287	275	561	13	76	22	0.62	228	48	20	33	68	7%	65	15%	2.51	-16.1	7	$1
Rand Var	+5	10 Proj	93	11	1	8	2	215			302	304	606	11	81	25	0.67	228	46	17	37	62	5%	57	12%	3.17	-6.7	17	$1

1-7-.197 in 76 AB at SD. MLB teams like left-handed pinch hitters who can draw walks and serve as defensive replacements, but fantasy teams don't. Hard to see upside when he can't even hit AAA pitching.

Maier,Mitch			AB	R	HR	RBI	SB	Avg	vL	vR	OB	Slg	OPS	bb%	ct%	h%	Eye	xBA	G	L	F	PX	hr/f	SX	SBO	RC/G	RAR	BPV	R$
Pos	89	05 aa	322	40	5	35	7	211			236	334	571	3	89	22	0.30	0				76		131	20%	2.63	-18.1	65	$4
Age	28	06 aa	543	70	10	68	10	257			297	385	681	5	86	28	0.40	0				78		91	19%	3.89	-10.9	47	$12
Bats	Left	07 aa	544	58	10	48	5	233			268	349	617	5	85	26	0.32	0				73		83	6%	3.06	-24.2	34	$6
Health	A	08 KC	* 436	54	6	41	9	279	273	293	320	387	707	6	87	31	0.46	276	48	22	30	71	6%	86	12%	4.20	-14.4	45	$11
PT/Exp	D	09 KC	* 387	48	4	39	10	245	299	224	330	339	669	11	78	31	0.58	224	42	18	40	65	3%	96	11%	3.95	-8.0	17	$7
Consist	B	1st Half	142	19	2	14	3	247			323	382	705	10	79	30	0.54	233	41	15	44	86	4%	112	13%	4.41	-1.0	42	$3
LIMA Plan	F	2nd Half	245	29	2	25	7	244			335	313	648	12	77	31	0.60	218	43	20	38	52	3%	71	10%	3.68	-7.0	-3	$5
Rand Var	-2	10 Proj	193	23	3	19	4	249			310	351	660	8	82	29	0.50	241	43	18	39	69	4%	86	12%	3.73	-6.1	29	$4

3-31-.243 in 341 AB at KC. If it takes an injury on a 97-loss team for a 27-year-old to gain PT, he's probably not destined to keep the PT. PX trend shows no pulse. With defense and speed, he can be a 4th OF.

Markakis,Nick			AB	R	HR	RBI	SB	Avg	vL	vR	OB	Slg	OPS	bb%	ct%	h%	Eye	xBA	G	L	F	PX	hr/f	SX	SBO	RC/G	RAR	BPV	R$
Pos	9	05 aa	120	19	3	28	0	325			413	533	946	13	78	40	0.69	0				158		65	3%	7.68	8.7	87	$6
Age	26	06 BAL	491	72	16	62	2	291	286	293	348	448	796	8	85	32	0.60	279	51	20	29	92	13%	67	1%	5.29	-5.0	53	$15
Bats	Left	07 BAL	637	97	23	112	18	300	274	311	361	485	846	9	82	33	0.54	286	45	18	37	120	12%	98	13%	5.94	7.8	75	$28
Health	A	08 BAL	599	106	20	88	10	304	297	310	403	487	890	14	81	35	0.87	287	46	21	33	126	12%	67	8%	6.86	24.9	75	$25
PT/Exp	A	09 BAL	642	94	18	101	6	293	262	314	350	453	803	8	85	32	0.57	266	43	17	41	100	8%	72	4%	5.41	1.4	59	$22
Consist	C	1st Half	312	46	8	52	2	298			356	458	814	8	85	33	0.60	274	41	19	40	102	8%	60	3%	5.58	2.1	58	$11
LIMA Plan	C	2nd Half	330	48	10	49	4	288			344	448	792	8	85	32	0.55	259	45	14	41	99	9%	72	5%	5.25	-0.8	56	$11
Rand Var	-1	10 Proj	622	97	19	99	5	289			360	461	820	10	83	32	0.65	275	44	18	38	111	10%	70	5%	5.73	6.6	64	$22

Your opponents think an off year presents a buying opportunity, but more FB didn't lead to more HRs. No power v LHP, SBs not likely to return, and he can't gain PT. Still young and talented, but has real flaws.

Marson,Lou			AB	R	HR	RBI	SB	Avg	vL	vR	OB	Slg	OPS	bb%	ct%	h%	Eye	xBA	G	L	F	PX	hr/f	SX	SBO	RC/G	RAR	BPV	R$
Pos	2	05	0	0	0	0	0	0							0			0						0					
Age	24	06	0	0	0	0	0	0							0			0						0					
Bats	Right	07	0	0	0	0	0	0							0			0						0					
Health	A	08 aa	322	41	4	34	2	276			374	363	737	13	84	32	0.94	0				62		36	5%	4.97	7.2	23	$7
PT/Exp	F	09 CLE	* 375	42	2	30	3	246	111	269	324	328	652	10	81	30	0.61	249	46	22	32	62	2%	61	4%	3.77	-5.5	15	$4
Consist	C	1st Half	178	20	1	15	2	248			320	314	634	9	81	30	0.56	299	40	40	20	51	3%	50	6%	3.47	-4.2	1	$2
LIMA Plan	F	2nd Half	197	23	1	16	1	245			329	340	669	11	81	30	0.66	239	48	16	35	72	2%	62	2%	4.04	-1.3	24	$2
Rand Var	0	10 Proj	247	29	2	22	2	247			335	328	663	12	82	29	0.74	246	47	21	32	61	3%	44	4%	3.96	-2.1	16	$3

0-4-.246 in 61 AB at PHI / CLE. Started 2/3 of games during Sept. call-up, so he has a shot at playing time. Still, only those in very deep leagues are looking for a catcher with about a .240 BA and no power, no speed.

Marte,Andy			AB	R	HR	RBI	SB	Avg	vL	vR	OB	Slg	OPS	bb%	ct%	h%	Eye	xBA	G	L	F	PX	hr/f	SX	SBO	RC/G	RAR	BPV	R$
Pos	3	05 ATL	* 446	53	20	76	0	262	174	118	362	468	830	14	82	28	0.88	256	35	13	52	130	10%	32	3%	5.99	5.1	72	$14
Age	26	06 CLE	* 521	69	19	69	1	246	227	225	310	433	742	8	78	28	0.42	250	34	17	48	125	9%	54	1%	4.66	-11.6	48	$11
Bats	Right	07 CLE	* 409	44	14	60	0	237	278	154	274	396	671	5	84	25	0.32	254	29	19	52	99	8%	35	0%	3.60	-20.3	37	$7
Health	A	08 CLE	235	21	3	17	1	221	293	198	265	315	580	6	78	27	0.27	206	34	16	49	69	3%	54	6%	2.51	-20.0	-4	$1
PT/Exp	D	09 CLE	* 455	58	20	77	2	263	167	244	311	463	774	7	84	28	0.43	257	31	16	53	117	10%	60	2%	4.90	-10.7	61	$14
Consist	D	1st Half	239	25	8	36	2	275			318	456	774	6	84	30	0.40	0				109		57	3%	4.91	-5.4	56	$7
LIMA Plan	F	2nd Half	216	32	12	41	0	249			304	470	773	7	83	25	0.45	261	31	16	53	125	12%	52	0%	4.88	-5.3	63	$7
Rand Var	-1	10 Proj	262	31	9	37	1	248			298	416	713	7	82	27	0.39	244	33	16	51	104	9%	52	2%	4.19	-10.1	41	$6

6-25-.232 in 155 AB at CLE. Lacks pop for 1B but if he returns to 3B (where he played in AAA), he's still on our radar. High FB% means BA-killing flyouts unless he can muscle more of them over the fences.

Martinez,Fernando			AB	R	HR	RBI	SB	Avg	vL	vR	OB	Slg	OPS	bb%	ct%	h%	Eye	xBA	G	L	F	PX	hr/f	SX	SBO	RC/G	RAR	BPV	R$
Pos	7	05	0	0	0	0	0	0							0			0						0					
Age	21	06	0	0	0	0	0	0							0			0						0					
Bats	Left	07 aa	236	31	3	20	2	278			333	380	713	8	85	32	0.54	0				68		67	12%	4.35	-5.9	30	$5
Health	D	08 aa	352	43	6	39	5	271			318	397	715	6	83	31	0.42	0				82		95	8%	4.29	-8.5	43	$9
PT/Exp	F	09 NYM	* 267	31	7	32	4	234	158	181	272	398	671	5	85	25	0.35	266	52	10	38	110	8%	84	11%	3.72	-14.9	65	$5
Consist	A	1st Half	265	31	7	32	4	235			274	401	676	5	85	25	0.35	267	52	11	37	111	9%	84	11%	3.77	-14.3	65	$6
LIMA Plan	D	2nd Half	2	0	0	0	0	0			0	0	0	0	100	0			50	0	50	0	0%				-0.6		($0)
Rand Var	+5	10 Proj	393	49	9	40	5	262			310	400	710	6	84	29	0.44	250	52	11	37	90	7%	80	11%	4.23	-14.3	49	$9

1-8-.176 in 91 AB at NYM. Torn knee cartilage wiped out 2H. Hitting too many GB for a guy with his power potential. Time is on his side, but he needs to spend more of it at Triple-A. Not ripe yet.

Martinez,Victor			AB	R	HR	RBI	SB	Avg	vL	vR	OB	Slg	OPS	bb%	ct%	h%	Eye	xBA	G	L	F	PX	hr/f	SX	SBO	RC/G	RAR	BPV	R$
Pos	23	05 CLE	547	73	20	80	0	305	274	320	377	475	852	10	86	33	0.81	278	48	21	32	106	13%	22	1%	6.08	30.8	57	$20
Age	31	06 CLE	572	82	16	93	0	316	290	332	392	465	857	11	86	35	0.91	274	44	22	34	92	9%	25	0%	6.23	27.9	51	$20
Bats	Both	07 CLE	562	78	25	114	0	301	289	307	370	505	876	10	86	31	0.82	300	42	20	38	126	13%	22	0%	6.31	31.2	75	$22
Health	C	08 CLE	266	30	2	35	0	278	339	260	338	365	703	8	88	31	0.75	262	45	22	33	64	3%	26	0%	4.37	1.4	29	$5
PT/Exp	B	09 2AL	588	88	23	108	1	303	273	316	382	480	861	11	87	32	1.01	288	43	21	35	101	13%	41	1%	6.25	31.8	67	$23
Consist	D	1st Half	300	53	14	57	0	313			398	523	921	12	86	33	1.02	302	45	21	34	120	16%	44	0%	6.99	22.0	81	$14
LIMA Plan	C	2nd Half	288	35	9	51	1	292			364	434	799	10	89	30	1.00	274	42	21	37	81	10%	34	1%	5.49	9.7	52	$10
Rand Var	-1	10 Proj	552	74	20	99	0	295			367	463	830	10	87	31	0.90	284	44	21	35	100	12%	25	0%	5.82	24.0	59	$19

Research show CA's hit better playing other positions. BOS says he'll catch full-time in '10:

Martinez	AB	OPS
2009 as CA	317	783
2009 as 1B	255	942

Adjust expectations accordingly.

Martin,Russell			AB	R	HR	RBI	SB	Avg	vL	vR	OB	Slg	OPS	bb%	ct%	h%	Eye	xBA	G	L	F	PX	hr/f	SX	SBO	RC/G	RAR	BPV	R$
Pos	2	05 aa	405	67	7	48	12	267			361	358	719	13	86	30	1.05	0				57		87	14%	4.74	10.0	44	$13
Age	27	06 LA	* 489	76	10	72	10	276	366	265	351	425	776	10	87	31	0.83	285	50	20	30	90	8%	92	12%	5.30	13.5	68	$16
Bats	Right	07 LA	540	87	19	87	21	293	357	273	371	469	839	11	84	32	0.75	284	48	18	34	108	12%	100	18%	5.99	24.0	74	$24
Health	A	08 LA	553	87	13	69	18	280	253	291	381	396	777	14	85	31	1.08	263	51	19	30	73	9%	79	12%	5.46	19.7	52	$21
PT/Exp	A	09 LA	505	63	7	53	11	250	275	243	340	329	668	12	84	28	0.86	246	49	21	31	54	5%	64	10%	4.05	-3.2	25	$11
Consist	B	1st Half	248	31	1	21	7	246			357	298	656	15	81	30	0.90	231	52	20	28	43	2%	63	12%	4.01	-1.9	7	$5
LIMA Plan	C	2nd Half	257	32	6	32	4	253			322	358	680	9	88	27	0.81	260	46	21	33	63	8%	58	8%	4.06	-1.6	39	$6
Rand Var	+1	10 Proj	493	70	10	61	9	266			354	377	731	12	85	30	0.90	261	49	20	31	71	8%	74	9%	4.80	7.8	44	$14

Wait, isn't he supposed to be peaking? XB hits in '09 were half of '07 totals, so both size & duration of power outage are worrisome. As a heavily used CA, are double-digit SB next? At least 2H gives a bit of hope.

MICHAEL WEDDELL

Mathis,Jeff

			AB	R	HR	RBI	SB	Avg	vL	vR	OB	Slg	OPS	bb%	ct%	h%	Eye	xBA	G	L	F	PX	hr/f	SX	SBO	RC/G	RAR	BPV	R$
Pos	2	05 aaa	427	59	16	56	3	246			296	420	717	7	86	25	0.52	0				105		76	8%	4.29	4.9	67	$11
Age	27	06 LAA *	439	57	6	41	2	241	133	150	285	364	650	6	83	28	0.37	211	29	12	59	85	3%	75	3%	3.52	-11.6	38	$5
Bats	Right	07 LAA *	421	57	8	45	3	214	242	203	265	332	597	6	78	26	0.32	227	42	13	45	87	5%	77	6%	2.77	-19.8	20	$4
Health	A	08 LAA	283	35	9	42	2	194	224	184	272	318	590	10	68	25	0.33	182	36	11	53	90	9%	52	6%	2.58	-14.5	-19	$4
PT/Exp	D	09 LAA	237	26	5	28	2	211	228	203	278	308	586	8	69	28	0.30	192	37	17	46	71	7%	47	8%	2.55	-12.8	-33	$2
Consist	A	1st Half	114	16	2	16	0	202			283	281	564	10	66	29	0.33	185	41	19	40	60	7%	47	3%	2.29	-7.1	-52	$1
LIMA Plan	D	2nd Half	123	10	3	12	2	220			273	333	606	7	72	28	0.26	199	33	16	51	80	7%	45	14%	2.77	-5.7	-17	$1
Rand Var	-2	10 Proj	308	36	7	37	3	211			275	322	597	8	72	27	0.32	198	36	15	49	80	7%	52	8%	2.70	-14.9	-14	$4

Does a great job calling pitches, but apparently can't read them when he's the one holding the bat. Two years of sub-.200 xBAs and negative BPVs offer little hope. More AB just means more damage to your BA.

Matsui,Hideki

			AB	R	HR	RBI	SB	Avg	vL	vR	OB	Slg	OPS	bb%	ct%	h%	Eye	xBA	G	L	F	PX	hr/f	SX	SBO	RC/G	RAR	BPV	R$
Pos	0	05 NYY	629	108	23	116	2	305	354	278	368	496	865	9	88	32	0.81	288	47	16	36	117	12%	64	2%	6.18	2.7	84	$26
Age	36	06 NYY	172	32	8	29	1	302	226	336	397	494	891	14	87	31	1.17	269	39	17	44	108	12%	49	2%	6.70	1.3	77	$7
Bats	Left	07 NYY	547	100	25	103	4	285	274	290	369	488	857	12	87	29	1.00	291	43	17	40	117	13%	83	3%	6.21	-0.4	91	$22
Health	D	08 NYY	337	43	9	45	0	294	315	284	365	424	790	10	86	32	0.81	257	47	19	34	82	9%	23	0%	5.36	4.1	39	$10
PT/Exp	B	09 NYY	456	62	28	90	0	274	282	271	363	509	872	12	84	27	0.85	286	38	20	42	130	17%	26	1%	6.32	15.0	73	$18
Consist	B	1st Half	206	23	10	28	0	248			340	466	806	12	83	26	0.81	278	40	18	42	129	14%	32	0%	5.62	2.7	70	$5
LIMA Plan	C	2nd Half	250	39	18	62	0	296			382	544	926	12	84	29	0.90	293	36	22	42	130	20%	21	1%	6.89	12.0	75	$13
Rand Var	+1	10 Proj	433	63	21	78	1	284			367	484	851	12	85	29	0.88	280	41	19	40	114	15%	40	1%	6.09	8.7	69	$16

Best PX and hr/f since 2004 despite ongoing issues from off-season knee surgery. Steady erosion of ct% means his .300 days are over, but health willing, there are still a productive few years in his bat.

Matsui,Kaz

			AB	R	HR	RBI	SB	Avg	vL	vR	OB	Slg	OPS	bb%	ct%	h%	Eye	xBA	G	L	F	PX	hr/f	SX	SBO	RC/G	RAR	BPV	R$
Pos	4	05 NYM	267	31	3	24	6	255	279	246	292	352	644	5	84	29	0.33	268	51	22	27	60	5%	123	11%	3.39	-9.2	32	$5
Age	34	06 2NL *	370	56	6	40	13	266	119	299	309	375	684	6	82	31	0.35	253	48	20	31	69	6%	121	15%	3.87	-7.8	33	$11
Bats	Both	07 COL	410	84	4	37	32	288	271	291	342	405	747	8	83	34	0.49	265	45	21	34	77	3%	169	31%	4.81	1.3	63	$18
Health	D	08 HOU	375	58	6	33	20	293	291	294	357	427	783	9	86	33	0.70	274	46	21	34	89	6%	124	22%	5.31	5.8	71	$15
PT/Exp	B	09 HOU	476	56	9	46	19	250	271	244	300	357	657	7	82	29	0.40	248	48	19	33	71	7%	107	18%	3.56	-13.7	33	$13
Consist	C	1st Half	189	24	2	18	6	249			297	333	630	6	81	30	0.36	239	49	19	32	60	4%	99	18%	3.24	-7.3	16	$4
LIMA Plan	C	2nd Half	287	32	7	28	13	251			302	373	675	7	83	28	0.43	254	47	19	34	78	9%	106	18%	3.77	-6.4	41	$8
Rand Var	+1	10 Proj	473	67	8	44	18	268			322	385	707	7	83	31	0.47	259	47	20	33	76	6%	122	17%	4.24	-5.2	47	$14

Second year in a row injuries have cut into his production, particularly his speed. And at his age, you can no longer count on a big rebound. As SB diminish, the rest of his game becomes more of a liability.

Matthews Jr.,Gary

			AB	R	HR	RBI	SB	Avg	vL	vR	OB	Slg	OPS	bb%	ct%	h%	Eye	xBA	G	L	F	PX	hr/f	SX	SBO	RC/G	RAR	BPV	R$
Pos	89	05 TEX	475	72	17	55	9	255	241	260	322	436	758	9	81	28	0.52	275	51	17	32	114	14%	116	9%	4.88	8.4	70	$14
Age	36	06 TEX	620	102	19	79	10	313	314	313	372	495	867	9	84	35	0.59	290	51	19	30	112	12%	97	9%	6.21	26.3	74	$23
Bats	Both	07 LAA	516	79	18	72	18	252	175	275	324	419	743	10	80	28	0.54	266	51	13	36	107	12%	110	16%	4.71	2.8	61	$17
Health	A	08 LAA	426	53	8	46	8	242	285	223	314	357	671	10	78	29	0.47	247	59	14	27	79	9%	94	9%	3.85	-19.2	24	$8
PT/Exp	B	09 LAA	316	44	4	50	4	250	221	261	334	361	695	11	77	32	0.54	233	42	19	39	81	4%	87	5%	4.29	-3.3	21	$7
Consist	B	1st Half	144	21	2	22	1	229			288	333	622	8	76	29	0.35	215	35	19	46	73	4%	86	3%	3.14	-6.5	7	$2
LIMA Plan	D	2nd Half	172	23	2	28	3	267			370	384	754	14	77	34	0.70	247	48	19	33	87	5%	74	7%	5.22	2.9	29	$5
Rand Var	0	10 Proj	282	39	6	39	5	252			330	381	711	10	78	31	0.53	248	49	17	34	89	7%	93	8%	4.43	-2.9	34	$7

Start with his 2006 line, and just follow the AB and xBA trends. Only above-average skill left in his toolbox is bb%, and he'd need to repeat 2H level to make it of value. Something for him to ponder as he sits on the bench.

Mauer,Joe

			AB	R	HR	RBI	SB	Avg	vL	vR	OB	Slg	OPS	bb%	ct%	h%	Eye	xBA	G	L	F	PX	hr/f	SX	SBO	RC/G	RAR	BPV	R$
Pos	2	05 MIN	489	61	9	55	13	294	232	323	373	411	784	11	87	32	0.95	288	52	24	24	75	9%	93	8%	5.42	19.0	60	$16
Age	27	06 MIN	521	86	13	84	8	347	331	356	433	507	940	13	90	37	1.46	311	49	25	26	94	11%	86	5%	7.38	40.0	88	$24
Bats	Left	07 MIN	406	62	7	60	7	293	283	299	380	426	806	12	87	32	1.12	294	55	18	28	87	7%	94	6%	5.80	17.1	74	$13
Health	B	08 MIN	536	98	9	85	1	328	361	312	419	451	871	14	91	35	1.68	294	49	23	28	76	7%	67	1%	6.66	34.9	73	$21
PT/Exp	A	09 MIN	523	94	28	96	4	365	345	376	446	587	1033	13	88	38	1.21	318	48	22	30	121	20%	59	2%	8.26	52.1	94	$31
Consist	C	1st Half	204	44	14	44	1	392			472	667	1139	13	86	41	1.11	322	48	19	33	148	24%	59	2%	9.52	25.7	110	$15
LIMA Plan	B+	2nd Half	319	50	14	52	3	348			429	536	965	12	89	36	1.29	315	48	25	28	104	18%	48	2%	7.48	26.2	81	$16
Rand Var	-5	10 Proj	536	93	20	90	5	332			418	512	930	13	89	35	1.28	308	50	22	29	104	15%	71	3%	7.16	41.0	86	$25

Finally found a way to hit for power without altering his basic stroke (16 HR to LF), though 2H PX and hr/f likely provide a more more realistic expectation. Add in some BA regression, and he'll probably fall short of $30 repeat.

Maxwell,Justin

			AB	R	HR	RBI	SB	Avg	vL	vR	OB	Slg	OPS	bb%	ct%	h%	Eye	xBA	G	L	F	PX	hr/f	SX	SBO	RC/G	RAR	BPV	R$
Pos	8	05	0	0	0	0	0	0							0			0						0					
Age	26	06	0	0	0	0	0	0							0			0						0					
Bats	Right	07	0	0	0	0	0	0							0			0						0					
Health	A	08 aa	146	27	5	21	10	191			301	348	649	14	84	19	1.01	0				89		148	37%	3.86	-5.7	82	$4
PT/Exp	F	09 WAS *	473	68	14	43	34	217	242	250	299	355	654	10	68	29	0.36	212	48	14	38	97	12%	141	35%	3.60	-16.8	14	$15
Consist	A	1st Half	241	30	8	24	14	192			282	329	611	11	64	26	0.35	207	62	8	31	103	16%	121	33%	3.01	-13.5	-1	$5
LIMA Plan	D	2nd Half	232	37	7	19	20	244			317	382	699	10	72	31	0.38	218	44	16	40	91	10%	152	36%	4.18	-3.9	27	$10
Rand Var	0	10 Proj	115	19	4	13	8	226			316	363	679	12	71	29	0.46	219	47	15	38	91	12%	131	33%	3.96	-2.6	23	$4

4-9-.247 in 89 AB at WAS.
PRO: Surprising speed for his size (6-5, 243 lbs), strong bb%, 153 PX in majors.
CON: ct% in the 60s could undermine everything.
Upside could be big. Watch him.

Maybin,Cameron

			AB	R	HR	RBI	SB	Avg	vL	vR	OB	Slg	OPS	bb%	ct%	h%	Eye	xBA	G	L	F	PX	hr/f	SX	SBO	RC/G	RAR	BPV	R$
Pos	8	05	0	0	0	0	0	0							0			0						0					
Age	23	06	0	0	0	0	0	0							0			0						0					
Bats	Right	07 DET *	69	17	4	10	5	203		200	298	436	733	12	61	26	0.35	246	54	4	43	191	22%	138	33%	4.97	0.9	65	$3
Health	A	08 FLA *	422	70	11	43	22	272	375	542	358	423	782	12	72	35	0.48	266	50	29	21	101	17%	144	22%	5.46	9.0	39	$17
PT/Exp	D	09 FLA *	474	69	7	47	8	281	254	248	352	424	776	10	78	35	0.50	261	55	17	28	100	7%	115	9%	5.30	7.7	47	$14
Consist	A	1st Half	245	34	3	19	6	273			348	412	760	10	77	34	0.50	246	55	13	32	94	5%	118	12%	5.14	2.9	42	$7
LIMA Plan	C+	2nd Half	229	35	4	28	2	288			356	437	792	9	79	35	0.49	272	55	19	26	106	9%	93	6%	5.47	4.8	48	$7
Rand Var	-1	10 Proj	407	63	8	42	12	278			354	425	779	11	76	35	0.49	262	54	19	27	101	10%	132	14%	5.37	8.1	46	$14

4-13-.250 in 176 AB at FLA.
Reasons to keep the faith:
- Three years of ct% growth
- .293 BA, 144 PX, .304 xBA in 92 AB in majors in Sept/Oct
- Youth is still on his side.
Breakout may not arrive 'til '11.

Maysonet,Edwin

			AB	R	HR	RBI	SB	Avg	vL	vR	OB	Slg	OPS	bb%	ct%	h%	Eye	xBA	G	L	F	PX	hr/f	SX	SBO	RC/G	RAR	BPV	R$
Pos	4	05	0	0	0	0	0	0							0			0						0					
Age	28	06	0	0	0	0	0	0							0			0						0					
Bats	Right	07 aa	341	26	4	30	4	222			249	296	545	4	82	26	0.21	0				49		71	8%	2.06	-24.0	-2	$2
Health	A	08 aa	406	40	5	23	3	215			270	299	569	7	86	24	0.53	0				57		58	7%	2.67	-27.3	22	$2
PT/Exp	F	09 HOU *	256	23	2	17	2	212	313	283	277	277	554	8	80	26	0.44	245	46	26	28	51	3%	49	3%	2.35	-17.2	-8	$1
Consist	A	1st Half	154	16	2	12	1	256			322	342	663	9	80	31	0.48	255	44	27	29	64	5%	40	2%	3.74	-3.5	2	$2
LIMA Plan	F	2nd Half	102	7	0	5	1	144			208	179	387	7	79	18	0.38	231	56	22	22	33	0%	51	5%	0.23	-14.7	-26	($2)
Rand Var	+2	10 Proj	98	9	1	6	1	204			259	269	528	7	82	24	0.41	252	48	25	27	48	4%	48	5%	2.05	-7.9	-3	$0

1-7-.290 in 69 AB at HOU.
Things we'd like to sell you if you think his HOU BA was legit:
- "Real estate" in Florida
- Shares in our Ponzi scheme
- An extended warranty
- Time share in Siberia

McCann,Brian

			AB	R	HR	RBI	SB	Avg	vL	vR	OB	Slg	OPS	bb%	ct%	h%	Eye	xBA	G	L	F	PX	hr/f	SX	SBO	RC/G	RAR	BPV	R$
Pos	2	05 ATL *	346	43	10	46	3	260	344	259	337	408	744	10	86	28	0.82	282	42	23	35	92	10%	55	7%	4.86	10.9	57	$9
Age	26	06 ATL	442	61	24	93	2	333	266	351	389	572	962	8	88	34	0.76	304	35	22	43	135	14%	38	2%	7.16	32.6	89	$23
Bats	Left	07 ATL	504	51	18	92	0	270	264	273	317	452	770	6	85	29	0.47	277	39	19	43	115	10%	18	1%	4.90	6.8	54	$14
Health	A	08 ATL	509	68	23	87	5	301	299	301	371	523	894	10	87	31	0.89	298	37	20	43	135	12%	67	3%	6.55	32.7	100	$22
PT/Exp	B	09 ATL	488	63	21	94	4	281	225	308	346	486	832	9	83	30	0.59	284	38	21	41	131	13%	60	4%	5.76	20.8	75	$20
Consist	C	1st Half	200	23	8	33	3	310			389	510	899	12	86	33	0.93	289	38	21	41	123	11%	62	6%	6.73	13.5	86	$9
LIMA Plan	C+	2nd Half	288	40	13	61	1	260			315	469	784	7	81	28	0.42	281	39	21	41	137	14%	45	2%	5.07	6.8	64	$11
Rand Var	0	10 Proj	510	64	25	104	4	286			350	509	860	9	85	30	0.65	295	38	21	42	137	14%	58	3%	6.06	25.9	86	$21

Tale of three seasons: blurred vision in April (.195 BA), got new glasses (.298 BA in May-July), seemed to tire down the stretch (.256 xBA after 8/1). His skills bounce around, but at the end of the day, still the NL's best CA.

BRANDON KRUSE

McCutchen,Andrew

	Year	AB	R	HR	RBI	SB	Avg	vL	vR	OB	Slg	OPS	bb%	ct%	h%	Eye	xBA	G	L	F	PX	hr/f	SX	SBO	RC/G	RAR	BPV	R$
Pos 8	05	0	0	0	0	0	0							0			0						0					
Age 23	06	0	0	0	0	0	0							0			0						0					
Bats Right	07 aa	513	68	9	47	19	260			316	373	688	8	86	29	0.57	0				72		103	17%	4.06	-7.1	48	$13
Health A	08 aa	512	66	7	44	30	270			345	371	716	10	86	30	0.80	0				67		97	32%	4.58	-7.3	48	$17
PT/Exp C	09 PIT	* 634	108	15	71	30	284	310	279	353	456	809	10	84	32	0.67	268	42	19	39	105	7%	151	20%	5.65	16.6	86	$27
Consist B	1st Half	314	51	4	35	12	283			328	433	761	6	88	31	0.55	276	46	19	34	85	4%	150	17%	4.96	2.1	79	$12
LIMA Plan B	2nd Half	320	57	11	36	18	284			376	478	854	13	80	33	0.73	268	41	18	41	126	11%	133	23%	6.34	14.8	89	$15
Rand Var -2	10 Proj	568	86	18	57	33	276			348	449	796	10	84	30	0.70	270	42	18	40	104	9%	132	28%	5.44	12.6	82	$24

12-54-22-.286 in 433 AB at PIT. Blue chipper dazzled in debut. 2H bb%, OB spikes say it only gets better from here. Power is there too; 125 PX in two of four months. He's a gem. UP: 20 HR, 40 SB

McDonald,Darnell

	Year	AB	R	HR	RBI	SB	Avg	vL	vR	OB	Slg	OPS	bb%	ct%	h%	Eye	xBA	G	L	F	PX	hr/f	SX	SBO	RC/G	RAR	BPV	R$
Pos 7	05 aaa	355	38	9	26	5	227			263	352	616	5	83	25	0.29	0				82		81	8%	2.95	-22.4	32	$5
Age 31	06 aaa	538	71	12	50	27	260			312	387	699	7	79	31	0.36	0				85		103	28%	4.05	-18.7	30	$16
Bats Right	07 aaa	491	65	7	67	31	269			328	381	708	8	78	33	0.39	0				80		130	27%	4.29	-13.0	31	$18
Health A	08 aaa	369	38	8	41	14	212			262	343	605	6	78	25	0.30	0				91		116	22%	2.85	-26.3	33	$6
PT/Exp D	09 CIN	* 385	43	10	39	7	254	365	170	285	418	703	4	77	31	0.19	257	47	18	35	114	9%	110	13%	4.02	-17.6	42	$9
Consist C	1st Half	161	16	3	15	3	212			254	352	605	5	77	26	0.24	251	55	16	29	91	9%	111	11%	2.82	-13.7	27	$2
LIMA Plan F	2nd Half	224	27	6	23	4	283			308	466	774	3	77	34	0.15	262	42	19	40	129	9%	102	13%	4.87	-4.4	51	$7
Rand Var 0	10 Proj	113	13	3	12	4	248			289	394	683	5	78	30	0.26	253	47	18	35	102	8%	113	23%	3.82	-5.6	39	$3

2-10-.267 in 105 AB at CIN. Top prospect from previous decade got first extended look. .500+ Slg w/CIN in 2H was coupled with 66% ct% and 3% bb%. Could have part-time role vs LHP, but that's his upside.

McDonald,John

	Year	AB	R	HR	RBI	SB	Avg	vL	vR	OB	Slg	OPS	bb%	ct%	h%	Eye	xBA	G	L	F	PX	hr/f	SX	SBO	RC/G	RAR	BPV	R$
Pos 6	05 2AL	166	18	0	16	6	277	298	253	322	325	647	6	86	32	0.46	252	55	21	24	36	0%	98	14%	3.55	-4.8	15	$4
Age 36	06 TOR	260	35	3	23	7	223	230	220	268	308	576	6	84	25	0.39	238	48	18	34	49	4%	128	15%	2.63	-14.3	28	$3
Bats Right	07 TOR	327	32	1	31	7	251	329	223	275	333	608	3	85	29	0.23	259	40	23	37	62	1%	95	13%	2.95	-13.0	28	$5
Health B	08 TOR	186	21	1	18	3	210	250	184	250	269	519	5	87	24	0.40	219	42	15	43	44	1%	75	10%	2.03	-13.4	16	$1
PT/Exp F	09 TOR	151	18	4	13	0	258	260	257	263	384	647	1	88	27	0.06	240	32	17	50	73	6%	46	7%	3.16	-5.7	28	$3
Consist C	1st Half	26	3	0	0	0	269			269	269	538	0	85	32	0.00	201	36	23	41	0	0%	63	14%	1.78	-2.1	-41	$0
LIMA Plan F	2nd Half	125	15	4	13	0	256			262	408	670	1	89	26	0.07	249	32	16	52	88	7%	46	5%	3.44	-3.7	43	$2
Rand Var -2	10 Proj	135	15	2	13	2	244			271	351	622	4	86	27	0.27	248	41	18	41	68	4%	92	11%	3.11	-5.2	37	$2

"Muscled up" for 4 HR while putting half his BIP in the air. Of course, he did walk once in 151 AB, so that's something. It's time for "Old McDonald" to head to the farm. (With a quack quack here...)

McGehee,Casey

	Year	AB	R	HR	RBI	SB	Avg	vL	vR	OB	Slg	OPS	bb%	ct%	h%	Eye	xBA	G	L	F	PX	hr/f	SX	SBO	RC/G	RAR	BPV	R$
Pos 54	05 aa	451	60	8	62	2	273			331	392	723	8	87	30	0.66	0				80		59	3%	4.53	-1.4	48	$12
Age 27	06 aaa	497	51	11	62	0	266			318	390	708	7	87	29	0.58	0				76		30	2%	4.27	-14.1	34	$9
Bats Right	07 a/a	436	45	9	48	1	229			283	355	639	7	83	26	0.44	0				85		48	4%	3.41	-24.4	30	$5
Health A	08 aaa	497	49	9	66	0	248			288	357	646	5	85	28	0.38	0				73		23	3%	3.41	-25.4	18	$8
PT/Exp D	09 MIL	355	58	16	66	0	301	303	301	362	499	861	9	81	33	0.51	274	38	22	40	125	14%	42	2%	6.07	9.1	56	$16
Consist C	1st Half	115	20	5	21	0	322			391	539	930	10	82	36	0.62	300	40	24	36	146	15%	31	0%	7.04	5.8	75	$6
LIMA Plan D+	2nd Half	240	38	11	45	0	292			349	479	828	8	81	32	0.46	262	37	20	42	114	13%	49	3%	5.60	3.1	47	$10
Rand Var -4	10 Proj	453	61	12	65	0	276			331	414	745	8	83	31	0.48	259	38	22	40	91	8%	42	2%	4.67	-7.7	35	$13

4 reasons to be cautious...
- BA inflated by fluky h%
- Ct% erosion
- PX came out of nowhere
- 2H PX, Eye regressions

This was his age 26 breakout. Don't expect age 27 follow-up.

McLouth,Nate

	Year	AB	R	HR	RBI	SB	Avg	vL	vR	OB	Slg	OPS	bb%	ct%	h%	Eye	xBA	G	L	F	PX	hr/f	SX	SBO	RC/G	RAR	BPV	R$
Pos 8	05 PIT	* 506	68	9	42	28	263	100	292	307	374	680	6	88	29	0.52	271	52	16	31	70	6%	121	29%	3.92	-9.7	58	$17
Age 28	06 PIT	270	50	7	16	10	233	260	227	281	385	666	6	78	27	0.31	259	39	25	35	99	9%	141	20%	3.63	-6.6	48	$6
Bats Left	07 PIT	329	62	13	38	22	258	269	256	337	459	796	11	77	30	0.51	246	31	16	53	132	10%	147	26%	5.47	9.1	79	$14
Health B	08 PIT	597	113	26	94	23	276	261	282	347	497	845	10	84	29	0.70	279	35	19	47	137	11%	134	17%	5.98	21.2	109	$28
PT/Exp B	09 2TM	507	86	20	70	19	256	230	269	344	436	780	12	80	28	0.69	256	40	16	43	112	11%	106	17%	5.28	8.9	69	$20
Consist B	1st Half	255	41	12	45	10	259			332	463	795	10	82	27	0.61	263	41	13	45	123	13%	107	16%	5.32	4.8	80	$11
LIMA Plan B	2nd Half	252	45	8	25	9	254			356	409	765	14	79	29	0.75	248	39	19	42	101	10%	97	17%	5.22	4.0	55	$8
Rand Var 0	10 Proj	562	100	18	72	24	260			339	429	768	11	81	29	0.63	253	37	18	45	109	9%	123	19%	5.12	6.4	72	$22

PROs:
- SX dip likely hammy-induced
- bb% spike in 2nd half

CONs:
- FB trend puts HRs at risk
- Deepening struggles vs LHP

20 SB a safer bet than 20 HR.

Michaels,Jason

	Year	AB	R	HR	RBI	SB	Avg	vL	vR	OB	Slg	OPS	bb%	ct%	h%	Eye	xBA	G	L	F	PX	hr/f	SX	SBO	RC/G	RAR	BPV	R$
Pos 7	05 PHI	289	54	4	31	3	304	323	289	396	415	812	13	84	35	0.98	269	41	25	35	75	5%	87	5%	5.89	4.4	52	$10
Age 34	06 CLE	494	77	9	55	9	267	291	252	326	391	717	8	80	32	0.43	250	40	23	38	87	6%	88	11%	4.37	-11.6	32	$12
Bats Right	07 CLE	267	43	7	39	3	270	287	252	321	397	718	7	81	31	0.40	238	37	17	46	82	7%	78	10%	4.27	-6.0	30	$8
Health A	08 2TM	286	28	8	53	2	224	187	241	291	360	651	9	77	26	0.42	233	38	19	43	92	8%	57	4%	3.49	-14.4	19	$5
PT/Exp D	09 HOU	135	17	4	16	1	237	268	215	318	430	748	11	72	30	0.42	249	31	21	48	151	9%	75	10%	4.99	-2.4	54	$3
Consist C	1st Half	68	4	0	5	1	176			243	294	537	8	72	24	0.32	215	37	12	51	119	0%	50	20%	2.15	-7.6	17	($1)
LIMA Plan F	2nd Half	67	13	4	11	0	299			390	567	957	13	72	36	0.53	276	25	29	46	183	18%	92	5%	7.87	4.3	88	$3
Rand Var 0	10 Proj	95	13	3	14	1	253			326	428	754	10	76	31	0.44	248	34	21	45	122	9%	85	8%	4.93	-1.5	47	$3

If he was 10 years younger, this box might have an UP projection given PX, bb% gains. In reality, he showed them only at home, where he had a .953 OPS in 59 AB. Ct% dive, PX history say don't bet on that again.

Miles,Aaron

	Year	AB	R	HR	RBI	SB	Avg	vL	vR	OB	Slg	OPS	bb%	ct%	h%	Eye	xBA	G	L	F	PX	hr/f	SX	SBO	RC/G	RAR	BPV	R$
Pos 4	05 COL	* 356	41	2	29	5	271	234	292	287	344	631	2	89	30	0.20	281	54	23	23	45	3%	105	8%	3.18	-14.1	29	$7
Age 33	06 STL	426	48	2	30	2	263	291	256	323	347	671	8	90	29	0.90	275	55	20	25	51	2%	78	2%	4.09	-6.3	43	$5
Bats Both	07 STL	414	55	2	32	2	290	286	292	330	348	678	6	90	32	0.63	258	54	18	28	39	2%	62	2%	3.96	-8.6	25	$8
Health C	08 STL	379	49	4	31	3	317	315	317	356	398	754	6	90	34	0.62	273	54	21	25	51	5%	70	5%	4.78	0.1	36	$12
PT/Exp D	09 CHC	* 244	23	0	11	4	189	206	179	220	239	459	4	86	22	0.28	244	50	20	30	40	0%	92	13%	1.27	-25.5	12	($1)
Consist F	1st Half	123	15	0	4	3	203			240	260	500	5	86	24	0.35	257	51	21	28	48	0%	91	13%	1.82	-10.4	22	$0
LIMA Plan F	2nd Half	121	8	0	7	1	174			198	218	416	3	85	20	0.20	215	47	17	37	31	0%	77	13%	0.70	-15.3	-4	($1)
Rand Var +5	10 Proj	134	14	1	8	1	239			274	303	577	5	88	27	0.40	257	53	20	27	43	2%	86	7%	2.71	-7.7	22	$1

0-5-.185 in 157 AB at CHC. Had fifth worst OPS of anyone with 100+ AB. And you wonder why CHC struggled? Injuries didn't help, but w/no power or speed, his only value comes in BA. And xBA gives little hope.

Millar,Kevin

	Year	AB	R	HR	RBI	SB	Avg	vL	vR	OB	Slg	OPS	bb%	ct%	h%	Eye	xBA	G	L	F	PX	hr/f	SX	SBO	RC/G	RAR	BPV	R$
Pos 30	05 BOS	449	57	9	50	0	272	246	283	350	399	749	11	84	31	0.73	243	34	20	46	87	5%	37	1%	4.94	-1.9	39	$10
Age 39	06 BAL	430	64	15	64	1	272	244	283	360	437	797	12	83	30	0.80	264	35	22	42	103	10%	38	1%	5.53	1.4	51	$12
Bats Right	07 BAL	476	63	17	63	1	254	250	256	357	420	777	14	80	28	0.81	253	29	20	51	109	9%	41	1%	5.36	1.4	50	$11
Health A	08 BAL	535	73	20	72	0	236	238	232	325	394	719	12	83	25	0.76	247	30	19	51	99	9%	28	1%	4.53	-11.9	44	$11
PT/Exp B	09 TOR	251	29	7	29	0	223	250	191	309	363	671	11	80	25	0.63	229	32	17	51	90	7%	24	0%	3.91	-13.7	25	$3
Consist B	1st Half	144	19	4	21	0	236			308	368	676	9	81	27	0.54	234	33	19	48	84	7%	31	0%	3.89	-7.9	20	$3
LIMA Plan F	2nd Half	107	10	3	8	0	206			309	355	664	13	80	23	0.76	223	31	14	55	99	6%	15	0%	3.94	-5.9	33	$0
Rand Var +2	10 Proj	123	15	4	15	0	236			327	387	714	12	81	26	0.72	240	31	18	51	98	8%	28	1%	4.50	-3.7	38	$2

The writing's on the wall...
- Steep PX decline
- Can't hit RHers
- Ominous xBA trend

It doesn't matter how well you can loft ball if your pop is MIA. Great clubhouse guy, though.

Milledge,Lastings

	Year	AB	R	HR	RBI	SB	Avg	vL	vR	OB	Slg	OPS	bb%	ct%	h%	Eye	xBA	G	L	F	PX	hr/f	SX	SBO	RC/G	RAR	BPV	R$
Pos 7	05 aa	193	27	3	20	9	316			354	446	800	6	81	38	0.32	0				99		86	29%	5.28	1.3	44	$9
Age 25	06 NYM	* 473	70	11	61	15	275	241	241	355	429	783	11	79	33	0.60	263	44	22	34	99	8%	102	20%	5.39	1.9	52	$15
Bats Right	07 NYM	* 246	41	10	40	8	289	317	250	330	472	801	6	78	34	0.27	283	47	24	29	113	18%	117	16%	5.21	-1.0	50	$11
Health A	08 WAS	523	65	14	61	24	268	258	272	317	402	719	7	82	31	0.40	256	45	20	35	85	9%	104	24%	4.28	-17.5	42	$19
PT/Exp C	09 2TM	* 383	35	4	30	15	270	327	265	309	358	667	5	82	32	0.31	240	41	21	38	65	3%	75	22%	3.64	-18.5	15	$9
Consist B	1st Half	103	10	0	4	6	216			238	263	500	3	77	28	0.12	228	50	21	29	43	0%	100	33%	1.38	-12.5	-19	$1
LIMA Plan D+	2nd Half	280	26	4	26	9	290			335	393	728	6	84	34	0.41	249	41	21	39	72	4%	61	19%	4.43	-6.9	26	$8
Rand Var 0	10 Proj	433	51	8	43	18	270			313	385	698	6	81	32	0.32	252	44	21	35	79	7%	94	22%	3.99	-15.5	28	$13

4-21-.279 in 244 AB at WAS and PIT. Broken finger sent PX to another low, but there's hope in 2H ct% and another year of more FB. Has LHers figured out too. Expect more downs than ups, but he's got time to grow.

STEPHEN NICKRAND

Miller,Corky			AB	R	HR	RBI	SB	Avg	vL	vR	OB	Slg	OPS	bb%	ct%	h%	Eye	xBA	G	L	F	PX	hr/f	SX	SBO	RC/G	RAR	BPV	R$
Pos	2	05 aaa	166	25	7	18	0	181			273	351	623	11	83	17	0.76	0				101		50	5%	3.31	-3.2	54	$2
Age	34	06 aaa	204	25	12	31	0	221			292	437	729	9	76	23	0.42	0				132		21	0%	4.39	0.1	37	$4
Bats	Right	07 aaa	181	10	4	20	4	179			260	278	538	10	85	19	0.74	0				63		45	9%	2.41	-11.4	27	($0)
Health	A	08 ATL	* 116	13	5	15	0	190			266	345	610	9	76	20	0.43	0				96		33	4%	2.87	-5.0	11	$1
PT/Exp	F	09 2TM	* 179	21	1	23	0	218	226	172	300	279	579	11	81	26	0.62	212	33	21	47	48	1%	33	0%	2.84	-7.8	-5	$1
Consist	A	1st Half	59	6	0	6	0	179			249	230	479	9	79	23	0.44	211	40	20	40	46	0%	36	0%	1.45	-5.3	-18	($0)
LIMA Plan	F	2nd Half	120	15	1	17	0	237			324	304	628	11	82	28	0.72	212	28	21	51	49	2%	31	0%	3.50	-2.7	2	$2
Rand Var	-2	10 Proj	63	7	1	8	0	206			286	302	588	10	80	24	0.56	221	34	20	46	62	6%	37	2%	2.80	-2.9	3	$1

1-15-.189 in 95 AB at CHW/CIN. How does a career .179 BA, .552 OPS hitter keep getting major league AB every year for nine seasons? Forget Scott Boras, we want this guy's agent.

Moeller,Chad			AB	R	HR	RBI	SB	Avg	vL	vR	OB	Slg	OPS	bb%	ct%	h%	Eye	xBA	G	L	F	PX	hr/f	SX	SBO	RC/G	RAR	BPV	R$
Pos	2	05 MIL	199	23	7	23	0	206	191	215	255	367	622	6	76	24	0.27	236	47	13	40	108	12%	54	0%	2.96	-5.1	20	$2
Age	35	06 MIL	* 230	17	4	19	0	183			239	270	508	7	76	22	0.31	0				59		24	4%	1.56	-20.7	-26	($1)
Bats	Right	07 2NL	* 141	16	4	18	0	220			281	348	629	8	71	28	0.29	0				92		28	0%	3.11	-5.7	-16	$2
Health	A	08 NYY	* 172	17	1	15	0	215			262	279	541	6	75	28	0.26	0				55		32	0%	1.99	-11.6	-32	$0
PT/Exp	F	09 BAL	* 207	11	2	18	0	206	160	297	244	307	551	5	81	24	0.27	237	33	21	45	73	3%	37	2%	2.25	-13.1	7	($0)
Consist	B	1st Half	115	5	1	6	0	183			226	275	501	5	83	21	0.32	232	35	21	44	61	2%	45	4%	1.71	-9.5	5	($1)
LIMA Plan	F	2nd Half	92	7	1	11	0	234			266	348	614	4	80	28	0.22	245	31	22	47	88	3%	18	0%	2.95	-3.6	6	$1
Rand Var	+3	10 Proj	99	8	1	10	0	212			257	313	569	6	78	26	0.27	218	41	17	42	77	4%	28	1%	2.38	-5.7	-7	$0

2-10-.258 in 89 AB at BAL. And here's a guy with 10 years of AB under his belt, despite a career .226 BA and .639 OPS. If you can't be a star, be a lefty reliever or a backup catcher. Or better yet, a lefty catcher.

Molina,Bengie			AB	R	HR	RBI	SB	Avg	vL	vR	OB	Slg	OPS	bb%	ct%	h%	Eye	xBA	G	L	F	PX	hr/f	SX	SBO	RC/G	RAR	BPV	R$
Pos	2	05 ANA	410	45	15	69	0	295	393	253	339	446	785	6	90	30	0.66	270	41	21	38	86	11%	18	2%	5.05	11.7	49	$14
Age	36	06 TOR	433	44	19	57	1	284	358	246	314	467	781	4	89	28	0.40	290	39	23	38	99	13%	37	2%	4.84	5.3	57	$12
Bats	Right	07 SF	497	38	19	81	0	276	271	277	297	433	729	3	89	28	0.28	265	37	19	44	85	10%	18	0%	4.20	-3.3	39	$13
Health	A	08 SF	530	47	16	95	0	292	297	291	317	445	762	3	93	29	0.50	263	35	18	47	90	7%	15	0%	4.72	7.4	56	$17
PT/Exp	B	09 SF	491	52	20	80	0	265	277	261	284	442	726	3	86	27	0.19	252	31	17	53	106	9%	32	0%	4.10	-2.3	46	$15
Consist	B	1st Half	270	26	10	46	0	259			267	430	697	1	88	26	0.09	250	28	17	55	100	8%	36	0%	3.73	-4.2	46	$7
LIMA Plan	D+	2nd Half	221	26	10	34	0	271			303	457	760	4	84	28	0.29	253	35	16	49	112	11%	23	0%	4.56	1.9	44	$7
Rand Var	0	10 Proj	483	48	19	79	0	263			288	440	728	3	88	26	0.30	262	32	18	50	102	9%	32	0%	4.21	-0.6	53	$14

Declines in bb%, ct% along with rise in FB% suggest that he's giving it all up to focus on the long ball. xBA, RC/G trends show the cost. There's value in the power, but know you're buying HR/RBI, not BA.

Molina,Jose			AB	R	HR	RBI	SB	Avg	vL	vR	OB	Slg	OPS	bb%	ct%	h%	Eye	xBA	G	L	F	PX	hr/f	SX	SBO	RC/G	RAR	BPV	R$
Pos	2	05 ANA	184	14	6	25	2	228	306	186	279	348	627	7	78	26	0.32	236	50	20	30	74	14%	39	4%	3.01	-5.6	-3	$3
Age	35	06 LAA	225	18	4	22	1	240	218	254	269	369	638	4	78	29	0.18	239	42	18	39	96	6%	38	2%	3.18	-8.3	11	$2
Bats	Right	07 2AL	191	18	1	19	2	257	360	220	276	340	616	3	77	33	0.12	252	48	23	29	73	2%	55	8%	2.84	-8.1	-8	$2
Health	C	08 NYY	268	32	3	18	0	216	188	230	250	313	563	4	81	26	0.23	244	48	19	33	75	4%	44	0%	2.32	-15.4	6	$1
PT/Exp	F	09 NYY	138	15	1	11	0	217	220	216	289	268	558	9	80	27	0.50	202	39	19	42	36	2%	30	0%	2.43	-7.8	-23	$0
Consist	A	1st Half	44	5	1	6	0	273			333	386	720	8	86	30	0.67	274	37	26	37	69	7%	23	0%	4.45	0.2	26	$1
LIMA Plan	F	2nd Half	94	10	0	5	0	191			269	213	482	10	77	25	0.45	168	40	15	45	19	0%	34	0%	1.40	-8.6	-47	($1)
Rand Var	0	10 Proj	151	15	1	12	1	225			269	300	569	6	78	28	0.27	221	45	19	36	57	3%	45	2%	2.37	-8.6	-16	$1

Do you think Jose ever feels like he got the genetic shaft? If the eyes were just a little bit sharper, or the hands just a little bit faster... But they aren't, and as xBA shows, it means he'll likely be the first Molina to retire.

Molina,Yadier			AB	R	HR	RBI	SB	Avg	vL	vR	OB	Slg	OPS	bb%	ct%	h%	Eye	xBA	G	L	F	PX	hr/f	SX	SBO	RC/G	RAR	BPV	R$
Pos	2	05 STL	385	36	8	49	2	252	299	231	294	358	653	6	92	26	0.77	273	51	18	31	62	7%	48	5%	3.70	-1.1	46	$7
Age	28	06 STL	417	29	6	49	1	216	213	217	262	321	583	6	90	23	0.63	252	42	18	39	67	4%	26	4%	2.94	-18.0	36	$2
Bats	Right	07 STL	353	30	6	40	1	275	288	269	339	368	707	9	88	30	0.79	249	46	19	35	58	6%	25	2%	4.38	-0.5	25	$7
Health	A	08 STL	444	37	7	56	0	304	323	296	351	392	743	7	93	31	1.10	257	46	21	33	53	5%	13	1%	4.77	6.9	35	$12
PT/Exp	B	09 STL	481	45	6	54	9	293	248	307	360	383	742	9	92	31	1.28	272	51	20	29	57	5%	60	7%	4.95	9.3	52	$14
Consist	A	1st Half	244	25	5	24	4	279			343	381	724	9	92	29	1.26	277	51	20	28	58	8%	66	6%	4.69	3.0	55	$7
LIMA Plan	D+	2nd Half	237	20	1	30	5	308			376	384	760	10	92	33	1.30	265	50	19	30	56	2%	48	8%	5.22	6.3	48	$7
Rand Var	-2	10 Proj	481	42	7	57	6	289			348	378	726	8	92	31	1.08	265	48	20	32	57	5%	48	6%	4.68	5.7	45	$12

Stole more bases last year than every previous year combined, thanks to highest OB of his career. Continued Eye and xBA growth, peak age... there's a lot to like here. Has quietly become a solid second-tier catcher.

Montero,Miguel			AB	R	HR	RBI	SB	Avg	vL	vR	OB	Slg	OPS	bb%	ct%	h%	Eye	xBA	G	L	F	PX	hr/f	SX	SBO	RC/G	RAR	BPV	R$
Pos	2	05 aa	108	10	2	10	1	225			264	323	588	5	81	26	0.28	0				53		97	4%	2.60	-4.3	7	$1
Age	27	06 a/a	439	38	15	66	1	269	333	231	338	426	764	9	87	28	0.81	241	38	15	46	91	9%	13	5%	5.02	8.2	46	$10
Bats	Left	07 ARI	214	30	10	37	0	224	286	218	291	397	688	9	84	22	0.57	244	39	14	47	97	12%	32	0%	3.93	-3.3	41	$5
Health	A	08 ARI	184	24	5	18	0	255	286	250	325	435	760	9	73	32	0.39	256	36	22	41	138	9%	49	0%	5.07	4.6	39	$4
PT/Exp	D	09 ARI	425	61	16	59	1	294	329	286	352	478	830	8	82	33	0.49	274	44	20	36	122	13%	36	3%	5.70	17.0	54	$16
Consist	B	1st Half	155	16	4	16	1	252			333	381	714	11	82	28	0.68	248	41	20	39	86	8%	35	2%	4.46	0.9	31	$3
LIMA Plan	D+	2nd Half	270	45	12	43	0	319			363	533	897	7	81	36	0.38	289	46	19	35	143	16%	36	3%	6.40	15.6	66	$13
Rand Var	-4	10 Proj	480	64	18	63	1	273			335	459	794	9	80	31	0.47	272	41	20	39	124	12%	46	2%	5.30	14.3	53	$14

Given his age and overall positive trends, it sure looks like he arrived in the 2nd half. Because of the sample size, we'll temper expecations for now, but don't be surprised if... UP: .300 BA, 25 HR, 85 RBI.

Morales,Jose			AB	R	HR	RBI	SB	Avg	vL	vR	OB	Slg	OPS	bb%	ct%	h%	Eye	xBA	G	L	F	PX	hr/f	SX	SBO	RC/G	RAR	BPV	R$
Pos	2	05	0	0	0	0	0	0							0			0						0					
Age	27	06	0	0	0	0	0	0							0			0						0					
Bats	Both	07 aaa	376	41	2	37	1	303			351	388	740	7	88	34	0.62	0				62		39	4%	4.72	3.7	29	$8
Health	A	08 aaa	197	14	3	12	0	262			283	344	627	3	86	29	0.21	0				49		36	2%	3.05	-6.6	4	$2
PT/Exp	F	09 MIN	* 330	38	2	28	1	293	412	300	361	367	729	10	85	34	0.73	264	49	24	27	52	2%	40	3%	4.71	4.0	17	$7
Consist	D	1st Half	169	23	0	10	1	271			341	328	669	10	86	31	0.77	273	46	28	26	41	0%	67	3%	4.05	-1.1	19	$3
LIMA Plan	F	2nd Half	161	15	2	18	0	317			382	409	791	10	85	37	0.69	248	52	20	28	64	5%	18	3%	5.41	5.0	17	$4
Rand Var	-3	10 Proj	98	9	1	8	0	276			325	354	679	7	86	37	0.53	263	50	23	27	56	4%	31	3%	3.94	-0.9	14	$2

0-7-.311 in 119 AB at MIN. That's seven straight catchers, folks. We pride ourselves on one-stop shopping! bb% and LD% are promising, but he needs to develop another skill to become more than a backup.

Morales,Kendry			AB	R	HR	RBI	SB	Avg	vL	vR	OB	Slg	OPS	bb%	ct%	h%	Eye	xBA	G	L	F	PX	hr/f	SX	SBO	RC/G	RAR	BPV	R$
Pos	3	05 aa	281	36	13	42	2	267			299	445	744	4	88	26	0.38	0				100		55	3%	4.41	-7.6	59	$9
Age	27	06 LAA	* 453	53	14	63	1	263	229	235	306	413	718	6	87	28	0.47	260	52	15	34	86	11%	46	6%	4.28	-15.2	45	$10
Bats	Both	07 LAA	* 374	48	8	47	0	302	241	311	335	445	779	5	87	33	0.37	254	47	11	42	96	6%	40	3%	4.95	-3.2	47	$11
Health	A	08 LAA	* 378	44	14	60	1	283	214	213	317	446	764	5	88	29	0.42	255	41	15	44	96	10%	29	5%	4.70	-6.2	50	$12
PT/Exp	C	09 LAA	566	86	34	108	3	306	296	309	358	569	927	8	79	33	0.39	292	42	17	41	162	18%	50	7%	6.82	17.5	79	$26
Consist	C	1st Half	264	35	13	41	0	280			338	527	864	8	79	31	0.42	287	39	18	43	156	14%	50	3%	6.15	3.3	74	$9
LIMA Plan	D+	2nd Half	302	51	21	67	3	328			375	606	981	7	79	36	0.37	297	44	16	40	168	22%	45	10%	7.41	13.8	82	$18
Rand Var	-4	10 Proj	591	81	30	101	2	296			339	517	856	6	83	31	0.40	281	43	16	41	133	15%	38	6%	5.82	5.5	66	$23

Traded nine points of ct% for 20 homers. Best. Trade. Ever. Only fly in the ointment? One HR every 14 AB vs. RH, one every 34 AB vs. LH. Otherwise, age and 2H skills make odds of a repeat look good.

Mora,Melvin			AB	R	HR	RBI	SB	Avg	vL	vR	OB	Slg	OPS	bb%	ct%	h%	Eye	xBA	G	L	F	PX	hr/f	SX	SBO	RC/G	RAR	BPV	R$
Pos	5	05 BAL	593	86	27	88	7	283	234	304	339	474	813	8	81	31	0.45	259	37	18	45	119	13%	66	7%	5.41	15.3	57	$22
Age	38	06 BAL	624	96	16	83	11	274	253	282	332	391	723	8	84	30	0.55	243	39	20	41	71	7%	87	7%	4.41	-10.7	37	$18
Bats	Right	07 BAL	467	67	14	58	9	274	254	280	340	418	758	9	82	31	0.57	258	40	19	42	93	9%	80	9%	4.89	0.2	47	$14
Health	B	08 BAL	513	77	23	104	3	285	314	272	333	483	816	7	86	29	0.53	293	42	21	37	117	14%	59	8%	5.40	7.7	72	$21
PT/Exp	B	09 BAL	450	44	8	48	3	260	242	270	312	358	670	7	87	29	0.57	245	43	19	38	61	5%	39	5%	3.82	-11.3	23	$8
Consist	C	1st Half	207	18	2	22	2	266			321	324	645	8	89	29	0.74	244	43	21	35	36	3%	38	6%	3.64	-6.3	13	$3
LIMA Plan	D+	2nd Half	243	26	6	26	1	255			304	387	691	7	85	28	0.46	247	43	16	41	83	7%	38	3%	3.99	-4.9	32	$4
Rand Var	0	10 Proj	422	52	10	58	4	265			319	391	711	7	85	29	0.54	257	42	19	39	78	7%	60	6%	4.28	-6.0	39	$10

2008 power outburst is starting to look like the last gasp of a dying career. ct% is up, but minus the power, it's just not enough to carry the day. He's old and tired; with 8-year-old quintuplets, you can see why.

BRNADON KRUSE

Morgan,Nyjer

		Year	AB	R	HR	RBI	SB	Avg	vL	vR	OB	Slg	OPS	bb%	ct%	h%	Eye	xBA	G	L	F	PX	hr/f	SX	SBO	RC/G	RAR	BPV	R$
Pos	78	05	0	0	0	0	0	0							0			0						0					
Age	30	06 aa	219	31	1	8	17	254			294	322	615	5	87	29	0.42	0				37		149	46%	3.16	-14.0	35	$6
Bats	Left	07 PIT	* 271	37	1	14	25	262	259	313	310	332	642	7	83	31	0.41	247	57	16	27	41	2%	152	45%	3.46	-15.6	24	$9
Health	B	08 PIT	* 482	67	1	33	42	264	240	304	297	331	628	5	84	31	0.30	263	50	25	26	51	1%	144	45%	3.21	-31.9	31	$17
PT/Exp	C	09 2NL	464	74	3	39	42	308	175	344	363	390	753	8	84	36	0.55	257	54	19	26	51	3%	145	37%	4.87	-9.1	39	$24
Consist	B	1st Half	278	39	2	27	18	277			345	356	701	9	82	33	0.59	242	52	19	29	46	3%	133	30%	4.32	-10.3	27	$10
LIMA Plan	C+	2nd Half	186	35	1	12	24	355			391	441	832	6	87	40	0.46	279	58	20	23	58	3%	150	48%	5.64	0.4	53	$13
Rand Var	-5	10 Proj	**502**	**77**	**2**	**34**	**33**	**273**			**318**	**348**	**666**	**6**	**85**	**32**	**0.43**	**261**	**55**	**20**	**25**	**49**	**2%**	**144**	**35%**	**3.76**	**-25.7**	**36**	**$17**

3 reasons to be cautious...
- OB surge fueled by fluky h%
- xBA says this is no .300 hitter
- Getting really bad vs LHers
He found something in that 1H bb%, but history says we can't expect that again. SB at risk.

Morneau,Justin

		Year	AB	R	HR	RBI	SB	Avg	vL	vR	OB	Slg	OPS	bb%	ct%	h%	Eye	xBA	G	L	F	PX	hr/f	SX	SBO	RC/G	RAR	BPV	R$
Pos	3	05 MIN	490	62	22	79	0	239	205	254	301	437	738	8	81	25	0.47	263	42	18	41	121	14%	56	2%	4.54	-8.0	56	$12
Age	29	06 MIN	592	97	34	130	3	321	315	325	377	559	936	8	84	34	0.57	298	36	24	41	137	17%	49	4%	6.85	22.8	80	$29
Bats	Left	07 MIN	590	84	31	111	1	271	228	294	343	492	834	10	85	28	0.70	291	45	16	39	130	16%	53	1%	5.77	8.6	79	$21
Health	A	08 MIN	623	97	23	129	0	300	284	310	376	499	875	11	86	32	0.89	293	43	19	38	124	11%	48	1%	6.43	19.9	83	$25
PT/Exp	A	09 MIN	508	85	30	100	0	274	277	272	364	516	880	12	83	28	0.84	282	41	16	43	139	17%	37	0%	6.45	10.7	82	$20
Consist	A	1st Half	298	54	19	64	0	309			391	574	964	12	83	32	0.80	295	41	16	43	152	18%	42	0%	7.44	14.0	93	$15
LIMA Plan	C+	2nd Half	210	31	11	36	0	224			326	433	760	13	83	22	0.89	263	43	15	42	121	15%	26	0%	5.05	-4.2	65	$5
Rand Var	+1	10 Proj	**590**	**92**	**34**	**114**	**0**	**281**			**363**	**522**	**884**	**11**	**84**	**29**	**0.80**	**291**	**42**	**17**	**41**	**140**	**17%**	**43**	**1%**	**6.45**	**16.1**	**85**	**$24**

Stress fracture in back cost him last few weeks and likely zapped 2H power. But FB uptick says he hasn't maxed out power yet. See 1st half.
UP: 40 HR

Moss,Brandon

		Year	AB	R	HR	RBI	SB	Avg	vL	vR	OB	Slg	OPS	bb%	ct%	h%	Eye	xBA	G	L	F	PX	hr/f	SX	SBO	RC/G	RAR	BPV	R$
Pos	97	05 aa	500	74	13	53	5	254			314	406	720	8	78	30	0.40	0				106		89	6%	4.40	-8.5	43	$12
Age	27	06 aa	508	66	11	72	7	271			336	416	752	9	81	32	0.51	0				99		75	9%	4.88	-4.9	45	$13
Bats	Left	07 aaa	493	59	13	70	3	276			347	452	800	10	73	35	0.41	0				140		46	6%	5.65	6.5	39	$13
Health	A	08 2TM	* 399	42	14	58	3	247	267	239	305	437	742	8	72	31	0.30	256	44	20	36	134	13%	87	6%	4.73	-6.5	39	$9
PT/Exp	D	09 PIT	385	47	7	41	1	236	232	237	298	364	662	8	78	29	0.40	243	45	20	36	88	7%	72	6%	3.69	-13.9	23	$6
Consist	B	1st Half	202	27	1	20	0	267			308	376	685	6	80	33	0.30	247	46	19	35	85	2%	69	0%	3.94	-5.4	22	$4
LIMA Plan	F	2nd Half	183	20	6	21	1	202			288	350	638	11	76	23	0.50	239	44	20	36	92	12%	70	13%	3.37	-8.9	22	$2
Rand Var	+2	10 Proj	**293**	**34**	**8**	**36**	**1**	**242**			**307**	**398**	**705**	**9**	**76**	**30**	**0.39**	**251**	**44**	**20**	**36**	**108**	**9%**	**70**	**6%**	**4.25**	**-6.4**	**30**	**$5**

Got first crack at regular MLB duty and stunk it up. H% tanked in 2H, but xBA confirms there's no BA upside here anyway. Owned by both LH and RH, so less exposure won't help. Neither will shaky glove in OF.

Murphy,Daniel

		Year	AB	R	HR	RBI	SB	Avg	vL	vR	OB	Slg	OPS	bb%	ct%	h%	Eye	xBA	G	L	F	PX	hr/f	SX	SBO	RC/G	RAR	BPV	R$
Pos	37	05	0	0	0	0	0	0							0			0						0					
Age	25	06	0	0	0	0	0	0							0			0						0					
Bats	Left	07 aa	361	48	11	56	12	271			333	432	765	8	89	28	0.84	0				97		84	18%	5.03	-7.0	78	$12
Health	A	08 NYM	* 492	72	13	73	12	283	400	306	350	443	793	7	86	31	0.76	313	41	33	25	100	12%	96	14%	5.42	-4.5	75	$18
PT/Exp	C	09 NYM	508	60	12	63	4	266	223	275	317	427	744	7	86	29	0.55	272	40	19	41	105	7%	78	5%	4.72	-26.4	69	$13
Consist	B	1st Half	215	28	5	24	1	242			315	358	673	10	88	26	0.88	245	41	17	41	69	6%	60	3%	4.04	-15.9	46	$4
LIMA Plan	C	2nd Half	293	32	7	39	3	283			318	478	796	5	85	31	0.35	291	39	20	41	132	7%	83	7%	5.22	-10.6	84	$9
Rand Var	0	10 Proj	**451**	**59**	**15**	**62**	**5**	**277**			**335**	**464**	**799**	**8**	**87**	**29**	**0.65**	**289**	**40**	**21**	**39**	**115**	**10%**	**73**	**8%**	**5.36**	**-10.7**	**78**	**$15**

PRO:
- PX trend, especially 2H
- FB uptick
CON:
- Eroding eye
- LHers handcuffed him
Still young, so HR could come.

Murphy,David

		Year	AB	R	HR	RBI	SB	Avg	vL	vR	OB	Slg	OPS	bb%	ct%	h%	Eye	xBA	G	L	F	PX	hr/f	SX	SBO	RC/G	RAR	BPV	R$
Pos	7	05 aa	480	59	12	63	11	257			311	394	705	7	85	28	0.52	0				87		92	14%	4.22	-11.6	54	$13
Age	28	06 a/a	490	59	10	61	6	259			327	422	749	9	85	29	0.67	0				106		80	9%	4.93	-4.1	69	$10
Bats	Left	07 2AL	* 512	56	10	51	7	267	409	325	318	405	723	7	85	30	0.49	290	42	26	32	89	7%	95	7%	4.45	-8.8	54	$10
Health	B	08 TEX	415	64	15	74	7	275	258	282	325	465	790	7	83	30	0.44	278	42	18	40	121	11%	102	9%	5.17	3.8	76	$15
PT/Exp	C	09 TEX	432	61	17	57	9	269	235	279	343	447	790	10	75	32	0.46	249	38	19	43	117	12%	75	11%	5.35	4.3	40	$14
Consist	A	1st Half	178	25	7	22	5	258			347	427	774	12	75	31	0.55	247	41	19	40	110	13%	60	17%	5.20	1.0	33	$6
LIMA Plan	C+	2nd Half	254	36	10	35	4	276			341	461	801	9	76	33	0.40	251	36	19	44	121	12%	78	6%	5.45	3.1	43	$9
Rand Var	-3	10 Proj	**448**	**62**	**20**	**72**	**8**	**268**			**331**	**472**	**803**	**9**	**80**	**30**	**0.47**	**272**	**40**	**19**	**41**	**128**	**14%**	**84**	**10%**	**5.38**	**5.3**	**66**	**$16**

3 reasons for optimism...
- Power skills remain strong
- Rising fly ball rate
- Solid skills vs RHers
Had a 130+ PX in regular duty in Aug + Sept. No pop vs lefties, but 25 HR potential remains.

Nady,Xavier

		Year	AB	R	HR	RBI	SB	Avg	vL	vR	OB	Slg	OPS	bb%	ct%	h%	Eye	xBA	G	L	F	PX	hr/f	SX	SBO	RC/G	RAR	BPV	R$
Pos	9	05 SD	326	40	13	43	2	261	323	220	307	439	746	6	79	29	0.33	269	44	20	36	112	14%	75	4%	4.54	-6.7	45	$9
Age	31	06 2NL	468	57	17	63	3	280	336	263	323	453	776	6	82	31	0.35	261	46	17	37	106	12%	52	5%	4.91	1.9	41	$14
Bats	Right	07 PIT	431	55	20	72	3	278	295	274	315	476	791	5	77	32	0.23	268	39	21	40	127	15%	60	4%	5.03	1.9	38	$15
Health	F	08 2TM	555	76	25	97	2	305	262	317	350	510	860	7	81	34	0.38	294	41	25	34	131	16%	52	2%	5.93	10.0	62	$23
PT/Exp	C	09 NYY	28	4	0	2	0	286	333	273	310	429	739	3	79	36	0.17	293	41	27	32	127	0%	44	0%	4.60	-0.6	38	$1
Consist	C	1st Half	28	4	0	2	0	286			310	429	739	3	79	36	0.17	293	41	27	32	127	0%	44	0%	4.60	-0.6	38	$1
LIMA Plan	F	2nd Half	0	0	0	0	0	0																					
Rand Var	+1	10 Proj	**263**	**34**	**10**	**40**	**1**	**281**			**325**	**459**	**784**	**6**	**80**	**32**	**0.33**	**271**	**43**	**21**	**37**	**112**	**13%**	**58**	**4%**	**5.00**	**-2.6**	**43**	**$8**

Bad elbow turned into a second Tommy John surgery. If healthy, pre-injury PX growth gives hope for even more power. But that's a big if. He doesn't loft ball well, so he'll be fighting that too. Big risk, moderate reward.

Napoli,Mike

		Year	AB	R	HR	RBI	SB	Avg	vL	vR	OB	Slg	OPS	bb%	ct%	h%	Eye	xBA	G	L	F	PX	hr/f	SX	SBO	RC/G	RAR	BPV	R$
Pos	2	05 aa	439	71	22	74	9	199			299	398	697	13	75	21	0.57	0				131		89	13%	4.14	3.3	57	$12
Age	28	06 LAA	* 346	57	18	51	3	225	185	241	337	434	770	14	65	29	0.48	217	34	14	52	155	15%	50	7%	5.47	11.3	29	$9
Bats	Right	07 LAA	219	40	10	34	5	247	291	232	345	443	788	13	71	30	0.52	248	36	19	46	139	14%	94	11%	5.52	8.0	52	$7
Health	B	08 LAA	227	39	20	49	7	273	286	270	370	586	956	13	69	31	0.50	272	31	17	52	209	24%	83	15%	7.80	23.8	98	$13
PT/Exp	D	09 LAA	382	60	20	56	3	272	330	253	341	492	833	9	73	32	0.39	259	38	19	43	145	17%	59	6%	5.90	18.0	47	$14
Consist	C	1st Half	183	25	10	29	2	295			368	514	881	10	74	35	0.44	261	43	18	39	142	19%	38	9%	6.55	11.8	43	$8
LIMA Plan	C	2nd Half	199	35	10	27	1	251			317	472	789	9	72	30	0.35	254	34	19	47	147	15%	78	2%	5.30	6.0	50	$6
Rand Var	-1	10 Proj	**364**	**61**	**22**	**60**	**4**	**261**			**345**	**499**	**843**	**11**	**71**	**31**	**0.45**	**257**	**35**	**18**	**47**	**160**	**18%**	**69**	**7%**	**6.14**	**20.2**	**59**	**$14**

'09 looks like '08, on surface. Deeper look shows this split:

	OB	Slg	OPS
vs. LHers	.417	.606	1.023
vs. RHers	.327	.455	.782

30 HR if 500 AB, but no chance w/bad defense and so-so v. RH.

Navarro,Dioner

		Year	AB	R	HR	RBI	SB	Avg	vL	vR	OB	Slg	OPS	bb%	ct%	h%	Eye	xBA	G	L	F	PX	hr/f	SX	SBO	RC/G	RAR	BPV	R$
Pos	2	05 LA	* 417	43	7	35	1	247	435	248	322	346	668	10	91	26	1.31	274	45	22	33	61	6%	29	4%	4.14	4.4	46	$6
Age	26	06 2TM	* 308	30	6	29	3	241	286	245	315	336	651	10	82	28	0.59	235	35	24	41	60	6%	47	4%	3.62	-6.9	11	$4
Bats	Both	07 TAM	388	46	9	44	3	227	226	227	287	356	643	8	83	25	0.49	250	42	17	41	74	7%	76	4%	3.47	-9.6	38	$5
Health	B	08 TAM	427	43	7	54	0	295	257	308	347	407	755	7	89	32	0.69	278	46	23	30	76	6%	17	3%	4.87	8.2	36	$11
PT/Exp	C	09 TAM	376	38	8	32	5	218	279	182	254	322	576	5	86	23	0.35	243	37	20	43	62	6%	64	9%	2.58	-19.7	26	$4
Consist	D	1st Half	226	23	4	21	1	212			233	305	538	3	85	24	0.17	231	39	18	43	58	5%	53	5%	1.98	-16.1	8	$1
LIMA Plan	D	2nd Half	150	15	4	11	4	227			284	347	631	7	89	23	0.75	260	35	22	43	68	7%	63	14%	3.45	-3.8	47	$2
Rand Var	+4	10 Proj	**359**	**37**	**8**	**35**	**4**	**242**			**293**	**353**	**646**	**7**	**87**	**26**	**0.55**	**257**	**40**	**21**	**39**	**69**	**6%**	**52**	**7%**	**3.53**	**-7.7**	**34**	**$6**

Need a backup CA? Start by scanning PX. Ok, nothing here. Next, limit BA damage by eyeing xBA. Not much to like there. He's young and makes good contact, so we can't write him off. But '08 clearly is the outlier here.

Nieves,Wil

		Year	AB	R	HR	RBI	SB	Avg	vL	vR	OB	Slg	OPS	bb%	ct%	h%	Eye	xBA	G	L	F	PX	hr/f	SX	SBO	RC/G	RAR	BPV	R$
Pos	2	05 aaa	380	34	3	29	1	240			258	318	576	2	91	26	0.27	0				52		59	2%	2.68	-13.9	30	$3
Age	33	06 aaa	321	24	5	28	2	221			255	298	553	4	91	23	0.49	0				45		40	4%	2.49	-18.6	22	$1
Bats	Right	07 NYY	* 151	11	1	14	1	199			234	265	499	4	86	22	0.33	230	52	13	35	44	2%	63	3%	1.75	-12.1	9	($0)
Health	A	08 WAS	* 201	18	1	22	1	250	304	242	301	324	625	7	83	30	0.42	245	54	20	26	55	2%	57	3%	3.26	-5.6	7	$2
PT/Exp	F	09 WAS	224	20	1	26	1	259	186	276	311	299	610	7	80	32	0.38	225	62	19	19	32	3%	37	1%	2.98	-8.3	-28	$3
Consist	B	1st Half	103	9	0	12	0	233			275	262	537	6	77	30	0.25	202	56	19	25	28	0%	27	0%	1.94	-7.2	-50	$1
LIMA Plan	F	2nd Half	121	11	1	14	1	244			341	331	671	8	83	33	0.52	241	66	20	15	35	7%	36	2%	3.83	-1.5	-12	$3
Rand Var	-5	10 Proj	**131**	**11**	**1**	**14**	**1**	**244**			**292**	**300**	**592**	**6**	**83**	**29**	**0.39**	**238**	**59**	**19**	**22**	**42**	**3%**	**38**	**2%**	**2.80**	**-5.7**	**-9**	**$1**

Post-peak #3 catcher for the worst team in baseball but still probably makes more money than you. His ridiculously low FB and PX rates have created the "Nieves Shift" where all OFers play on the edge of the grass.

STEPHEN NICKRAND

Nix,Jayson

Nix,Jayson			AB	R	HR	RBI	SB	Avg	vL	vR	OB	Slg	OPS	bb%	ct%	h%	Eye	xBA	G	L	F	PX	hr/f	SX	SBO	RC/G	RAR	BPV	R$
Pos	4	05 aa	501	52	10	36	8	219			252	327	579	4	86	24	0.32	0				72		70	15%	2.61	-27.1	33	$5
Age	28	06 aaa	358	29	2	19	11	235			283	293	576	6	88	26	0.56	0				39		81	16%	2.80	-17.1	22	$3
Bats	Right	07 aa	439	59	9	43	18	252			290	387	677	5	85	28	0.35	0				90		110	28%	3.78	-7.5	55	$12
Health	A	08 aa	264	41	12	34	7	251			297	460	757	6	82	26	0.37	0				131		100	24%	4.68	-1.2	.79	$9
PT/Exp	F	09 CHW	255	36	12	32	10	224	256	194	300	408	708	10	75	25	0.44	232	39	13	48	117	13%	85	19%	4.19	-5.8	40	$7
Consist	B	1st Half	82	12	5	10	4	232			300	488	788	9	83	22	0.57	288	38	14	48	151	15%	83	25%	5.15	0.5	97	$3
LIMA Plan	D	2nd Half	173	24	7	22	6	220			301	370	670	10	71	27	0.40	205	40	12	48	98	12%	76	17%	3.71	-6.5	8	$4
Rand Var	+1	10 Proj	226	32	9	26	8	235			294	408	701	8	80	26	0.42	242	39	13	48	110	10%	84	21%	4.06	-4.4	50	$6

Started with a bang upon callup, but got exposed with more AB in 2H: ct% plunged, power returned to earth. PX/FB combo carries potential, but ct% struggles offset that with BA risk.

Nix,Laynce

Nix,Laynce			AB	R	HR	RBI	SB	Avg	vL	vR	OB	Slg	OPS	bb%	ct%	h%	Eye	xBA	G	L	F	PX	hr/f	SX	SBO	RC/G	RAR	BPV	R$
Pos	7	05 TEX	* 265	34	8	36	2	249	333	232	289	419	708	5	82	28	0.31	267	49	17	34	105	11%	104	5%	4.10	-4.8	54	$6
Age	29	06 2TM	* 421	53	17	72	4	261	125	169	296	440	736	5	72	33	0.17	231	43	15	43	120	13%	82	5%	4.43	-9.6	19	$12
Bats	Left	07 a/a	358	49	20	63	4	226			279	447	726	7	70	26	0.24	0				154		75	5%	4.36	-9.1	42	$10
Health	B	08 aaa	380	43	16	41	4	223			273	407	680	6	80	24	0.34	0				116		71	10%	3.72	-16.6	47	$7
PT/Exp	F	09 CIN	309	42	15	46	0	239	156	249	290	476	766	7	74	28	0.27	275	38	20	43	171	15%	50	2%	4.91	-6.0	62	$9
Consist	B	1st Half	166	23	7	21	0	253			303	500	803	7	72	31	0.26	288	36	24	40	192	15%	57	0%	5.58	0.1	73	$5
LIMA Plan	D	2nd Half	143	19	8	25	0	224			275	448	722	7	76	24	0.29	257	39	15	46	148	16%	39	4%	4.20	-6.0	50	$4
Rand Var	+1	10 Proj	248	32	12	36	1	250			298	466	764	6	75	29	0.28	265	40	18	41	146	15%	61	5%	4.81	-4.8	51	$7

Massive PX will cover a lot of ills, but yearly trends say that this is not a skill he can count on regularly. Meanwhile, the warts (poor plate control, low h%) are much more sustainable.

Oeltjen,Trent

Oeltjen,Trent			AB	R	HR	RBI	SB	Avg	vL	vR	OB	Slg	OPS	bb%	ct%	h%	Eye	xBA	G	L	F	PX	hr/f	SX	SBO	RC/G	RAR	BPV	R$
Pos	7	05	0	0	0	0	0	0							0			0						0					
Age	27	06 aa	401	55	3	40	21	278			332	377	709	7	85	32	0.54	0				58		142	28%	4.36	-10.1	47	$13
Bats	Left	07 aaa	244	32	2	23	14	230			257	324	581	4	82	27	0.20	0				60		153	42%	2.53	-20.4	29	$5
Health	A	08 aa	442	60	5	48	12	287			318	419	737	4	87	32	0.34	0				81		133	18%	4.52	-7.8	62	$13
PT/Exp	D	09 ARI	* 512	71	11	53	20	267	158	275	301	445	746	5	80	31	0.25	258	45	15	40	113	7%	144	27%	4.61	-14.3	66	$17
Consist	C	1st Half	308	40	6	39	8	269			310	460	770	6	81	32	0.31	0				120		126	23%	5.02	-4.9	71	$9
LIMA Plan	F	2nd Half	204	30	6	14	11	264			287	423	709	3	79	31	0.15	247	45	15	40	102	9%	149	33%	3.98	-9.5	51	$7
Rand Var	-1	10 Proj	100	14	2	10	4	250			283	390	673	4	82	29	0.26	247	45	15	40	87	5%	147	30%	3.71	-5.3	54	$3

3-4-.243 with 3 SB in 70 AB at ARI. Emerging power makes a nice complement to primary speed skill, but flimsy ct%/bb% diminishes any optimism. Tough to exploit speed skills with these OBPs. Add to Esix Snead list.

Ojeda,Augie

Ojeda,Augie			AB	R	HR	RBI	SB	Avg	vL	vR	OB	Slg	OPS	bb%	ct%	h%	Eye	xBA	G	L	F	PX	hr/f	SX	SBO	RC/G	RAR	BPV	R$
Pos	465	05 aaa	310	32	2	25	3	186			247	247	494	8	90	20	0.78	0				44		62	7%	2.04	-23.0	29	($0)
Age	35	06 aaa	306	33	3	21	4	212			300	274	574	11	87	23	1.00	0				38		68	5%	3.02	-12.7	25	$1
Bats	Both	07 ARI	* 210	27	1	22	2	244	250	292	314	310	624	9	88	27	0.82	249	43	21	36	41	2%	86	3%	3.53	-7.3	30	$3
Health	A	08 ARI	231	27	0	17	0	242	250	240	319	299	618	10	90	27	1.08	247	50	20	31	38	0%	56	0%	3.61	-8.0	28	$2
PT/Exp	F	09 ARI	264	38	1	16	3	246	203	263	328	345	672	11	89	27	1.14	252	46	15	38	67	1%	94	5%	4.29	-1.9	63	$4
Consist	A	1st Half	137	14	1	4	2	234			305	314	619	9	90	25	1.00	246	41	19	40	58	2%	53	8%	3.55	-4.1	42	$1
LIMA Plan	D	2nd Half	127	24	0	12	1	260			352	378	730	12	89	29	1.29	260	52	12	36	78	0%	115	3%	5.09	2.1	79	$3
Rand Var	0	10 Proj	188	26	1	14	1	239			319	323	641	10	89	27	1.06	250	48	17	35	56	1%	89	3%	3.89	-4.1	50	$2

No power, below average speed, consistently low h%. Not exactly an imposing plate presence. So, it's ridiculous that he got non-intentionally walked more times than he struck out. Throw him a strike!

Olivo,Miguel

Olivo,Miguel			AB	R	HR	RBI	SB	Avg	vL	vR	OB	Slg	OPS	bb%	ct%	h%	Eye	xBA	G	L	F	PX	hr/f	SX	SBO	RC/G	RAR	BPV	R$
Pos	2	05 2TM	* 300	36	11	43	7	225	284	188	247	381	628	3	72	28	0.11	240	47	18	35	109	15%	103	17%	2.87	-9.5	14	$7
Age	32	06 FLA	430	52	16	58	2	263	273	258	278	440	717	2	76	31	0.09	250	42	19	39	112	13%	70	6%	3.99	-4.4	21	$11
Bats	Right	07 FLA	452	43	16	60	3	237	295	221	260	405	665	3	73	29	0.11	240	43	17	40	112	12%	75	6%	3.39	-14.1	11	$8
Health	A	08 KC	306	29	12	41	7	255	262	251	272	444	716	2	73	31	0.09	251	38	17	44	140	12%	73	14%	4.04	-1.3	33	$8
PT/Exp	C	09 KC	390	51	23	65	5	249	265	238	284	490	773	5	68	31	0.15	250	45	14	40	159	22%	105	10%	5.04	8.9	41	$13
Consist	B	1st Half	187	23	12	32	2	262			270	524	794	1	66	33	0.03	269	51	17	32	180	31%	92	11%	5.27	5.4	41	$7
LIMA Plan	D+	2nd Half	203	28	11	33	3	236			295	458	754	8	69	29	0.27	231	40	12	48	140	17%	108	9%	4.83	3.5	38	$6
Rand Var	-1	10 Proj	370	43	18	56	5	246			275	454	729	4	71	30	0.13	247	43	16	42	142	16%	94	10%	4.31	0.7	34	$10

1H hr/f spike cancelled out spike in GB%. Net is a legit HR source at a scarce position, and handful of SB never hurts. But at what price? xBA history sets BA expectation, and sub-.300 OBP is death in sim formats.

Ordonez,Magglio

Ordonez,Magglio			AB	R	HR	RBI	SB	Avg	vL	vR	OB	Slg	OPS	bb%	ct%	h%	Eye	xBA	G	L	F	PX	hr/f	SX	SBO	RC/G	RAR	BPV	R$
Pos	90	05 DET	305	38	8	46	0	302	308	300	364	436	800	9	89	32	0.86	276	44	23	34	84	9%	23	0%	5.45	6.2	48	$10
Age	36	06 DET	593	82	24	104	1	298	294	300	348	477	825	7	85	32	0.52	267	45	18	38	104	13%	35	3%	5.53	-2.2	51	$21
Bats	Right	07 DET	595	117	28	139	4	363	410	351	435	595	1030	11	87	39	0.96	319	42	19	39	146	14%	57	2%	8.22	40.5	106	$36
Health	B	08 DET	561	72	21	103	1	317	328	314	376	494	870	9	86	34	0.70	283	44	20	36	107	12%	36	3%	6.17	12.4	61	$23
PT/Exp	A	09 DET	465	54	9	50	3	310	352	289	378	428	806	10	86	35	0.78	274	51	21	28	73	8%	56	3%	5.58	3.2	41	$14
Consist	C	1st Half	246	29	3	24	3	260			331	333	664	10	84	30	0.65	238	58	15	27	48	5%	57	4%	3.85	-10.6	12	$5
LIMA Plan	D+	2nd Half	219	25	6	26	0	365			430	534	965	10	89	39	1.00	313	44	27	29	99	11%	45	1%	7.44	11.6	69	$9
Rand Var	-2	10 Proj	348	46	12	53	1	296			364	462	826	10	87	32	0.80	289	46	21	33	100	12%	46	3%	5.75	3.9	61	$12

Dramatic 1H/2H disparity not just due to h%. Nudged 2H bb%, ct%, gb% and PX to near prior levels. Full-season decline in hr/f is the troubling trend here: BA/OBP should hold up, but 20 HR level a thing of the past.

Ortiz,David

Ortiz,David			AB	R	HR	RBI	SB	Avg	vL	vR	OB	Slg	OPS	bb%	ct%	h%	Eye	xBA	G	L	F	PX	hr/f	SX	SBO	RC/G	RAR	BPV	R$
Pos	0	05 BOS	601	119	47	148	1	300	302	297	401	604	1005	15	79	31	0.82	307	31	23	46	189	21%	51	1%	8.13	34.8	115	$34
Age	34	06 BOS	558	115	54	137	1	287	278	292	412	636	1048	18	79	27	1.02	308	36	17	47	200	26%	51	1%	8.76	36.3	129	$31
Bats	Left	07 BOS	549	116	35	117	3	332	308	343	444	621	1065	17	81	36	1.08	320	38	17	45	188	17%	59	2%	9.09	41.2	129	$32
Health	B	08 BOS	416	74	23	89	1	264	221	279	370	507	878	14	82	27	0.95	291	37	19	45	152	15%	53	1%	6.58	19.8	97	$17
PT/Exp	A	09 BOS	541	77	28	99	0	238	212	250	330	462	792	12	75	27	0.55	256	32	17	50	145	14%	33	1%	5.43	4.2	53	$15
Consist	D	1st Half	258	29	8	36	0	225			317	391	709	12	74	27	0.51	240	27	22	51	117	8%	38	3%	4.42	-5.9	26	$4
LIMA Plan	B	2nd Half	283	48	20	63	0	251			342	526	868	12	77	26	0.59	271	37	13	50	170	19%	28	0%	6.32	9.5	77	$11
Rand Var	+3	10 Proj	505	86	29	93	1	246			349	493	843	14	78	26	0.74	279	35	18	48	158	15%	48	1%	6.12	11.2	84	$17

You pick the cause of decline: '08 wrist surgery, PED loss, age? 2H PX looks vintage, but multi-year decay in PX, xBA, BA vLH tell a different tale. Own him for the power, but be wary of the BA risk and overall trends.

Overbay,Lyle

Overbay,Lyle			AB	R	HR	RBI	SB	Avg	vL	vR	OB	Slg	OPS	bb%	ct%	h%	Eye	xBA	G	L	F	PX	hr/f	SX	SBO	RC/G	RAR	BPV	R$
Pos	3	05 MIL	537	80	19	72	1	276	270	278	367	449	816	13	82	31	0.80	290	51	21	27	114	16%	51	1%	5.81	3.2	61	$17
Age	33	06 TOR	581	82	22	92	5	312	284	322	371	508	879	9	83	34	0.57	295	46	22	32	124	14%	56	5%	6.32	14.2	69	$22
Bats	Left	07 TOR	425	49	10	44	2	240	287	224	316	391	706	10	82	27	0.60	284	49	21	31	105	9%	66	2%	4.37	-11.3	52	$6
Health	B	08 TOR	544	74	15	69	1	270	215	291	358	419	777	12	79	32	0.64	265	44	23	33	103	11%	47	2%	5.31	0.6	37	$14
PT/Exp	B	09 TOR	423	57	16	64	0	265	190	282	374	466	840	15	78	31	0.78	274	42	20	37	136	13%	29	0%	6.28	6.9	59	$12
Consist	B	1st Half	197	26	9	41	0	264			391	492	883	17	82	28	1.17	294	44	19	37	141	15%	34	0%	6.88	6.7	88	$7
LIMA Plan	C	2nd Half	226	31	7	23	0	265			359	442	802	13	73	33	0.55	257	41	21	38	131	11%	24	0%	5.76	0.3	33	$5
Rand Var	0	10 Proj	423	56	14	57	1	277			369	452	821	13	79	32	0.69	273	44	21	34	120	12%	40	1%	5.92	5.3	50	$12

What looks like some late-career growth (PX, FB%, bb%) is really just a shift in role: he's sitting v. LHPs now, rather than flailing against them. Limits him to 400-450 AB, but enhances value in daily trannie leagues.

Pagan,Angel

Pagan,Angel			AB	R	HR	RBI	SB	Avg	vL	vR	OB	Slg	OPS	bb%	ct%	h%	Eye	xBA	G	L	F	PX	hr/f	SX	SBO	RC/G	RAR	BPV	R$
Pos	87	05 aaa	509	57	6	32	23	244			297	338	635	7	81	29	0.41	0				61		121	29%	3.35	-16.8	26	$11
Age	29	06 CHC	170	28	5	18	4	247	196	272	308	394	702	8	84	27	0.54	255	51	15	34	81	10%	112	14%	4.18	-1.3	51	$4
Bats	Both	07 CHC	* 264	34	7	28	8	237	236	289	283	391	674	6	80	27	0.33	245	36	18	46	96	7%	126	18%	3.74	-6.3	51	$6
Health	F	08 NYM	91	12	0	13	4	275	250	294	353	374	727	11	80	34	0.61	240	36	23	41	79	0%	115	14%	4.79	0.1	42	$3
PT/Exp	F	09 NYM	343	54	6	32	14	306	280	316	353	487	840	7	84	35	0.45	275	41	21	38	111	5%	138	23%	5.90	11.2	80	$14
Consist	C	1st Half	42	7	0	3	4	333			429	405	833	14	79	42	0.78	251	55	21	24	67	0%	84	22%	6.32	1.7	23	$2
LIMA Plan	D	2nd Half	301	47	6	29	10	302			342	498	840	6	84	34	0.38	278	39	21	40	117	6%	133	23%	5.82	9.3	84	$12
Rand Var	-4	10 Proj	294	43	7	28	9	262			312	419	732	7	83	30	0.42	259	44	18	38	95	7%	138	20%	4.52	-1.4	64	$9

Consistent playing time agreed with him, but it was over his head and the AB won't happen again. Speed is his major skill but a sub-par SB success rate (66%) dates back to the minors and caps his potential.

RAY MURPHY

Parra,Gerardo

			AB	R	HR	RBI	SB	Avg	vL	vR	OB	Slg	OPS	bb%	ct%	h%	Eye	xBA	G	L	F	PX	hr/f	SX	SBO	RC/G	RAR	BPV	R$
Pos	78	05	0	0	0	0	0	0							0			0						0					
Age	23	06	0	0	0	0	0	0							0			0						0					
Bats	Left	07	0	0	0	0	0	0							0			0						0					
Health	A	08 aa	265	30	4	28	14	267			319	408	727	7	90	29	0.73	0				80		132	36%	4.62	-4.1	78	$8
PT/Exp	F	09 ARI *	563	78	8	70	11	300	220	310	351	417	768	7	82	35	0.44	258	53	18	29	74	6%	105	13%	4.99	-9.1	37	$20
Consist	A	1st Half	278	38	6	34	6	291			358	428	786	9	83	33	0.63	265	57	16	27	77	10%	104	17%	5.32	-2.0	48	$10
LIMA Plan	C+	2nd Half	285	40	2	36	5	309			343	407	750	5	81	38	0.28	252	50	19	30	71	3%	103	10%	4.66	-7.1	24	$10
Rand Var	-3	10 Proj	521	67	7	61	9	274			325	397	722	7	85	31	0.50	269	52	19	29	75	6%	105	16%	4.46	-15.5	47	$14

5-60-.290 with 5 SB in 455 AB at ARI. Lofty h% masked several weaknesses in debut: meager PX, high GB%, big-time struggles v. LHP (.470 OPS in 100 AB) all say next step is at best sideways, if not back.

Patterson,Eric

			AB	R	HR	RBI	SB	Avg	vL	vR	OB	Slg	OPS	bb%	ct%	h%	Eye	xBA	G	L	F	PX	hr/f	SX	SBO	RC/G	RAR	BPV	R$
Pos	7	05	0	0	0	0	0	0							0			0						0					
Age	27	06 a/a	508	79	11	59	46	270			339	411	750	9	81	32	0.54	0				85		159	39%	4.87	-5.1	60	$23
Bats	Left	07 aa	516	75	12	52	19	261			317	401	718	7	85	29	0.55	0				85		116	21%	4.40	-12.3	61	$15
Health	A	08 2TM *	445	54	8	50	24	242	217	187	294	361	656	7	79	29	0.35	232	39	18	43	84	5%	130	26%	3.55	-21.1	38	$13
PT/Exp	C	09 OAK *	560	77	8	50	35	247	375	269	308	368	676	8	84	28	0.56	239	34	20	46	74	4%	144	31%	3.97	-17.6	58	$16
Consist	B	1st Half	322	42	5	23	20	243			295	366	661	7	87	27	0.57	0				70		145	36%	3.80	-11.9	63	$9
LIMA Plan	D	2nd Half	238	34	4	27	15	252			323	372	695	10	81	30	0.55	243	38	21	41	79	5%	128	25%	4.22	-5.6	46	$8
Rand Var	0	10 Proj	161	22	3	17	10	248			309	376	685	8	82	29	0.49	246	39	20	42	80	5%	131	28%	4.02	-4.6	51	$5

1-11-.287 with 6 SB in 94 AB at OAK. Speed is legit, but OBP a question mark: strong in OAK (.380), but MLEs more skeptical. SBO says he knows how to use his one skill. Needs a role, if he gets one.... UP: 40 SB.

Paulino,Ronny

			AB	R	HR	RBI	SB	Avg	vL	vR	OB	Slg	OPS	bb%	ct%	h%	Eye	xBA	G	L	F	PX	hr/f	SX	SBO	RC/G	RAR	BPV	R$
Pos	2	05 a/a	436	54	14	46	5	265			312	412	724	6	87	28	0.51	0				89		79	4%	4.36	5.8	56	$11
Age	29	06 PIT *	471	39	6	59	1	306	339	300	356	390	747	7	82	36	0.42	242	47	23	31	58	5%	25	1%	4.68	4.4	-3	$12
Bats	Right	07 PIT	457	56	11	55	2	263	407	218	312	389	702	7	83	30	0.42	253	47	17	36	83	8%	44	3%	4.09	-4.5	26	$10
Health	A	08 PIT *	229	21	5	32	0	235	235	202	299	377	676	8	76	29	0.39	243	43	19	38	107	7%	38	3%	3.88	-2.3	21	$3
PT/Exp	D	09 FLA	239	24	8	27	1	272	290	250	341	423	764	9	80	31	0.52	252	39	21	39	96	11%	44	1%	4.95	4.7	31	$6
Consist	B	1st Half	121	11	4	14	1	264			331	413	744	9	78	31	0.44	236	36	20	44	93	10%	60	3%	4.68	1.5	24	$3
LIMA Plan	F	2nd Half	118	13	4	13	0	280			351	432	783	10	82	31	0.62	264	42	23	35	98	12%	17	0%	5.22	3.2	34	$3
Rand Var	-2	10 Proj	224	23	6	27	1	268			331	414	744	9	80	31	0.47	254	42	21	37	96	9%	45	2%	4.70	2.9	30	$5

May finally be finding a role as a bad-side platoon CA; about the only thing he's done consistently well in his career is hit LHPs. If used accordingly, this makes him a nice, low-risk, end-game pickup.

Pearce,Steven

			AB	R	HR	RBI	SB	Avg	vL	vR	OB	Slg	OPS	bb%	ct%	h%	Eye	xBA	G	L	F	PX	hr/f	SX	SBO	RC/G	RAR	BPV	R$
Pos	3	05	0	0	0	0	0	0							0			0						0					
Age	27	06	0	0	0	0	0	0							0			0						0					
Bats	Right	07 PIT *	480	74	15	78	12	293	429	259	342	482	823	7	87	31	0.57	309	48	20	32	117	11%	102	12%	5.59	-7.2	88	$19
Health	A	08 PIT *	495	45	13	64	11	229	321	222	274	378	652	6	82	26	0.34	245	38	21	41	100	7%	80	15%	3.44	-34.6	44	$10
PT/Exp	C	09 PIT *	438	48	13	57	3	227	268	174	300	393	693	9	81	25	0.55	257	38	19	43	113	9%	51	10%	4.15	-32.1	50	$8
Consist	C	1st Half	238	25	7	33	2	228			294	376	670	9	86	24	0.66	206	50	0	50	89	7%	52	16%	3.86	-19.8	49	$5
LIMA Plan	F	2nd Half	200	23	6	24	1	225			307	415	721	11	75	27	0.48	262	37	20	43	144	9%	60	2%	4.59	-11.7	57	$3
Rand Var	+3	10 Proj	226	25	7	30	3	248			307	415	722	8	81	28	0.46	261	38	19	43	112	8%	70	11%	4.43	-11.9	54	$5

4-16-.206 in 165 AB at PIT. At age where everything should be coming together, there's little to see here. Borderline ct%, PX unremarkable, SBs drying up. Optimism of a few years ago fading fast.

Pedroia,Dustin

			AB	R	HR	RBI	SB	Avg	vL	vR	OB	Slg	OPS	bb%	ct%	h%	Eye	xBA	G	L	F	PX	hr/f	SX	SBO	RC/G	RAR	BPV	R$
Pos	4	05 a/a	453	63	10	52	7	276			343	415	758	9	92	28	1.35	0				85		84	8%	5.12	10.1	83	$13
Age	27	06 BOS *	512	56	7	53	1	283	162	212	349	404	754	9	94	29	1.68	295	48	23	30	75	5%	39	4%	5.16	15.1	68	$10
Bats	Right	07 BOS	520	86	8	50	7	317	348	303	374	442	816	8	92	33	1.12	286	43	18	38	83	4%	80	5%	5.70	23.8	77	$17
Health	A	08 BOS	653	118	17	83	20	326	313	331	374	493	867	7	92	34	0.96	306	43	21	36	104	8%	112	11%	6.14	21.7	101	$30
PT/Exp	A	09 BOS	626	115	15	72	20	296	277	302	370	447	817	11	93	30	1.64	289	39	20	41	90	6%	93	14%	5.87	16.5	94	$24
Consist	A	1st Half	306	56	2	35	14	291			369	386	755	11	93	31	1.73	275	42	21	38	65	2%	94	19%	5.29	3.1	75	$11
LIMA Plan	A	2nd Half	320	59	13	37	6	300			371	506	877	10	93	29	1.57	303	37	19	44	114	10%	81	10%	6.42	13.3	109	$13
Rand Var	0	10 Proj	604	105	20	74	17	298			362	476	839	9	93	30	1.35	302	41	20	39	105	9%	94	13%	5.97	21.3	102	$25

Skill-wise, '09 was just about as good as 2008 MVP campaign. Swing is tailor made to Fenway (career OPS split: .896/.756), rise in FB could trade some BA for power, but h% recovery and elite ct% keep BA elite.

Pena,Brayan

			AB	R	HR	RBI	SB	Avg	vL	vR	OB	Slg	OPS	bb%	ct%	h%	Eye	xBA	G	L	F	PX	hr/f	SX	SBO	RC/G	RAR	BPV	R$
Pos	20	05 aaa	282	24	0	22	3	301			358	379	738	8	94	32	1.47	0				58		55	4%	4.95	8.1	57	$6
Age	28	06 ATL *	366	39	2	36	6	287	200	308	327	361	688	6	91	31	0.69	287	58	22	19	48	3%	63	11%	4.11	-2.4	36	$8
Bats	Both	07 aaa	345	38	5	43	5	284			317	387	705	5	90	31	0.48	0				66		60	14%	4.16	-2.0	41	$9
Health	A	08 aaa	234	26	5	25	6	267			328	405	733	8	93	27	1.39	0				85		77	13%	4.84	4.4	83	$6
PT/Exp	F	09 KC *	253	25	9	31	2	267	258	282	307	438	745	5	90	27	0.57	306	51	22	28	97	14%	53	5%	4.61	2.5	65	$6
Consist	A	1st Half	128	14	4	16	2	277			303	444	747	4	92	28	0.44	319	45	26	29	94	11%	72	10%	4.57	1.1	72	$4
LIMA Plan	D	2nd Half	125	11	5	15	0	256			311	432	743	7	88	26	0.67	280	53	20	27	100	17%	10	0%	4.65	1.4	52	$3
Rand Var	+2	10 Proj	281	29	10	37	3	285			330	460	790	6	91	29	0.74	311	51	21	27	99	14%	57	8%	5.18	7.4	75	$9

6-18-.273 in 165 AB at KC. Quietly adds league-average power to borderline-elite ct%, creating a CA with pop and a safe BA floor. High GB% limits breakout potential, but the lack of downside risk still has value.

Pena,Carlos

			AB	R	HR	RBI	SB	Avg	vL	vR	OB	Slg	OPS	bb%	ct%	h%	Eye	xBA	G	L	F	PX	hr/f	SX	SBO	RC/G	RAR	BPV	R$
Pos	3	05 DET *	517	73	28	82	3	254	146	255	342	462	804	12	70	31	0.45	240	38	18	45	146	17%	47	5%	5.66	8.7	37	$17
Age	32	06 BOS *	451	66	21	68	4	249	273	273	339	433	772	12	76	28	0.57	252	48	17	35	115	18%	58	3%	5.13	-3.8	40	$12
Bats	Left	07 TAM	490	99	46	121	1	282	271	286	406	627	1033	17	71	30	0.73	310	37	18	45	233	30%	46	1%	8.96	51.0	121	$28
Health	B	08 TAM	490	76	31	102	1	247	190	280	370	494	864	16	66	31	0.58	246	32	18	50	181	19%	49	1%	6.86	23.1	59	$18
PT/Exp	A	09 TAM	471	91	39	100	3	227	211	236	348	537	885	16	65	25	0.53	263	29	17	54	215	23%	68	5%	7.09	19.8	87	$19
Consist	A	1st Half	282	58	23	55	1	238			354	550	904	15	64	28	0.50	261	27	16	56	224	23%	67	3%	7.49	15.1	89	$12
LIMA Plan	C+	2nd Half	189	33	16	45	2	212			338	519	856	16	67	22	0.58	265	31	17	51	203	25%	71	8%	6.53	4.8	86	$7
Rand Var	+4	10 Proj	497	88	38	107	2	249			368	538	906	16	67	29	0.58	264	32	17	51	199	22%	55	3%	7.32	26.9	79	$21

Two broken fingers on HBP ended season a month early. Pushed PX and hr/f back near '07 peaks, threw in even more FB for good measure. H% suffered, but that and BA vRHP should bounce back some.

Pena,Ramiro

			AB	R	HR	RBI	SB	Avg	vL	vR	OB	Slg	OPS	bb%	ct%	h%	Eye	xBA	G	L	F	PX	hr/f	SX	SBO	RC/G	RAR	BPV	R$
Pos	65	05 aa	233	25	0	11	3	239			265	266	531	3	82	29	0.21	0				20		87	7%	1.90	-16.5	-19	$2
Age	25	06 aa	86	6	1	6	0	186			231	244	475	5	76	23	0.24	0				40		33	6%	1.05	-9.3	-43	($1)
Bats	Both	07 aa	203	23	0	10	7	246			317	291	608	9	84	29	0.64	0				34		92	16%	3.23	-7.0	10	$3
Health	A	08 aa	443	53	2	42	8	250			308	327	636	8	81	30	0.45	0				54		101	11%	3.42	-14.0	16	$7
PT/Exp	F	09 NYY *	271	33	3	19	9	242	120	333	297	336	633	7	83	28	0.45	247	37	24	39	65	3%	98	16%	3.37	-8.8	28	$5
Consist	A	1st Half	86	13	0	7	3	267			308	349	657	5	80	33	0.29	231	34	24	42	61	0%	121	18%	3.58	-2.2	19	$2
LIMA Plan	F	2nd Half	185	20	3	12	6	230			293	330	623	8	84	26	0.54	264	44	24	32	66	6%	74	15%	3.29	-6.5	29	$3
Rand Var	0	10 Proj	97	12	1	7	3	247			302	327	629	7	82	30	0.44	236	36	24	40	53	2%	99	14%	3.33	-3.1	18	$2

1-10-.287 with 4 SB in 115 AB at NYY. Despite swiping bags in NY, speed skills are well short of elite. Of course, that's a far sight better than any other tool in his bag. An unremarkable MI right out of Central Casting.

Pence,Hunter

			AB	R	HR	RBI	SB	Avg	vL	vR	OB	Slg	OPS	bb%	ct%	h%	Eye	xBA	G	L	F	PX	hr/f	SX	SBO	RC/G	RAR	BPV	R$
Pos	9	05	0	0	0	0	0	0							0			0						0					
Age	27	06 aa	523	81	24	79	15	254			317	471	788	8	82	27	0.51	0				124		126	16%	5.19	-0.3	84	$18
Bats	Right	07 HOU *	551	70	20	86	13	315	354	314	354	531	885	6	80	36	0.31	300	49	19	32	135	14%	116	13%	6.31	21.5	78	$24
Health	A	08 HOU	595	78	25	83	11	269	250	275	315	466	781	6	79	30	0.32	268	52	14	34	125	15%	88	15%	4.98	-3.6	58	$22
PT/Exp	A	09 HOU	585	76	25	72	14	282	294	279	347	472	819	9	81	31	0.53	272	53	15	33	115	16%	88	15%	5.58	11.8	64	$23
Consist	B	1st Half	277	43	10	32	8	310			386	502	888	11	84	34	0.77	283	53	14	33	115	13%	104	14%	6.58	13.1	83	$13
LIMA Plan	C+	2nd Half	308	33	15	40	6	256			310	445	755	7	79	28	0.37	261	53	15	33	115	19%	62	16%	4.64	-2.2	43	$10
Rand Var	0	10 Proj	591	77	27	80	10	271			326	481	807	8	81	30	0.42	281	52	15	33	128	17%	94	14%	5.37	6.9	70	$21

As disappointing a $23 season as you'll ever see. Lack of skills growth since MLB arrival, PX, SX, GB%, all trending the wrong way. At age where he should be improving, skill trends say next step likely backward.

RAY MURPHY

105

Pennington,Cliff

		Year	AB	R	HR	RBI	SB	Avg	vL	vR	OB	Slg	OPS	bb%	ct%	h%	Eye	xBA	G	L	F	PX	hr/f	SX	SBO	RC/G	RAR	BPV	R$
Pos	6	05	0	0	0	0	0	0							0			0						0					
Age	26	06	0	0	0	0	0	0							0			0						0					
Bats	Both	07 aa	271	34	2	17	7	222			302	294	595	10	89	24	1.08	0				48		90	11%	3.32	-8.7	45	$3
Health	A	08 OAK	* 539	80	1	34	27	233	289	213	334	284	617	13	87	27	1.14	213	36	19	46	36	0%	116	19%	3.65	-11.2	39	$11
PT/Exp	C	09 OAK	* 568	60	6	48	26	235	200	307	296	334	630	8	85	27	0.58	244	42	18	39	64	3%	109	25%	3.45	-17.5	41	$11
Consist	A	1st Half	269	26	1	23	17	227			296	304	600	9	90	25	0.95	0				51		112	28%	3.34	-9.1	53	$5
LIMA Plan	D+	2nd Half	299	34	5	26	9	241			297	360	657	7	80	29	0.40	240	42	18	39	77	5%	98	22%	3.61	-7.7	29	$6
Rand Var	0	10 Proj	414	51	3	31	18	244			320	324	644	10	86	28	0.79	236	41	18	40	53	2%	109	19%	3.76	-8.1	41	$8

4-21-.279 with 7 SB in 208 AB at OAK. Nice 2H line in OAK largely h%-driven (34%), with a bit of a PX spike (91) thrown in. Neither looks sustainable, so even if he is OAK's 2010 SS, expect some SB and little else.

Peralta,Jhonny

		Year	AB	R	HR	RBI	SB	Avg	vL	vR	OB	Slg	OPS	bb%	ct%	h%	Eye	xBA	G	L	F	PX	hr/f	SX	SBO	RC/G	RAR	BPV	R$
Pos	56	05 CLE	504	82	24	78	0	292	305	288	365	520	885	10	75	35	0.45	276	46	19	35	158	18%	59	1%	6.65	30.3	65	$19
Age	28	06 CLE	569	84	13	68	0	257	267	252	323	385	708	9	73	33	0.37	231	48	19	34	91	9%	57	1%	4.30	-11.9	3	$11
Bats	Right	07 CLE	574	87	21	72	4	270	275	269	340	430	770	10	75	33	0.42	255	47	19	35	111	14%	60	5%	5.07	3.3	26	$17
Health	A	08 CLE	605	104	23	89	3	276	247	285	329	473	802	7	79	32	0.38	280	44	20	36	132	13%	90	3%	5.35	8.1	66	$21
PT/Exp	A	09 CLE	582	57	11	83	0	254	235	261	314	375	689	8	77	31	0.38	240	50	19	31	86	8%	24	1%	4.01	-11.5	2	$10
Consist	B	1st Half	267	25	4	33	0	258			331	363	694	10	76	33	0.46	231	54	17	28	75	7%	32	0%	4.18	-3.9	-3	$4
LIMA Plan	C	2nd Half	315	32	7	50	0	251			300	384	684	7	77	30	0.31	251	47	21	32	95	9%	25	3%	3.85	-7.7	8	$6
Rand Var	0	10 Proj	546	71	15	77	1	264			324	416	740	8	77	32	0.38	257	47	19	33	105	11%	53	2%	4.64	-2.0	26	$13

PX crashed as GB% reached a new high. Should we expect a rebound? PRO: 2H GB% closer to historical norm, outlier hr/f should revert. CON: ct% and GB long-term issues, '08 PX now an outlier. Mild recovery only.

Perez,Fernando

		Year	AB	R	HR	RBI	SB	Avg	vL	vR	OB	Slg	OPS	bb%	ct%	h%	Eye	xBA	G	L	F	PX	hr/f	SX	SBO	RC/G	RAR	BPV	R$
Pos	8	05	0	0	0	0	0	0							0			0						0					
Age	27	06	0	0	0	0	0	0							0			0						0					
Bats	Both	07 aa	393	68	7	27	26	268			369	411	780	14	76	34	0.65	0				97		137	34%	5.56	12.4	51	$14
Health	F	08 TAM	* 571	85	7	36	39	245	188	321	309	339	648	9	73	33	0.34	257	41	38	22	64	8%	153	32%	3.51	-32.1	7	$17
PT/Exp	D	09 TAM	* 70	13	0	4	6	229	154	238	289	271	561	8	59	39	0.21	172	55	15	30	51	0%	121	53%	2.45	-5.0	-71	$2
Consist	D	1st Half	0	0	0	0	0	0																					
LIMA Plan	D	2nd Half	70	13	0	4	6	229			290	271	561	8	59	39	0.21	172	55	15	30	51	0%	121	53%	2.45	-5.0	-71	$2
Rand Var	-5	10 Proj	228	39	2	14	17	250			328	349	677	10	69	35	0.37	224	53	18	29	76	5%	147	40%	4.08	-5.0	4	$7

0-2-.206 in 34 AB at TAM. Spring wrist injury cost him most of the year. Owns elite speed, and '07 MLEs hint at some plate skills, but now at an age where we need more than just hints. Speculative end-game SB play.

Phillips,Brandon

		Year	AB	R	HR	RBI	SB	Avg	vL	vR	OB	Slg	OPS	bb%	ct%	h%	Eye	xBA	G	L	F	PX	hr/f	SX	SBO	RC/G	RAR	BPV	R$
Pos	4	05 aaa	459	60	10	35	5	222			270	340	610	6	85	24	0.42	0				76		78	11%	3.02	-18.8	37	$6
Age	29	06 CIN	536	65	17	75	25	276	299	268	320	427	748	6	84	30	0.40	266	46	19	35	90	11%	102	20%	4.58	-0.2	51	$20
Bats	Right	07 CIN	650	107	30	94	32	288	341	262	322	485	807	5	83	31	0.30	287	47	18	35	111	16%	133	25%	5.15	8.3	73	$31
Health	A	08 CIN	559	80	21	78	23	261	296	247	309	442	751	7	83	28	0.42	274	50	16	34	105	13%	128	25%	4.65	-2.0	71	$22
PT/Exp	A	09 CIN	584	78	20	98	25	276	301	267	326	447	773	7	87	29	0.59	284	50	17	33	101	12%	111	23%	4.99	7.7	79	$25
Consist	A	1st Half	260	38	11	52	11	269			340	469	810	10	90	27	1.04	297	51	15	34	111	14%	113	23%	5.59	8.1	102	$12
LIMA Plan	C+	2nd Half	324	40	9	46	14	281			315	429	744	5	85	31	0.33	273	49	18	33	92	10%	107	23%	4.49	-0.4	58	$13
Rand Var	+1	10 Proj	600	84	23	90	24	283			329	464	793	6	85	30	0.46	282	49	17	34	105	14%	115	21%	5.12	8.6	74	$26

Rock-solid skill set means you can ink in another 20/20. 2H slump likely due to wrist injury he played through. Ct% growth, 1H BB% and xBA, ongoing BA-xBA gap all point to BA upside... UP: .300 BA.

Pierre,Juan

		Year	AB	R	HR	RBI	SB	Avg	vL	vR	OB	Slg	OPS	bb%	ct%	h%	Eye	xBA	G	L	F	PX	hr/f	SX	SBO	RC/G	RAR	BPV	R$
Pos	7	05 FLA	656	96	2	47	57	276	284	267	319	354	672	6	93	29	0.91	307	55	25	20	43	2%	170	39%	4.05	-24.9	71	$27
Age	33	06 CHC	699	87	3	40	58	292	293	291	323	388	711	4	95	31	0.84	299	55	21	24	52	2%	147	41%	4.40	-17.1	75	$26
Bats	Left	07 LA	668	96	0	41	64	293	274	301	327	353	680	5	94	31	0.89	286	53	21	26	36	0%	147	40%	4.08	-24.5	62	$27
Health	A	08 LA	375	44	1	28	40	283	346	257	322	328	650	6	94	30	0.92	281	53	24	23	28	1%	126	45%	3.76	-18.3	48	$16
PT/Exp	B	09 LA	380	57	0	31	30	308	320	304	354	392	746	7	93	33	1.00	292	51	24	24	50	0%	153	35%	4.91	-7.0	73	$17
Consist	B	1st Half	245	37	0	24	22	322			369	408	777	7	92	35	0.95	294	49	25	26	58	0%	140	37%	5.24	-2.2	73	$13
LIMA Plan	C	2nd Half	135	20	0	7	8	281			326	363	689	6	94	30	1.13	288	55	23	22	35	0%	142	32%	4.32	-5.0	61	$4
Rand Var	-2	10 Proj	362	49	0	25	28	293			334	354	688	6	94	31	0.98	286	53	23	24	36	0%	141	35%	4.22	-13.1	59	$14

Demonstrated during Manny suspension that both his plate and speed skills are very much intact. Continue to expect 10 SB per 100 AB. Pencil him in for 30 SB, but if pressed into a full-time role... UP: 60 SB.

Pierzynski,A.J.

		Year	AB	R	HR	RBI	SB	Avg	vL	vR	OB	Slg	OPS	bb%	ct%	h%	Eye	xBA	G	L	F	PX	hr/f	SX	SBO	RC/G	RAR	BPV	R$
Pos	2	05 CHW	460	61	18	56	0	257	230	262	292	420	711	5	85	27	0.34	276	46	22	32	98	14%	35	2%	4.05	0.5	41	$11
Age	33	06 CHW	509	65	16	64	1	295	270	304	324	436	760	4	86	32	0.31	273	44	23	33	84	11%	43	1%	4.60	2.7	33	$14
Bats	Left	07 CHW	472	54	14	50	1	263	252	266	300	403	702	5	86	28	0.38	264	43	18	39	88	9%	37	2%	4.02	-3.7	37	$10
Health	A	08 CHW	534	66	13	60	1	281	286	279	306	416	721	3	87	30	0.27	262	44	18	38	86	7%	50	1%	4.18	-0.2	40	$13
PT/Exp	B	09 CHW	504	57	13	49	1	300	277	307	331	425	756	5	90	31	0.46	272	47	20	33	70	9%	38	1%	4.65	5.3	38	$14
Consist	A	1st Half	235	27	8	24	1	294			328	443	770	5	90	30	0.52	282	48	19	32	79	12%	52	2%	4.81	3.5	51	$7
LIMA Plan	C	2nd Half	269	30	5	25	0	305			335	409	743	4	89	33	0.41	264	46	21	33	63	6%	27	1%	4.51	1.8	26	$7
Rand Var	-2	10 Proj	512	60	12	54	1	277			308	398	706	4	88	30	0.37	265	46	19	35	73	7%	44	1%	4.08	-2.5	34	$11

Late-developing ct% skills continue to pay dividends in BA, although xBA reminds us that he's not really a .300 hitter. Declining FB and PX say quality of his contact dropping, but this is still a worthwhile CA profile.

Pie,Felix

		Year	AB	R	HR	RBI	SB	Avg	vL	vR	OB	Slg	OPS	bb%	ct%	h%	Eye	xBA	G	L	F	PX	hr/f	SX	SBO	RC/G	RAR	BPV	R$
Pos	78	05 aa	240	39	12	23	13	298			341	538	879	6	81	33	0.34	0				152		133	42%	6.19	8.2	98	$12
Age	25	06 aaa	559	78	17	57	18	295			350	468	818	8	81	34	0.44	0				107		107	20%	5.60	6.1	59	$20
Bats	Left	07 CHC	* 406	69	10	57	16	283	111	241	333	436	769	7	81	33	0.39	272	48	20	32	92	9%	137	22%	4.94	-4.9	54	$16
Health	A	08 CHC	* 418	51	9	51	11	249	91	264	290	381	671	5	83	28	0.33	255	49	17	34	83	8%	106	21%	3.68	-22.0	43	$11
PT/Exp	D	09 BAL	252	38	9	29	1	266	250	269	330	437	766	9	77	31	0.41	254	41	21	38	103	12%	82	6%	4.97	-0.3	34	$7
Consist	C	1st Half	107	14	2	8	1	234			299	355	654	9	75	29	0.37	229	40	22	38	74	7%	102	14%	3.58	-4.8	8	$1
LIMA Plan	D+	2nd Half	145	24	7	21	0	290			352	497	849	9	79	33	0.45	271	41	20	39	124	16%	56	0%	5.95	3.8	50	$5
Rand Var	-1	10 Proj	352	52	11	42	6	267			321	428	750	7	79	31	0.39	260	42	21	37	100	10%	100	14%	4.70	-2.8	45	$10

Small-sample 2H surge finally replicates potential shown in MLEs, puts him back on our radar. Only thing he didn't do was run, but if he blends that into newfound plate skills, then.. UP: 20 HR, 20 SB

Podsednik,Scott

		Year	AB	R	HR	RBI	SB	Avg	vL	vR	OB	Slg	OPS	bb%	ct%	h%	Eye	xBA	G	L	F	PX	hr/f	SX	SBO	RC/G	RAR	BPV	R$
Pos	78	05 CHW	507	80	0	25	59	290	330	284	350	349	699	8	85	34	0.63	264	56	20	23	49	0%	129	50%	4.31	-6.2	38	$24
Age	34	06 CHW	524	86	3	45	40	261	216	278	330	353	684	9	82	32	0.56	257	49	23	28	63	2%	146	38%	4.12	-16.9	41	$18
Bats	Left	07 CHW	* 287	40	3	16	14	244	279	229	296	363	659	7	82	29	0.41	277	53	19	28	83	4%	135	32%	3.69	-11.9	50	$6
Health	C	08 COL	162	22	1	15	12	253	167	264	320	333	654	9	83	30	0.57	265	51	24	24	58	3%	121	34%	3.73	-8.3	33	$5
PT/Exp	D	09 CHW	* 579	79	7	50	31	296	320	297	345	402	747	7	86	33	0.54	268	53	18	30	65	5%	119	25%	4.75	-4.2	48	$21
Consist	B	1st Half	261	30	3	22	13	293			346	387	733	8	89	32	0.76	260	53	15	32	56	4%	100	23%	4.67	-2.5	49	$9
LIMA Plan	C	2nd Half	318	49	4	28	18	299			344	415	759	6	84	35	0.42	272	53	19	28	73	5%	130	27%	4.85	-1.4	47	$12
Rand Var	-3	10 Proj	425	60	4	34	26	266			322	365	686	8	84	31	0.52	269	52	20	27	66	4%	128	32%	4.07	-11.3	45	$13

7-48-.304 with 30 SB in 537 AB at CHW. This rebirth was AB-based, as skills remained stable across-the-board (with a little help from h%). Age, health, opportunity questions conspire to make a repeat improbable.

Polanco,Placido

		Year	AB	R	HR	RBI	SB	Avg	vL	vR	OB	Slg	OPS	bb%	ct%	h%	Eye	xBA	G	L	F	PX	hr/f	SX	SBO	RC/G	RAR	BPV	R$
Pos	4	05 2TM	501	84	9	56	4	331	348	324	373	447	820	6	95	34	1.32	317	48	27	25	69	8%	78	4%	5.60	16.6	73	$20
Age	35	06 DET	461	58	4	52	1	295	272	305	320	364	685	4	94	31	0.63	272	51	21	28	42	3%	53	2%	3.98	-1.8	35	$10
Bats	Right	07 DET	587	105	9	67	7	341	326	345	380	458	838	6	95	35	1.23	309	45	24	31	72	5%	87	5%	5.79	27.4	77	$23
Health	A	08 DET	580	90	8	58	7	307	321	301	346	417	764	6	93	32	0.81	278	47	19	35	69	4%	93	5%	4.95	0.9	67	$18
PT/Exp	A	09 DET	618	82	10	72	7	285	266	294	324	396	721	6	93	30	0.78	273	43	20	37	64	5%	88	5%	4.46	-8.1	61	$16
Consist	B	1st Half	282	31	5	33	3	255			295	387	682	5	93	26	0.76	278	47	17	36	77	5%	76	6%	4.07	-7.1	67	$5
LIMA Plan	C+	2nd Half	336	51	5	39	4	310			348	405	753	6	93	32	0.80	269	40	23	37	53	4%	86	5%	4.80	-1.2	52	$11
Rand Var	0	10 Proj	524	77	7	58	5	294			333	398	731	6	93	31	0.86	280	45	21	34	63	4%	87	4%	4.61	-1.3	62	$15

Rough 1H was just a h%-driven nightmare, 2H production and skills look vintage. Uptick in FB closes door on any more 2007-like BA. Age, free agency make more 550+ AB seasons less likely, but BA still has value.

RAY MURPHY

Posada,Jorge			AB	R	HR	RBI	SB	Avg	vL	vR	OB	Slg	OPS	bb%	ct%	h%	Eye	xBA	G	L	F	PX	hr/f	SX	SBO	RC/G	RAR	BPV	R$
Pos	2	05 NYY	474	67	19	71	1	262	281	246	352	430	782	12	80	29	0.70	251	43	17	39	108	13%	39	1%	5.30	17.6	45	$14
Age	39	06 NYY	465	65	23	93	3	277	263	284	365	492	857	12	79	31	0.66	270	38	20	42	132	15%	63	2%	6.24	24.1	68	$17
Bats	Both	07 NYY	506	91	20	90	2	338	331	341	422	543	966	13	81	39	0.76	298	40	22	37	140	13%	58	1%	7.70	44.9	80	$24
Health	F	08 NYY	168	18	3	22	0	268	255	274	359	411	770	13	77	33	0.63	252	40	21	40	108	6%	38	0%	5.34	5.5	34	$3
PT/Exp	C	09 NYY	383	55	22	81	1	285	290	282	364	522	886	11	74	33	0.48	272	36	21	43	157	18%	34	1%	6.67	25.8	54	$16
Consist	D	1st Half	164	22	10	33	1	268			362	500	862	13	77	29	0.63	257	40	15	46	141	17%	32	2%	6.29	9.5	57	$6
LIMA Plan	D+	2nd Half	219	33	12	48	0	297			366	539	905	10	71	37	0.38	283	33	27	41	170	19%	23	0%	7.01	16.5	49	$10
Rand Var	-1	10 Proj	344	48	15	63	1	276			361	482	844	12	76	32	0.56	271	38	21	41	139	14%	49	1%	6.14	18.5	56	$12

Ct% and Eye continue to drop. However, he took advantage of bandbox of a home park with more fly balls and highest PX since 2000. Power will keep him in upper tier of AL catchers as long as health allows.

Posey,Buster			AB	R	HR	RBI	SB	Avg	vL	vR	OB	Slg	OPS	bb%	ct%	h%	Eye	xBA	G	L	F	PX	hr/f	SX	SBO	RC/G	RAR	BPV	R$
Pos	2	05	0	0	0	0	0	0							0			0						0					
Age	23	06	0	0	0	0	0	0							0			0						0					
Bats	Right	07	0	0	0	0	0	0							0			0						0					
Health	A	08	0	0	0	0	0	0							0			0						0					
PT/Exp	F	09 SF	* 148	19	4	19	0	277		167	344	426	769	9	84	31	0.63	248	62	8	31	94	10%	56	2%	5.07	3.4	48	$4
Consist	F	1st Half	0	0	0	0	0	0																					
LIMA Plan	F	2nd Half	148	19	4	19	0	277			344	426	769	9	84	31	0.63	248	62	8	31	94	10%	56	2%	5.07	3.4	48	$4
Rand Var	-2	10 Proj	283	40	7	40	0	269			343	421	764	10	82	30	0.63	250	62	8	31	100	10%	58	3%	5.07	6.7	48	$8

0-0-.118 in 17 AB at SF. Made jump from A to AAA look easy, with .902 OPS in 131 AB's. Power is still developing, but he appears ready to hit for BA right away. His long-term prospects are outstanding.

Powell,Landon			AB	R	HR	RBI	SB	Avg	vL	vR	OB	Slg	OPS	bb%	ct%	h%	Eye	xBA	G	L	F	PX	hr/f	SX	SBO	RC/G	RAR	BPV	R$
Pos	2	05	0	0	0	0	0	0							0			0						0					
Age	28	06 aa	41	4	1	4	0	244			295	317	613	7	68	33	0.23	0				43		21	0%	2.79	-1.9	-70	$1
Bats	Both	07 aa	236	38	11	32	1	240			318	419	738	10	83	25	0.68	0				103		64	1%	4.63	1.9	56	$6
Health	A	08 aaa	300	29	10	37	0	178			283	310	593	13	78	19	0.66	0				84		21	1%	2.87	-12.9	11	$1
PT/Exp	F	09 OAK	140	19	7	30	0	229	128	267	299	429	727	9	74	26	0.39	248	38	18	44	129	15%	28	0%	4.41	0.6	29	$4
Consist	D	1st Half	64	7	2	15	0	203			271	375	646	9	77	23	0.40	243	38	16	46	121	9%	26	0%	3.46	-1.6	30	$1
LIMA Plan	F	2nd Half	76	12	5	15	0	250			321	474	795	10	72	28	0.38	252	38	20	42	136	22%	29	0%	5.27	2.2	28	$3
Rand Var	+1	10 Proj	125	16	6	21	0	240			321	414	735	11	77	27	0.51	242	38	18	44	110	13%	28	1%	4.57	1.2	26	$3

7-30-.229 in 140 AB at OAK. Showed improved power, though the sample size is fairly small. With ct% heading south, and h% staying there, it's not likely his role or value will increase a great deal.

Prado,Martin			AB	R	HR	RBI	SB	Avg	vL	vR	OB	Slg	OPS	bb%	ct%	h%	Eye	xBA	G	L	F	PX	hr/f	SX	SBO	RC/G	RAR	BPV	R$
Pos	453	05 aa	143	15	1	10	3	259			329	336	665	9	90	28	1.00	0				50		76	14%	4.06	-1.2	42	$2
Age	26	06 ATL	* 459	48	4	45	4	270	310	154	315	349	664	6	85	31	0.44	224	49	14	37	49	3%	65	6%	3.70	-12.0	14	$8
Bats	Right	07 aaa	395	55	4	37	5	301			351	397	748	7	90	33	0.79	0				63		73	7%	4.84	5.4	50	$11
Health	B	08 ATL	228	36	2	33	3	320	283	349	378	461	838	8	87	36	0.72	281	42	23	35	93	3%	110	6%	5.99	7.4	75	$9
PT/Exp	D	09 ATL	450	64	11	49	1	307	301	309	358	464	822	7	87	33	0.61	281	44	20	37	107	8%	36	3%	5.63	13.6	61	$15
Consist	B	1st Half	141	19	4	15	0	305			368	482	850	9	91	31	1.08	294	49	17	34	114	9%	31	3%	6.08	6.0	84	$5
LIMA Plan	C+	2nd Half	309	45	7	34	1	307			353	456	810	7	85	34	0.48	274	41	21	38	104	7%	43	4%	5.42	7.6	52	$11
Rand Var	-3	10 Proj	512	72	15	58	4	301			355	473	828	8	88	32	0.69	291	44	21	36	107	9%	71	5%	5.71	15.4	76	$18

PX trending in right direction while maintaining high ct%. Remained productive when given full-time opportunity in 2H. Power may be at its peak, but high BA and multi-position eligibility help provide value.

Pujols,Albert			AB	R	HR	RBI	SB	Avg	vL	vR	OB	Slg	OPS	bb%	ct%	h%	Eye	xBA	G	L	F	PX	hr/f	SX	SBO	RC/G	RAR	BPV	R$
Pos	3	05 STL	591	129	41	117	16	330	300	340	424	609	1034	14	89	32	1.49	334	42	20	38	156	21%	106	9%	8.30	42.2	142	$41
Age	30	06 STL	535	119	49	137	7	331	336	329	429	671	1100	15	91	29	1.84	334	37	18	45	170	23%	67	5%	8.98	42.0	150	$38
Bats	Right	07 STL	565	99	32	103	2	327	367	313	428	568	996	15	90	32	1.71	313	42	19	39	133	16%	32	4%	7.98	28.1	107	$29
Health	A	08 STL	524	100	37	116	7	357	411	333	463	653	1116	17	90	35	1.93	341	40	22	37	167	21%	53	5%	9.43	49.4	143	$37
PT/Exp	A	09 STL	568	124	47	135	16	327	338	324	441	658	1099	17	89	30	1.80	335	39	16	46	186	20%	81	10%	9.21	40.8	164	$43
Consist	B	1st Half	267	61	30	77	10	337			462	745	1207	19	88	29	1.94	359	36	16	48	223	26%	68	13%	10.47	27.9	190	$25
LIMA Plan	C	2nd Half	301	63	17	58	6	319			421	581	1002	15	89	31	1.66	315	41	15	43	154	15%	87	7%	8.09	12.8	139	$18
Rand Var	+1	10 Proj	558	114	41	123	11	326			435	628	1062	16	89	31	1.79	332	40	18	42	168	20%	73	7%	8.76	38.3	148	$37

Other-worldly 1H performance, followed by typical, outstanding 2H. He even led his team in SB. Hard to find any flaws in this skill set.
UP: .350 BA and finally hits the 50 HR mark. Why not?

Punto,Nick			AB	R	HR	RBI	SB	Avg	vL	vR	OB	Slg	OPS	bb%	ct%	h%	Eye	xBA	G	L	F	PX	hr/f	SX	SBO	RC/G	RAR	BPV	R$
Pos	46	05 MIN	394	45	4	26	13	239	210	246	302	335	637	8	78	30	0.42	247	51	21	28	69	5%	113	20%	3.41	-8.7	20	$7
Age	32	06 MIN	459	73	1	45	17	290	331	267	356	373	728	9	85	34	0.69	259	46	24	30	53	1%	133	15%	4.72	7.8	44	$13
Bats	Both	07 MIN	472	53	1	25	16	210	175	226	292	271	563	10	81	26	0.61	226	51	15	35	46	1%	106	17%	2.67	-19.8	15	$3
Health	C	08 MIN	338	43	2	28	15	284	302	274	346	382	728	9	83	34	0.56	252	45	21	35	69	2%	117	20%	4.64	-2.5	42	$10
PT/Exp	C	09 MIN	359	56	1	38	16	228	236	225	340	284	625	15	81	28	0.87	228	48	19	33	43	1%	103	15%	3.61	-14.4	18	$7
Consist	C	1st Half	156	20	0	15	6	212			309	237	546	12	83	25	0.85	220	43	21	36	21	0%	80	14%	2.61	-11.3	1	$2
LIMA Plan	D	2nd Half	203	36	1	23	10	241			364	320	684	16	78	30	0.89	235	52	17	31	60	2%	110	16%	4.42	-3.1	29	$5
Rand Var	+1	10 Proj	392	55	2	35	17	242			333	315	648	12	81	29	0.72	237	48	19	33	53	1%	113	17%	3.81	-10.6	27	$8

Drew a lot of walks, which is important when the only thing you bring to the table is speed. But he's a batting average drag, so how desperate are you for stolen bases?

Quentin,Carlos			AB	R	HR	RBI	SB	Avg	vL	vR	OB	Slg	OPS	bb%	ct%	h%	Eye	xBA	G	L	F	PX	hr/f	SX	SBO	RC/G	RAR	BPV	R$
Pos	7	05 aaa	452	68	16	62	6	268			345	445	789	10	89	27	1.08	0				104		91	5%	5.43	5.2	90	$15
Age	28	06 ARI	* 484	74	16	72	5	262	171	280	331	469	800	9	86	28	0.72	290	46	16	38	125	10%	99	4%	5.51	3.6	93	$14
Bats	Right	07 ARI	* 344	52	9	52	2	242	172	230	294	400	694	7	80	28	0.37	261	43	16	41	110	8%	69	7%	4.03	-13.8	46	$7
Health	C	08 CHW	480	96	36	100	7	288	246	303	374	571	944	12	83	28	0.83	304	41	15	43	164	21%	78	7%	7.14	30.9	114	$26
PT/Exp	C	09 CHW	351	47	21	56	3	236	213	245	298	456	754	8	85	22	0.60	271	37	16	47	118	15%	54	4%	4.67	-3.5	70	$10
Consist	F	1st Half	131	20	8	20	1	229			289	458	747	8	87	21	0.65	292	39	19	42	122	17%	54	4%	4.60	-1.6	80	$4
LIMA Plan	C+	2nd Half	220	27	13	36	2	241			304	455	759	8	84	23	0.57	257	35	15	51	116	14%	44	4%	4.72	-1.9	61	$7
Rand Var	+4	10 Proj	477	74	27	80	5	268			335	493	827	9	84	27	0.64	279	39	16	45	129	15%	70	5%	5.62	9.0	81	$18

8 HR in April, then plantar fasciitis and low h% contributed to struggles the rest of the way. Underwent surgery to remove pin from wrist in October. 2008 PX still represents his upside, but don't pay full value for it.

Quinlan,Robb			AB	R	HR	RBI	SB	Avg	vL	vR	OB	Slg	OPS	bb%	ct%	h%	Eye	xBA	G	L	F	PX	hr/f	SX	SBO	RC/G	RAR	BPV	R$
Pos	7	05 ANA	134	17	5	14	0	231	289	137	270	403	672	5	81	25	0.27	269	51	18	30	114	15%	45	4%	3.58	-4.6	39	$2
Age	33	06 LAA	234	28	9	32	2	321	326	313	340	491	832	3	88	34	0.25	282	53	17	30	95	14%	60	5%	5.32	0.9	54	$9
Bats	Right	07 LAA	178	21	3	21	3	247	269	203	302	348	650	7	85	28	0.52	243	48	14	38	69	5%	60	11%	3.58	-7.8	29	$3
Health	A	08 LAA	164	15	1	11	4	262	282	244	320	311	631	8	83	31	0.50	217	48	18	34	26	2%	90	11%	3.35	-7.2	-3	$3
PT/Exp	F	09 LAA	115	13	2	14	1	243	257	220	275	339	614	4	74	31	0.17	229	55	18	27	70	9%	54	8%	2.80	-7.6	-22	$2
Consist	A	1st Half	61	5	0	4	1	213			238	279	517	3	72	30	0.12	212	47	19	35	63	0%	58	9%	1.56	-6.5	-35	$0
LIMA Plan	F	2nd Half	54	8	2	10	0	278			316	407	723	5	76	33	0.23	246	63	17	20	76	25%	48	7%	4.14	-1.4	-8	$2
Rand Var	-1	10 Proj	99	11	2	11	1	253			295	340	635	6	79	30	0.29	230	53	17	30	57	8%	53	9%	3.14	-5.4	-9	$2

Has managed to hang on to part-time role with Angels for 7 years, but doesn't have much to offer. AB continue to drop, and recent history of PX, xBA reveal that this gig is probably nearing an end.

Quintero,Humberto			AB	R	HR	RBI	SB	Avg	vL	vR	OB	Slg	OPS	bb%	ct%	h%	Eye	xBA	G	L	F	PX	hr/f	SX	SBO	RC/G	RAR	BPV	R$
Pos	2	05 HOU	* 254	23	6	31	1	220			244	346	590	3	84	24	0.21	285	61	20	18	82	16%	44	4%	2.60	-9.3	24	$3
Age	31	06 HOU	* 313	33	3	31	3	262			298	366	664	5	86	30	0.36	310	61	28	11	69	10%	77	4%	3.68	-6.0	33	$5
Bats	Right	07 HOU	* 230	17	3	16	0	240			254	336	590	2	85	27	0.12	303	55	30	15	63	11%	40	4%	2.57	-12.9	6	$1
Health	B	08 HOU	* 298	25	4	24	0	205	273	215	230	277	507	3	84	23	0.20	216	59	12	29	46	5%	43	3%	1.64	-24.1	-6	$0
PT/Exp	F	09 HOU	157	11	4	14	0	236	273	226	268	376	644	4	74	29	0.17	219	57	10	32	101	11%	36	0%	3.21	-4.9	-2	$2
Consist	C	1st Half	60	3	0	9	0	283			283	350	633	0	83	34	0.00	232	58	16	26	44	0%	56	0%	2.97	-2.2	-13	$1
LIMA Plan	F	2nd Half	97	8	4	5	0	206			260	392	651	7	68	26	0.23	198	57	6	37	144	16%	12	0%	3.42	-2.5	6	$1
Rand Var	-2	10 Proj	159	12	3	14	0	233			259	347	607	3	79	28	0.17	231	58	12	30	77	8%	52	2%	2.73	-7.3	3	$1

Has hit just .213 in 409 career AB vs RH. High GB% will make it hard to maintain PX, and h% should drop, as he can't beat out many of those GB's. He only holds on to a part-time job because of his defense.

BRIAN RUDD

Raburn,Ryan

			AB	R	HR	RBI	SB	Avg	vL	vR	OB	Slg	OPS	bb%	ct%	h%	Eye	xBA	G	L	F	PX	hr/f	SX	SBO	RC/G	RAR	BPV	R$
Pos	7	05 aaa	466	53	16	57	7	234			294	399	694	8	81	26	0.44	0				101		99	9%	4.02	-14.3	51	$10
Age	29	06 aaa	451	62	18	73	15	257			328	454	782	10	75	30	0.43	0				127		118	16%	5.25	0.5	59	$15
Bats	Right	07 DET *	453	81	19	84	14	277	259	338	353	489	842	11	78	32	0.54	283	41	19	39	141	13%	122	14%	6.05	13.2	84	$20
Health	A	08 DET	182	26	4	20	3	236	238	235	298	368	666	8	73	30	0.33	227	47	14	39	99	8%	92	9%	3.71	-6.3	17	$4
PT/Exp	D	09 DET *	308	53	20	52	7	279	278	298	345	535	880	9	76	31	0.42	266	38	14	47	152	18%	90	14%	6.34	11.8	74	$14
Consist	F	1st Half	145	28	9	26	4	246			326	500	826	11	74	27	0.46	261	39	11	49	163	18%	79	16%	5.77	3.3	74	$6
LIMA Plan	C	2nd Half	163	25	11	26	3	309			362	566	929	8	78	34	0.39	269	37	16	46	143	19%	89	13%	6.82	8.2	72	$8
Rand Var	-2	10 Proj	**355**	**57**	**17**	**54**	**8**	**270**			**336**	**484**	**819**	**9**	**76**	**31**	**0.41**	**258**	**42**	**15**	**43**	**135**	**15%**	**100**	**13%**	**5.64**	**6.9**	**62**	**$14**

16-45.291 in 261 AB at DET. Finally brought minor-league PX to the majors. 2008's PX drop may just be small sample mirage. If he can maintain '09 FB rate and find 400+ AB's... UP: 25 HR

Ramirez,Alexei

			AB	R	HR	RBI	SB	Avg	vL	vR	OB	Slg	OPS	bb%	ct%	h%	Eye	xBA	G	L	F	PX	hr/f	SX	SBO	RC/G	RAR	BPV	R$
Pos	6	05 CUB	331	50	14	46	8	302			347	492	840	6	89	31	0.62								11%	5.68			
Age	29	06 CUB	212	28	7	30	3	274			345	420	764	10	92	27	1.44								8%	5.15			
Bats	Right	07 CUB	340	51	20	68	7	335			418	562	979	12	89	33	1.30								8%	7.58			
Health	A	08 CHW	480	65	21	77	13	290	312	281	315	475	790	4	87	30	0.30	284	47	17	37	106	14%	88	20%	4.89	7.7	69	$20
PT/Exp	B	09 CHW	542	71	15	68	14	277	370	248	337	389	726	8	88	29	0.74	246	46	16	38	60	8%	77	11%	4.51	0.9	41	$17
Consist	D	1st Half	283	36	10	39	12	272			325	403	727	7	88	28	0.63	257	50	15	35	69	12%	80	18%	4.41	-0.3	46	$10
LIMA Plan	C+	2nd Half	259	35	5	29	2	282			350	375	724	9	88	30	0.87	234	42	17	41	51	5%	60	5%	4.60	1.1	32	$7
Rand Var	-2	10 Proj	**544**	**74**	**18**	**79**	**10**	**281**			**338**	**422**	**759**	**8**	**88**	**29**	**0.72**	**262**	**46**	**16**	**38**	**77**	**10%**	**79**	**10%**	**4.86**	**7.2**	**56**	**$18**

Patience improved in second MLB season, but where did his power go? 7 HR in June, PX under 70 in every other month. Ct% limits BA downside, should reach double digits in HR and SB. But '08 PX could be a fluke.

Ramirez,Aramis

			AB	R	HR	RBI	SB	Avg	vL	vR	OB	Slg	OPS	bb%	ct%	h%	Eye	xBA	G	L	F	PX	hr/f	SX	SBO	RC/G	RAR	BPV	R$
Pos	5	05 CHC	463	72	31	92	0	302	355	284	351	568	919	7	87	29	0.58	318	39	20	41	153	19%	28	1%	6.52	22.1	95	$23
Age	32	06 CHC	594	93	38	119	2	291	261	301	346	561	907	8	89	27	0.79	303	35	18	47	141	15%	66	2%	6.46	16.1	108	$27
Bats	Right	07 CHC	506	72	26	101	0	310	395	286	364	549	914	8	87	32	0.65	300	39	18	44	136	13%	47	0%	6.60	13.6	89	$22
Health	C	08 CHC	554	97	27	111	2	289	239	305	373	518	891	12	83	31	0.79	284	31	20	48	145	12%	56	2%	6.62	19.5	90	$25
PT/Exp	B	09 CHC	306	46	15	65	2	317	350	312	374	516	891	8	86	33	0.65	278	35	21	44	115	13%	59	3%	6.33	9.8	72	$16
Consist	A	1st Half	66	8	4	16	0	364			408	591	999	7	88	37	0.63	318	31	28	41	126	17%	10	0%	7.40	3.7	72	$4
LIMA Plan	C+	2nd Half	240	38	11	49	2	304			365	496	861	9	85	32	0.66	270	36	20	45	112	12%	65	4%	6.03	5.9	70	$12
Rand Var	-4	10 Proj	**542**	**83**	**28**	**114**	**2**	**303**			**365**	**526**	**891**	**9**	**86**	**31**	**0.69**	**290**	**34**	**21**	**45**	**130**	**14%**	**58**	**2%**	**6.38**	**16.5**	**84**	**$26**

Dealt with shoulder issues all season, which appears to have sapped some of his power. With off-season of rest, should bounce back there. Struggles vs LH in 2008 proved to be a fluke, so BA should stay high.

Ramirez,Hanley

			AB	R	HR	RBI	SB	Avg	vL	vR	OB	Slg	OPS	bb%	ct%	h%	Eye	xBA	G	L	F	PX	hr/f	SX	SBO	RC/G	RAR	BPV	R$
Pos	6	05 aa	461	57	5	45	22	258			308	360	668	7	89	28	0.65	0				64		122	29%	3.90	-5.0	59	$13
Age	26	06 FLA	633	119	17	59	51	292	307	288	350	480	830	8	80	34	0.44	274	44	21	35	118	10%	164	40%	5.83	26.6	81	$31
Bats	Right	07 FLA	639	125	29	81	51	332	399	312	382	562	944	8	85	36	0.55	299	40	18	42	137	13%	141	36%	6.98	43.8	109	$41
Health	A	08 FLA	589	125	33	67	35	301	258	313	395	540	935	14	79	33	0.75	287	46	17	37	148	19%	126	24%	7.29	44.2	102	$35
PT/Exp	A	09 FLA	576	101	24	106	27	342	316	352	405	543	948	10	82	38	0.60	280	39	20	42	131	12%	93	18%	7.21	38.7	84	$37
Consist	A	1st Half	290	50	13	58	12	348			409	572	982	9	84	38	0.65	299	38	21	41	146	13%	75	21%	7.57	22.3	97	$20
LIMA Plan	D+	2nd Half	286	51	11	48	15	336			401	514	915	10	81	39	0.56	261	40	19	42	115	11%	110	16%	6.83	16.3	69	$18
Rand Var	-5	10 Proj	**598**	**111**	**26**	**88**	**24**	**314**			**383**	**521**	**904**	**10**	**82**	**35**	**0.62**	**281**	**41**	**19**	**40**	**130**	**13%**	**112**	**18%**	**6.70**	**35.2**	**88**	**$33**

H% more inflated than usual, which led to batting title. SBO and SX still falling, meaning 30 SB no longer a lock. Series of nagging injuries may have been a factor. Another $40 season possibly still within reach.

Ramirez,Manny

			AB	R	HR	RBI	SB	Avg	vL	vR	OB	Slg	OPS	bb%	ct%	h%	Eye	xBA	G	L	F	PX	hr/f	SX	SBO	RC/G	RAR	BPV	R$
Pos	7	05 BOS	554	112	45	144	1	292	236	313	382	594	976	13	79	30	0.67	310	37	24	39	185	27%	56	1%	7.63	44.8	106	$32
Age	38	06 BOS	449	79	35	102	0	321	326	319	444	619	1064	18	77	35	0.98	299	36	22	42	181	24%	26	1%	9.19	48.1	100	$24
Bats	Right	07 BOS	483	84	20	88	0	296	344	279	386	493	879	13	81	33	0.77	286	38	22	41	129	13%	40	0%	6.58	20.5	67	$19
Health	A	08 2TM	552	102	37	121	3	332	308	339	423	601	1024	14	78	37	0.70	300	38	23	39	173	22%	61	2%	8.45	47.9	96	$33
PT/Exp	B	09 LA	352	62	19	63	0	290	270	295	409	531	940	17	77	33	0.88	288	33	25	42	160	17%	45	1%	7.62	20.3	85	$16
Consist	C	1st Half	92	22	6	20	0	348			492	641	1133	22	82	38	1.53	328	39	24	37	190	22%	28	0%	10.28	11.1	133	$6
LIMA Plan	C+	2nd Half	260	40	13	43	0	269			377	492	869	15	75	31	0.70	272	31	26	44	148	15%	55	1%	6.61	7.9	68	$10
Rand Var	+1	10 Proj	**485**	**90**	**27**	**97**	**0**	**301**			**411**	**544**	**955**	**16**	**78**	**34**	**0.86**	**292**	**36**	**24**	**40**	**157**	**17%**	**46**	**0%**	**7.71**	**29.9**	**86**	**$24**

Before 50-game suspension, his BPI's were otherworldly. After he he returned, BPIs reverted to his typical worldly level. From here, it becomes a yearly battle between skill versus age, health and motivation.

Ramirez,Max

			AB	R	HR	RBI	SB	Avg	vL	vR	OB	Slg	OPS	bb%	ct%	h%	Eye	xBA	G	L	F	PX	hr/f	SX	SBO	RC/G	RAR	BPV	R$
Pos	2	05	0	0	0	0	0	0							0			0						0					
Age	25	06	0	0	0	0	0	0							0			0						0					
Bats	Right	07	0	0	0	0	0	0							0			0						0					
Health	A	08 TEX *	326	49	18	52	2	289	71	281	361	515	876	10	78	32	0.52	262	33	17	50	141	14%	66	4%	6.34	19.7	69	$13
PT/Exp	F	09 aa	274	23	4	34	1	203			274	287	562	9	73	26	0.37	0				65		36	1%	2.32	-16.7	-24	$1
Consist	F	1st Half	214	18	3	25	0	206			260	292	551	7	73	27	0.27	0				67		24	0%	2.09	-14.5	-31	$1
LIMA Plan	F	2nd Half	60	5	1	9	1	192			322	272	594	16	74	24	0.74	0				58		34	5%	3.02	-2.4	-13	$0
Rand Var	0	10 Proj	**204**	**22**	**6**	**29**	**2**	**235**			**322**	**371**	**693**	**11**	**76**	**28**	**0.52**	**217**	**33**	**17**	**50**	**93**	**8%**	**41**	**4%**	**4.13**	**-0.7**	**14**	**$4**

Huge step back, as ct% decline was accompanied by big drop in power. Wrist injury may be partially to blame. Still young enough to bounce back, but future not looking as bright, and not much short-term value.

Ramirez,Wilkin

			AB	R	HR	RBI	SB	Avg	vL	vR	OB	Slg	OPS	bb%	ct%	h%	Eye	xBA	G	L	F	PX	hr/f	SX	SBO	RC/G	RAR	BPV	R$
Pos	7	05	0	0	0	0	0	0							0			0						0					
Age	24	06	0	0	0	0	0	0							0			0						0					
Bats	Right	07 aa	121	14	2	13	6	207			256	298	553	6	71	27	0.23	0				63		120	30%	2.05	-12.1	-15	$2
Health	A	08 a/a	469	62	15	59	22	258			311	426	737	7	75	31	0.31	0				112		126	32%	4.56	-8.1	44	$17
PT/Exp	F	09 aaa	434	61	15	45	29	239			297	402	698	8	71	30	0.28	0				110		146	39%	4.09	-16.0	32	$16
Consist	C	1st Half	250	38	8	23	22	243			306	388	694	8	70	32	0.30	0				96		153	43%	4.06	-9.4	22	$10
LIMA Plan	D	2nd Half	184	23	7	23	8	234			284	420	704	6	72	29	0.24	0				129		120	32%	4.12	-6.6	40	$5
Rand Var	0	10 Proj	**135**	**18**	**4**	**16**	**7**	**237**			**291**	**404**	**695**	**7**	**72**	**30**	**0.27**	**0**	**0**	**0**	**0**	**113**		**136**	**35%**	**4.03**	**-4.9**	**37**	**$4**

1-3-.364 in 11 AB at DET.
PRO: Intriguing power/speed combo, particularly for his age.
CON: Ct% low, and actually regressed in 2009.
Verdict: 20/20 potential down the road, but not ready yet.

Ransom,Cody

			AB	R	HR	RBI	SB	Avg	vL	vR	OB	Slg	OPS	bb%	ct%	h%	Eye	xBA	G	L	F	PX	hr/f	SX	SBO	RC/G	RAR	BPV	R$
Pos	5	05 aaa	262	25	5	23	5	191			236	292	528	6	71	25	0.20	0				73		88	11%	1.66	-24.9	-18	$1
Age	34	06 aaa	380	48	16	46	2	201			277	381	658	9	75	22	0.42	0				115		59	3%	3.54	-20.4	32	$5
Bats	Right	07 HOU *	538	53	19	56	13	170	333	192	225	317	542	7	69	21	0.23	210	35	15	50	107	10%	80	19%	1.83	-66.9	2	$3
Health	C	08 NYY *	466	62	22	62	7	212			279	409	688	8	71	25	0.32	0				136		81	11%	3.90	-14.3	38	$10
PT/Exp	D	09 NYY *	175	35	3	25	2	206	158	220	305	366	671	13	71	27	0.50	231	38	15	47	124	5%	123	5%	4.06	-3.4	49	$3
Consist	C	1st Half	102	14	2	15	1	200			258	361	620	7	72	26	0.28	236	44	12	44	127	5%	102	6%	3.17	-4.8	36	$1
LIMA Plan	F	2nd Half	73	21	1	10	1	214			362	372	734	19	71	28	0.80	214	17	25	58	119	4%	132	4%	5.18	1.1	59	$2
Rand Var	0	10 Proj	**93**	**16**	**3**	**12**	**1**	**204**			**292**	**377**	**669**	**11**	**71**	**26**	**0.43**	**229**	**34**	**17**	**49**	**126**	**8%**	**110**	**8%**	**3.88**	**-2.6**	**42**	**$2**

0-10-.190 in 79 AB at NYY. A pro since '98, he's got 4200+ AB in the minors and 262 AB in 7 years in the Majors. But his legacy will be as A-Rod's injury replacement for a month in 2009.

Rasmus,Colby

			AB	R	HR	RBI	SB	Avg	vL	vR	OB	Slg	OPS	bb%	ct%	h%	Eye	xBA	G	L	F	PX	hr/f	SX	SBO	RC/G	RAR	BPV	R$
Pos	8	05	0	0	0	0	0	0							0			0						0					
Age	24	06	0	0	0	0	0	0							0			0						0					
Bats	Left	07 aa	472	76	22	59	15	239			323	456	778	11	82	25	0.67	0				136		102	17%	5.20	9.6	89	$15
Health	A	08 a/a	331	44	8	28	12	218			298	329	627	10	83	24	0.69	0				71		86	18%	3.40	-17.0	39	$6
PT/Exp	D	09 STL	474	72	16	52	3	251	160	277	304	407	711	7	80	28	0.38	243	35	20	46	100	9%	79	3%	4.17	-7.9	40	$13
Consist	C	1st Half	233	33	8	29	1	270			306	455	761	5	81	30	0.27	261	34	19	48	124	9%	68	2%	4.70	-0.2	56	$7
LIMA Plan	C+	2nd Half	241	39	8	23	2	232			302	361	663	9	79	26	0.47	227	36	20	44	77	10%	80	5%	3.62	-8.1	21	$5
Rand Var	-2	10 Proj	**542**	**80**	**17**	**55**	**11**	**256**			**323**	**401**	**724**	**9**	**81**	**29**	**0.52**	**242**	**35**	**20**	**45**	**91**	**9%**	**91**	**10%**	**4.44**	**-3.9**	**45**	**$16**

Smooth transition to majors with impressive 1H. Different story in 2H, as Eye improved, but power tanked. .474 OPS vs LH shows he may not be ready for everyday role. Still has bright future, but may take some time.

BRIAN RUDD

Reddick,Josh			AB	R	HR	RBI	SB	Avg	vL	vR	OB	Slg	OPS	bb%	ct%	h%	Eye	xBA	G	L	F	PX	hr/f	SX	SBO	RC/G	RAR	BPV	R$
Pos	7	05	0	0	0	0	0	0							0			0						0					
Age	23	06	0	0	0	0	0	0							0			0						0					
Bats	Left	07	0	0	0	0	0	0							0			0						0					
Health	A	08 aa	117	18	4	20	2	199			262	354	616	8	83	21	0.51	0				91		112	13%	3.11	-7.5	56	$2
PT/Exp	F	09 BOS	* 386	49	13	36	5	231	200	167	295	415	709	8	78	26	0.42	242	31	17	52	117	8%	90	13%	4.26	-8.9	53	$7
Consist	C	1st Half	171	25	7	14	3	257			321	474	795	9	81	28	0.50	0				131		95	15%	5.32	1.6	78	$5
LIMA Plan	F	2nd Half	215	24	6	22	2	209			274	367	641	8	76	25	0.37	226	31	17	52	104	7%	79	11%	3.37	-11.1	30	$2
Rand Var	0	10 Proj	161	22	5	20	2	224			287	400	686	8	80	25	0.45	239	31	17	52	108	8%	103	13%	3.96	-5.0	56	$3

2-4-.169 in 59 AB at BOS. Has shown flashes of plus power (1H in AA, 125 PX in majors), but FB-heavy swing (51% in minors) limits his BA upside. Be patient and observe while he works out the kinks.

Redmond,Mike			AB	R	HR	RBI	SB	Avg	vL	vR	OB	Slg	OPS	bb%	ct%	h%	Eye	xBA	G	L	F	PX	hr/f	SX	SBO	RC/G	RAR	BPV	R$
Pos	2	05 MIN	148	17	1	26	0	311	345	289	338	392	730	4	91	34	0.43	280	53	24	23	59	3%	30	0%	4.41	1.6	28	$5
Age	39	06 MIN	179	20	0	23	0	341	443	275	355	413	769	2	90	38	0.22	284	46	27	27	57	0%	29	0%	4.73	1.5	20	$5
Bats	Right	07 MIN	272	23	1	38	0	294	330	277	338	353	691	6	92	32	0.78	253	44	21	35	43	1%	18	0%	4.18	-0.8	21	$5
Health	A	08 MIN	129	14	0	12	0	287	277	297	313	333	647	4	91	31	0.45	282	47	28	25	37	0%	31	0%	3.54	-2.4	14	$2
PT/Exp	F	09 MIN	135	9	0	7	0	237	320	188	295	289	583	8	86	28	0.58	249	55	21	24	36	0%	40	0%	2.92	-5.5	2	$0
Consist	B	1st Half	83	4	0	4	0	229			297	277	574	9	89	26	0.89	249	51	23	26	38	0%	9	0%	3.01	-3.2	9	($0)
LIMA Plan	F	2nd Half	52	5	0	3	0	250			291	308	599	5	81	31	0.30	235	62	17	21	33	0%	76	0%	2.84	-2.2	-15	$0
Rand Var	+3	10 Proj	113	10	0	10	0	257			298	321	619	6	88	29	0.48	264	52	22	26	44	0%	49	0%	3.27	-3.2	14	$1

Injuries took a bite out of ct% and LD%, and predictably, BA suffered. BA, OPS, RC/G... pick a metric and the trend pretty much suggests that it's time to walk away. And if he doesn't, you should.

Reed,Jeremy			AB	R	HR	RBI	SB	Avg	vL	vR	OB	Slg	OPS	bb%	ct%	h%	Eye	xBA	G	L	F	PX	hr/f	SX	SBO	RC/G	RAR	BPV	R$
Pos	7	05 SEA	488	61	3	45	12	254	200	269	321	352	673	9	85	29	0.65	256	49	19	33	73	2%	90	17%	4.04	-10.0	45	$9
Age	29	06 SEA	212	27	6	17	2	217		243	256	377	633	5	85	23	0.35	255	51	13	37	83	9%	115	13%	3.26	-12.7	55	$2
Bats	Left	07 aa	563	70	10	47	10	235			282	349	631	6	86	26	0.47	0				74		86	15%	3.34	-32.0	44	$8
Health	B	08 SEA	* 435	49	7	46	7	274	115	285	322	390	712	7	88	30	0.60	283	52	20	28	77	6%	74	9%	4.35	-6.2	51	$10
PT/Exp	D	09 NYM	161	9	0	9	0	242	400	232	303	304	607	8	78	31	0.39	228	57	19	24	47	0%	56	7%	3.04	-12.4	-17	$0
Consist	C	1st Half	78	5	0	3	0	282			317	346	663	5	73	39	0.19	228	52	24	24	51	0%	63	5%	3.59	-4.4	-36	$1
LIMA Plan	F	2nd Half	83	4	0	6	0	205			290	265	555	11	82	25	0.67	228	62	15	24	43	0%	54	9%	2.64	-7.8	2	($0)
Rand Var	-2	10 Proj	143	12	1	11	1	245			301	332	633	7	83	29	0.47	251	56	18	26	61	4%	66	9%	3.39	-9.0	16	$1

Does anyone still remember when he used to be a hot prospect? The Minor League Baseball Analyst ranked him the #19 prospect in 2004. That's not a knock on MLBA, just a reminder of the fragility of fame.

Reimold,Nolan			AB	R	HR	RBI	SB	Avg	vL	vR	OB	Slg	OPS	bb%	ct%	h%	Eye	xBA	G	L	F	PX	hr/f	SX	SBO	RC/G	RAR	BPV	R$
Pos	7	05	0	0	0	0	0	0							0			0						0					
Age	26	06	0	0	0	0	0	0							0			0						0					
Bats	Right	07 aa	186	24	10	28	2	271			324	501	825	7	79	30	0.37	0				150		45	12%	5.56	1.9	66	$6
Health	A	08 aa	507	73	22	70	6	252			322	441	764	9	86	26	0.75	0				111		76	7%	4.96	-2.5	76	$15
PT/Exp	D	09 BAL	* 467	67	23	69	14	299	271	284	381	517	898	12	79	34	0.62	275	48	14	37	134	17%	89	11%	6.74	22.4	73	$21
Consist	B	1st Half	248	38	17	44	6	320			398	590	988	11	81	34	0.68	291	48	13	39	156	22%	56	8%	7.70	17.9	90	$14
LIMA Plan	B	2nd Half	219	29	6	25	8	274			361	434	795	12	76	34	0.57	250	49	15	36	107	10%	100	14%	5.60	3.7	45	$7
Rand Var	-4	10 Proj	534	75	24	75	11	275			350	477	827	10	81	30	0.60	275	48	15	37	124	15%	81	10%	5.75	12.0	70	$19

15-45-.279 in 358 AB at BAL. 2H drop-off was likely part torn Achilles and part MLB pitchers making adjustments. Power skills are real, and with LD% more likely to go up than down, there's some BA potential here.

Renteria,Edgar			AB	R	HR	RBI	SB	Avg	vL	vR	OB	Slg	OPS	bb%	ct%	h%	Eye	xBA	G	L	F	PX	hr/f	SX	SBO	RC/G	RAR	BPV	R$
Pos	6	05 BOS	623	100	8	70	9	276	326	253	335	385	720	8	84	32	0.65	270	47	24	29	76	5%	99	7%	4.48	-1.4	44	$17
Age	35	06 ATL	598	100	14	70	17	293	333	281	359	436	796	9	85	33	0.70	282	47	22	31	90	9%	97	13%	5.43	18.0	62	$22
Bats	Right	07 ATL	494	87	12	57	11	332	349	323	389	470	859	9	84	38	0.60	285	46	23	31	89	9%	91	8%	6.09	21.3	55	$22
Health	B	08 DET	503	69	10	55	6	270	366	239	320	382	702	7	87	29	0.58	272	46	22	32	69	7%	81	6%	4.19	-2.0	44	$12
PT/Exp	B	09 SF	460	50	5	48	7	250	231	257	309	328	637	8	85	28	0.57	250	48	21	31	54	4%	75	7%	3.47	-16.1	23	$9
Consist	C	1st Half	256	31	2	36	5	266			326	340	666	8	85	31	0.59	253	47	22	31	56	3%	65	9%	3.85	-6.0	22	$7
LIMA Plan	D+	2nd Half	204	19	3	12	2	230			286	314	600	7	85	26	0.53	246	49	20	31	52	6%	69	4%	3.00	-10.2	20	$2
Rand Var	+2	10 Proj	438	57	7	45	7	267			324	367	690	8	85	30	0.57	262	47	22	31	65	6%	81	7%	4.08	-6.2	36	$11

Power and speed have been slipping away, dragging BA with them. Off-season elbow surgery may lead to a slight rebound, but age and the skill trends are more telling. Key stat: used to be a lefty killer.

Reyes,Jose			AB	R	HR	RBI	SB	Avg	vL	vR	OB	Slg	OPS	bb%	ct%	h%	Eye	xBA	G	L	F	PX	hr/f	SX	SBO	RC/G	RAR	BPV	R$
Pos	6	05 NYM	696	99	7	58	60	273	288	269	300	386	687	4	89	30	0.35	270	47	20	33	63	3%	182	44%	3.93	-0.5	70	$29
Age	27	06 NYM	647	122	19	81	64	300	330	288	353	487	840	8	87	32	0.65	288	45	21	34	98	10%	168	45%	5.85	27.4	96	$37
Bats	Both	07 NYM	681	119	12	57	78	280	318	266	354	421	775	10	89	30	0.99	270	42	19	40	81	5%	164	48%	5.33	17.6	91	$35
Health	F	08 NYM	688	113	16	68	56	297	280	303	358	475	833	9	88	32	0.80	294	44	23	33	100	8%	163	36%	5.90	24.8	101	$35
PT/Exp	A	09 NYM	147	18	2	15	11	279	400	248	358	395	752	11	87	31	0.95	252	41	19	40	71	4%	127	27%	5.09	1.8	67	$6
Consist	B	1st Half	147	18	2	15	11	279			358	395	752	11	87	31	0.95	252	41	19	40	71	4%	127	27%	5.09	1.8	67	$6
LIMA Plan	B+	2nd Half	0	0	0	0	0	0																					
Rand Var	-1	10 Proj	600	93	11	59	34	285			350	429	779	9	88	31	0.82	271	43	20	37	83	6%	151	27%	5.29	12.4	83	$25

News on the hammy appears good, and age gives hope he can pick up where he left off. But we won't really know until he hits the field, and his value is utterly tied to speed. A risky play coming off this kind of injury.

Reynolds,Mark			AB	R	HR	RBI	SB	Avg	vL	vR	OB	Slg	OPS	bb%	ct%	h%	Eye	xBA	G	L	F	PX	hr/f	SX	SBO	RC/G	RAR	BPV	R$
Pos	53	05	0	0	0	0	0	0							0			0						0					
Age	27	06 aa	114	20	8	18	0	264			322	528	849	8	70	31	0.29	0				177		48	4%	6.08	2.8	54	$4
Bats	Right	07 ARI	* 500	84	23	79	3	278	278	279	347	495	842	10	69	36	0.34	251	36	20	44	153	15%	92	4%	6.29	9.7	46	$18
Health	A	08 ARI	539	87	28	97	11	239	279	226	320	458	778	11	62	33	0.31	229	36	19	45	172	19%	109	10%	5.67	4.8	43	$20
PT/Exp	A	09 ARI	578	98	44	102	24	260	235	266	346	543	889	12	61	34	0.34	252	35	17	47	223	26%	93	22%	7.40	38.7	77	$31
Consist	C	1st Half	285	50	21	56	13	270			354	554	908	11	63	35	0.35	260	42	14	44	219	27%	103	24%	7.58	20.3	83	$17
LIMA Plan	B+	2nd Half	293	48	23	46	11	249			337	532	870	12	60	33	0.33	246	28	21	51	227	26%	76	20%	7.22	18.3	69	$14
Rand Var	-2	10 Proj	572	96	37	98	15	248			329	502	831	11	63	32	0.33	245	35	19	47	193	22%	103	15%	6.34	18.4	63	$25

Incredible season puts to rest any worries about job security, but doesn't erase concerns about BA. Slides in ct%, LD% create dangerous downside if power goes from superhuman back to merely elite.

Rios,Alex			AB	R	HR	RBI	SB	Avg	vL	vR	OB	Slg	OPS	bb%	ct%	h%	Eye	xBA	G	L	F	PX	hr/f	SX	SBO	RC/G	RAR	BPV	R$
Pos	98	05 TOR	481	71	10	59	14	262	249	271	303	397	700	6	79	31	0.28	255	49	19	31	90	8%	129	20%	4.02	-9.8	40	$14
Age	29	06 TOR	450	68	17	82	15	302	295	305	353	516	868	7	80	35	0.39	276	37	22	42	134	11%	123	18%	6.18	6.5	81	$20
Bats	Right	07 TOR	643	114	24	85	17	297	345	283	352	498	850	8	84	32	0.53	285	36	20	44	125	10%	125	12%	5.94	7.9	91	$27
Health	A	08 TOR	635	91	15	79	32	291	289	292	337	461	799	6	82	33	0.39	275	41	21	38	113	7%	134	25%	5.32	-0.8	76	$26
PT/Exp	A	09 2AL	582	63	17	71	24	247	261	242	292	395	688	6	82	28	0.35	251	43	16	41	92	9%	102	22%	3.86	-25.5	45	$16
Consist	C	1st Half	319	38	9	37	13	260			312	417	729	7	83	29	0.44	266	43	19	38	97	9%	104	19%	4.45	-8.2	56	$10
LIMA Plan	C+	2nd Half	263	25	8	34	11	232			268	369	637	5	80	26	0.25	231	42	13	45	86	8%	79	26%	3.13	-17.7	25	$6
Rand Var	+2	10 Proj	525	68	15	67	21	267			313	430	743	6	82	30	0.37	262	41	18	41	104	9%	115	22%	4.57	-11.9	60	$18

PRO: 2009 PX drop caused by slide in 2B and 3B, not HR; only 29, still owns '06/'07 skills; playing in HR-friendly park.
CON: Four-year PX slide, skills tanked even more at CHW.
Net: Hope for rebound, go xtra $.

Rivera,Juan			AB	R	HR	RBI	SB	Avg	vL	vR	OB	Slg	OPS	bb%	ct%	h%	Eye	xBA	G	L	F	PX	hr/f	SX	SBO	RC/G	RAR	BPV	R$
Pos	7	05 ANA	350	46	15	59	1	271	252	286	316	454	771	6	87	27	0.52	274	46	17	37	106	13%	43	12%	4.85	1.4	62	$11
Age	32	06 LAA	448	65	23	85	0	310	351	293	358	525	882	7	87	32	0.56	281	51	16	33	121	18%	23	3%	6.13	11.7	67	$18
Bats	Right	07 LAA	* 104	6	2	19	0	224	276	286	247	341	588	3	90	23	0.30	243	44	15	41	77	5%	10	0%	2.78	-7.1	31	$1
Health	D	08 LAA	256	31	12	45	1	246	233	253	290	438	728	6	87	24	0.48	261	37	14	48	111	11%	40	4%	4.33	-4.0	63	$7
PT/Exp	D	09 LAA	529	72	25	88	0	287	333	271	333	478	811	6	89	28	0.63	280	44	18	38	101	14%	31	1%	5.31	4.5	62	$19
Consist	C	1st Half	260	32	14	46	0	304			347	515	862	6	90	30	0.65	280	47	16	37	112	16%	17	0%	5.84	5.9	69	$11
LIMA Plan	D+	2nd Half	269	40	11	42	0	271			319	442	762	7	88	27	0.61	276	41	20	40	91	12%	51	1%	4.79	-1.7	58	$8
Rand Var	-1	10 Proj	490	60	21	84	0	273			315	454	769	6	88	27	0.53	272	42	17	41	101	12%	34	2%	4.82	-2.1	58	$15

Great season, but...
- PX, hr/f weren't as good as '06.
- Past his peak age
- One healthy season doesn't erase his recent injury history.
He can do this again. Just don't assume he will.

BRANDON KRUSE

Rivera,Mike			AB	R	HR	RBI	SB	Avg	vL	vR	OB	Slg	OPS	bb%	ct%	h%	Eye	xBA	G	L	F	PX	hr/f	SX	SBO	RC/G	RAR	BPV	R$
Pos	2	05 aaa	213	23	11	29	2	222			245	432	676	3	86	21	0.21	0				121		69	9%	3.53	-2.4	67	$5
Age	34	06 MIL	* 355	40	14	61	3	257	226	279	298	429	727	6	83	28	0.33	239	38	14	48	103	10%	43	7%	4.26	-0.8	38	$10
Bats	Right	07 aaa	349	29	15	48	4	178			222	346	568	5	79	18	0.27	0				103		42	17%	2.23	-24.4	25	$3
Health	A	08 MIL	62	8	1	14	2	306	176	356	368	435	803	9	84	35	0.60	275	44	23	33	94	6%	63	11%	5.51	2.2	49	$3
PT/Exp	F	09 MIL	114	10	2	14	1	228	267	214	318	342	660	12	72	30	0.47	208	33	18	49	94	5%	35	3%	3.79	-1.6	-2	$2
Consist	F	1st Half	46	2	0	2	1	261			292	348	639	4	76	34	0.18	209	33	17	50	84	0%	37	10%	3.28	-1.3	-7	$0
LIMA Plan	F	2nd Half	68	8	2	12	0	206			333	338	672	16	69	27	0.62	207	32	19	49	101	9%	20	0%	4.02	-0.5	-2	$1
Rand Var	-2	10 Proj	115	12	3	18	1	217			282	326	608	8	78	26	0.41	227	38	20	42	75	7%	45	5%	2.95	-4.6	6	$2

Remember when HE used to be a prospect too? You can't really tell from these small samples, but he still has a little pop. On a good day. Those two 2009 HR? They were both hit on August 13.

Roberts,Brian			AB	R	HR	RBI	SB	Avg	vL	vR	OB	Slg	OPS	bb%	ct%	h%	Eye	xBA	G	L	F	PX	hr/f	SX	SBO	RC/G	RAR	BPV	R$
Pos	4	05 BAL	561	92	18	73	27	314	273	332	387	515	902	11	85	34	0.81	298	35	27	37	128	10%	125	21%	6.78	41.0	104	$28
Age	33	06 BAL	563	85	10	55	36	286	235	308	350	410	760	9	88	31	0.83	271	44	21	35	77	6%	126	25%	5.04	14.8	72	$21
Bats	Both	07 BAL	621	103	12	57	50	290	268	299	379	432	810	13	84	33	0.90	260	36	20	45	95	5%	132	27%	5.83	32.2	79	$28
Health	A	08 BAL	614	107	9	57	40	295	313	289	379	448	827	12	83	34	0.80	280	40	24	36	107	5%	144	26%	6.05	20.1	87	$26
PT/Exp	A	09 BAL	632	110	16	79	30	283	294	278	358	451	809	10	82	32	0.66	273	36	22	42	114	7%	105	21%	5.67	13.4	75	$26
Consist	A	1st Half	309	57	7	36	16	278			354	434	787	10	83	32	0.68	256	32	21	48	104	6%	115	24%	5.41	4.3	72	$12
LIMA Plan	B	2nd Half	323	53	9	43	14	288			363	467	830	11	82	33	0.64	289	41	23	36	123	9%	93	18%	5.93	9.1	76	$13
Rand Var	-1	10 Proj	614	105	13	69	28	279			358	440	799	11	83	32	0.74	276	38	22	40	110	7%	122	20%	5.61	16.0	81	$23

A hitter in transition: note PX growth with ct% dip, and two-year SB/SBO declines. For now, it means cross-category value. But he'll never be a slugger, so as speed fades (in a year or 3), so will his value.

Roberts,Ryan			AB	R	HR	RBI	SB	Avg	vL	vR	OB	Slg	OPS	bb%	ct%	h%	Eye	xBA	G	L	F	PX	hr/f	SX	SBO	RC/G	RAR	BPV	R$
Pos	4	05 aa	338	48	14	39	5	248			344	437	780	13	70	32	0.48	0				138		92	5%	5.48	11.4	44	$9
Age	30	06 aaa	362	39	10	43	5	260			310	423	733	7	77	31	0.32	0				115		65	10%	4.51	1.6	36	$8
Bats	Right	07 aaa	337	37	10	38	1	220			309	361	670	11	77	25	0.57	0				93		40	3%	3.85	-5.2	20	$4
Health	A	08 aa	453	48	7	45	11	239			309	359	668	9	85	27	0.67	0				76		105	12%	3.95	-12.0	53	$8
PT/Exp	F	09 ARI	* 347	48	8	32	12	277	325	250	359	413	772	11	82	32	0.73	245	38	19	43	88	6%	102	14%	5.24	7.1	56	$12
Consist	B	1st Half	102	16	0	5	4	255			345	324	668	12	75	34	0.56	199	35	17	48	67	0%	84	12%	4.03	-1.5	7	$2
LIMA Plan	C	2nd Half	245	32	8	27	8	286			365	450	815	11	85	31	0.85	265	39	20	41	96	9%	101	14%	5.72	8.3	73	$9
Rand Var	-4	10 Proj	442	56	10	42	11	256			335	386	721	11	81	30	0.63	238	37	19	44	86	6%	101	11%	4.57	-0.6	46	$11

7-25-.279 in 351 AB at ARI. Why this "4-A" guy may stick:
- owns 2H skills, ct% growth
- more SBO netted SB
- another year or so at peak

Does his team believe? Don't ink in AB until after FA period.

Rodriguez,Alex			AB	R	HR	RBI	SB	Avg	vL	vR	OB	Slg	OPS	bb%	ct%	h%	Eye	xBA	G	L	F	PX	hr/f	SX	SBO	RC/G	RAR	BPV	R$
Pos	5	05 NYY	605	124	48	130	21	321	300	330	409	610	1019	13	77	35	0.65	293	45	16	40	179	26%	94	13%	8.29	61.9	108	$41
Age	35	06 NYY	572	113	35	121	15	290	294	289	387	523	909	14	76	33	0.65	267	42	18	40	143	20%	93	10%	6.99	31.9	74	$29
Bats	Right	07 NYY	583	143	54	156	24	314	272	327	410	645	1055	14	79	32	0.79	326	41	17	42	199	28%	98	15%	8.64	59.8	136	$45
Health	B	08 NYY	510	104	35	103	18	302	263	316	381	573	953	11	77	33	0.56	296	42	18	40	175	22%	94	14%	7.39	35.4	101	$31
PT/Exp	A	09 NYY	444	78	30	100	14	286	277	289	395	532	927	15	78	31	0.82	284	42	20	38	141	23%	85	10%	7.20	31.5	84	$24
Consist	B	1st Half	163	25	13	41	2	239			389	515	904	20	82	21	1.38	293	45	16	39	149	25%	37	3%	7.02	11.4	101	$7
LIMA Plan	B	2nd Half	281	53	17	59	12	313			399	541	940	12	76	36	0.59	275	41	22	37	136	22%	97	14%	7.33	20.3	69	$17
Rand Var	0	10 Proj	529	103	35	119	13	295			393	545	939	14	78	32	0.74	286	42	19	39	151	22%	86	9%	7.31	37.5	89	$30

Hip injury predictably took a small bite out of skills. But SX came back in 2H, and hr/f was as solid as ever. Now in his mid-30's, health likely stays an issue. But with the off-season to heal, a rebound is a good bet.

Rodriguez,Ivan			AB	R	HR	RBI	SB	Avg	vL	vR	OB	Slg	OPS	bb%	ct%	h%	Eye	xBA	G	L	F	PX	hr/f	SX	SBO	RC/G	RAR	BPV	R$
Pos	2	05 DET	504	71	14	50	7	276	294	271	291	444	736	2	82	31	0.12	284	48	22	30	111	11%	112	10%	4.26	3.4	55	$14
Age	38	06 DET	547	74	13	69	8	300	340	284	332	437	769	5	84	34	0.30	276	50	21	28	83	10%	96	8%	4.77	5.5	44	$17
Bats	Right	07 DET	502	50	11	63	2	281	302	274	294	420	714	2	81	33	0.09	275	52	19	28	96	10%	60	4%	3.97	-4.6	24	$11
Health	A	08 2AL	398	44	7	35	10	276	289	272	316	394	710	5	83	32	0.34	277	56	20	24	78	9%	103	11%	4.17	-0.3	39	$10
PT/Exp	B	09 2TM	425	55	10	47	1	249	283	240	280	384	663	4	78	30	0.20	258	54	18	28	91	11%	69	3%	3.46	-10.2	17	$8
Consist	A	1st Half	221	24	7	30	0	244			277	398	675	4	78	28	0.21	265	51	21	27	96	15%	63	4%	3.58	-4.5	19	$4
LIMA Plan	D	2nd Half	204	31	3	17	1	255			283	368	651	4	78	31	0.18	249	56	16	29	86	7%	69	2%	3.32	-5.6	13	$4
Rand Var	+1	10 Proj	365	45	7	38	1	266			295	389	684	4	80	31	0.21	262	54	19	27	85	8%	63	2%	3.74	-5.4	18	$7

The decline continues, and it's across the board. Saw an emotion-fueled surge upon return to TEX in August, but predictably, it didn't last. There's simply nothing left to recommend in these skills.

Rodriguez,Luis			AB	R	HR	RBI	SB	Avg	vL	vR	OB	Slg	OPS	bb%	ct%	h%	Eye	xBA	G	L	F	PX	hr/f	SX	SBO	RC/G	RAR	BPV	R$
Pos	64	05 MIN	* 305	34	3	34	2	260	233	276	328	358	686	9	88	29	0.84	258	43	21	36	66	3%	62	6%	4.25	-2.8	44	$5
Age	30	06 MIN	115	11	2	6	0	235	250	231	318	322	640	11	86	26	0.88	234	46	19	34	53	6%	19	0%	3.68	-2.5	16	$1
Bats	Both	07 MIN	155	18	2	12	1	219	226	218	275	303	579	7	91	23	0.86	250	54	13	34	49	4%	72	3%	2.99	-6.2	41	$1
Health	A	08 SD	* 298	30	1	18	1	273	238	309	319	344	663	6	94	29	1.23	266	49	19	31	47	1%	59	2%	4.03	-5.1	48	$4
PT/Exp	F	09 SD	208	18	2	16	1	202	294	172	322	260	582	15	89	22	1.61	223	41	18	40	38	3%	31	1%	3.39	-8.2	27	$0
Consist	B	1st Half	99	11	1	7	0	202			336	273	609	17	86	23	1.43	217	36	18	46	50	3%	22	0%	3.68	-3.0	25	$0
LIMA Plan	D	2nd Half	109	7	1	9	1	202			310	248	557	13	92	21	1.89	227	46	18	35	27	3%	28	3%	3.15	-5.2	26	$0
Rand Var	+3	10 Proj	187	18	2	14	1	225			310	299	610	11	91	24	1.33	244	46	18	36	46	3%	58	2%	3.58	-5.7	41	$1

Some odd stuff: superb ct% rendered useless by utter lack of PX, SX; 15% bb% somehow netting a .322 OB; and most bizarre, was actually a starting SS for a while. At least THAT won't happen again.

Rodriguez,Sean			AB	R	HR	RBI	SB	Avg	vL	vR	OB	Slg	OPS	bb%	ct%	h%	Eye	xBA	G	L	F	PX	hr/f	SX	SBO	RC/G	RAR	BPV	R$
Pos	4	05	0	0	0	0	0	0							0			0						0					
Age	25	06	0	0	0	0	0	0							0			0						0					
Bats	Right	07 aa	508	76	15	66	14	236			302	386	688	9	77	28	0.40	0				104		92	19%	3.97	-5.9	36	$13
Health	A	08 LAA	* 415	75	20	53	6	247	178	213	311	461	772	8	77	28	0.41	258	41	12	47	141	13%	103	8%	4.99	1.2	72	$13
PT/Exp	D	09 a/a	385	75	26	84	8	264			346	534	879	11	70	31	0.42	0				176		127	9%	6.67	21.7	84	$19
Consist	C	1st Half	232	38	18	56	6	240			299	518	817	8	69	26	0.27	274	70	0	30	181	38%	102	14%	5.58	5.9	69	$11
LIMA Plan	D	2nd Half	153	36	8	29	2	301			411	557	968	16	72	37	0.67	0				168		117	5%	8.24	14.8	90	$8
Rand Var	-1	10 Proj	188	36	10	32	3	261			339	490	829	11	74	30	0.45	251	38	13	49	150	14%	111	9%	5.89	6.8	72	$8

2-4-.200 in 25 AB at LAA. The key to the Scott Kazmir trade put on a HR display at AAA. Power is exciting for a MI, but ct% issues (122 K in 459 AB) suggest ML pitchers will find holes in his swing for a while.

Rolen,Scott			AB	R	HR	RBI	SB	Avg	vL	vR	OB	Slg	OPS	bb%	ct%	h%	Eye	xBA	G	L	F	PX	hr/f	SX	SBO	RC/G	RAR	BPV	R$
Pos	5	05 STL	196	28	5	28	1	235	237	234	321	383	704	11	86	25	0.89	272	35	23	42	95	7%	70	6%	4.47	-1.9	64	$4
Age	35	06 STL	521	94	22	95	7	296	259	310	364	518	882	10	87	31	0.81	289	33	20	48	133	10%	77	8%	6.42	13.6	98	$23
Bats	Right	07 STL	392	55	8	58	5	265	204	287	329	398	727	9	86	29	0.66	261	38	20	43	85	6%	81	7%	4.59	-11.6	54	$10
Health	D	08 TOR	408	58	11	50	5	262	250	266	337	431	768	10	83	29	0.65	267	36	21	44	113	7%	94	5%	5.14	3.1	71	$11
PT/Exp	B	09 2TM	475	76	11	67	5	305	374	283	365	455	820	9	87	33	0.73	278	37	23	41	97	7%	70	6%	5.69	10.2	66	$18
Consist	B	1st Half	255	43	6	30	4	333			388	494	883	8	89	36	0.79	305	34	29	37	106	7%	69	6%	6.39	9.9	78	$11
LIMA Plan	C	2nd Half	220	33	5	37	1	273			339	409	748	9	85	30	0.67	244	39	16	45	87	6%	62	6%	4.84	-0.4	48	$7
Rand Var	-3	10 Proj	408	62	10	58	4	279			346	434	781	9	85	31	0.70	269	37	21	43	100	7%	80	6%	5.25	2.8	66	$13

Bought 1H BA with atypical ct% and h%; 2H showed true level. Continued poor hr/f validates same trend, and shows HR power is gone. Add in health risk, and it all says to bid using 2007-08 value, not 2009.

Rollins,Jimmy			AB	R	HR	RBI	SB	Avg	vL	vR	OB	Slg	OPS	bb%	ct%	h%	Eye	xBA	G	L	F	PX	hr/f	SX	SBO	RC/G	RAR	BPV	R$
Pos	6	05 PHI	677	115	12	54	41	290	278	292	336	431	767	6	90	31	0.66	295	44	24	32	85	6%	166	26%	5.01	20.0	90	$29
Age	31	06 PHI	689	127	25	83	36	277	277	277	332	478	810	6	88	28	0.71	294	44	19	37	111	11%	149	24%	5.49	22.2	104	$30
Bats	Both	07 PHI	716	139	30	94	41	296	321	286	341	531	872	6	88	30	0.58	295	36	20	44	124	11%	169	27%	6.10	33.1	117	$37
Health	A	08 PHI	556	76	11	59	47	277	288	272	345	437	782	9	90	29	1.05	302	45	24	31	95	7%	156	32%	5.40	12.3	105	$25
PT/Exp	A	09 PHI	672	100	21	77	31	250	230	257	296	423	719	6	90	25	0.63	282	40	19	41	103	8%	132	27%	4.40	-5.3	95	$24
Consist	B	1st Half	307	41	6	27	11	205			247	319	566	5	89	21	0.50	249	42	16	42	71	5%	112	28%	2.64	-19.7	59	$5
LIMA Plan	A	2nd Half	365	59	15	50	20	288			337	510	846	7	90	29	0.75	307	38	22	41	130	11%	135	27%	5.85	12.3	121	$18
Rand Var	+4	10 Proj	641	100	23	74	38	278			329	479	808	7	89	28	0.73	298	41	21	38	115	11%	154	28%	5.45	16.1	112	$29

Q: Should we disregard 1H? The h%, LD%, PX, and hr/f all show total power outage; when other BPIs are solid, this cries "injury." We may never know. But 2H was as potent as ever. A: For now, we say "yes."

ROD TRUESDELL

Romero,Alex		AB	R	HR	RBI	SB	Avg	vL	vR	OB	Slg	OPS	bb%	ct%	h%	Eye	xBA	G	L	F	PX	hr/f	SX	SBO	RC/G	RAR	BPV	R$
Pos 79	05 aa	509	56	12	66	10	277			319	415	733	6	88	30	0.51	0				87		72	17%	4.50	-8.0	57	$15
Age 27	06 a/a	403	47	5	41	20	253			319	352	671	9	90	27	0.93	0				59		110	25%	4.08	-13.7	58	$10
Bats Left	07 aaa	533	66	5	52	10	278			317	378	695	5	92	30	0.67	0				63		89	15%	4.19	-15.6	56	$12
Health A	08 ARI	* 308	36	4	27	7	265	174	241	294	381	675	4	88	29	0.33	266	47	19	34	72	4%	112	14%	3.78	-14.7	53	$7
PT/Exp D	09 ARI	* 424	45	3	54	8	287	192	261	342	387	729	8	89	32	0.78	277	55	18	26	66	3%	87	10%	4.69	-10.4	53	$12
Consist B	1st Half	288	32	2	36	6	308			365	410	774	8	92	33	1.13	319	67	22	11	67	6%	78	11%	5.29	-2.2	64	$9
LIMA Plan F	2nd Half	136	13	1	18	2	243			295	338	633	7	83	29	0.43	254	55	18	27	63	3%	94	6%	3.38	-8.8	27	$2
Rand Var -2	10 Proj	98	11	1	11	2	265			311	366	677	6	88	29	0.55	268	52	19	29	64	4%	91	12%	3.96	-4.3	45	$2

1-18-.248 in 145 AB at ARI. BPV says there's consistency with his mediocrity. High ct% + bb% spike give hope of more, but MIA power and high GB% say he's a one trick SB pony at best. 2H tailspin big warning too.

Rosales,Adam		AB	R	HR	RBI	SB	Avg	vL	vR	OB	Slg	OPS	bb%	ct%	h%	Eye	xBA	G	L	F	PX	hr/f	SX	SBO	RC/G	RAR	BPV	R$
Pos 5	05	0	0	0	0	0	0							0			0						0					
Age 27	06	0	0	0	0	0	0							0			0						0					
Bats Right	07 aa	255	41	11	25	3	242			321	462	783	10	77	27	0.50	0				143		91	13%	5.27	0.2	72	$6
Health A	08 aaa	432	54	9	44	6	246			274	387	662	4	84	28	0.24	0				92		108	8%	3.51	-20.7	49	$9
PT/Exp F	09 CIN	* 339	44	9	35	4	242	255	200	315	381	696	10	82	27	0.60	246	45	16	40	90	8%	77	6%	4.20	-9.6	46	$7
Consist C	1st Half	214	32	6	26	3	259			312	400	712	7	82	29	0.43	238	41	15	45	93	7%	81	9%	4.24	-5.7	42	$6
LIMA Plan F	2nd Half	125	12	3	9	1	214			320	348	668	14	83	24	0.92	252	49	16	34	85	8%	59	3%	4.10	-4.0	47	$1
Rand Var 0	10 Proj	156	20	3	15	2	237			301	368	669	8	82	27	0.51	249	47	16	37	88	7%	84	7%	3.83	-6.7	42	$3

4-19-.213 in 230 AB at CIN. Has never been able to rekindle that '07 PX. As a 3Bman, that's a problem. Late year bb% jump says pitch recognition is fine. So he can work count, he just can't do anything after contact. Avoid.

Ross,Cody		AB	R	HR	RBI	SB	Avg	vL	vR	OB	Slg	OPS	bb%	ct%	h%	Eye	xBA	G	L	F	PX	hr/f	SX	SBO	RC/G	RAR	BPV	R$
Pos 89	05 aaa	388	49	14	40	3	201			258	353	611	7	83	21	0.45	0				92		71	8%	2.99	-17.5	43	$5
Age 29	06 2NL	* 319	45	16	52	1	244	245	216	317	447	764	10	76	27	0.45	253	36	21	43	122	15%	59	5%	4.91	4.5	41	$9
Bats Right	07 FLA	173	35	12	39	2	335	385	306	404	653	1057	10	78	37	0.53	333	41	21	38	211	23%	59	4%	8.71	18.9	121	$11
Health B	08 FLA	461	59	22	73	6	260	285	249	310	488	798	7	75	30	0.28	265	36	21	43	152	15%	101	7%	5.30	7.5	66	$16
PT/Exp C	09 FLA	559	73	24	90	5	270	284	266	312	469	781	6	78	31	0.28	259	33	19	48	134	12%	68	6%	4.96	3.7	54	$20
Consist D	1st Half	277	40	14	48	3	274			316	498	815	6	78	31	0.28	274	35	20	45	150	14%	60	7%	5.36	5.0	65	$11
LIMA Plan C+	2nd Half	282	33	10	42	2	266			308	440	747	6	78	31	0.27	244	31	19	50	118	9%	62	5%	4.56	-1.4	38	$9
Rand Var 0	10 Proj	521	73	25	87	5	269			319	488	807	7	77	30	0.33	270	35	20	45	146	14%	78	6%	5.37	10.3	66	$19

PROs:
- 30 HR pace in 1H
- Big FB jump in 2nd half

CONs:
- PX trend, especially in 2H
- Eye didn't recover from '08

Still good 25 HR, low BA target.

Ross,David		AB	R	HR	RBI	SB	Avg	vL	vR	OB	Slg	OPS	bb%	ct%	h%	Eye	xBA	G	L	F	PX	hr/f	SX	SBO	RC/G	RAR	BPV	R$
Pos 2	05 2NL	125	11	3	15	0	240	200	253	275	392	667	5	78	29	0.21	236	38	15	47	108	7%	52	0%	3.56	-0.9	23	$2
Age 33	06 CIN	247	37	21	52	0	255	316	228	352	579	931	13	70	28	0.49	276	32	17	51	211	24%	34	0%	7.44	22.4	86	$10
Bats Right	07 CIN	311	32	17	39	0	203	248	175	273	399	671	9	70	23	0.33	234	34	19	48	129	16%	14	0%	3.61	-7.9	9	$4
Health B	08 2TM	142	18	3	13	0	225	206	241	368	352	720	18	73	29	0.82	240	38	25	37	100	8%	25	2%	4.88	3.0	17	$2
PT/Exp F	09 ATL	128	18	7	20	0	273	250	284	376	508	884	14	70	34	0.54	260	30	22	49	175	16%	18	0%	6.97	9.9	53	$5
Consist D	1st Half	82	14	6	15	0	293			396	573	969	15	67	37	0.52	269	26	22	52	206	21%	21	0%	8.30	9.2	71	$4
LIMA Plan F	2nd Half	46	4	1	5	0	239			340	391	731	13	74	30	0.58	242	35	21	44	124	7%	12	0%	4.85	0.8	27	$1
Rand Var -4	10 Proj	144	19	8	21	0	243			339	464	803	13	70	29	0.49	251	33	20	47	156	17%	24	1%	5.67	6.1	41	$4

He'll be a popular backup CA choice in '10 since he shed Mendoza-ish BA, but elevated 1H h% is the reason. Power skills are real, though. Roster him in hopes that the front-liner goes down. Sad, but true.

Rowand,Aaron		AB	R	HR	RBI	SB	Avg	vL	vR	OB	Slg	OPS	bb%	ct%	h%	Eye	xBA	G	L	F	PX	hr/f	SX	SBO	RC/G	RAR	BPV	R$
Pos 8	05 CHW	578	77	13	69	16	270	303	259	308	407	715	5	80	32	0.28	267	52	21	28	92	10%	119	15%	4.18	-1.7	41	$17
Age 33	06 PHI	405	59	12	47	10	262	222	275	293	425	718	4	81	30	0.24	270	44	22	34	101	11%	110	16%	4.15	-3.5	49	$12
Bats Right	07 PHI	612	105	27	89	6	309	315	306	358	515	873	7	81	35	0.39	288	43	20	38	133	15%	65	5%	6.15	27.0	64	$26
Health B	08 SF	549	57	13	70	2	271	286	266	325	410	735	7	77	33	0.35	247	49	19	32	102	10%	31	4%	4.55	-2.9	16	$13
PT/Exp A	09 SF	499	61	15	64	4	261	213	276	302	419	721	6	75	32	0.24	242	45	16	39	114	10%	74	4%	4.28	-6.6	26	$13
Consist B	1st Half	268	38	8	33	4	299			347	474	821	7	76	37	0.31	262	44	19	37	130	11%	79	7%	5.67	7.0	46	$10
LIMA Plan D+	2nd Half	231	23	7	31	0	216			249	355	604	4	74	26	0.17	213	47	12	41	95	10%	47	0%	2.63	-14.9	-3	$3
Rand Var -1	10 Proj	465	58	12	61	2	254			299	396	695	6	77	31	0.28	244	46	17	36	102	9%	57	3%	3.95	-10.0	20	$11

Full-time work in jeopardy...
- ct%, Eye, BA, xBA in free fall
- Suddenly can't hit LHPs
- Bottom fell out in 2nd half

That '07 season is the obvious outlier, and SB upside is long gone too. Stay away.

Ruiz,Carlos		AB	R	HR	RBI	SB	Avg	vL	vR	OB	Slg	OPS	bb%	ct%	h%	Eye	xBA	G	L	F	PX	hr/f	SX	SBO	RC/G	RAR	BPV	R$
Pos 2	05 aaa	339	37	4	30	3	263			307	401	707	6	89	29	0.56	0				85		99	11%	4.34	4.4	67	$6
Age 31	06 PHI	* 437	58	20	76	4	289	263	260	354	488	842	9	85	30	0.68	286	47	19	34	113	16%	53	5%	5.85	18.5	67	$17
Bats Right	07 PHI	374	42	6	54	6	259	189	282	334	396	730	10	87	29	0.86	279	46	18	36	91	5%	81	7%	4.79	3.9	67	$8
Health A	08 PHI	320	47	4	31	1	219	212	220	313	300	613	12	88	24	1.16	248	54	17	29	54	5%	49	3%	3.55	-6.5	36	$3
PT/Exp C	09 PHI	322	32	9	43	3	255	293	242	350	425	775	13	88	27	1.21	282	42	19	39	111	8%	47	5%	5.44	11.2	82	$8
Consist D	1st Half	148	9	3	17	3	243			341	378	720	13	86	26	1.10	260	39	19	42	93	6%	34	11%	4.79	2.4	58	$3
LIMA Plan B	2nd Half	174	23	6	26	0	264			357	466	822	13	89	27	1.32	299	45	18	37	125	10%	42	0%	5.98	8.6	96	$5
Rand Var +2	10 Proj	402	47	15	61	3	261			347	449	796	12	88	27	1.08	290	46	18	36	114	12%	51	5%	5.55	15.3	83	$12

A precursor to a breakout?
- Eye spike
- Finally figured out LHPs
- PX surge, particularly in 2H

You won't find many CAs with a better bb% + ct% combo. Time to speculate. UP: 20-80-.280

Ruiz,Randy		AB	R	HR	RBI	SB	Avg	vL	vR	OB	Slg	OPS	bb%	ct%	h%	Eye	xBA	G	L	F	PX	hr/f	SX	SBO	RC/G	RAR	BPV	R$
Pos 0	05 aa	344	42	22	63	0	270			312	521	833	6	74	31	0.23	0				171		20	2%	5.63	-3.9	52	$13
Age 32	06 aa	491	46	18	56	2	199			242	360	602	5	71	24	0.20	0				112		54	2%	2.65	-58.4	4	$4
Bats Right	07 a/a	474	48	13	53	1	216			262	356	619	6	76	26	0.26	0				95		56	2%	2.94	-48.2	10	$5
Health B	08 MIN	* 478	55	12	55	1	249			281	389	670	4	71	33	0.15	0				109		55	3%	3.60	-18.8	-3	$9
PT/Exp C	09 TOR	* 577	77	27	85	1	255	286	322	303	471	775	6	78	28	0.31	263	49	11	40	138	15%	53	2%	4.92	-4.2	53	$16
Consist B	1st Half	332	36	11	47	0	248			287	438	724	5	80	28	0.27	0				127		34	0%	4.29	-8.6	43	$7
LIMA Plan D+	2nd Half	245	41	16	38	1	265			325	517	842	8	76	29	0.37	269	49	11	40	154	22%	62	3%	5.81	4.5	62	$9
Rand Var 0	10 Proj	357	45	18	48	1	261			305	475	780	6	75	30	0.25	254	49	11	40	142	17%	50	2%	4.97	-4.2	42	$10

10-17-.313 in 115 AB at TOR. Got first extended MLB look at age 31 and posted 3rd highest OPS among those w/100+ AB. Weak plate skills limit ceiling, but you can't ignore rising PX, especially in 2H. UP: 25 HR

Ryan,Brendan		AB	R	HR	RBI	SB	Avg	vL	vR	OB	Slg	OPS	bb%	ct%	h%	Eye	xBA	G	L	F	PX	hr/f	SX	SBO	RC/G	RAR	BPV	R$
Pos 6	05 aa	154	20	1	7	4	227			277	302	579	6	91	24	0.74	0				50		110	11%	2.97	-6.0	50	$2
Age 28	06 a/a	69	9	1	8	1	217			250	275	525	4	86	24	0.30	0				32		76	13%	1.92	-5.3	1	$1
Bats Right	07 STL	* 501	71	5	23	20	240	354	238	288	311	599	6	89	26	0.63	253	47	19	34	42	3%	118	20%	3.09	-20.6	41	$9
Health B	08 STL	197	30	0	10	7	244	261	229	300	289	590	8	84	29	0.52	240	52	19	28	39	0%	97	16%	2.92	-10.1	15	$4
PT/Exp D	09 STL	390	55	3	37	14	292	265	306	333	400	733	6	86	34	0.43	265	51	19	30	68	3%	130	19%	4.55	-1.2	50	$13
Consist D	1st Half	157	20	1	11	6	293			331	389	720	5	85	34	0.39	270	53	21	26	64	3%	112	20%	4.36	-1.4	39	$5
LIMA Plan D	2nd Half	233	35	2	26	8	292			335	408	742	6	86	33	0.45	262	51	17	32	71	3%	134	18%	4.68	0.1	55	$8
Rand Var -5	10 Proj	262	37	2	19	9	267			314	354	668	6	86	30	0.50	260	51	19	30	57	2%	128	18%	3.83	-5.7	44	$7

Rode h% to huge BA gain. As that corrects, so too will BA. The fallout? Fewer hits means fewer SB opps. He's been exposed in full-time work in the past. It will happen again.

Salazar,Oscar		AB	R	HR	RBI	SB	Avg	vL	vR	OB	Slg	OPS	bb%	ct%	h%	Eye	xBA	G	L	F	PX	hr/f	SX	SBO	RC/G	RAR	BPV	R$
Pos 7	05 MEX	264	35	5	30	2	246			323	348	672	10	87	27	0.86	0				63		67	5%	4.04	-7.8	40	$5
Age 32	06 VNZ	229	36	7	42	1	262			324	419	743	8	87	27	0.72	0				88		77	5%	4.75	-3.1	61	$7
Bats Right	07 aa	532	47	14	61	2	197			222	330	551	3	84	21	0.20	0				84		51	6%	2.15	-51.4	27	$3
Health A	08 BAL	* 527	66	15	76	6	250	211	349	308	409	716	8	87	26	0.65	276	40	19	40	100	8%	71	7%	4.41	-6.8	67	$13
PT/Exp D	09 2TM	* 338	40	14	59	0	305	357	265	352	506	858	7	86	32	0.50	273	48	13	39	119	12%	45	3%	5.92	5.9	66	$13
Consist D	1st Half	223	27	10	39	0	319			349	516	865	4	86	34	0.33	263	67	5	29	116	17%	39	4%	5.81	3.2	59	$10
LIMA Plan F	2nd Half	115	13	4	20	0	278			357	487	844	11	85	30	0.82	279	43	15	41	124	10%	62	0%	6.09	2.6	82	$4
Rand Var -5	10 Proj	130	15	4	20	1	262			316	436	753	7	86	28	0.57	268	44	15	41	106	9%	63	4%	4.78	-1.7	64	$3

5-25-.302 in 139 AB at BAL and SD. If he were 10 years younger, that PX trend would get our notice -- but this is a career minor leaguer. Don't pay for .300 BA; it was h% induced.

STEPHEN NICKRAND

Saltalamacchia,Jarrod

			AB	R	HR	RBI	SB	Avg	vL	vR	OB	Slg	OPS	bb%	ct%	h%	Eye	xBA	G	L	F	PX	hr/f	SX	SBO	RC/G	RAR	BPV	R$
Pos	2	05	0	0	0	0	0	0							0			0						0					
Age	25	06 aa	313	29	8	38	0	220			335	358	693	15	78	26	0.78	0				91		30	1%	4.36	-0.2	25	$3
Bats	Both	07 2TM	* 389	55	16	44	2	270	226	290	322	450	772	7	77	31	0.33	258	44	17	39	118	14%	62	2%	4.92	6.3	37	$11
Health	A	08 TEX	* 253	35	5	36	0	252	158	311	345	381	726	12	66	36	0.42	225	31	27	42	112	7%	51	3%	4.91	5.4	-5	$5
PT/Exp	D	09 TEX	283	34	9	34	0	233	229	235	289	371	660	7	66	32	0.23	217	36	23	41	104	12%	31	3%	3.61	-5.7	-28	$5
Consist	B	1st Half	210	25	6	27	0	248			298	376	674	7	63	37	0.19	215	35	26	39	103	12%	32	4%	3.93	-2.1	-41	$4
LIMA Plan	D	2nd Half	73	9	3	7	0	192			262	356	619	9	74	22	0.37	224	38	15	46	106	12%	31	0%	2.96	-3.0	10	$1
Rand Var	-1	10 Proj	**380**	**48**	**12**	**45**	**0**	**245**			**317**	**395**	**712**	**10**	**71**	**32**	**0.36**	**231**	**36**	**21**	**42**	**109**	**11%**	**45**	**2%**	**4.37**	**1.4**	**4**	**$7**

PX, xBA are going in the wrong direction, ct% is stagnantly awful... this is not encouraging. The pieces are there in his skill history, but will they ever come together? You can't bet more than a flyer on that possibility.

Sanchez,Freddy

			AB	R	HR	RBI	SB	Avg	vL	vR	OB	Slg	OPS	bb%	ct%	h%	Eye	xBA	G	L	F	PX	hr/f	SX	SBO	RC/G	RAR	BPV	R$
Pos	4	05 PIT	453	54	5	35	2	291	326	278	331	400	731	6	92	31	0.75	292	46	23	31	68	4%	73	3%	4.60	0.5	58	$11
Age	32	06 PIT	582	85	6	85	3	344	442	316	377	473	849	5	91	37	0.60	299	37	28	36	85	3%	60	3%	5.85	18.8	63	$23
Bats	Right	07 PIT	602	77	11	81	0	304	364	282	339	442	781	5	87	33	0.42	281	39	22	38	88	5%	49	1%	5.02	5.2	47	$17
Health	B	08 PIT	569	75	9	52	0	271	289	266	297	371	667	4	89	29	0.33	274	45	24	30	62	6%	56	1%	3.64	-18.4	31	$12
PT/Exp	A	09 2NL	457	56	7	41	5	293	323	282	326	416	741	5	83	34	0.29	272	45	24	31	85	6%	89	5%	4.50	-0.3	39	$13
Consist	C	1st Half	302	41	6	33	5	315			353	477	830	6	85	35	0.40	289	43	23	34	110	7%	97	8%	5.64	9.0	71	$11
LIMA Plan	C	2nd Half	155	15	1	8	0	252			270	297	567	3	80	31	0.13	237	50	26	25	34	3%	31	0%	2.19	-10.7	-36	$1
Rand Var	-2	10 Proj	**537**	**65**	**8**	**49**	**2**	**283**			**312**	**400**	**713**	**4**	**86**	**32**	**0.29**	**277**	**45**	**24**	**31**	**80**	**6%**	**67**	**2%**	**4.15**	**-7.2**	**36**	**$13**

1H PX was caused by huge number of doubles, 2H collapse was caused by knee, shoulder injuries. It's tempting to look at that first half and think there's another $20 season in his bat, but last two years say not likely.

Sanchez,Gaby

			AB	R	HR	RBI	SB	Avg	vL	vR	OB	Slg	OPS	bb%	ct%	h%	Eye	xBA	G	L	F	PX	hr/f	SX	SBO	RC/G	RAR	BPV	R$
Pos	3	05	0	0	0	0	0	0							0			0						0					
Age	27	06	0	0	0	0	0	0							0			0						0					
Bats	Right	07	0	0	0	0	0	0							0			0						0					
Health	A	08 aa	478	55	13	72	13	265			344	429	773	11	86	29	0.87	0				107		72	16%	5.25	-3.5	75	$15
PT/Exp	F	09 aaa	318	45	13	46	4	246			321	399	720	10	86	25	0.78	248	41	15	43	85	11%	64	4%	4.45	-15.6	53	$9
Consist	B	1st Half	190	27	6	25	4	257			322	397	719	9	82	28	0.55	0				85		70	7%	4.36	-9.7	38	$6
LIMA Plan	D	2nd Half	128	18	6	21	0	230			318	402	721	11	92	21	1.52	258	41	15	43	86	13%	28	0%	4.65	-5.6	68	$3
Rand Var	0	10 Proj	**219**	**29**	**8**	**33**	**3**	**251**			**330**	**408**	**738**	**11**	**87**	**26**	**0.91**	**255**	**41**	**15**	**43**	**91**	**10%**	**56**	**8%**	**4.76**	**-7.0**	**61**	**$6**

Has hit .276 with .552 Slg in the majors... in 29 career AB. Other than Eye, there's not much to get excited about here. Looks like he'll get another shot, but given his age and skills, this feels like too little, too late.

Sandoval,Pablo

			AB	R	HR	RBI	SB	Avg	vL	vR	OB	Slg	OPS	bb%	ct%	h%	Eye	xBA	G	L	F	PX	hr/f	SX	SBO	RC/G	RAR	BPV	R$
Pos	53	05	0	0	0	0	0	0							0			0						0					
Age	24	06	0	0	0	0	0	0							0			0						0					
Bats	Both	07	0	0	0	0	0	0							0			0						0					
Health	A	08 SF	* 320	50	9	57	0	328	237	383	350	491	841	3	90	34	0.35	311	45	26	29	99	11%	51	1%	5.54	1.4	65	$14
PT/Exp	D	09 SF	572	79	25	90	5	330	379	314	386	556	942	8	85	35	0.63	302	45	19	36	139	14%	72	6%	7.02	28.6	93	$28
Consist	C	1st Half	268	35	11	40	2	332			381	556	937	7	85	36	0.51	305	46	19	35	143	14%	63	5%	6.91	12.6	88	$13
LIMA Plan	C	2nd Half	304	44	14	50	3	329			391	556	947	9	86	35	0.74	298	44	18	38	135	14%	72	6%	7.11	16.0	95	$16
Rand Var	-2	10 Proj	**590**	**86**	**22**	**98**	**3**	**308**			**353**	**509**	**862**	**6**	**87**	**32**	**0.54**	**302**	**45**	**20**	**35**	**122**	**12%**	**72**	**5%**	**5.97**	**11.3**	**84**	**$25**

An impressive performance at age 23, with no signs of decline his second time around the league. ct%, LD% histories offer potential for improvement; for now, just be happy with more of the same.

Santiago,Ramon

			AB	R	HR	RBI	SB	Avg	vL	vR	OB	Slg	OPS	bb%	ct%	h%	Eye	xBA	G	L	F	PX	hr/f	SX	SBO	RC/G	RAR	BPV	R$
Pos	64	05 aaa	441	54	8	40	15	211			265	315	579	7	88	23	0.59	0				64		108	23%	2.82	-20.1	50	$7
Age	31	06 DET	* 163	20	1	14	3	227			267	294	562	5	80	28	0.27	230	58	15	27	47	3%	97	11%	2.32	-10.4	-1	$1
Bats	Both	07 DET	* 432	44	3	33	10	240	300	281	265	329	595	3	84	28	0.22	263	39	26	35	61	2%	105	21%	2.75	-20.3	26	$5
Health	B	08 DET	124	30	4	18	1	282	320	273	390	460	850	15	86	30	1.29	293	44	23	33	102	11%	112	2%	6.41	7.3	93	$5
PT/Exp	D	09 DET	262	29	7	35	1	267	270	267	312	385	697	6	78	32	0.30	231	47	17	35	69	10%	59	4%	3.93	-4.0	-0	$6
Consist	F	1st Half	117	17	6	24	0	291			331	496	826	6	75	34	0.24	239	52	7	40	123	17%	66	7%	5.52	3.6	32	$5
LIMA Plan	F	2nd Half	145	12	1	11	1	248			297	297	593	6	81	30	0.36	232	43	25	32	28	3%	62	2%	2.75	-7.3	-21	$1
Rand Var	-5	10 Proj	**226**	**32**	**5**	**27**	**1**	**252**			**311**	**373**	**684**	**8**	**82**	**29**	**0.47**	**252**	**46**	**20**	**34**	**73**	**8%**	**81**	**5%**	**3.95**	**-3.0**	**28**	**$5**

And the elite Eye disappears as quickly as it came. The power made a brief return appearance, but all he's proven is that he can catch lightning in a bottle once in a while. You can't invest based on samples this small.

Santos,Omir

			AB	R	HR	RBI	SB	Avg	vL	vR	OB	Slg	OPS	bb%	ct%	h%	Eye	xBA	G	L	F	PX	hr/f	SX	SBO	RC/G	RAR	BPV	R$
Pos	2	05 aa	401	36	9	40	0	218			234	317	552	2	82	24	0.12	0				65		33	1%	2.02	-23.2	-2	$3
Age	29	06 aa	324	27	4	33	1	233			270	314	584	5	78	29	0.22	0				60		38	1%	2.50	-18.2	-19	$2
Bats	Right	07 a/a	205	14	3	16	1	198			231	277	508	4	78	24	0.20	0				58		37	5%	1.51	-18.5	-21	($0)
Health	A	08 aaa	297	23	1	27	1	218			256	261	517	5	83	26	0.30	0				34		37	4%	1.84	-21.7	-19	$1
PT/Exp	F	09 NYM	281	28	7	40	0	260	218	283	297	391	689	5	84	29	0.34	259	40	22	38	84	8%	37	0%	3.86	-3.2	28	$6
Consist	C	1st Half	137	15	4	23	0	263			294	416	710	4	83	29	0.26	268	29	27	44	96	8%	50	0%	4.04	-0.9	35	$4
LIMA Plan	F	2nd Half	144	13	3	17	0	257			301	368	669	6	85	28	0.43	239	50	17	33	73	7%	19	0%	3.70	-2.3	19	$3
Rand Var	-1	10 Proj	**267**	**23**	**4**	**30**	**0**	**240**			**276**	**334**	**610**	**5**	**83**	**28**	**0.29**	**239**	**42**	**21**	**37**	**65**	**5%**	**32**	**2%**	**2.90**	**-10.8**	**3**	**$3**

2009 was the first year any team saw fit to give him more than 10 AB in the majors, and his MLEs show why. The Mets got lucky but we may have just witnessed his career year. Don't count on a strong follow-up.

Saunders,Michael

			AB	R	HR	RBI	SB	Avg	vL	vR	OB	Slg	OPS	bb%	ct%	h%	Eye	xBA	G	L	F	PX	hr/f	SX	SBO	RC/G	RAR	BPV	R$
Pos	7	05	0	0	0	0	0	0							0			0						0					
Age	23	06	0	0	0	0	0	0							0			0						0					
Bats	Left	07	0	0	0	0	0	0							0			0						0					
Health	A	08 aa	343	47	9	38	11	247			314	398	712	9	76	30	0.41	0				106		102	23%	4.32	-8.5	39	$10
PT/Exp	F	09 SEA	* 370	65	11	33	9	265	200	239	318	416	735	7	77	32	0.34	240	47	15	39	94	10%	122	13%	4.50	-5.5	35	$11
Consist	A	1st Half	198	44	9	23	4	278			344	475	819	9	82	30	0.56	0				115		107	11%	5.58	3.2	72	$8
LIMA Plan	C	2nd Half	172	21	2	10	5	250			287	349	636	5	71	34	0.18	203	47	15	39	66	4%	126	17%	3.21	-9.2	-14	$3
Rand Var	-2	10 Proj	**421**	**65**	**9**	**40**	**12**	**252**			**308**	**382**	**691**	**8**	**76**	**31**	**0.34**	**232**	**47**	**15**	**39**	**89**	**7%**	**114**	**18%**	**4.00**	**-12.3**	**25**	**$11**

0-4-.221 in 122 AB at SEA. Power skills were nowhere to be found in majors (34 PX), but MLEs suggest there's some pop in his bat. Speed skills are good, OB is not. Has potential, will need some time to reach it.

Scales,Bobby

			AB	R	HR	RBI	SB	Avg	vL	vR	OB	Slg	OPS	bb%	ct%	h%	Eye	xBA	G	L	F	PX	hr/f	SX	SBO	RC/G	RAR	BPV	R$
Pos	7	05 aaa	372	36	8	45	7	218			295	335	630	10	77	26	0.49	0				80		76	12%	3.30	-20.0	18	$5
Age	33	06 aaa	357	42	7	40	3	268			340	421	761	10	70	36	0.37	0				108		93	5%	5.20	-0.2	18	$7
Bats	Both	07 aaa	432	53	8	46	12	261			325	409	734	9	78	32	0.44	0				102		116	13%	4.66	-6.8	49	$10
Health	A	08 aaa	387	61	10	38	4	244			312	369	681	9	78	29	0.46	0				83		74	9%	3.90	-14.5	23	$9
PT/Exp	D	09 CHC	* 430	45	7	43	6	226	208	250	298	338	636	9	78	27	0.47	222	46	14	40	79	5%	74	12%	3.41	-28.8	18	$6
Consist	B	1st Half	202	28	6	21	3	229			306	390	696	10	79	26	0.53	239	42	14	44	104	9%	94	10%	4.16	-8.7	50	$4
LIMA Plan	F	2nd Half	228	17	1	22	3	223			291	292	583	9	77	29	0.42	205	49	14	37	57	1%	51	14%	2.73	-20.3	-11	$1
Rand Var	+1	10 Proj	**95**	**11**	**2**	**10**	**1**	**242**			**312**	**373**	**685**	**9**	**78**	**29**	**0.45**	**232**	**46**	**14**	**40**	**90**	**6%**	**90**	**11%**	**4.03**	**-4.1**	**30**	**$2**

3-15-.242 in 124 AB at CHC. It was a great story, getting his first major league AB at age 32. But unless your league has the category "rookies older than dirt" then he was not rosterable in '09 and won't be in '10 either.

Schafer,Jordan

			AB	R	HR	RBI	SB	Avg	vL	vR	OB	Slg	OPS	bb%	ct%	h%	Eye	xBA	G	L	F	PX	hr/f	SX	SBO	RC/G	RAR	BPV	R$
Pos	8	05	0	0	0	0	0	0							0			0						0					
Age	24	06	0	0	0	0	0	0							0			0						0					
Bats	Left	07	0	0	0	0	0	0							0			0						0					
Health	B	08 aa	297	38	8	42	10	242			334	404	738	12	75	30	0.56	0				110		110	19%	4.86	-1.7	49	$8
PT/Exp	F	09 ATL	* 202	23	4	10	4	202	212	200	302	301	603	13	65	29	0.41	193	44	18	39	84	8%	59	10%	2.97	-11.3	-29	$1
Consist	D	1st Half	202	23	4	10	4	202			302	301	603	13	65	29	0.41	193	44	18	39	84	8%	59	10%	2.97	-11.3	-29	$1
LIMA Plan	F	2nd Half	0	0	0	0	0	0																					
Rand Var	0	10 Proj	**197**	**23**	**4**	**17**	**5**	**234**			**328**	**357**	**685**	**12**	**69**	**32**	**0.46**	**215**	**44**	**18**	**39**	**95**	**8%**	**82**	**13%**	**4.17**	**-3.1**	**3**	**$4**

2-8-.204 in 167 AB at ATL. Following up PED suspension with a season this bad isn't the way to boost confidence in your future. Maybe it was bone spurs in his wrist. Maybe. Outlook is cloudier than it was a year ago.

BRANDON KRUSE

Schierholtz,Nate

			AB	R	HR	RBI	SB	Avg	vL	vR	OB	Slg	OPS	bb%	ct%	h%	Eye	xBA	G	L	F	PX	hr/f	SX	SBO	RC/G	RAR	BPV	R$
Pos	9	05	0	0	0	0	0	0							0			0						0					
Age	26	06 aa	470	56	14	55	8	270			310	445	755	5	83	30	0.33	0				103		108	10%	4.68	-7.3	59	$12
Bats	Left	07 SF	* 523	63	12	65	11	299	500	266	319	463	782	3	87	33	0.23	272	44	15	41	97	6%	114	14%	4.89	0.1	67	$17
Health	A	08 SF	* 425	65	14	67	8	294	333	315	326	503	828	5	87	31	0.38	328	46	30	24	121	16%	128	12%	5.51	3.8	96	$17
PT/Exp	D	09 SF	285	33	5	29	3	267	370	242	306	400	706	5	80	32	0.28	257	45	21	35	96	6%	83	6%	4.11	-6.4	33	$7
Consist	C	1st Half	126	15	3	12	2	302			328	444	773	4	81	35	0.21	256	46	18	36	95	8%	80	9%	4.79	-0.3	33	$4
LIMA Plan	C	2nd Half	159	18	2	17	1	239			288	365	653	6	79	29	0.32	257	43	22	34	97	5%	75	3%	3.55	-6.3	29	$2
Rand Var	0	10 Proj	405	51	12	49	6	281			316	463	779	5	83	31	0.30	285	45	21	34	114	11%	102	9%	4.93	-0.5	65	$13

There are some players who need consistent work to be productive, and this one just might be in that group. Huge BPI drop upon his first full year in the majors. Skill just doesn't disappear. Stay with him.

Schneider,Brian

			AB	R	HR	RBI	SB	Avg	vL	vR	OB	Slg	OPS	bb%	ct%	h%	Eye	xBA	G	L	F	PX	hr/f	SX	SBO	RC/G	RAR	BPV	R$
Pos	2	05 WAS	369	38	10	44	1	268	265	269	322	409	731	7	87	29	0.60	280	47	21	33	88	10%	46	1%	4.53	7.8	49	$9
Age	33	06 WAS	410	30	4	55	2	256	271	251	319	329	648	8	84	30	0.57	245	47	23	30	50	4%	28	3%	3.62	-8.7	2	$6
Bats	Left	07 WAS	408	33	6	54	0	235	212	244	328	336	663	12	86	26	1.00	237	48	15	36	66	5%	23	0%	4.08	-4.3	31	$4
Health	B	08 NYM	335	30	9	38	0	257	187	277	340	367	707	11	84	28	0.79	267	53	26	21	66	15%	12	0%	4.39	1.7	17	$6
PT/Exp	D	09 NYM	170	11	3	24	0	218		230	293	335	628	10	88	23	0.86	229	57	13	30	80	7%	11	0%	3.56	-3.6	39	$1
Consist	B	1st Half	66	6	2	17	0	242			342	424	766	13	91	24	1.67	273	53	15	32	116	10%	11	0%	5.43	2.3	88	$2
LIMA Plan	F	2nd Half	104	5	1	7	0	202			259	279	538	7	86	23	0.53	200	60	12	28	56	4%	10	0%	2.32	-6.3	6	($0)
Rand Var	+3	10 Proj	202	15	4	27	0	257			333	371	704	10	86	28	0.83	245	54	17	29	75	8%	14	0%	4.41	0.9	32	$4

Injuries and performance have successfully transformed him into a back-up CA. bb%/ct% combo means that he should be productive enough not to kill you, and certainly better than a .218 BA. But no bidding wars please.

Schumaker,Skip

			AB	R	HR	RBI	SB	Avg	vL	vR	OB	Slg	OPS	bb%	ct%	h%	Eye	xBA	G	L	F	PX	hr/f	SX	SBO	RC/G	RAR	BPV	R$
Pos	47	05 aaa	440	51	4	26	10	252			290	340	630	5	90	27	0.55	0				59		97	13%	3.41	-12.2	49	$7
Age	30	06 aaa	369	42	3	23	10	281			319	350	668	5	88	31	0.46	0				42		94	13%	3.75	-6.4	26	$8
Bats	Left	07 STL	* 409	42	6	40	3	272	375	327	317	385	702	6	86	30	0.48	275	54	19	27	73	6%	53	7%	4.18	-6.2	34	$8
Health	A	08 STL	540	87	8	46	8	302	168	340	358	406	763	8	89	33	0.78	291	58	22	20	62	8%	108	6%	5.02	3.7	55	$18
PT/Exp	B	09 STL	532	85	4	35	2	303	220	322	365	393	758	9	87	34	0.75	285	61	22	17	66	5%	56	2%	5.03	7.3	38	$15
Consist	A	1st Half	269	43	3	21	2	290			350	387	737	9	88	32	0.81	296	61	23	16	65	8%	72	5%	4.77	1.8	47	$7
LIMA Plan	D+	2nd Half	263	42	1	14	0	316			379	399	779	9	86	37	0.71	270	61	20	19	67	2%	36	0%	5.30	5.4	28	$7
Rand Var	-2	10 Proj	419	62	4	31	4	286			343	381	724	8	87	32	0.69	287	59	21	19	64	6%	78	4%	4.58	-0.5	42	$10

PRO: Established BA producer in a full-time role.
CON: Difficulties v LHP and inexperience at 2B might cost him playing time; owns neither power nor speed skills. More potential down than upside here.

Scott,Luke

			AB	R	HR	RBI	SB	Avg	vL	vR	OB	Slg	OPS	bb%	ct%	h%	Eye	xBA	G	L	F	PX	hr/f	SX	SBO	RC/G	RAR	BPV	R$
Pos	7	05 HOU	* 478	56	23	67	3	230	286	178	287	446	733	7	79	24	0.39	260	43	11	46	134	13%	82	6%	4.44	-13.1	66	$12
Age	32	06 HOU	* 532	79	26	85	7	287	240	366	369	517	887	11	81	31	0.68	285	36	24	40	133	15%	95	5%	6.58	19.9	84	$21
Bats	Left	07 HOU	369	49	18	64	3	255	271	252	348	504	852	13	74	30	0.56	285	41	19	40	167	16%	88	4%	6.36	10.9	84	$12
Health	A	08 BAL	476	67	23	65	2	256	215	269	331	471	801	10	79	28	0.52	268	39	17	44	139	14%	56	3%	5.43	8.1	64	$14
PT/Exp	B	09 BAL	449	61	25	77	0	258	260	257	339	488	827	11	77	28	0.53	265	40	17	43	143	17%	30	0%	5.78	10.1	54	$14
Consist	B	1st Half	201	35	15	40	0	299			379	572	951	11	79	31	0.60	287	39	19	42	160	22%	25	0%	7.27	12.5	74	$10
LIMA Plan	C	2nd Half	248	26	10	37	0	226			307	419	726	10	75	26	0.48	246	40	15	44	128	12%	31	0%	4.54	-3.6	37	$4
Rand Var	0	10 Proj	433	58	20	69	0	256			336	468	804	11	77	29	0.53	264	40	17	43	137	14%	48	1%	5.53	7.1	56	$12

Your opponents see consistent R$. You see him already is an older player with no defensive value coming off a poor 2H, and perceive PT risk. Doesn't fit on a rebuilding team like BAL. Don't bid past $10.

Scutaro,Marco

			AB	R	HR	RBI	SB	Avg	vL	vR	OB	Slg	OPS	bb%	ct%	h%	Eye	xBA	G	L	F	PX	hr/f	SX	SBO	RC/G	RAR	BPV	R$
Pos	6	05 OAK	381	48	9	37	5	247	171	262	312	391	703	9	87	26	0.75	274	43	21	36	90	7%	89	7%	4.34	-2.4	67	$8
Age	34	06 OAK	365	52	5	41	5	266	218	279	354	397	751	12	82	31	0.76	256	44	21	36	84	5%	111	5%	5.11	7.3	54	$8
Bats	Right	07 OAK	338	49	7	41	2	260	309	245	330	361	691	9	88	28	0.88	255	39	20	41	62	6%	53	3%	4.23	-0.6	39	$7
Health	A	08 TOR	517	76	7	60	7	267	268	267	340	356	696	10	87	29	0.88	260	43	23	35	59	4%	76	5%	4.34	0.2	41	$12
PT/Exp	B	09 TOR	574	100	12	60	14	282	269	287	380	409	789	14	87	31	1.20	257	37	19	44	80	6%	82	9%	5.64	19.4	65	$19
Consist	B	1st Half	319	58	6	33	7	279			382	414	796	14	87	30	1.33	258	41	16	43	86	5%	80	10%	5.79	12.3	73	$10
LIMA Plan	B	2nd Half	255	42	6	27	7	286			377	404	781	13	86	31	1.06	256	32	24	44	71	6%	75	9%	5.44	7.1	52	$9
Rand Var	-2	10 Proj	517	82	9	57	9	273			357	379	736	12	87	30	1.00	255	39	21	40	68	5%	79	7%	4.89	7.3	51	$14

Why 2009 is his career year:
- FB% and SBO% both peaked, yielding double digit HRs, SBs
- PX, SX show only modest skill
- xBA says he's a .260 hitter
- Plate discipline at likely peak
- New skills don't stick at 34.

Sheffield,Gary

			AB	R	HR	RBI	SB	Avg	vL	vR	OB	Slg	OPS	bb%	ct%	h%	Eye	xBA	G	L	F	PX	hr/f	SX	SBO	RC/G	RAR	BPV	R$
Pos	7	05 NYY	584	104	34	123	10	291	359	266	375	512	887	12	87	29	1.03	287	42	17	41	125	16%	75	6%	6.47	28.5	96	$29
Age	41	06 NYY	151	22	6	25	5	298	344	286	354	450	804	8	89	30	0.81	263	49	15	37	81	12%	73	13%	5.34	0.7	62	$6
Bats	Right	07 DET	494	107	25	75	22	265	245	271	372	462	834	15	86	27	1.18	281	41	17	42	112	14%	110	16%	6.04	14.4	96	$23
Health	D	08 DET	418	52	19	57	9	225	239	220	319	400	719	12	80	24	0.70	247	43	14	43	107	13%	66	9%	4.46	-5.0	53	$11
PT/Exp	B	09 NYM	268	44	10	43	2	276	294	268	370	451	822	13	83	30	0.87	263	47	15	38	107	12%	75	3%	5.88	2.4	67	$10
Consist	C	1st Half	173	36	10	30	2	289			394	514	909	15	82	30	0.97	280	51	13	35	131	20%	78	5%	6.94	6.7	88	$9
LIMA Plan	D	2nd Half	95	8	0	13	0	253			324	337	661	10	84	30	0.67	232	40	18	41	64	0%	49	0%	3.94	-4.5	24	$1
Rand Var	-2	10 Proj	286	42	9	43	1	259			348	407	755	12	83	28	0.82	248	44	16	40	91	9%	55	2%	5.02	-3.8	49	$8

Back, wrist and hamstring injuries during 2009. If you can figure out when he is healthy and not just playing through nagging injuries, there's about 100 useful AB per year. Then trade him because it won't last.

Shoppach,Kelly

			AB	R	HR	RBI	SB	Avg	vL	vR	OB	Slg	OPS	bb%	ct%	h%	Eye	xBA	G	L	F	PX	hr/f	SX	SBO	RC/G	RAR	BPV	R$
Pos	2	05 aaa	370	46	19	57	0	227			294	423	716	9	76	25	0.39	0				127		24	0%	4.22	3.5	33	$9
Age	30	06 CLE	* 188	18	6	25	0	247	314	213	298	409	708	7	63	36	0.20	207	43	15	42	137	12%	23	2%	4.51	0.6	-16	$3
Bats	Right	07 CLE	161	26	7	30	0	261	265	260	308	472	780	6	65	36	0.20	251	46	15	39	176	17%	41	0%	5.45	5.4	29	$5
Health	A	08 CLE	352	67	21	55	0	261	304	246	330	517	847	9	62	36	0.27	256	38	19	43	213	22%	43	0%	6.72	25.8	52	$13
PT/Exp	D	09 CLE	271	33	12	40	0	214	304	191	299	399	698	11	64	29	0.34	231	41	22	37	141	19%	23	0%	4.32	0.4	-1	$5
Consist	D	1st Half	145	20	6	19	0	200			270	372	643	9	64	26	0.27	232	40	24	36	131	18%	36	0%	3.41	-3.9	-8	$2
LIMA Plan	D+	2nd Half	126	13	6	21	0	230			331	429	760	13	63	31	0.41	227	41	20	39	152	19%	11	0%	5.36	4.1	7	$3
Rand Var	+4	10 Proj	352	50	17	55	0	253			326	460	785	10	64	34	0.30	239	41	19	39	163	19%	28	0%	5.64	14.4	17	$10

Career platoon split tells why he didn't become a starter:
v LHP: .295 BA, .999 OPS
v RHP: .224 BA, .704 OPS
Expect H%, BA to rebound, but HR are what you're bidding for, and role issues make them risky.

Sizemore,Grady

			AB	R	HR	RBI	SB	Avg	vL	vR	OB	Slg	OPS	bb%	ct%	h%	Eye	xBA	G	L	F	PX	hr/f	SX	SBO	RC/G	RAR	BPV	R$
Pos	8	05 CLE	640	111	22	81	22	289	245	308	342	484	827	8	79	34	0.39	284	44	24	31	125	14%	145	19%	5.70	25.8	78	$27
Age	28	06 CLE	655	134	28	76	22	290	214	329	366	533	898	11	77	34	0.51	269	33	20	47	158	12%	152	16%	6.86	40.6	102	$28
Bats	Left	07 CLE	628	118	24	78	33	277	284	274	377	462	839	14	75	33	0.65	252	33	21	47	125	11%	124	20%	6.22	30.7	69	$28
Health	B	08 CLE	634	101	33	90	38	268	224	286	366	502	868	13	79	29	0.75	276	35	19	46	147	14%	127	23%	6.44	20.1	103	$30
PT/Exp	A	09 CLE	436	73	18	64	13	248	216	262	339	445	784	12	79	28	0.65	249	36	16	48	116	11%	115	17%	5.35	9.4	69	$15
Consist	B	1st Half	237	32	10	40	7	219			305	414	718	11	75	25	0.49	248	34	20	46	123	12%	95	25%	4.43	-1.6	51	$6
LIMA Plan	B+	2nd Half	199	41	8	24	6	281			378	482	861	13	83	30	0.94	251	39	12	49	109	10%	132	10%	6.40	9.9	89	$8
Rand Var	+2	10 Proj	608	107	27	88	25	266			359	480	838	13	79	30	0.68	262	36	18	46	130	12%	129	18%	6.06	22.8	86	$26

Previously reliable "guaranteed" 600-AB guy suffered with elbow, abdominal injuries. With same plate skills and G/L/F, expect a return to the moderate BA, high HR model next year. Make believe 2009 never happened.

Smith,Seth

			AB	R	HR	RBI	SB	Avg	vL	vR	OB	Slg	OPS	bb%	ct%	h%	Eye	xBA	G	L	F	PX	hr/f	SX	SBO	RC/G	RAR	BPV	R$
Pos	7	05	0	0	0	0	0	0							0			0						0					
Age	28	06 aa	524	61	13	55	3	279			329	452	781	7	90	29	0.74	0				104		65	6%	5.19	-0.4	78	$12
Bats	Left	07 aa	451	50	14	61	5	275			320	447	767	6	86	30	0.47	0				104		83	8%	4.89	-4.0	66	$12
Health	A	08 COL	* 356	50	11	50	8	265		289	348	421	769	11	84	29	0.80	274	45	21	34	98	11%	89	8%	5.17	-2.5	66	$12
PT/Exp	D	09 COL	335	61	15	55	4	293	259	300	378	510	888	12	80	33	0.69	275	39	19	42	137	13%	104	5%	6.67	10.4	87	$15
Consist	B	1st Half	135	27	6	18	3	289			411	496	907	17	80	32	1.04	280	43	22	35	125	16%	110	6%	7.19	6.1	90	$6
LIMA Plan	C+	2nd Half	200	34	9	37	1	295			353	520	873	8	80	33	0.45	273	37	17	46	145	12%	85	4%	6.26	3.9	80	$9
Rand Var	-2	10 Proj	399	62	15	59	6	281			355	475	831	10	83	31	0.68	276	40	20	41	121	11%	99	6%	5.86	4.4	80	$15

Patient, powerful bat spent '09 miscast in a job share batting mostly in the leadoff or #2 slots. Might be overlooked due to age and PT concerns but lots to like as an unknown bat in COL:
UP: 25-90-.300 with 8 SB.

MICHAEL WEDDELL

Snider,Travis

		Year	AB	R	HR	RBI	SB	Avg	vL	vR	OB	Slg	OPS	bb%	ct%	h%	Eye	xBA	G	L	F	PX	hr/f	SX	SBO	RC/G	RAR	BPV	R$
Pos	79	05	0	0	0	0	0	0							0			0						0					
Age	22	06	0	0	0	0	0	0							0			0						0					
Bats	Left	07	0	0	0	0	0	0							0			0						0					
Health	A	08 TOR	*499	74	21	87	2	271	286	305	340	458	799	9	72	34	0.38	287	37	35	29	137	20%	47	2%	5.50	9.3	34	$17
PT/Exp	D	09 TOR	*416	58	20	59	3	268	225	244	347	486	833	11	72	33	0.44	255	44	15	41	146	16%	58	7%	6.01	12.1	48	$13
Consist	B	1st Half	139	13	3	13	1	231			287	346	633	7	73	29	0.30	209	44	14	42	84	7%	39	6%	3.20	-7.7	-11	$2
LIMA Plan	C	2nd Half	277	45	17	46	2	287			375	556	931	12	72	34	0.50	277	44	16	40	178	21%	67	8%	7.43	19.2	77	$12
Rand Var	-1	10 Proj	513	72	22	78	3	267			340	464	804	10	73	33	0.40	254	43	18	39	138	15%	51	5%	5.59	9.2	38	$16

9-29-.241 in 241 AB at TOR. Struck out in 20 of his 40 AB vs LH, but a lot of positives: 2H growth in bb%, xBA, PX, and hr/f. Expect continued ct% issues in short term, but power is ready now.

Snyder,Chris

		Year	AB	R	HR	RBI	SB	Avg	vL	vR	OB	Slg	OPS	bb%	ct%	h%	Eye	xBA	G	L	F	PX	hr/f	SX	SBO	RC/G	RAR	BPV	R$
Pos	2	05 ARI	326	24	6	28	0	202	260	185	290	301	590	11	73	26	0.46	219	51	19	29	75	9%	16	1%	2.76	-10.5	-18	$0
Age	29	06 ARI	184	19	6	32	0	277	246	294	354	424	778	11	79	32	0.56	250	45	22	33	93	13%	14	0%	5.20	4.5	17	$5
Bats	Right	07 ARI	326	37	13	47	0	252	316	215	333	433	766	11	79	28	0.60	249	40	15	45	117	11%	19	1%	5.05	5.9	41	$7
Health	D	08 ARI	334	47	16	64	0	237	250	231	346	452	798	14	70	29	0.55	248	38	18	44	158	16%	38	0%	5.76	15.5	48	$10
PT/Exp	D	09 ARI	165	20	6	22	0	200	161	220	330	352	681	16	72	24	0.68	215	37	17	46	109	11%	20	0%	4.12	-0.7	13	$2
Consist	C	1st Half	134	17	5	21	0	224			350	381	731	16	75	26	0.76	227	36	18	46	108	11%	19	0%	4.82	2.3	25	$3
LIMA Plan	F	2nd Half	31	3	1	1	0	97			243	226	469	16	58	12	0.46	166	44	11	44	112	12%	21	0%	0.66	-4.0	-38	($1)
Rand Var	+3	10 Proj	152	18	7	24	0	237			337	422	759	13	75	27	0.62	239	41	16	43	125	14%	20	0%	5.05	3.6	36	$4

Couldn't sustain 2008 PX, and lost starting job for good when bulging disk sent him to DL. He wasn't that bad vs LH, as he had 1.00 Eye and 18% h% vs them. Ct% keeps BA low, but power gives him a value base.

Soriano,Alfonso

		Year	AB	R	HR	RBI	SB	Avg	vL	vR	OB	Slg	OPS	bb%	ct%	h%	Eye	xBA	G	L	F	PX	hr/f	SX	SBO	RC/G	RAR	BPV	R$
Pos	7	05 TEX	637	102	36	104	30	268	257	272	304	512	816	5	80	28	0.26	278	34	19	47	155	15%	133	26%	5.29	10.4	97	$31
Age	34	06 WAS	647	119	46	95	41	277	293	271	345	560	904	9	75	30	0.42	272	29	20	51	175	18%	113	37%	6.70	27.6	96	$36
Bats	Right	07 CHC	579	97	33	70	19	299	254	311	334	560	894	5	78	34	0.24	288	34	20	46	166	16%	120	20%	6.35	15.9	91	$27
Health	D	08 CHC	453	76	29	75	19	280	351	252	343	532	875	9	77	31	0.42	275	29	23	48	160	17%	96	19%	6.23	10.5	86	$24
PT/Exp	B	09 CHC	477	64	20	55	9	241	184	256	300	423	723	8	75	28	0.34	241	33	19	48	124	12%	86	10%	4.33	-17.5	44	$14
Consist	C	1st Half	305	47	14	32	7	230			290	423	713	8	75	26	0.34	246	37	17	46	133	13%	85	14%	4.19	-12.7	49	$9
LIMA Plan	B	2nd Half	172	17	6	23	2	262			317	424	742	8	76	31	0.34	234	27	22	52	109	9%	63	5%	4.59	-4.8	28	$5
Rand Var	+2	10 Proj	518	75	26	71	8	266			321	484	805	7	77	30	0.34	260	31	21	49	142	14%	85	9%	5.35	-1.8	62	$19

Knee bothered him most of the year, leading to arthroscopic surgery in Sept. Is he likely to rebound? SX was in decline before injury, and age not on his side. PX was so consistent before 2009, should come back.

Soto,Geovany

		Year	AB	R	HR	RBI	SB	Avg	vL	vR	OB	Slg	OPS	bb%	ct%	h%	Eye	xBA	G	L	F	PX	hr/f	SX	SBO	RC/G	RAR	BPV	R$
Pos	2	05 aaa	288	24	3	32	0	230			323	306	630	12	80	28	0.69	0				58		18	1%	3.50	-3.6	-3	$2
Age	27	06 aaa	367	32	6	37	0	253			323	360	683	9	80	30	0.52	185	60	5	35	75	6%	18	1%	4.02	-3.8	6	$4
Bats	Right	07 CHC	*439	73	26	95	0	325	444	333	390	588	978	10	78	37	0.48	306	41	22	37	170	21%	45	0%	7.68	37.8	81	$23
Health	D	08 CHC	494	66	23	86	0	285	312	276	365	504	869	11	76	34	0.51	269	38	21	41	150	15%	36	1%	6.45	31.1	57	$19
PT/Exp	C	09 CHC	331	27	11	47	1	218	205	221	320	381	701	13	77	25	0.65	244	41	18	41	113	10%	37	1%	4.34	0.8	37	$5
Consist	D	1st Half	203	18	7	25	1	236			340	394	735	14	77	28	0.68	241	39	20	42	104	11%	44	2%	4.79	3.2	33	$4
LIMA Plan	C	2nd Half	128	9	4	22	0	187			288	359	647	12	77	21	0.60	234	44	16	41	127	10%	7	0%	3.63	-2.6	36	$1
Rand Var	+5	10 Proj	463	64	21	80	0	268			354	473	827	12	77	31	0.57	265	40	19	41	139	14%	40	1%	5.89	21.7	56	$16

Fought injuries all year, only healthy month may have been June, when he exploded for 6 HR, 203 PX. H% was a major factor in his struggles. Should bounce back, maybe even to 07-08 levels.

Span,Denard

		Year	AB	R	HR	RBI	SB	Avg	vL	vR	OB	Slg	OPS	bb%	ct%	h%	Eye	xBA	G	L	F	PX	hr/f	SX	SBO	RC/G	RAR	BPV	R$
Pos	879	05 aa	263	40	0	22	9	270			319	323	642	7	86	31	0.53	0				32		127	23%	3.56	-6.8	25	$7
Age	26	06 aa	536	75	2	42	23	272			319	332	651	6	86	32	0.48	0				37		122	22%	3.60	-14.9	24	$14
Bats	Left	07 aaa	487	58	3	54	25	261			313	345	658	7	81	32	0.40	0				57		120	29%	3.65	-12.9	22	$13
Health	A	08 MIN	*503	96	8	59	30	294	283	299	381	424	805	12	81	35	0.75	291	54	26	20	85	9%	141	26%	5.76	5.9	62	$23
PT/Exp	C	09 MIN	578	97	8	68	23	311	330	304	386	415	801	11	85	36	0.79	262	53	19	28	57	6%	126	15%	5.60	15.4	45	$24
Consist	C	1st Half	252	42	4	24	13	282			365	373	738	12	85	32	0.85	257	53	19	28	49	7%	121	20%	4.86	1.6	39	$9
LIMA Plan	C+	2nd Half	326	55	4	44	10	334			402	448	850	10	85	39	0.74	266	53	19	28	63	5%	121	12%	6.17	13.3	48	$15
Rand Var	-5	10 Proj	575	94	7	65	27	287			359	389	748	10	83	33	0.68	267	53	21	26	61	5%	133	21%	4.93	2.5	44	$21

PRO: Ct% higher than 07-08. .876 career OPS vs LH.
CON: SBO plummeted, and success rate dropped, which could affect future SB opps. BA/OBP are legit, but won't necessarily drive SB growth.

Spilborghs,Ryan

		Year	AB	R	HR	RBI	SB	Avg	vL	vR	OB	Slg	OPS	bb%	ct%	h%	Eye	xBA	G	L	F	PX	hr/f	SX	SBO	RC/G	RAR	BPV	R$
Pos	79	05 a/a	478	63	7	51	11	281			337	429	766	8	85	32	0.55	0				103		108	15%	5.06	0.4	71	$14
Age	31	06 COL	*436	62	8	46	11	295	323	267	348	422	770	7	85	33	0.53	274	51	21	29	78	7%	103	11%	5.01	-2.9	49	$14
Bats	Right	07 COL	*388	57	14	62	6	282	356	271	349	452	801	9	84	31	0.63	290	50	21	30	101	15%	81	9%	5.40	0.5	60	$14
Health	B	08 COL	233	38	6	36	7	313	326	306	410	468	877	14	82	36	0.93	287	55	21	24	100	13%	96	12%	6.70	8.3	68	$11
PT/Exp	D	09 COL	352	55	8	48	9	241	230	250	308	395	703	9	78	29	0.43	255	46	18	36	110	8%	114	17%	4.25	-13.9	52	$10
Consist	D	1st Half	207	34	6	29	8	261			329	430	759	9	78	31	0.46	263	42	20	38	120	10%	108	23%	4.96	-3.7	60	$8
LIMA Plan	C	2nd Half	145	21	2	19	1	214			278	345	623	8	77	26	0.39	244	53	14	33	95	5%	104	6%	3.25	-10.4	34	$2
Rand Var	+3	10 Proj	315	48	7	44	7	267			340	420	760	10	80	31	0.56	270	51	18	31	103	9%	105	12%	5.02	-4.1	57	$10

Finally started hitting some fly balls, but a low percentage of them left the park, and ct% suffered. Not able to sustain success vs LH, which resulted in fewer AB in 2H. Very little upside here, even in Colorado.

Stairs,Matt

		Year	AB	R	HR	RBI	SB	Avg	vL	vR	OB	Slg	OPS	bb%	ct%	h%	Eye	xBA	G	L	F	PX	hr/f	SX	SBO	RC/G	RAR	BPV	R$
Pos	9	05 KC	396	55	13	66	1	275	259	278	371	444	815	13	83	31	0.87	262	40	19	42	111	10%	42	2%	5.84	12.9	60	$12
Age	42	06 2AL	348	42	13	51	0	247	217	252	325	420	744	10	75	29	0.47	240	43	17	39	117	13%	22	0%	4.76	-9.2	24	$7
Bats	Left	07 TOR	357	58	21	64	2	289	289	288	367	549	916	11	82	30	0.67	308	40	18	42	166	17%	55	3%	6.86	13.6	99	$15
Health	A	08 2TM	337	46	13	49	1	252	235	254	335	409	745	11	73	31	0.47	238	43	20	37	105	14%	53	2%	4.78	-4.9	17	$9
PT/Exp	D	09 PHI	103	15	5	17	0	194		200	341	379	720	18	71	22	0.77	215	47	11	42	128	16%	23	0%	4.66	-0.7	31	$2
Consist	C	1st Half	55	9	3	12	0	291			400	491	891	15	71	36	0.63	241	46	18	36	136	21%	22	0%	7.01	3.3	32	$3
LIMA Plan	F	2nd Half	48	6	2	5	0	83			279	250	529	21	71	6	0.93	185	47	3	50	118	12%	23	0%	1.93	-5.1	30	($1)
Rand Var	+4	10 Proj	92	14	3	16	0	250			343	415	758	12	76	30	0.59	245	43	18	39	113	12%	39	1%	5.04	0.2	33	$3

Is he done? BA vs RHP now in freefall, although h% was a factor. Still has some pop, but along with AB, his xBA, ct% and age all show that long career is near its end.

Stavinoha,Nick

		Year	AB	R	HR	RBI	SB	Avg	vL	vR	OB	Slg	OPS	bb%	ct%	h%	Eye	xBA	G	L	F	PX	hr/f	SX	SBO	RC/G	RAR	BPV	R$
Pos	7	05	0	0	0	0	0	0							0			0						0					
Age	28	06 aa	417	43	9	57	2	255			292	383	675	5	83	29	0.31	0				81		60	3%	3.72	-18.3	28	$8
Bats	Right	07 aaa	499	37	9	36	5	206			241	287	528	4	86	22	0.32	0				49		56	6%	1.98	-50.1	9	$1
Health	A	08 aaa	427	50	11	54	2	274			298	403	701	3	90	28	0.35	0				75		63	3%	3.99	-14.0	48	$11
PT/Exp	D	09 STL	*346	34	9	57	3	224	262	200	267	368	635	5	84	24	0.36	243	34	18	49	95	7%	65	4%	3.27	-24.1	43	$7
Consist	C	1st Half	235	20	7	40	2	213			254	358	612	5	85	22	0.36	245	38	16	45	92	8%	45	4%	2.97	-18.8	39	$4
LIMA Plan	F	2nd Half	111	14	2	17	1	248			294	390	684	6	81	29	0.36	232	21	21	58	101	4%	79	4%	3.93	-5.3	45	$2
Rand Var	+2	10 Proj	100	10	2	14	2	240			277	358	635	5	85	26	0.34	231	29	19	52	76	5%	60	8%	3.24	-6.6	31	$2

2-17-.230 in 87 AB at STL. Free swinger with PX trending up, but still below average. Shuffled back and forth from STL to Memphis before hand fracture ended season in Aug. Won't have much of an impact.

Stewart,Ian

		Year	AB	R	HR	RBI	SB	Avg	vL	vR	OB	Slg	OPS	bb%	ct%	h%	Eye	xBA	G	L	F	PX	hr/f	SX	SBO	RC/G	RAR	BPV	R$
Pos	54	05	0	0	0	0	0	0							0			0						0					
Age	25	06 aa	462	58	9	55	2	255			312	424	736	8	84	29	0.51	0				109		80	11%	4.69	-7.8	64	$8
Bats	Left	07 COL	*457	63	14	63	9	284	100	242	346	442	788	9	81	33	0.48	270	46	19	35	101	11%	85	8%	5.24	-4.8	48	$15
Health	A	08 COL	*523	79	24	81	6	254	370	231	323	471	794	9	73	30	0.39	260	31	25	44	147	14%	103	8%	5.42	0.8	63	$18
PT/Exp	C	09 COL	425	74	25	70	7	228	178	244	318	464	782	12	68	27	0.41	243	40	14	46	168	19%	101	10%	5.42	3.6	60	$15
Consist	A	1st Half	209	35	14	39	5	215			281	474	754	8	71	23	0.32	251	36	11	53	174	18%	105	18%	4.74	-2.6	75	$8
LIMA Plan	B	2nd Half	216	39	11	31	2	241			352	454	805	15	64	32	0.47	235	45	17	38	160	21%	88	6%	6.10	6.3	42	$7
Rand Var	+1	10 Proj	439	75	27	82	6	246			325	506	831	10	72	28	0.42	269	39	17	44	173	20%	103	10%	5.91	8.5	82	$18

PRO: power is outstanding. Bb%, hr/f continue to improve.
CON: Ct% continues to drop, and reached dangerous level in 2H. Struggles vs LH further cloud his BA potential. Draft tactically; offset with BA booster.

BRIAN RUDD

Stubbs,Drew	Year	AB	R	HR	RBI	SB	Avg	vL	vR	OB	Slg	OPS	bb%	ct%	h%	Eye	xBA	G	L	F	PX	hr/f	SX	SBO	RC/G	RAR	BPV	R$
Pos 8	05	0	0	0	0	0	0							0			0						0					
Age 26	06	0	0	0	0	0	0							0			0						0					
Bats Right	07	0	0	0	0	0	0							0			0						0					
Health A	08 a/a	167	20	2	14	5	264			319	374	693	7	79	32	0.39	0				81		94	13%	4.08	-4.7	28	$4
PT/Exp F	09 CIN *	591	74	11	49	47	247	286	261	314	355	669	9	76	31	0.41	231	42	21	37	78	7%	119	37%	3.77	-17.2	22	$21
Consist A	1st Half	261	26	2	18	26	250			322	338	661	10	77	32	0.47	0				75		100	43%	3.78	-7.5	20	$9
LIMA Plan D	2nd Half	330	48	9	30	22	244			308	367	675	8	75	30	0.36	230	42	21	37	81	10%	127	31%	3.77	-9.6	21	$12
Rand Var -1	10 Proj	321	40	5	27	19	252			315	359	674	8	77	31	0.40	237	42	21	37	79	6%	113	27%	3.83	-8.1	25	$10

8-17-.267, 10 SB in 180 AB with CIN. MLB HR were likely a home venue anomaly, but speed is legit. Patience not a lost cause, but must improve ct%, BA to optimize wheels. Expect growing pains.

Sullivan,Cory	Year	AB	R	HR	RBI	SB	Avg	vL	vR	OB	Slg	OPS	bb%	ct%	h%	Eye	xBA	G	L	F	PX	hr/f	SX	SBO	RC/G	RAR	BPV	R$
Pos 7	05 COL	378	64	4	30	12	294	250	301	342	386	729	7	78	37	0.34	268	44	32	24	65	6%	136	13%	4.47	-9.2	20	$13
Age 31	06 COL	386	47	2	30	10	267	280	266	323	402	725	8	74	36	0.32	254	36	32	33	95	2%	119	16%	4.64	-6.9	25	$8
Bats Left	07 COL *	346	38	3	28	4	236	353	276	280	313	593	6	80	29	0.31	242	40	24	36	53	3%	87	8%	2.74	-27.4	4	$3
Health A	08 aa	381	43	4	29	8	248			284	357	640	5	87	28	0.38	0				75		85	19%	3.42	-19.7	44	$6
PT/Exp D	09 NYM *	422	43	4	31	9	228	167	263	294	311	604	9	88	25	0.78	251	47	20	34	50	3%	103	10%	3.27	-29.5	42	$5
Consist A	1st Half	246	22	2	16	2	221			274	283	557	7	89	24	0.69	0				44		45	6%	2.67	-21.9	22	$1
LIMA Plan F	2nd Half	176	20	2	15	7	237			320	349	668	11	86	26	0.88	253	47	20	34	59	4%	127	15%	4.11	-7.7	54	$4
Rand Var +4	10 Proj	153	17	1	12	6	242			298	336	634	7	85	28	0.54	265	41	27	32	59	4%	115	18%	3.46	-9.3	39	$3

2-15-.250, 7 SB in 136 AB at NYM. Improved ct%, patience give near-term hope, tempered by age and MLB track record. Zero pop, but 76% career MLB SB% still attractive. Next step more likely down than up.

Sutton,Drew	Year	AB	R	HR	RBI	SB	Avg	vL	vR	OB	Slg	OPS	bb%	ct%	h%	Eye	xBA	G	L	F	PX	hr/f	SX	SBO	RC/G	RAR	BPV	R$
Pos 4	05	0	0	0	0	0	0							0			0						0					
Age 27	06	0	0	0	0	0	0							0			0						0					
Bats Both	07 aa	480	65	8	42	19	232			297	333	629	9	84	26	0.58	0				68		103	20%	3.40	-14.0	40	$10
Health A	08 aa	520	72	15	49	14	260			329	418	747	9	85	28	0.67	0				99		94	16%	4.82	-0.1	67	$15
PT/Exp F	09 CIN *	238	36	6	26	1	217	167	217	303	367	670	11	76	26	0.50	237	37	19	44	109	7%	79	8%	3.90	-4.7	37	$4
Consist C	1st Half	145	23	5	15	1	209			310	381	691	13	78	24	0.67	0				117		79	8%	4.23	-1.4	58	$2
LIMA Plan F	2nd Half	93	13	1	12	0	230			290	346	636	8	71	31	0.30	215	37	19	44	95	3%	88	9%	3.38	-3.3	6	$1
Rand Var +1	10 Proj	127	18	3	13	2	236			308	381	689	9	79	28	0.50	243	37	19	44	100	6%	92	13%	4.11	-2.0	46	$3

1-9-.212 in 66 AB at CIN. Late bloomer flashing decent power and patience for a middle infielder. Ability to make MLB contact in question. Must play to keep growing, only watchable for now.

Suzuki,Ichiro	Year	AB	R	HR	RBI	SB	Avg	vL	vR	OB	Slg	OPS	bb%	ct%	h%	Eye	xBA	G	L	F	PX	hr/f	SX	SBO	RC/G	RAR	BPV	R$
Pos 9	05 SEA	679	111	15	68	33	303	352	284	349	436	785	7	90	32	0.73	296	54	21	24	71	10%	150	20%	5.17	8.9	78	$29
Age 36	06 SEA	695	110	9	49	45	322	352	312	367	416	783	7	90	35	0.69	273	51	22	28	50	5%	150	20%	5.15	-9.6	60	$30
Bats Left	07 SEA	678	111	6	68	37	351	331	358	395	431	825	7	89	39	0.64	283	56	20	24	48	4%	127	18%	5.62	2.2	47	$33
Health A	08 SEA	686	103	6	42	43	310	287	321	358	386	745	7	91	34	0.78	282	57	20	23	44	4%	139	20%	4.77	-11.0	55	$27
PT/Exp A	09 SEA	639	88	11	46	26	352	339	359	383	465	848	5	89	38	0.45	283	56	18	26	66	7%	101	17%	5.71	6.3	50	$28
Consist B	1st Half	304	38	6	18	16	368			396	493	890	4	92	39	0.56	293	59	16	25	69	9%	107	20%	6.15	6.3	65	$15
LIMA Plan D+	2nd Half	335	50	5	28	10	337			371	439	810	5	86	38	0.39	274	52	21	27	64	6%	86	13%	5.30	-0.3	35	$14
Rand Var -5	10 Proj	612	91	6	46	24	317			357	397	754	6	89	35	0.57	275	56	19	25	50	5%	106	15%	4.76	-9.8	42	$22

Like fine wine. As in '08, 2H leg issues curtailed his base-running, the only concession to age we see. Sacrificed bb% for pop while h% drove BA spike. Both will regress some, as risk rises a little more.

Suzuki,Kurt	Year	AB	R	HR	RBI	SB	Avg	vL	vR	OB	Slg	OPS	bb%	ct%	h%	Eye	xBA	G	L	F	PX	hr/f	SX	SBO	RC/G	RAR	BPV	R$
Pos 2	05	0	0	0	0	0	0							0			0						0					
Age 27	06 aa	376	52	6	45	4	250			333	366	699	11	89	27	1.10	0				74		68	6%	4.51	1.5	58	$7
Bats Right	07 OAK *	424	53	9	61	0	249	151	281	315	363	679	9	83	28	0.57	233	39	16	45	78	6%	29	0%	3.95	-4.2	22	$8
Health A	08 OAK	534	54	7	42	2	279	246	291	335	369	704	8	87	31	0.65	246	45	19	36	60	4%	37	3%	4.29	1.6	25	$10
PT/Exp B	09 OAK	570	74	15	88	8	274	250	283	308	421	729	5	90	28	0.47	284	44	19	36	88	8%	77	8%	4.40	2.2	63	$17
Consist A	1st Half	269	34	5	32	4	279			317	413	730	5	91	29	0.63	294	43	23	34	85	6%	63	9%	4.52	2.0	63	$7
LIMA Plan C	2nd Half	301	40	10	56	4	269			299	429	728	4	88	28	0.37	274	46	16	38	90	10%	85	6%	4.30	0.2	61	$10
Rand Var 0	10 Proj	555	68	12	74	5	268			317	395	712	7	88	29	0.59	267	44	19	37	79	7%	63	5%	4.32	1.1	49	$14

PRO: Doubled production by opening up for power while pushing up excellent ct%. CON: bb% trend, selectivity downturn are drags on BA. A very solid option among 2nd-tier catchers.

Sweeney,Mike	Year	AB	R	HR	RBI	SB	Avg	vL	vR	OB	Slg	OPS	bb%	ct%	h%	Eye	xBA	G	L	F	PX	hr/f	SX	SBO	RC/G	RAR	BPV	R$
Pos 0	05 KC	470	63	21	83	3	300	279	308	346	517	863	7	87	31	0.54	286	36	17	47	136	11%	54	3%	5.96	-0.8	88	$19
Age 37	06 KC	217	23	8	33	2	258	266	255	343	438	781	11	78	30	0.58	256	35	21	44	121	11%	40	3%	5.29	-7.2	45	$5
Bats Right	07 KC	265	26	7	38	0	260	301	242	305	404	709	6	89	27	0.59	272	35	20	45	88	7%	34	0%	4.25	-15.3	51	$5
Health F	08 OAK	126	13	2	12	0	286	321	260	323	397	720	5	95	29	1.17	259	42	17	41	70	4%	23	0%	4.52	-1.4	56	$3
PT/Exp F	09 SEA	242	25	8	34	0	281	235	340	328	442	770	7	87	30	0.55	263	38	18	44	96	9%	17	0%	4.92	-1.7	46	$6
Consist F	1st Half	114	9	3	15	0	263			300	404	704	5	89	27	0.50	265	32	21	47	84	6%	13	0%	4.13	-3.4	41	$2
LIMA Plan F	2nd Half	128	16	5	19	0	297			353	477	829	8	85	32	0.58	262	43	16	41	107	11%	21	0%	5.64	1.7	50	$4
Rand Var -2	10 Proj	164	17	5	22	0	274			321	422	744	6	89	29	0.62	263	39	18	43	90	8%	25	0%	4.65	-3.4	50	$4

Nice little comeback in part-time duty after usual back issues in 1H. Odd L/R BA splits - particularly given 7 HR vs. LHP. Given the age and health profile, this might well have been a last hurrah.

Sweeney,Ryan	Year	AB	R	HR	RBI	SB	Avg	vL	vR	OB	Slg	OPS	bb%	ct%	h%	Eye	xBA	G	L	F	PX	hr/f	SX	SBO	RC/G	RAR	BPV	R$
Pos 98	05 aa	426	54	1	39	4	281			327	348	675	6	90	31	0.72	0				47		68	9%	4.02	-11.8	35	$9
Age 25	06 CHW *	484	65	15	75	7	310			357	469	825	7	86	34	0.52	345	50	39	11	94	35%	66	10%	5.55	-1.5	54	$18
Bats Left	07 CHW *	442	52	13	50	7	263			339	397	737	10	85	29	0.77	319	60	28	13	84	27%	61	10%	4.74	-9.9	47	$11
Health B	08 OAK *	421	57	6	49	9	289	216	307	354	393	747	9	83	34	0.59	255	45	21	34	72	5%	96	7%	4.83	-6.2	39	$13
PT/Exp C	09 OAK	484	68	6	53	6	293	268	301	347	407	754	8	86	33	0.60	278	45	24	31	74	5%	78	8%	4.89	-6.0	45	$13
Consist A	1st Half	230	25	3	21	4	270			325	357	682	8	85	31	0.56	264	49	23	28	54	5%	70	9%	3.99	-9.0	22	$5
LIMA Plan D+	2nd Half	254	43	3	32	2	315			367	453	820	8	87	35	0.64	291	41	25	34	92	4%	80	7%	5.69	2.5	63	$9
Rand Var +1	10 Proj	468	64	7	54	7	286			346	400	745	8	85	32	0.62	273	45	23	32	74	6%	76	8%	4.79	-7.4	43	$13

Stayed healthy, hiked numbers vs. LHP. Elevated h%, FB% drove 2H performance and PX spike, but failed to produce HR up-tick. Age, size give hope, but hr/f shows zero growth. An asset if you need BA, defense.

Swisher,Nick	Year	AB	R	HR	RBI	SB	Avg	vL	vR	OB	Slg	OPS	bb%	ct%	h%	Eye	xBA	G	L	F	PX	hr/f	SX	SBO	RC/G	RAR	BPV	R$
Pos 93	05 OAK *	485	69	21	75	0	241	197	248	321	447	768	11	76	28	0.49	263	38	19	43	144	13%	39	2%	5.09	5.6	55	$12
Age 29	06 OAK	556	106	35	95	1	254	291	241	364	493	857	15	73	29	0.64	253	33	19	48	152	18%	55	2%	6.42	12.4	60	$20
Bats Both	07 OAK	539	84	22	78	3	262	291	250	377	455	832	16	76	31	0.76	260	37	18	46	136	12%	53	3%	6.19	10.8	60	$16
Health A	08 CHW	497	86	24	69	3	219	197	227	330	410	740	14	73	25	0.61	246	35	21	45	129	15%	63	4%	4.82	-8.3	44	$12
PT/Exp A	09 NYY	498	84	29	82	0	249	244	251	371	498	869	16	75	28	0.77	269	38	16	46	162	17%	35	0%	6.66	19.5	74	$16
Consist D	1st Half	239	42	14	39	0	238			370	494	864	17	74	27	0.79	267	40	14	46	168	17%	46	0%	6.66	9.5	80	$7
LIMA Plan C+	2nd Half	259	42	15	43	0	259			373	502	874	15	76	29	0.75	271	36	18	45	157	17%	23	0%	6.66	10.0	68	$9
Rand Var +1	10 Proj	475	79	27	74	0	251			365	486	851	15	74	28	0.70	266	37	18	45	156	17%	38	1%	6.35	14.1	66	$15

Incremental rebounds in ct%, patience and luck returned BA to a rosterable level, given his power. Apart from BA volatility, as stable a skill set as they come. Value spikes in OBP-oriented leagues.

Tatis,Fernando	Year	AB	R	HR	RBI	SB	Avg	vL	vR	OB	Slg	OPS	bb%	ct%	h%	Eye	xBA	G	L	F	PX	hr/f	SX	SBO	RC/G	RAR	BPV	R$
Pos 357	05	0	0	0	0	0	0							0			0						0					
Age 35	06 BAL *	382	47	8	41	7	260	286	214	329	387	716	9	80	31	0.51	230	44	15	41	83	7%	88	8%	4.41	-11.2	33	$8
Bats Right	07 aa	120	13	9	22	0	184			258	432	690	9	81	15	0.53	0				141		11	0%	3.85	-7.1	62	$2
Health A	08 NYM *	393	46	20	69	3	262	311	287	332	468	800	9	79	29	0.50	287	42	26	32	128	19%	56	3%	5.34	-4.4	57	$13
PT/Exp D	09 NYM	340	42	8	48	4	282	278	285	326	438	764	6	84	32	0.41	274	47	19	34	100	8%	95	6%	4.86	-15.8	59	$11
Consist B	1st Half	149	19	2	17	2	248			296	362	658	6	92	26	0.83	275	54	16	30	67	5%	98	8%	3.86	-11.7	65	$3
LIMA Plan D	2nd Half	191	23	6	31	2	309			350	497	847	6	78	37	0.29	273	40	23	38	130	11%	83	4%	5.89	-3.2	55	$8
Rand Var -3	10 Proj	226	27	8	35	2	270			326	453	779	8	82	30	0.46	278	45	21	34	113	13%	80	5%	5.05	-7.4	59	$7

Put together a fine h%-fueled 2H for deep-league owners after NYM lineup became a MASH unit. But at this age, he profiles as a versatile bench player with pop, unrosterable until the PT materializes.

JOCK THOMPSON

Taveras,Willy

			AB	R	HR	RBI	SB	Avg	vL	vR	OB	Slg	OPS	bb%	ct%	h%	Eye	xBA	G	L	F	PX	hr/f	SX	SBO	RC/G	RAR	BPV	R$
Pos	8	05 HOU	592	82	3	29	34	291	233	311	319	341	661	4	83	35	0.24	243	55	19	26	33	2%	134	25%	3.46	-18.6	7	$20
Age	28	06 HOU	529	83	1	30	33	278	254	285	321	338	660	6	83	33	0.39	244	56	18	27	40	1%	137	27%	3.64	-12.2	21	$16
Bats	Right	07 COL	372	64	2	24	33	320	371	304	356	382	738	5	85	37	0.38	245	52	17	32	41	2%	134	34%	4.50	-0.3	27	$18
Health	B	08 COL	479	64	1	26	68	251	266	245	303	296	599	7	84	30	0.46	238	52	20	28	34	1%	152	54%	2.96	-25.5	23	$22
PT/Exp	C	09 CIN	404	56	1	15	25	240	219	247	273	285	557	4	86	28	0.31	222	47	17	36	31	1%	133	31%	2.37	-28.9	18	$9
Consist	C	1st Half	245	38	1	11	15	237			278	298	576	5	83	28	0.33	226	49	16	35	46	1%	136	30%	2.59	-16.0	22	$6
LIMA Plan	D	2nd Half	159	18	0	4	10	245			264	264	528	2	90	27	0.25	215	44	18	37	10	0%	122	32%	2.07	-12.8	11	$3
Rand Var	0	10 Proj	361	50	1	16	23	247			283	290	573	5	86	29	0.35	230	49	18	33	29	1%	138	31%	2.59	-22.8	19	$9

Poor bb%, selectivity and FB spike started the plunge, 2H injuries (wrist, quad) sealed it. Outlier FB% suggests that he will rebound some, but speed remains his only skill. His AB will always be in jeopardy.

Teagarden,Taylor

			AB	R	HR	RBI	SB	Avg	vL	vR	OB	Slg	OPS	bb%	ct%	h%	Eye	xBA	G	L	F	PX	hr/f	SX	SBO	RC/G	RAR	BPV	R$
Pos	2	05	0	0	0	0	0	0							0			0						0					
Age	26	06	0	0	0	0	0	0							0			0						0					
Bats	Right	07 aa	102	16	6	14	0	266			318	466	784	7	68	34	0.24	0				137		31	0%	5.22	2.5	5	$3
Health	A	08 TEX *	293	34	13	33	1	202	91	389	278	382	660	10	71	24	0.37	235	25	25	50	122	12%	62	3%	3.56	-5.8	22	$4
PT/Exp	F	09 TEX	198	26	6	24	0	217	288	192	269	374	643	7	62	32	0.18	211	42	17	41	134	12%	38	0%	3.54	-4.4	-20	$3
Consist	B	1st Half	65	5	0	9	0	215			271	292	564	7	63	34	0.21	196	39	22	39	85	0%	22	0%	2.43	-3.7	-57	$0
LIMA Plan	F	2nd Half	133	21	6	15	0	218			268	414	681	6	61	31	0.17	220	44	15	41	159	18%	47	0%	4.11	-0.7	-0	$2
Rand Var	-1	10 Proj	258	33	10	31	0	233			292	403	695	8	66	31	0.25	224	42	18	40	129	14%	56	1%	4.15	-0.7	1	$5

No improvement. Already solid power ticked up with 2H PT, poor ct% deteriorated further with patience downturn. Age is on his side, more AB could spur growth, but he still seems to be at least a year away.

Teahen,Mark

			AB	R	HR	RBI	SB	Avg	vL	vR	OB	Slg	OPS	bb%	ct%	h%	Eye	xBA	G	L	F	PX	hr/f	SX	SBO	RC/G	RAR	BPV	R$
Pos	59	05 KC *	474	63	7	58	7	245	200	263	310	371	682	9	76	31	0.39	265	53	23	24	96	8%	105	8%	3.99	-7.1	32	$9
Age	29	06 KC *	472	83	20	82	10	298	274	296	374	527	900	11	80	34	0.60	283	49	16	35	136	15%	136	7%	6.78	23.0	92	$20
Bats	Left	07 KC	544	78	7	60	13	285	255	297	351	410	761	9	77	36	0.43	262	50	21	29	90	6%	120	11%	5.06	3.0	35	$15
Health	A	08 KC	572	66	15	59	4	255	262	252	311	402	713	7	77	31	0.35	260	49	21	31	101	11%	73	5%	4.26	-10.4	28	$12
PT/Exp	A	09 KC	524	69	12	50	8	271	287	262	319	408	727	7	77	33	0.30	260	51	20	29	97	10%	84	7%	4.42	-3.9	24	$13
Consist	A	1st Half	274	36	9	28	3	285			336	449	784	7	80	33	0.38	271	48	20	32	105	13%	72	4%	5.10	3.2	40	$8
LIMA Plan	D+	2nd Half	250	33	3	22	5	256			301	364	665	6	73	34	0.24	246	55	19	26	88	6%	77	10%	3.64	-7.6	1	$5
Rand Var	0	10 Proj	481	63	10	50	7	264			319	403	722	7	76	33	0.34	261	51	20	29	99	10%	95	8%	4.42	-4.9	30	$11

Stop us if you've heard this before: Too many GBs sap his power, not enough speed to make it work. Declining bb% rate just makes things worse. Even with his current club, his AB are more at risk than ever.

Teixeira,Mark

			AB	R	HR	RBI	SB	Avg	vL	vR	OB	Slg	OPS	bb%	ct%	h%	Eye	xBA	G	L	F	PX	hr/f	SX	SBO	RC/G	RAR	BPV	R$
Pos	3	05 TEX	644	112	43	144	4	301	292	301	372	575	946	10	80	32	0.58	305	40	21	38	168	22%	81	2%	7.14	36.1	104	$34
Age	30	06 TEX	628	99	33	110	2	282	302	275	371	514	885	12	80	31	0.70	281	39	20	41	146	16%	51	1%	6.61	21.0	77	$23
Bats	Both	07 2TM	494	86	30	105	0	306	357	282	394	563	957	13	77	34	0.64	294	39	20	41	165	19%	40	0%	7.56	25.1	81	$24
Health	A	08 2TM	574	102	33	121	2	308	303	311	408	552	961	14	84	32	1.04	305	43	21	36	149	19%	46	1%	7.58	32.3	99	$29
PT/Exp	A	09 NYY	609	103	39	122	2	292	305	287	375	565	940	12	81	30	0.71	300	36	20	44	161	18%	64	1%	7.18	24.9	98	$28
Consist	A	1st Half	284	51	20	60	1	278			375	567	942	13	83	27	0.90	305	40	16	44	169	19%	41	1%	7.24	12.3	107	$13
LIMA Plan	B	2nd Half	325	52	19	62	1	305			376	563	939	10	80	33	0.57	295	33	23	43	153	17%	67	1%	7.13	12.6	85	$15
Rand Var	+1	10 Proj	604	103	37	123	2	300			387	559	946	12	81	32	0.75	301	39	20	41	158	18%	58	1%	7.30	30.0	95	$29

Traded some patience for aggressiveness, lost some contact and a few BA points, added a few HR. Rock-solid MVP skill set, with triple-A reliability. It doesn't get much better than this.

Tejada,Miguel

			AB	R	HR	RBI	SB	Avg	vL	vR	OB	Slg	OPS	bb%	ct%	h%	Eye	xBA	G	L	F	PX	hr/f	SX	SBO	RC/G	RAR	BPV	R$
Pos	6	05 BAL	654	89	26	98	5	304	293	309	344	515	860	6	87	32	0.48	306	48	19	33	129	14%	85	4%	5.90	23.9	91	$25
Age	36	06 BAL	648	99	24	100	6	330	335	329	375	498	873	7	88	35	0.58	298	51	22	27	98	16%	61	4%	6.06	28.1	63	$27
Bats	Right	07 BAL	514	72	18	81	2	296	323	287	348	442	789	7	89	30	0.75	281	52	17	31	82	13%	49	2%	5.17	12.6	55	$18
Health	B	08 HOU	632	92	13	66	7	283	282	284	309	415	724	4	89	30	0.33	289	48	23	29	82	8%	84	9%	4.28	-6.4	55	$18
PT/Exp	A	09 HOU	635	83	14	86	5	313	326	310	333	455	788	3	92	32	0.40	298	49	20	31	89	8%	65	4%	4.99	5.6	69	$24
Consist	B	1st Half	305	43	6	42	2	331			350	475	826	3	92	34	0.39	299	51	19	30	95	7%	52	5%	5.39	5.9	69	$13
LIMA Plan	C	2nd Half	330	40	8	44	3	297			318	436	754	3	92	30	0.40	296	48	21	31	84	8%	70	4%	4.61	-0.5	66	$11
Rand Var	0	10 Proj	580	79	13	77	5	290			319	425	743	4	91	30	0.45	291	49	21	30	83	8%	79	5%	4.55	-0.3	63	$18

At age where most SS decline, he reverses 2-yr skid via ct% and hacking up-tick, and just enough pop to make it work. 2010 FA with splits to digest:
2008-9 Hm: .318 BA, 18 HR
2008-9 Rd: .278 BA, 9 HR

Thames,Marcus

			AB	R	HR	RBI	SB	Avg	vL	vR	OB	Slg	OPS	bb%	ct%	h%	Eye	xBA	G	L	F	PX	hr/f	SX	SBO	RC/G	RAR	BPV	R$
Pos	7	05 DET *	364	54	24	63	4	262	212	186	341	522	863	11	75	29	0.47	249	27	14	59	165	15%	89	5%	6.25	16.2	81	$14
Age	33	06 DET	348	61	26	60	1	256	238	266	327	549	876	10	74	27	0.40	262	26	15	59	185	17%	72	3%	6.38	12.3	85	$13
Bats	Right	07 DET	269	37	18	54	2	242	310	209	277	498	775	5	73	26	0.18	275	38	16	46	173	20%	54	7%	4.80	-1.9	59	$9
Health	C	08 DET	316	50	25	56	0	241	234	245	294	516	810	7	70	26	0.25	261	32	17	51	184	22%	34	5%	5.42	5.4	53	$12
PT/Exp	D	09 DET *	307	37	15	40	0	242	257	248	315	428	743	10	72	29	0.38	231	35	18	47	119	14%	36	2%	4.67	-3.1	15	$7
Consist	B	1st Half	142	16	7	16	0	228			299	412	711	9	72	27	0.36	226	35	17	48	114	14%	55	3%	4.22	-3.4	15	$3
LIMA Plan	D	2nd Half	165	21	8	24	0	255			328	442	770	10	72	31	0.39	234	35	18	47	123	14%	26	2%	5.06	0.2	16	$4
Rand Var	-1	10 Proj	303	42	18	48	0	248			310	479	789	8	72	28	0.32	249	34	17	49	151	17%	42	3%	5.21	2.2	39	$9

13-36-.252 in 258 AB at DET. Spent six weeks on DL (rib-cage muscle), hit 11 HR in June / July, finished with zero HR over final seven weeks. Age, health, PX plunge point to continued streakiness.

Theriot,Ryan

			AB	R	HR	RBI	SB	Avg	vL	vR	OB	Slg	OPS	bb%	ct%	h%	Eye	xBA	G	L	F	PX	hr/f	SX	SBO	RC/G	RAR	BPV	R$
Pos	6	05 aa	445	41	1	43	19	253			309	324	632	7	91	28	0.93	0				50		99	24%	3.67	-8.0	52	$9
Age	30	06 CHC *	414	71	3	35	26	294	346	317	358	399	756	9	88	33	0.81	290	50	27	24	62	3%	148	23%	5.06	8.2	65	$16
Bats	Right	07 CHC	537	80	3	45	28	266	286	260	328	346	674	8	91	29	0.98	279	49	21	30	54	2%	121	20%	4.14	-4.8	61	$15
Health	A	08 CHC	580	85	1	38	22	307	305	308	384	359	743	11	90	34	1.26	276	57	23	20	34	1%	97	15%	5.07	7.2	41	$19
PT/Exp	A	09 CHC	602	81	7	54	21	284	306	279	340	369	709	8	85	33	0.55	250	50	20	30	54	5%	105	16%	4.31	-6.1	30	$19
Consist	B	1st Half	287	40	7	29	9	286			337	418	755	7	83	32	0.46	261	49	19	33	83	9%	99	17%	4.76	0.8	46	$10
LIMA Plan	C+	2nd Half	315	41	0	25	12	283			343	324	667	8	86	33	0.64	241	52	20	27	27	0%	109	16%	3.91	-6.8	16	$9
Rand Var	-3	10 Proj	574	80	4	47	20	280			344	351	695	9	87	32	0.77	262	52	21	27	46	3%	109	16%	4.29	-4.6	39	$17

Traded some bb%, ct% for aggressiveness, lost some BA and OBP while picking up a handful of 1H HR. Running game props up his value. Still one of the better SS, but age is beginning to add to risk.

Thole,Josh

			AB	R	HR	RBI	SB	Avg	vL	vR	OB	Slg	OPS	bb%	ct%	h%	Eye	xBA	G	L	F	PX	hr/f	SX	SBO	RC/G	RAR	BPV	R$
Pos	2	05	0	0	0	0	0	0							0			0						0					
Age	23	06	0	0	0	0	0	0							0			0						0					
Bats	Left	07	0	0	0	0	0	0							0			0						0					
Health	A	08	0	0	0	0	0	0							0			0						0					
PT/Exp	F	09 NYM *	437	41	1	46	7	293	200	349	352	373	725	8	92	32	1.21	322	46	34	20	58	1%	65	9%	4.78	6.4	54	$11
Consist	F	1st Half	257	28	1	24	3	307			371	401	772	9	92	33	1.24	0				67		61	6%	5.33	7.6	60	$7
LIMA Plan	D	2nd Half	180	13	0	22	4	272			325	333	658	7	93	29	1.17	316	46	34	20	44	0%	68	13%	4.00	-1.4	45	$4
Rand Var	+2	10 Proj	258	22	0	29	5	271			330	342	671	8	93	29	1.20	268	51	19	30	51	1%	67	11%	4.18	-0.6	49	$5

0-9-.321 in 53 AB at NYM. Elite ct%, decent patience and zero power. .350 BA, six HR in 731 AA-AAA AB in 2008-9. Raw defensive skills leave PT uncertain, should be on your March watch list.

Thomas,Clete

			AB	R	HR	RBI	SB	Avg	vL	vR	OB	Slg	OPS	bb%	ct%	h%	Eye	xBA	G	L	F	PX	hr/f	SX	SBO	RC/G	RAR	BPV	R$
Pos	97	05	0	0	0	0	0	0							0			0						0					
Age	26	06	0	0	0	0	0	0							0			0						0					
Bats	Left	07 aa	528	91	7	49	16	261			331	373	704	9	80	32	0.52	0				77		122	18%	4.33	-13.5	38	$14
Health	A	08 DET *	407	43	8	45	25	234	368	268	310	366	676	10	75	29	0.44	235	40	19	41	97	6%	109	36%	3.94	-18.0	33	$11
PT/Exp	D	09 DET *	450	69	8	53	18	247	245	240	328	380	708	11	73	32	0.44	235	49	15	36	98	7%	125	17%	4.45	-11.8	30	$12
Consist	A	1st Half	287	40	5	31	15	251			328	390	718	10	76	32	0.47	246	55	11	34	101	7%	118	23%	4.54	-6.7	42	$8
LIMA Plan	F	2nd Half	163	29	3	22	3	239			329	362	691	12	67	34	0.41	214	44	19	37	90	7%	116	6%	4.31	-5.0	3	$4
Rand Var	-1	10 Proj	157	23	3	18	7	242			321	365	686	10	74	31	0.44	232	45	17	38	91	6%	108	21%	4.11	-5.9	23	$4

7-39-.240 in 275 AB at DET. 226 AB performance vs. RHP wasn't encouraging. Improving patience not helping dwindling ct%, average power. Speed under-utilized due to SBO. Not likely to see 275 AB in 2010.

JOCK THOMPSON

Thome,Jim

		Year	AB	R	HR	RBI	SB	Avg	vL	vR	OB	Slg	OPS	bb%	ct%	h%	Eye	xBA	G	L	F	PX	hr/f	SX	SBO	RC/G	RAR	BPV	R$
Pos	0	05 PHI	193	26	7	30	0	207	164	233	357	352	709	19	69	26	0.76	221	45	18	37	105	14%	21	0%	4.62	-8.4	8	$3
Age	40	06 CHW	490	108	42	109	0	288	236	321	415	598	1013	18	70	33	0.73	281	37	20	43	204	28%	30	0%	8.80	32.4	90	$26
Bats	Left	07 CHW	432	79	35	96	0	275	196	315	406	563	969	18	69	32	0.71	278	43	18	39	197	30%	21	1%	8.22	24.3	78	$21
Health	B	08 CHW	503	93	34	90	1	245	233	249	360	503	863	15	71	28	0.62	270	40	18	42	180	23%	43	1%	6.57	24.4	72	$19
PT/Exp	B	09 2TM	362	55	23	77	0	249	209	262	369	481	850	16	66	31	0.56	246	44	20	36	165	27%	20	0%	6.60	15.3	36	$14
Consist	B	1st Half	190	32	13	42	0	247			404	495	899	21	67	30	0.79	256	43	21	36	173	28%	19	0%	7.45	12.8	55	$8
LIMA Plan	C	2nd Half	172	23	10	35	0	250			325	465	790	10	65	32	0.32	236	46	18	36	156	25%	21	0%	5.56	2.0	14	$6
Rand Var	0	10 Proj	325	54	22	66	0	252			368	497	866	16	68	30	0.57	256	43	19	38	171	25%	28	0%	6.73	12.9	50	$13

Power-and-patience set is fading almost imperceptibly; ct% and BA are now issues, particularly vs. LHP. Likely to be a strict platoon player, AB will decline accordingly. Pay for 20 HR, .850 OPS.

Thurston,Joe

		Year	AB	R	HR	RBI	SB	Avg	vL	vR	OB	Slg	OPS	bb%	ct%	h%	Eye	xBA	G	L	F	PX	hr/f	SX	SBO	RC/G	RAR	BPV	R$
Pos	54	05 aaa	357	27	6	27	4	215			241	302	543	3	89	23	0.32	0				50		66	18%	2.26	-27.0	25	$2
Age	31	06 aaa	479	70	10	52	19	270			326	422	748	8	86	30	0.61	0				89		136	23%	4.83	-5.9	74	$15
Bats	Left	07 a/a	509	51	4	43	12	235			281	327	608	6	89	26	0.57	0				59		87	22%	3.20	-32.2	43	$6
Health	A	08 aaa	507	61	7	46	14	258			293	361	654	5	86	29	0.35	0				69		98	20%	3.52	-24.4	39	$11
PT/Exp	D	09 STL	267	27	1	25	4	225	196	231	310	330	640	11	79	28	0.59	257	45	25	30	79	2%	100	8%	3.66	-12.1	33	$3
Consist	A	1st Half	187	23	1	19	3	219			321	353	674	13	80	27	0.76	269	45	24	31	96	2%	108	10%	4.25	-5.2	58	$2
LIMA Plan	F	2nd Half	80	4	0	6	1	237			282	275	557	6	76	31	0.26	233	45	28	27	36	0%	33	5%	2.22	-7.0	-43	$0
Rand Var	+2	10 Proj	195	19	1	17	4	241			294	335	630	7	82	29	0.43	266	45	26	29	66	3%	91	14%	3.34	-11.4	26	$3

We have a choice in this book. We can continue to include analyses for these useless players in the interest of completeness, or use the space in a more productive way. Voice your preference. See p.10.

Tolbert,Matt

		Year	AB	R	HR	RBI	SB	Avg	vL	vR	OB	Slg	OPS	bb%	ct%	h%	Eye	xBA	G	L	F	PX	hr/f	SX	SBO	RC/G	RAR	BPV	R$
Pos	45	05	0	0	0	0	0	0							0			0						0					
Age	28	06 aa	248	29	3	31	5	234			308	333	641	10	82	27	0.60	0				69		85	9%	3.60	-5.7	31	$4
Bats	Both	07 aaa	417	63	6	51	11	283			336	408	744	7	86	32	0.58	0				78		124	12%	4.77	5.0	62	$13
Health	C	08 MIN	113	18	0	6	7	283	306	273	325	389	714	6	83	34	0.37	272	41	30	30	70	0%	156	27%	4.37	-1.7	49	$4
PT/Exp	F	09 MIN	* 434	55	4	36	11	235	321	193	286	324	609	7	84	27	0.45	243	49	17	34	54	3%	114	17%	3.10	-24.2	30	$7
Consist	B	1st Half	219	25	2	18	7	200			274	272	546	9	81	24	0.54	205	44	13	43	46	2%	99	20%	2.36	-18.1	11	$2
LIMA Plan	F	2nd Half	215	30	2	18	5	271			299	376	675	4	88	30	0.32	294	57	22	21	61	5%	123	13%	3.78	-7.1	46	$5
Rand Var	+2	10 Proj	196	27	2	17	7	260			309	360	668	7	84	30	0.45	267	45	24	31	63	3%	125	17%	3.82	-5.1	41	$5

2-19-.232 in 198 AB at MIN. 1H patience didn't work, 2H hacking did, due to better luck with h%. Zero power with plus speed, must find consistent balance of ct% and bb% to to land full-time gig.

Torrealba,Yorvit

		Year	AB	R	HR	RBI	SB	Avg	vL	vR	OB	Slg	OPS	bb%	ct%	h%	Eye	xBA	G	L	F	PX	hr/f	SX	SBO	RC/G	RAR	BPV	R$
Pos	2	05 2TM	201	32	3	15	1	234	314	209	290	338	629	7	75	30	0.32	238	60	14	26	84	8%	69	2%	3.19	-4.3	5	$3
Age	32	06 COL	* 259	23	7	44	4	234	246	247	273	407	680	5	79	27	0.25	271	63	13	25	112	14%	85	15%	3.76	-4.6	42	$5
Bats	Right	07 COL	396	47	8	47	2	255	264	252	314	376	690	8	82	30	0.47	261	53	18	29	81	8%	56	3%	4.04	-4.6	26	$7
Health	C	08 COL	236	19	6	31	0	246	279	234	282	394	676	5	81	28	0.27	251	50	17	33	103	10%	21	9%	3.69	-3.7	26	$4
PT/Exp	D	09 COL	213	27	2	31	1	291	220	318	355	380	735	9	80	36	0.50	251	50	23	28	66	4%	61	3%	4.68	2.5	13	$6
Consist	B	1st Half	61	7	2	7	0	230			299	344	643	9	77	27	0.43	230	47	21	32	70	13%	24	0%	3.31	-1.7	-8	$1
LIMA Plan	F	2nd Half	152	20	0	24	1	316			377	395	772	9	82	39	0.54	258	51	23	26	65	0%	69	4%	5.21	3.9	19	$5
Rand Var	-5	10 Proj	259	29	5	34	1	263			318	378	696	8	80	31	0.41	253	51	19	29	81	8%	54	4%	4.08	-1.3	18	$6

Exhibit A of what improved patience and a little luck can do, even during power outage. Took over starting job in late Aug, h% did the rest. Track record, age, position suggest regression, more part-time AB.

Torres,Andres

		Year	AB	R	HR	RBI	SB	Avg	vL	vR	OB	Slg	OPS	bb%	ct%	h%	Eye	xBA	G	L	F	PX	hr/f	SX	SBO	RC/G	RAR	BPV	R$
Pos	87	05 aa	82	13	0	2	5	244			303	317	620	8	71	34	0.29	0				63		147	32%	3.19	-3.1	-5	$2
Age	32	06 aaa	348	43	2	28	18	214			303	318	621	11	72	29	0.46	0				74		143	26%	3.34	-13.2	14	$5
Bats	Both	07 a/a	473	58	7	40	17	232			289	381	670	7	76	29	0.33	0				91		134	24%	3.82	-10.3	31	$9
Health	C	08 aaa	409	60	8	33	19	233			294	370	664	8	77	29	0.37	0				94		151	24%	3.72	-16.5	45	$10
PT/Exp	F	09 SF	* 195	37	7	25	7	272	338	210	330	508	838	8	67	37	0.26	230	34	16	49	159	11%	150	17%	6.43	9.5	57	$8
Consist	C	1st Half	82	15	3	12	5	264			343	497	840	11	68	36	0.38	235	43	11	46	153	11%	149	22%	6.49	4.2	63	$4
LIMA Plan	D	2nd Half	113	22	4	13	2	277			320	515	836	6	66	39	0.18	227	29	19	52	163	11%	134	13%	6.38	5.3	47	$4
Rand Var	-5	10 Proj	133	22	3	14	5	248			310	437	747	8	71	33	0.31	221	34	17	50	122	7%	147	21%	4.94	1.0	44	$4

6-23-.270 in 152 AB with SF. Zero power, poor ct%, injuries derailed speedster's career in '03. Bad hammy, ct% issues now back - with power flash after 43 minor league HR in 3,334 AB. Guess which return in 2010?

Towles,J.R.

		Year	AB	R	HR	RBI	SB	Avg	vL	vR	OB	Slg	OPS	bb%	ct%	h%	Eye	xBA	G	L	F	PX	hr/f	SX	SBO	RC/G	RAR	BPV	R$
Pos	2	05	0	0	0	0	0	0							0			0						0					
Age	26	06	0	0	0	0	0	0							0			0						0					
Bats	Right	07 HOU	* 299	52	11	54	9	293	333	387	347	466	813	8	87	31	0.64	284	34	24	42	99	10%	94	22%	5.46	8.9	73	$13
Health	A	08 HOU	* 314	30	10	36	3	198	222	118	259	335	594	8	79	22	0.39	214	41	11	48	86	8%	61	10%	2.72	-15.0	22	$3
PT/Exp	F	09 HOU	* 193	24	5	19	2	217	286	147	287	366	653	9	80	25	0.50	243	53	9	38	103	8%	78	4%	3.62	-3.8	46	$3
Consist	D	1st Half	119	16	2	13	2	238			314	364	678	10	82	28	0.63	215	29	14	57	88	3%	88	6%	4.07	-0.7	48	$2
LIMA Plan	F	2nd Half	74	8	3	6	0	184			243	368	611	7	77	20	0.34	236	60	8	32	129	16%	27	0%	2.88	-3.3	34	$0
Rand Var	+2	10 Proj	226	27	7	25	2	239			299	395	694	8	80	27	0.44	239	48	11	41	101	9%	68	8%	4.03	-1.5	40	$5

2-3-.187 in 48 AB at HOU. Still young enough to have an impact, but stagnating skill set looks more like 2008 than promising 2007. Ct%, LD% have fallen, seemingly can't get up. Avoid until they do.

Tracy,Chad

		Year	AB	R	HR	RBI	SB	Avg	vL	vR	OB	Slg	OPS	bb%	ct%	h%	Eye	xBA	G	L	F	PX	hr/f	SX	SBO	RC/G	RAR	BPV	R$
Pos	3	05 ARI	503	73	27	72	3	308	236	324	353	553	906	7	84	32	0.45	309	33	24	42	147	15%	77	3%	6.43	11.4	94	$23
Age	30	06 ARI	597	91	20	80	5	281	231	304	341	451	792	8	78	33	0.42	254	36	21	43	112	10%	63	4%	5.27	-12.3	41	$19
Bats	Left	07 ARI	227	30	7	35	0	264	174	287	348	454	801	11	81	30	0.67	269	37	18	45	125	8%	53	0%	5.61	-3.4	65	$6
Health	D	08 ARI	* 322	29	8	43	0	265	243	271	302	395	696	5	84	30	0.32	257	29	24	47	85	6%	18	0%	3.93	-16.7	20	$7
PT/Exp	D	09 ARI	* 292	32	8	42	1	238	146	258	306	381	687	9	85	26	0.64	245	35	18	48	91	7%	46	3%	4.08	-21.3	45	$6
Consist	B	1st Half	154	17	4	20	1	212			276	358	634	8	86	22	0.65	251	37	17	46	92	7%	65	6%	3.48	-14.5	57	$2
LIMA Plan	F	2nd Half	138	15	4	22	0	268			340	406	746	10	83	30	0.63	238	32	19	49	90	7%	19	0%	4.78	-6.9	30	$4
Rand Var	+2	10 Proj	284	32	8	41	0	257			318	411	730	8	83	28	0.54	254	33	20	47	99	7%	42	1%	4.53	-13.7	44	$7

8-39-.237 in 257 AB at ARI. Power hasn't resurfaced since '07 knee surgery, more injuries (oblique) cutting into PT. As 2010 FA, future is cloudy. Chase Field: .302/.360/.497 On the road: .259/.319/.413

Tulowitzki,Troy

		Year	AB	R	HR	RBI	SB	Avg	vL	vR	OB	Slg	OPS	bb%	ct%	h%	Eye	xBA	G	L	F	PX	hr/f	SX	SBO	RC/G	RAR	BPV	R$
Pos	6	05	0	0	0	0	0	0							0			0						0					
Age	25	06 COL	* 519	73	12	53	8	268	150	263	326	410	737	8	85	29	0.59	281	49	21	30	89	9%	78	10%	4.65	4.4	54	$13
Bats	Right	07 COL	609	104	24	99	7	291	333	278	351	479	831	9	79	34	0.44	271	42	20	38	119	13%	91	8%	5.76	22.5	56	$24
Health	B	08 COL	377	48	8	46	1	263	330	242	330	401	731	9	85	29	0.68	264	42	20	37	90	7%	53	7%	4.66	0.4	49	$9
PT/Exp	A	09 COL	543	101	32	92	20	297	269	307	380	552	932	12	79	32	0.65	287	42	18	40	153	19%	128	18%	7.15	38.4	104	$31
Consist	D	1st Half	245	40	12	31	11	249			348	461	809	13	78	28	0.67	256	40	16	44	131	14%	117	25%	5.68	7.7	78	$10
LIMA Plan	B	2nd Half	298	61	20	61	9	336			407	628	1035	11	81	36	0.63	311	44	21	36	170	23%	125	14%	8.31	28.9	121	$21
Rand Var	-3	10 Proj	534	88	23	81	12	287			360	494	853	10	81	32	0.61	279	42	19	38	126	14%	106	13%	6.10	23.3	80	$23

Spring FB spike morphed into elevated hr/f, h%, resulting in monster 2H. Some slight regression is likely across the board, including SB (64% SB%), but you still want these skills from your 25-year old SS.

Uggla,Dan

		Year	AB	R	HR	RBI	SB	Avg	vL	vR	OB	Slg	OPS	bb%	ct%	h%	Eye	xBA	G	L	F	PX	hr/f	SX	SBO	RC/G	RAR	BPV	R$
Pos	4	05 aa	495	62	16	61	11	251			305	420	725	7	82	28	0.44	0				110		90	17%	4.40	0.8	59	$14
Age	30	06 FLA	611	105	27	90	6	282	307	273	334	480	813	7	80	31	0.39	256	41	17	42	113	13%	95	8%	5.42	14.4	55	$23
Bats	Right	07 FLA	632	113	31	88	2	245	245	245	319	479	798	10	74	29	0.41	263	34	16	51	162	13%	78	2%	5.48	14.6	69	$19
Health	A	08 FLA	531	97	32	92	5	260	191	283	354	514	868	13	68	32	0.45	254	36	16	48	189	18%	68	7%	6.74	30.8	70	$22
PT/Exp	A	09 FLA	564	84	31	90	2	243	208	253	349	459	808	14	73	28	0.61	249	37	17	46	145	16%	49	2%	5.72	20.1	55	$19
Consist	C	1st Half	271	38	15	45	1	225			333	443	776	14	76	24	0.68	247	33	16	51	139	14%	51	1%	5.25	5.9	61	$8
LIMA Plan	C+	2nd Half	293	46	16	45	1	259			364	474	838	14	71	31	0.56	250	40	18	42	151	18%	36	2%	6.21	14.4	46	$11
Rand Var	+1	10 Proj	583	95	31	92	4	250			343	477	820	12	73	29	0.51	254	37	17	47	155	16%	67	4%	5.86	21.4	61	$20

PRO: Elite power+patience at MI spot; stable HR & RBI. CON: Ct%, sub-par BA, streakiness, slight FB erosion. Hate to keep bringing this up, but since the '08 All Star Game debacle, he's batted just .238.

JOCK THOMPSON

Upton,B.J.

Upton,B.J.		AB	R	HR	RBI	SB	Avg	vL	vR	OB	Slg	OPS	bb%	ct%	h%	Eye	xBA	G	L	F	PX	hr/f	SX	SBO	RC/G	RAR	BPV	R$
Pos 8	05 aaa	536	75	13	56	35	275			349	425	773	10	84	31	0.72	0				96		118	34%	5.21	12.5	72	$22
Age 26	06 TAM	* 573	90	8	50	56	258	298	227	345	357	702	12	79	31	0.63	248	54	19	27	65	7%	135	41%	4.38	-5.0	34	$23
Bats Right	07 TAM	474	86	24	82	22	300	281	306	384	508	892	12	68	40	0.42	257	43	20	38	156	20%	95	19%	7.13	34.7	49	$25
Health A	08 TAM	531	85	9	67	44	273	269	275	385	401	786	15	75	35	0.72	252	51	19	31	101	7%	111	31%	5.72	5.8	46	$24
PT/Exp A	09 TAM	560	79	11	55	42	241	190	262	311	373	684	9	73	31	0.38	227	44	15	40	96	7%	130	39%	4.03	-10.5	28	$19
Consist D	1st Half	293	52	7	31	29	246			336	386	722	12	71	32	0.47	227	45	15	40	105	8%	131	42%	4.67	0.2	33	$13
LIMA Plan C+	2nd Half	267	27	4	24	13	236			282	360	641	6	75	30	0.25	227	44	16	41	87	5%	117	34%	3.33	-10.9	18	$6
Rand Var +1	10 Proj	**530**	**78**	**12**	**61**	**37**	**260**			**341**	**401**	**743**	**11**	**74**	**33**	**0.47**	**241**	**46**	**17**	**37**	**103**	**9%**	**117**	**33%**	**4.88**	**1.5**	**36**	**$20**

Were 2008 playoffs a tease? Or was it off-season shoulder surgery? Did poor 2H bb% and selectivity derail June HR spike? Elite speed a given, power remains a mystery. Age keeps huge upside intact.

Upton,Justin

Upton,Justin		AB	R	HR	RBI	SB	Avg	vL	vR	OB	Slg	OPS	bb%	ct%	h%	Eye	xBA	G	L	F	PX	hr/f	SX	SBO	RC/G	RAR	BPV	R$
Pos 9	05	0	0	0	0	0	0							0			0						0					
Age 23	06	0	0	0	0	0	0							0			0						0					
Bats Right	07 ARI	* 399	59	15	57	10	278	200	230	350	486	836	10	81	31	0.58	265	36	16	48	127	9%	114	17%	5.95	12.4	81	$15
Health C	08 ARI	356	52	15	42	1	250	253	249	349	463	812	13	66	34	0.45	239	37	21	42	157	15%	83	5%	6.15	10.2	43	$9
PT/Exp C	09 ARI	526	84	26	86	20	300	377	277	367	532	899	9	74	36	0.40	275	45	19	36	155	19%	129	17%	6.81	28.3	80	$28
Consist A	1st Half	273	49	14	45	10	315			393	568	961	11	74	38	0.50	287	41	23	37	171	19%	126	14%	7.75	21.3	97	$16
LIMA Plan B+	2nd Half	253	35	12	41	10	285			337	494	831	7	74	34	0.30	261	50	15	35	138	19%	117	20%	5.78	6.5	56	$12
Rand Var -4	10 Proj	**563**	**85**	**27**	**91**	**21**	**277**			**354**	**505**	**859**	**11**	**72**	**34**	**0.43**	**265**	**43**	**19**	**39**	**154**	**17%**	**129**	**17%**	**6.40**	**23.3**	**74**	**$26**

HR spike in the face of rising GB%. Improved ct%, but bb% decline suggests next tick up could take a bit longer. 80% SB% indicates speed is fast tracking. Consolidation year in '10, but if not... UP: 30-30

Uribe,Juan

Uribe,Juan		AB	R	HR	RBI	SB	Avg	vL	vR	OB	Slg	OPS	bb%	ct%	h%	Eye	xBA	G	L	F	PX	hr/f	SX	SBO	RC/G	RAR	BPV	R$
Pos 564	05 CHW	481	58	16	71	4	252	311	234	301	412	713	7	84	27	0.44	258	38	19	42	98	9%	68	9%	4.21	-4.2	50	$12
Age 31	06 CHW	463	53	21	71	1	235	224	244	256	441	697	3	82	24	0.16	265	38	17	45	123	12%	58	3%	3.76	-17.4	53	$10
Bats Right	07 CHW	513	55	20	68	1	234	257	225	282	394	675	6	78	26	0.30	232	35	15	50	101	10%	39	9%	3.62	-19.6	19	$9
Health A	08 CHW	324	38	7	40	1	247	254	245	295	386	681	6	80	29	0.34	248	34	20	45	99	6%	55	6%	3.84	-10.1	32	$6
PT/Exp C	09 SF	398	50	16	55	3	289	255	299	331	495	826	6	79	33	0.30	275	39	21	40	134	13%	84	4%	5.55	4.6	64	$15
Consist B	1st Half	149	13	2	15	1	282			305	423	728	3	79	35	0.16	262	47	20	33	109	5%	64	6%	4.32	-3.5	29	$3
LIMA Plan D+	2nd Half	249	37	14	40	2	293			346	538	884	7	80	32	0.40	282	35	21	44	149	16%	90	3%	6.28	7.8	83	$11
Rand Var -4	10 Proj	**395**	**47**	**14**	**53**	**2**	**258**			**302**	**438**	**740**	**6**	**80**	**29**	**0.31**	**260**	**38**	**20**	**43**	**117**	**10%**	**70**	**6%**	**4.50**	**-9.0**	**48**	**$10**

More LDs are helping his BA as did an unsustainable h%, notably vs. RHP. AT&T Park offense (.346/.385/.582) was astounding. Attractive power, versatility, but bb% and pitch selection still a shaky base.

Utley,Chase

Utley,Chase		AB	R	HR	RBI	SB	Avg	vL	vR	OB	Slg	OPS	bb%	ct%	h%	Eye	xBA	G	L	F	PX	hr/f	SX	SBO	RC/G	RAR	BPV	R$
Pos 4	05 PHI	543	93	28	105	16	291	220	313	371	540	911	11	80	32	0.63	297	35	23	42	159	15%	125	12%	6.89	35.4	109	$29
Age 31	06 PHI	658	131	32	102	15	309	301	312	369	527	896	9	80	35	0.48	269	37	20	43	131	14%	111	10%	6.53	34.8	77	$32
Bats Left	07 PHI	530	104	22	103	9	332	318	340	390	566	956	9	83	37	0.56	301	38	20	42	147	12%	112	7%	7.27	35.8	104	$29
Health A	08 PHI	607	113	33	104	14	292	277	301	359	535	895	10	83	31	0.62	294	33	24	42	147	15%	117	10%	6.51	29.4	106	$31
PT/Exp A	09 PHI	571	112	31	93	23	282	288	279	378	508	886	13	81	30	0.80	267	34	18	48	137	14%	128	12%	6.62	33.6	99	$31
Consist A	1st Half	266	53	17	52	7	301			408	560	968	15	81	32	0.96	286	35	18	47	158	17%	92	7%	7.72	23.3	112	$16
LIMA Plan B+	2nd Half	305	59	14	41	16	266			351	462	813	12	80	29	0.67	250	33	19	48	118	12%	139	17%	5.65	9.8	83	$15
Rand Var 0	10 Proj	**590**	**114**	**30**	**100**	**19**	**280**			**360**	**508**	**869**	**11**	**82**	**30**	**0.68**	**278**	**35**	**20**	**45**	**140**	**14%**	**129**	**12%**	**6.31**	**28.2**	**101**	**$29**

FB%, bb% hikes say he was looking for pitches to drive. Less aggressive approach nicked ct% and BA slightly, but SBO trend keeps value intact. Remains Exhibit A for Elite consistency at 2B.

Valbuena,Luis

Valbuena,Luis		AB	R	HR	RBI	SB	Avg	vL	vR	OB	Slg	OPS	bb%	ct%	h%	Eye	xBA	G	L	F	PX	hr/f	SX	SBO	RC/G	RAR	BPV	R$
Pos 46	05	0	0	0	0	0	0							0			0						0					
Age 24	06	0	0	0	0	0	0							0			0						0					
Bats Left	07 aa	444	47	9	38	9	214			283	331	614	9	83	24	0.57	0				76		76	15%	3.19	-16.1	35	$5
Health A	08 SEA	* 501	75	9	50	15	267			339	373	712	10	86	30	0.76	0				69		88	16%	4.47	-6.2	47	$14
PT/Exp D	09 CLE	* 446	64	12	42	4	257	205	255	318	420	738	8	79	30	0.42	265	41	22	37	107	9%	81	10%	4.64	-3.9	43	$10
Consist B	1st Half	211	30	6	21	3	230			314	395	708	11	76	28	0.51	251	36	21	43	114	9%	76	15%	4.39	-3.5	42	$4
LIMA Plan C+	2nd Half	235	34	6	21	1	281			321	443	764	6	81	32	0.32	275	43	23	34	100	9%	88	5%	4.81	-0.8	45	$6
Rand Var 0	10 Proj	**530**	**74**	**17**	**50**	**9**	**260**			**324**	**425**	**748**	**9**	**82**	**29**	**0.52**	**274**	**41**	**22**	**37**	**103**	**11%**	**82**	**13%**	**4.75**	**0.8**	**54**	**$14**

10-31-.250 in 368 AB at CLE Hopeful start for growth-age MI. Decent pop with LD stroke and promising patience. Pitch selection, ct% are works-in-progress, but not hopeless. 39 MLB ABs vs. LHP tell us little.

Valdez,Wilson

Valdez,Wilson		AB	R	HR	RBI	SB	Avg	vL	vR	OB	Slg	OPS	bb%	ct%	h%	Eye	xBA	G	L	F	PX	hr/f	SX	SBO	RC/G	RAR	BPV	R$
Pos 6	05 2TM	* 298	19	1	20	8	196	143	227	245	261	506	6	84	23	0.39	262	60	20	20	45	2%	101	15%	1.85	-22.8	15	$0
Age 32	06 aaa	528	67	5	38	19	236			289	298	586	7	92	25	0.89	0				38		81	27%	3.07	-21.7	37	$8
Bats Right	07 aaa	361	51	3	18	9	235			289	299	589	7	89	26	0.72	0				42		93	15%	3.03	-14.8	35	$5
Health A	08 JPN	78	8	1	8	1	239			297	275	572	8	83	28	0.49	0				23		47	4%	2.59	-4.4	-18	$1
PT/Exp F	09 NYM	* 321	33	0	16	5	206	115	317	254	241	496	6	88	24	0.53	259	64	19	17	24	0%	90	10%	1.88	-28.1	11	$1
Consist B	1st Half	168	16	0	10	4	156			213	179	393	7	86	18	0.53	239	75	10	15	14	0%	105	14%	0.66	-22.4	4	($1)
LIMA Plan F	2nd Half	153	17	0	6	1	261			300	309	610	5	89	29	0.52	272	60	22	18	34	0%	67	6%	3.18	-6.7	17	$2
Rand Var +5	10 Proj	**84**	**10**	**0**	**4**	**2**	**226**			**276**	**273**	**549**	**6**	**88**	**25**	**0.59**	**266**	**62**	**20**	**18**	**35**	**2%**	**69**	**14%**	**2.51**	**-5.3**	**17**	**$1**

0-7-.256 in 86 AB at NYM. When a player has this little power and makes this much empty contact, eventually he should stop swinging so often. Consistency here isn't a good thing.

Varitek,Jason

Varitek,Jason		AB	R	HR	RBI	SB	Avg	vL	vR	OB	Slg	OPS	bb%	ct%	h%	Eye	xBA	G	L	F	PX	hr/f	SX	SBO	RC/G	RAR	BPV	R$
Pos 2	05 BOS	470	70	22	70	2	281	320	267	365	489	854	12	75	33	0.53	277	45	23	32	144	20%	57	1%	6.27	29.8	58	$17
Age 38	06 BOS	365	46	12	55	1	238	229	244	324	400	724	11	76	28	0.53	241	45	17	38	106	11%	55	3%	4.55	1.6	30	$7
Bats Both	07 BOS	435	57	17	68	1	255	264	252	360	421	780	14	72	32	0.58	238	42	18	40	112	14%	51	2%	5.45	14.8	23	$11
Health A	08 BOS	423	37	13	43	0	220	284	201	305	359	665	11	71	28	0.43	202	42	14	45	104	10%	14	1%	3.74	-5.9	-4	$4
PT/Exp B	09 BOS	364	41	14	51	0	209	231	200	311	390	701	13	75	24	0.60	235	38	15	47	123	11%	19	0%	4.31	0.4	33	$5
Consist C	1st Half	205	31	11	32	0	234			332	473	805	13	78	25	0.67	271	40	15	45	153	15%	27	0%	5.61	8.3	70	$5
LIMA Plan F	2nd Half	159	10	3	19	0	176			284	283	567	13	72	23	0.53	187	35	15	50	81	5%	8	0%	2.50	-9.1	-18	($1)
Rand Var +4	10 Proj	**153**	**16**	**5**	**20**	**0**	**222**			**319**	**376**	**696**	**12**	**73**	**27**	**0.53**	**222**	**40**	**16**	**45**	**109**	**10%**	**22**	**1%**	**4.21**	**-0.2**	**13**	**$2**

Hit 10 HR over first 2 months via aggressiveness, finished as an automatic out (.125 BA, zero HR) from August on. Contact issues, recent LD%s and 2H power plunge say that regular playing time is history.

Vazquez,Ramon

Vazquez,Ramon		AB	R	HR	RBI	SB	Avg	vL	vR	OB	Slg	OPS	bb%	ct%	h%	Eye	xBA	G	L	F	PX	hr/f	SX	SBO	RC/G	RAR	BPV	R$
Pos 64	05 2AL	* 169	18	0	9	1	201	250	203	250	254	504	6	80	25	0.32	229	53	19	28	43	0%	79	5%	1.70	-15.3	-8	($0)
Age 34	06 CLE	* 166	29	2	18	2	217	286	200	323	289	612	14	72	29	0.55	186	40	17	43	50	4%	95	5%	3.17	-6.4	-16	$2
Bats Left	07 TEX	* 432	58	9	36	3	212	184	246	283	344	626	9	76	26	0.42	250	43	21	36	91	8%	98	4%	3.23	-14.1	27	$4
Health A	08 TEX	300	44	6	40	0	290	188	310	370	430	800	11	78	36	0.58	277	46	27	26	98	10%	66	1%	5.63	10.9	35	$9
PT/Exp D	09 PIT	204	17	1	16	1	230	290	220	332	279	611	13	77	29	0.66	205	47	19	34	41	2%	31	1%	3.26	-8.6	-22	$1
Consist F	1st Half	90	10	0	8	1	244			346	256	602	13	73	33	0.58	190	37	25	37	11	0%	43	3%	3.06	-4.3	-56	$1
LIMA Plan F	2nd Half	114	7	1	8	0	219			321	298	619	13	80	27	0.74	200	53	15	32	62	3%	8	0%	3.42	-4.3	-0	$0
Rand Var 0	10 Proj	**185**	**21**	**2**	**17**	**1**	**238**			**327**	**326**	**654**	**12**	**77**	**30**	**0.58**	**233**	**46**	**21**	**32**	**65**	**5%**	**59**	**2%**	**3.75**	**-4.5**	**3**	**$2**

PRO: Excellent health, patience. CON: Everything else. A fluky 1H in '08 bought him a middling 2H in '08, and as if nobody noticed that middling 2H, he still got 204 AB in '09. But again, he's got that good health.

Velez,Eugenio

Velez,Eugenio		AB	R	HR	RBI	SB	Avg	vL	vR	OB	Slg	OPS	bb%	ct%	h%	Eye	xBA	G	L	F	PX	hr/f	SX	SBO	RC/G	RAR	BPV	R$
Pos 74	05	0	0	0	0	0	0							0			0						0					
Age 28	06	0	0	0	0	0	0							0			0						0					
Bats Both	07 aa	394	45	1	19	41	247			284	322	606	5	84	29	0.33	0				48		156	61%	3.00	-27.2	34	$12
Health A	08 SF	* 446	52	5	42	26	265	235	268	308	398	706	6	84	31	0.39	276	59	15	26	85	5%	144	39%	4.25	-15.8	62	$14
PT/Exp D	09 SF	* 467	63	7	52	24	261	200	286	300	391	690	5	83	30	0.33	268	54	17	29	84	6%	141	35%	3.97	-22.4	54	$15
Consist B	1st Half	138	15	2	8	10	227			265	338	604	5	85	25	0.36	256	54	14	32	71	5%	133	54%	2.97	-11.4	50	$3
LIMA Plan D+	2nd Half	329	49	5	44	14	275			314	412	727	5	82	32	0.32	270	54	18	29	89	6%	136	28%	4.41	-11.2	53	$12
Rand Var 0	10 Proj	**336**	**42**	**4**	**31**	**21**	**265**			**305**	**385**	**689**	**5**	**84**	**31**	**0.35**	**268**	**56**	**16**	**28**	**76**	**5%**	**145**	**40%**	**3.99**	**-15.0**	**52**	**$11**

5-31-.267 with 11 SB in 285 AB at SF. 2H gains from LD% and h% hikes, stagnant bb%, ct%, and pitch selection make this look like his ceiling. Elite speed still capped by marginal SB% (73% in MLB) and SBO trend.

JOCK THOMPSON

Venable,Will			AB	R	HR	RBI	SB	Avg	vL	vR	OB	Slg	OPS	bb%	ct%	h%	Eye	xBA	G	L	F	PX	hr/f	SX	SBO	RC/G	RAR	BPV	R$
Pos	9	05	0	0	0	0	0	0							0			0						0					
Age	27	06	0	0	0	0	0	0							0			0						0					
Bats	Left	07 aa	515	56	7	58	18	238			284	314	598	6	84	27	0.40	0				48		106	15%	2.86	-36.1	20	$10
Health	A	08 SD	* 552	72	12	57	7	245	324	237	305	374	679	8	78	29	0.39	232	49	13	37	86	8%	96	7%	3.87	-21.8	28	$11
PT/Exp	C	09 SD	* 493	63	20	60	7	234	225	266	291	417	708	7	73	28	0.30	242	44	16	40	123	14%	100	7%	4.14	-10.9	39	$13
Consist	B	1st Half	235	29	8	24	2	194			253	359	612	7	77	22	0.34	253	48	17	35	108	13%	91	4%	2.91	-14.6	38	$3
LIMA Plan	D+	2nd Half	258	34	12	36	5	271			326	469	795	8	70	34	0.27	240	43	16	41	137	16%	93	9%	5.40	3.9	36	$10
Rand Var	0	10 Proj	454	57	14	52	8	242			299	390	688	7	76	29	0.34	235	45	15	40	97	10%	100	9%	3.90	-14.5	30	$11

12-38-.256 in 293 AB at SD. Contact-for-pop tradeoff paid dividends, but only after h%, hr/f inflation in 2H. Ct% and bb% say fluke, not growth. Ct% trend is particularly damning. Exercise extreme caution.

Victorino,Shane			AB	R	HR	RBI	SB	Avg	vL	vR	OB	Slg	OPS	bb%	ct%	h%	Eye	xBA	G	L	F	PX	hr/f	SX	SBO	RC/G	RAR	BPV	R$
Pos	8	05 aaa	494	73	16	55	13	279			332	468	800	7	88	29	0.68	0				102		126	19%	5.37	13.6	90	$18
Age	29	06 PHI	415	70	6	46	4	287	273	293	326	414	740	5	87	32	0.44	266	45	21	34	72	5%	117	6%	4.60	1.9	53	$12
Bats	Both	07 PHI	456	78	12	46	37	281	291	276	335	423	758	8	86	30	0.60	273	47	17	36	85	8%	140	32%	4.85	4.2	72	$21
Health	A	08 PHI	570	102	14	58	36	293	282	298	345	447	792	7	88	31	0.65	276	45	19	36	90	8%	154	29%	5.28	8.8	86	$27
PT/Exp	A	09 PHI	620	102	10	62	25	292	314	283	354	445	800	9	89	32	0.85	288	45	22	33	93	5%	144	18%	5.55	14.3	91	$24
Consist	A	1st Half	302	52	5	34	13	295			362	440	803	10	87	32	0.84	285	45	23	33	91	6%	137	18%	5.61	7.5	85	$13
LIMA Plan	B+	2nd Half	318	50	5	28	12	289			347	450	797	8	90	31	0.85	292	46	21	34	94	5%	139	18%	5.49	6.9	94	$12
Rand Var	0	10 Proj	612	103	13	62	30	289			346	444	789	8	88	31	0.72	283	45	20	34	91	7%	152	23%	5.33	11.4	89	$25

SBO plunge likely a result of WBC play, nagging injuries (hip, knee, quad). SX gives hope for SB rebound. Steady ct% and PX, patience uptick provide additional reasons to own this stable skill set.

Vizquel,Omar			AB	R	HR	RBI	SB	Avg	vL	vR	OB	Slg	OPS	bb%	ct%	h%	Eye	xBA	G	L	F	PX	hr/f	SX	SBO	RC/G	RAR	BPV	R$
Pos	65	05 SF	568	66	3	45	24	271	253	279	337	350	687	9	90	30	0.97	273	44	24	32	53	2%	106	19%	4.30	5.7	54	$15
Age	43	06 SF	579	88	4	58	24	295	340	281	357	389	746	9	91	32	1.10	257	40	22	38	51	2%	132	16%	4.99	10.2	65	$19
Bats	Both	07 SF	513	54	4	51	14	246	243	247	305	316	621	8	91	26	0.92	243	41	18	40	43	2%	91	14%	3.50	-14.7	42	$9
Health	B	08 SF	266	24	0	23	5	222	121	250	286	267	553	8	89	25	0.83	235	42	21	37	34	0%	74	13%	2.74	-15.7	24	$2
PT/Exp	D	09 TEX	177	17	1	14	4	266	485	215	316	345	660	7	85	31	0.48	232	34	22	43	50	2%	96	8%	3.73	-3.7	23	$3
Consist	B	1st Half	74	10	0	7	4	297			342	378	720	6	91	33	0.71	235	38	17	45	52	0%	118	18%	4.55	0.2	54	$3
LIMA Plan	F	2nd Half	103	7	1	7	0	243			297	320	618	7	81	29	0.40	236	32	27	41	48	3%	42	0%	3.11	-4.1	-10	$1
Rand Var	-4	10 Proj	148	15	1	13	4	250			307	318	625	8	87	28	0.64	239	38	21	40	45	1%	81	11%	3.42	-4.3	27	$2

Ct% and speed cratered in 2H as PT increased. Glove, defensive versatility and LD stroke could land him final bench role, but he's running on empty. No longer an asset in our game, in any format.

Votto,Joey			AB	R	HR	RBI	SB	Avg	vL	vR	OB	Slg	OPS	bb%	ct%	h%	Eye	xBA	G	L	F	PX	hr/f	SX	SBO	RC/G	RAR	BPV	R$
Pos	3	05	0	0	0	0	0	0							0			0						0					
Age	27	06 aa	508	78	21	71	22	300			383	517	901	12	79	34	0.65	0				143		93	19%	6.86	16.3	86	$23
Bats	Left	07 CIN	* 580	77	26	99	16	284	269	345	359	469	828	10	81	32	0.59	270	28	26	46	112	12%	65	15%	5.74	-6.5	54	$24
Health	A	08 CIN	526	69	24	84	7	297	292	299	368	506	873	10	81	33	0.58	295	44	25	31	131	18%	69	8%	6.33	8.8	70	$22
PT/Exp	B	09 CIN	469	82	25	84	4	322	329	319	410	567	977	13	77	37	0.66	292	39	22	39	167	18%	63	3%	7.90	17.4	90	$25
Consist	C	1st Half	158	27	9	38	2	354			446	601	1047	14	80	40	0.81	307	42	25	33	161	21%	43	5%	8.75	9.0	91	$11
LIMA Plan	B	2nd Half	311	55	16	46	2	305			392	550	941	12	76	36	0.59	284	37	20	42	170	16%	66	2%	7.45	8.0	87	$15
Rand Var	-4	10 Proj	525	91	31	100	6	309			390	559	949	12	79	34	0.64	300	41	23	36	160	20%	64	6%	7.37	17.0	89	$28

Fought through 1H dizziness and personal issues to forge fine season. BA hike suspect due to h% and contact. With G/L/F in flux, PX spike needs validation. All minor stuff; this is a skill set well worth owning.

Weeks,Rickie			AB	R	HR	RBI	SB	Avg	vL	vR	OB	Slg	OPS	bb%	ct%	h%	Eye	xBA	G	L	F	PX	hr/f	SX	SBO	RC/G	RAR	BPV	R$
Pos	4	05 MIL	* 563	88	22	78	23	254	229	244	327	446	773	10	76	30	0.45	277	49	20	31	124	17%	151	18%	5.12	9.3	70	$22
Age	28	06 MIL	359	73	8	34	19	279	271	280	334	404	738	8	74	36	0.33	236	46	20	33	83	9%	141	23%	4.62	0.2	23	$14
Bats	Right	07 MIL	409	87	16	36	25	235	258	225	357	433	790	16	72	29	0.67	250	42	17	41	133	13%	157	21%	5.72	12.6	75	$15
Health	F	08 MIL	475	89	14	46	19	234	250	227	327	398	725	12	76	28	0.57	242	46	15	39	107	10%	151	18%	4.66	-1.6	61	$15
PT/Exp	C	09 MIL	147	28	9	24	2	272	276	271	327	517	844	8	73	31	0.31	261	38	19	44	154	19%	114	11%	5.90	5.8	69	$7
Consist	C	1st Half	147	28	9	24	2	272			327	517	844	8	73	31	0.31	261	37	19	44	154	19%	114	11%	5.90	5.8	69	$7
LIMA Plan	B	2nd Half	0	0	0	0	0	0																					
Rand Var	-2	10 Proj	477	93	15	56	19	264			344	426	770	11	74	33	0.47	239	42	18	40	108	11%	146	17%	5.20	8.0	50	$19

Enjoyed career-best start until wrist injury ended season in May. PX and SX history still project near elite HR-SB upside, but health hasn't cooperated and wrist issues can sap power. If 2009 was real... UP: 25/25.

Wells,Vernon			AB	R	HR	RBI	SB	Avg	vL	vR	OB	Slg	OPS	bb%	ct%	h%	Eye	xBA	G	L	F	PX	hr/f	SX	SBO	RC/G	RAR	BPV	R$
Pos	8	05 TOR	620	78	28	97	8	269	347	243	321	463	784	7	86	27	0.55	278	41	19	40	113	13%	82	7%	5.04	13.6	75	$21
Age	31	06 TOR	611	91	32	106	17	303	333	292	359	542	901	8	85	31	0.60	295	42	18	40	136	15%	105	13%	6.48	30.7	100	$28
Bats	Right	07 TOR	584	85	16	80	10	245	311	226	303	402	706	8	85	27	0.55	266	39	17	44	101	7%	103	10%	4.26	-4.7	68	$14
Health	B	08 TOR	427	63	20	78	4	300	333	290	344	496	841	6	89	30	0.63	294	47	17	36	111	15%	66	5%	5.65	3.6	80	$18
PT/Exp	A	09 TOR	630	84	15	66	17	260	206	278	313	400	713	7	86	28	0.56	254	43	15	42	85	6%	100	13%	4.33	-5.8	59	$17
Consist	C	1st Half	322	46	7	36	12	248			305	388	693	7	88	26	0.68	264	43	16	41	84	6%	119	16%	4.19	-4.3	73	$9
LIMA Plan	C+	2nd Half	308	38	8	30	5	273			321	412	734	7	84	30	0.46	243	42	14	44	86	7%	72	11%	4.49	-1.3	43	$8
Rand Var	0	10 Proj	618	85	20	83	12	272			323	437	760	7	87	29	0.56	269	43	16	41	98	9%	94	10%	4.82	0.7	69	$19

Now 2006 is looking like 5-year outlier. Power trending south along with patience and LD%. Improved health and likely hr/f, LHP improvements give hope, but trends and age suggest a ceiling. 81% SB% still a plus.

Werth,Jayson			AB	R	HR	RBI	SB	Avg	vL	vR	OB	Slg	OPS	bb%	ct%	h%	Eye	xBA	G	L	F	PX	hr/f	SX	SBO	RC/G	RAR	BPV	R$
Pos	9	05 LA	* 386	52	9	50	15	242	239	237	338	379	717	13	68	34	0.44	225	41	20	39	111	9%	109	15%	4.70	-6.4	19	$11
Age	31	06	0	0	0	0	0	0							0			0						0					
Bats	Right	07 PHI	255	43	8	49	7	298	375	257	401	459	860	15	71	39	0.60	255	40	27	33	109	13%	109	8%	6.71	12.9	37	$11
Health	B	08 PHI	418	73	24	67	20	273	303	255	360	498	858	12	72	33	0.48	259	39	23	38	147	21%	130	16%	6.37	14.1	69	$22
PT/Exp	B	09 PHI	571	98	36	99	20	268	302	256	369	506	875	14	73	31	0.58	261	36	20	44	159	20%	95	13%	6.61	28.6	76	$29
Consist	A	1st Half	275	52	15	43	10	265			361	484	844	13	76	30	0.62	263	41	17	42	141	17%	102	14%	6.12	10.0	75	$13
LIMA Plan	B	2nd Half	296	46	21	56	10	270			376	527	903	14	70	32	0.56	260	31	22	47	177	22%	71	11%	7.12	19.1	72	$16
Rand Var	+1	10 Proj	576	96	35	98	20	262			361	492	853	13	71	31	0.54	261	37	22	41	155	21%	98	12%	6.35	23.1	68	$27

FB% spike, patience say he looked for pitches to drive. HR spike and elite PX say he was successful. 87% SB% says SBO should keep coming. H% says he wasn't particularly lucky. We say pay it again.

Whitesell,Josh			AB	R	HR	RBI	SB	Avg	vL	vR	OB	Slg	OPS	bb%	ct%	h%	Eye	xBA	G	L	F	PX	hr/f	SX	SBO	RC/G	RAR	BPV	R$
Pos	3	05	0	0	0	0	0	0							0			0						0					
Age	28	06 aa	402	40	15	48	2	225			302	362	664	10	69	28	0.36	0				90		25	8%	3.62	-26.1	-21	$6
Bats	Left	07 aa	387	60	15	58	5	228			340	400	740	15	73	27	0.64	0				118		68	5%	4.88	-9.6	39	$9
Health	A	08 aa	475	67	22	86	1	289			368	496	864	11	75	35	0.50	0				145		30	2%	6.39	11.9	48	$19
PT/Exp	D	09 ARI	* 333	33	7	58	1	233	208	190	341	363	705	14	78	28	0.75	247	46	20	34	93	8%	36	2%	4.51	-20.1	29	$6
Consist	D	1st Half	217	21	5	39	0	259			372	398	770	15	80	30	0.89	282	44	29	27	96	12%	29	1%	5.41	-7.0	37	$5
LIMA Plan	F	2nd Half	116	12	2	19	1	186			282	298	580	12	75	23	0.54	208	47	11	42	89	5%	45	3%	2.75	-13.9	12	$1
Rand Var	+2	10 Proj	122	15	4	20	1	238			334	389	722	13	75	29	0.58	235	46	16	38	108	11%	36	3%	4.60	-5.8	25	$3

1-14-.194 in 108 AB at ARI. Upward power trend a thing of the past, leaving ultra-patient low-ct% hitter in its wake. '08 BA vanished with inflated h%. Punchlessness in the PCL and at Chase Field is a bad sign.

Whiteside,Eli			AB	R	HR	RBI	SB	Avg	vL	vR	OB	Slg	OPS	bb%	ct%	h%	Eye	xBA	G	L	F	PX	hr/f	SX	SBO	RC/G	RAR	BPV	R$
Pos	2	05 aaa	309	23	4	23	1	208			251	317	569	5	83	24	0.33	0				79		49	7%	2.51	-13.5	22	$0
Age	30	06 aaa	315	36	11	46	1	231			254	394	648	3	77	27	0.13	0				107		62	7%	3.17	-11.6	19	$5
Bats	Right	07 a/a	202	18	5	29	1	207			233	340	573	3	78	24	0.16	0				81		81	13%	2.28	-13.3	12	$2
Health	A	08 a/a	175	11	2	16	2	176			215	236	452	5	84	20	0.31	0				41		47	5%	1.08	-17.6	-6	($1)
PT/Exp	F	09 SF	* 243	27	6	31	0	211	83	262	243	354	596	4	71	27	0.14	221	41	17	42	105	9%	66	0%	2.57	-12.7	-1	$3
Consist	C	1st Half	146	17	4	20	0	208			239	356	595	4	70	27	0.14	209	35	15	50	110	8%	63	0%	2.54	-7.8	-2	$2
LIMA Plan	F	2nd Half	97	10	2	11	0	216			248	351	598	4	73	28	0.15	226	43	17	39	98	7%	67	0%	2.63	-4.9	1	$1
Rand Var	0	10 Proj	67	6	1	8	0	209			241	316	558	4	77	25	0.18	219	42	17	41	77	7%	44	4%	2.09	-4.5	-9	$0

2-13-.228 in 127 AB at SF. Minor league journeyman with 12 career MLB AB before '09. It's not difficult to figure out why. The real question is why was he given 127 more?

JOCK THOMPSON

Wieters,Matt

			AB	R	HR	RBI	SB	Avg	vL	vR	OB	Slg	OPS	bb%	ct%	h%	Eye	xBA	G	L	F	PX	hr/f	SX	SBO	RC/G	RAR	BPV	R$
Pos	2	05	0	0	0	0	0	0							0			0						0					
Age	24	06	0	0	0	0	0	0							0			0						0					
Bats	Both	07	0	0	0	0	0	0							0			0						0					
Health	A	08 aa	208	36	11	45	1	341			434	572	1006	14	88	35	1.42	0				131		53	1%	8.06	20.8	105	$12
PT/Exp	F	09 BAL	* 495	58	14	70	0	287	248	313	347	426	773	8	77	35	0.41	236	42	19	40	89	9%	35	0%	5.05	10.8	10	$14
Consist	F	1st Half	226	31	7	34	0	271			340	432	772	9	79	32	0.50	241	41	16	44	101	9%	56	0%	5.10	5.4	34	$6
LIMA Plan	C	2nd Half	269	27	7	36	0	301			354	420	774	8	76	38	0.34	224	42	19	38	79	9%	16	0%	5.01	5.5	-11	$8
Rand Var	-4	10 Proj	518	72	20	89	0	280			357	453	810	11	82	31	0.65	264	42	19	39	107	12%	46	0%	5.59	19.6	49	$17

9-43-.288 in 354 AB at BAL. Wrestled with pitch selection, patience and GB% for most of the season, still has work to do vs. LHP. H% shows promise, as did Sept up-tick (10% bb%, 99 PX). We think he's close.

Wigginton,Ty

			AB	R	HR	RBI	SB	Avg	vL	vR	OB	Slg	OPS	bb%	ct%	h%	Eye	xBA	G	L	F	PX	hr/f	SX	SBO	RC/G	RAR	BPV	R$
Pos	350	05 PIT	* 435	58	17	62	6	251	247	268	322	428	750	9	83	27	0.63	286	42	22	36	111	13%	66	11%	4.80	-10.5	63	$13
Age	33	06 TAM	444	55	24	79	4	275	316	260	324	498	821	7	78	30	0.33	271	40	19	41	138	17%	55	7%	5.46	0.6	55	$15
Bats	Right	07 2TM	547	71	22	67	3	278	284	276	328	459	787	7	79	32	0.36	267	44	18	38	119	13%	41	5%	5.09	-9.5	41	$16
Health	B	08 HOU	386	50	23	58	4	285	340	265	340	526	866	8	82	30	0.46	284	45	16	39	144	19%	50	10%	5.99	2.9	76	$16
PT/Exp	B	09 BAL	410	44	11	41	1	273	252	285	312	400	712	5	86	30	0.40	250	43	19	38	75	8%	32	3%	4.15	-18.4	27	$9
Consist	C	1st Half	192	16	6	22	1	266			299	401	700	4	88	28	0.39	247	41	16	43	76	8%	29	4%	3.97	-9.7	33	$4
LIMA Plan	D+	2nd Half	218	28	5	19	0	280			323	399	722	6	84	31	0.41	252	45	19	36	75	8%	34	2%	4.31	-8.7	22	$5
Rand Var	0	10 Proj	440	53	17	53	1	277			324	446	770	6	83	30	0.42	262	44	18	39	102	12%	31	5%	4.83	-8.3	40	$12

Effort to make more contact succeeded but power fell off a cliff. Uncharacteristic struggles vs. LHP (.333 Slg vs. .484 career). Steady FB% and hr/f plunge suggest he'll adjust. He's likely to fly under radars.

Willingham,Josh

			AB	R	HR	RBI	SB	Avg	vL	vR	OB	Slg	OPS	bb%	ct%	h%	Eye	xBA	G	L	F	PX	hr/f	SX	SBO	RC/G	RAR	BPV	R$
Pos	79	05 aaa	219	39	12	37	4	261			360	492	852	13	81	27	0.82	0				140		99	7%	6.22	7.6	95	$9
Age	31	06 FLA	502	62	26	74	2	277	299	269	347	496	843	10	78	31	0.50	262	43	16	41	132	16%	51	1%	5.92	9.6	56	$17
Bats	Right	07 FLA	521	75	21	89	8	265	218	281	348	463	810	11	77	31	0.54	265	36	21	43	130	12%	97	6%	5.68	4.8	64	$18
Health	B	08 FLA	351	54	15	51	3	254	242	258	343	470	813	12	77	29	0.59	265	39	19	42	140	13%	99	5%	5.77	3.6	74	$11
PT/Exp	B	09 WAS	427	70	24	61	4	260	300	251	352	496	849	13	76	29	0.59	278	36	22	42	161	17%	52	6%	6.18	7.8	74	$16
Consist	A	1st Half	153	31	9	18	1	288			394	549	943	15	76	32	0.75	285	36	18	46	180	17%	50	4%	7.57	8.7	97	$7
LIMA Plan	C+	2nd Half	274	39	15	43	3	245			328	467	795	11	75	27	0.50	275	36	24	40	150	18%	50	7%	5.39	-1.4	60	$9
Rand Var	+1	10 Proj	444	70	22	66	4	270			359	493	852	12	76	31	0.59	271	37	20	42	147	15%	76	5%	6.22	9.6	73	$17

Crowded OF limited April ABs, then personal issues and a virus wrecked his June. Aside from a h%-fueled Sept slump, he was outstanding. Stable power-and-patience profile, could shine with more AB.

Wilson,Jack

			AB	R	HR	RBI	SB	Avg	vL	vR	OB	Slg	OPS	bb%	ct%	h%	Eye	xBA	G	L	F	PX	hr/f	SX	SBO	RC/G	RAR	BPV	R$
Pos	6	05 PIT	587	60	8	52	7	257	255	256	294	363	657	5	90	27	0.53	267	48	18	34	62	4%	100	7%	3.69	-4.6	52	$11
Age	32	06 PIT	543	70	8	35	4	273	301	262	314	370	684	6	88	30	0.51	270	47	23	30	61	6%	60	5%	3.96	-6.3	32	$10
Bats	Right	07 PIT	477	67	12	56	2	296	320	289	348	440	788	7	90	31	0.83	275	39	19	42	86	7%	54	5%	5.25	10.7	63	$14
Health	C	08 PIT	305	24	1	22	2	272	228	282	302	348	649	4	91	30	0.48	259	41	22	37	54	1%	50	5%	3.61	-9.0	33	$4
PT/Exp	C	09 2TM	373	37	5	39	3	255	240	260	294	362	656	5	87	28	0.44	245	42	16	42	72	4%	63	5%	3.63	-10.2	38	$6
Consist	B	1st Half	208	24	3	25	2	284			313	413	727	4	89	31	0.39	269	41	19	40	86	4%	70	6%	4.40	-0.9	56	$5
LIMA Plan	D	2nd Half	165	13	2	14	1	218			271	297	568	7	85	25	0.48	210	43	13	44	54	3%	39	3%	2.60	-9.9	9	$1
Rand Var	0	10 Proj	406	40	5	38	3	254			295	353	648	6	88	28	0.51	251	42	18	40	66	4%	58	5%	3.57	-10.9	37	$6

Now near the end of his peak years, he's beginning to look like the new poster boy for good defense and empty hacking contact. Good only for the occasional h%-driven streak in daily leagues.

Wilson,Josh

			AB	R	HR	RBI	SB	Avg	vL	vR	OB	Slg	OPS	bb%	ct%	h%	Eye	xBA	G	L	F	PX	hr/f	SX	SBO	RC/G	RAR	BPV	R$
Pos	6	05 aaa	521	61	11	57	12	213			263	342	604	6	84	23	0.43	0				82		106	20%	2.99	-20.9	49	$8
Age	29	06 aaa	335	46	8	34	11	287			341	426	767	8	91	30	0.95	0				77		102	16%	5.06	6.5	74	$11
Bats	Right	07 2TM	282	28	2	24	6	238	256	230	281	333	614	6	80	29	0.30	219	43	13	44	69	2%	104	13%	3.03	-11.4	19	$3
Health	A	08 a/a	405	32	5	32	10	222			262	318	579	5	84	25	0.34	0				68		78	18%	2.66	-22.9	28	$4
PT/Exp	F	09 2TM	* 295	30	5	24	3	214	188	234	262	327	589	6	80	25	0.32	236	41	19	41	77	5%	81	9%	2.70	-17.1	21	$2
Consist	A	1st Half	116	7	1	10	1	185			257	271	528	9	84	21	0.60	207	43	11	46	59	2%	57	7%	2.26	-8.6	19	($1)
LIMA Plan	F	2nd Half	179	24	4	14	2	233			265	364	628	4	78	28	0.19	249	39	23	37	90	7%	91	11%	3.03	-8.3	20	$3
Rand Var	+2	10 Proj	165	16	2	14	3	224			269	333	603	6	82	26	0.34	235	41	17	42	75	4%	81	13%	2.91	-8.0	25	$2

3-13-.218 in 192 AB at ARI, SD and SEA. The past three years have been spent in BPV irrelevancy. They were also his peak skill years. Bad news.

Winn,Randy

			AB	R	HR	RBI	SB	Avg	vL	vR	OB	Slg	OPS	bb%	ct%	h%	Eye	xBA	G	L	F	PX	hr/f	SX	SBO	RC/G	RAR	BPV	R$
Pos	978	05 2TM	617	85	20	63	19	306	269	317	356	499	856	7	85	33	0.53	308	50	21	29	123	13%	107	18%	5.99	17.4	87	$25
Age	36	06 SF	573	82	11	56	10	262	219	278	319	396	715	8	89	28	0.76	272	50	17	33	79	6%	92	12%	4.48	-4.9	64	$13
Bats	Both	07 SF	593	73	14	65	15	300	351	277	349	445	794	7	86	33	0.52	287	51	19	31	94	9%	80	11%	5.24	6.0	58	$20
Health	A	08 SF	598	84	10	64	25	306	289	313	368	426	795	9	85	35	0.67	272	51	19	30	81	7%	111	14%	5.41	3.6	60	$24
PT/Exp	A	09 SF	538	65	2	51	16	262	158	292	321	353	675	8	83	31	0.51	255	46	22	32	68	1%	118	12%	3.97	-14.3	39	$13
Consist	B	1st Half	284	38	2	30	8	271			324	384	707	7	81	33	0.41	256	42	23	35	84	2%	120	12%	4.30	-4.7	44	$8
LIMA Plan	C	2nd Half	254	27	0	21	8	252			319	319	638	9	85	30	0.64	254	49	22	29	51	0%	102	12%	3.62	-9.4	30	$5
Rand Var	0	10 Proj	413	52	5	41	12	271			331	384	714	8	84	31	0.57	269	49	21	31	78	4%	111	12%	4.44	-6.3	52	$11

Power now almost completely gone, ct% showing age, even speed unable to exploit 2H GB spike. SB% remains excellent but .300 BA days are likely over. If LHP struggles persist, AB could dry up quickly.

Wise,Dewayne

			AB	R	HR	RBI	SB	Avg	vL	vR	OB	Slg	OPS	bb%	ct%	h%	Eye	xBA	G	L	F	PX	hr/f	SX	SBO	RC/G	RAR	BPV	R$
Pos	89	05 aaa	375	35	6	37	18	213			251	314	565	5	82	24	0.29	0				60		135	33%	2.39	-24.1	29	$7
Age	32	06 CIN	* 242	34	6	24	6	240			278	395	673	5	80	28	0.26	314	72	22	6	102	49%	110	16%	3.68	-5.6	46	$5
Bats	Left	07 aaa	207	27	6	16	6	211			235	382	617	3	73	26	0.12	0				113		150	26%	2.82	-11.1	38	$3
Health	C	08 CHW	* 320	49	14	35	20	251	154	268	306	450	755	7	80	28	0.38	268	35	23	42	122	13%	139	37%	4.72	-6.1	75	$13
PT/Exp	F	09 CHW	142	17	2	11	4	225	400	205	241	366	608	2	81	27	0.11	235	36	17	47	88	4%	138	41%	2.80	-8.3	42	$2
Consist	D	1st Half	68	6	0	3	2	191			225	279	505	4	75	25	0.18	194	37	16	47	55	0%	126	33%	1.55	-6.9	-8	($0)
LIMA Plan	F	2nd Half	74	11	2	8	2	257			257	446	703	0	86	27	0.00	273	36	17	47	114	7%	140	50%	3.83	-1.9	81	$2
Rand Var	+3	10 Proj	135	18	3	12	5	230			257	387	645	4	80	26	0.19	243	37	18	46	99	7%	138	37%	3.25	-6.5	50	$3

Age, 4/5 SB/CS takes shine from attractive speed. Even if running game rebounds, his problem is getting on base - and his bb% and ct% don't offer much hope.

Wood,Brandon

			AB	R	HR	RBI	SB	Avg	vL	vR	OB	Slg	OPS	bb%	ct%	h%	Eye	xBA	G	L	F	PX	hr/f	SX	SBO	RC/G	RAR	BPV	R$
Pos	5	05 aaa	19	1	0	1	0	263			263	421	684	0	58	45	0.00	0				133		54	0%	4.70	0.0	-44	$0
Age	25	06 aa	453	55	18	61	14	236			297	446	743	8	76	27	0.35	0				143		103	20%	4.67	-8.0	66	$12
Bats	Right	07 LAA	* 470	68	21	73	9	247			306	440	746	8	74	29	0.33	258	52	10	38	134	16%	90	9%	4.65	-3.1	49	$14
Health	A	08 LAA	* 545	81	30	83	9	247	94	229	300	457	757	7	76	28	0.31	245	36	14	50	135	14%	79	12%	4.67	-3.4	50	$18
PT/Exp	C	09 LAA	* 427	62	19	65	1	259	217	167	314	473	787	7	78	29	0.36	302	45	27	27	134	21%	67	2%	5.13	5.6	57	$13
Consist	A	1st Half	265	37	12	42	1	287			339	508	847	7	80	32	0.40	327	57	29	14	135	41%	62	3%	5.86	8.8	63	$10
LIMA Plan	C	2nd Half	162	25	7	23	0	215			271	417	688	7	75	24	0.31	282	40	27	33	133	17%	69	0%	3.89	-3.9	45	$3
Rand Var	+2	10 Proj	454	66	21	68	5	251			306	458	764	7	76	29	0.33	265	40	18	42	135	15%	84	7%	4.84	1.0	55	$14

1-3-.195 in 41 AB at LAA. Blocked in LAA, finally out of options, his time is now. Plus power with improving contact, 2H was interrupted by MLB stint as bat off the bench. In full-time role... UP: 25 HR, .265

Wright,David

			AB	R	HR	RBI	SB	Avg	vL	vR	OB	Slg	OPS	bb%	ct%	h%	Eye	xBA	G	L	F	PX	hr/f	SX	SBO	RC/G	RAR	BPV	R$
Pos	5	05 NYM	575	99	27	102	17	306	336	300	383	523	907	11	80	34	0.64	302	39	25	35	143	17%	86	13%	6.82	32.4	86	$31
Age	27	06 NYM	582	96	26	116	20	311	285	321	381	531	912	10	81	35	0.58	272	36	19	44	133	13%	110	14%	6.85	21.6	84	$30
Bats	Right	07 NYM	604	113	30	107	34	325	361	311	415	546	962	13	81	36	0.82	298	39	23	38	139	16%	99	18%	7.62	32.6	94	$37
Health	A	08 NYM	626	115	33	124	15	302	382	275	393	534	927	13	81	33	0.80	295	36	26	38	145	17%	92	10%	7.14	30.6	96	$34
PT/Exp	A	09 NYM	535	88	10	72	27	307	416	277	391	447	838	12	74	40	0.53	251	38	26	36	110	7%	109	19%	6.27	16.9	42	$26
Consist	B	1st Half	288	49	5	42	20	340			426	493	919	13	73	46	0.54	249	37	25	38	122	6%	122	25%	7.53	18.6	52	$18
LIMA Plan	B	2nd Half	247	39	5	30	7	267			349	393	742	11	75	34	0.51	253	40	26	34	97	8%	82	11%	4.86	-2.0	28	$8
Rand Var	-5	10 Proj	583	100	20	94	23	295			382	476	858	12	78	35	0.63	273	38	25	37	126	12%	106	16%	6.38	18.1	69	$28

HR / Slg splits say that power outage wasn't just due to new stadium. Ct% also down, year salvaged only by inflated h%, SBO and SB%. A normal hr/f reversion points to rebound, but Stud status is in jeopardy.

JOCK THOMPSON

Youkilis,Kevin			AB	R	HR	RBI	SB	Avg	vL	vR	OB	Slg	OPS	bb%	ct%	h%	Eye	xBA	G	L	F	PX	hr/f	SX	SBO	RC/G	RAR	BPV	R$
Pos	35	05 BOS *	231	33	7	29	1	284	300	265	390	474	865	15	82	32	0.96	295	32	28	40	133	9%	49	5%	6.61	10.1	81	$7
Age	31	06 BOS	569	100	13	72	5	279	270	283	379	429	808	14	79	33	0.76	251	31	24	45	104	6%	79	4%	5.85	6.9	52	$16
Bats	Right	07 BOS	528	85	16	83	4	288	290	287	379	453	831	13	80	33	0.73	265	34	21	45	113	8%	68	3%	6.04	11.5	58	$18
Health	A	08 BOS	538	91	29	115	3	312	288	318	383	569	952	10	80	35	0.57	298	34	22	44	166	15%	66	5%	7.34	30.5	95	$27
PT/Exp	A	09 BOS	491	99	27	94	7	305	309	304	400	548	948	14	75	36	0.62	275	35	21	44	160	17%	79	6%	7.63	25.8	79	$25
Consist	B	1st Half	226	49	14	47	4	314			424	593	1017	16	73	38	0.70	287	33	22	45	188	19%	84	6%	8.78	18.8	101	$13
LIMA Plan	B	2nd Half	265	50	13	47	3	298			378	509	887	11	76	35	0.53	265	36	20	44	138	15%	61	5%	6.66	7.0	57	$12
Rand Var	-4	10 Proj	525	96	30	107	5	301			389	555	943	13	77	34	0.63	289	34	21	44	164	17%	71	5%	7.40	27.8	89	$26

Power skills took a 2H dip, likely caused by 2H back spasms. Ct% dip appears due to even more Youkilidian patience (100 extra pitches in fewer PA) and should bounce back. With health, remains top drawer.

Young Jr.,Eric			AB	R	HR	RBI	SB	Avg	vL	vR	OB	Slg	OPS	bb%	ct%	h%	Eye	xBA	G	L	F	PX	hr/f	SX	SBO	RC/G	RAR	BPV	R$
Pos	4	05	0	0	0	0	0	0							0			0						0					
Age	25	06	0	0	0	0	0	0							0			0						0					
Bats	Both	07	0	0	0	0	0	0							0			0						0					
Health	A	08 aa	403	52	2	24	32	255			326	336	661	9	87	29	0.79	0				56		122	43%	3.97	-10.8	50	$13
PT/Exp	F	09 COL *	529	100	7	35	49	270	304	206	329	375	705	8	86	30	0.62	281	59	20	22	64	7%	164	44%	4.33	-3.2	62	$24
Consist	A	1st Half	298	57	3	20	36	267			332	361	693	9	87	30	0.75	0				60		163	52%	4.27	-2.3	65	$15
LIMA Plan	D	2nd Half	231	43	4	14	13	273			326	394	720	7	84	31	0.50	278	59	20	22	69	9%	153	34%	4.42	-0.8	54	$9
Rand Var	0	10 Proj	160	26	2	10	13	263			326	362	688	9	86	30	0.66	281	59	20	22	62	5%	146	43%	4.17	-2.2	57	$6

1-1-.246 in 57 AB at COL. He can flat out motor, but more here than just speed. The seeds of a legit leadoff man: solid bb%, contact GB/LD style, and yeah, the wheels. Now 25, let's see if he gets a shot... UP: 50 SB

Young,Chris			AB	R	HR	RBI	SB	Avg	vL	vR	OB	Slg	OPS	bb%	ct%	h%	Eye	xBA	G	L	F	PX	hr/f	SX	SBO	RC/G	RAR	BPV	R$
Pos	8	05 aa	462	78	24	61	25	249			330	489	819	11	78	27	0.54	0				161		126	29%	5.72	18.1	101	$20
Age	27	06 ARI *	472	67	18	66	14	241	360	178	307	440	747	9	86	25	0.66	289	42	20	37	116	12%	99	20%	4.78	4.9	85	$14
Bats	Right	07 ARI	569	85	32	68	27	237	246	234	291	467	758	7	75	26	0.30	259	37	15	48	146	15%	122	29%	4.71	3.2	70	$21
Health	A	08 ARI	625	85	22	85	14	248	285	236	316	443	759	9	74	30	0.38	251	38	19	43	137	11%	119	13%	4.99	4.6	60	$19
PT/Exp	A	09 ARI *	487	67	18	49	13	225	262	196	318	421	739	12	70	28	0.46	228	26	18	56	146	9%	109	15%	4.89	2.4	57	$12
Consist	A	1st Half	231	28	6	18	11	195			276	364	640	10	72	24	0.40	224	27	20	54	130	7%	125	28%	3.46	-9.3	51	$4
LIMA Plan	B+	2nd Half	256	39	12	31	2	252			354	473	827	14	69	32	0.51	232	26	17	58	162	11%	80	8%	6.21	11.3	59	$8
Rand Var	0	10 Proj	502	71	20	59	14	237			316	445	761	10	73	28	0.43	244	32	18	50	146	11%	117	17%	5.06	5.8	67	$15

15-42-.212 in 433 AB at ARI. Maddening! So many drool-inducing tools, so many gaping holes. No explosion's coming unless ct% trend reverses, and he gets a clue vs. RHP. There are no signs that'll happen soon.

Young,Delmon			AB	R	HR	RBI	SB	Avg	vL	vR	OB	Slg	OPS	bb%	ct%	h%	Eye	xBA	G	L	F	PX	hr/f	SX	SBO	RC/G	RAR	BPV	R$
Pos	7	05 a/a	558	75	21	81	28	292			321	463	784	4	88	30	0.35	0				96		120	32%	4.90	-2.2	74	$26
Age	25	06 TAM *	468	68	11	71	25	325	379	299	348	485	834	3	83	38	0.20	292	47	26	27	102	10%	136	26%	5.51	4.1	62	$22
Bats	Right	07 TAM	645	65	13	93	10	288	299	285	316	408	724	4	80	34	0.20	264	46	21	33	86	8%	63	8%	4.19	-15.4	19	$18
Health	A	08 MIN	575	80	10	69	14	290	300	286	331	405	736	6	82	34	0.33	261	55	17	28	77	8%	106	12%	4.48	-6.1	34	$18
PT/Exp	A	09 MIN	395	50	12	60	2	284	310	272	305	425	730	3	77	34	0.13	241	50	16	34	90	12%	63	7%	4.18	-9.4	5	$12
Consist	A	1st Half	176	18	2	23	2	256			276	318	594	3	69	36	0.09	196	54	15	31	49	6%	54	9%	2.47	-13.2	-62	$3
LIMA Plan	C	2nd Half	219	32	10	37	0	306			327	511	839	3	83	33	0.19	277	47	16	37	117	15%	65	6%	5.43	2.6	54	$9
Rand Var	-3	10 Proj	538	69	18	77	9	288			316	447	763	4	80	33	0.20	264	50	18	32	99	13%	82	11%	4.62	-5.3	33	$18

2H signs of a breakout to come? FB, PX gains; ct% turnaround Or, maybe not... bb% still tiny; speed skills MIA, xBA says no. 2H gives hope, but Hope tends to go for $5 over value at the draft table.

Young,Delwyn			AB	R	HR	RBI	SB	Avg	vL	vR	OB	Slg	OPS	bb%	ct%	h%	Eye	xBA	G	L	F	PX	hr/f	SX	SBO	RC/G	RAR	BPV	R$
Pos	49	05 a/a	526	54	15	55	1	253			285	394	679	4	84	28	0.28	0				92		31	4%	3.68	-10.3	28	$10
Age	28	06 aaa	532	58	14	75	2	233			277	378	654	6	85	25	0.39	0				92		40	7%	3.52	-13.6	37	$8
Bats	Both	07 LA *	524	85	16	77	4	281	333	421	322	470	791	6	80	33	0.30	274	34	21	45	129	8%	87	6%	5.18	7.1	62	$17
Health	B	08 LA	126	10	1	7	0	246	231	253	321	341	663	10	73	33	0.41	211	50	17	33	84	3%	16	0%	3.82	-3.5	-14	$1
PT/Exp	D	09 PIT	354	40	7	43	2	266	233	282	321	381	703	8	75	34	0.32	237	46	22	33	84	8%	67	2%	4.15	-3.9	3	$8
Consist	B	1st Half	107	14	2	15	2	318			387	411	798	10	73	42	0.41	223	45	22	32	70	8%	52	5%	5.56	2.9	-14	$4
LIMA Plan	F	2nd Half	247	26	5	28	0	243			292	368	660	6	75	30	0.28	241	46	21	33	90	8%	55	0%	3.55	-7.2	4	$4
Rand Var	-4	10 Proj	295	33	6	33	1	264			322	386	708	8	76	33	0.35	243	47	20	33	90	8%	60	3%	4.24	-3.3	11	$6

PIT gave him a real chance, and he tanked it. While the stats collapsed in 2H, in reality he was pretty bad all year, with 42% h% masking things early. In short, he's 27, has a career .713 OPS, and skills are going nowhere.

Young,Michael			AB	R	HR	RBI	SB	Avg	vL	vR	OB	Slg	OPS	bb%	ct%	h%	Eye	xBA	G	L	F	PX	hr/f	SX	SBO	RC/G	RAR	BPV	R$
Pos	5	05 TEX	668	114	24	91	5	331	340	327	384	513	898	8	86	36	0.64	304	45	26	29	111	14%	87	3%	6.47	34.7	78	$30
Age	33	06 TEX	691	93	14	103	7	314	295	320	359	459	817	6	86	35	0.50	296	48	25	27	94	9%	76	5%	5.52	9.5	57	$23
Bats	Right	07 TEX	639	80	9	94	13	315	309	316	362	418	779	7	86	37	0.44	290	48	27	24	74	7%	77	8%	5.07	3.5	31	$22
Health	A	08 TEX	645	102	12	82	10	284	305	276	340	402	742	8	83	33	0.50	270	47	23	31	80	7%	98	5%	4.67	-3.7	44	$20
PT/Exp	A	09 TEX	541	76	22	68	8	322	297	331	376	518	893	8	83	35	0.52	296	45	22	33	118	15%	73	7%	6.43	25.3	68	$23
Consist	C	1st Half	305	42	10	30	4	315			369	498	867	8	83	35	0.51	298	44	24	32	116	12%	71	6%	6.15	12.1	65	$11
LIMA Plan	C	2nd Half	236	34	12	38	4	331			385	542	928	8	83	36	0.54	293	46	21	34	120	18%	66	8%	6.78	13.2	68	$12
Rand Var	-3	10 Proj	581	84	18	79	7	305			358	466	824	8	84	34	0.51	288	46	23	31	101	12%	77	6%	5.61	13.5	56	$21

Why he's back: the move off SS and healthy fingers revived PX; rest of BPIs solid. Why there's some concern: Sept hammy strain may be first sign of PT mortality. Should follow up well, but can't ink 600 AB now.

Zaun,Gregg			AB	R	HR	RBI	SB	Avg	vL	vR	OB	Slg	OPS	bb%	ct%	h%	Eye	xBA	G	L	F	PX	hr/f	SX	SBO	RC/G	RAR	BPV	R$
Pos	2	05 TOR	434	61	11	61	2	251	278	241	359	373	732	14	84	28	1.04	250	46	19	35	77	9%	49	3%	4.91	11.5	43	$10
Age	39	06 TOR	290	39	12	40	0	272	373	251	363	462	825	12	86	28	0.98	275	38	20	42	113	11%	23	2%	5.88	12.2	66	$8
Bats	Both	07 TOR	331	43	10	52	0	242	290	229	343	411	754	13	83	26	0.93	272	42	17	41	113	9%	33	0%	5.13	8.3	63	$7
Health	C	08 TOR	245	29	6	30	2	237	163	255	339	359	698	13	84	26	1.00	240	44	15	40	79	7%	43	4%	4.47	2.0	43	$4
PT/Exp	D	09 2AL	262	34	8	27	0	260	217	269	338	416	754	11	82	29	0.65	254	42	18	40	101	9%	27	3%	4.93	5.1	39	$6
Consist	B	1st Half	142	19	3	9	0	239			333	366	700	12	85	26	0.91	249	43	18	39	83	6%	28	0%	4.46	0.8	39	$2
LIMA Plan	F	2nd Half	120	15	5	18	0	283			344	475	819	8	78	33	0.42	260	40	18	41	124	13%	29	6%	5.58	4.5	40	$4
Rand Var	-1	10 Proj	216	27	7	27	0	255			342	407	749	12	83	28	0.76	254	42	17	40	98	9%	32	3%	4.94	4.4	44	$5

The year-to-year fluctuations in skills are all well within ranges we'd expect to see. There aren't likely to be any surprises going forward, either. He's an end-game CA now, but as R$, RAR show, he's better than most.

Zimmerman,Ryan			AB	R	HR	RBI	SB	Avg	vL	vR	OB	Slg	OPS	bb%	ct%	h%	Eye	xBA	G	L	F	PX	hr/f	SX	SBO	RC/G	RAR	BPV	R$
Pos	5	05 WAS *	291	39	7	32	1	309	400	395	343	481	824	5	86	34	0.38	356	43	38	19	120	15%	41	10%	5.50	5.9	65	$10
Age	26	06 WAS	614	84	20	110	11	287	280	289	351	471	822	9	80	33	0.51	276	42	22	36	119	11%	78	11%	5.71	3.8	60	$23
Bats	Right	07 WAS	653	99	24	91	4	266	374	235	329	458	787	9	81	30	0.49	275	44	17	40	121	11%	85	3%	5.22	-7.3	65	$19
Health	B	08 WAS	428	51	14	51	1	283	333	259	331	442	773	7	83	31	0.44	268	46	20	34	100	12%	45	2%	4.92	-5.4	43	$12
PT/Exp	A	09 WAS	610	110	33	106	2	292	270	298	367	525	891	11	80	32	0.61	282	40	19	42	146	16%	73	1%	6.54	23.8	84	$28
Consist	B	1st Half	311	52	13	44	0	296			369	492	861	10	79	34	0.55	276	37	23	40	133	13%	32	0%	6.23	9.3	55	$13
LIMA Plan	C+	2nd Half	299	58	20	62	2	288			364	559	923	11	82	29	0.67	291	42	15	43	158	19%	93	2%	6.86	14.4	106	$16
Rand Var	-1	10 Proj	605	100	35	109	3	286			350	532	882	9	82	30	0.54	290	41	18	41	149	17%	72	3%	6.29	17.5	87	$27

Stayed healthy, and the power spike came -- and then some. 2H hr/f tough to repeat, but FB trend may offset a dip there. The rest of his skills took a nice, sustainable step up. Just hitting peak, so hop on for the ride.

Zobrist,Ben			AB	R	HR	RBI	SB	Avg	vL	vR	OB	Slg	OPS	bb%	ct%	h%	Eye	xBA	G	L	F	PX	hr/f	SX	SBO	RC/G	RAR	BPV	R$
Pos	49	05	0	0	0	0	0	0							0			0						0					
Age	29	06 TAM *	567	68	5	48	12	265	212	229	340	372	712	10	86	30	0.82	269	47	22	30	67	3%	103	13%	4.58	7.8	52	$10
Bats	Both	07 TAM *	319	47	8	29	10	226	182	147	320	358	677	12	81	26	0.74	259	43	20	37	85	8%	101	14%	4.08	0.8	50	$6
Health	C	08 TAM *	269	44	15	41	6	260	269	242	350	491	840	12	79	28	0.66	272	44	13	42	141	17%	96	9%	5.99	8.6	85	$11
PT/Exp	D	09 TAM	501	91	27	91	17	297	319	287	405	543	948	15	79	33	0.88	288	41	20	39	144	18%	118	13%	7.60	37.4	100	$26
Consist	D	1st Half	212	43	16	46	8	297			418	632	1050	17	78	32	0.94	316	40	18	42	198	23%	119	15%	9.00	24.2	142	$13
LIMA Plan	B+	2nd Half	289	48	11	45	9	298			396	478	873	14	80	34	0.82	269	42	21	37	106	13%	103	11%	6.59	13.4	67	$13
Rand Var	-4	10 Proj	510	84	23	77	15	275			372	486	858	13	80	30	0.79	277	42	19	39	127	14%	109	12%	6.35	24.3	85	$21

Can a career have a peak half? If so, 1H was it. Rigors of full-time play may have caught up to him, though some of the 1H BPIs (e.g., hr/f) would regress anyway. Skills support a solid, somewhat lesser follow-up.

ROD TRUESDELL

The Pitchers

QUALIFICATION: All pitchers who had at least 40 IP in the majors in 2009, and some with fewer than 40 IP have been included. The decision point is "potential impact in 2010." Those who may have a role but have battled injuries for several years are often not included, though an injury status update appears on page 194. All of these players will appear at Baseball HQ as roles become clearer.

THROWS: Right (RH) or left (LH). **ROLE:** Starters (projected 18+ batters faced per game) or Relievers (less than 18 BF/G). Each pitcher's **AGE** as of Opening Day is shown.

TYPE evaluates the extent to which a pitcher allows the ball to be put into play and his ground ball or flyball tendency. CON (contact) represents pitchers who allow the ball to be put into play a great deal. PWR (power) represents those with high strikeout and/or walk totals who keep the ball out of play. GB are those who have a ground ball rate more than 50%; xGB are those who have a GB rate more than 55%. FB are those who have a fly ball rate more than 40%; xFB are those who have a FB rate more than 45%.

RELIABILITY GRADES: An analysis of each player's forecast risk, on an A-F scale. High grades go to pitchers who have accumulated few disabled list days (Health), have a history of substantial and regular major league playing time (PT/Exp) and have displayed consistent performance over the past three years, using xERA (Consist).

LIMA PLAN GRADE: Rating that evaluates how well that pitcher would be a good fit for a team employing the LIMA Plan. Best grades will go to pitchers who have excellent base skills and had a 2009 Roto value less than $20. Lowest grades will go to poor skills and values more than $20.

RAND VAR: A score that measures the impact random variance had on the pitcher's 2009 stats and the probability that his 2010 performance will exceed or fall short of 2009. The variables tracked are levels for H%, S%, hr/f and xERA that would be prone to regression. Players are rated on a scale of –5 to +5 with positive scores indicating rebounds and negative scores indicating corrections.

PLAYER STAT LINES: The past five years' statistics represent the total accumulated in the majors as well as in Triple-A, Double-A ball and various foreign leagues during each year. All non-major league stats used have been converted to a major league equivalent (MLE) performance level. Minor league levels below AA are not included.

Nearly all baseball publications separate a player's statistical experiences in the major leagues from the minor leagues and outside leagues. While this may be appropriate for the sake of official record-keeping, it is not an accurate snapshot of a player's complete performance for the year.

Bill James has proven that minor league statistics (converted to MLEs), at Double-A level or above, provide as accurate a record of a player's performance as Major League statistics. Other researchers have also devised conversion factors for foreign leagues. Since these are accurate barometers, we include them in the pool of historical data.

TEAM DESIGNATIONS: An asterisk (*) appearing with a team name means that major league equivalent Triple-A and/or Double-A numbers are included in that year's stat line. A designation of "a/a" means the stats were accumulated at both levels that year. Other designations: JPN (Japan), MEX (Mexico), KOR (Korea), CUB (Cuba), VNZ (Venezuela) and ind (independent league). All these stats are converted to major league equivalents.

The designation "2TM" appears whenever a player was on more than one major league team, crossing leagues, in a season. "2AL" and "2NL" represent more than one team in the same league. Complete season stats are presented for players who crossed leagues during the season.

SABERMETRIC CATEGORIES: Descriptions of all the categories appear in the glossary. The decimal point has been suppressed on several categories to conserve space.
- Platoon data (vL, vR) and Ball-in-play data (G/L/F) are for major league performance only.
- The xERA2 and new BPV formulas are used when G/L/F data is available. The old formulas are used otherwise.

2010 FORECASTS: It is far too early to be making definitive projections for 2010, especially on playing time. Focus on the skill levels and trends, then consult Baseball HQ for playing time revisions as players change teams and roles become finalized. A free projections update will also be available online in March.

Forecasts are computed from a player's trends over the past five years. Adjustments were made for leading indicators and variances between skill and statistical output. After reviewing the leading indicators, you might opt to make further adjustments.

Although each year's numbers include all playing time at the Double-A level or above, the 2010 forecast only represents potential playing time at the major league level, and again is highly preliminary.

CAPSULE COMMENTARIES provide a brief analysis of each player's BPIs and the potential impact on performance in 2010. For those who played only a portion of 2009 in the Majors, and whose isolated MLB stats are significantly different from their full-season total, their MLB stats are listed here. Note that these commentaries generally look at performance related issues only. Playing time expectations may impact these analyses, so you will have to adjust accordingly. Upside (UP) and downside (DN) statistical potential appears for some players. These are less grounded in hard data and more speculative of skills potential.

DO-IT-YOURSELF ANALYSIS: Here are some data points you can look at in doing your own player analysis:
- Variance between vLH and vRH opposition batting avg
- Variance in 2009 hr/f rate from 10%
- Variance in 2009 hit rate (H%) from 30%
- Variance in 2009 strand rate (S%) to tolerances (65% - 75%)
- Variance between ERA and xERA each year
- Growth or decline in Base Performance Value (BPV)
- Spikes in innings pitched

Aardsma,David

		W	L	Sv	IP	K	ERA	WHIP	OBA	vL	vR	BF/G	H%	S%	xERA	G	L	F	Ctl	Dom	Cmd	hr/f	hr/9	RAR	BPV	R$
RH Reliever	05 aa	10	3	2	0	0	0.00	0.00				0.0			0.00				0.0	0.0				0.0	55	
Age 28	06 CHC *	5	3	8	89	81	4.24	1.38	239	190	225	5.2	29%	72%	4.44	37	19	44	4.4	8.2	1.8	9%	1.0	2.7	42	$10
Type Pwr xFB	07 CHW *	5	3	15	67	76	6.17	1.49	273			5.6	33%	63%	3.86	37	21	42	3.9	10.1	2.6	18%	1.9	-13.9	92	$9
Health B	08 BOS	4	2	0	49	49	5.54	1.72	263	289	250	4.8	34%	68%	4.64	44	18	38	6.5	9.1	1.4	8%	0.7	-7.2	10	$1
PT/Exp C	09 SEA	3	6	38	71	80	2.52	1.16	196	197	183	4.0	27%	80%	3.99	25	21	54	4.3	10.1	2.4	4%	0.5	17.0	69	$23
Consist B	1st Half	2	2	16	36	46	1.50	1.16	164			4.1	25%	88%	3.91	23	21	56	5.5	11.5	2.1	2%	0.2	13.2	59	$12
LIMA Plan C	2nd Half	1	4	22	35	34	3.58	1.16	226			3.9	28%	71%	4.07	27	21	52	3.1	8.7	2.8	6%	0.8	3.8	79	$11
Rand Var -5	10 Proj	4	4	30	65	69	4.14	1.38	233			4.5	30%	71%	4.21	33	20	47	4.7	9.5	2.0	7%	0.8	1.8	56	$16

Four reasons to be skeptical:
1. Gap between ERA and xERA
2. Favorable '09 h% and s%
3. Extreme fly-ball split
4. History of Ctl problems

2H Cmd a step, but this is not a stud-closer profile. Caution.

Accardo,Jeremy

		W	L	Sv	IP	K	ERA	WHIP	OBA	vL	vR	BF/G	H%	S%	xERA	G	L	F	Ctl	Dom	Cmd	hr/f	hr/9	RAR	BPV	R$
RH Reliever	05 SF *	4	5	7	73	59	3.45	1.19	234	182	265	4.9	29%	71%	3.85	39	23	38	3.0	7.3	2.5	5%	0.5	7.1	68	$10
Age 28	06 2TM	2	4	3	69	54	5.35	1.39	281	241	307	4.6	33%	62%	3.93	42	25	32	2.6	7.0	2.7	10%	0.9	-7.0	77	$4
Type Pwr	07 TOR	4	4	30	67	57	2.14	1.11	212	161	250	4.2	26%	83%	3.45	49	20	30	3.2	7.6	2.4	7%	0.5	19.6	78	$21
Health D	08 TOR	0	3	4	12	5	6.59	1.54	302	300	300	3.4	32%	56%	5.12	46	15	39	2.9	3.7	1.3	6%	0.7	-3.4	10	$1
PT/Exp C	09 TOR *	2	1	14	55	40	3.11	1.53	276	143	386	4.6	33%	80%	4.72	46	13	41	4.1	6.5	1.6	4%	0.5	9.1	31	$8
Consist C	1st Half	2	1	10	30	23	3.30	1.60	304			5.0	37%	79%	4.90	33	20	47	3.3	6.9	2.1	2%	0.3	4.3	46	$6
LIMA Plan C+	2nd Half	0	0	4	25	17	2.88	1.44	238			4.2	27%	82%	4.84	49	11	40	5.0	6.1	1.2	7%	0.7	4.8	1	$3
Rand Var -5	10 Proj	2	2	0	58	45	3.72	1.45	268			4.6	32%	75%	4.20	46	19	35	3.7	7.0	1.9	6%	0.6	1.7	49	$4

0-0, 2.55 ERA in 25 IP at TOR. A year removed from arm trouble but unable to regain promise of '06-'07, despite what ERA says. Taming Ctl is the first step back, but '09 2H is not encouraging.

Aceves,Alfredo

		W	L	Sv	IP	K	ERA	WHIP	OBA	vL	vR	BF/G	H%	S%	xERA	G	L	F	Ctl	Dom	Cmd	hr/f	hr/9	RAR	BPV	R$
RH Reliever	05 MEX	9	8	0	145	95	4.78	1.44	281			28.7	32%	68%	4.75				3.0	5.9	1.9		0.9	-8.5	49	$7
Age 27	06 MEX	8	5	0	124	90	4.86	1.28	271			27.4	31%	64%	4.54				2.1	6.5	3.1		1.2	-5.2	70	$10
Type xFB	07 MEX	11	5	0	106	65	4.33	1.32	254			25.0	29%	67%	3.97				3.2	5.5	1.7		0.7	1.7	53	$10
Health A	08 NYY *	5	5	0	123	78	3.66	1.27	265	238	213	22.4	29%	76%	4.27	42	17	41	2.3	5.7	2.5	10%	1.2	10.4	61	$10
PT/Exp C	09 NYY *	12	1	0	108	84	3.67	1.04	226	212	228	9.1	26%	69%	3.95	35	17	48	1.9	7.0	3.7	9%	1.1	10.5	87	$17
Consist A	1st Half	7	1	0	56	43	3.54	1.11	240			9.8	27%	74%	4.16	33	16	51	1.9	6.9	3.6	10%	1.3	6.3	83	$9
LIMA Plan C+	2nd Half	5	0	1	52	41	3.81	0.96	210			8.4	24%	62%	3.76	37	18	46	1.9	7.1	3.7	8%	0.9	4.1	91	$8
Rand Var -2	10 Proj	8	4	0	93	66	3.89	1.21	254			10.1	29%	71%	4.28	37	17	46	2.2	6.4	2.9	8%	1.1	1.8	70	$11

10-1, 3.54 ERA in 84 IP at NYY. PRO: Outstanding skills got better in 2H, proven results as both SP (minors) and RP (NYY). CON: Vulture Ws, NY hype and h% will inflate his value. Buy only at the right price.

Acosta,Manny

		W	L	Sv	IP	K	ERA	WHIP	OBA	vL	vR	BF/G	H%	S%	xERA	G	L	F	Ctl	Dom	Cmd	hr/f	hr/9	RAR	BPV	R$
RH Reliever	05	0	0	0	0	0	0.00	0.00							0.00											
Age 28	06 a/a	1	6	21	60	48	4.89	1.86	255			5.6	30%	75%	5.64				8.1	7.1	0.9		0.9	-2.8	37	$6
Type Pwr	07 ATL *	10	4	12	82	69	2.69	1.47	229	250	93	5.9	29%	81%	4.06	61	11	29	5.7	7.5	1.3	3%	0.2	17.6	20	$14
Health B	08 ATL	3	5	3	53	31	3.57	1.40	243	280	218	5.0	26%	79%	4.35	53	19	28	4.4	5.3	1.2	15%	1.2	4.6	7	$5
PT/Exp D	09 ATL *	2	4	0	59	47	4.12	1.64	287	297	302	5.3	33%	79%	4.61	44	19	37	4.6	7.2	1.6	12%	1.2	0.5	28	$1
Consist A	1st Half	1	3	0	37	27	3.05	1.40	248			6.0	27%	84%	4.38	47	17	36	4.3	6.5	1.5	13%	1.3	5.2	26	$2
LIMA Plan C	2nd Half	1	1	0	22	20	5.94	2.05	346			4.5	42%	72%	4.88	42	20	38	5.1	8.3	1.6	10%	1.1	-4.7	33	($1)
Rand Var 0	10 Proj	1	2	0	22	17	4.14	1.66	281			5.2	33%	76%	4.53	48	19	33	5.0	7.0	1.4	9%	0.8	-0.7	19	$1

1-1, 4.34 ERA in 38 IP at ATL. Ctl and Dom fluctuate, but the sub-2.0 Cmd never changes. Add that to a .299 OppBA in the majors in 09, and the future is not exactly bright. Keep the Triple-A shuttle warm.

Adams,Mike

		W	L	Sv	IP	K	ERA	WHIP	OBA	vL	vR	BF/G	H%	S%	xERA	G	L	F	Ctl	Dom	Cmd	hr/f	hr/9	RAR	BPV	R$
RH Reliever	05 MIL *	3	5	3	49	51	5.36	1.48	269			5.5	34%	64%	3.85	39	22	39	4.0	9.4	2.4	10%	0.9	-6.8	79	$3
Age 31	06 aaa	1	3	2	60	39	4.84	1.68	311			5.8	36%	70%	5.59				3.7	5.9	1.6		0.5	-2.4	47	$1
Type Pwr FB	07	0	0	0	0	0	0.00	0.00							0.00											
Health F	08 SD *	5	4	0	80	84	3.65	1.43	267	228	190	5.2	35%	76%	3.73	42	18	40	3.6	9.5	2.6	8%	0.8	6.0	94	$7
PT/Exp F	09 SD *	1	0	0	46	49	1.57	0.74	145	130	88	3.7	19%	84%	2.73	51	7	42	2.3	9.6	4.1	7%	0.6	14.9	138	$9
Consist B	1st Half	1	0	0	15	9	3.97	1.30	249			4.0	26%	75%	4.28	52	10	38	3.3	5.5	1.7	13%	1.4	0.4	41	$1
LIMA Plan A	2nd Half	0	0	0	31	40	0.38	0.46	82			3.6	13%	95%	2.05	50	7	43	1.9	11.6	6.1	3%	0.2	14.5	186	$8
Rand Var -5	10 Proj	2	2	0	58	56	3.10	1.16	223			4.5	28%	76%	3.51	46	13	41	3.1	8.7	2.8	8%	0.8	5.4	97	$6

0-0, 0.73 ERA in 37 IP at SD. Went from "fortunate" in the 1H to "deal with the devil" in the 2H, overshadowing significant skills growth. Use 2008 as base for 2010, but with 2 yrs of 90+ BPV, he's a sleeper saves candidate.

Affeldt,Jeremy

		W	L	Sv	IP	K	ERA	WHIP	OBA	vL	vR	BF/G	H%	S%	xERA	G	L	F	Ctl	Dom	Cmd	hr/f	hr/9	RAR	BPV	R$
LH Reliever	05 KC	0	2	0	49	39	5.30	1.73	288	263	283	4.7	35%	68%	4.29	53	22	25	5.3	7.1	1.3	8%	0.5	-5.7	16	($1)
Age 30	06 2TM	8	8	1	97	48	6.21	1.62	271	212	289	8.2	28%	63%	5.32	50	17	33	5.1	4.4	0.9	12%	1.2	-20.2	-30	$1
Type Pwr xGB	07 COL	4	3	0	59	46	3.51	1.36	220	250	211	3.4	27%	74%	4.21	53	14	33	5.0	7.0	1.4	6%	0.5	6.7	21	$6
Health A	08 CIN	1	1	0	78	80	3.33	1.32	261	269	255	4.5	33%	79%	3.03	54	18	28	2.9	9.2	3.2	15%	1.0	9.0	120	$6
PT/Exp C	09 SF	2	2	0	62	55	1.73	1.17	193	211	187	3.4	24%	87%	2.93	65	17	18	4.5	7.9	1.8	10%	0.4	18.9	65	$8
Consist B	1st Half	0	1	0	31	29	1.45	1.25	208			3.7	27%	89%	2.74	65	21	14	4.6	8.4	1.8	9%	0.3	10.5	69	$3
LIMA Plan C+	2nd Half	2	1	0	31	26	2.02	1.09	178			3.2	22%	84%	3.08	65	13	23	4.3	7.5	1.7	11%	0.6	8.4	61	$5
Rand Var -5	10 Proj	2	2	3	58	51	3.41	1.36	241			3.9	30%	76%	3.54	55	18	27	4.2	7.9	1.9	9%	0.6	5.2	62	$5

Others will bid on his improving ERA and WHIP. You bid on his extreme 2009 luck and return of Ctl problems. They win the bid; you move on. GB/Dom combo is enticing and limits implosion factor, but '08 Ctl seems a fluke.

Albaladejo,Jonathan

		W	L	Sv	IP	K	ERA	WHIP	OBA	vL	vR	BF/G	H%	S%	xERA	G	L	F	Ctl	Dom	Cmd	hr/f	hr/9	RAR	BPV	R$
RH Reliever	05	0	0	0	0	0	0.00	0.00							0.00											
Age 27	06 aa	1	2	1	36	22	5.41	1.55	332			8.9	36%	67%	6.40				1.3	5.6	4.3		1.3	-4.0	74	$1
Type GB	07 a/a	7	3	2	60	46	3.70	1.23	233			6.9	27%	72%	3.51				3.4	6.8	2.0		0.8	5.7	68	$9
Health A	08 NYY *	0	1	0	21	18	3.00	1.43	252			8.3	30%	82%	4.22				4.3	7.7	1.8		0.9	3.5	63	$1
PT/Exp F	09 NYY *	8	1	11	70	42	3.88	1.29	266	258	353	5.0	28%	76%	3.88	53	19	28	2.4	5.4	2.2	17%	1.4	5.0	62	$12
Consist B	1st Half	3	1	4	38	22	4.29	1.25	253			5.5	26%	71%	3.96	52	19	29	2.6	5.1	2.0	17%	1.4	0.7	52	$5
LIMA Plan B+	2nd Half	5	0	7	32	21	3.40	1.35	281			4.6	30%	82%	3.78	53	19	28	2.2	5.8	2.6	17%	1.4	4.2	74	$7
Rand Var +2	10 Proj	5	1	0	44	29	3.93	1.31	268			5.9	29%	75%	3.74	53	19	28	2.5	6.0	2.4	15%	1.2	3.8	72	$5

5-1, 5.24 ERA in 34 IP at NYY. Minor-league record shows a bit of promise, but skills have not translated to bigs (1.3 Cmd). 2009 xERA, unlucky hr/f and GB history warrant some interest. AL league reserve-list material.

Albers,Matt

		W	L	Sv	IP	K	ERA	WHIP	OBA	vL	vR	BF/G	H%	S%	xERA	G	L	F	Ctl	Dom	Cmd	hr/f	hr/9	RAR	BPV	R$
RH Reliever	05	0	0	0	0	0	0.00	0.00							0.00											
Age 27	06 HOU *	12	5	0	156	113	3.23	1.38	258	333	267	24.9	31%	77%	4.20	43	26	30	3.6	6.5	1.8	5%	0.5	24.2	41	$15
Type Pwr GB	07 HOU *	6	14	0	164	105	5.43	1.59	288	280	298	18.5	31%	69%	4.72	48	17	35	4.0	5.8	1.4	13%	1.4	-20.4	22	$1
Health C	08 BAL	3	3	0	49	26	3.49	1.33	237	163	312	7.4	26%	75%	4.53	53	12	34	4.0	4.8	1.2	7%	0.7	5.2	8	$4
PT/Exp C	09 BAL	3	6	0	67	49	5.51	1.73	297	342	273	5.6	35%	66%	4.71	48	20	31	4.8	6.6	1.4	4%	0.4	-8.7	14	($0)
Consist A	1st Half	1	2	0	31	23	3.46	1.60	285			5.6	34%	78%	4.92	40	19	41	4.3	6.5	1.5	2%	0.3	3.8	20	$2
LIMA Plan F	2nd Half	2	4	0	36	26	7.29	1.84	308			5.5	36%	58%	4.47	56	21	23	5.3	6.5	1.2	7%	0.5	-12.5	9	($2)
Rand Var +1	10 Proj	1	2	0	29	19	4.97	1.59	281			7.3	32%	68%	4.59	50	18	32	4.3	5.9	1.4	7%	0.6	-0.6	17	$1

No reported effects from 2008 shoulder injury, but this was not exactly a rebound. Problems w/ Ctl, LHB and runners on base cloud his future. Too young to write off, but window is closing.

Anderson,Brett

		W	L	Sv	IP	K	ERA	WHIP	OBA	vL	vR	BF/G	H%	S%	xERA	G	L	F	Ctl	Dom	Cmd	hr/f	hr/9	RAR	BPV	R$
LH Starter	05	0	0	0	0	0	0.00	0.00							0.00											
Age 22	06	0	0	0	0	0	0.00	0.00							0.00											
Type Pwr GB	07	0	0	0	0	0	0.00	0.00							0.00											
Health A	08 aa	2	1	0	31	34	2.49	1.14	240			21.0	32%	82%	3.30				2.2	9.8	4.4		0.8	7.0	133	$5
PT/Exp C	09 OAK	11	11	0	175	150	4.06	1.28	267	313	247	24.6	32%	71%	3.52	51	15	34	2.3	7.7	3.3	11%	1.0	8.6	105	$17
Consist A	1st Half	4	7	0	74	52	5.47	1.51	301			23.5	33%	68%	4.22	50	15	35	2.7	6.3	2.4	15%	1.6	-9.3	69	$2
LIMA Plan B	2nd Half	7	4	0	101	98	3.02	1.12	240			25.5	31%	75%	3.05	52	15	33	2.0	8.7	4.3	8%	0.6	17.8	131	$15
Rand Var +1	10 Proj	12	9	0	189	179	3.44	1.23	256			23.0	32%	75%	3.25	51	15	34	2.3	8.5	3.7	11%	1.0	27.4	121	$22

A rookie season nothing short of impressive. Solid skills in the 1H reached elite levels in 2H; serving up ground ball after ground ball. At his age, expect IP limits, but this may be his last 4.00 ERA for a while. Invest.

BRENT HERSHEY

Arias,Alberto

Arias,Alberto	Yr	W	L	Sv	IP	K	ERA	WHIP	OBA	vL	vR	BF/G	H%	S%	xERA	G	L	F	Ctl	Dom	Cmd	hr/f	hr/9	RAR	BPV	R$
RH Reliever	05	0	0	0	0	0	0.00	0.00							0.00											
Age 26	06 aa	8	6	0	111	71	5.67	1.47	278			10.0	29%	65%	5.64				3.5	5.7	**1.7**		1.6	-15.7	20	$4
Type xGB	07 aaa	3	2	0	34	17	4.24	1.65	305			9.7	34%	74%	5.47				3.7	4.5	**1.2**		0.5	1.0	31	$2
Health B	08 aaa	4	4	1	69	46	3.98	1.45	288			7.9	34%	72%	4.45				2.7	5.9	**2.2**		0.4	2.8	66	$5
PT/Exp F	09 HOU *	4	3	0	62	50	3.77	1.55	274	276	269	6.0	34%	74%	3.60	61	16	23	4.4	7.3	**1.7**	5%	0.3	3.2	52	$3
Consist B	1st Half	3	2	0	37	33	3.43	1.47	229			6.8	29%	77%	3.44	67	12	21	5.7	8.0	**1.4**	9%	0.5	3.5	36	$3
LIMA Plan B	2nd Half	1	1	0	25	17	4.30	1.67	333			5.2	40%	71%	3.70	58	19	24	2.4	6.1	**2.6**	0%	0.0	-0.3	81	$0
Rand Var 0	10 Proj	**3**	**3**	**0**	**49**	**33**	**4.08**	**1.57**	**294**			**7.0**	**35%**	**73%**	**3.78**	**60**	**17**	**23**	**3.5**	**6.1**	**1.7**	**5%**	**0.4**	**2.9**	**53**	**$2**

2-1, 3.35 ERA in 46 IP at HOU. 2H skills growth put him on the watch list, but health a concern after Aug hamstring injury and Sept knee surgery. GB split, 2.1 Cmd in the majors provide solid starting point.

Arredondo,Jose

Arredondo,Jose	Yr	W	L	Sv	IP	K	ERA	WHIP	OBA	vL	vR	BF/G	H%	S%	xERA	G	L	F	Ctl	Dom	Cmd	hr/f	hr/9	RAR	BPV	R$
RH Reliever	05	0	0	0	0	0	0.00	0.00							0.00											
Age 26	06 aa	2	3	0	60	41	6.58	1.71	328			25.3	37%	61%	6.52				3.0	6.1	**2.1**		1.0	-15.3	38	($2)
Type Pwr	07 aa	0	1	10	28	24	3.31	1.29	215			4.7	26%	76%	3.31				4.6	7.8	**1.7**		0.7	4.0	74	$6
Health A	08 LAA *	11	3	10	78	67	1.88	1.06	205	148	236	4.6	25%	86%	3.28	51	17	31	3.0	7.8	**2.6**	8%	0.6	23.8	87	$19
PT/Exp D	09 LAA	2	3	0	45	47	6.00	1.56	270	238	295	4.7	34%	63%	4.03	44	18	38	4.6	9.4	**2.0**	12%	1.2	-8.6	67	$1
Consist A	1st Half	1	3	0	24	27	5.60	1.66	292			4.4	41%	63%	3.51	49	25	26	4.5	10.1	**2.3**	0%	0.0	-3.4	87	$0
LIMA Plan B+	2nd Half	1	0	0	21	20	6.46	1.44	244			5.1	25%	63%	4.55	39	10	51	4.7	8.6	**1.8**	20%	2.6	-5.2	44	$1
Rand Var +5	10 Proj	**4**	**2**	**0**	**54**	**49**	**4.21**	**1.40**	**256**			**5.5**	**31%**	**74%**	**3.97**	**46**	**17**	**38**	**3.9**	**8.2**	**2.1**	**12%**	**1.2**	**3.1**	**68**	**$5**

Strand rate, along with 1H h%, 2H hr/f conspired to ruin 2009. Curiously, June elbow strain was followed by 2H FB% spike. If healthy, his numbers will improve, but future closer talk on hold for now.

Arroyo,Bronson

Arroyo,Bronson	Yr	W	L	Sv	IP	K	ERA	WHIP	OBA	vL	vR	BF/G	H%	S%	xERA	G	L	F	Ctl	Dom	Cmd	hr/f	hr/9	RAR	BPV	R$
RH Starter	05 BOS	14	10	0	205	100	4.52	1.30	269	286	234	24.7	29%	67%	4.81	38	18	44	2.4	4.4	**1.9**	7%	1.0	-3.7	31	$14
Age 33	06 CIN	14	11	0	240	184	3.30	1.19	247	282	206	28.2	28%	78%	4.05	38	21	41	2.4	6.9	**2.9**	11%	1.2	35.3	76	$26
Type	07 CIN	9	15	0	211	156	4.23	1.40	281	274	285	26.8	32%	73%	4.50	35	21	44	2.7	6.7	**2.5**	10%	1.2	5.1	61	$12
Health A	08 CIN	15	11	0	200	163	4.77	1.44	280	314	254	25.6	32%	70%	4.05	41	23	36	3.1	7.3	**2.4**	13%	1.3	-12.3	69	$12
PT/Exp A	09 CIN	15	13	0	220	127	3.84	1.27	256	278	236	27.9	27%	75%	4.29	45	19	37	2.7	5.2	**2.0**	12%	1.3	9.5	44	$17
Consist A	1st Half	8	7	0	98	52	5.69	1.52	285			27.2	29%	67%	4.87	45	18	37	3.6	4.8	**1.3**	16%	1.8	-18.2	13	$2
LIMA Plan D+	2nd Half	7	6	0	122	75	2.35	1.06	232			28.7	26%	82%	3.84	44	19	36	1.9	5.5	**2.9**	8%	0.8	27.7	70	$16
Rand Var 0	10 Proj	**13**	**12**	**0**	**203**	**135**	**4.27**	**1.37**	**274**			**27.1**	**30%**	**72%**	**4.31**	**42**	**20**	**38**	**2.7**	**6.0**	**2.2**	**11%**	**1.2**	**-1.3**	**55**	**$13**

Looked like toast in the 1H, but 2H skills rebound saved his season. His proven 200-IP track record has some value, but mediocre Dom, persistent carpal tunnel discomfort raise the risk. Don't overpay.

Ayala,Luis

Ayala,Luis	Yr	W	L	Sv	IP	K	ERA	WHIP	OBA	vL	vR	BF/G	H%	S%	xERA	G	L	F	Ctl	Dom	Cmd	hr/f	hr/9	RAR	BPV	R$
RH Reliever	05 WAS	8	7	1	71	40	2.66	1.25	273	350	230	4.4	30%	83%	4.05	43	23	34	1.8	5.1	**2.9**	9%	0.9	13.9	64	$10
Age 32	06 WAS	0	0	0	0	0	0.00	0.00							0.00											
Type FB	07 WAS	2	2	1	42	28	3.19	1.30	265	243	286	4.1	29%	80%	4.38	39	21	40	2.6	6.0	**2.3**	9%	1.1	6.4	55	$4
Health F	08 2NL	2	10	9	76	50	5.71	1.45	287	285	288	4.1	32%	61%	4.21	46	22	32	2.9	5.9	**2.1**	11%	1.1	-13.4	54	$3
PT/Exp C	09 2TM	1	5	0	40	28	5.63	1.60	307	396	279	4.8	35%	66%	4.84	37	19	43	3.2	6.3	**2.0**	9%	1.1	-6.5	44	($0)
Consist A	1st Half	1	2	0	32	21	4.21	1.43	296			5.0	33%	74%	4.49	39	19	42	2.2	5.9	**2.6**	9%	1.1	0.4	62	$1
LIMA Plan D+	2nd Half	0	3	0	8	7	11.39	2.28	350			4.1	42%	47%	6.29	31	19	50	6.8	8.0	**1.2**	7%	1.1	-6.9	-32	($2)
Rand Var +3	10 Proj	**1**	**2**	**0**	**29**	**19**	**4.66**	**1.38**	**281**			**4.3**	**32%**	**68%**	**4.45**	**39**	**21**	**41**	**2.5**	**5.9**	**2.4**	**8%**	**0.9**	**-0.4**	**56**	**$1**

Stats again affected by a nasty h%/s% combination. Consistent and passable skills, but other than ERA, there's very little upside. MLB GMs will be hard-pressed to give him another shot; this time, follow their lead.

Badenhop,Burke

Badenhop,Burke	Yr	W	L	Sv	IP	K	ERA	WHIP	OBA	vL	vR	BF/G	H%	S%	xERA	G	L	F	Ctl	Dom	Cmd	hr/f	hr/9	RAR	BPV	R$
RH Reliever	05	0	0	0	0	0	0.00	0.00							0.00											
Age 27	06	0	0	0	0	0	0.00	0.00							0.00											
Type Pwr xGB	07 aa	2	0	0	18	10	2.50	0.94	191			23.2	20%	80%	2.45				2.5	5.0	**2.0**		1.0	4.4	59	$3
Health D	08 FLA *	3	3	0	53	38	5.39	1.57	294	298	281	17.1	33%	67%	3.95	54	20	26	3.5	6.4	**1.8**	16%	1.2	-7.4	51	$1
PT/Exp D	09 FLA	7	4	0	72	57	3.75	1.32	259	250	269	8.7	31%	72%	3.43	54	20	26	3.0	7.1	**2.4**	9%	0.6	3.9	79	$7
Consist C	1st Half	5	3	0	44	29	3.48	1.34	266			9.4	30%	76%	3.82	50	23	27	2.9	5.9	**2.1**	11%	0.8	3.9	57	$5
LIMA Plan B	2nd Half	2	1	0	28	28	4.18	1.29	248			7.9	33%	66%	2.84	61	15	24	3.2	9.0	**2.8**	5%	0.3	0.0	114	$3
Rand Var 0	10 Proj	**6**	**4**	**0**	**73**	**58**	**3.95**	**1.41**	**272**			**10.5**	**32%**	**73%**	**3.52**	**56**	**19**	**25**	**3.2**	**7.2**	**2.2**	**11%**	**0.7**	**6.7**	**76**	**$6**

Career splits worth noting:

	Cmd	OppBA	ERA
as SP	1.4	.299	6.95
as RP	2.7	.254	3.28

If he can sustain 2H gains in GB% and Dom, he'll succeed in any role. Good speculative pick.

Baez,Danys

Baez,Danys	Yr	W	L	Sv	IP	K	ERA	WHIP	OBA	vL	vR	BF/G	H%	S%	xERA	G	L	F	Ctl	Dom	Cmd	hr/f	hr/9	RAR	BPV	R$
RH Reliever	05 TAM	5	4	41	72	51	2.87	1.33	245	268	215	4.6	28%	82%	4.15	47	20	33	3.7	6.4	**1.7**	10%	0.9	13.3	38	$21
Age 32	06 2NL	5	6	9	59	39	4.56	1.30	264	295	244	4.4	31%	64%	4.50	40	17	43	2.6	5.9	**2.3**	4%	0.5	-0.5	55	$8
Type GB	07 BAL	0	6	3	50	29	6.44	1.57	261	346	200	4.3	27%	61%	4.97	51	17	32	5.2	5.2	**1.0**	15%	1.4	-12.0	-17	($0)
Health F	08 BAL	0	0	0	0	0	0.00	0.00							0.00											
PT/Exp D	09 BAL	4	6	0	72	40	4.02	1.13	226	248	197	4.9	24%	67%	3.63	61	13	26	2.8	5.0	**1.8**	14%	1.0	3.8	55	$7
Consist C	1st Half	4	2	0	41	24	4.17	1.15	222			6.0	23%	67%	3.72	60	13	27	3.1	5.3	**1.7**	15%	1.1	1.4	50	$5
LIMA Plan C	2nd Half	0	4	0	31	16	3.81	1.11	231			4.0	25%	68%	3.50	63	14	24	2.3	4.7	**2.0**	13%	0.9	2.4	62	$2
Rand Var 0	10 Proj	**3**	**5**	**0**	**63**	**37**	**4.57**	**1.29**	**243**			**4.5**	**26%**	**66%**	**4.12**	**54**	**16**	**30**	**3.4**	**5.3**	**1.5**	**12%**	**1.0**	**2.4**	**35**	**$4**

Continues to slice up RHB, and extreme GB tilt covered up Dom deficiency. Between health issues, age, h% correction and sliding strikeout rate, it's hard to muster up faith in a repeat.

Bailey,Andrew

Bailey,Andrew	Yr	W	L	Sv	IP	K	ERA	WHIP	OBA	vL	vR	BF/G	H%	S%	xERA	G	L	F	Ctl	Dom	Cmd	hr/f	hr/9	RAR	BPV	R$
RH Reliever	05	0	0	0	0	0	0.00	0.00							0.00											
Age 25	06	0	0	0	0	0	0.00	0.00							0.00											
Type Pwr FB	07	0	0	0	0	0	0.00	0.00							0.00											
Health A	08 aa	5	9	0	110	89	4.73	1.47	263			13.1	31%	70%	4.73				4.2	7.3	**1.7**		1.0	-5.8	52	$5
PT/Exp D	09 OAK	6	3	26	83	91	1.84	0.88	173	146	185	4.7	23%	82%	3.07	42	13	45	2.6	9.8	**3.8**	6%	0.5	26.9	127	$26
Consist D	1st Half	4	1	8	47	57	2.10	1.02	179			5.2	26%	82%	3.21	39	14	46	3.6	10.9	**3.0**	6%	0.6	13.7	115	$12
LIMA Plan C+	2nd Half	2	2	18	36	34	1.49	0.69	164			4.1	21%	83%	2.88	46	11	43	1.2	8.5	**6.8**	5%	0.5	13.2	143	$14
Rand Var -5	10 Proj	**5**	**5**	**45**	**88**	**84**	**2.98**	**1.09**	**211**			**4.9**	**27%**	**75%**	**3.59**	**43**	**12**	**44**	**3.0**	**8.6**	**2.9**	**7%**	**0.7**	**9.2**	**96**	**$28**

A 16-1 K/BB line in the AFL was largely ignored but set the stage for this breakout. ERA received H% boost, but base skills trump fluke concerns. 2H growth is icing. No closer is swoon-proof, but all signs point to a repeat.

Bailey,Homer

Bailey,Homer	Yr	W	L	Sv	IP	K	ERA	WHIP	OBA	vL	vR	BF/G	H%	S%	xERA	G	L	F	Ctl	Dom	Cmd	hr/f	hr/9	RAR	BPV	R$
RH Starter	05	0	0	0	0	0	0.00	0.00							0.00											
Age 23	06 aa	7	1	0	68	68	2.02	1.25	230			21.8	31%	83%	2.79				3.7	9.0	**2.5**		0.1	21.0	111	$12
Type Pwr	07 CIN *	10	5	0	112	83	4.51	1.37	232	284	233	22.9	27%	67%	4.45	47	18	35	4.6	6.6	**1.4**	6%	0.6	-1.1	19	$9
Health A	08 CIN *	4	13	0	147	106	6.14	1.70	312	305	423	25.2	35%	65%	4.51	43	25	31	3.8	6.5	**1.7**	13%	1.2	-34.0	36	($4)
PT/Exp C	09 CIN *	16	10	0	203	158	4.09	1.47	276	283	248	26.2	32%	76%	4.26	43	21	37	3.6	7.0	**2.0**	11%	1.2	2.5	51	$13
Consist A	1st Half	9	5	0	98	77	4.03	1.53	282			27.3	32%	79%	4.61	41	15	44	3.8	7.0	**1.9**	11%	1.4	2.0	44	$7
LIMA Plan C+	2nd Half	7	5	0	104	81	4.15	1.42	271			25.1	32%	73%	4.15	43	21	36	3.4	7.0	**2.1**	9%	1.0	0.6	56	$7
Rand Var 0	10 Proj	**9**	**8**	**0**	**137**	**107**	**4.27**	**1.46**	**274**			**25.0**	**32%**	**73%**	**4.21**	**43**	**21**	**35**	**3.5**	**7.0**	**2.0**	**10%**	**1.0**	**1.0**	**52**	**$8**

8-5, 4.53 ERA in 113 IP at CIN. PRO: modest 2H growth; finally survived MLB hitters; age. CON: Three seasons, not one standout skill; 56 IP spike from 2008. Strong finish (2.08 Sep/Oct ERA); beware of overbids.

Baker,Scott

Baker,Scott	Yr	W	L	Sv	IP	K	ERA	WHIP	OBA	vL	vR	BF/G	H%	S%	xERA	G	L	F	Ctl	Dom	Cmd	hr/f	hr/9	RAR	BPV	R$
RH Starter	05 MIN *	8	11	0	187	125	3.60	1.23	263	221	257	24.3	29%	74%	4.12	40	19	41	2.0	6.0	**3.0**	9%	1.0	17.8	73	$17
Age 28	06 MIN *	10	12	0	167	119	5.19	1.54	310	349	299	26.6	35%	68%	4.79	34	19	47	2.4	6.4	**2.6**	8%	1.2	-13.0	62	$7
Type xFB	07 MIN *	12	11	1	186	134	4.39	1.29	282	323	257	25.3	32%	68%	4.21	35	22	43	1.7	6.5	**3.9**	7%	0.9	2.6	85	$16
Health B	08 MIN	11	4	0	172	141	3.45	1.18	249	263	230	25.2	29%	75%	3.98	33	21	46	2.2	7.4	**3.4**	9%	1.0	19.1	84	$20
PT/Exp A	09 MIN	15	9	0	194	160	4.36	1.19	252	221	271	24.9	29%	67%	4.05	34	19	47	2.1	7.4	**3.5**	10%	1.3	2.2	88	$21
Consist A	1st Half	6	6	0	92	74	4.99	1.14	251			24.9	27%	61%	4.00	33	20	47	1.8	7.2	**4.1**	13%	1.7	-6.1	93	$9
LIMA Plan C	2nd Half	9	3	0	102	86	3.79	1.23	252			24.9	30%	71%	4.09	35	19	46	2.5	7.6	**3.1**	7%	0.9	8.3	83	$12
Rand Var 0	10 Proj	**14**	**9**	**0**	**203**	**170**	**3.86**	**1.18**	**255**			**24.5**	**30%**	**71%**	**3.94**	**34**	**20**	**46**	**2.0**	**7.5**	**3.9**	**9%**	**1.1**	**12.4**	**95**	**$23**

Though ERA objects, a virtual repeat season with added IP. With outstanding Cmd, he again teeters on the cusp of frontline status, but FB and hr/9 are the enemy. Solid SP choice, but not (yet?) the anchor he could be.

BRENT HERSHEY

Balester,Collin

	Yr	W	L	Sv	IP	K	ERA	WHIP	OBA	vL	vR	BF/G	H%	S%	xERA	G	L	F	Ctl	Dom	Cmd	hr/f	hr/9	RAR	BPV	R$
RH Starter	05	0	0	0	0	0	0.00	0.00							0.00											
Age 23	06	0	0	0	0	0	0.00	0.00							0.00											
Type FB	07 a/a	4	10	0	150	103	4.45	1.40	280			24.0	32%	68%	4.57				2.7	6.2	2.3		0.7	0.2	63	$7
Health A	08 WAS *	12	10	0	158	107	4.85	1.41	280	278	298	22.8	31%	69%	4.41	40	22	39	2.8	6.1	2.2	12%	1.3	-11.2	52	$9
PT/Exp D	09 WAS *	8	14	0	137	81	5.90	1.71	322	315	254	23.6	36%	66%	5.36	37	17	47	3.3	5.3	1.6	7%	1.0	-28.9	20	($2)
Consist B	1st Half	6	7	0	85	48	5.18	1.65	316			24.3	36%	66%	5.36				3.1	5.1	1.7		0.3	-10.4	47	$1
LIMA Plan C+	2nd Half	2	7	0	52	33	7.06	1.82	331			22.5	35%	65%	5.47	37	17	47	3.8	5.7	1.5	14%	2.1	-18.5	15	($3)
Rand Var +2	10 Proj	2	4	0	44	28	5.17	1.56	302			24.4	33%	69%	4.90	38	19	44	3.1	5.8	1.9	9%	1.2	-3.4	36	$0

1-4, 6.82 ERA in 30 IP at WAS. Took a step back in just about every area. With only passable Dom, he needs either pinpoint Ctl or strong GB% to succeed. At 23, working on that task will be easier in AAA than in WAS.

Bale,John

	Yr	W	L	Sv	IP	K	ERA	WHIP	OBA	vL	vR	BF/G	H%	S%	xERA	G	L	F	Ctl	Dom	Cmd	hr/f	hr/9	RAR	BPV	R$
LH Reliever	05 JPN	2	1	24	54	68	3.93	1.24	237			4.4	28%	83%	5.12				3.3	11.4	3.4		2.5	2.5	74	$13
Age 35	06 JPN	1	2	6	43	44	3.64	1.44	285			6.3	34%	83%	5.73				2.9	9.1	3.2		1.7	4.7	68	$5
Type Pwr	07 KC *	1	2	0	57	52	3.95	1.49	285			6.8	36%	72%	4.47				3.3	8.2	2.5		0.3	3.9	90	$3
Health B	08 KC *	0	6	0	40	24	6.53	1.60	316			7.2	35%	58%	5.70				2.7	5.4	2.0		0.9	-10.7	39	($2)
PT/Exp D	09 KC	0	1	1	28	24	5.72	1.84	299	271	321	3.1	36%	69%	4.90	45	21	34	5.7	7.6	1.3	10%	1.0	-4.4	6	($1)
Consist C	1st Half	0	1	1	11	11	7.30	1.80	277			3.5	33%	61%	4.59	53	10	37	6.5	8.9	1.4	17%	1.6	-3.9	17	($0)
LIMA Plan D+	2nd Half	0	0	0	17	13	4.71	1.86	312			2.9	37%	74%	5.06	41	27	32	5.2	6.8	1.3	5%	0.5	-0.5	-0	($0)
Rand Var +3	10 Proj	0	1	0	29	25	4.66	1.59	294			4.7	35%	72%	4.13	45	21	34	3.7	7.8	2.1	10%	0.9	1.1	62	$0

Missed April and most of May with thyroid and back issues; hamstring woes wiped out Sept. Shoddy Ctl ruined the remaining 3 months. LH power arm will get another shot, but age, injury ills say to keep expecations low.

Balfour,Grant

	Yr	W	L	Sv	IP	K	ERA	WHIP	OBA	vL	vR	BF/G	H%	S%	xERA	G	L	F	Ctl	Dom	Cmd	hr/f	hr/9	RAR	BPV	R$
RH Reliever	05	0	0	0	0	0	0.00	0.00							0.00											
Age 32	06	0	0	0	0	0	0.00	0.00							0.00											
Type Pwr xFB	07 2TM *	2	3	7	68	81	4.57	1.55	255			5.3	36%	70%	3.79	42	22	36	5.2	10.7	2.0	7%	0.6	-0.9	71	$6
Health D	08 TAM *	7	2	12	82	113	1.23	0.86	131	120	159	4.7	21%	89%	2.87	29	19	52	3.9	12.4	3.2	5%	0.5	31.4	126	$24
PT/Exp D	09 TAM	5	4	4	67	69	4.81	1.37	237	240	232	4.0	30%	65%	4.11	36	21	43	4.4	9.2	2.1	8%	0.8	-3.0	61	$7
Consist C	1st Half	3	1	1	36	36	4.50	1.39	234			4.4	31%	67%	4.19	36	23	41	4.8	9.0	1.9	5%	0.5	-0.2	47	$4
LIMA Plan B+	2nd Half	2	3	3	31	33	5.18	1.34	241			3.5	30%	63%	4.01	36	18	46	4.0	9.5	2.4	10%	1.2	-2.8	76	$3
Rand Var +1	10 Proj	3	2	0	44	51	3.52	1.22	207			4.3	29%	72%	3.63	35	20	45	4.3	10.6	2.4	6%	0.6	4.3	85	$6

Monthly BPV, Apr through Sept highlight his inconsistency: (-104)/53/108/62/174/(-79). Still has the gas to close, though hurdles of Ctl, FB% remain. Given the unevenness, a risk best left for the end-game.

Bannister,Brian

	Yr	W	L	Sv	IP	K	ERA	WHIP	OBA	vL	vR	BF/G	H%	S%	xERA	G	L	F	Ctl	Dom	Cmd	hr/f	hr/9	RAR	BPV	R$
RH Starter	05 a/a	13	5	0	154	115	3.19	1.29	266			25.0	31%	77%	3.93				2.4	6.7	2.8		0.7	21.2	81	$17
Age 29	06 NYM *	5	4	0	68	40	4.78	1.52	285	286	185	21.6	31%	71%	5.22	40	15	45	3.6	5.3	1.5	9%	1.2	-2.5	16	$3
Type	07 KC *	13	10	0	185	87	3.84	1.22	254	281	219	24.7	27%	71%	4.66	41	19	40	2.4	4.2	1.8	8%	1.0	15.2	32	$18
Health B	08 KC	9	16	0	183	113	5.76	1.49	294	313	274	25.2	32%	64%	4.72	37	22	41	2.9	5.6	1.9	12%	1.4	-31.9	39	$4
PT/Exp B	09 KC	7	12	0	154	98	4.73	1.37	270	266	270	25.4	30%	66%	4.21	50	17	34	2.9	5.7	2.0	9%	0.9	-5.4	52	$8
Consist A	1st Half	5	6	0	84	53	3.95	1.31	261			25.4	29%	72%	4.23	47	18	35	2.8	5.7	2.0	8%	0.9	5.2	51	$7
LIMA Plan C	2nd Half	2	6	0	70	45	5.67	1.45	281			25.4	32%	61%	4.18	53	15	32	3.1	5.8	1.9	10%	0.9	-10.5	52	$1
Rand Var 0	10 Proj	9	12	0	166	102	4.66	1.40	276			24.7	30%	69%	4.44	45	18	37	2.9	5.5	1.9	9%	1.0	-0.2	45	$9

Shoulder fatigue ended season prematurely in Sept. BPV spike due to increased GB%. If he builds on that trend, marginal value may result. But realize that his upside is replacement level and nothing more.

Bard,Daniel

	Yr	W	L	Sv	IP	K	ERA	WHIP	OBA	vL	vR	BF/G	H%	S%	xERA	G	L	F	Ctl	Dom	Cmd	hr/f	hr/9	RAR	BPV	R$
RH Reliever	05	0	0	0	0	0	0.00	0.00							0.00											
Age 24	06	0	0	0	0	0	0.00	0.00							0.00											
Type Pwr	07	0	0	0	0	0	0.00	0.00							0.00											
Health A	08 aa	4	1	7	49	53	2.45	1.26	202			6.6	27%	82%	2.87				4.9	9.8	2.0		0.6	11.3	98	$10
PT/Exp F	09 BOS *	3	2	7	65	88	3.18	1.17	211	263	200	4.4	30%	78%	2.78	45	19	36	3.7	12.2	3.3	15%	1.1	10.2	141	$12
Consist A	1st Half	1	0	7	36	46	2.49	1.08	191			5.2	27%	81%	3.03	35	26	39	3.7	11.5	3.1	10%	0.7	8.7	119	$8
LIMA Plan B+	2nd Half	2	2	0	29	42	4.05	1.28	235			3.8	34%	75%	2.52	53	14	33	3.7	13.1	3.5	23%	1.6	1.4	166	$4
Rand Var +1	10 Proj	4	2	3	66	83	3.01	1.23	212			5.0	30%	80%	3.03	48	17	35	4.2	11.4	2.7	13%	1.0	11.4	116	$10

2-2, 3.65 ERA in 49 IP at BOS. Excellent debut; fluky 2H hr/f kept it from being better. Still needs to quiet LHP (.866 OPS), but with elite Dom and GB, he's a top setup guy already, and prime Papelbon insurance.

Bass,Brian

	Yr	W	L	Sv	IP	K	ERA	WHIP	OBA	vL	vR	BF/G	H%	S%	xERA	G	L	F	Ctl	Dom	Cmd	hr/f	hr/9	RAR	BPV	R$
RH Reliever	05 aa	12	8	0	165	86	5.40	1.50	300			27.0	33%	63%	4.96				2.6	4.7	1.8		0.6	-22.3	42	$5
Age 28	06 aa	5	6	0	59	24	7.08	1.85	350			21.7	36%	62%	7.54				3.0	3.7	1.2		1.3	-18.6	-5	($2)
Type xGB	07 aaa	7	3	1	103	64	5.11	1.44	294			12.1	33%	65%	5.09				2.4	5.6	2.4		0.9	-8.3	53	$5
Health A	08 2AL	4	4	1	89	45	4.84	1.44	280	240	310	8.0	29%	69%	4.09	58	17	25	3.1	4.5	1.5	16%	1.2	-5.4	33	$3
PT/Exp C	09 BAL	5	3	0	86	54	4.90	1.74	303	298	314	8.4	33%	74%	4.31	61	15	23	4.6	5.6	1.2	16%	1.1	-4.8	17	$1
Consist B	1st Half	4	2	0	48	30	3.75	1.48	278			8.4	29%	81%	3.72	65	13	22	3.6	5.6	1.6	23%	1.5	4.2	48	$4
LIMA Plan C+	2nd Half	1	1	0	38	24	6.34	2.06	333			8.3	38%	68%	5.09	57	19	24	5.9	5.6	1.0	9%	0.7	-8.9	-22	($3)
Rand Var +4	10 Proj	4	3	0	69	40	4.60	1.66	303			9.2	33%	75%	4.26	59	17	24	3.9	5.3	1.3	14%	1.1	1.4	25	$2

A soft-tosser with the GB% to succeed in the right role, but worsening Cmd negates the possibility. Baserunners galore plus gopheritis equals trouble in any pond. Go fishing elsewhere.

Batista,Miguel

	Yr	W	L	Sv	IP	K	ERA	WHIP	OBA	vL	vR	BF/G	H%	S%	xERA	G	L	F	Ctl	Dom	Cmd	hr/f	hr/9	RAR	BPV	R$
RH Reliever	05 TOR	5	8	31	74	54	4.12	1.44	277	256	282	4.6	31%	74%	4.10	48	19	33	3.3	6.5	2.0	12%	1.1	2.3	55	$15
Age 39	06 ARI	11	8	0	206	110	4.59	1.53	284	321	257	27.0	31%	71%	4.57	52	20	28	3.7	4.8	1.3	9%	0.8	-2.5	17	$7
Type Pwr	07 SEA	16	11	0	193	133	4.29	1.52	277	295	258	26.0	32%	73%	4.75	44	17	39	4.0	6.2	1.6	7%	0.8	5.1	27	$13
Health A	08 SEA	4	14	1	115	73	6.26	1.86	294	293	298	12.5	32%	69%	5.52	46	20	34	6.2	5.7	0.9	14%	1.5	-27.1	-40	($4)
PT/Exp B	09 SEA	7	4	1	71	52	4.04	1.65	282	331	242	5.8	33%	77%	4.83	47	18	35	4.9	6.6	1.3	9%	0.9	3.6	10	$5
Consist B	1st Half	4	2	0	41	27	2.85	1.51	262			6.1	31%	82%	4.63	51	16	33	4.6	5.9	1.3	5%	0.4	8.1	11	$4
LIMA Plan C	2nd Half	3	2	1	30	25	5.64	1.85	308			5.6	35%	73%	5.09	41	21	38	5.3	7.4	1.4	13%	1.5	-4.5	9	$1
Rand Var -2	10 Proj	4	4	0	55	39	4.93	1.70	290			7.9	33%	73%	4.93	46	19	36	4.9	6.4	1.3	11%	1.2	-3.4	6	$1

Got his Cmd back over 1.0 and the ERA gods were generous. But don't:
- let him start or close
- let him face LH batters
- expect a repeat
- let him near your roster

Beckett,Josh

	Yr	W	L	Sv	IP	K	ERA	WHIP	OBA	vL	vR	BF/G	H%	S%	xERA	G	L	F	Ctl	Dom	Cmd	hr/f	hr/9	RAR	BPV	R$
RH Starter	05 FLA	15	8	0	178	166	3.38	1.18	233	217	252	25.2	29%	73%	3.46	43	22	36	2.9	8.4	2.9	8%	0.7	18.9	92	$22
Age 29	06 BOS	16	11	0	204	158	5.02	1.30	249	251	248	26.1	27%	66%	4.09	45	17	38	3.3	7.0	2.1	16%	1.6	-11.8	60	$18
Type Pwr	07 BOS	20	7	0	201	194	3.27	1.14	250	255	235	27.2	32%	74%	3.21	47	16	37	1.8	8.7	4.9	8%	0.8	30.5	133	$31
Health B	08 BOS	12	10	0	174	172	4.03	1.19	260	260	252	26.5	33%	68%	3.15	41	25	34	1.8	8.9	5.1	11%	0.9	6.9	131	$20
PT/Exp A	09 BOS	17	6	0	212	199	3.86	1.19	249	258	226	27.3	30%	71%	3.26	47	21	32	2.3	8.4	3.6	13%	1.1	15.6	114	$26
Consist A	1st Half	9	3	0	105	99	3.68	1.23	243			27.2	30%	72%	3.33	47	24	30	2.9	8.5	2.9	10%	0.8	10.0	99	$13
LIMA Plan C+	2nd Half	8	3	0	107	100	4.03	1.16	254			27.3	30%	70%	3.19	48	19	34	1.8	8.4	4.8	16%	1.3	5.6	129	$13
Rand Var +2	10 Proj	17	8	0	210	199	3.64	1.18	251			27.0	31%	72%	3.27	45	21	34	2.1	8.5	4.0	11%	0.9	30.3	119	$27

2H hr/f obscured carbon-copy skill level from 2007 and 2008. Return of his GB% and injury-free season bodes well for his short-term outlook. Nary a chink here; bid with full confidence.

Bedard,Erik

	Yr	W	L	Sv	IP	K	ERA	WHIP	OBA	vL	vR	BF/G	H%	S%	xERA	G	L	F	Ctl	Dom	Cmd	hr/f	hr/9	RAR	BPV	R$
LH Starter	05 BAL	6	8	0	141	125	4.02	1.39	259	252	263	25.3	32%	72%	3.99	40	23	37	3.6	8.0	2.2	7%	0.6	6.2	63	$11
Age 31	06 BAL	15	11	0	196	171	3.76	1.35	262	200	272	25.4	32%	73%	3.62	49	21	30	3.2	7.8	2.5	9%	0.7	19.2	83	$21
Type Pwr	07 BAL	13	5	0	182	221	3.16	1.09	216	229	208	26.1	29%	75%	2.77	48	17	35	2.8	10.9	3.9	13%	0.9	30.1	146	$29
Health F	08 SEA	6	4	0	81	72	3.67	1.32	235	253	224	22.9	28%	76%	4.17	40	17	43	4.1	8.0	1.9	9%	1.0	6.8	51	$9
PT/Exp B	09 SEA	5	3	0	83	90	2.82	1.19	217	214	211	22.8	28%	80%	3.49	42	17	40	3.7	9.8	2.6	9%	0.9	16.7	96	$12
Consist C	1st Half	5	2	0	65	65	2.48	1.17	227			24.2	29%	83%	3.53	42	18	40	3.0	9.0	3.0	9%	0.8	15.8	99	$10
LIMA Plan B	2nd Half	0	1	0	18	25	4.04	1.29	180			18.7	26%	71%	3.32	44	14	42	6.1	12.6	2.1	13%	1.0	0.9	86	$2
Rand Var -3	10 Proj	5	5	0	102	112	3.46	1.21	216			22.1	28%	74%	3.46	43	17	40	3.9	9.9	2.5	10%	0.9	12.2	95	$12

Remained tough to hit, but the last two seasons, the even tougher challenge is getting on the field. Torn rotator cuff fixed in August, but beginning of 2010 in doubt. Purchase only at a steep discount.

BRENT HERSHEY

Beimel,Joe

		Yr	Tm	W	L	Sv	IP	K	ERA	WHIP	OBA	vL	vR	BF/G	H%	S%	xERA	G	L	F	Ctl	Dom	Cmd	hr/f	hr/9	RAR	BPV	R$
LH	Reliever	05	aaa	1	2	0	52	29	4.08	1.61	301			4.9	34%	74%	5.02				3.5	5.0	1.4		0.4	1.5	43	$1
Age	32	06	LA *	5	1	2	83	37	2.73	1.26	252	234	277	4.8	27%	81%	4.32	57	11	32	2.8	4.0	1.5	8%	0.8	18.0	33	$9
Type		07	LA	4	2	1	67	39	3.88	1.29	249	188	294	3.4	29%	67%	4.39	48	18	35	3.2	5.2	1.6	1%	0.1	4.5	33	$6
Health	A	08	LA	5	1	0	49	32	2.02	1.45	266	278	263	3.0	32%	85%	4.45	47	19	34	3.9	5.9	1.5	0%	0.0	13.6	27	$6
PT/Exp	D	09	2NL	1	6	1	55	35	3.58	1.37	268	258	282	3.3	30%	76%	4.73	39	15	46	3.1	5.7	1.8	6%	0.8	4.2	36	$3
Consist	A	1st Half		0	4	1	30	17	3.58	1.42	267			3.9	29%	78%	5.16	34	19	47	3.6	5.1	1.4	6%	0.9	2.3	7	$1
LIMA Plan	B	2nd Half		1	2	0	25	18	3.59	1.31	269			2.9	31%	74%	4.21	46	9	45	2.5	6.5	2.6	6%	0.7	1.9	72	$2
Rand Var	-3	10	Proj	2	3	0	48	30	3.94	1.38	266			3.3	30%	71%	4.52	45	15	40	3.2	5.6	1.8	5%	0.6	-1.5	38	$3

A southpaw reliever that's not real effective against LH hitters. Had five save opps as part of committee, converted only 1. With xERA trend, his age and mediocre skills, that's likely his last chance at relevance.

Belisario,Ronald

		Yr	Tm	W	L	Sv	IP	K	ERA	WHIP	OBA	vL	vR	BF/G	H%	S%	xERA	G	L	F	Ctl	Dom	Cmd	hr/f	hr/9	RAR	BPV	R$
RH	Reliever	05		0	0	0	0	0	0.00	0.00							0.00											
Age	27	06		0	0	0	0	0	0.00	0.00							0.00											
Type	Pwr GB	07	aa	1	0	0	25	21	3.96	1.60	269			6.3	31%	81%	5.67				5.0	7.6	1.5		1.4	1.6	35	$1
Health	B	08	aa	4	4	9	57	27	6.49	1.91	335			7.2	36%	66%	6.93				4.4	4.3	1.0		0.9	-15.4	8	$0
PT/Exp	D	09	LA	4	3	0	71	64	2.04	1.15	207	270	157	4.2	26%	84%	3.20	56	16	28	3.7	8.1	2.2	8%	0.5	18.8	81	$10
Consist	F	1st Half		1	2	0	47	46	1.91	1.10	203			4.6	27%	84%	2.88	59	15	26	3.4	8.8	2.6	6%	0.4	13.3	102	$6
LIMA Plan	C	2nd Half		3	1	0	24	18	2.30	1.23	214			3.5	25%	85%	3.88	50	19	31	4.2	6.9	1.6	10%	0.8	5.5	38	$4
Rand Var	-5	10	Proj	4	3	0	55	43	3.91	1.47	264			4.8	31%	75%	3.95	54	17	29	4.1	7.0	1.7	10%	0.8	2.2	48	$4

PRO: Fine overall debut, strong BPV and GB%, obviously earned manager's confidence. CON: ERA was h% aided and LA paid the 2H price for 47 1H IP. July elbow injury raises the risk considerably. Caution.

Bell,Heath

		Yr	Tm	W	L	Sv	IP	K	ERA	WHIP	OBA	vL	vR	BF/G	H%	S%	xERA	G	L	F	Ctl	Dom	Cmd	hr/f	hr/9	RAR	BPV	R$
RH	Reliever	05	NYM	1	3	0	46	43	5.65	1.49	301	303	288	4.9	38%	61%	3.52	45	24	31	2.5	8.4	3.3	7%	0.6	-8.0	105	$0
Age	32	06	NYM *	3	3	12	72	79	3.59	1.49	301	308	348	6.1	39%	78%	2.93	51	26	23	2.5	9.8	4.0	15%	0.9	8.0	139	$10
Type	Pwr	07	SD	6	4	2	94	102	2.02	0.96	185	216	157	4.5	26%	79%	2.43	59	19	23	2.9	9.8	3.4	6%	0.3	27.8	135	$18
Health	A	08	SD	6	6	0	78	71	3.58	1.21	231	207	254	4.3	29%	71%	3.56	46	20	35	3.2	8.2	2.5	7%	0.6	6.7	84	$9
PT/Exp	B	09	SD	6	4	42	70	79	2.71	1.12	216	275	138	4.1	30%	76%	2.94	48	18	35	3.1	10.2	3.3	5%	0.4	12.7	126	$25
Consist	B	1st Half		3	1	22	33	36	1.36	1.02	176			4.1	26%	85%	2.95	53	14	33	3.8	9.8	2.6	0%	0.0	11.6	104	$14
LIMA Plan	C+	2nd Half		3	3	20	37	43	3.95	1.21	248			4.2	34%	68%	2.92	43	21	36	2.5	10.6	4.3	9%	0.7	1.1	146	$11
Rand Var	-2	10	Proj	4	4	40	58	64	3.10	1.16	227			4.4	31%	75%	2.96	48	19	32	2.9	9.9	3.4	8%	0.6	9.3	126	$21

Seamless transition to stopper, and though his ERA more than doubled in the 2H, his skills got markedly better. Again, he devastated RH hitters. Expect this level to continue for at least a few more seasons.

Bergesen,Brad

		Yr	Tm	W	L	Sv	IP	K	ERA	WHIP	OBA	vL	vR	BF/G	H%	S%	xERA	G	L	F	Ctl	Dom	Cmd	hr/f	hr/9	RAR	BPV	R$
RH	Starter	05		0	0	0	0	0	0.00	0.00							0.00											
Age	24	06		0	0	0	0	0	0.00	0.00							0.00											
Type	Con	07		0	0	0	0	0	0.00	0.00							0.00											
Health	C	08	aa	15	6	0	148	61	4.07	1.33	290			26.2	31%	71%	4.58				1.6	3.7	2.3		0.8	4.2	43	$12
PT/Exp	D	09	BAL	7	5	0	123	65	3.43	1.28	266	263	267	27.3	29%	76%	4.19	50	18	32	2.3	4.7	2.0	8%	0.8	15.5	50	$11
Consist	A	1st Half		5	2	0	91	46	3.55	1.16	253			26.6	27%	72%	3.92	52	17	30	1.9	4.5	2.4	10%	0.9	10.1	61	$9
LIMA Plan	D+	2nd Half		2	3	0	32	19	3.08	1.62	301			29.1	34%	82%	4.98	44	18	38	3.6	5.3	1.5	5%	0.6	5.4	20	$2
Rand Var	-1	10	Proj	11	11	0	174	95	3.93	1.39	284			27.7	31%	74%	4.39	47	18	35	2.4	4.9	2.1	9%	1.0	1.0	50	$13

Decent debut cut short by a line drive off his shin on 7/30. Soft-looking skill set on the surface, but 42%/5% PQS DOM/DIS split, very good Ctl and GB% add some intrigue. Has to get Dom nearer to 5.6, though.

Bergmann,Jason

		Yr	Tm	W	L	Sv	IP	K	ERA	WHIP	OBA	vL	vR	BF/G	H%	S%	xERA	G	L	F	Ctl	Dom	Cmd	hr/f	hr/9	RAR	BPV	R$
RH	Reliever	05	a/a	5	2	7	74	66	2.31	1.12	212			7.3	26%	84%	2.92				3.3	8.0	2.4		0.9	18.2	87	$13
Age	28	06	WAS *	8	4	4	124	105	5.38	1.54	289	255	353	10.1	34%	67%	4.66	32	24	45	3.5	7.6	2.2	10%	1.2	-13.6	53	$6
Type	Pwr xFB	07	WAS *	8	7	0	139	103	4.02	1.23	238	263	200	22.2	27%	71%	4.58	33	16	50	3.1	6.7	2.1	9%	1.2	7.0	48	$13
Health	B	08	WAS *	4	13	0	169	118	4.94	1.43	277	309	243	21.0	30%	69%	4.81	30	24	46	3.1	6.3	2.0	11%	1.4	-14.0	37	$4
PT/Exp	D	09	WAS *	3	5	2	71	52	3.58	1.49	266	339	246	4.2	30%	79%	4.91	36	19	46	4.3	6.6	1.6	8%	1.0	5.3	17	$4
Consist	A	1st Half		1	2	2	37	20	3.70	1.46	269			4.9	29%	78%	5.20	32	26	43	3.8	4.9	1.3	8%	1.0	2.2	-5	$2
LIMA Plan	C+	2nd Half		2	3	0	34	32	3.45	1.53	262			3.6	32%	81%	4.56	37	15	47	4.8	8.5	1.8	9%	1.1	3.1	39	$2
Rand Var	-4	10	Proj	3	5	0	73	55	4.47	1.45	263			6.5	30%	73%	4.82	34	20	47	4.0	6.8	1.7	10%	1.2	-5.0	27	$3

2-4, 4.50 ERA in 48 IP at WAS. ERA says that switch to relief was positive, but xERA + BPV beg to differ. Ramped up the Dom in 2H, but Ctl also rose with it. Perhaps all you need to look at is his 5-year BPV trend.

Berken,Jason

		Yr	Tm	W	L	Sv	IP	K	ERA	WHIP	OBA	vL	vR	BF/G	H%	S%	xERA	G	L	F	Ctl	Dom	Cmd	hr/f	hr/9	RAR	BPV	R$
RH	Starter	05		0	0	0	0	0	0.00	0.00							0.00											
Age	26	06		0	0	0	0	0	0.00	0.00							0.00											
Type		07		0	0	0	0	0	0.00	0.00							0.00											
Health	A	08	aa	12	4	0	145	104	4.63	1.44	294			24.4	34%	68%	4.83				2.4	6.4	2.7		0.7	-5.8	69	$9
PT/Exp	D	09	BAL *	9	13	0	153	85	5.80	1.65	311	335	318	22.5	33%	67%	5.11	39	24	37	3.4	5.0	1.5	11%	1.3	-25.5	15	$1
Consist	A	1st Half		4	6	0	69	41	4.88	1.49	279			21.8	31%	68%	4.99	36	25	39	3.6	5.3	1.5	7%	0.8	-3.7	13	$3
LIMA Plan	C+	2nd Half		5	7	0	84	44	6.57	1.78	335			23.1	35%	66%	5.24	40	24	36	3.2	4.7	1.5	14%	1.7	-21.8	16	($3)
Rand Var	+2	10	Proj	4	4	0	58	35	5.12	1.50	291			23.3	31%	68%	4.72	39	24	37	3.1	5.4	1.8	11%	1.2	-2.0	31	$2

6-12, 6.54 ERA in 120 IP at BAL. After just 5 starts at AAA, the O's deemed him ready. MLB results suggested otherwise. Exhibit A of what happens when a low-Dom SP has neither high GB% nor pinpoint Ctl.

Betancourt,Rafael

		Yr	Tm	W	L	Sv	IP	K	ERA	WHIP	OBA	vL	vR	BF/G	H%	S%	xERA	G	L	F	Ctl	Dom	Cmd	hr/f	hr/9	RAR	BPV	R$
RH	Reliever	05	CLE	4	3	1	67	73	2.81	1.10	231	264	204	5.0	31%	77%	3.30	33	22	44	2.3	9.8	4.3	6%	0.7	12.9	126	$11
Age	34	06	CLE	3	4	3	56	48	3.84	1.12	247	221	254	4.5	29%	70%	4.20	26	17	57	1.8	7.7	4.4	8%	1.1	5.0	95	$8
Type	Pwr xFB	07	CLE	5	1	3	79	80	1.48	0.76	186	241	147	4.3	25%	84%	3.20	27	20	54	1.0	9.1	8.9	4%	0.5	29.6	141	$19
Health	C	08	CLE	3	4	4	71	64	5.07	1.42	275	252	295	4.5	32%	68%	4.40	29	21	50	3.2	8.1	2.6	10%	1.4	-6.3	67	$5
PT/Exp	C	09	2TM	4	3	2	56	61	2.73	1.11	210	265	169	3.7	28%	78%	3.74	30	16	54	3.2	9.8	3.1	5%	0.6	10.9	98	$9
Consist	B	1st Half		1	1	1	26	29	3.78	1.41	237			4.5	31%	76%	4.45	30	11	59	4.8	10.0	2.1	7%	1.0	1.7	57	$2
LIMA Plan	B+	2nd Half		3	2	1	30	32	1.81	0.84	184			3.1	26%	79%	3.13	30	21	49	1.8	9.7	5.3	3%	0.3	9.2	133	$7
Rand Var	-3	10	Proj	4	3	3	65	66	3.45	1.21	240			4.1	30%	76%	3.94	29	19	52	2.9	9.1	3.1	9%	1.1	3.2	93	$9

Excellent base skills translate into "wow" years when he gets hit-rate help. Yet as an extreme fly-baller, he's living on time borrowed against hr/f. '09 2H mirrored 2007, and we know how that followup worked out.

Billingsley,Chad

		Yr	Tm	W	L	Sv	IP	K	ERA	WHIP	OBA	vL	vR	BF/G	H%	S%	xERA	G	L	F	Ctl	Dom	Cmd	hr/f	hr/9	RAR	BPV	R$
RH	Starter	05	aa	13	6	0	146	136	3.64	1.16	229			21.3	29%	70%	3.11				2.9	8.4	2.9		0.7	12.0	98	$19
Age	25	06	LA *	13	7	0	160	128	3.79	1.47	247	328	213	22.7	29%	76%	4.48	48	16	36	4.9	7.2	1.5	8%	0.8	13.7	25	$13
Type	Pwr	07	LA	12	5	0	147	141	3.31	1.33	240	277	210	14.5	30%	78%	3.92	41	20	39	3.9	8.6	2.2	10%	0.9	20.3	69	$17
Health	A	08	LA	16	10	0	201	201	3.14	1.34	249	274	225	24.4	32%	78%	3.40	49	20	31	3.6	9.0	2.5	8%	0.6	28.0	92	$22
PT/Exp	A	09	LA	12	11	0	196	179	4.03	1.32	238	257	229	25.2	29%	71%	3.82	45	18	36	3.9	8.2	2.1	9%	0.8	3.8	65	$16
Consist	A	1st Half		9	4	0	112	110	3.13	1.26	222			27.5	29%	76%	3.73	44	17	39	4.1	8.8	2.2	5%	0.5	14.6	70	$13
LIMA Plan	C	2nd Half		3	7	0	84	69	5.24	1.40	259			22.7	30%	64%	3.95	47	20	33	3.7	7.4	2.0	13%	1.2	-10.9	57	$2
Rand Var	0	10	Proj	15	9	0	203	189	3.64	1.32	244			25.3	30%	74%	3.70	46	19	35	3.7	8.4	2.3	9%	0.8	14.1	76	$20

Unlucky 2H (s%, hr/f) made post-June dive seem worse than it was. Other rates remained strong. A virtual lock to return to a sub-4.00 ERA, and at 25, still has serious upside potential.

Blackburn,Nick

		Yr	Tm	W	L	Sv	IP	K	ERA	WHIP	OBA	vL	vR	BF/G	H%	S%	xERA	G	L	F	Ctl	Dom	Cmd	hr/f	hr/9	RAR	BPV	R$
RH	Starter	05	a/a	2	4	0	63	30	3.14	1.21	262			26.0	29%	74%	3.44				1.9	4.3	2.3		0.4	9.0	64	$5
Age	28	06	aa	7	8	0	132	66	6.38	1.70	327			20.3	35%	62%	6.44				2.9	4.5	1.5		1.0	-30.3	18	($2)
Type	Con	07	a/a	10	4	0	148	58	3.26	1.26	282			24.8	30%	75%	4.13				1.3	3.5	2.6		0.6	22.0	57	$14
Health	A	08	MIN	11	11	0	193	96	4.05	1.36	291	295	289	25.1	31%	73%	4.33	45	21	34	1.8	4.5	2.5	10%	1.1	7.1	54	$12
PT/Exp	A	09	MIN	11	11	0	206	98	4.03	1.37	293	300	277	26.7	31%	74%	4.51	46	18	37	1.8	4.3	2.4	9%	1.1	10.8	53	$13
Consist	A	1st Half		6	4	0	107	45	3.11	1.31	272			28.3	29%	79%	4.73	46	16	38	2.3	3.8	1.7	6%	0.8	17.7	31	$9
LIMA Plan	C	2nd Half		5	7	0	99	53	5.02	1.43	314			25.2	33%	69%	4.29	46	19	35	1.3	4.8	3.8	13%	1.5	-6.9	76	$4
Rand Var	0	10	Proj	10	10	0	189	90	4.20	1.36	294			25.2	31%	72%	4.44	45	19	35	1.7	4.3	2.5	10%	1.1	-0.1	54	$11

Hard to fathom that a pitcher with a consistent OppBA over .290 can sustain a near 4.00 ERA. But Ctl below 2.0 is a good start. Second half shows how fragile his perch is: hr/f hits, and he's gone. Low margin for error.

BRENT HERSHEY

Blanton,Joe

		Yr	Tm	W	L	Sv	IP	K	ERA	WHIP	OBA	vL	vR	BF/G	H%	S%	xERA	G	L	F	Ctl	Dom	Cmd	hr/f	hr/9	RAR	BPV	R$
RH	Starter	05	OAK	12	12	0	201	116	3.54	1.22	239	228	246	25.2	26%	75%	4.32	46	17	38	3.0	5.2	**1.7**	10%	1.0	20.7	36	$19
Age	29	06	OAK	16	12	0	194	107	4.82	1.54	306	314	304	27.1	34%	69%	4.78	43	20	37	2.7	5.0	**1.8**	7%	0.8	-6.3	38	$10
Type		07	OAK	14	10	0	230	140	3.95	1.22	270	291	248	28.0	31%	68%	3.85	47	21	32	1.6	5.5	**3.5**	7%	0.6	15.7	81	$22
Health	A	08	2TM	9	12	0	198	111	4.69	1.40	275	256	286	25.9	30%	68%	4.52	44	20	35	3.0	5.1	**1.7**	9%	1.0	-9.3	32	$8
PT/Exp	A	09	PHI	12	8	0	195	163	4.06	1.32	264	252	271	26.7	30%	74%	3.91	41	20	39	2.7	7.5	**2.8**	13%	1.4	3.2	80	$15
Consist	B	1st Half		4	4	0	88	80	5.10	1.47	289			25.8	33%	71%	4.00	39	21	40	3.0	8.2	**2.8**	17%	1.8	-9.9	84	$3
LIMA Plan	C	2nd Half		8	4	0	107	83	3.19	1.19	243			27.5	28%	77%	3.84	42	19	39	2.5	7.0	**2.8**	10%	1.0	13.2	78	$12
Rand Var	+1	10	Proj	**12**	**10**	**0**	**203**	**142**	**4.17**	**1.32**	**267**			**26.9**	**30%**	**72%**	**4.12**	**43**	**20**	**37**	**2.6**	**6.3**	**2.4**	**11%**	**1.1**	**3.7**	**64**	**$14**

PRO: Top team, bulldog mentality enhances W potential; sustained BPV for entire year. CON: Hr/f and hr/9 (especially in 1H) show home park risk. Age-28 Dom spike provides basis for guarded optimism.

Boggs,Mitchell

		Yr	Tm	W	L	Sv	IP	K	ERA	WHIP	OBA	vL	vR	BF/G	H%	S%	xERA	G	L	F	Ctl	Dom	Cmd	hr/f	hr/9	RAR	BPV	R$
RH	Starter	05		0	0	0	0	0	0.00	0.00							0.00											
Age	26	06		0	0	0	0	0	0.00	0.00							0.00											
Type	GB	07	aa	11	7	0	152	100	4.45	1.65	307			26.7	35%	75%	5.88				3.6	5.9	**1.6**		0.9	0.2	36	$6
Health	A	08	STL	* 12	5	0	159	79	4.68	1.44	267	321	283	23.9	28%	69%	4.53	52	19	29	3.7	4.4	**1.2**	10%	0.9	-8.0	9	$7
PT/Exp	D	09	STL	* 8	7	0	134	91	5.09	1.82	321	410	234	21.2	37%	72%	4.58	53	18	29	4.4	6.1	**1.4**	8%	0.7	-14.9	22	($1)
Consist	B	1st Half		4	4	0	72	50	5.66	1.84	331			22.9	38%	70%	4.86	45	20	35	4.0	6.2	**1.5**	8%	0.9	-13.1	26	($2)
LIMA Plan	C+	2nd Half		4	3	0	62	41	4.44	1.79	309			19.5	36%	75%	4.43	58	17	26	4.8	6.0	**1.3**	7%	0.5	-1.9	14	$0
Rand Var	+3	10	Proj	**5**	**3**	**0**	**73**	**48**	**4.47**	**1.50**	**274**			**21.4**	**31%**	**72%**	**4.19**	**54**	**18**	**28**	**4.0**	**6.0**	**1.5**	**11%**	**0.9**	**0.6**	**32**	**$3**

2-3, 4.19 ERA in 58 IP at STL. 7.1 Dom in majors is about only bright spot: surrendered 71 hits along with 5.1 Ctl, 5.00 xERA. Strong GBer but won't survive with this walk rate or the softballs he serves up to LH.

Bonderman,Jeremy

		Yr	Tm	W	L	Sv	IP	K	ERA	WHIP	OBA	vL	vR	BF/G	H%	S%	xERA	G	L	F	Ctl	Dom	Cmd	hr/f	hr/9	RAR	BPV	R$
RH	Reliever	05	DET	14	13	0	189	145	4.57	1.35	272	287	249	27.9	31%	68%	3.82	48	19	33	2.7	6.9	**2.5**	11%	1.0	-4.7	77	$15
Age	27	06	DET	14	8	0	214	202	4.08	1.30	262	284	235	26.6	33%	70%	3.41	48	20	32	2.7	8.5	**3.2**	9%	0.8	12.6	106	$23
Type		07	DET	11	9	0	174	145	5.01	1.38	282	268	291	26.8	33%	66%	3.76	48	18	34	2.5	7.5	**3.0**	12%	1.2	-10.8	94	$12
Health	F	08	DET	3	4	0	71	44	4.29	1.56	272	291	255	26.6	30%	75%	4.89	47	16	37	4.5	5.6	**1.2**	10%	1.1	0.5	3	$3
PT/Exp	C	09	DET	* 1	5	1	44	26	6.43	1.82	344	278	423	9.5	36%	69%	5.24	32	32	37	3.1	5.4	**1.7**	15%	1.9	-10.8	22	($2)
Consist	B	1st Half		1	2	0	24	12	5.73	1.70	326			27.7	33%	71%	5.22	33	33	33	3.1	4.4	**1.4**	17%	1.9	-3.8	8	($0)
LIMA Plan	C+	2nd Half		0	3	1	20	15	7.26	1.96	364			5.5	40%	66%	5.21	30	30	40	3.1	6.5	**2.1**	14%	1.8	-7.0	41	($2)
Rand Var	+5	10	Proj	**3**	**8**	**0**	**87**	**55**	**4.55**	**1.45**	**283**			**11.5**	**31%**	**71%**	**4.47**	**44**	**20**	**36**	**3.0**	**5.7**	**1.9**	**11%**	**1.1**	**-0.4**	**43**	**$4**

0-1, 8.71 ERA in 10 IP at DET. Return marred by h%, but skills showed understandable rust. Still several steps away (GB%, Dom) from regaining form. Can't be ruled out at 27 years old, but still a sizeable risk for 2010.

Bowden,Michael

		Yr	Tm	W	L	Sv	IP	K	ERA	WHIP	OBA	vL	vR	BF/G	H%	S%	xERA	G	L	F	Ctl	Dom	Cmd	hr/f	hr/9	RAR	BPV	R$
RH	Starter	05		0	0	0	0	0	0.00	0.00							0.00											
Age	23	06		0	0	0	0	0	0.00	0.00							0.00											
Type	FB	07	aa	8	6	0	96	69	5.33	1.60	308			22.9	36%	67%	5.71				3.1	6.5	**2.1**		0.8	-10.3	51	$4
Health	A	08	a/a	9	7	0	144	111	3.25	1.10	241			22.2	29%	72%	3.04				1.8	6.9	**3.8**		0.6	18.8	110	$18
PT/Exp	D	09	BOS	* 5	7	0	142	88	5.38	1.53	285	395	258	19.8	31%	66%	5.06	42	14	44	3.7	5.6	**1.5**	8%	1.1	-16.3	21	$2
Consist	F	1st Half		3	4	0	79	47	5.13	1.43	274			21.5	29%	67%	6.11	25	0	75	3.3	5.4	**1.6**	6%	1.3	-6.6	10	$3
LIMA Plan	B	2nd Half		2	3	0	63	41	5.71	1.66	299			18.1	34%	66%	5.14	43	15	42	4.1	5.8	**1.4**	7%	0.9	-9.8	15	($1)
Rand Var	0	10	Proj	**4**	**4**	**0**	**73**	**50**	**4.47**	**1.41**	**276**			**20.9**	**31%**	**71%**	**4.47**	**43**	**15**	**42**	**3.0**	**6.2**	**2.1**	**9%**	**1.1**	**-0.3**	**53**	**$5**

1-1, 9.56 ERA in 16 IP at BOS. Regression of base skills made him look a lot less ready than a year ago. Without a big Dom number, pinpoint Ctl will be a key. Still young, but mid-rotation starter looks like his upside.

Boyer,Blaine

		Yr	Tm	W	L	Sv	IP	K	ERA	WHIP	OBA	vL	vR	BF/G	H%	S%	xERA	G	L	F	Ctl	Dom	Cmd	hr/f	hr/9	RAR	BPV	R$
RH	Reliever	05	ATL	* 6	6	0	85	66	5.04	1.67	307	298	200	6.9	37%	69%	4.36	48	17	35	3.8	7.0	**1.8**	5%	0.5	-8.3	49	$2
Age	28	06	ATL	0	0	0	0	0	0.00	0.00				2.8		40%	0.00	67	0	33	45.0	0.0	**0.0**	0%	0.0	0.1		
Type	GB	07	aaa	4	3	2	73	51	5.71	2.02	310			17.2	37%	69%	6.14				6.7	6.3	**0.9**		0.1	-11.3	47	($2)
Health	A	08	ATL	2	6	1	72	67	5.88	1.36	264	271	256	4.1	32%	58%	3.72	46	16	38	3.1	8.4	**2.7**	13%	1.3	-14.3	90	$2
PT/Exp	D	09	2NL	0	2	0	55	29	4.11	1.39	266	240	290	4.9	31%	68%	3.77	60	19	21	3.3	4.8	**1.5**	3%	0.2	0.5	35	$1
Consist	C	1st Half		0	1	0	24	14	5.95	1.57	260			4.7	30%	59%	4.29	60	18	22	5.2	5.2	**1.0**	6%	0.4	-5.3	-9	($1)
LIMA Plan	C	2nd Half		0	1	0	31	15	2.66	1.25	271			5.1	31%	76%	3.39	61	19	20	1.8	4.4	**2.5**	0%	0.0	5.8	70	$2
Rand Var	-1	10	Proj	**1**	**2**	**0**	**44**	**25**	**4.55**	**1.49**	**277**			**5.5**	**31%**	**70%**	**4.29**	**54**	**18**	**28**	**3.7**	**5.2**	**1.4**	**10%**	**0.8**	**-0.2**	**25**	**$1**

Age and xERA point to some upside, but that was the sentiment last year, too. Now, the BPI swoon spearheaded by declining Dom and a 2-DFA season tips the scales towards "No thanks."

Braden,Dallas

		Yr	Tm	W	L	Sv	IP	K	ERA	WHIP	OBA	vL	vR	BF/G	H%	S%	xERA	G	L	F	Ctl	Dom	Cmd	hr/f	hr/9	RAR	BPV	R$
LH	Starter	05	aa	9	5	0	97	61	4.08	1.45	289			26.5	33%	71%	4.50				2.8	5.7	**2.0**		0.5	2.7	60	$7
Age	26	06	aa	0	0	0	3	2	18.00	3.00	515			17.8	55%	38%	16.54				0.0	6.0			3.0	-5.0	******	($1)
Type	FB	07	OAK	* 4	11	0	148	125	5.13	1.39	275	214	324	19.3	33%	64%	4.27	37	18	45	2.9	7.6	**2.7**	8%	0.9	-11.4	75	$7
Health	A	08	OAK	* 8	5	0	125	82	3.58	1.37	277	319	272	17.8	31%	78%	4.52	38	18	44	2.6	5.9	**2.3**	8%	1.1	11.8	53	$11
PT/Exp	C	09	OAK	8	9	0	137	81	3.88	1.36	272	203	290	26.6	31%	72%	4.77	36	21	43	2.8	5.3	**1.9**	5%	0.6	9.6	36	$10
Consist	A	1st Half		6	7	0	106	67	3.14	1.26	262			26.1	30%	76%	4.44	38	20	42	2.4	5.7	**2.4**	5%	0.6	17.2	54	$11
LIMA Plan	D+	2nd Half		2	2	0	31	14	6.47	1.70	306			28.3	33%	60%	6.00	31	24	45	4.1	4.1	**1.0**	4%	0.6	-7.6	-28	($1)
Rand Var	-3	10	Proj	**11**	**11**	**0**	**189**	**122**	**4.39**	**1.38**	**274**			**22.5**	**31%**	**70%**	**4.70**	**35**	**21**	**44**	**2.8**	**5.8**	**2.1**	**8%**	**1.0**	**-6.2**	**42**	**$12**

An ankle rash was eventually diagnosed as nerve irritation, and wiped out final two months. Again bested xERA by almost a run, though skills regressed. Likely ready for March, but beware looming ERA correction.

Breslow,Craig

		Yr	Tm	W	L	Sv	IP	K	ERA	WHIP	OBA	vL	vR	BF/G	H%	S%	xERA	G	L	F	Ctl	Dom	Cmd	hr/f	hr/9	RAR	BPV	R$
LH	Reliever	05	SD	* 2	2	0	77	62	3.04	1.30	243			5.3	30%	77%	3.87	46	20	34	3.6	7.3	**2.0**	5%	0.5	11.4	58	$6
Age	29	06	BOS	* 7	3	7	79	77	3.86	1.35	252			6.5	33%	71%	4.01	31	29	40	3.6	8.8	**2.4**	5%	0.5	6.8	70	$12
Type	Pwr xFB	07	aaa	2	3	1	68	59	5.84	1.72	318			6.4	38%	66%	6.29				3.6	7.8	**2.2**		1.0	-11.6	54	($0)
Health	A	08	2AL	0	2	1	47	39	1.91	1.13	204	183	221	3.9	26%	83%	3.95	42	17	42	3.6	7.5	**2.1**	2%	0.2	14.1	56	$6
PT/Exp	D	09	2AL	8	7	0	70	55	3.36	1.10	196	204	191	3.6	22%	74%	4.38	33	19	48	3.7	7.1	**1.9**	9%	1.0	9.4	37	$11
Consist	C	1st Half		1	4	0	30	25	4.20	1.23	199			3.3	23%	68%	4.67	32	19	49	4.8	7.5	**1.6**	8%	0.9	0.9	15	$3
LIMA Plan	D+	2nd Half		7	3	0	40	30	2.72	1.01	194			4.0	21%	80%	4.17	33	20	47	2.9	6.8	**2.3**	10%	1.1	8.5	54	$8
Rand Var	-5	10	Proj	**5**	**5**	**0**	**65**	**53**	**4.00**	**1.36**	**252**			**4.3**	**29%**	**74%**	**4.50**	**36**	**19**	**45**	**3.7**	**7.3**	**2.0**	**9%**	**1.1**	**-0.5**	**45**	**$6**

Mendoza-line OppBA for two straight seasons, but it's all hit-rate induced. Gets nice share of Ks, but walks too many. 2H is Ctl a step, but established history a downside. Let those who only see ERA bid him up.

Broxton,Jonathan

		Yr	Tm	W	L	Sv	IP	K	ERA	WHIP	OBA	vL	vR	BF/G	H%	S%	xERA	G	L	F	Ctl	Dom	Cmd	hr/f	hr/9	RAR	BPV	R$
RH	Reliever	05	aa	5	3	5	96	90	3.27	1.16	234			11.9	30%	71%	2.85				2.7	8.4	**3.1**		0.4	12.2	113	$13
Age	25	06	LA	* 5	1	8	87	113	2.27	1.18	213	244	196	4.5	31%	84%	3.10	39	20	40	3.7	11.6	**3.1**	9%	0.7	23.8	127	$16
Type	Pwr GB	07	LA	4	4	2	82	99	2.85	1.15	230	200	247	4.0	32%	77%	2.68	49	19	32	2.7	10.9	**4.0**	10%	0.7	15.9	148	$12
Health	A	08	LA	3	5	14	69	88	3.13	1.17	217	270	181	4.0	33%	72%	2.80	45	23	32	3.5	11.5	**3.3**	4%	0.3	9.7	134	$13
PT/Exp	B	09	LA	7	2	36	76	114	2.61	0.96	170	138	190	4.0	29%	74%	1.96	56	16	28	3.4	13.5	**3.9**	10%	0.5	14.9	184	$27
Consist	A	1st Half		6	0	19	37	62	2.18	0.78	132			3.9	26%	71%	1.42	57	22	21	3.1	15.0	**4.8**	8%	0.5	9.2	220	$16
LIMA Plan	C+	2nd Half		1	2	17	39	52	3.02	1.13	204			4.1	30%	76%	2.51	56	11	33	3.7	12.1	**3.3**	11%	0.7	5.6	151	$10
Rand Var	+1	10	Proj	**4**	**3**	**43**	**65**	**88**	**2.90**	**1.06**	**200**			**4.2**	**30%**	**75%**	**2.40**	**50**	**19**	**31**	**3.2**	**12.1**	**3.8**	**11%**	**0.7**	**15.0**	**161**	**$25**

Sparkling growth season all-around--Dom, GB, Opp BA--and fully supported by sub-2.00 xERA. As long as he's able to shake the 2-time NLCS ghosts, he looks like money right now.

Bruney,Brian

		Yr	Tm	W	L	Sv	IP	K	ERA	WHIP	OBA	vL	vR	BF/G	H%	S%	xERA	G	L	F	Ctl	Dom	Cmd	hr/f	hr/9	RAR	BPV	R$
RH	Reliever	05	ARI	1	3	12	46	51	7.43	1.98	302	280	314	4.8	39%	62%	4.72	41	22	37	6.8	10.0	**1.5**	12%	1.2	-18.1	14	$0
Age	28	06	NYY	* 2	3	3	37	48	4.84	1.69	245	115	229	5.0	34%	74%	4.47	35	18	47	7.0	11.6	**1.7**	12%	1.2	-1.3	32	$3
Type	Pwr xFB	07	NYY	3	2	0	50	39	4.68	1.62	238	303	209	3.9	28%	72%	5.87	31	17	52	6.7	7.0	**1.1**	7%	0.9	-1.1	-45	$2
Health	F	08	NYY	3	0	1	34	33	1.84	0.99	157	106	183	4.2	20%	84%	3.65	43	14	44	4.2	8.7	**2.1**	6%	0.5	10.6	63	$7
PT/Exp	F	09	NYY	5	0	0	39	36	3.92	1.51	247	214	269	3.9	29%	79%	4.98	32	16	52	5.3	8.3	**1.6**	11%	1.4	2.5	16	$4
Consist	D	1st Half		3	0	0	13	16	4.09	1.06	158			3.3	25%	57%	3.26	45	13	42	4.8	10.9	**2.3**	0%	0.0	0.6	91	$3
LIMA Plan	C+	2nd Half		2	0	0	26	20	3.84	1.74	285			4.3	30%	87%	5.91	27	17	56	5.6	7.0	**1.3**	13%	2.1	2.0	-20	$1
Rand Var	-2	10	Proj	**3**	**1**	**0**	**44**	**40**	**4.34**	**1.52**	**255**			**4.3**	**30%**	**75%**	**4.77**	**35**	**16**	**49**	**5.0**	**8.3**	**1.7**	**10%**	**1.2**	**-1.8**	**28**	**$3**

Returned to mediocrity with hit-rate correction. Big-Dom history a plus, but no Ctl and tons of fly balls endanger his ERA. Could be useful in a more forgiving home park, but nothing worth shedding your budget for.

BRENT HERSHEY

Buchholz,Clay

		Yr	Tm	W	L	Sv	IP	K	ERA	WHIP	OBA	vL	vR	BF/G	H%	S%	xERA	G	L	F	Ctl	Dom	Cmd	hr/f	hr/9	RAR	BPV	R$
RH Starter		05		0	0	0	0	0	0.00	0.00							0.00											
Age	25	06	aa	9	4	0	103	70	4.62	1.65	307			22.4	34%	75%	6.19				3.6	6.1	**1.7**		1.2	-1.3	28	$5
Type	Pwr GB	07	BOS	* 11	6	0	148	168	2.92	1.10	219	217	133	21.2	30%	75%	2.99	38	29	33	2.8	10.2	**3.7**	8%	0.6	28.9	125	$24
Health	A	08	BOS	* 7	11	0	134	122	5.14	1.52	276	293	305	22.1	34%	67%	3.85	48	21	31	4.0	8.2	**2.1**	11%	0.9	-13.1	66	$6
PT/Exp	C	09	BOS	* 14	6	0	191	144	3.93	1.30	249	284	228	24.4	28%	73%	3.71	54	18	29	3.3	6.8	**2.1**	13%	1.0	12.3	66	$18
Consist	B	1st Half		6	1	0	87	70	3.23	1.14	226			23.6	26%	75%	3.20				2.8	7.3	**2.6**		0.9	13.1	79	$12
LIMA Plan	C	2nd Half		8	5	0	104	74	4.52	1.44	268			25.1	30%	71%	4.01	54	18	29	3.6	6.4	**1.8**	14%	1.1	-0.8	49	$7
Rand Var	+1	10	Proj	**13**	**9**	**0**	**181**	**153**	**3.87**	**1.34**	**254**			**22.7**	**30%**	**74%**	**3.66**	**51**	**20**	**30**	**3.4**	**7.6**	**2.2**	**12%**	**0.9**	**17.4**	**73**	**$18**

7-4, 4.21 ERA in 92 IP at BOS. Improved GB% but DOM continued 3 year slide. Sept performance (84 BPV, 2.9 CMD in 38 IP) gives hope that he may be learning to pitch rather than throw.

Buckner,Billy

		Yr	Tm	W	L	Sv	IP	K	ERA	WHIP	OBA	vL	vR	BF/G	H%	S%	xERA	G	L	F	Ctl	Dom	Cmd	hr/f	hr/9	RAR	BPV	R$
RH Starter		05		0	0	0	0	0	0.00	0.00							0.00											
Age	26	06	aa	5	3	0	75	53	5.18	1.63	290			26.3	34%	68%	5.35				4.3	6.4	**1.5**		0.7	-6.1	44	$2
Type	Pwr	07	KC	* 11	12	0	158	98	5.18	1.53	302			18.5	33%	68%	5.76				2.8	5.6	**2.0**		1.2	-13.2	34	$7
Health	A	08	ARI	* 6	10	0	130	66	6.72	1.90	347			20.2	37%	65%	7.42				3.6	4.6	**1.3**		1.1	-39.2	6	($8)
PT/Exp	C	09	ARI	* 13	9	0	180	138	5.56	1.66	300	347	270	24.3	35%	67%	4.25	49	21	30	4.0	6.9	**1.7**	11%	0.9	-30.4	42	$2
Consist	F	1st Half		5	7	0	74	61	6.35	1.68	308			19.0	36%	64%	4.25	47	19	34	3.8	7.4	**1.9**	14%	1.3	-19.8	55	($1)
LIMA Plan	C+	2nd Half		8	2	0	106	77	5.00	1.64	295			30.2	35%	69%	4.16	51	24	25	4.2	6.5	**1.6**	9%	0.7	-10.6	33	$2
Rand Var	+4	10	Proj	**9**	**9**	**0**	**146**	**108**	**4.93**	**1.58**	**295**			**21.9**	**34%**	**70%**	**4.17**	**49**	**21**	**30**	**3.6**	**6.7**	**1.8**	**11%**	**1.0**	**1.6**	**48**	**$4**

4-6, 6.40 ERA in 77 IP at ARI. High H% and low S% say he was unlucky, but this is a multi-year trend for him. GB% intriguing, but needs to show that his MLB CMD (2.2) is sustainable.

Buehrle,Mark

		Yr	Tm	W	L	Sv	IP	K	ERA	WHIP	OBA	vL	vR	BF/G	H%	S%	xERA	G	L	F	Ctl	Dom	Cmd	hr/f	hr/9	RAR	BPV	R$
LH Starter		05	CHW	16	8	0	236	149	3.12	1.19	265	271	260	29.4	30%	76%	3.73	46	21	33	1.5	5.7	**3.7**	8%	0.8	36.3	85	$27
Age	31	06	CHW	12	13	0	204	98	4.99	1.45	300	238	322	27.8	31%	70%	4.70	44	19	37	2.1	4.3	**2.0**	13%	1.6	-10.8	43	$9
Type	Con	07	CHW	10	9	0	201	115	3.63	1.26	268	314	258	28.0	29%	74%	4.32	43	18	39	2.0	5.1	**2.6**	9%	1.0	21.8	60	$18
Health	A	08	CHW	15	12	0	219	140	3.79	1.34	280	293	277	27.4	31%	74%	3.88	50	19	31	2.1	5.8	**2.7**	10%	0.9	15.1	74	$19
PT/Exp	A	09	CHW	13	10	0	213	105	3.84	1.25	270	298	267	27.0	28%	73%	4.36	45	19	36	1.9	4.4	**2.3**	10%	1.1	16.1	52	$18
Consist	A	1st Half		7	2	0	99	61	3.27	1.16	246			27.0	27%	77%	4.08	44	20	37	2.2	5.5	**2.5**	11%	1.1	14.5	62	$12
LIMA Plan	D+	2nd Half		6	8	0	114	44	4.33	1.33	289			27.0	29%	71%	4.60	46	18	35	1.7	3.5	**2.1**	10%	1.2	1.7	42	$7
Rand Var	0	10	Proj	**13**	**11**	**0**	**218**	**120**	**3.97**	**1.30**	**277**			**27.8**	**30%**	**73%**	**4.23**	**46**	**19**	**35**	**2.0**	**5.0**	**2.5**	**10%**	**1.1**	**5.5**	**60**	**$17**

Nowhere to go but down after perfect game, but sudden loss in Dom (2.9 post perfect game) doomed his last two months. Assuming injury isn't a hidden cause, this is a stable skill set worth paying for.

Bulger,Jason

		Yr	Tm	W	L	Sv	IP	K	ERA	WHIP	OBA	vL	vR	BF/G	H%	S%	xERA	G	L	F	Ctl	Dom	Cmd	hr/f	hr/9	RAR	BPV	R$
RH Reliever		05	aaa	3	6	4	56	49	3.81	1.45	261			4.4	32%	74%	4.10				4.1	7.8	**1.9**		0.5	3.4	74	$5
Age	31	06	aaa	2	2	4	34	35	5.28	1.42	259			5.5	36%	59%	3.55				3.9	9.3	**2.4**		0.0	-3.2	109	$3
Type	Pwr FB	07	aaa	5	2	10	52	55	6.03	2.04	338			5.3	43%	70%	7.36				5.4	9.5	**1.8**		0.9	-10.1	56	$3
Health	A	08	LAA	* 4	0	16	59	69	2.75	1.53	238			5.1	33%	83%	3.85				5.8	10.5	**1.8**		0.5	11.7	95	$12
PT/Exp	D	09	LAA	6	1	1	66	68	3.56	1.16	199	196	217	4.2	25%	72%	3.68	43	14	43	4.1	9.3	**2.3**	10%	1.0	7.2	78	$10
Consist	D	1st Half		2	1	0	33	34	4.64	1.30	218			4.5	26%	68%	4.02	41	14	45	4.6	9.3	**2.0**	13%	1.4	-0.8	61	$3
LIMA Plan	B	2nd Half		4	0	1	33	34	2.48	1.01	178			3.9	24%	77%	3.33	46	14	41	3.6	9.4	**2.6**	6%	0.6	8.0	96	$7
Rand Var	-2	10	Proj	**4**	**3**	**3**	**65**	**69**	**3.72**	**1.36**	**237**			**4.6**	**31%**	**74%**	**3.87**	**44**	**14**	**42**	**4.4**	**9.5**	**2.2**	**7%**	**0.7**	**4.6**	**74**	**$8**

Minor league journeyman finally spent a full season in Majors. Maintained elite Dom while improving Ctl. Low H% says he got a bit lucky in '09, but if he can keep the Cmd gains, he's LIMA worthy.

Bumgarner,Madison

		Yr	Tm	W	L	Sv	IP	K	ERA	WHIP	OBA	vL	vR	BF/G	H%	S%	xERA	G	L	F	Ctl	Dom	Cmd	hr/f	hr/9	RAR	BPV	R$
LH Starter		05		0	0	0	0	0	0.00	0.00							0.00											
Age	20	06		0	0	0	0	0	0.00	0.00							0.00											
Type	Con xGB	07		0	0	0	0	0	0.00	0.00							0.00											
Health	A	08		0	0	0	0	0	0.00	0.00							0.00											
PT/Exp	F	09	SF	* 9	1	0	117	72	2.28	1.10	228	83	304	19.6	26%	82%	3.46	58	15	27	2.4	5.5	**2.3**	8%	0.6	27.6	70	$16
Consist	F	1st Half		6	1	0	53	39	2.10	1.10	227			23.7	28%	80%	2.43				2.4	6.6	**2.7**		0.2	13.6	102	$9
LIMA Plan	C+	2nd Half		3	0	0	64	33	2.42	1.11	229			17.2	24%	84%	3.66	58	15	27	2.4	4.7	**1.9**	12%	1.0	13.9	54	$7
Rand Var	-5	10	Proj	**7**	**4**	**0**	**131**	**79**	**4.00**	**1.34**	**268**			**25.3**	**30%**	**72%**	**3.78**	**58**	**15**	**27**	**2.8**	**5.4**	**2.0**	**11%**	**0.9**	**7.7**	**59**	**$8**

0-0, 1.80 ERA in 10 IP at SF. Loss of Dom (10.3 at A level in 2008) raises injury concerns but also shows he can succeed without the Ks. Excellent long term investment, but expect some bumps along the way.

Burke,Greg

		Yr	Tm	W	L	Sv	IP	K	ERA	WHIP	OBA	vL	vR	BF/G	H%	S%	xERA	G	L	F	Ctl	Dom	Cmd	hr/f	hr/9	RAR	BPV	R$
RH Reliever		05		0	0	0	0	0	0.00	0.00							0.00											
Age	27	06		0	0	0	0	0	0.00	0.00							0.00											
Type		07		0	0	0	0	0	0.00	0.00							0.00											
Health	A	08	aa	2	7	23	84	69	2.83	1.37	287			6.1	34%	82%	4.52				2.1	7.4	**3.5**		0.7	15.3	93	$15
PT/Exp	F	09	SD	* 6	3	7	62	43	3.77	1.39	249	346	208	4.4	29%	74%	4.34	48	17	35	4.1	6.3	**1.5**	8%	0.8	3.2	29	$8
Consist	A	1st Half		3	0	7	36	29	3.45	1.04	220			4.2	25%	71%	3.23	53	14	33	2.2	7.2	**3.3**	13%	1.1	3.3	102	$7
LIMA Plan	C+	2nd Half		3	3	0	26	14	4.20	1.87	286			4.6	32%	77%	6.05	43	19	37	6.7	4.9	**0.7**	3%	0.4	-0.0	-70	$1
Rand Var	-1	10	Proj	**3**	**3**	**0**	**44**	**31**	**3.93**	**1.47**	**273**			**5.0**	**32%**	**74%**	**4.40**	**46**	**18**	**36**	**3.7**	**6.4**	**1.7**	**6%**	**0.6**	**-0.7**	**39**	**$3**

3-3, 4.14 ERA in 46 IP at SD. xERA shows he fell apart in the 2H; only an abnormally low HR/FB rate protected him. Drop in Cmd could be a short term phenomenon, but wait to see a reversal before you buy.

Burnett,A.J.

		Yr	Tm	W	L	Sv	IP	K	ERA	WHIP	OBA	vL	vR	BF/G	H%	S%	xERA	G	L	F	Ctl	Dom	Cmd	hr/f	hr/9	RAR	BPV	R$
RH Starter		05	FLA	12	12	0	209	198	3.44	1.26	238	226	249	27.3	31%	73%	2.94	58	19	22	3.4	8.5	**2.5**	9%	0.5	20.6	98	$21
Age	33	06	TOR	10	8	0	135	118	3.99	1.31	266	261	267	27.2	32%	72%	3.42	50	20	29	2.6	7.9	**3.0**	12%	0.9	9.4	100	$15
Type	Pwr	07	TOR	10	8	0	166	176	3.75	1.19	219	200	231	27.2	27%	74%	3.05	55	15	30	3.6	9.6	**2.7**	18%	1.2	15.5	108	$21
Health	C	08	TOR	18	10	0	221	231	4.07	1.34	253	262	231	26.9	33%	71%	3.32	49	19	32	3.5	9.4	**2.7**	10%	0.8	7.7	101	$23
PT/Exp	A	09	NYY	13	9	0	207	195	4.04	1.40	248	217	282	27.1	30%	74%	4.09	43	18	39	4.2	8.5	**2.0**	11%	1.1	10.4	60	$18
Consist	B	1st Half		6	4	0	94	92	3.93	1.37	236			26.9	29%	76%	4.03	44	17	40	4.5	8.8	**2.0**	13%	1.2	6.1	59	$9
LIMA Plan	C	2nd Half		7	5	0	113	103	4.14	1.42	258			27.3	31%	73%	4.14	42	19	39	4.0	8.2	**2.1**	9%	1.0	4.3	60	$9
Rand Var	0	10	Proj	**14**	**9**	**0**	**203**	**194**	**4.17**	**1.36**	**246**			**27.1**	**30%**	**72%**	**3.75**	**47**	**18**	**35**	**3.9**	**8.6**	**2.2**	**11%**	**1.0**	**17.2**	**73**	**$19**

Managed to pitch 200+ innings two years in a row for the first time in his career, but posted lowest BPV since 2003. Could these be related? Rise in FB%, Ctl rates warn against going the extra buck.

Burnett,Sean

		Yr	Tm	W	L	Sv	IP	K	ERA	WHIP	OBA	vL	vR	BF/G	H%	S%	xERA	G	L	F	Ctl	Dom	Cmd	hr/f	hr/9	RAR	BPV	R$
LH Reliever		05	PIT	0	0	0	0	0	0.00	0.00							0.00				0.0	0.0						
Age	27	06	aaa	8	11	0	120	39	7.27	1.81	332			22.7	34%	60%	7.02				3.7	2.9	**0.8**		1.2	-40.7	-13	($6)
Type	Pwr GB	07	aaa	4	5	0	70	23	5.99	2.11	348			23.5	37%	71%	7.53				5.4	3.0	**0.6**		0.6	-13.2	-2	($5)
Health	B	08	PIT	* 2	2	3	74	53	3.94	1.51	248	171	328	4.7	28%	77%	4.63	48	19	33	5.3	6.5	**1.2**	11%	1.0	3.0	1	$4
PT/Exp	D	09	2NL	2	3	1	58	43	3.12	1.11	181	186	176	3.3	20%	76%	3.81	49	21	30	4.4	6.7	**1.5**	13%	0.9	7.6	30	$6
Consist	D	1st Half		1	2	1	33	23	3.25	1.14	197			3.5	21%	76%	4.20	41	23	36	4.1	6.2	**1.5**	12%	1.1	3.8	22	$3
LIMA Plan	C	2nd Half		1	1	0	25	20	2.94	1.06	158			3.0	18%	75%	3.20	61	18	21	4.8	7.3	**1.5**	15%	0.7	3.8	43	$3
Rand Var	-4	10	Proj	**3**	**3**	**0**	**65**	**49**	**3.86**	**1.43**	**252**			**4.7**	**29%**	**75%**	**4.08**	**51**	**20**	**29**	**4.3**	**6.8**	**1.6**	**10%**	**0.8**	**1.5**	**35**	**$4**

Extremely low H% helped ERA but xERA shows there are still some things to like: improved Ctl, rising Dom and 2H GB%. Still, this is nowhere near worthy of a low 3's ERA.

Burns,Mike

		Yr	Tm	W	L	Sv	IP	K	ERA	WHIP	OBA	vL	vR	BF/G	H%	S%	xERA	G	L	F	Ctl	Dom	Cmd	hr/f	hr/9	RAR	BPV	R$
RH Starter		05	HOU	* 2	1	13	61	47	3.75	1.09	240	328	156	4.7	26%	73%	3.21	47	25	27	1.8	6.9	**3.8**	21%	1.5	3.7	100	$10
Age	31	06	aaa	6	1	0	56	41	2.58	1.34	279			6.0	33%	83%	4.34				2.2	6.6	**2.9**		0.7	13.4	79	$8
Type	Con	07	aaa	4	9	3	112	62	6.98	1.79	344			15.1	37%	62%	7.51				2.7	5.0	**1.8**		1.5	-34.7	9	($4)
Health	A	08	aa	8	12	2	133	60	7.44	2.03	386			17.8	40%	66%	9.26				2.3	4.1	**1.8**		1.9	-51.5	-19	($10)
PT/Exp	D	09	MIL	* 11	8	0	144	94	4.04	1.37	287	295	293	21.3	32%	75%	4.51	33	24	44	2.1	5.9	**2.8**	9%	1.2	2.7	59	$10
Consist	F	1st Half		8	3	0	93	51	3.12	1.25	270			25.9	29%	79%	4.85	28	21	51	1.9	4.9	**2.6**	6%	0.9	12.3	43	$10
LIMA Plan	B	2nd Half		3	5	0	51	43	5.74	1.59	316			16.3	36%	68%	4.23	34	25	41	2.5	7.7	**3.1**	15%	1.8	-9.7	83	$0
Rand Var	0	10	Proj	**3**	**3**	**0**	**41**	**26**	**5.24**	**1.62**	**325**			**14.4**	**35%**	**72%**	**4.58**	**39**	**25**	**36**	**2.4**	**5.7**	**2.4**	**13%**	**1.5**	**-1.6**	**54**	**$1**

3-5, 5.75 ERA in 52 IP at MIL. PRO: Excellent Ctl, 2H Dom gains. CON: High LD%, historical trouble with H% suggests that he gets hit hard. Not worth the gamble.

BILL MACEY

Burton,Jared

		Yr	Tm	W	L	Sv	IP	K	ERA	WHIP	OBA	vL	vR	BF/G	H%	S%	xERA	G	L	F	Ctl	Dom	Cmd	hr/f	hr/9	RAR	BPV	R$
RH	Reliever	05		0	0	0	0	0	0.00	0.00							0.00											
Age	28	06	aa	6	5	1	74	50	5.27	1.58	296			6.3	34%	67%	5.51				3.5	6.1	1.7		0.9	-6.8	41	$3
Type	Pwr	07	CIN *	5	3	1	62	49	3.35	1.41	242	130	219	4.4	30%	75%	4.55	45	15	40	4.6	7.0	1.5	3%	0.3	8.2	25	$6
Health	C	08	CIN	5	1	0	59	58	3.22	1.38	253	247	250	4.7	32%	80%	3.62	51	14	36	3.8	8.9	2.3	10%	0.9	7.6	85	$6
PT/Exp	D	09	CIN	1	0	0	59	45	4.40	1.42	267	222	289	4.9	31%	70%	4.38	43	15	42	3.5	6.8	2.0	7%	0.8	-1.5	50	$2
Consist	B	1st Half		0	0	0	33	25	4.88	1.66	289			5.2	35%	69%	4.86	44	14	41	4.6	6.8	1.5	2%	0.3	-2.8	20	($1)
LIMA Plan	B	2nd Half		1	0	0	26	20	3.79	1.11	238			4.4	26%	72%	3.80	41	17	42	2.1	6.9	3.3	12%	1.4	1.3	87	$2
Rand Var	-1	10	Proj	2	2	0	51	40	4.26	1.36	259			4.7	30%	71%	4.14	46	15	40	3.4	7.1	2.1	10%	1.1	0.8	60	$3

A tale of two halves: xERA shows effect of improving Ctl while other skills remained the same. BA doesn't show it, but he's much more effective against RH (7.8 Dom) than LH (5.5 Dom).

Bush,David

		Yr	Tm	W	L	Sv	IP	K	ERA	WHIP	OBA	vL	vR	BF/G	H%	S%	xERA	G	L	F	Ctl	Dom	Cmd	hr/f	hr/9	RAR	BPV	R$
RH	Starter	05	TOR *	7	13	0	191	110	4.77	1.33	287	269	269	23.9	31%	67%	4.13	46	19	35	1.8	5.2	2.9	12%	1.3	-9.4	69	$9
Age	30	06	MIL	12	11	0	210	166	4.41	1.14	253	258	246	25.1	29%	64%	3.49	47	19	34	1.6	7.1	4.4	12%	1.1	1.9	109	$20
Type	FB	07	MIL	12	10	0	186	134	5.12	1.40	292	246	324	24.4	33%	66%	4.14	43	19	38	2.1	6.5	3.0	12%	1.3	-16.0	80	$10
Health	D	08	MIL	9	10	0	185	109	4.18	1.14	238	244	224	24.2	25%	69%	4.28	41	18	41	2.3	5.3	2.3	12%	1.4	2.0	51	$15
PT/Exp	A	09	MIL	5	9	0	114	89	6.38	1.47	289	293	295	22.8	32%	58%	4.48	34	21	45	2.9	7.0	2.4	12%	1.5	-30.9	60	$0
Consist	A	1st Half		3	4	0	81	59	5.67	1.35	267			23.0	28%	64%	4.42	35	21	44	2.9	6.6	2.3	16%	2.0	-14.8	53	$2
LIMA Plan	B+	2nd Half		2	5	0	33	30	8.11	1.77	338			22.3	42%	50%	4.62	33	21	46	3.0	8.1	2.7	2%	0.3	-16.1	76	($2)
Rand Var	+5	10	Proj	8	12	0	147	111	4.60	1.35	275			23.2	31%	69%	4.23	38	20	42	2.5	6.8	2.7	10%	1.2	0.6	71	$9

2H was the epitome of bad luck: More than 4 of every 10 batted balls fell for hits, and half of those runners scored. Teases us with solid BPIs that never translate to success. But always worth a token end game flyer.

Byrdak,Tim

		Yr	Tm	W	L	Sv	IP	K	ERA	WHIP	OBA	vL	vR	BF/G	H%	S%	xERA	G	L	F	Ctl	Dom	Cmd	hr/f	hr/9	RAR	BPV	R$
LH	Reliever	05	BAL *	3	3	12	64	67	3.30	1.43	234	214	300	3.6	30%	80%	3.60	51	19	30	5.1	9.4	1.8	12%	0.9	8.6	59	$10
Age	36	06	BAL	1	0	0	7	2	12.86	3.14	415			2.7	40%	60%	8.88	52	26	23	10.3	2.6	0.3	28%	2.6	-7.2	-202	($2)
Type	Pwr FB	07	DET	3	0	1	45	49	3.20	1.42	230			5.0	31%	79%	3.97	41	21	38	5.2	9.8	1.9	7%	0.6	7.2	55	$6
Health	A	08	HOU *	2	1	0	62	55	3.97	1.34	236	135	289	4.0	27%	76%	4.11	43	19	39	4.2	7.9	1.9	15%	1.4	2.3	50	$4
PT/Exp	D	09	HOU	1	2	0	61	58	3.23	1.22	184	184	172	3.3	20%	82%	4.19	42	14	45	5.3	8.5	1.6	15%	1.5	7.3	30	$5
Consist	A	1st Half		1	1	0	26	24	3.46	1.27	206			3.4	22%	82%	3.73	51	16	33	4.8	8.3	1.7	22%	1.7	2.3	48	$2
LIMA Plan	C	2nd Half		0	1	0	35	34	3.06	1.19	167			3.3	19%	81%	4.49	34	12	54	5.6	8.7	1.5	11%	1.3	4.9	17	$3
Rand Var	-5	10	Proj	1	2	0	58	53	4.19	1.47	245			3.9	29%	74%	4.36	43	17	40	5.0	8.2	1.7	11%	1.1	-0.7	35	$2

The flipside of "chicks diggin' the longball" is "managers diggin' the hard thrower." Doesn't matter if you can't find the plate or your defense always rescues you. High Ks and low ERAs = regular paydays.

Byrd,Paul

		Yr	Tm	W	L	Sv	IP	K	ERA	WHIP	OBA	vL	vR	BF/G	H%	S%	xERA	G	L	F	Ctl	Dom	Cmd	hr/f	hr/9	RAR	BPV	R$
RH	Starter	05	ANA	12	11	0	204	102	3.75	1.20	273	306	234	27.1	29%	72%	4.39	38	20	42	1.2	4.5	3.6	8%	1.0	15.7	63	$18
Age	39	06	CLE	10	9	0	179	88	4.88	1.51	315	369	256	25.6	33%	71%	4.79	39	24	37	1.9	4.4	2.3	11%	1.3	-7.1	45	$7
Type	Con FB	07	CLE	15	8	0	192	88	4.59	1.39	306	322	280	26.7	32%	70%	4.74	38	21	41	1.3	4.1	3.1	10%	1.3	-1.9	55	$13
Health	A	08	2AL	11	12	0	180	82	4.60	1.32	287	317	255	25.5	29%	71%	4.73	36	23	42	1.7	4.1	2.4	12%	1.6	-5.6	42	$11
PT/Exp	B	09	BOS	1	3	0	34	11	5.82	1.71	329	405	250	22.5	34%	67%	6.24	34	16	50	2.9	2.9	1.0	6%	1.1	-5.8	-14	($1)
Consist	B	1st Half		0	0	0	0	0	0.00	0.00							0.00											
LIMA Plan	D	2nd Half		1	3	0	34	11	5.83	1.71	329			22.5	34%	67%	6.25	34	16	50	2.9	2.9	1.0	6%	1.1	-5.8	-14	($1)
Rand Var	0	10	Proj	2	5	0	58	25	4.97	1.47	306			25.4	31%	70%	5.14	36	20	43	2.0	3.9	1.9	10%	1.4	-5.1	30	$1

If you're near 40something, you can relate... Suppose you're a marginal performer at a job requiring high caliber skill. You finally land a job after 9 months of sitting on your hands. In that context, '09 is no surprise at all.

Cahill,Trevor

		Yr	Tm	W	L	Sv	IP	K	ERA	WHIP	OBA	vL	vR	BF/G	H%	S%	xERA	G	L	F	Ctl	Dom	Cmd	hr/f	hr/9	RAR	BPV	R$
RH	Starter	05		0	0	0	0	0	0.00	0.00							0.00											
Age	22	06		0	0	0	0	0	0.00	0.00							0.00											
Type		07		0	0	0	0	0	0.00	0.00							0.00											
Health	A	08	aa	6	1	0	37	29	2.08	1.08	186			21.1	23%	83%	2.14				3.9	7.2	1.8		0.5	10.1	85	$8
PT/Exp	C	09	OAK	10	13	0	179	90	4.63	1.44	269	286	252	24.3	28%	72%	4.80	48	18	34	3.6	4.5	1.3	13%	1.4	-4.0	10	$8
Consist	F	1st Half		5	6	0	89	43	4.24	1.39	264			24.0	26%	75%	4.73	48	19	33	3.4	4.3	1.3	15%	1.5	2.3	11	$5
LIMA Plan	D+	2nd Half		5	7	0	90	47	5.02	1.48	273			24.7	29%	69%	4.87	48	17	35	3.8	4.7	1.2	11%	1.2	-6.3	8	$3
Rand Var	0	10	Proj	14	11	0	161	90	4.47	1.46	269			23.5	29%	71%	4.71	48	18	34	3.8	5.0	1.3	10%	1.0	-5.4	14	$11

Skipped AAA and only pitched a handful of IP at AA, so rough MLB debut wasn't surprising. Previous Dom in low minors (10.3 at A level in '07 and '08) and GB% offer hope, but look towards 2011 and beyond.

Cain,Matt

		Yr	Tm	W	L	Sv	IP	K	ERA	WHIP	OBA	vL	vR	BF/G	H%	S%	xERA	G	L	F	Ctl	Dom	Cmd	hr/f	hr/9	RAR	BPV	R$
RH	Starter	05	SF *	12	6	0	191	201	3.35	1.06	192	160	143	23.1	24%	72%	3.74	29	18	53	3.5	9.5	2.7	8%	0.9	21.2	83	$25
Age	25	06	SF	13	12	0	190	179	4.16	1.28	226	217	227	25.0	28%	69%	4.30	36	16	48	4.1	8.5	2.1	7%	0.9	7.6	55	$18
Type	Pwr FB	07	SF	7	16	0	200	163	3.65	1.26	235	248	224	26.1	28%	72%	4.29	39	16	45	3.6	7.3	2.1	5%	0.6	19.3	53	$17
Health	A	08	SF	8	14	0	218	186	3.76	1.36	251	268	235	27.4	30%	74%	4.38	33	23	44	3.8	7.7	2.0	7%	0.8	13.6	48	$14
PT/Exp	A	09	SF	14	8	0	218	171	2.89	1.18	231	233	231	27.1	27%	80%	4.04	39	19	42	3.0	7.1	2.3	8%	0.9	34.8	63	$24
Consist	A	1st Half		9	2	0	108	88	2.50	1.24	228			28.1	27%	85%	4.28	36	19	45	3.7	7.3	2.0	8%	0.9	22.6	47	$14
LIMA Plan	D+	2nd Half		5	6	0	110	83	3.29	1.12	233			26.0	27%	74%	3.82	41	19	40	2.4	6.8	2.9	9%	0.9	12.2	78	$11
Rand Var	-5	10	Proj	12	10	0	209	172	3.58	1.25	249			26.3	29%	74%	4.05	37	19	43	2.8	7.4	2.6	8%	0.9	5.4	73	$19

Yes, he benefited from some good luck, but there's still a lot to like here: note the 4 year trend in Ctl and FB%, and the AAA reliability rating. Loss of Dom the only concern.
UP: 2009 Repeat

Calero,Kiko

		Yr	Tm	W	L	Sv	IP	K	ERA	WHIP	OBA	vL	vR	BF/G	H%	S%	xERA	G	L	F	Ctl	Dom	Cmd	hr/f	hr/9	RAR	BPV	R$
RH	Reliever	05	OAK	4	1	1	55	52	3.26	1.14	224	319	162	3.9	27%	75%	3.80	34	19	47	2.9	8.5	2.9	9%	1.0	7.6	86	$8
Age	35	06	OAK	3	2	2	58	67	3.41	1.28	234	278	208	3.5	32%	74%	3.61	35	21	44	3.7	10.4	2.8	6%	0.6	8.2	99	$8
Type	Pwr xFB	07	OAK	1	5	1	41	31	5.75	1.65	286	245	315	4.0	34%	64%	5.25	34	20	47	4.6	6.9	1.5	5%	0.7	-6.2	10	$0
Health	B	08	aaa	3	4	1	39	33	7.85	2.18	313			5.8	36%	65%	7.94				8.1	7.6	0.9		1.6	-17.0	10	($3)
PT/Exp	D	09	FLA	2	2	0	60	69	1.95	1.10	175	187	176	3.6	26%	82%	3.70	32	16	52	4.5	10.4	2.3	1%	0.2	16.6	75	$9
Consist	F	1st Half		1	0	0	31	39	2.03	1.16	178			3.5	28%	81%	3.60	30	19	51	4.9	11.3	2.3	0%	0.0	8.3	79	$4
LIMA Plan	C	2nd Half		1	2	0	29	30	1.87	1.04	173			3.7	24%	83%	3.80	34	13	53	4.0	9.3	2.3	3%	0.3	8.3	71	$4
Rand Var	-5	10	Proj	3	5	3	73	73	4.10	1.39	236			4.1	30%	72%	4.35	34	18	49	4.7	9.1	1.9	7%	0.9	-0.8	47	$6

Aided by low H% and high S%. xERA shows how a high Dom covers other blemishes. Good track record of avoiding the long ball, but a 1% rate isn't repeatable, especially with a 50%+ fly ball rate.

Camp,Shawn

		Yr	Tm	W	L	Sv	IP	K	ERA	WHIP	OBA	vL	vR	BF/G	H%	S%	xERA	G	L	F	Ctl	Dom	Cmd	hr/f	hr/9	RAR	BPV	R$
RH	Reliever	05	KC *	4	10	1	116	62	5.26	1.62	319	407	274	10.6	35%	68%	4.30	57	14	29	2.7	4.8	1.8	10%	0.9	-12.8	47	$0
Age	34	06	TAM	7	4	4	75	53	4.68	1.49	305	370	284	4.4	35%	71%	3.58	57	18	24	2.3	6.4	2.8	15%	1.1	-1.1	88	$7
Type	xGB	07	TAM	0	3	0	40	36	7.20	2.03	358			4.0	42%	66%	3.86	57	21	22	4.1	8.1	2.0	23%	1.6	-13.3	72	($3)
Health	A	08	TOR *	4	1	4	49	41	3.29	1.14	246	356	204	4.3	31%	71%	3.06	54	19	27	2.0	7.6	3.8	5%	0.4	6.5	114	$8
PT/Exp	D	09	TOR	2	6	1	80	58	3.50	1.28	245	260	230	5.7	28%	75%	3.69	55	17	28	3.3	6.5	2.0	10%	0.8	9.4	63	$7
Consist	B	1st Half		0	3	0	35	25	4.11	1.37	256			5.6	30%	71%	3.52	62	16	22	3.6	6.4	1.8	13%	0.8	1.5	59	$2
LIMA Plan	B	2nd Half		2	3	1	45	33	3.02	1.21	236			5.8	27%	78%	3.80	50	18	33	3.0	6.6	2.2	9%	0.8	7.9	66	$5
Rand Var	0	10	Proj	2	4	0	58	45	3.88	1.34	265			4.9	31%	73%	3.53	55	18	27	2.9	7.0	2.4	11%	0.8	6.5	79	$4

Wasn't able to sustain Cmd improvement, but still owns outstanding GB rate. Solid LIMA option.

Capps,Matt

		Yr	Tm	W	L	Sv	IP	K	ERA	WHIP	OBA	vL	vR	BF/G	H%	S%	xERA	G	L	F	Ctl	Dom	Cmd	hr/f	hr/9	RAR	BPV	R$
RH	Reliever	05	aa	0	2	7	24	23	3.75	1.29	293			4.8	37%	72%	4.39				1.1	8.6	7.7		0.8	1.6	187	$4
Age	26	06	PIT	9	1	1	80	56	3.82	1.16	264	250	275	3.8	29%	73%	3.91	41	20	40	1.3	6.3	4.7	12%	1.3	6.6	95	$11
Type	FB	07	PIT	4	7	18	79	64	2.28	1.01	223	281	181	4.1	27%	80%	3.94	31	19	50	1.8	7.3	4.0	4%	0.6	20.9	91	$18
Health	B	08	PIT	2	3	21	54	39	3.02	0.97	237	222	245	4.3	27%	72%	3.75	31	23	46	0.8	6.5	7.8	7%	0.8	8.3	104	$14
PT/Exp	B	09	PIT	4	8	27	54	46	5.80	1.66	323	342	306	4.4	37%	69%	4.31	41	19	41	2.8	7.6	2.7	14%	1.7	-10.8	80	$9
Consist	A	1st Half		1	3	18	26	19	4.81	1.53	282			4.0	31%	72%	4.86	39	14	47	3.8	6.5	1.7	10%	1.4	-2.0	32	$6
LIMA Plan	B+	2nd Half		3	5	9	28	27	6.73	1.78	357			4.7	42%	66%	3.81	42	23	35	1.9	8.6	4.5	18%	1.9	-8.8	124	$3
Rand Var	+5	10	Proj	4	4	25	73	58	3.85	1.20	260			4.1	30%	73%	3.87	37	20	43	1.9	7.2	3.9	11%	1.2	3.5	95	$15

Returned to form in 2H with closer-worthy BPV after minor elbow injuries plagued his 1H. Gopheritis and H%/S% bad luck obscured that rebound. Odds are good he's going to be undervalued on draft day.

BILL MACEY

Carlson,Jesse

		Yr	Tm	W	L	Sv	IP	K	ERA	WHIP	OBA	vL	vR	BF/G	H%	S%	xERA	G	L	F	Ctl	Dom	Cmd	hr/f	hr/9	RAR	BPV	R$
LH	Reliever	05	a/a	4	3	5	57	50	3.91	1.39	291			4.1	34%	77%	5.18				2.1	8.0	3.8		1.3	2.8	85	$7
Age	29	06	a/a	6	5	3	69	41	5.77	1.69	323			6.0	35%	68%	6.71				3.2	5.3	1.7		1.4	-10.6	17	$2
Type	FB	07	aa	8	2	6	70	60	6.94	1.75	341			5.6	41%	59%	6.57				2.7	7.7	2.9		0.7	-21.4	72	$3
Health	A	08	TOR	7	2	2	60	55	2.25	1.03	195	205	186	3.4	23%	84%	3.74	34	21	45	3.2	8.3	2.6	9%	0.9	15.5	76	$12
PT/Exp	D	09	TOR	1	6	0	68	51	4.65	1.30	260	272	247	3.9	30%	65%	4.31	37	20	43	2.8	6.8	2.4	8%	0.9	-1.7	62	$4
Consist	D	1st Half		1	3	0	36	26	5.24	1.44	282			4.1	33%	62%	4.81	33	19	48	3.0	6.5	2.2	4%	0.5	-3.5	47	$1
LIMA Plan	B+	2nd Half		0	3	0	32	25	3.99	1.14	233			3.7	26%	71%	3.73	42	22	36	2.6	7.1	2.8	15%	1.4	1.8	79	$3
Rand Var	0	10	Proj	4	5	0	73	59	3.97	1.30	260			4.0	30%	73%	4.14	37	21	43	2.7	7.3	2.7	10%	1.1	2.7	73	$7

Aberrant 1st half H% and S% levels inflated his ERA and masked a solid skill set. 2H xERA and BPV track nicely with 2008 levels, making him an appealing LIMA option.

Carmona,Fausto

		Yr	Tm	W	L	Sv	IP	K	ERA	WHIP	OBA	vL	vR	BF/G	H%	S%	xERA	G	L	F	Ctl	Dom	Cmd	hr/f	hr/9	RAR	BPV	R$
RH	Starter	05	a/a	13	9	0	173	97	3.86	1.25	272			26.7	30%	70%	4.00				1.7	5.0	2.9		0.7	9.5	69	$15
Age	26	06	CLE *	2	13	0	102	85	5.75	1.55	294	299	298	10.4	35%	63%	3.64	60	13	27	3.4	7.5	2.2	12%	1.0	-15.0	80	$2
Type	xGB	07	CLE	19	8	0	215	137	3.06	1.21	247	275	216	27.7	28%	77%	3.27	64	14	22	2.6	5.7	2.2	11%	0.7	38.4	77	$27
Health	B	08	CLE	8	7	0	121	58	5.44	1.62	270	303	230	24.9	30%	65%	4.49	63	15	22	5.2	4.3	0.8	8%	0.5	-16.3	-22	$1
PT/Exp	B	09	CLE *	7	15	0	165	107	5.82	1.64	295	331	245	25.1	32%	66%	4.38	55	18	27	4.2	5.8	1.4	16%	1.3	-28.0	25	$0
Consist	B	1st Half		3	6	0	72	45	6.63	1.71	286			23.9	31%	63%	4.69	56	18	26	5.2	5.6	1.1	18%	1.4	-19.4	-8	($2)
LIMA Plan	C	2nd Half		4	9	0	93	62	5.20	1.59	302			26.2	34%	69%	4.16	54	17	28	3.3	6.0	1.8	14%	1.2	-8.6	51	$2
Rand Var	+4	10	Proj	8	11	0	149	98	4.30	1.41	262			23.0	30%	70%	3.83	59	16	25	3.7	5.9	1.6	10%	0.7	11.2	45	$9

5-12, 6.32 ERA in 125 IP at CLE. Home Plate - The Final Frontier. He had it in his scope prior to '08. The last two years, Ctl was in a different galaxy and base-runners unnerved him. But the intrinsic skill is still there. Flyer.

Carpenter,Chris

		Yr	Tm	W	L	Sv	IP	K	ERA	WHIP	OBA	vL	vR	BF/G	H%	S%	xERA	G	L	F	Ctl	Dom	Cmd	hr/f	hr/9	RAR	BPV	R$
RH	Starter	05	STL	21	5	0	241	213	2.84	1.06	231	264	199	29.1	28%	76%	2.83	55	19	26	1.9	7.9	4.2	10%	0.7	41.9	124	$35
Age	34	06	STL	15	8	0	221	184	3.09	1.07	237	266	210	27.6	28%	75%	3.08	53	18	28	1.7	7.5	4.3	12%	0.9	38.1	119	$30
Type	xGB	07	STL	0	1	0	6	3	7.50	1.67	347	375	300	27.5	39%	50%	2.82	65	26	9	1.5	4.5	3.0	0%	0.0	-2.3	84	($0)
Health	F	08	STL	0	1	0	15	7	1.76	1.31	271	158	351	16.2	31%	85%	4.01	51	24	24	2.4	4.1	1.8	0%	0.0	4.7	40	$1
PT/Exp	C	09	STL	17	4	0	193	144	2.24	1.01	223	239	214	27.0	27%	78%	3.08	55	17	28	1.8	6.7	3.8	4%	0.3	46.3	106	$30
Consist	C	1st Half		5	3	0	70	53	2.44	0.83	195			23.9	24%	71%	2.87	55	16	30	1.3	6.8	5.3	5%	0.4	15.2	120	$12
LIMA Plan	C	2nd Half		12	1	0	123	91	2.13	1.11	238			29.0	29%	81%	3.19	55	18	27	2.1	6.7	3.3	4%	0.3	31.1	98	$19
Rand Var	-4	10	Proj	13	7	0	183	141	3.15	1.14	246			28.6	29%	74%	3.05	56	21	23	2.0	6.9	3.4	9%	0.6	27.4	104	$22

This will be your true test of self-control. The skills are elite. The price tag will be high. But his track record of health and odds of a repeat carry incredible risk. The correct tactical move? Push the price but don't buy.

Carrasco,Carlos

		Yr	Tm	W	L	Sv	IP	K	ERA	WHIP	OBA	vL	vR	BF/G	H%	S%	xERA	G	L	F	Ctl	Dom	Cmd	hr/f	hr/9	RAR	BPV	R$
RH	Starter	05		0	0	0	0	0	0.00	0.00							0.00											
Age	23	06		0	0	0	0	0	0.00	0.00							0.00											
Type	Pwr	07	aa	6	4	0	70	44	5.50	1.63	263			22.8	28%	69%	5.58				5.6	5.7	1.0		1.3	-9.0	17	$2
Health	A	08	a/a	9	9	0	151	138	4.14	1.39	266			25.0	32%	72%	4.48				3.3	8.2	2.5		1.0	3.1	74	$12
PT/Exp	D	09	CLE *	11	14	0	179	152	5.69	1.42	283	367	431	25.1	33%	61%	3.48	48	27	25	2.7	7.6	2.8	17%	1.2	-27.5	90	$9
Consist	C	1st Half		5	7	0	92	78	5.59	1.48	297			25.3	35%	63%	5.24				2.6	7.6	2.9		1.0	-12.9	72	$3
LIMA Plan	B+	2nd Half		6	7	0	87	74	5.80	1.35	269			24.8	31%	58%	3.43	48	27	25	2.8	7.6	2.7	20%	1.3	-14.5	88	$5
Rand Var	+5	10	Proj	6	4	0	73	61	3.97	1.26	252			23.3	31%	69%	3.48	48	22	29	2.7	7.6	2.8	10%	0.7	8.6	89	$8

0-4, 8.87 ERA in 22 IP at CLE. Hit some pretty big speed bumps in his MLB debut, but there's a lot to like in the long term, particularly the Cmd and BPV trends. If they continue... UP: Rookie of the Year

Carrasco,D.J.

		Yr	Tm	W	L	Sv	IP	K	ERA	WHIP	OBA	vL	vR	BF/G	H%	S%	xERA	G	L	F	Ctl	Dom	Cmd	hr/f	hr/9	RAR	BPV	R$
RH	Reliever	05	KC *	9	10	0	141	66	4.36	1.55	282	286	292	19.7	30%	73%	4.49	54	22	24	3.9	4.2	1.1	10%	0.8	0.2	1	$5
Age	33	06	JPN	0	3	0	10	9	15.30	3.20	438			20.4	50%	52%	14.49				9.0	8.1	0.9		2.7	-13.3	-46	($4)
Type		07	aaa	5	14	0	137	89	7.81	2.13	365			20.4	40%	64%	8.62				4.6	5.8	1.3		1.3	-56.6	4	($14)
Health	A	08	CHW *	3	1	1	64	51	4.10	1.27	244	186	244	6.8	30%	66%	3.54	51	21	28	3.2	7.2	2.2	4%	0.3	2.0	71	$6
PT/Exp	D	09	CHW	5	1	0	93	62	3.76	1.41	281	317	251	8.3	33%	73%	4.19	47	20	33	2.8	6.0	2.1	5%	0.5	7.9	57	$7
Consist	F	1st Half		2	0	0	48	33	2.99	1.31	273			7.8	33%	76%	3.92	48	19	33	2.2	6.2	2.8	2%	0.2	8.7	76	$5
LIMA Plan	C+	2nd Half		3	1	0	45	29	4.59	1.53	290			8.7	33%	71%	4.48	47	21	33	3.4	5.8	1.7	8%	0.8	-0.8	37	$2
Rand Var	-2	10	Proj	5	3	0	87	59	4.34	1.39	271			9.1	31%	70%	4.05	49	20	30	3.1	6.1	2.0	9%	0.8	4.1	53	$6

Acceptable Cmd for two years now, and hr/f rate is impressive given home park, though will regress. High BF/G points to a long relief role where he's a better than average bet to pick up some vultured wins.

Casilla,Santiago

		Yr	Tm	W	L	Sv	IP	K	ERA	WHIP	OBA	vL	vR	BF/G	H%	S%	xERA	G	L	F	Ctl	Dom	Cmd	hr/f	hr/9	RAR	BPV	R$
RH	Reliever	05		0	0	0	0	0	0.00	0.00							0.00											
Age	29	06	OAK *	2	0	4	35	29	4.10	1.14	227	400		5.3	28%	63%	3.25	40	40	20	2.8	7.4	2.6	10%	0.5	2.0	76	$5
Type	Pwr	07	OAK *	5	2	5	75	73	4.75	1.38	235	212	230	4.7	29%	66%	4.52	33	16	51	4.7	8.8	1.9	7%	0.9	-2.3	43	$8
Health	B	08	OAK	2	1	2	50	43	3.94	1.59	297	308	291	4.4	36%	77%	4.19	43	20	36	3.6	7.7	2.2	9%	0.9	2.6	63	$3
PT/Exp	D	09	OAK	1	2	0	48	35	5.96	1.78	309	354	257	4.9	35%	68%	4.65	50	20	30	4.7	6.5	1.4	12%	1.1	-9.0	20	($1)
Consist	A	1st Half		1	2	0	28	20	5.74	1.42	246			4.7	26%	63%	4.38	51	16	33	4.5	6.4	1.4	18%	1.6	-4.5	23	$1
LIMA Plan	D	2nd Half		0	0	0	20	15	6.27	2.29	382			5.2	45%	71%	5.02	49	25	26	4.9	6.7	1.4	5%	0.4	-4.5	15	($2)
Rand Var	+5	10	Proj	1	1	0	44	34	4.55	1.52	273			4.7	32%	72%	4.31	46	20	33	4.1	7.0	1.7	11%	1.0	0.7	39	$2

PRO: xERA + h% say he's been very unlucky and the GB trend is encouraging.
CON: Ctl and Dom going in the wrong direction.
Yet to deliver on past flashes of dominance. Tread carefully.

Cecil,Brett

		Yr	Tm	W	L	Sv	IP	K	ERA	WHIP	OBA	vL	vR	BF/G	H%	S%	xERA	G	L	F	Ctl	Dom	Cmd	hr/f	hr/9	RAR	BPV	R$
LH	Starter	05		0	0	0	0	0	0.00	0.00							0.00											
Age	23	06		0	0	0	0	0	0.00	0.00							0.00											
Type	Pwr	07		0	0	0	0	0	0.00	0.00							0.00											
Health	A	08	a/a	8	5	0	108	98	3.75	1.39	263			19.4	33%	73%	3.99				3.4	8.2	2.4		0.5	7.5	86	$10
PT/Exp	D	09	TOR *	8	9	0	142	97	5.57	1.62	301	295	314	23.9	34%	67%	4.77	43	20	38	3.6	6.1	1.7	11%	1.2	-19.5	34	$2
Consist	B	1st Half		3	6	0	84	52	5.67	1.57	303			23.6	34%	64%	4.45	51	16	33	3.1	5.6	1.8	9%	1.0	-12.7	46	$0
LIMA Plan	C+	2nd Half		5	3	0	58	45	5.41	1.68	299			24.4	33%	72%	4.95	37	22	41	4.3	7.0	1.6	13%	1.5	-6.9	24	$2
Rand Var	+3	10	Proj	7	6	0	102	80	4.52	1.44	278			21.1	32%	71%	4.28	40	21	39	3.2	7.1	2.2	10%	1.1	1.9	60	$7

7-4, 5.30 ERA in 93 IP at TOR. Lost effectiveness as season wore on: PQS DOM/DIS was 14/57% in Aug-Sept vs. 50/ 30% in May-July. Tantalizing GB/Dom in minors, if that translates... UP: sub-4.00 ERA.

Chacin,Jhoulys

		Yr	Tm	W	L	Sv	IP	K	ERA	WHIP	OBA	vL	vR	BF/G	H%	S%	xERA	G	L	F	Ctl	Dom	Cmd	hr/f	hr/9	RAR	BPV	R$
RH	Reliever	05		0	0	0	0	0	0.00	0.00							0.00											
Age	22	06		0	0	0	0	0	0.00	0.00							0.00											
Type	Pwr FB	07		0	0	0	0	0	0.00	0.00							0.00											
Health	A	08		0	0	0	0	0	0.00	0.00							0.00											
PT/Exp	F	09	COL *	9	9	0	128	95	4.21	1.40	251	263	59	17.8	28%	73%	4.49	48	9	43	4.1	6.7	1.6	9%	1.1	-0.4	36	$8
Consist	F	1st Half		6	6	0	88	67	3.69	1.23	250			24.4	29%	72%	3.79				2.6	6.9	2.6		0.9	5.4	75	$8
LIMA Plan	C	2nd Half		3	3	0	40	28	5.36	1.76	253			11.7	27%	74%	5.79	48	9	43	7.3	6.3	0.9	14%	1.7	-5.8	-58	($0)
Rand Var	0	10	Proj	6	6	0	88	63	4.72	1.55	262			14.5	29%	73%	4.93	48	9	43	4.9	6.5	1.3	10%	1.2	-7.2	9	$3

0-1, 4.91 in 11 IP at COL. Used mainly as a RP, but future is at SP. High GB% rates in minors bode well given home ballpark. Ctl jumped when promoted to AAA, so likely needs additional seasoning.

Chamberlain,Joba

		Yr	Tm	W	L	Sv	IP	K	ERA	WHIP	OBA	vL	vR	BF/G	H%	S%	xERA	G	L	F	Ctl	Dom	Cmd	hr/f	hr/9	RAR	BPV	R$
RH	Starter	05		0	0	0	0	0	0.00	0.00							0.00											
Age	24	06		0	0	0	0	0	0.00	0.00							0.00											
Type	Pwr	07	NYY *	7	2	1	72	104	2.62	1.11	219	132	156	9.7	34%	80%	2.63	37	22	41	2.9	13.0	4.5	9%	0.7	16.8	171	$15
Health	A	08	NYY	4	3	0	100	118	2.60	1.26	235	247	219	10.0	33%	80%	2.98	52	14	34	3.5	10.6	3.0	6%	0.4	21.6	126	$13
PT/Exp	C	09	NYY	9	6	0	157	133	4.75	1.54	274	266	282	21.9	32%	72%	4.39	43	21	36	4.3	7.6	1.8	12%	1.2	-5.8	41	$8
Consist	B	1st Half		4	2	0	81	73	3.89	1.47	257			23.7	31%	76%	3.91	50	20	30	4.4	8.1	1.8	13%	1.0	5.6	54	$6
LIMA Plan	A	2nd Half		5	4	0	76	60	5.66	1.63	290			20.4	33%	68%	4.85	37	22	41	4.2	7.1	1.7	12%	1.4	-11.4	28	$2
Rand Var	+1	10	Proj	10	6	0	174	182	3.78	1.30	244			21.6	31%	73%	3.50	45	19	36	3.6	9.4	2.6	10%	0.9	20.2	96	$18

Struggled in SP role. Velocity may tell why. Avg fastball speed was 95.2 mph (2008), and 92.5 mph (2009). Role seems to matter, though '08 SP/RP BPIs were near identical. Rule #426B: Never reach for an enigma.

BILL MACEY

Chavez,Jesse

Chavez,Jesse		Yr	Tm	W	L	Sv	IP	K	ERA	WHIP	OBA	vL	vR	BF/G	H%	S%	xERA	G	L	F	Ctl	Dom	Cmd	hr/f	hr/9	RAR	BPV	R$
RH	Reliever	05	aa	4	3	1	57	23	7.42	1.91	343			8.9	34%	65%	8.20				3.9	3.6	0.9		2.1	-21.9	-34	($4)
Age	26	06	a/a	4	6	4	78	74	5.42	1.58	281			6.9	35%	65%	5.00				4.3	8.5	2.0		0.7	-8.7	71	$4
Type	FB	07	aa	3	3	2	80	51	4.97	1.64	333			7.9	38%	69%	5.87				2.1	5.8	2.7		0.5	-5.0	66	$2
Health	A	08	PIT *	2	7	14	83	69	5.53	1.53	287			5.6	33%	66%	5.47				3.6	7.5	2.1		1.2	-12.9	51	$5
PT/Exp	D	09	PIT	1	4	0	67	47	4.01	1.35	267	228	299	3.9	29%	76%	4.36	39	20	41	2.9	6.3	2.1	13%	1.5	1.5	51	$3
Consist	B	1st Half		0	3	0	34	26	3.44	1.26	244			3.7	28%	77%	4.28	37	19	44	3.2	6.9	2.2	9%	1.1	3.1	53	$2
LIMA Plan	C+	2nd Half		1	1	0	33	21	4.59	1.44	288			4.1	30%	76%	4.44	41	21	38	2.7	5.7	2.1	17%	1.9	-1.7	48	$1
Rand Var	0	10	Proj	2	4	3	73	52	4.47	1.42	276			4.9	31%	72%	4.42	40	20	40	3.1	6.5	2.1	11%	1.2	-1.4	50	$3

In the no-man's land that is the PIT bullpen, managed to best his MLEs by posting a solid Ctl rate and getting some H% and S% help. xERA sets your expectations for 2010 in TAM.

Chen,Bruce

Chen,Bruce		Yr	Tm	W	L	Sv	IP	K	ERA	WHIP	OBA	vL	vR	BF/G	H%	S%	xERA	G	L	F	Ctl	Dom	Cmd	hr/f	hr/9	RAR	BPV	R$
LH	Starter	05	BAL	13	10	0	197	133	3.84	1.27	252	324	224	24.3	27%	76%	4.29	39	21	40	2.9	6.1	2.1	14%	1.5	13.0	49	$18
Age	32	06	BAL	0	7	0	98	70	6.97	1.75	331	328	337	11.5	35%	67%	5.22	33	21	47	3.2	6.4	2.0	17%	2.6	-29.2	39	($5)
Type	xFB	07	TEX *	1	1	0	26	19	6.23	1.42	276			12.5	29%	61%	5.93				3.1	6.6	2.1		2.1	-5.5	21	$1
Health	F	08		0	0	0	0	0	0.00	0.00							0.00											
PT/Exp	D	09	KC *	5	8	0	144	97	5.14	1.38	267	292	305	20.0	29%	66%	5.02	31	17	51	3.2	6.0	1.9	9%	1.3	-12.2	32	$6
Consist	B	1st Half		4	3	0	88	60	4.71	1.15	238			23.9	26%	61%	4.94	24	14	62	2.5	6.1	2.5	6%	1.1	-2.8	45	$7
LIMA Plan	C	2nd Half		1	5	0	56	37	5.80	1.73	308			16.3	33%	71%	5.69	32	18	50	4.3	5.9	1.4	11%	1.8	-9.4	1	($1)
Rand Var	0	10	Proj	1	3	0	44	29	5.38	1.52	285			14.8	31%	68%	5.08	33	20	47	3.5	6.0	1.7	10%	1.4	-3.5	24	$1

1-6, 5.78 ERA in 62 IP at KC. Extreme FB pitchers with poor Cmd struggle to avoid disaster. Historical hr/9 shows he hasn't. Low S% shows he also has trouble pitching from the stretch. Lots of bad things here.

Choate,Randy

Choate,Randy		Yr	Tm	W	L	Sv	IP	K	ERA	WHIP	OBA	vL	vR	BF/G	H%	S%	xERA	G	L	F	Ctl	Dom	Cmd	hr/f	hr/9	RAR	BPV	R$
LH	Reliever	05	aaa	1	1	3	40	16	4.00	1.86	316			4.1	33%	81%	6.57				5.0	3.6	0.7		1.0	1.5	-1	$0
Age	34	06	aaa	6	0	8	45	37	2.72	1.26	267			4.4	34%	76%	3.24				2.1	7.4	3.5		0.0	10.0	120	$10
Type	xGB	07	aaa	3	1	3	62	45	4.60	1.78	343			5.4	40%	74%	6.63				2.7	6.5	2.4		0.7	-1.0	55	$2
Health	A	08	aaa	0	4	2	39	27	5.83	1.75	301			7.0	34%	67%	6.01				4.9	6.1	1.3		1.0	-7.3	29	($1)
PT/Exp	F	09	TAM *	4	0	5	55	40	3.98	1.22	231	141	321	2.8	27%	68%	3.34	65	10	25	3.3	6.6	2.0	10%	0.6	3.2	72	$8
Consist	D	1st Half		3	0	4	31	25	3.61	1.26	221			3.3	28%	70%	3.19	68	11	21	4.2	7.3	1.8	5%	0.3	3.2	65	$5
LIMA Plan	B	2nd Half		1	0	1	24	15	4.46	1.16	244			2.3	26%	64%	3.36	64	10	26	2.2	5.6	2.5	15%	1.1	-0.0	83	$2
Rand Var	+1	10	Proj	2	1	0	44	30	4.34	1.43	268			3.6	31%	71%	3.68	58	20	22	3.5	6.2	1.8	13%	0.8	4.0	52	$3

5 sv, 3.47 ERA in 36 IP at TAM. Long-time journeyman put up 94 BPV at TAM by being a lefty-killer (4.4 Cmd vL and (0.7 Cmd vR). Nice end-game pick that may get handful of saves as match-ups dictate.

Clippard,Tyler

Clippard,Tyler		Yr	Tm	W	L	Sv	IP	K	ERA	WHIP	OBA	vL	vR	BF/G	H%	S%	xERA	G	L	F	Ctl	Dom	Cmd	hr/f	hr/9	RAR	BPV	R$
RH	Reliever	05		0	0	0	0	0	0.00	0.00							0.00											
Age	25	06	aa	12	10	0	166	145	4.61	1.23	235			24.6	28%	64%	3.68				3.3	7.9	2.4		1.0	-1.8	77	$16
Type	Pwr xFB	07	NYY *	9	6	0	123	88	6.15	1.80	309			22.4	34%	69%	6.93				4.9	6.4	1.3		1.5	-24.9	13	($0)
Health	A	08	aaa	6	13	0	143	105	5.10	1.42	258			23.0	30%	64%	4.32				4.0	6.6	1.7		0.8	-14.0	54	$5
PT/Exp	D	09	WAS *	8	3	1	99	103	2.08	1.07	174	122	234	6.1	21%	87%	4.03	30	13	57	4.3	9.3	2.2	8%	1.0	25.8	61	$17
Consist	C	1st Half		4	1	1	42	39	1.50	1.02	186			6.4	23%	90%	3.74	33	22	44	3.4	8.4	2.4	6%	0.6	13.9	69	$8
LIMA Plan	C+	2nd Half		4	2	0	57	64	2.51	1.10	165			5.9	20%	85%	4.01	30	12	58	4.9	10.1	2.1	11%	1.3	11.9	57	$9
Rand Var	-5	10	Proj	5	4	8	73	70	4.59	1.42	252			10.2	30%	72%	4.68	30	12	58	4.2	8.7	2.1	9%	1.4	-3.8	50	$7

4-2, 2.69 ERA in 60 IP at WAS. PRO: Transition to RP resulted in Dom spike. CON: Still has Ctl problems and FB% dangerously high. H%, S%, xERA all warn against paying for a repeat.

Coffey,Todd

Coffey,Todd		Yr	Tm	W	L	Sv	IP	K	ERA	WHIP	OBA	vL	vR	BF/G	H%	S%	xERA	G	L	F	Ctl	Dom	Cmd	hr/f	hr/9	RAR	BPV	R$
RH	Reliever	05	CIN	4	1	1	58	26	4.50	1.64	339	337	348	4.6	36%	73%	4.26	51	23	26	1.7	4.0	2.4	9%	0.8	-1.8	55	$1
Age	29	06	CIN	6	7	8	78	60	3.58	1.44	279	347	242	4.2	33%	77%	3.79	52	21	27	3.1	6.9	2.2	10%	0.8	8.8	71	$10
Type	GB	07	CIN *	4	1	1	78	63	4.41	1.48	293	343	313	4.5	33%	75%	3.54	58	16	27	2.8	7.3	2.6	18%	1.4	0.1	91	$4
Health	A	08	2NL *	4	3	2	66	50	5.14	1.74	329			5.1	38%	73%	6.82				3.3	6.9	2.1		1.3	-7.1	36	$1
PT/Exp	D	09	MIL	4	4	2	84	65	2.90	1.16	244	282	223	4.4	28%	79%	3.37	52	17	31	2.3	7.0	3.1	11%	0.9	13.3	95	$10
Consist	F	1st Half		3	1	2	39	31	2.77	1.31	276			4.5	34%	80%	3.21	53	23	24	2.1	7.2	3.4	7%	0.5	6.8	103	$5
LIMA Plan	B+	2nd Half		1	3	0	45	34	3.02	1.03	212			4.3	23%	78%	3.48	52	11	37	2.4	6.8	2.8	13%	1.2	6.4	88	$5
Rand Var	-1	10	Proj	3	3	3	65	50	3.86	1.29	264			4.5	31%	72%	3.51	53	18	29	2.5	6.9	2.8	10%	0.8	6.1	88	$6

2008 looks like an aberration in what is an improving skill set over a 5-year period. If the trend continues, he could finally be worthy of the closer's role he seemed destined for so many years ago.

Coke,Phil

Coke,Phil		Yr	Tm	W	L	Sv	IP	K	ERA	WHIP	OBA	vL	vR	BF/G	H%	S%	xERA	G	L	F	Ctl	Dom	Cmd	hr/f	hr/9	RAR	BPV	R$
LH	Reliever	05		0	0	0	0	0	0.00	0.00							0.00											
Age	27	06		0	0	0	0	0	0.00	0.00							0.00											
Type	Pwr FB	07		0	0	0	0	0	0.00	0.00							0.00											
Health	A	08	NYY *	12	6	0	151	118	3.75	1.50	290			13.6	35%	76%	4.72				3.2	7.0	2.2		0.6	11.0	68	$12
PT/Exp	D	09	NYY	4	3	2	60	49	4.50	1.07	206	195	227	3.3	22%	63%	4.02	35	20	45	3.0	7.4	2.5	13%	1.5	-0.4	65	$8
Consist	B	1st Half		1	3	1	34	27	3.18	0.97	180			3.6	19%	75%	4.01	36	18	46	3.2	7.1	2.3	12%	1.3	5.3	57	$5
LIMA Plan	B	2nd Half		3	0	1	26	22	6.23	1.19	239			3.1	26%	50%	4.03	34	22	44	2.8	7.6	2.8	15%	1.7	-5.7	75	$3
Rand Var	0	10	Proj	5	2	0	58	48	4.19	1.31	262			4.8	30%	72%	4.21	35	20	45	2.8	7.4	2.7	10%	1.2	1.6	72	$6

FB tendency concerning given how New Yankee Stadium played (+26% HR). Struggled vs RH (0.9 Cmd); serviceable BPI in 1st full season earns him chances to address those issues and realize upside.

Colon,Bartolo

Colon,Bartolo		Yr	Tm	W	L	Sv	IP	K	ERA	WHIP	OBA	vL	vR	BF/G	H%	S%	xERA	G	L	F	Ctl	Dom	Cmd	hr/f	hr/9	RAR	BPV	R$
RH	Starter	05	ANA	21	8	0	222	157	3.48	1.16	255	250	258	27.5	29%	74%	3.81	44	17	39	1.7	6.4	3.7	10%	1.1	24.3	89	$28
Age	36	06	LAA	1	5	0	56	31	5.13	1.46	310	354	261	24.6	32%	70%	4.52	41	22	37	1.8	5.0	2.8	15%	1.8	-4.0	61	$1
Type	Con FB	07	LAA	6	8	0	99	76	6.34	1.62	320	313	325	23.7	36%	62%	4.46	42	18	40	2.6	6.9	2.6	11%	1.4	-22.5	73	$1
Health	F	08	BOS *	7	3	0	70	44	3.53	1.26	268	309	253	18.4	30%	75%	4.21	40	21	39	2.1	5.7	2.7	8%	0.9	7.1	63	$8
PT/Exp	C	09	CHW	3	6	0	62	38	4.19	1.44	282	288	273	22.7	29%	79%	4.68	44	16	40	3.0	5.5	1.8	16%	1.9	2.0	39	$3
Consist	A	1st Half		3	6	0	55	36	4.25	1.51	288			22.2	30%	80%	4.68	45	16	40	3.3	5.9	1.8	17%	2.0	1.4	40	$3
LIMA Plan	C+	2nd Half		0	0	0	7	2	3.75	0.97	228			28.0	21%	67%	4.61	43	14	43	1.2	2.5	2.0	10%	1.2	0.6	32	$1
Rand Var	0	10	Proj	3	3	0	44	25	4.76	1.49	290			24.0	31%	71%	4.85	42	17	40	3.1	5.2	1.7	10%	1.2	-2.2	30	$2

Hasn't been effective in several years despite acceptable Cmd, but now that has disappeared too. Two years running he has quit on his team and gone home late in season. Even if another chance comes, just say no.

Condrey,Clay

Condrey,Clay		Yr	Tm	W	L	Sv	IP	K	ERA	WHIP	OBA	vL	vR	BF/G	H%	S%	xERA	G	L	F	Ctl	Dom	Cmd	hr/f	hr/9	RAR	BPV	R$
RH	Reliever	05	aaa	7	8	0	132	57	5.32	1.71	344			24.5	36%	71%	6.78				2.1	3.9	1.9		1.1	-16.5	15	($1)
Age	34	06	PHI *	6	4	6	79	37	3.28	1.52	296			5.9	32%	79%	4.69	48	23	29	3.0	4.2	1.4	6%	0.6	11.8	19	$8
Type	Con xGB	07	PHI *	6	0	3	72	36	4.55	1.48	296	299	302	6.5	33%	68%	4.47	46	25	28	2.7	4.4	1.7	6%	0.5	-1.1	33	$5
Health	D	08	PHI	3	4	1	69	34	3.26	1.51	304	320	288	5.5	33%	81%	4.21	54	19	27	2.5	4.4	1.8	9%	0.8	8.6	45	$4
PT/Exp	D	09	PHI	6	2	1	42	25	3.00	1.21	238	172	267	3.9	26%	79%	3.66	55	20	24	3.0	5.4	1.8	13%	0.9	6.2	49	$6
Consist	A	1st Half		4	2	1	34	22	3.71	1.32	244			4.4	27%	76%	3.94	52	21	27	3.7	5.8	1.6	14%	1.1	2.0	35	$4
LIMA Plan	C	2nd Half		2	0	0	8	3	0.00	0.75	210			2.4	23%	100%	2.50	67	19	15	0.0	3.4		0%	0.0	4.1	105	$3
Rand Var	-2	10	Proj	5	2	0	58	32	4.03	1.47	284			5.8	31%	74%	3.95	57	20	23	3.1	5.0	1.6	11%	0.8	2.2	40	$4

Oblique strain cost him most of 2H. Health grade and annual drop in IP show that this is a growing concern. Encouraging jump in Dom, but at his age, it's more likely to be noise than a sudden improvement in skills.

Contreras,Jose

Contreras,Jose		Yr	Tm	W	L	Sv	IP	K	ERA	WHIP	OBA	vL	vR	BF/G	H%	S%	xERA	G	L	F	Ctl	Dom	Cmd	hr/f	hr/9	RAR	BPV	R$
RH	Starter	05	CHW	15	7	0	204	154	3.61	1.23	235	231	233	26.5	27%	74%	3.96	44	20	36	3.3	6.8	2.1	11%	1.0	19.1	55	$22
Age	38	06	CHW	13	9	0	196	134	4.27	1.27	260	267	248	27.4	29%	68%	4.17	45	16	39	2.5	6.2	2.4	8%	0.9	6.9	65	$18
Type	Pwr	07	CHW	10	17	0	189	113	5.57	1.56	303	333	270	26.4	33%	65%	4.68	45	19	36	3.0	5.4	1.8	9%	1.0	-24.9	40	$4
Health	C	08	CHW	7	6	0	121	70	4.54	1.36	276	286	258	25.9	30%	68%	4.04	51	19	30	2.6	5.2	2.0	10%	0.9	-2.8	52	$7
PT/Exp	B	09	2TM *	9	14	0	165	129	4.74	1.43	262	252	292	21.7	31%	68%	4.20	47	17	36	3.9	7.0	1.8	9%	0.9	-8.6	48	$8
Consist	A	1st Half		6	8	0	100	69	4.56	1.27	238			26.2	27%	65%	4.15	50	13	37	3.5	6.2	1.8	9%	0.9	-3.1	45	$7
LIMA Plan	C+	2nd Half		3	6	0	65	60	5.01	1.68	297			17.5	37%	71%	4.26	44	21	35	4.5	8.3	1.9	9%	0.9	-5.6	52	$1
Rand Var	0	10	Proj	5	10	0	116	83	4.68	1.48	269			23.1	31%	70%	4.38	47	19	34	4.0	6.5	1.6	10%	0.9	-0.5	34	$5

6-13, 4.92 ERA in 132 IP at CHW and COL. PQS split (39%/43%) says he's a feast or famine pitcher. Steady BPIs set stable yearly expectations amid that chaos, but at his age the ride gets bumpier from here.

BILL MACEY

Cook,Aaron

Cook,Aaron		Yr	Tm	W	L	Sv	IP	K	ERA	WHIP	OBA	vL	vR	BF/G	H%	S%	xERA	G	L	F	Ctl	Dom	Cmd	hr/f	hr/9	RAR	BPV	R$
RH Starter		05	COL	7	2	0	83	24	3.68	1.41	301	313	281	27.7	31%	76%	3.81	62	20	19	1.7	2.6	**1.5**	14%	0.9	5.8	40	$5
Age	31	06	COL	9	15	0	212	92	4.24	1.40	288	314	258	28.6	31%	70%	4.08	58	18	24	2.3	3.9	**1.7**	10%	0.7	6.4	43	$10
Type	Con xGB	07	COL	8	7	0	166	61	4.12	1.34	275	263	295	28.3	29%	71%	4.13	58	19	24	2.4	3.3	**1.4**	11%	0.8	6.3	31	$9
Health	D	08	COL	16	9	0	211	96	3.96	1.34	284	297	276	28.2	31%	70%	3.88	56	20	24	2.0	4.1	**2.0**	7%	0.6	8.1	52	$15
PT/Exp	A	09	COL	11	6	0	158	78	4.16	1.41	282	282	285	25.3	30%	73%	3.98	57	19	25	2.7	4.4	**1.7**	14%	1.1	0.6	42	$9
Consist	A	1st Half		8	3	0	98	50	3.77	1.33	264			26.0	28%	75%	3.86	58	18	24	2.8	4.6	**1.6**	15%	1.1	5.1	42	$8
LIMA Plan	C	2nd Half		3	3	0	60	28	4.80	1.53	310			24.3	33%	71%	4.17	55	19	26	2.4	4.2	**1.8**	13%	1.0	-4.5	44	$1
Rand Var	+1	10	Proj	13	9	0	207	92	4.18	1.39	288			26.2	31%	72%	3.98	57	19	24	2.3	4.0	1.8	11%	0.9	7.2	46	$11

Foot and shoulder problems truncated his 2H. Trend of disaster avoidance ended (21/26% DOM/DIS), continues to use elite GB% as lynchpin of otherwise-mediocre skill set. Like any SP, needs 2.0 Cmd.

Cordero,Francisco

Cordero,Francisco		Yr	Tm	W	L	Sv	IP	K	ERA	WHIP	OBA	vL	vR	BF/G	H%	S%	xERA	G	L	F	Ctl	Dom	Cmd	hr/f	hr/9	RAR	BPV	R$
RH Reliever		05	TEX	3	1	37	69	79	3.39	1.32	239	250	214	4.2	33%	76%	3.40	43	19	38	3.9	10.3	**2.6**	7%	0.7	8.3	101	$19
Age	34	06	2TM	10	5	22	75	84	3.72	1.34	246	286	219	4.2	33%	74%	3.60	40	21	39	3.8	10.1	**2.6**	9%	0.8	7.5	96	$18
Type	Pwr	07	MIL	0	4	44	63	86	2.99	1.11	226	225	212	3.9	34%	74%	2.74	41	17	42	2.6	12.2	**4.8**	7%	0.6	11.2	170	$22
Health	A	08	CIN	5	4	34	70	78	3.33	1.41	235	212	252	4.2	31%	78%	3.77	41	22	37	4.9	10.0	**2.1**	9%	0.8	8.2	67	$19
PT/Exp	A	09	CIN	2	6	39	67	58	2.16	1.32	236	228	256	4.2	30%	84%	3.98	41	23	36	4.0	7.8	**1.9**	3%	0.3	16.7	51	$20
Consist	B	1st Half		0	2	19	33	29	1.91	1.12	212			4.0	27%	83%	3.54	44	21	35	3.3	7.9	**2.4**	3%	0.3	9.3	76	$10
LIMA Plan	D+	2nd Half		2	4	20	34	29	2.40	1.51	258			4.3	33%	84%	4.42	38	25	36	4.8	7.7	**1.6**	3%	0.3	7.4	26	$10
Rand Var	-5	10	Proj	3	5	33	73	70	3.60	1.32	236			4.2	30%	74%	3.85	41	22	37	4.1	8.7	2.1	8%	0.7	3.7	64	$17

Outwardly impressive year, but warning signs abound: Dom and Cmd decline continued (Cmd free-fell in 2H). Outlier hr/f protected S% and in turn ERA. BPV trend and 2H xERA shine light on the hidden risk here.

Cormier,Lance

Cormier,Lance		Yr	Tm	W	L	Sv	IP	K	ERA	WHIP	OBA	vL	vR	BF/G	H%	S%	xERA	G	L	F	Ctl	Dom	Cmd	hr/f	hr/9	RAR	BPV	R$
RH Reliever		05	ARI	7	3	0	79	63	5.12	1.63	278	300	273	5.4	33%	69%	4.21	50	23	27	4.9	7.2	**1.5**	10%	0.8	-8.5	25	$3
Age	29	06	ATL *	8	8	0	127	66	5.23	1.77	323	271	351	15.7	35%	71%	4.96	50	21	29	3.8	4.7	**1.2**	10%	0.9	-11.7	8	($0)
Type	Con GB	07	ATL *	7	9	0	106	55	6.10	1.73	323			22.3	33%	69%	4.81	51	19	30	3.4	4.7	**1.4**	20%	1.9	-21.8	20	($1)
Health	A	08	BAL *	4	4	1	92	57	3.33	1.46	266	240	308	7.3	31%	77%	3.92	57	21	22	3.9	5.6	**1.4**	6%	0.4	11.5	29	$7
PT/Exp	D	09	TAM	3	3	2	77	36	3.26	1.29	256	239	261	6.1	27%	77%	4.35	52	17	30	2.9	4.2	**1.4**	8%	0.7	11.4	27	$7
Consist	B	1st Half		1	1	1	44	23	2.45	1.11	230			7.7	26%	77%	3.97	54	15	32	2.5	4.7	**1.9**	2%	0.2	10.8	50	$5
LIMA Plan	D+	2nd Half		2	2	1	33	13	4.32	1.53	288			4.9	29%	76%	4.86	51	20	28	3.5	3.5	**1.0**	15%	1.4	0.5	-2	$2
Rand Var	-2	10	Proj	2	2	0	44	21	4.14	1.47	277			7.1	30%	73%	4.50	53	19	28	3.5	4.3	1.2	10%	0.8	-0.4	14	$2

GB tilt remains his calling-card skill, but it's been four full years since he complemented that with an acceptable Dom. 2H Cmd says he's no closer to finding the right mix. Pass.

Corpas,Manny

Corpas,Manny		Yr	Tm	W	L	Sv	IP	K	ERA	WHIP	OBA	vL	vR	BF/G	H%	S%	xERA	G	L	F	Ctl	Dom	Cmd	hr/f	hr/9	RAR	BPV	R$
RH Reliever		05		0	0	0	0	0	0.00	0.00							0.00											
Age	27	06	COL *	3	3	19	77	63	2.22	1.06	238	281	290	4.0	29%	81%	3.38	45	20	34	1.6	7.3	**4.5**	5%	0.5	21.6	112	$17
Type	GB	07	COL	4	2	19	78	58	2.08	1.06	223	234	214	4.0	26%	84%	3.25	57	14	28	2.3	6.7	**2.9**	9%	0.7	22.6	94	$18
Health	A	08	COL	3	4	4	80	50	4.52	1.46	293	285	308	4.6	33%	70%	4.00	50	23	28	2.6	5.6	**2.2**	9%	0.8	-2.4	59	$4
PT/Exp	C	09	COL	1	3	1	34	24	5.88	1.51	316	400	267	4.3	37%	60%	3.79	49	22	30	1.9	6.4	**3.4**	9%	0.8	-7.0	92	$0
Consist	A	1st Half		1	3	1	31	23	5.48	1.47	313			4.2	37%	61%	3.62	49	23	28	1.7	6.6	**3.8**	7%	0.6	-5.0	100	$1
LIMA Plan	A	2nd Half		0	0	0	3	1	10.80	2.00	362			6.2	33%	50%	5.92	44	11	44	3.6	3.6	**1.0**	22%	3.6	-2.0	-10	($1)
Rand Var	+5	10	Proj	3	4	9	65	48	3.59	1.26	267			4.1	31%	74%	3.47	52	20	29	2.1	6.6	3.2	10%	0.8	6.4	93	$8

2H elbow surgeries (bone chips, subsequent infection) ended season. Others look at ERA and think he lost closer-in-waiting title, but you look at GB/Dom and Cmd gains, xERA and still see a developing closer.

Correia,Kevin

Correia,Kevin		Yr	Tm	W	L	Sv	IP	K	ERA	WHIP	OBA	vL	vR	BF/G	H%	S%	xERA	G	L	F	Ctl	Dom	Cmd	hr/f	hr/9	RAR	BPV	R$
RH Starter		05	SF *	5	7	7	104	74	5.21	1.57	277	311	242	10.0	30%	71%	4.86	37	24	39	4.4	6.4	**1.4**	13%	1.5	-12.4	10	$4
Age	29	06	SF	2	0	0	69	57	3.51	1.24	247	275	218	6.0	30%	73%	4.21	34	22	44	2.9	7.4	**2.6**	6%	0.7	8.3	68	$6
Type		07	SF	4	7	0	102	80	3.45	1.32	247	217	257	7.3	29%	76%	4.22	45	15	40	3.5	7.1	**2.0**	7%	0.8	12.2	55	$9
Health	B	08	SF *	4	8	0	122	76	5.74	1.63	307	307	312	20.6	34%	66%	4.89	38	25	37	3.5	5.6	**1.6**	10%	1.2	-22.1	24	($2)
PT/Exp	B	09	SD	12	11	0	198	142	3.91	1.30	258	247	269	25.3	30%	71%	4.04	45	19	36	2.9	6.5	**2.2**	8%	0.8	6.9	60	$15
Consist	B	1st Half		5	5	0	87	70	4.24	1.23	243			24.1	28%	68%	3.81	46	16	38	2.9	7.2	**2.5**	10%	1.0	-0.5	76	$7
LIMA Plan	C	2nd Half		7	6	0	111	72	3.65	1.36	269			26.4	31%	74%	4.22	44	21	35	2.9	5.8	**2.0**	6%	0.6	7.4	48	$8
Rand Var	0	10	Proj	9	11	0	193	141	4.10	1.38	270			15.1	31%	73%	4.23	42	20	37	3.1	6.6	2.1	10%	1.0	0.9	56	$11

What looks like a breakout is really just an extension of what he did in SF in '06-'07. GB and Dom look like basis of continued success, 2H Dom slide a yellow (not red) flag, Petco increases margin of error. Serviceable.

Crain,Jesse

Crain,Jesse		Yr	Tm	W	L	Sv	IP	K	ERA	WHIP	OBA	vL	vR	BF/G	H%	S%	xERA	G	L	F	Ctl	Dom	Cmd	hr/f	hr/9	RAR	BPV	R$
RH Reliever		05	MIN	12	5	1	79	25	2.73	1.14	215	194	225	4.3	22%	79%	4.89	46	16	37	3.3	2.8	**0.9**	6%	0.7	16.1	-13	$13
Age	28	06	MIN	4	5	1	76	60	3.54	1.27	269	259	263	4.7	32%	74%	3.22	55	21	24	2.1	7.1	**3.3**	11%	0.7	9.5	103	$9
Type	Pwr	07	MIN	1	2	0	16	10	5.52	1.41	292	269	308	3.9	29%	68%	4.30	48	14	38	2.2	5.5	**2.5**	19%	2.2	-2.0	66	$1
Health	D	08	MIN	5	4	0	63	50	3.59	1.37	260	250	261	4.1	31%	76%	4.28	41	17	42	3.4	7.2	**2.1**	8%	0.9	5.9	55	$6
PT/Exp	D	09	MIN *	8	4	1	67	61	4.28	1.47	246	297	221	4.4	31%	70%	4.46	43	16	41	4.9	8.2	**1.6**	4%	0.4	1.4	34	$7
Consist	A	1st Half		2	3	0	26	23	6.53	1.76	282			4.2	34%	63%	5.07	42	17	42	5.8	7.9	**1.4**	9%	1.0	-6.7	4	($0)
LIMA Plan	C	2nd Half		6	1	1	41	38	2.85	1.29	222			4.6	30%	75%	4.08	44	15	41	4.4	8.3	**1.9**	0%	0.0	8.1	53	$7
Rand Var	-2	10	Proj	6	4	0	58	47	4.19	1.43	252			4.4	30%	73%	4.42	44	16	40	4.3	7.3	1.7	9%	0.9	0.1	36	$6

Compare '09 skills to '06, and it is easy to see he isn't the same pitcher following '07 shoulder surgery. Cmd trend troubling, GBs no longer the great equalizer. Until further notice, treat him like '06 didn't happen.

Cruz,Juan

Cruz,Juan		Yr	Tm	W	L	Sv	IP	K	ERA	WHIP	OBA	vL	vR	BF/G	H%	S%	xERA	G	L	F	Ctl	Dom	Cmd	hr/f	hr/9	RAR	BPV	R$
RH Reliever		05	OAK *	5	4	0	107	111	4.03	1.32	235	283	296	11.1	31%	70%	3.54	45	19	35	4.0	9.3	**2.3**	9%	0.8	4.5	82	$10
Age	31	06	ARI	5	6	0	94	88	4.20	1.35	231	263	199	13.0	29%	69%	4.12	40	23	37	4.5	8.4	**1.9**	7%	0.7	3.3	48	$8
Type	Pwr xFB	07	ARI	6	1	0	61	87	3.10	1.26	207	269	143	4.8	31%	80%	3.23	35	19	47	4.7	12.8	**2.7**	12%	1.0	10.0	116	$10
Health	D	08	ARI	4	0	0	52	71	2.61	1.26	189	159	221	3.8	28%	83%	3.72	27	16	57	5.4	12.4	**2.3**	8%	0.9	10.6	82	$8
PT/Exp	D	09	KC	3	4	2	50	38	5.73	1.49	245	244	247	4.8	28%	62%	5.54	24	22	54	5.2	6.8	**1.3**	7%	1.1	-7.9	-16	$2
Consist	C	1st Half		3	2	2	33	24	4.91	1.36	225			4.9	25%	66%	5.63	16	23	61	4.9	6.5	**1.3**	7%	1.1	-1.9	-20	$3
LIMA Plan	C+	2nd Half		0	2	0	17	14	7.28	1.73	280			4.7	33%	57%	5.30	37	20	43	5.7	7.3	**1.3**	9%	1.0	-6.0	-8	($1)
Rand Var	+1	10	Proj	3	3	0	58	56	4.34	1.48	245			4.8	30%	73%	4.74	30	20	50	5.1	8.7	1.7	9%	1.1	-2.2	27	$4

Shoulder strain cost him most of the summer, 1H results and evaporation of Dom suggest he may have been pitching hurt even before he hit the DL. Even if Dom bounces back, Ctl and xFB combo can cause anxiety.

Cueto,Johnny

Cueto,Johnny		Yr	Tm	W	L	Sv	IP	K	ERA	WHIP	OBA	vL	vR	BF/G	H%	S%	xERA	G	L	F	Ctl	Dom	Cmd	hr/f	hr/9	RAR	BPV	R$
RH Starter		05		0	0	0	0	0	0.00	0.00							0.00											
Age	24	06		0	0	0	0	0	0.00	0.00							0.00											
Type	Pwr FB	07	a/a	8	4	0	83	88	3.41	1.15	261			24.1	33%	74%	3.92				1.3	9.6	**7.1**		1.0	10.8	179	$13
Health	A	08	CIN	9	14	0	174	158	4.81	1.41	266	249	275	24.3	31%	71%	4.09	39	21	41	3.5	8.2	**2.3**	14%	1.5	-11.6	69	$9
PT/Exp	B	09	CIN	11	11	0	171	132	4.41	1.36	263	250	274	24.4	30%	71%	4.22	42	18	41	3.2	6.9	**2.2**	11%	1.3	-4.7	58	$11
Consist	A	1st Half		8	4	0	103	78	2.70	1.12	224			26.1	25%	82%	3.94	42	16	42	2.8	6.8	**2.4**	10%	1.0	18.9	67	$14
LIMA Plan	C+	2nd Half		3	7	0	68	54	7.00	1.72	314			22.6	36%	61%	4.65	41	20	39	3.8	7.1	**1.9**	14%	1.6	-23.6	44	($3)
Rand Var	0	10	Proj	14	11	0	189	163	4.25	1.32	257			23.5	30%	72%	3.96	40	20	40	3.1	7.8	2.5	12%	1.2	6.9	76	$16

Essentially repeated rookie skills, but reminded us of the risks rather than the upside: 1H workload followed by 2H slide in Ctl, plus DL (shoulder) stint. Top '07 prospect still owns better skills. Patience.

Daley,Matt

Daley,Matt		Yr	Tm	W	L	Sv	IP	K	ERA	WHIP	OBA	vL	vR	BF/G	H%	S%	xERA	G	L	F	Ctl	Dom	Cmd	hr/f	hr/9	RAR	BPV	R$
RH Reliever		05		0	0	0	0	0	0.00	0.00							0.00											
Age	27	06		0	0	0	0	0	0.00	0.00							0.00											
Type	Pwr xFB	07	aa	2	6	0	95	68	5.36	1.44	295			9.6	32%	67%	5.89				2.3	6.4	**2.8**		1.7	-10.6	42	$2
Health	A	08	aaa	4	6	1	66	49	4.70	1.70	292			4.9	34%	74%	5.71				4.9	6.6	**1.4**		0.9	-3.2	37	$2
PT/Exp	D	09	COL	1	1	0	51	55	4.24	1.20	230	266	206	3.7	29%	67%	3.81	34	11	55	3.2	9.7	**3.1**	8%	1.1	-0.3	101	$4
Consist	C	1st Half		0	1	0	16	14	4.44	1.23	235			3.7	29%	63%	4.31	34	13	53	3.3	7.8	**2.3**	4%	0.6	-0.5	62	$1
LIMA Plan	B+	2nd Half		1	0	0	35	41	4.14	1.18	228			3.7	30%	69%	3.58	33	11	56	3.1	10.6	**3.4**	10%	1.3	0.2	118	$3
Rand Var	0	10	Proj	2	3	0	58	54	4.66	1.38	262			4.5	31%	70%	4.43	34	12	55	3.4	8.4	2.5	10%	1.4	-1.2	70	$3

Eye-popping 2H Dom, but the good news ends there. History doesn't support a Dom repeat xFB profile a monumentally bad approach for Coors. Talk him up as closer-in-waiting, then casually forget to bid.

RAY MURPHY

Danks,John

		Yr	Tm	W	L	Sv	IP	K	ERA	WHIP	OBA	vL	vR	BF/G	H%	S%	xERA	G	L	F	Ctl	Dom	Cmd	hr/f	hr/9	RAR	BPV	R$
LH	Starter	05	aa	4	10	0	98	77	6.82	1.67	322			25.0	37%	60%	6.51				3.0	7.0	2.4		1.4	-30.4	41	($3)
Age	24	06	a/a	9	9	0	140	140	5.69	1.59	296			23.4	35%	69%	6.45				3.6	9.0	2.5		1.9	-20.3	45	$5
Type		07	CHW	6	13	0	139	109	5.50	1.54	290	281	292	23.8	32%	69%	4.78	35	19	46	3.5	7.1	2.0	14%	1.8	-17.1	45	$4
Health	A	08	CHW	12	9	0	195	159	3.32	1.23	249	264	240	24.5	30%	75%	3.71	43	22	35	2.6	7.3	2.8	7%	0.7	24.6	82	$22
PT/Exp	A	09	CHW	13	11	0	200	149	3.77	1.28	246	244	246	26.3	27%	76%	4.26	44	15	41	3.3	6.7	2.0	11%	1.3	16.7	54	$19
Consist	B	1st Half		6	6	0	88	80	4.09	1.28	246			24.7	29%	72%	3.74	46	17	37	3.3	8.2	2.5	12%	1.1	4.0	83	$9
LIMA Plan	D+	2nd Half		7	5	0	112	69	3.53	1.28	246			27.7	26%	79%	4.68	43	14	44	3.3	5.5	1.7	11%	1.4	12.8	31	$11
Rand Var	0	10	Proj	12	12	0	203	158	4.17	1.36	265			25.6	30%	73%	4.22	42	18	40	3.1	7.0	2.2	11%	1.2	5.3	61	$16

Skill-wise, 1H was a worthy follow-up to 2008 breakout. Sudden Dom loss headlined 2H skill collapse, masked by h%. Two straight years of high IP at still-young age, coupled with Dom loss, casts shadow on '10.

Davies,Kyle

		Yr	Tm	W	L	Sv	IP	K	ERA	WHIP	OBA	vL	vR	BF/G	H%	S%	xERA	G	L	F	Ctl	Dom	Cmd	hr/f	hr/9	RAR	BPV	R$
RH	Starter	05	ATL	* 12	8	0	160	119	4.57	1.57	274	264	295	21.2	32%	72%	4.92	34	25	41	4.6	6.7	1.5	7%	0.8	-6.3	9	$7
Age	26	06	ATL	3	7	0	63	51	8.42	1.95	336	333	331	21.9	37%	59%	5.23	37	24	39	4.7	7.3	1.5	17%	2.0	-30.6	19	($5)
Type	Pwr FB	07	2TM	7	15	0	136	99	6.09	1.65	288	275	293	22.2	32%	66%	5.08	39	21	41	4.6	6.6	1.4	12%	1.5	-27.3	10	$0
Health	B	08	KC	* 15	9	0	170	101	3.70	1.46	275	251	300	23.3	31%	76%	4.84	39	22	40	3.5	5.3	1.5	6%	0.8	13.7	18	$14
PT/Exp	C	09	KC	* 12	11	0	169	120	4.63	1.55	276	239	284	25.2	31%	73%	4.90	42	17	41	4.3	6.4	1.5	10%	1.1	-3.7	19	$9
Consist	A	1st Half		6	7	0	98	68	4.77	1.45	254			25.3	28%	70%	4.83	43	17	40	4.4	6.2	1.4	11%	1.3	-3.8	13	$5
LIMA Plan	D+	2nd Half		6	4	0	71	52	4.43	1.69	304			25.2	35%	76%	5.01	42	15	43	4.2	6.6	1.6	7%	0.9	0.2	27	$3
Rand Var	0	10	Proj	9	11	0	158	114	4.78	1.53	274			25.1	31%	71%	4.80	40	19	41	4.2	6.5	1.6	10%	1.1	-7.2	23	$7

8-9, 5.27 ERA in 123 IP at KC. Failed to sustain Cmd gains from 2H 2008, and plunged right back into mediocrity. 2008 Ctl now an outlier, otherwise-consistent 4+ Ctl makes him unrosterable. xERA history says it all.

Davis,Doug

		Yr	Tm	W	L	Sv	IP	K	ERA	WHIP	OBA	vL	vR	BF/G	H%	S%	xERA	G	L	F	Ctl	Dom	Cmd	hr/f	hr/9	RAR	BPV	R$
LH	Starter	05	MIL	11	11	0	222	208	3.85	1.30	238	259	228	26.8	29%	74%	3.71	44	20	36	3.8	8.4	2.2	12%	1.1	10.9	72	$19
Age	34	06	MIL	11	11	0	203	159	4.92	1.52	265	307	253	26.5	31%	68%	4.56	44	20	36	4.5	7.0	1.6	9%	0.8	-10.8	27	$8
Type	Pwr	07	ARI	13	12	0	193	144	4.25	1.59	280	252	290	26.3	32%	75%	4.55	47	19	34	4.4	6.7	1.5	10%	1.0	4.2	26	$10
Health	A	08	ARI	6	8	0	146	112	4.32	1.53	280	321	269	25.0	33%	73%	4.21	47	22	31	3.9	6.9	1.8	9%	0.8	-0.8	43	$5
PT/Exp	A	09	ARI	9	14	0	203	146	4.12	1.51	261	264	268	26.5	29%	76%	4.60	43	22	35	4.6	6.5	1.4	11%	1.1	1.8	14	$8
Consist	A	1st Half		3	8	0	98	73	3.30	1.36	243			26.3	28%	80%	4.28	43	22	35	4.1	6.7	1.6	11%	1.0	10.8	31	$6
LIMA Plan	D+	2nd Half		6	6	0	105	73	4.88	1.64	278			26.6	31%	73%	4.91	43	22	36	5.0	6.3	1.3	12%	1.2	-9.0	-1	$2
Rand Var	0	10	Proj	10	12	0	196	144	4.32	1.50	265			26.2	30%	73%	4.47	45	21	34	4.4	6.6	1.5	10%	1.0	-5.0	24	$9

Hot start with hit/strand rates made him a popular 1H pickup, inflicted predictable damage in 2H. Slight GB bias does little to mitigate the "too many BB, too many HR" cocktail. Roster only with flame-retardant gear.

Davis,Wade

		Yr	Tm	W	L	Sv	IP	K	ERA	WHIP	OBA	vL	vR	BF/G	H%	S%	xERA	G	L	F	Ctl	Dom	Cmd	hr/f	hr/9	RAR	BPV	R$
RH	Starter	05		0	0	0	0	0	0.00	0.00							0.00											
Age	24	06		0	0	0	0	0	0.00	0.00							0.00											
Type	Pwr	07	aa	7	3	0	80	71	3.83	1.44	271			24.9	34%	72%	4.16				3.5	8.0	2.3		0.3	6.3	87	$8
Health	A	08	a/a	13	8	0	160	117	3.99	1.40	260			24.7	30%	73%	4.21				3.7	6.6	1.8		0.7	6.3	58	$13
PT/Exp	D	09	TAM	* 12	10	0	195	159	4.12	1.37	260	238	250	24.6	31%	71%	4.15	39	25	36	3.4	7.4	2.1	9%	0.8	8.0	57	$16
Consist	A	1st Half		8	4	0	95	70	3.51	1.44	270			24.4	32%	76%	4.28				3.6	6.6	1.8		0.6	11.1	62	$9
LIMA Plan	D+	2nd Half		4	6	0	100	89	4.70	1.31	251			24.7	30%	66%	3.87	39	25	36	3.3	8.1	2.5	12%	1.1	-3.1	74	$7
Rand Var	0	10	Proj	13	9	0	178	143	3.94	1.38	261			24.7	30%	74%	4.18	39	25	36	3.5	7.2	2.1	10%	1.0	5.6	53	$16

2-2, 3.72 ERA in 36 IP at TAM. Rays have taken their time in developing him, 2H Cmd spike and Sept success in TAM (87 BPV in MLB) suggest he's ready for the bigs.
UP: 3.50 ERA.

de la Rosa,Jorge

		Yr	Tm	W	L	Sv	IP	K	ERA	WHIP	OBA	vL	vR	BF/G	H%	S%	xERA	G	L	F	Ctl	Dom	Cmd	hr/f	hr/9	RAR	BPV	R$
LH	Starter	05	MIL	2	2	0	42	42	4.49	2.04	288	321	273	5.5	38%	76%	4.96	49	23	28	8.1	9.0	1.1	3%	0.2	-1.3	-31	($1)
Age	29	06	2TM	* 8	7	0	109	85	5.72	1.66	286	250	269	14.7	33%	67%	4.90	41	20	39	4.7	7.0	1.5	11%	1.2	-16.1	17	$3
Type	Pwr	07	KC	8	12	0	130	82	5.82	1.64	304	234	321	22.8	33%	67%	5.01	41	20	39	3.7	5.7	1.5	12%	1.4	-21.0	22	$2
Health	B	08	COL	* 13	8	0	152	145	4.56	1.47	263	289	253	20.9	33%	70%	3.90	46	20	34	4.2	8.6	2.1	9%	0.8	-5.4	65	$11
PT/Exp	B	09	COL	16	9	0	185	193	4.38	1.38	248	204	262	24.1	32%	70%	3.56	45	21	34	4.0	9.4	2.3	12%	1.0	-4.3	83	$16
Consist	B	1st Half		4	7	0	81	87	5.66	1.49	266			23.9	34%	63%	3.66	44	21	35	4.2	9.7	2.3	12%	1.0	-14.7	82	$2
LIMA Plan	C	2nd Half		12	2	0	104	106	3.38	1.29	233			24.3	29%	77%	3.48	45	22	34	3.9	9.2	2.4	12%	1.0	10.4	83	$14
Rand Var	+1	10	Proj	15	10	0	181	181	4.17	1.37	247			18.5	31%	71%	3.70	44	21	35	4.0	9.0	2.2	10%	0.9	12.6	75	$16

Elite Dom and healthy GB will play well anywhere, even Coors Field. Thin air may keep ERA from matching xERA, but strikeouts provide value, and trends say we haven't yet seen his best... UP: 18 W, 3.75 ERA.

Delcarmen,Manny

		Yr	Tm	W	L	Sv	IP	K	ERA	WHIP	OBA	vL	vR	BF/G	H%	S%	xERA	G	L	F	Ctl	Dom	Cmd	hr/f	hr/9	RAR	BPV	R$
RH	Reliever	05	a/a	7	5	5	59	62	3.20	1.44	248			5.7	33%	78%	3.84				4.6	9.5	2.1		0.5	8.0	92	$9
Age	28	06	BOS	* 2	1	0	70	62	4.62	1.44	283	319	302	5.1	36%	66%	3.69	45	26	30	3.0	8.0	2.7	3%	0.3	-0.6	86	$4
Type	Pwr	07	BOS	* 3	2	1	73	73	3.10	1.29	232	167	194	4.8	30%	77%	3.75	45	17	38	4.0	8.9	2.3	7%	0.6	12.7	77	$9
Health	A	08	BOS	1	2	2	74	72	3.27	1.12	208	190	218	4.1	27%	72%	3.28	52	13	35	3.4	8.7	2.6	7%	0.6	9.9	95	$9
PT/Exp	D	09	BOS	5	2	0	60	44	4.52	1.64	275	221	322	4.3	32%	73%	5.09	42	17	40	5.1	6.6	1.3	7%	0.8	-0.5	1	$3
Consist	C	1st Half		2	1	0	31	23	2.03	1.39	249			4.3	31%	84%	4.34	45	20	35	4.1	6.7	1.6	0%	0.0	9.3	34	$4
LIMA Plan	C+	2nd Half		3	1	0	29	21	7.21	1.92	302			4.2	33%	64%	5.95	40	15	46	6.3	6.6	1.1	11%	1.6	-9.8	-33	($1)
Rand Var	-2	10	Proj	3	2	0	51	43	4.08	1.42	255			4.3	31%	73%	4.23	45	17	39	4.1	7.6	1.9	9%	0.9	1.3	50	$4

Startling loss of Cmd derailed his march to closer-worthiness. Fewer GBs, big problems with RH batters, 2H Ctl jump all point to loss of stuff, possible physical issue. Worth an early season claim if issues resolved.

Dempster,Ryan

		Yr	Tm	W	L	Sv	IP	K	ERA	WHIP	OBA	vL	vR	BF/G	H%	S%	xERA	G	L	F	Ctl	Dom	Cmd	hr/f	hr/9	RAR	BPV	R$
RH	Starter	05	CHC	5	3	33	92	89	3.13	1.43	242	278	216	6.4	32%	78%	3.28	58	21	21	4.8	8.7	1.8	7%	0.4	12.7	63	$19
Age	32	06	CHC	1	9	24	75	67	4.80	1.51	267	310	226	4.5	33%	68%	3.94	52	18	30	4.3	8.0	1.9	7%	0.6	-2.9	58	$10
Type	Pwr	07	CHC	2	7	28	67	55	4.72	1.33	239	259	224	4.3	28%	67%	3.98	47	20	32	4.0	7.4	1.8	13%	1.1	-2.4	49	$13
Health	B	08	CHC	17	6	0	207	187	2.96	1.21	230	243	213	25.9	29%	77%	3.47	48	20	32	3.3	8.1	2.5	8%	0.6	33.4	83	$26
PT/Exp	A	09	CHC	11	9	0	200	172	3.65	1.31	258	281	241	27.3	31%	75%	3.65	47	18	34	2.9	7.7	2.6	11%	1.0	13.4	86	$17
Consist	A	1st Half		4	5	0	99	80	4.09	1.36	250			26.5	29%	73%	4.11	44	19	37	3.8	7.3	1.9	10%	1.0	1.2	50	$6
LIMA Plan	C+	2nd Half		7	4	0	101	92	3.21	1.25	266			28.1	32%	78%	3.23	50	17	32	2.0	8.2	4.0	12%	1.0	12.2	121	$11
Rand Var	0	10	Proj	13	10	0	199	175	3.57	1.27	249			26.9	30%	74%	3.54	48	19	32	3.0	7.9	2.6	10%	0.9	17.8	87	$19

Skill-wise, a carbon copy of 2008 breakout, just a few more hits and HR fell in. 2H GB% and Cmd spikes hint at old dog learning new tricks, at minimum show that he's ok with SP workload. Bid on a repeat.

Dessens,Elmer

		Yr	Tm	W	L	Sv	IP	K	ERA	WHIP	OBA	vL	vR	BF/G	H%	S%	xERA	G	L	F	Ctl	Dom	Cmd	hr/f	hr/9	RAR	BPV	R$
RH	Reliever	05	LA	1	2	0	65	37	3.59	1.26	255	236	254	9.7	28%	74%	3.98	50	19	31	2.6	5.1	1.9	9%	0.8	5.3	49	$4
Age	39	06	2TM	5	8	2	77	52	4.56	1.40	284	267	292	5.4	32%	69%	4.10	45	23	31	2.6	6.1	2.4	10%	0.9	-0.4	63	$6
Type	Con	07	2NL	* 5	2	0	60	41	4.95	1.32	274			10.6	31%	63%	4.48				2.3	6.2	2.7		0.9	-3.9	67	$4
Health	B	08	ATL	0	1	0	4	2	22.50	3.50	470			6.4	49%	31%	15.58				9.0	4.5	0.5		2.3	-9.0	-69	($3)
PT/Exp	F	09	NYM	* 3	2	11	68	35	3.16	1.15	230	193	228	5.0	24%	77%	4.73	38	14	48	2.7	4.7	1.7	7%	1.0	8.6	27	$10
Consist	F	1st Half		3	2	11	41	27	3.43	1.17	236			5.4	26%	74%	3.75	59	6	35	2.7	5.9	2.1	9%	0.9	3.8	69	$8
LIMA Plan	C	2nd Half		0	0	0	27	9	2.74	1.10	221			4.5	21%	81%	5.30	34	15	51	2.7	2.9	1.0	7%	1.1	4.8	-10	$2
Rand Var	-5	10	Proj	1	1	0	15	7	3.72	1.31	255			6.1	26%	76%	4.74	43	19	38	3.1	4.3	1.4	11%	1.2	-0.9	15	$1

0-0, 3.31 ERA in 33 IP at NYM. Back in 2002, went 7-8, 3.03 in 178 IP with CIN. He's been irrelevant basically ever since, despite the fact that he keeps finding work. Even that should be coming to an end soon.

Detwiler,Ross

		Yr	Tm	W	L	Sv	IP	K	ERA	WHIP	OBA	vL	vR	BF/G	H%	S%	xERA	G	L	F	Ctl	Dom	Cmd	hr/f	hr/9	RAR	BPV	R$
LH	Starter	05		0	0	0	0	0	0.00	0.00							0.00											
Age	24	06		0	0	0	0	0	0.00	0.00							0.00											
Type		07		0	0	0	0	0	0.00	0.00							0.00											
Health	A	08		0	0	0	0	0	0.00	0.00							0.00											
PT/Exp	D	09	WAS	* 5	11	0	152	103	4.50	1.64	303	288	289	22.3	35%	72%	4.55	43	25	32	3.7	6.1	1.6	5%	0.5	-5.9	30	$1
Consist	F	1st Half		0	7	0	71	53	4.80	1.56	295			22.8	35%	69%	4.31	43	22	34	3.4	6.7	2.0	6%	0.6	-5.3	50	($0)
LIMA Plan	C+	2nd Half		5	4	0	81	50	4.24	1.71	310			22.0	36%	74%	4.73	42	29	29	4.0	5.6	1.4	4%	0.3	-0.5	12	$1
Rand Var	0	10	Proj	5	9	0	137	92	4.60	1.51	278			23.3	32%	70%	4.47	43	26	32	3.8	6.0	1.6	9%	0.8	-3.4	27	$4

1-6, 5.00 ERA in 76 IP at WAS. Hot start got him a May callup, but skills didn't carry over (8.2 Dom in minors, 5.1 in majors). GB tilt and minors Dom suggest he may be worth waiting for, but more seasoning needed.

RAY MURPHY

Devine,Joey

		Yr	Tm	W	L	Sv	IP	K	ERA	WHIP	OBA	vL	vR	BF/G	H%	S%	xERA	G	L	F	Ctl	Dom	Cmd	hr/f	hr/9	RAR	BPV	R$
RH	Reliever	05	ATL *	1	2	5	26	28	5.88	1.96	297			5.3	36%	74%	7.19				6.9	9.7	**1.4**		1.7	-5.3	31	$1
Age	26	06	ATL *	2	0	0	17	28	5.26	1.64	212	333	286	4.6	35%	69%	4.03	13	38	50	7.9	14.7	**1.9**	12%	1.1	-1.6	43	$1
Type	Pwr FB	07	ATL *	6	4	20	65	72	2.27	1.30	235	300	211	4.6	33%	83%	3.24	57	9	35	3.9	9.9	**2.5**	4%	0.3	17.4	107	$17
Health	F	08	OAK	6	1	1	46	49	0.59	0.83	151	197	120	4.1	22%	92%	3.06	39	18	43	3.0	9.6	**3.3**	0%	0.0	21.2	111	$13
PT/Exp	D	09	OAK	0	0	0	0	0	0.00	0.00							0.00											
Consist	A	1st Half		0	0	0	0	0	0.00	0.00							0.00											
LIMA Plan	C+	2nd Half		0	0	0	0	0	0.00	0.00							0.00											
Rand Var		10	Proj	**6**	**2**	**0**	**54**	**49**	**3.50**	**1.33**	**247**			**4.6**	**30%**	**77%**	**4.07**	**41**	**18**	**42**	**3.7**	**8.2**	**2.2**	**9%**	**1.0**	**2.4**	**67**	**$7**

Full year lost to April TJ surgery. Working toward being ready for Opening Day, will likely be handled carefully, with role expanding as he demonstrates Cmd again. Still a closer-worthy skill set lurking here.

Dickey,R.A.

		Yr	Tm	W	L	Sv	IP	K	ERA	WHIP	OBA	vL	vR	BF/G	H%	S%	xERA	G	L	F	Ctl	Dom	Cmd	hr/f	hr/9	RAR	BPV	R$
RH	Reliever	05	TEX *	2	8	0	150	78	7.30	1.80	335	200	297	25.3	36%	59%	4.84	52	17	31	3.4	4.7	**1.4**	11%	1.1	-54.3	21	($11)
Age	35	06	aaa	9	8	1	131	50	7.87	1.77	327			28.0	32%	57%	7.53				3.6	3.5	**1.0**		1.9	-54.2	-26	($7)
Type		07	aaa	13	6	0	169	103	4.99	1.56	291			24.4	32%	70%	5.65				3.6	5.5	**1.5**		1.2	-10.9	26	$7
Health	A	08	SEA *	7	13	0	162	81	5.00	1.61	304	260	306	18.8	33%	70%	4.96	46	17	36	3.4	4.5	**1.3**	8%	1.0	-13.0	15	$2
PT/Exp	D	09	MIN *	3	2	0	97	56	5.19	1.64	305	246	326	11.1	34%	69%	4.89	47	18	35	3.6	5.2	**1.4**	8%	0.8	-8.9	20	$0
Consist	A	1st Half		1	0	0	45	33	2.39	1.33	248			8.0	28%	87%	4.03	51	16	33	3.6	6.6	**1.8**	11%	1.0	11.5	51	$5
LIMA Plan	C	2nd Half		2	2	0	52	23	7.61	1.91	347			15.8	37%	58%	5.85	39	23	39	3.7	4.0	**1.1**	5%	0.7	-20.4	-11	($4)
Rand Var	+1	10	Proj	**2**	**2**	**0**	**44**	**24**	**5.17**	**1.59**	**298**			**15.1**	**32%**	**69%**	**4.87**	**47**	**18**	**36**	**3.5**	**5.0**	**1.4**	**9%**	**1.0**	**-2.3**	**19**	**$1**

1-1, 4.62 ERA in 64 IP at MIN. Knuckleballer briefly found the magic formula for GBs and near-tolerable Cmd in 1H, but couldn't hold on to it. He's just an empty innings-eater in MLB, not worthy of same role for you.

DiFelice,Mark

		Yr	Tm	W	L	Sv	IP	K	ERA	WHIP	OBA	vL	vR	BF/G	H%	S%	xERA	G	L	F	Ctl	Dom	Cmd	hr/f	hr/9	RAR	BPV	R$
RH	Reliever	05	aaa	1	2	0	30	16	8.90	1.90	342			10.3	34%	57%	8.71				4.0	4.9	**1.2**		2.6	-17.0	-37	($4)
Age	33	06	ind	12	9	0	158	112	3.87	1.31	280			26.7	32%	72%	4.33				1.9	6.4	**3.3**		0.7	12.6	84	$15
Type	Pwr xFB	07	a/a	10	3	0	125	101	3.20	1.13	259			14.1	31%	74%	3.63				1.3	7.3	**5.7**		0.8	19.5	142	$17
Health	A	08	aaa	5	1	0	64	56	3.70	1.02	240			19.4	29%	65%	2.92				1.2	7.9	**6.7**		0.7	4.8	172	$9
PT/Exp	D	09	MIL	4	1	0	52	48	3.66	1.24	252	278	233	3.6	31%	74%	4.16	26	20	54	2.6	8.4	**3.2**	8%	1.0	3.4	84	$6
Consist	B	1st Half		4	0	0	30	28	1.79	0.86	198			3.8	24%	87%	3.30	35	17	48	1.5	8.4	**5.6**	8%	0.9	8.9	123	$7
LIMA Plan	C+	2nd Half		0	1	0	22	20	6.25	1.76	315			3.5	38%	66%	5.38	16	23	61	4.2	8.3	**2.0**	7%	1.2	-5.5	31	($1)
Rand Var	-1	10	Proj	**4**	**2**	**0**	**59**	**51**	**4.31**	**1.35**	**267**			**5.8**	**31%**	**73%**	**4.61**	**22**	**21**	**57**	**2.9**	**7.8**	**2.7**	**9%**	**1.4**	**-2.5**	**63**	**$4**

Elite minors BPIs carried over fairly well in first full MLB season. FB% got downright scary in 2H, will be his ongoing bugaboo. Cmd will keep him employed, but age works against any future saves opps.

Dolsi,Freddy

		Yr	Tm	W	L	Sv	IP	K	ERA	WHIP	OBA	vL	vR	BF/G	H%	S%	xERA	G	L	F	Ctl	Dom	Cmd	hr/f	hr/9	RAR	BPV	R$
RH	Reliever	05		0	0	0	0	0	0.00	0.00							0.00											
Age	27	06		0	0	0	0	0	0.00	0.00							0.00											
Type	GB	07		0	0	0	0	0	0.00	0.00							0.00											
Health	A	08	DET *	1	5	5	60	36	3.47	1.52	256	364	215	5.4	29%	77%	4.55	51	22	27	5.0	5.4	**1.1**	6%	0.5	6.5	-7	$4
PT/Exp	F	09	DET *	5	3	10	62	29	4.64	1.56	294	368	261	6.2	33%	68%	4.35	60	15	25	3.4	4.2	**1.2**	4%	0.3	-1.4	22	$6
Consist	A	1st Half		2	2	4	35	16	5.27	1.58	303			5.9	33%	64%	4.71	53	18	29	3.2	4.0	**1.3**	3%	0.3	-3.6	17	$2
LIMA Plan	C	2nd Half		3	1	6	27	14	3.80	1.53	282			6.6	32%	74%	4.03	65	13	22	3.8	4.6	**1.2**	5%	0.3	2.1	24	$4
Rand Var	-1	10	Proj	**2**	**2**	**0**	**29**	**15**	**4.34**	**1.48**	**275**			**5.8**	**30%**	**71%**	**4.37**	**54**	**20**	**26**	**3.7**	**4.7**	**1.3**	**8%**	**0.6**	**0.2**	**15**	**$2**

1-0, 1.69 ERA in 11 IP at DET. When GBs aren't enough: not enough K's yield terrible Cmd, has no answer for LH batters. And while not exactly old, it's getting a little late for him to suddenly become effective.

Dotel,Octavio

		Yr	Tm	W	L	Sv	IP	K	ERA	WHIP	OBA	vL	vR	BF/G	H%	S%	xERA	G	L	F	Ctl	Dom	Cmd	hr/f	hr/9	RAR	BPV	R$
RH	Reliever	05	OAK	1	2	7	15	16	3.58	1.39	190	269	107	4.3	23%	79%	4.72	24	26	50	6.6	9.5	**1.5**	11%	1.2	1.5	-4	$4
Age	36	06	NYY	0	0	0	10	7	10.80	2.90	390	333	414	4.2	43%	63%	8.46	37	20	44	9.9	6.3	**0.6**	12%	1.8	-7.7	-139	($3)
Type	Pwr xFB	07	2TM	2	1	11	31	41	4.10	1.34	251	265	225	4.0	35%	73%	3.25	38	16	46	3.5	12.0	**3.4**	12%	1.2	1.4	137	$7
Health	F	08	CHW	4	4	1	67	92	3.76	1.21	216	240	194	3.8	29%	77%	3.06	38	16	46	3.9	12.4	**3.2**	18%	1.6	4.8	133	$9
PT/Exp	C	09	CHW	3	3	0	62	75	3.32	1.44	235	268	226	4.4	32%	81%	4.19	30	19	51	5.2	10.8	**2.1**	9%	1.0	8.7	62	$6
Consist	B	1st Half		1	2	0	30	39	3.28	1.56	234			3.9	33%	82%	4.24	30	21	49	6.3	11.6	**1.9**	9%	0.9	4.4	48	$3
LIMA Plan	B+	2nd Half		2	1	0	32	36	3.36	1.34	236			5.1	31%	79%	4.14	29	17	54	4.2	10.1	**2.4**	9%	1.1	4.3	75	$4
Rand Var	-3	10	Proj	**4**	**3**	**8**	**65**	**77**	**3.86**	**1.35**	**230**			**4.2**	**30%**	**76%**	**3.87**	**34**	**18**	**48**	**4.6**	**10.6**	**2.3**	**12%**	**1.2**	**4.5**	**80**	**$10**

Can still blow it by hitters with regularity, but age-related cracks starting to show: see 1H Ctl, 2H FB issues; both part of longer-term trends. Still a worthwhile play if you're willing to trade a HR for a couple of K.

Downs,Scott

		Yr	Tm	W	L	Sv	IP	K	ERA	WHIP	OBA	vL	vR	BF/G	H%	S%	xERA	G	L	F	Ctl	Dom	Cmd	hr/f	hr/9	RAR	BPV	R$
LH	Reliever	05	TOR *	6	6	0	133	104	4.82	1.38	281	234	262	17.3	32%	68%	3.35	54	22	24	2.5	7.1	**2.8**	18%	1.2	-7.4	91	$7
Age	34	06	TOR	6	2	1	77	61	4.09	1.34	252	232	258	5.6	29%	72%	3.59	56	18	26	3.5	7.1	**2.0**	15%	1.1	4.4	67	$8
Type	Pwr xGB	07	TOR	4	2	1	58	57	2.17	1.22	223	209	238	3.0	29%	84%	2.94	60	18	22	3.7	8.8	**2.4**	9%	0.5	16.7	97	$9
Health	B	08	TOR	0	3	5	71	57	1.78	1.15	213	194	226	4.4	26%	86%	3.00	66	12	22	3.4	7.3	**2.1**	7%	0.4	22.4	81	$10
PT/Exp	C	09	TOR	1	3	9	47	43	3.08	1.26	259	263	246	4.1	32%	78%	2.99	56	21	24	2.5	8.3	**3.3**	13%	0.8	7.9	115	$8
Consist	A	1st Half		1	0	8	27	28	1.99	0.89	207			4.0	28%	78%	2.45	51	23	27	1.3	9.3	**7.0**	5%	0.3	8.2	160	$8
LIMA Plan	B+	2nd Half		0	3	1	20	15	4.59	1.79	320			4.2	36%	78%	3.78	62	18	20	4.1	6.9	**1.7**	23%	1.4	-0.3	52	$0
Rand Var	0	10	Proj	**2**	**5**	**10**	**73**	**63**	**3.23**	**1.32**	**255**			**4.2**	**31%**	**77%**	**3.15**	**60**	**18**	**23**	**3.2**	**7.8**	**2.4**	**10%**	**0.6**	**11.5**	**91**	**$10**

Briefly reclaimed closer role in 1H, before two DL stints (toe) cost him the job. xERA shows how good and consistent he's been for three years running. Set your expectations there and hope for another closer shot.

Duchscherer,Justin

		Yr	Tm	W	L	Sv	IP	K	ERA	WHIP	OBA	vL	vR	BF/G	H%	S%	xERA	G	L	F	Ctl	Dom	Cmd	hr/f	hr/9	RAR	BPV	R$
RH	Reliever	05	OAK	7	4	5	85	85	2.22	1.01	218	225	208	5.2	28%	82%	3.03	44	19	37	2.0	9.0	**4.5**	9%	0.7	22.6	130	$17
Age	32	06	OAK	2	1	9	55	51	2.93	1.11	250	248	241	4.2	31%	75%	3.34	37	26	38	1.5	8.3	**5.7**	7%	0.7	11.1	125	$11
Type		07	OAK	3	3	0	16	13	4.97	1.60	281	400	176	4.3	31%	74%	4.48	47	17	36	4.4	7.2	**1.6**	16%	1.7	-0.9	35	$2
Health	F	08	OAK	10	8	0	142	95	2.54	1.00	211	227	188	25.2	24%	78%	3.79	41	20	39	2.2	6.0	**2.8**	7%	0.7	31.6	70	$22
PT/Exp	D	09	OAK	0	0	0	0	0	0.00	0.00							0.00											
Consist	B	1st Half		0	0	0	0	0	0.00	0.00							0.00											
LIMA Plan	D	2nd Half		0	0	0	0	0	0.00	0.00							0.00											
Rand Var		10	Proj	**5**	**3**	**0**	**73**	**53**	**3.72**	**1.31**	**266**			**7.1**	**30%**	**75%**	**4.10**	**42**	**21**	**37**	**2.6**	**6.6**	**2.5**	**9%**	**1.0**	**3.0**	**68**	**$7**

Elbow injury cost him most of season, depression prevented a late-season comeback when arm was sound. Durability a major question mark, impacting his role. Skills not in doubt, pay for this line and hope for IP.

Duensing,Brian

		Yr	Tm	W	L	Sv	IP	K	ERA	WHIP	OBA	vL	vR	BF/G	H%	S%	xERA	G	L	F	Ctl	Dom	Cmd	hr/f	hr/9	RAR	BPV	R$
LH	Starter	05		0	0	0	0	0	0.00	0.00							0.00											
Age	27	06	aa	1	2	0	49	24	5.10	1.72	316			22.8	33%	74%	6.82				3.8	4.4	**1.2**		1.5	-3.5	-2	($1)
Type	Con	07	a/a	15	6	0	167	98	4.11	1.43	296			26.0	33%	73%	5.16				2.2	5.3	**2.4**		0.9	7.3	49	$13
Health	A	08	aaa	5	11	0	138	62	5.07	1.48	303			24.3	32%	67%	5.44				2.3	4.1	**1.8**		1.1	-12.9	24	$2
PT/Exp	D	09	MIN *	9	8	0	159	88	4.55	1.48	292	244	269	18.9	33%	69%	4.80	45	15	40	2.9	5.0	**1.7**	4%	0.5	-1.9	36	$7
Consist	A	1st Half		4	6	0	78	36	5.58	1.57	319			25.0	35%	62%	6.13	33	0	67	2.3	4.1	**1.8**	2%	0.4	-10.8	25	$1
LIMA Plan	C+	2nd Half		5	2	0	81	52	3.56	1.40	264			15.2	30%	76%	4.57	46	15	39	3.4	5.8	**1.7**	6%	0.7	9.0	35	$7
Rand Var	-2	10	Proj	**5**	**4**	**0**	**86**	**46**	**4.60**	**1.49**	**296**			**21.1**	**32%**	**71%**	**4.76**	**46**	**15**	**39**	**2.7**	**4.8**	**1.8**	**8%**	**0.9**	**-3.4**	**37**	**$4**

5-2, 3.64 ERA in 84 IP at MIN. Late-season savior of depleted MIN rotation did it with smoke and mirrors, not skill. Expect a correction in 2010, but Twins fans will thank him warmly for his contribution to Central title.

Duke,Zach

		Yr	Tm	W	L	Sv	IP	K	ERA	WHIP	OBA	vL	vR	BF/G	H%	S%	xERA	G	L	F	Ctl	Dom	Cmd	hr/f	hr/9	RAR	BPV	R$
LH	Starter	05	PIT *	20	5	0	192	117	2.49	1.21	260	150	273	26.5	30%	81%	3.61	48	26	26	2.0	5.5	**2.7**	7%	0.5	41.6	70	$26
Age	26	06	PIT	10	15	0	215	117	4.48	1.50	296	264	310	28.0	33%	71%	4.38	51	20	29	2.8	4.9	**1.7**	8%	0.7	0.3	40	$8
Type	Con	07	PIT	3	8	0	107	41	5.54	1.73	347	341	363	25.0	36%	70%	4.83	51	20	29	2.1	3.4	**1.6**	11%	1.2	-14.7	34	($3)
Health	B	08	PIT	5	14	0	185	87	4.82	1.50	306	279	308	26.4	33%	69%	4.48	48	21	31	2.3	4.2	**1.9**	9%	0.9	-12.5	41	$2
PT/Exp	A	09	PIT	11	16	0	213	106	4.06	1.31	278	284	285	28.2	30%	72%	4.22	48	20	33	2.1	4.5	**2.2**	10%	1.0	3.5	50	$12
Consist	A	1st Half		8	6	0	112	54	3.13	1.19	253			28.8	27%	77%	4.26	45	19	35	2.1	4.3	**2.1**	8%	0.9	14.6	45	$11
LIMA Plan	C	2nd Half		3	10	0	101	52	5.08	1.46	303			27.6	32%	67%	4.18	50	20	30	2.0	4.6	**2.3**	11%	1.1	-11.1	57	$1
Rand Var	0	10	Proj	**7**	**13**	**0**	**174**	**89**	**4.29**	**1.39**	**290**			**26.8**	**31%**	**71%**	**4.23**	**49**	**20**	**31**	**2.2**	**4.6**	**2.1**	**10%**	**1.0**	**0.6**	**51**	**$7**

First-half breakout was a H%-fueled mirage. Still, as xERA, BPV, and Cmd all trend in good directions, there may yet be something worthwhile here. But given the pace of that growth, check back in his 30s.

RAY MURPHY

Durbin,Chad

Durbin,Chad		Yr	Tm	W	L	Sv	IP	K	ERA	WHIP	OBA	vL	vR	BF/G	H%	S%	xERA	G	L	F	Ctl	Dom	Cmd	hr/f	hr/9	RAR	BPV	R$
RH	Reliever	05	aaa	4	5	0	115	82	5.93	1.53	287			19.7	31%	65%	5.82				3.5	6.4	**1.8**		1.6	-23.0	24	$0
Age	32	06	aaa	11	8	0	185	120	4.34	1.44	292			28.8	33%	72%	5.12				2.5	5.8	**2.4**		1.0	4.1	52	$12
Type	Pwr	07	DET	8	7	1	128	66	4.72	1.43	270	281	255	15.4	28%	71%	4.99	44	16	40	3.5	4.7	**1.3**	12%	1.5	-3.4	12	$7
Health	A	08	PHI	5	4	1	88	63	2.87	1.32	247	311	214	5.2	29%	79%	4.14	46	21	34	3.6	6.5	**1.8**	6%	0.5	15.1	43	$9
PT/Exp	C	09	PHI	2	2	2	70	62	4.39	1.48	222	223	218	5.2	26%	73%	4.75	39	18	42	6.1	8.0	**1.3**	10%	1.0	-1.7	-2	$3
Consist	B	1st Half		1	2	0	42	39	4.29	1.43	223			5.1	26%	74%	4.62	36	19	45	5.6	8.4	**1.5**	12%	1.3	-0.5	14	$2
LIMA Plan	C+	2nd Half		1	0	2	28	23	4.55	1.55	220			5.4	27%	71%	4.94	45	18	37	6.8	7.5	**1.1**	7%	0.6	-1.2	-27	$1
Rand Var	-2	10	Proj	**3**	**2**	**0**	**58**	**44**	**4.50**	**1.48**	**252**			**6.4**	**29%**	**72%**	**4.64**	**43**	**19**	**38**	**4.8**	**6.8**	**1.4**	**11%**	**1.1**	**-2.7**	**14**	**$2**

Complete loss of control overshadows Dom uptick. Shoulder injury that DL'd him in 2H may have been a factor much earlier in year. Career 1.4 Cmd in MLB says that even better health won't be enough.

Elbert,Scott

Elbert,Scott		Yr	Tm	W	L	Sv	IP	K	ERA	WHIP	OBA	vL	vR	BF/G	H%	S%	xERA	G	L	F	Ctl	Dom	Cmd	hr/f	hr/9	RAR	BPV	R$
LH	Reliever	05		0	0	0	0	0	0.00	0.00							0.00											
Age	24	06	aa	6	4	0	62	64	4.78	1.51	212			25.0	23%	75%	5.03				6.8	9.3	**1.4**		1.9	-2.0	40	$5
Type	Pwr	07	aa	0	1	0	14	21	4.50	1.64	233			21.3	39%	70%	3.77				7.1	13.5	**1.9**		0.0	-0.1	129	$1
Health	C	08	aa	4	1	0	41	41	2.71	1.08	176			6.6	23%	76%	1.98				4.3	8.9	**2.1**		0.5	8.1	103	$7
PT/Exp	D	09	LA *	6	4	0	116	126	4.87	1.61	286	222	282	13.4	37%	71%	3.87	44	17	39	4.3	9.8	**2.3**	10%	1.0	-9.7	83	$4
Consist	D	1st Half		4	4	0	79	92	4.90	1.56	286			20.9	38%	70%	3.91	32	23	45	3.9	10.5	**2.7**	8%	0.9	-7.0	94	$3
LIMA Plan	B	2nd Half		2	0	0	37	34	4.79	1.72	286			7.7	35%	74%	4.24	53	13	34	5.3	8.4	**1.6**	11%	1.1	-2.7	40	$0
Rand Var	+4	10	Proj	**7**	**4**	**0**	**108**	**107**	**4.08**	**1.34**	**240**			**23.0**	**30%**	**72%**	**3.66**	**49**	**14**	**36**	**4.1**	**8.9**	**2.2**	**10%**	**0.9**	**8.1**	**78**	**$9**

2-0, 5.03 ERA in 20 IP at LA. Dom shows the potential of a former 1st rounder, Ctl shows the refinement still needed. Cmd trend shows he's figuring it out. If he wins rotation spot, then... UP: 13 Wins, 3.50 ERA.

Embree,Alan

Embree,Alan		Yr	Tm	W	L	Sv	IP	K	ERA	WHIP	OBA	vL	vR	BF/G	H%	S%	xERA	G	L	F	Ctl	Dom	Cmd	hr/f	hr/9	RAR	BPV	R$
LH	Reliever	05	2AL	2	5	1	52	38	7.62	1.46	297	320	278	3.4	32%	48%	4.16	40	23	36	2.4	6.6	**2.7**	16%	1.7	-20.8	71	($1)
Age	40	06	SD	4	3	0	52	53	3.28	1.25	254	240	258	3.0	33%	75%	3.42	43	20	37	2.6	9.2	**3.5**	8%	0.7	7.7	116	$7
Type		07	OAK	1	2	17	68	51	3.97	1.26	259	205	278	4.2	31%	69%	4.34	34	20	45	2.5	6.8	**2.7**	5%	0.7	4.5	66	$11
Health	D	08	OAK	2	5	0	62	57	4.96	1.44	253	232	265	3.8	30%	68%	4.23	45	12	44	4.4	8.3	**1.9**	10%	1.2	-4.7	54	$3
PT/Exp	C	09	COL	2	2	0	25	12	5.83	1.62	287	326	264	3.1	30%	65%	5.32	41	23	36	4.4	4.4	**1.0**	10%	1.1	-5.0	-20	($0)
Consist	B	1st Half		1	2	0	21	11	6.82	1.80	312			3.2	33%	63%	5.49	41	24	36	4.7	4.7	**1.0**	11%	1.3	-6.9	-23	($1)
LIMA Plan	F	2nd Half		1	0	0	4	1	0.00	0.56	90			2.5	10%	100%	4.22	43	14	43	2.5	2.5	**1.0**	0%	0.0	1.9	-2	$1
Rand Var	+1	10	Proj	**2**	**3**	**0**	**44**	**28**	**4.97**	**1.56**	**277**			**3.5**	**30%**	**71%**	**5.01**	**40**	**20**	**40**	**4.3**	**5.8**	**1.3**	**11%**	**1.2**	**-4.0**	**5**	**$1**

Line drive broke his leg in July, ending his season. Age, loss of Dom, BPV trend all say that even if the liner didn't end his career, that day isn't far away. Steer clear.

Escobar,Kelvim

Escobar,Kelvim		Yr	Tm	W	L	Sv	IP	K	ERA	WHIP	OBA	vL	vR	BF/G	H%	S%	xERA	G	L	F	Ctl	Dom	Cmd	hr/f	hr/9	RAR	BPV	R$
RH	Starter	05	ANA	3	2	1	59	63	3.04	1.11	212	278	138	14.9	28%	74%	3.19	47	15	38	3.2	9.6	**3.0**	7%	0.6	9.7	111	$9
Age	34	06	LAA	11	14	0	189	147	3.62	1.28	265	258	270	26.5	31%	74%	3.86	45	19	36	2.4	7.0	**2.9**	8%	0.8	21.9	84	$20
Type	Pwr	07	LAA	18	7	0	196	160	3.40	1.27	248	264	233	27.3	30%	73%	3.96	44	17	39	3.0	7.4	**2.4**	5%	0.5	26.6	72	$25
Health	F	08	LAA	0	0	0	0	0	0.00	0.00							0.00											
PT/Exp	C	09	LAA *	0	1	0	10	6	7.09	2.21	359		571	25.7	41%	64%	6.27	54	0	46	5.7	5.3	**0.9**	0%	0.0	-3.3	-28	($1)
Consist	F	1st Half		0	1	0	10	6	7.09	2.21	359			25.7	41%	64%	6.27	54	0	46	5.7	5.3	**0.9**	0%	0.0	-3.3	-28	($1)
LIMA Plan	C	2nd Half		0	0	0	0	0	0.00	0.00						98%	0.00						**0.0**					
Rand Var	+3	10	Proj	**4**	**4**	**0**	**73**	**54**	**4.10**	**1.42**	**266**			**21.0**	**31%**	**73%**	**4.35**	**46**	**15**	**39**	**3.6**	**6.7**	**1.9**	**8%**	**0.9**	**0.8**	**48**	**$5**

Much spring optimism about return to health yielded another year lost to shoulder problems. Best case after two lost years is likely a successful return to bullpen work, with real chance that he falls short of even that.

Eveland,Dana

Eveland,Dana		Yr	Tm	W	L	Sv	IP	K	ERA	WHIP	OBA	vL	vR	BF/G	H%	S%	xERA	G	L	F	Ctl	Dom	Cmd	hr/f	hr/9	RAR	BPV	R$
LH	Starter	05	MIL *	11	5	1	140	108	3.79	1.44	270			13.6	33%	73%	3.69	51	25	25	3.6	6.9	**1.9**	6%	0.4	7.9	57	$11
Age	26	06	MIL *	6	8	0	132	135	4.43	1.35	243			19.4	32%	67%	3.51	44	27	29	3.9	9.2	**2.3**	9%	0.6	1.0	81	$10
Type	GB	07	aaa	2	0	0	33	16	4.64	1.76	301			11.9	34%	72%	4.97	55	20	25	4.9	4.4	**0.9**	3%	0.3	-0.7	-21	$0
Health	B	08	OAK	9	9	0	168	118	4.34	1.48	266	248	275	25.5	31%	70%	4.22	49	22	29	4.1	6.3	**1.5**	7%	0.5	0.2	29	$9
PT/Exp	C	09	OAK *	10	10	0	168	93	5.80	1.76	318	373	362	23.1	35%	67%	4.58	56	18	25	4.0	5.0	**1.2**	10%	0.8	-28.0	16	($1)
Consist	B	1st Half		8	3	0	93	54	4.75	1.69	298			23.9	33%	72%	4.69	56	16	28	4.5	5.2	**1.2**	8%	0.7	-3.5	6	$3
LIMA Plan	C	2nd Half		2	7	0	75	39	7.11	1.85	342			22.3	37%	61%	4.43	57	21	22	3.4	4.8	**1.4**	13%	1.0	-24.5	28	($5)
Rand Var	+4	10	Proj	**4**	**4**	**0**	**80**	**49**	**4.74**	**1.57**	**284**			**18.8**	**32%**	**70%**	**4.40**	**52**	**21**	**27**	**4.1**	**5.5**	**1.4**	**10%**	**0.8**	**0.3**	**20**	**$2**

Seems he's still not done paying back the karma gods for his h%-fueled "breakout" in 1H of 2008. Even with neutral luck, the Cmd is a non-starter and GB% isn't enough to cover that up. Forget that start to '08, shop elsewhere.

Eyre,Scott

Eyre,Scott		Yr	Tm	W	L	Sv	IP	K	ERA	WHIP	OBA	vL	vR	BF/G	H%	S%	xERA	G	L	F	Ctl	Dom	Cmd	hr/f	hr/9	RAR	BPV	R$
LH	Reliever	05	SF	2	2	0	68	65	2.64	1.09	200	182	213	3.2	26%	76%	3.66	38	18	43	3.4	8.6	**2.5**	4%	0.4	13.5	78	$9
Age	37	06	CHC	1	3	0	61	73	3.39	1.49	261	273	261	3.6	33%	85%	3.65	42	20	38	4.4	10.8	**2.4**	18%	1.6	8.3	94	$4
Type	Pwr FB	07	CHC	2	1	0	52	45	4.13	1.80	286	253	317	4.5	35%	77%	5.14	39	24	38	6.0	7.7	**1.3**	5%	0.5	1.9	-6	$1
Health	D	08	2NL	5	0	0	26	32	4.20	1.17	241	220	267	2.8	34%	64%	3.00	35	23	42	2.5	11.2	**4.6**	8%	0.7	0.2	149	$5
PT/Exp	D	09	PHI	2	1	0	30	22	1.50	1.27	206	210	200	3.0	23%	94%	4.79	33	21	46	4.8	6.6	**1.4**	8%	0.9	10.0	1	$4
Consist	D	1st Half		1	1	0	14	10	2.57	1.36	202			2.4	21%	88%	5.31	31	19	50	5.8	6.4	**1.1**	10%	1.3	2.8	-32	$1
LIMA Plan	C	2nd Half		1	0	0	16	12	0.56	1.19	210			3.9	25%	100%	4.33	36	22	42	3.9	6.7	**1.7**	5%	0.6	7.2	29	$3
Rand Var	-5	10	Proj	**2**	**1**	**0**	**44**	**34**	**4.55**	**1.52**	**260**			**3.9**	**30%**	**72%**	**4.87**	**35**	**22**	**43**	**4.8**	**7.0**	**1.5**	**9%**	**1.0**	**-3.3**	**12**	**$2**

Two DL stints (calf, elbow) cut his season short. In between he rode ridiculous hit/strand rates to an ERA three full runs below xERA. Considering retirement this offseason, which is one way to avoid the correction.

Farnsworth,Kyle

Farnsworth,Kyle		Yr	Tm	W	L	Sv	IP	K	ERA	WHIP	OBA	vL	vR	BF/G	H%	S%	xERA	G	L	F	Ctl	Dom	Cmd	hr/f	hr/9	RAR	BPV	R$
RH	Reliever	05	2TM	1	1	16	70	87	2.19	1.01	182	198	165	3.8	26%	82%	2.80	43	21	36	3.5	11.2	**3.2**	9%	0.6	18.3	128	$16
Age	33	06	NYY	3	6	6	66	75	4.36	1.36	250	215	264	3.9	33%	71%	3.76	34	22	44	3.8	10.2	**2.7**	11%	1.1	1.6	93	$8
Type	Pwr	07	NYY	2	1	0	60	48	4.80	1.45	262	273	242	4.1	30%	71%	4.95	30	19	51	4.1	7.2	**1.8**	10%	1.4	-2.2	29	$3
Health	A	08	2AL	2	3	1	60	61	4.48	1.53	292	275	318	4.4	34%	81%	4.11	35	19	46	3.3	9.1	**2.8**	18%	2.2	-1.0	88	$3
PT/Exp	D	09	KC	1	5	0	37	42	4.58	1.53	290	277	294	4.0	39%	70%	3.44	46	21	34	3.4	10.1	**3.0**	8%	0.7	-0.6	115	$2
Consist	B	1st Half		1	4	0	23	25	4.29	1.30	269			3.6	35%	68%	3.43	35	26	39	2.3	9.7	**4.2**	8%	0.8	0.5	125	$2
LIMA Plan	A+	2nd Half		0	1	0	14	17	5.07	1.90	322			4.9	44%	73%	3.28	63	12	24	5.1	10.8	**2.1**	10%	0.6	-1.1	98	($0)
Rand Var	+5	10	Proj	**3**	**4**	**0**	**58**	**59**	**3.88**	**1.31**	**252**			**3.9**	**31%**	**74%**	**3.60**	**43**	**18**	**39**	**3.3**	**9.2**	**2.8**	**11%**	**1.1**	**6.0**	**98**	**$6**

Quietly kicked up his skills amid hit rate punishment. 2007 Cmd looks like an outlier, leaving only elite Cmd history. Reduction in FBs plugs biggest hole in his skill set, if that sustains then... UP: a big step toward 2005.

Feldman,Scott

Feldman,Scott		Yr	Tm	W	L	Sv	IP	K	ERA	WHIP	OBA	vL	vR	BF/G	H%	S%	xERA	G	L	F	Ctl	Dom	Cmd	hr/f	hr/9	RAR	BPV	R$
RH	Starter	05	aa	1	2	14	61	35	3.10	1.21	229			5.5	26%	76%	3.15				3.4	5.2	**1.5**		0.6	9.1	54	$9
Age	27	06	TEX *	2	4	4	68	52	3.57	1.26	259	280	259	4.8	30%	76%	3.18	59	19	22	2.5	6.8	**2.7**	18%	1.1	8.3	93	$8
Type		07	TEX *	2	3	2	69	39	5.87	1.79	288			6.5	32%	66%	4.98	59	15	26	5.8	5.1	**0.9**	7%	0.5	-11.6	-29	($1)
Health	A	08	TEX *	8	8	0	164	77	5.33	1.42	274	291	269	23.7	28%	64%	4.87	44	19	37	3.2	4.2	**1.3**	11%	1.2	-19.8	11	$5
PT/Exp	C	09	TEX	17	8	0	190	113	4.08	1.28	250	226	277	23.4	27%	70%	4.26	47	21	33	3.1	5.4	**1.7**	9%	0.9	8.7	38	$18
Consist	A	1st Half		6	2	0	83	43	4.11	1.19	237			21.4	24%	69%	4.37	47	18	35	2.8	4.7	**1.7**	12%	1.2	3.5	32	$8
LIMA Plan	D	2nd Half		11	6	0	107	70	4.06	1.35	259			25.3	30%	70%	4.17	47	22	31	3.3	5.9	**1.8**	7%	0.6	5.2	42	$11
Rand Var	0	10	Proj	**12**	**9**	**0**	**189**	**122**	**4.34**	**1.34**	**261**			**13.2**	**29%**	**69%**	**4.14**	**48**	**20**	**32**	**3.1**	**5.8**	**1.9**	**10%**	**0.9**	**6.8**	**48**	**$14**

BPV captures the very real growth trend here, not that it merited these results. GB profile can support sub-par Cmd if everything goes right, which it did. But don't pay for anything close to a repeat.

Feliciano,Pedro

Feliciano,Pedro		Yr	Tm	W	L	Sv	IP	K	ERA	WHIP	OBA	vL	vR	BF/G	H%	S%	xERA	G	L	F	Ctl	Dom	Cmd	hr/f	hr/9	RAR	BPV	R$
LH	Reliever	05	JPN	3	2	0	37	38	4.83	1.31	236			4.2	26%	71%	4.84				3.9	9.2	**2.4**		2.0	-2.4	52	$3
Age	33	06	NYM	7	2	0	60	54	2.10	1.26	248	231	266	3.9	31%	86%	3.44	49	21	29	3.0	8.1	**2.7**	8%	0.6	17.7	92	$10
Type	Pwr GB	07	NYM	2	2	2	64	61	3.09	1.22	207	168	221	3.4	27%	75%	3.34	56	17	27	4.4	8.6	**2.0**	7%	0.4	10.5	70	$7
Health	A	08	NYM	3	4	2	53	50	4.05	1.56	275	210	357	2.8	33%	78%	3.69	53	19	27	4.4	8.4	**1.9**	16%	1.2	1.4	65	$3
PT/Exp	C	09	NYM	6	4	0	59	59	3.04	1.16	234	215	264	2.8	29%	79%	2.88	57	16	28	2.7	9.0	**3.3**	16%	1.1	8.4	122	$9
Consist	B	1st Half		2	2	0	31	28	2.60	0.96	200			2.9	23%	81%	2.71	59	16	25	2.3	8.1	**3.5**	19%	1.2	6.1	120	$5
LIMA Plan	A	2nd Half		4	2	0	28	31	3.52	1.39	268			2.6	35%	78%	3.07	54	15	31	3.2	9.9	**3.1**	12%	1.0	2.3	124	$4
Rand Var	0	10	Proj	**4**	**3**	**0**	**53**	**53**	**3.43**	**1.24**	**241**			**2.9**	**31%**	**74%**	**3.03**	**55**	**17**	**28**	**3.1**	**9.1**	**2.9**	**10%**	**0.7**	**8.0**	**113**	**$6**

RP ERAs bounce around due to sample size issues, but BPV shows that this was his best work. Fewer FBs clearing the fence would push ERA down. A nice LIMA play with vulture wins potential.

RAY MURPHY

Feliz,Neftali

Feliz,Neftali		Yr	Tm	W	L	Sv	IP	K	ERA	WHIP	OBA	vL	vR	BF/G	H%	S%	xERA	G	L	F	Ctl	Dom	Cmd	hr/f	hr/9	RAR	BPV	R$
RH	Reliever	05		0	0	0	0	0	0.00	0.00							0.00											
Age	21	06		0	0	0	0	0	0.00	0.00							0.00											
Type	Pwr xFB	07		0	0	0	0	0	0.00	0.00							0.00											
Health	A	08	aa	4	3	0	45	42	3.23	1.25	217			18.8	29%	72%	2.67				4.2	8.4	**2.0**		0.2	6.0	98	$6
PT/Exp	F	09	TEX *	5	6	2	108	104	3.50	1.20	232	155	85	9.9	30%	70%	4.15	38	5	57	3.2	8.7	**2.7**	2%	0.3	12.7	87	$13
Consist	C	1st Half		3	5	0	67	58	4.27	1.40	262			17.0	34%	67%	3.58				3.5	7.8	**2.2**		0.1	1.5	92	$5
LIMA Plan	C	2nd Half		2	1	2	41	46	2.23	0.89	176			5.6	24%	79%	3.33	38	5	57	2.6	10.0	**3.9**	6%	0.7	11.2	128	$8
Rand Var	-3	10	Proj	**9**	**7**	**0**	**138**	**120**	**4.12**	**1.36**	**254**			**24.6**	**29%**	**74%**	**4.62**	**38**	**5**	**57**	**3.6**	**7.8**	**2.2**	**9%**	**1.3**	**-3.1**	**61**	**$12**

1-0, 1.74 ERA with 2 Sv in 31 IP at TEX. Top SP prospect made debut in bullpen, shredded MLB hitters (152 BPV in TEX). Age, inexperience in high minors temper short-term expectations as SP, but worth waiting on.

Figueroa,Nelson

Figueroa,Nelson		Yr	Tm	W	L	Sv	IP	K	ERA	WHIP	OBA	vL	vR	BF/G	H%	S%	xERA	G	L	F	Ctl	Dom	Cmd	hr/f	hr/9	RAR	BPV	R$
RH	Starter	05		0	0	0	0	0	0.00	0.00							0.00											
Age	35	06	aaa	3	5	0	76	35	5.48	1.50	297			21.0	30%	67%	5.88				2.7	4.2	**1.5**		1.5	-9.0	8	$1
Type		07	MEX	8	6	0	153	84	4.46	1.39	286			34.8	31%	70%	4.89				2.3	4.9	**2.1**		0.9	-0.0	43	$8
Health	B	08	NYM *	7	10	0	159	107	5.65	1.71	316	371	200	20.4	35%	68%	4.89	41	21	39	3.6	6.1	**1.7**	10%	1.2	-26.9	31	($2)
PT/Exp	C	09	NYM *	10	13	0	182	130	3.32	1.36	277	274	294	23.6	32%	77%	4.22	37	24	39	2.5	6.4	**2.5**	6%	0.7	19.5	62	$14
Consist	A	1st Half		4	5	0	88	58	3.64	1.31	264			26.6	30%	74%	4.28	47	11	42	2.7	5.9	**2.2**	6%	0.7	5.9	60	$6
LIMA Plan	C+	2nd Half		6	8	0	94	71	3.02	1.40	287			21.4	34%	80%	4.13	36	25	38	2.4	6.8	**2.9**	6%	0.6	13.6	73	$8
Rand Var	-3	10	Proj	**3**	**4**	**0**	**58**	**38**	**4.34**	**1.50**	**291**			**23.3**	**32%**	**74%**	**4.63**	**38**	**23**	**39**	**3.1**	**5.9**	**1.9**	**9%**	**1.1**	**-2.6**	**39**	**$2**

3-8, 4.09 ERA in 70 IP at NYM. Late-career skill surge, especially driving Dom to tolerable level, promotes him from the ranks of unrosterables. But at 35, it's likely a brief visit above the waterline.

Fisher,Carlos

Fisher,Carlos		Yr	Tm	W	L	Sv	IP	K	ERA	WHIP	OBA	vL	vR	BF/G	H%	S%	xERA	G	L	F	Ctl	Dom	Cmd	hr/f	hr/9	RAR	BPV	R$
RH	Reliever	05		0	0	0	0	0	0.00	0.00							0.00											
Age	27	06		0	0	0	0	0	0.00	0.00							0.00											
Type	Pwr	07	aa	5	9	0	113	72	5.93	1.85	337			25.7	37%	70%	7.27				3.7	5.7	**1.5**		1.2	-20.4	17	($3)
Health	A	08	a/a	6	5	8	68	52	3.97	1.70	303			6.3	36%	77%	5.51				4.3	6.9	**1.6**		0.6	2.8	52	$6
PT/Exp	D	09	CIN *	3	1	2	70	65	3.99	1.40	242	337	204	5.8	31%	71%	4.03	44	18	38	4.5	8.4	**1.9**	5%	0.5	1.7	51	$5
Consist	D	1st Half		3	0	2	34	35	2.95	1.22	216			5.4	30%	73%	3.69	36	23	41	4.0	9.4	**2.3**	0%	0.0	5.2	75	$5
LIMA Plan	B	2nd Half		0	1	0	36	30	4.96	1.57	265			6.3	31%	70%	4.46	47	16	37	5.0	7.4	**1.5**	10%	1.0	-3.4	25	($0)
Rand Var	-1	10	Proj	**2**	**2**	**0**	**44**	**39**	**4.14**	**1.47**	**260**			**6.8**	**32%**	**73%**	**4.16**	**45**	**18**	**37**	**4.3**	**8.1**	**1.9**	**8%**	**0.8**	**0.6**	**51**	**$2**

1-1, 4.47 ERA in 52 IP at CIN. Flashed attractive Dom/GB combo in MLB debut, but Ctl issues make him flammable, especially once hr/f corrects. Problems vLH hitters preclude high-leverage work, for now.

Fister,Doug

Fister,Doug		Yr	Tm	W	L	Sv	IP	K	ERA	WHIP	OBA	vL	vR	BF/G	H%	S%	xERA	G	L	F	Ctl	Dom	Cmd	hr/f	hr/9	RAR	BPV	R$
RH	Starter	05		0	0	0	0	0	0.00	0.00							0.00											
Age	26	06		0	0	0	0	0	0.00	0.00							0.00											
Type	Con	07	aa	7	8	0	131	74	5.52	1.64	328			24.9	36%	68%	6.39				2.4	5.1	**2.1**		1.1	-17.2	32	$1
Health	A	08	aa	6	14	0	134	88	6.43	1.70	321			20.0	36%	61%	6.07				3.2	5.9	**1.8**		0.8	-35.1	39	($3)
PT/Exp	D	09	SEA *	10	8	0	173	104	4.69	1.52	324	237	298	22.0	35%	72%	4.51	41	20	39	1.5	5.4	**3.5**	10%	1.2	-5.2	75	$7
Consist	B	1st Half		5	1	0	76	53	4.61	1.45	329			19.6	38%	69%	5.57				0.6	6.3	**10.1**		0.9	-1.4	213	$5
LIMA Plan	B	2nd Half		5	7	0	97	50	4.76	1.58	320			24.2	34%	74%	4.90	41	20	39	2.2	4.7	**2.1**	12%	1.5	-3.7	43	$2
Rand Var	+2	10	Proj	**3**	**5**	**0**	**65**	**40**	**4.55**	**1.53**	**311**			**20.8**	**34%**	**74%**	**4.61**	**41**	**20**	**39**	**2.3**	**5.5**	**2.4**	**10%**	**1.2**	**-1.4**	**55**	**$2**

3-4, 4.13 ERA in 61 IP at SEA. Ctl artist saw his marginal Dom fall below acceptable threshold in MLB debut. This profile could work with more GBs or better Dom, but until he shows one of those, he's just a watch-list guy.

Floyd,Gavin

Floyd,Gavin		Yr	Tm	W	L	Sv	IP	K	ERA	WHIP	OBA	vL	vR	BF/G	H%	S%	xERA	G	L	F	Ctl	Dom	Cmd	hr/f	hr/9	RAR	BPV	R$
RH	Starter	05	PHI *	7	11	0	163	103	7.33	1.67	297	283	283	24.1	33%	55%	5.05	42	19	39	4.2	5.7	**1.3**	8%	1.0	-62.0	7	($7)
Age	27	06	PHI *	11	7	0	169	105	6.81	1.74	317	306	323	28.1	34%	62%	5.19	39	24	37	3.9	5.6	**1.4**	13%	1.5	-48.5	13	($4)
Type		07	CHW *	8	8	0	176	134	4.70	1.44	285	314	286	23.3	32%	72%	4.33	42	17	41	2.8	6.8	**2.4**	13%	1.5	-4.2	67	$10
Health	A	08	CHW	17	8	0	206	145	3.84	1.26	246	259	226	26.1	27%	75%	4.22	41	19	40	3.1	6.3	**2.1**	12%	1.3	12.9	51	$21
PT/Exp	A	09	CHW	11	11	0	193	163	4.06	1.23	246	232	256	26.7	29%	69%	3.64	44	22	33	2.8	7.6	**2.8**	11%	1.0	9.4	85	$19
Consist	A	1st Half		6	5	0	102	81	4.14	1.33	254			27.2	30%	70%	3.89	45	24	31	3.3	7.1	**2.1**	9%	0.7	3.9	61	$9
LIMA Plan	C	2nd Half		5	6	0	91	82	3.96	1.11	238			26.2	28%	69%	3.39	43	20	36	2.1	8.1	**3.9**	14%	1.3	5.5	112	$11
Rand Var	+1	10	Proj	**14**	**8**	**0**	**203**	**164**	**3.95**	**1.30**	**258**			**26.0**	**30%**	**73%**	**3.92**	**43**	**21**	**36**	**2.9**	**7.3**	**2.5**	**11%**	**1.1**	**12.9**	**74**	**$20**

On the surface, a predictable step back from 2008... but skill growth tells a different story. Others see that 2008 line as a career year, you see it as a level he can regain or even surpass... UP: 3.50 ERA.

Fogg,Josh

Fogg,Josh		Yr	Tm	W	L	Sv	IP	K	ERA	WHIP	OBA	vL	vR	BF/G	H%	S%	xERA	G	L	F	Ctl	Dom	Cmd	hr/f	hr/9	RAR	BPV	R$
RH	Reliever	05	PIT	6	11	0	169	85	5.06	1.47	291	340	249	21.8	30%	69%	4.82	41	21	38	2.8	4.5	**1.6**	12%	1.4	-16.9	24	$2
Age	33	06	COL	11	9	0	172	93	5.49	1.55	298	309	291	24.8	32%	67%	4.96	43	20	37	3.1	4.9	**1.6**	11%	1.3	-21.4	23	$4
Type	FB	07	COL	10	9	0	166	94	4.94	1.53	293	279	305	24.6	31%	70%	4.99	40	20	40	3.2	5.1	**1.6**	10%	1.2	-10.6	23	$5
Health	C	08	CIN	2	7	0	78	45	7.59	1.58	305	299	305	16.0	31%	54%	5.09	38	19	43	3.1	5.2	**1.7**	15%	2.0	-32.0	25	($4)
PT/Exp	C	09	COL *	3	3	0	86	39	6.07	1.54	278	221	176	12.0	27%	66%	5.30	48	10	42	4.1	4.1	**1.0**	15%	2.0	-19.9	-10	($2)
Consist	A	1st Half		3	2	0	57	20	5.26	1.38	266			13.7	25%	67%	5.27	48	8	44	3.3	3.2	**1.0**	13%	1.8	-7.5	-5	$1
LIMA Plan	F	2nd Half		0	1	0	29	19	7.69	1.85	302			9.7	31%	63%	5.48	48	11	40	5.7	5.9	**1.0**	19%	2.3	-12.3	-22	($3)
Rand Var	+2	10	Proj	**2**	**3**	**0**	**58**	**32**	**5.28**	**1.60**	**294**			**13.8**	**31%**	**71%**	**5.19**	**43**	**16**	**41**	**3.9**	**5.0**	**1.3**	**12%**	**1.6**	**-6.6**	**5**	**($0)**

0-2, 3.74 ERA in 46 IP at COL. Boosted his GB% and almost completely avoided LDs... and still pushed his BPV into the red. Too bad; prior to '09, he had the most consistent set of bad BPIs around. Now they're worse.

Francisco,Frank

Francisco,Frank		Yr	Tm	W	L	Sv	IP	K	ERA	WHIP	OBA	vL	vR	BF/G	H%	S%	xERA	G	L	F	Ctl	Dom	Cmd	hr/f	hr/9	RAR	BPV	R$
RH	Reliever	05	TEX	0	0	0	0	0	0.00	0.00							0.00				0.0	0.0						
Age	30	06	TEX *	0	1	0	22	25	3.26	1.22	243		444	4.4	31%	79%	3.10	50	13	38	2.9	10.2	**3.6**	14%	1.2	3.5	134	$2
Type	Pwr xFB	07	TEX	1	1	0	59	49	4.55	1.60	254	221	286	4.5	31%	71%	5.15	35	22	43	5.8	7.4	**1.3**	4%	0.5	-0.3	-9	$2
Health	F	08	TEX	3	5	5	63	83	3.13	1.15	208	193	207	4.4	30%	77%	3.20	33	19	48	3.7	11.8	**3.2**	10%	1.0	9.5	123	$11
PT/Exp	C	09	TEX	2	3	25	49	57	3.83	1.12	223	238	186	3.9	29%	69%	3.45	29	21	50	2.7	10.4	**3.8**	10%	1.1	3.8	121	$15
Consist	C	1st Half		2	1	12	23	26	2.33	1.03	206			3.8	26%	86%	3.69	18	25	57	2.7	10.1	**3.7**	9%	1.2	6.1	104	$8
LIMA Plan	B+	2nd Half		0	2	13	26	31	5.17	1.19	238			4.0	32%	57%	3.20	40	18	43	2.8	10.7	**3.9**	11%	1.0	-2.3	136	$6
Rand Var	0	10	Proj	**2**	**4**	**38**	**58**	**67**	**3.57**	**1.16**	**223**			**4.1**	**29%**	**73%**	**3.45**	**33**	**20**	**47**	**3.1**	**10.4**	**3.4**	**10%**	**1.1**	**7.1**	**114**	**$20**

In between two DL stints (shoulder, pneumonia), handled first season as closer capably. Continued improvement in Ctl raises our confidence; health and FB% are only warts, but the latter could be deadly in TEX.

Francis,Jeff

Francis,Jeff		Yr	Tm	W	L	Sv	IP	K	ERA	WHIP	OBA	vL	vR	BF/G	H%	S%	xERA	G	L	F	Ctl	Dom	Cmd	hr/f	hr/9	RAR	BPV	R$
LH	Reliever	05	COL	14	12	0	183	128	5.70	1.63	306	285	317	25.2	34%	67%	4.65	40	22	38	3.4	6.3	**1.8**	11%	1.3	-32.8	39	$3
Age	29	06	COL	13	11	0	199	117	4.16	1.29	250	241	252	26.2	28%	69%	4.49	45	19	36	3.1	5.3	**1.7**	8%	0.8	8.0	34	$14
Type		07	COL	17	9	0	215	165	4.22	1.38	278	242	289	27.2	32%	72%	4.07	44	18	37	2.6	6.9	**2.6**	10%	1.0	5.4	75	$18
Health	F	08	COL	4	10	0	144	94	5.01	1.48	288	248	295	26.4	31%	69%	4.46	44	20	36	3.1	5.9	**1.9**	12%	1.3	-13.1	45	$2
PT/Exp	B	09	COL	0	0	0	0	0	0.00	0.00							0.00											
Consist	A	1st Half		0	0	0	0	0	0.00	0.00							0.00											
LIMA Plan	D	2nd Half		0	0	0	0	0	0.00	0.00							0.00											
Rand Var		10	Proj	**7**	**7**	**0**	**120**	**77**	**4.50**	**1.43**	**276**			**26.1**	**31%**	**71%**	**4.45**	**44**	**20**	**37**	**3.2**	**5.8**	**1.8**	**10%**	**1.1**	**-2.8**	**41**	**$6**

February surgery to repair torn labrum cost him entire season. Skill set from 2007 (last healthy season) sits out there as his upside, but a lot has to go right to even sniff those levels. Set your sights considerably lower.

Franklin,Ryan

Franklin,Ryan		Yr	Tm	W	L	Sv	IP	K	ERA	WHIP	OBA	vL	vR	BF/G	H%	S%	xERA	G	L	F	Ctl	Dom	Cmd	hr/f	hr/9	RAR	BPV	R$
RH	Reliever	05	SEA	8	15	0	190	93	5.11	1.44	283	266	295	25.9	29%	67%	4.96	42	16	42	2.9	4.4	**1.5**	10%	1.3	-17.3	20	$5
Age	37	06	2NL	6	7	0	77	43	4.55	1.54	283	265	294	5.2	30%	75%	4.91	47	18	35	3.9	5.0	**1.3**	14%	1.5	-0.6	11	$4
Type		07	STL	4	4	1	80	44	3.04	1.01	237	238	231	4.6	25%	74%	3.71	48	18	34	1.2	5.0	**4.0**	9%	0.9	13.7	82	$10
Health	A	08	STL	6	6	17	79	51	3.55	1.47	279	268	285	4.7	31%	80%	4.61	43	19	38	3.4	5.8	**1.7**	10%	1.1	7.0	33	$12
PT/Exp	B	09	STL	4	3	38	61	44	1.92	1.20	222	196	238	4.1	27%	85%	3.98	46	20	34	3.5	6.5	**1.8**	3%	0.3	17.1	45	$21
Consist	B	1st Half		2	0	18	30	21	0.90	0.80	183			3.8	21%	95%	3.27	44	20	35	1.5	6.3	**4.2**	7%	0.6	12.2	95	$12
LIMA Plan	F	2nd Half		2	3	20	31	23	2.90	1.58	255			4.2	32%	80%	4.72	47	20	34	5.5	6.7	**1.2**	0%	0.0	4.9	-4	$9
Rand Var	-5	10	Proj	**5**	**5**	**23**	**73**	**48**	**3.85**	**1.46**	**271**			**4.7**	**30%**	**77%**	**4.50**	**45**	**19**	**36**	**3.7**	**6.0**	**1.6**	**10%**	**1.0**	**-2.1**	**30**	**$12**

Combined borderline closer-worthy skills with absurd hit/strand rate luck through July, then everything came crashing down. Should enter 2010 with closer gig, but don't expect him to hold it. Extreme caution here.

RAY MURPHY

Frasor,Jason		Yr	Tm	W	L	Sv	IP	K	ERA	WHIP	OBA	vL	vR	BF/G	H%	S%	xERA	G	L	F	Ctl	Dom	Cmd	hr/f	hr/9	RAR	BPV	R$
RH Reliever		05	TOR	3	5	1	74	62	3.27	1.28	243	236	257	4.7	29%	78%	3.66	50	18	32	3.4	7.5	2.2	12%	1.0	10.0	71	$8
Age	32	06	TOR *	6	3	1	70	81	4.50	1.49	265	211	262	4.5	34%	73%	3.56	43	23	34	4.2	10.4	2.5	16%	1.3	0.5	94	$7
Type	Pwr	07	TOR	1	5	3	57	59	4.58	1.23	226	245	200	4.6	30%	61%	3.45	45	19	36	3.6	9.3	2.6	6%	0.5	-0.5	93	$6
Health	A	08	TOR	1	2	0	47	42	4.19	1.44	213	266	174	4.2	26%	72%	4.62	38	24	38	6.1	8.0	1.3	8%	0.8	0.9	-4	$3
PT/Exp	C	09	TOR	7	3	11	58	56	2.50	1.02	209	274	140	3.7	27%	78%	3.47	38	18	43	2.5	8.7	3.5	6%	0.6	13.9	106	$15
Consist	C	1st Half		5	1	2	27	23	1.99	0.99	207			3.4	26%	81%	3.88	29	23	48	2.3	7.6	3.3	3%	0.3	8.3	81	$7
LIMA Plan	B	2nd Half		2	2	9	31	33	2.95	1.05	211			4.0	27%	76%	3.09	47	14	39	2.7	9.7	3.7	10%	0.9	5.6	128	$8
Rand Var	-5	10	Proj	5	4	25	73	72	3.35	1.13	227			4.0	29%	73%	3.43	41	20	39	2.7	8.9	3.3	9%	0.9	9.0	106	$18

Accepted battlefield promotion to closer role in 2H and ran with it. Despite '08 outlier, history shows this success didn't just come out of nowhere. May end up sharing closer role, but skills say he can do it alone if asked.

French,Luke		Yr	Tm	W	L	Sv	IP	K	ERA	WHIP	OBA	vL	vR	BF/G	H%	S%	xERA	G	L	F	Ctl	Dom	Cmd	hr/f	hr/9	RAR	BPV	R$
LH Starter		05		0	0	0	0	0	0.00	0.00							0.00											
Age	24	06		0	0	0	0	0	0.00	0.00							0.00											
Type	xFB	07		0	0	0	0	0	0.00	0.00							0.00											
Health	A	08	aa	9	11	0	170	76	4.58	1.63	314			28.7	33%	73%	5.83				3.1	4.0	1.3		0.9	-5.8	18	$3
PT/Exp	D	09	2AL *	8	9	0	149	104	4.55	1.48	291	322	310	23.3	33%	72%	4.94	29	23	48	2.9	6.3	2.2	8%	1.1	-1.7	42	$8
Consist	B	1st Half		4	4	0	81	62	3.99	1.29	271			26.3	32%	70%	4.09				2.2	6.9	3.1		0.8	4.6	84	$7
LIMA Plan	C+	2nd Half		4	5	0	67	42	5.22	1.71	314			20.8	34%	73%	5.60	29	23	48	3.7	5.6	1.5	10%	1.5	-6.3	7	$1
Rand Var	-1	10	Proj	5	6	0	87	56	4.66	1.51	294			24.1	32%	72%	5.10	29	23	48	3.0	5.8	1.9	8%	1.1	-7.2	30	$4

4-5, 5.21 ERA in 67 IP at DET and SEA. Nice Cmd gains in 1H in minors, but couldn't bring it to the Show. Problems with RH batters (.937 OPS) suggest best role for now is as a specialist.

Fuentes,Brian		Yr	Tm	W	L	Sv	IP	K	ERA	WHIP	OBA	vL	vR	BF/G	H%	S%	xERA	G	L	F	Ctl	Dom	Cmd	hr/f	hr/9	RAR	BPV	R$
LH Reliever		05	COL	2	5	31	74	91	2.91	1.26	220	167	236	4.0	31%	79%	3.19	38	26	36	4.1	11.1	2.7	9%	0.7	12.2	103	$18
Age	34	06	COL	3	4	30	65	73	3.46	1.17	214	186	217	4.0	28%	75%	3.71	35	16	50	3.6	10.1	2.8	10%	1.1	8.3	97	$18
Type	Pwr xFB	07	COL	3	5	20	61	56	3.08	1.13	210	204	207	3.9	25%	76%	3.88	36	21	43	3.4	8.2	2.4	9%	0.9	10.2	71	$14
Health	B	08	COL	1	5	30	63	82	2.73	1.10	210	184	211	3.8	32%	76%	3.04	33	22	46	3.2	11.8	3.7	5%	0.4	11.9	137	$19
PT/Exp	B	09	LAA	1	5	48	55	46	3.93	1.40	255	239	261	3.7	30%	75%	4.60	36	17	47	3.9	7.5	1.9	8%	1.0	3.6	43	$20
Consist	C	1st Half		0	2	22	27	30	3.65	1.25	246			3.8	33%	72%	3.58	38	17	46	3.0	10.0	3.3	6%	0.7	2.7	114	$10
LIMA Plan	C	2nd Half		1	3	26	28	16	4.19	1.54	262			3.6	28%	77%	5.71	34	17	48	4.8	5.2	1.1	9%	1.3	0.9	-25	$10
Rand Var	-1	10	Proj	2	4	30	58	57	3.88	1.31	241			3.8	30%	73%	4.07	35	19	46	3.7	8.8	2.4	8%	0.9	2.6	72	$15

Gaudy save total masked skill set issues: xERA and BPV detail the problem, 2H Dom and Cmd collapses provide the exclamation point. Despite longer-term history, must treat him as a diminished commodity.

Fulchino,Jeff		Yr	Tm	W	L	Sv	IP	K	ERA	WHIP	OBA	vL	vR	BF/G	H%	S%	xERA	G	L	F	Ctl	Dom	Cmd	hr/f	hr/9	RAR	BPV	R$
RH Reliever		05	aaa	11	7	0	153	91	4.81	1.60	298			23.9	33%	72%	5.58				3.7	5.4	1.5		1.0	-9.6	28	$5
Age	30	06	aaa	6	10	0	140	96	4.84	1.54	285			25.0	33%	69%	5.03				3.7	6.2	1.7		0.7	-5.5	48	$5
Type		07	aaa	6	2	0	88	42	8.13	2.20	370			28.2	39%	64%	9.23				4.9	4.2	0.9		1.6	-39.8	-24	($10)
Health	A	08	aaa	3	4	6	64	42	7.89	2.24	375			12.3	43%	62%	8.02				4.9	5.8	1.2		0.4	-28.3	29	($6)
PT/Exp	D	09	HOU	6	4	0	82	71	3.40	1.18	232	261	209	5.5	28%	73%	3.62	47	14	38	3.0	7.8	2.6	8%	0.8	8.0	86	$9
Consist	F	1st Half		2	3	0	32	22	2.52	1.06	203			5.8	23%	81%	3.88	46	17	37	3.1	6.2	2.0	9%	0.8	6.6	52	$4
LIMA Plan	C+	2nd Half		4	1	0	50	49	3.97	1.26	250			5.4	32%	69%	3.46	48	13	39	2.9	8.8	3.1	7%	0.7	1.4	107	$5
Rand Var	-1	10	Proj	4	3	0	58	42	4.19	1.41	268			8.4	31%	72%	4.29	47	15	38	3.4	6.5	1.9	9%	0.9	-0.2	50	$4

Emerged from obscurity with a sudden Dom spike to augment his GB tendency. Ensuing skill profile reached closer-worthy levels in 2H. He'll have to repeat to convince us, but if he does he's a deep sleeper for Saves.

Galarraga,Armando		Yr	Tm	W	L	Sv	IP	K	ERA	WHIP	OBA	vL	vR	BF/G	H%	S%	xERA	G	L	F	Ctl	Dom	Cmd	hr/f	hr/9	RAR	BPV	R$
RH Starter		05	aa	3	3	0	71	47	6.13	1.46	299			26.0	33%	59%	5.52				2.3	5.9	2.5		1.3	-16.0	44	$0
Age	28	06	aa	1	6	0	41	31	7.63	2.05	379			22.7	43%	64%	8.98				3.0	6.9	2.3		1.6	-15.7	20	($4)
Type		07	aa	11	8	0	152	104	5.98	1.68	308			25.9	34%	66%	6.32				3.8	6.1	1.6		1.2	-28.5	26	$1
Health	A	08	DET	13	7	0	179	126	3.73	1.19	232	267	174	24.5	25%	75%	4.11	44	17	40	3.1	6.3	2.1	13%	1.4	13.7	53	$19
PT/Exp	B	09	DET	6	10	0	144	95	5.64	1.57	281	309	257	22.2	30%	67%	4.97	40	22	39	4.2	5.9	1.4	13%	1.5	-21.0	12	$2
Consist	D	1st Half		5	7	0	86	55	5.34	1.58	284			24.2	30%	71%	4.96	42	21	37	4.2	5.8	1.4	15%	1.7	-9.4	10	$2
LIMA Plan	C	2nd Half		1	3	0	58	40	6.08	1.54	276			19.8	31%	62%	4.98	37	22	41	4.2	6.2	1.5	11%	1.2	-11.6	13	($0)
Rand Var	+2	10	Proj	6	7	0	123	82	4.92	1.52	279			22.7	31%	71%	4.80	41	20	39	3.8	6.0	1.6	11%	1.3	-5.5	24	$4

2009's skills only incrementally worse than the year before, showing the tight-rope act that 2008 really was. We tend to remember those long shots that pay off, but 2009 represents the more typical outcome.

Gallagher,Sean		Yr	Tm	W	L	Sv	IP	K	ERA	WHIP	OBA	vL	vR	BF/G	H%	S%	xERA	G	L	F	Ctl	Dom	Cmd	hr/f	hr/9	RAR	BPV	R$
RH Reliever		05		0	0	0	0	0	0.00	0.00							0.00											
Age	24	06	aa	7	5	0	86	84	4.28	1.81	280			27.2	36%	77%	5.52				6.5	8.8	1.4		0.6	2.5	62	$4
Type	Pwr FB	07	CHC *	10	3	1	116	81	4.50	1.47	269			18.8	31%	69%	4.89	39	16	45	3.9	6.3	1.6	5%	0.6	-1.1	26	$8
Health	D	08	2TM *	7	9	0	144	129	4.80	1.44	257	266	259	22.5	31%	68%	4.38	36	22	43	4.2	8.0	1.9	8%	0.9	-8.8	46	$7
PT/Exp	D	09	SD *	4	2	0	40	27	3.86	1.39	254	323	327	9.1	30%	70%	4.72	34	25	40	3.9	6.0	1.6	2%	0.2	1.6	16	$3
Consist	A	1st Half		2	2	0	34	23	4.49	1.33	257			13.2	30%	64%	4.42	35	27	37	3.2	5.9	1.9	2%	0.3	-1.3	34	$2
LIMA Plan	D+	2nd Half		2	0	0	6	4	-0.00	1.79	240			3.3	30%	100%	6.43	31	19	50	8.0	6.4	0.8	0%	0.0	2.9	-92	$1
Rand Var	-4	10	Proj	8	5	0	113	86	4.56	1.48	264			18.3	31%	71%	4.82	34	21	45	4.2	6.9	1.7	8%	1.0	-7.8	23	$6

3-2, 5.95 ERA in 20 IP at OAK and SD. Has flashed elements of a worthwhile skill set at times. Durability a concern, but FB bias will play well in Petco. If he can get there and get healthy... UP: sub-4.00 ERA.

Gallardo,Yovani		Yr	Tm	W	L	Sv	IP	K	ERA	WHIP	OBA	vL	vR	BF/G	H%	S%	xERA	G	L	F	Ctl	Dom	Cmd	hr/f	hr/9	RAR	BPV	R$
RH Starter		05		0	0	0	0	0	0.00	0.00							0.00											
Age	24	06	aa	5	2	0	77	80	2.22	1.15	214			24.1	29%	81%	2.52				3.4	9.3	2.7		0.3	21.8	115	$12
Type	Pwr	07	MIL *	17	8	0	188	211	3.56	1.19	232	247	244	23.4	32%	71%	3.30	38	24	38	3.1	10.1	3.3	7%	0.6	20.1	115	$26
Health	F	08	MIL *	0	1	0	39	37	3.33	1.42	280	324	204	24.3	34%	81%	4.10	40	12	48	2.9	8.4	2.9	9%	1.1	4.5	91	$2
PT/Exp	C	09	MIL	13	12	0	186	204	3.73	1.31	223	213	225	26.2	29%	75%	3.52	45	19	36	4.6	9.9	2.2	12%	1.0	10.5	78	$18
Consist	B	1st Half		8	5	0	104	114	2.76	1.15	201			26.5	26%	81%	3.20	47	20	34	4.0	9.8	2.5	13%	1.0	18.3	95	$15
LIMA Plan	C+	2nd Half		5	7	0	82	90	4.97	1.52	249			25.9	32%	69%	3.95	43	19	38	5.3	9.9	1.9	12%	1.1	-7.8	57	$4
Rand Var	+1	10	Proj	12	10	0	189	199	3.63	1.34	242			25.1	31%	76%	3.68	42	18	40	3.9	9.5	2.4	10%	0.9	13.6	86	$18

Fulfilled ace-level expectations in 1H, although xERA shows 1H/2H split wasn't as dramatic as it looks. MIL handled him reasonably, should be more prepared for 2010 workload. If so... UP: two halves like 1H '09.

Garcia,Freddy		Yr	Tm	W	L	Sv	IP	K	ERA	WHIP	OBA	vL	vR	BF/G	H%	S%	xERA	G	L	F	Ctl	Dom	Cmd	hr/f	hr/9	RAR	BPV	R$
RH Starter		05	CHW	14	8	0	228	146	3.87	1.25	259	268	249	28.8	29%	72%	3.82	49	21	31	2.4	5.8	2.4	12%	1.0	14.2	67	$20
Age	33	06	CHW	17	9	0	216	135	4.54	1.28	272	262	271	27.5	29%	68%	4.32	41	18	41	2.0	5.6	2.8	11%	1.3	0.5	66	$20
Type		07	PHI	1	5	0	58	50	5.90	1.60	312	292	339	23.9	35%	68%	4.28	36	27	38	2.9	7.8	2.6	17%	1.9	-10.5	74	($0)
Health	C	08	DET	1	1	0	15	12	4.20	1.13	206	100	265	20.3	21%	71%	4.11	40	14	45	3.6	7.2	2.0	16%	1.8	0.3	51	$2
PT/Exp	D	09	CHW *	3	7	0	73	50	5.30	1.34	280	196	316	25.9	32%	60%	4.26	45	14	41	2.2	6.2	2.8	7%	0.9	-7.6	74	$3
Consist	A	1st Half		0	2	0	11	4	10.59	1.93	330			26.6	33%	44%	7.94				4.8	3.5	0.7		1.9	-8.3	-33	($2)
LIMA Plan	C+	2nd Half		3	5	0	62	46	4.36	1.24	270			25.8	32%	65%	3.94	45	14	41	1.7	6.6	3.8	6%	0.7	0.7	95	$5
Rand Var	+3	10	Proj	6	6	0	102	72	4.26	1.37	278			27.2	31%	72%	4.28	41	19	40	2.6	6.4	2.5	10%	1.2	1.9	65	$8

3-4, 4.34 ERA in 56 IP at CHW. On the long road back from '07 shoulder surgery, in 2H he showed flashes of recapturing former skills. Sample is small and durability an open question, but... UP: 15 Wins, 3.75 ERA.

Garland,Jon		Yr	Tm	W	L	Sv	IP	K	ERA	WHIP	OBA	vL	vR	BF/G	H%	S%	xERA	G	L	F	Ctl	Dom	Cmd	hr/f	hr/9	RAR	BPV	R$
RH Starter		05	CHW	18	10	0	221	115	3.50	1.17	254	267	242	28.3	27%	74%	3.96	47	21	32	1.9	4.7	2.4	11%	1.1	23.7	58	$24
Age	30	06	CHW	18	7	0	211	112	4.52	1.36	293	290	297	27.4	31%	69%	4.47	42	20	38	1.7	4.8	2.7	9%	1.1	1.0	59	$17
Type	Con	07	CHW	10	13	0	208	98	4.23	1.33	272	259	281	27.6	29%	69%	4.75	39	23	38	2.5	4.2	1.7	7%	0.8	7.0	27	$13
Health	A	08	LAA	14	8	0	197	90	4.90	1.50	299	300	307	27.2	32%	69%	4.42	50	22	28	2.7	4.1	1.5	12%	1.1	-13.3	29	$7
PT/Exp	A	09	2NL	11	13	0	204	109	4.01	1.40	281	271	293	26.7	30%	74%	4.47	46	19	35	2.7	4.8	1.8	10%	1.1	4.4	38	$10
Consist	A	1st Half		4	8	0	95	35	4.83	1.54	289			26.5	30%	70%	5.32	44	18	38	3.5	3.3	0.9	8%	0.9	-7.5	-13	$1
LIMA Plan	D+	2nd Half		7	5	0	109	74	3.31	1.27	274			26.9	31%	79%	3.77	47	21	32	2.0	6.1	3.1	12%	1.1	11.9	82	$10
Rand Var	0	10	Proj	12	11	0	203	105	4.30	1.39	283			27.4	30%	72%	4.43	46	21	33	2.5	4.7	1.8	10%	1.0	-4.2	39	$10

Year after year, it's the same: 200 IP, mid-4's xERA, no K's, double-digit Wins. And often there's also a half season with solid ERA/BPIs that teases us into thinking there may be more. But there's never any more.

RAY MURPHY

Garza,Matt

Garza,Matt		W	L	Sv	IP	K	ERA	WHIP	OBA	vL	vR	BF/G	H%	S%	xERA	G	L	F	Ctl	Dom	Cmd	hr/f	hr/9	RAR	BPV	R$
RH Starter	05	0	0	0	0	0	0.00	0.00							0.00											
Age 26	06 MIN *	12	9	0	141	123	4.15	1.30	255	245	356	23.8	31%	68%	4.03	35	25	40	3.0	7.8	2.6	6%	0.6	7.2	73	$16
Type Pwr FB	07 MIN *	9	13	0	175	144	4.53	1.59	300	314	276	24.7	36%	72%	4.29	48	15	38	3.4	7.4	2.1	7%	0.7	-0.4	66	$8
Health A	08 TAM	11	9	0	185	128	3.70	1.24	246	244	245	25.6	28%	73%	4.19	42	18	40	2.9	6.2	2.2	8%	0.9	14.7	54	$18
PT/Exp A	09 TAM	8	12	0	203	189	3.95	1.26	236	196	271	26.5	28%	72%	3.96	40	18	43	3.5	8.4	2.4	10%	1.1	12.7	74	$19
Consist A	1st Half	6	5	0	104	88	3.46	1.18	216			26.7	25%	76%	3.96	43	17	40	3.6	7.6	2.1	12%	1.2	12.8	60	$12
LIMA Plan C+	2nd Half	2	7	0	99	101	4.46	1.34	256			26.4	32%	69%	3.95	36	18	46	3.4	9.2	2.7	9%	1.0	-0.1	89	$7
Rand Var 0	10 Proj	12	9	0	203	184	3.72	1.26	248			25.0	30%	73%	3.86	40	18	42	3.0	8.2	2.7	9%	0.9	14.4	85	$21

Via wins and ERA, unable to sustain 2008. But xERA and BPV chronicle his improvement. Monitor his 2H FB%, but 2H skills spike, durability, and 50/6% PQS split point to a repeat in 2010. At least.

Gaudin,Chad

Gaudin,Chad		W	L	Sv	IP	K	ERA	WHIP	OBA	vL	vR	BF/G	H%	S%	xERA	G	L	F	Ctl	Dom	Cmd	hr/f	hr/9	RAR	BPV	R$
RH Starter	05 TOR *	10	11	0	163	117	4.64	1.36	285	481	462	24.9	32%	68%	3.86	40	29	31	2.2	6.5	3.0	12%	1.0	-5.4	76	$11
Age 27	06 OAK *	7	2	2	88	58	2.45	1.31	210	253	201	6.3	25%	81%	5.05	39	16	45	5.0	5.9	1.2	3%	0.3	22.9	-11	$12
Type Pwr	07 OAK	11	13	0	199	154	4.43	1.53	267	282	250	26.1	31%	73%	4.24	51	19	30	4.5	7.0	1.5	12%	0.9	2.0	32	$11
Health A	08 2TM	9	5	0	90	71	4.40	1.32	266	273	258	7.6	31%	69%	4.08	39	21	40	2.7	7.1	2.6	10%	1.1	-1.0	72	$9
PT/Exp A	09 2TM	6	10	0	147	139	4.64	1.51	260	296	224	21.0	32%	70%	4.13	44	20	36	4.6	8.5	1.8	9%	0.9	-6.0	49	$7
Consist A	1st Half	4	6	0	70	74	5.00	1.40	238			23.3	31%	64%	3.81	43	19	38	4.6	9.5	2.1	9%	0.8	-6.0	67	$4
LIMA Plan C	2nd Half	2	4	0	77	65	4.32	1.61	279			19.4	33%	75%	4.43	44	21	35	4.7	7.6	1.6	10%	0.9	-0.1	33	$2
Rand Var 0	10 Proj	6	6	0	106	89	4.44	1.45	263			14.0	31%	71%	4.19	44	20	36	4.0	7.6	1.9	10%	0.9	2.0	50	$6

If we could fuse 2009's Dom, 2008's Ctl, and 2007's GB%, then we'd have something. Six of eight starts from 6/17 to 7/26 were PQS-DOM. Five of next eight starts were PQS-0. Flip a coin (and cross your fingers).

Geer,Josh

Geer,Josh		W	L	Sv	IP	K	ERA	WHIP	OBA	vL	vR	BF/G	H%	S%	xERA	G	L	F	Ctl	Dom	Cmd	hr/f	hr/9	RAR	BPV	R$
RH Starter	05	0	0	0	0	0	0.00	0.00							0.00											
Age 26	06	0	0	0	0	0	0.00	0.00							0.00											
Type Con	07 aa	17	6	0	177	89	4.01	1.31	288			27.8	32%	69%	4.32				1.6	4.5	2.9		0.5	9.8	70	$17
Health A	08 aaa	8	9	0	166	82	5.54	1.66	325			27.2	34%	68%	6.40				2.7	4.4	1.6		1.2	-25.2	15	($1)
PT/Exp D	09 SD *	3	12	0	155	70	5.69	1.46	301	290	286	24.2	30%	66%	4.85	42	18	40	2.2	4.0	1.8	14%	1.8	-28.6	34	($2)
Consist D	1st Half	2	4	0	87	43	5.48	1.38	288			23.4	29%	66%	4.72	42	16	42	2.2	4.4	2.0	14%	1.9	-13.9	41	$0
LIMA Plan C+	2nd Half	1	8	0	68	27	5.95	1.56	318			25.3	31%	66%	4.89	44	22	34	2.2	3.5	1.6	16%	1.8	-14.7	25	($2)
Rand Var +3	10 Proj	2	4	0	58	27	4.66	1.45	297			25.3	31%	71%	4.81	43	19	39	2.3	4.2	1.8	10%	1.2	-3.9	33	$1

1-7, 5.96 ERA in 103 IP at SD. February to-do list:
1. Limit hits (173 in 2009)
2. Develop strikeout pitch
3. Do better w/ runners on base

Still time, but history in minors suggests tasks will remain.

Gervacio,Sammy

Gervacio,Sammy		W	L	Sv	IP	K	ERA	WHIP	OBA	vL	vR	BF/G	H%	S%	xERA	G	L	F	Ctl	Dom	Cmd	hr/f	hr/9	RAR	BPV	R$
RH Reliever	05	0	0	0	0	0	0.00	0.00							0.00											
Age 25	06	0	0	0	0	0	0.00	0.00							0.00											
Type Pwr xGB	07 aa	3	2	0	23	22	2.74	1.35	217			7.6	27%	83%	3.61				5.1	8.6	1.7		0.8	4.9	75	$4
Health A	08 aa	3	5	5	73	80	4.19	1.50	283			6.4	37%	74%	5.07				3.4	9.8	2.9		1.0	1.0	87	$6
PT/Exp F	09 HOU *	3	3	0	73	73	4.50	1.28	238	250	208	4.5	30%	65%	3.10	57	15	28	3.6	8.9	2.5	11%	0.8	-2.8	100	$5
Consist D	1st Half	2	1	0	39	33	6.46	1.51	267			6.2	32%	56%	4.81				4.4	7.6	1.7		0.9	-10.9	56	($0)
LIMA Plan A	2nd Half	1	2	0	34	40	2.26	1.01	203			3.4	28%	80%	2.43	57	15	28	2.7	10.4	3.9	10%	0.6	8.1	151	$5
Rand Var +3	10 Proj	2	3	0	58	61	3.57	1.24	234			4.8	30%	73%	2.94	57	15	28	3.4	9.5	2.8	12%	0.8	9.4	114	$5

1-1, 2.14 ERA in 21 IP at HOU. Fantastic 2H, MLB success may entice some to think "closer." Delivery, slight build and Ks via change of speeds, not heat, are strikes against. Follow for now and keep eye on usage pattern.

Gonzalez,Edgar

Gonzalez,Edgar		W	L	Sv	IP	K	ERA	WHIP	OBA	vL	vR	BF/G	H%	S%	xERA	G	L	F	Ctl	Dom	Cmd	hr/f	hr/9	RAR	BPV	R$
RH Reliever	05 aaa	1	5	0	160	100	4.50	1.36	289			25.3	32%	69%	4.81				1.9	5.6	3.0		1.0	-3.9	63	$5
Age 27	06 ARI *	6	12	0	180	122	4.49	1.33	286	259	288	21.9	32%	68%	4.50	38	15	47	1.7	6.1	3.5	7%	0.9	-0.1	78	$10
Type FB	07 ARI	8	4	0	102	62	5.03	1.35	277	313	237	13.6	29%	68%	4.47	45	15	40	2.5	5.5	2.2	13%	1.6	-7.6	54	$6
Health C	08 ARI	1	3	0	48	32	6.00	1.65	300	259	336	12.9	33%	66%	5.10	38	20	43	3.9	6.0	1.5	12%	1.5	-10.2	17	($1)
PT/Exp C	09 OAK *	3	6	0	105	59	5.62	1.69	310	351	230	14.6	35%	66%	5.32	41	18	41	3.8	5.1	1.3	5%	0.6	-15.1	8	($1)
Consist A	1st Half	3	3	0	65	40	5.89	1.67	312			16.7	36%	63%	5.13	40	18	41	3.5	5.5	1.6	4%	0.6	-11.6	24	($0)
LIMA Plan C	2nd Half	0	3	0	39	19	5.18	1.72	306			12.1	33%	70%	5.68	42	18	40	4.3	4.3	1.0	6%	0.8	-3.5	-18	($1)
Rand Var +1	10 Proj	1	3	0	44	26	5.38	1.59	298			14.0	32%	68%	5.05	41	18	41	3.5	5.4	1.5	10%	1.2	-3.3	21	$0

0-4, 5.51 ERA in 65 IP at OAK. Three September starts, all PQS-0; history says it's time to end that experiment. H% points to improvement, but Cmd, s% and xERA trends scuttle that idea. Onward.

Gonzalez,Gio

Gonzalez,Gio		W	L	Sv	IP	K	ERA	WHIP	OBA	vL	vR	BF/G	H%	S%	xERA	G	L	F	Ctl	Dom	Cmd	hr/f	hr/9	RAR	BPV	R$
LH Starter	05	0	0	0	0	0	0.00	0.00							0.00											
Age 24	06 aa	7	12	0	154	139	6.36	1.64	281			26.0	32%	65%	6.41				4.8	8.1	1.7		1.9	-35.0	25	$1
Type Pwr	07 aa	9	7	0	150	165	4.44	1.35	251			23.7	33%	69%	4.19				3.7	9.9	2.7		0.9	0.4	94	$13
Health A	08 OAK *	9	11	0	157	140	5.27	1.46	251	194	260	20.8	30%	66%	4.32	42	18	40	4.6	8.0	1.7	11%	1.2	-17.8	39	$8
PT/Exp D	09 OAK *	10	8	0	160	167	4.56	1.53	260	340	271	22.2	33%	72%	3.97	46	18	36	4.9	9.4	1.9	12%	1.0	-2.1	62	$11
Consist A	1st Half	4	3	0	78	79	3.69	1.47	249			21.4	32%	77%	4.03	44	20	36	4.8	9.1	1.9	9%	0.8	7.4	55	$7
LIMA Plan C	2nd Half	6	5	0	82	88	5.39	1.59	270			23.0	34%	68%	3.94	47	18	36	4.9	9.7	2.0	14%	1.2	-9.5	67	$4
Rand Var +2	10 Proj	10	9	0	145	145	4.34	1.41	245			21.7	31%	71%	3.88	45	18	37	4.5	9.0	2.0	11%	1.0	9.9	65	$13

6-7, 5.75 ERA in 99 IP at OAK. Terrific arm is unquestioned, but we'd like to see some Ctl growth. Due some h% and hr/f luck (see 2H) and if GB% sticks, he could dominate. Likely a couple seasons away, though.

Gonzalez,Mike

Gonzalez,Mike		W	L	Sv	IP	K	ERA	WHIP	OBA	vL	vR	BF/G	H%	S%	xERA	G	L	F	Ctl	Dom	Cmd	hr/f	hr/9	RAR	BPV	R$
LH Reliever	05 PIT	1	3	3	50	58	2.70	1.32	199	156	223	4.2	28%	80%	3.30	53	18	30	5.6	10.4	1.9	6%	0.4	9.5	68	$6
Age 31	06 PIT	3	4	24	54	64	2.17	1.35	216	163	227	4.3	32%	83%	3.70	37	27	36	5.2	10.7	2.1	2%	0.2	15.5	67	$16
Type Pwr FB	07 ATL	2	0	2	17	13	1.59	1.35	238	333	189	4.0	30%	87%	4.55	39	20	41	4.2	6.9	1.6	0%	0.0	6.0	26	$3
Health F	08 ATL *	1	3	15	45	52	3.47	1.31	257	259	196	4.2	34%	79%	3.53	31	25	44	3.1	10.5	3.4	11%	1.2	4.4	114	$9
PT/Exp D	09 ATL	5	4	10	74	90	2.42	1.20	211	194	218	3.8	29%	84%	3.35	38	18	44	4.0	10.9	2.7	9%	0.8	16.2	105	$14
Consist B	1st Half	2	0	9	37	50	2.68	1.22	229			3.9	33%	83%	3.04	38	15	47	3.4	12.2	3.6	10%	1.0	6.9	143	$8
LIMA Plan B+	2nd Half	3	4	1	37	40	2.17	1.18	192			3.7	25%	85%	3.68	38	20	42	4.6	9.7	2.1	8%	0.7	9.3	66	$6
Rand Var -5	10 Proj	3	4	25	65	77	3.31	1.26	220			4.0	30%	77%	3.48	38	20	42	4.1	10.6	2.6	10%	1.0	6.3	95	$15

Though he avoided the DL, back, forearm and elbow issues dogged him all season. Here is the big question: Will he get 35 saves or 35 IP? Cast your vote. Winners placed in drawing for a free 2011 book. Details on p. 10.

Gorzelanny,Tom

Gorzelanny,Tom		W	L	Sv	IP	K	ERA	WHIP	OBA	vL	vR	BF/G	H%	S%	xERA	G	L	F	Ctl	Dom	Cmd	hr/f	hr/9	RAR	BPV	R$
LH Reliever	05 aa	8	5	0	129	102	3.88	1.36	264			24.0	32%	71%	3.84				3.1	7.1	2.3		0.4	6.8	80	$11
Age 27	06 PIT *	8	10	0	160	120	3.53	1.20	227	239	223	24.5	27%	70%	3.90	49	18	33	3.4	6.7	2.0	5%	0.4	18.8	57	$16
Type FB	07 PIT	14	10	0	202	135	3.88	1.40	273	217	284	27.2	31%	74%	4.51	42	18	40	3.0	6.0	2.0	7%	0.8	13.5	47	$15
Health A	08 PIT *	9	10	0	140	91	5.74	1.65	284	261	299	22.9	31%	67%	5.34	40	16	44	4.8	5.9	1.2	10%	1.4	-25.5	-5	$0
PT/Exp B	09 2NL *	11	6	0	134	105	4.21	1.45	276	244	252	15.8	33%	71%	4.26	41	21	38	3.4	7.1	2.1	6%	0.6	-0.4	54	$9
Consist B	1st Half	6	3	0	70	55	3.87	1.34	258			15.0	32%	69%	3.87	46	21	33	3.2	7.1	2.2	3%	0.3	2.8	65	$6
LIMA Plan C	2nd Half	5	3	0	64	50	4.59	1.58	294			16.8	34%	73%	4.49	40	22	39	3.6	7.0	1.9	9%	1.1	-3.2	46	$3
Rand Var -1	10 Proj	11	8	0	145	108	4.22	1.42	270			24.2	31%	73%	4.40	41	19	40	3.4	6.7	2.0	9%	1.1	-2.5	48	$10

7-3, 5.55 ERA in 47 IP at PIT, CHC. Why there's still hope:
- Dominated at AAA (2.48 ERA)
- Repeated skills upon callup (9.0 Dom, 2.8 Cmd, 90 BPV)
- Still 27, fresh start with CHC

Tiny sample but could surprise.

Grabow,John

Grabow,John		W	L	Sv	IP	K	ERA	WHIP	OBA	vL	vR	BF/G	H%	S%	xERA	G	L	F	Ctl	Dom	Cmd	hr/f	hr/9	RAR	BPV	R$
LH Reliever	05 PIT	2	3	0	52	42	4.85	1.37	239	219	250	3.5	28%	66%	4.03	47	20	33	4.3	7.3	1.7	12%	1.0	-3.9	39	$2
Age 31	06 PIT	4	2	0	69	66	4.16	1.42	258	275	251	4.2	32%	73%	3.78	49	18	34	3.9	8.6	2.2	11%	0.9	2.8	76	$5
Type Pwr	07 PIT	3	2	1	52	42	4.53	1.45	278	238	303	3.6	33%	71%	3.95	50	17	33	3.3	7.3	2.2	11%	1.0	-0.6	70	$3
Health A	08 PIT	6	3	4	76	62	2.84	1.28	219	239	207	4.3	25%	83%	4.32	40	20	41	4.4	7.3	1.7	10%	1.1	13.4	31	$10
PT/Exp C	09 2NL	3	0	0	72	57	3.36	1.41	233	222	238	4.2	28%	77%	4.60	43	15	41	5.0	7.1	1.4	6%	0.6	7.4	15	$5
Consist A	1st Half	3	0	0	36	32	3.75	1.56	256			4.6	32%	77%	4.60	41	17	41	5.3	8.0	1.5	7%	0.8	2.0	22	$2
LIMA Plan C+	2nd Half	0	0	0	36	25	2.98	1.27	209			3.8	24%	77%	4.59	45	13	42	4.7	6.2	1.3	5%	0.5	5.4	8	$2
Rand Var -4	10 Proj	3	1	0	65	52	4.00	1.41	246			4.1	29%	74%	4.40	44	17	39	4.4	7.2	1.6	9%	1.0	-1.1	32	$4

On the one hand, a sharp ERA the last two seasons makes him a safe RP choice. But on the other hand, xERA history warns to stay clear. Ctl, Cmd trends strongly lean towards the latter.

BRENT HERSHEY

Green,Sean

		Yr	Tm	W	L	Sv	IP	K	ERA	WHIP	OBA	vL	vR	BF/G	H%	S%	xERA	G	L	F	Ctl	Dom	Cmd	hr/f	hr/9	RAR	BPV	R$
RH	Reliever	05	a/a	4	3	15	73	51	4.37	1.53	253			6.0	30%	70%	4.00				5.2	6.3	1.2		0.3	-0.6	60	$8
Age	30	06	SEA	0	0	0	32	15	4.50	1.47	274			5.9	30%	69%	4.31	58	19	24	3.7	4.2	1.2	8%	0.6	0.2	13	$1
Type	Pwr xGB	07	SEA *	7	3	1	85	60	3.73	1.64	285	329	286	5.2	34%	76%	3.93	61	19	20	4.7	6.4	1.4	4%	0.2	8.2	28	$6
Health	A	08	SEA	4	5	1	79	62	4.67	1.47	264	299	233	4.8	32%	66%	3.36	63	17	20	4.1	7.1	1.7	6%	0.3	-3.2	58	$4
PT/Exp	C	09	NYM	1	4	1	70	54	4.52	1.43	246	223	250	3.8	29%	68%	3.40	66	14	20	4.6	7.0	1.5	12%	0.6	-2.8	44	$2
Consist	A	1st Half		1	2	0	34	29	5.26	1.49	272			4.1	32%	66%	3.42	63	13	24	3.9	7.6	1.9	16%	1.1	-4.5	71	$0
LIMA Plan	B	2nd Half		0	2	1	36	25	3.80	1.38	219			3.6	26%	71%	3.32	70	15	15	5.3	6.3	1.2	6%	0.3	1.7	18	$2
Rand Var	+2	10	Proj	2	4	3	73	54	4.34	1.48	255			4.4	30%	70%	3.55	64	16	20	4.6	6.7	1.5	9%	0.5	6.4	39	$3

How can a guy have a 5.0+ Ctl and a sub-4.00 ERA? That 2H GB% is how. While it helps to prevent those BB from turning into ER via HR, a sub-2.0 Cmd continues to make him a fringe middle man. Use 2H as upside.

Gregerson,Luke

		Yr	Tm	W	L	Sv	IP	K	ERA	WHIP	OBA	vL	vR	BF/G	H%	S%	xERA	G	L	F	Ctl	Dom	Cmd	hr/f	hr/9	RAR	BPV	R$
RH	Reliever	05		0	0	0	0	0	0.00	0.00							0.00											
Age	25	06		0	0	0	0	0	0.00	0.00							0.00											
Type	Pwr	07		0	0	0	0	0	0.00	0.00							0.00											
Health	A	08	aa	7	6	10	75	64	3.78	1.28	250			5.5	31%	71%	3.63				3.0	7.6	2.5		0.6	4.8	85	$12
PT/Exp	D	09	SD	2	4	1	75	93	3.24	1.24	227	285	161	4.3	33%	73%	2.94	46	21	33	3.7	11.2	3.0	5%	0.4	8.8	124	$8
Consist	B	1st Half		0	3	0	34	35	3.17	1.44	238			5.0	32%	77%	3.72	46	24	30	5.0	9.2	1.8	4%	0.3	4.3	55	$2
LIMA Plan	A	2nd Half		2	1	1	41	58	3.30	1.08	217			3.9	34%	69%	2.38	45	19	36	2.6	12.8	4.8	6%	0.4	4.5	182	$6
Rand Var	0	10	Proj	4	5	5	73	79	3.35	1.24	236			4.7	32%	73%	3.21	46	21	34	3.4	9.8	2.9	6%	0.5	9.4	110	$10

You don't see growth like this often. Huge Dom jump and 2H Ctl gains point to big things in '10. Missing piece is an out pitch vs. LHers. But with this Dom + Cmd + GB%, he just needs opportunity. UP: 30 SV

Gregg,Kevin

		Yr	Tm	W	L	Sv	IP	K	ERA	WHIP	OBA	vL	vR	BF/G	H%	S%	xERA	G	L	F	Ctl	Dom	Cmd	hr/f	hr/9	RAR	BPV	R$
RH	Reliever	05	ANA *	4	3	0	98	81	4.65	1.50	282	267	279	10.9	33%	70%	3.99	48	19	33	3.5	7.4	2.1	10%	0.9	-3.3	64	$4
Age	31	06	LAA	3	4	0	78	71	4.15	1.40	285	298	268	10.5	34%	74%	4.12	36	18	46	2.4	8.2	3.4	9%	1.2	3.9	96	$6
Type	Pwr FB	07	FLA	0	5	32	84	87	3.54	1.23	210	162	247	4.7	27%	73%	4.25	29	16	55	4.3	9.3	2.2	6%	0.8	9.2	59	$18
Health	A	08	FLA	7	8	29	69	58	3.41	1.28	208	181	222	4.0	26%	73%	4.13	45	20	35	4.8	7.6	1.6	5%	0.4	7.3	29	$18
PT/Exp	A	09	CHC	5	6	23	69	71	4.72	1.31	236	195	257	4.0	28%	70%	3.85	38	18	44	3.9	9.3	2.4	16%	1.7	-4.5	77	$13
Consist	A	1st Half		2	2	14	35	35	3.85	1.34	238			4.0	28%	78%	3.86	40	19	40	4.1	9.0	2.2	16%	1.5	1.5	69	$8
LIMA Plan	C+	2nd Half		3	4	9	34	36	5.62	1.28	234			4.0	27%	61%	3.85	35	16	49	3.7	9.6	2.6	16%	1.9	-5.9	86	$5
Rand Var	+3	10	Proj	5	6	15	73	73	3.97	1.27	230			4.4	28%	73%	3.86	38	18	44	3.8	9.1	2.4	12%	1.2	3.6	76	$12

Blame aberrant 2H S% and hr/f for loss of closer role, not skills. Both these should regress to the mean; xERA tells the real tale. As FB pitcher w/control issues, he'll continue to be volatile. But w/ another chance... UP: 30 SV

Greinke,Zack

		Yr	Tm	W	L	Sv	IP	K	ERA	WHIP	OBA	vL	vR	BF/G	H%	S%	xERA	G	L	F	Ctl	Dom	Cmd	hr/f	hr/9	RAR	BPV	R$
RH	Starter	05	KC	5	17	0	183	114	5.80	1.56	311	340	279	24.9	34%	64%	4.61	39	23	37	2.6	5.6	2.2	10%	1.1	-32.3	48	($0)
Age	26	06	KC *	9	3	0	111	87	4.69	1.23	260	400	200	22.0	30%	63%	3.70	35	35	30	2.2	7.0	3.2	11%	0.9	-1.8	81	$12
Type	Pwr FB	07	KC	7	7	1	122	106	3.69	1.30	262	266	263	9.9	32%	74%	4.15	32	22	46	2.7	7.8	2.9	7%	0.9	12.3	79	$13
Health	A	08	KC	13	10	0	202	183	3.47	1.28	261	287	232	26.5	32%	76%	3.63	43	19	38	2.5	8.1	3.3	9%	0.9	21.9	100	$22
PT/Exp	A	09	KC	16	8	0	229	242	2.16	1.07	232	250	211	27.7	31%	81%	3.18	40	19	41	2.0	9.5	4.7	5%	0.4	64.9	135	$38
Consist	A	1st Half		10	3	0	115	114	1.95	1.03	236			28.4	32%	81%	3.09	41	20	38	1.4	8.9	6.3	3%	0.2	35.5	142	$22
LIMA Plan	C	2nd Half		6	5	0	114	128	2.36	1.12	228			27.1	31%	82%	3.27	39	18	43	2.6	10.1	3.9	6%	0.6	29.4	128	$18
Rand Var	-5	10	Proj	14	10	0	218	217	3.10	1.20	250			21.3	32%	77%	3.47	39	20	41	2.3	9.0	3.9	8%	0.8	25.9	116	$28

A year for the ages. Surging Cmd says repeat is possible, but elevated S% and low hr/f suggest ERA is headed toward 3.00. That still makes him an ace, just not one about to go on a late '90s vintage Pedro run.

Grilli,Jason

		Yr	Tm	W	L	Sv	IP	K	ERA	WHIP	OBA	vL	vR	BF/G	H%	S%	xERA	G	L	F	Ctl	Dom	Cmd	hr/f	hr/9	RAR	BPV	R$
RH	Reliever	05	aaa	1	9	0	160	86	5.38	1.63	308			27.0	33%	69%	6.00				3.3	4.9	1.5		1.2	-21.2	17	($3)
Age	33	06	DET	2	3	0	62	31	4.21	1.39	259	292	249	5.2	28%	71%	4.91	47	15	38	3.6	4.5	1.2	8%	0.9	2.7	8	$3
Type	Pwr FB	07	DET	5	3	0	80	62	4.74	1.42	265	237	275	6.1	32%	66%	4.33	45	16	39	3.6	7.0	1.9	5%	0.6	-2.3	51	$5
Health	A	08	2TM	3	3	1	75	69	3.00	1.40	241	237	242	5.4	31%	78%	4.01	42	23	34	4.6	8.3	1.8	3%	0.2	12.1	46	$7
PT/Exp	C	09	2TM	2	3	1	46	49	5.32	1.68	280	262	289	4.0	37%	68%	4.58	34	21	46	5.3	9.6	1.8	7%	0.8	-5.7	42	$1
Consist	A	1st Half		0	2	1	27	26	4.96	1.80	307			4.3	38%	74%	4.89	34	21	45	5.0	8.6	1.7	8%	1.0	-2.2	33	($0)
LIMA Plan	C+	2nd Half		2	1	0	19	23	5.84	1.51	235			3.7	34%	59%	4.14	32	20	48	5.8	11.2	1.9	5%	0.5	-3.5	54	$1
Rand Var	+2	10	Proj	3	3	0	51	51	4.43	1.50	251			4.8	32%	71%	4.27	39	20	41	5.0	9.0	1.8	7%	0.7	0.5	46	$3

ERA surge was the product of inflated H% and bad control. Surging Dom won't matter if he can't fix latter. FB% spike says there's HR risk too, a flammable combo for someone w/bad Ctl. Risk still outweighs reward here.

Guardado,Eddie

		Yr	Tm	W	L	Sv	IP	K	ERA	WHIP	OBA	vL	vR	BF/G	H%	S%	xERA	G	L	F	Ctl	Dom	Cmd	hr/f	hr/9	RAR	BPV	R$
LH	Reliever	05	SEA	2	3	36	56	48	2.73	1.19	247	231	242	4.0	29%	83%	3.93	35	19	46	2.4	7.7	3.2	9%	1.1	11.4	87	$18
Age	39	06	2TM	1	3	13	37	39	3.89	1.54	297	239	324	3.8	34%	87%	4.33	33	14	54	3.2	9.5	3.0	17%	2.4	2.9	96	$7
Type	xFB	07	CIN	0	0	0	14	8	7.23	1.46	293	333	273	4.0	31%	50%	5.19	23	29	48	2.6	5.3	2.0	9%	1.3	-4.7	25	($1)
Health	F	08	2AL	4	4	4	56	33	4.16	1.23	240	210	268	3.6	27%	66%	5.03	25	22	53	3.0	5.3	1.7	4%	0.6	1.3	16	$6
PT/Exp	D	09	TEX	1	2	0	38	20	4.46	1.41	265	333	228	3.5	26%	76%	5.15	37	21	42	3.5	4.7	1.3	15%	1.9	-0.1	4	$1
Consist	A	1st Half		1	1	0	22	12	4.86	1.53	293			3.4	30%	73%	5.33	32	23	45	3.2	4.9	1.5	12%	1.6	-1.1	10	$1
LIMA Plan	C	2nd Half		0	1	0	16	8	3.91	1.24	223			3.5	19%	81%	4.83	44	19	38	3.9	4.5	1.1	21%	2.2	1.1	-3	$1
Rand Var	-1	10	Proj	1	2	0	30	16	5.10	1.40	255			3.7	26%	68%	5.34	32	22	46	3.9	4.8	1.2	11%	1.5	-3.3	-9	$1

4 reasons why the end is near...
- Cmd dropping like a rock
- Another 5.00+ ERA
- Owned by LHers 2 of last 3 yrs
- No more flashes of good Dom

Add poor health to the mix, and you can see retirement lurking.

Guerrier,Matt

		Yr	Tm	W	L	Sv	IP	K	ERA	WHIP	OBA	vL	vR	BF/G	H%	S%	xERA	G	L	F	Ctl	Dom	Cmd	hr/f	hr/9	RAR	BPV	R$
RH	Reliever	05	MIN	0	3	0	71	46	3.41	1.33	261	279	247	7.0	30%	76%	4.15	47	19	34	3.0	5.8	1.9	8%	0.8	8.4	48	$4
Age	31	06	MIN	1	0	1	69	37	3.38	1.43	286	333	256	7.7	30%	81%	4.65	45	18	37	2.7	4.8	1.8	10%	1.2	10.0	36	$4
Type	Con	07	MIN	2	4	1	88	68	2.35	1.05	222	264	187	4.8	26%	83%	3.55	47	16	36	2.1	7.0	3.2	10%	0.9	23.4	93	$13
Health	A	08	MIN	6	9	1	76	59	5.19	1.59	281	282	272	4.5	32%	71%	4.45	47	18	35	4.4	7.0	1.6	14%	1.4	-7.9	32	$3
PT/Exp	C	09	MIN	5	1	1	76	47	2.26	0.94	211	194	213	3.7	22%	84%	3.84	42	18	40	1.7	5.6	3.4	10%	1.1	20.5	76	$13
Consist	B	1st Half		3	0	0	35	24	2.82	0.94	208			3.5	22%	79%	3.79	42	16	42	1.8	6.2	3.4	12%	1.3	7.1	82	$6
LIMA Plan	C+	2nd Half		2	1	1	41	23	1.77	0.94	213			4.0	23%	88%	3.88	42	20	38	1.6	5.1	3.3	9%	0.9	13.4	70	$7
Rand Var	-5	10	Proj	4	3	0	68	45	3.71	1.24	262			4.4	29%	74%	4.04	44	18	38	2.1	6.0	2.8	10%	1.1	3.3	72	$7

Reasons ERA will spike in '10...
- Hit rates don't get any luckier
- S% will drop as H% corrects
- Fly ball jump

And with marginal Dom, his margin for error is bigger than it seems. Use xERA as guide.

Guthrie,Jeremy

		Yr	Tm	W	L	Sv	IP	K	ERA	WHIP	OBA	vL	vR	BF/G	H%	S%	xERA	G	L	F	Ctl	Dom	Cmd	hr/f	hr/9	RAR	BPV	R$
RH	Starter	05	aaa	12	10	0	136	84	5.39	1.57	301			24.4	34%	66%	5.41				3.2	5.6	1.7		0.9	-18.2	38	$4
Age	31	06	CLE *	9	5	0	142	88	4.61	1.55	275			21.2	32%	70%	4.62	50	19	31	4.3	5.6	1.3	6%	0.5	-1.0	13	$7
Type	Con FB	07	BAL	7	5	0	175	123	3.70	1.21	250	255	243	22.6	28%	74%	4.05	42	19	38	2.4	6.3	2.6	11%	1.2	17.5	69	$17
Health	A	08	BAL	10	12	0	191	120	3.63	1.23	247	241	243	26.4	27%	75%	4.20	44	18	38	2.7	5.7	2.1	11%	1.1	16.8	50	$17
PT/Exp	A	09	BAL	10	17	0	200	110	5.04	1.42	284	289	274	26.3	29%	69%	5.09	35	19	47	2.7	5.0	1.8	11%	1.6	-14.5	29	$8
Consist	B	1st Half		6	7	0	91	57	5.13	1.39	278			24.6	29%	68%	4.76	38	17	44	2.8	5.6	2.0	13%	1.7	-7.6	43	$5
LIMA Plan	C	2nd Half		4	10	0	109	53	4.96	1.44	289			27.9	30%	70%	5.36	32	20	48	2.6	4.4	1.7	10%	1.5	-6.9	17	$3
Rand Var	0	10	Proj	10	13	0	189	112	4.63	1.43	285			25.6	30%	72%	4.81	38	19	43	2.8	5.3	1.9	11%	1.5	-8.8	38	$10

The ERA spike we all saw coming. Eroding Cmd says the damage isn't done, and spiking FB% confirms high hr/9 wasn't a fluke. With this BPV trend, we can't even hope for a 4.00 ERA anymore.

Gutierrez,Juan

		Yr	Tm	W	L	Sv	IP	K	ERA	WHIP	OBA	vL	vR	BF/G	H%	S%	xERA	G	L	F	Ctl	Dom	Cmd	hr/f	hr/9	RAR	BPV	R$
RH	Reliever	05		0	0	0	0	0	0.00	0.00							0.00											
Age	26	06	aa	8	4	0	103	87	3.78	1.42	277			22.4	33%	76%	4.81				3.1	7.6	2.5		1.0	9.5	68	$10
Type	Pwr	07	aaa	5	10	0	156	86	5.22	1.61	295			27.2	32%	70%	5.89				3.8	5.0	1.3		1.2	-14.6	17	$1
Health	A	08	aaa	5	11	0	116	69	8.86	2.14	379			23.5	42%	58%	8.69				3.8	5.4	1.4		1.2	-65.3	5	($15)
PT/Exp	D	09	ARI	4	3	9	71	66	4.06	1.37	251	297	207	4.7	33%	68%	3.96	40	20	39	3.8	8.4	2.2	3%	0.3	1.2	66	$8
Consist	F	1st Half		1	2	1	38	42	4.71	1.49	281			5.1	38%	66%	3.79	32	28	40	3.5	9.9	2.8	2%	0.2	-2.5	93	$2
LIMA Plan	B	2nd Half		3	1	8	33	24	3.29	1.22	213			4.2	26%	72%	4.14	50	12	38	4.1	6.6	1.6	3%	0.3	3.6	35	$6
Rand Var	-2	10	Proj	4	4	25	71	64	3.94	1.41	265			5.1	33%	73%	4.00	43	18	39	3.6	8.1	2.3	7%	0.8	2.3	71	$13

PRO:
- 1H Dom spike
- GB pitcher in 2nd half

CON:
- Can't get LHers out
- Marginal Ctl

Transition to relief needs time.

STEPHEN NICKRAND

Guzman,Angel

	Yr	Tm	W	L	Sv	IP	K	ERA	WHIP	OBA	vL	vR	BF/G	H%	S%	xERA	G	L	F	Ctl	Dom	Cmd	hr/f	hr/9	RAR	BPV	R$
RH Reliever	05		0	0	0	0	0	0.00	0.00							0.00											
Age 28	06	CHC *	4	10	0	131	128	6.31	1.66	295	305	309	20.0	36%	62%	4.52	32	28	40	4.3	8.8	2.0	10%	1.1	-29.5	51	($1)
Type Pwr	07	CHC *	0	3	0	40	33	5.85	1.55	294			11.2	36%	61%	5.17				3.4	7.4	2.2		0.7	-7.0	67	($0)
Health A	08	CHC *	1	0	0	22	23	3.27	1.32	253			8.5	34%	75%	3.62				3.3	9.4	2.9		0.4	2.7	109	$2
PT/Exp D	09	CHC	3	3	1	61	47	2.95	1.05	192	189	194	4.4	21%	79%	3.78	48	13	39	3.4	6.9	2.0	12%	1.2	9.3	59	$8
Consist B	1st Half		2	1	1	32	27	2.53	1.00	189			4.5	23%	77%	3.35	51	14	35	3.1	7.6	2.5	7%	0.6	6.5	82	$5
LIMA Plan C+	2nd Half		1	2	0	29	20	3.41	1.10	196			4.3	18%	81%	4.25	45	12	43	3.7	6.2	1.7	17%	1.9	2.8	34	$3
Rand Var -5	10	Proj	2	4	0	65	53	4.00	1.32	246			6.7	28%	73%	4.12	44	16	40	3.6	7.3	2.0	10%	1.1	1.1	56	$4

ERA trend would seem to tell the story, or does it? A deflated H% and inflated S% drove this sub-3.00 ERA. We know his arm is good, but lingering triceps issues make him a health risk again. Don't bet on a repeat.

Haeger,Charlie

	Yr	Tm	W	L	Sv	IP	K	ERA	WHIP	OBA	vL	vR	BF/G	H%	S%	xERA	G	L	F	Ctl	Dom	Cmd	hr/f	hr/9	RAR	BPV	R$
RH Starter	05		0	0	0	0	0	0.00	0.00							0.00											
Age 26	06		0	0	0	0	0	0.00	0.00							0.00											
Type	07	aaa	5	16	0	147	112	5.63	1.62	288			27.9	32%	68%	6.06				4.3	6.8	1.6		1.5	-21.1	28	$1
Health A	08	aaa	10	13	0	178	103	5.87	1.57	285			28.6	31%	63%	5.24				4.0	5.2	1.3		0.9	-34.4	29	$1
PT/Exp D	09	LA *	12	7	0	163	95	4.76	1.63	291	125	222	26.5	31%	74%	5.03	48	13	39	4.3	5.2	1.2	11%	1.4	-11.5	6	$4
Consist B	1st Half		8	5	0	103	53	3.96	1.45	267			28.2	29%	75%	4.75				3.8	4.7	1.2		1.0	3.0	26	$6
LIMA Plan C	2nd Half		4	2	0	60	42	6.14	1.94	328			24.3	35%	73%	5.27	48	13	39	5.1	6.3	1.2	16%	2.0	-14.5	2	($3)
Rand Var 0	10	Proj	2	2	0	29	18	4.97	1.66	294			26.5	32%	73%	5.00	48	13	39	4.3	5.6	1.3	11%	1.2	-2.6	9	$0

1-1, 3.32 ERA in 19 IP at LA. He's at the mercy of his knuckleball. When it's dancing, he can be baffling. Given this skill history, he's danced alone more often than not. There's no reason to speculate here.

Halladay,Roy

	Yr	Tm	W	L	Sv	IP	K	ERA	WHIP	OBA	vL	vR	BF/G	H%	S%	xERA	G	L	F	Ctl	Dom	Cmd	hr/f	hr/9	RAR	BPV	R$
RH Starter	05	TOR	12	4	0	141	108	2.42	0.96	229	217	235	28.9	27%	78%	2.60	61	18	21	1.1	6.9	6.0	13%	0.7	34.0	132	$24
Age 32	06	TOR	16	5	0	220	132	3.19	1.10	251	259	244	27.6	28%	74%	3.18	57	21	22	1.4	5.4	3.9	12%	0.8	37.1	95	$29
Type GB	07	TOR	16	7	0	225	139	3.72	1.24	267	265	270	30.3	30%	71%	3.70	53	18	29	1.9	5.6	2.9	7%	0.6	22.0	79	$23
Health B	08	TOR	20	11	0	246	206	2.78	1.05	241	243	230	28.7	29%	76%	2.88	54	19	27	1.4	7.5	5.3	9%	0.7	47.5	129	$37
PT/Exp A	09	TOR	17	10	0	239	208	2.79	1.13	258	240	278	30.2	31%	79%	3.04	50	20	29	1.3	7.8	5.9	11%	0.8	49.1	134	$34
Consist A	1st Half		10	2	0	109	95	2.56	1.05	245			28.8	30%	78%	2.68	56	21	24	1.2	7.8	6.8	10%	0.6	25.4	144	$19
LIMA Plan C	2nd Half		7	8	0	130	113	2.98	1.19	268			31.4	32%	80%	3.33	46	20	34	1.5	7.8	5.4	11%	1.0	23.7	125	$16
Rand Var -1	10	Proj	18	9	0	218	180	2.94	1.12	254			29.3	31%	77%	3.06	52	20	28	1.4	7.4	5.1	10%	0.7	36.8	125	$31

This $20 lock has evolved into a $30+ one. Spiking Dom and continuing pinpoint Ctl suggest there's even sub-2.50 ERA upside here, as confirmed in 1H. His only real risk is injury, given four straight 220+ IP seasons.

Hamels,Cole

	Yr	Tm	W	L	Sv	IP	K	ERA	WHIP	OBA	vL	vR	BF/G	H%	S%	xERA	G	L	F	Ctl	Dom	Cmd	hr/f	hr/9	RAR	BPV	R$
LH Starter	05	aa	2	0	0	19	18	2.84	1.32	183			26.8	22%	83%	3.17				6.2	8.5	1.4		0.9	3.4	70	$3
Age 26	06	PHI *	11	8	0	155	177	3.59	1.15	228	207	244	24.3	30%	73%	3.34	39	18	43	2.8	10.2	3.6	11%	1.1	17.1	125	$21
Type	07	PHI	15	5	0	183	177	3.39	1.12	240	247	236	26.5	29%	76%	3.36	42	19	39	2.1	8.7	4.1	13%	1.2	23.5	119	$25
Health A	08	PHI	14	10	0	227	196	3.09	1.08	231	262	215	27.6	27%	77%	3.52	40	22	39	2.1	7.8	3.7	11%	1.1	33.1	101	$28
PT/Exp A	09	PHI	10	11	0	194	168	4.32	1.29	274	242	282	25.5	32%	69%	3.67	40	21	39	2.0	7.8	3.9	11%	1.1	-3.1	105	$14
Consist A	1st Half		4	5	0	85	77	4.98	1.47	309			24.9	37%	68%	3.59	41	26	33	1.9	8.2	4.3	12%	1.2	-8.2	114	$3
LIMA Plan B+	2nd Half		6	6	0	109	91	3.81	1.14	244			26.0	29%	70%	3.72	40	17	43	2.1	7.5	3.6	10%	1.1	5.1	98	$11
Rand Var +1	10	Proj	16	9	0	218	194	3.56	1.18	253			26.2	30%	74%	3.54	40	20	39	2.0	8.0	4.0	11%	1.1	19.4	109	$24

Former ace will be underbid in some leagues due to ERA and WHIP spikes. Blame those issues on 1H H% uptick, in most part vs. RHers. Four years of 100+ BPV confirms this remains an ace. Plenty of profit here.

Hammel,Jason

	Yr	Tm	W	L	Sv	IP	K	ERA	WHIP	OBA	vL	vR	BF/G	H%	S%	xERA	G	L	F	Ctl	Dom	Cmd	hr/f	hr/9	RAR	BPV	R$
RH Starter	05	a/a	11	4	0	136	106	3.38	1.32	260			26.2	31%	76%	3.97				2.9	7.0	2.4		0.7	15.6	74	$14
Age 27	06	TAM *	5	15	0	171	132	6.10	1.62	311	372	299	23.5	36%	62%	4.44	44	19	38	3.1	6.9	2.2	9%	1.0	-32.5	63	$1
Type	07	TAM *	7	10	0	161	129	5.50	1.52	278	310	277	19.3	33%	64%	4.64	41	16	43	3.9	7.2	1.8	7%	0.9	-19.7	43	$5
Health A	08	TAM	4	4	2	78	44	4.60	1.51	273	281	265	8.7	29%	73%	4.67	47	21	32	4.0	5.1	1.3	13%	1.3	-2.4	7	$4
PT/Exp B	09	COL	10	8	0	177	133	4.33	1.39	289	289	290	22.4	34%	70%	3.72	46	23	31	2.1	6.8	3.2	10%	0.9	-3.0	88	$10
Consist A	1st Half		5	4	0	80	56	3.93	1.36	285			21.4	33%	73%	3.88	44	23	32	2.1	6.3	2.9	8%	0.8	2.6	78	$6
LIMA Plan B	2nd Half		5	4	0	97	77	4.66	1.41	293			23.2	35%	68%	3.58	48	22	30	2.1	7.2	3.3	11%	0.9	-5.6	97	$5
Rand Var +2	10	Proj	11	9	0	192	143	3.99	1.37	284			24.9	33%	73%	3.81	46	22	32	2.3	6.7	3.0	11%	1.0	10.8	84	$13

Why he'll be a late round steal...
- Cracked sub-4.00 xERA
- Solidified now as GB pitcher
- Elite BPV nobody knows about

Ctl was good all year; repeating those gains will determine how much growth we'll see. Sleeper.

Hampton,Mike

	Yr	Tm	W	L	Sv	IP	K	ERA	WHIP	OBA	vL	vR	BF/G	H%	S%	xERA	G	L	F	Ctl	Dom	Cmd	hr/f	hr/9	RAR	BPV	R$
LH Starter	05	ATL	5	3	0	69	27	3.52	1.33	275	338	263	24.5	29%	75%	4.33	51	20	29	2.3	3.5	1.5	7%	0.7	6.2	29	$5
Age 37	06	ATL	0	0	0	0	0	0.00	0.00							0.00											
Type GB	07	ATL	0	0	0	0	0	0.00	0.00							0.00											
Health F	08	ATL *	3	5	0	91	49	4.65	1.45	278	339	267	23.4	30%	71%	4.19	53	22	26	3.3	4.8	1.5	15%	1.2	-4.2	30	$2
PT/Exp D	09	HOU	7	10	0	112	74	5.30	1.55	288	238	316	23.9	32%	67%	4.22	51	20	29	3.7	5.9	1.6	12%	1.0	-15.4	36	$2
Consist A	1st Half		4	5	0	73	49	4.44	1.40	264			24.2	30%	70%	4.03	51	19	30	3.5	6.0	1.8	12%	1.0	-2.2	45	$4
LIMA Plan C	2nd Half		3	5	0	39	25	6.92	1.85	329			23.2	37%	63%	4.59	51	22	27	4.2	5.8	1.4	13%	1.2	-13.1	20	($2)
Rand Var +2	10	Proj	1	1	0	15	8	4.97	1.59	294			21.8	31%	71%	4.47	52	21	27	3.7	5.0	1.3	15%	1.2	-0.4	18	$0

Had some value in the 1H, but it was fleeting. With these mediocre skills, his high GB% can only help so much. Surgery in Sept for torn rotator cuff and labrum damage might finally end career, if skills don't do it for him.

Hanrahan,Joel

	Yr	Tm	W	L	Sv	IP	K	ERA	WHIP	OBA	vL	vR	BF/G	H%	S%	xERA	G	L	F	Ctl	Dom	Cmd	hr/f	hr/9	RAR	BPV	R$
RH Reliever	05	aa	9	8	0	111	82	5.26	1.64	291			22.1	33%	71%	5.88				4.3	6.7	1.5		1.3	-13.1	29	$3
Age 28	06	a/a	11	5	0	140	91	4.32	1.57	260			24.2	29%	74%	4.81				5.2	5.9	1.1		0.8	3.4	37	$8
Type Pwr	07	WAS *	10	7	0	126	101	5.24	1.67	276	267	305	21.5	31%	72%	5.33	31	25	44	5.4	7.2	1.3	12%	1.4	-12.6	-6	$4
Health A	08	WAS	6	3	9	84	93	3.95	1.36	235	228	237	5.2	31%	74%	3.61	43	22	36	4.5	9.9	2.2	12%	1.0	3.3	78	$11
PT/Exp C	09	2NL	1	4	5	64	72	4.78	1.67	288	269	293	4.4	39%	70%	4.07	36	25	39	4.8	10.1	2.1	4%	0.4	-4.7	68	$2
Consist C	1st Half		0	3	5	33	36	7.59	1.96	353			4.6	45%	60%	3.96	42	25	32	3.8	9.8	2.6	9%	0.8	-13.9	93	($2)
LIMA Plan B+	2nd Half		1	1	0	31	36	1.75	1.36	202			4.1	30%	86%	4.21	27	23	50	5.8	10.5	1.8	0%	0.0	9.3	37	$4
Rand Var +3	10	Proj	3	4	10	73	76	4.10	1.42	250			5.6	33%	72%	3.92	37	23	39	4.3	9.4	2.2	8%	0.7	3.1	68	$8

Why he's a saves sleeper again:
- Dom increase continues
- ERA spike due to insane H%
- xERA well south of 5.00 again.

Sustaining those 1H Ctl gains would let him go here, if given opportunity... UP: 25 SV

Hanson,Tommy

	Yr	Tm	W	L	Sv	IP	K	ERA	WHIP	OBA	vL	vR	BF/G	H%	S%	xERA	G	L	F	Ctl	Dom	Cmd	hr/f	hr/9	RAR	BPV	R$
RH Starter	05		0	0	0	0	0	0.00	0.00							0.00											
Age 23	06		0	0	0	0	0	0.00	0.00							0.00											
Type Pwr FB	07		0	0	0	0	0	0.00	0.00							0.00											
Health A	08	aa	8	4	0	98	99	3.49	1.21	220			22.5	28%	74%	3.25				3.8	9.1	2.4		0.8	9.9	91	$12
PT/Exp D	09	ATL *	14	7	0	194	195	2.51	1.10	215	256	192	24.3	28%	80%	3.42	40	18	42	2.9	9.1	3.1	7%	0.7	40.2	102	$28
Consist A	1st Half		7	3	0	95	97	1.99	1.08	205			23.8	26%	86%	3.62	33	20	47	3.2	9.2	2.9	7%	0.8	25.8	90	$15
LIMA Plan C	2nd Half		7	4	0	99	98	3.01	1.11	225			24.9	29%	75%	3.35	43	17	40	2.6	8.9	3.4	7%	0.6	14.4	110	$13
Rand Var -4	10	Proj	15	8	0	204	203	3.41	1.22	234			24.8	29%	75%	3.62	41	18	41	3.2	9.0	2.8	9%	0.9	16.1	93	$23

11-4, 2.89 ERA in 127 IP at ATL. Elite at age 22? High S% gets some of the credit. But RHers have no chance against him. He sustained elite skills all year too. xERA says his ERA will go north, but this already is an ace.

Happ,J.A.

	Yr	Tm	W	L	Sv	IP	K	ERA	WHIP	OBA	vL	vR	BF/G	H%	S%	xERA	G	L	F	Ctl	Dom	Cmd	hr/f	hr/9	RAR	BPV	R$
LH Starter	05		0	0	0	0	0	0.00	0.00							0.00											
Age 27	06	a/a	7	2	0	80	71	3.70	1.35	252			26.3	32%	72%	3.70				3.6	8.0	2.2		0.4	8.1	86	$9
Type Pwr FB	07	aaa	4	6	0	118	100	6.40	1.72	293			22.8	35%	63%	6.06				5.0	7.6	1.5		1.1	-28.2	40	($2)
Health A	08	PHI *	9	7	0	167	153	4.52	1.39	261	209	247	22.5	31%	71%	4.21	31	27	43	3.5	8.2	2.3	11%	1.2	-5.1	62	$10
PT/Exp C	09	PHI	12	4	0	166	119	2.93	1.23	241	216	253	19.7	27%	82%	4.28	38	19	43	3.0	6.5	2.1	9%	1.1	25.8	51	$18
Consist B	1st Half		5	0	0	66	45	3.00	1.23	222			14.4	24%	81%	4.69	36	16	48	3.8	6.1	1.6	9%	1.1	9.7	21	$7
LIMA Plan D	2nd Half		7	4	0	100	74	2.88	1.24	254			26.0	29%	82%	4.02	40	20	40	2.5	6.7	2.6	10%	1.1	16.2	70	$11
Rand Var -5	10	Proj	11	6	0	174	135	4.19	1.36	255			21.3	29%	72%	4.42	38	19	43	3.5	7.0	2.0	10%	1.1	-3.3	46	$12

Speaking of strong rookie SP debuts, this was another. But his sub-3.00 was a fluke. Low H%, high S% drove down both ERA and WHIP. Dom and Ctl were more marginal than exciting. Regression to the mean here.

STEPHEN NICKRAND

Harang,Aaron

Harang,Aaron		Yr	Tm	W	L	Sv	IP	K	ERA	WHIP	OBA	vL	vR	BF/G	H%	S%	xERA	G	L	F	Ctl	Dom	Cmd	hr/f	hr/9	RAR	BPV	R$
RH Starter		05	CIN	11	13	0	211	163	3.84	1.27	267	253	279	27.6	31%	72%	3.89	39	22	39	2.2	6.9	**3.2**	9%	0.9	10.7	83	$17
Age	31	06	CIN	16	11	0	234	216	3.77	1.27	268	267	270	27.3	33%	74%	3.71	39	22	40	2.2	8.3	**3.9**	10%	1.1	20.8	108	$24
Type	Pwr FB	07	CIN	16	6	0	232	218	3.73	1.14	246	237	246	27.7	30%	71%	3.52	40	18	42	2.0	8.5	**4.2**	10%	1.1	19.9	116	$27
Health	C	08	CIN	6	17	0	184	153	4.79	1.38	283	298	274	26.4	32%	71%	4.20	34	22	44	2.4	7.5	**3.1**	14%	1.7	-11.7	81	$8
PT/Exp	A	09	CIN	6	14	0	162	142	4.21	1.41	289	285	289	27.0	34%	75%	4.00	35	24	41	2.4	7.9	**3.3**	12%	1.3	-0.5	90	$8
Consist	A	1st Half		5	8	0	98	80	3.95	1.39	294			26.4	34%	76%	4.03	35	23	42	1.9	7.3	**3.8**	10%	1.2	2.9	93	$6
LIMA Plan	B+	2nd Half		1	6	0	64	62	4.62	1.45	281			28.1	33%	73%	3.95	34	25	41	3.1	8.7	**2.8**	14%	1.5	-3.4	85	$2
Rand Var	+2	10	Proj	**13**	**11**	**0**	**203**	**180**	**3.86**	**1.28**	**264**			**26.6**	**31%**	**75%**	**3.87**	**36**	**22**	**42**	**2.4**	**8.0**	**3.3**	**11%**	**1.2**	**10.0**	**92**	**$18**

Skills aren't quite as good as they were in 2006-07, but main difference has been run support and a few more hr/f. Guy who earned $8 in '09 isn't that far off from guy who earned $24 in '06. UP: 15 wins, 3.75 ERA.

Harden,Rich

Harden,Rich		Yr	Tm	W	L	Sv	IP	K	ERA	WHIP	OBA	vL	vR	BF/G	H%	S%	xERA	G	L	F	Ctl	Dom	Cmd	hr/f	hr/9	RAR	BPV	R$
RH Starter		05	OAK	10	5	0	128	121	2.53	1.06	205	179	221	23.2	26%	78%	3.22	43	26	31	3.0	8.5	**2.8**	7%	0.5	29.1	93	$21
Age	28	06	OAK	4	0	0	46	49	4.29	1.23	192	176	211	21.3	24%	67%	3.62	43	24	32	5.1	9.5	**1.9**	14%	1.0	1.6	57	$6
Type	Pwr FB	07	OAK	1	2	0	26	27	2.45	1.13	199	292	98	14.9	25%	85%	3.60	39	19	42	3.9	9.5	**2.5**	11%	1.1	6.5	83	$4
Health	F	08	2TM	10	2	0	148	181	2.07	1.06	187	200	167	23.6	26%	84%	3.34	30	21	49	3.7	11.0	**3.0**	7%	0.7	40.9	106	$26
PT/Exp	B	09	CHC	9	9	0	141	171	4.09	1.34	235	251	220	23.1	30%	75%	3.54	38	18	44	4.3	10.9	**2.6**	15%	1.5	1.8	97	$13
Consist	A	1st Half		5	4	0	67	76	4.57	1.40	250			24.1	31%	74%	3.71	38	19	42	4.2	10.2	**2.5**	17%	1.7	-3.1	88	$5
LIMA Plan	B	2nd Half		4	5	0	74	95	3.65	1.28	220			22.2	30%	76%	3.39	37	17	45	4.4	11.6	**2.6**	13%	1.2	4.9	105	$8
Rand Var	+2	10	Proj	**10**	**6**	**0**	**145**	**170**	**3.41**	**1.23**	**214**			**23.1**	**28%**	**76%**	**3.52**	**37**	**20**	**44**	**4.2**	**10.6**	**2.5**	**11%**	**1.1**	**13.2**	**92**	**$17**

Basically, gap between '07 and '08 comes down to the three BPIs most subject to random fluctuations: H%, S%, and hr/f. That means there's a buying opportunity here, though you still can't pay for a full season.

Haren,Dan

Haren,Dan		Yr	Tm	W	L	Sv	IP	K	ERA	WHIP	OBA	vL	vR	BF/G	H%	S%	xERA	G	L	F	Ctl	Dom	Cmd	hr/f	hr/9	RAR	BPV	R$
RH Starter		05	OAK	14	12	0	217	163	3.73	1.22	257	252	258	26.4	29%	73%	3.57	48	20	32	2.2	6.8	**3.1**	12%	1.1	17.1	88	$22
Age	29	06	OAK	14	13	0	223	176	4.12	1.21	263	246	268	27.1	30%	70%	3.63	45	19	36	1.8	7.1	**3.9**	13%	1.3	12.1	102	$24
Type	Pwr	07	OAK	15	9	0	223	192	3.07	1.21	254	230	264	27.0	30%	79%	3.63	44	17	38	2.2	7.8	**3.5**	10%	1.0	39.4	102	$28
Health	A	08	ARI	16	8	0	216	206	3.33	1.13	251	241	253	26.5	31%	73%	3.14	44	21	35	1.7	8.6	**5.2**	9%	0.8	25.0	132	$27
PT/Exp	A	09	ARI	14	10	0	229	223	3.14	1.00	229	229	219	27.3	28%	74%	3.00	43	20	37	1.5	8.8	**5.9**	12%	1.1	29.7	138	$31
Consist	A	1st Half		7	5	0	115	113	2.19	0.81	194			26.8	24%	79%	2.75	43	20	37	1.2	8.8	**7.5**	10%	0.9	28.3	149	$21
LIMA Plan	C	2nd Half		7	5	0	114	110	4.09	1.20	261			27.7	32%	70%	3.26	43	20	36	1.8	8.7	**4.8**	13%	1.3	1.3	128	$11
Rand Var	0	10	Proj	**17**	**8**	**0**	**223**	**212**	**3.23**	**1.11**	**245**			**27.2**	**30%**	**74%**	**3.18**	**44**	**20**	**36**	**1.7**	**8.6**	**4.9**	**10%**	**0.9**	**29.9**	**129**	**$29**

Cmd, xERA, and BPV trends all show a pitcher who just keeps getting better. He's healthy, consistent, and returning to NL has been good for his Dom. Upside remains 20 wins and a Cy Young Award.

Harrison,Matt

Harrison,Matt		Yr	Tm	W	L	Sv	IP	K	ERA	WHIP	OBA	vL	vR	BF/G	H%	S%	xERA	G	L	F	Ctl	Dom	Cmd	hr/f	hr/9	RAR	BPV	R$
LH Starter		05		0	0	0	0	0	0.00	0.00							0.00											
Age	24	06	aa	3	4	0	77	48	5.14	1.57	319			26.6	36%	68%	5.76				2.2	5.6	**2.5**		0.8	-5.9	53	$1
Type	Con	07	aa	5	7	0	116	67	4.34	1.49	296			25.6	33%	70%	4.92				2.7	5.2	**1.9**		0.5	1.8	51	$5
Health	F	08	TEX *	15	6	0	168	88	4.73	1.55	298	310	297	25.0	32%	71%	4.90	40	23	36	3.2	4.7	**1.5**	9%	1.0	-7.9	17	$8
PT/Exp	D	09	TEX	4	5	0	63	34	6.11	1.64	312	210	351	26.3	33%	64%	4.75	47	23	31	3.3	4.8	**1.5**	13%	1.3	-13.0	24	($0)
Consist	A	1st Half		4	5	0	63	34	6.13	1.65	313			26.2	33%	64%	4.75	47	23	31	3.3	4.8	**1.5**	13%	1.3	-13.1	24	($0)
LIMA Plan	D	2nd Half		0	0	0	0	0	0.00	0.00							0.00											
Rand Var	+5	10	Proj	**4**	**4**	**0**	**65**	**37**	**4.83**	**1.50**	**295**			**26.2**	**33%**	**68%**	**4.50**	**45**	**23**	**32**	**2.9**	**5.1**	**1.8**	**8%**	**0.8**	**-0.5**	**37**	**$3**

PRO: ERA bloated by S%, xERA trend suggests there's been slight improvement. CON: Cmd falling apart, hr/9 trend suggests he's making a lot of mistakes, poor health. Observe from a safe distance.

Hart,Kevin

Hart,Kevin		Yr	Tm	W	L	Sv	IP	K	ERA	WHIP	OBA	vL	vR	BF/G	H%	S%	xERA	G	L	F	Ctl	Dom	Cmd	hr/f	hr/9	RAR	BPV	R$
RH Reliever		05		0	0	0	0	0	0.00	0.00							0.00											
Age	27	06		0	0	0	0	0	0.00	0.00							0.00											
Type	Pwr	07	aa	12	6	0	158	105	5.28	1.55	301			26.2	33%	69%	6.05				3.1	6.0	**1.9**		1.4	-15.9	28	$6
Health	A	08	aaa	4	2	5	60	50	3.49	1.22	224			9.2	28%	71%	3.00				3.7	7.5	**2.1**		0.5	6.1	84	$8
PT/Exp	D	09	2NL *	7	12	3	133	95	5.10	1.64	285	335	278	15.2	32%	71%	4.82	43	20	37	4.6	6.4	**1.4**	11%	1.2	-15.0	12	$2
Consist	F	1st Half		3	3	3	55	48	3.85	1.36	241			9.5	28%	76%	3.57	62	8	31	4.2	7.7	**1.9**	15%	1.2	2.3	66	$5
LIMA Plan	C+	2nd Half		4	9	0	78	47	5.99	1.84	314			24.7	34%	69%	5.41	42	21	37	4.9	5.4	**1.1**	11%	1.2	-17.2	-15	($3)
Rand Var	0	10	Proj	**3**	**3**	**0**	**44**	**32**	**4.55**	**1.49**	**268**			**13.7**	**31%**	**72%**	**4.52**	**43**	**20**	**37**	**4.1**	**6.6**	**1.6**	**10%**	**1.0**	**-1.4**	**28**	**$2**

4-9, 5.44 ERA in 81 IP at CHC/PIT. 2nd half line represents nearly all his work in the majors last year, and it wasn't pretty. 2008 skills had some promise, but he has to prove himself in the bigs before you can invest.

Hawkins,LaTroy

Hawkins,LaTroy		Yr	Tm	W	L	Sv	IP	K	ERA	WHIP	OBA	vL	vR	BF/G	H%	S%	xERA	G	L	F	Ctl	Dom	Cmd	hr/f	hr/9	RAR	BPV	R$
RH Reliever		05	2NL	2	8	6	56	43	3.85	1.46	268	228	297	3.7	31%	77%	4.34	44	17	39	3.9	6.9	**1.8**	10%	1.1	2.7	42	$5
Age	37	06	BAL	3	2	0	60	27	4.49	1.46	301	323	285	4.4	33%	69%	4.73	44	21	35	2.2	4.0	**1.8**	5%	0.6	0.5	34	$3
Type		07	COL	2	5	0	55	29	3.42	1.23	250	237	266	3.7	27%	76%	3.51	63	16	21	2.6	4.7	**1.8**	16%	1.0	6.9	56	$5
Health	B	08	2TM	3	1	1	62	48	3.92	1.21	233	293	189	4.5	28%	67%	3.88	46	17	37	3.2	7.0	**2.2**	5%	0.4	3.0	63	$6
PT/Exp	C	09	HOU	1	4	11	63	45	2.13	1.20	252	203	303	4.0	28%	88%	3.66	45	24	31	2.3	6.4	**2.8**	12%	1.0	16.1	77	$10
Consist	A	1st Half		1	2	10	35	29	2.56	1.25	250			4.1	29%	85%	3.81	41	22	37	2.8	7.4	**2.6**	11%	1.0	7.0	76	$7
LIMA Plan	C+	2nd Half		0	2	1	28	16	1.60	1.13	253			3.9	27%	93%	3.44	49	27	24	1.6	5.1	**3.2**	14%	1.0	9.0	76	$3
Rand Var	-5	10	Proj	**2**	**4**	**5**	**73**	**48**	**3.48**	**1.21**	**250**			**4.1**	**28%**	**74%**	**3.76**	**49**	**21**	**30**	**2.5**	**6.0**	**2.4**	**10%**	**0.9**	**4.5**	**67**	**$7**

Cmd shows he's finding a way to stay relevant in the face of advancing age and inconsistent Dom. ERA repeat is a long shot due to incredibly high S%, but veteran status will ensure more save opps get thrown his way.

Hawksworth,Blake

Hawksworth,Blake		Yr	Tm	W	L	Sv	IP	K	ERA	WHIP	OBA	vL	vR	BF/G	H%	S%	xERA	G	L	F	Ctl	Dom	Cmd	hr/f	hr/9	RAR	BPV	R$
RH Reliever		05		0	0	0	0	0	0.00	0.00							0.00											
Age	27	06	aa	4	2	0	79	55	3.98	1.43	270			26.5	31%	75%	4.70				3.5	6.3	**1.8**		0.9	5.2	48	$5
Type	GB	07	aaa	4	13	0	129	74	6.31	1.66	323			23.7	34%	65%	6.97				2.9	5.2	**1.8**		1.7	-29.4	9	($3)
Health	A	08	aaa	5	7	0	88	64	7.37	1.95	349			23.9	40%	63%	7.63				4.0	6.5	**1.6**		1.2	-33.3	21	($6)
PT/Exp	D	09	STL *	9	4	0	113	63	3.55	1.24	248	246	176	11.2	28%	71%	4.04	54	14	32	2.8	5.0	**1.8**	5%	0.4	8.8	45	$11
Consist	F	1st Half		5	4	0	69	44	4.68	1.29	261			18.2	30%	63%	4.12	52	10	38	2.7	5.7	**2.1**	5%	0.5	-4.2	60	$5
LIMA Plan	C+	2nd Half		4	0	0	44	19	1.78	1.17	226			6.9	25%	85%	4.21	54	16	30	3.1	3.9	**1.3**	3%	0.3	13.0	19	$6
Rand Var	-2	10	Proj	**3**	**2**	**0**	**44**	**26**	**4.76**	**1.49**	**285**			**13.7**	**32%**	**69%**	**4.27**	**54**	**15**	**31**	**3.3**	**5.4**	**1.6**	**9%**	**0.8**	**-0.1**	**40**	**$2**

4-0, 2.03 ERA in 40 IP at STL. Success w/Cards was a fluke: 1.3 Cmd, 23 BPV, 4.62 xERA. AAA 1H is only time he's shown anything resembling potential, and at his age, it's very late. Don't expect an encore.

Heilman,Aaron

Heilman,Aaron		Yr	Tm	W	L	Sv	IP	K	ERA	WHIP	OBA	vL	vR	BF/G	H%	S%	xERA	G	L	F	Ctl	Dom	Cmd	hr/f	hr/9	RAR	BPV	R$
RH Reliever		05	NYM	5	3	5	108	106	3.17	1.15	222	208	236	8.3	29%	73%	3.18	46	24	31	3.1	8.8	**2.9**	7%	0.5	14.4	100	$14
Age	31	06	NYM	4	5	0	87	73	3.62	1.16	229	231	231	4.8	28%	69%	3.77	45	17	38	2.9	7.6	**2.6**	5%	0.5	9.3	81	$9
Type	Pwr	07	NYM	7	7	1	86	63	3.03	1.07	229	234	218	4.2	26%	75%	3.62	45	21	34	2.1	6.6	**3.2**	9%	0.8	14.8	85	$13
Health	A	08	NYM	3	8	3	76	80	5.21	1.59	259	308	222	4.4	33%	69%	4.15	41	24	35	5.4	9.5	**1.7**	14%	1.2	-8.8	42	$3
PT/Exp	C	09	CHC	4	4	1	72	65	4.11	1.41	250	210	288	4.5	30%	74%	4.13	41	21	39	4.2	8.1	**1.9**	11%	1.1	0.7	50	$5
Consist	A	1st Half		2	3	0	34	31	3.95	1.64	255			4.9	31%	77%	4.63	43	22	35	6.1	8.2	**1.3**	9%	0.8	1.0	4	$1
LIMA Plan	B+	2nd Half		2	1	1	38	34	4.25	1.21	246			4.1	28%	70%	3.72	39	19	41	2.6	8.0	**3.1**	13%	1.4	-0.3	92	$4
Rand Var	0	10	Proj	**4**	**5**	**0**	**78**	**71**	**3.92**	**1.31**	**247**			**4.5**	**30%**	**73%**	**3.81**	**42**	**21**	**37**	**3.5**	**8.2**	**2.4**	**11%**	**1.0**	**4.4**	**74**	**$6**

Finally found himself again over the last two months: 3.38 ERA, 1.5 Ctl, 6.0 Cmd. Not enough to disregard the lousy year and four months that preceeded it, but you can certainly justify an end-game or reserve pick.

Hendrickson,Mark

Hendrickson,Mark		Yr	Tm	W	L	Sv	IP	K	ERA	WHIP	OBA	vL	vR	BF/G	H%	S%	xERA	G	L	F	Ctl	Dom	Cmd	hr/f	hr/9	RAR	BPV	R$
LH Reliever		05	TAM	11	8	0	178	89	5.91	1.55	311	258	328	25.7	33%	63%	4.54	46	22	32	2.5	4.5	**1.8**	12%	1.2	-33.8	38	$2
Age	35	06	2TM	6	15	0	164	99	4.22	1.43	272	287	264	23.0	30%	72%	4.59	48	16	36	3.4	5.4	**1.6**	9%	0.9	6.1	32	$8
Type	Con	07	LA	4	8	0	123	92	5.21	1.39	291	258	300	13.6	33%	64%	3.89	44	23	33	2.1	6.7	**3.2**	12%	1.1	-11.8	86	$4
Health	A	08	FLA	7	8	0	134	81	5.45	1.47	282	248	296	16.3	31%	64%	4.55	44	20	35	3.2	5.5	**1.7**	11%	1.1	-19.5	33	$3
PT/Exp	B	09	BAL	6	5	1	105	61	4.37	1.42	281	275	282	8.6	30%	74%	4.52	45	20	35	2.8	5.2	**1.8**	13%	1.4	1.0	40	$6
Consist	A	1st Half		3	4	0	51	33	5.11	1.64	308			11.1	33%	73%	4.92	40	22	38	3.5	5.8	**1.7**	14%	1.6	-4.1	28	$1
LIMA Plan	C	2nd Half		3	1	1	54	28	3.67	1.21	255			6.9	27%	74%	4.14	49	18	33	2.2	4.7	**2.2**	12%	1.2	5.2	52	$5
Rand Var	0	10	Proj	**6**	**6**	**0**	**116**	**70**	**4.73**	**1.41**	**281**			**10.9**	**30%**	**70%**	**4.40**	**45**	**20**	**35**	**2.8**	**5.4**	**1.9**	**12%**	**1.2**	**0.5**	**45**	**$6**

For his career...
As SP: 5.28 ERA, 1.8 Cmd
As RP: 3.40 ERA, 2.8 Cmd
So at least you know how to use him, even if MLB teams don't. Could be a LIMA candidate if some team gets smart.

BRANDON KRUSE

Herges,Matt

		Yr/Tm	W	L	Sv	IP	K	ERA	WHIP	OBA	vL	vR	BF/G	H%	S%	xERA	G	L	F	Ctl	Dom	Cmd	hr/f	hr/9	RAR	BPV	R$
RH Reliever		05 2NL *	2	3	0	58	35	3.88	1.71	320	256	333	5.0	34%	83%	5.02	39	22	39	3.4	5.4	1.6	12%	1.6	2.6	23	$1
Age	40	06 FLA	2	3	0	71	36	4.31	1.72	319	300	340	5.0	35%	75%	5.03	47	22	31	3.5	4.6	1.3	6%	0.6	1.6	11	$0
Type		07 COL *	7	2	1	84	55	2.60	1.13	224	216	184	5.1	25%	81%	4.10	46	15	38	2.9	5.9	2.0	8%	0.8	18.8	53	$12
Health	A	08 COL	3	4	0	64	46	5.04	1.60	303	280	326	5.0	35%	68%	4.48	40	26	34	3.4	6.4	1.9	7%	0.7	-6.1	43	$1
PT/Exp	D	09 2TM *	7	5	4	63	46	3.73	1.31	263	277	219	4.9	30%	75%	4.08	47	14	39	2.7	6.6	2.4	9%	1.0	4.5	70	$8
Consist	A	1st Half	3	3	4	35	24	4.45	1.42	281			4.8	32%	69%	4.40	46	14	40	2.9	6.1	2.1	7%	0.8	-0.6	56	$4
LIMA Plan	B	2nd Half	4	2	0	28	22	2.81	1.16	238			5.1	27%	83%	3.65	48	14	38	2.5	7.3	2.9	13%	1.3	5.1	89	$5
Rand Var	0	10 Proj	4	3	0	44	31	4.14	1.38	273			5.1	31%	73%	4.18	44	20	36	2.9	6.4	2.2	10%	1.0	0.9	59	$4

3-1, 3.38 ERA in 35 IP at CLE/COL. The crazy life of a reliever: gets 64 IP in 2008 despite bad ERA and poor skills; in 2009, with good ERA and better skills, gets released mid-season. He's flyer material at best.

Hernandez,David

		Yr/Tm	W	L	Sv	IP	K	ERA	WHIP	OBA	vL	vR	BF/G	H%	S%	xERA	G	L	F	Ctl	Dom	Cmd	hr/f	hr/9	RAR	BPV	R$
RH Starter		05	0	0	0	0	0	0.00	0.00							0.00											
Age	24	06	0	0	0	0	0	0.00	0.00							0.00											
Type	Pwr xFB	07	0	0	0	0	0	0.00	0.00							0.00											
Health	A	08 aa	10	4	0	141	141	3.42	1.45	251			22.8	32%	78%	4.24				4.5	9.0	2.0		0.8	15.4	77	$13
PT/Exp	D	09 BAL *	7	12	0	162	136	5.21	1.49	276	280	297	22.4	30%	71%	4.92	29	18	53	3.7	7.5	2.0	13%	1.9	-15.2	43	$6
Consist	B	1st Half	4	4	0	76	76	4.72	1.42	273			22.0	34%	68%	4.06	37	18	46	3.3	9.0	2.8	8%	1.0	-2.5	88	$5
LIMA Plan	C	2nd Half	3	8	0	86	60	5.64	1.54	279			22.6	27%	74%	5.52	27	18	55	4.1	6.3	1.5	17%	2.7	-12.7	8	$1
Rand Var	+1	10 Proj	5	6	0	102	86	4.52	1.47	267			22.3	30%	74%	4.92	29	18	54	4.0	7.6	1.9	10%	1.5	-6.0	36	$6

4-10, 5.42 ERA in 101 IP at BAL. Lots to like in 1H, but 2H covers most of his time in the majors, where he had 5.84 xERA, 4 BPV and most importantly, 6.0 Dom. Until those minor-league Ks show up, he's going to struggle.

Hernandez,Felix

		Yr/Tm	W	L	Sv	IP	K	ERA	WHIP	OBA	vL	vR	BF/G	H%	S%	xERA	G	L	F	Ctl	Dom	Cmd	hr/f	hr/9	RAR	BPV	R$
RH Starter		05 SEA *	13	8	0	172	187	2.35	1.04	194	164	224	22.0	27%	78%	2.26	67	14	19	3.3	9.8	3.0	10%	0.4	42.8	133	$30
Age	24	06 SEA	12	14	0	191	176	4.52	1.34	266	281	241	26.2	32%	69%	3.11	58	18	25	2.8	8.3	2.9	17%	1.1	0.8	109	$18
Type	Pwr GB	07 SEA	14	7	0	190	165	3.93	1.38	280	299	262	27.3	34%	74%	3.08	61	16	23	2.5	7.8	3.1	15%	0.9	13.6	112	$19
Health	A	08 SEA	9	11	0	201	175	3.45	1.39	259	275	242	27.9	32%	77%	3.59	52	18	29	3.6	7.8	2.2	10%	0.8	22.1	75	$17
PT/Exp	A	09 SEA	19	5	0	239	217	2.49	1.14	229	228	226	28.5	29%	80%	3.17	53	17	30	2.7	8.2	3.1	8%	0.6	57.8	106	$36
Consist	A	1st Half	8	3	0	109	107	2.55	1.17	238			27.9	31%	80%	3.15	51	17	32	2.6	8.8	3.3	7%	0.6	25.6	117	$16
LIMA Plan	C	2nd Half	11	2	0	130	110	2.43	1.10	222			29.0	27%	80%	3.20	55	17	28	2.7	7.6	2.8	8%	0.6	32.3	98	$21
Rand Var	-3	10 Proj	17	7	0	225	207	3.04	1.23	244			27.4	31%	77%	3.17	55	17	28	2.8	8.3	2.9	10%	0.7	35.2	105	$29

Season everyone was waiting for, though as the skills show, this was just 2007 with better H%, S%, and more IP. Dom fell to 6.4 over last 7 GS (fatigue?), but he still managed 80 BPV, 3.27 xERA. The mark of an ace.

Hernandez,Livan

		Yr/Tm	W	L	Sv	IP	K	ERA	WHIP	OBA	vL	vR	BF/G	H%	S%	xERA	G	L	F	Ctl	Dom	Cmd	hr/f	hr/9	RAR	BPV	R$
RH Starter		05 WAS	15	10	0	246	147	3.99	1.43	279	290	278	30.6	31%	74%	4.48	40	26	34	3.1	5.4	1.8	9%	0.9	7.9	31	$14
Age	35	06 2NL	13	13	0	216	128	4.83	1.50	288	302	275	28.1	31%	71%	5.11	37	20	44	3.3	5.3	1.6	9%	1.2	-9.2	23	$9
Type	Con	07 ARI	11	11	0	204	90	4.93	1.60	300	295	320	28.0	30%	73%	5.50	38	21	41	3.5	4.0	1.1	11%	1.5	-12.8	-6	$3
Health	A	08 2TM	13	11	0	180	67	6.05	1.67	336	340	344	26.6	34%	65%	5.04	44	22	34	2.2	3.4	1.6	11%	1.3	-38.7	25	($2)
PT/Exp	A	09 2NL	9	12	0	184	102	5.44	1.56	298	287	330	26.6	33%	66%	4.87	41	22	37	3.3	5.0	1.5	8%	0.9	-28.3	20	$1
Consist	A	1st Half	5	3	0	93	49	4.06	1.39	276			26.8	29%	74%	4.67	42	20	38	2.9	4.7	1.6	9%	1.1	1.5	27	$5
LIMA Plan	C	2nd Half	4	9	0	91	53	6.86	1.73	320			26.3	36%	59%	5.08	39	25	36	3.7	5.3	1.4	7%	0.8	-29.8	12	($4)
Rand Var	0	10 Proj	6	12	0	148	74	5.55	1.60	309			26.7	33%	67%	5.01	41	22	37	3.1	4.5	1.5	9%	1.1	-13.6	18	($1)

Little known fact: There a point where negative RAR adds up enough to cancel out the rest of your career and create a statistical black hole. Even if you just stare at his numbers, you risk getting pulled into the abyss.

Herrera,Daniel

		Yr/Tm	W	L	Sv	IP	K	ERA	WHIP	OBA	vL	vR	BF/G	H%	S%	xERA	G	L	F	Ctl	Dom	Cmd	hr/f	hr/9	RAR	BPV	R$
LH Reliever		05	0	0	0	0	0	0.00	0.00							0.00											
Age	25	06	0	0	0	0	0	0.00	0.00							0.00											
Type		07	0	0	0	0	0	0.00	0.00							0.00											
Health	A	08 a/a	7	4	6	72	52	3.24	1.16	248			5.1	29%	73%	3.31				2.1	6.5	3.1		0.6	9.5	90	$12
PT/Exp	D	09 CIN	4	4	0	62	44	3.06	1.41	266	183	361	3.8	31%	80%	3.98	50	20	30	3.5	6.4	1.8	9%	0.7	8.6	49	$5
Consist	B	1st Half	1	3	0	30	23	2.09	1.36	260			4.0	32%	85%	3.58	53	21	26	3.3	6.9	2.1	4%	0.3	7.8	66	$3
LIMA Plan	C+	2nd Half	3	1	0	32	21	4.00	1.46	271			3.6	30%	76%	4.35	47	20	33	3.7	6.0	1.6	12%	1.1	0.7	33	$2
Rand Var	-3	10 Proj	5	4	0	65	46	3.45	1.32	258			4.2	30%	76%	3.87	49	20	30	3.0	6.3	2.1	10%	0.8	3.2	60	$6

ERA got a big boost from S%, but a glance at 1H GB% and Dom, as well as 2008 Ctl and BPV, tells you he's a pitcher worth tracking. League seemed to figure him out in 2H; how he adjusts this year is crucial.

Hill,Rich

		Yr/Tm	W	L	Sv	IP	K	ERA	WHIP	OBA	vL	vR	BF/G	H%	S%	xERA	G	L	F	Ctl	Dom	Cmd	hr/f	hr/9	RAR	BPV	R$
LH Starter		05 a/a	10	4	0	122	152	4.34	1.23	246			24.2	31%	73%	4.54				2.8	11.2	4.0		1.8	-0.6	104	$15
Age	30	06 CHC *	13	8	0	199	205	3.34	1.12	222	262	220	25.1	28%	74%	3.83	30	18	52	2.8	9.3	3.3	8%	0.9	28.2	99	$26
Type	Pwr xFB	07 CHC	11	8	0	195	183	3.92	1.19	236	191	247	25.1	28%	72%	3.82	36	21	43	2.9	8.4	2.9	12%	1.2	12.1	88	$20
Health	F	08 CHC *	3	4	0	46	37	6.45	2.10	250	154	200	19.1	28%	71%	7.49	33	17	50	10.4	7.2	0.7	10%	1.4	-12.3	******	($3)
PT/Exp	C	09 BAL *	4	4	0	71	57	6.78	1.76	272	267	303	19.5	32%	61%	5.76	31	21	48	6.3	7.2	1.1	8%	1.0	-20.3	-32	($1)
Consist	F	1st Half	4	3	0	53	48	5.96	1.68	259			20.4	31%	65%	5.27	34	21	45	6.2	8.1	1.3	9%	1.0	-9.9	-11	$1
LIMA Plan	C+	2nd Half	0	1	0	18	9	9.26	2.00	308			17.2	33%	52%	7.23	26	23	52	6.7	4.6	0.7	6%	1.0	-10.4	-93	($3)
Rand Var	+3	10 Proj	3	4	0	73	57	4.84	1.48	266			18.7	30%	70%	4.94	30	21	49	4.1	7.1	1.7	9%	1.2	-4.5	25	$3

3-3, 7.80 ERA in 58 IP at BAL. Still paying burnout price for that 2006 IP jump. First it was loss of Dom, then back injury and labrum tear finished the job. Nice speculative end-game pick IF he gets a clean bill of health.

Hochevar,Luke

		Yr/Tm	W	L	Sv	IP	K	ERA	WHIP	OBA	vL	vR	BF/G	H%	S%	xERA	G	L	F	Ctl	Dom	Cmd	hr/f	hr/9	RAR	BPV	R$
RH Starter		05	0	0	0	0	0	0.00	0.00							0.00											
Age	26	06	0	0	0	0	0	0.00	0.00							0.00											
Type		07 KC *	4	10	0	165	121	6.03	1.59	310	273	208	23.9	35%	64%	3.68	63	10	27	2.9	6.6	2.3	18%	1.4	-31.0	83	$0
Health	B	08 KC *	7	13	0	146	82	5.28	1.44	276	314	244	25.5	30%	64%	4.36	52	17	32	3.3	5.0	1.5	9%	0.9	-16.8	31	$4
PT/Exp	C	09 KC *	12	14	0	191	134	5.39	1.46	290	292	289	25.3	32%	65%	4.25	47	18	36	2.8	6.3	2.3	11%	1.2	-22.1	63	$8
Consist	A	1st Half	8	4	0	93	49	3.41	1.26	250			24.3	27%	74%	4.19	54	13	32	2.8	4.7	1.7	7%	0.7	11.9	41	$10
LIMA Plan	B	2nd Half	4	10	0	98	85	7.27	1.65	324			26.3	37%	58%	4.18	43	20	38	2.7	7.8	2.9	15%	1.7	-34.0	89	($2)
Rand Var	+3	10 Proj	7	11	0	137	102	4.60	1.36	272			24.5	31%	68%	3.95	49	17	34	2.8	6.7	2.4	11%	1.1	8.1	71	$9

7-13, 6.55 ERA in 143 IP at KC. Developed a splitter in 2H and bam! Great Dom, elite Cmd. S%, hr/f rained on the parade, but xERA says this is a pitcher worth owning. And ERA says you can do it at a bargain price.

Hoffman,Trevor

		Yr/Tm	W	L	Sv	IP	K	ERA	WHIP	OBA	vL	vR	BF/G	H%	S%	xERA	G	L	F	Ctl	Dom	Cmd	hr/f	hr/9	RAR	BPV	R$
RH Reliever		05 SD	1	6	43	57	54	2.99	1.12	244	291	179	3.9	31%	74%	3.44	37	21	42	1.9	8.5	4.5	4%	0.5	8.9	117	$20
Age	42	06 SD	0	2	46	63	50	2.14	0.97	213	194	214	3.8	25%	84%	3.82	32	22	45	1.9	7.1	3.8	8%	0.9	18.2	89	$24
Type	Pwr xFB	07 SD	4	5	42	57	44	2.98	1.12	233	299	169	3.8	29%	73%	4.31	31	18	52	2.4	6.9	2.9	2%	0.3	10.2	69	$22
Health	B	08 SD	3	6	30	45	46	3.77	1.04	229	291	165	3.7	27%	72%	3.33	39	14	47	1.8	9.1	5.1	14%	1.6	2.8	133	$16
PT/Exp	B	09 MIL	3	2	37	54	48	1.83	0.91	187	222	149	3.8	24%	81%	3.49	39	14	46	2.3	8.0	3.4	3%	0.3	15.7	98	$22
Consist	B	1st Half	1	1	18	23	19	1.95	0.95	207			3.7	27%	77%	3.28	44	20	36	1.9	7.4	3.8	0%	0.0	6.4	102	$10
LIMA Plan	C	2nd Half	2	1	19	31	29	1.75	0.87	171			3.8	22%	84%	3.63	36	9	55	2.6	8.4	3.2	5%	0.6	9.3	95	$12
Rand Var	-5	10 Proj	3	4	35	51	44	3.37	1.12	231			3.9	28%	72%	3.95	35	16	49	2.5	7.8	3.1	6%	0.7	2.0	86	$18

Another age-defying year, but...
- Hit the trifecta on H%, S%, hr/f
- 5.4 Dom, 1.1 Cmd in June/July
- 62% FB after August 1st

There are some cracks in the foundation. At his age, you have to take that seriously.

Holland,Derek

		Yr/Tm	W	L	Sv	IP	K	ERA	WHIP	OBA	vL	vR	BF/G	H%	S%	xERA	G	L	F	Ctl	Dom	Cmd	hr/f	hr/9	RAR	BPV	R$
LH Starter		05	0	0	0	0	0	0.00	0.00							0.00											
Age	23	06	0	0	0	0	0	0.00	0.00							0.00											
Type	Pwr	07	0	0	0	0	0	0.00	0.00							0.00											
Health	A	08 aa	3	0	0	26	24	1.38	0.96	188			25.2	24%	88%	1.72				2.8	8.3	3.0		0.3	9.4	120	$6
PT/Exp	D	09 TEX	8	13	0	138	107	6.12	1.50	291	287	289	18.5	32%	62%	4.37	41	19	39	3.1	7.0	2.3	15%	1.7	-28.4	62	$3
Consist	F	1st Half	1	5	0	49	39	6.23	1.61	313			14.8	35%	64%	4.27	45	19	36	2.9	7.1	2.4	15%	1.6	-10.8	73	($1)
LIMA Plan	B+	2nd Half	7	8	0	89	68	6.05	1.43	278			21.6	30%	61%	4.42	39	20	41	3.1	6.9	2.2	15%	1.7	-17.6	56	$4
Rand Var	+5	10 Proj	12	14	0	174	140	4.81	1.43	280			23.7	32%	69%	4.19	42	19	39	3.0	7.2	2.4	11%	1.2	5.3	69	$11

Promising debut gets buried by S% and hr/f. xERA shows he can be a good fit for the back of your rotation, and top prospect pedigree suggests big upside once he cuts down on the bad pitches. He's a growth stock.

BRANDON KRUSE

Howell,J.P.

Howell,J.P.			W	L	Sv	IP	K	ERA	WHIP	OBA	vL	vR	BF/G	H%	S%	xERA	G	L	F	Ctl	Dom	Cmd	hr/f	hr/9	RAR	BPV	R$
LH Reliever	05	KC *	8	6	0	127	99	5.16	1.48	263	229	271	22.4	31%	65%	3.72	58	19	24	4.3	7.0	1.6	12%	0.8	-12.3	45	$6
Age 26	06	TAM *	9	8	0	133	103	4.60	1.53	298	400	281	22.8	36%	70%	3.99	45	26	29	3.0	7.0	2.3	7%	0.6	-0.7	68	$8
Type Pwr GB	07	TAM *	8	14	0	179	177	5.43	1.45	286	296	325	25.2	35%	66%	3.50	46	23	31	2.9	8.9	3.1	17%	1.4	-20.4	106	$9
Health A	08	TAM	6	1	3	89	92	2.22	1.13	198	188	197	5.7	26%	83%	3.08	54	17	30	3.9	9.3	2.4	9%	0.6	23.5	93	$15
PT/Exp C	09	TAM	7	5	17	67	79	2.83	1.20	200	284	158	4.0	27%	81%	3.18	49	16	35	4.5	10.7	2.4	13%	0.9	13.3	99	$17
Consist A	1st Half		4	2	6	38	46	1.65	1.10	194			3.9	29%	85%	2.77	51	20	29	3.8	10.8	2.9	4%	0.2	13.2	122	$10
LIMA Plan C+	2nd Half		3	3	11	29	33	4.42	1.33	207			4.0	24%	75%	3.76	46	12	42	5.4	10.4	1.9	21%	1.9	0.1	67	$7
Rand Var -2	10	Proj	5	4	28	65	70	3.31	1.27	227			5.6	29%	79%	3.34	50	16	33	4.0	9.7	2.4	14%	1.1	8.8	94	$18

PRO: Continued Dom growth, 3 years of closer-worthy BPVs.
CON: Growing Ctl issues and gopher ball problems.
Add in bias against LH closers, and these saves feel a little dicey. His leash may be short.

Howry,Bob

Howry,Bob			W	L	Sv	IP	K	ERA	WHIP	OBA	vL	vR	BF/G	H%	S%	xERA	G	L	F	Ctl	Dom	Cmd	hr/f	hr/9	RAR	BPV	R$
RH Reliever	05	CLE	7	4	3	73	48	2.47	0.89	192	186	198	3.5	22%	74%	3.76	40	19	41	2.0	5.9	3.0	5%	0.5	17.2	71	$14
Age 36	06	CHC	4	5	5	76	71	3.19	1.14	246	247	244	3.7	30%	76%	3.66	38	18	44	2.0	8.4	4.2	8%	0.9	12.2	113	$11
Type xFB	07	CHC	6	7	8	81	72	3.32	1.17	249	192	283	4.3	30%	75%	3.94	32	20	48	2.1	8.0	3.8	7%	0.9	11.1	97	$13
Health A	08	CHC	7	5	1	71	59	5.35	1.46	311	328	297	4.3	35%	68%	4.22	35	18	47	1.7	7.5	4.5	12%	1.7	-9.4	103	$4
PT/Exp C	09	SF	2	6	0	64	46	3.39	1.15	218	225	207	4.1	25%	72%	4.51	33	16	51	3.2	6.5	2.0	5%	0.7	6.3	40	$6
Consist A	1st Half		0	4	0	28	17	3.86	1.32	255			4.0	29%	71%	4.84	35	17	47	3.2	5.5	1.7	5%	0.6	1.1	25	$1
LIMA Plan C+	2nd Half		2	2	0	36	29	3.03	1.01	186			4.2	22%	73%	4.24	30	15	55	3.3	7.3	2.2	6%	0.8	5.1	51	$5
Rand Var -5	10	Proj	3	5	3	58	44	4.19	1.31	258			4.2	29%	71%	4.51	34	17	49	2.9	6.8	2.3	8%	1.1	-1.8	55	$5

Falling Dom, rising FB% and walk rate... days as a LIMA pick appear to be coming to an end. xERA trend shows the gradual deterioration. He could rebound a little, but odds are against as he pushes past 35.

Hudson,Daniel

Hudson,Daniel			W	L	Sv	IP	K	ERA	WHIP	OBA	vL	vR	BF/G	H%	S%	xERA	G	L	F	Ctl	Dom	Cmd	hr/f	hr/9	RAR	BPV	R$
RH Starter	05		0	0	0	0	0	0.00	0.00							0.00											
Age 23	06		0	0	0	0	0	0.00	0.00							0.00											
Type Pwr xFB	07		0	0	0	0	0	0.00	0.00							0.00											
Health A	08		0	0	0	0	0	0.00	0.00							0.00											
PT/Exp F	09	CHW *	10	1	0	99	91	2.82	1.17	238	194	257	20.2	30%	77%	4.24	30	12	58	2.6	8.3	3.1	4%	0.5	19.8	86	$16
Consist F	1st Half		1	0	0	18	18	5.47	1.33	261			25.6	34%	57%	3.73				3.0	9.0	3.0		0.5	-2.3	105	$1
LIMA Plan C+	2nd Half		9	1	0	81	73	2.23	1.14	233			19.3	29%	83%	4.23	30	12	58	2.6	8.1	3.2	4%	0.6	22.1	85	$14
Rand Var -4	10	Proj	3	2	0	58	46	4.19	1.38	258			22.7	31%	71%	4.65	36	15	49	3.6	7.1	2.0	6%	0.8	-1.5	46	$4

1-1, 3.37 ERA in 19 IP at CHW. Pitched at every level of the organization, from Low A to the majors, in one season. Skills were impressive in minors, less so in majors (4.3 Ctl, 1.6 Cmd, 5.54 xERA). Give him time.

Hudson,Tim

Hudson,Tim			W	L	Sv	IP	K	ERA	WHIP	OBA	vL	vR	BF/G	H%	S%	xERA	G	L	F	Ctl	Dom	Cmd	hr/f	hr/9	RAR	BPV	R$
RH Starter	05	ATL	14	9	0	192	115	3.52	1.35	264	285	240	28.3	29%	77%	3.56	59	21	21	3.0	5.4	1.8	16%	0.9	17.3	51	$16
Age 34	06	ATL	13	12	0	218	141	4.87	1.44	276	281	265	27.2	31%	68%	3.86	58	18	24	3.3	5.8	1.8	15%	1.0	-10.3	52	$10
Type xGB	07	ATL	16	10	0	224	132	3.33	1.22	259	261	261	27.3	30%	72%	3.34	62	17	22	2.1	5.3	2.5	6%	0.4	30.3	78	$23
Health F	08	ATL	11	7	0	142	85	3.17	1.16	238	255	223	25.2	27%	75%	3.38	59	19	22	2.5	5.4	2.1	11%	0.7	19.3	66	$16
PT/Exp B	09	ATL	2	1	0	42	30	3.62	1.47	291	329	271	26.5	34%	78%	3.29	62	18	20	2.8	6.4	2.3	14%	0.9	3.0	80	$2
Consist A	1st Half		0	0	0	0	0	0.00	0.00																		
LIMA Plan B+	2nd Half		2	1	0	42	30	3.62	1.47	291			26.5	34%	78%	3.29	62	18	20	2.8	6.4	2.3	14%	0.9	3.0	80	$2
Rand Var +2	10	Proj	12	7	0	181	116	3.53	1.33	268			26.6	30%	75%	3.42	61	18	22	2.7	5.8	2.1	11%	0.7	18.8	70	$15

Return from TJS was quite successful, as skills remained intact and Dom even flourished (though IP sample was small). BPV, xERA say he's still a front-end starter, and maybe one you can land for a back-end price.

Huff,David

Huff,David			W	L	Sv	IP	K	ERA	WHIP	OBA	vL	vR	BF/G	H%	S%	xERA	G	L	F	Ctl	Dom	Cmd	hr/f	hr/9	RAR	BPV	R$
LH Starter	05		0	0	0	0	0	0.00	0.00							0.00											
Age 25	06		0	0	0	0	0	0.00	0.00							0.00											
Type FB	07		0	0	0	0	0	0.00	0.00							0.00											
Health A	08	a/a	11	5	0	146	123	3.37	1.16	250			22.1	30%	74%	3.64				2.0	7.6	3.9		1.0	16.9	103	$18
PT/Exp D	09	CLE *	16	9	0	167	94	5.50	1.53	296	317	292	24.8	32%	65%	5.08	38	20	42	3.1	5.0	1.6	9%	1.1	-21.6	23	$7
Consist C	1st Half		8	4	0	85	55	5.73	1.48	282			23.4	31%	63%	5.05	35	18	47	3.3	5.8	1.8	10%	1.4	-13.5	28	$4
LIMA Plan C	2nd Half		8	5	0	82	39	5.25	1.58	309			26.5	33%	67%	5.19	39	21	39	2.8	4.3	1.5	7%	0.9	-8.1	17	$3
Rand Var 0	10	Proj	10	11	0	160	106	4.46	1.39	280			23.7	31%	71%	4.50	38	21	41	2.6	6.0	2.3	9%	1.1	-1.3	54	$11

11-8, 5.61 ERA in 128 IP at CLE Couldn't find a strikeout pitch in majors, and it only got worse second time around the league. MLEs suggest he can turn this around; for now, that's enough to justify an end-game pick.

Hughes,Phil

Hughes,Phil			W	L	Sv	IP	K	ERA	WHIP	OBA	vL	vR	BF/G	H%	S%	xERA	G	L	F	Ctl	Dom	Cmd	hr/f	hr/9	RAR	BPV	R$
RH Reliever	05		0	0	0	0	0	0.00	0.00							0.00											
Age 23	06	aa	10	3	0	116	120	2.96	1.02	206			21.8	28%	71%	2.18				2.6	9.3	3.6		0.4	22.4	132	$20
Type Pwr FB	07	NYY *	9	4	0	108	93	3.88	1.18	224	264	210	22.1	27%	68%	4.09	37	18	45	3.3	7.7	2.3	6%	0.7	8.4	65	$14
Health F	08	NYY *	1	4	0	63	51	6.57	1.71	313	333	299	20.9	37%	61%	4.70	34	27	39	3.9	7.3	1.9	7%	0.9	-17.3	39	($2)
PT/Exp D	09	NYY *	11	3	3	105	112	3.00	1.14	231	257	184	7.9	30%	78%	3.48	34	22	44	2.7	9.6	3.6	9%	0.9	18.9	113	$18
Consist B	1st Half		6	2	0	66	63	3.94	1.27	252			15.4	30%	74%	3.90	37	19	45	2.9	8.6	3.0	12%	1.4	4.2	92	$8
LIMA Plan B+	2nd Half		5	1	3	39	49	1.39	0.93	192			4.1	29%	86%	2.80	31	26	43	2.3	11.4	4.9	3%	0.2	14.6	151	$11
Rand Var -1	10	Proj	6	3	2	73	76	3.35	1.12	230			9.4	30%	72%	3.40	34	24	42	2.5	9.4	3.8	8%	0.7	9.2	115	$12

8-3, 3.03 ERA in 86 IP at NYY. The usage breakdown for '09...
SP: 5.45 ERA, 2.1 Cmd, 1.6 hr/9
RP: 1.40 ERA, 5.0 Cmd, 0.4 hr/9
In one role, a LIMA stud, even Rivera insurance. In the other... well, we don't know yet, do we?

Hunter,Tommy

Hunter,Tommy			W	L	Sv	IP	K	ERA	WHIP	OBA	vL	vR	BF/G	H%	S%	xERA	G	L	F	Ctl	Dom	Cmd	hr/f	hr/9	RAR	BPV	R$
RH Starter	05		0	0	0	0	0	0.00	0.00							0.00											
Age 23	06		0	0	0	0	0	0.00	0.00							0.00											
Type Con FB	07		0	0	0	0	0	0.00	0.00							0.00											
Health A	08	aa	8	4	0	105	48	3.77	1.36	285			28.1	30%	76%	4.80				2.1	4.1	1.9		1.0	7.0	32	$8
PT/Exp D	09	TEX *	13	8	0	183	107	4.54	1.45	290	288	228	25.0	32%	71%	4.85	37	20	42	2.6	5.2	2.0	8%	1.0	-1.9	39	$11
Consist A	1st Half		3	3	0	82	48	5.15	1.64	324			25.0	36%	70%	5.26	35	19	47	2.6	5.3	2.0	7%	1.0	-7.0	37	$1
LIMA Plan C	2nd Half		9	5	0	101	59	4.04	1.29	260			24.9	28%	71%	4.63	38	21	42	2.6	5.2	2.0	8%	1.0	5.1	39	$10
Rand Var -1	10	Proj	10	9	0	160	85	4.63	1.40	287			26.5	31%	70%	4.85	37	20	42	2.4	4.8	2.0	9%	1.1	-8.1	36	$9

9-6, 4.10 ERA in 112 IP at TEX. Any optimism you gain from his MLB surface stats should be tempered by his high xERAs. Flyball prone soft-tossers are not a good match for Texas. DN: ERA soars, back to AAA.

Jackson,Edwin

Jackson,Edwin			W	L	Sv	IP	K	ERA	WHIP	OBA	vL	vR	BF/G	H%	S%	xERA	G	L	F	Ctl	Dom	Cmd	hr/f	hr/9	RAR	BPV	R$
RH Starter	05	LA *	11	13	0	145	78	5.57	1.53	277	333	236	21.5	29%	65%	5.38	36	19	46	4.0	4.8	1.2	9%	1.2	-23.8	-8	$3
Age 26	06	TAM *	3	7	5	109	83	6.60	1.86	314	233	333	11.6	37%	64%	4.76	52	17	31	5.1	6.8	1.3	9%	0.8	-27.5	15	($2)
Type FB	07	TAM	5	15	0	161	128	5.76	1.76	300	313	285	23.5	35%	68%	4.82	45	19	36	4.9	7.2	1.5	10%	1.1	-24.9	19	($1)
Health A	08	TAM	14	11	0	183	108	4.42	1.51	278	295	268	25.4	30%	74%	4.97	39	21	40	3.8	5.3	1.4	9%	1.1	-1.6	11	$10
PT/Exp A	09	DET	13	9	0	214	161	3.62	1.26	249	247	248	27.1	28%	76%	4.27	39	18	42	2.9	6.8	2.3	10%	1.1	22.0	59	$21
Consist A	1st Half		6	4	0	108	84	2.50	1.05	216			26.8	26%	78%	3.94	39	17	45	2.4	7.0	2.9	5%	0.6	26.1	77	$16
LIMA Plan F	2nd Half		7	5	0	106	77	4.76	1.48	280			27.4	30%	74%	4.62	39	20	40	3.5	6.5	1.9	15%	1.7	-4.0	41	$6
Rand Var -1	10	Proj	13	11	0	209	147	4.23	1.41	272			26.6	30%	74%	4.52	40	19	41	3.2	6.3	2.0	10%	1.2	-2.2	45	$15

PRO: Strong 1st half, Ctl growth trend, first year with plus Cmd.
CON: Four and a half years of mediocrity, 1H ERA/xERA gap, FB% trend, 2nd half slide.
This was a step forward, but he's not really a $20 pitcher yet.

Jackson,Steven

Jackson,Steven			W	L	Sv	IP	K	ERA	WHIP	OBA	vL	vR	BF/G	H%	S%	xERA	G	L	F	Ctl	Dom	Cmd	hr/f	hr/9	RAR	BPV	R$
RH Reliever	05		0	0	0	0	0	0.00	0.00							0.00											
Age 28	06	aa	8	11	0	149	105	4.00	1.49	290			27.4	34%	73%	4.73				3.0	6.3	2.1		0.5	9.6	63	$9
Type	07	a/a	4	9	1	90	52	7.79	2.08	362			16.1	39%	64%	8.71				4.3	5.2	1.2		1.6	-36.9	-8	($8)
Health A	08	a/a	4	3	6	79	68	6.19	1.67	300			7.4	37%	61%	5.42				4.2	7.8	1.9		0.6	-18.4	62	$2
PT/Exp D	09	PIT *	3	3	1	75	41	4.19	1.53	285	216	253	5.7	32%	72%	4.92	44	19	38	3.6	4.9	1.3	4%	0.5	-0.0	11	$2
Consist D	1st Half		3	1	1	32	17	4.30	1.53	284			5.7	31%	73%	4.30	58	14	28	3.7	4.8	1.3	10%	0.9	-0.4	24	$2
LIMA Plan C	2nd Half		0	2	0	43	24	4.12	1.53	285			5.6	33%	71%	5.14	37	21	42	3.6	5.0	1.4	2%	0.2	0.4	7	$0
Rand Var -3	10	Proj	2	2	0	44	28	5.17	1.63	302			7.3	35%	68%	4.85	43	19	38	3.7	5.8	1.6	5%	0.6	-3.2	25	$0

2-3, 3.14 ERA in 43 IP at PIT. Do NOT be fooled by MLB ERA.
- xERA in majors was 5.72
- Had more walks than K's
- Inconsistent; low ceiling
But 3.14 will buy him another shot in the bigs. For you? Bid $0.

BRANDON KRUSE

Jakubauskas,Chris

Jakubauskas,Chris	Yr	Tm	W	L	Sv	IP	K	ERA	WHIP	OBA	vL	vR	BF/G	H%	S%	xERA	G	L	F	Ctl	Dom	Cmd	hr/f	hr/9	RAR	BPV	R$
RH Reliever	05		0	0	0	0	0	0.00	0.00							0.00											
Age 31	06		0	0	0	0	0	0.00	0.00							0.00											
Type Con	07	aa	0	4	0	51	28	7.28	1.99	339			15.6	38%	62%	7.10				4.9	4.9	**1.0**		0.7	-17.7	18	($5)
Health A	08	a/a	8	1	0	88	49	2.86	1.60	313			22.1	35%	85%	5.68				2.9	5.0	**1.7**		0.8	15.7	34	$7
PT/Exp D	09	SEA	6	7	0	93	47	5.32	1.27	258	275	235	11.1	26%	61%	4.65	45	14	41	2.6	4.5	**1.7**	12%	1.5	-10.0	35	$5
Consist C	1st Half		4	5	0	61	29	5.46	1.28	255			13.5	26%	59%	4.92	42	14	44	2.8	4.3	**1.5**	9%	1.2	-7.6	22	$3
LIMA Plan C	2nd Half		2	2	0	32	18	5.06	1.25	262			8.3	26%	67%	4.12	51	14	35	2.2	5.1	**2.3**	19%	2.0	-2.4	59	$2
Rand Var +2	10	Proj	**3**	**3**	**0**	**54**	**29**	**4.67**	**1.48**	**293**			**10.3**	**31%**	**71%**	**4.72**	**47**	**14**	**38**	**2.8**	**4.8**	**1.7**	**10%**	**1.2**	**-1.9**	**36**	**$2**

Late season shoulder soreness ended year early, but that was a good thing. Soft-tossers need pinpoint Ctl and high GB rate to have any value. Small signs of that in 2H, but not nearly enough to invest in.

Janssen,Casey

Janssen,Casey	Yr	Tm	W	L	Sv	IP	K	ERA	WHIP	OBA	vL	vR	BF/G	H%	S%	xERA	G	L	F	Ctl	Dom	Cmd	hr/f	hr/9	RAR	BPV	R$
RH Reliever	05	aa	3	3	0	43	39	4.63	1.62	350			21.7	43%	73%	6.35				0.9	8.2	**9.3**		0.9	-1.7	202	$2
Age 28	06	TOR *	7	15	0	136	72	5.64	1.40	295	292	261	21.0	32%	60%	4.16	53	16	31	2.0	4.7	**2.4**	11%	1.1	-18.2	62	$5
Type Con GB	07	TOR	2	3	6	73	39	2.35	1.20	246	257	241	4.3	28%	82%	4.13	49	18	33	2.5	4.8	**2.0**	5%	0.5	19.3	47	$10
Health F	08	TOR	0	0	0	0	0	0.00	0.00							0.00											
PT/Exp D	09	TOR	2	4	1	40	24	5.85	1.83	343	313	367	9.0	38%	69%	4.52	50	24	26	3.2	5.4	**1.7**	13%	1.1	-6.9	40	($1)
Consist A	1st Half		2	3	0	26	11	6.23	1.81	353			24.6	37%	67%	5.11	42	28	31	2.4	3.8	**1.6**	13%	1.4	-5.7	23	($1)
LIMA Plan D	2nd Half		0	1	1	14	13	5.14	1.86	325			4.2	40%	72%	3.28	67	17	17	4.5	8.4	**1.9**	13%	0.6	-1.2	74	($0)
Rand Var +5	10	Proj	**2**	**4**	**0**	**44**	**24**	**4.55**	**1.47**	**294**			**12.7**	**32%**	**70%**	**4.13**	**53**	**20**	**27**	**2.7**	**5.0**	**1.8**	**10%**	**0.8**	**1.6**	**48**	**$2**

Was not fully recovered from '08 labrum surgery, but BPIs show he was not far off from previous skill levels either. 2010 will be better, but stop looking at 2007 because that wasn't real. You don't chase BPVs in the 40s.

Jenks,Bobby

Jenks,Bobby	Yr	Tm	W	L	Sv	IP	K	ERA	WHIP	OBA	vL	vR	BF/G	H%	S%	xERA	G	L	F	Ctl	Dom	Cmd	hr/f	hr/9	RAR	BPV	R$
RH Reliever	05	CHW *	2	3	25	80	89	3.12	1.37	247	105	298	5.1	34%	78%	3.30	45	26	30	4.1	10.0	**2.5**	6%	0.5	12.3	93	$16
Age 29	06	CHW	3	4	41	69	80	4.03	1.40	253	227	268	4.5	35%	72%	2.81	59	19	22	4.0	10.4	**2.6**	13%	0.7	4.5	115	$20
Type Pwr GB	07	CHW	3	5	40	65	56	2.77	0.89	197	237	169	3.8	25%	68%	2.91	54	16	31	1.8	7.8	**4.3**	4%	0.3	13.9	123	$24
Health A	08	CHW	3	1	30	62	38	2.63	1.10	227	219	241	4.4	26%	77%	3.51	58	14	28	2.5	5.5	**2.2**	6%	0.4	13.1	68	$18
PT/Exp B	09	CHW	3	4	29	53	49	3.71	1.28	257	309	202	4.3	30%	78%	3.46	49	18	33	2.7	8.3	**3.1**	18%	1.5	4.8	103	$15
Consist A	1st Half		2	2	18	28	28	3.21	1.07	233			4.0	27%	80%	2.86	54	14	32	1.9	9.0	**4.7**	21%	1.6	4.3	142	$10
LIMA Plan C+	2nd Half		1	2	11	25	21	4.27	1.50	282			4.7	32%	76%	4.15	43	23	34	3.6	7.5	**2.1**	15%	1.4	0.6	59	$5
Rand Var +2	10	Proj	**3**	**3**	**28**	**58**	**49**	**3.57**	**1.29**	**255**			**4.4**	**30%**	**75%**	**3.55**	**51**	**18**	**31**	**2.9**	**7.6**	**2.6**	**11%**	**0.9**	**6.3**	**87**	**$15**

Nagging injuries limited work, while concerns about stamina grew. Skills are elite; ERA uptick was product of inflated hr/f. Has handcuffed LHers in past, so he could make gains there. Saves at risk due to shape, not skill.

Jennings,Jason

Jennings,Jason	Yr	Tm	W	L	Sv	IP	K	ERA	WHIP	OBA	vL	vR	BF/G	H%	S%	xERA	G	L	F	Ctl	Dom	Cmd	hr/f	hr/9	RAR	BPV	R$
RH Reliever	05	COL	6	9	0	122	75	5.02	1.57	274	269	279	27.4	31%	69%	4.52	48	25	27	4.6	5.5	**1.2**	10%	0.8	-11.6	2	$2
Age 31	06	COL	9	13	0	212	142	3.78	1.37	256	254	261	28.4	29%	74%	4.53	44	19	37	3.6	6.0	**1.7**	7%	0.7	18.5	33	$14
Type Pwr FB	07	HOU	2	9	0	99	71	6.45	1.55	299	309	295	23.3	32%	61%	4.81	35	21	44	3.1	6.5	**2.1**	13%	1.7	-24.8	46	($2)
Health C	08		0	0	0	0	0	0.00	0.00							0.00											
PT/Exp D	09	TEX	2	4	1	61	44	4.13	1.56	280	327	257	6.2	32%	76%	4.70	44	19	38	4.1	6.5	**1.6**	10%	1.0	2.4	27	$3
Consist A	1st Half		2	3	1	42	28	3.63	1.40	261			7.0	30%	75%	4.36	47	20	33	3.6	6.0	**1.6**	7%	0.6	4.3	35	$4
LIMA Plan C+	2nd Half		0	1	0	19	16	5.27	1.91	320			5.0	36%	78%	5.42	37	16	47	5.3	7.7	**1.5**	14%	1.9	-1.9	11	($1)
Rand Var -1	10	Proj	**2**	**6**	**0**	**87**	**63**	**4.86**	**1.54**	**279**			**9.0**	**31%**	**72%**	**4.76**	**41**	**19**	**40**	**4.0**	**6.5**	**1.6**	**12%**	**1.3**	**-3.5**	**27**	**$2**

Lost 2008 to forearm tendon surgery. Showed some promise in '09, but was released late in the year after a miserable July and August. Minor signs of life here, but needs to show he is healthy.

Jepsen,Kevin

Jepsen,Kevin	Yr	Tm	W	L	Sv	IP	K	ERA	WHIP	OBA	vL	vR	BF/G	H%	S%	xERA	G	L	F	Ctl	Dom	Cmd	hr/f	hr/9	RAR	BPV	R$
RH Reliever	05		0	0	0	0	0	0.00	0.00							0.00											
Age 25	06		0	0	0	0	0	0.00	0.00							0.00											
Type Pwr xGB	07		0	0	0	0	0	0.00	0.00							0.00											
Health A	08	aa	3	4	13	54	46	2.27	1.44	233			5.9	29%	86%	3.72				5.2	7.6	**1.4**		0.5	13.6	69	$10
PT/Exp F	09	LAA *	7	4	3	73	63	7.02	1.92	334	373	208	5.2	41%	62%	4.16	57	16	27	4.6	7.8	**1.7**	10%	0.8	-23.0	53	($1)
Consist A	1st Half		3	2	2	30	21	12.76	2.92	434			6.3	48%	55%	5.55	61	20	20	6.8	6.4	**0.9**	22%	1.6	-30.8	-30	($8)
LIMA Plan B+	2nd Half		4	2	1	43	42	2.96	1.22	240			4.4	32%	75%	3.12	55	14	30	3.0	8.9	**3.0**	3%	0.2	7.9	113	$7
Rand Var +5	10	Proj	**5**	**4**	**8**	**65**	**58**	**3.72**	**1.33**	**252**			**5.0**	**31%**	**73%**	**3.37**	**57**	**16**	**27**	**3.4**	**8.0**	**2.3**	**10%**	**0.7**	**8.6**	**86**	**$9**

6-4, 4.94 ERA in 54 IP at LAA. Why there's tons of profit here...
- H%, S% inflated ERA, WHIP
- Electric 2H + still extreme GBer

Early season back problems sabotaged 1H. Out pitch vs. LH is missing piece. UP: 25 Saves

Jimenez,Ubaldo

Jimenez,Ubaldo	Yr	Tm	W	L	Sv	IP	K	ERA	WHIP	OBA	vL	vR	BF/G	H%	S%	xERA	G	L	F	Ctl	Dom	Cmd	hr/f	hr/9	RAR	BPV	R$
RH Starter	05	aa	2	5	0	63	45	7.43	1.60	283			23.7	28%	59%	6.86				4.4	6.4	**1.5**		2.6	-24.3	-10	($3)
Age 26	06	a/a	14	4	0	151	128	4.88	1.48	254			25.6	31%	67%	4.37				4.7	7.6	**1.6**		0.7	-6.7	63	$11
Type Pwr GB	07	COL *	12	9	0	185	145	6.51	1.67	285	244	212	25.0	33%	61%	4.77	46	17	37	4.9	7.0	**1.4**	10%	1.1	-47.6	19	($0)
Health A	08	COL	12	12	0	199	172	3.99	1.43	245	248	241	25.4	31%	72%	3.80	54	18	28	4.7	7.8	**1.7**	7%	0.5	7.0	47	$13
PT/Exp A	09	COL	15	12	0	218	198	3.47	1.23	229	251	206	27.4	29%	72%	3.31	53	20	28	3.5	8.2	**2.3**	8%	0.5	19.4	83	$23
Consist B	1st Half		6	7	0	103	85	3.75	1.33	250			27.4	31%	71%	3.49	53	21	26	3.5	7.4	**2.1**	5%	0.3	5.5	70	$8
LIMA Plan C	2nd Half		9	5	0	115	113	3.21	1.14	210			27.4	27%	74%	3.15	52	18	30	3.5	8.9	**2.5**	10%	0.7	13.9	94	$15
Rand Var 0	10	Proj	**16**	**9**	**0**	**210**	**198**	**3.34**	**1.25**	**230**			**25.8**	**29%**	**74%**	**3.33**	**53**	**18**	**29**	**3.7**	**8.5**	**2.3**	**9%**	**0.6**	**24.2**	**84**	**$24**

High strikeout rate? Check. Improving control? Check. Strong GB tendency? Check. Stable H% and S%? Check. Humidor still working? Check. It's true, it's real and it's getting better.

Johnson,Jim

Johnson,Jim	Yr	Tm	W	L	Sv	IP	K	ERA	WHIP	OBA	vL	vR	BF/G	H%	S%	xERA	G	L	F	Ctl	Dom	Cmd	hr/f	hr/9	RAR	BPV	R$
RH Reliever	05		0	0	0	0	0	0.00	0.00							0.00											
Age 26	06	aa	13	6	0	156	108	6.30	1.72	320			26.8	36%	63%	6.36				3.5	6.2	**1.8**		1.0	-34.3	35	$1
Type GB	07	aaa	6	12	0	148	95	5.72	1.70	326			26.3	36%	68%	6.66				3.0	5.8	**1.9**		1.2	-22.9	28	($1)
Health A	08	BAL	2	4	1	69	38	2.23	1.19	218	227	212	5.2	26%	79%	3.90	59	14	27	3.7	5.0	**1.4**	0%	0.0	18.0	27	$8
PT/Exp C	09	BAL	4	6	10	70	49	4.11	1.37	270	262	278	4.7	30%	73%	3.91	52	18	30	3.0	6.3	**2.1**	12%	1.0	2.9	63	$9
Consist C	1st Half		3	3	1	37	24	2.90	1.26	250			4.7	28%	80%	3.81	55	17	29	2.9	5.8	**2.0**	9%	0.7	7.1	59	$5
LIMA Plan C+	2nd Half		1	3	9	33	25	5.49	1.49	291			4.7	33%	66%	4.01	49	20	31	3.0	6.9	**2.3**	15%	1.4	-4.2	69	$4
Rand Var +1	10	Proj	**3**	**5**	**15**	**73**	**51**	**3.97**	**1.39**	**268**			**6.1**	**31%**	**73%**	**3.89**	**54**	**17**	**29**	**3.2**	**6.3**	**2.0**	**11%**	**0.9**	**4.9**	**59**	**$10**

Fell into Sv opps because BAL had nothing better. Average skills get energized by high GB%. With neither flashes of elite Dom nor pinpoint Ctl, he'll be far from a Sv lock. If you bid, bet on '09 surface stats, not '08.

Johnson,Josh

Johnson,Josh	Yr	Tm	W	L	Sv	IP	K	ERA	WHIP	OBA	vL	vR	BF/G	H%	S%	xERA	G	L	F	Ctl	Dom	Cmd	hr/f	hr/9	RAR	BPV	R$
RH Starter	05	FLA *	1	4	0	151	112	4.71	1.56	288			22.5	35%	68%	4.55				3.8	6.7	**1.8**		0.2	-8.6	68	$1
Age 26	06	FLA	12	7	0	157	133	3.10	1.30	235	246	227	21.4	28%	79%	4.02	46	19	36	3.9	7.6	**2.0**	9%	0.8	27.0	56	$18
Type Pwr	07	FLA	0	3	0	16	14	7.45	2.42	370	419	361	21.0	45%	68%	5.69	44	22	33	6.9	8.0	**1.2**	5%	0.6	-5.9	-19	($2)
Health F	08	FLA *	8	2	0	106	89	3.73	1.38	279	288	259	26.9	34%	74%	3.63	48	21	31	2.6	7.5	**2.9**	8%	0.7	7.1	90	$9
PT/Exp C	09	FLA	15	5	0	209	191	3.23	1.16	238	242	231	25.8	30%	73%	3.20	50	18	32	2.5	8.2	**3.3**	8%	0.6	24.7	109	$25
Consist C	1st Half		7	1	0	114	97	2.76	1.13	232			27.2	29%	76%	3.17	53	18	29	2.5	7.7	**3.0**	6%	0.5	20.1	101	$14
LIMA Plan C	2nd Half		8	4	0	95	94	3.79	1.19	245			24.4	31%	70%	3.23	47	18	36	2.5	8.9	**3.6**	9%	0.8	4.6	118	$11
Rand Var 0	10	Proj	**13**	**5**	**0**	**183**	**161**	**3.54**	**1.28**	**254**			**24.8**	**31%**	**73%**	**3.53**	**48**	**19**	**33**	**2.9**	**7.9**	**2.8**	**7%**	**0.6**	**16.5**	**91**	**$18**

Why he's on the verge of a Cy...
- Cmd trend, especially in 2H
- Solidified '08 Ctl gains
- Rising GB rate
- Handcuffs LH and RH equally.

Why it may not be in 2010...
- Huge '09 IP spike. Be careful.

Johnson,Randy

Johnson,Randy	Yr	Tm	W	L	Sv	IP	K	ERA	WHIP	OBA	vL	vR	BF/G	H%	S%	xERA	G	L	F	Ctl	Dom	Cmd	hr/f	hr/9	RAR	BPV	R$
LH Starter	05	NYY	17	8	0	225	211	3.80	1.13	246	185	257	26.8	29%	72%	3.28	45	17	38	1.9	8.4	**4.5**	13%	1.3	16.0	124	$29
Age 46	06	NYY	17	11	0	205	172	5.00	1.24	251	194	259	25.8	29%	62%	3.96	42	16	43	2.6	7.6	**2.9**	11%	1.2	-11.3	85	$20
Type Pwr FB	07	ARI	4	3	0	57	72	3.81	1.15	245	182	257	23.1	34%	71%	2.83	40	19	40	2.1	11.4	**5.5**	12%	1.1	4.3	168	$8
Health F	08	ARI	11	10	0	184	173	3.91	1.24	262	215	267	25.5	32%	73%	3.61	40	18	42	2.2	8.5	**3.9**	11%	1.2	8.1	112	$17
PT/Exp B	09	SF	8	6	0	96	86	4.88	1.33	264	268	260	18.6	30%	70%	3.65	45	19	35	2.9	8.1	**2.8**	19%	1.8	-8.1	90	$7
Consist A	1st Half		8	5	0	88	78	4.70	1.32	255			23.3	29%	69%	3.65	47	19	34	3.2	8.0	**2.5**	17%	1.5	-5.6	83	$7
LIMA Plan B	2nd Half		0	1	0	8	8	6.75	1.50	347			5.9	35%	75%	3.56	30	26	44	0.0	9.0		34%	4.5	-2.5	170	($0)
Rand Var +5	10	Proj	**6**	**4**	**0**	**77**	**66**	**4.59**	**1.36**	**266**			**14.2**	**31%**	**70%**	**4.06**	**38**	**21**	**41**	**3.1**	**7.8**	**2.5**	**12%**	**1.3**	**1.9**	**73**	**$6**

Tear in rotator cuff wiped out 2H. But BPIs were already into their gentle decline. Rise in hr/f% and decline vs LH are cracks in the once-formidable armor. The only question - does the HOF voting start in 2014 or 2015?

STEPHEN NICKRAND

Jurrjens,Jair		Yr	Tm	W	L	Sv	IP	K	ERA	WHIP	OBA	vL	vR	BF/G	H%	S%	xERA	G	L	F	Ctl	Dom	Cmd	hr/f	hr/9	RAR	BPV	R$
RH Starter		05		0	0	0	0	0	0.00	0.00							0.00											
Age	24	06	aa	4	3	0	67	48	4.22	1.52	300			24.8	34%	75%	5.50				2.8	6.5	2.3		1.0	2.5	52	$4
Type		07	DET	* 10	6	0	143	94	4.47	1.42	284	262	167	23.9	32%	69%	4.70	38	18	44	2.7	5.9	2.2	6%	0.8	0.6	50	$10
Health	A	08	ATL	13	10	0	188	139	3.68	1.37	261	261	260	26.1	31%	73%	3.75	52	22	27	3.3	6.6	2.0	7%	0.5	13.7	59	$15
PT/Exp	A	09	ATL	14	10	0	215	152	2.60	1.21	235	264	212	26.1	27%	81%	4.13	43	18	39	3.1	6.4	2.0	6%	0.6	42.3	51	$24
Consist	B	1st Half		6	6	0	102	74	2.73	1.24	236			25.0	28%	79%	4.27	41	16	42	3.3	6.5	1.9	5%	0.5	18.3	46	$11
LIMA Plan	D+	2nd Half		8	4	0	113	78	2.47	1.19	234			27.3	27%	82%	4.00	44	19	36	2.9	6.2	2.1	7%	0.7	23.9	55	$14
Rand Var	-5	10	Proj	15	10	0	209	150	3.50	1.30	256			25.9	30%	75%	3.99	46	20	34	3.0	6.5	2.1	8%	0.7	7.0	59	$19

On surface, continued growth. But not so fast. Sub-3.00 ERA was product of H% and S% support. Marginal Ctl and Dom haven't caught up to him...yet. Lower GB% another warning sign. Don't bid full value.

Karstens,Jeff		Yr	Tm	W	L	Sv	IP	K	ERA	WHIP	OBA	vL	vR	BF/G	H%	S%	xERA	G	L	F	Ctl	Dom	Cmd	hr/f	hr/9	RAR	BPV	R$
RH Reliever		05	aa	12	11	0	169	123	4.95	1.54	313			26.9	36%	69%	5.59				2.3	6.6	2.9		1.0	-13.5	63	$7
Age	27	06	NYY	* 13	6	0	189	108	4.33	1.40	277	253	233	24.8	30%	72%	5.18	33	16	51	2.8	5.1	1.8	7%	1.1	5.2	28	$14
Type	xFB	07	NYY	* 5	4	0	51	31	5.06	1.69	309			16.7	34%	73%	5.78	27	21	52	3.8	5.4	1.4	8%	1.3	-3.5	-0	$2
Health	F	08	PIT	* 8	10	0	120	68	4.61	1.38	288	265	293	24.5	31%	70%	4.48	42	20	39	2.1	5.1	2.4	11%	1.3	-4.9	53	$6
PT/Exp	D	09	PIT	4	6	0	108	52	5.42	1.48	274	263	294	12.2	29%	64%	5.38	39	16	46	3.8	4.3	1.2	7%	1.0	-16.3	-7	$0
Consist	C	1st Half		3	4	0	67	27	4.69	1.43	270			17.2	28%	69%	5.43	41	14	45	3.5	3.6	1.0	8%	1.1	-4.1	-10	$2
LIMA Plan	C	2nd Half		1	2	0	41	25	6.62	1.57	281			8.3	31%	57%	5.30	35	19	46	4.2	5.5	1.3	6%	0.9	-12.2	-1	($1)
Rand Var	0	10	Proj	4	5	0	73	41	4.97	1.49	281			13.9	30%	70%	5.15	37	18	45	3.5	5.1	1.5	10%	1.4	-8.0	13	$2

Guys like this have no business taking IP away from promising arms. Sinking Dom, shaky Ctl is a flammable combination. RHers have touched him up for two straight years, meaning short-relief isn't in cards either.

Kawakami,Kenshin		Yr	Tm	W	L	Sv	IP	K	ERA	WHIP	OBA	vL	vR	BF/G	H%	S%	xERA	G	L	F	Ctl	Dom	Cmd	hr/f	hr/9	RAR	BPV	R$
RH Starter		05	JPN	11	8	0	180	131	4.66	1.30	282			30.4	31%	70%	5.17				1.7	6.5	3.8		1.7	-7.8	67	$12
Age	34	06	JPN	17	7	0	215	184	3.12	1.05	227			29.5	25%	80%	3.66				2.0	7.7	3.8		1.5	37.1	90	$32
Type		07	JPN	12	8	0	167	138	4.42	1.30	285			27.1	32%	72%	5.26				1.5	7.4	4.8		1.6	0.9	95	$15
Health	C	08	JPN	9	5	0	117	106	2.87	1.17	244			23.9	28%	84%	4.03				2.4	8.2	3.4		1.4	20.8	85	$16
PT/Exp	A	09	ATL	7	12	1	156	105	3.86	1.34	258	252	268	20.8	29%	73%	4.39	42	19	39	3.3	6.0	1.8	8%	0.9	6.4	40	$10
Consist	B	1st Half		4	6	0	78	60	4.26	1.34	251			23.8	29%	70%	4.34	41	17	42	3.6	6.9	1.9	8%	0.9	-0.7	47	$5
LIMA Plan	C+	2nd Half		3	6	1	78	45	3.45	1.34	264			18.5	29%	77%	4.43	44	21	36	3.0	5.2	1.7	8%	0.8	7.1	34	$5
Rand Var	-1	10	Proj	9	9	0	149	106	4.29	1.37	267			22.8	30%	72%	4.29	42	19	38	3.1	6.4	2.1	11%	1.1	-0.5	53	$9

Elite skills from Japan didn't carry over to MLB. Even though ERA improved as year went along, credit high 2H S% for that. Dom erosion over same period suggests he wasn't fooling guys. Keep bidding under $10.

Kazmir,Scott		Yr	Tm	W	L	Sv	IP	K	ERA	WHIP	OBA	vL	vR	BF/G	H%	S%	xERA	G	L	F	Ctl	Dom	Cmd	hr/f	hr/9	RAR	BPV	R$
LH Starter		05	TAM	10	9	0	186	174	3.77	1.46	247	174	268	25.5	31%	75%	4.20	42	20	38	4.8	8.4	1.7	6%	0.6	13.7	41	$15
Age	26	06	TAM	10	8	0	144	163	3.25	1.28	245	227	242	25.2	32%	78%	3.37	42	19	39	3.2	10.2	3.1	10%	0.9	23.3	115	$20
Type	Pwr xFB	07	TAM	13	9	0	207	239	3.48	1.38	252	217	263	26.1	34%	77%	3.57	43	16	41	3.9	10.4	2.7	8%	0.8	26.1	104	$24
Health	C	08	TAM	12	8	0	152	166	3.49	1.27	223	198	227	23.6	28%	79%	3.92	31	20	49	4.1	9.8	2.4	12%	1.4	16.2	74	$19
PT/Exp	A	09	2AL	10	9	0	147	117	4.89	1.42	264	261	258	24.6	31%	67%	4.71	34	19	48	3.7	7.1	2.0	8%	1.0	-7.9	42	$9
Consist	B	1st Half		4	4	0	50	40	7.35	1.87	311			24.1	36%	62%	5.39	39	18	43	5.4	7.2	1.3	11%	1.4	-17.9	1	($2)
LIMA Plan	B	2nd Half		6	5	0	97	77	3.61	1.18	237			24.9	28%	71%	4.37	31	19	50	2.8	7.1	2.6	6%	0.7	10.0	62	$11
Rand Var	0	10	Proj	12	10	0	174	155	3.98	1.33	253			24.7	30%	74%	4.24	35	19	46	3.4	8.0	2.3	10%	1.1	4.2	66	$17

Why there's still a $20 SP here...
- Significant 2H Ctl gains
- 62/23% PQS DOM/DIS%
- Bad 1H due to quad, forearm

Overall skill decline, continued health risk, FB approach temper optimism. High risk, high reward.

Kelley,Shawn		Yr	Tm	W	L	Sv	IP	K	ERA	WHIP	OBA	vL	vR	BF/G	H%	S%	xERA	G	L	F	Ctl	Dom	Cmd	hr/f	hr/9	RAR	BPV	R$
RH Reliever		05		0	0	0	0	0	0.00	0.00							0.00											
Age	25	06		0	0	0	0	0	0.00	0.00							0.00											
Type	xFB	07		0	0	0	0	0	0.00	0.00							0.00											
Health	B	08	aa	3	1	9	42	38	2.47	1.27	231			6.1	29%	82%	3.19				3.8	8.1	2.1		0.4	9.6	89	$9
PT/Exp	F	09	SEA	5	4	0	46	41	4.50	1.17	258	209	303	4.6	29%	69%	3.98	31	17	51	1.8	8.0	4.6	13%	1.8	-0.3	106	$6
Consist	B	1st Half		1	1	0	11	11	1.61	1.07	258			4.5	30%	100%	3.59	29	16	55	0.8	8.8	11.0	12%	1.6	3.9	144	$2
LIMA Plan	A	2nd Half		4	3	0	35	30	5.43	1.21	257			4.6	28%	60%	4.10	32	17	50	2.1	7.8	3.8	14%	1.8	-4.2	94	$4
Rand Var	+1	10	Proj	6	4	3	58	52	3.88	1.19	255			5.1	30%	73%	4.03	31	17	52	2.0	8.1	4.0	10%	1.4	2.9	100	$9

Why there's an elite RP here...
- Fantastic command
- RHP who handcuffs LHers
- 2H ERA spike due to low S%

The risk is HR/9, given extreme FB tendency. With pinpoint Ctl, it's one worth taking. UP: 20 SV

Kendrick,Kyle		Yr	Tm	W	L	Sv	IP	K	ERA	WHIP	OBA	vL	vR	BF/G	H%	S%	xERA	G	L	F	Ctl	Dom	Cmd	hr/f	hr/9	RAR	BPV	R$
RH Starter		05		0	0	0	0	0	0.00	0.00							0.00											
Age	25	06		0	0	0	0	0	0.00	0.00							0.00											
Type	Con	07	PHI	* 14	11	0	202	91	3.88	1.33	283	321	241	26.8	30%	73%	4.38	47	21	32	1.9	4.0	2.1	9%	0.9	13.7	45	$15
Health	A	08	PHI	11	9	0	156	68	5.49	1.61	306	334	271	22.8	32%	68%	4.88	44	27	29	3.3	3.9	1.2	14%	1.3	-23.5	4	$1
PT/Exp	B	09	PHI	* 12	8	0	169	66	4.08	1.35	278	267	278	21.9	29%	70%	4.00	56	22	22	2.4	3.5	1.5	9%	0.6	2.4	32	$10
Consist	B	1st Half		5	6	0	98	40	4.54	1.46	288			23.9	30%	70%	4.62	50	20	30	2.9	3.6	1.3	9%	0.8	-4.2	16	$3
LIMA Plan	C	2nd Half		7	2	0	71	27	3.44	1.20	263			19.6	28%	71%	3.70	57	22	21	1.8	3.4	1.9	6%	0.4	6.6	48	$7
Rand Var	0	10	Proj	6	4	0	83	36	4.45	1.42	287			22.5	30%	70%	4.45	47	25	28	2.6	3.9	1.5	10%	0.9	-1.9	25	$4

3-1, 3.42 ERA in 26 IP at PHI. Sinking Dom shows he doesn't miss many bats, an issue offset partially by his elite GB%. But he's at the mercy of his defense. Window shop only until he sustains at least a 2.0 Cmd.

Kennedy,Ian		Yr	Tm	W	L	Sv	IP	K	ERA	WHIP	OBA	vL	vR	BF/G	H%	S%	xERA	G	L	F	Ctl	Dom	Cmd	hr/f	hr/9	RAR	BPV	R$
RH Starter		05		0	0	0	0	0	0.00	0.00							0.00											
Age	25	06		0	0	0	0	0	0.00	0.00							0.00											
Type	Pwr xFB	07	NYY	* 7	2	0	102	91	3.00	1.13	209	161	216	23.0	26%	74%	4.25	26	23	51	3.4	8.0	2.3	4%	0.5	19.0	56	$15
Health	A	08	NYY	* 5	7	0	109	87	4.89	1.43	266	236	397	20.5	32%	66%	4.54	41	12	48	3.6	7.2	2.0	6%	0.8	-7.2	50	$6
PT/Exp	D	09	NYY	* 1	0	0	23	22	2.35	1.35	253			19.6	34%	81%	3.19				3.5	8.6	2.4		0.0	6.0	107	$3
Consist	B	1st Half		1	0	0	22	21	2.43	1.31	260			23.5	35%	79%	3.18				2.8	8.5	3.0		0.0	5.5	117	$3
LIMA Plan	B	2nd Half		0	0	0	1	1	0.00	0.00				4.3			0.00				22.5	11.2	0.5			0.4	133	
Rand Var	-4	10	Proj	4	2	0	73	64	3.85	1.26	241			21.6	30%	71%	4.18	38	14	48	3.2	7.9	2.5	6%	0.7	2.3	71	$7

0-0, 0.00 ERA in 1 IP at NYY. Aneurysm in throwing shoulder wiped out nearly entire season. He's still young enough to bring back elite prospect talk; Triple-A skills have been really solid for awhile now. If healthy, sleeper.

Keppel,Bobby		Yr	Tm	W	L	Sv	IP	K	ERA	WHIP	OBA	vL	vR	BF/G	H%	S%	xERA	G	L	F	Ctl	Dom	Cmd	hr/f	hr/9	RAR	BPV	R$
RH Reliever		05		0	0	0	0	0	0.00	0.00							0.00											
Age	27	06		0	0	0	0	0	0.00	0.00							0.00											
Type	Con	07	aa	8	10	0	138	51	8.33	2.07	360			26.5	37%	59%	8.38				4.3	3.3	0.8		1.3	-65.9	-20	($14)
Health	A	08	aa	9	11	0	159	68	7.93	2.11	373			28.6	38%	64%	9.03				3.9	3.8	1.0		1.8	-71.2	-29	($16)
PT/Exp	D	09	MIN	* 3	4	1	108	53	3.91	1.43	286	314	286	8.0	32%	72%	4.39	51	20	29	2.7	4.4	1.6	5%	0.4	7.2	35	$5
Consist	F	1st Half		3	3	1	61	28	2.63	1.32	267			10.4	30%	79%	3.45	73	7	20	2.6	4.1	1.6	3%	0.2	13.8	55	$6
LIMA Plan	C+	2nd Half		0	1	0	47	25	5.60	1.59	310			6.2	34%	64%	4.54	49	21	30	2.9	4.8	1.7	8%	0.8	-6.6	35	($1)
Rand Var	-2	10	Proj	2	2	0	44	22	4.97	1.61	313			11.6	34%	71%	4.57	50	21	29	2.9	4.6	1.6	11%	1.0	-0.7	32	$1

1-1, 4.83 ERA in 54 IP at MIN.
PRO:
- BPV greater than 0
- Next to Kershaw in book

CON: No matter how good Kershaw is, ink proximity is not all it's cut out to be.

Kershaw,Clayton		Yr	Tm	W	L	Sv	IP	K	ERA	WHIP	OBA	vL	vR	BF/G	H%	S%	xERA	G	L	F	Ctl	Dom	Cmd	hr/f	hr/9	RAR	BPV	R$
LH Starter		05		0	0	0	0	0	0.00	0.00							0.00											
Age	22	06		0	0	0	0	0	0.00	0.00							0.00											
Type	Pwr	07	aa	1	2	0	24	26	4.88	1.63	228			21.8	26%	76%	5.57				7.1	9.8	1.4		1.9	-1.2	40	$1
Health	A	08	LA	* 7	8	0	169	157	3.48	1.30	240	250	269	20.4	30%	74%	3.57	48	21	31	3.7	8.4	2.2	8%	0.6	16.4	76	$14
PT/Exp	C	09	LA	8	8	0	171	185	2.79	1.23	198	173	208	22.9	27%	77%	3.74	39	19	42	4.8	9.7	2.0	4%	0.4	29.5	63	$19
Consist	C	1st Half		5	5	0	87	88	3.51	1.32	204			23.1	27%	74%	4.07	41	19	40	5.4	9.1	1.7	6%	0.5	7.3	38	$8
LIMA Plan	C	2nd Half		3	3	0	84	97	2.04	1.13	192			22.6	28%	82%	3.41	38	20	43	4.2	10.4	2.5	2%	0.2	22.2	90	$12
Rand Var	-4	10	Proj	10	8	0	203	209	3.41	1.30	225			21.9	29%	75%	3.73	42	20	38	4.3	9.3	2.2	8%	0.7	13.3	71	$19

Despite sub-3.00 ERA, don't put him in class of Tommy Hanson yet. Electric Dom offset by wobbly Ctl. Touch of H% and S% support, combined with low hr/f, suggests his ERA is headed north. He'll be gem, but not yet.

STEPHEN NICKRAND

Kuo,Hong-Chih

		Yr	Tm	W	L	Sv	IP	K	ERA	WHIP	OBA	vL	vR	BF/G	H%	S%	xERA	G	L	F	Ctl	Dom	Cmd	hr/f	hr/9	RAR	BPV	R$
LH	Reliever	05	aa	1	2	3	33	49	3.82	1.48	250			5.6	40%	74%	4.02				4.9	13.4	2.7		0.5	2.0	126	$4
Age	28	06	LA *	5	8	1	112	123	3.70	1.45	255	241	246	9.6	34%	75%	3.67	44	21	34	4.3	9.9	2.3	8%	0.6	10.8	83	$9
Type	Pwr	07	LA *	1	5	0	50	49	6.32	1.61	290	240	296	15.2	36%	60%	4.69	31	20	49	4.2	8.8	2.1	7%	0.9	-11.8	54	($1)
Health	F	08	LA	5	3	1	80	96	2.14	1.01	210	202	205	7.5	30%	81%	2.63	46	20	34	2.4	10.8	4.6	6%	0.5	21.0	155	$14
PT/Exp	D	09	LA	2	0	0	30	32	3.00	1.13	199	152	219	3.5	27%	75%	3.35	46	15	39	3.9	9.6	2.5	7%	0.6	4.4	91	$4
Consist	C	1st Half		1	0	0	5	4	7.06	1.76	258			3.4	28%	63%	4.88	56	13	31	7.1	7.1	1.0	21%	1.8	-1.8	-29	$0
LIMA Plan	A+	2nd Half		1	0	0	25	28	2.17	1.00	186			3.5	26%	79%	3.08	43	16	41	3.3	10.1	3.1	4%	0.4	6.2	115	$4
Rand Var	-3	10	Proj	2	3	0	54	59	3.03	1.21	230			6.1	31%	76%	3.24	46	17	37	3.4	9.9	3.0	6%	0.5	6.7	112	$6

Glass half full, or half empty? Another 100+ BPV half season, but missed the other half with -- cue the ominous music -- more elbow pain. Clearly a LIMA & Holds stud when healthy. But the Health grade enunciates the risk.

Kuroda,Hiroki

		Yr	Tm	W	L	Sv	IP	K	ERA	WHIP	OBA	vL	vR	BF/G	H%	S%	xERA	G	L	F	Ctl	Dom	Cmd	hr/f	hr/9	RAR	BPV	R$
RH	Starter	05	JPN	15	12	0	213	157	3.94	1.17	246			30.0	27%	71%	3.84				2.2	6.6	3.0		1.2	9.7	73	$22
Age	35	06	JPN	13	6	1	189	137	2.31	1.10	254			29.2	29%	85%	3.58				1.2	6.5	5.2		0.9	51.6	125	$28
Type	Con GB	07	JPN	12	8	0	180	117	4.41	1.34	271			29.5	28%	74%	5.23				2.6	5.8	2.2		1.7	1.2	33	$13
Health	D	08	LA	9	10	0	183	116	3.73	1.22	259	260	246	24.5	30%	70%	3.65	51	20	29	2.1	5.7	2.8	8%	0.6	12.2	76	$15
PT/Exp	A	09	LA	8	7	0	117	87	3.76	1.14	250	233	253	22.7	29%	70%	3.47	49	17	33	1.8	6.7	3.6	10%	0.9	6.2	98	$12
Consist	B	1st Half		2	4	0	43	35	3.77	1.00	229			24.1	27%	64%	3.02	54	14	32	1.5	7.3	5.0	10%	0.8	2.2	124	$5
LIMA Plan	B	2nd Half		6	3	0	74	52	3.75	1.22	261			22.0	30%	72%	3.73	47	19	34	2.1	6.3	3.1	10%	1.0	4.0	83	$7
Rand Var	0	10	Proj	11	9	0	170	119	3.81	1.19	255			24.9	29%	71%	3.57	50	18	31	2.0	6.3	3.1	11%	1.0	14.4	87	$16

His injuries (an oblique strain, a liner off the noggin) weren't arm-related, and when he was out there, he saw a healthy skills bump. Another step up unlikely at age 35, but two solid years make a strong case for another.

Lackey,John

		Yr	Tm	W	L	Sv	IP	K	ERA	WHIP	OBA	vL	vR	BF/G	H%	S%	xERA	G	L	F	Ctl	Dom	Cmd	hr/f	hr/9	RAR	BPV	R$
RH	Starter	05	ANA	14	5	0	209	199	3.44	1.33	261	274	241	26.9	33%	75%	3.50	45	23	33	3.1	8.6	2.8	7%	0.6	23.9	94	$22
Age	31	06	LAA	13	11	0	217	190	3.56	1.27	249	263	231	27.6	31%	72%	3.84	43	18	39	3.0	7.9	2.6	6%	0.6	26.6	82	$25
Type		07	LAA	19	9	0	224	179	3.01	1.21	257	280	229	28.0	31%	77%	3.68	45	19	36	2.1	7.2	3.4	7%	0.7	41.2	96	$30
Health	C	08	LAA	12	5	0	163	130	3.75	1.23	259	221	301	28.2	29%	76%	3.62	45	20	35	2.2	7.2	3.3	15%	1.4	12.1	93	$18
PT/Exp	A	09	LAA	11	8	0	176	139	3.83	1.27	263	276	247	27.4	31%	72%	3.79	45	20	35	2.4	7.1	3.0	9%	0.9	13.6	86	$17
Consist	A	1st Half		2	3	0	53	42	5.08	1.53	306			26.2	36%	68%	3.92	45	24	31	2.5	7.1	2.8	11%	1.0	-4.1	83	$2
LIMA Plan	C+	2nd Half		9	5	0	123	97	3.29	1.16	242			27.9	29%	74%	3.72	45	18	37	2.3	7.1	3.0	8%	0.8	17.7	87	$16
Rand Var	0	10	Proj	13	8	0	189	148	3.72	1.27	263			27.3	31%	74%	3.77	45	20	35	2.4	7.1	3.0	10%	1.0	15.4	86	$19

That's two years in a row with a minor but IP-cutting arm malady. Otherwise, a Gibraltar of skills consistency. So it's all in the IP; upside is 2007, downside the last two years. Unless of course, the next malady is less minor.

Laffey,Aaron

		Yr	Tm	W	L	Sv	IP	K	ERA	WHIP	OBA	vL	vR	BF/G	H%	S%	xERA	G	L	F	Ctl	Dom	Cmd	hr/f	hr/9	RAR	BPV	R$
LH	Starter	05		0	0	0	0	0	0.00	0.00							0.00											
Age	24	06	aa	8	3	0	112	54	4.34	1.54	305			26.3	33%	73%	5.37				2.7	4.3	1.6		0.7	2.6	32	$5
Type	Con GB	07	CLE *	17	6	0	180	115	3.79	1.29	271	322	271	24.5	31%	70%	3.17	62	19	19	2.1	5.7	2.7	8%	0.4	15.9	86	$20
Health	B	08	CLE *	11	9	0	155	85	4.88	1.54	302	244	292	25.6	33%	68%	4.37	51	19	30	2.9	4.9	1.7	7%	0.7	-10.2	40	$6
PT/Exp	C	09	CLE *	7	11	1	139	68	5.22	1.74	305	255	310	21.6	33%	70%	5.21	49	21	30	4.5	4.4	1.0	7%	0.7	-13.2	-15	($0)
Consist	C	1st Half		3	3	1	51	28	6.25	1.86	307			16.3	34%	65%	5.17	53	21	26	5.5	4.9	0.9	7%	0.5	-11.4	-30	($1)
LIMA Plan	C	2nd Half		4	8	0	88	40	4.62	1.67	304			26.8	33%	73%	5.16	47	21	32	3.9	4.1	1.1	8%	0.8	-1.8	-6	$1
Rand Var	0	10	Proj	10	9	0	149	78	4.85	1.59	299			25.8	33%	69%	4.63	50	20	30	3.5	4.7	1.4	7%	0.7	-3.5	20	$5

7-9, 4.44 ERA in 122 IP at CLE.
PRO:
- Still young, owns 2007 skills
CON:
- Walks up, GB% & K's down
Until the latter trends reverse, you may safely ignore the PRO.

Lannan,John

		Yr	Tm	W	L	Sv	IP	K	ERA	WHIP	OBA	vL	vR	BF/G	H%	S%	xERA	G	L	F	Ctl	Dom	Cmd	hr/f	hr/9	RAR	BPV	R$
LH	Starter	05		0	0	0	0	0	0.00	0.00							0.00											
Age	25	06		0	0	0	0	0	0.00	0.00							0.00											
Type	Con GB	07	WAS *	8	5	0	109	43	3.31	1.38	257	273	273	24.6	28%	76%	4.98	51	14	35	3.6	3.6	1.0	5%	0.5	14.9	-5	$9
Health	A	08	WAS	9	15	0	182	117	3.91	1.34	251	259	250	25.0	27%	75%	3.93	54	19	27	3.6	5.8	1.6	15%	1.1	8.2	40	$12
PT/Exp	A	09	WAS	9	13	0	206	89	3.88	1.35	265	290	259	26.7	28%	74%	4.42	52	18	30	3.0	3.9	1.3	10%	1.0	7.8	20	$10
Consist	B	1st Half		5	5	0	99	47	3.45	1.35	258			26.4	27%	79%	4.44	51	19	30	3.4	4.3	1.3	12%	1.1	9.0	15	$6
LIMA Plan	D	2nd Half		4	8	0	107	42	4.28	1.34	272			26.9	28%	69%	4.41	53	17	30	2.6	3.5	1.4	9%	0.8	-1.2	24	$4
Rand Var	0	10	Proj	9	13	0	189	94	4.20	1.40	269			26.3	29%	72%	4.36	53	18	29	3.2	4.5	1.4	10%	0.9	-2.1	24	$9

Again saw well-aimed GB hit a lot of gloves, and broke 4 ERA by barest of margins. But with Cmd this poor, he's living on the very edge. Just a little bit worse H% and S% luck away from: DN: 5.00 ERA.

Latos,Mat

		Yr	Tm	W	L	Sv	IP	K	ERA	WHIP	OBA	vL	vR	BF/G	H%	S%	xERA	G	L	F	Ctl	Dom	Cmd	hr/f	hr/9	RAR	BPV	R$
RH	Starter	05		0	0	0	0	0	0.00	0.00							0.00											
Age	22	06		0	0	0	0	0	0.00	0.00							0.00											
Type	Pwr xFB	07		0	0	0	0	0	0.00	0.00							0.00											
Health	A	08		0	0	0	0	0	0.00	0.00							0.00											
PT/Exp	F	09	SD *	9	6	0	98	79	3.32	1.11	216	271	200	20.7	26%	71%	4.00	36	19	45	2.9	7.3	2.5	6%	0.6	10.5	66	$13
Consist	F	1st Half		4	1	0	42	34	2.14	1.00	218			20.6	28%	76%	1.90				1.9	7.3	3.8		0.0	10.6	134	$7
LIMA Plan	C	2nd Half		5	5	0	56	45	4.20	1.18	215			20.8	24%	68%	4.24	36	19	45	3.7	7.3	2.0	10%	1.1	-0.1	45	$6
Rand Var	-4	10	Proj	7	8	0	95	75	4.17	1.38	260			22.7	30%	73%	4.49	36	19	45	3.5	7.1	2.0	9%	1.1	-2.6	47	$7

4-5, 4.62 ERA in 51 IP at SD. Enticing debut from the talented 21-y/o, but don't hyperventilate yet. Only 84 IP above A-ball, and SD is still limiting IP. So time in minors or pen probable. Keeper gold, but likely overvalued in '10.

League,Brandon

		Yr	Tm	W	L	Sv	IP	K	ERA	WHIP	OBA	vL	vR	BF/G	H%	S%	xERA	G	L	F	Ctl	Dom	Cmd	hr/f	hr/9	RAR	BPV	R$
RH	Reliever	05	TOR *	5	4	0	98	50	6.57	1.67	314	333	269	11.6	33%	62%	4.12	60	19	21	3.4	4.5	1.3	21%	1.4	-26.7	28	($3)
Age	27	06	TOR *	4	4	9	96	66	2.80	1.33	275	276	178	6.4	33%	78%	2.68	73	13	14	2.3	6.2	2.6	7%	0.3	20.9	99	$13
Type	Pwr xGB	07	TOR	0	0	0	12	7	6.15	2.22	365			4.3	41%	72%	5.03	59	18	23	5.4	5.4	1.0	10%	0.8	-2.4	-11	($1)
Health	C	08	TOR *	3	5	3	67	50	3.78	1.45	274	263	200	5.8	32%	75%	2.98	67	19	14	3.5	6.7	1.9	17%	0.7	4.7	70	$5
PT/Exp	D	09	TOR	3	6	0	75	76	4.58	1.24	255	270	245	4.6	32%	65%	2.89	56	18	26	2.5	9.2	3.6	15%	1.0	-1.2	130	$7
Consist	C	1st Half		1	3	0	36	33	5.48	1.27	256			4.6	31%	57%	3.34	51	19	30	2.7	8.2	3.0	13%	1.0	-4.6	103	$2
LIMA Plan	A	2nd Half		2	3	0	39	43	3.73	1.22	254			4.7	33%	72%	2.48	60	17	23	2.3	10.0	4.3	17%	0.9	3.4	156	$5
Rand Var	+5	10	Proj	5	3	0	73	65	3.10	1.21	247			5.4	31%	76%	2.91	59	18	23	2.6	8.1	3.1	11%	0.6	13.6	112	$9

Elite skills masked by aberrant hr/f, S%. BPV, xERA tell the true story. The closest '09 comp for this extreme GB, Power profile? Some guy named Broxton. Similarly, with the opportunity... UP: Broxton-esque save totals.

LeBlanc,Wade

		Yr	Tm	W	L	Sv	IP	K	ERA	WHIP	OBA	vL	vR	BF/G	H%	S%	xERA	G	L	F	Ctl	Dom	Cmd	hr/f	hr/9	RAR	BPV	R$
LH	Starter	05		0	0	0	0	0	0.00	0.00							0.00											
Age	25	06		0	0	0	0	0	0.00	0.00							0.00											
Type	xFB	07	aa	7	3	0	57	47	4.23	1.34	257			20.2	29%	74%	4.82				3.3	7.4	2.3		1.5	1.6	51	$7
Health	A	08	SD *	12	12	0	160	127	6.40	1.53	291			22.9	33%	60%	5.85				3.3	7.1	2.1		1.5	-42.0	39	$3
PT/Exp	D	09	SD *	7	10	0	167	111	4.01	1.20	244	235	203	20.9	27%	70%	4.45	36	17	47	2.7	6.0	2.3	8%	1.0	3.7	50	$12
Consist	C	1st Half		2	6	0	74	52	4.52	1.33	263			19.7	29%	69%	4.66	29	24	47	2.9	6.2	2.1	8%	1.1	-3.1	41	$3
LIMA Plan	C+	2nd Half		5	4	0	93	60	3.60	1.10	228			22.0	25%	71%	4.32	37	16	47	2.4	5.8	2.4	8%	1.0	6.8	53	$9
Rand Var	-2	10	Proj	8	7	0	116	85	4.58	1.37	270			21.6	30%	70%	4.56	36	17	47	2.9	6.6	2.2	9%	1.2	-4.3	53	$7

3-1, 3.69 ERA in 46 IP at SD. Stats bested compadre Latos', but a deeper look shows skills that lack oomph. Cmd is far from awful, true. But xERA shows the result when 2H H% regresses. He's short a plus pitch right now.

Lee,Cliff

		Yr	Tm	W	L	Sv	IP	K	ERA	WHIP	OBA	vL	vR	BF/G	H%	S%	xERA	G	L	F	Ctl	Dom	Cmd	hr/f	hr/9	RAR	BPV	R$
LH	Starter	05	CLE	18	5	0	202	143	3.79	1.22	254	293	237	26.1	29%	72%	4.22	35	21	44	2.3	6.4	2.8	8%	1.0	14.6	66	$23
Age	31	06	CLE	14	11	0	200	129	4.41	1.41	284	261	282	26.3	31%	73%	4.90	33	19	48	2.6	5.8	2.2	9%	1.3	3.8	45	$15
Type		07	CLE *	7	11	0	143	109	5.73	1.59	283	327	267	22.3	32%	65%	5.20	35	15	50	4.3	6.8	1.6	8%	1.1	-21.6	19	$3
Health	B	08	CLE	22	3	0	223	170	2.54	1.11	254	272	245	29.0	31%	78%	3.43	46	19	35	1.4	6.9	5.0	5%	0.5	49.8	110	$34
PT/Exp	A	09	2TM	14	13	0	232	181	3.22	1.24	273	241	283	28.4	33%	76%	3.70	41	22	36	1.7	7.0	4.2	7%	0.7	31.1	101	$24
Consist	C	1st Half		4	7	0	114	82	3.39	1.38	288			28.8	34%	77%	3.92	44	23	33	2.1	6.5	3.0	6%	0.6	12.9	81	$8
LIMA Plan	C	2nd Half		10	6	0	118	99	3.06	1.11	257			27.9	31%	75%	3.50	39	22	40	1.2	7.6	6.2	7%	0.7	18.2	120	$16
Rand Var	-1	10	Proj	16	10	0	222	170	3.49	1.23	264			27.1	31%	74%	3.85	41	20	39	1.9	6.9	3.5	8%	0.9	13.4	90	$24

Key is that shiny new elite Cmd, and improved FB%. Impressive. But Dom isn't strong enough to offset even '06 Ctl, so this level isn't set in stone. Add in xERA's warning of some ERA pad, and it's clear there's risk in a full bid.

ROD TRUESDELL

Lehr,Justin

Lehr,Justin		Yr	Tm	W	L	Sv	IP	K	ERA	WHIP	OBA	vL	vR	BF/G	H%	S%	xERA	G	L	F	Ctl	Dom	Cmd	hr/f	hr/9	RAR	BPV	R$
RH Starter		05	MIL *	8	8	1	122	78	4.35	1.62	301	211	270	11.1	34%	75%	4.50	49	19	32	3.7	5.7	1.5	9%	0.9	-1.6	30	$4
Age	32	06	aaa	4	7	0	112	73	5.74	1.73	332			27.4	36%	71%	7.27				2.9	5.9	2.0		1.7	-16.8	15	($1)
Type	Con	07	aaa	7	1	1	119	39	6.69	2.29	386			23.0	40%	70%	9.06				4.6	2.9	0.6		0.9	-32.7	-18	($12)
Health	A	08	aaa	6	2	1	64	34	2.66	1.15	256			16.3	28%	81%	3.66				1.6	4.8	3.0		0.9	13.0	68	$9
PT/Exp	D	09	CIN *	18	6	0	182	83	4.84	1.39	277	234	324	25.4	28%	68%	4.93	40	20	40	2.8	4.1	1.5	10%	1.3	-14.5	17	$11
Consist	F	1st Half		11	3	0	94	39	4.73	1.39	284			23.8	29%	68%	4.96				2.4	3.7	1.5		1.1	-6.3	20	$6
LIMA Plan	C	2nd Half		7	3	0	88	44	4.95	1.40	270			27.2	28%	68%	4.90	40	20	40	3.2	4.5	1.4	12%	1.4	-8.2	13	$4
Rand Var	0	10	Proj	3	2	0	44	21	4.55	1.49	294			21.3	31%	72%	4.95	41	20	39	2.9	4.3	1.5	8%	1.0	-3.7	19	$2

5-3, 5.37 ERA in 65 IP at CIN. If you are an extreme, pitch-to-contact hurler, you must have extreme control, extreme GB tendency, and extremely good defense behind you. Failing that, you could be extremely bad.

Lester,Jon

Lester,Jon		Yr	Tm	W	L	Sv	IP	K	ERA	WHIP	OBA	vL	vR	BF/G	H%	S%	xERA	G	L	F	Ctl	Dom	Cmd	hr/f	hr/9	RAR	BPV	R$
LH Starter		05	aa	1	6	0	148	139	3.40	1.30	244			24.1	31%	75%	3.64				3.5	8.4	2.4		0.7	16.5	87	$11
Age	26	06	BOS *	10	6	0	127	100	4.39	1.64	283	397	271	22.3	33%	75%	4.83	41	22	38	4.8	7.1	1.5	8%	0.9	2.7	16	$8
Type	Pwr	07	BOS *	9	5	0	140	97	4.69	1.52	270	231	267	23.1	31%	70%	5.20	34	19	47	4.3	6.2	1.4	7%	0.9	-3.1	8	$7
Health	C	08	BOS	16	6	0	210	152	3.21	1.27	254	217	273	26.7	30%	76%	3.81	47	21	32	2.8	6.5	2.3	7%	0.6	29.5	66	$23
PT/Exp	A	09	BOS	15	8	0	203	225	3.41	1.23	245	257	237	26.4	32%	75%	3.11	48	18	34	2.8	10.0	3.5	11%	0.9	26.2	129	$27
Consist	C	1st Half		7	6	0	99	114	4.36	1.31	264			26.2	34%	70%	3.10	48	17	35	2.7	10.4	3.8	14%	1.2	1.1	138	$10
LIMA Plan	C+	2nd Half		8	2	0	104	111	2.50	1.15	226			26.5	30%	81%	3.12	48	18	34	2.9	9.6	3.3	8%	0.6	25.0	119	$17
Rand Var	0	10	Proj	16	6	0	210	210	3.30	1.20	242			24.8	31%	76%	3.31	46	19	35	2.7	9.0	3.3	10%	0.9	29.3	112	$28

Avoided '07 to '08 workload spike concerns while cranking Dom up to superb levels. PQS splits were great too: 69% / 13% including stretch of 8 consecutive DOM starts in Aug & Sept. Behold the newest elite starter.

Lewis,Jensen

Lewis,Jensen		Yr	Tm	W	L	Sv	IP	K	ERA	WHIP	OBA	vL	vR	BF/G	H%	S%	xERA	G	L	F	Ctl	Dom	Cmd	hr/f	hr/9	RAR	BPV	R$
RH Reliever		05		0	0	0	0	0	0.00	0.00							0.00											
Age	25	06	aa	1	2	0	39	39	4.83	1.51	299			24.7	38%	69%	5.32				2.8	9.0	3.3		0.9	-1.5	90	$2
Type	Pwr xFB	07	CLE *	4	1	2	81	89	2.10	1.11	216			5.5	30%	83%	3.55	32	19	48	3.0	9.9	3.3	4%	0.4	24.1	107	$14
Health	A	08	CLE *	1	6	14	86	70	4.19	1.44	264	267	264	6.1	31%	74%	4.42	35	25	40	3.9	7.3	1.9	10%	1.0	1.7	41	$8
PT/Exp	D	09	CLE	2	4	1	66	62	4.62	1.37	249	299	205	6.1	28%	73%	4.33	37	16	48	3.9	8.4	2.1	15%	1.8	-1.3	60	$4
Consist	A	1st Half		2	3	1	39	36	5.06	1.43	266			6.1	29%	72%	4.27	42	12	46	3.7	8.3	2.3	17%	2.1	-3.0	69	$3
LIMA Plan	B	2nd Half		0	1	0	27	26	3.97	1.29	223			6.0	26%	74%	4.40	29	21	50	4.3	8.6	2.0	11%	1.3	1.6	46	$2
Rand Var	+2	10	Proj	1	2	0	44	41	4.14	1.36	251			6.4	30%	74%	4.20	35	20	45	3.7	8.5	2.3	11%	1.2	1.3	65	$3

Troubles with FB%, exacerbated by inflated hr/f, saw balls going yard with wanton abandon in 1H. That, and marginal Ctl are only things holding him back from excelling. Under radar again; could reward token bid.

Lewis,Scott

Lewis,Scott		Yr	Tm	W	L	Sv	IP	K	ERA	WHIP	OBA	vL	vR	BF/G	H%	S%	xERA	G	L	F	Ctl	Dom	Cmd	hr/f	hr/9	RAR	BPV	R$
LH Reliever		05		0	0	0	0	0	0.00	0.00							0.00											
Age	26	06		0	0	0	0	0	0.00	0.00							0.00											
Type	xFB	07	aa	7	9	0	134	105	4.73	1.49	301			21.9	35%	69%	5.36				2.5	7.0	2.8		0.9	-4.4	69	$7
Health	F	08	CLE *	12	4	0	121	84	3.18	1.17	262	130	254	23.6	30%	75%	4.26	36	12	51	1.5	6.3	4.1	5%	0.7	17.4	86	$16
PT/Exp	D	09	CLE *	0	1	0	14	11	5.66	1.47	284	500	353	15.7	31%	67%	5.12	19	25	56	3.1	6.9	2.2	12%	1.9	-2.1	36	$0
Consist	B	1st Half		0	0	0	11	7	4.10	1.42	267			16.3	28%	78%	5.44	19	25	56	3.5	5.9	1.7	10%	1.6	0.5	6	$0
LIMA Plan	C+	2nd Half		0	1	0	3	4	11.55	1.65	342			13.7	41%	28%	8.42				1.7	10.9	6.6		3.0	-2.6	101	($0)
Rand Var	+1	10	Proj	10	6	0	119	86	4.03	1.27	271			22.5	31%	72%	4.43	36	12	51	2.0	6.5	3.3	8%	1.1	0.1	79	$12

0-0, 8.31 ERA in 4 IP at CLE Strained forearm in April; on DL until August, then in minors. Lost season shouldn't distract from fine '07-'08 BPIs. Long balls always a concern for FB pitcher, but otherwise solid skills.

Lidge,Brad

Lidge,Brad		Yr	Tm	W	L	Sv	IP	K	ERA	WHIP	OBA	vL	vR	BF/G	H%	S%	xERA	G	L	F	Ctl	Dom	Cmd	hr/f	hr/9	RAR	BPV	R$
RH Reliever		05	HOU	4	4	42	70	103	2.31	1.15	227	244	202	4.1	36%	83%	2.25	47	23	30	2.9	13.2	4.5	11%	0.6	16.8	183	$25
Age	33	06	HOU	1	5	32	75	104	5.28	1.40	246	286	201	4.2	35%	64%	2.99	44	23	33	4.3	12.5	2.9	17%	1.2	-7.3	130	$15
Type	Pwr	07	HOU	5	3	19	67	88	3.36	1.25	222	184	243	4.2	31%	79%	3.18	42	15	43	4.3	11.8	2.9	13%	1.2	8.8	124	$15
Health	B	08	PHI	2	0	41	69	92	1.95	1.23	204	273	105	4.0	32%	84%	2.89	46	22	32	4.5	11.9	2.6	4%	0.3	19.9	117	$24
PT/Exp	B	09	PHI	0	8	31	59	61	7.21	1.81	303	319	285	4.1	37%	62%	4.55	39	19	42	5.2	9.4	1.8	15%	1.7	-21.8	45	$6
Consist	B	1st Half		0	3	14	27	28	7.64	1.96	320			4.4	37%	65%	4.92	38	16	45	5.6	9.3	1.6	18%	2.3	-11.5	31	$2
LIMA Plan	B	2nd Half		0	5	17	32	33	6.84	1.68	288			3.9	36%	59%	4.22	40	21	39	4.8	9.4	1.9	11%	1.1	-10.3	57	$4
Rand Var	+5	10	Proj	3	3	28	58	65	4.19	1.43	245			4.0	32%	73%	3.75	42	19	39	4.7	10.1	2.2	10%	0.9	3.6	76	$13

Early season knee injury may explain part of this debacle. High H%, low S% explains another part. Signs of life in post-season beg for some rebound, but BPIs - especially Ctl - are a huge red warning flag.

Lilly,Ted

Lilly,Ted		Yr	Tm	W	L	Sv	IP	K	ERA	WHIP	OBA	vL	vR	BF/G	H%	S%	xERA	G	L	F	Ctl	Dom	Cmd	hr/f	hr/9	RAR	BPV	R$
LH Starter		05	TOR	10	11	0	126	96	5.57	1.53	275	336	248	22.4	30%	68%	4.72	37	22	41	4.1	6.9	1.7	14%	1.6	-18.6	26	$5
Age	34	06	TOR	15	13	0	181	160	4.32	1.43	259	202	265	24.7	30%	75%	4.40	38	19	43	4.0	7.9	2.0	12%	1.4	5.3	50	$17
Type	xFB	07	CHC	15	8	0	207	174	3.83	1.14	237	258	230	24.7	27%	71%	4.07	34	17	49	2.4	7.6	3.2	10%	1.2	15.3	83	$24
Health	B	08	CHC	17	9	0	205	184	4.09	1.23	245	307	219	25.0	28%	72%	3.95	34	22	44	2.8	8.1	2.9	12%	1.4	4.6	81	$21
PT/Exp	A	09	CHC	12	9	0	177	151	3.10	1.06	232	219	233	26.1	27%	76%	3.84	32	17	51	1.8	7.7	4.2	9%	1.1	23.8	99	$23
Consist	A	1st Half		7	6	0	104	88	3.37	1.13	244			26.4	28%	77%	4.00	32	17	52	2.0	7.6	3.8	10%	1.4	10.6	93	$12
LIMA Plan	C	2nd Half		5	3	0	73	63	2.72	0.95	214			25.6	26%	75%	3.60	33	19	49	1.6	7.8	4.8	6%	0.7	13.2	107	$11
Rand Var	-1	10	Proj	15	10	0	203	175	3.77	1.19	247			25.3	29%	73%	3.99	33	19	48	2.3	7.8	3.3	10%	1.2	6.9	87	$22

Only a DL stint could slow him down. Outstanding Cmd, but...
- Had assist from 2H H%
- Got away with high FB%
- Displayed career-best Ctl

No question he's good, but xERA doubts he's this good.

Lincecum,Tim

Lincecum,Tim		Yr	Tm	W	L	Sv	IP	K	ERA	WHIP	OBA	vL	vR	BF/G	H%	S%	xERA	G	L	F	Ctl	Dom	Cmd	hr/f	hr/9	RAR	BPV	R$
RH Starter		05		0	0	0	0	0	0.00	0.00							0.00											
Age	25	06		0	0	0	0	0	0.00	0.00							0.00											
Type	Pwr	07	SF *	11	5	0	177	188	3.35	1.20	214	214	238	25.2	29%	73%	3.45	47	15	38	3.9	9.5	2.5	7%	0.6	23.5	92	$22
Health	A	08	SF	18	5	0	227	265	2.62	1.17	221	221	221	27.3	31%	78%	3.06	44	21	35	3.3	10.5	3.2	6%	0.4	46.3	121	$33
PT/Exp	A	09	SF	15	7	0	225	261	2.48	1.05	209	209	203	27.9	30%	77%	2.75	48	19	33	2.7	10.4	3.8	6%	0.4	47.6	140	$34
Consist	A	1st Half		8	2	0	114	132	2.37	1.07	226			28.4	32%	78%	2.73	45	21	34	2.2	10.4	4.7	4%	0.3	25.6	151	$18
LIMA Plan	C	2nd Half		7	5	0	111	129	2.59	1.02	191			27.4	27%	76%	2.76	50	17	33	3.2	10.4	3.2	7%	0.5	22.0	128	$17
Rand Var	-2	10	Proj	17	5	0	224	256	2.82	1.11	212			27.3	30%	75%	2.88	48	19	33	3.1	10.3	3.3	6%	0.4	38.0	127	$32

Small improvements in GB%, Ctl show he's not done growing; PQS split of 81% / 6% shows how rarely he has a bad outing. Has been fortunate with low hr/f, and lots of IP on young arm, but those are only blemishes.

Lindstrom,Matt

Lindstrom,Matt		Yr	Tm	W	L	Sv	IP	K	ERA	WHIP	OBA	vL	vR	BF/G	H%	S%	xERA	G	L	F	Ctl	Dom	Cmd	hr/f	hr/9	RAR	BPV	R$
RH Reliever		05	aa	2	5	0	73	44	6.43	2.26	341			10.8	37%	74%	8.53				7.3	5.4	0.7		1.5	-19.2	-10	($8)
Age	30	06	aa	2	4	11	40	40	6.18	1.89	341			5.5	43%	66%	6.66				3.9	9.0	2.3		0.5	-8.2	74	$3
Type		07	FLA	3	4	0	67	62	3.09	1.30	259	263	255	4.0	34%	75%	3.59	47	16	36	2.8	8.3	3.0	3%	0.3	11.0	99	$7
Health	B	08	FLA	3	3	5	57	43	3.14	1.45	261	324	214	3.8	32%	77%	4.16	46	23	30	4.1	6.8	1.7	2%	0.2	8.0	36	$6
PT/Exp	C	09	FLA	2	1	15	47	39	5.90	1.65	288	278	284	4.0	34%	64%	4.46	45	20	35	4.6	7.4	1.6	10%	1.0	-10.0	33	$4
Consist	A	1st Half		2	1	14	29	26	6.52	1.90	300			4.4	37%	64%	4.44	54	18	27	6.2	8.1	1.3	8%	0.6	-8.3	10	$3
LIMA Plan	B+	2nd Half		0	0	1	18	13	4.92	1.26	269			3.5	29%	65%	4.33	31	21	48	2.0	6.4	3.3	11%	1.5	-1.6	71	$1
Rand Var	+5	10	Proj	3	3	10	73	58	4.10	1.30	258			3.9	30%	71%	3.88	43	21	36	2.9	7.2	2.5	10%	1.0	3.4	74	$8

Strained rotator cuff during WBC, and elbow sprain in June, so that horrific 1H Ctl probably injury related. Small 2H sample says that he still owns the skills. We're gonna go with that. A little.

Linebrink,Scott

Linebrink,Scott		Yr	Tm	W	L	Sv	IP	K	ERA	WHIP	OBA	vL	vR	BF/G	H%	S%	xERA	G	L	F	Ctl	Dom	Cmd	hr/f	hr/9	RAR	BPV	R$
RH Reliever		05	SD	8	1	1	73	70	1.84	1.07	210	195	223	4.0	27%	85%	3.45	39	21	41	2.8	8.6	3.0	5%	0.5	21.7	95	$14
Age	33	06	SD	7	4	2	75	68	3.35	1.22	248	204	294	4.3	30%	75%	3.83	39	19	42	2.6	8.1	3.1	10%	1.1	8.3	93	$10
Type	Pwr	07	2NL	5	6	1	70	50	3.71	1.32	255	215	284	4.2	27%	79%	4.27	42	21	37	3.2	6.4	2.0	15%	1.5	6.2	49	$7
Health	B	08	CHW	2	2	1	46	40	3.69	1.08	239	200	263	3.7	27%	74%	3.55	39	18	43	1.7	7.8	4.4	14%	1.6	3.7	110	$6
PT/Exp	C	09	CHW	3	7	2	56	55	4.66	1.66	307	297	310	4.5	37%	76%	4.24	37	24	39	3.7	8.8	2.4	13%	1.4	-1.4	75	$3
Consist	B	1st Half		2	4	1	29	30	2.17	1.41	262			4.3	33%	92%	3.98	36	21	43	3.7	9.3	2.5	12%	1.2	8.2	81	$4
LIMA Plan	B+	2nd Half		1	3	1	27	25	7.33	1.93	350			4.7	41%	64%	4.50	39	26	35	3.7	8.3	2.3	15%	1.7	-9.6	68	($1)
Rand Var	+4	10	Proj	3	4	0	51	46	4.43	1.36	263			4.2	31%	71%	3.96	39	22	39	3.2	8.2	2.6	12%	1.2	3.0	77	$4

Wild swings in 1H to 2H H% and S% shouldn't obscure real story: sagging Ctl and ongoing gopheritis. Taken together, they mean lots of three-run homers. xERAs show the likely range, with '06 as an upside.

JOSHUA RANDALL

Liriano,Francisco

				W	L	Sv	IP	K	ERA	WHIP	OBA	vL	vR	BF/G	H%	S%	xERA	G	L	F	Ctl	Dom	Cmd	hr/f	hr/9	RAR	BPV	R$
LH	Starter	05	MIN	*13	9	0	190	220	3.41	1.12	226	222	221	23.3	31%	71%	2.72	50	19	31	2.7	10.4	3.9	9%	0.6	22.6	143	$27
Age	26	06	MIN	12	3	1	121	144	2.16	1.00	207	202	206	16.9	29%	82%	2.29	55	21	23	2.4	10.7	4.5	13%	0.7	35.8	162	$26
Type	Pwr	07	MIN	0	0	0	0	0	0.00	0.00							0.00											
Health	F	08	MIN	*16	6	0	194	160	3.85	1.30	256	217	266	24.8	31%	71%	3.98	42	18	40	3.0	7.4	2.5	6%	0.7	11.9	73	$20
PT/Exp	C	09	MIN	5	13	0	137	122	5.79	1.55	276	255	287	21.1	32%	65%	4.48	40	19	41	4.3	8.0	1.9	12%	1.4	-22.6	47	$3
Consist	A	1st Half		4	8	0	89	80	5.65	1.52	272			24.8	32%	65%	4.32	43	18	39	4.2	8.1	1.9	12%	1.2	-13.2	52	$3
LIMA Plan	B+	2nd Half		1	5	0	48	42	6.06	1.60	283			16.5	32%	66%	4.76	35	19	45	4.4	8.0	1.8	14%	1.7	-9.4	39	($0)
Rand Var	+3	10	Proj	12	10	0	180	160	3.96	1.31	253			23.0	30%	73%	3.92	42	19	39	3.3	8.0	2.5	10%	1.1	11.5	76	$18

Continued skill erosion says stay away, but there are hints of hope. He's electric at home...

	Ctl	Dom	Cmd
Home	1.8	8.2	4.6
Away	6.2	7.9	1.3

Good pre-'09 Ctl too, so buy low.

Litsch,Jesse

				W	L	Sv	IP	K	ERA	WHIP	OBA	vL	vR	BF/G	H%	S%	xERA	G	L	F	Ctl	Dom	Cmd	hr/f	hr/9	RAR	BPV	R$
RH	Starter	05		0	0	0	0	0	0.00	0.00							0.00											
Age	25	06	aa	3	4	0	69	47	7.29	1.74	352			26.8	40%	57%	7.03				1.8	6.1	3.4		1.0	-23.6	61	($3)
Type	Con FB	07	TOR	*15	11	0	187	98	3.42	1.29	264	308	229	24.6	28%	77%	4.36	48	18	34	2.5	4.7	1.8	9%	1.0	25.2	42	$19
Health	F	08	TOR	13	9	0	176	99	3.58	1.23	264	270	250	25.2	28%	75%	3.94	49	20	32	2.0	5.1	2.5	11%	1.0	16.7	64	$18
PT/Exp	C	09	TOR	0	1	0	9	8	9.00	1.67	356	261	471	20.6	37%	55%	4.34	34	16	50	1.0	8.0	8.0	25%	4.0	-5.0	129	($1)
Consist	A	1st Half		0	1	0	9	8	9.00	1.67	356			20.6	37%	55%	4.34	34	16	50	1.0	8.0	8.0	25%	4.0	-5.0	129	($1)
LIMA Plan	C	2nd Half		0	0	0	0	0	0.00	0.00							0.00											
Rand Var	+5	10	Proj	2	2	0	28	17	4.50	1.43	301			24.4	33%	70%	4.46	42	17	40	1.9	5.5	2.8	8%	1.0	-0.1	67	$2

Elbow problems plagued him early, then he had Tommy John surgery in May. Prior to that, low Dom, high GB profile suggested low risk more than high upside type. Given major surgery, keep him off your radar until 2H.

Lohse,Kyle

				W	L	Sv	IP	K	ERA	WHIP	OBA	vL	vR	BF/G	H%	S%	xERA	G	L	F	Ctl	Dom	Cmd	hr/f	hr/9	RAR	BPV	R$
RH	Starter	05	MIN	9	13	0	178	86	4.19	1.43	296	291	305	25.0	31%	74%	4.50	44	22	34	2.2	4.3	2.0	10%	1.1	3.9	40	$9
Age	31	06	2TM	*7	11	0	150	106	5.30	1.48	287	288	304	17.4	33%	65%	4.44	43	20	37	3.1	6.4	2.1	9%	1.0	-14.4	52	$5
Type	Con	07	2NL	9	12	0	193	122	4.62	1.37	276	276	282	24.3	31%	68%	4.61	37	22	41	2.7	5.7	2.1	8%	1.0	-4.7	46	$10
Health	C	08	STL	15	6	0	200	119	3.78	1.30	272	254	285	25.6	30%	73%	4.05	46	22	32	2.2	5.4	2.4	9%	0.8	12.1	61	$17
PT/Exp	A	09	STL	6	10	0	118	77	4.74	1.37	274	251	285	21.9	30%	68%	4.22	45	19	36	2.8	5.9	2.1	12%	1.2	-8.0	54	$5
Consist	A	1st Half		4	4	0	56	39	4.01	1.23	251			23.3	28%	70%	3.79	46	23	32	2.6	6.3	2.4	11%	1.0	1.2	67	$5
LIMA Plan	C+	2nd Half		2	6	0	62	38	5.41	1.49	293			20.9	31%	67%	4.61	44	17	40	2.9	5.6	1.9	12%	1.5	-9.2	43	$0
Rand Var	+1	10	Proj	11	11	0	174	109	4.50	1.37	277			22.6	30%	70%	4.29	44	20	36	2.6	5.6	2.2	10%	1.1	-0.6	53	$10

Bitten by forearm, groin injuries. His ability to post 4.00-ish ERA depends on near 2.5 Cmd; see '08 and 1H '09. Given history of marginal Cmd, that's not a level we can count on. If you bid, you better be in a deep league.

Looper,Braden

				W	L	Sv	IP	K	ERA	WHIP	OBA	vL	vR	BF/G	H%	S%	xERA	G	L	F	Ctl	Dom	Cmd	hr/f	hr/9	RAR	BPV	R$
RH	Starter	05	NYM	4	7	28	59	27	3.96	1.47	281	336	210	4.3	29%	76%	4.47	51	21	27	3.4	4.1	1.2	12%	1.1	2.1	13	$12
Age	35	06	STL	9	3	0	73	41	3.57	1.31	269	287	272	4.5	31%	72%	4.15	49	20	30	2.5	5.0	2.1	4%	0.4	8.3	52	$9
Type	Con	07	STL	12	12	0	175	87	4.94	1.34	271	279	261	24.0	28%	65%	4.66	42	21	36	2.6	4.5	1.7	10%	1.1	-11.0	30	$10
Health	A	08	STL	12	14	0	199	108	4.16	1.31	278	279	279	25.5	30%	72%	4.10	48	20	32	2.0	4.9	2.4	12%	1.1	2.7	59	$13
PT/Exp	A	09	MIL	14	7	0	195	100	5.22	1.49	292	302	278	25.3	29%	71%	4.71	46	17	36	3.0	4.6	1.6	16%	1.8	-24.8	28	$5
Consist	B	1st Half		6	4	0	90	54	4.90	1.40	281			24.3	29%	71%	4.33	46	19	35	2.7	5.4	2.0	16%	1.7	-7.9	48	$4
LIMA Plan	C	2nd Half		8	3	0	105	46	5.50	1.57	301			26.1	30%	70%	5.04	47	16	37	3.2	4.0	1.2	16%	1.9	-16.9	10	$1
Rand Var	+2	10	Proj	13	10	0	189	99	4.73	1.43	284			17.1	30%	70%	4.53	47	19	35	2.8	4.7	1.7	11%	1.2	-6.2	35	$8

As a low Dom, GB type, he's at the mercy of his defense more often than not. 2H implosion was self-induced, as confirmed by xERA. Without the inability to crack a 5.0+ Dom, these kind of stretches will become the norm.

Loux,Shane

				W	L	Sv	IP	K	ERA	WHIP	OBA	vL	vR	BF/G	H%	S%	xERA	G	L	F	Ctl	Dom	Cmd	hr/f	hr/9	RAR	BPV	R$
RH	Reliever	05		0	0	0	0	0	0.00	0.00							0.00											
Age	30	06	aaa	2	5	2	54	19	8.58	1.97	372			8.5	40%	53%	7.37				2.6	3.2	1.2		0.4	-27.1	14	($6)
Type	Con	07		0	0	0	0	0	0.00	0.00							0.00											
Health	C	08	LAA	*12	6	0	154	54	5.98	1.97	365			26.0	38%	71%	7.83				3.2	3.2	1.0		1.1	-31.0	-12	($6)
PT/Exp	D	09	LAA	*3	5	0	83	31	5.40	1.73	319	385	291	14.9	34%	69%	5.43	47	21	33	3.7	3.3	0.9	7%	0.8	-9.8	-14	($2)
Consist	F	1st Half		2	5	0	48	16	6.55	2.07	359			21.8	38%	67%	6.15	45	21	34	4.4	3.0	0.7	5%	0.6	-12.4	-40	($4)
LIMA Plan	F	2nd Half		1	0	0	35	15	3.84	1.27	255			9.8	26%	72%	4.48	49	21	30	2.7	3.8	1.4	10%	0.9	2.7	21	$2
Rand Var	0	10	Proj	2	2	0	44	15	5.38	1.70	325			14.4	33%	70%	5.27	47	21	32	3.1	3.1	1.0	9%	1.0	-4.5	-3	($1)

2-3, 5.86 ERA in 58 IP at LAA. This is no joke. I am absolutely convinced that, if you put me up on a mound, I could strike out one batter every three innings. I have refined an off-speed pitch. Granted, they're all off speed.

Lowe,Derek

				W	L	Sv	IP	K	ERA	WHIP	OBA	vL	vR	BF/G	H%	S%	xERA	G	L	F	Ctl	Dom	Cmd	hr/f	hr/9	RAR	BPV	R$
RH	Starter	05	LA	12	15	0	222	146	3.61	1.25	263	296	219	26.5	29%	76%	3.12	64	15	21	2.2	5.9	2.7	19%	1.1	17.5	88	$18
Age	36	06	LA	16	8	0	218	123	3.63	1.27	264	270	255	26.1	30%	72%	3.18	67	16	17	2.3	5.1	2.2	11%	0.6	23.0	75	$20
Type	Con xGB	07	LA	12	14	0	199	147	3.88	1.27	257	271	239	25.3	30%	72%	3.03	65	16	19	2.7	6.6	2.5	17%	0.9	13.3	91	$18
Health	A	08	LA	14	11	0	211	147	3.24	1.13	246	251	240	25.2	29%	72%	3.07	60	17	23	1.9	6.3	3.3	10%	0.6	26.8	99	$23
PT/Exp	A	09	ATL	15	10	0	195	111	4.67	1.52	297	300	303	25.4	33%	70%	4.02	56	18	26	2.9	5.1	1.8	9%	0.7	-11.5	48	$8
Consist	A	1st Half		7	6	0	101	55	4.45	1.40	273			25.7	31%	67%	4.17	55	16	29	3.1	4.9	1.6	5%	0.4	-3.3	37	$5
LIMA Plan	C+	2nd Half		8	4	0	94	56	4.90	1.63	321			25.1	35%	72%	3.84	58	20	22	2.7	5.4	2.0	15%	1.1	-8.2	60	$2
Rand Var	+2	10	Proj	13	10	0	183	111	3.89	1.33	268			25.1	30%	72%	3.57	60	17	23	2.7	5.5	2.1	10%	0.7	15.7	64	$14

Even pitching in LA wouldn't have kept sub-4 ERA with this skill erosion. Partial 2H rebound was obscured by elevated H%. GB profile remains strong, so it's all about the Cmd. 2nd half and history provide some hope.

Lowe,Mark

				W	L	Sv	IP	K	ERA	WHIP	OBA	vL	vR	BF/G	H%	S%	xERA	G	L	F	Ctl	Dom	Cmd	hr/f	hr/9	RAR	BPV	R$
RH	Reliever	05		0	0	0	0	0	0.00	0.00							0.00											
Age	26	06	SEA	*1	1	3	32	28	1.98	1.13	225	167	205	5.4	29%	83%	3.43	49	19	33	2.8	7.8	2.8	3%	0.3	10.2	91	$6
Type	Pwr	07	SEA	0	0	0	3	3	6.67	1.85	208			3.2	18%	75%	7.35				10.0	10.0	1.0	50%	3.3	-0.7	-6	($0)
Health	C	08	SEA	1	5	1	64	55	5.37	1.76	303	354	250	5.2	37%	70%	4.53	45	21	35	4.8	7.8	1.6	9%	0.8	-8.0	33	($0)
PT/Exp	D	09	SEA	2	7	3	80	69	3.26	1.25	239	253	213	4.4	29%	76%	4.00	39	21	40	3.3	7.8	2.4	8%	0.8	11.7	68	$9
Consist	D	1st Half		1	4	0	35	27	3.32	1.42	255			4.5	31%	77%	4.41	38	28	34	4.1	6.9	1.7	5%	0.5	4.9	30	$3
LIMA Plan	C+	2nd Half		1	3	3	45	42	3.21	1.12	227			4.4	28%	76%	3.69	40	15	45	2.6	8.4	3.2	9%	1.0	6.8	99	$6
Rand Var	-2	10	Proj	3	3	0	65	58	3.86	1.38	255			4.8	31%	74%	4.03	42	20	38	3.7	8.0	2.1	8%	0.8	3.2	63	$5

Huge ERA and WHIP gains driven by good health and sharp 2H skill growth, along with new out pitch vs. LHers. Given health and consistency issues, the safe bet is to assume regression. But he's still young, so watch him.

Lyon,Brandon

				W	L	Sv	IP	K	ERA	WHIP	OBA	vL	vR	BF/G	H%	S%	xERA	G	L	F	Ctl	Dom	Cmd	hr/f	hr/9	RAR	BPV	R$
RH	Reliever	05	ARI	0	2	14	29	17	6.49	1.86	349	317	364	4.3	37%	69%	4.93	42	23	35	3.1	5.3	1.7	16%	1.9	-8.1	32	$2
Age	30	06	ARI	2	4	0	69	46	3.91	1.30	259	244	270	4.3	29%	72%	4.19	43	24	33	2.9	6.0	2.1	10%	0.9	4.9	51	$5
Type		07	ARI	6	4	2	74	40	2.68	1.24	251	233	267	4.2	29%	78%	4.50	43	19	38	2.7	4.9	1.8	2%	0.2	16.0	36	$10
Health	A	08	ARI	3	5	26	59	44	4.70	1.48	310	278	321	4.3	36%	70%	4.15	40	22	38	2.0	6.7	3.4	9%	1.1	-3.2	85	$11
PT/Exp	C	09	DET	6	5	3	77	56	2.92	1.12	205	207	209	4.9	23%	77%	4.00	46	17	36	3.5	6.5	1.9	9%	0.8	14.5	48	$12
Consist	A	1st Half		3	3	0	38	21	4.03	1.21	207			5.2	21%	71%	4.48	49	19	32	4.3	5.0	1.2	14%	1.2	2.0	2	$4
LIMA Plan	C	2nd Half		3	2	3	39	35	1.85	1.03	203			4.5	26%	84%	3.56	43	15	41	2.8	8.1	2.9	5%	0.5	12.5	92	$8
Rand Var	-5	10	Proj	4	6	3	73	52	3.97	1.31	258			4.6	30%	72%	4.17	43	19	37	3.0	6.5	2.2	8%	0.9	2.4	57	$7

Rebounded well after Apr/May flop ended saves chances. But take a look at that H% and 2H S%, and then at xERA. That's the true level of his performance, not ERA. When those regress, ERA and WHIP are headed up.

MacDougal,Mike

				W	L	Sv	IP	K	ERA	WHIP	OBA	vL	vR	BF/G	H%	S%	xERA	G	L	F	Ctl	Dom	Cmd	hr/f	hr/9	RAR	BPV	R$
RH	Reliever	05	KC	5	6	21	70	72	3.34	1.33	259	240	270	4.4	33%	77%	3.03	57	15	28	3.1	9.2	3.0	11%	0.8	8.9	118	$15
Age	33	06	2AL	1	1	1	29	21	1.55	0.93	204	281	171	3.9	25%	85%	2.48	64	21	15	1.9	6.5	3.5	8%	0.3	10.8	109	$6
Type	Pwr xGB	07	CHW	2	5	0	42	39	6.81	1.96	295	298	288	3.8	37%	64%	4.63	56	18	26	7.0	8.3	1.2	9%	0.6	-12.0	-6	($2)
Health	C	08	aaa	0	4	4	49	55	5.21	1.87	299			6.2	40%	71%	5.84				6.0	10.1	1.7		0.6	-5.5	74	$0
PT/Exp	D	09	2TM	1	1	20	54	34	4.31	1.66	254	286	232	4.4	29%	74%	4.48	62	17	21	6.3	5.6	0.9	8%	0.5	0.0	-28	$7
Consist	C	1st Half		0	0	3	18	10	3.96	1.81	260			4.3	30%	76%	5.30	59	19	22	7.4	4.9	0.7	0%	0.0	0.8	-75	$1
LIMA Plan	D+	2nd Half		1	1	17	36	24	4.49	1.58	250			4.4	28%	72%	4.09	64	16	20	5.7	6.0	1.0	14%	0.7	-0.8	-5	$6
Rand Var	0	10	Proj	1	2	3	45	33	4.77	1.66	261			4.5	31%	71%	4.26	60	18	22	6.0	6.6	1.1	10%	0.6	0.5	-5	$1

Chaconian: Having the ability to post many saves despite sub-Mendoza BPIs. His ERA wasn't that bad, which may draw some end-game speculation, but has anybody heard from Shawn lately?

STEPHEN NICKRAND

Madson,Ryan		Yr	Tm	W	L	Sv	IP	K	ERA	WHIP	OBA	vL	vR	BF/G	H%	S%	xERA	G	L	F	Ctl	Dom	Cmd	hr/f	hr/9	RAR	BPV	R$
RH Reliever		05	PHI	6	5	0	87	79	4.14	1.25	255	292	233	4.7	31%	70%	3.19	48	25	27	2.6	8.2	3.2	16%	1.1	1.2	103	$8
Age	29	06	PHI	11	9	2	134	99	5.70	1.69	318	306	336	12.4	36%	68%	4.61	43	22	35	3.4	6.6	2.0	12%	1.3	-20.1	50	$3
Type	Pwr	07	PHI	2	2	1	56	43	3.05	1.27	233	170	275	6.2	27%	79%	3.96	47	21	32	3.7	6.9	1.9	10%	0.8	9.5	50	$6
Health	B	08	PHI	4	2	1	83	67	3.05	1.23	253	268	243	4.5	31%	77%	3.44	51	19	30	2.5	7.3	2.9	8%	0.7	12.5	93	$9
PT/Exp	C	09	PHI	5	5	10	77	78	3.26	1.23	251	257	245	4.1	32%	76%	3.16	46	22	32	2.6	9.1	3.5	10%	0.8	8.9	118	$12
Consist	A	1st Half		2	3	4	38	40	2.84	1.29	235			4.1	31%	80%	3.42	45	20	35	3.8	9.5	2.5	9%	0.7	6.3	91	$6
LIMA Plan	B+	2nd Half		3	2	6	39	38	3.66	1.17	265			4.0	33%	71%	2.92	47	23	30	1.4	8.7	6.3	12%	0.9	2.5	144	$7
Rand Var	0	10	Proj	3	3	15	58	56	3.10	1.16	245			4.5	31%	76%	3.09	47	21	31	2.2	8.7	4.0	10%	0.8	8.4	123	$12

The makings of an elite closer?
- Spiking strikeout rate
- No control erosion
- Electric 2nd half
- Ground ball profile
- Improving xERA trend

All that he needs is opportunity.

Mahay,Ron		Yr	Tm	W	L	Sv	IP	K	ERA	WHIP	OBA	vL	vR	BF/G	H%	S%	xERA	G	L	F	Ctl	Dom	Cmd	hr/f	hr/9	RAR	BPV	R$
LH Reliever		05	TEX *	1	5	1	59	52	7.02	1.73	308	302	322	7.2	36%	62%	4.08	48	23	29	4.3	7.9	1.9	20%	1.7	-19.3	54	($2)
Age	38	06	TEX	1	3	0	57	56	3.95	1.44	251	240	258	4.0	31%	76%	4.07	41	21	38	4.4	8.8	2.0	12%	1.1	4.3	58	$4
Type	Pwr FB	07	2TM *	3	1	1	77	62	3.45	1.51	252	189	242	5.2	30%	78%	4.44	49	17	34	5.0	7.2	1.4	7%	0.6	9.6	22	$5
Health	B	08	KC	5	0	0	65	49	3.48	1.39	251	255	250	4.9	29%	77%	4.48	40	19	41	4.0	6.8	1.7	8%	0.8	6.9	32	$6
PT/Exp	D	09	2AL	2	1	0	50	41	4.32	1.68	305	265	327	4.1	34%	81%	4.77	40	17	43	4.0	7.4	1.9	15%	1.8	0.8	44	$1
Consist	A	1st Half		1	0	0	24	23	4.46	1.74	312			4.5	37%	79%	4.62	38	17	44	4.1	8.6	2.1	12%	1.5	-0.0	60	$1
LIMA Plan	C+	2nd Half		1	1	0	26	18	4.19	1.63	299			3.8	31%	83%	4.90	42	17	41	3.8	6.3	1.6	17%	2.1	0.8	29	$1
Rand Var	0	10	Proj	1	2	0	44	34	4.55	1.52	273			4.4	31%	73%	4.60	42	18	40	4.1	7.0	1.7	11%	1.2	-0.9	35	$2

Blame H%, hr/f spikes for the inflated ERA but his Dom was a 4-year high. xERA trend shows BPI erosion. Growing concerns vs both LH and RH bats, and rising FB% signal the end may be soon.

Maholm,Paul		Yr	Tm	W	L	Sv	IP	K	ERA	WHIP	OBA	vL	vR	BF/G	H%	S%	xERA	G	L	F	Ctl	Dom	Cmd	hr/f	hr/9	RAR	BPV	R$
LH Starter		05	PIT *	10	4	0	158	107	3.30	1.31	258	87	232	23.9	30%	75%	3.57	55	20	25	3.0	6.1	2.1	7%	0.5	18.5	63	$14
Age	27	06	PIT	8	10	0	176	117	4.76	1.61	289	233	313	26.6	33%	72%	4.36	53	20	27	4.1	6.0	1.4	12%	1.0	-5.8	27	$4
Type	GB	07	PIT	10	15	0	178	105	5.01	1.42	289	238	305	26.6	31%	67%	4.07	53	17	30	2.5	5.3	2.1	12%	1.1	-12.9	60	$7
Health	A	08	PIT	9	9	0	206	139	3.71	1.28	257	183	279	27.9	29%	74%	3.69	54	19	28	2.7	6.1	2.2	12%	0.9	14.3	67	$15
PT/Exp	A	09	PIT	8	9	0	195	119	4.44	1.44	287	182	316	27.4	32%	69%	4.06	52	18	30	2.8	5.5	2.0	7%	0.6	-6.0	54	$7
Consist	A	1st Half		5	4	0	99	63	4.36	1.42	279			26.9	32%	68%	4.13	50	18	32	3.0	5.7	1.9	5%	0.5	-2.1	51	$4
LIMA Plan	C+	2nd Half		3	5	0	96	56	4.52	1.46	295			27.9	33%	70%	3.99	54	18	28	2.5	5.3	2.1	10%	0.8	-3.9	58	$2
Rand Var	0	10	Proj	9	10	0	199	128	4.07	1.37	275			26.7	31%	72%	3.87	53	18	29	2.7	5.8	2.2	10%	0.8	9.6	63	$11

Tweaked knee in first start of season and never found '08 groove. Big step back vs. RHB didn't help either. Given pre-'09 Cmd, xERA trends, there's a rebound coming. Just use a 4.00 ERA as your baseline.

Maine,John		Yr	Tm	W	L	Sv	IP	K	ERA	WHIP	OBA	vL	vR	BF/G	H%	S%	xERA	G	L	F	Ctl	Dom	Cmd	hr/f	hr/9	RAR	BPV	R$
RH Starter		05	BAL *	8	14	0	168	121	5.78	1.50	283	227	275	22.5	32%	63%	4.27	46	21	34	3.5	6.5	1.9	13%	1.2	-29.2	46	$4
Age	28	06	NYM *	9	10	0	146	112	4.14	1.31	250	231	191	23.8	29%	71%	4.57	38	15	47	3.3	6.9	2.1	8%	1.0	6.2	49	$12
Type	Pwr FB	07	NYM	15	10	0	191	180	3.91	1.27	238	237	234	25.0	29%	73%	4.05	37	18	45	3.5	8.5	2.4	10%	1.1	12.1	72	$20
Health	F	08	NYM	10	8	0	140	122	4.18	1.35	236	238	229	23.9	28%	72%	4.20	41	20	39	4.3	7.8	1.8	10%	1.0	1.6	43	$11
PT/Exp	B	09	NYM	7	6	0	81	55	4.43	1.29	226	159	304	22.8	25%	67%	4.75	35	21	44	4.2	6.1	1.4	8%	0.9	-2.4	9	$6
Consist	A	1st Half		5	4	0	61	42	4.56	1.39	228			24.0	25%	69%	5.02	35	21	44	5.0	6.2	1.2	9%	1.0	-2.8	-11	$4
LIMA Plan	C	2nd Half		2	2	0	20	13	4.03	0.99	220			19.7	26%	58%	3.98	35	21	44	1.8	5.8	3.3	4%	0.4	0.4	70	$3
Rand Var	-3	10	Proj	8	9	0	135	98	4.35	1.37	248			23.1	28%	71%	4.63	37	20	43	3.9	6.6	1.7	10%	1.1	-6.1	27	$8

Shoulder woes of '08 got worse in '09, making him even more of a health risk. When healthy, he had a marginal skill profile to begin with. '07 breakout is the clear outlier here. Eroding Cmd, xERA confirm lower ceiling.

Maloney,Matt		Yr	Tm	W	L	Sv	IP	K	ERA	WHIP	OBA	vL	vR	BF/G	H%	S%	xERA	G	L	F	Ctl	Dom	Cmd	hr/f	hr/9	RAR	BPV	R$
LH Starter		05		0	0	0	0	0	0.00	0.00							0.00											
Age	26	06		0	0	0	0	0	0.00	0.00							0.00											
Type	xFB	07	a/a	13	10	0	170	151	4.65	1.31	259			25.7	30%	68%	4.57				2.9	8.0	2.7		1.3	-4.0	71	$15
Health	A	08	aaa	11	5	0	140	115	5.72	1.46	293			24.5	34%	64%	5.60				2.6	7.4	2.9		1.5	-24.4	57	$6
PT/Exp	D	09	CIN *	11	13	0	191	137	4.27	1.37	295	286	280	27.3	33%	73%	4.55	34	13	53	1.7	6.5	3.8	8%	1.2	-1.8	83	$11
Consist	C	1st Half		5	7	0	104	74	3.67	1.27	279			27.3	31%	76%	4.67	26	15	58	1.6	6.4	4.0	7%	1.2	6.6	76	$8
LIMA Plan	A	2nd Half		6	6	0	87	63	4.98	1.49	313			27.3	35%	70%	4.50	40	11	49	1.8	6.6	3.6	9%	1.3	-8.5	87	$3
Rand Var	0	10	Proj	3	2	0	44	33	4.55	1.33	281			26.4	31%	71%	4.43	36	12	52	2.1	6.8	3.3	10%	1.4	-0.9	81	$3

2-4, 4.87 ERA in 40 IP at CIN.
PRO:
- Surging Cmd, strong BPV

CON:
- Dipping Dom, FB% w/CIN

His blowup risk is low w/pinpoint Ctl, but so is upside. Good LIMA.

Marcum,Shaun		Yr	Tm	W	L	Sv	IP	K	ERA	WHIP	OBA	vL	vR	BF/G	H%	S%	xERA	G	L	F	Ctl	Dom	Cmd	hr/f	hr/9	RAR	BPV	R$
RH Reliever		05	a/a	13	5	0	157	115	5.50	1.38	298			25.0	33%	64%	5.57				1.7	6.6	4.0		1.6	-23.2	70	$9
Age	28	06	TOR *	7	4	0	130	117	4.90	1.48	283	303	256	14.7	33%	71%	4.40	36	18	46	3.3	8.1	2.4	12%	1.5	-5.6	70	$8
Type	Pwr FB	07	TOR	12	6	1	159	122	4.13	1.25	249	259	237	17.4	27%	73%	4.15	40	18	42	2.8	6.9	2.5	13%	1.5	7.3	68	$17
Health	F	08	TOR	9	7	0	151	123	3.39	1.16	228	244	200	24.7	26%	77%	3.82	43	17	40	3.0	7.3	2.5	12%	1.2	17.9	73	$18
PT/Exp	B	09	TOR	0	0	0	0	0	0.00	0.00																		
Consist	A	1st Half		0	0	0	0	0	0.00	0.00																		
LIMA Plan	D	2nd Half		0	0	0	0	0	0.00	0.00																		
Rand Var		10	Proj	9	5	0	145	119	4.10	1.32	263			22.0	30%	73%	4.13	40	18	42	2.9	7.4	2.6	11%	1.2	5.5	74	$13

Missed all of '09 after Sept '08 Tommy John surgery. Before that, there were several reasons for optimism: xERA trend, GB% increase, lights out vs. RHers. He's not a legit sub-3.50 ERA guy yet, but w/health, he's close.

Marmol,Carlos		Yr	Tm	W	L	Sv	IP	K	ERA	WHIP	OBA	vL	vR	BF/G	H%	S%	xERA	G	L	F	Ctl	Dom	Cmd	hr/f	hr/9	RAR	BPV	R$
RH Reliever		05	aa	3	4	0	81	62	4.77	1.55	266			25.9	30%	73%	5.38				4.8	6.9	1.4		1.4	-4.7	30	$2
Age	27	06	CHC *	8	9	0	138	117	5.21	1.59	252	229	263	19.5	30%	68%	5.52	29	18	53	5.8	7.6	1.3	7%	1.0	-12.2	-12	$4
Type	Pwr xFB	07	CHC *	9	2	1	110	134	2.87	1.14	200	209	146	6.7	28%	77%	3.58	31	16	52	3.9	10.9	2.8	6%	0.7	21.1	101	$18
Health	A	08	CHC	2	4	7	87	114	2.68	0.93	140	180	98	4.1	18%	77%	3.20	35	10	55	4.2	11.8	2.8	10%	1.0	17.1	110	$16
PT/Exp	C	09	CHC	2	4	15	74	93	3.41	1.46	171	136	200	4.1	26%	75%	4.45	36	16	48	7.9	11.3	1.4	3%	0.2	7.2	4	$10
Consist	B	1st Half		2	1	3	37	41	3.88	1.59	167			4.1	24%	74%	5.29	36	19	45	9.2	9.9	1.1	3%	0.2	1.4	-56	$3
LIMA Plan	D+	2nd Half		0	3	12	37	52	2.93	1.33	175			4.1	29%	77%	3.71	36	12	52	6.6	12.7	1.9	3%	0.2	5.7	64	$7
Rand Var	-5	10	Proj	2	4	20	73	88	3.97	1.41	209			4.9	28%	74%	4.17	34	14	51	6.0	10.9	1.8	9%	1.0	0.9	48	$12

Got back into saves picture late in season, but there's plenty to worry about here. Control is a disaster. xFB tendency was hidden due to tiny hr/f. Exercise extreme caution.
DN: 5.00+ ERA, Marmol who?

Marquis,Jason		Yr	Tm	W	L	Sv	IP	K	ERA	WHIP	OBA	vL	vR	BF/G	H%	S%	xERA	G	L	F	Ctl	Dom	Cmd	hr/f	hr/9	RAR	BPV	R$
RH Starter		05	STL	13	14	0	207	100	4.13	1.33	261	238	280	26.6	27%	73%	4.30	52	17	31	3.0	4.3	1.4	14%	1.3	2.9	28	$13
Age	31	06	STL	14	16	0	194	96	6.03	1.52	288	288	291	26.1	29%	64%	5.23	43	17	40	3.5	4.5	1.3	13%	1.6	-36.9	7	$3
Type	Con GB	07	CHC	12	9	0	192	109	4.60	1.39	260	274	242	24.3	28%	69%	4.51	50	17	33	3.6	5.1	1.4	11%	1.0	-4.1	23	$11
Health	A	08	CHC	11	9	0	167	91	4.53	1.45	268	244	287	25.2	29%	70%	4.64	48	20	33	3.8	4.9	1.3	8%	0.8	-5.3	12	$8
PT/Exp	A	09	COL	15	13	0	216	115	4.04	1.38	264	275	258	28.1	29%	71%	4.13	56	17	27	3.3	4.8	1.4	8%	0.6	3.9	30	$13
Consist	A	1st Half		10	5	0	109	51	3.88	1.31	258			28.8	28%	72%	4.04	58	16	26	3.0	4.2	1.4	9%	0.7	4.2	31	$9
LIMA Plan	D	2nd Half		5	8	0	107	64	4.21	1.45	269			27.5	31%	70%	4.22	53	18	29	3.7	5.4	1.5	6%	0.5	-0.3	28	$4
Rand Var	0	10	Proj	12	11	0	189	102	4.34	1.41	265			26.3	29%	70%	4.39	52	18	31	3.5	4.9	1.4	9%	0.8	-2.9	23	$10

The only reason he has a BPV over zero is because of his GB rate. Watch how BPV tracks GB each year. So his one chief weapon is GB rate. GB rate and consistency. His TWO chief weapons are GB rate, consiste..

Marshall,Sean		Yr	Tm	W	L	Sv	IP	K	ERA	WHIP	OBA	vL	vR	BF/G	H%	S%	xERA	G	L	F	Ctl	Dom	Cmd	hr/f	hr/9	RAR	BPV	R$
LH Reliever		05	aa	0	1	0	25	20	4.55	1.14	239			25.4	28%	60%	3.23				2.3	7.2	3.2		0.8	-0.7	94	$2
Age	27	06	CHC *	6	11	0	146	95	5.48	1.55	271	256	273	23.4	29%	67%	4.89	47	17	36	4.6	5.8	1.3	12%	1.3	-17.9	7	$2
Type	Pwr	07	CHC *	9	8	0	128	79	3.65	1.36	264	203	280	21.8	29%	77%	4.38	48	16	36	3.1	5.6	1.8	11%	1.2	12.3	43	$7
Health	A	08	CHC *	4	6	1	97	76	4.01	1.28	255	269	236	9.9	30%	72%	4.09	41	17	42	2.8	7.1	2.6	9%	1.1	3.2	72	$7
PT/Exp	D	09	CHC	3	7	0	85	68	4.33	1.44	274	243	289	6.8	32%	73%	3.77	49	23	28	3.4	7.2	2.1	14%	1.1	-1.4	65	$3
Consist	A	1st Half		3	6	0	55	37	4.41	1.32	258			10.2	28%	71%	4.02	48	20	32	3.1	6.0	1.9	15%	1.3	-1.5	51	$3
LIMA Plan	B+	2nd Half		0	1	0	30	31	4.17	1.66	303			4.3	39%	75%	3.27	51	29	20	3.9	9.2	2.4	11%	0.6	0.1	90	$0
Rand Var	+2	10	Proj	5	4	0	91	73	3.88	1.36	263			7.7	31%	74%	3.77	47	22	31	3.2	7.3	2.3	11%	0.9	5.5	70	$7

Four years of steady xERA growth and occasional flashes of something greater (see 2H) make him very intriguing. Cmd isn't quite where it needs to be, and role is uncertain, but he's worth a speculative investment.

STEPHEN NICKRAND

Martinez,Pedro		Yr	W	L	Sv	IP	K	ERA	WHIP	OBA	vL	vR	BF/G	H%	S%	xERA	G	L	F	Ctl	Dom	Cmd	hr/f	hr/9	RAR	BPV	R$
RH Starter		05 NYM	15	8	0	217	208	2.82	0.95	206	215	192	27.1	26%	74%	3.30	38	17	45	1.9	8.6	**4.4**	8%	0.8	38.2	119	$33
Age	38	06 NYM	9	8	0	132	137	4.49	1.11	225	231	211	23.2	27%	63%	3.53	36	19	44	2.7	9.3	**3.5**	12%	1.3	-0.1	110	$15
Type	FB	07 NYM	3	1	0	28	32	2.57	1.43	295	319	261	24.4	41%	80%	3.59	31	24	44	2.3	10.3	**4.6**	0%	0.0	6.4	134	$4
Health	F	08 NYM	5	6	0	109	87	5.61	1.57	292	304	282	24.5	33%	68%	4.34	41	24	35	3.6	7.2	**2.0**	16%	1.6	-18.1	50	$1
PT/Exp	C	09 PHI	5	1	0	45	37	3.62	1.25	276	276	268	20.7	32%	78%	3.92	29	27	44	1.6	7.4	**4.6**	12%	1.4	3.1	98	$5
Consist	B	1st Half	0	0	0	0	0	0.00	0.00							0.00											
LIMA Plan	B+	2nd Half	5	1	0	45	37	3.62	1.25	276			20.7	32%	78%	3.92	29	27	44	1.6	7.5	**4.6**	12%	1.4	3.1	98	$5
Rand Var	0	10 Proj	**9**	**5**	**0**	**116**	**97**	**3.88**	**1.23**	**260**			**22.9**	**30%**	**73%**	**3.90**	**35**	**23**	**42**	**2.2**	**7.5**	**3.5**	**11%**	**1.2**	**5.2**	**90**	**$12**

Surprising return, flashing Cmd of old. But not all is so rosy:
- Ctl will be tough to repeat
- LD and FB rates mounting
- This was just two months
- Not getting younger or healthier

DN: DL and/or another 5+ ERA

Martin,J.D.		Yr	W	L	Sv	IP	K	ERA	WHIP	OBA	vL	vR	BF/G	H%	S%	xERA	G	L	F	Ctl	Dom	Cmd	hr/f	hr/9	RAR	BPV	R$
RH Starter		05 aa	3	1	0	56	55	2.88	0.98	229			21.9	30%	71%	2.39				1.3	8.8	**6.9**		0.5	9.9	192	$9
Age	27	06	0	0	0	0	0	0.00	0.00							0.00											
Type	Con xFB	07 aa	2	3	0	42	20	5.40	1.60	299			21.1	32%	67%	5.62				3.6	4.3	**1.2**		0.9	-4.9	19	$0
Health	A	08 a/a	12	3	0	89	67	3.29	1.37	282			10.9	33%	79%	4.58				2.3	6.7	**2.9**		0.8	11.2	74	$11
PT/Exp	D	09 WAS *	13	7	0	165	89	3.93	1.27	273	307	252	22.3	29%	72%	4.62	37	17	46	1.9	4.9	**2.6**	7%	1.0	5.3	52	$14
Consist	B	1st Half	8	2	0	84	51	2.76	1.08	256			22.4	29%	75%	3.07				1.0	5.5	**5.5**		0.4	14.8	140	$12
LIMA Plan	C+	2nd Half	5	5	0	81	38	5.14	1.46	290			22.2	29%	69%	5.22	37	17	46	2.8	4.2	**1.5**	11%	1.6	-9.5	15	$2
Rand Var	-2	10 Proj	**8**	**4**	**0**	**102**	**63**	**4.17**	**1.34**	**278**			**17.3**	**30%**	**74%**	**4.63**	**37**	**17**	**46**	**2.3**	**5.6**	**2.4**	**10%**	**1.3**	**-4.6**	**53**	**$8**

5-4, 4.44 ERA in 77 IP at WAS. Skill history looks like it belongs to four different pitchers. That inconsistency, along with 5.51 xERA in majors, says avoid him. But MLEs, particularly Cmd, say you can't write him off just yet.

Martis,Shairon		Yr	W	L	Sv	IP	K	ERA	WHIP	OBA	vL	vR	BF/G	H%	S%	xERA	G	L	F	Ctl	Dom	Cmd	hr/f	hr/9	RAR	BPV	R$
RH Starter		05	0	0	0	0	0	0.00	0.00							0.00											
Age	23	06	0	0	0	0	0	0.00	0.00							0.00											
Type	Con FB	07	0	0	0	0	0	0.00	0.00							0.00											
Health	A	08 a/a	5	6	0	116	87	3.62	1.35	262			23.6	31%	73%	3.81				3.1	6.8	**2.2**		0.4	9.9	76	$9
PT/Exp	D	09 WAS *	9	7	0	160	71	5.55	1.50	289	315	182	25.2	30%	64%	5.30	40	15	44	3.2	4.0	**1.3**	8%	1.2	-26.8	5	$1
Consist	C	1st Half	5	3	0	85	34	5.28	1.43	257			24.7	26%	65%	5.55	40	15	44	4.1	3.6	**0.9**	9%	1.2	-11.5	-28	$2
LIMA Plan	C+	2nd Half	4	4	0	75	37	5.86	1.57	322			25.8	34%	64%	6.09				2.1	4.4	**2.1**		1.1	-15.4	28	($1)
Rand Var	0	10 Proj	**3**	**3**	**0**	**58**	**33**	**4.81**	**1.45**	**284**			**25.3**	**30%**	**70%**	**4.90**	**40**	**15**	**44**	**2.9**	**5.1**	**1.7**	**9%**	**1.2**	**-4.6**	**31**	**$2**

5-3, 5.25 ERA in 86 IP at WAS. 0.9 Cmd, -27 BPV, and 6.04 xERA in MLB. Dom didn't come back in return to AAA either. Ctl skill could make him passable, but that's not really a ringing endorsement, is it?

Masset,Nick		Yr	W	L	Sv	IP	K	ERA	WHIP	OBA	vL	vR	BF/G	H%	S%	xERA	G	L	F	Ctl	Dom	Cmd	hr/f	hr/9	RAR	BPV	R$
RH Reliever		05 aa	7	12	0	157	88	8.27	1.94	352			26.3	38%	57%	7.83				3.7	5.1	**1.4**		1.5	-76.8	-0	($14)
Age	27	06 a/a	6	7	3	115	88	5.32	1.75	314			16.8	38%	68%	5.79				4.1	6.9	**1.7**		0.5	-11.4	54	$2
Type	Pwr GB	07 CHW *	2	7	0	84	50	6.75	1.79	325			10.5	35%	63%	5.32	43	17	40	3.8	5.3	**1.4**	9%	1.2	-23.4	12	($4)
Health	A	08 2TM	2	0	1	62	43	3.92	1.56	289	262	316	6.6	33%	78%	4.14	53	20	28	3.8	6.2	**1.7**	12%	1.0	3.0	41	$3
PT/Exp	D	09 CIN	5	1	0	76	70	2.37	1.03	201	219	194	4.1	25%	81%	3.07	54	14	32	2.8	8.3	**2.9**	9%	0.7	17.1	105	$12
Consist	C	1st Half	4	0	0	30	26	1.79	0.89	150			4.6	19%	81%	3.06	58	13	29	3.6	7.7	**2.2**	5%	0.3	8.9	79	$7
LIMA Plan	B	2nd Half	1	1	0	46	44	2.75	1.11	232			3.8	29%	80%	3.08	52	14	34	2.4	8.6	**3.7**	12%	1.0	8.1	122	$5
Rand Var	-5	10 Proj	**4**	**2**	**2**	**73**	**62**	**3.60**	**1.30**	**252**			**5.7**	**30%**	**75%**	**3.52**	**52**	**17**	**31**	**3.1**	**7.7**	**2.5**	**11%**	**0.9**	**6.7**	**85**	**$7**

Reportedly found success by adding a cutter to his repertoire, and 2H Cmd suggests he really found a comfort zone. Can't ignore previous four seasons, but growth trends in xERA, Dom make it feel like he earned this.

Masterson,Justin		Yr	W	L	Sv	IP	K	ERA	WHIP	OBA	vL	vR	BF/G	H%	S%	xERA	G	L	F	Ctl	Dom	Cmd	hr/f	hr/9	RAR	BPV	R$
RH Reliever		05	0	0	0	0	0	0.00	0.00							0.00											
Age	25	06	0	0	0	0	0	0.00	0.00							0.00											
Type	Pwr GB	07 aa	4	3	0	58	43	6.21	1.50	287			25.6	34%	57%	4.98				3.3	6.6	**2.0**		0.7	-12.5	57	$1
Health	A	08 BOS *	8	8	0	136	106	3.79	1.29	236	238	196	11.9	28%	72%	3.63	54	18	27	3.8	7.0	**1.9**	10%	0.7	9.4	57	$13
PT/Exp	C	09 2AL	4	10	0	129	119	4.52	1.45	260	323	203	13.5	32%	70%	3.77	54	15	31	4.2	8.3	**2.0**	10%	0.8	-1.2	68	$7
Consist	B	1st Half	2	2	0	61	54	4.28	1.39	271			12.0	33%	70%	3.54	53	18	30	3.1	8.0	**2.6**	9%	0.7	1.3	90	$4
LIMA Plan	B	2nd Half	2	8	0	68	65	4.74	1.51	249			15.1	31%	70%	3.98	54	13	33	5.1	8.6	**1.7**	11%	0.9	-2.5	48	$3
Rand Var	+1	10 Proj	**7**	**11**	**0**	**160**	**136**	**4.23**	**1.37**	**254**			**14.0**	**31%**	**70%**	**3.69**	**54**	**16**	**30**	**3.7**	**7.7**	**2.1**	**10%**	**0.8**	**14.6**	**69**	**$12**

For second year in a row, better skills as RP (2.9 Ctl, 3.3 Cmd) than SP (4.7 Ctl, 1.6 Cmd). Dom growth has come in both roles, and GB% has held up across the board, so there's still room for cautious optimism.

Mathis,Doug		Yr	W	L	Sv	IP	K	ERA	WHIP	OBA	vL	vR	BF/G	H%	S%	xERA	G	L	F	Ctl	Dom	Cmd	hr/f	hr/9	RAR	BPV	R$
RH Reliever		05	0	0	0	0	0	0.00	0.00							0.00											
Age	26	06	0	0	0	0	0	0.00	0.00							0.00											
Type	Con	07	0	0	0	0	0	0.00	0.00							0.00											
Health	A	08	0	0	0	0	0	0.00	0.00							0.00											
PT/Exp	F	09 TEX *	4	3	1	100	57	3.59	1.44	294	250	239	12.4	33%	77%	4.22	50	19	31	2.4	5.1	**2.2**	8%	0.7	10.6	56	$6
Consist	F	1st Half	4	3	0	69	36	3.74	1.60	314			18.4	35%	78%	4.80	56	4	40	2.8	4.7	**1.7**	5%	0.7	6.1	43	$3
LIMA Plan	B+	2nd Half	0	0	1	31	21	3.25	1.08	246			6.8	28%	73%	3.33	47	26	26	1.5	6.2	**4.2**	12%	0.9	4.5	97	$3
Rand Var	-2	10 Proj	**1**	**1**	**0**	**44**	**27**	**3.72**	**1.29**	**273**			**9.2**	**31%**	**73%**	**3.80**	**48**	**23**	**28**	**2.1**	**5.6**	**2.7**	**10%**	**0.8**	**3.4**	**71**	**$3**

0-1, 3.16 ERA in 43 IP at TEX. Really clicked in 2H as Dom passed 5.6 tipping point, even if it did cost him a few GB. That pitcher has LIMA upside, but given sample size and lack of history, might be best to wait.

Matsuzaka,Daisuke		Yr	W	L	Sv	IP	K	ERA	WHIP	OBA	vL	vR	BF/G	H%	S%	xERA	G	L	F	Ctl	Dom	Cmd	hr/f	hr/9	RAR	BPV	R$
RH Starter		05 JPN	14	13	0	215	238	2.86	1.14	233			31.2	31%	79%	3.28				2.5	10.0	**3.9**		0.9	38.3	123	$30
Age	29	06 JPN	17	5	0	186	211	2.64	1.02	220			29.4	29%	80%	2.96				2.0	10.2	**5.0**		1.0	43.2	146	$34
Type	Pwr FB	07 BOS	15	12	0	205	201	4.40	1.32	249	238	253	27.1	31%	70%	3.96	38	18	44	3.5	8.8	**2.5**	10%	1.1	2.7	80	$20
Health	F	08 BOS	18	3	0	168	154	2.90	1.32	213	225	195	24.5	27%	80%	4.33	39	18	43	5.0	8.3	**1.6**	6%	0.6	30.0	29	$23
PT/Exp	A	09 BOS	4	6	0	59	54	5.77	1.87	326	340	304	23.7	39%	72%	4.99	34	23	43	4.6	8.2	**1.8**	12%	1.5	-9.6	37	($0)
Consist	B	1st Half	1	5	0	35	34	8.23	2.20	374			22.4	44%	65%	5.28	30	27	43	4.6	8.7	**1.9**	15%	2.1	-16.3	40	($4)
LIMA Plan	D	2nd Half	3	1	0	24	20	2.22	1.40	243			26.2	29%	88%	4.52	41	16	42	4.4	7.4	**1.7**	7%	0.7	6.7	32	$4
Rand Var	+5	10 Proj	**13**	**10**	**0**	**176**	**163**	**4.51**	**1.45**	**255**			**24.7**	**31%**	**71%**	**4.35**	**37**	**20**	**43**	**4.3**	**8.3**	**1.9**	**10%**	**1.1**	**1.8**	**49**	**$14**

Easy to look at 1H/2H surface stats and think shoulder rehab did the trick, but Dom and Cmd know better. We're three years into this experiment, and his skills keep getting worse. Does this look like an ace to you?

Matusz,Brian		Yr	W	L	Sv	IP	K	ERA	WHIP	OBA	vL	vR	BF/G	H%	S%	xERA	G	L	F	Ctl	Dom	Cmd	hr/f	hr/9	RAR	BPV	R$
LH Starter		05	0	0	0	0	0	0.00	0.00							0.00											
Age	23	06	0	0	0	0	0	0.00	0.00							0.00											
Type	xFB	07	0	0	0	0	0	0.00	0.00							0.00											
Health	A	08	0	0	0	0	0	0.00	0.00							0.00											
PT/Exp	F	09 BAL *	12	2	0	91	77	3.47	1.30	264	200	315	23.9	32%	76%	4.26	31	21	48	2.6	7.6	**3.0**	7%	0.9	11.0	77	$13
Consist	F	1st Half	3	0	0	18	18	0.99	1.05	203			24.0	28%	89%	1.72				3.0	9.0	**3.0**		0.0	7.7	131	$5
LIMA Plan	C	2nd Half	9	2	0	73	59	4.09	1.36	278			23.9	32%	73%	4.40	31	21	48	2.5	7.3	**3.0**	8%	1.1	3.3	74	$8
Rand Var	-2	10 Proj	**12**	**8**	**0**	**154**	**121**	**4.32**	**1.34**	**263**			**24.3**	**30%**	**71%**	**4.51**	**31**	**21**	**48**	**3.0**	**7.1**	**2.4**	**9%**	**1.2**	**-1.4**	**56**	**$14**

5-2, 4.63 ERA in 45 IP at BAL. Top prospect put up 2.7 Cmd rate in first exposure to the bigs. That's an awfully good place to start. But FB% is a concern, and with less than 100 IP as a pro, he's no sure thing yet.

Mazzaro,Vince		Yr	W	L	Sv	IP	K	ERA	WHIP	OBA	vL	vR	BF/G	H%	S%	xERA	G	L	F	Ctl	Dom	Cmd	hr/f	hr/9	RAR	BPV	R$
RH Starter		05	0	0	0	0	0	0.00	0.00							0.00											
Age	23	06	0	0	0	0	0	0.00	0.00							0.00											
Type	FB	07	0	0	0	0	0	0.00	0.00							0.00											
Health	A	08 aa	15	6	0	171	112	2.84	1.25	265			25.5	31%	77%	3.44				2.1	5.9	**2.8**		0.3	30.9	88	$20
PT/Exp	D	09 OAK *	6	11	0	148	97	4.27	1.48	284	321	316	24.1	32%	73%	4.74	39	21	40	3.3	5.9	**1.8**	7%	0.9	3.3	35	$7
Consist	C	1st Half	4	5	0	92	66	2.73	1.11	226			23.3	27%	75%	3.92	42	21	37	2.6	6.4	**2.4**	3%	0.3	19.7	65	$12
LIMA Plan	C	2nd Half	2	6	0	55	31	6.86	2.11	364			25.2	39%	70%	6.05	37	21	41	4.4	5.1	**1.1**	13%	1.8	-16.4	-12	($5)
Rand Var	-1	10 Proj	**8**	**9**	**0**	**144**	**97**	**4.06**	**1.34**	**269**			**23.7**	**30%**	**73%**	**4.44**	**38**	**21**	**40**	**2.7**	**6.1**	**2.2**	**9%**	**1.1**	**-0.1**	**51**	**$11**

4-9, 5.32 ERA in 91 IP at BAL. His season divided into 3 parts:
1. 2.56 ERA in 8 AAA starts
2. PQS 4/5 in 5 of first 6 MLB starts with a 2.95 ERA.
3. PQS 0/1 in 8 of next 11 starts with 6.91 ERA... and shut down.

BRANDON KRUSE

McCarthy,Brandon

McCarthy,Brandon				W	L	Sv	IP	K	ERA	WHIP	OBA	vL	vR	BF/G	H%	S%	xERA	G	L	F	Ctl	Dom	Cmd	hr/f	hr/9	RAR	BPV	R$
RH	Starter	05	CHW *	10	9	0	186	165	4.31	1.19	249	182	276	23.9	28%	70%	3.73	35	23	42	2.3	8.0	3.5	14%	1.5	1.5	95	$18
Age	26	06	CHW	4	7	0	84	69	4.70	1.31	245	197	270	6.7	26%	71%	4.40	38	15	47	3.5	7.4	2.1	15%	1.8	-1.5	54	$7
Type	FB	07	TEX	5	10	0	102	59	4.87	1.56	279	292	263	19.8	31%	69%	5.52	36	17	47	4.2	5.2	1.2	6%	0.8	-4.5	-7	$3
Health	F	08	TEX	1	1	0	22	10	4.09	1.27	244	293	195	18.4	25%	72%	5.27	24	30	46	3.3	4.1	1.3	9%	1.2	0.7	-12	$1
PT/Exp	C	09	TEX	7	4	0	97	65	4.62	1.36	259	264	246	24.5	28%	69%	4.65	39	19	42	3.3	6.0	1.8	10%	1.2	-2.1	35	$7
Consist	A	1st Half		5	2	0	64	44	4.92	1.44	268			25.4	29%	70%	4.96	34	19	46	3.7	6.2	1.7	12%	1.5	-3.7	25	$4
LIMA Plan	C	2nd Half		2	2	0	33	21	4.05	1.20	242			22.9	28%	66%	4.03	48	18	34	2.7	5.7	2.1	6%	0.5	1.6	55	$3
Rand Var	0	10	Proj	6	7	0	105	72	4.55	1.37	268			23.6	30%	70%	4.57	36	21	43	3.0	6.2	2.1	10%	1.2	-1.7	44	$7

PRO: Cut FB% and found Ctl in 2H, still only 26.
CON: Nearly 300 DL days in last 3 years, hasn't fully rebuilt Dom, Cmd remains shaky.
Worth a flyer, though by now it's hard not to feel like a sucker.

McClellan,Kyle

McClellan,Kyle				W	L	Sv	IP	K	ERA	WHIP	OBA	vL	vR	BF/G	H%	S%	xERA	G	L	F	Ctl	Dom	Cmd	hr/f	hr/9	RAR	BPV	R$
RH	Reliever	05		0	0	0	0	0	0.00	0.00							0.00											
Age	25	06		0	0	0	0	0	0.00	0.00							0.00											
Type	Pwr	07	aa	2	0	0	30	25	2.77	1.09	239			5.0	29%	77%	3.06				1.8	7.5	4.1		0.6	6.3	119	$4
Health	C	08	STL	2	7	1	76	59	4.04	1.39	270	238	291	4.8	32%	72%	3.83	48	21	31	3.1	7.0	2.3	10%	0.8	2.1	69	$4
PT/Exp	D	09	STL	4	4	3	67	51	3.37	1.35	229	198	252	4.3	27%	76%	4.07	50	19	31	4.6	6.9	1.5	7%	0.5	6.7	28	$7
Consist	B	1st Half		2	2	1	36	27	2.99	1.27	210			4.6	24%	79%	4.21	48	18	34	4.7	6.7	1.4	9%	0.7	5.3	19	$4
LIMA Plan	C+	2nd Half		2	2	2	31	24	3.82	1.44	252			4.0	31%	72%	3.87	53	21	26	4.4	7.1	1.6	4%	0.3	1.4	39	$3
Rand Var	-2	10	Proj	4	5	3	73	57	4.10	1.37	250			4.6	30%	71%	3.89	50	20	30	3.8	7.1	1.8	9%	0.7	3.3	51	$6

Ctl continues to implode, though this time H% and S% helped hide the damage. BPV says one-time future closer is no longer fit for the job. That 2007 skill sample is looking awfully small these days.

McClung,Seth

McClung,Seth				W	L	Sv	IP	K	ERA	WHIP	OBA	vL	vR	BF/G	H%	S%	xERA	G	L	F	Ctl	Dom	Cmd	hr/f	hr/9	RAR	BPV	R$
RH	Reliever	05	TAM *	9	11	0	127	108	6.23	1.54	265	294	197	14.2	30%	62%	4.67	37	21	42	4.7	7.6	1.6	13%	1.5	-29.1	24	$3
Age	29	06	TAM	6	12	6	103	59	6.29	1.83	292	299	289	12.5	31%	67%	6.15	37	20	43	5.9	5.2	0.9	9%	1.2	-22.0	-52	($0)
Type	Pwr FB	07	MIL *	3	6	5	89	92	2.58	1.47	227			6.6	30%	84%	3.96	53	13	34	5.8	9.3	1.6	8%	0.6	20.3	42	$10
Health	B	08	MIL	6	6	0	105	87	4.02	1.41	238	251	235	12.3	28%	73%	4.36	44	18	38	4.7	7.4	1.6	9%	0.9	3.3	29	$7
PT/Exp	C	09	MIL	3	3	0	62	40	4.94	1.63	262	291	243	6.9	27%	74%	5.60	37	19	45	5.7	5.8	1.0	12%	1.6	-5.7	-34	$0
Consist	B	1st Half		3	1	0	45	30	3.58	1.48	248			6.9	27%	80%	5.13	38	19	43	5.0	6.0	1.2	10%	1.2	3.4	-11	$3
LIMA Plan	C	2nd Half		0	2	0	17	10	8.57	2.02	297			6.9	29%	62%	6.94	33	18	49	7.5	5.4	0.7	18%	2.7	-9.1	-95	($3)
Rand Var	0	10	Proj	2	4	0	57	42	5.05	1.67	265			8.2	30%	72%	5.42	38	18	44	5.8	6.6	1.1	10%	1.3	-8.1	-22	($0)

S%-aided 1H ERA likely means he'll keep getting work, even as xERA trend (including horrific 2H) suggests his reign of terror should be ended. If a -95 BPV can't finish him off, maybe he's indestructable. Or a zombie.

McCutchen,Daniel

McCutchen,Daniel				W	L	Sv	IP	K	ERA	WHIP	OBA	vL	vR	BF/G	H%	S%	xERA	G	L	F	Ctl	Dom	Cmd	hr/f	hr/9	RAR	BPV	R$
RH	Starter	05		0	0	0	0	0	0.00	0.00							0.00											
Age	27	06		0	0	0	0	0	0.00	0.00							0.00											
Type	Con	07	aa	3	2	0	41	27	3.90	1.36	262			25.0	30%	72%	4.22				3.2	5.9	1.9		0.7	2.8	55	$4
Health	A	08	a/a	11	12	0	171	113	4.85	1.45	303			26.7	33%	72%	5.86				2.0	6.0	2.9		1.6	-11.5	44	$8
PT/Exp	D	09	PIT *	14	8	0	179	105	4.31	1.41	295	262	280	25.7	33%	71%	4.45	40	20	40	2.0	5.3	2.6	7%	0.8	-2.6	59	$11
Consist	D	1st Half		7	5	0	84	53	5.51	1.48	299			24.7	33%	63%	5.19				2.5	5.7	2.3		0.9	-13.7	51	$3
LIMA Plan	C+	2nd Half		7	3	0	94	52	3.23	1.35	292			26.8	32%	78%	4.39	40	20	40	1.7	5.0	3.0	6%	0.8	11.2	64	$8
Rand Var	-1	10	Proj	8	10	0	144	86	4.45	1.38	287			25.7	31%	71%	4.45	40	20	40	2.2	5.4	2.5	10%	1.2	-3.4	56	$7

1-2, 4.21 ERA in 36 IP at PIT. Cmd makes him one to watch, even if the rest of the package is fairly underwhelming. As a starter, could be a decent back-end guy, but it may be best just to monitor the skills for now.

McDonald,James

McDonald,James				W	L	Sv	IP	K	ERA	WHIP	OBA	vL	vR	BF/G	H%	S%	xERA	G	L	F	Ctl	Dom	Cmd	hr/f	hr/9	RAR	BPV	R$
RH	Reliever	05		0	0	0	0	0	0.00	0.00							0.00											
Age	25	06		0	0	0	0	0	0.00	0.00							0.00											
Type	Pwr	07	aa	7	2	0	52	56	1.72	1.19	238			21.4	30%	93%	3.70				2.8	9.7	3.5		1.0	17.6	108	$11
Health	A	08	a/a	7	4	0	141	124	3.75	1.32	248			22.1	30%	75%	4.12				3.5	7.9	2.3		1.1	9.7	69	$12
PT/Exp	D	09	LA *	6	5	0	93	90	3.78	1.40	238	213	282	7.9	30%	75%	4.02	44	17	39	4.7	8.7	1.9	8%	0.8	4.7	53	$7
Consist	A	1st Half		3	1	0	54	51	4.34	1.39	224			12.3	28%	70%	4.29	44	13	43	5.2	8.4	1.6	8%	0.8	-1.0	34	$3
LIMA Plan	C+	2nd Half		3	4	0	39	39	3.01	1.41	257			5.3	33%	81%	3.72	44	19	36	3.9	9.0	2.3	8%	0.7	5.7	79	$4
Rand Var	-1	10	Proj	10	7	0	137	131	4.01	1.32	244			10.2	30%	72%	3.75	44	18	38	3.7	8.6	2.3	10%	0.9	8.6	78	$12

5-5, 4.00 ERA in 63 IP at LA. Skills finally took a step in right direction in 2H while working out of the pen. Future as a SP, and with Dom this good, he certainly belongs on your radar, if not yet on your roster.

McGowan,Dustin

McGowan,Dustin				W	L	Sv	IP	K	ERA	WHIP	OBA	vL	vR	BF/G	H%	S%	xERA	G	L	F	Ctl	Dom	Cmd	hr/f	hr/9	RAR	BPV	R$
RH	Reliever	05	TOR *	1	5	0	80	62	5.91	1.54	297	243	301	18.8	33%	66%	4.16	47	17	36	3.2	7.0	2.2	18%	1.8	-15.2	65	($0)
Age	28	06	TOR *	5	7	1	111	96	6.32	1.76	292	327	283	13.3	35%	64%	4.67	43	26	31	5.4	7.8	1.4	10%	0.9	-24.1	14	($0)
Type	Pwr	07	TOR *	12	12	0	192	169	3.85	1.23	234	257	198	24.8	29%	69%	3.46	53	16	31	3.3	7.9	2.4	8%	0.7	15.4	85	$21
Health	F	08	TOR	6	7	0	111	85	4.37	1.37	268	295	252	25.2	32%	69%	4.14	41	21	38	3.1	6.9	2.2	7%	0.7	-0.3	60	$8
PT/Exp	C	09	TOR	0	0	0	0	0	0.00	0.00							0.00											
Consist	B	1st Half		0	0	0	0	0	0.00	0.00							0.00											
LIMA Plan	D	2nd Half		0	0	0	0	0	0.00	0.00							0.00											
Rand Var		10	Proj	2	3	0	52	42	4.72	1.42	256			17.2	30%	68%	4.15	45	20	35	4.0	7.3	1.8	9%	0.9	1.8	47	$3

Labrum surgery followed by knee surgery has him facing a long road back to the majors. Add in the fact that his history contains one good season and three so-so ones, and it's clear he's way too much of a gamble.

Meche,Gil

Meche,Gil				W	L	Sv	IP	K	ERA	WHIP	OBA	vL	vR	BF/G	H%	S%	xERA	G	L	F	Ctl	Dom	Cmd	hr/f	hr/9	RAR	BPV	R$
RH	Starter	05	SEA	10	8	0	143	83	5.09	1.57	275	266	285	22.2	30%	70%	5.23	40	20	40	4.5	5.2	1.2	9%	1.1	-12.8	-10	$4
Age	31	06	SEA	11	8	0	186	156	4.50	1.43	258	240	271	25.3	30%	72%	4.30	43	18	38	4.1	7.5	1.9	11%	1.2	1.4	47	$14
Type	Pwr	07	KC	9	13	0	216	156	3.67	1.30	264	242	284	26.8	30%	74%	3.98	47	18	35	2.6	6.5	2.5	9%	0.9	22.3	72	$19
Health	B	08	KC	14	11	0	210	183	3.98	1.32	256	238	273	26.2	31%	71%	3.92	39	22	39	3.1	7.8	2.5	8%	0.8	9.5	74	$20
PT/Exp	A	09	KC	6	10	0	129	95	5.09	1.57	284	268	292	25.2	32%	70%	4.46	49	17	34	4.0	6.6	1.6	12%	1.2	-10.2	37	$4
Consist	A	1st Half		4	8	0	98	76	4.22	1.46	269			25.3	32%	71%	4.13	50	17	33	3.8	7.0	1.9	7%	0.6	2.9	52	$6
LIMA Plan	B	2nd Half		2	2	0	31	19	7.89	1.92	326			24.8	32%	65%	5.57	45	17	39	5.0	5.6	1.1	24%	2.9	-13.1	-11	($2)
Rand Var	+1	10	Proj	11	12	0	188	148	4.27	1.40	268			24.5	31%	72%	4.14	45	18	37	3.3	7.1	2.2	10%	1.0	6.9	62	$14

Reasons he'll be undervalued:
- 3.0 Cmd, 3.60 xERA in April buried by injury-marred season
- Gap between ERA and xERA
- Pitches for the Royals

Health is the key, but a return to promise of '06-07 seems viable.

Medders,Brandon

Medders,Brandon				W	L	Sv	IP	K	ERA	WHIP	OBA	vL	vR	BF/G	H%	S%	xERA	G	L	F	Ctl	Dom	Cmd	hr/f	hr/9	RAR	BPV	R$
RH	Reliever	05	ARI *	7	3	8	66	71	2.33	1.25	225	239	161	4.4	30%	84%	3.41	44	19	37	3.8	9.6	2.5	8%	0.7	15.7	92	$13
Age	30	06	ARI	5	3	0	71	47	3.67	1.46	275	348	196	5.2	32%	76%	4.69	42	20	38	3.5	5.9	1.7	6%	0.6	7.2	31	$5
Type	Pwr	07	aaa	5	3	5	48	27	7.23	2.21	363			7.0	40%	67%	8.39				5.4	5.1	0.9		0.9	-16.4	6	($2)
Health	A	08	aaa	1	2	0	38	23	12.37	2.52	381			8.0	42%	49%	9.98				7.1	5.5	0.8		1.5	-38.0	-16	($10)
PT/Exp	D	09	SF	5	1	1	69	58	3.01	1.38	245	258	242	4.8	30%	81%	4.32	34	27	39	4.2	7.6	1.8	8%	0.8	10.0	36	$7
Consist	F	1st Half		2	1	0	31	28	3.17	1.57	273			4.7	33%	83%	4.43	35	27	38	4.6	8.1	1.8	9%	0.9	3.9	34	$2
LIMA Plan	D+	2nd Half		3	0	1	38	30	2.88	1.23	221			5.0	26%	79%	4.22	33	27	40	3.8	7.2	1.9	7%	0.7	6.1	37	$5
Rand Var	-4	10	Proj	4	2	0	58	43	5.28	1.60	272			5.6	31%	69%	4.95	38	24	38	5.0	6.7	1.3	10%	1.1	-4.9	2	$1

Case #425G: Middle reliever with lousy skills clutters up the basepaths and is rescued by subsequent pitchers, thereby inflating his strand rate and preserving his ERA. In year #2, the rescuers stop showing up.

Medlen,Kris

Medlen,Kris				W	L	Sv	IP	K	ERA	WHIP	OBA	vL	vR	BF/G	H%	S%	xERA	G	L	F	Ctl	Dom	Cmd	hr/f	hr/9	RAR	BPV	R$
RH	Reliever	05		0	0	0	0	0	0.00	0.00							0.00											
Age	24	06		0	0	0	0	0	0.00	0.00							0.00											
Type	Pwr	07		0	0	0	0	0	0.00	0.00							0.00											
Health	A	08	aa	7	8	1	120	102	4.17	1.39	291			14.4	36%	70%	4.53				2.1	7.6	3.7		0.6	2.0	101	$9
PT/Exp	D	09	ATL *	8	5	0	105	111	3.26	1.22	229	183	328	9.7	31%	73%	3.36	41	23	36	3.4	9.5	2.8	5%	0.4	12.0	98	$13
Consist	C	1st Half		7	3	0	63	64	3.28	1.14	205			16.0	28%	70%	3.64	39	17	44	3.7	9.1	2.5	3%	0.3	7.1	82	$9
LIMA Plan	B+	2nd Half		1	2	0	42	47	3.24	1.34	263			6.1	36%	77%	3.11	42	28	30	3.0	10.1	3.4	9%	0.6	4.9	121	$3
Rand Var	-1	10	Proj	7	7	0	123	121	3.89	1.25	245			23.2	31%	70%	3.41	41	25	33	3.0	8.9	3.0	9%	0.7	12.9	98	$12

3-5, 4.26 ERA in 67 IP at ATL. Overshadowed by Hanson, but he's electric in his own right. 2H growth under radar since it came as RP. Missing piece to bigger role is out pitch vs. RH. Target his skills, not role. LIMA gem.

BRANDON KRUSE

Meek,Evan

		Yr	Tm	W	L	Sv	IP	K	ERA	WHIP	OBA	vL	vR	BF/G	H%	S%	xERA	G	L	F	Ctl	Dom	Cmd	hr/f	hr/9	RAR	BPV	R$
RH	Reliever	05		0	0	0	0	0	0.00	0.00							0.00											
Age	26	06		0	0	0	0	0	0.00	0.00							0.00											
Type	Pwr GB	07	aa	2	1	1	67	58	5.51	1.87	319			7.3	40%	68%	6.03				4.9	7.8	**1.6**		0.3	-8.7	62	($1)
Health	B	08	a/a	1	1	4	57	39	3.50	1.32	260			7.6	31%	73%	3.65				3.0	6.1	**2.0**		0.4	5.7	72	$5
PT/Exp	D	09	PIT	1	1	0	47	42	3.45	1.34	204	250	176	4.9	26%	74%	3.89	52	19	29	5.6	8.0	**1.4**	6%	0.4	4.3	25	$3
Consist	C	1st Half		0	0	0	28	18	2.87	1.38	193			5.3	22%	81%	4.76	53	18	30	6.4	5.7	**0.9**	8%	0.6	4.6	-38	$1
LIMA Plan	B+	2nd Half		1	1	0	19	24	4.31	1.28	221			4.4	34%	63%	2.75	51	22	27	4.3	11.5	**2.7**	0%	0.0	-0.3	120	$2
Rand Var	-3	10	Proj	**2**	**2**	**0**	**73**	**64**	**3.97**	**1.41**	**247**			**5.8**	**31%**	**72%**	**3.72**	**52**	**20**	**28**	**4.3**	**7.9**	**1.8**	**9%**	**0.6**	**4.8**	**56**	**$4**

Oblique injury ended season in August. 2H Dom should put him on your radar, even with shaky Ctl. As a GBer, he's got more room for error than most. 2H gains hidden by H% and S%. Watch him.

Meredith,Cla

		Yr	Tm	W	L	Sv	IP	K	ERA	WHIP	OBA	vL	vR	BF/G	H%	S%	xERA	G	L	F	Ctl	Dom	Cmd	hr/f	hr/9	RAR	BPV	R$
RH	Reliever	05	a/a	3	5	19	61	46	5.16	1.46	300			5.2	35%	65%	5.10				2.2	6.8	**3.1**		0.9	-6.4	73	$8
Age	26	06	SD *	8	1	2	96	70	1.96	0.96	221	281	107	4.8	26%	83%	2.37	69	16	15	1.4	6.5	**4.7**	14%	0.6	29.9	127	$18
Type	xGB	07	SD	5	6	0	80	59	3.50	1.39	295	286	303	4.3	35%	76%	2.61	72	14	14	1.9	6.7	**3.5**	16%	0.7	9.1	118	$7
Health	A	08	SD	0	3	0	70	49	4.10	1.47	285	351	258	4.2	33%	73%	3.17	67	16	17	3.1	6.3	**2.0**	15%	0.8	1.5	75	$2
PT/Exp	C	09	2TM	4	2	0	65	37	4.00	1.50	284	280	305	4.5	32%	73%	3.81	63	16	21	3.4	5.1	**1.5**	9%	0.6	2.5	40	$3
Consist	B	1st Half		4	1	0	32	16	3.66	1.59	307			4.8	34%	76%	3.82	65	16	19	3.1	4.5	**1.5**	5%	0.3	2.6	40	$2
LIMA Plan	B	2nd Half		0	1	0	33	21	4.32	1.41	260			4.2	29%	70%	3.80	61	16	23	3.8	5.7	**1.5**	12%	0.8	-0.1	39	$1
Rand Var	0	10	Proj	**2**	**2**	**0**	**58**	**36**	**4.03**	**1.43**	**275**			**4.4**	**31%**	**72%**	**3.45**	**65**	**16**	**19**	**3.3**	**5.6**	**1.7**	**11%**	**0.6**	**6.4**	**56**	**$3**

Declines don't get more steep...
- Rising control rate
- Eroding strikeout rate
- Surging xERA

As an extreme GBer, he doesn't need elite skills to survive. But w/o Cmd, sub-4 ERA is history.

Meyer,Dan

		Yr	Tm	W	L	Sv	IP	K	ERA	WHIP	OBA	vL	vR	BF/G	H%	S%	xERA	G	L	F	Ctl	Dom	Cmd	hr/f	hr/9	RAR	BPV	R$
LH	Reliever	05	aaa	2	8	0	89	54	5.66	1.67	301			21.5	32%	69%	6.31				4.1	5.5	**1.3**		1.5	-14.9	10	($2)
Age	28	06	aaa	3	3	0	49	25	5.54	1.79	331			23.2	34%	74%	7.59				3.5	4.5	**1.3**		1.8	-6.2	-12	($1)
Type	Pwr xFB	07	aaa	8	2	0	119	79	4.69	1.70	296			25.0	33%	76%	6.23				4.6	6.0	**1.3**		1.3	-3.3	20	$3
Health	A	08	aaa	10	5	0	122	77	5.68	1.64	296			25.3	33%	65%	5.45				4.1	5.7	**1.4**		0.8	-20.7	35	$2
PT/Exp	D	09	FLA	3	2	2	58	56	3.09	1.17	222	228	211	3.4	27%	79%	3.86	36	16	48	3.2	8.6	**2.7**	9%	1.1	7.9	82	$7
Consist	C	1st Half		2	0	1	32	31	1.96	0.90	181			3.2	21%	88%	3.55	36	11	54	2.5	8.7	**3.4**	9%	1.1	8.8	102	$6
LIMA Plan	C+	2nd Half		1	2	1	26	25	4.47	1.49	268			3.5	33%	72%	4.23	36	22	42	4.1	8.6	**2.1**	9%	1.0	-0.9	57	$1
Rand Var	-3	10	Proj	**3**	**3**	**3**	**58**	**50**	**4.03**	**1.38**	**262**			**6.1**	**31%**	**74%**	**4.34**	**36**	**18**	**46**	**3.4**	**7.8**	**2.3**	**9%**	**1.1**	**-0.5**	**61**	**$5**

The light came on after years of mediocrity in high-minors. Skill trends are headed in right direction, but that 2H Ctl says not so fast, especially given prior chronic wildness. Use 2H ERA and WHIP as baselines.

Mickolio,Kam

		Yr	Tm	W	L	Sv	IP	K	ERA	WHIP	OBA	vL	vR	BF/G	H%	S%	xERA	G	L	F	Ctl	Dom	Cmd	hr/f	hr/9	RAR	BPV	R$
RH	Reliever	05		0	0	0	0	0	0.00	0.00							0.00											
Age	25	06		0	0	0	0	0	0.00	0.00							0.00											
Type	Pwr	07	aa	6	4	3	53	48	3.31	1.38	248			7.1	31%	76%	3.84				4.0	8.0	**2.0**		0.5	7.5	80	$8
Health	A	08	a/a	3	1	3	58	53	4.64	1.58	271			5.8	35%	69%	4.43				4.8	8.3	**1.7**		0.3	-2.4	77	$3
PT/Exp	F	09	BAL *	3	5	0	57	58	4.31	1.29	239	43	370	5.2	30%	69%	3.69	39	24	37	3.7	9.1	**2.5**	11%	1.0	1.0	82	$5
Consist	B	1st Half		2	3	0	33	31	4.38	1.34	257			5.2	32%	68%	4.04				3.3	8.3	**2.5**		0.8	0.3	82	$3
LIMA Plan	B	2nd Half		1	2	0	24	27	4.20	1.23	213			5.2	27%	69%	3.45	39	24	37	4.2	10.2	**2.4**	14%	1.2	0.7	88	$2
Rand Var	+1	10	Proj	**4**	**4**	**5**	**64**	**62**	**4.11**	**1.35**	**248**			**5.5**	**31%**	**72%**	**3.84**	**39**	**24**	**37**	**3.8**	**8.8**	**2.3**	**11%**	**1.0**	**4.7**	**72**	**$8**

0-2, 2.63 ERA in 13 IP at BAL. Elbow inflammation ended year early. Before that, Ctl + Dom gains showed he has the tools for an increased role. Especially with that 2H Dom. Watch his Ctl; if it stabilizes... UP: 20 SV

Mijares,Jose

		Yr	Tm	W	L	Sv	IP	K	ERA	WHIP	OBA	vL	vR	BF/G	H%	S%	xERA	G	L	F	Ctl	Dom	Cmd	hr/f	hr/9	RAR	BPV	R$
LH	Reliever	05		0	0	0	0	0	0.00	0.00							0.00											
Age	25	06		0	0	0	0	0	0.00	0.00							0.00											
Type	Pwr xFB	07	a/a	5	4	9	69	66	5.07	1.66	229			6.2	27%	73%	5.25				7.4	8.6	**1.2**		1.4	-5.2	42	$6
Health	A	08	MIN *	1	2	2	26	20	2.77	1.15	223			5.0	26%	79%	2.94				3.1	6.9	**2.2**		0.7	5.1	78	$4
PT/Exp	D	09	MIN	2	2	0	62	55	2.33	1.17	220	147	283	3.6	26%	86%	4.16	37	12	51	3.4	8.0	**2.4**	8%	1.0	16.1	69	$8
Consist	D	1st Half		0	1	0	23	18	2.35	1.43	245			3.6	28%	90%	4.89	41	10	49	4.7	7.0	**1.5**	9%	1.2	6.0	19	$2
LIMA Plan	B	2nd Half		2	1	0	39	37	2.33	1.01	204			3.6	25%	83%	3.76	35	13	52	2.6	8.6	**3.4**	8%	0.9	10.2	98	$6
Rand Var	-5	10	Proj	**2**	**2**	**0**	**51**	**46**	**3.90**	**1.30**	**243**			**4.3**	**29%**	**75%**	**4.29**	**37**	**12**	**51**	**3.5**	**8.2**	**2.3**	**10%**	**1.2**	**0.9**	**67**	**$5**

A full year of H% and S% help made him look like one of MLB's best LH RP. xERA confirms his true level was much worse. There is optimism in that 2H growth, but w/o solution for RH bats, his upside is limited.

Miller,Andrew

		Yr	Tm	W	L	Sv	IP	K	ERA	WHIP	OBA	vL	vR	BF/G	H%	S%	xERA	G	L	F	Ctl	Dom	Cmd	hr/f	hr/9	RAR	BPV	R$
LH	Starter	05		0	0	0	0	0	0.00	0.00							0.00											
Age	24	06	DET	0	1	0	10	6	6.24	1.78	219			5.9	26%	61%	4.85	64	24	12	8.9	5.3	**0.6**	0%	0.0	-2.1	-103	($0)
Type	Pwr	07	DET *	7	5	0	100	85	4.67	1.56	275	175	312	23.6	33%	71%	4.11	49	21	30	4.4	7.6	**1.7**	11%	0.9	-2.0	46	$6
Health	C	08	FLA	6	10	0	107	89	5.87	1.64	284	226	307	16.9	35%	63%	4.40	46	22	33	4.7	7.5	**1.6**	6%	0.6	-21.2	31	$0
PT/Exp	C	09	FLA *	4	7	0	98	79	5.05	1.62	266	309	261	18.5	32%	68%	4.45	48	22	30	5.4	7.3	**1.3**	8%	0.6	-10.4	10	$1
Consist	A	1st Half		2	4	0	70	55	4.36	1.44	256			21.9	31%	68%	4.08	48	21	31	4.2	7.1	**1.7**	5%	0.4	-1.5	39	$3
LIMA Plan	C	2nd Half		2	3	0	28	24	6.80	2.09	290			13.9	34%	69%	5.46	48	25	27	8.4	7.8	**0.9**	17%	1.3	-8.9	-61	($2)
Rand Var	0	10	Proj	**3**	**5**	**0**	**58**	**48**	**4.97**	**1.60**	**262**			**16.4**	**31%**	**69%**	**4.30**	**50**	**22**	**28**	**5.4**	**7.4**	**1.4**	**10%**	**0.8**	**-0.3**	**15**	**$1**

3-5, 4.84 ERA in 80 IP at FLA. Flashes of good things in 1H went up into flames in 2H. Was even worse after demotion. Still young, but eroding Ctl and Dom give no hope in short-term. He's at a crossroads.

Miller,Justin

		Yr	Tm	W	L	Sv	IP	K	ERA	WHIP	OBA	vL	vR	BF/G	H%	S%	xERA	G	L	F	Ctl	Dom	Cmd	hr/f	hr/9	RAR	BPV	R$
RH	Reliever	05	aaa	3	1	2	50	46	3.09	1.27	255			7.5	32%	77%	3.61				2.7	8.2	**3.0**		0.6	7.5	99	$6
Age	32	06	JPN	0	1	0	12	10	13.04	2.64	363			5.6	38%	54%	12.35				9.3	7.8	**0.8**		3.7	-12.6	-65	($4)
Type	Pwr FB	07	FLA *	5	0	6	76	90	3.41	1.36	248	324	184	4.3	35%	76%	3.54	43	14	43	3.9	10.7	**2.7**	6%	0.6	9.5	108	$10
Health	B	08	FLA	4	2	0	47	43	4.24	1.41	259	310	224	4.4	32%	71%	4.32	32	24	44	3.9	8.3	**2.2**	7%	0.8	0.2	55	$4
PT/Exp	D	09	SF	3	3	0	57	36	3.17	1.31	227	241	233	5.4	24%	81%	4.76	41	16	43	4.3	5.7	**1.3**	10%	1.1	7.1	6	$5
Consist	B	1st Half		1	1	0	31	20	2.31	1.22	214			5.2	23%	88%	4.67	40	15	45	4.0	5.8	**1.4**	10%	1.2	7.2	13	$3
LIMA Plan	C	2nd Half		2	2	0	26	16	4.24	1.41	242			5.8	26%	73%	4.87	42	18	40	4.6	5.6	**1.2**	10%	1.1	-0.1	-2	$2
Rand Var	-5	10	Proj	**3**	**2**	**0**	**44**	**30**	**4.34**	**1.47**	**264**			**5.3**	**30%**	**73%**	**4.87**	**38**	**19**	**43**	**4.1**	**6.2**	**1.5**	**9%**	**1.0**	**-3.3**	**16**	**$2**

Hoping for another sub-4 ERA? No chance. H% and S% drove this one. Cmd freefall means his ERA is headed towards 5.00, a risk made evident by xERA trend. Off-season elbow surgery clouds '10 even more.

Miller,Trever

		Yr	Tm	W	L	Sv	IP	K	ERA	WHIP	OBA	vL	vR	BF/G	H%	S%	xERA	G	L	F	Ctl	Dom	Cmd	hr/f	hr/9	RAR	BPV	R$
LH	Reliever	05	TAM	2	2	0	44	35	4.08	1.68	266	267	289	3.3	31%	77%	4.96	40	25	35	5.9	7.1	**1.2**	9%	0.8	1.6	-13	$2
Age	36	06	HOU	2	3	1	50	56	3.05	1.10	229	224	225	2.9	29%	79%	3.45	33	18	49	2.3	10.0	**4.3**	11%	1.3	8.9	128	$7
Type	Pwr FB	07	HOU	0	0	1	46	46	4.86	1.47	256	209	289	2.7	32%	69%	4.45	34	18	48	4.5	8.9	**2.0**	10%	1.2	-2.5	52	$2
Health	A	08	TAM	2	0	2	43	44	4.16	1.36	242	209	286	2.7	32%	68%	4.05	32	25	44	4.2	9.1	**2.2**	4%	0.4	1.0	62	$4
PT/Exp	D	09	STL	4	1	0	44	46	2.06	0.96	201	135	295	2.4	25%	86%	3.21	35	20	45	2.3	9.5	**4.2**	10%	1.0	11.5	122	$8
Consist	B	1st Half		2	0	0	21	24	2.56	1.09	212			2.6	27%	85%	3.43	33	16	51	3.0	10.2	**3.4**	11%	1.3	4.2	114	$4
LIMA Plan	B+	2nd Half		2	1	0	23	22	1.59	0.84	191			2.3	24%	88%	2.97	38	23	39	1.6	8.8	**5.5**	9%	0.8	7.2	130	$5
Rand Var	-5	10	Proj	**3**	**1**	**0**	**51**	**52**	**3.72**	**1.26**	**243**			**2.7**	**31%**	**74%**	**3.75**	**34**	**21**	**44**	**3.2**	**9.2**	**2.9**	**10%**	**1.1**	**3.2**	**92**	**$5**

Skills completely support a sub-3.00 ERA. What they don't support is a near-2.00 ERA. A near-20% jump in strand rate won't maintain and FB tendency keeps him risky in this role. LIMA fodder, but don't reach.

Millwood,Kevin

		Yr	Tm	W	L	Sv	IP	K	ERA	WHIP	OBA	vL	vR	BF/G	H%	S%	xERA	G	L	F	Ctl	Dom	Cmd	hr/f	hr/9	RAR	BPV	R$
RH	Starter	05	CLE	9	11	0	192	146	2.86	1.22	252	269	227	26.5	29%	81%	3.66	46	21	33	2.4	6.8	**2.8**	10%	0.9	35.8	82	$21
Age	35	06	TEX	16	12	0	215	157	4.52	1.31	273	285	258	26.7	31%	67%	3.91	45	21	34	2.2	6.6	**3.0**	10%	1.0	1.0	81	$20
Type		07	TEX	10	14	0	173	123	5.16	1.62	304	288	311	25.3	35%	69%	4.42	46	21	32	3.5	6.4	**1.8**	10%	1.0	-13.9	46	$5
Health	C	08	TEX	9	10	0	169	125	5.07	1.59	316	273	354	26.3	37%	69%	4.23	41	25	34	2.6	6.7	**2.6**	9%	1.0	-15.0	68	$5
PT/Exp	A	09	TEX	13	10	0	199	123	3.67	1.34	258	240	272	27.3	28%	77%	4.56	42	19	39	3.2	5.6	**1.7**	11%	1.2	19.2	34	$17
Consist	A	1st Half		8	5	0	119	74	2.80	1.24	245			29.1	27%	83%	4.38	42	19	38	2.9	5.6	**1.9**	10%	1.1	24.3	42	$14
LIMA Plan	D	2nd Half		5	5	0	80	49	4.97	1.48	277			25.1	30%	70%	4.84	42	19	39	3.6	5.5	**1.5**	12%	1.4	-5.1	22	$3
Rand Var	-1	10	Proj	**12**	**12**	**0**	**194**	**126**	**4.47**	**1.46**	**284**			**26.5**	**31%**	**72%**	**4.47**	**43**	**21**	**36**	**3.1**	**5.9**	**1.9**	**10%**	**1.1**	**-0.9**	**43**	**$11**

New TEX pitching coach, Mike Maddux is being credited with turning the staff around. But there's no evidence of BPI gains here. Random gauges (H%, S%) are what has improved. Does not bode well for 2010.

STEPHEN NICKRAND

Miner,Zach		Yr	Tm	W	L	Sv	IP	K	ERA	WHIP	OBA	vL	vR	BF/G	H%	S%	xERA	G	L	F	Ctl	Dom	Cmd	hr/f	hr/9	RAR	BPV	R$
RH Reliever		05	a/a	5	9	1	140	87	4.88	1.73	305			24.2	34%	72%	5.79				4.5	5.6	**1.2**		0.8	-10.0	31	($0)
Age	28	06	DET *	13	6	0	144	94	4.44	1.42	271	320	245	17.3	31%	70%	4.30	47	21	32	3.3	5.9	**1.8**	9%	0.8	2.1	41	$12
Type		07	DET *	4	8	0	107	63	4.97	1.51	276	207	317	10.1	31%	67%	4.32	56	16	27	3.9	5.3	**1.4**	8%	0.7	-6.1	24	$3
Health	B	08	DET	8	5	0	118	62	4.27	1.39	262	269	256	11.3	29%	70%	4.66	45	20	35	3.5	4.7	**1.3**	7%	0.8	1.1	14	$8
PT/Exp	C	09	DET	7	5	1	92	61	4.12	1.55	273	250	294	8.2	31%	76%	4.79	46	18	36	4.4	6.0	**1.4**	10%	1.0	3.7	12	$6
Consist	A	1st Half		5	1	0	46	35	4.10	1.56	282			9.8	33%	75%	4.21	52	17	31	4.1	6.8	**1.7**	9%	0.8	2.0	43	$4
LIMA Plan	C	2nd Half		2	4	1	46	26	4.14	1.54	263			7.0	28%	77%	5.37	39	20	41	4.7	5.1	**1.1**	10%	1.2	1.7	-18	$2
Rand Var	-1	10	Proj	**6**	**7**	**0**	**108**	**65**	**4.42**	**1.50**	**271**			**9.5**	**30%**	**73%**	**4.77**	**46**	**19**	**35**	**4.1**	**5.4**	**1.3**	**10%**	**1.0**	**-4.5**	**11**	**$5**

Fanalytically irrelevant. No real skills worth chasing and his almost-rosterable ERAs are unsupported. Slight GB tendency is the only thing keeping his BPVs above zero.

Misch,Pat		Yr	Tm	W	L	Sv	IP	K	ERA	WHIP	OBA	vL	vR	BF/G	H%	S%	xERA	G	L	F	Ctl	Dom	Cmd	hr/f	hr/9	RAR	BPV	R$
LH Reliever		05	a/a	7	11	0	163	92	5.80	1.62	322			26.4	35%	66%	6.20				2.5	5.1	**2.0**		1.2	-30.1	28	($1)
Age	28	06	a/a	9	6	0	168	110	3.94	1.46	305			26.3	35%	75%	5.25				2.0	5.9	**3.0**		0.8	12.0	67	$11
Type	Con	07	SF *	2	9	1	107	81	4.13	1.42	281			8.9	33%	71%	4.06	43	24	33	2.9	6.8	**2.4**	7%	0.6	3.9	67	$5
Health	A	08	SF *	6	8	0	139	77	7.27	1.76	335	281	270	18.6	35%	61%	5.01	44	19	36	3.1	5.0	**1.6**	16%	1.9	-51.5	29	($8)
PT/Exp	D	09	2NL *	7	6	1	114	50	4.38	1.43	291	325	263	11.3	31%	71%	4.82	42	20	38	2.4	3.9	**1.6**	7%	0.9	-2.7	26	$5
Consist	B	1st Half		3	1	1	41	18	4.37	1.58	312			8.5	34%	70%	4.76	48	19	32	2.7	3.9	**1.4**	2%	0.2	-0.9	23	$1
LIMA Plan	C+	2nd Half		4	5	0	73	32	4.39	1.34	279			14.1	29%	71%	4.72	41	20	39	2.2	4.0	**1.8**	10%	1.2	-1.8	30	$4
Rand Var	-1	10	Proj	**2**	**3**	**0**	**44**	**23**	**4.55**	**1.43**	**285**			**12.6**	**31%**	**70%**	**4.63**	**43**	**20**	**37**	**2.7**	**4.8**	**1.8**	**9%**	**1.0**	**-2.0**	**34**	**$2**

3-4, 4.48 ERA in 62 IP at NYM/SF. Well, that was discouraging. Dom rate continues free-fall; when Ctl waffles, he's tossing batting practice. No better vs LHB, so he can't even fall back on situational work.

Mitre,Sergio		Yr	Tm	W	L	Sv	IP	K	ERA	WHIP	OBA	vL	vR	BF/G	H%	S%	xERA	G	L	F	Ctl	Dom	Cmd	hr/f	hr/9	RAR	BPV	R$
RH Starter		05	CHC *	7	11	0	130	85	5.04	1.42	276	294	235	16.6	31%	66%	3.43	66	11	22	3.1	5.9	**1.9**	17%	1.1	-12.8	66	$5
Age	29	06	FLA	1	5	0	41	31	5.71	1.56	276	344	232	12.2	30%	67%	4.23	52	20	28	4.4	6.8	**1.6**	20%	1.5	-6.2	34	($0)
Type	Con xGB	07	FLA	5	8	0	149	80	4.65	1.48	300	271	332	24.3	33%	68%	3.85	60	17	23	2.5	4.8	**2.0**	8%	0.5	-4.1	58	$4
Health	F	08	FLA	0	0	0	0	0	0.00	0.00							0.00											
PT/Exp	C	09	NYY *	6	4	0	97	60	5.33	1.47	312	421	246	22.3	34%	66%	3.60	58	18	24	1.7	5.6	**3.3**	18%	1.3	-10.5	90	$4
Consist	A	1st Half		2	1	0	30	19	4.82	1.36	307			25.8	34%	66%	5.04				1.0	5.6	**5.8**		1.0	-1.4	119	$2
LIMA Plan	B	2nd Half		4	3	0	67	41	5.56	1.52	314			21.1	34%	67%	3.71	58	18	24	2.0	5.6	**2.7**	20%	1.5	-9.1	81	$2
Rand Var	+5	10	Proj	**5**	**6**	**0**	**102**	**63**	**4.52**	**1.38**	**283**			**19.0**	**32%**	**68%**	**3.69**	**57**	**18**	**25**	**2.4**	**5.6**	**2.3**	**11%**	**0.8**	**9.3**	**71**	**$6**

3-3, 6.79 ERA in 52 IP at NYY. Lost '08 to TJS, then 50 games to PED penalty. So these BPIs? Stunning. xERA calls for better stats, but sub-2 Ctl doesn't fit history. Still, xGBer could help the right team.

Mock,Garrett		Yr	Tm	W	L	Sv	IP	K	ERA	WHIP	OBA	vL	vR	BF/G	H%	S%	xERA	G	L	F	Ctl	Dom	Cmd	hr/f	hr/9	RAR	BPV	R$
RH Reliever		05		0	0	0	0	0	0.00	0.00							0.00											
Age	26	06	aa	4	12	0	147	104	7.31	1.83	335			25.9	38%	60%	7.19				3.7	6.3	**1.7**		1.3	-50.7	24	($8)
Type	Pwr	07	aa	1	5	0	51	32	7.05	2.10	351			23.3	39%	66%	7.89				5.2	5.7	**1.1**		0.9	-16.3	14	($5)
Health	A	08	WAS *	7	6	0	145	125	3.56	1.32	262	279	207	13.7	32%	75%	3.79	45	19	36	2.9	7.8	**2.7**	8%	0.7	12.8	83	$12
PT/Exp	D	09	WAS *	8	11	2	142	112	4.84	1.51	282	344	271	15.4	34%	68%	4.07	50	17	33	3.6	7.1	**1.9**	7%	0.7	-11.5	57	$6
Consist	F	1st Half		4	3	2	56	42	4.76	1.33	252			9.5	31%	62%	3.90	54	11	35	3.4	6.7	**2.0**	4%	0.3	-3.9	61	$4
LIMA Plan	C+	2nd Half		4	8	0	86	70	4.90	1.62	300			24.5	35%	71%	4.16	49	18	33	3.8	7.3	**1.9**	10%	0.9	-7.6	57	$1
Rand Var	+1	10	Proj	**6**	**9**	**0**	**120**	**93**	**4.28**	**1.38**	**263**			**15.6**	**31%**	**71%**	**3.98**	**49**	**17**	**34**	**3.4**	**7.0**	**2.1**	**10%**	**1.0**	**4.2**	**61**	**$7**

3-10, 5.62 ERA in 91 IP at WAS. Threw better than stats would suggest, and continued solid Dom is a nice building block. GB bump also encouraging. If that trend holds, plus '08 Cmd: UP: 10+ Wins, sub-4 ERA

Moehler,Brian		Yr	Tm	W	L	Sv	IP	K	ERA	WHIP	OBA	vL	vR	BF/G	H%	S%	xERA	G	L	F	Ctl	Dom	Cmd	hr/f	hr/9	RAR	BPV	R$
RH Starter		05	FLA	6	12	0	158	95	4.55	1.52	308	320	305	19.0	34%	71%	4.24	44	25	31	2.4	5.4	**2.3**	9%	0.9	-6.0	55	$4
Age	38	06	FLA	7	11	0	122	58	6.57	1.66	323	351	297	19.2	34%	62%	4.96	45	22	33	2.8	4.3	**1.5**	13%	1.4	-31.3	25	($2)
Type	Con	07	HOU	1	4	1	60	36	4.07	1.41	285	303	268	6.2	31%	75%	4.13	52	16	32	2.6	5.4	**2.1**	13%	1.2	2.6	59	$3
Health	B	08	HOU	11	8	0	150	82	4.56	1.35	282	307	255	20.6	30%	69%	4.34	44	21	35	2.2	4.9	**2.3**	11%	1.2	-5.4	52	$9
PT/Exp	B	09	HOU	8	12	0	155	91	5.47	1.54	300	280	316	23.8	32%	66%	4.59	44	20	36	3.0	5.3	**1.8**	11%	1.2	-24.4	38	$1
Consist	A	1st Half		5	4	0	67	45	5.64	1.55	305			23.0	33%	68%	4.58	41	19	40	2.8	6.0	**2.1**	14%	1.7	-12.0	51	$1
LIMA Plan	C+	2nd Half		3	8	0	88	46	5.34	1.53	296			24.4	32%	65%	4.59	47	21	32	3.1	4.7	**1.5**	8%	0.8	-12.4	27	($0)
Rand Var	+2	10	Proj	**7**	**10**	**0**	**140**	**79**	**4.77**	**1.44**	**288**			**16.0**	**31%**	**69%**	**4.45**	**45**	**20**	**34**	**2.7**	**5.1**	**1.9**	**11%**	**1.2**	**-3.2**	**42**	**$5**

Small signs of erosion, most notably Ctl, which was actually his worst in a full season since 1997. Not good, as Ctl is about all he's got left. Near the age at which a drop-off can come fast. DN: Another 5+ ERA, <100 IP

Morales,Franklin		Yr	Tm	W	L	Sv	IP	K	ERA	WHIP	OBA	vL	vR	BF/G	H%	S%	xERA	G	L	F	Ctl	Dom	Cmd	hr/f	hr/9	RAR	BPV	R$
LH Reliever		05		0	0	0	0	0	0.00	0.00							0.00											
Age	24	06		0	0	0	0	0	0.00	0.00							0.00											
Type	Pwr FB	07	COL *	8	6	0	152	109	4.46	1.48	262	129	273	23.8	30%	71%	4.07	55	19	27	4.3	6.5	**1.5**	11%	0.8	-0.6	34	$8
Health	B	08	COL *	11	7	0	135	80	6.18	1.76	278	200	295	24.4	30%	66%	5.83	40	20	40	6.0	5.3	**0.9**	9%	1.1	-31.9	-50	($2)
PT/Exp	D	09	COL *	5	4	7	81	72	4.11	1.48	259	205	265	7.4	31%	74%	4.76	27	23	50	4.4	8.0	**1.8**	7%	0.9	0.8	29	$7
Consist	C	1st Half		3	2	0	49	40	3.67	1.36	261			21.0	30%	78%	5.21	9	23	68	3.3	7.3	**2.2**	7%	1.3	3.2	30	$4
LIMA Plan	C	2nd Half		2	2	7	32	32	4.78	1.66	256			3.9	34%	69%	4.89	31	24	45	6.2	9.0	**1.5**	2%	0.3	-2.3	4	$3
Rand Var	-2	10	Proj	**4**	**3**	**2**	**65**	**52**	**4.69**	**1.56**	**267**			**7.9**	**31%**	**72%**	**4.81**	**37**	**22**	**41**	**4.8**	**7.2**	**1.5**	**10%**	**1.1**	**-4.4**	**14**	**$3**

3-2, 4.50, 7 Sv in 40 IP at COL.
Why he won't get 7 Sv again:
- Lefty; bad Ctl, way too risky
Why he might:
- Teams love power closers
- H. Street not so durable
We bet he won't, though.

Morrow,Brandon		Yr	Tm	W	L	Sv	IP	K	ERA	WHIP	OBA	vL	vR	BF/G	H%	S%	xERA	G	L	F	Ctl	Dom	Cmd	hr/f	hr/9	RAR	BPV	R$
RH Reliever		05		0	0	0	0	0	0.00	0.00							0.00											
Age	25	06		0	0	0	0	0	0.00	0.00							0.00											
Type	Pwr xFB	07	SEA	3	4	0	63	66	4.12	1.67	239	278	221	4.8	32%	75%	5.13	35	18	47	7.1	9.4	**1.3**	4%	0.4	3.0	-10	$3
Health	A	08	SEA *	4	6	10	95	104	3.77	1.21	191	198	149	6.9	24%	73%	3.99	33	16	51	4.9	9.9	**2.0**	11%	1.1	6.7	57	$14
PT/Exp	D	09	SEA *	7	7	6	125	99	4.06	1.48	252	277	212	15.2	30%	74%	4.85	37	20	43	4.8	7.1	**1.5**	8%	0.9	6.1	14	$10
Consist	B	1st Half		0	3	6	35	38	5.14	1.83	283			8.3	37%	73%	4.76	40	19	41	6.4	9.8	**1.5**	10%	1.0	-3.0	20	$2
LIMA Plan	D+	2nd Half		7	4	0	90	61	3.63	1.35	239			23.9	27%	75%	4.92	35	21	45	4.1	6.1	**1.5**	7%	0.8	9.0	10	$9
Rand Var	-2	10	Proj	**7**	**9**	**0**	**145**	**134**	**4.28**	**1.45**	**247**			**23.5**	**30%**	**73%**	**4.54**	**36**	**18**	**46**	**4.7**	**8.3**	**1.8**	**10%**	**1.1**	**-1.9**	**36**	**$10**

2-4, 4.39 ERA in 70 IP at SEA.
How to screw up a young P:
2007: 22-year-old SP to RP
2008: SP to RP to closer to SP
2009: SP to closer to SP
And 2010... who knows? Still upside, but has gained no skill.

Morton,Charlie		Yr	Tm	W	L	Sv	IP	K	ERA	WHIP	OBA	vL	vR	BF/G	H%	S%	xERA	G	L	F	Ctl	Dom	Cmd	hr/f	hr/9	RAR	BPV	R$
RH Starter		05		0	0	0	0	0	0.00	0.00							0.00											
Age	26	06		0	0	0	0	0	0.00	0.00							0.00											
Type		07	aa	4	6	0	79	55	5.62	1.72	300			9.0	36%	65%	5.40				4.6	6.3	**1.4**		0.4	-11.3	51	($0)
Health	A	08	ATL *	9	10	0	154	111	4.27	1.34	241	306	245	22.6	29%	68%	4.08	50	18	31	4.0	6.5	**1.6**	6%	0.5	-0.1	38	$10
PT/Exp	D	09	PIT *	12	11	0	168	112	3.76	1.32	259	316	236	24.6	30%	72%	4.02	49	18	33	3.0	6.0	**2.0**	6%	0.5	9.0	54	$14
Consist	B	1st Half		7	3	0	82	56	2.92	1.17	252			24.0	30%	76%	4.14	35	22	43	2.0	6.2	**3.1**	4%	0.4	12.9	70	$10
LIMA Plan	C	2nd Half		5	8	0	86	56	4.56	1.46	266			25.1	30%	68%	4.31	51	17	32	3.9	5.9	**1.5**	7%	0.6	-3.9	28	$4
Rand Var	-1	10	Proj	**9**	**10**	**0**	**145**	**100**	**4.28**	**1.40**	**260**			**19.0**	**30%**	**69%**	**4.17**	**50**	**18**	**32**	**3.7**	**6.2**	**1.7**	**7%**	**0.6**	**1.6**	**41**	**$9**

5-9, 4.55 ERA in 97 IP at PIT. Baby steps. Has yet to master Ctl issues in ML, but 1H MLEs give hope. Far from a finished product, far from a sure thing. But still has #3 starter upside, and there are worse staff fillers.

Mota,Guillermo		Yr	Tm	W	L	Sv	IP	K	ERA	WHIP	OBA	vL	vR	BF/G	H%	S%	xERA	G	L	F	Ctl	Dom	Cmd	hr/f	hr/9	RAR	BPV	R$
RH Reliever		05	FLA	2	2	2	67	60	4.70	1.45	256	243	262	5.2	32%	67%	4.24	41	19	41	4.3	8.1	**1.9**	6%	0.7	-3.8	48	$3
Age	36	06	2TM	4	3	0	55	46	4.57	1.43	261	252	261	4.6	29%	75%	4.71	34	18	48	3.9	7.5	**1.9**	14%	1.8	-0.3	41	$4
Type	FB	07	NYM *	2	3	0	67	52	6.26	1.52	291	235	284	5.0	33%	60%	4.32	44	18	38	3.2	7.1	**2.2**	11%	1.2	-15.0	62	($0)
Health	B	08	MIL	5	6	1	57	50	4.11	1.40	244	287	216	4.2	29%	74%	4.03	45	22	33	4.4	7.9	**1.8**	13%	1.1	1.2	46	$5
PT/Exp	D	09	LA	3	4	0	65	39	3.45	1.18	223	202	238	4.4	24%	73%	4.69	36	17	47	3.3	5.4	**1.6**	6%	0.8	6.0	22	$6
Consist	A	1st Half		3	2	0	35	21	4.11	1.31	245			4.6	27%	70%	4.37	46	19	34	3.6	5.4	**1.5**	8%	0.8	0.3	24	$3
LIMA Plan	C	2nd Half		0	2	0	30	18	2.67	1.02	197			4.1	21%	79%	4.96	24	14	62	3.0	5.3	**1.8**	6%	0.9	5.7	18	$3
Rand Var	-5	10	Proj	**3**	**4**	**0**	**58**	**40**	**4.03**	**1.31**	**252**			**4.5**	**28%**	**72%**	**4.53**	**38**	**18**	**44**	**3.3**	**6.2**	**1.9**	**9%**	**1.1**	**-1.9**	**40**	**$4**

Gap between his surface stats and skills is going to wreak havoc on teams both real and fanalytic in 2010. Dom loss is a bad sign for a pitcher who has always lived and died by the K. DN: 5.00+ ERA, 1.50+ WHIP

ROD TRUESDELL

Motte,Jason

		Yr	Tm	W	L	Sv	IP	K	ERA	WHIP	OBA	vL	vR	BF/G	H%	S%	xERA	G	L	F	Ctl	Dom	Cmd	hr/f	hr/9	RAR	BPV	R$
RH	Reliever	05		0	0	0	0	0	0.00	0.00							0.00											
Age	27	06		0	0	0	0	0	0.00	0.00							0.00											
Type	Pwr xFB	07	aa	3	3	8	49	50	2.45	1.38	243			4.7	32%	84%	3.88				4.3	9.1	**2.1**		0.6	12.2	87	$9
Health	A	08	aaa	4	3	9	66	82	4.06	1.61	298			4.8	41%	76%	5.36				3.8	11.1	**3.0**		0.8	2.0	101	$7
PT/Exp	D	09	STL	4	4	0	57	54	4.76	1.41	263	341	214	3.6	31%	71%	4.11	38	17	45	3.7	8.6	**2.3**	14%	1.6	-4.0	72	$3
Consist	C	1st Half		2	2	0	29	24	4.95	1.34	254			3.4	29%	66%	4.15	43	15	43	3.4	7.4	**2.2**	11%	1.2	-2.7	62	$2
LIMA Plan	A	2nd Half		2	2	0	28	30	4.57	1.49	271			3.7	32%	77%	4.07	33	19	48	3.9	9.8	**2.5**	16%	2.0	-1.3	82	$2
Rand Var	+2	10	Proj	**4**	**4**	**0**	**58**	**62**	**3.88**	**1.33**	**248**			**4.0**	**31%**	**75%**	**3.79**	**37**	**17**	**46**	**3.6**	**9.6**	**2.7**	**11%**	**1.2**	**3.3**	**92**	**$6**

How does an Opening Day closer not record a single save? Monthly BPVs ranged from -26 to 202, so consistency was an issue. Skills aren't that bad; if opportunity arises again, he may be up to the challenge.

Moyer,Jamie

		Yr	Tm	W	L	Sv	IP	K	ERA	WHIP	OBA	vL	vR	BF/G	H%	S%	xERA	G	L	F	Ctl	Dom	Cmd	hr/f	hr/9	RAR	BPV	R$
LH	Starter	05	SEA	13	7	0	200	102	4.28	1.39	285	294	278	26.9	30%	72%	4.77	37	22	41	2.3	4.6	**2.0**	8%	1.0	2.4	34	$12
Age	47	06	2TM	11	14	0	211	108	4.31	1.32	277	251	285	27.1	29%	72%	4.66	40	21	39	2.2	4.6	**2.1**	12%	1.4	5.6	42	$14
Type	Con	07	PHI	14	12	0	199	133	5.01	1.45	283	309	279	26.4	31%	69%	4.59	39	21	39	3.0	6.0	**2.0**	12%	1.4	-14.4	45	$10
Health	A	08	PHI	16	7	0	196	123	3.71	1.33	264	240	270	25.3	29%	75%	4.27	44	21	35	2.8	5.6	**2.0**	9%	0.9	13.5	47	$17
PT/Exp	A	09	PHI	12	10	0	162	94	4.94	1.36	279	243	290	23.1	29%	68%	4.49	41	19	40	2.4	5.2	**2.2**	13%	1.5	-15.1	49	$8
Consist	A	1st Half		6	6	0	83	50	6.06	1.52	305			24.6	31%	65%	4.70	40	18	42	2.5	5.4	**2.2**	16%	2.1	-19.2	48	$1
LIMA Plan	C	2nd Half		6	4	0	79	44	3.76	1.19	250			21.6	27%	71%	4.25	42	20	38	2.3	5.0	**2.2**	8%	0.9	4.1	49	$7
Rand Var	+1	10	Proj	**5**	**4**	**0**	**72**	**40**	**4.63**	**1.43**	**285**			**8.2**	**30%**	**71%**	**4.67**	**41**	**20**	**38**	**2.8**	**5.0**	**1.8**	**11%**	**1.3**	**-3.6**	**35**	**$3**

Fluctuations in S% and hr/f continue to cause unpredictable swings in ERA. The concern is that at his age, this kind of inconsistency may lead teams to stop trusting him.
DN: Stays in the bullpen.

Moylan,Peter

		Yr	Tm	W	L	Sv	IP	K	ERA	WHIP	OBA	vL	vR	BF/G	H%	S%	xERA	G	L	F	Ctl	Dom	Cmd	hr/f	hr/9	RAR	BPV	R$
RH	Reliever	05		0	0	0	0	0	0.00	0.00							0.00											
Age	31	06	ATL *	1	7	1	71	60	8.33	2.02	323			7.0	39%	57%	4.61	58	17	25	6.1	7.5	**1.2**	11%	0.8	-33.7	8	($7)
Type	Pwr xGB	07	ATL	5	3	1	90	63	1.80	1.07	204	242	184	4.5	24%	87%	3.30	62	13	25	3.1	6.3	**2.0**	9%	0.6	29.2	70	$14
Health	F	08	ATL	0	1	1	6	5	1.58	1.05	237	273	167	3.2	27%	100%	2.47	67	11	22	1.6	7.9	**5.0**	28%	1.6	1.9	144	$1
PT/Exp	D	09	ATL	6	2	0	73	61	2.84	1.37	240	309	211	3.6	31%	77%	3.24	62	18	20	4.3	7.5	**1.7**	0%	0.0	12.2	59	$8
Consist	B	1st Half		2	2	0	30	25	4.19	1.46	234			3.2	30%	68%	3.35	65	19	16	5.4	7.5	**1.4**	0%	0.0	0.0	32	$2
LIMA Plan	B	2nd Half		4	0	0	43	36	1.89	1.31	244			3.9	31%	84%	3.15	61	18	22	3.6	7.6	**2.1**	0%	0.0	12.2	78	$6
Rand Var	-4	10	Proj	**5**	**3**	**8**	**73**	**59**	**3.60**	**1.31**	**241**			**4.2**	**30%**	**73%**	**3.19**	**64**	**15**	**21**	**3.7**	**7.3**	**2.0**	**9%**	**0.5**	**9.6**	**73**	**$9**

PRO: Strong xERA, improved Cmd in 2H, didn't allow a HR.
CON: Ctl is still an issue. BPV says that he's not closer material, but a an extreme GB rate like that makes him too intriguing to ignore.

Mujica,Edward

		Yr	Tm	W	L	Sv	IP	K	ERA	WHIP	OBA	vL	vR	BF/G	H%	S%	xERA	G	L	F	Ctl	Dom	Cmd	hr/f	hr/9	RAR	BPV	R$
RH	Reliever	05	aa	2	1	10	34	29	3.43	1.35	299			5.4	37%	75%	4.43				1.3	7.7	**5.8**		0.5	3.7	147	$6
Age	25	06	CLE *	4	2	13	69	53	2.21	1.28	275	324	341	6.6	34%	83%	4.60	26	18	55	1.9	6.9	**3.5**	2%	0.3	20.1	75	$14
Type	xFB	07	CLE *	2	1	14	50	47	6.63	1.39	294			4.9	35%	52%	4.41	26	16	58	2.0	8.4	**4.3**	8%	1.3	-13.2	102	$6
Health	A	08	CLE *	3	4	4	65	51	6.26	1.58	307	277	318	5.7	36%	60%	4.68	30	23	46	2.9	7.1	**2.4**	7%	1.0	-15.3	57	$2
PT/Exp	D	09	SD	3	5	2	94	76	3.94	1.28	277	300	247	5.9	32%	75%	3.92	39	17	44	1.8	7.3	**4.0**	11%	1.3	2.9	99	$7
Consist	B	1st Half		2	3	1	38	33	2.83	1.15	240			4.4	29%	80%	3.95	33	18	49	2.4	7.8	**3.3**	8%	0.9	6.4	88	$5
LIMA Plan	A	2nd Half		1	2	1	56	43	4.69	1.37	299			7.4	33%	71%	3.90	42	17	41	1.5	7.0	**4.8**	14%	1.6	-3.5	106	$2
Rand Var	0	10	Proj	**3**	**3**	**0**	**73**	**60**	**4.22**	**1.28**	**276**			**5.5**	**32%**	**71%**	**4.01**	**36**	**19**	**46**	**1.9**	**7.4**	**4.0**	**10%**	**1.2**	**2.3**	**98**	**$5**

2H reduction in FB% was very encouraging, as that would complete his skill package. hr/9 splits (0.7 home, 2.2 away) worth noting in daily leagues. Good LIMA candidate for now, possible closer in the future.

Mulvey,Kevin

		Yr	Tm	W	L	Sv	IP	K	ERA	WHIP	OBA	vL	vR	BF/G	H%	S%	xERA	G	L	F	Ctl	Dom	Cmd	hr/f	hr/9	RAR	BPV	R$
RH	Starter	05		0	0	0	0	0	0.00	0.00							0.00											
Age	24	06		0	0	0	0	0	0.00	0.00							0.00											
Type		07	aa	12	10	0	157	98	3.72	1.31	270			24.6	32%	70%	3.72				2.4	5.6	**2.3**		0.2	14.4	77	$15
Health	A	08	aaa	7	9	0	148	99	4.38	1.49	291			24.2	33%	73%	5.15				3.0	6.0	**2.0**		1.0	-1.3	46	$6
PT/Exp	D	09	2TM *	5	11	0	173	111	5.09	1.54	291	228	400	24.2	33%	68%	4.44	40	31	29	3.4	5.8	**1.7**	10%	0.9	-16.6	29	$2
Consist	C	1st Half		3	5	0	95	63	4.83	1.59	299			26.8	35%	69%	5.15				3.5	6.0	**1.7**		0.6	-6.1	50	$1
LIMA Plan	C+	2nd Half		2	6	0	78	48	5.40	1.48	283			21.5	31%	66%	4.42	40	31	29	3.3	5.5	**1.7**	15%	1.3	-10.5	27	$1
Rand Var	+1	10	Proj	**1**	**1**	**0**	**15**	**9**	**4.34**	**1.38**	**268**			**20.8**	**31%**	**68%**	**4.23**	**40**	**31**	**29**	**3.1**	**5.6**	**1.8**	**7%**	**0.6**	**0.2**	**35**	**$1**

0-3, 8.14 ERA in 24 IP at MIN/ARI. There's no growth in these skills, just a trend of becoming more overmatched at each new level. That's a good way to earn a regular seat on the MLB/AAA shuttle.

Myers,Brett

		Yr	Tm	W	L	Sv	IP	K	ERA	WHIP	OBA	vL	vR	BF/G	H%	S%	xERA	G	L	F	Ctl	Dom	Cmd	hr/f	hr/9	RAR	BPV	R$
RH	Reliever	05	PHI	13	8	0	215	208	3.72	1.21	241	241	233	26.1	29%	75%	3.22	46	23	31	2.8	8.7	**3.1**	17%	1.3	13.8	104	$22
Age	29	06	PHI	12	7	0	198	189	3.91	1.30	258	259	254	26.9	31%	75%	3.60	46	18	36	2.9	8.6	**3.0**	14%	1.3	14.1	101	$19
Type	Pwr	07	PHI	5	7	21	69	83	4.32	1.28	239	183	274	5.7	32%	70%	3.11	46	19	35	3.5	10.9	**3.1**	15%	1.2	0.9	124	$14
Health	F	08	PHI	10	13	0	190	163	4.55	1.38	269	235	293	27.2	31%	71%	3.72	47	20	32	3.1	7.7	**2.5**	16%	1.4	-6.5	81	$11
PT/Exp	B	09	PHI	4	3	0	71	50	4.84	1.37	271	233	320	16.9	27%	75%	4.05	47	18	35	2.9	6.4	**2.2**	23%	2.3	-5.6	61	$3
Consist	A	1st Half		4	3	0	63	46	4.70	1.36	270			27.1	27%	77%	4.00	47	18	35	2.8	6.6	**2.3**	24%	2.4	-4.0	66	$4
LIMA Plan	A	2nd Half		0	0	0	8	4	6.00	1.47	274			4.1	29%	60%	4.44	48	24	29	3.6	4.8	**1.3**	14%	1.2	-1.7	15	($0)
Rand Var	+5	10	Proj	**11**	**11**	**0**	**174**	**147**	**3.98**	**1.31**	**257**			**23.7**	**30%**	**74%**	**3.66**	**47**	**21**	**32**	**3.0**	**7.6**	**2.5**	**14%**	**1.2**	**12.9**	**81**	**$14**

If we give him a pass on injury-decimated season, he's still a peak age hurler with consistent skills who has been plagued by hr/f issues. Can't pay what you would have a year ago, but you can still covet the upside.

Narveson,Chris

		Yr	Tm	W	L	Sv	IP	K	ERA	WHIP	OBA	vL	vR	BF/G	H%	S%	xERA	G	L	F	Ctl	Dom	Cmd	hr/f	hr/9	RAR	BPV	R$
LH	Reliever	05	aaa	4	6	0	118	65	5.11	1.46	271			22.5	29%	67%	4.93				3.7	5.0	**1.4**		1.1	-11.7	25	$2
Age	28	06	aaa	8	5	0	80	50	3.60	1.46	269			23.4	29%	79%	4.97				3.8	5.6	**1.5**		1.1	9.1	32	$8
Type	Pwr xFB	07	aaa	3	2	0	45	28	7.30	1.60	282			22.7	30%	54%	5.76				4.4	5.6	**1.3**		1.3	-15.8	19	($1)
Health	A	08	aaa	6	13	0	136	110	6.00	1.57	289			21.8	33%	65%	5.91				3.8	7.3	**1.9**		1.6	-28.5	34	$1
PT/Exp	D	09	MIL *	6	4	5	122	113	4.19	1.28	248	313	224	10.9	31%	68%	4.11	31	21	47	3.2	8.3	**2.6**	6%	0.7	-0.0	72	$11
Consist	B	1st Half		3	3	5	47	44	4.96	1.24	244			7.8	30%	61%	3.84	35	22	43	3.0	8.4	**2.8**	9%	1.0	-4.5	84	$5
LIMA Plan	B	2nd Half		3	1	0	75	68	3.71	1.31	250			14.4	31%	72%	4.21	31	21	48	3.3	8.2	**2.5**	5%	0.6	4.5	66	$6
Rand Var	-1	10	Proj	**5**	**5**	**0**	**87**	**74**	**4.66**	**1.40**	**266**			**14.5**	**31%**	**69%**	**4.47**	**31**	**21**	**47**	**3.4**	**7.7**	**2.2**	**9%**	**1.1**	**-2.2**	**55**	**$5**

2-0, 3.83 ERA in 47 IP at MIL. Late-blooming swingman now has three years of Cmd growth and a 0 BB/10K start vs. Cubs under his belt. Posted 8.8 Dom in majors. Has the makings of a sleeper if you're feeling bold.

Nathan,Joe

		Yr	Tm	W	L	Sv	IP	K	ERA	WHIP	OBA	vL	vR	BF/G	H%	S%	xERA	G	L	F	Ctl	Dom	Cmd	hr/f	hr/9	RAR	BPV	R$
RH	Reliever	05	MIN	7	4	43	70	94	2.70	0.97	189	160	206	3.9	28%	75%	2.82	37	12	50	2.8	12.1	**4.3**	7%	0.6	14.4	157	$28
Age	35	06	MIN	7	0	36	68	95	1.59	0.79	165	193	130	4.0	27%	82%	2.36	36	22	42	2.1	12.6	**5.9**	5%	0.4	25.0	183	$29
Type	Pwr FB	07	MIN	4	2	37	72	77	1.88	1.02	211	221	199	4.2	29%	84%	3.09	40	21	39	2.4	9.7	**4.1**	6%	0.5	23.2	128	$26
Health	A	08	MIN	1	2	39	68	74	1.33	0.90	184	167	192	3.8	25%	91%	2.69	47	19	33	2.4	9.8	**4.1**	9%	0.7	25.2	138	$25
PT/Exp	A	09	MIN	2	2	47	67	87	2.15	0.93	175	145	187	3.7	24%	84%	2.82	41	12	47	3.0	11.7	**4.0**	11%	0.9	19.0	150	$28
Consist	A	1st Half		1	1	21	31	39	1.45	0.77	170			3.5	25%	86%	2.47	44	13	43	1.7	11.3	**6.5**	7%	0.6	11.5	179	$14
LIMA Plan	C+	2nd Half		1	1	26	36	48	2.76	1.06	179			4.0	24%	82%	3.12	39	11	50	4.0	12.0	**3.0**	13%	1.3	7.5	125	$14
Rand Var	-5	10	Proj	**2**	**2**	**40**	**65**	**75**	**2.48**	**1.07**	**203**			**4.0**	**27%**	**83%**	**3.17**	**42**	**16**	**42**	**3.2**	**10.3**	**3.3**	**11%**	**1.0**	**10.2**	**121**	**$23**

Bone chips likely account for drastic 2H upticks in Ctl and FB%, and the fact that he still managed a 12.0 Dom and 125 BPV just reinforces what you already know: he's good. As safe as closer investments get.

Nelson,Joe

		Yr	Tm	W	L	Sv	IP	K	ERA	WHIP	OBA	vL	vR	BF/G	H%	S%	xERA	G	L	F	Ctl	Dom	Cmd	hr/f	hr/9	RAR	BPV	R$
RH	Reliever	05	a/a	0	3	7	59	58	5.14	1.65	273			6.1	32%	74%	5.97				5.3	8.8	**1.6**		1.7	-6.1	36	$2
Age	35	06	KC *	3	3	16	76	76	3.72	1.27	219	180	252	4.8	27%	75%	4.04	34	23	43	4.3	9.0	**2.1**	11%	1.1	7.9	58	$13
Type	Pwr FB	07		0	0	0	0	0	0.00	0.00							0.00											
Health	D	08	FLA *	4	2	12	79	88	2.30	1.18	224	227	189	4.2	30%	84%	3.28	40	23	38	3.3	10.0	**3.0**	8%	0.7	19.3	109	$15
PT/Exp	F	09	TAM *	5	2	3	57	49	4.87	1.66	257	212	216	4.8	29%	76%	5.50	32	17	50	6.1	7.7	**1.3**	13%	1.7	-2.9	-17	$4
Consist	F	1st Half		2	0	2	32	30	4.49	1.37	230			4.3	25%	76%	4.61	31	19	49	4.8	8.4	**1.8**	16%	2.0	-0.1	32	$2
LIMA Plan	C+	2nd Half		3	2	1	25	19	5.36	2.02	290			5.4	32%	77%	6.80	36	9	55	7.9	6.8	**0.9**	9%	1.4	-2.8	-76	$0
Rand Var	0	10	Proj	**4**	**3**	**0**	**64**	**60**	**4.25**	**1.50**	**251**			**4.8**	**30%**	**76%**	**4.58**	**36**	**19**	**45**	**5.0**	**8.5**	**1.7**	**11%**	**1.3**	**-1.1**	**33**	**$5**

3-0, 4.02, 3 Sv in 40 IP at TAM. Horrible for three months (1.0 Cmd, -62 BPV); awesome for one (9.0 Cmd, 120 BPV). Sent down in August. No reports of injury, but until he fixes that Ctl spike, you can't rely on him.

BRANDON KRUSE

Neshek,Pat

		Yr	Tm	W	L	Sv	IP	K	ERA	WHIP	OBA	vL	vR	BF/G	H%	S%	xERA	G	L	F	Ctl	Dom	Cmd	hr/f	hr/9	RAR	BPV	R$
RH	Reliever	05	aa	6	4	24	82	75	2.92	1.37	275			6.4	33%	84%	4.66				2.7	8.2	3.1		1.1	14.0	80	$17
Age	29	06	MIN *	10	4	14	97	125	2.65	1.02	219	244	140	5.9	29%	84%	3.07	32	14	54	2.1	11.6	5.5	13%	1.4	22.8	162	$25
Type	Pwr xFB	07	MIN	7	2	0	70	74	2.94	1.01	182	181	185	3.7	23%	75%	3.71	32	16	52	3.5	9.5	2.7	8%	0.9	13.5	87	$13
Health	F	08	MIN	0	1	0	13	15	4.74	1.20	242	250	233	3.7	31%	64%	3.33	31	28	42	2.7	10.2	3.8	14%	1.4	-0.6	118	$1
PT/Exp	D	09	MIN	0	0	0	0	0	0.00	0.00							0.00											
Consist	A	1st Half		0	0	0	0	0	0.00	0.00							0.00											
LIMA Plan	D	2nd Half		0	0	0	0	0	0.00	0.00							0.00											
Rand Var		10	Proj	4	2	0	44	44	3.93	1.24	241			5.2	30%	73%	3.88	31	22	47	3.1	9.1	2.9	11%	1.2	3.0	89	$6

Tore up elbow May 2008; TJS November 2008. Should be on track for spring training. Will need time to shake the rust off, but young enough to bounce back to being high-Dom RP with propensity for the long ball.

Niemann,Jeff

		Yr	Tm	W	L	Sv	IP	K	ERA	WHIP	OBA	vL	vR	BF/G	H%	S%	xERA	G	L	F	Ctl	Dom	Cmd	hr/f	hr/9	RAR	BPV	R$
RH	Starter	05	aa	0	1	0	10	12	5.40	1.30	199			7.0	30%	54%	2.36				5.4	10.8	2.0		0.0	-1.4	122	$0
Age	27	06	aa	5	5	0	77	70	4.09	1.39	252			23.7	31%	73%	4.34				4.0	8.2	2.1		1.0	4.1	68	$7
Type		07	aaa	12	6	0	131	108	5.43	1.72	321			24.3	38%	70%	6.48				3.4	7.4	2.2		1.1	-15.6	48	$4
Health	A	08	aaa	9	5	0	133	110	4.17	1.23	233			23.0	27%	69%	3.75				3.3	7.4	2.2		1.1	2.2	67	$13
PT/Exp	C	09	TAM	13	6	0	181	125	3.93	1.35	266	274	258	24.9	30%	73%	4.40	41	20	39	2.9	6.2	2.1	8%	0.8	11.5	51	$16
Consist	D	1st Half		7	4	0	79	45	3.98	1.41	256			22.9	28%	74%	5.20	39	16	45	4.0	5.1	1.3	7%	0.9	4.6	2	$6
LIMA Plan	C	2nd Half		6	2	0	102	80	3.90	1.30	274			26.8	32%	72%	3.81	42	23	35	2.1	7.1	3.3	8%	0.8	6.9	90	$9
Rand Var	-1	10	Proj	15	8	0	201	155	3.80	1.33	266			23.7	31%	74%	4.12	41	20	39	2.7	6.9	2.5	9%	1.0	7.9	70	$20

Struggled out of the gate, then blossomed in 2H, showing the kind of growth you want to see from a rookie. Nice Ctl trend, too. Overshadowed by bigger names in TAM rotation, he could be a draft day bargain.

Niese,Jonathon

		Yr	Tm	W	L	Sv	IP	K	ERA	WHIP	OBA	vL	vR	BF/G	H%	S%	xERA	G	L	F	Ctl	Dom	Cmd	hr/f	hr/9	RAR	BPV	R$
LH	Starter	05		0	0	0	0	0	0.00	0.00							0.00											
Age	23	06		0	0	0	0	0	0.00	0.00							0.00											
Type		07		0	0	0	0	0	0.00	0.00							0.00											
Health	C	08	aa	11	8	0	164	124	3.68	1.38	270			24.3	32%	73%	4.08				3.1	6.8	2.2		0.5	12.7	74	$14
PT/Exp	D	09	NYM *	6	7	0	120	94	4.62	1.40	283	333	242	24.6	34%	67%	3.79	48	19	33	2.5	7.0	2.8	7%	0.6	-6.4	84	$6
Consist	A	1st Half		4	6	0	91	79	5.38	1.46	298			25.0	36%	63%	3.57	50	18	32	2.4	7.8	3.3	8%	0.6	-13.5	105	$2
LIMA Plan	C+	2nd Half		2	1	0	29	14	2.18	1.20	233			23.5	26%	82%	4.36	47	19	34	3.1	4.5	1.5	3%	0.3	7.1	22	$3
Rand Var	+2	10	Proj	7	6	0	116	81	3.96	1.34	265			24.7	30%	72%	4.02	47	19	34	2.9	6.3	2.2	8%	0.8	3.5	61	$8

1-1, 4.21 ERA in 25 IP at NYM. Torn hamstring ended his season in August. Otherwise, high GB% plus solid Dom is a good foundation to build upon. BA vs LH came in small sample; normally no significant splits.

Nieve,Fernando

		Yr	Tm	W	L	Sv	IP	K	ERA	WHIP	OBA	vL	vR	BF/G	H%	S%	xERA	G	L	F	Ctl	Dom	Cmd	hr/f	hr/9	RAR	BPV	R$
RH	Starter	05	a/a	8	7	0	167	142	4.58	1.43	273			26.9	32%	70%	4.74				3.3	7.7	2.3		1.0	-5.7	64	$9
Age	27	06	HOU	3	3	0	96	70	4.21	1.33	243	262	224	10.2	26%	75%	4.64	41	15	44	3.8	6.6	1.7	14%	1.7	3.2	33	$6
Type	xFB	07	aaa	1	3	0	22	12	6.55	2.18	340			22.4	37%	70%	7.81				6.5	4.9	0.8		0.8	-5.7	8	($2)
Health	C	08	HOU *	2	6	6	83	59	6.93	1.85	344			8.4	38%	66%	7.92				3.3	6.4	1.9		1.8	-27.3	10	($3)
PT/Exp	D	09	NYM *	6	4	0	79	55	4.52	1.48	264	200	351	20.4	30%	71%	4.98	36	18	46	4.3	6.3	1.5	7%	0.8	-3.2	12	$4
Consist	D	1st Half		6	2	0	66	46	4.57	1.42	260			20.5	30%	68%	4.64	43	14	43	3.9	6.3	1.6	6%	0.7	-3.1	30	$4
LIMA Plan	C+	2nd Half		0	2	0	13	9	4.25	1.81	281			20.0	31%	81%	6.21	22	27	51	6.4	6.4	1.0	10%	1.4	-0.1	-58	($0)
Rand Var	-1	10	Proj	4	3	0	73	53	4.72	1.43	274			12.6	30%	71%	4.75	33	20	47	3.4	6.6	2.0	10%	1.4	-4.3	39	$3

3-3, 2.95 ERA in 36 IP at NYM. Quad injury in July was another bump in long road back from '07 TJS. MLB data suggest better fit in bullpen (14.2 IP, 8.0 Cmd) than rotation (69.1 IP, 1.1 Cmd), making value role-driven.

Nippert,Dustin

		Yr	Tm	W	L	Sv	IP	K	ERA	WHIP	OBA	vL	vR	BF/G	H%	S%	xERA	G	L	F	Ctl	Dom	Cmd	hr/f	hr/9	RAR	BPV	R$
RH	Reliever	05	aa	8	3	0	117	84	3.07	1.36	258			27.8	31%	77%	3.73				3.4	6.4	1.9		0.4	17.8	70	$11
Age	28	06	ARI *	13	10	0	150	123	6.11	1.69	317	333	375	25.7	37%	64%	4.10	56	12	32	3.4	7.4	2.1	11%	1.0	-30.0	73	$2
Type	Pwr	07	ARI *	1	4	0	81	74	6.15	1.49	256	238	290	7.8	31%	59%	4.28	38	28	34	4.7	8.2	1.7	12%	1.1	-17.3	36	($0)
Health	F	08	TEX *	9	7	0	135	86	5.98	1.73	320	263	354	19.6	35%	68%	5.09	37	24	39	3.7	5.7	1.6	11%	1.4	-27.1	19	($1)
PT/Exp	D	09	TEX	5	3	0	70	54	3.87	1.33	246	257	231	14.8	29%	73%	4.38	41	18	41	3.7	7.0	1.9	8%	0.9	5.0	44	$7
Consist	B	1st Half		1	1	0	17	10	3.92	1.38	221			14.8	22%	76%	4.18				5.2	5.0	1.0		1.3	1.1	22	$1
LIMA Plan	C+	2nd Half		4	2	0	53	44	3.86	1.32	253			14.8	31%	72%	4.10	41	18	41	3.3	7.6	2.3	7%	0.8	3.9	68	$5
Rand Var	-1	10	Proj	5	4	0	80	64	4.06	1.38	258			14.3	30%	73%	4.25	40	21	38	3.6	7.2	2.0	10%	1.0	1.9	51	$7

Struggled with shoulder and rib cage injuries at beginning of season. As long as he remains consistently inconsistent as SP (50% / 40% PQS split), he'll be relegated to swing-man role. 2H Cmd a positive sign, though.

Ni,Fu-Te

		Yr	Tm	W	L	Sv	IP	K	ERA	WHIP	OBA	vL	vR	BF/G	H%	S%	xERA	G	L	F	Ctl	Dom	Cmd	hr/f	hr/9	RAR	BPV	R$
LH	Reliever	05		0	0	0	0	0	0.00	0.00							0.00											
Age	27	06		0	0	0	0	0	0.00	0.00							0.00											
Type	xFB	07	TWN	7	12	4	122	119	4.40	1.34	257			11.8	29%	75%	5.18				3.3	8.7	2.7		1.8	1.0	57	$12
Health	A	08	TWN	5	12	0	145	125	4.16	1.56	308			26.0	37%	75%	5.55				2.7	7.8	2.9		0.9	2.6	73	$6
PT/Exp	B	09	DET *	3	0	0	65	47	3.11	1.21	241	115	289	4.5	27%	80%	4.70	32	13	55	2.8	6.5	2.3	8%	1.1	10.8	52	$7
Consist	B	1st Half		3	0	0	36	30	3.57	1.36	282			6.0	32%	81%	4.78	20	20	60	2.3	7.5	3.3	9%	1.5	3.9	71	$4
LIMA Plan	B	2nd Half		0	0	0	29	17	2.52	1.01	182			3.4	20%	78%	4.87	33	13	55	3.5	5.3	1.5	4%	0.6	6.8	13	$3
Rand Var	-5	10	Proj	2	3	0	58	43	4.19	1.40	275			7.2	31%	75%	4.89	33	13	55	2.9	6.7	2.3	9%	1.4	-3.2	51	$4

0-0, 2.61 ERA in 31 IP at DET. Murdered LH batters (.466 OPS against); not so against RHB (.791). Unfortunately, you pay for both. Declining Dom trend worrisome, and xERA says expect closer to 5.00 than 3.00.

Nolasco,Ricky

		Yr	Tm	W	L	Sv	IP	K	ERA	WHIP	OBA	vL	vR	BF/G	H%	S%	xERA	G	L	F	Ctl	Dom	Cmd	hr/f	hr/9	RAR	BPV	R$
RH	Starter	05	aa	1	3	0	161	152	3.74	1.41	281			25.8	35%	76%	4.72				2.7	8.5	3.1		0.9	11.2	86	$9
Age	27	06	FLA	11	11	0	140	99	4.82	1.41	285	338	240	17.3	32%	69%	4.46	39	21	40	2.6	6.4	2.4	11%	1.3	-5.8	60	$9
Type	Pwr FB	07	FLA *	1	5	0	39	26	10.18	1.96	361	293	350	19.2	39%	48%	5.43	37	19	44	3.3	6.0	1.8	14%	2.1	-28.0	35	($6)
Health	C	08	FLA	15	8	0	212	186	3.52	1.10	243	238	239	25.1	28%	73%	3.57	39	19	42	1.8	7.9	4.4	11%	1.2	19.7	111	$25
PT/Exp	B	09	FLA	13	9	0	185	195	5.06	1.25	265	251	268	24.9	34%	61%	3.33	38	22	40	2.1	9.5	4.4	11%	1.1	-19.8	129	$15
Consist	C	1st Half		5	6	0	76	70	6.02	1.46	302			23.8	36%	59%	3.95	35	23	43	2.1	8.3	3.9	10%	1.2	-17.2	104	$2
LIMA Plan	B+	2nd Half		8	3	0	109	125	4.38	1.11	236			25.8	31%	63%	2.91	41	21	37	2.2	10.3	4.8	13%	1.1	-2.6	148	$12
Rand Var	+5	10	Proj	15	9	0	203	204	3.81	1.20	254			22.6	31%	72%	3.42	38	21	41	2.1	9.0	4.3	11%	1.2	21.2	122	$22

Pummeled by unfavorable H% and S%, but BPIs were better in almost every way than '08. And he was stupendous in 2H, with an 86% / 14% PQS split in 17 GS. Avoided another IP spike, lessening that worry. Buy!

Norris,Bud

		Yr	Tm	W	L	Sv	IP	K	ERA	WHIP	OBA	vL	vR	BF/G	H%	S%	xERA	G	L	F	Ctl	Dom	Cmd	hr/f	hr/9	RAR	BPV	R$
RH	Starter	05		0	0	0	0	0	0.00	0.00							0.00											
Age	25	06		0	0	0	0	0	0.00	0.00							0.00											
Type	Pwr FB	07		0	0	0	0	0	0.00	0.00							0.00											
Health	A	08	aa	3	8	0	80	70	4.29	1.59	300			19.0	36%	75%	5.50				3.4	7.9	2.3		0.9	0.1	63	$3
PT/Exp	D	09	HOU *	10	12	0	176	151	3.64	1.47	265	200	323	25.7	32%	77%	4.42	37	20	43	4.0	7.7	1.9	7%	0.8	12.0	45	$12
Consist	C	1st Half		3	6	0	93	79	3.10	1.48	262			27.3	32%	81%	4.42				4.4	7.6	1.8		0.7	12.5	65	$6
LIMA Plan	C+	2nd Half		7	6	0	83	72	4.24	1.45	269			24.1	32%	73%	4.31	37	20	43	3.7	7.8	2.1	9%	1.0	-0.6	56	$6
Rand Var	-2	10	Proj	8	12	0	149	129	4.17	1.42	262			21.5	31%	73%	4.31	37	20	43	3.7	7.8	2.1	9%	1.0	-0.9	54	$9

6-3, 4.53 in 55 IP at HOU. Huge workload increase raises concerns, as does lack of improvement in Ctl. Only has two good pitches, so he either develops third or moves to 'pen. Expect some growing pains.

Nunez,Leo

		Yr	Tm	W	L	Sv	IP	K	ERA	WHIP	OBA	vL	vR	BF/G	H%	S%	xERA	G	L	F	Ctl	Dom	Cmd	hr/f	hr/9	RAR	BPV	R$
RH	Reliever	05	KC *	4	2	4	66	44	6.53	1.59	308	374	298	5.6	34%	61%	4.80	37	21	42	3.0	6.0	2.0	12%	1.5	-17.6	42	$1
Age	26	06	KC *	3	4	8	72	55	3.62	1.44	272	211	355	7.0	31%	79%	4.12	41	30	30	3.5	6.9	2.0	14%	1.1	8.3	48	$8
Type	FB	07	KC *	4	6	0	87	64	3.17	1.11	236	275	248	14.6	26%	78%	4.24	32	19	49	2.1	6.6	3.1	10%	1.3	14.3	71	$11
Health	D	08	KC	4	1	0	48	26	2.98	1.24	248	272	230	4.5	28%	76%	4.66	39	18	43	2.8	4.8	1.7	3%	0.4	8.1	29	$6
PT/Exp	C	09	FLA	4	6	26	69	60	4.06	1.25	233	234	225	3.8	26%	75%	4.02	41	15	44	3.5	7.9	2.2	15%	1.7	1.1	65	$14
Consist	B	1st Half		2	3	4	35	33	3.86	1.23	215			3.6	25%	74%	3.87	42	16	41	4.1	8.5	2.1	13%	1.3	1.4	62	$5
LIMA Plan	C	2nd Half		2	3	22	34	27	4.27	1.28	252			4.0	26%	77%	4.18	40	14	46	2.9	7.2	2.5	17%	2.1	-0.3	68	$10
Rand Var	0	10	Proj	4	5	10	73	56	3.97	1.34	260			4.8	29%	75%	4.32	39	17	44	3.1	7.0	2.2	10%	1.2	-0.5	59	$9

Would you want to roster him without the 26 saves from last year? xERA has yet to crack 4.00, even in years when he's healthy. Hard thrower should have better hr/f luck next year, but doesn't own closer's skills.

JOSHUA RANDALL

O'Day,Darren

		Yr	W	L	Sv	IP	K	ERA	WHIP	OBA	vL	vR	BF/G	H%	S%	xERA	G	L	F	Ctl	Dom	Cmd	hr/f	hr/9	RAR	BPV	R$
RH	Reliever	05	0	0	0	0	0	0.00	0.00							0.00											
Age	27	06	0	0	0	0	0	0.00	0.00							0.00											
Type	Pwr	07 aa	3	4	10	29	18	5.21	1.66	291			4.6	32%	70%	5.74				4.6	5.6	**1.2**		1.0	-2.7	27	$4
Health	B	08 LAA *	2	3	7	76	52	4.43	1.41	285	275	290	6.5	33%	68%	3.73	55	17	28	2.6	6.2	**2.4**	8%	0.6	-0.8	75	$6
PT/Exp	D	09 2TM	2	1	2	59	56	1.84	1.01	199	239	180	3.4	26%	84%	3.43	41	17	42	2.8	8.6	**3.1**	5%	0.5	17.9	99	$10
Consist	C	1st Half	2	0	1	28	27	1.28	1.03	209			3.5	26%	96%	3.45	41	16	43	2.6	8.6	**3.4**	9%	1.0	10.5	105	$6
LIMA Plan	B+	2nd Half	0	1	1	31	29	2.35	0.98	188			3.3	26%	73%	3.40	42	18	41	2.9	8.5	**2.9**	0%	0.0	7.4	94	$4
Rand Var	-5	10 Proj	**4**	**4**	**3**	**65**	**55**	**3.59**	**1.21**	**243**			**4.3**	**29%**	**73%**	**3.70**	**46**	**17**	**37**	**2.8**	**7.6**	**2.8**	**9%**	**0.8**	**5.2**	**86**	**$8**

Nice end-gamer, but that's it:
PRO: Love 3.0+ Cmd!
CON: Sidearmers (due to platoon splits) rarely become closers, has partially torn labrum in his history, xERA tells us not to get too excited.

O'Flaherty,Eric

		Yr	W	L	Sv	IP	K	ERA	WHIP	OBA	vL	vR	BF/G	H%	S%	xERA	G	L	F	Ctl	Dom	Cmd	hr/f	hr/9	RAR	BPV	R$
LH	Reliever	05	0	0	0	0	0	0.00	0.00							0.00											
Age	25	06 SEA *	3	2	7	54	44	1.83	1.52	283			5.7	35%	89%	4.37				3.7	7.3	**2.0**		0.3	18.1	74	$9
Type	GB	07 SEA	7	1	0	52	36	4.47	1.24	234	183	277	3.9	28%	61%	4.25	45	18	37	3.4	6.2	**1.8**	2%	0.2	0.2	41	$7
Health	A	08 SEA *	1	1	2	25	23	9.00	2.24	373			5.9	45%	58%	8.59				5.0	8.3	**1.6**		1.1	-14.3	32	($3)
PT/Exp	D	09 ATL	2	1	0	56	39	3.04	1.24	247	215	282	3.0	29%	75%	3.59	55	17	28	2.9	6.2	**2.2**	4%	0.3	8.0	68	$5
Consist	F	1st Half	1	1	0	29	16	3.72	1.14	241			2.9	28%	66%	3.88	51	16	33	2.2	5.0	**2.3**	3%	0.3	1.7	60	$2
LIMA Plan	B	2nd Half	1	0	0	27	23	2.31	1.36	252			3.2	32%	83%	3.21	60	18	22	3.6	7.6	**2.1**	6%	0.3	6.3	77	$3
Rand Var	-2	10 Proj	**4**	**1**	**0**	**58**	**42**	**3.41**	**1.29**	**248**			**3.6**	**29%**	**75%**	**3.83**	**52**	**18**	**31**	**3.3**	**6.5**	**2.0**	**7%**	**0.6**	**3.1**	**59**	**$6**

Extreme groundballer who can thrive with Dom of "only" 6.0, especially when he faces RHB only half of the time. Got lucky in one respect last year:
2008: 2 HR in 7 IP (in majors)
2009: 2 HR in 56 IP

O'Sullivan,Sean

		Yr	W	L	Sv	IP	K	ERA	WHIP	OBA	vL	vR	BF/G	H%	S%	xERA	G	L	F	Ctl	Dom	Cmd	hr/f	hr/9	RAR	BPV	R$
RH	Starter	05	0	0	0	0	0	0.00	0.00							0.00											
Age	22	06	0	0	0	0	0	0.00	0.00							0.00											
Type	Con FB	07	0	0	0	0	0	0.00	0.00							0.00											
Health	A	08	0	0	0	0	0	0.00	0.00							0.00											
PT/Exp	F	09 LAA *	11	8	0	139	81	6.22	1.45	299	263	324	21.0	32%	59%	4.84	37	20	44	2.3	5.2	**2.3**	11%	1.4	-30.3	48	$4
Consist	F	1st Half	8	4	0	86	54	6.07	1.50	310			23.8	34%	60%	4.85	38	15	47	2.1	5.7	**2.7**	8%	1.2	-17.2	61	$3
LIMA Plan	C+	2nd Half	3	4	0	53	27	6.46	1.38	280			17.5	28%	56%	4.95	36	22	42	2.6	4.6	**1.8**	14%	1.9	-13.1	28	$1
Rand Var	+5	10 Proj	**4**	**4**	**0**	**58**	**32**	**4.97**	**1.43**	**294**			**19.4**	**31%**	**70%**	**4.86**	**36**	**21**	**43**	**2.3**	**5.0**	**2.1**	**12%**	**1.6**	**-3.0**	**41**	**$3**

4-2, 5.92 ERA in 52 IP at LAA. Let's recap his 2009 season: 5.30 ERA in AA, 5.48 in AAA, then 5.92 in majors. Next promotion, Mars? A RHP who throws only 90 mph needs time to develop other pitches.

Ohka,Tomo

		Yr	W	L	Sv	IP	K	ERA	WHIP	OBA	vL	vR	BF/G	H%	S%	xERA	G	L	F	Ctl	Dom	Cmd	hr/f	hr/9	RAR	BPV	R$
RH	Starter	05 2NL	11	9	0	180	98	4.05	1.35	271	258	277	24.1	29%	73%	4.50	42	22	37	2.7	4.9	**1.8**	10%	1.1	4.4	34	$11
Age	34	06 MIL	4	5	0	97	50	4.82	1.37	264	265	266	23.1	28%	67%	4.99	39	21	40	3.2	4.6	**1.4**	9%	1.1	-4.0	13	$4
Type	Con FB	07 TOR *	2	10	0	97	33	8.47	1.97	360	376	348	27.9	36%	58%	5.91	44	20	36	3.5	3.1	**0.9**	14%	1.8	-47.4	-16	($11)
Health	B	08 aaa	5	11	0	135	95	5.75	1.63	323			22.0	34%	72%	7.30				2.5	6.3	**2.5**		2.2	-24.0	14	($0)
PT/Exp	D	09 CLE *	4	8	0	123	54	5.28	1.37	287	256	299	19.6	28%	67%	5.08	38	17	45	2.1	3.9	**1.9**	12%	1.8	-12.6	31	$3
Consist	D	1st Half	3	5	0	79	32	4.92	1.45	301			24.7	30%	70%	4.96	44	17	39	2.1	3.6	**1.7**	12%	1.5	-4.5	30	$2
LIMA Plan	C+	2nd Half	1	3	0	44	22	5.93	1.23	262			14.0	24%	58%	4.91	34	17	49	2.0	4.5	**2.2**	15%	2.2	-8.0	38	$1
Rand Var	+1	10 Proj	**1**	**3**	**0**	**44**	**22**	**5.17**	**1.49**	**302**			**19.2**	**31%**	**69%**	**5.00**	**39**	**19**	**42**	**2.5**	**4.6**	**1.8**	**11%**	**1.4**	**-3.0**	**32**	**$0**

1-5, 5.96 ERA in 71 IP at CLE. Chronic gopheritis for three years makes him unrosterable. That's not just bad luck: in 18 games in CLE last year, gave up more FB than GB 17 times, plus he strikes out few batters.

Ohlendorf,Ross

		Yr	W	L	Sv	IP	K	ERA	WHIP	OBA	vL	vR	BF/G	H%	S%	xERA	G	L	F	Ctl	Dom	Cmd	hr/f	hr/9	RAR	BPV	R$
RH	Starter	05	0	0	0	0	0	0.00	0.00							0.00											
Age	27	06 a/a	10	8	0	182	111	4.33	1.40	305			28.1	34%	70%	5.07				1.5	5.5	**3.7**		0.8	4.3	80	$11
Type	FB	07 aaa	3	4	0	68	41	6.67	1.93	356			15.0	39%	66%	7.80				3.3	5.4	**1.6**		1.2	-18.6	14	($4)
Health	A	08 2TM *	6	8	0	132	98	5.66	1.72	327	370	273	14.5	37%	69%	4.40	43	24	33	3.1	6.7	**2.1**	12%	1.2	-21.9	58	($1)
PT/Exp	C	09 PIT	11	10	0	177	109	3.92	1.23	249	286	221	25.3	26%	73%	4.39	41	17	42	2.7	5.6	**2.1**	11%	1.3	5.8	46	$14
Consist	D	1st Half	7	6	0	96	52	4.41	1.24	258			25.0	27%	69%	4.34	43	19	38	2.3	4.9	**2.1**	12%	1.3	-2.6	46	$7
LIMA Plan	D+	2nd Half	4	4	0	81	57	3.35	1.23	238			25.7	26%	78%	4.46	37	16	47	3.1	6.4	**2.0**	10%	1.2	8.4	45	$7
Rand Var	-2	10 Proj	**9**	**10**	**0**	**174**	**116**	**4.50**	**1.39**	**276**			**25.9**	**30%**	**71%**	**4.46**	**41**	**19**	**41**	**2.8**	**6.0**	**2.1**	**10%**	**1.2**	**-4.3**	**50**	**$9**

Huge reversal of fortune for H% was the big story for 2009. Might grow a bit in his 2nd full season as MLB starter given 2H Dom, prior GB% tendencies. But he's likely a year too soon to target.

Okajima,Hideki

		Yr	W	L	Sv	IP	K	ERA	WHIP	OBA	vL	vR	BF/G	H%	S%	xERA	G	L	F	Ctl	Dom	Cmd	hr/f	hr/9	RAR	BPV	R$
LH	Reliever	05 JPN	1	0	0	53	53	6.54	1.56	283			5.7	31%	67%	6.96				4.0	9.0	**2.3**		2.8	-14.6	15	($1)
Age	34	06 JPN	2	2	4	55	60	2.85	1.21	241			4.1	30%	84%	4.09				2.8	9.8	**3.4**		1.4	11.4	97	$8
Type	Pwr xFB	07 BOS	3	2	5	69	63	2.22	0.97	204	236	182	4.1	25%	82%	3.34	45	15	41	2.2	8.2	**3.7**	8%	0.8	19.5	111	$13
Health	A	08 BOS	3	2	1	62	60	2.61	1.16	219	184	234	4.0	27%	82%	3.88	32	20	48	3.3	8.7	**2.6**	8%	0.9	13.3	77	$9
PT/Exp	C	09 BOS	6	0	0	61	53	3.39	1.26	246	167	309	3.8	29%	78%	4.45	30	16	54	3.1	7.8	**2.5**	8%	1.2	8.0	66	$8
Consist	B	1st Half	3	0	0	34	36	3.44	1.12	213			3.8	27%	74%	3.98	27	14	59	3.2	9.5	**3.0**	8%	1.1	4.2	91	$5
LIMA Plan	C+	2nd Half	3	0	0	27	17	3.33	1.44	283			3.7	31%	83%	5.07	34	17	49	3.0	5.7	**1.9**	9%	1.3	3.7	33	$3
Rand Var	-3	10 Proj	**4**	**1**	**0**	**58**	**49**	**3.88**	**1.29**	**252**			**4.0**	**30%**	**74%**	**4.36**	**34**	**17**	**49**	**3.1**	**7.6**	**2.5**	**8%**	**1.1**	**0.6**	**65**	**$6**

Evolving from LIMA reliever to generic LHP. RHB clobbered him for a .901 OPS in 2009. xERA trend, especially 2H spike, looks ominous. Let others pay for his ERA history: he's not a safe pick anymore.

Oliver,Darren

		Yr	W	L	Sv	IP	K	ERA	WHIP	OBA	vL	vR	BF/G	H%	S%	xERA	G	L	F	Ctl	Dom	Cmd	hr/f	hr/9	RAR	BPV	R$
LH	Reliever	05 aaa	1	3	0	31	15	10.93	2.50	441			24.1	46%	56%	11.58				2.4	4.4	**1.8**		1.8	-25.5	-24	($7)
Age	39	06 NYM	4	1	0	81	60	3.44	1.12	235	208	244	7.3	25%	77%	3.72	48	17	35	2.3	6.7	**2.9**	16%	1.4	10.4	83	$9
Type		07 LAA	3	1	0	64	51	3.78	1.26	242	289	209	4.4	29%	71%	4.01	48	12	40	3.2	7.1	**2.2**	7%	0.7	5.8	68	$6
Health	A	08 LAA	7	1	0	72	48	2.88	1.15	248	229	271	5.4	29%	77%	3.82	47	16	37	2.0	6.0	**3.0**	6%	0.6	13.1	79	$10
PT/Exp	C	09 LAA	5	1	0	73	65	2.71	1.14	229	263	217	4.7	28%	78%	3.67	44	14	41	2.7	8.0	**3.0**	6%	0.6	15.7	93	$11
Consist	A	1st Half	2	0	0	34	23	2.91	1.32	262			5.5	31%	79%	4.36	44	15	40	2.9	6.1	**2.1**	5%	0.5	6.5	53	$4
LIMA Plan	C+	2nd Half	3	1	0	39	42	2.54	0.97	197			4.1	26%	77%	3.11	44	14	42	2.5	9.7	**3.8**	8%	0.7	9.2	128	$7
Rand Var	-3	10 Proj	**2**	**3**	**0**	**58**	**44**	**3.57**	**1.29**	**255**			**5.2**	**29%**	**75%**	**4.07**	**46**	**15**	**39**	**2.9**	**6.8**	**2.3**	**9%**	**0.9**	**2.6**	**67**	**$5**

Big Dom increase in 2H led to him being used in high pressure situations. If that sticks, wins and occasional saves would be his... if he was 10 years younger. But the odds of him maintaining these elite level skills is remote.

Olsen,Scott

		Yr	W	L	Sv	IP	K	ERA	WHIP	OBA	vL	vR	BF/G	H%	S%	xERA	G	L	F	Ctl	Dom	Cmd	hr/f	hr/9	RAR	BPV	R$
LH	Starter	05 FLA *	7	5	0	100	106	4.68	1.47	277	333	238	23.1	35%	70%	3.85	41	14	45	3.5	9.5	**2.7**	9%	1.1	-5.3	96	$6
Age	26	06 FLA	12	10	0	180	166	4.05	1.30	239	182	255	24.6	29%	73%	3.88	45	18	37	3.7	8.3	**2.2**	12%	1.1	9.8	71	$17
Type	Pwr FB	07 FLA	10	15	0	177	133	5.81	1.76	312	331	311	25.1	35%	70%	5.03	38	24	39	4.3	6.8	**1.6**	13%	1.5	-30.1	21	($1)
Health	F	08 FLA	8	11	0	202	113	4.19	1.31	255	187	266	25.8	27%	73%	4.78	37	20	42	3.1	5.0	**1.6**	11%	1.3	1.9	23	$11
PT/Exp	A	09 WAS	2	4	0	63	42	6.03	1.72	319	309	324	26.5	35%	68%	5.04	37	22	41	3.6	6.0	**1.7**	12%	1.6	-14.2	26	($2)
Consist	A	1st Half	1	4	0	48	36	6.56	1.75	328			24.9	37%	64%	4.84	35	24	41	3.4	6.8	**2.0**	12%	1.5	-14.0	43	($3)
LIMA Plan	D	2nd Half	1	0	0	15	6	4.29	1.63	291			33.5	28%	81%	5.69	42	16	42	4.3	3.7	**0.9**	14%	1.8	-0.2	-30	$0
Rand Var	+4	10 Proj	**6**	**9**	**0**	**131**	**100**	**4.76**	**1.49**	**278**			**24.0**	**32%**	**71%**	**4.55**	**39**	**20**	**41**	**3.7**	**6.9**	**1.9**	**11%**	**1.2**	**-4.7**	**42**	**$4**

Reasons to avoid for 2010:
- Labrum surgery in July
- 2006 was a long time ago.

Reasons for a reserve pick:
- Bum shoulder might explain loss of velocity in '08 & '09
- Was good once upon a time.

Olson,Garrett

		Yr	W	L	Sv	IP	K	ERA	WHIP	OBA	vL	vR	BF/G	H%	S%	xERA	G	L	F	Ctl	Dom	Cmd	hr/f	hr/9	RAR	BPV	R$
LH	Reliever	05	0	0	0	0	0	0.00	0.00							0.00											
Age	26	06 aa	6	5	0	84	76	4.71	1.51	286			26.6	36%	69%	4.85				3.4	8.1	**2.4**		0.6	-2.0	77	$5
Type	Pwr FB	07 BAL *	10	10	0	160	133	5.11	1.42	260			24.0	30%	66%	4.68	34	17	49	3.8	7.5	**2.0**	9%	1.2	-11.9	43	$10
Health	A	08 BAL *	10	12	0	169	117	5.97	1.69	304	310	309	23.6	35%	65%	4.91	42	19	39	4.1	6.2	**1.5**	8%	1.0	-33.8	21	$0
PT/Exp	C	09 SEA *	5	8	0	127	80	5.43	1.39	251	275	251	13.7	26%	64%	5.16	34	19	47	4.0	5.7	**1.4**	11%	1.5	-15.3	5	$4
Consist	A	1st Half	5	4	0	74	42	4.27	1.15	221			15.9	22%	68%	5.03	30	17	53	3.2	5.1	**1.6**	9%	1.3	1.6	15	$7
LIMA Plan	C	2nd Half	0	4	0	53	37	7.04	1.72	289			11.7	31%	61%	5.24	39	23	38	5.1	6.4	**1.2**	15%	1.7	-16.9	-7	($3)
Rand Var	0	10 Proj	**4**	**5**	**0**	**82**	**58**	**5.08**	**1.50**	**272**			**10.9**	**30%**	**68%**	**4.83**	**38**	**20**	**42**	**4.0**	**6.4**	**1.6**	**10%**	**1.2**	**-3.9**	**24**	**$3**

3-5, 5.60 ERA in 80 IP at SEA. "Common wisdom" states that lefties take longer to mature than righties. "Common wisdom" also states that you have to wait at least an hour after a meal before you can go swimming.

MICHAEL WEDDELL

Ortiz,Russ

		Yr	Tm	W	L	Sv	IP	K	ERA	WHIP	OBA	vL	vR	BF/G	H%	S%	xERA	G	L	F	Ctl	Dom	Cmd	hr/f	hr/9	RAR	BPV	R$
RH	Starter	05	ARI	5	11	0	115	46	6.89	1.84	312	329	296	24.9	32%	64%	6.09	37	26	37	5.1	3.6	0.7	11%	1.4	-37.5	-58	($8)
Age	35	06	2TM *	1	8	0	83	53	6.96	1.89	324	378	299	13.4	34%	67%	5.67	37	24	39	4.9	5.7	1.2	17%	2.1	-25.1	-15	($6)
Type	Pwr	07	SF *	3	4	0	65	36	5.28	1.54	298	346	259	17.1	33%	65%	4.82	42	22	35	3.1	4.9	1.6	7%	0.7	-6.9	25	$1
Health	F	08		0	0	0	0	0	0.00	0.00							0.00											
PT/Exp	D	09	HOU *	5	8	0	117	82	5.31	1.68	284	272	305	18.5	33%	69%	4.64	48	22	30	5.0	6.3	1.3	10%	0.9	-16.1	5	($1)
Consist	A	1st Half		3	3	0	64	47	3.37	1.45	252			15.6	29%	79%	4.28	48	21	31	4.5	6.6	1.5	10%	0.8	6.5	23	$4
LIMA Plan	F	2nd Half		2	5	0	53	35	7.66	1.95	320			23.3	36%	59%	4.98	49	26	26	5.6	6.0	1.1	11%	0.9	-22.5	-17	($5)
Rand Var	+1	10	Proj	2	3	0	44	27	5.79	1.77	302			18.5	33%	68%	5.19	43	24	33	5.0	5.6	1.1	10%	1.0	-5.0	-13	($1)

3-6, 5.57 ERA in 85 IP at HOU. Returned from '08 TJS, but needn't have bothered. From the moment he reached AA-ball in 1996. he has never achieved a 2.0 Cmd ratio. Never.

Oswalt,Roy

		Yr	Tm	W	L	Sv	IP	K	ERA	WHIP	OBA	vL	vR	BF/G	H%	S%	xERA	G	L	F	Ctl	Dom	Cmd	hr/f	hr/9	RAR	BPV	R$
RH	Starter	05	HOU	20	12	0	241	184	2.95	1.21	263	279	247	28.4	31%	78%	3.35	49	22	29	1.8	6.9	3.8	8%	0.7	38.6	102	$29
Age	32	06	HOU	15	8	0	220	166	2.98	1.17	262	264	262	27.3	31%	77%	3.47	49	20	31	1.6	6.8	4.4	9%	0.7	40.8	107	$27
Type		07	HOU	14	7	0	212	154	3.18	1.33	270	272	259	27.3	32%	77%	3.75	53	16	31	2.5	6.5	2.6	7%	0.6	32.5	80	$21
Health	B	08	HOU	17	10	0	209	165	3.54	1.18	253	262	243	26.7	29%	74%	3.33	50	20	29	2.0	7.1	3.5	13%	1.0	18.9	102	$23
PT/Exp	A	09	HOU	8	6	0	181	138	4.12	1.24	264	279	252	25.1	31%	69%	3.73	43	21	36	2.1	6.9	3.3	10%	0.9	1.6	88	$13
Consist	A	1st Half		4	4	0	105	83	4.02	1.30	265			26.1	31%	73%	3.93	40	22	38	2.6	7.1	2.8	11%	1.1	2.1	77	$7
LIMA Plan	B	2nd Half		4	2	0	76	55	4.25	1.15	261			23.9	30%	63%	3.46	48	20	33	1.4	6.5	4.6	8%	0.7	-0.6	104	$6
Rand Var	0	10	Proj	12	7	0	198	144	3.74	1.25	261			25.7	30%	73%	3.69	48	20	32	2.2	6.6	2.9	10%	0.9	14.0	84	$17

Can he return to $20+ form? PRO: Unusually high 1H FB% reverted in 2H, Dom unchanged year-over-year, excellent Ctl CON: 2H Dom slip, herniated disk (opted out of surgery) VERDICT: Not quite.

Outman,Josh

		Yr	Tm	W	L	Sv	IP	K	ERA	WHIP	OBA	vL	vR	BF/G	H%	S%	xERA	G	L	F	Ctl	Dom	Cmd	hr/f	hr/9	RAR	BPV	R$
LH	Starter	05		0	0	0	0	0	0.00	0.00							0.00											
Age	25	06		0	0	0	0	0	0.00	0.00							0.00											
Type	Pwr FB	07	aa	2	3	0	42	28	5.52	1.62	272			27.2	30%	68%	5.67				5.1	6.0	1.2		1.3	-5.5	22	$0
Health	D	08	OAK *	8	6	1	124	89	3.69	1.49	278			11.4	33%	75%	4.30				3.6	6.5	1.8		0.4	10.1	64	$9
PT/Exp	D	09	OAK	4	1	0	67	53	3.48	1.16	218	123	238	19.6	24%	75%	4.19	38	19	43	3.3	7.1	2.1	11%	1.2	8.1	53	$8
Consist	B	1st Half		4	1	0	67	53	3.49	1.16	219			19.6	24%	75%	4.19	38	19	43	3.4	7.1	2.1	11%	1.2	8.0	53	$8
LIMA Plan	D+	2nd Half		0	0	0	0	0	0.00	0.00							0.00											
Rand Var	-3	10	Proj	1	1	0	15	11	4.34	1.45	255			21.1	29%	74%	4.76	38	19	43	4.3	6.8	1.6	11%	1.2	-0.6	21	$1

Ctl, Dom, and xERA improving, though PQS split of 50/33% (in 12 GS) shows dangers of young pitchers. Tore UCL June 19, had TJS late June, and may miss all of '10. He's one to tuck away for next season.

Owings,Micah

		Yr	Tm	W	L	Sv	IP	K	ERA	WHIP	OBA	vL	vR	BF/G	H%	S%	xERA	G	L	F	Ctl	Dom	Cmd	hr/f	hr/9	RAR	BPV	R$
RH	Starter	05		0	0	0	0	0	0.00	0.00							0.00											
Age	27	06	a/a	16	2	0	162	112	4.41	1.54	301			26.8	35%	71%	5.12				2.9	6.2	2.1		0.6	2.2	59	$12
Type	Pwr FB	07	ARI	8	8	0	153	106	4.30	1.28	253	265	240	22.1	28%	70%	4.44	37	20	42	2.9	6.2	2.1	10%	1.2	2.3	48	$11
Health	B	08	ARI	6	9	0	105	87	5.93	1.38	260	268	242	20.5	30%	58%	4.38	34	23	43	3.5	7.5	2.1	10%	1.2	-21.5	51	$3
PT/Exp	B	09	CIN	7	12	1	120	68	5.34	1.59	272	272	271	20.8	29%	69%	5.45	37	21	42	4.8	5.1	1.1	11%	1.4	-17.0	-23	$1
Consist	B	1st Half		5	8	0	83	50	4.65	1.56	273			24.9	29%	74%	5.17	40	19	41	4.5	5.4	1.2	11%	1.3	-4.7	-7	$2
LIMA Plan	C	2nd Half		2	4	1	37	18	6.90	1.64	270			15.1	27%	59%	6.10	29	26	45	5.4	4.4	0.8	11%	1.5	-12.2	-60	($1)
Rand Var	0	10	Proj	7	10	0	116	75	5.20	1.56	272			20.0	30%	69%	5.26	34	23	43	4.6	5.8	1.3	10%	1.2	-14.3	-7	$2

Any chance of a rebound was quashed by even worse Ctl than in '08. Shoulder tightness in late July and perforated ear-drum in Sept (HBP in head) raise injury warning flag. 47% PQS DIS is nail in coffin.

Padilla,Vicente

		Yr	Tm	W	L	Sv	IP	K	ERA	WHIP	OBA	vL	vR	BF/G	H%	S%	xERA	G	L	F	Ctl	Dom	Cmd	hr/f	hr/9	RAR	BPV	R$
RH	Starter	05	PHI	9	12	0	147	103	4.71	1.50	260	297	222	24.0	28%	72%	4.47	46	22	32	4.5	6.3	1.4	15%	1.3	-8.5	15	$6
Age	32	06	TEX	15	10	0	200	156	4.50	1.38	268	305	228	26.1	31%	69%	4.05	44	22	34	3.2	7.0	2.2	10%	0.9	1.4	63	$17
Type		07	TEX	6	10	0	120	71	5.76	1.63	301	329	271	23.8	33%	66%	4.84	46	21	34	3.7	5.3	1.4	11%	1.2	-18.6	18	$1
Health	C	08	TEX	14	8	0	171	127	4.74	1.46	277	312	240	25.8	31%	71%	4.35	43	19	38	3.4	6.7	2.0	13%	1.4	-8.2	49	$11
PT/Exp	A	09	2TM	12	6	0	147	97	4.46	1.43	273	303	246	24.6	31%	71%	4.22	48	20	32	3.3	5.9	1.8	11%	1.0	-2.7	44	$10
Consist	A	1st Half		6	4	0	83	45	4.77	1.52	273			26.3	30%	69%	4.70	50	20	31	4.1	4.9	1.2	8%	0.8	-4.6	4	$3
LIMA Plan	C	2nd Half		6	2	0	64	52	4.07	1.31	273			22.6	31%	73%	3.65	47	20	34	2.2	7.3	3.3	14%	1.3	2.0	95	$6
Rand Var	0	10	Proj	11	9	0	160	112	4.40	1.45	278			24.9	31%	73%	4.25	46	20	34	3.3	6.3	1.9	11%	1.1	1.7	49	$10

Season marred by shoulder strain in May, bruised hand early July, and swine flu late July. But he was excellent in 2H, with 7 DOM, 0 DIS in 11 GS. Color us skeptical. You might eke out some profit, if you dare.

Palmer,Matt

		Yr	Tm	W	L	Sv	IP	K	ERA	WHIP	OBA	vL	vR	BF/G	H%	S%	xERA	G	L	F	Ctl	Dom	Cmd	hr/f	hr/9	RAR	BPV	R$
RH	Reliever	05	aa	0	1	1	27	19	3.00	1.33	247			10.4	29%	79%	3.78				3.7	6.3	1.7		0.7	4.3	60	$2
Age	31	06	a/a	11	7	0	153	85	4.26	1.54	305			22.8	34%	74%	5.44				2.7	5.0	1.9		0.8	5.0	39	$8
Type	GB	07	aaa	11	8	0	155	69	6.75	1.91	346			25.0	36%	66%	7.76				3.8	4.0	1.1		1.4	-43.7	-9	($7)
Health	A	08	aaa	6	10	0	142	91	7.01	2.18	349			27.8	39%	67%	7.92				6.0	5.8	1.0		0.9	-47.4	12	($13)
PT/Exp	C	09	LAA	11	2	0	121	69	3.93	1.32	235	279	197	12.9	25%	72%	4.55	51	16	34	4.1	5.1	1.3	9%	0.9	7.8	11	$12
Consist	C	1st Half		7	1	0	68	42	5.02	1.42	259			22.8	29%	66%	4.73	46	17	37	4.0	5.6	1.4	9%	0.9	-4.8	16	$5
LIMA Plan	D	2nd Half		4	1	0	53	27	2.54	1.18	202			8.1	21%	83%	4.29	57	14	29	4.2	4.6	1.1	11%	0.8	12.6	3	$7
Rand Var	-3	10	Proj	4	2	0	58	32	4.81	1.62	288			15.5	31%	72%	4.87	52	15	32	4.3	5.0	1.1	11%	1.1	-3.1	3	$2

Was 6-0 on June 12, but 1.5 Cmd was a warning. 15 ER in next 16 IP got him demoted to pen, where he was worse (1.1 Cmd). Low H% obscured truth, but that's what xERA is for. Like The Who, don't get fooled again.

Papelbon,Jonathan

		Yr	Tm	W	L	Sv	IP	K	ERA	WHIP	OBA	vL	vR	BF/G	H%	S%	xERA	G	L	F	Ctl	Dom	Cmd	hr/f	hr/9	RAR	BPV	R$
RH	Reliever	05	BOS *	9	5	1	148	125	3.11	1.14	233	190	319	15.9	27%	77%	3.79	35	25	40	2.6	7.6	2.9	10%	1.0	23.0	79	$19
Age	29	06	BOS	4	2	35	68	75	0.93	0.78	172	203	128	4.3	24%	92%	2.89	37	17	46	1.7	9.9	5.8	4%	0.4	30.5	147	$28
Type	Pwr xFB	07	BOS	1	3	37	58	84	1.85	0.77	154	104	200	3.6	24%	83%	2.56	29	16	55	2.3	13.0	5.6	8%	0.8	19.1	178	$25
Health	A	08	BOS	5	4	41	69	77	2.34	0.95	229	235	210	4.0	31%	77%	2.43	49	20	31	1.0	10.0	9.6	7%	0.5	17.2	179	$26
PT/Exp	A	09	BOS	1	1	38	68	76	1.85	1.15	220	187	242	4.2	30%	88%	3.73	27	21	52	3.2	10.1	3.2	6%	0.7	21.8	100	$23
Consist	B	1st Half		1	1	20	35	34	1.80	1.34	233			4.3	29%	93%	4.41	30	21	49	4.4	8.7	2.0	9%	1.0	11.4	47	$11
LIMA Plan	C+	2nd Half		0	0	18	33	42	1.91	0.94	205			4.1	31%	80%	3.09	23	21	56	1.9	11.5	6.0	2%	0.3	10.4	155	$12
Rand Var	-5	10	Proj	2	2	38	58	66	2.64	1.07	220			4.3	30%	79%	3.29	33	20	47	2.5	10.2	4.1	7%	0.8	8.2	129	$21

Uncharacteristically poor Ctl in 1H; recovered in 2H, so this looks like a blip. But after a year of inducing GB, he turned back into a FB pitcher. That'll lead to more dingers if hr/f strays near 10%. He'll still be great, though.

Park,Chan Ho

		Yr	Tm	W	L	Sv	IP	K	ERA	WHIP	OBA	vL	vR	BF/G	H%	S%	xERA	G	L	F	Ctl	Dom	Cmd	hr/f	hr/9	RAR	BPV	R$
RH	Reliever	05	2TM	12	8	0	155	113	5.74	1.68	292	305	279	23.8	34%	65%	4.43	50	21	29	4.6	6.6	1.4	7%	0.6	-27.6	21	$2
Age	36	06	SD	7	7	0	136	96	4.82	1.40	275	266	278	24.5	30%	69%	4.35	44	18	38	2.9	6.3	2.2	12%	1.3	-5.6	57	$7
Type	Pwr	07	aa	6	14	0	135	86	8.38	1.97	365			27.5	38%	61%	9.29				3.1	5.7	1.8		2.4	-65.3	-18	($12)
Health	B	08	LA	4	4	2	95	79	3.40	1.40	265	301	237	7.6	31%	80%	3.73	51	19	30	3.4	7.5	2.2	14%	1.1	10.2	71	$8
PT/Exp	C	09	PHI	3	3	0	83	73	4.43	1.40	263	280	248	8.0	33%	68%	3.82	44	24	33	3.6	7.9	2.2	6%	0.5	-2.5	68	$4
Consist	F	1st Half		3	2	0	53	44	6.09	1.62	292			11.0	35%	62%	4.32	42	24	34	4.1	7.4	1.8	9%	0.8	-12.5	44	($0)
LIMA Plan	B	2nd Half		0	1	0	30	29	1.49	1.03	206			5.2	28%	84%	2.98	48	23	29	2.7	8.7	3.2	0%	0.0	10.0	109	$4
Rand Var	0	10	Proj	2	2	0	44	36	4.55	1.45	268			8.6	32%	69%	3.96	47	21	32	3.7	7.4	2.0	10%	0.8	1.6	58	$2

Starter or reliever?

	IP	ERA	Ctl	Dom
SP	33	7.29	4.6	5.7
RP	50	2.52	2.9	9.4

It's no contest. But he's 36, & he isn't a closer or closer-in-waiting, so value is limited regardless.

Parnell,Bobby

		Yr	Tm	W	L	Sv	IP	K	ERA	WHIP	OBA	vL	vR	BF/G	H%	S%	xERA	G	L	F	Ctl	Dom	Cmd	hr/f	hr/9	RAR	BPV	R$
RH	Reliever	05		0	0	0	0	0	0.00	0.00							0.00											
Age	25	06		0	0	0	0	0	0.00	0.00							0.00											
Type	Pwr	07	aa	5	5	0	89	62	5.63	1.70	311			24.2	36%	67%	6.12				3.9	6.3	1.6		0.9	-12.8	36	$0
Health	A	08	a/a	12	8	0	148	93	5.70	1.66	299			23.4	33%	66%	5.65				4.1	5.7	1.4		0.9	-25.4	31	$2
PT/Exp	D	09	NYM	4	8	1	88	74	5.30	1.66	289	270	290	6.0	35%	68%	4.50	47	16	37	4.7	7.5	1.6	8%	0.8	-12.1	34	$1
Consist	B	1st Half		2	3	0	29	24	5.26	1.96	339			3.6	41%	73%	5.17	38	19	43	4.6	7.4	1.6	5%	0.6	-3.8	24	($1)
LIMA Plan	C+	2nd Half		2	5	1	59	50	5.32	1.52	261			9.1	31%	65%	4.15	52	14	34	4.7	7.6	1.6	10%	0.9	-8.3	39	$1
Rand Var	+2	10	Proj	5	6	0	87	68	4.45	1.48	266			8.5	31%	73%	4.38	46	16	38	4.1	7.0	1.7	11%	1.1	-1.3	39	$4

If you're going to bet on a "one skill away" guy, hoping that a healthy hard thrower finds some Ctl is a decent gamble. Will need to earn his next audition as a starter after 7.93 ERA in 8 GS during 2008. Late reserve pick.

JOSHUA RANDALL

Parra,Manny

		Yr	Tm	W	L	Sv	IP	K	ERA	WHIP	OBA	vL	vR	BF/G	H%	S%	xERA	G	L	F	Ctl	Dom	Cmd	hr/f	hr/9	RAR	BPV	R$
LH	Starter	05	aa	5	6	0	91	75	4.55	1.58	324			25.6	40%	70%	5.33				2.1	7.4	3.6		0.4	-2.7	98	$4
Age	27	06	aa	3	0	0	31	25	4.18	1.36	273			22.2	35%	66%	3.61				2.7	7.3	2.7		0.0	1.3	101	$3
Type	Pwr	07	MIL	* 10	5	0	133	119	3.34	1.32	254	174	280	21.6	33%	74%	4.17	33	23	44	3.3	8.1	2.5	2%	0.3	17.8	68	$14
Health	A	08	MIL	10	8	0	166	147	4.39	1.54	279	233	288	23.1	34%	74%	3.74	52	22	27	4.1	8.0	2.0	13%	1.0	-2.5	63	$8
PT/Exp	C	09	MIL	* 12	13	0	164	132	5.93	1.75	299	287	311	24.8	35%	67%	4.59	48	18	34	5.0	7.3	1.5	11%	1.0	-35.3	23	($1)
Consist	B	1st Half		4	10	0	88	71	6.44	1.76	289			24.4	34%	63%	4.82	47	17	36	5.5	7.3	1.3	9%	0.9	-24.6	7	($3)
LIMA Plan	C+	2nd Half		8	3	0	76	61	5.34	1.74	310			25.2	36%	71%	4.36	49	19	32	4.3	7.2	1.7	13%	1.2	-10.8	42	$2
Rand Var	+4	10	Proj	12	9	0	160	134	4.63	1.52	278			23.6	33%	71%	3.98	49	20	31	3.9	7.6	1.9	10%	0.8	5.5	57	$8

11-11, 6.36 ERA in 140 IP at MIL. The best we can do is blame his shoulder, even though it was never bad enough for the DL. There is huge talent here, but BPI trends are frightening. Dare you to resist when $1 is tossed.

Paulino,Felipe

		Yr	Tm	W	L	Sv	IP	K	ERA	WHIP	OBA	vL	vR	BF/G	H%	S%	xERA	G	L	F	Ctl	Dom	Cmd	hr/f	hr/9	RAR	BPV	R$
RH	Starter	05		0	0	0	0	0	0.00	0.00							0.00											
Age	26	06		0	0	0	0	0	0.00	0.00							0.00											
Type	Pwr	07	aa	4	5	0	112	90	4.47	1.53	276			22.6	33%	70%	4.73				4.1	7.2	1.8		0.6	-0.1	63	$5
Health	F	08	HOU	0	0	0	0	0	0.00	0.00							0.00											
PT/Exp	D	09	HOU	* 5	12	0	132	117	5.70	1.70	304	354	286	20.3	36%	69%	4.45	42	19	39	4.2	8.0	1.9	13%	1.4	-24.5	51	($1)
Consist	A	1st Half		3	4	0	62	56	4.63	1.47	283			19.5	34%	71%	4.03	41	19	40	3.2	8.1	2.5	11%	1.2	-3.4	78	$3
LIMA Plan	C+	2nd Half		2	8	0	70	62	6.64	1.90	321			21.0	37%	68%	4.82	44	18	38	5.1	7.9	1.6	15%	1.7	-21.1	27	($4)
Rand Var	+5	10	Proj	11	9	0	181	159	4.54	1.48	269			23.4	32%	72%	4.21	42	19	39	4.0	7.9	2.0	11%	1.1	1.2	55	$10

3-11, 6.27 ERA in 98 IP at HOU. Also 8.5 Dom, 3.4 Ctl at HOU and no arm injuries, unlike '08. There is something special, and deeply hidden here. If he can solve LHB, then UP: 3.70 ERA, 15 Wins

Pavano,Carl

		Yr	Tm	W	L	Sv	IP	K	ERA	WHIP	OBA	vL	vR	BF/G	H%	S%	xERA	G	L	F	Ctl	Dom	Cmd	hr/f	hr/9	RAR	BPV	R$
RH	Starter	05	NYY	4	6	0	100	56	4.77	1.47	314	335	294	25.8	33%	72%	4.07	50	19	31	1.6	5.0	3.1	15%	1.5	-4.9	75	$3
Age	34	06	a/a	2	0	0	17	15	1.59	1.12	250			17.2	33%	84%	2.62				1.6	7.9	5.0		0.0	6.1	158	$3
Type	Con	07	NYY	1	0	0	11	4	4.78	1.24	274	208	350	23.5	28%	62%	4.56	46	18	36	1.6	3.2	2.0	7%	0.8	-0.4	38	$1
Health	F	08	NYY	* 5	3	0	48	26	5.40	1.47	295	324	283	21.2	30%	68%	4.84	40	17	42	2.6	4.8	1.9	13%	1.7	-6.3	35	$2
PT/Exp	C	09	2AL	14	12	0	199	147	5.10	1.37	295	271	317	25.9	33%	65%	3.98	43	19	37	1.8	6.6	3.8	11%	1.2	-16.0	93	$13
Consist	B	1st Half		6	7	0	92	68	5.57	1.41	301			24.9	35%	61%	3.80	48	19	33	1.8	6.6	3.8	11%	1.1	-12.7	98	$4
LIMA Plan	C+	2nd Half		8	5	0	107	79	4.70	1.34	289			26.9	33%	68%	4.13	39	20	41	1.8	6.6	3.8	11%	1.3	-3.3	89	$8
Rand Var	+4	10	Proj	12	9	0	183	122	4.62	1.32	282			23.5	31%	68%	4.10	44	19	38	1.9	6.0	3.1	11%	1.2	7.6	78	$13

TJS survivor showed he's back with 200 IP and no 2H fade. No one believes he's quite that good, but with average luck, xERA near 4.00 shows his upside. That said, who knows how long until his next injury?

Peavy,Jake

		Yr	Tm	W	L	Sv	IP	K	ERA	WHIP	OBA	vL	vR	BF/G	H%	S%	xERA	G	L	F	Ctl	Dom	Cmd	hr/f	hr/9	RAR	BPV	R$
RH	Starter	05	SD	13	7	0	203	216	2.88	1.04	221	223	212	26.8	29%	76%	2.93	44	20	35	2.2	9.6	4.3	10%	0.8	34.2	135	$29
Age	28	06	SD	11	14	0	202	215	4.10	1.23	247	242	243	26.2	32%	69%	3.58	38	18	44	2.8	9.6	3.5	10%	1.0	9.7	114	$20
Type	Pwr	07	SD	19	6	0	223	240	2.54	1.06	212	242	174	26.1	29%	78%	3.16	44	17	39	2.7	9.7	3.5	6%	0.5	52.0	122	$37
Health	F	08	SD	10	11	0	174	166	2.85	1.18	230	263	194	26.4	28%	80%	3.54	41	21	38	3.1	8.6	2.8	10%	0.9	30.4	91	$21
PT/Exp	A	09	2TM	9	6	0	102	110	3.45	1.12	218	249	178	25.7	29%	71%	3.26	42	18	40	3.0	9.7	3.2	8%	0.7	10.8	114	$15
Consist	A	1st Half		6	6	0	81	92	3.99	1.19	232			25.7	31%	68%	3.26	41	19	40	3.1	10.2	3.3	8%	0.8	3.2	119	$10
LIMA Plan	B+	2nd Half		3	0	0	21	18	1.32	0.83	160			25.6	20%	88%	3.20	46	17	38	2.6	7.9	3.0	5%	0.4	7.6	95	$5
Rand Var	0	10	Proj	14	9	0	174	174	3.93	1.23	239			26.7	30%	70%	3.52	43	19	38	3.1	9.0	2.9	9%	0.9	17.8	99	$20

Stud with terrific xERA history, but what are the risks? Last year's ankle injury adds to '08 elbow injury history. He'll miss the pitcher's best friend, Petco. Swinging strike % dropped in 2009. That's a lot of warnings.

Pelfrey,Mike

		Yr	Tm	W	L	Sv	IP	K	ERA	WHIP	OBA	vL	vR	BF/G	H%	S%	xERA	G	L	F	Ctl	Dom	Cmd	hr/f	hr/9	RAR	BPV	R$
RH	Starter	05		0	0	0	0	0	0.00	0.00							0.00											
Age	26	06	NYM	* 7	3	0	95	84	4.16	1.57	279	278	326	23.7	35%	73%	4.00	49	23	29	4.3	7.9	1.9	6%	0.5	3.9	55	$6
Type	GB	07	NYM	* 6	14	0	147	92	5.16	1.60	292	321	279	22.9	33%	68%	4.54	48	23	28	4.0	5.6	1.4	9%	0.7	-13.4	20	$2
Health	A	08	NYM	13	11	0	201	110	3.72	1.36	270	307	245	26.8	30%	73%	4.20	50	21	30	2.9	4.9	1.7	6%	0.5	13.6	39	$14
PT/Exp	A	09	NYM	10	12	0	184	107	5.03	1.51	291	284	294	26.4	32%	67%	4.31	51	19	30	3.2	5.2	1.6	10%	0.9	-19.1	36	$4
Consist	A	1st Half		6	3	0	88	43	4.29	1.45	281			25.7	31%	70%	4.30	54	19	27	3.2	4.4	1.4	7%	0.6	-1.0	26	$4
LIMA Plan	C+	2nd Half		4	9	0	96	64	5.71	1.57	300			27.0	33%	65%	4.32	49	19	32	3.3	6.0	1.8	11%	1.1	-18.1	46	($0)
Rand Var	+1	10	Proj	13	11	0	194	122	4.45	1.44	280			25.7	31%	70%	4.15	50	20	30	3.1	5.7	1.8	10%	0.9	2.7	46	$10

Seems to have found his level -- a durable, reliable, humdrum level. As a GBer with poor Cmd, results seem tied to swings of fortune. But he's shown better; if 2H Dom is a sign he's tapping into lost skills, there's upside.

Pena,Tony

		Yr	Tm	W	L	Sv	IP	K	ERA	WHIP	OBA	vL	vR	BF/G	H%	S%	xERA	G	L	F	Ctl	Dom	Cmd	hr/f	hr/9	RAR	BPV	R$
RH	Reliever	05	aa	7	13	0	148	83	5.58	1.59	318			26.7	34%	67%	6.13				2.5	5.1	2.0		1.3	-23.2	27	$0
Age	28	06	ARI	* 8	5	14	76	53	3.33	1.22	266			4.8	30%	75%	4.07	39	22	39	1.8	6.2	3.5	7%	0.8	10.9	81	$15
Type		07	ARI	5	4	2	85	63	3.27	1.10	208	245	176	4.6	24%	73%	3.99	48	12	40	3.3	6.6	2.0	8%	0.8	12.2	57	$11
Health	A	08	ARI	3	2	3	73	52	4.33	1.33	281	296	267	4.3	33%	67%	3.79	47	20	32	2.1	6.4	3.1	7%	0.6	-0.6	84	$5
PT/Exp	C	09	2TM	6	5	2	70	55	3.99	1.44	291	288	280	4.2	34%	74%	3.83	46	23	31	2.6	7.1	2.8	10%	0.9	2.8	82	$6
Consist	A	1st Half		5	3	1	33	26	4.36	1.55	301			4.2	36%	73%	3.97	48	21	31	3.0	7.1	2.4	9%	0.8	-0.2	72	$3
LIMA Plan	B+	2nd Half		1	2	1	37	29	3.65	1.35	282			4.3	33%	76%	3.69	44	25	31	2.2	7.1	3.2	11%	1.0	3.0	90	$3
Rand Var	+2	10	Proj	5	4	0	73	56	3.97	1.31	268			4.5	31%	72%	3.77	46	21	33	2.5	7.0	2.8	9%	0.9	5.2	82	$6

Platoon split problem is growing:

2009	OPS	Ctl	Dom
v LHB	874	5.4	6.0
v RHB	654	0.6	7.8

Excellent slider is a weapon only vs. RHB. Can't close w/o finding an out pitch for lefties.

Penny,Brad

		Yr	Tm	W	L	Sv	IP	K	ERA	WHIP	OBA	vL	vR	BF/G	H%	S%	xERA	G	L	F	Ctl	Dom	Cmd	hr/f	hr/9	RAR	BPV	R$
RH	Starter	05	LA	7	9	0	175	122	3.91	1.29	273	263	276	25.4	31%	72%	3.80	47	20	34	2.1	6.3	3.0	9%	0.9	7.3	81	$12
Age	31	06	LA	16	9	0	189	148	4.33	1.38	279	275	283	23.9	33%	70%	4.03	44	20	36	2.6	7.0	2.7	9%	0.9	3.6	79	$16
Type		07	LA	16	4	0	208	135	3.03	1.31	253	229	286	26.6	30%	77%	4.09	49	20	31	3.2	5.8	1.8	4%	0.4	35.8	47	$22
Health	C	08	LA	6	9	0	95	51	6.27	1.63	295	328	284	22.7	31%	62%	4.80	49	20	31	4.0	4.8	1.2	13%	1.2	-23.4	7	($1)
PT/Exp	A	09	2TM	11	9	0	173	109	4.88	1.40	281	259	299	24.9	31%	67%	4.42	44	18	39	2.6	5.7	2.1	10%	1.1	-12.2	52	$9
Consist	B	1st Half		6	3	0	82	55	4.82	1.52	297			24.3	33%	70%	4.64	42	17	41	3.0	6.0	2.0	9%	1.1	-5.1	49	$4
LIMA Plan	C	2nd Half		5	6	0	91	54	4.94	1.28	266			25.5	29%	64%	4.22	45	19	36	2.4	5.3	2.3	11%	1.2	-7.1	55	$5
Rand Var	0	10	Proj	8	7	0	116	72	4.50	1.42	280			24.0	31%	70%	4.37	46	19	35	2.9	5.6	1.9	10%	1.0	-0.5	45	$7

Three straight years of a soft skill set, plus he has a wonky shoulder. Don't lose sight of the big picture just because his H% was lucky during his September return to the NL. Let others bet on full health.

Percival,Troy

		Yr	Tm	W	L	Sv	IP	K	ERA	WHIP	OBA	vL	vR	BF/G	H%	S%	xERA	G	L	F	Ctl	Dom	Cmd	hr/f	hr/9	RAR	BPV	R$
RH	Reliever	05	DET	1	3	8	25	20	5.76	1.20	212	173	250	4.0	19%	61%	4.77	27	14	59	4.0	7.2	1.8	17%	2.5	-4.3	28	$4
Age	40	06		0	0	0	0	0	0.00	0.00							0.00											
Type	Pwr xFB	07	STL	* 3	0	0	46	43	1.79	0.97	181	220	136	4.5	23%	85%	3.95	33	12	55	3.1	8.3	2.7	5%	0.6	15.0	78	$8
Health	F	08	TAM	2	1	28	46	38	4.53	1.23	184	185	171	3.8	18%	70%	5.24	23	10	67	5.3	7.5	1.4	11%	1.8	-1.0	-8	$13
PT/Exp	D	09	TAM	0	1	6	11	7	6.37	1.68	305	478	130	3.7	31%	69%	5.86	23	23	54	4.0	5.6	1.4	14%	2.4	-2.7	-6	$2
Consist	B	1st Half		0	1	6	11	7	6.49	1.71	309			3.7	31%	69%	5.89	23	23	54	4.1	5.7	1.4	15%	2.4	-2.8	-6	$1
LIMA Plan	C	2nd Half		0	0	0	0	0	0.00	0.00							0.00											
Rand Var	+2	10	Proj	0	0	3	7	6	4.97	1.24	197			4.3	22%	63%	4.95	26	16	58	5.0	7.4	1.5	9%	1.2	-0.5	4	$1

Widely expected that he'll retire soon. There's not much of a market for 40-year-olds who spend most of the season on the DL and post negative BPVs during the infrequent times they can pitch anyway.

Perdomo,Luis

		Yr	Tm	W	L	Sv	IP	K	ERA	WHIP	OBA	vL	vR	BF/G	H%	S%	xERA	G	L	F	Ctl	Dom	Cmd	hr/f	hr/9	RAR	BPV	R$
RH	Reliever	05		0	0	0	0	0	0.00	0.00							0.00											
Age	25	06		0	0	0	0	0	0.00	0.00							0.00											
Type	Pwr GB	07		0	0	0	0	0	0.00	0.00							0.00											
Health	A	08	aa	4	2	2	33	31	4.58	1.40	265			6.0	33%	68%	4.39				3.4	8.5	2.5		0.9	-1.1	79	$4
PT/Exp	D	09	SD	1	0	0	60	55	4.80	1.52	252	293	198	7.6	29%	74%	3.92	52	18	30	5.1	8.3	1.6	22%	1.7	-4.5	41	$1
Consist	A	1st Half		1	0	0	27	15	4.33	1.15	208			6.9	21%	67%	4.22	48	20	32	3.7	5.0	1.4	15%	1.3	-0.5	17	$2
LIMA Plan	B+	2nd Half		0	0	0	33	40	5.18	1.82	284			8.2	36%	77%	3.61	57	16	27	6.3	10.9	1.7	29%	1.9	-4.0	62	($1)
Rand Var	+5	10	Proj	3	1	0	58	55	4.19	1.43	258			6.8	32%	73%	3.56	53	18	29	4.0	8.5	2.1	12%	0.9	5.0	75	$4

Rule 5 rook with a GB/Dom combination worth following. Still work to do, particularly in Ctl, but both hr/f and 2H h% made the '09 road bumpy. Can already handle right-handed hitters, a good first step.

MICHAEL WEDDELL

Perez,Chris

Perez,Chris		W	L	Sv	IP	K	ERA	WHIP	OBA	vL	vR	BF/G	H%	S%	xERA	G	L	F	Ctl	Dom	Cmd	hr/f	hr/9	RAR	BPV	R$
RH Reliever	05	0	0	0	0	0	0.00	0.00							0.00											
Age 24	06	0	0	0	0	0	0.00	0.00							0.00											
Type Pwr xFB	07 aa	2	1	36	54	68	3.33	1.19	141			4.1	19%	75%	2.29				6.5	11.3	**1.7**		0.8	7.5	106	$19
Health A	08 STL *	4	4	18	67	74	3.51	1.36	223	220	231	4.3	28%	79%	3.89	39	20	41	5.0	10.0	**2.0**	13%	1.2	6.3	62	$13
PT/Exp D	09 2TM	1	2	2	57	68	4.26	1.19	203	188	207	3.8	26%	68%	3.56	35	18	47	4.3	10.7	**2.5**	13%	1.3	0.3	91	$6
Consist B	1st Half	1	1	1	24	30	5.60	1.45	218			3.5	30%	63%	3.90	37	22	42	6.0	11.2	**1.9**	13%	1.1	-3.8	55	$1
LIMA Plan A	2nd Half	0	1	1	33	38	3.28	1.00	192			4.2	24%	75%	3.33	34	14	51	3.0	10.4	**3.5**	13%	1.4	4.2	118	$4
Rand Var 0	10 Proj	**2**	**2**	**13**	**58**	**68**	**3.88**	**1.19**	**220**			**4.0**	**29%**	**71%**	**3.44**	**36**	**18**	**45**	**3.6**	**10.6**	**3.0**	**11%**	**1.1**	**6.5**	**108**	**$10**

Began to fulfill potential with terrific 2H. An ERA risk as long as his FB% hovers around 50%, but has the gas and Cmd to overcome. With a fragile closer incumbent in CLE, the BPIs are a worthy speculative investment.

Perez,Oliver

Perez,Oliver		W	L	Sv	IP	K	ERA	WHIP	OBA	vL	vR	BF/G	H%	S%	xERA	G	L	F	Ctl	Dom	Cmd	hr/f	hr/9	RAR	BPV	R$
LH Starter	05 PIT	7	5	0	103	97	5.85	1.67	260	313	255	23.6	29%	70%	5.10	34	17	49	6.1	8.5	**1.4**	16%	2.0	-20.4	-1	$1
Age 28	06 2NL *	5	18	0	163	152	7.08	1.71	288	260	300	23.6	33%	61%	5.07	30	23	47	5.1	8.4	**1.7**	14%	1.8	-52.2	22	($5)
Type Pwr xFB	07 NYM	15	10	0	177	174	3.56	1.31	235	206	235	25.8	29%	77%	4.28	33	17	50	4.0	8.8	**2.2**	9%	1.1	18.9	62	$20
Health F	08 NYM	10	7	0	194	180	4.22	1.40	234	158	258	24.7	28%	73%	4.54	32	22	46	4.9	8.4	**1.7**	10%	1.1	1.2	29	$13
PT/Exp A	09 NYM	3	4	0	66	62	6.82	1.92	270	200	306	22.8	31%	67%	6.07	28	20	52	7.9	8.5	**1.1**	12%	1.6	-21.4	-55	($4)
Consist B	1st Half	1	2	0	21	20	10.19	2.31	319			22.2	39%	54%	6.80	23	29	48	8.9	8.5	**1.0**	9%	1.3	-15.7	-87	($4)
LIMA Plan F	2nd Half	2	2	0	45	42	5.22	1.74	245			23.2	28%	75%	5.73	31	15	54	7.4	8.4	**1.1**	13%	1.8	-5.7	-40	($0)
Rand Var +1	10 Proj	**7**	**10**	**0**	**145**	**137**	**4.97**	**1.57**	**260**			**23.2**	**31%**	**72%**	**4.87**	**30**	**21**	**50**	**5.2**	**8.5**	**1.7**	**11%**	**1.4**	**-10.8**	**22**	**$4**

Battled knee problems, and pretty much everything else, all season long. Consistent Dom a tease, but always saddled w/ high FB% and erratic Ctl. 2007 (passable Ctl and hr/f) was the perfect storm; it will not return.

Perez,Rafael

Perez,Rafael		W	L	Sv	IP	K	ERA	WHIP	OBA	vL	vR	BF/G	H%	S%	xERA	G	L	F	Ctl	Dom	Cmd	hr/f	hr/9	RAR	BPV	R$
LH Reliever	05 aa	4	3	1	66	39	2.10	1.12	249			17.8	28%	85%	3.29				1.7	5.3	**3.1**		0.7	18.0	82	$9
Age 27	06 CLE *	4	8	0	106	90	3.65	1.28	246			10.4	31%	71%	3.57	58	9	33	3.2	7.6	**2.4**	5%	0.4	11.9	85	$11
Type Pwr GB	07 CLE *	4	5	1	107	90	2.97	1.19	252	145	213	8.5	31%	77%	3.30	53	17	30	2.2	7.6	**3.4**	9%	0.7	20.3	107	$13
Health A	08 CLE	4	4	2	76	86	3.54	1.18	237	222	243	4.3	31%	73%	2.54	57	19	24	2.7	10.1	**3.7**	17%	0.9	7.6	144	$10
PT/Exp D	09 CLE	4	3	0	48	32	7.31	1.90	328	412	277	4.3	37%	60%	4.84	49	24	27	4.7	6.0	**1.3**	11%	0.9	-16.9	8	($2)
Consist D	1st Half	1	2	0	23	20	9.35	2.34	356			4.2	43%	58%	5.59	44	26	30	7.0	7.8	**1.1**	8%	0.8	-14.0	-27	($4)
LIMA Plan D+	2nd Half	3	1	0	25	12	5.42	1.49	299			4.4	32%	65%	4.20	53	22	25	2.5	4.3	**1.7**	14%	1.1	-3.0	41	$1
Rand Var +5	10 Proj	**3**	**2**	**0**	**44**	**34**	**4.34**	**1.40**	**264**			**4.8**	**31%**	**70%**	**3.74**	**52**	**22**	**26**	**3.5**	**7.0**	**2.0**	**11%**	**0.8**	**3.8**	**61**	**$3**

Easy to say that he was done in by bad luck, but skills collapse more mysterious. Notice the Dom dive and struggles against LH. Worth a flier because of consistency of pre-2009 skills, little other reason for optimism.

Perkins,Glen

Perkins,Glen		W	L	Sv	IP	K	ERA	WHIP	OBA	vL	vR	BF/G	H%	S%	xERA	G	L	F	Ctl	Dom	Cmd	hr/f	hr/9	RAR	BPV	R$
LH Starter	05 aa	4	4	0	79	58	6.04	1.62	292			25.6	35%	60%	4.98				4.1	6.6	**1.6**		0.5	-16.9	56	($0)
Age 27	06 a/a	4	12	0	121	113	5.50	1.64	294			23.0	36%	68%	5.72				4.2	8.4	**2.0**		1.0	-14.6	57	$2
Type Con	07 MIN *	0	2	0	42	27	5.04	1.43	246	250	222	7.9	25%	70%	5.12	39	18	44	4.6	5.8	**1.3**	14%	1.8	-2.7	-3	$1
Health D	08 MIN *	14	5	0	184	96	4.26	1.48	292	352	288	24.5	31%	76%	4.91	38	22	40	2.8	4.7	**1.6**	11%	1.3	2.0	23	$11
PT/Exp C	09 MIN	6	7	0	96	45	5.89	1.48	306	333	295	23.6	32%	62%	4.80	47	14	39	2.1	4.2	**2.0**	10%	1.2	-17.1	43	$2
Consist A	1st Half	4	4	0	74	35	4.38	1.27	277			25.8	30%	67%	4.50	47	13	40	1.7	4.3	**2.5**	7%	0.9	0.7	55	$5
LIMA Plan C+	2nd Half	2	3	0	22	10	10.90	2.20	389			19.0	39%	51%	5.83	48	17	35	3.6	4.0	**1.1**	18%	2.4	-17.7	0	($4)
Rand Var +3	10 Proj	**7**	**8**	**0**	**116**	**62**	**4.97**	**1.55**	**301**			**17.3**	**32%**	**72%**	**4.92**	**44**	**18**	**38**	**3.0**	**4.8**	**1.6**	**12%**	**1.4**	**-6.9**	**27**	**$4**

Late-season disagreement w/ MIN on extent of shoulder injury and service time is one caution, but Dom slide, hittability and thick xERA is more troubling. Not worth the risk at this point.

Perry,Ryan

Perry,Ryan		W	L	Sv	IP	K	ERA	WHIP	OBA	vL	vR	BF/G	H%	S%	xERA	G	L	F	Ctl	Dom	Cmd	hr/f	hr/9	RAR	BPV	R$
RH Reliever	05	0	0	0	0	0	0.00	0.00							0.00											
Age 23	06	0	0	0	0	0	0.00	0.00							0.00											
Type Pwr	07	0	0	0	0	0	0.00	0.00							0.00											
Health A	08	0	0	0	0	0	0.00	0.00							0.00											
PT/Exp F	09 DET *	1	1	3	76	71	3.69	1.49	247	294	206	5.5	30%	78%	4.40	42	19	39	5.1	8.4	**1.7**	10%	1.0	7.2	33	$5
Consist F	1st Half	1	1	1	35	30	3.58	1.50	225			5.0	27%	79%	4.92	40	18	42	6.1	7.8	**1.3**	10%	1.0	3.8	-7	$3
LIMA Plan C+	2nd Half	0	0	2	41	41	3.78	1.49	265			6.0	34%	77%	3.98	43	20	37	4.2	9.0	**2.1**	9%	0.9	3.4	69	$3
Rand Var -2	10 Proj	**1**	**1**	**5**	**58**	**55**	**3.88**	**1.40**	**248**			**5.4**	**30%**	**76%**	**4.05**	**42**	**19**	**39**	**4.2**	**8.5**	**2.0**	**11%**	**1.1**	**2.8**	**60**	**$6**

0-1, 3.79 ERA in 62 IP at DET. Nice debut by high draft pick with solid 2H growth. Too early to tell whether he'll be able to rein in Ctl, which looks like the difference-maker. If harnessed, UP: 35 saves.

Petit,Yusmeiro

Petit,Yusmeiro		W	L	Sv	IP	K	ERA	WHIP	OBA	vL	vR	BF/G	H%	S%	xERA	G	L	F	Ctl	Dom	Cmd	hr/f	hr/9	RAR	BPV	R$
RH Reliever	05 a/a	9	6	0	132	133	3.65	1.03	234			21.7	28%	70%	3.38				1.5	9.1	**6.1**		1.3	10.6	152	$18
Age 25	06 FLA *	5	7	0	122	88	5.27	1.39	293	381	400	16.5	33%	65%	4.59	29	24	46	2.0	6.5	**3.2**	10%	1.4	-11.8	70	$5
Type Pwr xFB	07 ARI *	11	8	0	150	93	4.91	1.40	268	274	250	21.0	28%	70%	5.23	33	15	52	3.4	5.6	**1.7**	10%	1.6	-9.0	20	$8
Health B	08 ARI *	6	8	0	116	100	5.44	1.25	273	231	205	16.2	31%	61%	4.03	33	17	50	1.7	7.8	**4.5**	12%	1.6	-16.8	104	$6
PT/Exp C	09 ARI	3	10	0	90	74	5.82	1.52	287	282	269	17.3	32%	67%	4.68	31	20	49	3.4	7.4	**2.2**	14%	1.9	-18.0	50	$0
Consist B	1st Half	0	3	0	24	19	8.18	1.78	326			18.9	34%	60%	5.05	32	22	46	3.7	7.1	**1.9**	21%	3.0	-11.9	37	($2)
LIMA Plan B	2nd Half	3	7	0	66	55	4.95	1.42	272			16.7	31%	70%	4.55	30	20	50	3.3	7.6	**2.3**	11%	1.5	-6.1	55	$3
Rand Var +3	10 Proj	**6**	**13**	**0**	**146**	**117**	**5.06**	**1.46**	**283**			**17.7**	**32%**	**70%**	**4.64**	**32**	**20**	**49**	**3.1**	**7.2**	**2.3**	**12%**	**1.6**	**-6.9**	**55**	**$5**

Annoucing this year's winning Science Fair project: Take any xFB pitcher, even one with 2.0+ Cmd. Measure out a higher than normal hr/f rate. Combine both in a bandbox. Duck.

Pettitte,Andy

Pettitte,Andy		W	L	Sv	IP	K	ERA	WHIP	OBA	vL	vR	BF/G	H%	S%	xERA	G	L	F	Ctl	Dom	Cmd	hr/f	hr/9	RAR	BPV	R$
LH Starter	05 HOU	17	9	0	222	171	2.39	1.03	231	200	239	26.6	27%	80%	3.06	50	23	27	1.7	6.9	**4.2**	10%	0.7	50.8	108	$33
Age 37	06 HOU	14	13	0	214	178	4.20	1.44	283	259	290	25.9	33%	74%	3.71	50	22	29	2.9	7.5	**2.5**	14%	1.1	7.5	83	$15
Type	07 NYY	15	9	0	215	141	4.05	1.43	282	298	282	26.0	32%	72%	4.23	48	19	33	2.9	5.9	**2.0**	7%	0.7	12.0	54	$16
Health A	08 NYY	14	14	0	204	158	4.54	1.41	288	203	325	26.8	34%	69%	3.59	51	20	29	2.4	7.0	**2.9**	10%	0.8	-4.9	89	$14
PT/Exp A	09 NYY	14	8	0	195	148	4.16	1.38	260	282	249	26.2	30%	72%	4.31	43	19	38	3.5	6.8	**1.9**	9%	0.9	7.0	49	$16
Consist B	1st Half	8	3	0	97	66	4.26	1.50	285			26.8	32%	75%	4.52	45	18	36	3.4	6.1	**1.8**	10%	1.1	2.3	41	$7
LIMA Plan D+	2nd Half	6	5	0	98	82	4.06	1.26	234			25.5	28%	69%	4.10	40	20	40	3.6	7.6	**2.1**	7%	0.7	4.8	57	$10
Rand Var 0	10 Proj	**13**	**9**	**0**	**189**	**141**	**4.30**	**1.40**	**268**			**26.3**	**31%**	**71%**	**4.11**	**46**	**20**	**34**	**3.3**	**6.7**	**2.0**	**10%**	**1.0**	**7.6**	**57**	**$14**

ERA rebounded, but skills dropped off to 2007 levels. Dips in Ctl and GB more pronounced than before. Durability, guile and NYY offense are plusses. Look forward, though--not back--when setting his value.

Pineiro,Joel

Pineiro,Joel		W	L	Sv	IP	K	ERA	WHIP	OBA	vL	vR	BF/G	H%	S%	xERA	G	L	F	Ctl	Dom	Cmd	hr/f	hr/9	RAR	BPV	R$
RH Starter	05 SEA	7	11	0	189	107	5.62	1.48	296	295	305	27.7	32%	63%	4.41	45	22	33	2.7	5.1	**1.9**	11%	1.1	-29.1	43	$3
Age 31	06 SEA	8	13	1	165	87	6.37	1.65	310	287	332	18.9	33%	62%	4.76	47	23	29	3.5	4.7	**1.4**	13%	1.3	-37.0	17	($1)
Type Con GB	07 2TM	7	5	0	98	60	4.33	1.39	285	250	308	10.0	31%	73%	4.22	49	17	34	2.4	5.5	**2.3**	13%	1.3	1.6	61	$7
Health B	08 STL	7	7	1	149	81	5.14	1.45	300	297	304	25.0	32%	67%	4.17	49	22	30	2.1	4.9	**2.3**	14%	1.3	-16.0	58	$4
PT/Exp A	09 STL	15	12	0	214	105	3.49	1.14	265	272	266	27.2	29%	69%	3.34	60	16	24	1.1	4.4	**3.9**	6%	0.5	18.5	87	$21
Consist A	1st Half	6	9	0	99	42	3.45	1.18	273			27.1	30%	69%	3.41	62	16	22	1.1	3.8	**3.5**	4%	0.3	9.0	79	$9
LIMA Plan D+	2nd Half	9	3	0	115	63	3.52	1.11	259			27.3	29%	69%	3.28	59	16	25	1.2	4.9	**4.2**	9%	0.6	9.4	94	$12
Rand Var 0	10 Proj	**11**	**10**	**0**	**183**	**97**	**4.03**	**1.31**	**280**			**20.9**	**30%**	**71%**	**3.83**	**54**	**18**	**28**	**1.9**	**4.8**	**2.6**	**10%**	**0.9**	**9.7**	**68**	**$12**

Significant jump in GB and Ctl fueled this surprise, and xERA says it was legit. But poor Dom, fortunate hr/9 and past health issues provide little room for error. Could have a window, but history says bet against.

Pinto,Renyel

Pinto,Renyel		W	L	Sv	IP	K	ERA	WHIP	OBA	vL	vR	BF/G	H%	S%	xERA	G	L	F	Ctl	Dom	Cmd	hr/f	hr/9	RAR	BPV	R$
LH Reliever	05 a/a	11	5	0	152	129	4.50	1.53	258			24.2	32%	69%	4.19				5.0	7.6	**1.5**		0.4	-3.6	69	$9
Age 27	06 FLA *	8	2	1	124	123	3.40	1.46	234			12.1	30%	78%	4.27	45	16	39	5.4	8.9	**1.7**	8%	0.7	16.6	39	$12
Type Pwr FB	07 FLA	2	4	1	59	56	3.68	1.31	214	210	227	4.4	26%	76%	4.29	37	19	44	4.9	8.6	**1.8**	10%	1.1	5.4	37	$5
Health C	08 FLA	2	5	0	65	56	4.45	1.41	222	264	203	4.2	25%	72%	4.36	46	17	37	5.4	7.8	**1.4**	14%	1.3	-1.4	18	$3
PT/Exp C	09 FLA	4	1	0	61	58	3.23	1.60	235	277	208	3.8	30%	81%	4.81	43	14	42	6.6	8.5	**1.3**	6%	0.6	7.3	-4	$4
Consist A	1st Half	3	1	0	27	25	3.31	1.62	238			4.0	30%	81%	5.32	32	17	51	6.6	8.3	**1.3**	5%	0.7	3.0	-20	$2
LIMA Plan C	2nd Half	1	0	0	34	33	3.17	1.58	232			3.7	30%	81%	4.33	53	12	34	6.6	8.7	**1.3**	6%	0.5	4.3	10	$2
Rand Var -5	10 Proj	**2**	**3**	**0**	**58**	**54**	**4.34**	**1.53**	**238**			**4.3**	**29%**	**73%**	**4.58**	**44**	**16**	**40**	**5.9**	**8.4**	**1.4**	**9%**	**0.9**	**-2.3**	**13**	**$2**

Solid Dom, dreadful Ctl, low LD%, and mastery over RHB are constants. G/L/F and HR metrics swing year-to-year, often 1H-to-2H. ERA very sensitive to H% and S% ticks. If you take this ride, close your eyes.

BRENT HERSHEY

Ponson,Sidney

Ponson,Sidney			W	L	Sv	IP	K	ERA	WHIP	OBA	vL	vR	BF/G	H%	S%	xERA	G	L	F	Ctl	Dom	Cmd	hr/f	hr/9	RAR	BPV	R$
RH	Starter	05 BAL	7	11	0	130	68	6.23	1.73	325	360	299	26.3	35%	65%	4.56	53	20	27	3.3	4.7	1.4	12%	1.1	-29.8	26	($3)
Age	33	06 2TM	4	5	0	85	48	6.25	1.69	311	304	328	20.6	34%	63%	4.80	51	18	31	3.8	5.1	1.3	11%	1.1	-18.1	18	($1)
Type	Con GB	07 MIN	2	5	0	37	23	7.02	1.91	340	265	410	25.7	36%	66%	4.77	54	17	29	4.1	5.6	1.4	18%	1.7	-11.5	22	($2)
Health	C	08 2AL *	9	7	0	163	69	5.00	1.66	312	344	269	24.1	33%	71%	4.67	54	19	26	3.5	3.8	1.1	12%	1.0	-13.1	8	$1
PT/Exp	D	09 KC *	3	8	0	92	48	5.74	1.65	319	372	284	21.0	35%	65%	4.60	49	22	29	3.0	4.7	1.6	9%	0.8	-14.6	32	($1)
Consist	A	1st Half	1	6	0	61	32	6.55	1.73	334			18.9	36%	61%	4.52	54	19	27	2.8	4.7	1.7	10%	0.9	-15.8	39	($3)
LIMA Plan	C	2nd Half	2	2	0	31	17	4.13	1.50	287			27.0	32%	73%	4.83	37	31	33	3.3	4.9	1.5	6%	0.6	1.2	14	$2
Rand Var	+4	10 Proj	3	4	0	58	30	5.28	1.64	309			24.0	33%	69%	4.64	51	21	29	3.4	4.7	1.4	10%	0.9	-1.5	20	$0

1-7, 7.36 ERA in 58 IP at KC. xERA, Reliability Grade say he puts up consistently bad BPIs and consistently underperforms them. His ongoing ability to find MLB work indicts pitching coaches everywhere.

Porcello,Rick

Porcello,Rick			W	L	Sv	IP	K	ERA	WHIP	OBA	vL	vR	BF/G	H%	S%	xERA	G	L	F	Ctl	Dom	Cmd	hr/f	hr/9	RAR	BPV	R$
RH	Starter	05	0	0	0	0	0	0.00	0.00							0.00											
Age	21	06	0	0	0	0	0	0.00	0.00							0.00											
Type	Con GB	07	0	0	0	0	0	0.00	0.00							0.00											
Health	A	08	0	0	0	0	0	0.00	0.00							0.00											
PT/Exp	D	09 DET	14	9	0	165	81	4.04	1.35	270	281	255	23.5	28%	74%	4.20	54	17	28	2.7	4.4	1.6	14%	1.2	8.5	38	$14
Consist	F	1st Half	8	5	0	83	44	3.90	1.42	275			24.0	29%	77%	4.09	57	18	25	3.1	4.8	1.5	17%	1.3	5.6	36	$7
LIMA Plan	D+	2nd Half	6	4	0	82	37	4.17	1.27	264			22.9	27%	70%	4.29	52	16	32	2.3	4.1	1.8	11%	1.1	2.8	41	$7
Rand Var	+1	10 Proj	15	10	0	189	99	4.15	1.38	278			23.8	30%	72%	4.15	54	17	29	2.6	4.7	1.8	11%	1.0	6.5	46	$14

Fine rookie campaign for 20-yr-old. Four months of 5+ Dom suggests it was inconsistent, not MIA. Good velocity says K's will kick in as he learns new tricks. GB% will keep his head above water in interim.

Poreda,Aaron

Poreda,Aaron			W	L	Sv	IP	K	ERA	WHIP	OBA	vL	vR	BF/G	H%	S%	xERA	G	L	F	Ctl	Dom	Cmd	hr/f	hr/9	RAR	BPV	R$
LH	Reliever	05	0	0	0	0	0	0.00	0.00							0.00											
Age	23	06	0	0	0	0	0	0.00	0.00							0.00											
Type	Pwr GB	07	0	0	0	0	0	0.00	0.00							0.00											
Health	A	08 aa	3	4	0	87	64	4.03	1.39	285			25.0	33%	72%	4.54				2.4	6.6	2.8		0.7	3.0	74	$5
PT/Exp	D	09 2TM *	6	7	0	120	105	3.97	1.53	224	333	143	15.7	29%	72%	4.63	53	9	38	6.4	7.9	1.2	2%	0.2	5.1	-1	$7
Consist	A	1st Half	6	4	0	69	67	3.00	1.43	238			18.8	32%	78%	3.72	58	8	33	4.9	8.7	1.8	2%	0.1	11.2	60	$8
LIMA Plan	C+	2nd Half	0	3	0	51	38	5.27	1.66	204			13.0	25%	66%	5.82	50	9	41	8.4	6.7	0.8	3%	0.4	-6.1	-80	($1)
Rand Var	-3	10 Proj	2	2	0	44	35	4.30	1.39	248			17.2	29%	70%	4.20	52	9	39	4.1	7.2	1.8	8%	0.8	0.8	48	$3

1-0, 2.70 ERA in 13 IP at CHW and SD. Solid Dom-and-GB combination, but once-steady Ctl spiked upward after AAA and MLB promotions. Nice potential as Petco stud, but likely at least a year away.

Price,David

Price,David			W	L	Sv	IP	K	ERA	WHIP	OBA	vL	vR	BF/G	H%	S%	xERA	G	L	F	Ctl	Dom	Cmd	hr/f	hr/9	RAR	BPV	R$
LH	Starter	05	0	0	0	0	0	0.00	0.00							0.00											
Age	24	06	0	0	0	0	0	0.00	0.00							0.00											
Type	Pwr	07	0	0	0	0	0	0.00	0.00							0.00											
Health	A	08 TAM *	8	1	0	89	74	2.73	1.22	242	158	188	20.5	29%	81%	3.68	50	13	38	2.9	7.5	2.6	8%	0.8	17.8	84	$13
PT/Exp	D	09 TAM *	11	11	0	162	133	4.49	1.37	248	236	242	22.5	28%	71%	4.33	41	19	39	4.0	7.4	1.8	12%	1.3	-0.7	44	$13
Consist	B	1st Half	3	6	0	70	68	4.35	1.52	244			20.8	29%	77%	4.53	37	24	40	5.5	8.7	1.6	16%	1.5	0.9	23	$4
LIMA Plan	D+	2nd Half	8	5	0	92	65	4.59	1.26	251			24.1	28%	66%	4.20	43	17	39	2.8	6.4	2.2	10%	1.1	-1.6	59	$9
Rand Var	+1	10 Proj	14	9	0	189	158	4.01	1.33	246			21.6	29%	73%	4.12	43	18	39	3.7	7.5	2.1	11%	1.1	7.3	57	$18

10-7, 4.42 ERA in 128 IP at TAM. Poor Ctl, hr/f spike hurt 1H, S% issues derailed 2H. Chalk up reversals to normal growing pains, should build on 2H in 2010. Work-in-progress will pay off this year or next.

Purcey,David

Purcey,David			W	L	Sv	IP	K	ERA	WHIP	OBA	vL	vR	BF/G	H%	S%	xERA	G	L	F	Ctl	Dom	Cmd	hr/f	hr/9	RAR	BPV	R$
LH	Starter	05 aa	4	3	0	43	39	4.53	1.65	258			24.6	32%	73%	4.74				6.0	8.1	1.3		0.6	-1.2	61	$2
Age	27	06 a/a	6	12	0	140	106	8.02	2.03	326			24.7	37%	61%	7.72				6.0	6.8	1.1		1.5	-60.4	11	($11)
Type	Pwr xFB	07 aa	3	5	0	62	42	7.42	1.67	329			25.9	38%	53%	6.19				2.6	6.1	2.4		0.8	-22.6	52	($2)
Health	A	08 TOR *	11	12	0	182	154	4.37	1.40	268	284	261	25.4	32%	71%	4.38	32	23	45	3.3	7.6	2.3	8%	1.0	-0.6	57	$13
PT/Exp	D	09 TOR *	10	9	0	187	128	5.28	1.67	277	156	329	26.0	32%	68%	5.75	32	19	49	5.3	6.2	1.2	5%	0.6	-19.2	-22	$3
Consist	D	1st Half	2	4	0	94	68	5.22	1.68	272			25.5	32%	68%	5.76	31	20	49	5.6	6.5	1.1	3%	0.5	-8.9	-27	($0)
LIMA Plan	C	2nd Half	8	5	0	93	61	5.35	1.66	282			26.5	32%	68%	5.75	32	19	49	4.9	5.9	1.2	6%	0.8	-10.3	-18	$3
Rand Var	-2	10 Proj	5	7	0	102	75	4.70	1.52	276			25.0	31%	72%	5.03	32	21	47	4.0	6.7	1.7	9%	1.2	-7.5	22	$4

1-3, 6.19 ERA in 48 IP at TOR. Unable to sustain '08 Dom gains, 1H Ctl plunge was followed by weak 2H bounce. FB% spike, hr/f says it could have been worse. His future now looks very much in doubt.

Putz,J.J.

Putz,J.J.			W	L	Sv	IP	K	ERA	WHIP	OBA	vL	vR	BF/G	H%	S%	xERA	G	L	F	Ctl	Dom	Cmd	hr/f	hr/9	RAR	BPV	R$
RH	Reliever	05 SEA	6	5	1	60	45	3.60	1.35	255	321	197	4.0	29%	78%	3.68	55	17	28	3.5	6.8	2.0	16%	1.2	5.7	61	$7
Age	33	06 SEA	4	1	36	78	104	2.30	0.92	211	211	204	4.2	32%	76%	2.17	51	16	33	1.5	12.0	8.0	7%	0.5	21.7	204	$27
Type	Pwr	07 SEA	6	1	40	72	82	1.38	0.70	155	148	158	3.8	21%	89%	2.56	42	17	41	1.6	10.3	6.3	9%	0.8	27.6	161	$32
Health	F	08 SEA	6	5	15	46	56	3.89	1.60	261	258	253	4.5	36%	77%	3.92	40	20	40	5.4	10.9	2.0	8%	0.8	2.6	67	$10
PT/Exp	C	09 NYM	1	4	2	29	19	5.22	1.64	260	296	220	4.6	31%	66%	5.11	47	19	34	5.8	5.8	1.0	3%	0.3	-3.7	-28	$0
Consist	C	1st Half	1	4	2	29	19	5.26	1.65	261			4.6	31%	66%	5.12	47	19	34	5.9	5.9	1.0	3%	0.3	-3.8	-28	$0
LIMA Plan	C+	2nd Half	0	0	0	0	0	0.00	0.00							0.00											
Rand Var	-1	10 Proj	4	4	3	48	43	4.31	1.44	245			4.5	30%	71%	4.13	46	18	36	4.7	8.1	1.7	8%	0.8	0.8	42	$4

June surgery for bone spur on elbow, then frayed tendon on same elbow ended season. Dom plunge suggests he was pitching hurt from the get-go. Latest injury puts Dom and Ctl in jeopardy. A TJS candidate.

Qualls,Chad

Qualls,Chad			W	L	Sv	IP	K	ERA	WHIP	OBA	vL	vR	BF/G	H%	S%	xERA	G	L	F	Ctl	Dom	Cmd	hr/f	hr/9	RAR	BPV	R$
RH	Reliever	05 HOU	6	4	0	79	60	3.30	1.21	246	218	275	4.3	29%	75%	3.05	58	21	20	2.6	6.8	2.6	15%	0.8	9.3	88	$9
Age	31	06 HOU	7	3	0	88	56	3.78	1.18	234	229	251	4.5	26%	71%	3.58	60	14	26	2.9	5.7	2.0	14%	1.0	7.7	64	$10
Type	xGB	07 HOU	6	5	5	83	78	3.05	1.32	265	248	289	4.4	32%	82%	3.20	57	14	29	2.7	8.5	3.1	14%	1.1	14.1	114	$11
Health	B	08 ARI	4	8	9	74	71	2.81	1.07	227	220	229	3.8	29%	75%	2.62	58	19	23	2.2	8.7	3.9	9%	0.5	13.3	133	$13
PT/Exp	C	09 ARI	2	2	24	52	45	3.63	1.15	265	298	214	4.2	32%	71%	2.71	57	20	23	1.2	7.8	6.4	14%	0.9	3.6	142	$13
Consist	A	1st Half	1	1	13	30	28	4.17	1.26	285			4.2	35%	69%	2.36	65	17	18	1.2	8.3	7.0	18%	0.9	0.1	161	$6
LIMA Plan	B+	2nd Half	1	1	11	22	17	2.89	1.01	236			4.1	28%	75%	3.12	45	24	30	1.2	7.0	5.7	10%	0.8	3.5	116	$6
Rand Var	+2	10 Proj	4	5	35	76	66	3.21	1.14	249			4.1	31%	74%	2.87	56	19	25	1.8	7.8	4.4	11%	0.7	13.0	127	$21

Ugly knee ligament tear ended season in August, expected to be ready to go in February. Was enjoying good first year as closer, marred only by 1H H% and 2H injury. If healthy, still an upper-echelon closer.

Ramirez,Ramon

Ramirez,Ramon			W	L	Sv	IP	K	ERA	WHIP	OBA	vL	vR	BF/G	H%	S%	xERA	G	L	F	Ctl	Dom	Cmd	hr/f	hr/9	RAR	BPV	R$
RH	Reliever	05 a/a	9	9	0	141	107	4.73	1.43	274			20.5	31%	71%	5.12				3.3	6.8	2.1		1.4	-7.5	43	$8
Age	28	06 COL	4	3	0	67	61	3.48	1.26	234	274	194	4.6	29%	74%	4.13	41	14	45	3.6	8.2	2.3	6%	0.7	8.3	68	$7
Type	Pwr FB	07 COL *	12	3	1	91	83	4.83	1.49	264	240	357	5.9	32%	69%	4.78	31	17	52	4.3	8.2	1.9	7%	1.0	-4.5	41	$9
Health	A	08 KC	3	2	1	72	70	2.64	1.23	220	300	153	4.2	32%	78%	3.55	46	19	35	3.9	8.8	2.3	3%	0.3	15.1	77	$9
PT/Exp	D	09 BOS	7	4	0	70	52	2.84	1.33	237	244	220	4.2	27%	83%	4.82	35	18	48	4.1	6.7	1.6	7%	0.9	13.9	22	$9
Consist	C	1st Half	5	2	0	35	22	1.80	0.94	175			3.9	18%	90%	4.42	35	16	48	3.1	5.7	1.8	8%	1.0	11.4	32	$8
LIMA Plan	C	2nd Half	2	2	0	35	30	3.89	1.73	290			4.6	35%	79%	5.20	34	19	47	5.2	7.8	1.5	6%	0.8	2.4	12	$2
Rand Var	-5	10 Proj	5	3	0	58	49	3.57	1.38	245			4.7	29%	77%	4.47	38	18	44	4.2	7.6	1.8	8%	0.9	-0.3	40	$6

H% saved flagging Dom in 1H, Ctl dive, reversal in H% luck hurt 2H, S% helped all year. 2H Dom rebound bodes well, but Ctl, unstable BPIs remain suspect. Don't count on another sub-3 ERA.

Rauch,Jon

Rauch,Jon			W	L	Sv	IP	K	ERA	WHIP	OBA	vL	vR	BF/G	H%	S%	xERA	G	L	F	Ctl	Dom	Cmd	hr/f	hr/9	RAR	BPV	R$
RH	Reliever	05 WAS *	3	5	0	51	43	3.53	1.16	234	255	186	9.5	27%	74%	4.17	26	23	51	2.6	7.6	2.9	8%	1.1	4.5	69	$6
Age	31	06 WAS	4	5	2	91	86	3.36	1.25	233	254	216	4.5	28%	79%	4.23	30	21	49	3.6	8.5	2.4	11%	1.3	12.7	65	$10
Type	xFB	07 WAS	8	4	4	87	71	3.61	1.10	234	208	249	4.0	28%	69%	4.16	33	13	53	2.2	7.3	3.4	5%	0.7	8.8	85	$13
Health	A	08 2NL	4	8	18	72	66	4.14	1.19	254	268	242	4.0	30%	70%	3.77	31	23	46	2.0	8.3	4.1	12%	1.4	1.1	104	$13
PT/Exp	C	09 2TM	7	3	2	69	49	3.64	1.34	264	239	284	4.0	30%	75%	4.50	37	20	43	3.0	6.4	2.1	6%	0.8	5.8	48	$8
Consist	B	1st Half	0	0	2	35	23	4.60	1.39	261			4.0	29%	69%	4.87	36	19	45	3.6	5.9	1.6	8%	1.0	-1.3	23	$1
LIMA Plan	B	2nd Half	7	3	0	34	26	2.64	1.29	267			4.0	32%	81%	4.11	37	22	41	2.4	6.9	2.9	5%	0.5	7.0	75	$6
Rand Var	-2	10 Proj	5	3	0	51	40	3.90	1.24	255			4.1	29%	72%	4.19	34	20	46	2.5	7.1	2.9	9%	1.1	1.0	73	$6

9.31 ERA, -39 BPV in April, then righted the ship. PRO: 2H BPV. Cmd history. CON: Ctl, Dom erosion. Heavy workload. FB% track record. He is probably riskier than his ERA history would suggest.

JOCK THOMPSON

Ray,Chris		Yr	Tm	W	L	Sv	IP	K	ERA	WHIP	OBA	vL	vR	BF/G	H%	S%	xERA	G	L	F	Ctl	Dom	Cmd	hr/f	hr/9	RAR	BPV	R$
RH	Reliever	05	BAL *	2	5	18	77	77	2.12	1.05	203	284	174	4.3	25%	87%	3.45	35	23	41	2.9	9.0	**3.1**	11%	1.1	21.5	95	$18
Age	28	06	BAL	4	4	33	66	51	2.73	1.09	195	184	202	4.3	21%	84%	4.37	35	16	48	3.7	7.0	**1.9**	11%	1.4	14.9	39	$20
Type	Pwr	07	BAL	5	6	16	43	44	4.43	1.24	225	233	212	4.1	28%	67%	3.57	45	18	38	3.8	9.3	**2.4**	12%	1.1	0.4	87	$11
Health	F	08	BAL	0	0	0	0	0	0.00	0.00							0.00				0.0	0.0						
PT/Exp	D	09	BAL *	0	5	1	58	53	6.02	1.75	305	449	279	4.8	36%	67%	4.62	41	21	38	4.6	8.2	**1.8**	11%	1.2	-11.3	41	($1)
Consist	C	1st Half		0	2	1	35	37	6.67	1.71	298			5.1	38%	61%	4.44	33	25	42	4.6	9.5	**2.1**	9%	1.0	-9.6	57	($1)
LIMA Plan	C+	2nd Half		0	3	0	23	16	5.04	1.81	314			4.4	34%	76%	4.99	47	18	35	4.7	6.2	**1.3**	15%	1.6	-1.7	11	($1)
Rand Var	+5	10	Proj	5	5	5	68	61	4.37	1.41	256			4.4	31%	72%	4.14	42	19	39	4.0	8.1	2.0	10%	1.1	2.5	58	$7

0-4, 7.27 ERA in 43 IP at BAL. Still finding himself after TJ surgery, as evidenced by Ctl. Dom started strong, but faded in 2H, though he regained GB tendencies. Needs to improve Cmd if he is to have any value.

Redding,Tim		Yr	Tm	W	L	Sv	IP	K	ERA	WHIP	OBA	vL	vR	BF/G	H%	S%	xERA	G	L	F	Ctl	Dom	Cmd	hr/f	hr/9	RAR	BPV	R$
RH	Reliever	05	2TM *	3	9	0	92	61	7.02	1.70	323			19.4	36%	58%	6.33				3.2	5.9	**1.9**		1.1	-30.8	32	($4)
Age	32	06	aaa	12	10	0	187	118	4.91	1.50	292			28.5	31%	72%	5.84				3.1	5.7	**1.9**		1.6	-9.0	23	$9
Type	FB	07	WAS *	12	11	0	173	95	5.54	1.68	315	245	282	24.9	34%	68%	5.26	38	22	39	3.4	4.9	**1.5**	8%	1.0	-23.7	14	$2
Health	B	08	WAS	10	11	0	182	120	4.95	1.43	275	277	274	24.0	30%	69%	4.61	40	20	40	3.2	5.9	**1.8**	11%	1.3	-15.1	38	$7
PT/Exp	B	09	NYM	3	6	0	120	76	5.10	1.43	265	278	247	17.4	28%	68%	5.05	36	16	48	3.8	5.7	**1.5**	10%	1.4	-13.5	15	$2
Consist	B	1st Half		1	3	0	45	30	6.39	1.49	274			24.8	30%	58%	5.17	33	15	51	3.8	6.0	**1.6**	9%	1.4	-12.2	17	($1)
LIMA Plan	C	2nd Half		2	3	0	75	46	4.33	1.40	259			14.7	28%	73%	4.97	37	17	46	3.7	5.5	**1.5**	10%	1.3	-1.3	14	$3
Rand Var	0	10	Proj	4	8	0	98	61	5.17	1.49	280			20.5	30%	68%	4.98	37	18	44	3.5	5.6	1.6	10%	1.3	-8.6	22	$2

3.41 ERA in Aug-Sept doesn't make up for a career of "keep him off your roster" production. Cmd has been sub-par since the Clinton administration, and now he is giving up more fly balls as well. Avoid vigorously.

Reyes,Dennys		Yr	Tm	W	L	Sv	IP	K	ERA	WHIP	OBA	vL	vR	BF/G	H%	S%	xERA	G	L	F	Ctl	Dom	Cmd	hr/f	hr/9	RAR	BPV	R$
LH	Reliever	05	SD	3	2	0	43	35	5.21	2.06	319	208	359	6.0	38%	74%	4.21	65	17	18	6.7	7.3	**1.1**	11%	0.6	-5.1	-6	($1)
Age	32	06	MIN *	6	0	0	68	59	0.80	1.01	208	148	244	3.8	26%	95%	2.52	69	11	20	2.4	7.8	**3.2**	8%	0.4	31.6	122	$15
Type	Pwr xGB	07	MIN	2	1	0	29	21	3.99	1.88	292	273	364	2.8	35%	78%	4.56	64	13	22	6.5	6.5	**1.0**	5%	0.3	1.9	-16	$1
Health	B	08	MIN	3	0	0	46	39	2.33	1.19	235	202	276	2.5	28%	84%	3.02	60	17	23	2.9	7.6	**2.6**	13%	0.8	11.5	95	$7
PT/Exp	B	09	STL	0	2	1	41	33	3.29	1.37	232	207	276	2.3	29%	76%	3.94	53	16	31	4.6	7.2	**1.6**	5%	0.4	4.5	37	$2
Consist	C	1st Half		0	1	1	20	19	4.46	1.34	240			2.3	30%	68%	3.93	41	19	40	4.0	8.5	**2.1**	9%	0.9	-0.7	63	$1
LIMA Plan	B	2nd Half		0	1	0	21	14	2.16	1.39	225			2.4	28%	83%	3.82	66	12	22	5.2	6.1	**1.2**	0%	0.0	5.2	12	$1
Rand Var	-2	10	Proj	2	1	0	44	35	3.52	1.38	246			2.8	30%	75%	3.60	59	15	26	4.1	7.2	1.8	9%	0.6	3.6	56	$3

Ctl has been a roller coaster ride, while Dom has remained fairly steady. Still-elite GB rate trending down, and he remains extremely tough on LHers. Ctl holds the key to his ratios, but role restricts value.

Rhodes,Arthur		Yr	Tm	W	L	Sv	IP	K	ERA	WHIP	OBA	vL	vR	BF/G	H%	S%	xERA	G	L	F	Ctl	Dom	Cmd	hr/f	hr/9	RAR	BPV	R$
LH	Reliever	05	CLE	3	1	0	43	43	2.09	1.04	214	286	155	3.6	28%	81%	3.18	41	23	36	2.5	9.0	**3.6**	5%	0.4	12.1	113	$8
Age	40	06	PHI	0	5	4	45	48	5.38	1.70	269	290	246	3.8	36%	67%	4.68	36	22	41	6.0	9.6	**1.6**	4%	0.4	-5.0	25	$1
Type	Pwr FB	07	SEA	0	0	0	0	0	0.00	0.00							0.00											
Health	F	08	2TM	4	1	2	35	40	2.04	1.25	220	157	309	2.4	32%	82%	3.75	27	28	45	4.1	10.2	**2.5**	0%	0.0	9.9	78	$7
PT/Exp	D	09	CIN	1	1	0	53	48	2.53	1.07	198	141	245	3.2	25%	78%	3.70	41	17	42	3.4	8.1	**2.4**	5%	0.5	10.9	73	$6
Consist	A	1st Half		0	0	0	27	22	1.65	0.96	173			3.1	20%	88%	3.70	45	14	42	3.3	7.3	**2.2**	7%	0.7	8.5	64	$4
LIMA Plan	C	2nd Half		1	1	0	26	26	3.45	1.19	222			3.4	30%	70%	3.68	36	22	42	3.4	9.0	**2.6**	3%	0.3	2.4	82	$3
Rand Var	-5	10	Proj	2	2	0	46	40	3.74	1.33	241			3.2	30%	72%	4.23	36	22	42	3.9	7.9	2.0	5%	0.6	0.2	50	$4

LHers still can't touch him. Dom drop not drastic, and offset by Ctl, GB improvement. ERA likely to rise. Age has to catch up at some point, but still looking like a solid LIMA option. Just don't expect a more visible role.

Richard,Clayton		Yr	Tm	W	L	Sv	IP	K	ERA	WHIP	OBA	vL	vR	BF/G	H%	S%	xERA	G	L	F	Ctl	Dom	Cmd	hr/f	hr/9	RAR	BPV	R$
LH	Reliever	05		0	0	0	0	0	0.00	0.00							0.00											
Age	26	06		0	0	0	0	0	0.00	0.00							0.00											
Type		07		0	0	0	0	0	0.00	0.00							0.00											
Health	A	08	CHW *	14	11	0	175	102	4.19	1.27	274	274	320	22.2	31%	67%	3.70	50	23	27	1.8	5.3	**2.9**	8%	0.6	3.3	74	$16
PT/Exp	C	09	2TM	9	5	0	153	114	4.41	1.47	263	229	279	17.7	30%	72%	4.32	48	18	34	4.2	6.7	**1.6**	11%	1.0	-1.9	34	$8
Consist	B	1st Half		3	1	0	68	52	4.49	1.51	275			13.7	31%	73%	4.28	49	17	34	4.0	6.9	**1.7**	12%	1.2	-1.5	44	$3
LIMA Plan	C+	2nd Half		6	4	0	85	62	4.35	1.44	253			23.1	29%	71%	4.35	48	19	33	4.3	6.6	**1.5**	9%	0.8	-0.4	27	$5
Rand Var	0	10	Proj	10	10	0	174	123	4.14	1.39	267			23.4	30%	72%	4.08	48	19	33	3.2	6.4	2.0	10%	0.9	5.8	54	$12

Enjoyed his new home park after trade to SD, with 2.00 ERA in 6 starts at Petco. GB rate, rising Dom, success vs LH show promise. If he splits difference between 08-09 Ctl... UP:14 Wins, sub-4.00 ERA

Richmond,Scott		Yr	Tm	W	L	Sv	IP	K	ERA	WHIP	OBA	vL	vR	BF/G	H%	S%	xERA	G	L	F	Ctl	Dom	Cmd	hr/f	hr/9	RAR	BPV	R$
RH	Starter	05		0	0	0	0	0	0.00	0.00							0.00											
Age	30	06		0	0	0	0	0	0.00	0.00							0.00											
Type	Pwr xFB	07		0	0	0	0	0	0.00	0.00							0.00											
Health	B	08	a/a	6	11	0	137	84	6.80	1.77	327			26.8	34%	66%	7.50				3.6	5.5	**1.5**		2.0	-42.2	-5	($6)
PT/Exp	D	09	TOR	8	11	0	139	117	5.52	1.49	273	292	233	22.6	30%	68%	4.62	34	22	45	3.8	7.6	**2.0**	14%	1.8	-18.2	45	$6
Consist	F	1st Half		6	5	0	85	71	3.70	1.20	231			21.9	25%	77%	4.05	38	20	42	3.2	7.5	**2.4**	15%	1.6	7.9	66	$10
LIMA Plan	C	2nd Half		2	6	0	54	46	8.40	1.94	332			23.7	37%	59%	5.54	28	24	48	4.9	7.7	**1.6**	14%	2.0	-26.1	13	($5)
Rand Var	+2	10	Proj	6	10	0	116	88	4.97	1.52	284			23.4	32%	72%	4.86	31	23	46	3.6	6.8	1.9	12%	1.6	-6.1	36	$5

Reasons not to get excited about 1H performance:
- 2H performance
- That ugly 2008 line
- FB rate
- Career OPS vs RHers of .967

Risk easily exceeds reward.

Rivera,Mariano		Yr	Tm	W	L	Sv	IP	K	ERA	WHIP	OBA	vL	vR	BF/G	H%	S%	xERA	G	L	F	Ctl	Dom	Cmd	hr/f	hr/9	RAR	BPV	R$
RH	Reliever	05	NYY	7	4	43	78	80	1.38	0.87	185	177	176	4.2	25%	85%	2.50	57	14	29	2.1	9.2	**4.4**	4%	0.2	28.8	145	$31
Age	40	06	NYY	5	5	34	75	55	1.80	0.96	224	194	248	4.6	27%	83%	3.13	54	16	30	1.3	6.6	**5.0**	5%	0.4	25.5	115	$25
Type	Pwr GB	07	NYY	3	4	30	71	74	3.16	1.12	253	255	241	4.3	33%	72%	2.69	53	19	29	1.5	9.3	**6.2**	7%	0.5	11.9	158	$20
Health	A	08	NYY	6	5	39	71	77	1.40	0.66	171	147	183	4.0	23%	84%	2.12	55	15	31	0.8	9.8	**12.8**	8%	0.5	25.7	188	$30
PT/Exp	A	09	NYY	3	3	44	66	72	1.76	0.90	204	182	211	3.8	26%	89%	2.43	51	22	27	1.6	9.8	**6.0**	16%	1.0	22.0	161	$27
Consist	A	1st Half		1	2	20	32	40	2.80	0.96	236			3.9	31%	81%	2.16	49	22	28	0.8	11.2	**13.3**	22%	1.4	6.6	206	$12
LIMA Plan	C+	2nd Half		2	1	24	34	32	0.79	0.85	172			3.8	22%	96%	2.70	53	21	26	2.4	8.4	**3.6**	9%	0.5	15.4	119	$16
Rand Var	-5	10	Proj	4	3	35	65	63	3.03	1.06	227			4.2	29%	73%	2.84	53	19	28	2.1	8.7	4.2	10%	0.7	12.8	131	$21

Yet another dominant season. Allowed most HR since 1995, and despite ERA, skills dipped just a bit in 2H. But that is just nitpicking. Age raises the risk, but every reason to think he will be among the top closers again.

Rivera,Saul		Yr	Tm	W	L	Sv	IP	K	ERA	WHIP	OBA	vL	vR	BF/G	H%	S%	xERA	G	L	F	Ctl	Dom	Cmd	hr/f	hr/9	RAR	BPV	R$
RH	Reliever	05	aa	3	3	9	76	50	3.27	1.53	304			8.5	35%	79%	4.92				2.7	5.9	**2.2**		0.4	9.7	62	$7
Age	32	06	WAS *	4	1	2	88	61	3.01	1.52	264	194	290	5.9	31%	81%	4.75	46	19	35	4.6	6.2	**1.3**	5%	0.5	16.1	12	$7
Type	GB	07	WAS	4	6	3	93	64	3.68	1.40	251	271	244	4.7	30%	71%	4.31	50	18	32	4.1	6.2	**1.5**	1%	0.1	8.6	29	$7
Health	A	08	WAS	5	6	0	84	65	3.96	1.49	275	271	284	4.9	34%	72%	3.77	54	21	25	3.8	7.0	**1.9**	5%	0.3	3.2	56	$5
PT/Exp	C	09	WAS *	3	8	2	84	48	5.41	1.89	333	296	321	6.7	37%	72%	4.73	56	17	27	4.3	5.1	**1.2**	10%	0.9	-12.6	9	($3)
Consist	B	1st Half		1	6	1	42	29	5.25	1.99	350			6.7	40%	74%	4.52	53	23	25	4.2	6.1	**1.5**	10%	0.9	-5.5	28	($2)
LIMA Plan	C	2nd Half		2	2	1	41	19	5.58	1.79	314			6.7	33%	69%	4.95	57	15	28	4.5	4.1	**0.9**	10%	0.9	-7.0	-12	($1)
Rand Var	+3	10	Proj	3	4	0	61	39	4.56	1.57	282			5.7	32%	71%	4.34	53	19	28	4.1	5.7	1.4	9%	0.7	-0.6	23	$1

1-3, 6.10 ERA in 38 IP at WAS. H% has plagued him, some FB finally left the park, and ERA suffered as a result. GB% is strong, but Dom not high enough to overcome shaky Ctl. Check back only if Cmd clears 2.0.

Robertson,David		Yr	Tm	W	L	Sv	IP	K	ERA	WHIP	OBA	vL	vR	BF/G	H%	S%	xERA	G	L	F	Ctl	Dom	Cmd	hr/f	hr/9	RAR	BPV	R$
RH	Reliever	05		0	0	0	0	0	0.00	0.00							0.00											
Age	25	06		0	0	0	0	0	0.00	0.00							0.00											
Type	Pwr FB	07		0	0	0	0	0	0.00	0.00							0.00											
Health	A	08	NYY *	8	0	3	84	101	3.34	1.22	211	259	254	6.3	30%	72%	3.30	43	16	41	4.2	10.9	**2.6**	5%	0.4	10.4	103	$14
PT/Exp	F	09	NYY *	2	4	3	58	84	3.11	1.33	227	189	237	4.6	36%	78%	3.09	36	23	41	4.5	13.1	**2.9**	8%	0.6	9.6	127	$8
Consist	A	1st Half		1	3	2	31	47	2.59	1.28	214			4.9	35%	82%	2.99	41	14	46	4.6	13.5	**2.9**	7%	0.6	7.2	138	$5
LIMA Plan	B+	2nd Half		1	1	1	27	37	3.72	1.39	242			4.4	37%	74%	3.23	33	28	39	4.4	12.5	**2.8**	8%	0.7	2.4	117	$3
Rand Var	0	10	Proj	4	3	5	73	95	3.35	1.21	209			5.0	30%	74%	3.18	37	23	41	4.2	11.8	2.8	9%	0.7	11.2	113	$12

2-1, 3.30 ERA in 43 IP at NYY. Still has some issues with his Ctl, but makes up for it with elite Dom. Showed significant improvement vs LH in '09. Skills say he could end up as the eventual Rivera successor.

BRIAN RUDD

Robertson,Nate

LH	Reliever	Yr	Tm	W	L	Sv	IP	K	ERA	WHIP	OBA	vL	vR	BF/G	H%	S%	xERA	G	L	F	Ctl	Dom	Cmd	hr/f	hr/9	RAR	BPV	R$
Age	32	05	DET	7	16	0	196	122	4.50	1.36	267	244	272	26.2	29%	71%	4.07	49	20	30	3.0	5.6	1.9	15%	1.3	-3.0	48	$10
Type	Pwr	06	DET	13	13	0	208	137	3.85	1.31	260	181	284	27.5	28%	75%	4.13	47	20	33	2.9	5.9	2.0	13%	1.3	18.2	53	$19
Health	D	07	DET	9	13	0	178	119	4.76	1.47	284	296	278	26.0	32%	70%	4.51	45	18	37	3.2	6.0	1.9	10%	1.1	-5.6	45	$9
PT/Exp	B	08	DET	7	11	0	169	108	6.35	1.66	314	323	311	24.1	34%	63%	4.71	44	19	37	3.3	5.8	1.7	12%	1.4	-41.6	37	($2)
Consist	A	09	DET	2	3	0	50	35	5.43	1.75	296	295	295	8.3	34%	69%	5.35	41	18	41	5.1	6.3	1.3	6%	0.7	-6.0	-4	($0)
LIMA Plan	D	1st Half		1	0	0	21	17	7.71	1.86	297			4.8	35%	57%	5.24	43	20	37	6.0	7.3	1.2	8%	0.9	-8.5	-10	($1)
Rand Var	0	2nd Half		1	3	0	29	18	3.76	1.67	296			18.8	34%	78%	5.42	39	17	44	4.4	5.6	1.3	5%	0.6	2.4	0	$1
		10	Proj	**4**	**7**	**0**	**102**	**68**	**5.23**	**1.66**	**295**			**12.6**	**33%**	**70%**	**4.99**	**43**	**18**	**39**	**4.3**	**6.0**	**1.4**	**9%**	**1.1**	**-7.0**	**14**	**$1**

Landed on DL in May with back strain, then missed 2 months following elbow surgery. Skills were marginal to begin with, and have been in decline for some time. Now add health risk to the list of reasons to avoid him.

Rodney,Fernando

RH	Reliever	Yr	Tm	W	L	Sv	IP	K	ERA	WHIP	OBA	vL	vR	BF/G	H%	S%	xERA	G	L	F	Ctl	Dom	Cmd	hr/f	hr/9	RAR	BPV	R$
Age	33	05	DET	2	3	9	44	42	2.86	1.27	239	265	219	4.7	29%	82%	3.53	40	28	31	3.5	8.6	2.5	13%	1.0	8.2	79	$8
Type	Pwr GB	06	DET	7	4	7	71	65	3.54	1.19	203	202	192	4.6	25%	72%	3.51	57	12	31	4.3	8.2	1.9	10%	0.8	8.9	66	$13
Health	F	07	DET	2	6	1	51	54	4.26	1.32	243	247	231	4.5	32%	69%	3.48	45	19	35	3.7	9.6	2.6	11%	0.9	1.5	95	$5
PT/Exp	C	08	DET	0	6	13	40	49	4.91	1.59	230	256	186	4.8	32%	69%	3.98	40	26	33	6.7	10.9	1.6	9%	0.7	-2.8	34	$5
Consist	A	09	DET	2	4	37	73	60	4.33	1.43	244	265	219	4.4	29%	72%	3.99	57	11	31	4.7	7.4	1.6	12%	1.0	1.1	42	$16
LIMA Plan	D	1st Half		0	1	17	33	27	4.36	1.39	244			4.2	29%	70%	4.09	53	12	35	4.4	7.4	1.7	9%	0.8	0.4	46	$7
Rand Var	+1	2nd Half		2	3	20	40	33	4.31	1.46	243			4.6	28%	74%	3.90	60	11	28	5.0	7.5	1.5	15%	1.1	0.7	38	$9
		10	Proj	**2**	**7**	**25**	**73**	**65**	**4.59**	**1.48**	**250**			**4.6**	**30%**	**70%**	**4.03**	**51**	**17**	**32**	**4.8**	**8.1**	**1.7**	**10%**	**0.9**	**3.6**	**43**	**$12**

GB rate is the only thing - ONLY THING - that kept this season afloat. Bad Ctl, lowest Dom since 2002, even .219 BA vs RH was backed by only a 1.0 Cmd. Just 1 BSv, but only 10 of 37 saves were clean (no H or BB).

Rodriguez,Francisco

RH	Reliever	Yr	Tm	W	L	Sv	IP	K	ERA	WHIP	OBA	vL	vR	BF/G	H%	S%	xERA	G	L	F	Ctl	Dom	Cmd	hr/f	hr/9	RAR	BPV	R$
Age	28	05	ANA	2	5	45	67	91	2.68	1.15	192	213	153	4.1	28%	81%	2.83	46	17	38	4.3	12.2	2.8	13%	0.9	14.0	128	$25
Type	Pwr FB	06	LAA	2	3	47	73	98	1.73	1.10	202	215	179	4.2	30%	89%	3.01	39	14	47	3.5	12.1	3.5	8%	0.7	25.5	141	$28
Health	A	07	LAA	5	2	40	67	90	2.81	1.25	209	187	217	4.2	32%	78%	3.13	43	17	40	4.5	12.0	2.6	5%	0.4	14.1	115	$24
PT/Exp	A	08	LAA	2	3	62	68	77	2.24	1.29	219	227	205	3.8	30%	85%	3.51	42	20	38	4.5	10.1	2.3	6%	0.5	17.8	82	$29
Consist	A	09	NYM	3	6	35	68	73	3.71	1.31	210	185	223	4.1	27%	74%	4.06	35	19	46	5.0	9.7	1.9	9%	0.9	4.1	51	$17
LIMA Plan	C	1st Half		1	2	21	37	39	1.21	1.16	167			4.1	23%	90%	4.11	29	22	48	5.3	9.4	1.8	2%	0.2	13.7	34	$12
Rand Var	0	2nd Half		2	4	14	31	34	6.72	1.49	257			4.1	31%	58%	3.97	41	15	44	4.7	9.9	2.1	16%	1.8	-9.6	72	$5
		10	Proj	**3**	**5**	**38**	**73**	**80**	**3.97**	**1.38**	**233**			**4.2**	**30%**	**74%**	**3.88**	**40**	**18**	**43**	**4.7**	**9.9**	**2.1**	**10%**	**1.0**	**3.5**	**69**	**$18**

Uh-oh. Dom dropping, Ctl, FB rate rising. RH had .750 OPS against him, the highest of his career. Still racking up saves, but BPV, xERA trends tell the story. He will be over-valued on draft day.

Rodriguez,Wandy

LH	Starter	Yr	Tm	W	L	Sv	IP	K	ERA	WHIP	OBA	vL	vR	BF/G	H%	S%	xERA	G	L	F	Ctl	Dom	Cmd	hr/f	hr/9	RAR	BPV	R$
Age	31	05	HOU	* 14	12	0	177	118	5.42	1.50	279	275	273	23.1	30%	67%	4.33	46	23	31	3.7	6.0	1.6	16%	1.4	-25.6	31	$6
Type	Pwr	06	HOU	* 11	12	0	161	110	5.97	1.65	294	262	298	21.0	33%	65%	4.79	45	22	33	4.3	6.1	1.4	11%	1.1	-29.6	17	$1
Health	B	07	HOU	9	13	0	183	158	4.58	1.32	258	252	254	25.0	31%	68%	3.99	41	19	40	3.1	7.8	2.5	10%	1.1	-3.5	77	$13
PT/Exp	A	08	HOU	9	7	0	137	131	3.54	1.31	260	282	248	23.2	32%	76%	3.62	40	23	36	2.9	8.6	3.0	10%	0.9	12.4	95	$13
Consist	A	09	HOU	14	12	0	206	193	3.02	1.24	249	192	264	25.9	31%	79%	3.50	45	18	37	2.8	8.4	3.1	10%	0.9	29.7	101	$23
LIMA Plan	C+	1st Half		6	6	0	96	90	3.37	1.34	253			25.6	31%	79%	3.87	42	18	40	3.5	8.4	2.4	11%	1.1	9.8	78	$9
Rand Var	-2	2nd Half		8	6	0	110	103	2.71	1.15	245			26.2	31%	79%	3.19	48	18	34	2.1	8.5	4.0	9%	0.7	20.0	120	$15
		10	Proj	**16**	**10**	**0**	**213**	**200**	**3.22**	**1.23**	**252**			**25.9**	**31%**	**78%**	**3.47**	**43**	**20**	**37**	**2.5**	**8.5**	**3.4**	**10%**	**1.0**	**20.9**	**106**	**$25**

Other than a few more GB, it was a carbon copy of 2008. And 2H performance was elite. Huge improvement vs LH, as he held them to .502 OPS. Cmd, BPV, xERA all trending in right direction, so invest.

Romero,J.C.

LH	Reliever	Yr	Tm	W	L	Sv	IP	K	ERA	WHIP	OBA	vL	vR	BF/G	H%	S%	xERA	G	L	F	Ctl	Dom	Cmd	hr/f	hr/9	RAR	BPV	R$
Age	33	05	MIN	4	3	0	57	48	3.47	1.56	237	198	268	3.8	28%	81%	4.36	55	14	31	6.2	7.6	1.2	12%	0.9	6.3	3	$4
Type	Pwr xGB	06	LAA	1	2	0	48	31	6.74	1.77	296	202	382	3.5	34%	60%	4.70	57	16	27	5.2	5.8	1.1	7%	0.6	-12.9	-2	($2)
Health	C	07	2TM	2	2	1	56	42	1.92	1.40	197	208	198	3.3	24%	88%	4.41	60	11	29	6.4	6.7	1.1	7%	0.5	17.7	-14	$6
PT/Exp	D	08	PHI	4	4	1	59	52	2.75	1.34	198	102	282	3.1	24%	82%	3.59	62	16	22	5.8	7.9	1.4	14%	0.8	11.1	26	$7
Consist	C	09	PHI	0	0	0	17	12	2.69	1.56	216	308	156	3.6	24%	88%	4.87	54	15	30	7.0	6.5	0.9	14%	1.1	3.1	-40	$1
LIMA Plan	C	1st Half		0	0	0	11	7	3.24	1.89	223			4.5	25%	85%	6.45	52	16	32	9.7	5.7	0.6	9%	0.8	1.3	******	($0)
Rand Var	-5	2nd Half		0	0	0	6	5	1.61	0.89	202			2.4	22%	100%	2.54	60	13	27	1.6	8.0	5.0	25%	1.6	1.8	139	$1
		10	Proj	**2**	**2**	**0**	**44**	**33**	**3.93**	**1.61**	**255**			**3.4**	**30%**	**77%**	**4.35**	**58**	**14**	**27**	**5.8**	**6.8**	**1.2**	**11%**	**0.8**	**-0.5**	**3**	**$2**

Returned from suspension with awful BPI's, before missing 2 months with forearm strain. Still has a nice GB rate, but that's like telling the ugliest girl in the room that she has nice elbows. She does... but still.

Romero,Ricky

LH	Starter	Yr	Tm	W	L	Sv	IP	K	ERA	WHIP	OBA	vL	vR	BF/G	H%	S%	xERA	G	L	F	Ctl	Dom	Cmd	hr/f	hr/9	RAR	BPV	R$
Age	25	05		0	0	0	0	0	0.00	0.00							0.00											
Type	Pwr GB	06		0	0	0	0	0	0.00	0.00							0.00											
Health	A	07	aa	3	6	0	88	68	6.03	1.87	313			23.5	36%	69%	6.78				5.3	6.9	1.3		1.1	-17.0	28	($3)
PT/Exp	C	08	a/a	8	8	0	164	96	5.65	1.76	312			27.4	35%	68%	6.08				4.3	5.3	1.2		0.8	-27.2	25	($3)
Consist	C	09	TOR	13	9	0	178	141	4.30	1.52	277	297	278	27.3	33%	74%	3.91	54	19	27	4.0	7.1	1.8	12%	0.9	3.4	52	$12
LIMA Plan	C	1st Half		6	3	0	72	61	2.87	1.25	245			27.3	29%	83%	3.52	52	17	31	3.0	7.6	2.5	14%	1.1	14.1	86	$10
Rand Var	+1	2nd Half		7	6	0	106	80	5.27	1.71	297			27.2	35%	69%	4.18	55	21	24	4.7	6.8	1.5	11%	0.8	-10.7	29	$2
		10	Proj	**11**	**10**	**0**	**185**	**142**	**4.54**	**1.51**	**276**			**25.5**	**32%**	**71%**	**3.90**	**54**	**19**	**27**	**3.9**	**6.9**	**1.8**	**12%**	**0.9**	**12.1**	**51**	**$10**

Post-hype prospect started off strong, as 9 of first 11 starts were PQS-4/5. Unfortunately, only 2 of last 18 fell into that category. GB%, '09 Dom are intriguing, if he can maintain that combo... UP: 3.75 ERA.

Romo,Sergio

RH	Reliever	Yr	Tm	W	L	Sv	IP	K	ERA	WHIP	OBA	vL	vR	BF/G	H%	S%	xERA	G	L	F	Ctl	Dom	Cmd	hr/f	hr/9	RAR	BPV	R$
Age	27	05		0	0	0	0	0	0.00	0.00							0.00											
Type	Pwr xFB	06		0	0	0	0	0	0.00	0.00							0.00											
Health	B	07		0	0	0	0	0	0.00	0.00							0.00											
PT/Exp	D	08	SF	* 4	4	11	67	61	3.31	0.99	203	83	176	4.7	26%	67%	3.81	33	14	53	2.4	8.2	3.4	4%	0.6	7.9	92	$13
Consist	A	09	SF	5	2	2	34	41	3.97	1.21	238	188	259	3.1	35%	65%	3.48	32	15	53	2.9	10.9	3.7	2%	0.3	0.9	127	$6
LIMA Plan	A	1st Half		2	0	0	10	14	2.65	1.27	258			3.6	38%	83%	3.41	29	7	64	2.6	12.4	4.7	6%	0.9	1.9	157	$2
Rand Var	0	2nd Half		3	2	2	24	27	4.54	1.18	230			3.0	33%	57%	3.48	33	18	48	3.0	10.2	3.4	0%	0.0	-1.0	113	$4
		10	Proj	**7**	**5**	**3**	**68**	**76**	**3.44**	**1.13**	**226**			**3.5**	**30%**	**72%**	**3.62**	**32**	**14**	**55**	**2.8**	**10.1**	**3.6**	**6%**	**0.8**	**5.4**	**116**	**$11**

Missed first 2 months due to sprained right elbow. Unlucky H%, S% balanced out by just 1 HR allowed, despite high FB rate. That won't happen again. Though 34 IP is a small sample, BPV gives him saves potential.

Rosales,Leo

RH	Reliever	Yr	Tm	W	L	Sv	IP	K	ERA	WHIP	OBA	vL	vR	BF/G	H%	S%	xERA	G	L	F	Ctl	Dom	Cmd	hr/f	hr/9	RAR	BPV	R$
Age	28	05		0	0	0	0	0	0.00	0.00							0.00											
Type	FB	06	aa	5	6	0	61	43	4.58	1.47	285			5.1	32%	71%	5.09				3.1	6.4	2.0		1.0	-0.4	50	$4
Health	A	07	aaa	1	1	14	24	21	4.70	1.71	305			4.7	36%	76%	6.36				4.3	7.8	1.8		1.3	-0.7	40	$5
PT/Exp	F	08	ARI	* 3	3	9	66	39	5.68	1.80	319	286	263	5.6	35%	70%	5.26	45	18	37	4.3	5.3	1.2	11%	1.3	-11.5	1	$1
Consist	B	09	ARI	* 4	2	3	64	42	3.78	1.18	233	235	238	5.3	26%	70%	4.53	34	19	47	2.9	5.9	2.0	7%	0.8	3.3	38	$7
LIMA Plan	C+	1st Half		3	1	3	34	18	2.94	1.23	229			5.5	25%	78%	4.88	35	22	43	3.5	4.7	1.3	5%	0.6	5.3	3	$5
Rand Var	-4	2nd Half		1	1	0	30	24	4.74	1.13	237			5.0	27%	60%	4.06	33	18	49	2.3	7.2	3.2	9%	1.1	-2.0	80	$2
		10	Proj	**2**	**2**	**0**	**44**	**29**	**4.55**	**1.40**	**273**			**5.2**	**30%**	**71%**	**4.70**	**37**	**19**	**45**	**3.1**	**6.0**	**1.9**	**10%**	**1.2**	**-2.3**	**39**	**$2**

2-1, 4.76 ERA in 45 IP at ARI. PRO: 2H gains in both Ctl and Dom. Improved vs LH and RH. CON: Shaky Cmd history. FB% heading in wrong direction. Verdict: ERA will rise, it's just a matter of how much.

Rowland-Smith,Ryan

LH	Starter	Yr	Tm	W	L	Sv	IP	K	ERA	WHIP	OBA	vL	vR	BF/G	H%	S%	xERA	G	L	F	Ctl	Dom	Cmd	hr/f	hr/9	RAR	BPV	R$
Age	27	05	aa	6	7	0	122	93	5.16	1.67	305			17.0	36%	68%	5.45				3.9	6.9	1.8		0.6	-12.9	54	$1
Type	FB	06	aa	1	3	4	41	42	3.84	1.63	286			8.1	37%	76%	4.97				4.5	9.1	2.0		0.5	3.5	82	$3
Health	C	07	SEA	* 4	4	1	80	85	4.29	1.49	262			6.9	34%	72%	4.25	34	21	46	4.4	9.5	2.2	6%	0.7	2.2	64	$6
PT/Exp	D	08	SEA	* 7	3	2	136	88	3.50	1.36	251	311	224	11.7	28%	78%	4.74	39	19	42	3.8	5.8	1.5	8%	1.0	14.3	20	$12
Consist	A	09	SEA	* 10	7	0	152	85	4.01	1.25	263	195	253	25.4	29%	70%	4.58	39	18	43	2.2	5.0	2.3	7%	0.8	8.4	48	$13
LIMA Plan	C	1st Half		2	3	0	38	17	5.60	1.75	332			22.3	36%	68%	5.96	47	0	53	3.1	3.9	1.2	4%	0.7	-5.4	10	($1)
Rand Var	-2	2nd Half		8	4	0	114	68	3.47	1.08	236			26.9	26%	71%	4.21	38	19	42	1.9	5.4	2.8	7%	0.9	13.8	62	$14
		10	Proj	**8**	**8**	**0**	**154**	**99**	**4.38**	**1.39**	**270**			**22.9**	**30%**	**71%**	**4.72**	**38**	**19**	**43**	**3.1**	**5.8**	**1.9**	**8%**	**1.1**	**-5.3**	**37**	**$10**

5-4, 3.74 ERA in 96 IP at SEA. Triceps tendinitis cost him much of the season. Improved vs LH, Ctl dropping, but Dom hasn't carried over to new role (8.6 career as SP, 4.8 as RP). Expect more ERA erosion if SP.

BRIAN RUDD

Ryan,B.J.

Ryan,B.J.			W	L	Sv	IP	K	ERA	WHIP	OBA	vL	vR	BF/G	H%	S%	xERA	G	L	F	Ctl	Dom	Cmd	hr/f	hr/9	RAR	BPV	R$
LH Reliever	05	BAL	1	4	36	70	100	2.44	1.14	215	211	206	4.1	34%	80%	2.48	45	21	34	3.3	12.8	**3.8**	8%	0.5	16.7	164	$22
Age 34	06	TOR	2	2	38	72	86	1.37	0.86	171	120	182	4.2	25%	86%	2.85	37	20	43	2.5	10.7	**4.3**	4%	0.4	28.3	140	$27
Type Pwr FB	07	TOR	0	2	3	4	3	12.56	2.56	366	333	333	4.7	40%	50%	7.54	24	35	41	8.4	6.3	**0.8**	15%	2.1	-4.3	-111	($0)
Health F	08	TOR	2	4	32	58	58	2.95	1.28	220	230	211	4.1	28%	79%	3.91	39	19	42	4.3	9.0	**2.1**	6%	0.6	10.0	61	$17
PT/Exp D	09	TOR	1	1	2	21	13	6.52	1.88	274	250	333	4.0	27%	71%	6.77	35	14	51	7.4	5.7	**0.8**	15%	2.2	-5.3	-85	($0)
Consist F	1st Half		1	0	2	20	13	5.40	1.80	271			3.9	28%	75%	6.41	34	15	51	6.8	5.9	**0.9**	12%	1.8	-2.3	-65	$0
LIMA Plan D	2nd Half		0	1	0	1	0	0.00	0.00				5.0		0%	0.00	50	0	50	25.7	0.0	**0.0**	67%	12.8	0.4	-665	$0
Rand Var +1	10	Proj	**1**	**1**	**3**	**29**	**25**	**4.97**	**1.52**	**255**			**4.3**	**30%**	**70%**	**4.76**	**37**	**18**	**44**	**5.0**	**7.8**	**1.6**	**11%**	**1.2**	**-1.2**	**21**	**$2**

Velocity was down, while Dom and Ctl were way off. He was released by TOR and CHC. Days as a dominant closer are behind him. There is very little reason for optimism, no matter where he latches on.

Rzepczynski,Marc

Rzepczynski,Marc			W	L	Sv	IP	K	ERA	WHIP	OBA	vL	vR	BF/G	H%	S%	xERA	G	L	F	Ctl	Dom	Cmd	hr/f	hr/9	RAR	BPV	R$
LH Starter	05		0	0	0	0	0	0.00	0.00							0.00											
Age 24	06		0	0	0	0	0	0.00	0.00							0.00											
Type Pwr GB	07		0	0	0	0	0	0.00	0.00							0.00											
Health A	08		0	0	0	0	0	0.00	0.00							0.00											
PT/Exp F	09	TOR	* 11	9	0	149	147	3.43	1.52	267	220	226	24.5	35%	78%	3.67	51	20	28	4.4	8.9	**2.0**	7%	0.5	18.8	70	$14
Consist F	1st Half		9	5	0	88	87	3.27	1.65	291			25.1	39%	79%	4.68				4.4	8.9	**2.0**		0.1	12.8	89	$8
LIMA Plan B	2nd Half		2	4	0	61	60	3.67	1.32	228			23.6	28%	76%	3.51	51	20	28	4.4	8.8	**2.0**	15%	1.0	5.9	69	$6
Rand Var 0	10	Proj	**7**	**7**	**0**	**116**	**114**	**4.19**	**1.40**	**246**			**23.8**	**31%**	**71%**	**3.52**	**51**	**20**	**28**	**4.3**	**8.8**	**2.1**	**10%**	**0.7**	**13.0**	**73**	**$10**

2-4, 3.67 ERA in 61 IP at TOR. As was the case during minor league career, combined high GB% and strong Dom. Ctl still needs work, but 73/18 PQS split is indication that early success can be maintained.

Sabathia,CC

Sabathia,CC			W	L	Sv	IP	K	ERA	WHIP	OBA	vL	vR	BF/G	H%	S%	xERA	G	L	F	Ctl	Dom	Cmd	hr/f	hr/9	RAR	BPV	R$
LH Starter	05	CLE	15	10	0	196	161	4.04	1.26	251	248	248	26.4	30%	70%	3.53	49	20	31	2.8	7.4	**2.6**	11%	0.9	8.1	84	$20
Age 29	06	CLE	12	11	0	192	172	3.23	1.18	251	271	242	28.1	31%	75%	3.43	45	19	36	2.1	8.1	**3.9**	9%	0.8	31.5	112	$25
Type Pwr	07	CLE	19	7	0	241	209	3.21	1.14	259	203	275	28.8	32%	74%	3.36	45	18	37	1.4	7.8	**5.6**	8%	0.7	38.5	126	$33
Health A	08	2TM	17	10	0	253	251	2.70	1.11	238	205	247	29.2	31%	78%	3.00	47	22	32	2.1	8.9	**4.3**	9%	0.7	50.0	129	$35
PT/Exp A	09	NYY	19	8	0	230	197	3.37	1.15	233	198	242	27.5	28%	72%	3.65	43	20	37	2.6	7.7	**2.9**	7%	0.7	30.8	89	$31
Consist B	1st Half		7	4	0	109	78	3.55	1.09	223			27.3	26%	69%	3.98	41	19	40	2.6	6.4	**2.5**	7%	0.7	12.1	66	$13
LIMA Plan C	2nd Half		12	4	0	121	119	3.20	1.20	242			27.7	31%	75%	3.36	44	21	35	2.7	8.9	**3.3**	8%	0.7	18.7	109	$18
Rand Var -1	10	Proj	**17**	**8**	**0**	**218**	**196**	**3.19**	**1.15**	**241**			**27.7**	**30%**	**75%**	**3.40**	**45**	**20**	**35**	**2.3**	**8.1**	**3.6**	**9%**	**0.8**	**27.8**	**107**	**$30**

1H wasn't up his typical level, but 2H was vintage. Yankees managed their investment well, as evidenced by drop in BF/G, lowest since 2005. Rel grades speak to workhorse status. Bid with confidence.

Saito,Takashi

Saito,Takashi			W	L	Sv	IP	K	ERA	WHIP	OBA	vL	vR	BF/G	H%	S%	xERA	G	L	F	Ctl	Dom	Cmd	hr/f	hr/9	RAR	BPV	R$
RH Reliever	05	JPN	3	4	0	106	98	4.75	1.46	285			22.1	33%	73%	5.64				3.1	8.3	**2.7**		1.7	-5.8	54	$4
Age 40	06	LA	6	2	24	78	107	2.07	0.91	179	229	129	4.2	28%	78%	2.73	36	16	49	2.7	12.3	**4.7**	4%	0.3	23.2	164	$24
Type Pwr xFB	07	LA	2	1	39	64	78	1.40	0.72	154	186	114	3.7	21%	88%	2.44	46	13	41	1.8	10.9	**6.0**	9%	0.7	24.0	171	$27
Health B	08	LA	4	4	18	47	60	2.49	1.19	232	244	209	4.3	35%	78%	2.81	47	17	36	3.1	11.5	**3.8**	2%	0.2	10.3	149	$14
PT/Exp B	09	BOS	3	3	2	56	52	2.42	1.35	241	195	304	4.2	30%	87%	4.52	31	17	52	4.0	8.4	**2.1**	7%	1.0	13.9	51	$7
Consist C	1st Half		2	1	2	27	26	3.31	1.29	246			3.9	30%	78%	4.24	27	22	51	3.3	8.6	**2.6**	8%	1.0	3.8	71	$4
LIMA Plan C	2nd Half		1	2	0	29	26	1.58	1.40	237			4.6	29%	95%	4.78	34	12	54	4.7	8.2	**1.7**	7%	0.9	10.1	32	$4
Rand Var -5	10	Proj	**2**	**4**	**0**	**51**	**45**	**4.08**	**1.44**	**255**			**4.6**	**30%**	**75%**	**4.54**	**37**	**16**	**47**	**4.3**	**8.0**	**1.9**	**9%**	**1.1**	**-0.6**	**44**	**$3**

ERA remained low, but lots of reasons to not expect it again:
- Huge jump in FB rate
- Ctl, Dom heading wrong way
- Benefited from lucky S%, hr/f
- All of these a little worse in 2H

Not likely to be as lucky again.

Samardzija,Jeff

Samardzija,Jeff			W	L	Sv	IP	K	ERA	WHIP	OBA	vL	vR	BF/G	H%	S%	xERA	G	L	F	Ctl	Dom	Cmd	hr/f	hr/9	RAR	BPV	R$
RH Reliever	05		0	0	0	0	0	0.00	0.00							0.00											
Age 25	06		0	0	0	0	0	0.00	0.00							0.00											
Type	07	aa	3	3	0	34	17	4.22	1.38	283			24.4	26%	84%	6.52				2.4	4.5	**1.9**		2.6	1.0	-14	$3
Health A	08	CHC	* 8	6	1	141	95	4.47	1.53	261	167	276	13.1	30%	72%	4.67	46	22	32	4.8	6.1	**1.3**	9%	0.8	-3.4	4	$6
PT/Exp D	09	CHC	* 7	9	0	124	82	5.97	1.63	313	361	304	14.8	34%	67%	4.76	41	18	40	3.1	6.0	**1.9**	13%	1.6	-27.1	42	($1)
Consist B	1st Half		5	3	0	71	50	4.67	1.54	302			16.7	33%	74%	4.74	40	13	47	2.9	6.3	**2.2**	10%	1.4	-4.2	53	$3
LIMA Plan C+	2nd Half		2	6	0	52	32	7.73	1.76	328			12.9	35%	58%	5.05	41	19	39	3.4	5.5	**1.6**	15%	1.9	-22.9	26	($4)
Rand Var +4	10	Proj	**4**	**7**	**0**	**87**	**56**	**4.97**	**1.46**	**283**			**14.1**	**31%**	**69%**	**4.54**	**42**	**20**	**38**	**3.1**	**5.8**	**1.9**	**11%**	**1.2**	**-3.0**	**41**	**$2**

1-3, 7.53 ERA in 34 IP at CHC. A starter during minor league career, but just 2 starts with CHC. Probably wasn't ready for callup, as hr/9 and BA vL show. For now, just a thrower lacking upside in any role.

Sampson,Chris

Sampson,Chris			W	L	Sv	IP	K	ERA	WHIP	OBA	vL	vR	BF/G	H%	S%	xERA	G	L	F	Ctl	Dom	Cmd	hr/f	hr/9	RAR	BPV	R$
RH Reliever	05	aa	4	12	4	150	63	5.28	1.61	339			21.2	36%	68%	6.30				1.4	3.8	**2.6**		1.0	-18.0	35	($0)
Age 31	06	aaa	12	3	4	125	54	3.17	1.19	274			19.0	29%	78%	4.20				1.1	3.9	**3.6**		1.0	20.9	69	$17
Type Con xGB	07	HOU	7	8	0	122	51	4.59	1.38	287	291	292	21.8	29%	72%	4.70	47	17	36	2.2	3.8	**1.7**	13%	1.5	-2.4	33	$6
Health C	08	HOU	6	4	0	117	61	4.22	1.20	263	273	261	9.0	29%	65%	3.73	56	15	29	1.8	4.7	**2.7**	7%	0.6	0.7	71	$8
PT/Exp B	09	HOU	4	2	3	55	33	5.05	1.57	297	315	272	5.1	34%	66%	4.30	52	20	28	3.4	5.4	**1.6**	4%	0.3	-5.8	34	$2
Consist B	1st Half		4	1	3	44	24	2.66	1.18	239			4.9	28%	76%	4.04	49	19	32	2.7	4.9	**1.8**	2%	0.2	8.3	44	$7
LIMA Plan B	2nd Half		0	1	0	11	9	14.34	3.10	459			5.7	53%	50%	5.16	60	22	18	6.4	7.2	**1.1**	11%	0.8	-14.1	-5	($4)
Rand Var +1	10	Proj	**4**	**2**	**0**	**58**	**30**	**4.03**	**1.31**	**272**			**9.4**	**30%**	**70%**	**3.88**	**55**	**19**	**26**	**2.3**	**4.7**	**2.0**	**10%**	**0.8**	**2.7**	**54**	**$4**

PRO: GB% remains a strength. Dom rising. Just 2 HR allowed. CON: Cmd still declined, as Ctl nearly doubled. Not dominant vs LH or RH. Lucky hr/f. Verdict: ERA should improve, but little upside in these BPI's.

Sanches,Brian

Sanches,Brian			W	L	Sv	IP	K	ERA	WHIP	OBA	vL	vR	BF/G	H%	S%	xERA	G	L	F	Ctl	Dom	Cmd	hr/f	hr/9	RAR	BPV	R$
RH Reliever	05	aaa	4	3	1	80	57	4.62	1.54	298			7.1	33%	74%	5.69				3.1	6.4	**2.1**		1.3	-3.1	39	$3
Age 31	06	aaa	3	2	19	43	41	3.14	1.12	215			4.8	27%	74%	2.81				3.1	8.5	**2.7**		0.7	7.4	100	$13
Type Pwr xFB	07	aaa	2	3	16	47	40	6.72	1.70	350			6.0	41%	61%	7.11				1.7	7.7	**4.6**		1.3	-13.1	89	$4
Health A	08	aaa	2	1	13	33	34	3.01	1.17	236			4.2	31%	76%	3.12				2.7	9.3	**3.4**		0.6	5.3	117	$9
PT/Exp B	09	FLA	* 5	3	4	74	68	2.68	1.34	246	245	227	5.0	31%	83%	4.31	33	17	50	3.8	8.3	**2.2**	6%	0.8	13.7	60	$9
Consist F	1st Half		2	2	4	34	32	2.32	1.35	252			4.4	32%	85%	4.16	36	17	47	3.6	8.4	**2.3**	5%	0.6	7.9	68	$5
LIMA Plan B+	2nd Half		3	1	0	39	36	2.99	1.33	241			5.5	29%	81%	4.38	32	17	51	3.9	8.3	**2.1**	7%	0.9	5.8	54	$4
Rand Var -5	10	Proj	**3**	**2**	**0**	**54**	**50**	**4.00**	**1.31**	**255**			**5.0**	**31%**	**72%**	**4.20**	**33**	**17**	**50**	**3.2**	**8.3**	**2.6**	**8%**	**1.0**	**0.4**	**76**	**$4**

4-2, 2.56 ERA in 56 IP at FLA. PRO: Strong Dom carried over to majors. BA vs RHB CON: Ctl wavered. High FB%, benefited from low hr/f, S%. Verdict: Dom likely to repeat, but probably not his ERA.

Sanchez,Anibal

Sanchez,Anibal			W	L	Sv	IP	K	ERA	WHIP	OBA	vL	vR	BF/G	H%	S%	xERA	G	L	F	Ctl	Dom	Cmd	hr/f	hr/9	RAR	BPV	R$
RH Starter	05	aa	3	5	0	57	54	4.41	1.38	281			22.3	35%	70%	4.65				2.5	8.5	**3.4**		0.9	-0.8	92	$4
Age 26	06	FLA	* 13	9	0	199	155	3.48	1.33	252	229	202	25.7	30%	76%	4.31	45	14	41	3.5	7.0	**2.0**	7%	0.8	24.8	55	$19
Type Pwr	07	FLA	2	1	0	30	14	4.80	2.07	337	329	357	24.9	36%	78%	6.41	45	15	40	5.7	4.2	**0.7**	7%	0.9	-1.4	-55	($1)
Health F	08	FLA	2	5	0	52	50	5.57	1.57	270	340	188	23.2	33%	66%	4.09	40	27	32	4.7	8.7	**1.9**	14%	1.2	-8.3	48	$1
PT/Exp D	09	FLA	4	8	0	86	71	3.87	1.51	257	231	276	23.8	30%	78%	4.50	42	20	38	4.8	7.4	**1.5**	10%	1.0	3.4	24	$4
Consist A	1st Half		1	4	0	35	28	5.63	1.79	312			23.7	35%	72%	4.90	39	23	39	4.6	7.2	**1.6**	13%	1.5	-6.2	21	($1)
LIMA Plan C+	2nd Half		3	4	0	51	43	2.66	1.32	214			23.9	26%	83%	4.20	45	18	37	5.0	7.6	**1.5**	8%	0.7	9.6	26	$5
Rand Var -1	10	Proj	**8**	**8**	**0**	**124**	**106**	**4.43**	**1.49**	**259**			**23.8**	**31%**	**73%**	**4.35**	**42**	**21**	**37**	**4.6**	**7.7**	**1.7**	**10%**	**1.0**	**-1.3**	**35**	**$7**

Missed more than half of the season with shoulder issues. 2H ERA a result of a lot of things going his way. 2H Dom and GB% show promise, but Ctl, injury history reveal that he comes with a great deal of risk.

Sanchez,Jonathan

Sanchez,Jonathan			W	L	Sv	IP	K	ERA	WHIP	OBA	vL	vR	BF/G	H%	S%	xERA	G	L	F	Ctl	Dom	Cmd	hr/f	hr/9	RAR	BPV	R$
LH Starter	05		0	0	0	0	0	0.00	0.00							0.00											
Age 27	06	SF	* 7	4	2	95	96	3.79	1.22	210	256	248	8.6	28%	67%	4.01	36	20	45	4.3	9.1	**2.1**	3%	0.3	8.2	62	$12
Type Pwr FB	07	SF	* 1	5	0	72	84	5.03	1.54	269	197	321	8.3	36%	69%	3.84	39	22	39	4.5	10.5	**2.3**	11%	1.0	-5.3	83	$2
Health B	08	SF	9	12	0	158	157	5.01	1.45	257	235	263	23.8	33%	66%	3.96	41	21	37	4.3	8.9	**2.1**	8%	0.8	-14.5	65	$8
PT/Exp B	09	SF	8	12	0	163	177	4.24	1.37	227	223	220	21.9	29%	72%	3.91	41	16	43	4.8	9.8	**2.0**	11%	1.0	-1.1	63	$12
Consist A	1st Half		2	8	0	67	67	5.49	1.74	273			20.9	34%	69%	4.90	38	16	45	6.2	9.0	**1.5**	8%	0.9	-10.8	12	($1)
LIMA Plan B	2nd Half		6	4	0	96	110	3.37	1.10	191			22.7	24%	74%	3.26	43	16	41	3.9	10.3	**2.6**	13%	1.1	9.7	100	$12
Rand Var 0	10	Proj	**12**	**11**	**0**	**195**	**210**	**3.97**	**1.32**	**234**			**15.6**	**30%**	**72%**	**3.72**	**40**	**19**	**41**	**4.2**	**9.7**	**2.3**	**10%**	**0.9**	**13.0**	**81**	**$18**

Elite dominance and 2H surge fuel owner hopes, but the sum of his up-tick was greater than the parts. Ctl is still the issue here, and 2H H% will regress. Improvement, yes; imminent breakout? We don't think so.

BRIAN RUDD

Santana,Ervin

Santana,Ervin	Yr	Tm	W	L	Sv	IP	K	ERA	WHIP	OBA	vL	vR	BF/G	H%	S%	xERA	G	L	F	Ctl	Dom	Cmd	hr/f	hr/9	RAR	BPV	R$
RH Starter	05	ANA	* 18	9	0	191	140	4.14	1.34	264	261	271	24.7	30%	72%	4.43	37	19	44	3.0	6.6	2.2	8%	1.0	5.5	53	$18
Age 27	06	LAA	16	8	0	204	141	4.28	1.23	239	254	229	25.7	27%	67%	4.47	38	17	44	3.1	6.2	2.0	8%	0.9	7.0	45	$21
Type FB	07	LAA	* 9	15	0	182	152	5.94	1.60	302	284	292	24.9	35%	65%	4.69	36	19	46	3.4	7.5	2.2	11%	1.5	-32.3	57	$4
Health C	08	LAA	16	7	0	219	214	3.49	1.12	243	240	234	27.6	30%	72%	3.36	39	20	42	1.9	8.8	4.6	9%	0.9	23.1	123	$29
PT/Exp A	09	LAA	8	8	0	140	107	5.03	1.47	288	323	248	25.6	32%	70%	4.50	38	20	42	3.0	6.9	2.3	13%	1.5	-9.9	59	$7
Consist C	1st Half		1	3	0	31	21	7.52	1.86	339			24.8	38%	59%	5.34	33	26	41	3.8	6.1	1.6	9%	1.2	-11.8	19	($2)
LIMA Plan C+	2nd Half		7	5	0	109	86	4.31	1.36	271			25.8	30%	75%	4.26	40	18	43	2.8	7.1	2.5	14%	1.7	1.9	70	$9
Rand Var +1	10	Proj	12	8	0	174	141	4.19	1.37	272			25.7	31%	73%	4.24	37	20	42	2.8	7.3	2.6	10%	1.2	4.3	70	$15

2008 now outlier due to elbow injury, slow 1H return skewed bottom line. Lost 3-4 mph off fastball, sharp slider, pinpoint Ctl. Results seen in hr/9 spike, Cmd collapse. Dom, velocity still pluses, but now a TJS risk.

Santana,Johan

Santana,Johan	Yr	Tm	W	L	Sv	IP	K	ERA	WHIP	OBA	vL	vR	BF/G	H%	S%	xERA	G	L	F	Ctl	Dom	Cmd	hr/f	hr/9	RAR	BPV	R$
LH Starter	05	MIN	16	7	0	231	238	2.88	0.97	216	256	200	27.3	28%	74%	3.11	40	17	43	1.8	9.3	5.3	9%	0.9	42.5	137	$38
Age 31	06	MIN	19	6	0	233	245	2.78	1.00	220	254	206	26.9	28%	77%	3.06	41	20	40	1.8	9.5	5.2	10%	0.9	51.2	140	$41
Type Pwr FB	07	MIN	15	13	0	219	235	3.33	1.07	229	197	234	26.5	28%	76%	3.26	38	18	44	2.1	9.7	4.5	13%	1.4	31.8	132	$33
Health B	08	NYM	16	7	0	234	206	2.54	1.15	238	247	227	28.0	29%	83%	3.52	41	22	36	2.4	7.9	3.3	10%	0.9	50.1	96	$30
PT/Exp A	09	NYM	13	9	0	167	146	3.13	1.21	249	267	235	27.6	30%	79%	3.96	36	17	48	2.5	7.9	3.2	9%	1.1	21.8	88	$19
Consist A	1st Half		9	6	0	102	104	3.35	1.26	248			26.7	31%	78%	3.88	32	19	49	3.0	9.2	3.1	9%	1.1	10.6	94	$12
LIMA Plan C+	2nd Half		4	3	0	65	42	2.79	1.13	251			29.1	28%	80%	4.08	41	14	45	1.7	5.9	3.5	8%	1.0	11.2	79	$8
Rand Var -3	10	Proj	13	8	0	189	167	3.39	1.20	248			27.7	29%	76%	3.78	39	18	43	2.4	8.0	3.3	10%	1.1	11.3	95	$21

Elbow surgery (bone chips) ended season, raises risk. Cmd, xERA, BA vs. LHB all trending south, FB% at new high, and durability now an issue. Big strikeout years are likely gone.

Saunders,Joe

Saunders,Joe	Yr	Tm	W	L	Sv	IP	K	ERA	WHIP	OBA	vL	vR	BF/G	H%	S%	xERA	G	L	F	Ctl	Dom	Cmd	hr/f	hr/9	RAR	BPV	R$
LH Starter	05	a/a	10	7	0	160	88	4.00	1.47	290			26.0	32%	73%	4.74				2.8	5.0	1.7		0.6	6.1	44	$9
Age 28	06	LAA	* 17	7	0	205	132	3.48	1.27	254	220	274	25.3	29%	75%	4.05	48	20	32	2.8	5.8	2.1	8%	0.8	27.2	54	$23
Type Con	07	LAA	* 12	12	0	193	131	5.78	1.58	313	274	304	27.2	35%	64%	4.37	45	21	34	2.7	6.1	2.3	10%	1.1	-30.5	61	$5
Health A	08	LAA	17	7	0	198	103	3.41	1.21	251	260	250	26.4	27%	75%	4.32	47	15	38	2.4	4.7	1.9	9%	1.0	22.9	44	$22
PT/Exp A	09	LAA	16	7	0	186	101	4.60	1.43	278	257	287	26.1	29%	72%	4.66	47	17	36	3.1	4.9	1.6	13%	1.4	-3.3	29	$12
Consist A	1st Half		8	5	0	102	59	4.24	1.30	256			26.9	26%	74%	4.54	46	14	39	3.0	5.2	1.7	14%	1.6	2.7	37	$9
LIMA Plan D+	2nd Half		8	2	0	84	42	5.04	1.58	303			25.2	32%	70%	4.81	48	20	32	3.2	4.5	1.4	11%	1.2	-6.0	20	$3
Rand Var 0	10	Proj	13	11	0	196	109	4.23	1.42	280			26.5	30%	73%	4.52	47	18	36	2.9	5.0	1.8	10%	1.1	-2.1	38	$13

Overachieving again until June shoulder issue. DL stint and cortisone helped him win 7 of last 8 starts. Sub-par Dom, wrings max from GB%, Ctl, and 23% PQS-DOM. Team context is key for these pitchers.

Scherzer,Max

Scherzer,Max	Yr	Tm	W	L	Sv	IP	K	ERA	WHIP	OBA	vL	vR	BF/G	H%	S%	xERA	G	L	F	Ctl	Dom	Cmd	hr/f	hr/9	RAR	BPV	R$
RH Starter	05		0	0	0	0	0	0.00	0.00							0.00											
Age 25	06		0	0	0	0	0	0.00	0.00							0.00											
Type Pwr	07	aa	4	4	0	73	65	5.20	1.62	272			23.7	34%	67%	4.84				5.1	8.0	1.6		0.5	-6.6	66	$2
Health A	08	ARI	* 1	5	0	109	133	3.39	1.24	229	319	167	15.6	32%	74%	2.98	42	28	30	3.6	10.9	3.0	10%	0.7	11.8	118	$10
PT/Exp C	09	ARI	9	11	0	170	174	4.12	1.34	257	265	239	24.2	32%	72%	3.65	42	18	40	3.3	9.2	2.8	11%	1.1	1.4	95	$13
Consist C	1st Half		5	5	0	83	83	3.35	1.40	257			23.9	33%	76%	3.76	43	18	38	3.8	9.0	2.4	9%	0.9	5.2	81	$7
LIMA Plan B+	2nd Half		4	6	0	87	91	4.54	1.30	257			24.5	32%	68%	3.54	40	18	42	2.9	9.4	3.3	12%	1.2	-3.8	109	$6
Rand Var 0	10	Proj	9	9	0	196	210	3.82	1.30	245			24.3	32%	73%	3.48	42	21	38	3.4	9.7	2.8	10%	0.9	18.9	100	$17

2H FB and hr/f hikes, S% slide hurt ERA. Ctl gains say he's better than this. Elite Dom, BPV point to bright future. Inefficiency is an issue (note BF/G), affects Wins. 1.5 hr/9 at Chase Field needs work.

Schlereth,Daniel

Schlereth,Daniel	Yr	Tm	W	L	Sv	IP	K	ERA	WHIP	OBA	vL	vR	BF/G	H%	S%	xERA	G	L	F	Ctl	Dom	Cmd	hr/f	hr/9	RAR	BPV	R$
LH Reliever	05		0	0	0	0	0	0.00	0.00							0.00											
Age 23	06		0	0	0	0	0	0.00	0.00							0.00											
Type Pwr xGB	07		0	0	0	0	0	0.00	0.00							0.00											
Health A	08		0	0	0	0	0	0.00	0.00							0.00											
PT/Exp F	09	ARI	* 1	4	3	45	53	3.38	1.48	210	222	220	4.7	30%	77%	3.59	59	9	33	6.6	10.5	1.6	6%	0.4	4.5	49	$4
Consist F	1st Half		0	2	3	27	33	3.00	1.38	193			4.9	28%	78%	2.94	73	0	27	6.4	10.9	1.7	6%	0.3	4.0	74	$3
LIMA Plan B+	2nd Half		1	2	0	18	20	3.96	1.62	236			4.5	32%	75%	4.05	54	11	34	6.8	10.0	1.5	6%	0.5	0.5	28	$1
Rand Var -2	10	Proj	2	5	0	51	58	4.26	1.42	218			4.6	30%	71%	3.50	57	10	33	5.7	10.3	1.8	10%	0.7	4.8	66	$3

1-4, 5.89 ERA in 18 IP at ARI. Experience, Ctl are the only hurdles for closer-in-waiting, though the latter (15 MLB BB) seems daunting in short-term. Dom, GB% already Elite, allowed only two HR all year.

Schoeneweis,Scott

Schoeneweis,Scott	Yr	Tm	W	L	Sv	IP	K	ERA	WHIP	OBA	vL	vR	BF/G	H%	S%	xERA	G	L	F	Ctl	Dom	Cmd	hr/f	hr/9	RAR	BPV	R$
LH Reliever	05	TOR	3	4	1	57	43	3.32	1.39	251	188	306	3.1	31%	75%	3.60	59	17	24	3.9	6.8	1.7	5%	0.3	7.4	52	$5
Age 36	06	2TM	4	2	4	51	29	4.92	1.41	250	236	257	3.1	28%	65%	4.28	58	16	26	4.2	5.1	1.2	9%	0.7	-2.5	13	$4
Type	07	NYM	0	2	2	59	41	5.03	1.53	271	204	316	3.7	30%	70%	4.36	51	19	30	4.3	6.3	1.5	14%	1.2	-4.4	27	$1
Health B	08	NYM	2	6	1	57	34	3.33	1.38	256	178	333	3.3	28%	80%	4.32	50	19	31	3.7	5.4	1.5	12%	1.1	6.6	26	$4
PT/Exp D	09	ARI	1	2	0	24	14	7.13	1.75	300	276	302	2.5	30%	64%	5.27	44	20	36	4.9	5.3	1.1	20%	2.3	-8.7	-15	($1)
Consist B	1st Half		0	0	0	12	7	4.43	1.64	289			2.1	29%	82%	4.99	41	26	33	4.4	5.2	1.2	22%	2.2	-0.4	-7	($0)
LIMA Plan D	2nd Half		1	2	0	12	7	9.91	1.86	311			3.0	31%	47%	5.55	48	13	40	5.3	5.3	1.0	18%	2.3	-8.3	-23	($1)
Rand Var +5	10	Proj	2	3	0	44	27	4.34	1.47	273			3.4	30%	73%	4.48	48	18	33	3.7	5.6	1.5	11%	1.0	-1.2	26	$2

Personal tragedy wrecked his season and affected his profile in ways impossible to analyze. Situational lefty GBer will likely work again, but marginal Dom, poor Ctl and now GB trend will keep him off fantasy rosters.

Seay,Bobby

Seay,Bobby	Yr	Tm	W	L	Sv	IP	K	ERA	WHIP	OBA	vL	vR	BF/G	H%	S%	xERA	G	L	F	Ctl	Dom	Cmd	hr/f	hr/9	RAR	BPV	R$
LH Reliever	05	COL	* 1	0	0	38	36	4.97	1.82	314			4.7	38%	75%	4.19	47	21	32	4.7	8.5	1.8	13%	1.2	-3.4	51	($1)
Age 31	06	DET	* 1	2	0	39	24	6.23	1.51	281			4.5	31%	59%	4.82	37	28	35	3.7	5.5	1.5	11%	1.2	-8.0	15	$0
Type Pwr FB	07	DET	3	0	1	46	38	2.33	1.14	225	209	250	3.2	29%	79%	4.02	38	18	44	2.9	7.4	2.5	2%	0.2	12.4	70	$7
Health A	08	DET	1	2	0	56	58	4.48	1.49	271	303	252	4.1	35%	70%	3.96	38	21	40	4.0	9.3	2.3	6%	0.6	-0.9	75	$3
PT/Exp D	09	DET	6	3	0	49	37	4.25	1.29	251	261	239	3.1	30%	67%	4.47	37	16	47	3.1	6.8	2.2	4%	0.6	1.2	53	$6
Consist A	1st Half		1	1	0	24	15	3.36	0.95	200			2.7	24%	61%	4.14	40	14	46	2.2	5.6	2.5	0%	0.0	3.2	59	$3
LIMA Plan C+	2nd Half		5	2	0	25	22	5.12	1.63	295			3.5	35%	70%	4.77	34	19	47	4.0	8.0	2.0	8%	1.1	-2.0	48	$3
Rand Var -2	10	Proj	5	2	0	53	45	4.25	1.34	254			3.5	31%	69%	4.27	37	19	44	3.4	7.6	2.3	6%	0.7	1.1	61	$5

Benefitted from unusually good Ctl and fortunate h% in 1H that both reverted in 2H. Continued swings in Dom, Ctl, while GLF, xERA remain relatively stable. Increasingly marginal middle reliever and LIMA option.

Sheets,Ben

Sheets,Ben	Yr	Tm	W	L	Sv	IP	K	ERA	WHIP	OBA	vL	vR	BF/G	H%	S%	xERA	G	L	F	Ctl	Dom	Cmd	hr/f	hr/9	RAR	BPV	R$
RH Reliever	05	MIL	10	9	0	156	141	3.34	1.07	244	234	241	28.3	29%	74%	3.40	37	21	42	1.4	8.1	5.6	10%	1.1	17.4	122	$20
Age 31	06	MIL	6	7	0	106	116	3.82	1.09	260	248	266	25.0	34%	66%	2.99	40	19	40	0.9	9.8	10.5	8%	0.8	8.7	170	$13
Type FB	07	MIL	12	5	0	141	106	3.82	1.24	257	200	300	24.5	29%	73%	4.23	37	19	45	2.4	6.8	2.9	9%	1.1	10.5	72	$15
Health F	08	MIL	13	9	0	198	158	3.09	1.15	245	256	226	26.0	29%	76%	3.79	41	18	41	2.1	7.2	3.4	7%	0.8	29.0	90	$23
PT/Exp B	09		0	0	0	0	0	0.00	0.00							0.00											
Consist A	1st Half		0	0	0	0	0	0.00	0.00							0.00											
LIMA Plan C+	2nd Half		0	0	0	0	0	0.00	0.00							0.00											
Rand Var	10	Proj	8	6	0	116	85	4.11	1.26	260			26.9	30%	70%	4.15	39	19	42	2.4	6.6	2.7	9%	1.0	2.8	71	$10

Missed the entire season due to surgery on torn tendon in throwing arm, Opening Day readiness still up in the air. Skills remain Elite, Health remains an F - and our projections reflect both.

Sherrill,George

Sherrill,George	Yr	Tm	W	L	Sv	IP	K	ERA	WHIP	OBA	vL	vR	BF/G	H%	S%	xERA	G	L	F	Ctl	Dom	Cmd	hr/f	hr/9	RAR	BPV	R$
LH Reliever	05	SEA	* 5	6	7	43	54	3.98	1.14	219	116	273	3.4	31%	67%	2.98	42	16	42	3.1	11.3	3.6	9%	0.8	2.1	139	$9
Age 32	06	SEA	2	4	1	40	42	4.28	1.43	210	143	297	2.4	30%	67%	4.71	30	19	51	6.1	9.5	1.6	0%	0.0	1.4	14	$4
Type Pwr xFB	07	SEA	2	0	3	46	56	2.36	0.98	178	156	212	2.4	25%	80%	3.40	25	21	55	3.3	11.0	3.3	7%	0.8	12.1	111	$9
Health A	08	BAL	3	5	31	53	58	4.73	1.50	238	190	254	4.1	31%	70%	4.52	34	13	53	5.6	9.8	1.8	8%	1.0	-2.5	38	$13
PT/Exp B	09	2TM	1	1	21	69	61	1.70	1.12	214	128	244	3.9	27%	88%	3.89	37	18	45	3.1	8.0	2.5	5%	0.5	22.3	74	$16
Consist B	1st Half		0	1	17	32	31	2.52	1.15	216			4.0	27%	82%	4.12	28	18	54	3.4	8.7	2.6	7%	0.8	7.1	71	$9
LIMA Plan C	2nd Half		1	0	4	37	30	0.98	1.08	212			3.8	27%	92%	3.64	45	19	36	2.9	7.3	2.5	3%	0.2	15.2	76	$7
Rand Var -5	10	Proj	3	3	5	73	71	3.48	1.26	230			3.6	29%	75%	4.04	35	17	48	3.7	8.8	2.4	8%	0.9	2.7	71	$9

PRO: LH don't have much of a chance vs him. Ctl rebounded. GB% improved.
CON: Dom heading south. Still a FB pitcher.
Verdict: '09 luck can't continue, ERA will rise toward xERA.

JOCK THOMPSON

Shields,James

Shields,James	Yr	W	L	Sv	IP	K	ERA	WHIP	OBA	vL	vR	BF/G	H%	S%	xERA	G	L	F	Ctl	Dom	Cmd	hr/f	hr/9	RAR	BPV	R$
RH Starter	05 a/a	8	5	0	115	94	3.13	1.23	253			26.5	31%	74%	3.32				2.5	7.4	2.9		0.4	16.7	98	$13
Age 28	06 TAM *	9	10	0	185	159	4.37	1.38	289	266	309	25.7	34%	71%	3.70	43	23	34	2.1	7.7	3.6	11%	1.0	4.3	102	$15
Type	07 TAM	12	8	0	215	184	3.85	1.11	250	243	250	27.9	29%	70%	3.50	43	16	40	1.5	7.7	5.1	11%	1.2	17.3	119	$26
Health A	08 TAM	14	8	0	215	160	3.56	1.15	255	255	253	26.5	29%	73%	3.63	46	16	37	1.7	6.7	4.0	10%	1.0	20.9	100	$24
PT/Exp A	09 TAM	11	12	0	220	167	4.14	1.32	278	272	279	28.3	32%	73%	3.97	42	20	37	2.1	6.8	3.2	11%	1.2	8.5	86	$17
Consist A	1st Half	6	6	0	115	84	3.52	1.28	275			28.4	31%	77%	3.94	43	20	38	1.9	6.6	3.5	10%	1.1	13.3	88	$11
LIMA Plan C+	2nd Half	5	6	0	105	83	4.82	1.38	282			28.1	32%	68%	3.99	42	21	37	2.4	7.1	3.0	12%	1.3	-4.8	83	$6
Rand Var 0	10 Proj	13	9	0	218	170	3.85	1.26	268			27.5	31%	73%	3.79	43	19	37	2.0	7.0	3.5	11%	1.1	17.3	94	$21

Continues to provide plenty of innings at a skill level worth owning. However, the 3-year negative trend in Cmd, BPV, xERA, and BA vs LH, RH is reason to be a little wary. xERA is your guide; don't overreact.

Shields,Scot

Shields,Scot	Yr	W	L	Sv	IP	K	ERA	WHIP	OBA	vL	vR	BF/G	H%	S%	xERA	G	L	F	Ctl	Dom	Cmd	hr/f	hr/9	RAR	BPV	R$
RH Reliever	05 ANA	10	11	7	91	98	2.76	1.13	204	202	203	4.7	28%	77%	2.91	54	17	28	3.7	9.7	2.6	8%	0.5	18.1	108	$18
Age 34	06 LAA	7	7	2	87	84	2.89	1.08	222	207	227	4.7	28%	77%	3.10	52	15	33	2.5	8.7	3.5	10%	0.8	17.9	119	$15
Type Pwr	07 LAA	4	5	2	77	77	3.86	1.23	222	214	226	4.5	28%	70%	3.60	45	19	36	3.9	9.0	2.3	10%	0.8	6.2	80	$9
Health F	08 LAA	6	4	4	63	64	2.70	1.34	239	209	262	4.2	30%	84%	3.37	54	16	31	4.1	9.1	2.2	11%	0.9	12.9	84	$10
PT/Exp D	09 LAA	1	3	1	18	12	6.61	1.75	243	250	229	4.1	28%	60%	6.28	37	19	44	7.6	6.1	0.8	4%	0.5	-4.7	-81	($0)
Consist D	1st Half	1	3	1	17	12	6.80	1.80	248			4.1	29%	60%	6.35	37	19	44	7.8	6.3	0.8	4%	0.5	-5.0	-84	($0)
LIMA Plan D+	2nd Half	0	0	0	1	0	0.00	0.00							0.00											
Rand Var +1	10 Proj	4	6	0	58	53	3.88	1.38	248			4.3	30%	74%	3.95	46	17	37	4.0	8.2	2.0	10%	0.9	3.4	63	$6

Struggled in the early going, then patellar tendinits ended season in late May. Prior to '09, skills were consistently strong, so there's a good chance you can get '07-'08 production at a reduced cost.

Shouse,Brian

Shouse,Brian	Yr	W	L	Sv	IP	K	ERA	WHIP	OBA	vL	vR	BF/G	H%	S%	xERA	G	L	F	Ctl	Dom	Cmd	hr/f	hr/9	RAR	BPV	R$
LH Reliever	05 TEX	3	2	0	53	35	5.25	1.37	269	209	337	3.6	29%	64%	3.72	54	21	25	3.1	5.9	1.9	17%	1.2	-5.8	57	$2
Age 41	06 2TM	1	3	2	38	23	4.02	1.52	271	238	309	2.6	30%	76%	4.55	51	20	29	4.3	5.4	1.3	11%	0.9	2.4	12	$2
Type Con xGB	07 MIL	1	1	1	48	32	3.02	1.26	255	214	295	2.7	31%	73%	3.51	55	21	24	2.6	6.0	2.3	0%	0.0	8.3	71	$4
Health C	08 MIL	5	1	2	51	33	2.81	1.17	241	180	301	3.0	27%	80%	3.13	62	19	19	2.5	5.8	2.4	16%	0.9	9.3	78	$8
PT/Exp D	09 TAM	1	1	0	28	17	4.50	1.36	282	224	356	2.7	30%	73%	3.20	61	23	16	2.3	5.5	2.4	33%	1.6	-0.2	77	$2
Consist A	1st Half	1	1	0	14	9	3.83	1.42	299			3.2	33%	78%	2.70	71	17	13	1.9	5.7	3.0	33%	1.3	1.1	101	$1
LIMA Plan B	2nd Half	0	0	0	14	8	5.18	1.29	263			2.3	26%	67%	3.66	51	29	20	2.6	5.2	2.0	33%	1.9	-1.2	52	$0
Rand Var +5	10 Proj	3	2	0	51	30	4.08	1.36	267			2.9	30%	71%	3.59	59	22	19	3.0	5.3	1.8	12%	0.7	5.3	51	$4

Still tough on LH, but that's all he does; it took 45 appearances to reach 28 IP. Skills remain consistent, and excellent GB rate suggests HR issues were a fluke. ERA rebound likely, but at 41, could fall off cliff at any time.

Silva,Carlos

Silva,Carlos	Yr	W	L	Sv	IP	K	ERA	WHIP	OBA	vL	vR	BF/G	H%	S%	xERA	G	L	F	Ctl	Dom	Cmd	hr/f	hr/9	RAR	BPV	R$
RH Reliever	05 MIN	9	8	0	188	71	3.44	1.17	286	302	277	28.5	29%	76%	3.94	49	20	31	0.4	3.4	7.9	12%	1.2	21.5	77	$16
Age 30	06 MIN	11	15	0	180	70	5.95	1.54	326	329	320	22.3	32%	66%	4.83	44	22	34	1.6	3.5	2.2	16%	1.9	-30.9	41	$2
Type Con	07 MIN	13	14	0	202	89	4.19	1.31	287	294	280	25.9	30%	70%	4.36	48	19	34	1.6	4.0	2.5	8%	0.9	7.9	54	$15
Health F	08 SEA	4	15	0	153	69	6.46	1.60	330	348	312	24.7	35%	60%	4.68	44	23	33	1.9	4.1	2.2	10%	1.2	-39.9	44	($4)
PT/Exp B	09 SEA	1	3	0	30	10	8.61	1.72	324	380	250	17.6	32%	49%	5.47	45	22	33	3.3	3.0	0.9	13%	1.5	-15.6	-12	($3)
Consist B	1st Half	1	3	0	28	10	8.62	1.67	323			21.6	32%	48%	5.23	46	21	33	2.9	3.2	1.1	14%	1.6	-14.5	4	($2)
LIMA Plan D	2nd Half	0	0	0	2	0	8.57	2.38	336			5.6	34%	60%	9.23	38	25	38	8.6	0.0	0.0	0%	0.0	-1.1	******	($0)
Rand Var +5	10 Proj	6	11	0	126	55	5.08	1.47	299			24.0	31%	68%	4.71	46	21	33	2.4	3.9	1.6	11%	1.2	-4.2	29	$3

Shoulder cost him most of the season, and was both bad and unlucky when he pitched. LH's just crush him, and Dom is always in dangerous territory, so even a healthy shoulder probably won't do much good.

Sipp,Tony

Sipp,Tony	Yr	W	L	Sv	IP	K	ERA	WHIP	OBA	vL	vR	BF/G	H%	S%	xERA	G	L	F	Ctl	Dom	Cmd	hr/f	hr/9	RAR	BPV	R$
LH Reliever	05	0	0	0	0	0	0.00	0.00							0.00											
Age 26	06 aa	4	2	3	60	69	4.01	1.25	237			8.6	33%	66%	3.07				3.4	10.3	3.0		0.3	3.8	124	$8
Type Pwr xFB	07	0	0	0	0	0	0.00	0.00							0.00											
Health D	08 aa	0	3	1	22	27	4.50	1.41	262			6.0	33%	77%	5.51				3.7	11.0	3.0		2.0	-0.5	71	$1
PT/Exp F	09 CLE *	3	0	1	57	67	3.35	1.36	225	208	179	4.2	30%	79%	4.01	35	14	51	4.9	10.6	2.2	9%	1.0	7.7	72	$7
Consist C	1st Half	1	0	1	28	33	3.91	1.48	236			5.0	31%	78%	4.29	35	13	52	5.5	10.7	1.9	11%	1.3	1.9	57	$3
LIMA Plan B+	2nd Half	2	0	0	29	34	2.81	1.25	213			3.6	30%	79%	3.77	35	15	50	4.4	10.6	2.4	6%	0.6	5.8	86	$4
Rand Var -2	10 Proj	3	1	0	44	51	3.93	1.31	227			5.3	30%	73%	3.84	35	14	50	4.3	10.6	2.4	9%	1.0	3.2	86	$5

2-0, 2.92 ERA in 40 IP at CLE.
PRO: Tough on both LH and RH. Outstanding Dom.
CON: High FB rate. Shaky Ctl heading in wrong direction. Two years after TJ surgery, a repeat of 2H xERA is within reach.

Slowey,Kevin

Slowey,Kevin	Yr	W	L	Sv	IP	K	ERA	WHIP	OBA	vL	vR	BF/G	H%	S%	xERA	G	L	F	Ctl	Dom	Cmd	hr/f	hr/9	RAR	BPV	R$
RH Starter	05	0	0	0	0	0	0.00	0.00							0.00											
Age 25	06 aa	4	3	0	59	44	4.42	1.29	268			27.6	30%	69%	4.56				2.3	6.7	2.9		1.2	0.8	67	$5
Type xFB	07 MIN *	14	6	0	200	134	3.42	1.26	281	267	309	25.3	32%	76%	4.53	29	21	50	1.4	6.0	4.2	6%	0.9	26.7	77	$22
Health D	08 MIN	12	11	0	160	123	3.99	1.15	263	277	246	24.2	30%	70%	3.86	36	19	45	1.3	6.9	5.1	10%	1.2	7.1	102	$18
PT/Exp B	09 MIN	10	3	0	91	75	4.86	1.41	306	354	267	24.6	35%	70%	4.26	32	20	48	1.5	7.4	5.0	11%	1.5	-4.6	104	$8
Consist B	1st Half	10	3	0	87	71	4.44	1.40	305			25.1	35%	73%	4.24	32	20	47	1.4	7.3	5.1	10%	1.4	0.2	103	$9
LIMA Plan A	2nd Half	0	0	0	4	4	15.42	1.71	336			16.2	41%	0%	4.67	20	10	70	2.6	10.3	4.0	13%	2.6	-4.7	114	($1)
Rand Var +3	10 Proj	13	7	0	160	124	3.78	1.17	265			25.1	30%	73%	4.01	33	20	47	1.4	7.0	5.0	10%	1.3	8.3	99	$19

Bone chip in wrist ended year in early July. Gaudy career Cmd of 17.1 vs RH. '09 troubles vs LH exaggerated by 42% H%. Dom keeps going up, and Ctl is elite. If healthy, a few more GB could mean... UP: 3.25 ERA.

Smith,Chris

Smith,Chris	Yr	W	L	Sv	IP	K	ERA	WHIP	OBA	vL	vR	BF/G	H%	S%	xERA	G	L	F	Ctl	Dom	Cmd	hr/f	hr/9	RAR	BPV	R$
RH Reliever	05 aa	4	3	0	72	38	7.48	1.86	369			24.7	39%	61%	8.15				1.9	4.7	2.4		1.7	-28.3	11	($5)
Age 29	06 a/a	10	7	0	149	84	5.65	1.55	311			24.7	34%	63%	5.63				2.5	5.0	2.0		0.9	-20.9	39	$4
Type xFB	07 a/a	6	9	1	109	63	6.15	2.10	371			17.1	41%	72%	8.45				3.9	5.2	1.3		1.1	-22.6	7	($6)
Health A	08 aaa	1	5	15	59	42	4.17	1.32	285			6.8	32%	71%	4.59				1.8	6.4	3.6		1.0	1.0	83	$8
PT/Exp D	09 MIL *	2	0	17	88	77	2.91	1.17	238	232	232	5.7	27%	84%	4.08	32	17	51	2.6	7.8	3.0	11%	1.5	13.9	81	$14
Consist F	1st Half	2	0	12	47	42	1.80	1.11	232			6.4	28%	91%	4.34	20	17	63	2.3	7.9	3.4	6%	1.0	14.0	77	$11
LIMA Plan B	2nd Half	0	0	5	41	35	4.20	1.23	244			5.1	26%	76%	4.05	37	17	47	2.9	7.7	2.7	17%	2.0	-0.0	75	$4
Rand Var -5	10 Proj	2	3	0	69	51	4.20	1.34	272			7.3	30%	74%	4.55	33	17	50	2.6	6.7	2.6	10%	1.4	-2.4	61	$4

0-0, 4.11 ERA in 46 IP at MIL. Dom continues to trend in right direction, while keeping Ctl at very reasonable level. HR/9 issues probably aren't going away, but BPV says he should stick in majors this time around.

Smith,Joe

Smith,Joe	Yr	W	L	Sv	IP	K	ERA	WHIP	OBA	vL	vR	BF/G	H%	S%	xERA	G	L	F	Ctl	Dom	Cmd	hr/f	hr/9	RAR	BPV	R$
RH Reliever	05	0	0	0	0	0	0.00	0.00							0.00											
Age 26	06	0	0	0	0	0	0.00	0.00							0.00											
Type Pwr xGB	07 NYM *	3	2	2	53	50	3.38	1.50	268	298	266	3.8	34%	78%	3.23	62	17	21	4.2	8.4	2.0	9%	0.5	6.9	78	$5
Health C	08 NYM	6	3	0	63	52	3.55	1.30	222	320	192	3.3	27%	73%	3.18	63	20	18	4.4	7.4	1.7	13%	0.6	5.6	55	$7
PT/Exp D	09 CLE	0	0	0	34	30	3.44	1.26	238	355	198	3.8	28%	77%	3.38	55	17	28	3.4	7.9	2.3	15%	1.1	4.2	83	$3
Consist A	1st Half	0	0	0	17	18	4.21	1.64	261			4.3	35%	74%	3.69	52	26	22	5.8	9.5	1.6	10%	0.5	0.5	44	$0
LIMA Plan A+	2nd Half	0	0	0	17	12	2.66	0.89	214			3.4	22%	83%	3.07	58	8	33	1.1	6.4	6.0	18%	1.6	3.7	123	$2
Rand Var +1	10 Proj	3	1	0	64	55	3.52	1.23	243			3.5	30%	73%	3.10	59	17	24	3.0	7.7	2.6	11%	0.7	10.5	97	$7

Shoulder and knee woes each cost him a month, but retained effectiveness in between. GB% and Dom are raw elements of a sustainable profile, but BA vL trend is disturbing, and needs to be solved for continued success.

Smoltz,John

Smoltz,John	Yr	W	L	Sv	IP	K	ERA	WHIP	OBA	vL	vR	BF/G	H%	S%	xERA	G	L	F	Ctl	Dom	Cmd	hr/f	hr/9	RAR	BPV	R$
RH Starter	05 ATL	14	7	0	229	169	3.06	1.15	245	252	233	28.3	29%	76%	3.44	48	22	30	2.1	6.6	3.2	9%	0.7	33.4	89	$26
Age 42	06 ATL	16	9	0	232	211	3.49	1.19	253	278	226	27.2	31%	74%	3.37	46	20	33	2.1	8.2	3.8	10%	0.9	28.5	114	$27
Type	07 ATL	14	8	0	206	197	3.11	1.18	253	262	237	26.4	32%	76%	3.30	45	20	35	2.1	8.6	4.2	9%	0.8	33.5	122	$26
Health F	08 ATL	3	2	0	28	36	2.57	1.18	240	226	234	19.1	35%	81%	2.71	49	14	38	2.6	11.6	4.5	8%	0.6	5.9	165	$5
PT/Exp C	09 2TM *	4	9	0	97	83	6.13	1.39	292	342	256	22.0	34%	57%	3.97	40	18	42	2.1	7.7	3.7	10%	1.2	-21.7	100	$2
Consist B	1st Half	1	2	0	28	17	5.48	1.22	260			19.4	29%	53%	3.85	48	21	31	2.1	5.4	2.6	8%	0.7	-4.0	68	$1
LIMA Plan B+	2nd Half	3	7	0	69	66	6.39	1.46	304			23.3	37%	58%	3.88	38	18	44	2.1	8.6	4.1	12%	1.4	-17.7	115	$1
Rand Var +5	10 Proj	7	6	0	116	94	4.21	1.27	261			24.2	31%	69%	3.83	44	18	38	2.5	7.3	2.9	10%	1.0	7.3	86	$10

3-8, 6.35 ERA in 78 IP at BOS and STL. BPIs say he pitched better than bottom line. Poor S%, H% did him in, but so did LHB and gopheritis. Worth a flyer, but Sept tendinitis, age and health grade point south.

BRIAN RUDD

Snell,Ian

		Yr	Tm	W	L	Sv	IP	K	ERA	WHIP	OBA	vL	vR	BF/G	H%	S%	xERA	G	L	F	Ctl	Dom	Cmd	hr/f	hr/9	RAR	BPV	R$
RH	Starter	05	PIT	* 12	5	0	154	122	4.32	1.21	245	304	239	19.3	28%	67%	3.99	37	21	42	2.6	7.1	**2.7**	9%	1.1	-1.5	72	$15
Age	28	06	PIT	14	11	0	186	169	4.74	1.46	274	305	251	25.5	32%	72%	4.04	43	21	36	3.6	8.2	**2.3**	15%	1.4	-5.8	71	$13
Type	Pwr	07	PIT	9	12	0	208	177	3.76	1.33	263	284	245	27.6	31%	75%	3.88	46	17	37	2.9	7.7	**2.6**	9%	1.0	17.0	82	$17
Health	A	08	PIT	7	12	0	164	135	5.42	1.77	303	314	295	24.8	36%	70%	4.88	38	25	37	4.9	7.4	**1.5**	9%	1.0	-23.4	17	($1)
PT/Exp	A	09	2TM	* 9	12	0	182	126	4.12	1.52	261	265	267	24.5	30%	74%	4.98	38	22	40	4.7	6.2	**1.3**	6%	0.7	4.4	1	$8
Consist	B	1st Half		3	8	0	94	70	4.59	1.50	264			24.5	31%	70%	4.69	40	22	38	4.4	6.7	**1.5**	6%	0.7	-3.2	19	$3
LIMA Plan	C+	2nd Half		6	4	0	88	56	3.61	1.54	258			24.5	29%	78%	5.31	37	22	41	5.1	5.7	**1.1**	6%	0.7	7.6	-19	$5
Rand Var	-2	10	Proj	**7**	**13**	**0**	**181**	**127**	**4.87**	**1.59**	**272**			**24.8**	**31%**	**71%**	**5.03**	**39**	**22**	**39**	**4.9**	**6.3**	**1.3**	**9%**	**1.0**	**-15.2**	**-0**	**$4**

7-10, 4.84 ERA in 145 IP at PIT and SEA. ERA rebound due mostly to S%, H% and hr/f fortunes. '07 Ctl, GB% haven't returned, now are outliers. Dom trend suggests he's living on the edge of disaster.

Sonnanstine,Andy

		Yr	Tm	W	L	Sv	IP	K	ERA	WHIP	OBA	vL	vR	BF/G	H%	S%	xERA	G	L	F	Ctl	Dom	Cmd	hr/f	hr/9	RAR	BPV	R$
RH	Starter	05		0	0	0	0	0	0.00	0.00							0.00											
Age	27	06	aa	15	8	0	185	127	4.11	1.27	274			27.7	31%	70%	4.36				1.9	6.2	**3.2**		1.0	9.4	77	$18
Type	Con FB	07	TAM	* 12	14	0	202	155	5.09	1.31	283	318	266	25.8	32%	64%	4.09	39	18	43	1.8	6.9	**3.9**	10%	1.2	-14.5	93	$14
Health	A	08	TAM	13	9	0	193	124	4.38	1.29	280	265	289	25.4	31%	68%	4.16	42	17	41	1.7	5.8	**3.4**	8%	1.0	-0.7	78	$15
PT/Exp	B	09	TAM	* 11	12	0	157	91	6.32	1.62	323	275	367	23.0	35%	63%	4.82	43	19	38	2.5	5.2	**2.1**	11%	1.4	-36.1	48	$1
Consist	A	1st Half		7	7	0	87	53	6.41	1.54	311			24.3	33%	61%	4.57	44	19	37	2.4	5.5	**2.3**	13%	1.5	-21.0	56	$1
LIMA Plan	C	2nd Half		4	5	0	70	38	6.21	1.73	338			21.6	37%	65%	5.28	37	20	43	2.6	4.9	**1.9**	8%	1.2	-15.1	33	($1)
Rand Var	+5	10	Proj	**11**	**11**	**0**	**167**	**105**	**4.59**	**1.36**	**283**			**23.8**	**31%**	**69%**	**4.39**	**42**	**18**	**40**	**2.2**	**5.7**	**2.6**	**10%**	**1.2**	**0.9**	**63**	**$11**

6-9, 6.77 ERA in 99 IP at TAM. Poor H% and S% hurt, but Cmd slide and inability to improve GB% were the killers. Must halt dominance drift and regain fine Ctl to have any shot at returning to relevance.

Soriano,Rafael

		Yr	Tm	W	L	Sv	IP	K	ERA	WHIP	OBA	vL	vR	BF/G	H%	S%	xERA	G	L	F	Ctl	Dom	Cmd	hr/f	hr/9	RAR	BPV	R$
RH	Reliever	05	SEA	0	0	0	7	9	2.54	0.99	231	571	100	4.0	35%	71%	2.84	32	16	53	1.3	11.4	**9.0**	0%	0.0	1.6	181	$1
Age	30	06	SEA	1	2	2	60	65	2.25	1.08	206	244	179	4.5	27%	85%	3.77	27	19	54	3.2	9.8	**3.1**	7%	0.9	17.1	96	$10
Type	Pwr xFB	07	ATL	3	3	9	72	70	3.00	0.86	188	164	197	3.8	21%	76%	3.41	33	16	51	1.9	8.8	**4.7**	13%	1.5	12.7	118	$14
Health	F	08	ATL	0	1	3	14	16	2.57	1.14	151	222	103	4.1	20%	80%	4.30	23	16	61	5.8	10.3	**1.8**	5%	0.6	2.9	30	$3
PT/Exp	C	09	ATL	1	6	27	76	102	2.97	1.06	199	258	138	3.9	30%	74%	2.97	31	21	48	3.2	12.1	**3.8**	8%	0.7	11.4	140	$18
Consist	C	1st Half		1	1	6	36	49	1.24	0.91	164			4.0	26%	88%	2.75	34	19	47	3.2	12.2	**3.8**	3%	0.2	13.2	144	$9
LIMA Plan	B	2nd Half		0	5	21	40	53	4.56	1.19	229			3.9	32%	64%	3.16	28	23	49	3.2	12.1	**3.8**	11%	1.1	-1.8	137	$10
Rand Var	0	10	Proj	**4**	**3**	**30**	**73**	**85**	**3.48**	**1.14**	**230**			**4.1**	**30%**	**74%**	**3.41**	**31**	**19**	**50**	**2.7**	**10.6**	**3.9**	**10%**	**1.1**	**7.6**	**125**	**$19**

Avoided DL, earned preferred closer status by July, put up Elite numbers. 2H ERA hurt by poor H%, S% luck and hr/f regression, and FB% can be a problem. But health (shoulder, elbow) is only real red flag.

Soria,Joakim

		Yr	Tm	W	L	Sv	IP	K	ERA	WHIP	OBA	vL	vR	BF/G	H%	S%	xERA	G	L	F	Ctl	Dom	Cmd	hr/f	hr/9	RAR	BPV	R$
RH	Reliever	05	MEX	5	0	0	66	55	4.91	1.74	301			10.3	35%	75%	6.18				4.8	7.5	**1.6**		1.2	-4.9	36	$2
Age	25	06	MEX	0	0	15	37	28	4.38	1.43	277			4.1	33%	70%	4.60				3.2	6.8	**2.2**		0.7	0.6	64	$6
Type	Pwr FB	07	KC	2	3	17	69	75	2.48	0.94	191	167	200	4.3	26%	74%	3.06	39	20	40	2.5	9.8	**3.9**	4%	0.4	17.3	126	$17
Health	B	08	KC	2	3	42	67	66	1.60	0.86	170	167	171	4.0	22%	87%	3.10	45	14	41	2.5	8.8	**3.5**	7%	0.7	22.8	113	$26
PT/Exp	B	09	KC	3	2	30	53	69	2.21	1.13	227	224	213	4.6	33%	85%	2.90	40	18	42	2.7	11.7	**4.3**	10%	0.8	14.7	155	$19
Consist	A	1st Half		2	0	10	18	23	1.98	1.15	214			4.1	31%	85%	2.74	48	21	31	3.5	11.4	**3.3**	8%	0.5	5.6	137	$7
LIMA Plan	B	2nd Half		1	2	20	35	46	2.33	1.12	234			4.8	33%	86%	2.97	35	16	48	2.3	11.9	**5.1**	10%	1.0	9.1	165	$12
Rand Var	-5	10	Proj	**3**	**2**	**40**	**58**	**71**	**2.64**	**1.05**	**220**			**4.4**	**30%**	**80%**	**2.85**	**42**	**17**	**41**	**2.3**	**11.0**	**4.7**	**11%**	**0.9**	**11.3**	**155**	**$23**

Hiked Dom and BPV to super-Elite levels in season marred only by shoulder soreness and three-week DL stint in May. FB, hr/9 creeping upward, but only health can prevent him from improving save totals.

Sosa,Jorge

		Yr	Tm	W	L	Sv	IP	K	ERA	WHIP	OBA	vL	vR	BF/G	H%	S%	xERA	G	L	F	Ctl	Dom	Cmd	hr/f	hr/9	RAR	BPV	R$
RH	Reliever	05	ATL	13	3	0	134	85	2.55	1.39	244	247	235	13.1	27%	85%	4.89	35	24	41	4.3	5.7	**1.3**	7%	0.8	28.0	-0	$15
Age	32	06	2NL	3	11	4	118	75	5.42	1.51	293	326	270	11.6	30%	72%	5.00	35	21	44	3.1	5.7	**1.9**	17%	2.3	-13.5	34	$2
Type	Pwr FB	07	NYM	* 13	8	0	145	87	3.93	1.39	275	326	202	13.3	31%	73%	4.83	38	19	43	2.9	5.4	**1.9**	6%	0.7	8.9	34	$12
Health	A	08	aa	2	2	4	36	27	5.28	1.89	300			6.4	34%	75%	6.83				6.2	6.8	**1.1**		1.5	-4.3	15	$1
PT/Exp	D	09	WAS	* 3	3	5	70	61	4.60	1.47	281	344	293	8.1	33%	71%	4.45	32	20	47	3.3	7.8	**2.4**	8%	1.0	-3.6	61	$4
Consist	F	1st Half		1	2	0	35	28	4.32	1.50	309			15.5	36%	72%	5.32				2.2	7.1	**3.3**		0.8	-0.6	80	$1
LIMA Plan	C+	2nd Half		2	1	5	35	33	4.88	1.43	250			5.5	30%	69%	4.44	32	20	47	4.4	8.5	**1.9**	11%	1.3	-3.0	44	$3
Rand Var	+1	10	Proj	**2**	**2**	**0**	**44**	**34**	**4.97**	**1.56**	**281**			**7.8**	**32%**	**71%**	**4.83**	**35**	**21**	**44**	**4.1**	**7.0**	**1.7**	**10%**	**1.2**	**-3.0**	**28**	**$1**

2-1, 6.45 ERA in 22 IP at WAS. Dom is spiking upward, Cmd hit a career high, but the good ends there. Gopheritis is always lurking, Ctl remains erratic, and LHers demolish him. 5 saves? Only on the Nationals.

Sowers,Jeremy

		Yr	Tm	W	L	Sv	IP	K	ERA	WHIP	OBA	vL	vR	BF/G	H%	S%	xERA	G	L	F	Ctl	Dom	Cmd	hr/f	hr/9	RAR	BPV	R$
LH	Starter	05	a/a	6	1	0	88	65	2.25	1.11	262			25.4	31%	84%	3.45				1.0	6.6	**6.5**		0.7	22.3	158	$13
Age	26	06	CLE	* 16	5	0	185	83	2.62	1.23	253	225	259	26.5	27%	80%	4.29	48	21	30	2.4	4.0	**1.7**	6%	0.5	44.2	33	$24
Type	Con FB	07	CLE	* 5	11	0	164	79	5.56	1.57	315	206	338	26.2	34%	65%	5.23	40	16	44	2.5	4.3	**1.8**	6%	0.9	-21.3	29	$0
Health	A	08	CLE	* 8	12	0	181	102	4.68	1.47	290	258	303	24.8	31%	71%	4.54	42	24	34	2.8	5.0	**1.8**	11%	1.1	-7.4	34	$7
PT/Exp	C	09	CLE	* 8	13	0	160	74	4.85	1.48	280	291	277	24.3	30%	67%	5.40	38	19	43	3.4	4.2	**1.2**	5%	0.7	-7.9	-2	$5
Consist	B	1st Half		4	7	0	83	48	4.47	1.50	286			24.5	32%	71%	4.90	41	20	40	3.3	5.2	**1.6**	7%	0.9	-0.2	25	$4
LIMA Plan	C	2nd Half		4	6	0	77	26	5.26	1.47	274			24.2	29%	63%	5.88	36	18	46	3.6	3.0	**0.8**	4%	0.6	-7.7	-30	$2
Rand Var	-2	10	Proj	**5**	**7**	**0**	**102**	**50**	**4.70**	**1.46**	**285**			**24.7**	**30%**	**69%**	**5.05**	**39**	**20**	**41**	**3.0**	**4.4**	**1.5**	**8%**	**1.0**	**-7.7**	**16**	**$4**

6-11, 5.25 ERA in 123 IP at CLE. Very hittable, losing any chance at success as long as his GB% and Ctl trend in the wrong direction. Scary Dom, things could have been worse if not for hr/f. Avoid.

Springer,Russ

		Yr	Tm	W	L	Sv	IP	K	ERA	WHIP	OBA	vL	vR	BF/G	H%	S%	xERA	G	L	F	Ctl	Dom	Cmd	hr/f	hr/9	RAR	BPV	R$
RH	Reliever	05	HOU	4	4	0	59	54	4.73	1.19	228	209	231	3.9	26%	64%	3.81	40	16	44	3.2	8.2	**2.6**	13%	1.4	-3.5	80	$5
Age	41	06	HOU	1	1	0	59	46	3.50	1.05	216	253	187	3.3	23%	75%	4.44	27	15	58	2.4	7.0	**2.9**	10%	1.5	7.2	65	$6
Type	Pwr xFB	07	STL	8	1	0	66	66	2.18	0.91	181	235	158	3.3	24%	77%	3.55	30	20	51	2.6	9.0	**3.5**	4%	0.4	18.3	100	$14
Health	A	08	STL	2	1	0	50	45	2.33	1.13	216	277	176	2.9	27%	83%	4.08	30	20	49	3.2	8.1	**2.5**	6%	0.7	12.1	66	$6
PT/Exp	D	09	2AL	1	4	1	57	58	4.11	1.49	297	350	263	3.4	36%	78%	4.61	19	19	62	2.7	9.2	**3.4**	9%	1.4	2.4	90	$4
Consist	B	1st Half		0	1	0	28	34	5.11	1.77	329			3.9	43%	76%	4.53	20	21	58	3.5	10.9	**3.1**	10%	1.6	-2.3	99	($0)
LIMA Plan	B	2nd Half		1	3	1	29	24	3.12	1.22	263			3.0	30%	81%	4.65	18	17	65	1.9	7.5	**4.0**	7%	1.2	4.7	81	$4
Rand Var	0	10	Proj	**2**	**3**	**0**	**58**	**50**	**4.50**	**1.36**	**265**			**3.3**	**31%**	**71%**	**4.69**	**25**	**19**	**57**	**3.1**	**7.8**	**2.5**	**9%**	**1.4**	**-1.8**	**58**	**$4**

Ageless wonder continues to dominate, control his walks, work around high FB%, and outpitch his xERA. Hurt by ridiculously poor 1H h%, but rebounded in strong 2H. Age, BA vs. LHB are red flags.

Stammen,Craig

		Yr	Tm	W	L	Sv	IP	K	ERA	WHIP	OBA	vL	vR	BF/G	H%	S%	xERA	G	L	F	Ctl	Dom	Cmd	hr/f	hr/9	RAR	BPV	R$
RH	Starter	05		0	0	0	0	0	0.00	0.00							0.00											
Age	26	06		0	0	0	0	0	0.00	0.00							0.00											
Type	Con	07		0	0	0	0	0	0.00	0.00							0.00											
Health	A	08	a/a	4	5	0	81	53	5.03	1.45	286			23.6	34%	63%	4.36				2.9	5.9	**2.1**		0.3	-7.3	66	$3
PT/Exp	D	09	WAS	* 8	9	0	146	60	4.33	1.25	268	290	247	23.4	27%	68%	4.32	47	21	32	2.0	3.7	**1.9**	11%	1.1	-2.5	38	$8
Consist	A	1st Half		5	5	0	84	34	3.97	1.24	267			23.4	28%	71%	4.25	50	19	32	1.9	3.6	**1.9**	10%	1.0	2.3	41	$6
LIMA Plan	C+	2nd Half		3	4	0	62	26	4.83	1.27	270			23.4	27%	65%	4.36	45	22	33	2.0	3.8	**1.9**	13%	1.3	-4.9	36	$3
Rand Var	0	10	Proj	**6**	**12**	**0**	**160**	**72**	**4.51**	**1.40**	**288**			**23.8**	**30%**	**70%**	**4.51**	**46**	**21**	**32**	**2.4**	**4.1**	**1.7**	**9%**	**1.0**	**-4.9**	**34**	**$5**

4-7, 5.11 ERA in 105 IP at WAS. 1H / 2H splits reveal the fine line he walked. S%, GB% down-ticks and hr/f, hr/9 hikes killed 2H ERA. Could struggle big-time if Dom doesn't rebound

Stauffer,Tim

		Yr	Tm	W	L	Sv	IP	K	ERA	WHIP	OBA	vL	vR	BF/G	H%	S%	xERA	G	L	F	Ctl	Dom	Cmd	hr/f	hr/9	RAR	BPV	R$
RH	Reliever	05	SD	* 5	11	0	147	99	5.57	1.54	305	289	283	24.3	35%	64%	4.40	41	23	36	2.8	6.1	**2.2**	8%	0.9	-24.0	54	$0
Age	27	06	aaa	7	12	0	153	78	5.35	1.65	320			25.0	35%	68%	6.05				2.9	4.6	**1.6**		0.9	-15.7	25	$1
Type		07	aa	8	5	0	130	76	5.76	1.74	336			24.3	37%	68%	6.72				2.8	5.2	**1.8**		1.0	-20.8	28	($1)
Health	F	08	SD	0	0	0	0	0	0.00	0.00							0.00											
PT/Exp	D	09	SD	* 7	8	1	115	74	3.17	1.30	247	239	279	16.2	28%	78%	4.30	44	20	36	3.4	5.8	**1.7**	8%	0.8	14.5	35	$10
Consist	F	1st Half		2	1	1	34	18	3.04	1.22	258			9.4	29%	76%	3.63				2.1	4.8	**2.3**		0.6	4.8	62	$4
LIMA Plan	C	2nd Half		5	7	0	81	56	3.22	1.34	243			23.0	27%	79%	4.34	44	20	36	3.9	6.2	**1.6**	9%	0.9	9.7	28	$7
Rand Var	-3	10	Proj	**7**	**8**	**0**	**124**	**75**	**4.35**	**1.46**	**281**			**18.7**	**31%**	**72%**	**4.56**	**43**	**21**	**36**	**3.2**	**5.4**	**1.7**	**9%**	**1.0**	**-4.6**	**33**	**$6**

4-7, 3.58 ERA in 73 IP at SD. SD's #1 pick in 2003 returns from shoulder woes. Aided by H%, Dom and decent GB%, but deteriorating Ctl is a red flag. Consistency, health are still concerns, even in Petco.

JOCK THOMPSON

Stetter,Mitch			W	L	Sv	IP	K	ERA	WHIP	OBA	vL	vR	BF/G	H%	S%	xERA	G	L	F	Ctl	Dom	Cmd	hr/f	hr/9	RAR	BPV	R$
LH	Reliever	05 a/a	3	4	8	77	59	3.49	1.29	263			5.5	30%	76%	4.15				2.5	6.9	**2.7**		1.0	7.7	72	$9
Age	29	06 aaa	2	5	0	38	32	5.97	1.64	297			3.4	35%	64%	5.71				4.1	7.5	**1.8**		1.0	-6.8	51	$0
Type	Pwr xFB	07 a/a	1	0	1	16	17	5.63	0.97	181			2.4	24%	38%	1.99				3.1	9.6	**3.1**		0.6	-2.3	122	$2
Health	A	08 MIL *	6	4	0	54	56	3.17	1.22	200			3.8	26%	77%	3.08				4.7	9.3	**2.0**		0.8	7.4	88	$8
PT/Exp	D	09 MIL	4	1	1	45	44	3.60	1.42	226	178	259	2.8	28%	77%	4.57	36	14	50	5.4	8.8	**1.6**	7%	0.8	3.3	26	$5
Consist	C	1st Half	2	0	1	26	34	2.41	0.92	150			2.7	22%	77%	3.06	38	7	55	3.8	11.7	**3.1**	7%	0.7	5.7	125	$5
LIMA Plan	B	2nd Half	2	1	0	19	10	5.24	2.12	310			2.8	34%	76%	7.17	34	21	46	7.6	4.8	**0.6**	7%	1.0	-2.4	-108	($1)
Rand Var	-3	10 Proj	**4**	**3**	**0**	**44**	**38**	**4.34**	**1.52**	**251**			**3.2**	**30%**	**74%**	**4.89**	**35**	**17**	**48**	**5.2**	**7.9**	**1.5**	**8%**	**1.0**	**-3.4**	**15**	**$3**

H% aided strong 1H. 2H Dom and Ctl swings, ongoing issues vs. RHB limited 2H role to situational lefty. Hard thrower, but spiking Ctl trend is scary.
vL: 24 IP, 2.6 Cmd, 1.46 ERA
vR: 20 IP, 0.9 Cmd, 6.20 ERA

Stokes,Brian			W	L	Sv	IP	K	ERA	WHIP	OBA	vL	vR	BF/G	H%	S%	xERA	G	L	F	Ctl	Dom	Cmd	hr/f	hr/9	RAR	BPV	R$
RH	Reliever	05 aa	4	5	0	85	50	4.86	1.54	297			25.3	33%	69%	5.24				3.2	5.2	**1.7**		0.9	-5.9	36	$2
Age	30	06 TAM *	8	7	0	157	99	5.51	1.66	308			21.2	35%	66%	5.25	40	15	45	3.6	5.6	**1.5**	5%	0.7	-18.4	21	$2
Type		07 TAM	2	7	0	62	35	7.08	1.85	339	346	341	5.0	36%	63%	5.12	48	17	35	3.6	5.1	**1.4**	14%	1.6	-19.8	20	($4)
Health	A	08 NYM *	11	8	1	164	89	6.22	1.78	323	316	250	16.3	36%	64%	5.38	39	24	38	3.9	4.9	**1.3**	6%	0.8	-39.3	-0	($4)
PT/Exp	C	09 NYM	2	4	0	70	45	3.97	1.56	266	330	219	4.6	30%	76%	4.90	44	22	35	4.9	5.8	**1.2**	8%	0.8	1.9	-6	$2
Consist	A	1st Half	1	2	0	31	15	4.05	1.41	285			4.6	31%	73%	4.50	44	24	32	2.6	4.3	**1.7**	9%	0.9	0.5	30	$1
LIMA Plan	C	2nd Half	1	2	0	39	30	3.90	1.68	251			4.5	30%	78%	5.25	43	19	37	6.7	6.9	**1.0**	7%	0.7	1.4	-35	$1
Rand Var	-2	10 Proj	**2**	**4**	**0**	**58**	**35**	**4.97**	**1.59**	**281**			**6.2**	**31%**	**70%**	**4.93**	**44**	**20**	**35**	**4.3**	**5.4**	**1.3**	**9%**	**0.9**	**-4.8**	**3**	**$0**

Journeyman middle reliever benefitted from 2.21 ERA and 0.5 hr/9 in friendly confines of Citi Field. Poor Cmd, MIA BPV continue to decline, and he still gets crushed by LHBs. ERA repeat would be a shocker.

Street,Huston			W	L	Sv	IP	K	ERA	WHIP	OBA	vL	vR	BF/G	H%	S%	xERA	G	L	F	Ctl	Dom	Cmd	hr/f	hr/9	RAR	BPV	R$
RH	Reliever	05 OAK	5	1	23	78	72	1.73	1.01	194	224	172	4.6	25%	84%	3.38	45	17	38	3.0	8.3	**2.8**	4%	0.3	25.5	91	$21
Age	26	06 OAK	4	4	37	70	67	3.33	1.10	244	274	211	4.1	31%	70%	3.42	37	21	42	1.7	8.6	**5.2**	5%	0.5	10.6	125	$22
Type	Pwr FB	07 OAK	5	2	16	50	63	2.88	0.94	199	224	162	4.0	28%	74%	2.77	40	15	45	2.2	11.3	**5.3**	10%	0.9	10.0	164	$16
Health	B	08 OAK	7	5	18	71	70	3.80	1.23	231	200	250	4.6	29%	70%	3.71	36	23	41	3.4	8.9	**2.6**	8%	0.8	4.8	81	$15
PT/Exp	B	09 COL	4	1	35	62	70	3.06	0.91	198	167	217	3.7	26%	71%	2.86	38	19	43	1.9	10.2	**5.4**	11%	1.0	8.6	149	$22
Consist	B	1st Half	2	1	19	34	39	2.91	1.12	226			3.8	29%	82%	3.25	34	21	45	2.6	10.3	**3.9**	13%	1.3	5.4	126	$11
LIMA Plan	C+	2nd Half	2	0	16	28	31	3.25	0.65	161			3.5	22%	50%	2.38	45	15	40	1.0	10.1	**10.3**	8%	0.6	3.2	178	$11
Rand Var	-1	10 Proj	**5**	**2**	**40**	**65**	**73**	**3.17**	**1.01**	**220**			**4.0**	**29%**	**72%**	**2.99**	**39**	**19**	**42**	**1.9**	**10.1**	**5.2**	**9%**	**0.8**	**10.3**	**146**	**$24**

Stayed healthy, regained Dom, pinpoint Ctl and closer role, all in the least likely of venues. 4.08 home ERA says he is surviving Coors, 2H GB tick is promising, BPV speaks to overall excellence. He's back.

Stults,Eric			W	L	Sv	IP	K	ERA	WHIP	OBA	vL	vR	BF/G	H%	S%	xERA	G	L	F	Ctl	Dom	Cmd	hr/f	hr/9	RAR	BPV	R$
LH	Starter	05 a/a	7	10	0	146	94	4.80	1.52	313			24.0	35%	71%	5.76				2.1	5.8	**2.7**		1.2	-9.0	49	$4
Age	30	06 LA *	11	11	0	170	110	4.50	1.49	274			23.5	31%	70%	4.98	40	19	41	3.9	5.8	**1.5**	6%	0.7	-0.3	18	$9
Type	xFB	07 LA *	6	11	0	128	89	9.14	2.28	390			20.1	44%	60%	5.74	39	21	39	4.3	6.3	**1.5**	10%	1.5	-74.3	15	($18)
Health	F	08 LA *	9	10	0	156	104	4.91	1.65	313	314	233	26.4	34%	74%	4.91	38	22	41	3.3	6.0	**1.8**	11%	1.4	-12.2	35	$2
PT/Exp	D	09 LA *	9	7	0	114	66	5.43	1.76	318	262	270	24.3	36%	69%	5.68	35	17	48	4.0	5.2	**1.3**	4%	0.7	-17.4	-3	($0)
Consist	B	1st Half	4	3	0	48	34	5.12	1.66	280			22.0	33%	67%	5.53	33	18	49	5.1	6.3	**1.2**	3%	0.4	-5.5	-13	$1
LIMA Plan	C	2nd Half	5	4	0	66	32	5.65	1.84	343			26.2	37%	70%	4.98	57	7	36	3.3	4.4	**1.3**	7%	0.9	-11.9	25	($2)
Rand Var	0	10 Proj	**4**	**4**	**0**	**58**	**36**	**5.28**	**1.62**	**300**			**23.9**	**33%**	**70%**	**5.23**	**37**	**18**	**45**	**3.7**	**5.6**	**1.5**	**9%**	**1.2**	**-6.9**	**15**	**$1**

4-3, 4.86 ERA in 50 IP at LA. Dom and GB% both trending the wrong way, Ctl hasn't been anything special for a while. Five-year h% suggests he's far too hittable, only hr/f keeps this profile from looking worse.

Suppan,Jeff			W	L	Sv	IP	K	ERA	WHIP	OBA	vL	vR	BF/G	H%	S%	xERA	G	L	F	Ctl	Dom	Cmd	hr/f	hr/9	RAR	BPV	R$
RH	Starter	05 STL	16	10	0	194	114	3.57	1.39	273	271	279	26.1	30%	78%	4.26	46	21	32	2.9	5.3	**1.8**	12%	1.1	16.2	41	$16
Age	35	06 STL	12	7	0	190	104	4.12	1.45	279	302	257	26.0	30%	74%	4.56	47	23	31	3.3	4.9	**1.5**	11%	1.0	8.6	25	$11
Type	Con	07 MIL	12	12	0	207	114	4.62	1.50	294	334	271	26.9	32%	70%	4.68	45	20	35	3.0	5.0	**1.7**	7%	0.8	-4.8	33	$8
Health	B	08 MIL	10	10	0	178	90	4.96	1.54	292	288	308	25.6	30%	72%	4.79	44	23	32	3.4	4.6	**1.3**	15%	1.5	-15.2	13	$4
PT/Exp	A	09 MIL	7	12	0	162	80	5.29	1.69	305	311	306	24.9	32%	72%	5.06	49	18	33	4.1	4.5	**1.1**	13%	1.4	-21.9	-4	($2)
Consist	A	1st Half	5	6	0	87	47	4.86	1.66	304			24.9	32%	74%	4.87	50	16	34	3.8	4.9	**1.3**	12%	1.3	-7.2	12	$1
LIMA Plan	F	2nd Half	2	6	0	75	33	5.78	1.74	306			24.9	31%	69%	5.28	48	20	31	4.5	4.0	**0.9**	14%	1.4	-14.7	-23	($3)
Rand Var	+1	10 Proj	**5**	**11**	**0**	**135**	**68**	**5.02**	**1.61**	**298**			**25.4**	**31%**	**72%**	**4.89**	**47**	**20**	**33**	**3.7**	**4.6**	**1.2**	**13%**	**1.3**	**-10.4**	**8**	**$0**

Five-year ERA, xERA and RAR are trending in a straight line to oblivion. Gopheritis has gone from acute to chronic. 2nd half BPIs were on life support. But he gives you innings, always takes his turn, like it's a good thing.

Swarzak,Anthony			W	L	Sv	IP	K	ERA	WHIP	OBA	vL	vR	BF/G	H%	S%	xERA	G	L	F	Ctl	Dom	Cmd	hr/f	hr/9	RAR	BPV	R$
RH	Starter	05	0	0	0	0	0	0.00	0.00							0.00											
Age	24	06	0	0	0	0	0	0.00	0.00							0.00											
Type	Con xFB	07 aa	5	4	0	86	62	3.87	1.30	266			24.2	31%	71%	4.02				2.5	6.5	**2.6**		0.6	6.3	76	$8
Health	A	08 a/a	8	8	0	146	84	5.23	1.63	312			24.7	34%	69%	5.90				3.2	5.2	**1.6**		1.0	-16.7	28	$1
PT/Exp	D	09 MIN *	7	12	0	138	71	4.88	1.49	297	331	292	24.4	32%	69%	5.18	36	19	45	2.7	4.6	**1.7**	7%	1.0	-7.4	25	$5
Consist	C	1st Half	6	6	0	92	53	3.12	1.26	257			25.7	29%	76%	4.58	42	16	43	2.5	5.2	**2.0**	5%	0.6	15.2	44	$10
LIMA Plan	C+	2nd Half	1	6	0	46	18	8.43	1.96	367			22.4	37%	59%	6.26	32	21	47	2.9	3.5	**1.2**	12%	2.1	-22.5	-6	($5)
Rand Var	-1	10 Proj	**4**	**7**	**0**	**87**	**48**	**5.07**	**1.51**	**304**			**24.1**	**32%**	**70%**	**5.09**	**34**	**21**	**45**	**2.5**	**5.0**	**2.0**	**10%**	**1.4**	**-7.0**	**34**	**$2**

3-7, 6.25 ERA in 59 IP at MIN. Has displayed better Dom in the minors. FB% says he isn't likely to succeed without it, as noted in 2H performance. Ctl, age offer hope, H% past says he's too hittable to roster.

Tallet,Brian			W	L	Sv	IP	K	ERA	WHIP	OBA	vL	vR	BF/G	H%	S%	xERA	G	L	F	Ctl	Dom	Cmd	hr/f	hr/9	RAR	BPV	R$
LH	Starter	05 aaa	6	5	0	97	49	4.48	1.40	288			19.1	30%	73%	5.29				2.4	4.6	**1.9**		1.4	-2.1	23	$5
Age	32	06 TOR *	4	2	3	79	53	5.36	1.65	282	220	246	5.7	31%	70%	5.26	41	18	41	4.9	6.1	**1.2**	10%	1.2	-7.8	-4	$2
Type	Pwr FB	07 TOR	2	4	0	62	54	3.47	1.24	218	247	194	5.4	28%	70%	4.11	40	19	40	4.0	7.8	**1.9**	1%	0.1	8.0	50	$6
Health	A	08 TOR	1	2	0	56	47	2.88	1.31	247	257	230	4.7	30%	80%	3.94	43	22	36	3.5	7.5	**2.1**	7%	0.6	10.2	61	$5
PT/Exp	C	09 TOR	7	9	0	161	120	5.32	1.50	272	290	259	19.2	31%	66%	4.84	36	21	43	4.0	6.7	**1.7**	9%	1.1	-17.2	26	$5
Consist	B	1st Half	5	5	0	94	71	4.49	1.34	234			21.1	27%	68%	4.71	37	20	44	4.3	6.8	**1.6**	8%	1.0	-0.4	21	$7
LIMA Plan	C+	2nd Half	2	4	0	67	49	6.50	1.73	319			17.2	36%	64%	5.02	36	22	42	3.7	6.6	**1.8**	10%	1.4	-16.8	35	($2)
Rand Var	0	10 Proj	**3**	**4**	**0**	**87**	**72**	**4.45**	**1.45**	**268**			**7.6**	**31%**	**72%**	**4.38**	**39**	**21**	**41**	**3.7**	**7.4**	**2.0**	**10%**	**1.1**	**0.5**	**50**	**$5**

Marginal-but-improving skills overexposed once pressed into rotation after injuries and demotions. Revival possible with return to pen, though '07-'08 ERAs aren't likely. GB% and rebound vs. LHB are keys.

Tavarez,Julian			W	L	Sv	IP	K	ERA	WHIP	OBA	vL	vR	BF/G	H%	S%	xERA	G	L	F	Ctl	Dom	Cmd	hr/f	hr/9	RAR	BPV	R$
RH	Reliever	05 STL	2	3	4	65	47	3.45	1.33	270	294	271	3.7	31%	77%	3.65	51	21	28	2.6	6.5	**2.5**	10%	0.8	6.4	74	$6
Age	36	06 BOS	5	4	1	98	56	4.49	1.57	284	248	327	7.6	31%	73%	4.35	57	17	26	4.0	5.1	**1.3**	12%	0.9	0.8	19	$4
Type	Pwr	07 BOS	7	11	0	135	77	5.14	1.50	284	260	300	17.5	31%	66%	4.39	54	16	30	3.4	5.1	**1.5**	10%	0.9	-10.6	32	$5
Health	A	08 2TM	1	5	0	55	51	5.10	1.85	321	374	270	5.0	40%	73%	3.76	53	27	21	4.6	8.4	**1.8**	14%	0.8	-5.4	57	($1)
PT/Exp	C	09 WAS	3	7	1	35	32	4.89	1.74	256	315	207	3.9	33%	70%	4.70	50	18	32	6.9	8.2	**1.2**	3%	0.3	-3.0	-11	$1
Consist	B	1st Half	3	6	1	31	29	4.34	1.51	222			3.7	29%	70%	4.23	52	17	31	6.4	8.4	**1.3**	4%	0.3	-0.6	9	$3
LIMA Plan	C	2nd Half	0	1	0	4	3	9.23	3.59	450			5.1	53%	71%	9.11	41	24	35	11.5	6.9	**0.6**	0%	0.0	-2.4	-168	($1)
Rand Var	0	10 Proj	**2**	**3**	**0**	**29**	**22**	**4.66**	**1.55**	**268**			**5.4**	**31%**	**71%**	**4.32**	**48**	**22**	**30**	**4.7**	**6.8**	**1.5**	**11%**	**0.9**	**-0.2**	**24**	**$1**

Being cut by WAS (after a 14.73 ERA and .521 OBA in July) and finding no buyers for his skills hints at issues. GB% piques interest, but BBs now at levels that rising Dom can't help.

Tazawa,Junichi			W	L	Sv	IP	K	ERA	WHIP	OBA	vL	vR	BF/G	H%	S%	xERA	G	L	F	Ctl	Dom	Cmd	hr/f	hr/9	RAR	BPV	R$
RH	Starter	05	0	0	0	0	0	0.00	0.00							0.00											
Age	23	06	0	0	0	0	0	0.00	0.00							0.00											
Type	Con xFB	07	0	0	0	0	0	0.00	0.00							0.00											
Health	A	08	0	0	0	0	0	0.00	0.00							0.00											
PT/Exp	F	09 BOS *	11	10	0	134	94	4.35	1.39	284	323	440	22.3	32%	70%	4.95	25	23	53	2.5	6.3	**2.5**	6%	0.9	1.6	49	$11
Consist	F	1st Half	7	5	0	82	67	4.06	1.37	271			23.4	32%	72%	4.39				2.9	7.4	**2.6**		0.9	4.0	73	$8
LIMA Plan	C+	2nd Half	4	5	0	52	27	4.81	1.43	302			20.7	33%	67%	5.35	25	23	53	1.9	4.6	**2.5**	5%	0.9	-2.3	35	$3
Rand Var	-2	10 Proj	**5**	**5**	**0**	**58**	**37**	**4.50**	**1.38**	**284**			**20.8**	**31%**	**71%**	**5.03**	**25**	**23**	**53**	**2.3**	**5.7**	**2.5**	**8%**	**1.2**	**-4.2**	**43**	**$5**

2-3, 7.46 ERA in 25 IP at BOS. Didn't bring K's, did bring too many LD and FB contact in AL hitter parks during MLB debut. Fine Ctl, 8.1 Dom at AAA say skills are there, but 2011 payoff is more likely.

JOCK THOMPSON

Tejeda,Robinson

Tejeda,Robinson	Yr	W	L	Sv	IP	K	ERA	WHIP	OBA	vL	vR	BF/G	H%	S%	xERA	G	L	F	Ctl	Dom	Cmd	hr/f	hr/9	RAR	BPV	R$
RH Reliever	05 PHI *	6	3	0	113	96	3.34	1.36	220	210	226	15.6	28%	75%	4.57	36	21	43	5.1	7.6	1.5	4%	0.4	12.7	14	$10
Age 28	06 TEX *	11	7	0	153	108	4.52	1.56	271	331	250	23.7	30%	74%	5.20	37	18	45	4.6	6.3	1.4	10%	1.2	0.6	6	$9
Type Pwr xFB	07 TEX *	6	12	0	114	84	7.49	1.96	313	317	264	23.1	35%	62%	6.15	35	14	51	6.1	6.7	1.1	9%	1.3	-41.8	-31	($7)
Health B	08 2AL *	3	3	1	78	74	3.49	1.12	191	225	115	8.1	24%	70%	4.03	33	20	47	4.1	8.5	2.1	7%	0.7	8.3	53	$10
PT/Exp D	09 KC	4	2	0	74	87	3.54	1.26	171	209	125	8.8	24%	72%	4.13	35	15	50	6.1	10.6	1.7	5%	0.5	8.3	39	$9
Consist C	1st Half	0	0	0	19	26	4.26	1.68	241			6.2	38%	72%	4.00	43	17	40	7.1	12.3	1.7	0%	0.0	0.4	50	$1
LIMA Plan B+	2nd Half	4	2	0	55	61	3.29	1.12	144			10.5	19%	72%	4.16	32	14	54	5.8	10.0	1.7	6%	0.7	7.8	35	$8
Rand Var -5	10 Proj	4	3	0	87	90	4.24	1.45	227			10.0	30%	71%	4.52	36	16	48	5.6	9.3	1.7	5%	0.6	-0.9	30	$6

3-1, 2.74 ERA as SP in Sept built on 19% H% and 5.7 Ctl. Throws very hard but often can't find home plate with a GPS. BA vs RH and hr/f are begging for a correction, especially with his FB rate. Risk level is toxic.

Thatcher,Joe

Thatcher,Joe	Yr	W	L	Sv	IP	K	ERA	WHIP	OBA	vL	vR	BF/G	H%	S%	xERA	G	L	F	Ctl	Dom	Cmd	hr/f	hr/9	RAR	BPV	R$
LH Reliever	05	0	0	0	0	0	0.00	0.00							0.00											
Age 28	06	0	0	0	0	0	0.00	0.00							0.00											
Type Pwr	07 a/a	4	1	1	46	53	1.64	1.23	262			4.2	38%	85%	3.11				2.1	10.4	5.1		0.0	16.1	171	$9
Health A	08 aaa	5	2	3	39	32	3.61	1.61	310			4.8	37%	78%	5.35				3.1	7.3	2.4		0.6	3.3	70	$5
PT/Exp F	09 SD *	2	2	1	64	74	2.67	1.30	240	182	267	3.8	34%	80%	3.28	44	18	38	3.7	10.4	2.8	5%	0.4	12.0	111	$7
Consist F	1st Half	1	1	0	29	27	3.24	1.63	288			4.6	35%	84%	4.15	45	20	35	4.4	8.3	1.9	10%	1.0	3.4	54	$1
LIMA Plan A	2nd Half	1	1	1	35	47	2.20	1.02	195			3.3	32%	76%	2.59	43	17	39	3.0	12.2	4.0	-1%	-0.1	8.5	158	$6
Rand Var -2	10 Proj	4	2	0	58	61	3.41	1.24	241			4.0	31%	75%	3.37	44	18	38	3.1	9.5	3.1	9%	0.8	6.4	109	$7

1-0, 2.80 ERA in 45 IP at SD. Fine 2H BPIs across the board paced by eye-opening Dom spike. 3.26 ERA, one HR on the road says this isn't just a PETCO creation. Needs to do it again, but future looks bright.

Thompson,Brad

Thompson,Brad	Yr	W	L	Sv	IP	K	ERA	WHIP	OBA	vL	vR	BF/G	H%	S%	xERA	G	L	F	Ctl	Dom	Cmd	hr/f	hr/9	RAR	BPV	R$
RH Reliever	05 STL *	6	1	1	68	39	3.04	1.19	235	224	228	5.7	26%	77%	3.62	58	17	25	2.9	5.1	1.8	11%	0.8	10.2	50	$8
Age 28	06 STL *	3	2	0	98	61	3.11	1.28	265	284	256	7.3	30%	77%	3.63	55	21	24	2.4	5.6	2.3	9%	0.6	16.7	69	$8
Type Con GB	07 STL	8	6	0	129	53	4.73	1.52	301	343	267	13.1	30%	74%	4.89	49	17	34	2.8	3.7	1.3	15%	1.6	-4.9	19	$4
Health B	08 STL *	7	4	0	77	35	5.94	1.57	315	279	303	11.9	33%	63%	4.52	51	20	29	2.5	4.1	1.6	12%	1.1	-15.9	34	$1
PT/Exp C	09 STL	2	6	0	80	34	4.84	1.35	274	255	289	10.7	29%	65%	4.28	53	19	28	2.6	3.8	1.5	10%	0.9	-6.4	30	$2
Consist A	1st Half	2	4	0	48	15	4.69	1.27	266			13.4	27%	64%	4.21	57	17	26	2.3	2.8	1.3	11%	0.9	-2.9	24	$2
LIMA Plan C+	2nd Half	0	2	0	32	19	5.06	1.47	285			8.3	32%	66%	4.35	47	21	32	3.1	5.3	1.7	9%	0.8	-3.4	37	($0)
Rand Var +1	10 Proj	2	2	0	44	21	4.76	1.45	290			10.0	31%	69%	4.37	51	19	30	2.7	4.3	1.6	11%	1.0	-0.6	35	$1

ERA / xERA track H% and GB% - his primary skill. And good Ctl doesn't compensate for sub-standard dominance when you're this hittable. Not rosterable until he learns a new trick.

Thornton,Matt

Thornton,Matt	Yr	W	L	Sv	IP	K	ERA	WHIP	OBA	vL	vR	BF/G	H%	S%	xERA	G	L	F	Ctl	Dom	Cmd	hr/f	hr/9	RAR	BPV	R$
LH Reliever	05 SEA	0	4	0	57	57	5.21	1.68	251	262	235	4.8	28%	76%	4.76	43	15	42	6.6	9.0	1.4	20%	2.1	-5.9	4	($0)
Age 33	06 CHW	5	3	2	54	49	3.33	1.24	232	211	240	3.6	28%	76%	3.55	49	19	32	3.5	8.2	2.3	10%	0.8	8.2	80	$8
Type Pwr	07 CHW	4	4	2	56	55	4.80	1.51	271	283	260	3.7	35%	68%	3.89	47	19	34	4.2	8.8	2.1	7%	0.6	-2.0	71	$5
Health A	08 CHW	5	3	1	67	77	2.67	1.00	202	170	218	3.6	28%	76%	2.48	53	20	27	2.5	10.3	4.1	11%	0.7	13.9	148	$12
PT/Exp C	09 CHW	6	3	4	72	87	2.74	1.08	221	208	223	4.1	31%	77%	2.79	46	17	36	2.5	10.8	4.4	8%	0.6	15.3	152	$14
Consist B	1st Half	4	2	0	31	39	2.88	1.19	221			4.0	31%	79%	2.86	51	14	35	3.5	11.3	3.3	12%	0.9	6.0	138	$6
LIMA Plan B+	2nd Half	2	1	4	41	48	2.63	1.00	222			4.2	31%	74%	2.73	43	20	37	1.8	10.5	6.0	5%	0.4	9.2	163	$8
Rand Var -1	10 Proj	5	3	28	65	74	3.03	1.12	227			3.9	30%	76%	2.89	48	18	34	2.6	10.2	3.9	11%	0.8	12.5	139	$20

Outstanding Dom in three-year upswing, consolidated once-spotty Ctl, avoids HR via solid GB%. Two straight years of elite closer skills on verge of opportunity despite handedness. If not, a solid LIMA call.

Tillman,Chris

Tillman,Chris	Yr	W	L	Sv	IP	K	ERA	WHIP	OBA	vL	vR	BF/G	H%	S%	xERA	G	L	F	Ctl	Dom	Cmd	hr/f	hr/9	RAR	BPV	R$
RH Starter	05	0	0	0	0	0	0.00	0.00							0.00											
Age 21	06	0	0	0	0	0	0.00	0.00							0.00											
Type Pwr xFB	07	0	0	0	0	0	0.00	0.00							0.00											
Health A	08 aa	11	4	0	135	141	3.74	1.37	248			20.7	32%	74%	3.97				4.0	9.4	2.3		0.8	9.4	88	$14
PT/Exp D	09 BAL *	10	11	0	162	130	4.19	1.35	272	254	341	23.1	31%	73%	4.32	37	18	45	2.7	7.2	2.7	10%	1.2	5.3	72	$13
Consist A	1st Half	6	5	0	80	76	3.38	1.16	244			21.8	31%	72%	3.17				2.3	8.5	3.8		0.6	10.6	119	$11
LIMA Plan C	2nd Half	4	6	0	82	54	4.98	1.54	297			24.4	32%	73%	4.96	37	18	45	3.1	6.0	1.9	13%	1.7	-5.3	38	$3
Rand Var 0	10 Proj	11	10	0	174	146	4.34	1.32	258			21.7	30%	70%	4.23	37	18	45	3.0	7.6	2.5	10%	1.2	4.5	70	$15

2-5, 5.40 ERA in 65 IP at BAL. Plagued by HR ball (2.1 hr/9) and struggled to put away RHB (3.5 Dom) in MLB debut. Minor league history (9.9 Dom) says he's better than this, age says he'll suffer growing pains.

Todd,Jess

Todd,Jess	Yr	W	L	Sv	IP	K	ERA	WHIP	OBA	vL	vR	BF/G	H%	S%	xERA	G	L	F	Ctl	Dom	Cmd	hr/f	hr/9	RAR	BPV	R$
RH Reliever	05	0	0	0	0	0	0.00	0.00							0.00											
Age 23	06	0	0	0	0	0	0.00	0.00							0.00											
Type Pwr FB	07	0	0	0	0	0	0.00	0.00							0.00											
Health• A	08 aa	5	6	0	125	86	3.38	1.10	231			24.0	26%	73%	3.30				2.3	6.2	2.7		1.0	14.3	72	$13
PT/Exp D	09 CLE *	4	3	25	75	80	3.96	1.35	272	408	304	5.0	35%	72%	3.63	32	28	41	2.6	9.6	3.6	8%	0.8	4.6	111	$16
Consist A	1st Half	3	1	18	41	45	2.84	1.19	251			5.0	34%	78%	2.68	67	0	33	2.2	9.8	4.5	8%	0.7	8.2	163	$12
LIMA Plan B+	2nd Half	1	2	7	34	35	5.33	1.54	296			5.0	37%	67%	4.05	29	30	41	3.2	9.3	2.9	10%	1.1	-3.6	88	$3
Rand Var +2	10 Proj	3	3	0	59	53	4.15	1.28	260			7.2	31%	71%	3.94	29	30	41	2.6	8.2	3.1	10%	1.1	3.6	83	$5

0-1, 7.66 ERA in 22 IP at CLE. 25 saves at AAA, maintained Dom in MLB debut, ended with 7 scoreless IP. MLB struggles tied to h%, inexperience. If he resolves LHB issues (4 HR in 10 IP), he could come fast.

Tomko,Brett

Tomko,Brett	Yr	W	L	Sv	IP	K	ERA	WHIP	OBA	vL	vR	BF/G	H%	S%	xERA	G	L	F	Ctl	Dom	Cmd	hr/f	hr/9	RAR	BPV	R$
RH Reliever	05 SF	8	15	1	190	114	4.50	1.38	277	282	264	24.8	30%	69%	4.46	40	22	38	2.7	5.4	2.0	8%	0.9	-5.9	42	$9
Age 37	06 LA	8	7	0	112	76	4.74	1.36	280	300	258	10.9	31%	69%	4.56	37	18	45	2.3	6.1	2.6	10%	1.4	-3.4	62	$8
Type Con FB	07 2NL	4	12	0	131	105	5.55	1.50	287	276	291	14.5	33%	65%	4.35	41	20	39	3.3	7.2	2.2	11%	1.2	-18.2	60	$2
Health C	08 2TM	2	7	0	70	49	6.30	1.44	296	283	298	13.9	33%	58%	4.16	44	19	37	2.3	6.3	2.7	13%	1.4	-17.2	73	$0
PT/Exp C	09 2AL	5	3	0	57	33	3.77	1.10	236	218	252	11.0	23%	76%	4.52	35	17	48	2.0	5.2	2.5	14%	1.9	4.8	51	$7
Consist A	1st Half	0	2	0	16	10	5.59	1.30	248			5.7	24%	65%	5.16	30	16	54	3.4	5.6	1.7	15%	2.2	-2.3	18	$0
LIMA Plan C	2nd Half	5	1	0	41	23	3.06	1.02	232			18.0	22%	82%	4.27	37	18	45	1.5	5.0	3.3	14%	1.7	7.1	64	$7
Rand Var -3	10 Proj	4	6	0	73	42	4.72	1.38	279			11.5	30%	70%	4.77	38	19	43	2.6	5.2	2.0	11%	1.4	-3.0	40	$4

Limited RP role before July release by NYY, brief success as OAK SP before nerve damage ended season in Sept. H% fueled '09 ERA, Dom now trending south, gopheritis now chronic. Age, health say avoid.

Troncoso,Ramon

Troncoso,Ramon	Yr	W	L	Sv	IP	K	ERA	WHIP	OBA	vL	vR	BF/G	H%	S%	xERA	G	L	F	Ctl	Dom	Cmd	hr/f	hr/9	RAR	BPV	R$
RH Reliever	05	0	0	0	0	0	0.00	0.00							0.00											
Age 27	06	0	0	0	0	0	0.00	0.00							0.00											
Type Pwr xGB	07 aa	7	3	7	52	32	3.83	1.54	294			6.6	34%	75%	5.02				3.3	5.6	1.7		0.5	4.1	49	$7
Health A	08 LA *	5	1	0	68	52	5.16	1.74	317	254	278	5.9	38%	69%	3.57	61	22	18	3.9	6.9	1.8	8%	0.4	-7.5	57	$1
PT/Exp D	09 LA	5	4	6	83	55	2.72	1.41	262	289	251	4.9	31%	81%	3.91	55	19	26	3.7	6.0	1.6	4%	0.3	15.0	41	$9
Consist B	1st Half	2	0	4	51	30	1.94	1.22	230			5.9	26%	85%	3.85	54	19	26	3.4	5.3	1.6	5%	0.4	14.1	37	$7
LIMA Plan C	2nd Half	3	4	2	32	25	3.97	1.73	309			4.0	38%	76%	4.01	56	18	26	4.3	7.1	1.7	4%	0.3	0.8	47	$2
Rand Var -5	10 Proj	5	3	0	65	47	4.14	1.46	267			5.0	31%	71%	3.77	57	19	24	3.9	6.5	1.7	8%	0.6	3.9	47	$4

PRO: Outstanding GB%, 2H Dom spike, RHB killer (1 HR)
CON: 1H overuse, 2H H% tracks history, poor Ctl trend. It won't be as easy his second time around.

Uehara,Koji

Uehara,Koji	Yr	W	L	Sv	IP	K	ERA	WHIP	OBA	vL	vR	BF/G	H%	S%	xERA	G	L	F	Ctl	Dom	Cmd	hr/f	hr/9	RAR	BPV	R$
RH Starter	05 JPN	9	12	0	187	138	4.12	1.09	250			27.8	26%	72%	4.39				1.3	6.6	5.0		1.9	4.2	93	$18
Age 35	06 JPN	8	9	0	168	143	3.99	1.16	262			28.5	28%	78%	5.04				1.4	7.7	5.5		2.1	10.9	100	$18
Type xFB	07 JPN	4	3	32	62	63	2.16	0.89	224			4.3	28%	83%	2.65				0.7	9.1	12.6		1.0	17.6	301	$23
Health F	08 JPN	6	5	1	90	68	4.72	1.29	276			14.6	30%	70%	5.23				2.0	6.8	3.4		1.8	-4.6	58	$7
PT/Exp C	09 BAL	2	4	0	67	48	4.05	1.24	274	273	266	23.1	31%	70%	4.48	30	17	53	1.6	6.5	4.0	6%	0.9	3.3	81	$5
Consist D	1st Half	2	4	0	66	48	4.08	1.25	276			23.0	32%	70%	4.48	30	17	53	1.6	6.5	4.0	6%	1.0	3.0	82	$5
LIMA Plan B+	2nd Half	0	0	0	1	0	0.00	0.00							0.00											
Rand Var -1	10 Proj	3	3	5	58	44	3.88	1.24	268			5.9	30%	75%	4.40	30	17	53	1.9	6.8	3.7	10%	1.4	0.2	81	$7

Shelved by elbow woes in late June after MLB debut as SP. Will likely move to pen where limited durability and skills play better. Fine Cmd fueled by outstanding Ctl, but FBs an issue in AL East, Camden Yards.

JOCK THOMPSON

Valdez,Merkin	Yr	Tm	W	L	Sv	IP	K	ERA	WHIP	OBA	vL	vR	BF/G	H%	S%	xERA	G	L	F	Ctl	Dom	Cmd	hr/f	hr/9	RAR	BPV	R$
RH Reliever	05	aa	5	6	0	107	79	4.34	1.50	277			19.7	33%	71%	4.58				3.8	6.6	1.7		0.6	-0.4	57	$5
Age 28	06	aaa	0	4	5	49	41	6.40	1.87	288			5.1	34%	66%	6.30				6.6	7.5	1.1		1.1	-11.4	33	($1)
Type Pwr	07	SF	0	0	0	0	0	0.00	0.00							0.00											
Health F	08	SF	1	0	0	16	13	1.69	1.31	237			4.0	29%	90%	3.55				3.9	7.3	1.9		0.6	5.1	74	$2
PT/Exp D	09	SF	2	1	0	49	38	5.66	1.72	291	250	324	4.8	34%	68%	4.63	45	24	31	5.1	6.9	1.4	10%	0.9	-8.9	10	($1)
Consist C	1st Half		2	0	0	23	18	3.52	1.39	217			4.5	27%	74%	4.12	52	20	28	5.5	7.0	1.3	6%	0.4	1.9	9	$2
LIMA Plan D	2nd Half		0	1	0	26	20	7.53	2.02	345			5.0	39%	63%	5.04	40	27	33	4.8	6.8	1.4	13%	1.4	-10.8	12	($3)
Rand Var +3	10	Proj	1	1	0	29	23	4.66	1.52	262			5.1	31%	71%	4.31	44	25	31	4.7	7.1	1.5	11%	0.9	-0.2	25	$1

Once-heralded power arm now scuffling in middle relief after 2006 TJS surgery. Still has solid Dom, but can't control walks, while other BPIs are all over the map. Still young, must tame Ctl, show consistency.

Valverde,Jose	Yr	Tm	W	L	Sv	IP	K	ERA	WHIP	OBA	vL	vR	BF/G	H%	S%	xERA	G	L	F	Ctl	Dom	Cmd	hr/f	hr/9	RAR	BPV	R$
RH Reliever	05	ARI	3	4	15	66	75	2.45	1.07	215	168	241	4.3	29%	80%	3.14	38	19	43	2.7	10.2	3.8	7%	0.7	14.6	126	$15
Age 32	06	ARI	2	3	18	49	69	5.87	1.47	265	323	192	4.9	39%	61%	3.26	35	24	41	4.0	12.6	3.1	12%	1.1	-8.3	132	$8
Type Pwr FB	07	ARI	1	4	47	64	78	2.66	1.12	202	202	189	4.0	27%	82%	3.37	36	17	47	3.6	10.9	3.0	10%	1.0	14.0	112	$24
Health C	08	HOU	6	3	44	72	83	3.38	1.18	234	190	252	4.0	30%	77%	3.22	39	20	41	2.9	10.4	3.6	13%	1.3	8.0	126	$25
PT/Exp A	09	HOU	4	2	25	54	56	2.33	1.13	208	281	144	4.2	27%	84%	3.59	41	13	46	3.5	9.3	2.7	8%	0.8	12.4	92	$16
Consist A	1st Half		0	2	6	16	20	3.91	1.12	223			3.8	26%	79%	3.15	34	17	49	2.8	11.2	4.0	21%	2.2	0.5	138	$3
LIMA Plan B	2nd Half		4	0	19	38	36	1.66	1.13	202			4.4	27%	86%	3.78	43	11	45	3.8	8.5	2.3	2%	0.2	11.8	73	$13
Rand Var -5	10	Proj	4	4	40	73	82	3.23	1.20	233			4.1	30%	78%	3.41	39	16	45	3.1	10.2	3.3	11%	1.1	7.6	116	$22

Lost 7 weeks in 1H due to leg injury, finished year converting final 19 save opps. Lost some Cmd and hr/9, threw more GBs after returning, but bottom line traced recent years. Remains on our Elite closer short list.

VandenHurk,Rick	Yr	Tm	W	L	Sv	IP	K	ERA	WHIP	OBA	vL	vR	BF/G	H%	S%	xERA	G	L	F	Ctl	Dom	Cmd	hr/f	hr/9	RAR	BPV	R$
RH Starter	05		0	0	0	0	0	0.00	0.00							0.00											
Age 24	06		0	0	0	0	0	0.00	0.00							0.00											
Type Pwr xFB	07		0	0	0	0	0	0.00	0.00							0.00											
Health C	08	aa	5	4	0	73	68	4.96	1.41	257			22.6	30%	69%	4.84				3.9	8.4	2.1		1.4	-5.9	57	$5
PT/Exp B	09	FLA *	8	4	0	118	95	3.74	1.20	238	273	224	22.1	27%	72%	4.32	27	23	50	2.8	7.3	2.6	8%	1.1	6.5	59	$12
Consist B	1st Half		3	1	0	38	33	3.30	0.99	212			21.4	27%	65%	2.03				2.1	7.8	3.7		0.2	4.2	129	$5
LIMA Plan C+	2nd Half		5	3	0	80	62	3.95	1.29	250			22.4	28%	76%	4.57	27	23	50	3.2	7.0	2.2	11%	1.5	2.3	46	$6
Rand Var -1	10	Proj	9	5	0	125	108	4.18	1.27	252			21.8	29%	72%	4.31	27	23	50	2.9	7.8	2.7	10%	1.3	-0.7	67	$11

3-2, 4.30 ERA in 58 IP at FLA. Still shows promise even with Dom slide matching drop in Ctl. With Cmd on upswing, biggest issues are durability (elbow, back) and gopheritis, notably vs. LHBs (2.0 hr/9). Watch.

Vargas,Claudio	Yr	Tm	W	L	Sv	IP	K	ERA	WHIP	OBA	vL	vR	BF/G	H%	S%	xERA	G	L	F	Ctl	Dom	Cmd	hr/f	hr/9	RAR	BPV	R$
RH Reliever	05	2NL *	11	11	0	160	124	5.10	1.44	276	268	288	23.3	31%	69%	4.42	35	23	41	3.3	6.9	2.1	14%	1.6	-16.8	49	$7
Age 31	06	ARI	12	10	0	167	123	4.84	1.42	282	275	272	23.4	31%	70%	4.47	40	18	42	2.8	6.6	2.4	12%	1.5	-7.4	61	$10
Type FB	07	MIL	11	6	1	134	107	5.09	1.54	288	320	255	20.7	32%	71%	4.74	34	22	44	3.6	7.2	2.0	12%	1.5	-11.1	43	$7
Health D	08	NYM *	8	4	0	80	46	6.15	1.73	325	323	178	19.6	35%	66%	4.80	49	17	34	3.3	5.2	1.6	11%	1.3	-18.5	30	($0)
PT/Exp C	09	2NL *	1	0	1	54	39	2.50	1.13	227	203	159	5.1	25%	84%	4.09	40	16	44	2.7	6.5	2.4	9%	1.1	11.3	63	$6
Consist A	1st Half		0	0	1	13	9	4.89	1.63	353			8.4	38%	80%	8.04				0.8	6.5	7.9		2.4	-1.1	117	$0
LIMA Plan C+	2nd Half		1	0	0	41	30	1.74	0.97	177			4.5	20%	86%	4.01	40	16	44	3.3	6.5	2.0	6%	0.7	12.5	47	$6
Rand Var -5	10	Proj	3	2	0	44	31	4.34	1.40	268			10.4	30%	73%	4.54	38	19	42	3.3	6.4	1.9	10%	1.2	-1.5	43	$3

1-0, 1.74 ERA in 41 IP at LA and MIL. May find niche as RP after years of mediocrity as SP. But '09 2H was fueled by charmed H%, hr/f, nothing more. Basis for biggest issue - gopheritis - remains intact.

Vargas,Jason	Yr	Tm	W	L	Sv	IP	K	ERA	WHIP	OBA	vL	vR	BF/G	H%	S%	xERA	G	L	F	Ctl	Dom	Cmd	hr/f	hr/9	RAR	BPV	R$
LH Starter	05	FLA *	6	5	0	92	79	3.90	1.36	249	192	269	19.7	30%	73%	4.43	31	21	47	3.8	7.7	2.0	6%	0.8	3.9	45	$8
Age 27	06	FLA *	4	8	0	112	71	7.55	1.89	328	262	302	21.6	36%	61%	6.15	32	17	51	4.7	5.7	1.2	9%	1.5	-42.4	-13	($8)
Type xFB	07	NYM *	9	8	0	135	92	6.67	1.70	325		370	24.1	36%	61%	5.74	27	13	60	3.1	6.1	2.0	7%	1.2	-37.5	30	($2)
Health F	08		0	0	0	0	0	0.00	0.00							0.00											
PT/Exp D	09	SEA *	7	9	0	143	94	4.32	1.32	271	290	277	18.9	30%	71%	4.50	37	21	42	2.5	5.9	2.4	10%	1.2	2.4	54	$10
Consist B	1st Half		4	4	0	75	52	3.48	1.30	265			21.2	29%	78%	4.41	37	19	43	2.5	6.3	2.5	10%	1.2	9.0	59	$7
LIMA Plan C	2nd Half		3	5	0	68	41	5.25	1.35	277			17.0	30%	63%	4.59	36	24	41	2.4	5.5	2.3	10%	1.2	-6.6	47	$3
Rand Var 0	10	Proj	5	6	0	87	59	4.45	1.43	281			13.0	31%	73%	4.74	34	21	45	2.9	6.1	2.1	10%	1.3	-3.3	44	$5

3-6, 4.91 ERA in 91 IP at SEA. Back after injuries (elbow spur, hip surgery) canceled his '08. Shaved FB% significantly, but unable to cut into toxic hr/9. Dom too light for GB%, skills better suited for bullpen.

Vasquez,Esmerling	Yr	Tm	W	L	Sv	IP	K	ERA	WHIP	OBA	vL	vR	BF/G	H%	S%	xERA	G	L	F	Ctl	Dom	Cmd	hr/f	hr/9	RAR	BPV	R$
RH Reliever	05		0	0	0	0	0	0.00	0.00							0.00											
Age 26	06		0	0	0	0	0	0.00	0.00							0.00											
Type Pwr FB	07	aa	10	6	0	165	129	3.93	1.29	244			23.9	29%	71%	3.83				3.4	7.0	2.1		0.8	10.8	69	$15
Health A	08	aaa	3	6	0	83	48	9.25	2.12	297			17.4	31%	56%	7.54				8.3	5.3	0.6		1.6	-50.6	-8	($12)
PT/Exp D	09	ARI	3	3	0	53	45	4.42	1.53	258	196	304	4.4	31%	71%	4.54	43	17	40	4.9	7.6	1.6	6%	0.7	-1.5	25	$2
Consist F	1st Half		1	2	0	26	22	5.17	1.69	290			5.0	34%	71%	4.57	47	14	39	4.8	7.6	1.6	10%	1.0	-3.2	31	($0)
LIMA Plan C	2nd Half		2	1	0	27	23	3.68	1.38	225			4.0	28%	72%	4.50	38	20	42	5.0	7.7	1.5	3%	0.3	1.7	19	$2
Rand Var -1	10	Proj	2	2	0	44	34	4.97	1.56	268			7.0	31%	70%	4.76	42	17	41	4.8	7.0	1.5	9%	1.0	-2.7	18	$1

Solid dominance, lousy Ctl, otherwise unstable BPIs. Survived 2H via unsustainable hr/f and deflated h%. Torched by LHB (1.4 hr/9) and at Chase Field (6.23 ERA). Avoid until he settles down.

Vazquez,Javier	Yr	Tm	W	L	Sv	IP	K	ERA	WHIP	OBA	vL	vR	BF/G	H%	S%	xERA	G	L	F	Ctl	Dom	Cmd	hr/f	hr/9	RAR	BPV	R$
RH Starter	05	ARI	11	15	0	215	192	4.43	1.25	269	244	285	27.2	31%	70%	3.38	43	23	34	1.9	8.0	4.2	16%	1.5	-5.0	114	$17
Age 33	06	CHW	11	12	0	202	184	4.85	1.30	265	256	261	25.8	32%	64%	3.81	40	20	41	2.5	8.2	3.3	10%	1.0	-7.3	98	$17
Type Pwr	07	CHW	15	8	0	217	213	3.74	1.14	244	230	253	27.5	30%	72%	3.49	40	17	43	2.1	8.8	4.3	11%	1.2	20.5	121	$28
Health A	08	CHW	12	16	0	208	200	4.67	1.32	267	259	266	26.8	33%	67%	3.73	38	20	42	2.6	8.6	3.3	10%	1.1	-8.2	101	$17
PT/Exp A	09	ATL	15	10	0	219	238	2.87	1.03	226	235	212	27.0	30%	76%	2.83	42	24	35	1.8	9.8	5.4	10%	0.8	35.6	147	$32
Consist B	1st Half		5	7	0	106	125	3.05	1.06	231			26.4	31%	75%	2.70	42	24	34	1.9	10.6	5.4	11%	0.8	14.9	158	$14
LIMA Plan C	2nd Half		10	3	0	113	113	2.71	0.99	222			27.6	28%	76%	2.95	41	24	35	1.7	9.0	5.4	10%	0.8	20.7	136	$18
Rand Var 0	10	Proj	14	9	0	203	206	3.64	1.14	243			27.5	31%	71%	3.24	40	21	38	2.1	9.1	4.4	10%	1.0	25.7	127	$24

More forgiving NL lineups and venue fueled Cmd spike and career year. A few more GBs also fed into the effort here. Not likely to improve or repeat at this age, but should be fine. ATL looks like a comfort zone.

Veras,Jose	Yr	Tm	W	L	Sv	IP	K	ERA	WHIP	OBA	vL	vR	BF/G	H%	S%	xERA	G	L	F	Ctl	Dom	Cmd	hr/f	hr/9	RAR	BPV	R$
RH Reliever	05	aaa	3	5	24	61	62	4.26	1.63	286			4.9	37%	74%	5.02				4.6	9.1	2.0		0.6	0.3	77	$10
Age 29	06	aaa	5	3	21	59	55	3.07	1.31	256			5.0	32%	78%	3.84				3.1	8.4	2.7		0.6	10.6	93	$15
Type Pwr FB	07	NYY	0	0	2	9	7	5.81	1.40	186			4.5	24%	54%	5.20	41	19	41	6.8	6.8	1.0	0%	0.0	-1.5	-42	$1
Health A	08	NYY *	5	3	9	71	80	3.33	1.34	236	217	254	4.1	31%	79%	3.60	41	18	41	4.2	10.2	2.4	11%	1.0	8.9	88	$12
PT/Exp D	09	2AL	4	3	0	50	40	5.19	1.39	228	259	198	4.6	25%	66%	4.92	36	16	47	5.0	7.2	1.4	12%	1.4	-4.6	8	$3
Consist C	1st Half		3	1	0	27	20	5.96	1.40	238			4.2	25%	61%	5.07	33	19	48	4.6	6.6	1.4	13%	1.7	-5.0	5	$2
LIMA Plan C+	2nd Half		1	2	0	23	20	4.29	1.39	216			5.2	25%	72%	4.72	41	13	46	5.5	7.8	1.4	10%	1.2	0.5	12	$2
Rand Var 0	10	Proj	2	2	0	35	32	4.17	1.42	248			4.7	30%	73%	4.35	39	17	44	4.4	8.3	1.9	9%	1.0	0.4	48	$3

4-3, 5.19 ERA in 50 IP at CLE and NYY. Terrific dominance, but erratic Ctl and gopheritis have made bad years as likely as good ones. So whither his 2010? Our projections are splitting the baby.

Verlander,Justin	Yr	Tm	W	L	Sv	IP	K	ERA	WHIP	OBA	vL	vR	BF/G	H%	S%	xERA	G	L	F	Ctl	Dom	Cmd	hr/f	hr/9	RAR	BPV	R$
RH Starter	05	DET *	2	2	0	43	35	2.08	0.88	181			18.2	22%	78%	1.46				2.3	7.3	3.2		0.4	12.2	117	$8
Age 27	06	DET	17	9	0	186	124	3.63	1.33	263	279	253	26.3	29%	76%	4.27	42	23	35	2.9	6.0	2.1	10%	1.0	21.3	49	$21
Type Pwr FB	07	DET	18	6	0	202	183	3.66	1.23	241	232	234	26.2	29%	73%	3.78	41	19	40	3.0	8.2	2.7	9%	0.9	21.1	85	$26
Health A	08	DET	11	17	0	201	163	4.84	1.40	256	254	254	26.3	30%	66%	4.39	40	18	42	3.9	7.3	1.9	7%	0.8	-12.1	44	$12
PT/Exp A	09	DET	19	9	0	240	269	3.45	1.18	244	248	237	28.1	33%	73%	3.31	36	21	43	2.4	10.1	4.3	7%	0.8	29.7	132	$33
Consist B	1st Half		8	4	0	109	130	3.55	1.20	238			26.4	33%	72%	3.29	35	22	43	2.9	10.7	3.7	8%	0.7	12.2	128	$15
LIMA Plan C	2nd Half		11	5	0	131	139	3.37	1.15	250			29.6	33%	73%	3.33	37	20	43	1.9	9.6	5.0	7%	0.8	17.5	135	$19
Rand Var 0	10	Proj	17	11	0	225	233	3.56	1.20	245			26.4	31%	73%	3.45	39	20	41	2.5	9.3	3.7	9%	0.9	27.2	116	$29

What we've been waiting for: Breakout fully supported by skills (Cmd spike), driven by consistency: 1H/2H splits nearly identical, just two DIS starts all year. If he can re-introduce more GBs... UP: 20 W, sub-3.00 ERA.

JOCK THOMPSON

Villanueva,Carlos

Villanueva,Carlos		Yr	Tm	W	L	Sv	IP	K	ERA	WHIP	OBA	vL	vR	BF/G	H%	S%	xERA	G	L	F	Ctl	Dom	Cmd	hr/f	hr/9	RAR	BPV	R$
RH Reliever		05	aa	1	3	0	21	13	8.14	1.57	280			23.6	29%	48%	5.90				4.3	5.6	1.3		1.7	-9.9	8	($1)
Age	26	06	MIL	*13	8	0	181	146	4.22	1.22	246	226	204	23.5	28%	69%	4.00	43	16	41	2.7	7.2	2.7	11%	1.1	6.0	77	$18
Type	Pwr	07	MIL	8	5	1	114	99	3.94	1.35	239	250	227	8.3	28%	75%	4.51	36	17	47	4.2	7.8	1.9	11%	1.3	6.9	42	$11
Health	A	08	MIL	4	7	1	108	93	4.07	1.31	268	227	300	9.7	31%	75%	3.63	47	19	35	2.5	7.7	3.1	16%	1.5	2.6	96	$8
PT/Exp	B	09	MIL	4	10	3	96	83	5.34	1.43	274	257	278	6.5	32%	65%	4.04	40	22	38	3.3	7.8	2.4	12%	1.2	-13.7	69	$4
Consist	B	1st Half		2	4	3	36	35	4.99	1.25	250			4.3	32%	60%	3.66	37	21	42	2.7	8.7	3.2	7%	0.7	-3.5	98	$3
LIMA Plan	B+	2nd Half		2	6	0	60	48	5.56	1.54	287			9.2	32%	67%	4.27	42	23	36	3.6	7.2	2.0	15%	1.5	-10.1	52	$0
Rand Var	+3	10	Proj	4	6	0	82	70	4.20	1.36	263			7.9	31%	72%	3.99	41	20	39	3.2	7.7	2.4	11%	1.1	2.7	72	$5

Hmmm, which role suits him best? Check the career splits:

	ERA	Cmd	hr/9
SP:	4.81	1.8	1.7
RP:	3.96	2.9	1.1

He's a strong bounceback candidate if he stays in pen.

Villone,Ron

Villone,Ron		Yr	Tm	W	L	Sv	IP	K	ERA	WHIP	OBA	vL	vR	BF/G	H%	S%	xERA	G	L	F	Ctl	Dom	Cmd	hr/f	hr/9	RAR	BPV	R$
LH Reliever		05	2TM	5	5	1	64	70	4.08	1.44	240	222	258	3.5	32%	72%	3.70	43	22	35	4.9	9.8	2.0	7%	0.6	1.8	66	$6
Age	40	06	NYY	3	3	0	80	72	5.06	1.57	249	179	289	5.1	30%	69%	5.15	31	21	48	5.7	8.1	1.4	8%	1.0	-4.9	-0	$3
Type	Pwr FB	07	NYY	0	0	0	42	25	4.26	1.28	232			4.8	25%	69%	4.91	37	19	43	3.8	5.3	1.4	9%	1.1	1.3	8	$2
Health	A	08	STL	1	2	1	50	50	4.68	1.64	242	176	300	3.1	31%	72%	4.80	38	22	40	6.7	9.0	1.4	7%	0.7	-2.5	-2	$1
PT/Exp	D	09	WAS	5	6	1	49	33	4.25	1.70	282	293	272	3.6	32%	78%	5.39	39	20	42	5.4	6.1	1.1	9%	1.1	-0.4	-18	$2
Consist	A	1st Half		3	5	0	22	12	2.84	1.58	251			3.4	28%	82%	5.73	37	20	43	5.7	4.9	0.9	3%	0.4	3.7	-50	$2
LIMA Plan	C	2nd Half		2	1	1	27	21	5.43	1.81	306			3.7	34%	74%	5.10	40	19	41	5.1	7.1	1.4	14%	1.7	-4.1	9	$0
Rand Var	-3	10	Proj	2	3	0	36	23	4.97	1.71	281			3.7	31%	74%	5.57	38	20	42	5.5	5.7	1.0	10%	1.2	-5.8	-29	$0

Recent Cmd history makes one wonder how he keeps finding a job every year. He couldn't even get LH out in 2009, removing his last shred of usefulness. The end of the road appears to be very near.

Volquez,Edinson

Volquez,Edinson		Yr	Tm	W	L	Sv	IP	K	ERA	WHIP	OBA	vL	vR	BF/G	H%	S%	xERA	G	L	F	Ctl	Dom	Cmd	hr/f	hr/9	RAR	BPV	R$
RH Starter		05	TEX	*1	9	0	72	53	6.88	1.68	316			20.7	36%	60%	6.41				3.4	6.6	2.0		1.4	-22.2	31	($3)
Age	26	06	TEX	*7	12	0	153	127	5.40	1.68	273			24.3	32%	70%	5.56				5.6	7.5	1.3		1.2	-16.0	36	$3
Type	Pwr	07	TEX	*16	3	0	143	133	3.72	1.25	233	222	299	23.9	28%	73%	3.93	38	22	40	3.6	8.3	2.3	10%	1.0	13.9	69	$20
Health	F	08	CIN	17	6	0	196	206	3.21	1.33	232	248	214	25.2	31%	77%	3.54	46	20	34	4.3	9.5	2.2	8%	0.6	25.5	79	$23
PT/Exp	B	09	CIN	4	2	0	50	47	4.35	1.33	195	202	181	23.5	23%	70%	4.07	45	21	34	5.8	8.5	1.5	14%	1.1	-1.0	20	$4
Consist	A	1st Half		4	2	0	49	47	4.39	1.34	197			23.3	23%	70%	4.07	45	21	34	5.9	8.6	1.5	14%	1.1	-1.2	20	$4
LIMA Plan	C	2nd Half		0	0	0	1	0	0.00	0.00							0.00											
Rand Var	-1	10	Proj	3	2	0	44	38	4.55	1.49	246			24.0	30%	70%	4.33	45	21	35	5.2	7.9	1.5	9%	0.8	-0.4	24	$2

Not able to repeat previous year's success, as Ctl reached unacceptable level. Now he will probably miss at least half of 2010, following August TJ surgery. Strong Dom points to a bright (but delayed) future.

Volstad,Chris

Volstad,Chris		Yr	Tm	W	L	Sv	IP	K	ERA	WHIP	OBA	vL	vR	BF/G	H%	S%	xERA	G	L	F	Ctl	Dom	Cmd	hr/f	hr/9	RAR	BPV	R$
RH Starter		05		0	0	0	0	0	0.00	0.00							0.00											
Age	23	06		0	0	0	0	0	0.00	0.00							0.00											
Type	GB	07	aa	4	2	0	42	23	3.63	1.33	279			25.6	30%	75%	4.53				2.1	4.9	2.3		0.9	4.4	51	$4
Health	A	08	FLA	*10	8	0	175	102	3.39	1.36	258	243	236	25.0	30%	73%	4.15	53	18	29	3.4	5.2	1.5	2%	0.2	19.1	33	$13
PT/Exp	C	09	FLA	9	13	0	159	107	5.21	1.43	274	255	302	23.9	29%	68%	4.21	49	17	34	3.3	6.1	1.8	17%	1.6	-20.0	46	$5
Consist	A	1st Half		5	7	0	95	70	4.64	1.28	257			25.0	28%	68%	3.77	51	16	34	2.7	6.6	2.4	15%	1.4	-5.3	74	$6
LIMA Plan	C	2nd Half		4	6	0	64	37	6.06	1.66	297			22.5	30%	68%	4.89	48	18	34	4.2	5.2	1.2	19%	2.0	-14.7	6	($1)
Rand Var	+3	10	Proj	11	10	0	162	103	4.50	1.42	274			24.2	30%	71%	4.23	50	17	33	3.2	5.7	1.8	11%	1.1	0.7	44	$9

Took big step forward in 1H, but was a little unlucky. August struggles resulted in demotion. The seeds are there, as GB%, 1H Dom, Ctl show. It may take some time, but if he puts it all together... UP: 15 W, 3.75 ERA.

Wagner,Billy

Wagner,Billy		Yr	Tm	W	L	Sv	IP	K	ERA	WHIP	OBA	vL	vR	BF/G	H%	S%	xERA	G	L	F	Ctl	Dom	Cmd	hr/f	hr/9	RAR	BPV	R$
LH Reliever		05	PHI	4	3	38	77	87	1.52	0.84	171	128	173	3.9	23%	88%	2.62	46	19	35	2.3	10.1	4.4	10%	0.7	26.0	143	$28
Age	38	06	NYM	3	2	40	72	94	2.25	1.11	225	161	234	4.2	32%	85%	2.47	53	16	31	2.6	11.7	4.5	13%	0.9	19.9	171	$25
Type	Pwr FB	07	NYM	2	2	34	68	80	2.64	1.13	222	241	209	4.2	30%	80%	3.28	37	18	45	2.9	10.5	3.6	8%	0.8	15.1	126	$20
Health	F	08	NYM	0	1	27	47	52	2.30	0.89	194	220	174	4.0	26%	79%	2.91	38	20	42	1.9	10.0	5.2	8%	0.8	11.4	144	$16
PT/Exp	C	09	2TM	1	1	0	16	26	1.72	1.02	153	111	176	3.6	28%	87%	2.79	23	15	62	4.6	14.9	3.3	6%	0.6	5.0	146	$3
Consist	A	1st Half		0	0	0	0	0	0.00	0.00							0.00											
LIMA Plan	A+	2nd Half		1	1	0	16	26	1.72	1.02	153			3.6	28%	87%	2.79	23	15	62	4.6	14.9	3.3	6%	0.6	5.0	146	$3
Rand Var	-5	10	Proj	2	2	25	51	67	2.66	1.06	201			4.0	30%	78%	2.92	38	18	45	3.2	11.9	3.7	8%	0.7	8.9	143	$16

Didn't pitch until August, as he recovered from TJ surgery. It's a small sample size, but he is showing no signs of slowing down. If health cooperates, still has the goods to be a top-flight closer.

Wainwright,Adam

Wainwright,Adam		Yr	Tm	W	L	Sv	IP	K	ERA	WHIP	OBA	vL	vR	BF/G	H%	S%	xERA	G	L	F	Ctl	Dom	Cmd	hr/f	hr/9	RAR	BPV	R$
RH Starter		05	aaa	9	10	0	176	123	4.86	1.48	301			27.7	35%	68%	5.12				2.4	6.3	2.6		0.8	-12.0	63	$7
Age	28	06	STL	2	1	3	75	72	3.12	1.15	232	301	182	5.0	29%	75%	3.34	48	17	35	2.6	8.6	3.3	8%	0.7	12.7	110	$10
Type	Pwr	07	STL	14	12	0	202	136	3.70	1.40	271	249	283	27.2	31%	74%	4.24	48	18	34	3.1	6.1	1.9	6%	0.6	18.1	51	$16
Health	C	08	STL	11	3	0	132	91	3.20	1.18	247	264	234	27.1	28%	76%	3.83	46	19	35	2.3	6.2	2.7	9%	0.8	17.4	73	$15
PT/Exp	A	09	STL	19	8	0	233	212	2.63	1.21	247	275	217	28.3	31%	81%	3.21	51	19	30	2.5	8.2	3.2	9%	0.7	44.9	107	$30
Consist	B	1st Half		8	5	0	114	101	3.32	1.32	250			28.4	30%	78%	3.68	47	19	34	3.4	8.0	2.3	11%	0.9	12.3	77	$11
LIMA Plan	C+	2nd Half		11	3	0	119	111	1.97	1.11	245			28.2	32%	83%	2.78	55	19	27	1.7	8.4	4.8	6%	0.4	32.6	137	$19
Rand Var	-3	10	Proj	17	7	0	218	187	3.23	1.23	253			22.6	31%	76%	3.43	49	19	32	2.5	7.7	3.1	9%	0.8	22.5	99	$25

Reasons breakout was legit:
- Excellent Dom in starting role
- A few more ground balls
- Held RH to .545 OPS
- Everything better in 2H

Workload spike makes burnout biggest threat to a repeat.

Wakefield,Tim

Wakefield,Tim		Yr	Tm	W	L	Sv	IP	K	ERA	WHIP	OBA	vL	vR	BF/G	H%	S%	xERA	G	L	F	Ctl	Dom	Cmd	hr/f	hr/9	RAR	BPV	R$
RH Starter		05	BOS	16	12	0	225	151	4.16	1.24	249	202	278	28.3	27%	72%	4.26	41	17	42	2.7	6.0	2.2	12%	1.4	5.9	55	$21
Age	43	06	BOS	7	11	0	140	90	4.63	1.33	255	221	265	25.9	28%	68%	4.72	39	16	44	3.3	5.8	1.8	10%	1.2	-1.2	33	$10
Type	xFB	07	BOS	17	12	0	189	110	4.76	1.35	264	247	276	26.0	29%	67%	4.80	39	19	42	3.0	5.2	1.7	8%	1.0	-6.0	29	$15
Health	D	08	BOS	10	11	0	181	117	4.13	1.18	232	244	218	24.8	25%	69%	4.59	36	16	49	3.0	5.8	2.0	9%	1.2	4.9	38	$16
PT/Exp	A	09	BOS	11	5	0	130	72	4.58	1.44	272	280	263	26.9	30%	69%	5.25	36	17	47	3.5	5.0	1.4	6%	0.8	-2.0	10	$8
Consist	A	1st Half		10	3	0	94	50	4.20	1.37	259			26.9	29%	69%	5.13	38	18	45	3.4	4.8	1.4	4%	0.6	2.9	9	$8
LIMA Plan	D+	2nd Half		1	2	0	36	22	5.58	1.63	305			26.9	33%	69%	5.56	32	16	52	3.5	5.6	1.6	9%	1.5	-4.9	15	($0)
Rand Var	-2	10	Proj	7	8	0	120	68	5.10	1.51	282			26.6	30%	69%	5.33	36	17	47	3.6	5.1	1.4	9%	1.4	-13.3	8	$4

Lingering back issues limited his innings in 2H, but skills were fading before that. He posted highest Ctl since 2001, and lowest Dom since 1993. Just an innings eater at this point, and that's if he's healthy.

Walker,Tyler

Walker,Tyler		Yr	Tm	W	L	Sv	IP	K	ERA	WHIP	OBA	vL	vR	BF/G	H%	S%	xERA	G	L	F	Ctl	Dom	Cmd	hr/f	hr/9	RAR	BPV	R$
RH Reliever		05	SF	6	4	23	61	54	4.26	1.55	283	284	278	4.1	33%	77%	4.30	42	18	41	4.0	7.9	2.0	12%	1.3	-0.1	55	$12
Age	33	06	2TM	1	4	10	25	19	7.17	1.55	276	333	226	4.3	33%	50%	4.78	35	28	37	4.3	6.8	1.6	3%	0.4	-8.2	19	$3
Type	FB	07	SF	*3	2	7	37	26	4.46	1.63	299	182	308	4.8	33%	77%	5.22	35	18	48	3.8	6.3	1.6	10%	1.4	-0.1	23	$4
Health	D	08	SF	5	8	0	53	49	4.56	1.28	238	319	186	3.4	28%	67%	3.53	48	21	31	3.5	8.3	2.3	15%	1.2	-1.9	79	$5
PT/Exp	D	09	PHI	*4	2	3	54	43	2.68	0.97	209	229	230	4.5	24%	77%	3.76	38	15	48	2.0	7.1	3.5	7%	0.8	10.1	90	$9
Consist	B	1st Half		2	1	3	28	20	1.99	0.81	189			4.8	21%	84%	3.56	40	13	47	1.3	6.5	4.8	8%	1.0	7.6	98	$6
LIMA Plan	B+	2nd Half		2	1	0	26	23	3.42	1.14	229			4.3	28%	71%	3.92	37	15	48	2.7	7.9	2.9	6%	0.7	2.5	82	$3
Rand Var	-5	10	Proj	5	4	0	59	48	3.69	1.18	250			4.1	29%	73%	3.78	40	18	41	2.2	7.4	3.4	10%	1.1	3.5	93	$7

2-1, 3.06 ERA in 35 IP at PHI. Second straight season with impressive skills, highlighted by best Ctl, Cmd of career. Had H%, hr/f working in his favor, so ERA should rise. But '08-'09 xERA level looks legitimate.

Wang,Chien-Ming

Wang,Chien-Ming		Yr	Tm	W	L	Sv	IP	K	ERA	WHIP	OBA	vL	vR	BF/G	H%	S%	xERA	G	L	F	Ctl	Dom	Cmd	hr/f	hr/9	RAR	BPV	R$
RH Reliever		05	NYY	*10	6	0	150	65	4.21	1.30	271	258	254	26.4	29%	69%	3.68	64	14	22	2.3	3.9	1.7	11%	0.8	3.0	50	$10
Age	30	06	NYY	19	6	1	218	76	3.63	1.31	275	275	279	27.1	29%	72%	3.83	63	17	20	2.1	3.1	1.5	8%	0.5	24.9	39	$21
Type	xGB	07	NYY	19	7	0	199	104	3.70	1.29	261	286	242	28.0	29%	71%	3.78	58	18	23	2.7	4.7	1.8	6%	0.4	19.7	49	$21
Health	F	08	NYY	8	2	0	95	54	4.07	1.32	251	261	238	26.8	29%	68%	3.83	55	22	23	3.3	5.1	1.5	6%	0.4	3.2	36	$8
PT/Exp	B	09	NYY	1	6	0	42	29	9.64	2.02	358	394	329	17.3	40%	51%	4.66	53	20	27	4.1	6.2	1.5	17%	1.5	-26.9	33	($6)
Consist	A	1st Half		1	6	0	36	28	10.19	2.15	370			16.7	42%	51%	4.66	53	21	26	4.5	7.0	1.6	17%	1.5	-25.6	35	($6)
LIMA Plan	D	2nd Half		0	0	0	6	1	6.21	1.21	268			23.9	25%	50%	4.54	58	11	32	1.6	1.6	1.0	15%	1.6	-1.3	22	($0)
Rand Var	+5	10	Proj	7	7	0	100	57	4.88	1.57	300			22.3	33%	69%	4.19	57	17	26	3.3	5.2	1.6	10%	0.8	3.0	39	$4

March hip injury preceded July surgery for torn ligament in pitching shoulder. '10 readiness in doubt, durability issues over last two years cloud skill profile, which was light-Dom'd to begin with. Be careful here.

BRIAN RUDD

Washburn,Jarrod		Yr	Tm	W	L	Sv	IP	K	ERA	WHIP	OBA	vL	vR	BF/G	H%	S%	xERA	G	L	F	Ctl	Dom	Cmd	hr/f	hr/9	RAR	BPV	R$
LH	Starter	05	ANA	8	8	0	177	94	3.20	1.33	269	266	276	25.9	29%	80%	4.64	39	21	40	2.6	4.8	1.8	8%	1.0	25.6	33	$14
Age	35	06	SEA	8	14	0	187	103	4.67	1.35	273	317	257	25.8	29%	68%	4.78	40	18	42	2.6	5.0	1.9	10%	1.2	-2.6	36	$11
Type	Con FB	07	SEA	10	15	0	194	114	4.32	1.38	269	213	288	26.1	29%	71%	4.96	37	18	45	3.1	5.3	1.7	8%	1.1	4.4	26	$12
Health	A	08	SEA	5	14	1	154	87	4.68	1.46	286	252	299	24.0	31%	70%	4.86	36	23	41	2.9	5.1	1.7	9%	1.1	-6.4	27	$5
PT/Exp	A	09	2AL	9	9	0	176	100	3.78	1.19	244	178	268	25.8	26%	73%	4.56	38	20	43	2.5	5.1	2.0	10%	1.2	14.5	40	$16
Consist	A	1st Half		4	6	0	96	66	3.37	1.20	247			26.4	28%	76%	4.19	38	22	40	2.4	6.2	2.5	9%	1.0	12.8	61	$10
LIMA Plan	D	2nd Half		5	3	0	80	34	4.28	1.18	240			25.2	24%	68%	5.01	37	17	46	2.6	3.8	1.5	10%	1.4	1.7	14	$7
Rand Var	-3	10	Proj	8	11	0	174	96	4.45	1.36	272			25.7	29%	71%	4.84	37	20	43	2.7	5.0	1.8	10%	1.2	-8.6	31	$10

OF defense in SEA helped cut H%. Add better-than-usual Ctl to get formula for WHIP and ERA gains. Trade, knee injury and Dom skid all factored into poor 2H finish. BPIs say he's the same pitcher, just older.

Weathers,David		Yr	Tm	W	L	Sv	IP	K	ERA	WHIP	OBA	vL	vR	BF/G	H%	S%	xERA	G	L	F	Ctl	Dom	Cmd	hr/f	hr/9	RAR	BPV	R$
RH	Reliever	05	CIN	7	4	15	77	61	3.96	1.30	246	265	226	4.5	29%	71%	3.62	50	21	28	3.4	7.1	2.1	11%	0.8	2.7	65	$12
Age	40	06	CIN	4	4	12	73	50	3.57	1.30	228	219	230	4.6	24%	80%	4.56	45	17	38	4.2	6.1	1.5	14%	1.5	8.3	20	$11
Type		07	CIN	2	6	33	78	48	3.59	1.21	234	254	218	4.6	27%	70%	4.64	36	21	43	3.1	5.6	1.8	4%	0.5	8.0	29	$17
Health	A	08	CIN	4	6	0	69	46	3.25	1.53	280	245	296	4.3	32%	81%	4.52	44	24	32	3.9	6.0	1.5	8%	0.8	8.7	24	$4
PT/Exp	C	09	2NL	4	6	1	62	37	3.92	1.31	233	218	241	3.9	24%	76%	4.71	44	15	41	4.1	5.4	1.3	13%	1.5	2.1	9	$5
Consist	A	1st Half		0	1	1	26	17	2.40	1.11	196			3.4	23%	79%	4.51	39	14	46	3.8	5.8	1.5	3%	0.3	5.8	21	$3
LIMA Plan	C	2nd Half		4	5	0	36	20	5.03	1.45	257			4.2	24%	74%	4.84	47	16	37	4.3	5.0	1.2	21%	2.3	-3.7	0	$2
Rand Var	-2	10	Proj	3	5	3	58	36	4.34	1.48	272			4.3	30%	73%	4.77	43	19	38	3.9	5.6	1.4	10%	1.1	-3.6	17	$3

Chronic overachiever will turn 40 this season, has outpitched xERA now for 4 straight years. Fortunate h% did the trick in '09, elevated S% and Dom in '08. Tough to bet against, but his risk has never been higher.

Weaver,Jeff		Yr	Tm	W	L	Sv	IP	K	ERA	WHIP	OBA	vL	vR	BF/G	H%	S%	xERA	G	L	F	Ctl	Dom	Cmd	hr/f	hr/9	RAR	BPV	R$
RH	Reliever	05	LA	14	11	0	224	157	4.22	1.17	258	297	208	27.0	28%	69%	3.83	41	21	38	1.7	6.3	3.7	13%	1.4	0.7	86	$20
Age	33	06	2TM	8	14	0	172	107	5.76	1.51	305	340	267	24.6	32%	66%	4.65	39	23	38	2.5	5.6	2.3	15%	1.8	-26.2	51	$3
Type	Pwr	07	SEA	7	13	0	147	80	6.20	1.53	315	324	306	24.2	33%	61%	5.12	36	17	47	2.1	4.9	2.3	9%	1.4	-30.6	44	$1
Health	A	08	aaa	4	6	0	84	49	8.78	1.94	353			18.6	37%	57%	8.56				3.6	5.3	1.5		2.1	-46.4	-17	($9)
PT/Exp	C	09	LA	6	4	0	79	64	3.65	1.52	281	286	277	12.5	34%	78%	4.27	41	23	36	3.8	7.3	1.9	8%	0.8	5.3	49	$5
Consist	F	1st Half		4	2	0	37	29	3.63	1.59	291			12.9	35%	79%	4.53	39	24	38	3.9	7.0	1.8	7%	0.7	2.6	38	$3
LIMA Plan	C	2nd Half		2	2	0	42	35	3.66	1.46	272			12.2	33%	77%	4.02	43	23	34	3.7	7.5	2.1	9%	0.9	2.7	58	$3
Rand Var	-1	10	Proj	4	5	0	73	55	4.84	1.50	281			15.3	32%	70%	4.50	39	21	39	3.6	6.8	1.9	10%	1.1	-2.1	43	$3

Reborn as swingman, Dom & GB surge, and limited exposure kept him surprisingly effective all season. Unsustainable S% and hr/9 say he won't repeat. This isn't the Weaver you want to draft.

Weaver,Jered		Yr	Tm	W	L	Sv	IP	K	ERA	WHIP	OBA	vL	vR	BF/G	H%	S%	xERA	G	L	F	Ctl	Dom	Cmd	hr/f	hr/9	RAR	BPV	R$
RH	Starter	05	aa	3	3	0	43	39	4.19	1.49	275			23.7	33%	75%	4.93				3.8	8.2	2.2		1.0	0.6	63	$3
Age	27	06	LAA *	17	3	0	200	184	2.43	1.02	222	250	174	25.4	27%	82%	3.78	30	18	52	1.9	8.3	4.4	8%	1.0	52.5	106	$36
Type	Pwr xFB	07	LAA	13	7	0	161	115	3.91	1.39	282	291	269	24.8	32%	74%	4.60	36	17	47	2.5	6.4	2.6	7%	1.0	11.8	61	$15
Health	A	08	LAA	11	10	0	177	152	4.33	1.28	258	243	266	24.8	31%	69%	4.11	33	22	46	2.8	7.7	2.8	8%	1.0	0.4	76	$16
PT/Exp	A	09	LAA	16	8	0	211	174	3.75	1.24	248	276	208	26.6	29%	74%	4.38	31	19	50	2.8	7.4	2.6	8%	1.1	18.2	66	$23
Consist	A	1st Half		8	3	0	107	86	3.11	1.13	226			27.1	26%	76%	4.27	31	19	50	2.8	7.2	2.6	7%	0.9	17.7	64	$15
LIMA Plan	D+	2nd Half		8	5	0	104	88	4.42	1.36	269			26.1	31%	71%	4.49	31	18	51	2.9	7.6	2.7	9%	1.3	0.4	69	$9
Rand Var	-1	10	Proj	15	9	0	206	170	3.94	1.29	258			25.5	30%	74%	4.34	32	19	49	2.8	7.4	2.7	9%	1.2	2.5	70	$21

Better off-speed stuff reduced pitch counts, raised his effectiveness. Increased BF/G, IP and wins fell into place. Solid Dom, stable skill set, hr/9 will always be the issue here. An xFBer you can live with.

Webb,Brandon		Yr	Tm	W	L	Sv	IP	K	ERA	WHIP	OBA	vL	vR	BF/G	H%	S%	xERA	G	L	F	Ctl	Dom	Cmd	hr/f	hr/9	RAR	BPV	R$
RH	Starter	05	ARI	14	12	0	229	172	3.54	1.26	262	298	228	29.0	31%	74%	2.74	65	19	16	2.3	6.8	2.9	18%	0.8	20.0	102	$21
Age	30	06	ARI	16	8	0	235	178	3.10	1.13	246	261	231	28.9	29%	74%	2.63	66	17	16	1.9	6.8	3.6	13%	0.6	40.2	115	$29
Type	xGB	07	ARI	18	10	0	236	194	3.01	1.19	239	272	199	28.6	29%	75%	2.93	62	18	20	2.7	7.4	2.7	9%	0.5	41.3	99	$29
Health	F	08	ARI	22	7	0	227	183	3.30	1.20	244	265	219	27.4	30%	73%	2.86	64	15	20	2.6	7.3	2.8	10%	0.5	27.3	103	$28
PT/Exp	A	09	ARI	0	0	0	4	2	13.50	2.00	347	222	500	19.7	30%	33%	5.32	53	13	33	4.5	4.5	1.0	39%	4.5	-4.6	-9	($1)
Consist	C	1st Half		0	0	0	4	2	13.50	2.00	347			19.7	30%	33%	5.32	53	13	33	4.5	4.5	1.0	39%	4.5	-4.6	-9	($1)
LIMA Plan	C+	2nd Half		0	0	0	0	0	0.00	0.00							0.00											
Rand Var	+5	10	Proj	15	9	0	189	143	3.68	1.26	252			29.2	30%	72%	3.26	60	16	24	2.8	6.8	2.4	10%	0.6	23.4	85	$19

Shoulder woes ended season, but surgery removed debris, found no damage. The word is that he's good to go for spring training, and if he is, grab him. Durability is the only issue for one of the NL's premier studs.

Wellemeyer,Todd		Yr	Tm	W	L	Sv	IP	K	ERA	WHIP	OBA	vL	vR	BF/G	H%	S%	xERA	G	L	F	Ctl	Dom	Cmd	hr/f	hr/9	RAR	BPV	R$
RH	Starter	05	CHC *	5	3	1	85	72	4.55	1.56	264	234	284	11.2	31%	73%	4.44	47	15	38	5.0	7.6	1.5	9%	1.0	-3.2	28	$4
Age	31	06	2TM	1	4	1	78	54	4.15	1.51	236	208	265	7.5	27%	73%	5.01	49	14	37	5.8	6.2	1.1	7%	0.7	3.6	-17	$3
Type	FB	07	2TM	3	3	0	79	60	4.54	1.48	256	311	200	10.9	29%	73%	4.79	40	18	41	4.5	6.8	1.5	11%	1.2	-0.8	18	$4
Health	C	08	STL	13	9	0	192	134	3.71	1.25	248	256	237	25.0	27%	75%	4.25	39	21	40	2.9	6.3	2.2	11%	1.2	13.3	52	$17
PT/Exp	B	09	STL	7	10	0	122	78	5.89	1.77	317	351	305	20.5	35%	69%	5.35	37	21	42	4.2	5.7	1.4	11%	1.4	-25.6	5	($3)
Consist	B	1st Half		6	7	0	88	55	5.71	1.71	309			25.5	34%	68%	5.32	37	20	43	4.1	5.6	1.4	8%	1.1	-16.6	6	($1)
LIMA Plan	F	2nd Half		1	3	0	34	23	6.33	1.94	338			13.8	36%	72%	5.39	38	23	39	4.5	6.1	1.4	17%	2.1	-9.0	4	($2)
Rand Var	+2	10	Proj	5	6	0	102	67	4.97	1.56	281			15.1	31%	71%	4.95	39	20	41	4.1	5.9	1.5	11%	1.3	-8.6	14	$2

DOM/DIS of 19/ 38% sent him to pen in July, more elbow woes sent him to DL in Aug. '08 IP spike is a factor, but Ctl, hr/9 were hardly rock-solid. Dicey health, Dom and FB% trending badly. Avoid.

Wells,Kip		Yr	Tm	W	L	Sv	IP	K	ERA	WHIP	OBA	vL	vR	BF/G	H%	S%	xERA	G	L	F	Ctl	Dom	Cmd	hr/f	hr/9	RAR	BPV	R$
RH	Reliever	05	PIT	8	18	0	182	132	5.09	1.57	266	288	249	24.7	30%	69%	4.58	47	20	33	4.9	6.5	1.3	12%	1.1	-19.0	10	$3
Age	32	06	2TM	2	5	0	44	20	6.53	1.86	329	353	323	23.4	36%	63%	5.30	51	20	29	4.3	4.1	1.0	6%	0.6	-10.9	-13	($2)
Type	Pwr GB	07	STL	7	17	0	163	122	5.70	1.62	288	287	287	21.7	33%	66%	4.49	48	19	33	4.3	6.7	1.6	11%	1.1	-25.5	31	$1
Health	F	08	2TM	1	3	0	38	31	6.21	1.83	268	266	286	7.2	32%	66%	4.94	53	17	29	7.2	7.4	1.0	12%	1.0	-8.8	-29	($2)
PT/Exp	C	09	2NL	2	5	2	73	43	5.32	1.38	226	248	212	9.5	25%	61%	4.66	49	18	33	5.0	5.3	1.1	8%	0.7	-10.2	-11	$2
Consist	A	1st Half		0	2	2	26	18	6.55	1.57	238			5.1	28%	55%	4.95	50	16	34	6.2	6.2	1.0	4%	0.3	-7.6	-28	($1)
LIMA Plan	C	2nd Half		2	3	0	47	25	4.64	1.27	220			19.5	23%	65%	4.49	49	19	32	4.2	4.8	1.1	11%	1.0	-2.6	-1	$2
Rand Var	+1	10	Proj	2	5	0	58	39	4.81	1.48	255			9.5	29%	69%	4.49	50	18	32	4.7	6.1	1.3	10%	0.9	-1.6	11	$1

Age, GB% and occasionally flashing dominance keep him in opportunities. Ctl, ERA and health keep him moving from team to team. xERA says he's better than his results, but not even close to being rosterable.

Wells,Randy		Yr	Tm	W	L	Sv	IP	K	ERA	WHIP	OBA	vL	vR	BF/G	H%	S%	xERA	G	L	F	Ctl	Dom	Cmd	hr/f	hr/9	RAR	BPV	R$
RH	Starter	05		0	0	0	0	0	0.00	0.00							0.00											
Age	27	06	a/a	9	7	0	131	97	5.17	1.63	318			23.8	37%	69%	5.98				2.8	6.7	2.4		0.9	-10.5	53	$4
Type		07	aaa	5	6	2	95	77	6.30	1.84	324			11.3	37%	68%	7.25				4.4	7.2	1.6		1.5	-21.6	24	($2)
Health	A	08	aaa	10	4	0	118	76	5.16	1.69	326			20.2	36%	73%	6.69				3.0	5.8	1.9		1.4	-12.5	23	$3
PT/Exp	D	09	CHC *	15	10	0	191	119	3.20	1.29	262	310	221	25.1	30%	77%	4.03	48	19	33	2.6	5.6	2.2	7%	0.7	23.3	57	$18
Consist	D	1st Half		6	3	0	89	60	2.94	1.16	243			24.2	28%	76%	3.69	49	19	32	2.3	6.1	2.7	6%	0.5	13.7	75	$10
LIMA Plan	C	2nd Half		9	7	0	102	59	3.43	1.40	278			26.0	31%	78%	4.32	48	19	34	2.8	5.2	1.8	9%	0.9	9.6	43	$9
Rand Var	-2	10	Proj	13	9	0	174	115	4.34	1.43	280			19.4	31%	72%	4.21	48	19	33	3.0	5.9	2.0	11%	1.0	1.2	52	$11

12-10, 3.05 ERA in 165 IP at CHC. Fine rookie year fueled by GB% and solid Ctl, but 1H xERA has no precedent. Past also says Ctl, hr/9 repeats aren't likely. Set expectations against 2H xERA.

Westbrook,Jake		Yr	Tm	W	L	Sv	IP	K	ERA	WHIP	OBA	vL	vR	BF/G	H%	S%	xERA	G	L	F	Ctl	Dom	Cmd	hr/f	hr/9	RAR	BPV	R$
RH	Reliever	05	CLE	15	15	0	210	119	4.50	1.30	269	275	255	26.1	30%	66%	3.32	62	19	19	2.4	5.1	2.1	15%	0.8	-3.2	67	$15
Age	32	06	CLE	15	10	0	211	109	4.18	1.43	293	290	300	28.7	32%	71%	3.75	61	17	22	2.3	4.6	2.0	9%	0.6	9.9	59	$15
Type	Con xGB	07	CLE	6	9	0	152	93	4.32	1.41	271	288	263	26.3	30%	70%	4.05	54	20	27	3.3	5.5	1.7	10%	0.8	3.4	43	$9
Health	F	08	CLE	1	2	0	35	19	3.11	1.15	252	238	273	28.3	26%	80%	3.61	55	17	28	1.8	4.9	2.7	16%	1.3	5.3	73	$3
PT/Exp	C	09	aa *	0	1	0	9	5	3.00	1.22	262			12.4	28%	80%	4.05				2.0	5.0	2.5		1.0	1.5	55	$1
Consist	A	1st Half		0	0	0	7	3	0.00	1.01	230			13.7	26%	100%	2.06				1.5	4.4	2.9		0.0	3.7	96	$1
LIMA Plan	C+	2nd Half		0	1	0	2	2	13.49	1.97	356			9.8	34%	32%	11.04				3.7	7.2	1.9		4.5	-2.3	-67	($0)
Rand Var	-5	10	Proj	3	5	0	80	39	4.42	1.40	275			28.6	30%	69%	4.01	58	18	24	2.9	4.4	1.5	11%	0.8	3.2	36	$3

Comeback from '08 TJS ended in AA, reportedly set to go for '10. Hip surgery ups durability concerns for xGBer with sub-par Dom. Needs both defense and run support from rebuilding team to be an asset.

JOCK THOMPSON

West,Sean

		Yr	Tm	W	L	Sv	IP	K	ERA	WHIP	OBA	vL	vR	BF/G	H%	S%	xERA	G	L	F	Ctl	Dom	Cmd	hr/f	hr/9	RAR	BPV	R$
LH	Starter	05		0	0	0	0	0	0.00	0.00							0.00											
Age	23	06		0	0	0	0	0	0.00	0.00							0.00											
Type	Pwr	07		0	0	0	0	0	0.00	0.00							0.00											
Health	A	08		0	0	0	0	0	0.00	0.00							0.00											
PT/Exp	D	09	FLA	* 15	9	0	167	127	5.34	1.62	294	338	267	23.7	33%	70%	4.73	40	19	41	4.0	6.8	**1.7**	11%	1.3	-23.8	33	$5
Consist	F	1st Half		7	4	0	86	70	5.20	1.60	276			24.4	31%	72%	5.03	34	19	47	4.8	7.3	**1.5**	13%	1.7	-10.8	14	$3
LIMA Plan	C	2nd Half		8	5	0	81	58	5.49	1.64	313			23.1	36%	67%	4.48	45	19	36	3.2	6.4	**2.0**	8%	0.9	-13.0	51	$2
Rand Var	+2	10	Proj	13	8	0	145	112	4.90	1.52	280			23.0	32%	70%	4.52	41	19	40	3.8	7.0	1.8	11%	1.2	-4.7	41	$7

8-6, 4.79 ERA in 103 IP at FLA. MLB debut after only 64 IP above High-A guarantees MLB growing pains, even for the best prospects. Good Dom potential, Ctl is improving, Cmd should be much better in 2011.

Wheeler,Dan

		Yr	Tm	W	L	Sv	IP	K	ERA	WHIP	OBA	vL	vR	BF/G	H%	S%	xERA	G	L	F	Ctl	Dom	Cmd	hr/f	hr/9	RAR	BPV	R$
RH	Reliever	05	HOU	2	3	3	73	69	2.22	0.98	205	206	204	4.0	25%	83%	3.40	38	18	44	2.3	8.5	**3.6**	8%	0.9	18.3	106	$12
Age	32	06	HOU	3	5	9	71	68	2.53	1.15	224	273	183	3.9	29%	81%	3.79	37	20	44	3.0	8.6	**2.8**	6%	0.6	17.2	87	$13
Type	xFB	07	2TM	1	9	11	75	82	5.30	1.30	260	260	253	4.5	33%	62%	3.61	37	18	45	2.8	9.9	**3.6**	12%	1.3	-7.7	118	$8
Health	A	08	TAM	5	6	13	66	53	3.12	1.00	191	215	163	3.7	20%	77%	4.21	28	17	54	3.0	7.2	**2.4**	10%	1.4	10.0	55	$14
PT/Exp	A	09	TAM	4	5	2	58	45	3.28	0.87	201	305	156	3.2	20%	74%	3.91	31	13	56	1.4	7.0	**5.0**	12%	1.7	8.4	97	$10
Consist	A	1st Half		2	1	0	27	20	3.65	1.11	239			3.4	26%	73%	4.25	32	17	51	2.0	6.6	**3.3**	10%	1.3	2.7	76	$3
LIMA Plan	C+	2nd Half		2	4	2	31	25	2.94	0.65	165			3.0	14%	77%	3.61	30	9	61	0.9	7.4	**8.3**	15%	2.1	5.7	117	$7
Rand Var	-4	10	Proj	3	5	5	58	45	4.03	1.26	262			3.8	29%	73%	4.46	32	15	53	2.3	7.0	3.0	10%	1.4	-0.2	73	$7

Why the bottom could drop out:
- Spiking FB and HR trends
- Decline in Dom last two years
- Absurd hit rates WILL correct.

Cmd keeps him eminently rosterable but save opps will be limited.

White,Sean

		Yr	Tm	W	L	Sv	IP	K	ERA	WHIP	OBA	vL	vR	BF/G	H%	S%	xERA	G	L	F	Ctl	Dom	Cmd	hr/f	hr/9	RAR	BPV	R$
RH	Reliever	05	aa	2	5	0	50	28	5.29	1.41	267			27.1	30%	60%	3.99				3.4	4.9	**1.5**		0.4	-6.1	50	$1
Age	28	06	aa	5	6	1	102	58	6.95	2.18	371			24.8	42%	66%	7.94				4.6	5.1	**1.1**		0.4	-30.7	23	($9)
Type	Con	07	SEA	* 2	3	0	48	24	5.06	1.50	262			11.8	29%	65%	4.43				4.5	4.5	**1.0**		0.6	-3.3	34	$1
Health	A	08	aa	6	11	0	125	39	7.37	2.28	397			29.6	41%	68%	9.32				3.8	2.8	**0.7**		1.0	-47.3	-23	($16)
PT/Exp	D	09	SEA	3	2	1	64	28	2.80	1.09	216	191	238	5.0	23%	75%	4.43	48	16	36	2.8	3.9	**1.4**	4%	0.4	13.1	21	$8
Consist	F	1st Half		2	1	1	36	16	2.49	1.27	222			5.2	24%	82%	4.75	50	18	31	4.2	4.0	**0.9**	6%	0.5	8.7	-14	$4
LIMA Plan	C	2nd Half		1	1	0	28	12	3.19	0.85	209			4.6	23%	61%	4.02	46	13	41	1.0	3.8	**4.0**	3%	0.3	4.4	67	$4
Rand Var	-5	10	Proj	3	3	0	58	26	4.19	1.43	288			8.4	30%	74%	4.80	48	15	37	2.6	4.0	1.5	9%	1.1	-2.6	27	$3

Soft-tossing groundballer rode depressed H% to career year. Ctl trend is promising, but 2H gains don't look sustainble. Inability to induce swings-and-misses makes risk / reward for middle reliever easy to ignore.

Willis,Dontrelle

		Yr	Tm	W	L	Sv	IP	K	ERA	WHIP	OBA	vL	vR	BF/G	H%	S%	xERA	G	L	F	Ctl	Dom	Cmd	hr/f	hr/9	RAR	BPV	R$
LH	Starter	05	FLA	22	10	0	236	170	2.63	1.14	242	222	247	28.2	29%	77%	3.56	45	24	32	2.1	6.5	**3.1**	5%	0.4	47.0	83	$33
Age	28	06	FLA	12	12	0	223	160	3.87	1.42	271	231	281	28.5	31%	75%	4.21	48	20	33	3.3	6.5	**1.9**	9%	0.8	16.9	51	$15
Type	Pwr	07	FLA	10	15	0	205	146	5.17	1.60	294	123	320	26.5	33%	70%	4.47	46	21	32	3.8	6.4	**1.7**	13%	1.3	-18.9	37	$4
Health	F	08	DET	* 3	3	0	52	36	7.27	2.06	276	125	242	18.5	31%	65%	6.84	43	12	46	8.8	6.2	**0.7**	9%	1.2	-18.7	-106	($4)
PT/Exp	C	09	DET	* 3	6	0	64	33	7.03	1.90	281	306	289	23.7	30%	62%	6.01	52	17	31	7.2	4.6	**0.6**	9%	0.9	-20.3	-81	($4)
Consist	D	1st Half		2	5	0	51	27	6.71	1.87	285			24.6	30%	64%	5.76	52	17	31	6.7	4.8	**0.7**	12%	1.1	-14.3	-65	($3)
LIMA Plan	C	2nd Half		1	1	0	12	5	8.34	2.04	266			20.5	30%	55%	5.27				9.2	3.8	**0.4**		0.0	-6.0	33	($1)
Rand Var	+3	10	Proj	2	3	0	44	29	5.17	1.70	281			25.1	31%	71%	5.04	48	19	33	5.4	6.0	1.1	11%	1.0	-3.3	-12	$0

1-4, 7.49 ERA in 33 IP at DET. PQS-DOM vs. TEX in May got hearts fluttering, but it was his last DOM of the year. Hasn't shown any Ctl now for 2 years, with dominance ticking down. Don't even think about it.

Wilson,Brian

		Yr	Tm	W	L	Sv	IP	K	ERA	WHIP	OBA	vL	vR	BF/G	H%	S%	xERA	G	L	F	Ctl	Dom	Cmd	hr/f	hr/9	RAR	BPV	R$
RH	Reliever	05	a/a	1	1	8	27	35	2.00	1.00	155			4.4	25%	78%	1.06				4.3	11.7	**2.7**		0.0	7.7	150	$7
Age	28	06	SF	* 3	6	8	58	50	4.50	1.60	252			4.8	31%	72%	4.56	45	26	29	5.9	7.8	**1.3**	8%	0.6	-0.1	3	$5
Type	Pwr	07	SF	* 2	4	17	58	47	2.66	1.38	220	304	145	4.5	28%	80%	4.03	56	15	29	5.2	7.3	**1.4**	2%	0.2	12.6	24	$11
Health	A	08	SF	3	2	41	62	67	4.62	1.44	261	202	320	4.3	34%	70%	3.34	52	19	30	4.0	9.7	**2.4**	14%	1.0	-2.7	95	$18
PT/Exp	B	09	SF	5	6	38	72	83	2.74	1.20	227	189	255	4.4	32%	77%	3.10	46	18	36	3.4	10.3	**3.1**	5%	0.4	12.9	119	$22
Consist	A	1st Half		2	4	21	36	39	3.50	1.25	234			4.3	32%	72%	3.27	48	16	36	3.5	9.8	**2.8**	6%	0.5	3.1	107	$11
LIMA Plan	C+	2nd Half		3	2	17	36	44	1.98	1.16	221			4.5	32%	83%	2.93	44	20	36	3.2	10.9	**3.4**	3%	0.2	9.9	131	$12
Rand Var	-2	10	Proj	4	5	35	73	77	3.45	1.26	237			4.4	31%	74%	3.39	45	19	36	3.5	9.5	2.8	9%	0.7	7.9	101	$19

His first year entering the Elite Closers Club. It's an exclusive group of 100+ BPV performers, but you have to stay over 100 to keep membership. With GB rate declining and Ctl/Dom likely at peak, it may be a short stay.

Wilson,C.J.

		Yr	Tm	W	L	Sv	IP	K	ERA	WHIP	OBA	vL	vR	BF/G	H%	S%	xERA	G	L	F	Ctl	Dom	Cmd	hr/f	hr/9	RAR	BPV	R$
LH	Reliever	05	TEX	* 1	11	1	92	65	6.49	1.72	327	290	339	11.9	36%	64%	3.64	60	20	20	3.2	6.4	**2.0**	23%	1.4	-24.1	66	($3)
Age	29	06	TEX	2	4	1	44	43	4.08	1.29	239	155	292	4.2	28%	74%	3.42	49	21	30	3.7	8.8	**2.4**	20%	1.4	2.6	86	$5
Type	Pwr GB	07	TEX	2	1	12	68	63	3.03	1.22	206	112	275	4.3	26%	76%	3.51	49	24	27	4.3	8.3	**1.9**	8%	0.5	12.4	59	$12
Health	B	08	TEX	2	2	24	46	41	6.03	1.64	273	265	269	4.2	31%	66%	4.36	49	16	35	5.2	8.0	**1.5**	17%	1.6	-9.6	29	$8
PT/Exp	B	09	TEX	5	6	14	74	84	2.81	1.33	241	206	249	4.2	34%	79%	2.91	55	20	25	3.9	10.3	**2.6**	6%	0.4	14.9	113	$15
Consist	C	1st Half		4	3	7	33	29	2.73	1.36	256			4.2	32%	81%	3.29	59	18	23	3.5	7.9	**2.2**	9%	0.5	7.0	83	$7
LIMA Plan	B	2nd Half		1	3	7	41	55	2.87	1.30	229			4.3	36%	77%	2.62	52	22	26	4.2	12.2	**2.9**	4%	0.2	7.9	136	$7
Rand Var	-1	10	Proj	4	5	13	73	74	3.48	1.31	236			4.3	31%	74%	3.28	52	20	28	4.0	9.2	2.3	9%	0.6	10.3	89	$12

Health finally cooperated. Dom and GB spiked, hr/f reverted, but he was unable to hold Ctl gains of 1H. Handedness, Ctl and durability will likely always limit his saves opps, but he's an option at this point in time.

Wolf,Randy

		Yr	Tm	W	L	Sv	IP	K	ERA	WHIP	OBA	vL	vR	BF/G	H%	S%	xERA	G	L	F	Ctl	Dom	Cmd	hr/f	hr/9	RAR	BPV	R$
LH	Starter	05	PHI	6	4	0	80	61	4.39	1.41	278	238	293	26.7	31%	75%	4.36	35	23	42	2.9	6.9	**2.3**	13%	1.6	-1.4	58	$5
Age	33	06	PHI	4	0	0	56	44	5.60	1.71	284	86	323	21.7	30%	73%	5.33	37	19	44	5.3	7.0	**1.3**	17%	2.1	-7.7	-1	$1
Type	FB	07	LA	9	6	0	103	94	4.73	1.45	275	250	278	24.9	34%	68%	4.09	41	19	40	3.4	8.2	**2.4**	8%	0.9	-3.9	75	$8
Health	C	08	2NL	12	12	0	190	162	4.30	1.38	262	283	258	24.8	31%	71%	4.10	39	23	39	3.4	7.7	**2.3**	10%	1.0	-0.8	64	$13
PT/Exp	A	09	LA	11	7	0	214	160	3.23	1.10	228	159	246	25.3	26%	75%	3.91	40	18	42	2.4	6.7	**2.8**	9%	1.0	25.3	73	$23
Consist	A	1st Half		3	3	0	102	74	3.61	1.19	238			24.7	26%	75%	4.20	37	19	44	2.7	6.5	**2.4**	11%	1.3	7.2	59	$8
LIMA Plan	D+	2nd Half		8	4	0	112	86	2.89	1.02	218			26.0	26%	75%	3.66	42	18	40	2.2	6.9	**3.2**	7%	0.7	18.0	86	$15
Rand Var	-3	10	Proj	12	9	0	196	152	3.95	1.30	259			25.0	30%	73%	4.12	39	20	41	2.8	7.0	2.5	9%	1.1	3.4	68	$16

Improved Ctl, fortunate H% and another healthy year yield formula for ERA and WHIP surprise. Strong finish bodes well, but BPIs, age and health history say there's no upside, enough downside for caution.

Wood,Kerry

		Yr	Tm	W	L	Sv	IP	K	ERA	WHIP	OBA	vL	vR	BF/G	H%	S%	xERA	G	L	F	Ctl	Dom	Cmd	hr/f	hr/9	RAR	BPV	R$
RH	Reliever	05	CHC	3	4	0	66	77	4.23	1.18	218	220	211	12.9	26%	73%	3.34	34	24	42	3.5	10.5	**3.0**	21%	1.9	0.1	105	$7
Age	32	06	CHC	1	2	0	19	13	4.22	1.41	260	206	293	20.8	25%	82%	5.06	39	10	51	3.8	6.1	**1.6**	16%	2.3	0.6	26	$1
Type	Pwr FB	07	CHC	1	1	0	24	24	3.33	1.28	208	148	233	4.6	29%	71%	4.31	34	18	48	4.8	8.9	**1.8**	0%	0.0	3.3	42	$2
Health	F	08	CHC	5	4	34	66	84	3.26	1.09	224	209	227	4.1	33%	70%	2.82	39	20	41	2.4	11.4	**4.7**	5%	0.4	8.3	157	$22
PT/Exp	C	09	CLE	3	3	20	55	63	4.25	1.38	236	255	208	4.1	31%	72%	3.85	40	15	45	4.6	10.3	**2.3**	11%	1.1	1.3	80	$12
Consist	C	1st Half		2	3	9	27	30	5.31	1.51	246			3.9	30%	69%	4.14	40	18	42	5.3	10.0	**1.9**	17%	1.7	-2.9	54	$5
LIMA Plan	B	2nd Half		1	0	11	28	33	3.23	1.25	226			4.3	31%	76%	3.58	40	12	48	3.9	10.6	**2.8**	6%	0.6	4.2	105	$7
Rand Var	+1	10	Proj	4	4	33	73	82	3.85	1.30	230			4.6	30%	73%	3.71	39	17	45	4.1	10.2	2.5	10%	1.1	6.5	89	$19

Horrendous 1H fueled by Ctl issues and hr/f spike, rebound began when they subsided. With G/L/F swings and suspect Ctl, he's likely to remain fairly erratic in-season. Only the saves and Ks seem reliable.

Wright,Jamey

		Yr	Tm	W	L	Sv	IP	K	ERA	WHIP	OBA	vL	vR	BF/G	H%	S%	xERA	G	L	F	Ctl	Dom	Cmd	hr/f	hr/9	RAR	BPV	R$
RH	Reliever	05	COL	8	16	0	171	101	5.47	1.65	294	314	279	23.0	32%	68%	4.49	53	20	27	4.3	5.3	**1.2**	14%	1.2	-25.9	11	($1)
Age	35	06	SF	6	10	0	156	79	5.19	1.48	275	261	300	20.2	29%	66%	4.27	58	18	23	3.7	4.6	**1.2**	13%	0.9	-13.6	18	$3
Type	Pwr xGB	07	TEX	* 6	6	0	97	48	4.29	1.59	286	268	253	18.2	31%	75%	4.71	55	17	28	4.1	4.5	**1.1**	10%	0.9	2.6	2	$4
Health	B	08	TEX	8	7	0	84	60	5.12	1.52	281	286	280	5.0	33%	65%	3.46	62	20	19	3.7	6.4	**1.7**	10%	0.5	-8.1	54	$5
PT/Exp	C	09	KC	3	5	0	79	60	4.33	1.48	247	200	285	5.3	29%	72%	3.96	59	17	24	5.0	6.8	**1.4**	14%	0.9	1.2	25	$4
Consist	B	1st Half		0	2	0	35	26	4.11	1.40	273			5.4	31%	75%	3.40	58	21	21	3.1	6.7	**2.2**	22%	1.3	1.5	74	$2
LIMA Plan	C	2nd Half		3	3	0	44	34	4.50	1.55	225			5.3	27%	71%	4.45	60	13	27	6.5	7.0	**1.1**	9%	0.6	-0.3	-14	$2
Rand Var	+1	10	Proj	4	5	0	73	50	4.47	1.53	266			6.5	31%	71%	4.02	59	18	23	4.6	6.2	1.4	11%	0.7	3.7	25	$3

As GB% and - occasionally - Dom suggests, good stuff but his bottom lines have rarely matched the skill components. Ctl has always been his most consistent problem. At age 35, why bet on things changing?

JOCK THOMPSON

Wright,Wesley

Wright,Wesley		W	L	Sv	IP	K	ERA	WHIP	OBA	vL	vR	BF/G	H%	S%	xERA	G	L	F	Ctl	Dom	Cmd	hr/f	hr/9	RAR	BPV	R$
LH Reliever	05	0	0	0	0	0	0.00	0.00							0.00											
Age 25	06 aa	1	1	1	21	25	5.14	1.33	202			6.0	26%	64%	3.81				5.6	10.7	1.9		1.3	-1.6	81	$2
Type Pwr	07 a/a	7	4	2	78	75	4.50	1.68	272			8.2	33%	75%	5.51				5.7	8.7	1.5		1.0	-0.4	54	$5
Health A	08 HOU	4	3	1	56	57	5.01	1.42	223	207	220	3.4	27%	68%	4.17	40	21	39	5.5	9.2	1.7	14%	1.3	-5.1	35	$4
PT/Exp D	09 HOU *	5	5	0	64	64	4.95	1.63	275	359	265	4.7	34%	73%	4.14	43	23	34	5.1	9.0	1.8	14%	1.3	-5.9	46	$2
Consist B	1st Half	3	2	0	32	34	4.55	1.58	275			4.8	35%	72%	4.09	35	27	37	4.6	9.4	2.0	9%	0.8	-1.4	58	$2
LIMA Plan B	2nd Half	2	3	0	32	31	5.35	1.68	274			4.5	32%	73%	4.25	48	20	33	5.6	8.7	1.6	20%	1.7	-4.5	31	$0
Rand Var +4	10 Proj	6	5	0	73	73	4.97	1.57	258			4.4	32%	70%	4.22	42	22	36	5.3	9.1	1.7	12%	1.1	0.3	39	$4

3-4, 5.44 ERA in 44 IP at HOU. Dominating stuff, would excite us more if the strike zone wasn't such an elusive concept. His 5.2 Ctl career minor league mark suggests this may be a long wait. Batters: Just don't swing.

Wuertz,Mike

Wuertz,Mike		W	L	Sv	IP	K	ERA	WHIP	OBA	vL	vR	BF/G	H%	S%	xERA	G	L	F	Ctl	Dom	Cmd	hr/f	hr/9	RAR	BPV	R$
RH Reliever	05 CHC	6	2	0	75	89	3.83	1.33	221	260	197	4.3	30%	72%	3.52	43	17	40	4.8	10.7	2.2	8%	0.7	3.9	83	$8
Age 31	06 CHC *	9	1	10	81	98	2.61	1.22	241	184	245	4.7	33%	83%	2.75	54	16	30	2.9	10.8	3.7	13%	0.9	18.9	148	$17
Type Pwr	07 CHC	2	3	0	72	79	3.49	1.37	239	238	233	4.2	31%	78%	3.76	44	15	41	4.4	9.8	2.3	10%	1.0	8.4	81	$6
Health A	08 CHC *	1	2	4	65	55	3.74	1.48	247	230	288	4.6	29%	78%	4.16	46	25	29	5.0	7.6	1.5	13%	1.0	4.3	26	$4
PT/Exp C	09 OAK	6	1	4	79	102	2.63	0.95	190	183	193	4.1	28%	75%	2.63	45	14	40	2.6	11.7	4.4	9%	0.7	17.7	162	$17
Consist B	1st Half	4	1	2	36	41	2.74	0.97	197			3.9	27%	73%	2.91	43	18	39	2.5	10.2	4.1	6%	0.5	7.6	138	$8
LIMA Plan B	2nd Half	2	0	2	43	61	2.54	0.94	184			4.3	28%	78%	2.39	48	10	42	2.7	12.9	4.7	11%	0.8	10.1	184	$9
Rand Var 0	10 Proj	4	2	3	73	83	3.35	1.19	218			4.3	29%	75%	3.21	45	17	38	3.6	10.3	2.9	10%	0.9	10.9	112	$11

Dom, Ctl trends made abrupt turnaround, BPIs again appear closer-worthy. Who is this guy really?? 1H / 2H consistency bodes well, but don't buy into last year's numbers just yet. He'll need to do it again.

Young,Chris

Young,Chris		W	L	Sv	IP	K	ERA	WHIP	OBA	vL	vR	BF/G	H%	S%	xERA	G	L	F	Ctl	Dom	Cmd	hr/f	hr/9	RAR	BPV	R$
RH Starter	05 TEX	12	7	0	164	137	4.28	1.26	259	281	220	22.1	30%	69%	4.19	33	18	49	2.5	7.5	3.0	8%	1.0	2.0	79	$16
Age 30	06 SD	11	5	0	179	164	3.47	1.13	210	175	234	23.4	24%	77%	4.39	25	18	56	3.5	8.2	2.4	10%	1.4	22.5	58	$22
Type Pwr xFB	07 SD	9	8	0	173	167	3.12	1.10	195	231	155	23.2	25%	72%	4.16	29	16	54	3.7	8.7	2.3	4%	0.5	27.8	62	$22
Health F	08 SD	7	6	0	102	93	3.96	1.29	226	259	189	23.9	27%	73%	4.62	22	25	53	4.2	8.2	1.9	9%	1.1	3.9	33	$9
PT/Exp B	09 SD	4	6	0	76	50	5.21	1.45	246	210	297	23.7	26%	67%	5.41	30	18	52	4.7	5.9	1.3	10%	1.4	-9.6	-13	$2
Consist B	1st Half	4	6	0	76	50	5.21	1.45	246			23.7	26%	67%	5.41	30	18	52	4.7	5.9	1.3	10%	1.4	-9.6	-13	$2
LIMA Plan C+	2nd Half	0	0	0	0	0	0.00	0.00							0.00											
Rand Var -1	10 Proj	8	9	0	145	122	4.41	1.37	247			23.9	28%	72%	4.76	28	19	53	4.0	7.6	1.9	10%	1.4	-8.9	35	$9

Season ended in mid-June due to surgery for frayed labrum. Outlook clouded by two years of arm issues, poorly-trending Ctl. Dom likely to bounce with better health, but Petco is best reason to own a xFB hurler.

Zambrano,Carlos

Zambrano,Carlos		W	L	Sv	IP	K	ERA	WHIP	OBA	vL	vR	BF/G	H%	S%	xERA	G	L	F	Ctl	Dom	Cmd	hr/f	hr/9	RAR	BPV	R$
RH Starter	05 CHC	14	6	0	223	202	3.27	1.15	213	212	212	27.5	26%	74%	3.30	50	20	30	3.5	8.1	2.3	12%	0.8	26.9	81	$26
Age 28	06 CHC	16	7	0	214	210	3.41	1.29	212	247	174	27.3	27%	76%	3.89	47	17	36	4.8	8.8	1.8	10%	0.8	28.5	53	$24
Type Pwr	07 CHC	18	13	0	216	177	3.95	1.33	235	268	200	27.0	27%	73%	4.15	47	17	37	4.2	7.4	1.8	10%	1.0	12.6	44	$21
Health B	08 CHC	14	6	0	189	130	3.91	1.29	244	235	247	26.5	28%	72%	4.15	47	18	35	3.4	6.2	1.8	9%	0.9	8.4	44	$16
PT/Exp A	09 CHC	9	7	0	169	152	3.77	1.38	245	258	235	26.0	31%	73%	3.98	45	18	37	4.1	8.1	1.9	6%	0.5	8.7	56	$12
Consist A	1st Half	4	3	0	83	66	3.69	1.33	243			27.1	29%	74%	4.26	41	18	41	3.8	7.2	1.9	7%	0.8	5.1	46	$6
LIMA Plan C	2nd Half	5	4	0	86	86	3.86	1.43	247			25.0	33%	72%	3.70	48	19	33	4.5	9.0	2.0	4%	0.3	3.5	66	$6
Rand Var -1	10 Proj	10	8	0	174	147	4.03	1.39	252			26.8	30%	73%	4.04	46	18	36	4.0	7.6	1.9	9%	0.8	4.8	54	$12

Once wrote that the excessive innings would have him hawking burgers by time he's 28. Well, here we are and he's not working at Hardees yet. No, his BPIs and IP are just eroding when they should be peaking.

Zavada,Clay

Zavada,Clay		W	L	Sv	IP	K	ERA	WHIP	OBA	vL	vR	BF/G	H%	S%	xERA	G	L	F	Ctl	Dom	Cmd	hr/f	hr/9	RAR	BPV	R$
LH Reliever	05	0	0	0	0	0	0.00	0.00							0.00											
Age 25	06	0	0	0	0	0	0.00	0.00							0.00											
Type Pwr xFB	07	0	0	0	0	0	0.00	0.00							0.00											
Health A	08	0	0	0	0	0	0.00	0.00							0.00											
PT/Exp F	09 ARI *	4	3	0	68	66	3.39	1.32	233	284	205	4.8	28%	79%	4.34	28	21	51	4.2	8.8	2.1	9%	1.1	6.7	50	$6
Consist F	1st Half	2	1	0	35	33	1.71	1.20	210			4.8	26%	91%	4.16	33	16	51	4.0	8.6	2.1	7%	0.9	10.7	56	$5
LIMA Plan C+	2nd Half	2	2	0	33	33	5.18	1.45	256			4.8	31%	67%	4.49	25	24	51	4.4	9.0	2.1	11%	1.4	-4.0	47	$1
Rand Var -3	10 Proj	3	2	0	51	49	4.43	1.48	259			5.0	31%	74%	4.63	27	22	51	4.4	8.7	2.0	9%	1.2	-2.3	42	$3

3-3, 3.35 ERA in 51 IP at ARI. Minor league Dom translated just fine at MLB level, Ctl barely good enough. GB% ebbed with promotions, was charmed at Chase Field (22 IP, 0 hr/f). Don't go overboard in 2010.

Ziegler,Brad

Ziegler,Brad		W	L	Sv	IP	K	ERA	WHIP	OBA	vL	vR	BF/G	H%	S%	xERA	G	L	F	Ctl	Dom	Cmd	hr/f	hr/9	RAR	BPV	R$
RH Reliever	05 aa	2	1	0	21	18	7.71	1.67	329			24.1	40%	52%	6.08				2.6	7.7	3.0		0.9	-8.8	73	($0)
Age 30	06 a/a	9	7	0	162	74	4.78	1.71	336			27.8	35%	75%	6.89				2.6	4.1	1.6		1.3	-5.3	8	$2
Type xGB	07 aa	12	3	2	78	44	3.47	1.40	288			6.8	34%	73%	4.02				2.4	5.1	2.1		0.0	9.6	73	$11
Health A	08 OAK *	5	0	19	85	43	0.88	1.14	222	280	198	5.1	25%	93%	3.39	65	16	19	3.0	4.5	1.5	4%	0.2	36.2	43	$19
PT/Exp D	09 OAK	2	4	7	73	54	3.07	1.50	284	336	265	4.7	34%	79%	3.44	62	18	20	3.4	6.6	1.9	4%	0.2	12.5	67	$7
Consist A	1st Half	1	3	6	36	25	3.25	1.53	293			5.0	35%	78%	3.33	69	11	19	3.3	6.3	1.9	4%	0.3	5.3	72	$4
LIMA Plan B	2nd Half	1	1	1	37	29	2.90	1.47	276			4.4	34%	80%	3.54	55	25	20	3.6	7.0	1.9	4%	0.2	7.2	61	$3
Rand Var -1	10 Proj	4	3	3	73	51	3.10	1.35	263			5.4	31%	78%	3.30	62	18	20	3.1	6.3	2.0	9%	0.5	10.1	70	$8

Dom spike partially offset by Ctl tumble, but it was the H% return to earth that ended the closer fantasies. GB% and hr/9 still make this a viable skill set, particularly for 4X4 owners needing ERA.

Zimmermann,Jordan

Zimmermann,Jordan		W	L	Sv	IP	K	ERA	WHIP	OBA	vL	vR	BF/G	H%	S%	xERA	G	L	F	Ctl	Dom	Cmd	hr/f	hr/9	RAR	BPV	R$
RH Starter	05	0	0	0	0	0	0.00	0.00							0.00											
Age 23	06	0	0	0	0	0	0.00	0.00							0.00											
Type Pwr	07	0	0	0	0	0	0.00	0.00							0.00											
Health C	08 aa	7	2	0	106	86	3.22	1.21	237			22.0	29%	75%	3.26				3.1	7.3	2.4		0.6	14.2	84	$12
PT/Exp D	09 WAS	3	5	0	91	92	4.63	1.36	270	279	263	24.4	34%	68%	3.37	44	24	32	2.9	9.1	3.2	12%	1.0	-5.0	108	$5
Consist A	1st Half	3	3	0	75	75	4.55	1.30	266			24.4	33%	67%	3.29	42	25	32	2.5	9.0	3.6	12%	1.0	-3.3	114	$5
LIMA Plan A+	2nd Half	0	2	0	16	17	5.03	1.61	284			24.3	36%	71%	3.72	49	19	33	4.5	9.5	2.1	13%	1.1	-1.7	77	($0)
Rand Var +4	10 Proj	1	1	0	15	14	4.34	1.24	241			20.1	31%	65%	3.36	46	21	32	3.1	8.7	2.8	8%	0.6	1.6	97	$1

Had season-ending TJS in August. Expected to miss all of 2010, but BPV says he's worth a late-season flyer. Great pick if playing for 2011, better even for 2012. TJS arms often come back stronger, which is scary.

Zito,Barry

Zito,Barry		W	L	Sv	IP	K	ERA	WHIP	OBA	vL	vR	BF/G	H%	S%	xERA	G	L	F	Ctl	Dom	Cmd	hr/f	hr/9	RAR	BPV	R$
LH Starter	05 OAK	14	13	0	228	171	3.87	1.20	223	215	223	26.9	25%	71%	4.07	42	21	37	3.5	6.7	1.9	11%	1.0	14.2	46	$23
Age 31	06 OAK	16	10	0	221	151	3.83	1.40	253	260	257	28.1	28%	76%	4.92	38	17	45	4.0	6.1	1.5	9%	1.1	19.9	18	$20
Type Pwr FB	07 SF	11	13	0	197	131	4.53	1.35	247	242	244	24.7	27%	69%	4.70	39	20	41	3.8	6.0	1.6	10%	1.1	-2.5	22	$12
Health A	08 SF	10	17	0	180	120	5.15	1.60	268	213	285	25.4	30%	68%	5.27	36	23	40	5.1	6.0	1.2	7%	0.8	-19.5	-15	$3
PT/Exp A	09 SF	10	13	0	192	154	4.03	1.35	248	230	256	24.9	29%	73%	4.30	38	22	40	3.8	7.2	1.9	9%	1.0	3.8	43	$13
Consist B	1st Half	4	7	0	89	66	4.55	1.42	255			25.7	29%	70%	4.48	40	21	39	4.0	6.7	1.7	11%	1.1	-4.0	29	$4
LIMA Plan D+	2nd Half	6	6	0	103	88	3.58	1.30	243			24.2	29%	75%	4.15	35	23	42	3.6	7.7	2.1	8%	0.9	7.7	55	$9
Rand Var 0	10 Proj	10	14	0	189	140	4.34	1.43	262			25.6	30%	72%	4.58	38	22	41	3.9	6.7	1.7	9%	1.1	-7.4	32	$10

3.35 ERA in May, 1.93 ERA in August got everyone excited, but at the end of the day, BPIs were not significantly different from the past. Remember - a half run of ERA in 200 IP comes out to just one ER every 4 starts.

Zumaya,Joel

Zumaya,Joel		W	L	Sv	IP	K	ERA	WHIP	OBA	vL	vR	BF/G	H%	S%	xERA	G	L	F	Ctl	Dom	Cmd	hr/f	hr/9	RAR	BPV	R$
RH Reliever	05 a/a	9	5	0	151	181	3.46	1.25	212			24.2	30%	73%	3.00				4.4	10.8	2.4		0.6	15.7	110	$18
Age 25	06 DET	6	3	1	83	97	1.95	1.18	193	183	188	5.5	27%	87%	3.66	34	21	45	4.5	10.5	2.3	7%	0.6	26.7	78	$15
Type Pwr xFB	07 DET	2	3	1	34	27	4.27	1.19	195	271	135	4.9	23%	65%	4.56	36	16	48	4.5	7.2	1.6	7%	0.8	1.0	22	$4
Health F	08 DET	0	2	1	23	22	3.48	1.97	268	161	317	5.4	32%	86%	5.76	40	20	40	8.5	8.5	1.0	11%	1.2	2.5	-58	$0
PT/Exp D	09 DET	3	3	1	31	30	4.94	1.81	280	344	206	5.1	34%	76%	5.44	34	14	52	6.4	8.7	1.4	11%	1.5	-1.8	-3	$1
Consist B	1st Half	3	2	1	26	25	4.14	1.61	261			4.9	31%	79%	5.03	34	14	52	5.5	8.6	1.6	10%	1.4	1.0	18	$3
LIMA Plan B	2nd Half	0	1	0	5	5	9.18	2.86	367			5.7	44%	69%	7.90	38	13	50	11.0	9.2	0.8	12%	1.8	-2.9	******	($1)
Rand Var 0	10 Proj	3	4	0	44	44	4.14	1.45	241			5.9	30%	75%	4.40	37	16	47	5.0	9.1	1.8	11%	1.2	0.2	45	$4

It's been a long time since consistent 100 mph outings and serious closer talk. BPIs have taken a 3-year beating and shoulder surgery shelved him yet again. Are you feelin' lucky? Or desperate? Must pick one.

JOCK THOMPSON

Batter Consistency Charts

by Dylan Hedges

The definition of consistency is the achievement of a level of performance that does not vary greatly in quality over time. Few things are as valuable to head-to-head points league success as filling your roster with players who can produce a solid weekly baseline of stats, week in and week out. In traditional leagues, while consistency is not as important — all we really care about are the end-of-season aggregate numbers — populating your fantasy team with consistent players can make roster management easier.

Consistent batters have good plate discipline, walk rates and on base percentages. These are foundation skills. Those who add power to the mix are obviously more valuable, however, the ability to hit home runs consistently is rare.

We can *track* consistency — and we do so in the accompanying charts — but *predicting* it is difficult. Many fantasy leaguers will try to predict a batter's hot or cold streaks, but that is typically a fool's errand. The best we can do is find players who demonstrate seasonal consistency over time; in-season, we want to manage players and consistency tactically.

For this process, we use the Base Performance Value (BPV) gauge. This primarily measures batting eye, batting average and power. BPV levels of 50 or above in a given week are defined as "DOMinating" weeks. Levels less than zero are defined as "DISaster" weeks. By comparing the DOM and DIS levels in individual weeks, we can analyze batters similarly to how we evaluate starting pitchers.

Note that all BPV levels now use the new version of the formula and all historical consistency ratings have been updated as well.

There are three elements to the process:

First, you want players who provide some **base level production**. This is no different than any other skills evaluation process. You want batters on your team that are projected to be highly productive. *Consistent* production in this context is almost secondary.

The second element is **risk mitigation**. Batters who perform poorly in individual weeks can have a much greater negative impact on a team's overall performance than the positive impact of batters doing well. The Quality-Consistency Score (QC) described earlier in the book reflects this by giving negative outcomes double the weight. We use this formula in the charts: (DOM−(2xDIS)) x 2

Third is the application of the DOM/DIS rates for use in **comparison of players** to uncover hidden value. The minimum level benchmark is a DOM/DIS split of 50/20. While this equates to a QC score of only 20, it keeps the available talent pool open while focusing on the best skills.

An example: Derek Lee and Kendry Morales put up nearly identical aggregate statistics in 2009. Lee went 35-111 -.306 and Morales went 34-108-.306. Both were valued at $23 (the values in this book are higher due to a different definition of the player pool.) However, in terms of quality and consistency, these players' values are much further apart. Lee's DOM/DIS split was 70/15 for a QC score of 80. Morales was 59/19 for a QC score of 42. If you played in a head-to-head league, Lee would have been a more valuable player for your team despite the nearly identical seasonal stat lines.

The following charts include:
- Up to four years of data for all batters who had at least five weeks of stats in 2009
- Base Performance Value for the year (BPV)
- Total number of weeks he accumulated stats (#Wks)
- Domination and Disaster percentages (DOM, DIS)
- Quality-Consistency Score (QC)
- The final chart lists the top individual QC scores, by year, for each of the past four years

Some other observations...

Evidence that seasonal stat lines alone are not sufficient for H2H play... **Lance Berkman** had an off year in 2009, both with his stat line as well as BPV (91 vs 121 in 2008). But his DOM/DIS split showed 2009 to be more consistent (72/8% vs 59/11%), leading to a better QC score (112 vs 74).

Only two players in this entire chart have maintained QC levels in excess of 100 for four straight years. **Albert Pujols** is one of them. Who is the other? *Answer below.*

As **Ryan Braun** ascends the ADP charts, his QC score is in a three-year tailspin (100, 90, 30).

While **Matt Kemp** breaks into our Top 5 for 2010, he's got a ways to go for H2H purposes. His QC trend (-154, -90, -44, +8) is heading in the right direction, though.

Adam LaRoche has become the poster boy for slow starts and fast finishes. That inconsistency is aptly reflected in his DOM/DIS and QC scores. Last three years: 37/37% (-74), 46/35% (-48), 52/41% (-60). His seasonal stat line makes him look quite draftable until you take consistency into account.

As great a pair of seasons as **Evan Longoria** has posted, his consistency is not there yet (QC's of –90 and 0).

Dustin Pedroia had his MVP year in 2008 and a slight regression in 2009. QC begs to differ (108, 140).

Four straight years of 100+ QCs? Pujols and **Carlos Lee**.

One player has managed to post a QC level less than –200 for four straight years. Perhaps equally amazing is that **Paul Bako** got at-bats in 91 of those 104 weeks!

How many batters had four straight years of positive QC's? It's a tough feat. Only 21.

BATTER CONSISTENCY

Name	Yr	BPV	#Wk	DOM	DIS	QC
Abreu,Bobby	06	65	27	48%	22%	8
	07	75	27	59%	26%	14
	08	75	27	56%	22%	24
	09	56	27	44%	33%	-44
Abreu,Tony	07	48	13	46%	23%	0
Alfonzo,Eliezer	06	23	18	50%	39%	-56
	07	-44	11	9%	73%	-274
	09	-60	12	8%	67%	-252
Allen,Brandon	09	4	7	43%	57%	-142
Amezaga,Alfredo	06	30	27	33%	37%	-82
	07	47	27	37%	22%	-14
	08	44	26	38%	46%	-108
	09	-28	5	0%	60%	-240
Anderson,Brian	06	17	27	41%	41%	-82
	08	54	27	33%	44%	-110
	09	-4	22	18%	55%	-184
Anderson,Garret	06	36	26	31%	31%	-62
	07	76	19	58%	21%	32
	08	49	27	37%	30%	-46
	09	32	26	35%	23%	-22
Anderson,Josh	07	24	5	40%	60%	-160
	08	32	9	33%	44%	-110
	09	30	25	28%	56%	-168
Andino,Robert	06	-51	7	0%	71%	-284
	08	-41	19	21%	63%	-210
	09	-15	26	19%	73%	-254
Andrus,Elvis	09	49	27	37%	37%	-74
Ankiel,Rick	07	69	9	44%	33%	-44
	08	69	24	42%	38%	-68
	09	25	25	20%	56%	-184
Antonelli,Matt	08	-1	5	0%	40%	-160
Atkins,Garrett	06	96	27	70%	7%	112
	07	62	27	56%	26%	8
	08	50	27	37%	33%	-58
	09	23	26	35%	50%	-130
Aubrey,Michael	08	26	5	20%	60%	-200
	09	74	8	50%	13%	48
Aurilia,Rich	06	79	25	72%	16%	80
	07	35	24	38%	46%	-108
	08	36	27	37%	37%	-74
	09	-24	24	8%	67%	-252
Ausmus,Brad	06	1	27	19%	44%	-138
	07	15	27	26%	48%	-140
	08	-4	27	30%	52%	-148
	09	-18	25	24%	64%	-208
Avila,Alex	09	82	9	56%	33%	-20
Aviles,Mike	08	66	19	47%	21%	10
	09	-17	14	14%	86%	-316
Aybar,Erick	06	-3	14	14%	79%	-288
	07	-2	21	10%	52%	-188
	08	52	22	41%	27%	-26
	09	57	27	37%	30%	-46
Aybar,Willy	06	40	16	44%	25%	-12
	08	58	21	43%	19%	10
	09	38	27	41%	33%	-50
Bailey,Jeff	08	20	11	36%	64%	-184
	09	47	7	43%	43%	-86
Baker,Jeff	06	172	5	40%	0%	80
	07	-10	24	17%	67%	-234
	08	55	26	46%	50%	-108
	09	25	19	32%	47%	-124
Baker,John	08	30	13	46%	31%	-32
	09	20	27	33%	37%	-82
Bako,Paul	06	-86	22	0%	82%	-328
	07	-62	26	19%	73%	-254
	08	-17	26	23%	69%	-230
	09	-17	12	12%	71%	-260
Baldelli,Rocco	06	85	17	59%	35%	-22
	07	19	7	14%	29%	-88
	08	30	8	50%	50%	-100
	09	26	24	33%	54%	-150
Balentien,Wladimir	08	-17	16	19%	69%	-238
	09	24	26	38%	50%	-124
Barajas,Rod	06	39	26	38%	35%	-64
	07	49	22	36%	45%	-108
	08	37	24	42%	29%	-32
	09	34	27	41%	37%	-66
Barden,Brian	07	-22	9	22%	56%	-180
	08	-179	5	0%	80%	-320
	09	13	11	18%	55%	-184
Bard,Josh	06	58	26	50%	42%	-68
	07	43	25	32%	24%	-32
	08	9	16	13%	44%	-150
	09	23	25	32%	40%	-96
Barfield,Josh	06	58	27	52%	19%	28
	07	7	27	19%	59%	-198
	09	-68	7	14%	71%	-256
Barker,Kevin	09	-13	9	44%	56%	-136
Barmes,Clint	06	34	27	37%	30%	-46
	07	-44	10	20%	60%	-200
	08	69	23	52%	22%	16
	09	54	26	50%	31%	-24
Bartlett,Jason	06	34	17	35%	29%	-46
	07	52	26	46%	35%	-48
	08	27	24	29%	46%	-126
	09	74	24	58%	25%	16
Barton,Daric	08	26	27	26%	48%	-140
	09	63	13	54%	23%	16
Bautista,Jose	06	29	22	36%	45%	-108
	07	56	25	48%	24%	0
	08	24	27	30%	59%	-176
	09	44	27	22%	48%	-148
Bay,Jason	06	70	27	59%	19%	42
	07	31	27	37%	44%	-102
	08	89	27	63%	30%	6
	09	85	27	67%	26%	30
Beckham,Gordon	09	72	19	58%	32%	-12
Belliard,Ronnie	06	30	27	41%	30%	-38
	07	48	27	56%	30%	-8
	08	61	20	50%	45%	-80
	09	46	26	35%	46%	-114
Beltran,Carlos	06	133	27	85%	15%	110
	07	100	26	65%	19%	54
	08	109	27	78%	11%	112
	09	89	17	47%	6%	70
Beltre,Adrian	06	67	27	48%	37%	-52
	07	79	27	56%	26%	8
	08	68	25	64%	8%	96
	09	32	21	29%	29%	-58
Berkman,Lance	06	99	27	67%	4%	118
	07	75	27	52%	30%	-16
	08	121	27	59%	11%	74
	09	91	25	72%	8%	112
Berroa,Angel	06	3	27	15%	56%	-194
	08	10	17	29%	41%	-106
	09	-19	14	14%	71%	-256
Betancourt,Y.	06	53	27	44%	15%	28
	07	61	26	50%	31%	-24
	08	58	27	48%	15%	36
	09	44	24	21%	13%	-10
Betemit,Wilson	06	33	27	52%	41%	-60
	07	33	27	44%	37%	-60
	08	5	22	32%	45%	-116
	09	-3	9	44%	33%	-44
Bixler,Brian	08	-56	14	7%	79%	-302
	09	-41	8	13%	75%	-274
Blake,Casey	06	53	22	41%	36%	-62
	07	46	27	41%	33%	-50
	08	53	27	44%	19%	12
	09	54	27	52%	26%	0
Blalock,Hank	06	35	26	35%	31%	-54
	07	103	11	73%	9%	110
	08	81	14	50%	21%	16
	09	53	27	41%	44%	-94
Blanco,Andres	06	10	12	25%	50%	-150
	09	34	16	38%	25%	-24
Blanco,Gregor	08	5	26	12%	54%	-192
	09	-7	6	17%	67%	-234
Blanco,Henry	06	36	27	41%	44%	-94
	07	-32	13	8%	54%	-200
	08	-3	25	28%	56%	-168
	09	16	23	35%	48%	-122
Blanks,Kyle	09	54	11	45%	36%	-54
Bloomquist,Willie	06	21	27	26%	44%	-124
	07	-14	27	19%	59%	-198
	08	-6	18	17%	61%	-210
	09	30	27	15%	52%	-178
Blum,Geoff	06	12	27	26%	37%	-96
	07	29	27	30%	30%	-60
	08	47	26	35%	38%	-82
	09	21	24	33%	38%	-86
Bonifacio,Emilio	07	19	5	20%	40%	-120
	08	8	14	29%	57%	-170
	09	6	27	19%	70%	-242
Boone,Aaron	06	32	25	36%	44%	-104
	07	28	13	38%	38%	-76
	08	19	23	26%	48%	-140
	09	-59	6	0%	33%	-132
Borbon,Julio	09	31	10	20%	50%	-160
Bourgeois,Jason	09	9	9	11%	56%	-202
Bourn,Michael	06	-68	6	17%	50%	-166
	07	56	22	32%	45%	-116
	08	4	27	7%	59%	-222
	09	34	27	30%	37%	-88
Bowker,John	08	21	24	25%	42%	-118
	09	27	11	27%	27%	-54
Bradley,Milton	06	61	19	42%	16%	20
	07	86	19	53%	47%	-62
	08	83	27	56%	30%	-8
	09	25	24	33%	46%	-118
Brantley,Michael	09	-11	6	0%	67%	-268
Branyan,Russell	06	44	26	50%	31%	-24
	07	25	24	29%	46%	-126
	08	102	13	62%	31%	0
	09	55	21	48%	24%	0
Braun,Ryan	07	110	20	80%	15%	100
	08	100	27	67%	11%	90
	09	91	27	59%	22%	30
Brignac,Reid	09	48	11	27%	27%	-54
Brown,Dusty	09	377	5	20%	60%	-200
Bruce,Jay	08	36	19	47%	42%	-74
	09	75	18	56%	33%	-20
Bruntlett,Eric	06	11	23	26%	61%	-192
	07	-5	17	24%	53%	-164
	08	38	27	30%	48%	-132
	09	-4	27	30%	63%	-192
Buck,John	06	15	26	35%	54%	-146
	07	34	26	50%	42%	-68
	08	15	27	30%	48%	-132
	09	48	22	32%	59%	-172
Buck,Travis	07	70	19	58%	16%	52
	08	47	10	40%	50%	-120
	09	11	11	27%	64%	-202
Burke,Chris	06	36	25	32%	40%	-96
	07	50	24	42%	29%	-32
	08	22	26	27%	58%	-178
	09	21	8	25%	63%	-202
Burke,Jamie	07	28	25	32%	48%	-128
	08	26	25	24%	36%	-96
	09	-98	8	0%	100%	-400
Burrell,Pat	06	57	27	56%	41%	-52
	07	73	27	59%	26%	14
	08	82	26	54%	27%	0
	09	5	24	25%	67%	-218
Burriss,Emmanuel	08	37	22	36%	45%	-108
	09	-6	11	0%	64%	-256
Buscher,Brian	07	-3	10	10%	60%	-220
	08	3	18	17%	44%	-142
	09	-16	20	20%	65%	-220
Butler,Billy	07	45	18	33%	33%	-66
	08	33	23	30%	39%	-96
	09	62	27	48%	26%	-8
Byrd,Marlon	06	18	15	33%	53%	-146
	07	38	19	37%	32%	-54
	08	77	24	54%	21%	24
	09	64	26	46%	19%	16
Byrnes,Eric	06	84	27	67%	19%	58
	07	82	26	58%	31%	-8
	08	61	11	64%	36%	-16
	09	72	18	39%	39%	-78
Cabrera,Asdrubal	07	45	9	44%	22%	0
	08	18	23	17%	57%	-194
	09	56	23	52%	26%	0
Cabrera,Everth	09	35	20	30%	35%	-80
Cabrera,Melky	06	58	22	55%	18%	38
	07	56	27	37%	37%	-74
	08	27	24	17%	42%	-134
	09	63	27	56%	30%	-8
Cabrera,Miguel	06	87	27	67%	22%	46
	07	78	27	56%	22%	24
	08	73	27	59%	30%	-2
	09	72	27	56%	15%	52
Cabrera,Orlando	06	76	26	62%	8%	92
	07	55	26	50%	12%	52
	08	49	27	37%	22%	-14
	09	50	27	41%	19%	6
Cairo,Miguel	06	45	22	41%	41%	-82
	07	40	22	23%	50%	-154
	08	43	26	23%	38%	-106
	09	62	12	25%	50%	-150
Callaspo,Alberto	06	13	7	29%	29%	-58
	07	22	15	33%	40%	-94
	08	47	20	35%	40%	-90
	09	80	27	56%	11%	68
Cameron,Mike	06	70	24	50%	29%	-16
	07	53	27	41%	37%	-66
	08	66	23	39%	35%	-62
	09	52	27	41%	26%	-22
Cano,Robinson	06	74	22	55%	14%	54
	07	73	26	46%	19%	16
	08	52	27	48%	33%	-36
	09	82	27	63%	19%	50

BATTER CONSISTENCY

Name	Yr	BPV	#Wk	DOM	DIS	QC
Cantu,Jorge	06	18	22	27%	32%	-74
	07	7	19	37%	42%	-94
	08	68	27	48%	30%	-24
	09	55	26	46%	15%	32
Carlin,Luke	08	-40	17	12%	65%	-236
	09	-20	7	0%	86%	-344
Carp,Mike	09	48	8	50%	38%	-52
Carroll,Brett	07	-65	7	14%	71%	-256
	08	33	8	0%	63%	-252
	09	29	23	26%	52%	-156
Carroll,Jamey	06	45	26	27%	27%	-54
	07	38	27	30%	56%	-164
	08	19	26	15%	46%	-154
	09	5	21	33%	57%	-162
Casilla,Alexi	07	5	13	8%	46%	-168
	08	40	19	42%	37%	-64
	09	25	21	24%	57%	-180
Castillo,Luis	06	51	27	44%	19%	12
	07	51	26	50%	19%	24
	08	46	20	30%	40%	-100
	09	33	27	41%	30%	-38
Castro,Juan	06	17	27	22%	44%	-132
	07	-35	15	7%	80%	-306
	08	1	15	20%	40%	-120
	09	-23	23	17%	57%	-194
Castro,Ramon	06	-11	17	35%	59%	-166
	07	54	23	43%	48%	-106
	08	31	20	40%	45%	-100
	09	20	25	36%	48%	-120
Catalanotto,Frank	06	74	26	65%	8%	98
	07	86	24	58%	21%	32
	08	61	23	57%	30%	-6
	09	39	18	22%	44%	-132
Cedeno,Ronny	06	0	27	22%	56%	-180
	07	19	14	29%	64%	-198
	08	19	27	30%	41%	-104
	09	10	24	25%	67%	-218
Cervelli,Francisco	09	14	16	31%	44%	-114
Chavez,Endy	06	60	27	52%	22%	16
	07	50	15	40%	53%	-132
	08	43	27	33%	30%	-54
	09	23	11	18%	45%	-144
Chavez,Eric	06	64	27	44%	30%	-32
	07	62	17	47%	18%	22
	08	29	6	33%	50%	-134
Chavez,Raul	06	-45	11	9%	73%	-274
	08	3	19	26%	58%	-180
	09	8	23	22%	78%	-268
Choo,Shin-Soo	06	38	12	42%	33%	-48
	08	95	18	61%	22%	34
	09	60	26	58%	23%	24
Church,Ryan	06	66	18	50%	39%	-56
	07	57	26	42%	27%	-24
	08	27	18	39%	33%	-54
	09	42	24	38%	42%	-92
Cintron,Alex	06	43	27	37%	44%	-102
	07	6	22	23%	64%	-210
	08	21	19	26%	47%	-136
	09	-84	6	0%	67%	-268
Clark,Tony	06	-12	20	25%	50%	-150
	07	51	27	52%	44%	-72
	08	-45	26	12%	73%	-268
	09	40	10	50%	50%	-100
Clement,Jeff	08	-14	15	27%	53%	-158
Coghlan,Chris	09	62	23	39%	22%	-10
Conrad,Brooks	09	30	10	20%	50%	-160
Cora,Alex	06	29	27	33%	37%	-82
	07	63	26	46%	31%	-32
	08	51	23	43%	35%	-54
	09	37	18	39%	28%	-34
Coste,Chris	06	40	20	30%	35%	-80
	07	15	15	33%	60%	-174
	08	31	27	44%	41%	-76
	09	-16	25	28%	56%	-168
Counsell,Craig	06	44	22	41%	18%	10
	07	31	26	31%	42%	-106
	08	34	27	33%	37%	-82
	09	59	27	44%	26%	-16
Crawford,Carl	06	81	26	69%	4%	122
	07	64	25	60%	36%	-24
	08	63	21	38%	33%	-56
	09	66	26	50%	27%	-8
Crede,Joe	06	74	26	62%	8%	92
	07	12	10	30%	40%	-100
	08	73	19	58%	5%	96
	09	49	22	59%	18%	46
Crisp,Coco	06	50	18	50%	11%	56
	07	59	27	37%	22%	-14
	08	54	28	46%	36%	-52
	09	89	10	50%	30%	-20
Crosby,Bobby	06	13	20	25%	45%	-130
	07	29	17	29%	35%	-82
	08	37	27	37%	37%	-74
	09	38	26	31%	35%	-78
Crowe,Trevor	09	22	19	32%	47%	-124
Cruz,Luis	08	44	5	40%	20%	0
	09	-6	14	7%	43%	-158
Cruz,Nelson	06	6	11	36%	45%	-108
	07	9	21	24%	62%	-200
	08	105	6	83%	0%	166
	09	78	25	44%	20%	8
Cuddyer,Michael	06	77	27	63%	19%	50
	07	55	26	46%	38%	-60
	08	52	15	40%	27%	-28
	09	86	27	59%	30%	-2
Cunningham,Aaron	09	-35	8	0%	75%	-300
Cust,Jack	07	48	22	41%	50%	-118
	08	39	28	46%	46%	-92
	09	8	27	26%	44%	-124
Damon,Johnny	06	93	27	67%	19%	58
	07	65	27	52%	15%	44
	08	77	25	56%	16%	48
	09	88	27	67%	15%	74
Davis,Chris	08	74	15	67%	27%	26
	09	-5	21	19%	57%	-190
Davis,Rajai	06	18	7	29%	43%	-114
	07	59	18	50%	44%	-76
	08	39	25	28%	60%	-184
	09	56	27	41%	30%	-38
De Aza,Alejandro	07	-8	12	25%	50%	-150
	09	0	7	43%	57%	-142
DeJesus,David	06	71	22	59%	23%	26
	07	58	26	42%	15%	24
	08	63	25	48%	28%	-16
	09	53	25	56%	12%	64
Delgado,Carlos	06	78	26	62%	27%	16
	07	47	26	35%	31%	-54
	08	76	27	59%	19%	42
	09	76	6	83%	17%	98
Dellucci,David	06	70	26	58%	38%	-36
	07	43	14	29%	43%	-114
	08	39	26	31%	54%	-154
	09	-43	9	33%	44%	-110
DeRosa,Mark	06	42	25	40%	40%	-80
	07	32	27	30%	37%	-88
	08	76	26	46%	35%	-48
	09	39	26	27%	42%	-114
Desmond,Ian	09	109	5	40%	40%	-80
DeWitt,Blake	08	32	23	39%	52%	-130
	09	51	13	38%	38%	-76
Diaz,Matt	06	39	26	27%	46%	-130
	07	38	27	41%	41%	-82
	08	-40	10	0%	80%	-320
	09	47	26	38%	38%	-76
Diaz,Robinzon	09	28	15	40%	33%	-52
Dickerson,Chris	08	121	6	50%	17%	32
	09	19	21	33%	62%	-182
Dillon,Joe	07	59	10	50%	30%	-20
	08	-10	18	17%	67%	-234
	09	12	9	22%	22%	-44
Dobbs,Greg	06	75	10	20%	30%	-80
	07	58	27	37%	30%	-46
	08	60	26	54%	35%	-32
	09	20	24	21%	63%	-210
Doumit,Ryan	06	11	15	33%	47%	-122
	07	54	19	53%	47%	-82
	08	71	25	44%	16%	24
	09	47	16	50%	31%	-24
Drew,J.D.	06	79	26	65%	15%	70
	07	57	26	46%	31%	-32
	08	102	23	65%	26%	26
	09	80	27	56%	19%	36
Drew,Stephen	06	46	13	23%	54%	-170
	07	46	27	41%	41%	-82
	08	82	27	59%	26%	14
	09	68	25	44%	24%	-8
Duffy,Chris	06	15	16	19%	38%	-114
	07	40	13	31%	31%	-62
	09	-85	6	0%	83%	-332
Dukes,Elijah	07	54	12	50%	25%	0
	08	74	16	44%	25%	-12
	09	39	23	30%	35%	-80
Duncan,Chris	06	80	18	61%	28%	10
	07	37	24	42%	46%	-100
	08	12	16	31%	50%	-138
	09	18	16	19%	56%	-186
Duncan,Shelley	07	69	11	45%	45%	-90
	08	7	8	25%	63%	-202
	09	-121	5	0%	100%	-400
Dunn,Adam	06	54	27	52%	30%	-16
	07	93	26	54%	31%	-16
	08	77	27	67%	15%	74
	09	62	27	52%	22%	16
Dye,Jermaine	06	102	26	65%	12%	82
	07	67	26	54%	23%	16
	08	89	28	54%	25%	8
	09	45	27	33%	37%	-82
Eckstein,David	06	27	22	27%	18%	-18
	07	56	24	38%	21%	-8
	08	42	24	46%	21%	8
	09	43	25	40%	20%	0
Ellis,A.J.	09	-39	7	0%	43%	-172
Ellis,Mark	06	44	24	38%	29%	-40
	07	61	27	48%	26%	-8
	08	65	23	48%	17%	28
	09	52	19	37%	26%	-30
Ellsbury,Jacoby	07	76	9	56%	22%	24
	08	61	28	39%	39%	-78
	09	68	27	56%	11%	68
Encarnacion,Edwin	06	63	24	42%	25%	-16
	07	46	26	38%	35%	-64
	08	68	27	48%	15%	36
	09	41	18	39%	33%	-54
Erstad,Darin	06	28	11	27%	55%	-166
	07	30	19	26%	32%	-76
	08	-2	26	27%	50%	-146
	09	28	24	33%	58%	-166
Escobar,Alcides	09	15	9	22%	56%	-180
Escobar,Yunel	07	53	19	47%	32%	-34
	08	46	25	40%	32%	-48
	09	62	27	52%	15%	44
Ethier,Andre	06	46	23	39%	39%	-78
	07	54	27	56%	22%	24
	08	89	27	52%	15%	44
	09	88	27	52%	22%	16
Evans,Nick	08	34	16	44%	50%	-112
	09	10	9	33%	44%	-110
Everett,Adam	06	42	27	44%	26%	-16
	07	26	13	38%	46%	-108
	08	49	16	50%	31%	-24
	09	17	27	22%	41%	-120
Everidge,Tommy	09	31	5	40%	60%	-160
Feliz,Pedro	06	45	27	59%	19%	42
	07	54	27	41%	19%	6
	08	48	23	48%	22%	8
	09	38	27	33%	22%	-22
Fielder,Prince	06	57	27	56%	26%	8
	07	119	26	73%	8%	114
	08	70	27	59%	26%	14
	09	107	27	74%	7%	120
Fields,Josh	07	38	18	44%	56%	-136
	08	-143	7	0%	100%	-400
	09	-16	22	23%	73%	-246
Figgins,Chone	06	52	26	42%	31%	-40
	07	50	22	36%	27%	-36
	08	15	23	13%	39%	-130
	09	46	27	33%	33%	-66
Fiorentino,Jeff	06	55	5	40%	20%	0
	09	-45	6	0%	67%	-268
Flores,Jesus	07	-10	27	37%	52%	-134
	08	4	20	25%	55%	-170
	09	36	6	33%	33%	-66
Flowers,Tyler	09	-80	5	20%	80%	-280
Fontenot,Mike	07	42	19	21%	58%	-190
	08	83	26	50%	35%	-40
	09	31	26	38%	46%	-108
Fowler,Dexter	08	-40	5	0%	60%	-240
	09	50	26	42%	38%	-68
Fox,Jake	09	39	20	40%	40%	-80
Francisco,Ben	07	45	11	36%	64%	-184
	08	53	23	35%	26%	-34
	09	68	27	52%	33%	-28
Francoeur,Jeff	06	30	27	37%	30%	-46
	07	32	27	33%	44%	-110
	08	23	27	26%	44%	-124
	09	44	26	46%	27%	-16
Frandsen,Kevin	06	17	14	14%	50%	-172
	07	51	25	48%	32%	-32
	09	15	9	22%	44%	-132

BATTER CONSISTENCY

Name	Yr	BPV	#Wk	DOM	DIS	QC
Freel,Ryan	06	42	25	36%	36%	-72
	07	41	14	43%	43%	-86
	08	24	10	30%	40%	-100
	09	-44	13	0%	85%	-340
Fukudome,Kosuke	08	44	26	23%	38%	-106
	09	62	26	54%	23%	16
Fuld,Sam	07	-131	5	40%	60%	-160
	09	76	14	43%	29%	-30
Furcal,Rafael	06	67	26	35%	15%	10
	07	49	24	38%	8%	44
	08	126	7	86%	14%	116
	09	46	26	35%	31%	-54
Gamel,Mat	09	0	16	25%	69%	-226
Garciaparra,Nomar	06	99	23	74%	4%	132
	07	33	24	25%	25%	-50
	08	95	14	71%	7%	114
	09	13	22	18%	50%	-164
Gardner,Brett	08	14	12	25%	67%	-218
	09	55	21	33%	48%	-126
Garko,Ryan	06	38	10	40%	40%	-80
	07	47	27	44%	22%	0
	08	26	27	41%	44%	-94
	09	40	27	30%	26%	-44
Gathright,Joey	06	12	26	19%	54%	-178
	07	-1	17	18%	59%	-200
	08	6	23	17%	52%	-174
	09	-48	11	27%	64%	-202
Gentry,Craig	09	-14	5	20%	40%	-120
German,Esteban	06	60	27	41%	30%	-38
	07	47	27	44%	33%	-44
	08	35	27	26%	48%	-140
	09	38	8	25%	13%	-2
Gerut,Jody	08	75	20	40%	20%	0
	09	49	27	30%	33%	-72
Getz,Chris	08	0	5	0%	100%	-400
	09	45	24	33%	38%	-86
Giambi,Jason	06	109	27	74%	19%	72
	07	35	18	39%	33%	-54
	08	76	27	67%	30%	14
	09	33	22	36%	18%	0
Giles,Brian	06	72	27	63%	4%	110
	07	63	22	50%	9%	64
	08	86	27	56%	7%	84
	09	26	11	27%	45%	-126
Gimenez,Chris	09	-32	16	25%	63%	-202
Glaus,Troy	06	76	26	62%	19%	48
	07	47	23	48%	39%	-60
	08	69	27	56%	30%	-8
Gload,Ross	06	68	24	38%	38%	-76
	07	62	22	32%	36%	-80
	08	32	25	32%	36%	-80
	09	51	27	44%	37%	-60
Gomes,Jonny	06	41	21	43%	52%	-122
	07	42	24	38%	38%	-76
	08	48	23	43%	52%	-122
	09	67	20	65%	25%	30
Gomez,Carlos	07	-3	12	17%	42%	-134
	08	15	27	33%	48%	-126
	09	28	27	33%	44%	-110
Gonzalez,Adrian	06	45	27	48%	30%	-24
	07	63	27	56%	26%	8
	08	60	27	44%	30%	-32
	09	100	27	67%	15%	74
Gonzalez,Alberto	07	52	6	17%	50%	-166
	08	40	17	35%	35%	-70
	09	42	24	38%	29%	-40
Gonzalez,Alex	06	33	24	38%	33%	-56
	07	51	23	35%	43%	-102
	09	22	23	35%	30%	-50
Gonzalez,Andy	07	-50	21	10%	76%	-284
	08	22	6	17%	83%	-298
	09	-9	6	17%	67%	-234
Gonzalez,Carlos	08	7	17	29%	53%	-154
	09	88	18	56%	33%	-20
Gonzalez,Edgar	08	-2	20	20%	60%	-200
	09	32	21	29%	52%	-150
Gordon,Alex	07	40	27	41%	44%	-94
	08	53	24	46%	33%	-40
	09	22	13	31%	46%	-122
Gorecki,Reid	09	-137	8	0%	100%	-400
Granderson,Curtis	06	37	27	33%	48%	-126
	07	100	27	70%	15%	80
	08	88	24	75%	13%	98
	09	64	27	56%	26%	8
Greene,Khalil	06	50	25	32%	40%	-96
	07	67	27	52%	11%	60
	08	2	18	22%	44%	-132
	09	29	21	33%	52%	-142
Greene,Tyler	09	-24	11	18%	82%	-292
Green,Nick	06	-40	19	26%	74%	-244
	09	6	24	21%	46%	-142
Griffey Jr.,Ken	06	55	21	52%	24%	8
	07	78	25	64%	20%	48
	08	58	27	56%	26%	8
	09	47	27	41%	30%	-38
Gross,Gabe	06	44	26	31%	46%	-122
	07	77	24	50%	38%	-52
	08	50	27	41%	41%	-82
	09	13	27	33%	56%	-158
Guerrero,Vladimir	06	92	26	77%	8%	122
	07	98	26	77%	4%	138
	08	87	26	73%	15%	86
	09	47	18	56%	28%	0
Guillen,Carlos	06	93	27	63%	26%	22
	07	87	27	63%	22%	38
	08	71	22	55%	27%	2
	09	47	17	29%	29%	-58
Guillen,Jose	06	46	15	33%	27%	-42
	07	44	27	44%	30%	-32
	08	46	27	44%	30%	-32
	09	14	16	25%	50%	-150
Gutierrez,Franklin	06	-4	11	27%	45%	-126
	07	48	21	38%	48%	-116
	08	37	27	33%	37%	-82
	09	29	27	37%	33%	-58
Guzman,Cristian	06	62	11	36%	27%	-36
	08	58	26	42%	23%	-8
	09	33	26	31%	50%	-138
Guzman,Jesus	09	-59	7	0%	86%	-344
Gwynn,Tony	06	-15	9	33%	44%	-110
	07	9	18	22%	61%	-200
	08	-1	9	22%	44%	-132
	09	28	21	24%	38%	-104
Hafner,Travis	06	125	22	73%	9%	110
	07	56	27	48%	22%	8
	08	3	13	15%	69%	-246
	09	49	22	41%	27%	-26
Hairston,Jerry	06	0	27	7%	63%	-238
	07	37	21	24%	38%	-104
	08	87	20	50%	25%	0
	09	58	27	41%	41%	-82
Hairston,Scott	06	-4	5	20%	80%	-280
	07	68	23	43%	35%	-54
	08	64	22	45%	41%	-74
	09	59	23	48%	17%	28
Hall,Bill	06	80	27	59%	22%	30
	07	26	24	42%	46%	-100
	08	19	26	27%	50%	-146
	09	-16	27	30%	59%	-176
Hamilton,Josh	07	86	17	71%	24%	46
	08	83	27	63%	22%	38
	09	34	18	28%	39%	-100
Hanigan,Ryan	08	29	8	38%	50%	-124
	09	19	26	23%	42%	-122
Hannahan,Jack	07	25	8	25%	50%	-150
	08	0	26	27%	58%	-178
	09	0	24	33%	58%	-166
Hardy,J.J.	06	26	7	43%	29%	-30
	07	65	27	52%	11%	60
	08	67	27	41%	19%	6
	09	20	25	36%	40%	-88
Harris,Brendan	06	19	10	30%	50%	-140
	07	47	26	38%	35%	-64
	08	25	27	30%	52%	-148
	09	6	27	26%	48%	-140
Harris,Willie	06	33	14	14%	57%	-200
	07	48	23	35%	43%	-102
	08	71	26	42%	35%	-56
	09	74	25	40%	40%	-80
Hart,Corey	06	35	24	33%	46%	-118
	07	99	27	63%	11%	82
	08	77	27	63%	22%	38
	09	49	21	43%	29%	-30
Hawpe,Brad	06	64	27	52%	37%	-44
	07	70	27	63%	19%	50
	08	54	26	50%	35%	-40
	09	69	27	59%	22%	30
Hayes,Brett	09	156	8	25%	50%	-150
Headley,Chase	08	10	16	31%	56%	-162
	09	26	27	30%	37%	-88
Helms,Wes	06	67	27	52%	33%	-28
	07	3	27	26%	59%	-184
	08	-17	26	27%	62%	-194
	09	-18	27	19%	67%	-230
Helton,Todd	06	86	26	69%	15%	78
	07	82	27	74%	11%	104
	08	42	16	31%	25%	-38
	09	72	26	62%	15%	64
Hermida,Jeremy	06	18	21	10%	43%	-152
	07	52	21	62%	24%	28
	08	27	26	23%	42%	-122
	09	20	23	26%	57%	-176
Hernandez,Andrsn	06	-11	9	33%	56%	-158
	08	25	7	29%	43%	-114
	09	24	26	35%	54%	-146
Hernandez,Diory	09	-31	11	9%	82%	-310
Hernandez,Luis	07	-1	9	11%	33%	-110
	08	-9	9	0%	56%	-224
	09	-63	13	8%	77%	-292
Hernandez,Michel	09	32	17	18%	41%	-128
Hernandez,Ramon	06	66	26	50%	19%	24
	07	28	22	36%	41%	-92
	08	43	27	44%	26%	-16
	09	40	17	41%	29%	-34
Hester,John	09	30	6	50%	50%	-100
Hill,Aaron	06	40	27	41%	19%	6
	07	59	26	50%	27%	-8
	08	31	9	33%	44%	-110
	09	71	27	48%	11%	52
Hill,Koyie	07	4	12	17%	50%	-166
	09	-26	26	23%	73%	-246
Hinske,Eric	06	53	27	44%	41%	-76
	07	58	27	41%	48%	-110
	08	71	27	52%	33%	-28
	09	38	27	41%	52%	-126
Hoffpauir,Micah	08	43	11	36%	55%	-148
	09	50	23	43%	30%	-34
Holliday,Matt	06	95	27	70%	19%	64
	07	105	27	63%	11%	82
	08	97	24	58%	21%	32
	09	83	27	52%	19%	28
Howard,Ryan	06	87	27	63%	22%	38
	07	82	26	69%	23%	46
	08	78	27	48%	33%	-36
	09	92	26	58%	15%	56
Hudson,Orlando	06	72	27	52%	15%	44
	07	64	23	52%	30%	-16
	08	62	19	47%	26%	-10
	09	54	27	37%	30%	-46
Huff,Aubrey	06	64	25	60%	28%	8
	07	55	26	54%	23%	16
	08	103	27	70%	19%	64
	09	34	27	37%	37%	-74
Hulett,Tug	08	-68	9	22%	78%	-268
	09	-75	7	0%	86%	-344
Hundley,Nick	08	-11	14	7%	50%	-186
	09	28	20	30%	50%	-140
Hunter,Torii	06	62	25	40%	16%	16
	07	84	27	70%	19%	64
	08	71	27	48%	11%	52
	09	70	22	55%	27%	2
Hu,Chin-lung	07	48	6	17%	33%	-98
	08	4	15	27%	60%	-186
Iannetta,Chris	06	21	5	40%	20%	0
	07	4	24	21%	54%	-174
	08	69	27	56%	33%	-20
	09	61	24	54%	42%	-60
Ibanez,Raul	06	72	27	67%	15%	74
	07	61	25	44%	28%	-24
	08	63	27	44%	37%	-60
	09	99	25	56%	20%	32
Infante,Omar	06	39	25	28%	48%	-136
	07	17	24	29%	58%	-174
	08	50	20	45%	20%	10
	09	28	16	38%	31%	-48
Inge,Brandon	06	54	27	52%	22%	16
	07	13	27	33%	52%	-142
	08	34	26	27%	38%	-98
	09	3	27	26%	63%	-200
Inglett,Joe	06	22	16	25%	38%	-102
	08	58	25	44%	20%	8
	09	-3	16	31%	54%	-200
Iribarren,Hernan	09	14	5	40%	60%	-160
Ishikawa,Travis	06	45	5	40%	40%	-80
	08	17	8	38%	50%	-124
	09	1	26	15%	54%	-186
Iwamura,Akinori	07	34	23	35%	35%	-70
	08	27	27	26%	44%	-124
	09	36	14	21%	21%	-42

BATTER CONSISTENCY

Name	Yr	BPV	#Wk	DOM	DIS	QC
Izturis,Cesar	06	33	11	45%	36%	-54
	07	41	27	33%	22%	-22
	08	47	25	32%	16%	0
	09	37	22	50%	41%	-64
Izturis,Maicer	06	76	22	59%	23%	26
	07	59	21	38%	19%	0
	08	62	19	47%	32%	-34
	09	75	26	58%	23%	24
Jackson,Conor	06	47	27	44%	22%	0
	07	79	27	52%	26%	0
	08	81	26	58%	19%	40
	09	20	6	17%	17%	-34
Jacobs,Mike	06	54	26	50%	27%	-8
	07	42	23	39%	39%	-78
	08	72	27	44%	22%	0
	09	0	27	26%	52%	-156
Janish,Paul	08	-33	11	27%	64%	-202
	09	41	27	33%	26%	-38
Jaramillo,Jason	09	29	22	32%	55%	-156
Jeter,Derek	06	66	27	48%	15%	36
	07	52	27	52%	22%	16
	08	43	26	35%	27%	-38
	09	56	27	41%	26%	-22
Johjima,Kenji	06	60	27	52%	26%	0
	07	52	26	42%	15%	24
	08	42	27	37%	37%	-74
	09	48	22	36%	45%	-108
Johnson,Kelly	06	65	27	37%	30%	-46
	08	59	27	44%	22%	0
	09	71	25	48%	40%	-64
Johnson,Nick	06	96	25	72%	4%	128
	08	78	7	71%	14%	86
	09	41	26	46%	31%	-32
Johnson,Reed	06	60	26	54%	12%	60
	07	8	16	19%	63%	-214
	08	21	26	31%	46%	-122
	09	60	18	39%	39%	-78
Johnson,Rob	08	-25	5	0%	60%	-240
	09	14	27	30%	52%	-148
Jones,Adam	06	-26	10	10%	70%	-260
	07	21	10	40%	60%	-160
	08	27	23	22%	52%	-164
	09	56	22	36%	36%	-72
Jones,Andruw	06	79	27	52%	33%	-28
	07	48	26	35%	42%	-98
	08	-41	15	13%	73%	-266
	09	74	25	48%	44%	-80
Jones,Chipper	06	107	23	65%	9%	94
	07	124	25	80%	12%	112
	08	98	26	54%	12%	60
	09	66	27	63%	37%	-22
Jones,Garrett	07	4	11	27%	45%	-126
	09	96	15	53%	20%	26
Kapler,Gabe	06	44	17	35%	53%	-142
	08	76	24	50%	29%	0
	09	76	27	41%	37%	-66
Kata,Matt	07	23	22	27%	36%	-90
	09	-11	11	0%	55%	-220
Kearns,Austin	06	53	26	58%	27%	8
	07	41	27	41%	26%	-22
	08	9	16	31%	50%	-138
	09	1	18	17%	67%	-234
Kelly,Don	07	-15	12	0%	25%	-100
	09	27	11	27%	45%	-126
Kemp,Matt	06	26	13	31%	54%	-154
	07	47	20	35%	40%	-90
	08	52	27	44%	33%	-44
	09	64	27	48%	22%	8
Kendall,Jason	06	30	27	30%	26%	-44
	07	30	27	33%	41%	-98
	08	52	27	37%	15%	14
	09	29	27	33%	33%	-66
Kendrick,Howie	06	42	14	36%	29%	-44
	07	36	16	38%	31%	-48
	08	40	19	32%	47%	-124
	09	47	25	44%	20%	8
Kennedy,Adam	06	42	27	41%	26%	-22
	07	29	19	26%	42%	-116
	08	47	27	30%	48%	-132
	09	42	23	26%	35%	-88
Keppinger,Jeff	06	50	6	67%	17%	66
	07	90	16	69%	6%	114
	08	56	21	38%	5%	56
	09	53	26	35%	31%	-54
Kinsler,Ian	06	68	22	68%	18%	64
	07	79	23	57%	22%	26
	08	107	21	57%	5%	94
	09	110	26	69%	8%	106

BATTER CONSISTENCY

Name	Yr	BPV	#Wk	DOM	DIS	QC
Konerko,Paul	06	71	26	50%	19%	24
	07	73	27	56%	19%	36
	08	66	24	58%	21%	32
	09	68	26	54%	23%	16
Kotchman,Casey	06	-4	6	17%	67%	-234
	07	88	26	65%	23%	38
	08	66	26	58%	12%	68
	09	44	26	42%	23%	-8
Kotsay,Mark	06	53	27	41%	15%	22
	07	43	12	42%	42%	-84
	08	57	23	39%	35%	-62
	09	39	18	39%	28%	-34
Kottaras,George	09	33	22	36%	50%	-128
Kouzmanoff,Kevin	06	21	5	40%	60%	-160
	07	45	27	41%	37%	-66
	08	27	27	41%	44%	-94
	09	31	25	28%	40%	-104
Kubel,Jason	06	17	21	14%	52%	-180
	07	64	27	44%	22%	0
	08	60	27	52%	41%	-60
	09	71	27	56%	22%	24
Laird,Gerald	06	51	27	48%	48%	-96
	07	13	26	35%	50%	-130
	08	30	22	32%	18%	-8
	09	33	27	22%	41%	-120
Langerhans,Ryan	06	11	27	41%	48%	-110
	07	-10	24	17%	71%	-250
	08	49	18	50%	39%	-56
	09	30	12	25%	58%	-182
LaPorta,Matt	09	52	12	50%	25%	0
Larish,Jeff	08	-19	12	25%	58%	-182
	09	51	9	33%	56%	-158
LaRoche,Adam	06	71	26	62%	15%	64
	07	43	27	37%	37%	-74
	08	65	26	46%	35%	-48
	09	55	27	52%	41%	-60
LaRoche,Andy	07	9	9	22%	56%	-180
	08	12	17	24%	41%	-116
	09	52	27	48%	26%	-8
LaRue,Jason	06	8	24	29%	63%	-194
	07	-33	25	20%	60%	-200
	08	49	25	44%	40%	-72
	09	-15	25	20%	56%	-184
Lee,Carlos	06	104	26	73%	8%	114
	07	99	27	70%	0%	140
	08	103	19	74%	5%	128
	09	79	27	67%	7%	106
Lee,Derrek	06	48	12	33%	42%	-102
	07	67	27	52%	19%	28
	08	65	27	52%	26%	0
	09	97	27	70%	15%	80
Lewis,Fred	06	-7	5	20%	60%	-200
	07	42	15	40%	33%	-52
	08	49	24	38%	38%	-76
	09	30	26	42%	42%	-84
Lillibridge,Brent	08	22	13	31%	54%	-154
	09	-40	16	13%	69%	-250
Lind,Adam	06	79	6	67%	33%	2
	07	21	18	28%	50%	-144
	08	46	18	39%	39%	-78
	09	82	26	65%	15%	70
Loney,James	06	118	13	62%	31%	0
	07	70	17	47%	35%	-46
	08	57	27	52%	26%	0
	09	54	27	44%	26%	-16
Longoria,Evan	08	83	22	45%	45%	-90
	09	80	27	44%	22%	0
Lopez,Felipe	06	33	27	26%	37%	-96
	07	34	27	26%	30%	-68
	08	33	27	33%	33%	-66
	09	43	27	44%	26%	-16
Lopez,Jose	06	44	27	30%	37%	-88
	07	26	27	22%	41%	-120
	08	60	27	48%	15%	36
	09	65	27	56%	15%	52
Loretta,Mark	06	34	27	37%	37%	-74
	07	42	27	26%	37%	-96
	08	38	27	33%	30%	-54
	09	17	27	30%	33%	-72
Lowell,Mike	06	80	27	63%	15%	66
	07	72	27	59%	26%	14
	08	66	23	52%	30%	-16
	09	63	24	50%	21%	16
Lowrie,Jed	08	41	17	29%	47%	-130
	09	-29	10	20%	60%	-200
Ludwick,Ryan	07	54	22	50%	27%	-8
	08	100	27	67%	22%	46
	09	40	26	35%	50%	-130

BATTER CONSISTENCY

Name	Yr	BPV	#Wk	DOM	DIS	QC
Lugo,Julio	06	53	24	42%	33%	-48
	07	58	27	41%	30%	-38
	08	10	16	6%	56%	-212
	09	58	23	48%	39%	-60
Macias,Drew	08	44	15	40%	40%	-80
	09	35	15	47%	33%	-38
Maier,Mitch	08	-35	9	0%	56%	-224
	09	15	26	23%	54%	-170
Markakis,Nick	06	54	26	35%	31%	-54
	07	74	26	62%	12%	76
	08	76	27	59%	19%	42
	09	59	27	52%	22%	16
Marson,Lou	09	1	7	29%	43%	-114
Marte,Andy	06	51	11	45%	45%	-90
	07	19	8	38%	25%	-24
	08	-4	24	13%	71%	-258
	09	35	11	36%	45%	-108
Martinez,Fernando	09	36	6	33%	50%	-134
Martinez,Victor	06	51	26	50%	23%	8
	07	74	25	64%	8%	96
	08	29	16	31%	19%	-14
	09	67	27	67%	19%	58
Martin,Russell	06	68	22	59%	14%	62
	07	75	27	59%	22%	30
	08	53	27	48%	22%	8
	09	24	26	27%	38%	-98
Mathis,Jeff	06	16	10	30%	30%	-60
	07	9	13	31%	62%	-186
	08	-18	26	27%	73%	-238
	09	-32	27	19%	67%	-230
Matsui,Hideki	06	77	10	70%	20%	60
	07	90	24	63%	8%	94
	08	40	18	39%	28%	-34
	09	73	27	56%	7%	84
Matsui,Kaz	06	31	15	27%	27%	-54
	07	63	21	48%	14%	40
	08	73	20	55%	15%	50
	09	32	25	24%	40%	-112
Matthews Jr.,Gary	06	75	25	56%	8%	80
	07	60	26	50%	19%	24
	08	23	27	22%	44%	-132
	09	22	27	30%	44%	-116
Mauer,Joe	06	89	27	74%	7%	120
	07	74	21	52%	10%	64
	08	73	27	63%	19%	50
	09	94	24	67%	13%	82
Maxwell,Justin	07	13	5	20%	40%	-120
	09	41	10	30%	70%	-220
Mayberry,John	09	30	12	33%	50%	-134
Maybin,Cameron	07	-8	8	25%	63%	-202
	09	31	12	50%	50%	-100
Maysonet,Edwin	09	-40	14	7%	71%	-270
McCann,Brian	06	87	26	50%	15%	40
	07	54	26	50%	23%	8
	08	102	27	67%	19%	58
	09	75	26	58%	19%	40
McCutchen,Andrew	09	84	19	63%	16%	62
McDonald,Darnell	09	1	13	23%	62%	-202
McDonald,John	06	28	25	16%	44%	-144
	07	28	26	27%	42%	-114
	08	16	23	22%	57%	-184
	09	29	27	15%	56%	-194
McGehee,Casey	09	56	27	37%	44%	-102
McLouth,Nate	06	46	19	37%	32%	-54
	07	80	27	48%	41%	-68
	08	111	27	67%	11%	90
	09	70	25	56%	12%	64
Michaels,Jason	06	32	25	36%	32%	-56
	07	29	27	37%	44%	-102
	08	20	27	33%	56%	-158
	09	53	26	38%	54%	-140
Mientkiewicz,Doug	06	51	17	41%	24%	-14
	07	59	14	50%	29%	-16
	08	60	27	44%	33%	-44
	09	-73	8	13%	88%	-326
Miles,Aaron	06	43	27	41%	26%	-22
	07	25	27	37%	37%	-74
	08	36	27	30%	30%	-60
	09	24	19	16%	53%	-180
Millar,Kevin	06	51	26	54%	27%	0
	07	49	27	44%	33%	-44
	08	44	27	44%	30%	-32
	09	26	25	40%	44%	-96
Milledge,Lastings	06	11	14	14%	57%	-200
	07	38	15	27%	20%	-26
	08	43	24	25%	33%	-82
	09	5	13	23%	54%	-170

Name	Yr	BPV	#Wk	DOM	DIS	QC
Miller,Corky	07	40	8	38%	38%	-76
	08	-50	19	21%	63%	-210
	09	-18	15	27%	47%	-134
Moeller,Chad	06	-38	14	14%	64%	-228
	07	-56	16	6%	56%	-212
	08	13	19	26%	42%	-116
	09	53	15	47%	53%	-118
Molina,Bengie	06	53	26	58%	27%	8
	07	39	26	35%	19%	-6
	08	57	27	44%	22%	0
	09	45	26	46%	31%	-32
Molina,Jose	06	11	26	31%	50%	-138
	07	-9	26	23%	58%	-186
	08	6	27	30%	48%	-132
	09	-21	19	32%	63%	-188
Molina,Yadier	06	34	27	37%	30%	-46
	07	26	22	32%	50%	-136
	08	36	26	35%	19%	-6
	09	52	27	44%	33%	-44
Monroe,Craig	06	60	27	56%	26%	8
	07	6	27	30%	52%	-148
	08	31	18	39%	50%	-122
	09	-8	11	18%	55%	-184
Montanez,Lou	08	37	10	30%	50%	-140
	09	2	8	25%	50%	-150
Montero,Miguel	07	42	27	44%	37%	-60
	08	41	24	38%	58%	-156
	09	53	27	52%	26%	0
Morales,Jose	09	-8	17	29%	53%	-154
Morales,Kendry	06	45	13	46%	31%	-32
	07	49	18	33%	44%	-110
	08	59	7	29%	43%	-114
	09	80	27	59%	19%	42
Mora,Melvin	06	37	27	30%	37%	-88
	07	47	24	42%	21%	0
	08	73	26	54%	27%	0
	09	23	26	19%	35%	-102
Morgan,Nyjer	07	43	6	50%	33%	-32
	08	24	14	21%	50%	-158
	09	39	21	29%	29%	-58
Morneau,Justin	06	81	27	74%	7%	120
	07	79	27	59%	22%	30
	08	83	27	56%	15%	52
	09	82	23	61%	13%	70
Morse,Mike	06	43	11	18%	64%	-220
	07	8	5	20%	80%	-280
	09	23	8	38%	38%	-76
Moss,Brandon	07	57	7	43%	57%	-142
	08	33	18	33%	50%	-134
	09	23	27	41%	44%	-94
Murphy,Daniel	08	57	10	50%	50%	-100
	09	68	27	52%	30%	-16
Murphy,David	06	58	6	33%	50%	-134
	07	83	11	55%	27%	2
	08	76	19	68%	21%	52
	09	41	27	44%	41%	-76
Murton,Matt	06	55	27	52%	26%	0
	07	48	22	36%	32%	-56
	08	-26	9	11%	67%	-246
	09	35	11	27%	64%	-202
Nady,Xavier	06	39	25	44%	36%	-56
	07	39	27	33%	44%	-110
	08	62	26	58%	15%	56
Napoli,Mike	06	43	22	50%	45%	-80
	07	51	21	43%	43%	-86
	08	97	22	59%	23%	26
	09	48	27	44%	33%	-44
Navarro,Dioner	06	9	19	26%	37%	-96
	07	38	27	30%	37%	-88
	08	37	24	63%	25%	26
	09	27	26	27%	46%	-130
Nelson,Brad	09	-151	6	0%	100%	-400
Nieves,Wil	06	-65	5	0%	60%	-240
	07	9	14	7%	50%	-186
	08	10	23	26%	43%	-120
	09	-27	25	16%	72%	-256
Nix,Jayson	08	-57	6	0%	83%	-332
	09	40	23	39%	39%	-78
Nix,Laynce	06	-109	6	0%	100%	-400
	09	61	26	50%	35%	-40
Norton,Greg	06	51	24	50%	42%	-68
	07	-2	21	38%	52%	-132
	08	45	25	48%	28%	-16
	09	-39	23	22%	65%	-216
Oeltjen,Trent	09	80	6	33%	33%	-66
Ojeda,Augie	07	40	17	29%	41%	-106
	08	29	27	30%	33%	-72
	09	63	27	33%	19%	-10

Name	Yr	BPV	#Wk	DOM	DIS	QC
Olivo,Miguel	06	19	26	31%	58%	-170
	07	12	26	27%	58%	-178
	08	33	25	36%	52%	-136
	09	42	26	38%	42%	-92
Ordonez,Magglio	06	51	27	48%	11%	52
	07	105	27	81%	11%	118
	08	61	25	48%	20%	16
	09	41	27	30%	30%	-60
Orr,Pete	06	4	26	23%	46%	-138
	07	-35	20	5%	65%	-250
	08	-14	15	13%	60%	-214
	09	2	7	29%	71%	-226
Ortiz,David	06	129	27	89%	7%	150
	07	127	27	67%	19%	58
	08	97	21	67%	24%	38
	09	54	27	44%	37%	-60
Overbay,Lyle	06	69	27	59%	30%	-2
	07	52	22	36%	36%	-72
	08	37	24	44%	33%	-44
	09	60	27	52%	41%	-60
Padilla,Jorge	09	-93	10	10%	70%	-260
Pagan,Angel	06	49	17	29%	29%	-58
	07	58	14	43%	36%	-58
	08	44	7	43%	57%	-142
	09	79	18	61%	17%	54
Parra,Gerardo	09	24	22	32%	45%	-116
Patterson,Corey	06	58	26	46%	31%	-32
	07	56	23	52%	22%	16
	08	54	27	33%	41%	-98
	09	-156	8	0%	88%	-352
Patterson,Eric	08	-19	12	8%	67%	-252
	09	20	11	18%	64%	-220
Paulino,Ronny	06	-7	24	17%	46%	-150
	07	27	27	41%	37%	-66
	08	-6	13	15%	46%	-154
	09	30	27	26%	67%	-216
Pearce,Steve	07	45	6	50%	50%	-100
	08	35	12	33%	50%	-134
	09	41	15	53%	33%	-26
Pedroia,Dustin	06	42	7	43%	29%	-30
	07	76	27	63%	11%	82
	08	101	28	68%	7%	108
	09	95	27	78%	4%	140
Pena,Brayan	06	40	8	50%	25%	0
	07	9	9	11%	67%	-246
	08	26	5	20%	0%	40
	09	55	22	50%	27%	-8
Pena,Carlos	06	-2	6	33%	50%	-134
	07	119	27	70%	19%	64
	08	59	24	54%	29%	-8
	09	89	23	48%	26%	-8
Pena,Ramiro	09	27	21	19%	57%	-190
Pena,Tony	06	12	13	23%	54%	-170
	07	22	27	22%	44%	-132
	08	-28	26	4%	62%	-240
	09	-64	11	18%	55%	-184
Pence,Hunter	07	73	21	57%	19%	38
	08	60	27	52%	26%	0
	09	63	27	44%	15%	28
Pennington,Cliff	08	12	8	25%	50%	-150
	09	37	11	36%	36%	-72
Peralta,Jhonny	06	3	27	19%	56%	-186
	07	25	26	31%	42%	-106
	08	66	27	56%	30%	-8
	09	2	27	26%	59%	-184
Perez,Fernando	08	57	5	60%	0%	120
	09	-100	6	0%	83%	-332
Petit,Gregorio	08	-44	7	14%	71%	-256
	09	-45	5	0%	60%	-240
Pettit,Chris	09	-21	5	0%	80%	-320
Phillips,Brandon	06	50	26	42%	19%	8
	07	74	26	58%	23%	24
	08	72	24	50%	21%	16
	09	78	27	59%	19%	42
Phillips,Paul	06	14	9	22%	67%	-224
	07	53	5	20%	40%	-120
	09	59	10	40%	40%	-80
Pierre,Juan	06	74	27	67%	7%	106
	07	62	27	48%	11%	52
	08	49	25	32%	24%	-32
	09	72	27	44%	22%	0
Pierzynski,A.J.	06	34	27	22%	22%	-44
	07	37	26	27%	23%	-38
	08	39	27	48%	30%	-24
	09	38	26	42%	35%	-56
Pie,Felix	07	32	18	22%	56%	-180
	08	-37	10	20%	70%	-240
	09	35	25	32%	56%	-160

Name	Yr	BPV	#Wk	DOM	DIS	QC
Podsednik,Scott	06	41	26	31%	35%	-78
	07	60	16	38%	31%	-48
	08	35	24	29%	54%	-158
	09	50	24	38%	33%	-56
Polanco,Placido	06	35	23	39%	26%	-26
	07	76	27	52%	4%	88
	08	67	26	54%	19%	32
	09	61	27	59%	26%	14
Posada,Jorge	06	68	27	56%	30%	-8
	07	79	26	50%	19%	24
	08	34	11	36%	45%	-108
	09	55	24	50%	29%	-16
Powell,Landon	09	30	25	40%	44%	-96
Prado,Martin	06	30	7	57%	43%	-58
	07	10	9	33%	56%	-158
	08	77	20	45%	25%	-10
	09	60	27	48%	19%	20
Pujols,Albert	06	147	25	88%	4%	160
	07	108	27	74%	11%	104
	08	145	26	92%	0%	184
	09	163	27	85%	7%	142
Punto,Nick	06	44	27	44%	30%	-32
	07	14	27	15%	44%	-146
	08	42	22	36%	41%	-92
	09	18	26	31%	46%	-122
Quentin,Carlos	06	94	12	58%	8%	84
	07	21	19	32%	47%	-124
	08	114	23	87%	0%	174
	09	70	20	50%	25%	0
Quinlan,Robb	06	54	26	42%	38%	-68
	07	29	26	35%	42%	-98
	08	-3	24	21%	54%	-174
	09	-21	26	15%	65%	-230
Quintanilla,Omar	06	-10	6	17%	50%	-166
	07	-21	8	38%	63%	-176
	08	13	21	33%	62%	-182
	09	-110	24	13%	79%	-290
Quintero,Humberto	06	20	6	33%	50%	-134
	07	-58	12	0%	83%	-332
	08	-21	16	6%	81%	-312
	09	-2	25	24%	44%	-128
Raburn,Ryan	07	74	14	36%	43%	-100
	08	17	26	31%	46%	-122
	09	70	25	48%	40%	-64
Ramirez,Alexei	08	70	27	44%	19%	12
	09	42	27	41%	33%	-50
Ramirez,Aramis	06	105	27	78%	4%	140
	07	90	26	62%	15%	64
	08	92	27	52%	22%	16
	09	71	18	50%	28%	-12
Ramirez,Hanley	06	79	27	52%	26%	0
	07	110	27	78%	11%	112
	08	105	26	65%	15%	70
	09	83	26	62%	27%	16
Ramirez,Manny	06	100	24	67%	21%	50
	07	66	24	50%	25%	0
	08	97	27	59%	26%	14
	09	84	19	68%	16%	72
Ramirez,Max	08	-8	8	25%	63%	-202
Ramirez,Wilkin	09	159	7	43%	43%	-86
Ransom,Cody	07	38	5	40%	60%	-160
	08	113	8	50%	50%	-100
	09	35	9	44%	56%	-136
Rasmus,Colby	09	39	27	33%	48%	-126
Reddick,Josh	09	1	9	22%	56%	-180
Redmond,Mike	06	20	26	31%	42%	-106
	07	20	21	19%	52%	-170
	08	14	22	18%	45%	-144
	09	2	22	27%	50%	-146
Reed,Jeremy	06	55	14	36%	29%	-44
	08	31	19	42%	32%	-44
	09	-16	27	22%	59%	-192
Reimold,Nolan	09	56	19	53%	26%	2
Renteria,Edgar	06	61	26	54%	19%	32
	07	55	23	43%	26%	-18
	08	45	27	44%	33%	-44
	09	24	25	25%	42%	-118
Repko,Jason	06	42	17	29%	41%	-106
	08	-103	6	17%	67%	-234
	09	-157	6	0%	67%	-268
Reyes,Jose	06	94	26	77%	12%	106
	07	91	27	74%	7%	120
	08	102	27	70%	4%	124
	09	67	7	57%	14%	58
Reynolds,Mark	07	33	21	43%	52%	-122
	08	45	27	30%	52%	-148
	09	76	27	63%	22%	38
Richard,Chris	09	-106	5	0%	80%	-320

BATTER CONSISTENCY

Name	Yr	BPV	#Wk	DOM	DIS	QC
Riggans,Shawn	06	-35	5	20%	80%	-280
	08	39	23	30%	43%	-112
	09	38	5	20%	40%	-120
Rios,Alex	06	81	24	54%	33%	-24
	07	90	27	70%	11%	96
	08	76	27	41%	26%	-22
	09	45	27	41%	37%	-66
Rivera,Juan	06	68	24	54%	13%	56
	08	63	25	28%	44%	-120
	09	63	26	54%	12%	60
Rivera,Mike	06	14	17	57%	36%	-30
	08	50	17	35%	35%	-70
	09	-1	23	17%	61%	-210
Roberts,Brian	06	72	24	63%	8%	94
	07	79	26	65%	8%	98
	08	87	27	63%	15%	66
	09	76	27	63%	19%	50
Roberts,Ryan	07	-165	5	0%	100%	-400
	09	52	24	29%	50%	-142
Rodriguez,Alex	06	75	26	62%	12%	76
	07	135	27	70%	11%	96
	08	101	25	60%	24%	24
	09	84	23	57%	26%	10
Rodriguez,Ivan	06	44	27	44%	30%	-32
	07	23	26	23%	50%	-154
	08	40	27	41%	41%	-82
	09	15	26	31%	46%	-122
Rodriguez,Luis	06	16	24	25%	42%	-118
	07	40	23	30%	22%	-28
	08	43	14	36%	14%	16
	09	27	23	22%	52%	-164
Rodriguez,Sean	08	-13	15	13%	73%	-266
	09	30	6	17%	50%	-166
Rohlinger,Ryan	08	2	8	0%	50%	-200
	09	-71	6	17%	67%	-234
Rolen,Scott	06	96	27	74%	4%	132
	07	55	22	27%	32%	-74
	08	71	22	45%	23%	-2
	09	67	25	56%	20%	32
Rollins,Jimmy	06	102	27	74%	0%	148
	07	119	27	78%	0%	156
	08	107	24	67%	4%	118
	09	94	26	58%	12%	68
Romero,Alex	08	45	22	32%	45%	-116
	09	27	15	27%	33%	-78
Rosales,Adam	08	-15	8	13%	50%	-174
	09	14	22	23%	59%	-190
Ross,Cody	06	37	24	38%	46%	-108
	07	123	17	82%	12%	116
	08	69	27	48%	22%	8
	09	53	25	52%	32%	-24
Ross,David	06	82	25	68%	24%	40
	07	10	25	28%	56%	-168
	08	18	20	25%	65%	-210
	09	53	22	41%	36%	-62
Rowand,Aaron	06	47	20	45%	25%	-10
	07	65	27	44%	26%	-16
	08	17	27	30%	44%	-116
	09	25	27	33%	41%	-98
Ruiz,Carlos	06	45	11	36%	36%	-72
	07	68	27	48%	15%	36
	08	37	26	35%	31%	-54
	09	81	24	58%	21%	32
Ruiz,Randy	08	-45	8	13%	88%	-326
	09	87	9	56%	33%	-20
Ryal,Rusty	09	107	8	38%	50%	-124
Ryan,Brendan	07	60	17	41%	29%	-34
	08	16	21	29%	48%	-134
	09	49	25	52%	36%	-40
Ryan,Dusty	08	14	5	40%	60%	-160
	09	-107	7	14%	86%	-316
Salazar,Jeff	06	23	5	40%	40%	-80
	07	35	11	27%	55%	-166
	08	6	22	36%	64%	-184
	09	-77	7	14%	71%	-256
Salazar,Oscar	08	74	8	50%	38%	-52
	09	72	18	39%	44%	-98
Saltalamacchia,J	07	12	23	30%	52%	-148
	08	-25	19	21%	58%	-190
	09	-26	20	15%	70%	-250
Sammons,Clint	08	-46	10	10%	70%	-260
	09	-80	5	0%	100%	-400
Sanchez,Freddy	06	61	27	48%	15%	36
	07	47	25	40%	28%	-32
	08	32	27	19%	22%	-50
	09	39	23	39%	43%	-94
Sanchez,Gaby	09	73	8	25%	38%	-102

BATTER CONSISTENCY

Name	Yr	BPV	#Wk	DOM	DIS	QC
Sandoval,Pablo	08	60	8	50%	38%	-52
	09	92	27	67%	19%	58
Santiago,Ramon	06	-13	21	10%	62%	-228
	07	48	8	38%	38%	-76
	08	92	21	48%	43%	-76
	09	0	27	19%	56%	-186
Santos,Omir	08	-81	5	0%	40%	-160
	09	28	25	32%	32%	-64
Sardinha,Dane	08	-45	10	10%	80%	-300
	09	-157	8	0%	100%	-400
Saunders,Michael	09	-53	12	8%	67%	-252
Scales,Bobby	09	34	12	25%	58%	-182
Schafer,Jordan	09	-42	9	22%	78%	-268
Schierholtz,Nate	07	19	10	30%	60%	-180
	08	88	5	60%	20%	40
	09	32	25	32%	52%	-144
Schneider,Brian	06	1	26	15%	46%	-154
	07	31	26	27%	50%	-146
	08	18	26	23%	54%	-170
	09	38	21	43%	38%	-66
Schumaker,Skip	06	20	9	22%	33%	-88
	07	49	18	44%	33%	-44
	08	56	27	30%	26%	-44
	09	38	27	37%	19%	-2
Scott,Luke	06	106	13	69%	31%	14
	07	86	27	56%	26%	8
	08	65	27	63%	30%	6
	09	55	26	46%	42%	-76
Scutaro,Marco	06	54	26	38%	27%	-32
	07	39	26	35%	23%	-22
	08	42	27	26%	30%	-68
	09	65	25	48%	12%	48
Sheffield,Gary	06	62	9	33%	22%	-22
	07	95	26	64%	32%	0
	08	52	24	38%	33%	-56
	09	66	22	59%	32%	-10
Shoppach,Kelly	06	-49	20	25%	70%	-230
	07	28	26	50%	42%	-68
	08	53	27	37%	48%	-118
	09	0	26	35%	54%	-146
Sizemore,Grady	06	102	27	63%	11%	82
	07	67	27	59%	22%	30
	08	103	27	70%	22%	52
	09	70	19	63%	26%	22
Smith,Jason	06	-9	15	27%	67%	-214
	07	-13	20	30%	60%	-180
	08	-54	9	22%	67%	-224
	09	-141	6	0%	67%	-268
Smith,Seth	08	49	17	41%	47%	-106
	09	86	27	70%	30%	20
Snider,Travis	08	7	6	17%	33%	-98
	09	18	15	27%	40%	-106
Snyder,Chris	06	15	26	31%	58%	-170
	07	42	26	38%	35%	-64
	08	49	24	42%	33%	-48
	09	13	15	33%	60%	-174
Soriano,Alfonso	06	92	27	63%	19%	50
	07	92	25	44%	8%	56
	08	88	21	62%	19%	48
	09	43	22	41%	36%	-62
Soto,Geovany	07	88	7	43%	29%	-30
	08	59	26	50%	23%	8
	09	36	24	38%	54%	-140
Span,Denard	08	70	17	56%	24%	34
	09	46	26	42%	38%	-68
Spilborghs,Ryan	06	46	17	41%	41%	-82
	07	65	20	50%	35%	-40
	08	70	20	50%	35%	-40
	09	51	27	52%	37%	-44
Stairs,Matt	06	25	25	48%	28%	-16
	07	98	26	54%	27%	0
	08	18	27	41%	33%	-50
	09	31	27	37%	52%	-134
Stavinoha,Nick	08	-47	8	0%	75%	-300
	09	35	10	40%	30%	-40
Stewart,Ian	07	-19	8	25%	50%	-150
	08	28	17	35%	53%	-142
	09	59	27	48%	48%	-96
Stinnett,Kelly	06	-84	19	11%	84%	-314
	07	-38	9	22%	78%	-268
Stubbs,Drew	09	31	8	13%	38%	-126
Sullivan,Cory	06	24	27	22%	48%	-148
	07	21	17	24%	59%	-188
	08	-4	5	20%	60%	-200
	09	54	11	27%	55%	-166
Sutton,Drew	09	17	15	40%	33%	-52

BATTER CONSISTENCY

Name	Yr	BPV	#Wk	DOM	DIS	QC
Suzuki,Ichiro	06	60	27	52%	7%	76
	07	47	27	33%	26%	-38
	08	55	27	33%	19%	-10
	09	51	26	38%	31%	-48
Suzuki,Kurt	07	41	17	53%	29%	-10
	08	25	28	29%	39%	-98
	09	64	27	63%	26%	22
Sweeney,Mike	06	45	13	46%	31%	-32
	07	50	18	50%	22%	12
	08	57	11	64%	27%	20
	09	46	25	48%	36%	-48
Sweeney,Ryan	06	-76	6	0%	100%	-400
	08	32	26	27%	42%	-114
	09	45	25	32%	40%	-96
Swisher,Nick	06	60	27	56%	22%	24
	07	60	27	52%	30%	-16
	08	44	27	33%	48%	-126
	09	74	27	56%	26%	8
Tatis,Fernando	06	74	12	58%	25%	16
	08	53	19	58%	32%	-12
	09	58	26	42%	31%	-40
Tatum,Craig	09	-8	11	18%	45%	-144
Taveras,Willy	06	20	27	41%	41%	-82
	07	27	22	27%	41%	-110
	08	24	26	31%	50%	-138
	09	18	22	18%	45%	-144
Teagarden,Taylor	08	191	6	67%	33%	2
	09	-18	27	33%	52%	-142
Teahen,Mark	06	85	20	55%	35%	-30
	07	34	25	32%	32%	-64
	08	28	27	33%	48%	-126
	09	25	26	31%	42%	-106
Teixeira,Mark	06	77	27	52%	19%	28
	07	80	22	59%	23%	26
	08	100	27	70%	11%	96
	09	100	27	63%	15%	66
Tejada,Miguel	06	63	27	48%	15%	36
	07	54	24	42%	25%	-16
	08	56	27	44%	19%	12
	09	68	27	52%	15%	44
Thames,Marcus	06	86	26	54%	27%	0
	07	58	24	42%	25%	-16
	08	53	27	48%	37%	-52
	09	26	19	42%	53%	-128
Theriot,Ryan	06	112	15	60%	27%	12
	07	62	26	54%	19%	32
	08	42	27	26%	22%	-36
	09	29	27	30%	41%	-104
Thole,Josh	09	35	6	50%	17%	32
Thomas,Clete	08	29	11	27%	45%	-126
	09	23	20	30%	40%	-100
Thome,Jim	06	90	27	56%	33%	-20
	07	77	24	58%	21%	32
	08	73	27	63%	11%	82
	09	38	27	33%	56%	-158
Thurston,Joe	06	20	6	0%	50%	-200
	09	33	27	30%	44%	-116
Tolbert,Matt	08	49	12	42%	42%	-84
	09	17	15	27%	47%	-134
Toregas,Wyatt	09	-56	11	9%	64%	-238
Torrealba,Yorvit	06	49	15	47%	20%	14
	07	26	27	33%	41%	-98
	08	27	22	41%	41%	-82
	09	12	22	27%	45%	-126
Torres,Andres	09	80	20	35%	40%	-90
Towles,J.R.	07	124	5	20%	0%	40
	08	-17	18	11%	72%	-266
	09	-3	5	13%	88%	-326
Tracy,Andy	09	-13	5	20%	80%	-280
Tracy,Chad	06	39	27	48%	26%	-8
	07	66	18	50%	17%	32
	08	25	19	26%	42%	-116
	09	50	23	52%	39%	-52
Tulowitzki,Troy	06	-30	5	0%	60%	-240
	07	57	27	44%	26%	-16
	08	50	19	37%	26%	-30
	09	103	26	62%	23%	32
Turner,Justin	09	-20	5	40%	40%	-80
Uggla,Dan	06	53	27	63%	22%	38
	07	70	27	52%	30%	-16
	08	72	26	50%	35%	-40
	09	54	27	41%	37%	-66
Upton,B.J.	06	-19	10	0%	60%	-240
	07	48	22	41%	41%	-82
	08	46	27	33%	33%	-66
	09	29	26	31%	50%	-138

BATTER CONSISTENCY

Name	Yr	BPV	#Wk	DOM	DIS	QC
Upton,Justin	07	26	10	30%	60%	-180
	08	46	21	43%	38%	-66
	09	79	25	60%	28%	8
Uribe,Juan	06	52	26	54%	27%	0
	07	19	27	22%	44%	-132
	08	31	24	29%	50%	-142
	09	63	27	44%	33%	-44
Utley,Chase	06	75	27	63%	11%	82
	07	105	23	65%	13%	78
	08	107	26	65%	15%	70
	09	99	26	65%	19%	54
Valbuena,Luis	08	15	5	20%	60%	-200
	09	39	23	48%	30%	-24
Valdez,Wilson	07	13	11	18%	55%	-184
	09	39	12	25%	42%	-118
Varitek,Jason	06	30	23	48%	35%	-44
	07	22	27	37%	48%	-118
	08	-4	28	32%	61%	-180
	09	34	27	48%	33%	-36
Vazquez,Ramon	06	-29	14	14%	57%	-200
	07	26	21	33%	52%	-142
	08	35	27	37%	48%	-118
	09	-21	27	22%	67%	-224
Velez,Eugenio	08	60	21	33%	48%	-126
	09	44	18	28%	50%	-144
Venable,Will	08	41	6	33%	33%	-66
	09	30	18	28%	44%	-120
Victorino,Shane	06	52	27	41%	41%	-82
	07	73	25	60%	12%	72
	08	88	24	58%	17%	48
	09	91	27	70%	22%	52
Vizquel,Omar	06	64	27	52%	19%	28
	07	42	27	41%	22%	-6
	08	25	22	27%	50%	-146
	09	24	25	36%	52%	-136
Votto,Joey	07	72	5	60%	20%	40
	08	72	27	41%	22%	-6
	09	89	24	54%	25%	8
Walker,Neil	09	-54	6	17%	67%	-234
Weeks,Rickie	06	23	17	41%	35%	-58
	07	76	25	36%	52%	-136
	08	63	24	46%	25%	-8
	09	68	7	43%	29%	-30
Wells,Vernon	06	100	27	70%	19%	64
	07	67	25	44%	20%	8
	08	80	20	65%	10%	90
	09	60	27	44%	19%	12
Werth,Jayson	07	38	22	32%	59%	-172
	08	71	26	46%	31%	-32
	09	75	27	44%	44%	-88
Whitesell,Josh	09	-1	12	33%	58%	-166
Whiteside,Eli	09	-1	20	20%	60%	-200
Wieters,Matt	09	-5	20	25%	65%	-210
Wigginton,Ty	06	55	23	43%	30%	-34
	07	40	27	33%	26%	-38
	08	78	23	52%	22%	16
	09	27	26	38%	31%	-48
Willingham,Josh	06	53	26	54%	31%	-16
	07	65	25	44%	28%	-24
	08	76	20	45%	40%	-70
	09	73	27	52%	37%	-44
Willits,Reggie	06	-1	12	25%	75%	-250
	07	19	26	23%	46%	-138
	08	-10	23	9%	70%	-262
	09	-12	17	12%	59%	-212
Wilson,Bobby	09	60	6	17%	83%	-298
Wilson,Jack	06	31	27	33%	37%	-82
	07	64	26	58%	27%	8
	08	34	18	33%	22%	-22
	09	36	21	29%	38%	-94
Wilson,Josh	07	19	26	31%	54%	-154
	09	7	19	16%	53%	-180
Winn,Randy	06	63	26	62%	19%	48
	07	59	27	48%	22%	8
	08	61	27	37%	30%	-46
	09	38	27	22%	44%	-132
Wise,DeWayne	06	-15	9	11%	67%	-246
	08	60	17	29%	41%	-106
	09	42	20	35%	45%	-110
Woodward,Chris	06	-7	25	20%	52%	-168
	07	3	27	19%	56%	-186
	09	-53	13	8%	77%	-292
Wood,Brandon	07	-61	9	22%	78%	-268
	08	-17	12	8%	67%	-252
	09	-87	9	11%	78%	-290

BATTER CONSISTENCY

Name	Yr	BPV	#Wk	DOM	DIS	QC
Wright,David	06	82	27	56%	15%	52
	07	94	27	63%	19%	50
	08	99	27	52%	7%	76
	09	42	25	40%	36%	-64
Youkilis,Kevin	06	53	26	31%	15%	2
	07	58	26	46%	35%	-48
	08	95	28	64%	29%	12
	09	80	26	62%	31%	0
Young Jr.,Eric	09	-7	7	43%	57%	-142
Young,Chris	06	40	8	38%	38%	-76
	07	72	26	46%	31%	-32
	08	62	27	52%	22%	16
	09	48	26	35%	38%	-82
Young,Delmon	06	37	6	33%	33%	-66
	07	18	27	22%	44%	-132
	08	34	27	30%	44%	-116
	09	6	25	28%	56%	-168
Young,Delwyn	06	-78	5	0%	40%	-160
	07	89	7	43%	43%	-86
	08	-13	21	29%	62%	-190
	09	2	26	19%	46%	-146
Young,Michael	06	57	27	44%	26%	-16
	07	30	26	27%	35%	-86
	08	44	27	37%	41%	-90
	09	69	24	50%	29%	-16
Zaun,Gregg	06	67	26	58%	19%	40
	07	62	21	43%	29%	-30
	08	43	24	33%	50%	-134
	09	40	27	44%	48%	-104
Zimmerman,Ryan	06	58	27	52%	19%	28
	07	66	27	52%	19%	28
	08	44	19	37%	26%	-30
	09	83	27	52%	22%	16
Zobrist,Ben	06	16	10	20%	30%	-80
	07	-26	9	22%	67%	-224
	08	99	17	71%	18%	70
	09	101	27	59%	26%	14

BATTER CONSISTENCY

Top QC by Year	Yr	BPV	#Wk	DOM	DIS	QC
Pujols,Albert	09	163	27	85%	7%	142
Pedroia,Dustin		95	27	78%	4%	140
Fielder,Prince		107	27	74%	7%	120
Berkman,Lance		91	25	72%	8%	112
Kinsler,Ian		110	26	69%	8%	106
Lee,Carlos		79	27	67%	6%	106
Matsui,Hideki		73	27	56%	7%	84
Mauer,Joe		94	24	67%	13%	82
Pujols,Albert	08	145	26	92%	0%	184
Quentin,Carlos		114	23	87%	0%	174
Lee,Carlos		103	19	74%	5%	128
Reyes,Jose		102	27	70%	4%	124
Rollins,Jimmy		107	24	67%	4%	118
Garciaparra,Nomar		95	14	71%	7%	114
Beltran,Carlos		109	27	78%	11%	112
Pedroia,Dustin		101	28	68%	7%	108
Granderson,Curtis		88	24	75%	13%	98
Teixeira,Mark		100	27	70%	11%	96
Crede,Joe		73	19	58%	5%	96
Beltre,Adrian		68	25	64%	8%	96
Kinsler,Ian		107	21	57%	5%	94
McLouth,Nate		111	27	67%	11%	90
Wells,Vernon		80	20	65%	10%	90
Braun,Ryan		100	27	67%	11%	90
Guerrero,Vladimir		87	26	73%	15%	86
Giles,Brian		86	27	56%	7%	84
Thome,Jim		73	27	63%	11%	82
Rollins,Jimmy	07	119	27	78%	0%	156
Lee,Carlos		99	27	70%	0%	140
Guerrero,Vladimir		98	26	77%	4%	138
Reyes,Jose		91	27	74%	7%	120
Ordonez,Magglio		105	27	81%	11%	118
Ross,Cody		123	17	82%	12%	116
Fielder,Prince		119	26	73%	8%	114
Keppinger,Jeff		90	16	69%	6%	114
Jones,Chipper		124	25	80%	12%	112
Ramirez,Hanley		110	27	78%	11%	112
Blalock,Hank		103	11	73%	9%	110
Pujols,Albert		108	27	74%	11%	104
Bonds,Barry		137	25	76%	12%	104
Helton,Todd		82	27	74%	11%	104
Braun,Ryan		110	20	80%	15%	100
Roberts,Brian		79	26	65%	8%	98
Martinez,Victor		74	25	64%	8%	96
Rodriguez,Alex		135	27	70%	11%	96
Rios,Alex		90	27	70%	11%	96
Matsui,Hideki		90	24	63%	8%	94
Polanco,Placido		76	27	52%	4%	88
Kent,Jeff		81	26	73%	15%	86
Hart,Corey		99	27	63%	11%	82
Pedroia,Dustin		76	27	63%	11%	82
Holliday,Matt		105	27	63%	11%	82
Bonds,Barry	06	125	27	89%	4%	162
Pujols,Albert		147	25	88%	4%	160
Ortiz,David		129	27	89%	7%	150
Rollins,Jimmy		102	27	74%	0%	148
Ramirez,Aramis		105	27	78%	4%	140
Garciaparra,Nomar		99	23	74%	4%	132
Rolen,Scott		96	27	74%	4%	132
Johnson,Nick		96	25	72%	4%	128
Crawford,Carl		81	26	69%	4%	122
Guerrero,Vladimir		92	26	77%	8%	122
Alou,Moises		107	21	81%	10%	122
Morneau,Justin		81	27	74%	7%	120
Mauer,Joe		89	27	74%	7%	120
Berkman,Lance		99	27	67%	4%	118
Lee,Carlos		104	26	73%	8%	114
Atkins,Garrett		96	27	70%	7%	112
Giles,Brian		72	27	63%	4%	110
Hafner,Travis		125	22	73%	9%	110
Beltran,Carlos		133	27	85%	15%	110
Reyes,Jose		94	26	77%	12%	106
Pierre,Juan		74	27	67%	7%	106
Barrett,Michael		80	21	71%	10%	102
Gonzalez,Luis		78	27	63%	7%	98
Catalanotto,Frank		74	26	65%	8%	98
Roberts,Brian		72	24	63%	8%	94
Jones,Chipper		107	23	65%	9%	94
Crede,Joe		74	26	62%	8%	92
Cabrera,Orlando		76	27	62%	8%	92
Batista,Tony		42	11	64%	9%	92
Quentin,Carlos		94	12	58%	8%	84
Hatteberg,Scott		70	26	58%	8%	84
Utley,Chase		75	27	63%	11%	82
Durham,Ray		104	26	65%	12%	82
Sizemore,Grady		102	27	63%	11%	82
Dye,Jermaine		102	26	65%	12%	82
Thomas,Frank		83	26	65%	12%	82

Starting Pitcher Consistency Charts

We've always approached performance measures on an aggregate basis. Each individual event that our statistics chronicle gets dumped into a huge pool of data. We then use our formulas to try to sort and slice and manipulate the data into more usable information.

Pure Quality Starts (PQS) take a different approach (see *Glossary for complete definition*). It says that the smallest unit of measure should not be the "event" but instead be the "game." Within that game, we can accumulate all the strikeouts, hits and walks, and evaluate that outing as a whole. After all, when a pitcher takes the mound, he is either "on" or "off" his game; he is either dominant or struggling, or somewhere in between.

PQS captures the array of events and slaps an evaluative label on that outing, on a scale of 0 to 5. It doesn't matter if a few extra balls got through the infield, or the pitcher was given the hook in the fourth or sixth inning, or the bullpen was able to strand their inherited baserunners. When we look at performance in the aggregate, *those events do matter*, and will affect a pitcher's BPIs and ERA. But with PQS, the minutia is less relevant than the overall performance.

In the end, a dominating performance is a dominating performance, whether Zach Greinke is hurling a 1-hit shutout or giving up 4 runs while striking out 8 in 7 IP. And a disaster is still a disaster, whether Armando Galarraga gets a first inning hook after giving up 5 runs, or "takes one for the team" getting shelled for 8 runs in 5.2 IP.

With Gene McCaffrey's Domination and Disaster percentages, we can sort out the PQS scores even more.

Domination Percentage (DOM%) measures the portion of a pitcher's starts that scored a 4 or 5 on the PQS scale.

Disaster Percentage (DIS%) measures the portion of a pitcher's starts that scored a 0 or 1 on the PQS scale.

DOM/DIS percentages open up a new perspective, providing us with two separate scales of performance. In tandem, they measure consistency.

This is important because a pitcher might possess incredible skill but be unable to sustain it on a start-by-start basis. For instance, a pitcher who posts PQS scores of 5,0,5,0,5 might have an ERA that is identical to one who posts scores of 3,3,3,3,3 — less skill, but more consistent. ERAs, WHIPs, and even BPIs don't capture that subtle difference. DOM/DIS *does* capture that difference, and in

doing so, helps us identify pitchers who might be better or worse than their stats — and sabermetrics — indicate.

The final step is to convert a pitcher's DOM/DIS split back to an equivalent ERA. By creating a grid of individual DOM and DIS levels, we can determine the average ERA at each cross point. The result is an ERA based purely on PQS, and so we can call it the PQS ERA, or qERA.

The following charts include:

· Up to six years of data for all pitchers who had at least five starts in 2009
· Total number of starts in that year (#)
· Average pitch counts for all starts (PC)
· Domination and Disaster percentages (DOM, DIS) for first half, second half and total season
· Quality-Consistency Score (QC)
· PQS Earned Run Average (qERA)

Some observations...

The ability to maintain positive QC scores is rarer than we would think. That's why you have to take notice of a pitcher like **Bronson Arroyo**, who has posted positive QC scores in five of the last six years. Take note of his last two 2nd halves — 64/0% in 2008 and 73/0% in 2009.

After four full seasons in the Majors, you have to like **Matt Cain's** qERA trend (4.50, 4.10, 3.68. 3.50) and his consistency (QC scores of 12, 36, 76, 86).

For those who consider 2009 a breakout season for **Scott Feldman**, note that his 35% DOM rate was nothing to write home about, and his 4.41 qERA was only marginally better than 2008's 4.75 level.

Yovani Gallardo's 13-12 record might scare off H2H gamers as being too inconsistent, but his 63/3% DOM/DIS split and 114 QC make him much more of a good target.

Cole Hamels had an off-year in 2009, but you wouldn't be able to tell from his BPIs alone, which were nearly identical to 2008. His PQS record shows where things fell apart. His splits were 70/6% with a 116 QC and 3.25 qERA in 2008; 53/25% with a 6 QC and 4.61 qERA in 2009.

Kevin Millwood improved his ERA by 1.40 runs in 2009 (5.07 to 3.67), but qERA says this was the same pitcher both years (4.53, 4.40), and not such a great one.

Mike Pelfrey looks like he lost something in 2009, his ERA jumping from 3.72 to 5.03, but he too was the same mediocre pitcher both years (qERA's of 4.90, 4.82).

STARTING PITCHER CONSISTENCY CHART

				First Half		Second Half		Full Season			
Pitcher	Yr	#	PC	DOM	DIS	DOM	DIS	DOM	DIS	QC	qERA
Anderson,Brett	09	30	94	38%	38%	64%	0%	50%	20%	20	4.50
Arroyo,Bronson	04	29	95	57%	14%	60%	13%	59%	14%	62	3.97
	05	32	101	53%	18%	27%	27%	41%	22%	-6	4.56
	06	34	110	79%	11%	47%	13%	65%	12%	82	3.61
	07	34	101	50%	11%	44%	13%	47%	12%	46	4.28
	08	34	101	40%	30%	64%	0%	50%	18%	28	4.37
	09	33	103	22%	33%	73%	0%	45%	18%	18	4.40
Bailey,Homer	07	9	90	17%	33%	33%	0%	22%	22%	-44	4.75
	08	8	85	25%	50%	0%	50%	13%	50%	-174	7.08
	09	20	101	50%	25%	25%	19%	30%	20%	-20	4.71
Baker,Scott	05	9	90	100%	0%	50%	13%	56%	11%	68	3.97
	06	16	90	22%	56%	0%	43%	13%	50%	-174	7.08
	07	23	90	22%	22%	43%	7%	35%	13%	18	4.41
	08	28	96	43%	14%	57%	14%	50%	14%	44	4.23
	09	32	99	53%	18%	67%	13%	59%	16%	54	4.10
Balester,Collin	08	15	90	0%	33%	42%	17%	33%	20%	-14	4.71
	09	7	73			29%	57%	29%	57%	-170	7.14
Bannister,Brian	06	6	100	40%	20%	100%	0%	50%	17%	32	4.37
	07	27	96	38%	15%	36%	29%	37%	22%	-14	4.64
	08	32	98	42%	21%	31%	46%	38%	31%	-48	5.00
	09	26	97	44%	6%	30%	20%	38%	12%	28	4.41
Bastardo,Antonio	09	5	87	40%	40%			40%	40%	-80	5.21
Bazardo,Yorman	09	6	75			0%	83%	0%	83%	-332	12.14
Beckett,Josh	04	26	94	54%	23%	62%	15%	58%	19%	40	4.10
	05	29	97	81%	19%	69%	8%	76%	14%	96	3.41
	06	33	98	56%	17%	47%	13%	52%	15%	44	4.37
	07	30	103	63%	13%	86%	0%	73%	7%	118	3.25
	08	27	100	65%	12%	80%	10%	70%	11%	96	3.51
	09	32	105	89%	11%	64%	0%	78%	6%	132	3.13
Bedard,Erik	04	26	100	33%	27%	45%	45%	38%	35%	-64	5.13
	05	24	103	67%	11%	40%	20%	50%	17%	32	4.37
	06	33	100	47%	32%	71%	7%	58%	21%	32	4.23
	07	28	105	74%	11%	78%	0%	75%	7%	122	3.13
	08	15	91	40%	27%			40%	27%	-28	4.74
	09	15	97	46%	15%	0%	100%	40%	27%	-28	4.74
Bergesen,Brad	09	19	98	44%	6%	33%	0%	42%	5%	64	4.11
Berken,Jason	09	24	85	11%	33%	7%	60%	8%	50%	-184	7.26
Billingsley,Chad	06	16	95	0%	60%	36%	18%	25%	31%	-74	5.13
	07	20	95	25%	50%	50%	13%	45%	20%	10	4.53
	08	32	101	58%	5%	54%	8%	56%	6%	88	3.68
	09	32	100	68%	0%	54%	23%	63%	9%	90	3.50
Blackburn,Nick	08	33	87	47%	21%	29%	50%	39%	33%	-54	5.00
	09	33	94	28%	17%	33%	40%	30%	27%	-48	4.90
Blanton,Joe	05	33	93	35%	29%	56%	6%	45%	18%	18	4.40
	06	31	101	28%	22%	23%	8%	26%	16%	-12	4.62
	07	34	102	63%	0%	40%	13%	53%	6%	82	3.85
	08	33	98	30%	15%	38%	23%	33%	18%	-6	4.60
	09	31	105	47%	18%	64%	14%	55%	16%	46	4.10
Boggs,Mitchell	08	6	89	20%	20%	0%	100%	17%	33%	-98	5.29
	09	9	94	25%	50%	0%	20%	11%	33%	-110	5.37
Bonderman,J	04	32	90	41%	18%	53%	20%	47%	19%	18	4.40
	05	29	98	56%	6%	55%	27%	55%	14%	54	3.97
	06	34	97	61%	11%	38%	25%	50%	18%	28	4.37
	07	28	97	81%	0%	33%	33%	61%	14%	66	3.71
	08	12	98	33%	25%			33%	25%	-34	4.90
Bonser,Boof	06	18	87	43%	43%	45%	9%	44%	22%	0	4.56
	07	30	92	39%	11%	25%	42%	33%	23%	-26	4.71
	08	12	89	42%	25%			42%	25%	-16	4.74
Braden,Dallas	07	14	85	25%	75%	10%	60%	14%	64%	-228	8.46
	08	10	89			40%	20%	40%	20%	0	4.56
	09	22	97	50%	0%	0%	25%	41%	5%	62	4.11
Buchholz,Clay	08	15	91	22%	33%	17%	50%	20%	40%	-120	5.50
	09	16	95			38%	25%	38%	25%	-24	4.82
Buckner,Billy	09	13	93	29%	14%	67%	17%	46%	15%	32	4.40
Buehrle,Mark	04	35	106	58%	11%	44%	6%	51%	9%	66	3.85
	05	33	105	56%	0%	40%	7%	48%	3%	84	3.68
	06	32	97	28%	11%	21%	43%	25%	25%	-50	4.93
	07	30	103	41%	6%	31%	15%	37%	10%	34	4.41
	08	34	100	47%	11%	60%	20%	53%	15%	46	4.37
	09	33	97	39%	11%	27%	27%	33%	18%	-6	4.60
Burnett,A.J.	04	19	94	50%	38%	55%	0%	53%	16%	42	4.37
	05	32	103	65%	6%	60%	13%	63%	9%	90	3.50
	06	21	103	33%	33%	67%	13%	57%	19%	38	4.10
	07	25	106	60%	27%	70%	0%	64%	16%	64	3.83
	08	34	107	50%	20%	71%	0%	59%	12%	70	3.97
	09	33	105	59%	12%	56%	13%	58%	12%	68	3.97
Burns,Mike	09	8	83	25%	50%	25%	50%	25%	50%	-150	6.56
Bush,David	04	16	92	50%	0%	50%	21%	50%	19%	24	4.37
	05	24	88	30%	50%	43%	36%	38%	42%	-92	5.25
	06	32	93	63%	11%	46%	23%	56%	16%	48	4.10
	07	31	95	59%	6%	36%	21%	48%	13%	44	4.28
	08	29	92	35%	24%	42%	8%	38%	17%	8	4.52
	09	21	88	36%	21%	29%	57%	33%	33%	-66	5.08
Byrd,Paul	04	19	88	50%	25%	33%	13%	37%	16%	10	4.52
	05	31	94	35%	6%	43%	21%	39%	13%	26	4.41
	06	31	92	53%	18%	7%	43%	32%	29%	-52	4.90
	07	31	91	38%	6%	7%	27%	23%	16%	-18	4.63
	08	30	84	39%	44%	33%	8%	37%	30%	-46	5.00
	09	6	86			0%	33%	0%	33%	-132	5.53

STARTING PITCHER CONSISTENCY CHART

				First Half		Second Half		Full Season			
Pitcher	Yr	#	PC	DOM	DIS	DOM	DIS	DOM	DIS	QC	qERA
Cabrera,Daniel	04	27	92	25%	8%	7%	47%	15%	30%	-90	5.29
	05	29	99	47%	24%	33%	25%	41%	24%	-14	4.56
	06	26	103	33%	20%	45%	36%	38%	27%	-32	4.82
	07	34	105	58%	11%	40%	20%	50%	15%	40	4.37
	08	30	101	30%	20%	10%	50%	23%	30%	-74	5.21
	09	9	90	13%	63%	0%	0%	11%	56%	-202	7.77
Cahill,Trevor	09	32	94	28%	33%	14%	36%	22%	34%	-92	5.21
Cain,Matt	05	7	102			57%	0%	57%	0%	114	3.38
	06	31	106	38%	38%	67%	7%	52%	23%	12	4.50
	07	32	105	53%	12%	60%	27%	56%	19%	36	4.10
	08	34	106	60%	10%	50%	7%	56%	9%	76	3.68
	09	33	102	61%	11%	60%	7%	61%	9%	86	3.50
Carmona,Fausto	06	7	87	33%	33%	25%	25%	29%	29%	-58	4.93
	07	32	98	53%	12%	47%	0%	50%	6%	76	3.85
	08	22	92	10%	40%	25%	25%	18%	32%	-92	5.29
	09	24	94	8%	25%	25%	25%	17%	25%	-66	5.03
Carpenter,Chris	04	28	96	53%	6%	45%	27%	50%	14%	44	4.23
	05	33	103	89%	6%	60%	7%	76%	6%	128	3.13
	06	32	102	65%	0%	67%	7%	66%	3%	120	3.14
	09	28	95	77%	8%	67%	0%	71%	4%	126	2.99
Carrasco,Carlos	09	5	80			0%	80%	0%	80%	-320	12.14
Cecil,Brett	09	17	94	38%	38%	33%	44%	35%	41%	-94	5.25
Chamberlain,J	08	12	94	50%	38%	75%	25%	58%	33%	-16	4.55
	09	31	88	41%	41%	36%	64%	39%	52%	-130	6.25
Chen,Bruce	04	7	102			29%	14%	29%	14%	2	4.50
	05	32	95	59%	12%	47%	20%	53%	16%	42	4.37
	06	12	91	10%	60%	0%	0%	8%	50%	-184	7.26
	09	9	93	25%	50%	20%	20%	22%	33%	-88	5.21
Colon,Bartolo	04	34	100	28%	33%	69%	19%	47%	26%	-10	4.67
	05	33	98	67%	6%	67%	0%	67%	3%	122	3.14
	06	10	85	14%	14%	33%	33%	20%	20%	-40	4.75
	07	18	88	36%	29%	25%	50%	33%	33%	-66	5.08
	08	7	83	50%	17%	0%	0%	43%	14%	30	4.32
	09	12	83	18%	27%	100%	0%	25%	25%	-50	4.93
Contreras,Jose	04	31	97	43%	36%	47%	24%	45%	29%	-26	4.67
	05	32	99	47%	18%	53%	0%	50%	9%	64	3.85
	06	30	101	50%	6%	36%	21%	43%	13%	34	4.32
	07	30	97	35%	12%	46%	31%	40%	20%	0	4.56
	08	20	95	37%	26%	0%	100%	35%	30%	-50	5.00
	09	23	93	50%	25%	27%	64%	39%	43%	-94	5.25
Cook,Aaron	04	16	92	9%	18%	20%	20%	13%	19%	-50	4.66
	05	13	91			8%	31%	8%	31%	-108	5.45
	06	32	97	39%	6%	21%	21%	31%	13%	10	4.49
	07	25	96	32%	11%	67%	0%	40%	8%	48	4.11
	08	32	96	25%	0%	25%	17%	25%	6%	26	4.48
	09	27	89	22%	22%	22%	33%	22%	26%	-60	4.98
Correia,Kevin	05	11	82	0%	50%	44%	44%	36%	45%	-108	5.75
	07	8	88			63%	13%	63%	13%	74	3.71
	08	19	90	40%	40%	33%	22%	37%	32%	-54	5.00
	09	33	96	50%	17%	53%	13%	52%	15%	44	4.37
Cueto,Johnny	08	31	98	47%	21%	42%	25%	45%	23%	-2	4.53
	09	30	97	56%	17%	33%	17%	47%	17%	26	4.40
Danks,John	07	26	93	25%	25%	20%	40%	23%	31%	-78	5.21
	08	33	95	58%	16%	50%	29%	55%	21%	26	4.23
	09	32	100	65%	12%	33%	13%	50%	13%	48	4.23
Davies,Kyle	05	14	98	18%	27%	67%	0%	29%	21%	-26	4.73
	06	14	89	25%	38%	17%	67%	21%	50%	-158	6.74
	07	28	88	31%	50%	17%	50%	25%	50%	-150	6.56
	08	21	94	11%	33%	33%	33%	24%	33%	-84	5.21
	09	22	99	36%	43%	50%	13%	41%	32%	-46	4.92
Davis,Doug	04	34	100	47%	16%	60%	13%	53%	15%	46	4.37
	05	35	106	58%	26%	63%	13%	60%	20%	40	3.95
	06	34	103	21%	16%	47%	13%	32%	15%	4	4.60
	07	33	102	44%	22%	40%	27%	42%	24%	-12	4.56
	08	26	95	58%	17%	36%	43%	46%	31%	-32	4.82
	09	34	102	47%	21%	27%	20%	38%	21%	-8	4.64
Davis,Wade	09	6	100			33%	17%	33%	17%	-2	4.60
de la Rosa,Jorge	04	5	82			0%	40%	0%	40%	-160	5.90
	06	13	84	0%	100%	10%	30%	8%	46%	-168	6.53
	07	23	91	33%	28%	0%	60%	26%	35%	-88	5.27
	08	23	92	27%	45%	58%	17%	43%	30%	-34	4.92
	09	32	95	47%	24%	53%	13%	50%	19%	24	4.37
Dempster,Ryan	05	6	99	67%	17%			67%	17%	66	3.73
	08	33	101	55%	5%	77%	0%	64%	3%	116	3.29
	09	31	102	65%	12%	64%	0%	65%	6%	106	3.38
Detwiler,Ross	09	14	88	40%	30%	25%	25%	36%	29%	-44	4.82
Dinardo,Lenny	09	5	91			0%	60%	0%	60%	-240	9.02
Duchscherer,J	08	22	93	63%	6%	17%	17%	50%	9%	64	3.85
Duensing,Brian	09	9	89			33%	33%	33%	33%	-66	5.08
Duke,Zach	05	14	91	100%	0%	42%	33%	50%	29%	-16	4.61
	06	34	96	32%	21%	33%	13%	32%	18%	-8	4.60
	07	19	88	6%	41%	0%	50%	5%	42%	-158	5.80
	08	31	94	21%	26%	50%	8%	32%	19%	-12	4.60
	09	32	96	56%	11%	29%	29%	44%	19%	12	4.44
Eaton,Adam	04	33	99	56%	6%	47%	13%	52%	9%	68	3.85
	05	22	100	50%	14%	38%	13%	45%	14%	34	4.28
	06	13	87			31%	31%	31%	31%	-62	5.08
	07	30	92	33%	22%	8%	50%	23%	33%	-86	5.21
	08	19	92	21%	26%			21%	26%	-62	4.98
	09	8	100	13%	50%			13%	50%	-174	7.08

STARTING PITCHER CONSISTENCY CHART

				First Half		Second Half		Full Season			
Pitcher	Yr	#	PC	DOM	DIS	DOM	DIS	DOM	DIS	QC	qERA
Escobar,Kelvim	04	33	104	41%	6%	63%	6%	52%	6%	80	3.85
	05	7	91	57%	14%			57%	14%	58	3.97
	06	30	97	53%	12%	69%	15%	60%	13%	68	3.71
	07	30	101	69%	13%	50%	21%	60%	17%	52	3.83
Eveland,Dana	06	5	97	0%	40%			0%	40%	-160	5.90
	08	29	93	32%	21%	30%	40%	31%	28%	-50	4.90
	09	9	86	17%	67%	0%	67%	11%	67%	-246	9.15
Feldman,Scott	08	25	94	21%	21%	27%	18%	24%	20%	-32	4.75
	09	31	98	13%	7%	56%	19%	35%	13%	18	4.41
Figueroa,Nelson	08	6	98	33%	33%			33%	33%	-66	5.08
	09	10	99	0%	0%	44%	22%	40%	20%	0	4.56
Fister,Doug	09	10	94			50%	20%	50%	20%	20	4.50
Floyd,Gavin	06	11	91	9%	55%			9%	55%	-202	7.99
	07	10	96	0%	100%	67%	22%	60%	30%	0	4.39
	08	33	98	39%	17%	47%	7%	42%	12%	36	4.32
	09	30	99	44%	11%	67%	17%	53%	13%	54	4.23
Fogg,Josh	04	32	87	12%	35%	27%	13%	19%	25%	-62	5.03
	05	28	93	47%	18%	9%	27%	32%	21%	-20	4.71
	06	31	89	18%	18%	29%	43%	23%	29%	-70	4.98
	07	29	91	33%	20%	21%	29%	28%	24%	-40	4.73
	08	14	81	33%	50%	13%	63%	21%	57%	-186	7.36
Francis,Jeff	04	7	93			14%	29%	14%	29%	-88	5.08
	05	33	95	33%	17%	33%	40%	33%	27%	-42	4.90
	06	32	99	35%	18%	33%	13%	34%	16%	4	4.60
	07	34	103	56%	6%	50%	13%	53%	9%	70	3.85
	08	24	99	35%	24%	71%	14%	46%	21%	8	4.53
French,Luke	09	12	91	50%	50%	10%	30%	17%	33%	-98	5.29
Galarraga,A	08	28	97	27%	7%	38%	15%	32%	11%	20	4.49
	09	25	93	33%	33%	29%	29%	32%	32%	-64	5.08
Gallardo,Yovani	07	17	96	67%	0%	64%	14%	65%	12%	82	3.61
	09	30	107	61%	6%	67%	0%	63%	3%	114	3.29
Garcia,Freddy	04	31	106	67%	6%	62%	8%	65%	6%	106	3.38
	05	33	103	50%	11%	27%	27%	39%	18%	6	4.52
	06	33	101	44%	17%	60%	0%	52%	9%	68	3.85
	07	11	95	36%	36%			36%	36%	-72	5.13
	09	9	92			67%	11%	67%	11%	90	3.61
Garland,Jon	04	33	103	35%	18%	25%	6%	30%	12%	12	4.49
	05	32	104	47%	0%	33%	13%	41%	6%	58	4.11
	06	32	104	35%	18%	53%	7%	44%	13%	36	4.32
	07	32	103	29%	6%	40%	27%	34%	16%	4	4.60
	08	32	100	16%	16%	15%	31%	16%	22%	-56	4.77
	09	33	99	44%	17%	53%	13%	48%	15%	36	4.40
Garza,Matt	06	9	89			22%	56%	22%	56%	-180	7.36
	07	15	95	100%	0%	29%	36%	33%	33%	-66	5.08
	08	30	98	41%	29%	31%	15%	37%	23%	-18	4.64
	09	32	107	50%	0%	50%	14%	50%	6%	76	3.85
Gaudin,Chad	07	34	97	33%	28%	38%	44%	35%	35%	-70	5.13
	08	6	93	67%	17%			67%	17%	66	3.73
	09	25	93	43%	14%	36%	45%	40%	28%	-32	4.74
Geer,Joshua	08	5	94			0%	20%	0%	20%	-80	4.83
	09	17	91	36%	21%	33%	67%	35%	29%	-46	4.82
Gonzalez,Edgar	04	10	81	0%	100%	11%	56%	10%	60%	-220	8.46
	06	5	94	100%	0%	67%	0%	80%	0%	160	2.69
	07	12	79	25%	13%	0%	75%	17%	33%	-98	5.29
	08	6	81	0%	50%			0%	50%	-200	7.46
	09	6	81	50%	0%	25%	75%	33%	50%	-134	6.37
Gonzalez,Gio	08	7	89			29%	57%	29%	57%	-170	7.14
	09	17	94	33%	33%	43%	29%	41%	29%	-34	4.74
Gorzelanny,Tom	06	11	92	0%	50%	56%	22%	45%	27%	-18	4.67
	07	32	104	50%	6%	36%	14%	44%	9%	52	4.11
	08	21	91	6%	35%	25%	75%	10%	43%	-152	5.70
	09	7	77			43%	29%	43%	29%	-30	4.74
Greinke,Zack	04	24	95	56%	0%	53%	13%	54%	8%	76	3.85
	05	33	94	22%	33%	33%	33%	27%	33%	-78	5.13
	07	14	86	29%	29%	29%	43%	29%	36%	-86	5.27
	08	32	101	58%	16%	77%	8%	66%	13%	80	3.61
	09	33	105	83%	0%	93%	0%	88%	0%	176	2.54
Guthrie,Jeremy	07	26	96	77%	0%	23%	38%	50%	19%	24	4.37
	08	30	102	50%	5%	50%	20%	50%	10%	60	4.23
	09	33	102	28%	22%	27%	20%	27%	21%	-30	4.73
Halladay,Roy	04	21	98	47%	6%	25%	75%	43%	19%	10	4.44
	05	19	101	68%	5%			68%	5%	116	3.38
	06	32	95	56%	0%	57%	14%	56%	6%	88	3.68
	07	31	107	50%	13%	47%	7%	48%	10%	56	4.28
	08	33	107	68%	0%	86%	0%	76%	0%	152	2.84
	09	32	106	82%	12%	73%	0%	78%	6%	132	3.13
Hamels,Cole	06	23	95	22%	33%	64%	14%	48%	22%	8	4.53
	07	28	100	61%	6%	70%	10%	64%	7%	100	3.50
	08	33	104	70%	5%	69%	8%	70%	6%	116	3.25
	09	32	97	53%	35%	53%	13%	53%	25%	6	4.61
Hammel,Jason	06	9	89	0%	50%	14%	57%	11%	56%	-202	7.77
	07	14	89			21%	36%	21%	36%	-102	5.36
	08	5	89	40%	20%			40%	20%	0	4.56
	09	30	88	53%	33%	47%	13%	50%	23%	8	4.50
Hampton,Mike	04	29	94	18%	29%	33%	33%	24%	31%	-76	5.21
	05	12	85	33%	22%	0%	100%	25%	42%	-118	5.40
	08	13	92			46%	23%	46%	23%	0	4.53
	09	21	88	33%	33%	17%	33%	29%	33%	-74	5.13
Hanson,Tommy	09	21	95	29%	14%	71%	7%	57%	10%	74	3.97
Happ,J.A.	09	23	100	60%	20%	31%	15%	43%	17%	18	4.44

STARTING PITCHER CONSISTENCY CHART

				First Half		Second Half		Full Season			
Pitcher	Yr	#	PC	DOM	DIS	DOM	DIS	DOM	DIS	QC	qERA
Harang,Aaron	04	28	97	50%	14%	36%	14%	43%	14%	30	4.32
	05	32	107	59%	6%	40%	0%	50%	3%	88	3.47
	06	34	106	63%	11%	47%	7%	56%	9%	76	3.68
	07	34	106	58%	5%	67%	7%	62%	6%	100	3.50
	08	29	103	53%	21%	60%	30%	55%	24%	14	4.23
	09	26	103	53%	26%	71%	0%	58%	19%	40	4.10
Harden,Rich	04	31	102	44%	19%	67%	7%	55%	13%	58	3.97
	05	19	99	73%	9%	75%	0%	74%	5%	128	3.25
	06	9	89	33%	33%	33%	67%	33%	44%	-110	5.29
	08	25	98	79%	7%	64%	0%	72%	4%	128	2.99
	09	26	96	50%	36%	67%	17%	58%	27%	8	4.39
Haren,Dan	04	5	89	0%	100%	25%	0%	20%	20%	-40	4.75
	05	34	99	53%	21%	47%	13%	50%	18%	28	4.37
	06	34	103	53%	5%	53%	7%	53%	6%	82	3.85
	07	34	107	68%	0%	80%	7%	74%	3%	136	2.99
	08	33	101	89%	5%	71%	14%	82%	9%	128	3.00
	09	33	105	89%	0%	67%	0%	79%	0%	158	2.84
Harrison,Matt	08	15	91	0%	50%	23%	38%	20%	40%	-120	5.50
	09	11	97	27%	45%			27%	45%	-126	5.98
Hart,Kevin	09	14	98	0%	0%	38%	23%	36%	21%	-12	4.64
Hendrickson,Mark	04	30	94	24%	29%	46%	31%	33%	30%	-54	5.08
	05	31	91	0%	25%	33%	27%	16%	26%	-72	5.03
	06	25	98	33%	13%	30%	40%	32%	24%	-32	4.71
	07	15	83	30%	30%	20%	40%	27%	33%	-78	5.13
	08	19	93	32%	37%			32%	37%	-84	5.19
	09	11	77	14%	86%	0%	25%	9%	64%	-238	8.72
Hernandez,David	09	19	98	0%	20%	36%	50%	26%	42%	-116	5.40
Hernandez,Felix	05	12	102			83%	8%	83%	8%	134	3.00
	06	31	99	47%	18%	50%	7%	48%	13%	44	4.28
	07	30	100	36%	14%	50%	0%	43%	7%	58	4.11
	08	31	103	59%	12%	57%	14%	58%	13%	64	3.97
	09	34	107	72%	11%	75%	6%	74%	9%	112	3.25
Hernandez,Livan	04	35	112	58%	5%	56%	6%	57%	6%	90	3.68
	05	34	114	26%	16%	40%	20%	32%	18%	-8	4.60
	06	34	103	16%	11%	40%	7%	26%	9%	16	4.48
	07	33	102	22%	22%	20%	33%	21%	27%	-66	4.98
	08	31	90	35%	30%	18%	36%	29%	32%	-70	5.13
	09	31	96	18%	24%	50%	29%	32%	26%	-40	4.90
Hill,Rich	06	16	101	0%	50%	67%	17%	50%	25%	0	4.61
	07	32	96	47%	12%	53%	13%	50%	13%	48	4.23
	08	5	71	20%	40%			20%	40%	-120	5.50
	09	13	85	27%	55%	0%	100%	23%	62%	-202	7.98
Hochevar,Luke	08	22	94	44%	31%	17%	17%	36%	27%	-36	4.82
	09	25	94	20%	40%	47%	27%	36%	32%	-56	5.00
Holland,Derek	09	21	90	29%	14%	14%	43%	19%	33%	-94	5.29
Hudson,Tim	04	27	102	40%	13%	33%	8%	37%	11%	30	4.41
	05	29	100	29%	36%	40%	0%	34%	17%	0	4.60
	06	35	98	32%	21%	31%	19%	31%	20%	-18	4.71
	07	34	93	53%	21%	47%	7%	50%	15%	40	4.37
	08	22	91	45%	25%	50%	0%	45%	23%	-2	4.53
	09	7	86			29%	29%	29%	29%	-58	4.93
Huff,David	09	23	98	18%	36%	17%	25%	17%	30%	-86	5.29
Hughes,Phil	07	13	95	50%	50%	36%	27%	38%	31%	-48	5.00
	08	8	79	17%	83%	50%	50%	25%	75%	-250	9.46
	09	7	89	43%	43%			43%	43%	-86	5.21
Hunter,Tommy	09	19	91	25%	25%	40%	20%	37%	21%	-10	4.64
Jackson,Edwin	04	5	71	0%	33%	0%	100%	0%	60%	-240	9.02
	05	6	88			0%	33%	0%	33%	-132	5.53
	07	31	95	44%	38%	40%	20%	42%	29%	-32	4.74
	08	31	97	33%	17%	23%	38%	29%	26%	-46	4.93
	09	33	105	78%	0%	20%	27%	52%	12%	56	4.23
Jakubauskas,C	09	8	90	25%	50%			25%	50%	-150	6.56
Janssen,Casey	09	5	85	0%	40%			0%	40%	-160	5.90
Jimenez,Ubaldo	07	15	90			40%	33%	40%	33%	-52	4.92
	08	34	99	40%	20%	71%	7%	53%	15%	46	4.37
	09	33	108	72%	17%	87%	7%	79%	12%	110	3.41
Johnson,Josh	06	24	99	58%	0%	67%	17%	63%	8%	94	3.50
	08	14	101	0%	0%	54%	0%	50%	0%	100	3.47
	09	33	100	79%	11%	57%	21%	70%	15%	80	3.63
Johnson,Randy	04	35	104	89%	0%	94%	0%	91%	0%	182	2.39
	05	34	101	74%	11%	73%	13%	74%	12%	100	3.51
	06	33	99	58%	26%	57%	7%	58%	18%	44	4.10
	07	10	91	60%	20%			60%	20%	40	3.95
	08	30	97	47%	24%	62%	8%	53%	17%	38	4.37
	09	17	85	29%	35%			29%	35%	-82	5.27
Jurrjens,Jair	07	7	68			14%	43%	14%	43%	-144	5.70
	08	31	99	56%	11%	46%	15%	52%	13%	52	4.23
	09	34	97	47%	11%	60%	7%	53%	9%	70	3.85
Karstens,Jeff	06	6	86			17%	17%	17%	17%	-34	4.65
	08	9	92			22%	22%	22%	22%	-44	4.75
	09	13	80	10%	30%	0%	67%	8%	38%	-136	5.63
Kawakami,Kenshir	09	25	91	50%	31%	33%	22%	44%	28%	-24	4.74
Kazmir,Scott	04	7	83			29%	43%	29%	43%	-114	5.40
	05	32	103	50%	28%	71%	21%	59%	25%	18	4.39
	06	24	101	47%	16%	100%	0%	58%	13%	64	3.97
	07	34	106	47%	11%	80%	7%	62%	9%	88	3.50
	08	27	102	57%	14%	62%	23%	59%	19%	42	4.10
	09	26	101	42%	42%	79%	7%	62%	23%	32	3.95
Kendrick,Kyle	07	20	88	20%	0%	33%	27%	30%	20%	-20	4.71
	08	30	87	26%	32%	9%	64%	20%	43%	-132	5.50

STARTING PITCHER CONSISTENCY CHART

				First Half		Second Half		Full Season			
Pitcher	Yr	#	PC	DOM	DIS	DOM	DIS	DOM	DIS	QC	qERA
Kennedy,Ian	08	9	82	25%	50%	0%	100%	22%	56%	-180	7.36
Kershaw,Clayton	08	21	88	13%	38%	62%	31%	43%	33%	-46	4.92
	09	30	100	44%	17%	58%	33%	50%	23%	8	4.50
Kuroda,Hiroki	08	31	88	41%	18%	71%	21%	55%	19%	34	4.10
	09	20	89	44%	11%	64%	18%	55%	15%	50	4.10
Lackey,John	04	32	100	41%	18%	20%	13%	31%	16%	-2	4.60
	05	33	106	39%	6%	73%	0%	55%	3%	98	3.38
	06	33	106	61%	11%	60%	27%	61%	18%	50	3.83
	07	33	103	61%	6%	60%	7%	61%	6%	98	3.50
	08	24	101	82%	0%	38%	8%	58%	4%	100	3.38
	09	27	102	50%	25%	67%	20%	59%	22%	30	4.23
Laffey,Aaron	07	9	80			11%	22%	11%	22%	-66	4.79
	08	16	93	43%	7%	0%	100%	38%	19%	0	4.52
	09	19	95	0%	20%	14%	21%	11%	21%	-62	4.79
Lannan,John	07	6	94			0%	17%	0%	17%	-68	4.69
	08	31	95	28%	17%	31%	23%	29%	19%	-18	4.62
	09	33	95	17%	17%	40%	20%	27%	18%	-18	4.62
Latos,Mat	09	10	87			30%	50%	30%	50%	-140	6.37
LeBlanc,Wade	09	9	86	0%	100%	29%	0%	22%	22%	-44	4.75
Lee,Cliff	04	33	96	56%	11%	33%	47%	45%	27%	-18	4.67
	05	32	97	56%	22%	79%	0%	66%	13%	80	3.61
	06	33	102	39%	11%	40%	27%	39%	18%	6	4.52
	07	16	97	23%	23%	33%	33%	25%	25%	-50	4.93
	08	31	106	72%	6%	62%	0%	68%	3%	124	3.14
	09	34	104	58%	5%	60%	13%	59%	9%	82	3.68
Lehr,Justin	09	11	97			36%	18%	36%	18%	0	4.52
Lester,Jon	06	15	101	33%	17%	0%	22%	13%	20%	-54	4.79
	07	11	97			36%	27%	36%	27%	-36	4.82
	08	33	100	50%	15%	69%	8%	58%	12%	68	3.97
	09	32	106	61%	11%	79%	14%	69%	13%	86	3.61
Lilly,Ted	04	32	103	39%	6%	36%	7%	38%	6%	52	4.29
	05	25	86	24%	35%	25%	50%	24%	40%	-112	5.50
	06	32	100	50%	22%	50%	14%	50%	19%	24	4.37
	07	34	95	78%	17%	50%	19%	65%	18%	58	3.73
	08	34	95	55%	30%	86%	7%	68%	21%	52	3.85
	09	27	99	72%	0%	78%	11%	74%	4%	132	2.99
Lincecum,Tim	07	24	99	58%	33%	75%	8%	67%	21%	50	3.85
	08	33	109	74%	0%	86%	14%	79%	6%	134	3.13
	09	32	107	83%	6%	79%	7%	81%	6%	138	3.00
Liriano,Francisco	06	16	89	80%	0%	50%	33%	69%	13%	86	3.61
	08	14	91	0%	67%	64%	18%	50%	29%	-16	4.61
	09	24	92	39%	28%	33%	50%	38%	33%	-56	5.00
Litsch,Jesse	07	20	89	20%	60%	27%	20%	25%	30%	-70	5.13
	08	28	97	28%	17%	50%	10%	36%	14%	16	4.41
Lohse,Kyle	04	34	98	22%	17%	13%	38%	18%	26%	-68	5.03
	05	30	95	33%	20%	20%	33%	27%	27%	-54	4.93
	06	19	89	25%	63%	45%	18%	37%	37%	-74	5.13
	07	32	94	39%	22%	36%	29%	38%	25%	-24	4.82
	08	33	96	50%	15%	54%	15%	52%	15%	44	4.37
	09	22	89	45%	45%	45%	36%	45%	41%	-74	5.14
Looper,Braden	07	30	93	19%	19%	57%	36%	37%	27%	-34	4.82
	08	33	98	32%	26%	50%	14%	39%	21%	-6	4.64
	09	34	96	28%	22%	19%	6%	24%	15%	-12	4.63
Lopez,Rodrigo	09	5	85	100%	0%	33%	33%	60%	20%	40	3.95
Loux,Shane	09	6	88	17%	33%			17%	33%	-98	5.29
Lowe,Derek	04	33	93	18%	35%	25%	38%	21%	36%	-102	5.36
	05	35	95	42%	11%	56%	19%	49%	14%	42	4.28
	06	34	96	32%	26%	47%	20%	38%	24%	-20	4.64
	07	32	94	53%	16%	62%	31%	56%	22%	24	4.23
	08	34	92	65%	5%	64%	14%	65%	9%	94	3.38
	09	34	95	32%	21%	20%	27%	26%	24%	-44	4.73
Lowry,Noah	04	14	95	33%	33%	45%	9%	43%	14%	30	4.32
	05	33	107	50%	22%	67%	0%	58%	12%	68	3.97
	06	27	97	15%	23%	43%	36%	30%	30%	-60	5.08
	07	26	98	35%	12%	22%	33%	31%	19%	-14	4.60
Maholm,Paul	05	6	102			50%	17%	50%	17%	32	4.37
	06	30	97	28%	28%	42%	0%	33%	17%	-2	4.60
	07	29	91	39%	28%	36%	18%	38%	24%	-20	4.64
	08	31	98	56%	17%	46%	8%	52%	13%	52	4.23
	09	31	98	33%	17%	23%	8%	29%	13%	6	4.50
Maine,John	05	8	79			0%	50%	0%	50%	-200	7.46
	06	15	100	0%	33%	42%	8%	33%	13%	14	4.49
	07	32	102	76%	18%	33%	33%	56%	25%	12	4.39
	08	25	102	63%	21%	17%	33%	52%	24%	8	4.50
	09	15	92	36%	27%	25%	50%	33%	33%	-66	5.08
Maloney,Matt	09	7	93	67%	0%	25%	0%	43%	0%	86	3.89
Manship,Jeff	09	5	80			0%	60%	0%	60%	-240	9.02
Marcum,Shaun	06	14	88			21%	50%	21%	50%	-158	6.74
	07	25	91	45%	18%	43%	29%	44%	24%	-8	4.56
	08	25	93	67%	7%	30%	50%	52%	24%	8	4.50
Marquis,Jason	04	32	104	35%	12%	33%	13%	34%	13%	16	4.49
	05	32	100	33%	17%	21%	21%	28%	19%	-20	4.62
	06	33	93	28%	22%	27%	40%	27%	30%	-66	5.13
	07	33	91	44%	17%	40%	33%	42%	24%	-12	4.56
	08	28	94	29%	18%	18%	18%	25%	18%	-22	4.62
	09	33	98	33%	17%	40%	27%	36%	21%	-12	4.64
Marshall,Sean	06	24	86	35%	35%	0%	71%	25%	46%	-134	5.98
	07	19	84	67%	22%	30%	50%	47%	37%	-54	4.98
	08	7	87	67%	33%	50%	25%	57%	29%	-2	4.39
	09	9	86	38%	13%	0%	100%	33%	22%	-22	4.71

STARTING PITCHER CONSISTENCY CHART

				First Half		Second Half		Full Season			
Pitcher	Yr	#	PC	DOM	DIS	DOM	DIS	DOM	DIS	QC	qERA
Martin,J.D.	09	15	86			20%	40%	20%	40%	-120	5.50
Martinez,Joe	09	5	84			0%	40%	0%	40%	-160	5.90
Martinez,Pedro	04	33	106	72%	11%	73%	7%	73%	9%	110	3.25
	05	31	98	89%	0%	62%	8%	77%	3%	142	2.84
	06	23	92	88%	6%	29%	43%	70%	17%	72	3.63
	07	5	92			40%	0%	40%	0%	80	3.89
	08	20	94	11%	33%	36%	9%	25%	20%	-30	4.73
	09	9	81			22%	44%	22%	44%	-132	5.50
Martis,Shairon	09	15	91	7%	27%			7%	27%	-94	5.13
Masterson,Justin	08	9	96	56%	0%			56%	0%	112	3.38
	09	16	97	50%	0%	30%	40%	38%	25%	-24	4.82
Matsuzaka,D	07	32	109	72%	0%	50%	14%	63%	6%	102	3.50
	08	29	100	44%	13%	54%	15%	48%	14%	40	4.28
	09	12	92	13%	50%	50%	0%	25%	33%	-82	5.13
Matusz,Brian	09	8	93			25%	13%	25%	13%	-2	4.50
Mazzaro,Vince	09	17	98	63%	25%	0%	67%	29%	47%	-130	5.98
McCarthy,B	05	10	95	40%	60%	60%	0%	50%	30%	-20	4.71
	07	22	84	23%	38%	22%	44%	23%	41%	-118	5.50
	08	5	75			40%	60%	40%	60%	-160	7.05
	09	17	93	27%	27%	33%	33%	29%	29%	-58	4.93
McCutchen,D	09	6	95			33%	17%	33%	17%	-2	4.60
McGowan,Dustin	05	7	89			14%	43%	14%	43%	-144	5.70
	07	27	100	42%	17%	67%	7%	56%	11%	68	3.97
	08	19	95	42%	21%			42%	21%	0	4.56
Meche,Gil	04	23	101	30%	40%	46%	8%	39%	22%	-10	4.64
	05	26	98	33%	28%	0%	50%	23%	35%	-94	5.36
	06	32	103	56%	11%	43%	36%	50%	22%	12	4.50
	07	34	105	58%	11%	47%	13%	53%	12%	58	4.23
	08	34	105	45%	10%	86%	0%	62%	6%	100	3.50
	09	23	99	47%	26%	0%	75%	39%	35%	-62	5.13
Miller,Andrew	07	13	94	17%	0%	0%	57%	8%	31%	-108	5.45
	08	20	91	30%	40%			30%	40%	-100	5.29
	09	14	91	31%	31%	0%	100%	29%	36%	-86	5.27
Millwood,Kevin	04	25	94	67%	17%	57%	43%	64%	24%	32	3.95
	05	30	99	40%	13%	53%	0%	47%	7%	66	3.98
	06	34	97	56%	11%	63%	13%	59%	12%	70	3.97
	07	31	95	40%	20%	38%	25%	39%	23%	-14	4.64
	08	29	93	33%	17%	73%	27%	48%	21%	12	4.53
	09	31	106	53%	11%	33%	33%	45%	19%	14	4.40
Milton,Eric	09	5	81	0%	40%			0%	40%	-160	5.90
Miner,Zach	06	16	89	43%	14%	11%	44%	25%	31%	-74	5.13
	08	13	95			46%	23%	46%	23%	0	4.53
	09	5	85	0%	25%	0%	100%	0%	40%	-160	5.90
Misch,Pat	08	7	88	29%	43%			29%	43%	-114	5.40
	09	7	80			0%	29%	0%	29%	-116	5.18
Mitre,Sergio	09	9	85			11%	56%	11%	56%	-202	7.77
Mock,Garrett	09	15	94			33%	20%	33%	20%	-14	4.71
Moehler,Brian	05	25	86	27%	33%	20%	50%	24%	40%	-112	5.50
	06	21	81	27%	47%	0%	67%	19%	52%	-170	6.90
	08	26	84	42%	17%	36%	21%	38%	19%	0	4.52
	09	29	87	33%	20%	21%	43%	28%	31%	-68	5.13
Morales,Franklin	07	8	74			63%	38%	63%	38%	-26	4.53
	08	5	97	0%	40%			0%	40%	-160	5.90
Morris,Matt	04	32	96	44%	6%	36%	29%	41%	16%	18	4.44
	05	31	93	69%	13%	27%	20%	48%	16%	32	4.40
	06	33	99	44%	17%	47%	20%	45%	18%	18	4.40
	07	32	95	24%	12%	27%	27%	25%	19%	-26	4.62
	08	5	92	0%	100%			0%	100%	-400	15.00
Morrow,Brandon	08	5	101			40%	40%	40%	40%	-80	5.21
	09	10	85	17%	67%	25%	0%	20%	40%	-120	5.50
Mortensen,Claytor	09	6	87			0%	50%	0%	50%	-200	7.46
Morton,Charlie	08	15	88	33%	17%	33%	44%	33%	33%	-66	5.08
	09	18	89	40%	40%	38%	23%	39%	28%	-34	4.82
Moyer,Jamie	04	33	102	39%	22%	13%	33%	27%	27%	-54	4.93
	05	32	102	33%	28%	43%	14%	38%	22%	-12	4.64
	06	33	99	39%	6%	27%	27%	33%	15%	6	4.60
	07	33	95	39%	22%	33%	13%	36%	18%	0	4.52
	08	33	96	32%	16%	29%	7%	30%	12%	12	4.49
	09	25	96	35%	29%	38%	13%	36%	24%	-24	4.64
Myers,Brett	04	31	90	31%	38%	27%	27%	29%	32%	-70	5.13
	05	34	102	61%	11%	56%	13%	59%	12%	70	3.97
	06	31	104	56%	19%	73%	7%	65%	13%	78	3.61
	08	30	101	29%	29%	77%	15%	50%	23%	8	4.50
	09	10	102	30%	20%			30%	20%	-20	4.71
Niemann,Jeff	09	30	95	19%	44%	64%	14%	40%	30%	-40	4.92
Niese,Jonathon	09	5	80	50%	50%	0%	33%	20%	40%	-120	5.50
Nieve,Fernando	09	7	87	33%	33%	0%	100%	29%	43%	-114	5.40
Nippert,Dustin	08	6	97			33%	33%	33%	33%	-66	5.08
	09	10	90	0%	100%	63%	25%	50%	40%	-60	5.03
Nolasco,Ricky	06	22	87	30%	40%	25%	33%	27%	36%	-90	5.27
	08	32	99	61%	33%	79%	0%	69%	19%	62	3.73
	09	31	98	44%	25%	73%	13%	58%	19%	40	4.10
Norris,Bud	09	10	90			50%	10%	50%	10%	60	4.23
O Sullivan,Sean	09	10	87	50%	25%	17%	67%	30%	50%	-140	6.37
Ohka,Tomo	09	6	89	0%	50%	0%	0%	0%	33%	-132	5.53
Ohlendorf,Ross	08	5	86			0%	60%	0%	60%	-240	9.02
	09	29	93	28%	11%	55%	9%	38%	10%	36	4.41

STARTING PITCHER CONSISTENCY CHART

				First Half		Second Half		Full Season			
Pitcher	Yr	#	PC	DOM	DIS	DOM	DIS	DOM	DIS	QC	qERA
Olsen,Scott	06	31	93	50%	19%	60%	13%	55%	16%	46	4.10
	07	33	93	26%	21%	21%	43%	24%	30%	-72	5.21
	08	33	94	42%	21%	36%	14%	39%	18%	6	4.52
	09	11	95	27%	36%			27%	36%	-90	5.27
Olson,Garrett	07	7	92	0%	100%	17%	50%	14%	57%	-200	7.77
	08	26	89	21%	36%	25%	42%	23%	38%	-106	5.36
	09	11	79	50%	0%	0%	100%	36%	27%	-36	4.82
Ortiz,Russ	05	22	94	7%	43%	13%	75%	9%	55%	-202	7.99
	06	11	74	0%	75%	0%	100%	0%	82%	-328	12.14
	07	8	87	20%	20%	0%	33%	13%	25%	-74	5.08
	09	13	91	20%	30%	33%	67%	23%	38%	-106	5.36
Oswalt,Roy	04	35	102	68%	5%	69%	19%	69%	11%	94	3.61
	05	35	103	68%	5%	63%	6%	66%	6%	108	3.38
	06	32	101	41%	6%	73%	0%	56%	3%	100	3.38
	07	32	103	60%	0%	50%	17%	56%	6%	88	3.68
	08	32	97	58%	16%	69%	0%	63%	9%	90	3.50
	09	30	93	68%	5%	45%	18%	60%	10%	80	3.71
Outman,Josh	09	12	89	50%	33%			50%	33%	-32	4.71
Owings,Micah	07	27	90	43%	29%	54%	31%	48%	30%	-24	4.82
	08	18	93	53%	24%	0%	100%	50%	28%	-12	4.61
	09	19	95	38%	38%	0%	100%	32%	47%	-124	5.83
Padilla,Vicente	04	20	89	40%	10%	50%	30%	45%	20%	10	4.53
	05	27	95	8%	46%	57%	21%	33%	33%	-66	5.08
	06	33	100	56%	17%	33%	13%	45%	15%	30	4.40
	07	23	89	13%	40%	50%	25%	26%	35%	-88	5.27
	08	29	100	22%	17%	27%	9%	24%	14%	-8	4.51
	09	25	97	13%	13%	60%	0%	32%	8%	32	4.48
Palmer,Matt	09	13	93	27%	36%	0%	0%	23%	31%	-78	5.21
Park,Chan Ho	04	16	95	38%	38%	13%	38%	25%	38%	-102	5.27
	05	29	97	47%	24%	8%	42%	31%	31%	-62	5.08
	06	21	101	31%	6%	20%	40%	29%	14%	2	4.50
	08	5	87	60%	40%			60%	40%	-40	4.67
	09	7	92	29%	43%			29%	43%	-114	5.40
Parnell,Bobby	09	8	92			25%	50%	25%	50%	-150	6.56
Parra,Manny	08	29	93	44%	39%	45%	18%	45%	31%	-34	4.82
	09	27	95	29%	36%	31%	23%	30%	30%	-60	5.08
Paulino,Felipe	09	17	89	40%	50%	29%	14%	35%	35%	-70	5.13
Pavano,Carl	04	31	102	71%	6%	50%	7%	61%	6%	98	3.50
	05	17	91	29%	29%			29%	29%	-58	4.93
	08	7	81			0%	43%	0%	43%	-172	5.90
	09	33	94	56%	17%	47%	20%	52%	18%	32	4.37
Peavy,Jake	04	27	99	55%	9%	69%	0%	63%	4%	110	3.29
	05	30	105	71%	6%	69%	0%	70%	3%	128	2.99
	06	32	105	59%	12%	60%	13%	59%	13%	66	3.97
	07	34	106	72%	0%	81%	6%	76%	3%	140	2.84
	08	27	106	73%	20%	50%	17%	63%	19%	50	3.83
	09	16	98	69%	8%	100%	0%	75%	6%	126	3.13
Pelfrey,Mike	07	13	94	13%	25%	40%	20%	23%	23%	-46	4.75
	08	32	104	33%	28%	36%	21%	34%	25%	-32	4.90
	09	31	102	35%	29%	36%	21%	35%	26%	-34	4.82
Penny,Brad	04	24	95	67%	6%	33%	33%	58%	13%	64	3.97
	05	29	96	53%	13%	50%	29%	52%	21%	20	4.50
	06	33	98	61%	6%	20%	13%	42%	9%	48	4.11
	07	33	98	56%	11%	33%	13%	45%	12%	42	4.28
	08	17	98	40%	20%	0%	50%	35%	24%	-26	4.64
	09	30	98	29%	18%	54%	23%	40%	20%	0	4.56
Perez,Oliver	04	30	104	60%	7%	87%	7%	73%	7%	118	3.25
	05	20	94	40%	33%	20%	60%	35%	40%	-90	5.25
	06	22	96	40%	47%	43%	43%	41%	45%	-98	5.67
	07	29	104	73%	13%	57%	21%	66%	17%	64	3.73
	08	34	99	42%	26%	73%	13%	56%	21%	28	4.23
	09	14	94	17%	67%	25%	13%	21%	36%	-102	5.36
Perkins,Glen	08	26	91	46%	23%	15%	31%	31%	27%	-46	4.90
	09	17	85	46%	15%	0%	50%	35%	24%	-26	4.64
Petit,Yusmeiro	07	10	79	33%	0%	29%	57%	30%	40%	-100	5.29
	08	8	79	100%	0%	43%	43%	50%	38%	-52	4.87
	09	17	81	14%	57%	40%	40%	29%	47%	-130	5.98
Pettitte,Andy	04	15	90	70%	20%	20%	0%	53%	13%	54	4.23
	05	33	97	76%	0%	88%	0%	82%	0%	164	2.69
	06	35	100	35%	20%	47%	13%	40%	17%	12	4.44
	07	34	99	39%	22%	50%	13%	44%	18%	16	4.44
	08	33	99	45%	20%	46%	23%	45%	21%	6	4.53
	09	32	103	39%	22%	57%	7%	47%	16%	30	4.40
Pineiro,Joel	04	21	107	56%	11%	67%	33%	57%	14%	58	3.97
	05	30	98	27%	27%	33%	27%	30%	27%	-48	4.90
	06	25	96	33%	33%	14%	43%	28%	36%	-88	5.27
	07	11	90			36%	36%	36%	36%	-72	5.13
	08	25	87	27%	20%	20%	30%	24%	24%	-48	4.75
	09	32	92	29%	6%	60%	13%	44%	9%	52	4.11
Ponson,Sidney	04	33	100	28%	28%	33%	0%	30%	15%	0	4.60
	05	23	90	28%	33%	0%	80%	22%	43%	-128	5.50
	06	16	82	23%	31%	33%	67%	25%	38%	-102	5.27
	07	7	90	14%	57%			14%	57%	-200	7.77
	08	24	90	42%	33%	17%	50%	29%	42%	-110	5.40
	09	9	91	33%	33%	33%	67%	33%	44%	-110	5.29
Porcello,Rick	09	30	88	38%	38%	36%	29%	37%	33%	-58	5.00
Price,David	09	23	99	22%	44%	50%	14%	39%	26%	-26	4.82
Purcey,David	08	12	93	0%	100%	60%	20%	50%	33%	-32	4.71
	09	9	98	20%	60%	0%	25%	11%	44%	-154	5.70

STARTING PITCHER CONSISTENCY CHART

				First Half		Second Half		Full Season			
Pitcher	Yr	#	PC	DOM	DIS	DOM	DIS	DOM	DIS	QC	qERA
Redding,Tim	04	17	90	7%	57%	33%	67%	12%	59%	-212	7.77
	05	7	71	17%	50%	0%	100%	14%	57%	-200	7.77
	07	15	93	0%	0%	31%	23%	27%	20%	-26	4.73
	08	33	95	35%	15%	23%	46%	30%	27%	-48	4.90
	09	17	93	22%	44%	50%	0%	35%	24%	-26	4.64
Reyes,Anthony	06	17	85	33%	17%	45%	36%	41%	29%	-34	4.74
	07	20	88	42%	17%	50%	25%	45%	20%	10	4.53
	08	6	87			17%	17%	17%	17%	-34	4.65
	09	8	85	38%	38%			38%	38%	-76	5.13
Reyes,Jo-Jo	07	10	82	0%	100%	22%	33%	20%	40%	-120	5.50
	08	22	85	43%	36%	13%	75%	32%	50%	-136	6.37
	09	5	81	20%	40%			20%	40%	-120	5.50
Richard,Clayton	08	8	81			38%	63%	38%	63%	-176	7.25
	09	26	91	25%	58%	36%	21%	31%	38%	-90	5.19
Richmond,Scott	08	5	87			40%	0%	40%	0%	80	3.89
	09	24	95	38%	23%	18%	55%	29%	38%	-94	5.27
Robertson,Nate	04	32	93	47%	18%	47%	20%	47%	19%	18	4.40
	05	32	92	41%	18%	20%	7%	31%	13%	10	4.49
	06	32	97	39%	17%	36%	7%	38%	13%	24	4.41
	07	30	96	20%	27%	60%	13%	40%	20%	0	4.56
	08	28	90	26%	16%	33%	44%	29%	25%	-42	4.93
	09	6	79			33%	50%	33%	50%	-134	6.37
Rodriguez,Wandy	05	22	92	11%	22%	31%	23%	23%	23%	-46	4.75
	06	24	92	37%	26%	20%	40%	33%	29%	-50	4.90
	07	31	98	59%	0%	36%	29%	48%	13%	44	4.28
	08	25	91	46%	31%	42%	33%	44%	32%	-40	4.92
	09	33	102	67%	22%	67%	13%	67%	18%	62	3.73
Romero,Ricky	09	29	103	69%	15%	13%	25%	38%	21%	-8	4.64
Rowland-Smith,R	08	12	99	0%	50%	40%	20%	33%	25%	-34	4.90
	09	15	100	0%	100%	57%	14%	53%	20%	26	4.50
Rzepczynski,Marc	09	11	99	100%	0%	67%	22%	73%	18%	74	3.63
Sabathia,C.C.	04	30	104	47%	12%	46%	8%	47%	10%	54	4.28
	05	31	102	44%	25%	67%	7%	55%	16%	46	4.10
	06	28	105	64%	21%	71%	7%	68%	14%	80	3.61
	07	34	105	74%	5%	73%	0%	74%	3%	136	2.99
	08	35	109	70%	15%	80%	0%	74%	9%	112	3.25
	09	34	106	58%	11%	60%	7%	59%	9%	82	3.68
Sadowski,Ryan	09	6	82	33%	0%	0%	100%	17%	50%	-166	6.90
Sanchez,Anibal	06	17	99	0%	50%	60%	13%	53%	18%	34	4.37
	07	6	95	0%	17%			0%	17%	-68	4.69
	08	10	88			40%	20%	40%	20%	0	4.56
	09	16	92	29%	43%	56%	22%	44%	31%	-36	4.92
Sanchez,Jonathan	08	29	98	53%	21%	30%	50%	45%	31%	-34	4.82
	09	29	96	21%	36%	60%	13%	41%	24%	-14	4.56
Santana,Ervin	05	23	98	38%	50%	60%	20%	52%	30%	-16	4.71
	06	33	97	50%	11%	27%	33%	39%	21%	-6	4.64
	07	26	97	56%	33%	38%	13%	50%	27%	-8	4.61
	08	32	107	79%	0%	69%	0%	75%	0%	150	2.84
	09	23	99	13%	50%	67%	7%	48%	22%	8	4.53
Santana,Johan	04	34	101	79%	16%	100%	0%	88%	9%	140	2.88
	05	33	101	78%	0%	80%	7%	79%	3%	146	2.84
	06	34	102	74%	0%	80%	7%	76%	3%	140	2.84
	07	33	101	89%	0%	60%	7%	76%	3%	140	2.84
	08	34	106	79%	0%	80%	7%	79%	3%	146	2.84
	09	25	103	56%	6%	57%	0%	56%	4%	96	3.38
Saunders,Joe	06	13	89			54%	31%	54%	31%	-16	4.71
	07	18	99	20%	0%	23%	8%	22%	6%	20	4.49
	08	31	97	39%	11%	23%	23%	32%	16%	0	4.60
	09	31	97	28%	22%	15%	23%	23%	23%	-46	4.75
Scherzer,Max	08	7	94	33%	33%	50%	0%	43%	14%	30	4.32
	09	30	102	53%	24%	46%	15%	50%	20%	20	4.50
Sheets,Ben	04	34	105	89%	6%	88%	0%	88%	3%	164	2.54
	05	22	104	62%	0%	89%	0%	73%	0%	146	2.99
	06	17	92	50%	25%	85%	8%	76%	12%	104	3.41
	07	24	94	67%	11%	50%	50%	63%	21%	42	3.95
	08	31	99	72%	0%	54%	15%	65%	6%	106	3.38
Shields,James	06	21	95	50%	0%	46%	15%	48%	10%	56	4.28
	07	31	102	61%	0%	77%	8%	68%	3%	124	3.14
	08	33	95	63%	11%	50%	7%	58%	9%	80	3.68
	09	33	101	63%	5%	43%	7%	55%	6%	86	3.68
Silva,Carlos	04	33	88	17%	33%	7%	7%	12%	21%	-60	4.79
	05	27	85	38%	6%	64%	9%	48%	7%	68	3.98
	06	31	84	13%	33%	31%	38%	23%	35%	-94	5.36
	07	33	93	33%	17%	40%	20%	36%	18%	0	4.52
	08	28	88	35%	25%	0%	63%	25%	36%	-94	5.27
	09	6	86	17%	83%			17%	83%	-298	10.80
Silva,Walter	09	6	81	17%	67%			17%	67%	-234	8.85
Slowey,Kevin	07	11	94	0%	29%	75%	0%	27%	18%	-18	4.62
	08	27	93	50%	21%	46%	15%	48%	19%	20	4.40
	09	16	89	44%	31%			44%	31%	-36	4.92
Smoltz,John	05	33	100	42%	11%	93%	0%	64%	6%	104	3.50
	06	35	101	74%	5%	75%	13%	74%	9%	112	3.25
	07	32	96	82%	12%	73%	7%	78%	9%	120	3.13
	08	5	87	80%	20%			80%	20%	80	3.55
	09	15	88	25%	25%	45%	18%	40%	20%	0	4.56
Snell,Ian	05	5	80			0%	40%	0%	40%	-160	5.90
	06	32	95	39%	28%	50%	0%	44%	16%	24	4.44
	07	32	98	65%	0%	53%	13%	59%	6%	94	3.68
	08	31	97	39%	33%	38%	31%	39%	32%	-50	5.00
	09	27	94	27%	20%	17%	17%	22%	19%	-32	4.63

Pitcher	Yr	#	PC	First Half DOM	First Half DIS	Second Half DOM	Second Half DIS	Full Season DOM	Full Season DIS	QC	qERA
Sonnanstine,Andy	07	22	95	57%	0%	33%	27%	41%	18%	10	4.44
	08	32	91	32%	11%	54%	15%	41%	13%	30	4.32
	09	18	88	40%	40%	0%	67%	33%	44%	-110	5.29
Sowers,Jeremy	06	14	91	33%	33%	55%	18%	50%	21%	16	4.50
	07	13	82	8%	50%	100%	0%	15%	46%	-154	6.25
	08	22	92	11%	67%	23%	23%	18%	41%	-128	5.60
	09	22	90	30%	30%	8%	42%	18%	36%	-108	5.45
Stammen,Craig	09	19	83	40%	20%	22%	44%	32%	32%	-64	5.08
Stauffer,Tim	09	14	90	100%	0%	31%	38%	36%	36%	-72	5.13
Stults,Eric	07	5	87			40%	60%	40%	60%	-160	7.05
	08	7	89	60%	20%	0%	100%	43%	43%	-86	5.21
	09	10	88	44%	33%	100%	0%	50%	30%	-20	4.71
Suppan,Jeff	04	31	98	47%	12%	14%	21%	32%	16%	0	4.60
	05	32	95	17%	22%	50%	14%	31%	19%	-14	4.60
	06	32	96	6%	41%	40%	27%	22%	34%	-92	5.21
	07	34	94	32%	11%	27%	7%	29%	9%	22	4.48
	08	31	91	28%	28%	8%	31%	19%	29%	-78	5.03
	09	30	91	22%	39%	8%	42%	17%	40%	-126	5.60
Swarzak,Anthony	09	12	88	17%	50%	0%	50%	8%	50%	-184	7.26
Tallet,Brian	09	25	93	41%	18%	25%	38%	36%	24%	-24	4.64
Tejeda,Robinson	05	13	88	50%	33%	57%	14%	54%	23%	16	4.50
	06	14	90	0%	60%	33%	33%	21%	43%	-130	5.50
	07	19	94	12%	41%	0%	50%	11%	42%	-146	5.70
	09	6	92			50%	17%	50%	17%	32	4.37
Thompson,Brad	07	17	82	20%	10%	14%	43%	18%	24%	-60	4.77
	08	6	74	33%	33%	33%	33%	33%	33%	-66	5.08
	09	8	76	13%	38%			13%	38%	-126	5.54
Tillman,Chris	09	12	97			0%	33%	0%	33%	-132	5.53
Tomko,Brett	04	31	101	25%	31%	47%	20%	35%	26%	-34	4.82
	05	30	100	35%	18%	46%	15%	40%	17%	12	4.44
	06	15	95	33%	33%			33%	33%	-66	5.08
	07	19	90	50%	38%	36%	18%	42%	26%	-20	4.74
	08	10	96	30%	30%			30%	30%	-60	5.08
	09	6	94			50%	33%	50%	33%	-32	4.71
Torres,Carlos	09	5	79			40%	40%	40%	40%	-80	5.21
Uehara,Koji	09	12	88	33%	17%			33%	17%	-2	4.60
VandenHurk,Rick	09	11	91			36%	18%	36%	18%	0	4.52
Vargas,Jason	09	14	90	18%	36%	0%	67%	14%	43%	-144	5.70
Vasquez,Virgil	09	7	83	25%	50%	0%	67%	14%	57%	-200	7.77
Vazquez,Javier	04	32	100	50%	0%	29%	36%	41%	16%	18	4.44
	05	33	101	67%	11%	53%	13%	61%	12%	74	3.71
	06	32	103	47%	6%	53%	20%	50%	13%	48	4.23
	07	32	108	82%	0%	67%	0%	75%	0%	150	2.84
	08	33	102	53%	16%	50%	29%	52%	21%	20	4.50
	09	32	104	83%	0%	86%	0%	84%	0%	168	2.69
Verlander,Justin	06	30	99	47%	6%	38%	23%	43%	13%	34	4.32
	07	32	105	76%	6%	67%	13%	72%	9%	108	3.25
	08	33	107	50%	10%	46%	31%	48%	18%	24	4.40
	09	35	112	79%	11%	75%	0%	77%	6%	130	3.13
Villanueva,Carlos	06	6	99	33%	33%	33%	0%	33%	17%	-2	4.60
	07	6	87	100%	0%	40%	0%	50%	0%	100	3.47
	08	9	96	11%	22%			11%	22%	-66	4.79
	09	6	78			17%	50%	17%	50%	-166	6.90
Volquez,Edinson	06	8	81			13%	63%	13%	63%	-226	8.46
	07	6	99			33%	17%	33%	17%	-2	4.60
	08	32	105	74%	11%	54%	8%	66%	9%	96	3.38
	09	9	94	44%	33%			44%	33%	-44	4.92
Volstad,Chris	08	14	92	100%	0%	31%	15%	36%	14%	16	4.41
	09	29	89	50%	22%	9%	64%	34%	38%	-84	5.19
Wainwright,Adam	07	32	99	18%	12%	60%	7%	38%	9%	40	4.29
	08	20	98	62%	0%	43%	14%	55%	5%	90	3.68
	09	34	106	53%	0%	80%	0%	65%	0%	130	3.14
Wakefield,Tim	04	30	98	31%	13%	21%	36%	27%	23%	-38	4.73
	05	33	103	44%	11%	47%	27%	45%	18%	18	4.40
	06	23	98	61%	6%	0%	60%	48%	17%	28	4.40
	07	31	93	35%	18%	36%	29%	35%	23%	-22	4.64
	08	30	93	42%	11%	45%	36%	43%	20%	6	4.56
	09	21	96	35%	12%	50%	25%	38%	14%	20	4.41
Wang,Chien-Ming	05	17	90	33%	17%	40%	20%	35%	18%	-2	4.52
	06	33	92	26%	26%	21%	14%	24%	21%	-36	4.75
	07	30	95	40%	7%	53%	13%	47%	10%	54	4.28
	08	15	94	33%	13%			33%	13%	14	4.49
	09	9	70	0%	67%			0%	67%	-268	9.80
Washburn,Jarrod	04	25	97	35%	18%	50%	25%	40%	20%	0	4.56
	05	29	93	33%	28%	27%	9%	31%	21%	-22	4.71
	06	31	99	50%	28%	31%	23%	42%	26%	-20	4.74
	07	32	102	35%	24%	47%	27%	41%	25%	-18	4.74
	08	26	100	39%	22%	25%	38%	35%	27%	-38	4.82
	09	28	97	59%	6%	18%	36%	43%	18%	14	4.44
Weaver,Jeff	05	34	99	68%	21%	60%	0%	65%	12%	82	3.61
	06	31	93	38%	31%	33%	40%	35%	35%	-70	5.13
	07	27	89	0%	58%	20%	40%	22%	48%	-148	6.12
	09	7	73	20%	20%	50%	50%	29%	29%	-58	4.93
Weaver,Jered	06	19	102	100%	0%	38%	15%	58%	11%	72	3.97
	07	28	98	50%	29%	50%	14%	50%	21%	16	4.50
	08	30	101	63%	16%	45%	18%	57%	17%	46	4.10
	09	33	103	67%	6%	47%	27%	58%	15%	56	4.10
Webb,Brandon	04	35	98	42%	5%	38%	25%	40%	14%	24	4.32
	05	33	102	61%	0%	67%	7%	64%	3%	116	3.29
	06	33	101	74%	0%	50%	7%	64%	3%	116	3.29
	07	34	101	53%	0%	80%	0%	65%	0%	130	3.14
	08	34	99	75%	10%	57%	14%	68%	12%	88	3.61
Wellemeyer,Todd	07	11	77	25%	38%	67%	33%	36%	36%	-72	5.13
	08	32	97	67%	11%	57%	0%	63%	6%	102	3.50
	09	21	93	22%	28%	0%	100%	19%	38%	-114	5.45
Wells,Kip	05	33	94	53%	32%	21%	43%	39%	36%	-66	5.13
	06	9	86	0%	75%	0%	60%	11%	67%	-246	9.15
	07	26	94	40%	27%	36%	45%	38%	35%	-64	5.13
	09	7	90			29%	29%	29%	29%	-58	4.93
Wells,Randy	09	27	94	75%	8%	27%	33%	48%	22%	8	4.53
West,Sean	09	20	85	20%	50%	30%	50%	25%	50%	-150	6.56
Westbrook,Jake	04	30	99	21%	7%	38%	6%	30%	7%	32	4.48
	05	34	94	42%	21%	33%	13%	38%	18%	4	4.52
	06	32	102	61%	17%	21%	14%	44%	16%	24	4.44
	07	25	99	44%	33%	31%	6%	36%	16%	8	4.52
	08	5	101	20%	0%			20%	0%	40	4.47
Willis,Dontrelle	04	32	98	33%	33%	57%	7%	44%	22%	0	4.56
	05	34	105	78%	6%	56%	13%	68%	9%	100	3.38
	06	34	106	33%	17%	44%	19%	38%	18%	4	4.52
	07	35	100	47%	11%	19%	38%	34%	23%	-24	4.71
	08	7	71	0%	75%	0%	33%	0%	57%	-228	8.24
	09	7	88	14%	57%			14%	57%	-200	7.77
Wolf,Randy	04	23	92	50%	21%	44%	22%	48%	22%	8	4.53
	05	13	100	38%	8%			38%	8%	44	4.29
	06	12	88			17%	33%	17%	33%	-98	5.29
	07	18	99	33%	11%			33%	11%	22	4.49
	08	33	96	60%	30%	38%	23%	52%	27%	-4	4.61
	09	34	97	53%	11%	80%	0%	65%	6%	106	3.38
Young,Chris	04	7	95			43%	43%	43%	43%	-86	5.21
	05	31	92	44%	28%	38%	38%	42%	32%	-44	4.92
	06	31	98	61%	11%	46%	31%	55%	19%	34	4.10
	07	30	96	65%	24%	62%	23%	63%	23%	34	3.95
	08	18	97	60%	20%	63%	13%	61%	17%	54	3.83
	09	14	93	43%	36%			43%	36%	-58	5.07
Zambrano,Carlos	04	31	112	71%	12%	79%	0%	74%	6%	124	3.25
	05	33	108	61%	22%	67%	7%	64%	15%	68	3.83
	06	33	110	68%	11%	71%	14%	70%	12%	92	3.51
	07	34	109	68%	16%	47%	13%	59%	15%	58	4.10
	08	30	101	56%	6%	33%	33%	47%	17%	26	4.40
	09	28	102	56%	13%	50%	25%	54%	18%	36	4.37
Zimmermann,J	09	16	98	60%	7%	0%	0%	56%	6%	88	3.68
Zito,Barry	04	34	108	44%	22%	50%	6%	47%	15%	34	4.40
	05	35	109	58%	5%	75%	19%	66%	11%	88	3.61
	06	34	108	47%	5%	33%	20%	41%	12%	34	4.32
	07	33	103	22%	22%	60%	27%	39%	24%	-18	4.64
	08	32	100	26%	42%	31%	23%	28%	34%	-80	5.13
	09	33	97	33%	22%	67%	27%	48%	24%	0	4.53

Bullpen Indicator Charts

Closer Volatility Chart

CLOSERS DRAFTED refers to the number of saves sources purchased in both LABR and Tout Wars experts leagues each year. These only include relievers drafted for at least $10, specifically for saves speculation. **AVG R$** refers to the average purchase price of these pitchers in the AL-only and NL-only leagues. **FAILED** is the number (and percentage) of closers drafted that did not return at least 50% of their value that year. The Failures include those that lost their value due to ineffectiveness, injury or managerial decision. **NEW SOURCES** are arms that were drafted for less than $10 (if they were drafted at all) but finished with at least double-digit saves.

Bullpen Indicators Chart

These charts offer insight for those looking to speculate on future closer candidates. The charts help focus on many of the statistical and situational factors that might go into a manager's decision to grant any individual pitcher a save opportunity. It's not all-encompassing, but it's a good start. The chart provides a five-year scan for nearly all pitchers who posted at least one save and/or three holds in 2009.

Saves Percentage: What it says is simple... "Who is getting it done?" Intuitively, this percentage should be a major factor in determining which closers might be in danger of losing their jobs. However, a Doug Dennis study showed little correlation between saves success rate alone and future opportunity. Better to prospect for pitchers who have *both* a high saves percentage (80% or better) *and* high skills, as measured by base performance value.

Base Performance Value: The components of BPV are evaluated in many ways. Big league managers tend to look for a pitcher who can strike out eight or nine batters per 9 IP, sometimes even if he's also walking that many. In using BPV, we set a benchmark of 75 as the minimum necessary for success. BPV's more than 100 are much better, however.

Situational Performance is the last piece of the puzzle. The chart includes opposition batting averages for each pitcher versus right-handed and left-handed hitters, with runners on base, in his first 15 pitches, etc. which are all good indicators. We'll set a benchmark of a .250 BA; anything over and the risk level increases.

There are other variables that come into play as well. Left-handed relievers rarely move into a closer's role unless the team's bullpen has sufficient southpaw depth. Some managers do see the value of having a high-skills arm available for the middle innings, so those pitchers don't get promoted into a closer's role either.

The tools are here. Whether or not a manager will make a decision reflective of this information remains to be seen. But the data can help us increase our odds of uncovering those elusive saves and minimizing some of the risk.

NOTE: In the Bullpen Indicators Chart, BPV values for 2006-07 use the previous version of the BPV formula. 2008-09 values use the new version.

2009 Closer Volatility Report

Closer values dropped 22 cents in 2009 but are still essentially on a four-year plateau. While 2009's $17.56 value is a new all-time low, the range has been within 24 cents since 2006. The percentage of closers that failed also remained close to 33% for the fourth straight year.

While the rate of failed closers remained steady, the raw number of failures dropped below double-digits for the first time in seven years. The number of new sources of 10+ saves was at a four-year high.

Only three drafted closers managed to return 30% or more in profit: Brian Wilson ($22 return on $13 average draft price), Trevor Hoffman ($22 on $13) and Heath Bell ($25 on $15). Only eight closers total (29%) returned any type of profit, the same rate as last year. Five returned $0 on their investments (which averaged $13.60) — Joey Devine, Joel Hanrahan, B.J. Ryan, Matt Lindstrom and Chris Ray. In all, 20 of 28 pitchers drafted for saves (71%) realized a loss on their purchase price. Saves remain extremely high risk investments.

The accompanying chart lists the nine 2009 closers who returned less than 50% of their draft value; these are classified as the "failures." However, the list does not include others who also lost their jobs but managed to return at least half their value. These pitchers were George Sherrill, Bobby Jenks, Mike Gonzalez and Chad Qualls. So, in some sense, the failure rate was even greater than indicated.

Of the 13 new sources that amassed at least 10 saves in 2009, nearly half would be considered strong front-line closer candidates for 2010. However, shaky arms on teams with few alternatives, like Franklin and Rodney, and higher skilled arms on teams with more alternatives, like Frasor and Howell, are by no means guarantees.

As we go to press, there are six unsettled bullpen situations in the American League, and five in the National League. While that represents far less uncertainty than in recent years, that's still nearly a dozen potential new sources of saves that will be speculated on over the winter.

Six potential closers are free agents — Rafael Soriano, Mike Gonzalez, Kevin Gregg, Jose Valverde, Billy Wagner and J.J. Putz. There is no guarantee that all these arms will find closing jobs, and in fact, several are good bets to end up in other roles. Still, their signings may create possible ripple effects for all closers.

There will always be volatility here, but this winter likely will not have nearly as much impact as recent seasons. As such, it is reasonable to expect closer prices to rise somewhat in 2010.

CLOSER VOLATILITY CHART

FAILURES

2003	2004	2005	2006	2007	2008	2009
Alfonseca	Biddle	Adams	Benitez	Benitez	Accardo	Capps
Anderson,M	Borowski	Affeldt	Dempster	Dotel	Isringhausen	Devine
Benitez	Guardado	Benitez	Foulke	Fuentes	Jones,T	Hanrahan
Dejean	Koch	Dotel	Gagne	Gagne	Soriano,R	Lidge
Embree	Lopez,Aq	Foulke	Guardado	Gonzalez,M	Borowski	Lindstrom
Escobar	MacDougal	Gagne	MacDougal	Gordon	Corpas	Marmol
Hoffman	Mantei	Graves	Orvella	Ray	Cordero,C	Motte
Isringhausen	Nen	Kolb	Reitsma	Ryan	Gagne	Perez,C
Jimenez	Rhodes	Mota	Turnbow	Torres	Putz	Ryan,BJ
Koch	Riske	Percival	Valverde	Wickman	Wilson,CJ	Wood
Mesa	Wagner	Speier				
Nen		Takatsu				
Sasaki						
Stewart						
Urbina						
Williams,M						
Williamson						

NEW SOURCES

2003	2004	2005	2006	2007	2008	2009
Beck	Affeldt	Brazoban	Burgos	Accardo	Broxton	Aardsma
Biddle	Aquino	Bruney	Duchscherer	Capps	Franklin,R	Bailey,A
Borowski	Chacon	Dempster	Julio,J	Corpas	Fuentes	Franklin
Carter,L	Cordero	Farnsworth	Nelson,J	Embree	Gonzalez,M	Frasor
Cordero,F	Frasor	Fuentes	Otsuka	Gregg	Lewis,J	Hawkins
Gordon	Herges	Hermanson	Papelbon	Hennessy	Morrow	Howell,JP
Hasegawa	Hermanson	Jones,T	Putz	Myers,B	Rauch	Johnson,J
Kolb,D	Hawkins	Lyon	Saito,T	Reyes,A	Rodney	MacDougal
Lopez,Aq	Lidge	MacDougal	Timlin	Soria	Torres,S	Madson
MacDougal	Putz	Reitsma	Torres,S	Wheeler	Wheeler	Nunez,L
Marte	Rodriguez,Fr	Rodney	Walker,T	Wilson,CJ	Ziegler	Rodney
Politte	Takatsu	Street	Wheeler			Soriano,R
Tavarez	Wickman	Turnbow				Wilson,CJ
Worrell	Worrell	Walker,T				
	Yan	Weathers				

SUMMARY

NUMBER OF CLOSERS

YEAR	Drafted	Avg R$	Failed	Failure %	New Sources
1996	24	$30	3	13%	2
1997	26	$30	5	19%	8
1998	25	$32	11	44%	9
1999	23	$25	5	22%	7
2000	27	$25	10	37%	9
2001	25	$26	7	28%	7
2002	28	$22	8	29%	12
2003	29	$21.97	17	59%	14
2004	29	$19.78	11	38%	15
2005	28	$20.79	12	43%	15
2006	30	$17.80	10	33%	12
2007	28	$17.67	10	36%	11
2008	32	$17.78	10	31%	11
2009	28	$17.56	9	32%	13

BULLPEN INDICATORS

Pitcher			Tm	BPIs			Results		Runners		Pitch Ct		Platoon	
				IP/g	bpv	S%	Sv%	Eff%	Emp	On	1-15	16-30	vLH	vRH
Aardsma,David	R	06	CHC	1.2	41	75%	0%	100%	189	247	219	197	190	225
		07	CHW	1.3	66	63%	0%	56%	262	338	274	356	283	310
		08	BOS	1.0	4	68%	0%	73%	202	298	223	316	253	245
		09	SEA	1.0	63	80%	90%	82%	185	180	178	185	190	175
Accardo,Jeremy	R	05	SF	1.0	48	67%	0%	45%	239	222	203	313	182	265
		06	TOR	1.1	72	62%	38%	62%	226	364	286	276	241	307
		07	TOR	1.1	85	83%	86%	80%	201	211	181	290	161	250
		08	TOR	0.8	13	56%	67%	55%	450	200	326	143	300	300
		09	TOR	0.9	-29	87%	100%	100%	310	222	288	235	139	381
Aceves,Alfredo	R	09	NYY	2.0	100	69%	50%	89%	201	265	190	281	216	229
Acosta,Manny	R	07	ATL	1.1	87	84%	0%	83%	159	171	190	105	250	93
		08	ATL	1.2	7	79%	60%	59%	257	247	255	227	289	220
		09	ATL	1.0	34	77%	0%	75%	254	333	293	344	286	304
Adams,Mike	R	05	MIL	1.0	46	90%	50%	60%	231	240	278	167	200	258
		08	SD	1.2	130	82%	0%	71%	158	273	220	188	225	181
		09	SD	1.0	170	90%	0%	94%	98	158	110	150	138	91
Affeldt,Jeremy	L	05	KC	1.0	55	68%	0%	86%	300	259	293	268	263	283
		06	COL	1.8	9	62%	33%	58%	165	315	260	180	213	240
		07	COL	0.8	58	74%	0%	65%	240	213	241	129	250	211
		08	CIN	1.1	116	79%	0%	75%	268	258	277	224	269	261
		09	SF	0.8	62	87%	0%	95%	226	182	187	281	207	198
Albaladejo,Jonatl	R	09	NYY	1.1	16	73%	0%	75%	284	317	272	351	258	338
Albers,Matt	R	08	BAL	1.8	10	75%	0%	64%	226	233	203	227	159	292
		09	BAL	1.2	11	66%	0%	57%	321	306	296	358	342	289
Aquino,Greg	R	09	CLE	1.6	-88	74%	0%	50%	265	174	241	222	182	257
Arias,Alberto	R	09	HOU	1.1	74	76%	0%	79%	319	241	276	276	276	269
Arredondo,Jose	R	08	LAA	1.2	86	87%	0%	74%	175	206	205	161	155	228
		09	LAA	1.0	62	62%	0%	82%	260	282	290	200	244	290
Ascanio,Jose	R	09	PIT	1.1	70	77%	0%	33%	268	379	333	318	522	213
Badenhop,Burke	R	09	FLA	2.1	78	72%	0%	64%	257	253	231	277	257	254
Baez,Danys	R	09	BAL	1.2	56	67%	0%	70%	196	265	200	306	250	205
Bailey,Andrew	R	09	OAK	1.2	124	82%	87%	83%	180	157	174	173	149	188
Bale,John	L	09	KC	0.7	2	69%	20%	69%	245	333	333	0	276	315
Balfour,Grant	R	08	TAM	1.1	128	86%	80%	89%	120	169	100	213	122	156
		09	TAM	0.9	56	65%	44%	75%	197	275	226	246	242	235
Bard,Daniel	R	09	BOS	1.0	115	74%	25%	76%	222	238	262	156	263	202
Bass,Brian	R	08	BAL	1.8	35	69%	50%	62%	368	233	287	237	279	309
		09	BAL	1.8	15	74%	0%	67%	311	302	281	339	298	314
Batista,Miguel	R	09	SEA	1.3	8	77%	20%	73%	309	259	284	293	328	247
Bautista,Denny	R	08	PIT	1.2	-40	70%	0%	74%	286	274	288	230	284	278
		09	PIT	1.0	65	67%	0%	50%	160	450	273	364	286	292
Beimel,Joe	L	06	LA	1.1	26	79%	100%	93%	258	267	286	185	232	279
		07	LA	0.8	42	67%	100%	91%	250	256	256	235	188	294
		08	LA	0.7	25	85%	0%	94%	268	260	265	250	278	250
		09	COL	0.8	36	76%	17%	58%	263	269	232	412	244	282
Belisario,Ronald	R	09	LA	1.0	78	84%	0%	62%	218	178	184	250	268	156
Belisle,Matt	R	09	COL	1.3	95	62%	0%	80%	246	315	333	162	241	308
Bell,Heath	R	07	SD	1.2	134	79%	33%	84%	162	214	182	206	216	157
		08	SD	1.1	83	71%	0%	69%	234	197	234	159	197	242
		09	SD	1.0	122	76%	88%	83%	241	175	239	141	278	132
Bennett,Jeff	R	08	ATL	1.4	38	73%	75%	72%	229	239	249	228	273	212
		09	TAM	1.1	-43	77%	0%	50%	361	333	377	256	386	313
Bergmann,Jason	R	09	WAS	0.9	19	75%	0%	71%	329	242	234	372	339	252
Betancourt,Rafae	R	05	CLE	1.2	129	77%	33%	75%	215	238	233	200	264	204
		06	CLE	1.1	104	71%	50%	65%	214	278	248	236	221	254
		07	CLE	1.2	223	84%	50%	91%	190	173	191	157	239	148
		08	CLE	1.0	64	68%	50%	70%	275	270	303	200	243	295
		09	COL	0.9	94	78%	33%	79%	242	184	238	143	268	174
Bowden,Michael	R	09	BOS	2.0	49	46%	0%	67%	143	476	222	182	370	200
Boyer,Blaine	R	08	ATL	0.9	89	58%	20%	63%	228	313	230	357	271	256
		09	ARI	1.1	36	68%	0%	67%	206	327	263	345	240	288
Bradford,Chad	R	05	BOS	0.8	64	72%	0%	83%	308	315	297	389	409	282
		06	NYM	0.9	108	73%	67%	84%	284	224	238	333	262	251
		07	BAL	0.8	36	75%	29%	68%	273	312	291	310	321	282
		08	TAM	0.9	34	85%	0%	83%	280	264	268	318	303	259
		09	TAM	0.5	78	83%	0%	75%	313	486	426	500	800	391
Breslow,Craig	L	08	MIN	1.0	56	83%	50%	67%	214	200	196	229	190	224
		09	OAK	0.9	36	74%	0%	72%	224	160	190	220	206	185
Broxton,Jonathar	R	06	LA	1.1	106	83%	43%	79%	253	172	234	192	244	196
		07	LA	1.0	137	77%	25%	79%	228	220	245	152	200	247
		08	LA	1.0	130	72%	64%	70%	173	255	199	238	260	177
		09	LA	1.0	176	74%	86%	85%	151	196	149	232	142	194
Bruney,Brian	R	05	ARI	1.0	55	62%	75%	71%	227	364	277	339	280	314
		06	NYY	1.1	87	96%	0%	83%	195	182	184	200	115	229
		07	NYY	0.9	31	72%	0%	69%	256	232	262	204	303	209
		08	NYY	1.1	60	84%	50%	94%	105	212	192	71	119	179
		09	NYY	0.9	12	79%	0%	95%	200	327	259	192	224	269
Bulger,Jason	R	09	LAA	1.0	73	72%	25%	80%	241	170	213	196	192	223
Burke,Greg	R	09	SD	1.0	19	75%	0%	72%	276	266	293	176	346	208
Burnett,Sean	L	09	WAS	0.8	28	76%	33%	74%	198	161	176	217	186	176
Burton,Jared	R	07	CIN	0.9	68	79%	0%	75%	195	176	179	222	130	219
		08	CIN	1.1	83	80%	0%	84%	250	257	284	190	242	262
		09	CIN	1.1	48	70%	0%	100%	235	285	284	250	227	289

BULLPEN INDICATORS

Pitcher			Tm	BPIs			Results		Runners		Pitch Ct		Platoon	
				IP/g	bpv	S%	Sv%	Eff%	Emp	On	1-15	16-30	vLH	vRH
Byrdak,Tim	L	05	BAL	0.6	85	77%	100%	92%	250	260	247	261	214	300
		06	BAL	0.4	-56	60%	0%	100%	412	467	444	400	381	545
		07	DET	1.2	80	79%	50%	92%	231	230	193	290	176	268
		08	HOU	0.9	28	78%	0%	91%	232	218	235	105	138	295
		09	HOU	0.8	26	82%	0%	71%	180	176	177	208	186	171
Calero,Kiko	R	09	FLA	0.9	69	82%	0%	67%	214	147	185	178	194	174
Cameron,Kevin	R	09	OAK	1.7	72	70%	100%	100%	184	267	314	148	240	209
Camp,Shawn	R	06	TAM	1.0	64	71%	67%	79%	316	310	300	365	370	284
		07	TAM	0.8	54	66%	0%	69%	382	362	397	212	370	368
		08	TOR	1.0	92	67%	0%	91%	228	301	279	167	356	204
		09	TOR	1.4	62	75%	100%	60%	256	237	243	273	268	228
Capps,Matt	R	06	PIT	1.0	95	72%	10%	70%	265	268	266	288	250	275
		07	PIT	1.0	99	80%	86%	79%	228	207	197	364	281	181
		08	PIT	1.1	106	72%	81%	74%	233	253	248	235	229	253
		09	PIT	1.0	79	69%	84%	71%	353	294	311	380	339	311
Caridad,Esmailin	R	09	CHC	1.4	119	83%	0%	100%	229	250	182	231	222	250
Carlson,Jesse	L	08	TOR	0.9	73	84%	100%	93%	202	185	188	220	200	189
		09	TOR	0.9	61	65%	0%	59%	276	234	247	304	270	248
Carlyle,Buddy	R	09	ATL	1.3	-33	62%	0%	67%	441	345	405	346	316	426
Casilla,Santiago	R	07	OAK	1.1	73	68%	40%	81%	216	233	208	266	212	230
		08	OAK	1.0	60	77%	67%	85%	344	257	328	230	308	291
		09	OAK	1.1	17	68%	0%	75%	250	354	326	178	366	243
Castillo,Alberto	L	09	BAL	0.6	54	81%	0%	100%	308	308	324	0	292	333
Chavez,Jesse	R	09	TAM	0.9	50	76%	0%	67%	256	277	270	255	230	301
Choate,Randy	L	09	TAM	0.6	94	71%	100%	100%	213	210	213	200	149	306
Clippard,Tyler	R	09	WAS	1.5	53	85%	0%	70%	165	190	186	197	114	247
Coffey,Todd	R	09	MIL	1.1	95	79%	33%	80%	226	273	258	206	292	213
Coke,Phil	L	09	NYY	0.8	63	63%	29%	77%	235	184	196	243	197	229
Colon,Roman	R	09	KC	1.2	7	69%	0%	57%	202	312	252	250	272	243
Condrey,Clay	R	07	PHI	1.3	32	67%	100%	100%	290	309	322	206	299	302
		08	PHI	1.2	46	81%	100%	56%	293	314	340	191	317	292
		09	PHI	0.9	49	79%	50%	82%	181	317	246	143	175	268
Corcoran,Roy	R	09	HOU	1.2	-128	72%	0%	80%	267	425	383	333	345	366
Cordero,Francisc	R	05	TEX	1.0	98	76%	82%	82%	231	236	249	194	250	214
		06	MIL	1.0	90	74%	67%	75%	229	266	260	231	286	219
		07	MIL	1.0	156	74%	86%	80%	187	260	191	340	225	212
		08	CIN	1.0	61	78%	85%	80%	213	261	245	203	212	252
		09	CIN	1.0	48	84%	91%	80%	241	253	230	327	230	260
Cormier,Lance	R	09	TAM	1.5	29	77%	100%	79%	287	209	278	196	245	255
Corpas,Manny	R	06	COL	0.9	91	76%	0%	67%	282	291	311	150	281	290
		07	COL	1.0	90	84%	86%	89%	211	245	213	300	234	214
		08	COL	1.0	59	70%	31%	67%	275	295	271	315	267	301
		09	COL	1.0	93	60%	33%	64%	286	369	348	217	400	267
Cotts,Neal	L	05	CHW	0.9	90	82%	0%	89%	171	188	196	114	206	155
		06	CHW	0.8	21	75%	25%	76%	295	287	285	309	263	314
		08	CHC	0.7	117	77%	0%	69%	319	175	250	267	254	250
		09	CHC	0.6	-33	70%	0%	40%	389	259	333	250	318	304
Crain,Jesse	R	05	MIN	1.1	15	79%	25%	75%	218	219	228	185	209	225
		06	MIN	1.1	91	74%	25%	65%	243	289	250	256	259	263
		07	MIN	0.9	47	68%	0%	78%	200	440	224	500	269	308
		08	MIN	0.9	55	76%	0%	76%	276	233	256	255	247	258
		09	MIN	0.9	26	67%	0%	73%	255	241	243	275	296	218
Cruz,Juan	R	07	ARI	1.2	120	80%	0%	91%	198	211	219	208	269	143
		08	ARI	0.9	74	83%	0%	86%	141	243	163	231	160	207
		09	KC	1.1	-19	62%	33%	60%	242	255	259	238	247	250
Daley,Matt	R	09	COL	0.9	97	67%	0%	76%	178	280	216	256	260	198
Delcarmen,Mann	R	06	BOS	1.1	91	66%	0%	80%	273	345	283	371	319	302
		07	BOS	1.0	93	85%	50%	92%	193	169	195	143	164	196
		08	BOS	1.0	92	72%	40%	81%	199	215	209	200	197	214
		09	BOS	0.9	-2	73%	0%	69%	288	252	229	361	221	322
Dickey,R.A.	R	09	MIN	1.8	16	74%	0%	67%	293	304	321	269	257	331
DiFelice,Mark	R	09	MIL	0.9	82	74%	0%	87%	255	233	230	324	278	233
Donnelly,Brendar	R	05	ANA	1.0	65	74%	0%	76%	258	228	260	194	213	274
		06	ANA	1.0	51	74%	0%	94%	234	246	256	194	290	204
		07	BOS	0.8	66	71%	0%	91%	235	234	225	300	212	250
		08	CLE	0.9	-73	61%	0%	100%	269	407	286	545	300	364
		09	FLA	0.8	87	87%	100%	100%	333	160	243	222	262	220
Dotel,Octavio	R	05	OAK	1.0	52	79%	64%	57%	143	212	175	273	269	107
		07	ATL	0.9	117	73%	73%	74%	322	164	278	133	265	225
		08	CHW	0.9	127	77%	20%	76%	242	188	235	167	250	201
		09	CHW	1.0	56	81%	0%	76%	228	250	238	232	268	226
Downs,Scott	L	06	TOR	1.3	54	72%	25%	72%	246	134	199	203	177	208
		07	TOR	0.7	97	84%	25%	85%	198	250	233	184	209	238
		08	TOR	1.1	82	86%	56%	81%	200	229	209	203	194	226
		09	TOR	1.0	114	78%	69%	74%	295	205	259	222	263	246
Duensing,Brian	L	09	MIN	3.5	36	75%	0%	75%	266	286	341	220	227	303
Dumatrait,Phil	L	09	PIT	0.9	-101	70%	0%	25%	269	261	250	333	304	231
Durbin,Chad	R	09	PHI	1.2	-8	73%	67%	80%	210	240	207	276	229	217
Elbert,Scott	L	09	LA	1.0	105	68%	0%	100%	282	206	243	240	206	282
Embree,Alan	L	09	COL	0.7	-20	65%	0%	62%	300	286	284	333	326	264
Escalona,Sergio	L	09	PHI	1.0	45	59%	0%	100%	261	143	167	500	182	231

BULLPEN INDICATORS

				BPIs			Results		Runners		Pitch Ct		Platoon	
Pitcher			Tm	IP/g	bpv	S%	Sv%	Eff%	Emp	On	1-15	16-30	vLH	vRH
Eyre,Scott	L	05	SF	0.8	92	76%	0%	89%	233	167	188	239	182	213
		06	CHC	0.8	67	85%	0%	76%	280	248	298	179	281	255
		07	CHC	1.0	41	77%	0%	58%	258	321	271	339	253	317
		08	PHI	0.7	142	64%	0%	87%	293	216	200	471	220	286
		09	PHI	0.7	-2	94%	0%	94%	292	130	225	150	203	209
Farnsworth,Kyle	R	09	KC	0.9	111	70%	0%	46%	232	353	288	289	277	294
Feliciano,Pedro	L	06	NYM	0.9	87	86%	0%	77%	255	242	270	173	231	266
		07	NYM	0.8	87	75%	67%	88%	233	165	199	208	168	221
		08	NYM	0.6	60	78%	50%	81%	292	268	297	115	198	368
		09	NYM	0.7	120	79%	0%	83%	274	184	228	238	216	264
Feliz,Neftali	R	09	TEX	1.6	152	79%	67%	92%	134	114	154	93	161	87
Fisher,Carlos	R	09	CIN	1.3	22	71%	0%	60%	267	239	248	265	321	200
Flores,Randy	L	05	STL	0.8	93	76%	33%	83%	280	194	228	310	176	300
		06	STL	0.6	58	68%	0%	90%	286	293	306	182	258	329
		07	STL	0.8	72	71%	50%	95%	261	360	307	333	326	299
		08	STL	0.6	-56	75%	33%	89%	273	344	286	435	314	316
		09	COL	0.4	164	64%	0%	91%	320	250	268	375	273	313
Fogg,Josh	R	09	COL	1.9	15	73%	0%	33%	173	206	167	196	203	175
Francisco,Frank	R	07	TEX	1.0	42	71%	0%	96%	309	220	245	284	221	286
		08	TEX	1.1	117	77%	45%	65%	189	212	196	216	193	205
		09	TEX	1.0	116	69%	86%	82%	167	300	203	250	240	190
Franklin,Ryan	R	07	STL	1.2	92	74%	17%	77%	227	244	256	172	238	231
		08	STL	1.1	33	80%	68%	72%	269	284	283	278	258	287
		09	STL	1.0	44	85%	88%	84%	231	192	221	182	194	230
Frasor,Jason	R	05	TOR	1.1	63	78%	33%	73%	248	246	250	244	236	257
		06	TOR	1.0	75	71%	0%	83%	207	293	248	235	211	262
		07	TOR	1.1	93	61%	50%	50%	217	222	213	224	245	200
		08	TOR	1.0	-10	72%	0%	63%	230	186	194	267	266	174
		09	TOR	0.9	104	78%	79%	79%	198	227	217	186	274	140
Fuentes,Brian	L	05	COL	1.0	101	79%	91%	83%	261	171	235	182	164	237
		06	COL	1.0	86	75%	83%	77%	240	173	216	184	183	218
		07	COL	1.0	82	76%	74%	72%	167	271	190	275	204	207
		08	COL	0.9	131	76%	88%	80%	188	235	180	300	184	210
		09	LAA	0.8	41	75%	87%	80%	264	247	268	205	229	271
Fulchino,Jeff	R	09	HOU	1.3	84	73%	0%	72%	226	233	235	280	254	208
Geary,Geoff	R	05	PHI	1.5	58	73%	0%	71%	222	277	212	313	192	294
		06	PHI	1.1	81	79%	25%	85%	337	234	303	253	348	249
		07	PHI	1.2	35	72%	0%	71%	318	259	290	263	248	309
		08	HOU	1.2	29	79%	0%	74%	203	175	191	151	216	174
		09	HOU	1.3	-9	61%	0%	38%	368	348	451	259	375	346
Gervacio,Sammy	R	09	HOU	0.7	130	83%	0%	78%	150	296	203	286	235	200
Gonzalez,Mike	L	05	PIT	1.0	91	80%	100%	86%	225	169	207	173	152	223
		06	PIT	1.0	102	83%	100%	88%	168	267	223	184	163	227
		07	ATL	0.9	51	87%	100%	100%	290	200	235	300	333	189
		08	ATL	0.9	115	71%	88%	74%	221	205	253	77	269	200
		09	ATL	0.9	98	84%	59%	74%	258	142	233	138	198	219
Gorzelanny,Tom	L	09	CHC	2.1	90	59%	0%	69%	100	318	83	438	235	171
Grabow,John	L	05	PIT	0.8	48	66%	0%	80%	217	257	242	237	219	250
		06	PIT	1.0	70	73%	0%	79%	223	307	259	214	275	251
		07	PIT	0.8	63	71%	50%	80%	263	291	293	231	238	303
		08	PIT	1.0	28	83%	50%	79%	259	176	228	227	239	214
		09	CHC	1.0	11	77%	0%	93%	200	265	254	154	213	242
Gray,Jeff	R	09	OAK	1.1	115	74%	0%	50%	263	273	260	296	304	236
Green,Sean	R	06	SEA	1.3	33	69%	0%	75%	273	286	250	294	190	325
		07	SEA	1.1	57	75%	0%	78%	300	297	292	324	329	286
		08	SEA	1.1	56	66%	25%	73%	292	233	272	215	306	229
		09	NYM	0.9	41	68%	33%	73%	212	287	249	200	228	259
Gregerson,Luke	R	09	SD	1.0	119	73%	14%	75%	214	239	233	200	291	162
Gregg,Kevin	R	07	FLA	1.1	76	73%	89%	81%	194	220	166	276	162	247
		08	CHC	1.0	27	73%	76%	70%	182	228	206	200	179	224
		09	CHC	1.0	73	70%	77%	69%	242	212	233	222	195	257
Grilli,Jason	R	06	DET	1.2	27	71%	0%	79%	239	290	223	319	292	249
		07	DET	1.4	52	66%	0%	76%	245	280	305	226	237	275
		08	COL	1.3	41	78%	50%	67%	252	220	262	229	227	242
		09	TEX	0.9	36	68%	100%	77%	278	281	279	295	262	295
Guardado,Eddie	L	05	SEA	1.0	80	83%	88%	83%	234	244	240	239	231	242
		06	CIN	0.9	47	87%	72%	67%	303	288	308	250	234	327
		08	MIN	0.9	18	66%	80%	87%	257	233	277	108	213	268
		09	TEX	0.8	5	76%	0%	60%	241	305	272	226	333	228
Guerrier,Matt	R	06	MIN	1.8	31	81%	100%	100%	304	273	276	318	337	258
		07	MIN	1.2	92	83%	25%	71%	218	224	232	195	264	187
		08	MIN	1.0	30	71%	20%	68%	266	287	264	273	280	272
		09	MIN	1.0	70	84%	25%	91%	250	165	224	160	198	221
Gutierrez,Juan	R	09	ARI	1.1	63	68%	90%	83%	211	301	264	240	297	212
Guzman,Angel	R	09	CHC	1.1	58	79%	100%	86%	198	181	203	179	189	194
Hanrahan,Joel	R	08	WAS	1.2	72	74%	69%	72%	215	252	257	230	228	237
		09	PIT	1.0	61	70%	50%	63%	293	279	302	274	271	297
Hawkins,LaTroy	R	05	SF	0.9	45	77%	40%	58%	203	370	236	345	228	297
		06	BAL	1.0	44	69%	0%	76%	313	287	314	278	323	285
		07	COL	0.9	53	76%	0%	67%	262	237	222	433	237	266
		08	HOU	1.1	62	67%	50%	89%	178	303	219	250	287	185
		09	HOU	1.0	77	88%	73%	79%	279	198	266	167	204	289
Hawksworth,Blak	R	09	STL	1.3	23	83%	0%	100%	228	196	220	231	262	174

BULLPEN INDICATORS

				BPIs			Results		Runners		Pitch Ct		Platoon	
Pitcher			Tm	IP/g	bpv	S%	Sv%	Eff%	Emp	On	1-15	16-30	vLH	vRH
Heilman,Aaron	R	05	NYM	2.0	98	73%	83%	79%	198	216	207	213	185	225
		06	NYM	1.2	85	69%	0%	76%	205	267	228	239	231	231
		07	NYM	1.1	87	75%	17%	71%	197	261	211	237	234	218
		08	NYM	1.0	38	69%	38%	62%	216	309	262	240	308	225
		09	CHC	1.0	47	74%	14%	60%	257	256	270	261	214	286
Hendrickson,Marl	L	09	BAL	2.0	42	74%	33%	56%	292	240	232	305	247	283
Henn,Sean	L	09	BAL	0.7	-26	60%	0%	29%	226	333	256	333	323	208
Herges,Matt	R	05	ARI	1.0	-23	59%	0%	80%	317	288	346	154	256	333
		06	FLA	1.1	35	75%	0%	61%	318	323	296	386	300	340
		07	COL	1.4	61	73%	0%	73%	170	250	223	164	216	184
		08	COL	1.1	41	68%	0%	44%	273	328	306	313	282	318
		09	COL	1.2	91	78%	0%	67%	215	286	247	233	270	222
Herrera,Daniel	L	09	CIN	0.9	48	80%	0%	76%	263	291	261	360	185	362
Hinckley,Mike	L	08	WAS	1.0	78	100%	0%	100%	273	63	172	222	214	167
		09	TEX	0.7	-209	78%	0%	80%	313	200	190	250	77	389
Hoffman,Trevor	R	05	SD	1.0	131	74%	93%	83%	240	230	235	235	298	179
		06	SD	1.0	98	84%	90%	87%	257	122	212	133	194	214
		07	SD	0.9	70	73%	86%	79%	215	247	230	211	299	169
		08	SD	0.9	130	72%	88%	77%	211	268	217	333	299	170
		09	MIL	1.0	97	81%	90%	87%	180	200	209	43	227	151
Howell,J.P.	L	08	TAM	1.4	90	83%	60%	88%	207	178	215	116	188	197
		09	TAM	1.0	93	81%	68%	68%	197	196	204	176	280	159
Howry,Bob	R	05	CLE	0.9	84	74%	60%	87%	181	212	201	148	180	198
		06	CHC	0.9	110	76%	56%	77%	240	250	253	224	247	244
		07	CHC	1.0	95	75%	67%	77%	196	317	269	162	192	283
		08	CHC	1.0	102	68%	20%	72%	319	288	305	304	336	282
		09	SF	1.0	40	72%	0%	57%	180	261	165	297	216	210
Hughes,Dustin	L	09	KC	1.8	54	68%	0%	50%	222	190	357	111	250	182
Hughes,Phil	R	09	NYY	1.7	110	76%	50%	83%	170	145	161	143	182	143
Jackson,Steven	R	09	PIT	1.1	-23	78%	0%	60%	250	228	198	293	205	268
Jakubauskas,Chr	R	09	SEA	2.7	36	61%	0%	53%	192	309	175	292	202	263
Janssen,Casey	R	09	TOR	1.9	41	69%	100%	56%	259	379	268	385	158	405
Jenks,Bobby	R	05	CHW	1.2	118	80%	75%	77%	224	227	221	268	105	298
		06	CHW	1.0	97	72%	91%	85%	241	266	254	261	227	268
		07	CHW	1.0	131	68%	87%	80%	149	269	202	176	237	169
		08	CHW	1.1	69	77%	88%	87%	244	209	244	156	219	240
		09	CHW	1.0	101	78%	83%	76%	268	224	265	190	309	202
Jepsen,Kevin	R	09	LAA	1.0	91	65%	50%	83%	263	296	280	292	356	204
Johnson,Jim	R	08	BAL	1.3	27	79%	100%	85%	236	200	198	250	227	212
		09	BAL	1.1	63	73%	63%	70%	285	239	278	224	248	279
Karstens,Jeff	R	09	PIT	2.8	-5	64%	0%	45%	182	406	250	277	274	266
Kawakami,Kensh	R	09	ATL	4.9	40	73%	100%	0%	250	333	318	273	263	300
Kelley,Shawn	R	09	SEA	1.1	105	69%	0%	64%	255	263	254	259	209	307
Kensing,Logan	R	08	FLA	1.2	21	75%	0%	67%	212	257	254	224	208	259
		09	WAS	1.1	-12	57%	33%	43%	367	363	387	317	317	400
Keppel,Bobby	R	09	MIN	1.5	30	69%	0%	71%	297	276	333	226	299	275
Kilby,Brad	L	09	OAK	1.5	130	100%	0%	100%	139	263	171	250	227	152
Kinney,Josh	R	09	STL	0.9	-61	59%	0%	75%	370	333	304	471	219	484
Kuo,Hong-Chih	L	08	LA	1.9	149	81%	33%	78%	204	181	214	188	167	207
		09	LA	0.9	87	75%	0%	94%	236	167	209	167	156	225
Laffey,Aaron	L	09	CLE	4.9	-8	73%	100%	0%	200	286	130	353	176	276
Leach,Brent	L	09	LA	0.5	27	60%	0%	100%	216	211	224	125	256	156
League,Brandon	R	08	TOR	1.1	46	85%	100%	78%	246	211	235	219	250	210
		09	TOR	1.1	128	65%	0%	57%	252	258	239	296	263	246
Lewis,Jensen	R	07	CLE	1.1	107	83%	0%	86%	222	246	274	188	244	229
		08	CLE	1.3	39	77%	93%	77%	283	254	264	235	265	272
		09	CLE	1.4	57	73%	20%	47%	258	243	220	247	312	198
Lidge,Brad	R	05	HOU	1.0	154	83%	91%	85%	239	205	235	186	244	202
		06	HOU	1.0	100	64%	84%	78%	224	256	242	236	286	201
		07	HOU	1.0	116	79%	70%	74%	223	212	213	234	184	243
		08	PHI	1.0	109	84%	100%	100%	209	170	207	137	261	108
		09	PHI	0.9	39	62%	74%	63%	279	336	316	286	322	289
Lincoln,Mike	R	08	CIN	1.1	76	69%	0%	67%	253	248	243	284	225	270
		09	CIN	1.2	-117	66%	0%	67%	405	255	357	267	405	269
Lindstrom,Matt	R	07	FLA	0.9	87	75%	0%	79%	230	289	247	280	263	255
		08	FLA	0.9	34	77%	83%	85%	276	270	288	152	327	218
		09	FLA	0.9	30	64%	88%	89%	267	299	270	310	276	287
Linebrink,Scott	R	05	SD	1.0	101	85%	17%	85%	227	186	208	200	197	221
		06	SD	1.0	81	75%	18%	78%	258	224	248	230	204	294
		07	MIL	1.0	54	79%	12%	68%	268	232	251	258	215	284
		08	CHW	0.9	111	74%	25%	81%	204	250	217	237	179	256
		09	CHW	1.0	71	76%	50%	57%	341	260	306	286	303	307
Logan,Boone	L	06	CHW	0.8	37	59%	50%	75%	194	378	302	176	357	244
		07	CHW	0.7	40	71%	0%	81%	301	295	248	465	221	357
		08	CHW	0.8	97	67%	0%	56%	264	371	315	379	291	351
		09	ATL	0.9	8	69%	0%	67%	290	278	316	111	237	345
Lowe,Mark	R	08	SEA	1.1	30	70%	20%	25%	317	297	309	314	358	258
		09	SEA	1.1	67	76%	23%	65%	234	221	215	270	259	200
Lyon,Brandon	R	05	ARI	0.9	12	69%	93%	83%	382	311	356	320	317	364
		06	ARI	1.0	52	72%	0%	69%	290	226	294	143	244	270
		07	ARI	1.0	39	78%	40%	86%	294	210	278	146	233	267
		08	ARI	1.0	85	70%	84%	76%	294	318	301	314	283	323
		09	DET	1.2	46	78%	50%	75%	203	207	206	153	209	201

BULLPEN INDICATORS

				BPIs			Results		Runners		Pitch Ct		Platoon	
Pitcher			Tm	IP/g	bpv	S%	Sv%	Eff%	Emp	On	1-15	16-30	vLH	vRH
MacDougal,Mike	R	09	WAS	1.0	-32	74%	95%	91%	256	267	274	240	294	226
Madson,Ryan	R	05	PHI	1.1	81	70%	0%	76%	247	273	304	160	292	233
		06	PHI	2.7	41	68%	50%	63%	344	256	342	235	296	311
		07	PHI	1.5	64	79%	50%	77%	198	280	222	200	170	275
		08	PHI	1.1	92	77%	33%	85%	244	258	267	225	257	244
		09	PHI	1.0	116	76%	63%	79%	277	220	247	268	259	243
Mahay,Ron	L	05	TEX	1.2	24	65%	100%	78%	314	313	326	370	302	322
		06	TEX	0.9	62	76%	0%	71%	248	252	245	254	240	258
		07	ATL	1.2	62	82%	50%	92%	227	210	210	203	189	242
		08	KC	1.1	31	77%	0%	96%	248	246	217	299	250	245
		09	MIN	0.9	45	81%	0%	89%	294	299	320	265	265	324
Marmol,Carlos	R	07	CHC	1.2	123	89%	50%	92%	183	154	150	208	209	146
		08	CHC	1.1	103	77%	78%	87%	126	151	128	162	187	94
		09	CHC	0.9	-6	75%	79%	85%	221	131	175	162	138	201
Marshall,Sean	L	08	CHC	1.9	74	74%	50%	54%	269	150	242	95	219	217
		09	CHC	1.6	63	73%	0%	59%	276	235	260	310	230	277
Marte,Damaso	L	05	CHW	0.7	69	81%	50%	78%	222	291	269	222	267	244
		06	PIT	0.8	78	75%	0%	56%	257	230	238	206	225	258
		07	PIT	0.7	107	79%	0%	100%	202	197	211	160	94	271
		08	NYY	0.9	86	67%	71%	88%	197	224	220	146	235	197
		09	NYY	0.6	52	39%	0%	60%	286	290	286	300	130	414
Masset,Nick	R	08	CIN	1.5	39	78%	33%	71%	327	263	346	176	263	311
		09	CIN	1.0	102	81%	0%	89%	168	255	223	104	217	198
Masterson,Justin	R	09	CLE	3.1	65	70%	0%	48%	210	284	219	250	316	198
Mathis,Doug	R	09	TEX	1.8	68	76%	100%	67%	236	191	254	209	259	185
McClellan,Kyle	R	08	STL	1.1	67	72%	17%	73%	298	238	280	253	238	291
		09	STL	1.0	26	76%	50%	76%	187	265	219	210	186	244
McClung,Seth	R	09	MIL	1.5	-36	74%	0%	67%	270	239	245	281	284	227
McDonald,James	R	09	LA	1.4	26	75%	0%	67%	265	257	293	226	212	291
Medders,Brandor	R	09	SF	1.1	33	81%	25%	78%	278	226	228	312	260	247
Medlen,Kris	R	09	ATL	1.8	79	70%	0%	36%	247	284	280	231	165	373
Meek,Evan	R	09	PIT	1.1	20	74%	0%	71%	225	189	192	261	250	176
Meredith,Cla	R	06	SD	1.1	153	91%	0%	88%	216	114	161	200	281	107
		07	SD	1.0	97	76%	0%	58%	267	327	295	262	286	303
		08	SD	1.0	74	73%	0%	55%	299	285	281	298	352	260
		09	BAL	1.0	40	73%	0%	62%	274	323	297	275	286	311
Messenger,Rand	R	06	FLA	1.0	44	66%	0%	58%	299	293	265	338	333	267
		07	SF	1.1	17	75%	20%	64%	314	343	357	292	342	320
		08	SEA	1.0	-1	80%	100%	100%	381	200	310	273	250	333
		09	SEA	0.9	100	80%	0%	50%	346	214	300	333	333	250
Meyer,Dan	L	09	FLA	0.8	79	79%	100%	93%	177	271	209	243	235	198
Mickolio,Kam	R	09	BAL	1.2	54	78%	0%	50%	160	280	214	222	43	370
Mijares,Jose	L	09	MIN	0.9	67	86%	0%	91%	248	168	217	188	122	280
Miller,Justin	R	07	FLA	1.0	108	72%	0%	88%	242	213	252	148	324	184
		08	FLA	1.0	51	71%	0%	79%	289	232	256	261	310	224
		09	SF	1.3	5	81%	0%	57%	263	210	229	267	241	233
Miller,Trever	L	05	TAM	0.7	44	77%	0%	72%	239	308	282	257	267	289
		06	HOU	0.7	113	79%	33%	75%	271	176	234	161	221	228
		07	HOU	0.6	61	69%	33%	87%	205	290	242	333	209	289
		08	TAM	0.6	56	68%	67%	94%	313	173	248	250	209	299
		09	STL	0.6	120	86%	0%	89%	188	188	184	231	121	293
Miner,Zach	R	07	DET	1.6	44	80%	0%	67%	326	222	318	210	219	312
		08	DET	2.6	14	70%	0%	64%	222	274	281	175	247	250
		09	DET	1.8	12	76%	20%	64%	285	230	299	214	261	260
Morales,Franklin	L	09	COL	1.0	26	72%	88%	85%	182	263	225	185	152	253
Moreno,Edwin	R	09	SD	1.2	-43	78%	0%	56%	370	250	333	296	352	250
Morrow,Brandon	R	07	SEA	1.1	58	75%	0%	78%	222	265	277	187	278	221
		08	SEA	1.4	65	78%	83%	73%	125	174	131	185	200	99
		09	SEA	2.7	3	76%	75%	60%	275	243	300	259	311	188
Mota,Guillermo	R	05	FLA	1.2	68	67%	50%	82%	231	279	283	211	243	262
		06	NYM	1.1	32	75%	0%	81%	261	253	237	300	252	261
		07	NYM	1.1	65	59%	0%	62%	225	317	264	215	235	284
		08	MIL	1.0	43	74%	25%	65%	236	253	229	291	291	210
		09	LA	1.1	22	73%	0%	45%	185	283	230	207	207	239
Motte,Jason	R	08	STL	0.9	185	88%	100%	100%	111	167	130	143	71	188
		09	STL	0.8	69	71%	0%	73%	315	202	250	316	341	208
Moylan,Peter	R	07	ATL	1.1	76	87%	50%	78%	215	199	223	171	242	184
		08	ATL	0.8	144	100%	50%	71%	273	167	217	0	273	167
		09	ATL	0.8	56	77%	0%	82%	242	246	263	167	304	211
Mujica,Edward	R	09	SD	1.4	99	75%	67%	73%	284	223	293	195	285	238
Nathan,Joe	R	05	MIN	1.0	143	75%	90%	85%	165	215	171	224	158	206
		06	MIN	1.1	188	82%	95%	96%	168	141	176	63	193	130
		07	MIN	1.1	129	84%	90%	87%	174	262	209	207	221	199
		08	MIN	1.0	133	91%	87%	83%	211	130	191	163	175	191
		09	MIN	1.0	146	84%	90%	88%	184	153	162	191	156	190
Nelson,Joe	R	08	FLA	0.9	93	88%	20%	75%	198	219	232	150	237	183
		09	TAM	1.0	-13	79%	75%	93%	138	317	170	273	212	216
Ni,Fu-Te	L	09	DET	0.9	32	79%	0%	60%	250	150	197	95	119	289
Nippert,Dustin	R	09	TEX	3.5	42	73%	0%	67%	167	241	182	182	125	296
Nunez,Leo	R	08	FLA	1.1	29	76%	0%	73%	231	253	246	237	266	221
		09	FLA	0.9	63	75%	79%	77%	253	204	246	196	236	229
O'Day,Darren	R	09	TEX	0.9	97	84%	100%	96%	180	221	194	194	246	174
O'Flaherty,Eric	L	09	ATL	0.7	67	75%	0%	85%	221	290	234	379	219	293

BULLPEN INDICATORS

				BPIs			Results		Runners		Pitch Ct		Platoon	
Pitcher			Tm	IP/g	bpv	S%	Sv%	Eff%	Emp	On	1-15	16-30	vLH	vRH
Okajima,Hideki	L	07	BOS	1.0	112	82%	71%	90%	230	168	219	155	236	182
		08	BOS	1.0	75	82%	11%	73%	182	269	213	241	188	242
		09	BOS	0.9	63	78%	0%	94%	199	305	229	294	167	309
Oliver,Darren	L	06	NYM	1.8	57	77%	0%	88%	215	259	259	161	208	244
		07	LAA	1.1	63	71%	0%	92%	222	263	219	221	289	209
		08	LAA	1.3	80	77%	0%	86%	252	263	247	229	231	275
		09	LAA	1.2	91	78%	0%	93%	235	235	271	186	250	222
Olson,Garrett	L	09	SEA	2.6	4	67%	0%	62%	250	268	244	350	333	213
Owings,Micah	R	09	CIN	4.6	-24	69%	100%	0%	139	143	53	83	87	185
Papelbon,Jonath:	R	05	BOS	2.0	64	87%	0%	78%	262	259	262	292	200	308
		06	BOS	1.2	169	92%	85%	83%	199	112	180	132	203	128
		07	BOS	1.0	189	82%	92%	87%	123	187	161	83	104	200
		08	BOS	1.0	178	77%	89%	84%	186	263	206	255	227	202
		09	BOS	1.0	96	88%	93%	91%	258	177	257	123	192	246
Park,Chan Ho	R	09	PHI	1.9	65	68%	0%	80%	175	301	196	315	269	204
Parnell,Bobby	R	09	NYM	1.3	31	68%	20%	64%	253	272	253	280	250	270
Pena,Tony	R	06	ARI	1.2	39	66%	100%	60%	253	356	309	289	382	179
		07	ARI	1.1	65	73%	40%	84%	209	205	211	205	245	176
		08	ARI	1.0	84	67%	38%	81%	264	277	279	230	280	260
		09	CHW	1.0	81	74%	50%	75%	290	276	284	279	288	279
Peralta,Joel	R	09	COL	0.9	26	61%	0%	60%	318	245	250	273	348	216
Percival,Troy	R	05	DET	1.0	6	61%	73%	60%	206	207	211	200	176	244
		07	STL	1.2	106	84%	0%	100%	161	186	218	30	214	138
		08	TAM	0.9	-11	70%	88%	87%	165	218	190	167	188	179
		09	TAM	0.8	-7	69%	100%	86%	385	200	300	333	478	130
Perez,Chris	R	08	STL	1.0	46	78%	64%	70%	267	169	202	258	245	207
		09	CLE	0.9	85	68%	40%	67%	163	242	193	245	185	209
Perez,Rafael	L	07	CLE	1.4	137	86%	50%	82%	185	191	147	254	145	213
		08	CLE	1.0	140	73%	29%	78%	202	276	230	236	216	244
		09	CLE	0.9	7	60%	0%	71%	312	348	322	414	392	283
Perry,Ryan	R	09	DET	1.2	23	78%	0%	60%	250	257	252	277	306	210
Pinto,Renyel	L	06	FLA	1.1	66	84%	100%	100%	156	217	207	222	150	215
		07	FLA	1.0	71	76%	17%	68%	271	167	228	200	210	227
		08	FLA	1.0	14	72%	0%	73%	236	214	259	148	258	206
		09	FLA	0.8	-10	81%	0%	77%	295	188	220	229	275	200
Putz,J.J.	R	05	SEA	0.9	46	78%	25%	78%	236	276	225	364	321	197
		06	SEA	1.1	226	76%	84%	85%	176	257	200	229	211	204
		07	SEA	1.1	194	89%	95%	94%	180	109	173	26	148	158
		08	SEA	1.0	61	77%	65%	62%	239	274	279	222	261	250
		09	NYM	1.0	-30	66%	50%	68%	228	286	263	242	296	220
Qualls,Chad	R	05	HOU	1.0	72	75%	0%	88%	263	234	251	242	218	275
		06	HOU	1.1	46	71%	0%	77%	242	242	258	181	227	253
		07	HOU	1.0	96	82%	50%	76%	292	252	264	333	248	289
		08	ARI	1.0	131	75%	53%	69%	212	248	242	176	225	234
		09	ARI	1.0	142	71%	83%	79%	223	295	281	150	298	214
Ramirez,Ramon	R	06	COL	1.1	76	74%	0%	74%	241	218	265	141	274	194
		07	COL	0.8	51	44%	0%	71%	321	308	316	300	240	357
		08	KC	1.0	73	78%	20%	81%	218	225	226	222	294	157
		09	BOS	1.0	20	83%	0%	70%	248	220	217	276	244	220
Ramirez,Ramon	R	09	CIN	1.1	42	70%	0%	100%	174	83	185	0	200	120
Rauch,Jon	R	06	WAS	1.1	63	79%	40%	75%	215	252	257	180	254	216
		07	WAS	1.0	81	69%	40%	82%	200	278	230	232	208	249
		08	ARI	1.0	103	70%	75%	67%	233	296	252	267	268	242
		09	MIN	0.9	47	75%	40%	81%	270	256	283	215	241	282
Ray,Chris	R	05	BAL	1.0	74	85%	0%	56%	208	237	218	261	284	174
		06	BAL	1.1	41	84%	87%	80%	188	202	221	119	184	202
		07	BAL	1.0	90	67%	80%	68%	190	276	218	216	233	212
		09	BAL	0.9	32	66%	0%	46%	346	337	367	286	442	265
Reyes,Dennys	L	05	SD	1.4	39	74%	0%	100%	192	237	219	190	136	262
		06	MIN	0.8	105	96%	0%	95%	229	151	205	143	148	244
		07	MIN	0.6	38	78%	0%	91%	302	319	293	455	273	364
		08	MIN	0.6	95	84%	0%	87%	222	250	240	182	198	284
		09	STL	0.5	34	76%	100%	90%	205	254	234	125	202	268
Rhodes,Arthur	L	05	CLE	0.9	117	81%	0%	83%	220	188	200	235	286	155
		06	PHI	0.8	79	67%	57%	77%	224	305	243	333	286	248
		08	FLA	0.6	73	82%	67%	94%	206	250	219	333	162	309
		09	CIN	0.8	71	78%	0%	90%	182	227	204	167	141	245
Rincon,Juan	R	05	MIN	1.0	111	79%	0%	74%	229	219	207	278	218	228
		06	MIN	1.0	97	77%	33%	91%	273	266	260	313	222	303
		07	MIN	0.9	50	70%	0%	77%	270	277	272	292	313	236
		08	CLE	1.2	27	66%	0%	67%	254	348	259	359	330	264
		09	COL	1.1	-4	54%	0%	71%	270	186	253	237	241	213
Rivera,Mariano	R	05	NYY	1.1	142	85%	91%	86%	166	194	166	179	177	176
		06	NYY	1.2	132	83%	92%	83%	258	174	237	194	192	250
		07	NYY	1.1	168	72%	88%	80%	245	252	257	208	255	241
		08	NYY	1.1	186	84%	98%	88%	178	149	178	130	155	183
		09	NYY	1.0	158	89%	96%	90%	243	139	194	224	185	213
Rivera,Saul	R	06	WAS	1.1	46	78%	33%	87%	232	263	275	209	194	290
		07	WAS	1.1	48	71%	60%	76%	298	215	275	231	271	244
		08	WAS	1.1	54	72%	0%	65%	306	250	333	156	271	284
		09	WAS	1.3	35	65%	0%	43%	261	380	299	359	333	312
Robertson,David	R	09	NYY	1.0	111	78%	100%	89%	198	231	177	276	203	222

BULLPEN INDICATORS

Pitcher			Tm	BPIs			Results		Runners		Pitch Ct		Platoon	
				IP/g	bpv	S%	Sv%	Eff%	Emp	On	1-15	16-30	vLH	vRH
Rodney,Fernand	R	05	DET	1.1	73	82%	60%	61%	273	207	283	130	265	219
		06	DET	1.1	67	72%	64%	80%	185	208	176	214	202	192
		07	DET	1.1	92	69%	33%	65%	200	276	262	207	247	231
		08	DET	1.1	25	69%	68%	60%	222	237	261	186	260	197
		09	DET	1.0	32	72%	97%	87%	252	230	238	260	261	213
Rodriguez,Franci	R	05	ANA	1.0	105	81%	90%	82%	190	173	184	154	213	153
		06	ANA	1.1	124	89%	92%	88%	201	191	202	176	215	179
		07	LAA	1.1	116	78%	87%	85%	205	204	230	138	187	217
		08	LAA	0.9	75	85%	90%	86%	252	183	235	160	228	208
		09	NYM	1.0	45	74%	83%	75%	233	171	219	169	186	223
Rodriguez,Rafael	R	09	LAA	1.7	15	71%	0%	40%	410	304	339	326	377	333
Romero,J.C.	L	05	MIN	0.8	43	81%	0%	79%	248	223	244	214	198	268
		06	ANA	0.7	41	60%	0%	73%	225	363	300	333	202	382
		07	PHI	0.8	57	88%	50%	90%	250	158	209	176	208	198
		08	PHI	0.7	21	82%	20%	78%	228	174	209	138	101	287
		09	PHI	0.8	-45	88%	0%	86%	208	235	283	0	308	156
Romo,Sergio	R	08	SF	1.2	109	76%	0%	89%	123	186	100	242	91	188
		09	SF	0.8	122	65%	100%	89%	210	277	229	261	188	263
Rosa,Carlos	R	09	KC	1.5	21	75%	100%	0%	385	278	368	0	200	438
Rosales,Leo	R	09	ARI	1.4	59	60%	0%	80%	216	254	216	255	210	250
Russell,Adam	R	09	SD	0.8	-22	79%	0%	88%	222	333	379	125	316	269
Saito,Takashi	R	06	LA	1.1	161	78%	92%	90%	159	206	170	164	227	129
		07	LA	1.0	192	88%	91%	89%	143	169	155	135	186	114
		08	LA	1.0	143	78%	82%	73%	188	288	226	255	250	213
		09	BOS	1.0	48	87%	50%	62%	265	222	254	224	200	297
Sampson,Chris	R	08	HOU	2.2	73	65%	0%	74%	203	256	179	295	303	183
		09	HOU	1.1	35	66%	50%	81%	241	349	265	350	315	272
Sanches,Brian	R	09	FLA	1.2	42	85%	0%	72%	255	208	236	236	242	224
Sarfate,Dennis	R	07	HOU	1.2	392	83%	0%	100%	105	300	211	125	182	167
		08	BAL	1.4	-3	71%	0%	58%	181	207	224	138	165	220
		09	BAL	1.2	1	69%	0%	50%	143	441	205	364	278	275
Schoeneweis,Sc	L	05	TOR	0.7	67	75%	25%	78%	238	252	246	240	188	306
		06	CIN	0.7	35	65%	67%	87%	200	310	233	364	236	257
		07	NYM	0.8	43	70%	67%	81%	319	221	243	373	204	316
		08	NYM	0.8	25	80%	20%	64%	227	299	238	342	172	336
		09	ARI	0.5	-16	64%	0%	58%	313	280	301	200	276	325
Seay,Bobby	L	07	DET	0.8	74	79%	50%	93%	284	165	209	333	209	250
		08	DET	0.9	71	70%	0%	82%	271	283	315	186	302	250
		09	DET	0.7	52	67%	0%	83%	245	244	245	240	255	229
Sherrill,George	L	05	SEA	0.7	98	53%	0%	81%	188	200	204	182	156	273
		06	SEA	0.6	89	67%	100%	83%	194	232	217	158	143	297
		07	SEA	0.6	122	80%	43%	87%	222	143	174	208	156	212
		08	BAL	0.9	31	70%	84%	76%	233	242	259	176	194	257
		09	LA	1.0	72	88%	81%	85%	238	181	222	188	132	250
Shields,Scot	R	05	ANA	1.2	99	77%	54%	75%	186	220	205	202	199	203
		06	ANA	1.2	101	77%	25%	75%	217	218	232	174	207	227
		07	LAA	1.1	88	70%	25%	77%	199	243	242	170	214	226
		08	LAA	1.0	81	84%	44%	82%	299	184	259	200	216	267
		09	LAA	0.9	-86	60%	25%	57%	233	243	246	200	250	229
Shouse,Brian	L	05	TEX	0.8	41	64%	0%	78%	200	340	247	342	209	337
		06	MIL	0.6	31	76%	40%	75%	200	333	244	429	238	309
		07	MIL	0.7	68	73%	25%	85%	260	255	275	167	214	295
		08	MIL	0.7	78	80%	40%	85%	220	250	247	150	173	301
		09	TAM	0.6	78	73%	0%	85%	333	216	258	400	227	357
Sipp,Tony	L	09	CLE	0.9	48	83%	0%	100%	229	172	206	188	211	190
Smith,Joe	R	07	NYM	0.8	83	79%	0%	87%	203	327	274	257	298	266
		08	NYM	0.8	53	73%	0%	80%	195	262	212	293	340	196
		09	CLE	0.9	81	77%	0%	91%	210	262	253	208	355	198
Soria,Joakim	R	07	KC	1.1	131	74%	81%	80%	173	211	168	246	167	200
		08	KC	1.1	112	87%	93%	88%	154	209	146	267	169	171
		09	KC	1.1	150	85%	91%	87%	252	181	236	163	224	213
Soriano,Rafael	R	06	SEA	1.1	97	85%	33%	78%	214	192	232	121	244	179
		07	ATL	1.0	132	76%	75%	84%	165	221	190	154	164	197
		08	ATL	1.0	23	80%	75%	60%	200	111	152	143	222	103
		09	ATL	1.0	134	74%	87%	77%	220	155	201	170	258	138
Sosa,Jorge	R	09	WAS	1.2	0	69%	100%	88%	364	261	333	300	344	293
Springer,Russ	R	05	HOU	1.0	62	64%	0%	67%	205	247	206	286	209	231
		06	HOU	0.8	57	75%	0%	91%	220	198	221	156	253	187
		07	STL	0.9	112	77%	0%	86%	191	167	178	175	235	158
		08	STL	0.7	63	83%	0%	85%	256	184	214	240	281	179
		09	TAM	0.8	87	78%	33%	73%	313	274	324	143	350	263
Stetter,Mitch	L	08	MIL	0.8	20	77%	0%	78%	149	194	193	130	167	170
		09	MIL	0.6	21	77%	50%	93%	209	228	222	208	182	263
Stokes,Brian	R	07	TAM	1.1	12	63%	0%	53%	354	333	341	344	346	341
		08	NYM	1.4	83	79%	33%	75%	263	286	295	269	333	220
		09	NYM	1.0	-7	76%	0%	67%	281	248	251	380	327	219
Street,Huston	R	05	OAK	1.2	98	84%	85%	85%	192	197	194	195	224	172
		06	OAK	1.0	144	70%	77%	74%	205	276	238	242	274	211
		07	OAK	1.0	164	74%	76%	79%	179	213	184	222	224	162
		08	COL	1.1	76	71%	72%	72%	217	250	228	219	200	250
		09	COL	1.0	146	71%	95%	93%	151	303	205	143	172	218

BULLPEN INDICATORS

Pitcher			Tm	BPIs			Results		Runners		Pitch Ct		Platoon	
				IP/g	bpv	S%	Sv%	Eff%	Emp	On	1-15	16-30	vLH	vRH
Tejeda,Robinson	R	09	KC	2.1	32	72%	0%	75%	138	250	158	250	235	150
Thatcher,Joe	L	08	SD	1.0	1	61%	0%	42%	400	364	343	405	387	380
		09	SD	0.9	117	77%	0%	91%	200	263	223	227	184	271
Thayer,Dale	R	09	TAM	1.2	88	75%	100%	0%	333	292	296	364	250	345
Thornton,Matt	L	05	SEA	1.0	21	76%	0%	50%	292	213	262	167	262	235
		06	CHW	0.9	73	76%	40%	81%	223	235	213	316	211	240
		07	CHW	0.8	71	68%	29%	72%	245	289	303	146	283	260
		08	CHW	0.9	145	76%	17%	76%	148	248	188	186	176	211
		09	CHW	1.0	147	77%	44%	81%	218	222	219	230	208	227
Todd,Jess	R	09	CLE	1.1	54	62%	0%	50%	325	405	345	348	429	300
Troncoso,Ramon	R	09	LA	1.1	40	81%	86%	83%	281	246	290	226	285	251
Valdez,Merkin	R	09	SF	1.0	7	68%	0%	60%	300	286	312	274	250	324
Valverde,Jose	R	05	ARI	1.1	120	80%	88%	81%	222	200	236	172	168	241
		06	ARI	1.1	109	61%	82%	75%	245	268	270	246	323	192
		07	ARI	1.0	112	82%	87%	81%	197	194	203	173	202	189
		08	HOU	1.0	122	77%	86%	83%	231	200	228	190	174	253
		09	HOU	1.0	89	84%	86%	83%	238	151	230	93	279	129
Vargas,Claudio	R	09	MIL	1.1	47	86%	0%	86%	184	172	212	119	211	156
Vasquez,Esmerli	R	09	ARI	1.0	22	71%	0%	50%	247	268	270	232	198	309
Veal,Donnie	L	09	PIT	0.9	-129	69%	0%	100%	333	167	258	278	118	300
Veras,Jose	R	07	NYY	1.0	48	54%	100%	100%	250	111	130	125	154	190
		08	NYY	1.0	69	78%	0%	75%	250	214	248	174	202	256
		09	CLE	1.1	4	66%	0%	77%	158	299	223	242	263	196
Villanueva,Carlos	R	07	MIL	1.9	57	75%	33%	78%	209	278	229	219	230	243
		08	MIL	2.3	95	75%	100%	70%	238	185	211	260	206	228
		09	MIL	1.5	67	65%	38%	52%	221	293	233	306	242	254
Villone,Ron	L	09	WAS	0.8	-20	78%	25%	59%	301	275	320	128	303	271
Wade,Cory	R	08	LA	1.3	84	81%	0%	85%	198	200	203	205	208	191
		09	LA	1.0	31	60%	0%	50%	175	370	241	321	283	238
Wagner,Billy	L	05	PHI	1.0	131	88%	93%	88%	176	147	174	143	128	173
		06	NYM	1.0	138	85%	89%	86%	248	171	250	136	161	234
		07	NYM	1.0	119	80%	87%	84%	229	198	223	150	241	209
		08	NYM	1.0	142	79%	79%	77%	143	250	170	250	233	169
		09	BOS	0.9	135	87%	0%	88%	148	200	189	0	125	194
Walker,Tyler	R	05	SF	0.9	50	77%	82%	78%	231	343	292	241	287	276
		06	TAM	1.0	63	50%	71%	60%	350	224	253	364	333	226
		07	SF	1.0	55	88%	0%	90%	182	308	238	500	182	308
		08	SF	0.8	78	67%	0%	67%	239	239	238	242	329	189
		09	PHI	1.1	78	78%	0%	75%	227	254	276	182	239	241
Weathers,David	R	05	CIN	1.1	62	71%	79%	79%	229	258	244	222	265	226
		06	CIN	1.1	24	80%	63%	69%	234	216	230	239	219	230
		07	CIN	1.1	42	70%	85%	74%	222	248	247	188	254	218
		08	CIN	1.0	24	81%	0%	70%	331	215	288	232	235	296
		09	MIL	0.9	8	76%	20%	72%	237	213	220	225	218	234
Webb,Ryan	R	09	SD	0.9	49	77%	0%	89%	298	234	234	304	233	294
Wheeler,Dan	R	05	HOU	1.0	101	83%	60%	81%	205	202	225	145	204	204
		06	HOU	1.0	92	81%	75%	82%	204	245	232	200	273	183
		07	TAM	1.1	103	62%	61%	65%	179	371	239	284	260	253
		08	TAM	0.9	53	77%	72%	80%	170	214	204	114	217	166
		09	TAM	0.8	98	74%	33%	71%	202	205	206	182	310	160
White,Sean	R	09	SEA	1.2	23	75%	33%	83%	200	231	233	167	191	238
Williams,Randy	L	09	CHW	0.7	54	70%	0%	75%	148	250	196	182	162	269
Wilson,Brian	R	06	SF	1.0	55	67%	50%	64%	404	177	280	294	348	235
		07	SF	1.0	90	77%	86%	84%	218	133	178	182	304	145
		08	SF	1.0	92	70%	87%	85%	234	271	240	288	194	308
		09	SF	1.1	114	77%	84%	77%	238	213	247	175	192	259
Wilson,C.J.	L	05	TEX	2.0	41	58%	100%	46%	140	270	213	286	178	204
		06	TEX	1.0	60	74%	50%	67%	218	247	241	238	155	292
		07	TEX	1.0	84	76%	86%	91%	171	248	209	243	112	275
		08	TEX	0.9	26	66%	86%	82%	240	301	266	262	260	271
		09	TEX	1.0	107	79%	78%	79%	242	228	281	125	207	249
Wood,Kerry	R	09	CLE	0.9	74	72%	77%	72%	212	263	247	200	257	213
Wood,Tim	R	09	FLA	1.2	29	83%	0%	100%	268	282	291	263	219	313
Wright,Jamey	R	09	KC	1.2	22	72%	0%	65%	207	287	221	284	200	285
Wright,Wesley	L	08	HOU	0.8	29	68%	100%	86%	198	242	194	308	207	230
		09	HOU	0.9	50	74%	0%	60%	315	293	318	216	356	276
Wuertz,Mike	R	05	CHC	1.0	89	72%	0%	83%	208	232	218	231	260	197
		06	CHC	1.0	78	85%	0%	82%	200	253	207	231	184	245
		07	CHC	1.0	84	78%	0%	77%	255	210	246	203	241	232
		08	CHC	1.0	23	77%	0%	50%	216	357	309	209	233	306
		09	OAK	1.1	157	75%	67%	92%	215	165	222	113	183	200
Zavada,Clay	L	09	ARI	1.0	52	78%	0%	70%	204	278	244	240	292	207
Ziegler,Brad	R	08	OAK	1.3	36	93%	85%	92%	283	159	237	222	286	175
		09	OAK	1.1	65	79%	70%	77%	294	295	309	238	343	262
Zumaya,Joel	R	06	DET	1.3	92	87%	17%	82%	162	207	174	228	183	188
		07	DET	1.2	56	65%	20%	61%	141	241	200	156	271	135
		08	DET	1.1	-67	86%	20%	50%	275	255	276	241	161	317
		09	DET	1.1	-10	76%	14%	55%	300	250	321	172	344	206

Injuries

Off-Season Injury Report

by Rick Wilton

This time last year, baseball was coming off a record-breaking 431 players landing on the disabled list. The volume of players injured in September (but not landing on the DL also) was a huge concern. This past season, "only" 408 players hit the DL. As comforting as that may sound, it is the second-highest number of players since 2000 and most likely since the beginning of DL records kept by MLB.

This past season, we saw an apparent epidemic of hip injuries. Players like Chase Utley, Mike Lowell. Alex Rodriquez, Alex Gordon, Carlos Delgado, Brett Myers and others attempted to come back from hip surgery, which almost always included damage to the labrum. It remains to be seen if this is a trend or aberration.

We have learned this: younger players like Utley, Rodriguez and Gordon all were able to return on schedule and without any setbacks. Lowell and Delgado, both into their mid-to-late 30's, struggled to bounce back as quickly as their younger counterparts did. That was not unexpected considering their age. What we can conclude is it's probable that players will return on schedule and perform close to their prior level once activated.

Off-season updates…

Adrian Beltre (3B, SEA) missed about half the season due to bone chips in his left shoulder and a severely bruised testicle. A late season activation erased most of the doubts concerning his left shoulder entering spring training 2010.

Carlos Beltran (OF, NYM) struggled to bounce back from a bone bruise in his right knee. If he can avoid the need for microfracture surgery, he should return to form in 2010.

Exploratory surgery on **Erik Bedard's** (LHP, SEA) left shoulder in August revealed a torn labrum and casts a cloud over both the 2010 season and his career. He should start the season on the disabled list.

Jeremy Bonderman (RHP, DET) struggled to recover from thoracic outlet syndrome surgery in '09. This rare condition, combined with '08 elbow issues, have cost him most of 2008-09. The Tigers plan on him making their '10 rotation, but he has to prove he can stay healthy.

Boof Bonser (RHP, MIN) underwent surgery in February to repair both a torn rotator cuff and labrum in his pitching shoulder. His career is still in jeopardy due to the extent of the surgery even if the reports that he is recovering ahead of schedule are true.

Russell Branyan (1B, SEA) was diagnosed with a herniated disc in August, a malady that plagued him for the entire second half of the season. The big question for 2010 is, can he avoid more back issues?

Eric Chavez' (3B, OAK) career is in a downward spiral due to a nerve irritation problem (repaired by surgery in August '09), elbow irritation and surgery to repair a torn labrum in his throwing shoulder. His career is about over due to five surgeries since September 2007.

For the third year in a row, **Joe Crede** (3B, MIN) had back surgery to remove fluid and repair another herniated disc. Kudos for Crede for completing multiple rehabs, but eventually it will catch up with him and cause his retirement. That could happen this off-season.

Carlos Delgado (1B, NYM) underwent surgery in May to repair an impingement in his right hip, an injury that had plagued him for some time. He never made it back in 2009, further complicated by a strained oblique. He is looking all of his 37 years, and he may be ready for a DH role.

Ryan Doumit (C, PIT) continues to solidify his reputation as an injury-prone catcher. A fractured right wrist that required surgery to repair the damage cost him about half the season. He has now landed on the disabled list four straight years.

A myriad of maladies has cast a cloud over **Justin Duchscherer's** (RHP, OAK) career. Even though his surgery in late March did not find any major damage, he ended up missing all of 2009 due to the elbow. He also dealt with clinical depression late in the year.

Edwin Encarnacion (3B, TOR) lost the early part of the season due to a chipped bone in his left wrist. After he returned and was traded to the Blue Jays, he developed a sore left knee. He should enter spring training healthy.

Jeff Francis (LHP, COL) missed all of 2009 due to labrum surgery in February. It remains to be seen if he can bounce back in 2010 from this difficult injury.

Troy Glaus (3B, STL) missed all but 14 games in 2009 due to a torn pectoral muscle in his right shoulder. A strained oblique late in the season did not help. Glaus has battled numerous injuries recently and he is definitely injury prone at this stage of his career.

Khalil Greene (SS, STL) missed considerable time due to an anxiety disorder. Without specifics, and with the fact that each player (and patient) needs to be treated differently, it is hard to judge his immediate future. He and the Cardinals' medical staff have the off-season to work on a program to help him cope with the situation. That said, his future is questionable as far as 2010 is concerned.

Vlad Guerrero (OF, LAA) is 34 years old; the wear-and-tear is starting to take its toll. A torn right pectoral muscle and inflammation in his left knee cost him time last season.

Travis Hafner (DH, CLE) continues to look for the magic formula to regain his home run swing. Sadly, he will not find it, as the strength in his right shoulder has declined in recent seasons, and he may never get it back.

After playing in 156 games in 2008, **Josh Hamilton** (OF, TEX) missed a good portion of the 2009 season due to a sports hernia and lower back pain. Which player will show up this year? The healthy one or injury-prone one? I would bet on the injury-prone one.

Tim Hudson (RHP, ATL) will be roughly 20 months removed from Tommy John surgery on Opening Day.

Barring a setback, Hudson is primed for a solid comeback season similar to 2005.

Jason Isringhausen (RHP, TAM) underwent Tommy John surgery in July 2009 and is not expected back until late in the 2010 season.

Conor Jackson (1B, ARI) contracted Valley Fever early in the 2009 season. This malady cost him the rest of the year as he battled the symptoms, including overall fatigue. Even though he was impressive at times in winter ball, he is at risk for a relapse.

Randy Johnson's (LHP, SF) career could be over by the end of spring training due to a strained left shoulder he suffered in 2009.

Hong-Chih Kuo (LHP, LA) has a long history of elbow issues dating back to his days in Japan. He also has a high pain tolerance and has pitched with pain almost from the beginning of his MLB career. If his elbow woes are behind him he could rebound, but that is a big "if".

Francisco Liriano (LHP, MIN) continues to struggle to return to his pre-Tommy John surgery levels of 2006. He had problems with soreness in his left elbow last year, and that may have been scar tissue. He has yet to regain the bite on his slider, and that may be due to the elbow surgery.

Jed Lowrie (SS, BOS) continues to battle through a sore left wrist that cost him the shortstop job in Boston last year. He saw a hand specialist in the fall who gave him the green light for this season. That still does not guarantee a healthy and pain-free left wrist in 2010.

A pinched nerve and right shoulder weakness limited **John Maine's** (RHP, NYM) playing time last season. By season's end he was back on the mound, but he remains a risky investment due to past shoulder issues that were never repaired via surgery.

It has been 18 months since **Shaun Marcum** (RHP, TOR) had Tommy John surgery. Barring any setbacks over the winter or in March, he should be able to resume his career, though it will take some time to regain his effectiveness.

Justin Morneau (1B, MIN) was shut down in September due to a stress fracture in his L5 vertebrae. If the development of the fracture was just a freak occurrence, he should pick up where he left off when healthy last season.

Dustin Moseley (RHP, TOR) lost the 2009 season due to tightness in his pitching forearm and a late season left hip injury. He had surgery in September, and is expected to be healthy at the start of spring training.

Xavier Nady (OF, NYY) underwent Tommy John surgery on his throwing elbow in July. The Yanks expect him back by the end of April at the latest.

Roy Oswalt (RHP, HOU) developed a herniated disc in his lower back during the 2nd half of the season. It looks like he will avoid surgery for the time being, but if more back problems surface, surgery is the likely outcome.

Left elbow inflammation and shoulder tightness hindered **Glen Perkins** (LHP, MIN) almost all of 2009. Reportedly, his injuries are not serious enough to warrant surgery, and he is expected to be ready at the start of spring training.

A fraying of a tendon in **J.J. Putz's** (RHP, NYM) right forearm shut him down for the year in August. No surgery was planned, and he should be ready in March.

Chad Qualls (RHP, ARI) suffered a torn patellar ligament in his left knee that was surgically repaired in August. The D'backs say he will be ready when camp opens up. We believe he may struggle in March and get off to a slow start.

A book could be written about **Jose Reyes'** (SS, NYM) hamstring and leg woes last season. He had surgery in October to repair scar tissue in his upper right hamstring tendon. The medical staff indicates he will be ready by the start of spring training. We'll see, as we were taken on a long roller coaster ride last season.

Anibal Sanchez (RHP, FLA) is a talented but injury-prone pitcher who is still trying to come back from surgery to repair a torn labrum in his right shoulder in 2007. Be wary of his past medical issues.

Johan Santana (LHP, NYM) had several bone chips removed from his left elbow in September. He is expected to be very close to 100% by Opening Day. Still, hedge your bidding on him on draft day.

Ben Sheets (RHP, FA) had surgery in February 2009 to repair a damaged flexor tendon in his right forearm. With good health in the right situation, he could surprise in 2010.

Grady Sizemore (OF, CLE) had surgery on his left elbow to clean out some inflamed tissue. He also had a tear in his abdominal wall. Both surgeries were "minor," and the Indians believe he will avoid starting the year on the DL.

Kevin Slowey's (RHP, MIN) September surgery on his right wrist turned out to be more involved than first thought. He needed two permanent screws inserted to stabilize the wrist. The Twins indicate he will be ready for spring training; that is an overly optimistic viewpoint.

According to the Cubs, a troublesome left knee and torn cartilage were the reasons **Alfonso Soriano** (OF, CHC) struggled in 2009, and not a slow bat. Depending how well his knee bounced back, he should be ready for the start of the season, but it is not written in stone.

Edison Volquez (RHP, CIN) underwent Tommy John surgery in August and will likely miss all of 2010.

Tim Wakefield (RHP, BOS) had surgery to repair a damaged disc in his lower back. He struggled with loss of sensation and weakness in his left leg due to the sciatica that plagued him last season. Boston expects him back at the start of spring training.

Chien-Ming Wang (RHP, NYY) will likely miss all of 2010 due to a long recovery from surgery to repair ligament damage in his right shoulder capsule.

Surgery to clean out **Brandon Webb's** (RHP, ARI) right shoulder in August was deemed a success. He expects to be ready for spring training without any restrictions. He still may get off to a slow start, including the possibility he will need a short DL stint at the beginning of the year.

The Brewers believe **Rickie Weeks'** (2B, MIL) left wrist is completely healed from his May surgery. Weeks is injury prone and can't seem to shake the wrist/hand injury bug.

The Tigers believe **Joel Zumaya** (RHP, DET) will return to form in 2010. History says he will not.

Hidden Injuries: 2010 Speculations

by Ray Murphy

Rick Wilton's reports tell only part of the story. There is another category of injured players: those who didn't (fully) disclose their injuries. Some will tell us about them next spring, but others may only be detected in their diminished 2009 performance. Here is a speculative list of players who may have been negatively impacted by injury in 2009, and what it might mean for them in 2010.

Under-reported injuries

BJ Upton (OF, TAM) pushed through his rehab from off-season shoulder surgery, missing only the opening week of the season. He started slowly and never came around. Late in the season, Upton complained about getting moved from the leadoff role, rekindling the whispers of attitude problems. But when considering the shoulder injury and those maturity issues, which is the chicken and which is the egg? It remains possible, even likely, that his shoulder wasn't right all year, with his frustration just a by-product.

Kevin Kouzmanoff (3B, SD) was in a nearly identical situation to Upton — off-season shoulder surgery, slow start to the season. In this case, though, his PX spiked in the 2nd half, signaling a return to health. There is upside beyond the power levels we have seen thus far in his career; combine that with a possible move out of Petco and 30 HR's could be attainable in the right situation.

Geovany Soto (C, SD) started 2009 fighting a shoulder problem. Then in July he landed on the DL with an oblique strain. In between, he posted one good month: a .900 OPS/6 HR surge in June. It's an unfortunate reality that catchers get dinged up all the time; in between dings, Soto showed that his skills were intact. Fewer dings in 2010 is all that is needed to recapture 2008's .285/20 HR levels.

Mike Napoli (C, LAA) also started 2009 recovering from a shoulder issue; in his case it was off-season surgery. A traditionally streaky hitter, Napoli flashed his potent bat at times in '09. Interestingly, his production seemed to worsen when he got more consistent playing time at catcher. When he was sitting a few days a week or mixing in DH ABs, especially in the first half, he was more productive. This suggests lingering shoulder trouble. His late-season fade would further support this idea. A winter's rest and the possibility of more DH AB's make his outlook optimistic.

Strange half-season splits

Magglio Ordonez (OF, DET) had been very consistent from 2006-08: 20+ HR, 100+ RBI, .298+ BA. He cratered in the first half of 2009 to .264 and 3 HR. He spiked his GB% in that time, further indicating that something was amiss with his swing. But he recovered in the 2nd half, including a reduction in that GB% (58%-44%). Age is a factor (36 in '10), but not enough to write him off. Don't pay for full recovery, but buy cheap and look for .290 with double-digit HRs.

Jonathan Papelbon's (RHP, BOS) comparatively shaky first-half performance triggered some whispers that he was already falling down the far side of the usually short peak period in a closer's lifespan. His Cmd (2.0) and pitch selection were both unusually shaky amid those early-season struggles. But he answered the bell in the 2nd half, spiking his Cmd (11.1) and BPV back to a near-vintage 147. This looks to have been a case of a player successfully navigating a minor injury, or simply pacing himself for the grind of the long season. Either way, our level of concern for 2010 is minimal.

Jimmy Rollins (SS, PHI) has been plagued by extreme half-season splits a few times in his career, perhaps none more glaring than 2009. After a .207/6 HR/10 SB first half, Rollins caught fire and made his season-ending numbers downright respectable, thanks to a second half .285/15 HR/21 SB surge. But what was the root cause for the anemic start? It was a multiple-day benching in late June that turned his season around. Rollins credited an adjustment to his batting stance, but there were also reports of a lingering back problem in spring training, which could have been a contributing factor as well.

Kerry Wood's (RHP, CLE) transition to closing in 2008 was a smashing success. What changed in 2009? His Dom rate was still strong, but he walked an extra two hitters per 9 IP. That issue was mostly confined to the first half, and although his 2nd half save total was only 11, his skills (100 BPV) were back to being closer-worthy. Given that Wood had some health issues late in 2008 with the Cubs, there may have been a carryover into early 2009 before he righted himself. His strong finish increases confidence for 2010.

Unexplained down years

A.J. Burnett (RHP, NYY) had an erratic season, colored (perhaps excessively) by some brutal starts that poisoned his ERA. Notable in his split stats, though, is that his ERA was more than a run higher when he pitched on the normal four days rest, as opposed to when he got an extra day or two (4.50 vs. 3.42). This could suggest that he was fighting some physical problem all year, and the extra time between starts was allowing him to stay ahead of that issue.

Matt Capps (RHP, PIT) entered 2009 as a nicely skilled reliever at the lower end of the closer pool. But after three years worth of closer-worthy BPVs (95-99-173 from 2006-08), Capps' BPV fell to 31 in the first half. His skills did rebound later in the year (2H BPV: 124), although his results got worse (6.83 ERA in 28 IP). Small sample sizes with relievers often lead to random variation, but it's also worth considering that Capps was not the same pitcher physically. Remember those prior years' strong skills, and the possibility of a health-related rebound in 2010.

Alex Rios (OF, CHW) entered 2009 with a track record of inconsistency: he had flashed big half-seasons, but never put two together. He managed two consistent halves in 2009; unfortunately both were bad. His profile showed a skill set in line with his prior, better seasons, except both his PX and SX collapsed. That combination strongly points to a nagging injury, perhaps a back problem, hampering him all year. It's difficult to project 2010 without more information, but Rios' longer-term track record suggests that Chicago's waiver claim on him may yet pay dividends.

Is health a skill?

by Bill Macey

Injuries are unavoidable in baseball; it's a demanding game and even the healthiest player can get hurt. Each year many do – approximately 33% of batters and 37% of pitchers landed on the disabled list (DL) in 2008.

In preparing for the upcoming season it's useful to know if the players injured in the previous year are more likely to be injured in the upcoming year. Injuries may be unavoidable, but can a fanalytic owner mitigate these risks?

Using data from the 2003-2007 seasons, the following tables present the percentage of batters and pitchers on the disabled list in the year following a year in which they were also on the DL.

	Batters on the DL	Also on the DL	
Year	Year 1	Year 2	Percent
2003	78	30	38%
2004	97	35	36%
2005	105	40	38%
2006	118	45	38%
2007	170	66	39%
TOTAL	568	216	38%

	Pitchers on the DL	Also on the DL	
Year	Year 1	Year 2	Percent
2003	68	24	35%
2004	86	37	43%
2005	99	41	41%
2006	141	80	57%
2007	222	85	38%
TOTAL	616	267	43%

For both batters and pitchers, players appearing on the disabled list are more likely to appear on the disabled list during the following year. However, the rate is greater for pitchers: 43% of pitchers on the DL in one year appear on the DL the following year compared to 38% of batters.

Previously injured players also tend to spend a longer time on the disabled list. During the period 2003-2008, the average number of days on the DL for batters was 51 days, and 73 days for pitchers. For the subset of players injured in the previous year, the average number of days on the DL the following year was 58 days for batters and 88 days for pitchers.

We also considered whether older players were more likely to become re-injured. The following tables divide the pools of batters and pitchers into those under 30 and those 30 and older.

	Batters <30 the DL	Also on the DL	
Year	Year 1	Year 2	Percent
2003	60	18	30%
2004	62	20	32%
2005	66	20	30%
2006	68	28	41%
2007	94	40	43%
TOTAL	350	126	36%

	Batters >30 the DL	Also on the DL	
Year	Year 1	Year 2	Percent
2003	18	12	67%
2004	35	15	43%
2005	39	20	51%
2006	50	17	34%
2007	75	26	35%
TOTAL	217	90	41%

	Pitchers <30 the DL	Also on the DL	
Year	Year 1	Year 2	Percent
2003	46	16	35%
2004	58	30	52%
2005	67	29	43%
2006	92	49	53%
2007	138	55	40%
TOTAL	401	179	45%

	Pitchers >30 the DL	Also on the DL	
Year	Year 1	Year 2	Percent
2003	22	8	36%
2004	28	7	25%
2005	32	12	38%
2006	49	31	63%
2007	81	29	36%
TOTAL	212	87	41%

In aggregate, batters who were 30 and older when on the DL were more likely to appear on the DL the following year than batters under 30. The opposite trend holds for pitchers; those 30 and older appearing on the DL were less likely to appear on the DL again the following year. However, there is enough year-to-year variance in the data to suggest this may just be noise.

Does the risk of injury further increase for players placed on the disabled list in two consecutive years?

	Batters the DL	Also on the DL	
Years	Both Years	Year 3	Percent
2003 & 2004	30	13	43%
2004 & 2005	35	20	57%
2005 & 2006	40	22	55%
2006 & 2007	45	26	58%
TOTAL	150	81	54%

	Pitchers the DL	Also on the DL	
Years	Both Years	Year 3	Percent
2003 & 2004	24	10	42%
2004 & 2005	37	10	27%
2005 & 2006	41	25	61%
2006 & 2007	80	30	38%
TOTAL	182	75	41%

For batters, 54% of those on the disabled list in two consecutive years also appeared on the disabled list in the third year. This suggests that chronically injured batters do continue to get injured and should be discounted accordingly during the draft or auction.

Only 41% of the pitchers on the disabled list in two consecutive years also appeared on the disabled list in the third year.

There are two possible reasons for this difference between batters and pitchers. First, pitcher injuries tend to be more traumatic. For example, a pitcher requiring Tommy John surgery mid-season will likely miss the remainder of the season as well as at least part of the next season. Being on the disabled list in two consecutive years may represent two unique injuries more often for a batter than for a pitcher, and thus may be a better gauge of chronic injury.

A second related explanation is that players no longer on an active major league roster won't appear on a disabled list. Those pitchers on the disabled list in two consecutive years may be more likely to find themselves out of major league baseball entirely.

Conclusions

A general analysis like this isn't meant to replace specific injury analyses. Every player is different, and specific information regarding a player's injury should take precedence.

However, from a high-level draft preparation perspective, the lessons are:

- Players appearing on the disabled list are more likely to appear on the disabled list during the following year.
- DL trips for previously injured players last longer.
- Pitchers are more likely to become injured than batters and spend longer on the DL than do batters.
- Batters injured in two consecutive years are substantially more likely to be injured in the third year than injury-free players.

5-Year Injury Log

The following chart details the disabled list stints for all players during the past five years. For each injury, the number of days the player missed during the season is listed. A few DL stints are for fewer than 15 days; these are cases when a player was placed on the DL prior to Opening Day (only in-season time lost is listed).

There are a few abbreviations used in this table:

Lt = left
Rt = right
fx = fractured
R/C = rotator cuff
str = strained
surg = surgery
TJS = Tommy John (ulnar collateral ligament reconstruction) surgery
x 2 = two occurrences of the same injury
x 3 = three occurrences of the same injury

All data provided by Rick Wilton of Baseball-Injury-Report.com and Fanball.com

FIVE-YEAR INJURY LOG

FIVE-YEAR INJURY LOG

BATTERS	Yr	Days	Injury
Abreu,Tony	08	184	Hip surgery 5/08
Amezaga,Alfredo	09	148	Strained left knee; lower back
Anderson,Brian	09	18	Strained right oblique
Anderson,Garret	07	96	Hip flexor x 2; right elbow
	09	15	Strained left quad muscle
Anderson,Marlon	08	47	Strained left hip x 2
Ankiel,Rick	06	182	Torn patella tendon
	09	19	Bruised shoulder
Atkins,Garrett	05	22	Strained right hamstring
Aurilia,Rich	05	18	Strained left hamstring
	06	15	Strained right groin
	07	25	Strained right hamstring; neck
	09	37	Tendinitis left ankle; infected toe
Aviles,Mike	09	134	Strained right forearm
Aybar,Erick	07	49	Strained left hamstring; bruised hand
	08	28	Dislocated right pinkie finger
Aybar,Willy	08	49	Strained left hamstring
Bailey,Jeff	09	58	High ankle sprain left ankle
Baker,Jeff	07	21	Concussion
	09	66	Sprained left hand
Bako,Paul	05	128	Left knee surgery
	06	31	Partially torn right oblique
Baldelli,Rocco	05	182	Recovery from left knee surgery
	06	65	Left hamstring strain
	07	167	Strained left hamstring; Right groin
	08	133	Mitochondrial disorder
	09	31	Strained left hamstring; bruised left ankle
Barajas,Rod	07	29	Strained right groin
Bard,Josh	07	15	Strained right groin
	08	93	Sprained right ankle; strained right triceps
Barfield,Josh	08	82	Strained middle finger - left hand
Barrett,Michael	06	29	Intrascrotal hematoma
	07	21	Concussion
	08	135	Facial surgery; Strained right elbow
	09	79	Torn muscle - right shoulder
Bartlett,Jason	08	20	Sprained right knee
	09	21	Sprained left ankle
Barton,Brian	08	55	Strained right oblique; Bruised right hand
Barton,Daric	08	17	Strained neck
	09	25	Strained right hamstring
Bates,Aaron	09	6	Sprained left ankle
Bautista,José	07	17	Puncture wound-left hand
Belliard,Ronnie	08	40	Strained left calf, Right groin
Beltran,Carlos	07	16	Strained abdominal muscle
	09	78	Bone bruise, right knee
Beltre,Adrian	09	69	Surgery - right Shoulder; bruised testicle x 2
Berkman,Lance	05	31	Right knee soreness
	09	20	Strained left calf
Bernadina,Roger	09	169	Fractured right ankle
Betancourt,Yuniesky	09	20	Strained right hamstring x 2
Betemit,Wilson	08	34	Strained right hamstring
Blake,Casey	06	48	Sprained right ankle; oblique
Blalock,Hank	07	107	Thoracic Outlet Syndrome
	08	108	Carpal tunnel right wrist; Inflam. right shoulder
Blanco,Andres	09	28	Strained left calf
Blanco,Henry	07	82	Herniated disc - neck
	09	24	Strained right hamstring
Blanks,Kyle	09	37	Strained arch-right foot
Bloomquist,Willie	08	51	Strained right hamstring
Blum,Geoff	05	18	Left chest contusion
	09	15	Strained left hamstring
Boggs,Brandon	09	34	Dislocated left shoulder
Boone,Aaron	07	98	Sprained MCL - left knee
	09	144	Heart surgery - aortic value repair
Bourn,Michael	07	41	Sprained right ankle
Bradley,Milton	05	94	Ligament tear right finger; patella tendon
	06	79	Sprained right knee; Left shoulder
	07	66	Calf; hamstring; wrist; oblique
Branyan,Russell	05	32	Fractured left middle finger
	08	42	Strained right oblique muscle
	09	31	Herniated disc-lower back
Bruce,Jay	09	64	Fractured right wrist
Buck,John	09	36	Herniated disc lower back
Buck,Travis	07	59	Strained left hamstring; Right thumb
	08	20	Shin splints
	09	15	Strained left oblique
Burke,Chris	06	15	Dislocated left shoulder
Burrell,Pat	09	32	Strained neck
Burriss,Emmanuel	09	34	Fractured left toe
Buscher,Brian	07	16	Infection - right leg
Bynum,Freddie	06	57	Right shoulder inflammation
	07	44	Strained left hamstring
	08	39	Recovery from right knee surgery
Byrd,Marlon	05	29	Broken right ring finger
	08	27	Inflammation left knee
Byrnes,Eric	08	118	Strained right hamstring x 2
	09	71	Fractured left hand
Cabrera,Asdrubal	09	26	AC Joint sprain left shoulder
Cabrera,Everth	09	60	Fractured hamate bone - left hand
Cabrera,Orlando	05	15	Inflammation of the right elbow
Cairo,Miguel	05	17	Strained left hamstring
	06	36	Strained left hamstring
Callaspo,Jolbert	08	56	Unspecific medical condition
Cameron,Mike	05	83	Multiple facial fractures; Left wrist
	06	20	Strained left oblique
Cano,Robinson	06	43	Strained left hamstring
Cantu,Jorge	06	43	Broken bone, left foot
Carroll,Brett	08	100	Separated right shoulder
Carroll,Jamey	09	36	Fractured left hand
Casilla,Alexi	08	23	Torn ligament right thumb
Castillo,Luis	08	53	Strained left hip flexor
Castillo,Wilkin	09	106	Torn labrum right shoulder
Castro,Juan	05	22	Strained left knee
	07	84	Tendinitis right elbow x 2
Castro,Ramon	05	18	Strained right quadriceps
	06	62	Strained left oblique
	07	49	Arthritis - lower back
	08	56	Strained right hamstring x 2
Catalanotto,Frank	07	22	Acute strain - right biceps muscle
Chavez,Endy	07	82	Strained left hamstring
	09	107	Torn ACL right knee
Chavez,Eric	07	66	Lower back spasms
	08	155	Inflammation of right shoulder; Back spasms
	09	163	Strained right forearm/elbow
Choo,Shin-Soo	08	61	Recovery from surgery on left elbow
Church,Ryan	05	35	Right rib cage sprain; fractured toe
	08	70	Concussion x 2
	09	15	Strained right hamstring
Clark,Tony	06	39	Right shoulder strain
	09	45	Strained ligament right wrist
Copeland,Ben	09	30	Sprained right shoulder
Cora,Alex	08	25	Sore right elbow
	09	68	Torn lig. Right thumb; surgery both thumbs
Costa,Shane	06	20	Strained left hamstring
	08	28	Recovery from surgery on his wrist
Coste,Chris	07	7	Strained hamstring
Cota,Humberto	05	23	Strained oblique
	07	27	Strained left shoulder
Counsell,Craig	06	38	Right rib fracture
Crawford,Carl	08	47	Dislocated right index finger
Crede,Joe	05	15	Stress fracture - right index finger
	07	118	Inflammation lower back
	08	34	Inflammation lower back
	09	17	Strained lower back
Crisp,Coco	05	15	Sprained right thumb
	06	49	Fractured left finger
	09	114	Sore right shoulder
Crosby,Bobby	05	77	Fractured rib; Left ankle
	06	59	Lower back strain x 2
	07	68	Fractured left hand
	08	14	Strained left hamstring
	09	15	Strained left calf
Crowe,Trevor	09	18	Strained right oblique
Cruz,Nelson	09	16	sprained left ankle
Cuddyer,Michael	05	17	Bone bruise in right hand
	07	15	Torn ligament-left thumb
	08	96	Dislocated right finger; Fx left foot; Left finger
Damon,Johnny	08	14	Sprained A/C joint right shoulder
De Aza,Alejandro	07	114	Sprained right ankle
	08	184	High ankle sprain left ankle
DeJesus,David	06	40	Strained left hamstring
Delgado,Carlos	05	16	Sore left elbow
	09	147	Right hip impingement
Dellucci,David	07	79	Severely strained left hamstring
	09	26	Strained left calf muscle

BATTERS	Yr	Days	Injury
Denorfia,Chris	07	183	Pending surgery - right elbow
	08	73	Lower back stiffness
DeRosa,Mark	06	15	Sprained left foot
	09	17	Sprained left wrist
Diaz,Matt	05	37	Strained oblique
	08	119	Strained ligament left knee
Dickerson,Chris	09	52	Bruised right R/C; sprained left ankle
Dobbs,Greg	09	25	Strained right calf
Doumit,Ryan	06	100	Strained left hamstring x 2
	07	46	High ankle sprain; Left wrist sprain
	08	23	Fractured tip of left thumb
	09	80	Fractured scaphoid bone right wrist
Drew,J.D.	05	91	Broken left wrist
	08	21	Herniated disc
Drew,Stephen	09	17	Strained left hamstring
Dukes,Elijah	08	88	Right hamstring; Right knee; Right calf
	09	15	Strained left hamstring
Duncan,Chris	08	70	Pinched nerve -cervical spine
Duran,German	09	43	Appendectomy
Eckstein,David	06	27	Torn oblique muscle
	07	28	Lower back spasms
	08	20	Strained right hip flexor
	09	22	Strained right hamstring
Ellis,Mark	06	30	Broken right thumb
	08	9	Torn labrum - right shoulder
	09	60	Strained left calf
Encarnacion,Edwin	06	29	Sprained left ankle
	09	81	Fractured left wrist; left knee soreness
Erstad,Darin	06	75	Right ankle irritation x 2
	07	59	Sprained left ankle x 2
	09	19	Strained left hamstring
Everett,Adam	07	94	Fractured left fibula
	08	87	Strained right shoulder; tend. right shoulder
Feliz,Pedro	08	26	Inflammation lower back
Figgins,Chone	07	29	Fracture of two fingers - right hand
	08	37	Strained right hamstring x 2
Flores,Jesus	08	15	Sprained left ankle
	09	139	Torn labrum & bruised right shoulder
Floyd,Cliff	06	47	Left Achilles; Left ankle
	08	32	Torn cartilage - right knee (surgery)
	09	55	Strained right shoulder
Fowler,Dexter	09	15	Bruised left knee
Frandsen,Kevin	06	15	Broken jaw
	08	181	Torn left Achilles tendon
Freel,Ryan	05	51	Left foot inflammation; Right knee
	07	94	Torn cartilage right knee; neck bruise
	08	181	Strained right hamstring
	09	45	Concussion; strained left hamstring
Furcal,Rafael	07	12	Sprained left ankle
	08	141	Back surgery 7/08
Garciaparra,Nomar	05	106	Torn left groin muscle
	06	34	Right knee sprain; ribcage
	07	21	Strained left calf
	08	97	Strained left knee; torn MCL left knee
	09	42	Strained right calf x 2
Gardner,Brett	09	43	Fractured left thumb
Gathright,Joey	08	28	Bruised right shoulder
German,Esteban	09	18	Strained right groin
Getz,Chris	09	20	Strained right oblique
Giambi,Jason	07	68	Torn Plantar fascia tendon - Left foot
	09	18	Strained right quad
Giles,Brian	09	108	Bruised right knee
Glaus,Troy	07	32	Left foot surgery; heel
	09	149	Recovery from surgery on rt pectoral muscle
Gload,Ross	05	83	Left shoulder inflammation
	07	47	Torn right quad muscle
Gomes,Jonny	06	41	Right shoulder surgery
Gomez,Carlos	07	64	Fractured hamate bone - left hand
Gonzalez,Alberto	08	27	Strained left hamstring
Gonzalez,Alex	06	15	Oblique strain
	08	184	Compression fx left lower leg/surgery
	09	35	Bone chips - right elbow
Gonzalez,Edgar	09	44	Concussion
Gordon,Alex	08	20	Torn right quadriceps
	09	91	Torn labrum - right hip / surgery
Gotay,Ruben	08	15	Strained left hamstring
Granderson,Curtis	08	24	Fractured 3rd metacarpal, right Hand

BATTERS	Yr	Days	Injury
Greene,Khalil	05	37	Fractured right finger; left toe
	06	16	Torn left middle finger ligament
	08	61	Fractured left hand
	09	53	Anxiety related disorder
Griffey Jr.,Ken	06	28	Strained biceps tendon in right knee
Guerrero,Vladimir	05	20	Partial dislocation of left shoulder
	09	64	Torn right pectoral muscle; sore left knee
Guillen,Carlos	05	68	Sore right knee; Left hamstring
	09	80	Inflammation right shoulder
Guillen,Jose	06	90	Left hamstring strain; Right elbow
	09	72	Torn left LCL; str rt. hamstring; torn rt hip flexo
Gutierrez,Franklin	07	12	Strained left hamstring
Guzman,Christian	06	182	Right shoulder surgery
	07	122	Strained left hamstring; left thumb
	09	15	Strained left hamstring
Gwynn,Tony,Jr.	08	19	Strained left hamstring
Hafner,Travis	05	18	Post-concussion syndrome
	08	102	Strained right shoulder
	09	26	Sore and weak right shoulder
Hairston Jr.,Jerry	05	15	Left elbow ligament injury
	07	73	Lower back soreness; neck
	08	50	Fractured rt hamstring x 2; Fractured lt thumb
Hairston,Scott	05	31	Torn labrum
	06	39	Left biceps strain
	07	29	Strained left oblique muscle
	08	32	Torn ligament - left thumb
	09	20	Strained left biceps
Hall,Bill	07	19	Sprained right ankle
Hamilton,Josh	07	51	Sprained right wrist; stomach ailment
	09	52	Strained ribcage; abdominal wall
Hanigan,Ryan	09	16	Concussion
Hardy,J.J.	06	138	Right ankle surgery
Harris,Willie	09	15	Strained left oblique
Hart,Corey	09	37	Appendicitis
Hawpe,Brad	05	52	Strained left hamstring
	08	16	Strained right hamstring
Helton,Todd	05	15	Left calf strain
	06	15	Stomach ailment
	08	71	Sore lower back
Hermida,Jeremy	06	40	Sore right hip flexor, groin strain
	07	43	Bruised right patellar
	08	9	Tight left hamstring
Hernandez,Anderson	09	8	Strained left hamstring
Hernandez,Ramon	05	58	Sprained Left wrist; surgery
	07	33	Groin contusion; oblique
	09	64	Left knee surgery
Hill,Aaron	08	123	Post concussion syndrome symptoms
Holliday,Matt	05	40	Fractured right pinkie finger
	08	16	Strained left hamstring
Hollimon,Michael	09	36	Recovery from right shoulder surgery
Howard,Ryan	07	15	Strained left quad muscle
Hudson,Orlando	08	51	Dislocated left wrist
Huff,Aubrey	06	23	Left knee sprain
Hundley,Nick	09	55	Bruised Left wrist
Hunter,Torii	05	65	Fractured left ankle
	06	15	Stress fracture, left foot
	09	39	strained right adductor
Iannetta,Chris	09	16	Strained right hamstring
Ibanez,Raul	09	22	Strained left groin
Infante,Omar	08	54	Strained left hamstring; Fractured left hand
	09	82	Fractured 5th metacarpal left hand
Inge,Brandon	08	17	Strained left oblique
Ingett,Joe	07	17	Strained left hamstring
Iwamura,Akinori	07	34	Strained right oblique
	09	96	Torn ACL left knee
Izturis,Cesar	05	72	Lower back sprain; hamstring
	06	93	Post elbow surgery; hamstring
	08	15	Strained right hamstring
	09	37	Appendicitis
Izturis,Maicer	05	53	Sprained MCL, left knee
	06	46	Strained left hamstring
	07	63	Strained right hamstring x 2
	08	61	Strained back; torn thumb ligament
Jackson,Conor	09	146	Valley fever
Jacobs,Mike	07	40	Fractured right thumb
Johjima,Kenji	09	46	Strained right hamstring; Fractured toe
Johnson,Kelly	06	182	Right elbow surgery
	09	20	Tendinitis - right wrist

FIVE-YEAR INJURY LOG

BATTERS	Yr	Days	Injury
Johnson, Nick	05	29	Right heel contusion
	07	183	Fractured right femur + surgery x 2
	08	138	Torn tendon - right wrist
	09	16	Strained right hamstring
Johnson, Reed	07	85	Herniated disc lower back
	08	15	Lower back spasms
	09	68	Fractured left foot; back spasms
Jones, Adam	08	29	Fractured left foot
	09	33	Sprained left ankle
Jones, Andruw	08	82	Tendinitis - right patellar tendon
	09	15	Strained left hamstring
Jones, Chipper	05	42	Ligament strain, left foot
	06	44	Right ankle; oblique x 2
	07	20	Bone bruise right wrist/hand
	08	15	Strained left hamstring
Kearns, Austin	08	78	Stress fx left foot; surgery right elbow
	09	62	Bruised right thumb
Kemp, Matt	07	17	Separated right shoulder
Kendrick, Howie	07	78	Fx index finger left hand x 2
	08	78	Strained left hamstring x 2
Kennedy, Adam	05	27	Recovery from right knee surgery
	07	50	Torn cartilage - right knee
Keppinger, Jeff	05	23	Left knee (tibia plate) fracture
	07	21	Fractured right index finger
	08	39	Fractured left patellar (kneecap)
Kinsler, Ian	06	43	Dislocated left thumb
	07	29	Stress fracture left foot
	08	43	Sports hernia
	09	16	Strained left hamstring
Konerko, Paul	08	23	Strained left oblique
Kotchman, Casey	06	146	Mononucleosis
	09	15	Bruised right lower leg
Kotsay, Mark	07	108	Lower back spasms; surgery
	08	36	Strained lower back
	09	58	Recovery from herniated disc surgery
Kottaras, George	09	33	Strained lower back
Kubel, Jason	05	182	Left knee surgery
Laird, Gerald	08	35	Strained left hamstring
Larish, Jeff	09	32	Recover from right wrist surgery
LaRoche, Adam	08	17	Right intercostal strain
LaRoche, Andy	08	34	Surgery right thumb
LaRue, Jason	06	15	Right knee surgery
	07	15	Contusion left shoulder
Lee, Carlos	08	51	Fractured left pink finger
Lee, Derrek	06	101	Inflammation, fx right wrist
Lewis, Fred	07	20	Strained right oblique
Longoria, Evan	08	29	Fractured right hand
Lowell, Mike	08	42	Strained right oblique muscle; Right thumb
	09	19	Strained right hip
Lowrie, Jed	09	119	Fractured and strained left wrist
Ludwick, Ryan	09	15	Strained right hamstring
Lugo, Julio	06	31	Strained abdominal muscle
	08	80	Strained left quad
	09	22	Surgery to repair torn meniscus - right knee
Marte, Andy	07	26	Strained left hamstring
Martinez, Fernando	09	93	Inflammation behind right knee
Martinez, Ramon	09	124	Fractured pinkie finger left hand
Martinez, Victor	08	78	Surgery - right elbow
Matsui, Hideki	06	123	Broken left wrist
	07	15	Strained left hamstring
	08	56	Inflammation left knee
Matsui, Kaz	05	52	Bruised left knee
	06	17	Sprained MCL, right knee
	07	36	Strained lower back
	08	54	Strained rt hamstr; Anal fissures; Inflam disc
	09	21	Strained right hamstring
Matthews Jr., Gary	05	24	Strained left hamstring
	06	9	Ribcage strain
Mauer, Joe	07	34	Strained left quad muscle
	09	26	Inflamed right sacroiliac joint
McCann, Brian	06	16	Sprained right ankle
	09	15	Left eye infection
McDonald, John	06	15	Groin injury
	08	31	Sprained right ankle
McLouth, Nate	06	51	Left ankle sprain
	09	19	Strained-left hamstring
Metcalf, Travis	07	15	Strained left hamstring

FIVE-YEAR INJURY LOG

BATTERS	Yr	Days	Injury
Mientkiewicz, Doug	05	49	Bruised lower back; hamstring
	06	68	Lower back strain
	07	91	Fractured right wrist
	09	138	Dislocated right shoulder
Miles, Aaron	05	33	Right intercostal strain
	09	60	Strained right shoulder; right elbow
Milledge, Lastings	08	27	Strained right groin
Molina, Bengie	05	25	Strained right quadriceps
Molina, Jose	09	61	Grade two strain of the left hamstring
Molina, Yadier	05	40	Hairline fracture, left pinkie finger
	07	29	Fractured left wrist
Montanez, Lou	09	119	Torn ligaments right thumb
Montero, Miguel	08	24	Fractured index finger right hand
Mora, Melvin	07	23	Sprained left foot
	09	15	Strained left hamstring
Morales, Jose	07	22	Sprained left ankle
Morgan, Nyjer	09	38	Fractured left hand
Morneau, Justin	05	15	Concussion
Moss, Brandon	08	21	Appendectomy
Murphy, David	08	54	Sprained posterior cruciate ligament - rt knee
Murphy, Donnie	05	15	Fractured finger - right hand
	07	15	Strained oblique
	08	32	Inflammation right elbow
Nady, Xavier	06	19	Appendectomy
	09	172	Torn ligament - right elbow
Napoli, Mike	07	51	Strained right hamstring; ankle
	08	32	Inflammation right shoulder
Navarro, Dioner	06	41	Bruised right wrist
	08	17	Lacerations of two fingers on right Hand
Nelson, Chris	09	27	Torn ligament right wrist
Nix, Jayson	09	26	Strained right quad muscle
Nix, Laynce	09	15	Herniated disc-cervical spine
Norton, Greg	07	46	Torn meniscus - right knee (surgery)
	09	31	Strained right hamstring
Ordonez, Magglio	05	79	Hernia surgery
	08	18	Strained right oblique
Ortiz, David	08	54	Torn tendon sheath - left wrist
Overbay, Lyle	07	38	Fractured right hand
Owens, Jerry	06	15	Sprained right ankle
	08	20	Surgery to repair torn R/C right shoulder
Ozuna, Pablo	07	126	Fractured right fibula, torn ligament
Pagan, Angel	06	75	Torn left hamstring
	07	54	Colitis
	08	140	Bruised labrum left shoulder
	09	80	Strained right groin; Right elbow surgery
Paul, Xavier	09	137	Skin infection - left leg
Pena, Brayan	07	15	Concussion
	08	18	Lower back strain
Pena, Carlos	08	23	Fractured index finger left hand
	09	27	Fractured left index and ring finger
Pena, Tony	09	30	Fractured hamate bone left hand
Pence, Hunter	07	29	Chip fracture - right wrist
Perez, Fernando	09	149	Dislocated left wrist
Phillips, Brandon	08	18	Fractured right index finger & surgery
Pierre, Juan	08	25	Sprained medial collateral ligament - lt knee
Podsednik, Scott	05	16	Strained left adductor muscle
	07	89	Strained left rib cage muscle; adductor
	08	25	Fractured left pinky finger
Polanco, Placido	05	15	Strained left hamstring
	06	37	Separated left shoulder
Posada, Jorge	08	108	Torn subscapularis muscle - right shoulder
	09	24	Strained right hamstring
Prado, Martin	08	59	Sprained left thumb
Pujols, Albert	06	18	Strained right oblique
	08	15	Strained left calf
Punto, Nick	05	30	Pulled right hamstring
	08	40	Strained left hamstring x 2
	09	15	Strained right groin
Quentin, Carlos	07	45	Strained hamstring; torn labrum
	09	55	Plantar Fasciitis left foot
Quinlan, Robb	05	53	Bulging disc in neck
Quintanilla, Omar	06	19	Right shin contusion
	08	20	Concussion
Quintero, Humberto	09	17	Strained right shoulder
Rabelo, Mike	08	12	Sprained left knee
Ramirez, Aramis	05	39	Strained left quadriceps
	07	15	Tendinitis - left patellar
	09	58	Dislocated left shoulder

BATTERS	Yr	Days	Injury
Ransom,Cody	09	60	Strained right quad muscle
Reed,Jeremy	06	91	Fractured right thumb
Reimold,Nolan	09	17	Tendinitis left Achilles tendon
Renteria,Edgar	07	34	Sprained right ankle x 2
Reyes,Jose	09	137	Tendinitis right calf
Richar,Danny	08	60	Stress fracture of Rib
	09	94	Torn labrum, right shoulder
Riggans,Shawn	07	119	Tendinitis - throwing elbow
	08	22	Surgery - right knee
	09	106	Tendinitis - right shoulder
Rios,Alex	06	30	Staph infection in lower left leg
Rivera,Juan	06	21	Rib cage tightness
	07	154	Fractured left leg (1/07), surgery
Rivera,Mike	09	15	Sprained left ankle
Roberts,Brian	06	24	Strained groin
Robles,Oscar	07	15	Torn tendon - left wrist
Rodriguez,Alex	08	19	Grade 2 strain of right quad muscle
	09	33	Surgery to repair torn labrum - right hip
Rodriguez,Luis	09	28	Sprained left ankle
Rolen,Scott	05	111	Sprained left shoulder; tendinitis
	07	33	Sore left shoulder
	08	41	Fractured finger; Inflammation right shoulder
	09	15	Postconcussion syndrome
Rolins,Jimmy	08	19	Sprained right ankle
Ross,Cody	06	24	Bruised left pinky finger
	07	74	Strained left hamstring
Ross,David	06	18	Lower abdominal strain
	07	15	Concussion
	08	24	Back Spasms
	09	12	Strained left groin
Rowand,Aaron	06	56	Fx left ankle; Fx nose
Ruiz,Carlos	09	21	Strained right oblique
Ryan,Brendan	08	24	Strained ribcage
	09	15	Strained left hamstring
Saltalamacchia,J	09	18	Numbness rt arm (Thoracic Outlet Syndrome)
Sanchez,Angel	07	183	Strained elbow
	08	28	Sprained finger left hand
Sanchez,Freddy	07	6	Sprained MCL right knee
	09	20	Strained left shoulder
Santiago,Ramon	08	33	Separated left shoulder
Schafer,Jordan	09	30	Rehab from surgery right wrist
Schierholtz,Nate	09	16	Strained left hip
Schneider,Brian	06	15	Strained left hamstring
	09	42	Strained back muscle
Scott,Luke	09	16	Strained left shoulder
Sheffield,Gary	06	129	Left wrist contusion; surgery
	07	15	Sore right shoulder
	08	28	Strained left oblique
	09	15	Strained right hamstring
Sizemore,Grady	09	54	Inflamed left elbow; torn ab. wall
Snyder,Chris	08	19	Left testicular fracture
	09	81	Strained lower back x 2
Soriano,Alfonso	07	22	Strained right quad muscle
	08	56	Fx metacarpal - left hand; Strained right calf
	09	31	Surgery left knee
Soto,Geovany	09	90	Strained left oblique
Span,Denard	09	15	Right ear infection
Spilborghs,Ryan	08	54	Strained left oblique
Suzuki,Ichiro	09	10	Bleeding ulcer
Sweeney,Mark	07	11	Bruised right foot
	08	23	Strained right hamstring
Sweeney,Mike	05	15	Sprained left wrist and elbow
	06	98	Bulging disc in upper back
	07	74	Cartilage damage right knee
	08	97	Inflammation - surgery on both knees
	09	15	Back spasms
Sweeney,Ryan	08	29	Sprained thumb; Bruised left foot
	09	15	Sprained left knee
Swisher,Nick	05	23	Sprained right shoulder
Taveras,Willy	07	47	Strained right quad muscle
	09	34	Strained right quadriceps
Teahen,Mark	05	21	Lower back strain
	07	15	Strained left forearm
Teixeira,Mark	07	34	Strained left quad muscle
Tejada,Miguel	07	35	Fractured radius left wrist
Thames,Marcus	07	21	Strained left hamstring
	09	46	Strained right oblique

BATTERS	Yr	Days	Injury
Thomas,Clete	08	15	Sprained right ankle
Thome,Jim	05	114	Back strain; Right elbow surgery
	07	22	Strained right ribcage
Tolbert,Matt	08	109	Torn ligament left thumb
Torrealba,Yorvit	06	82	Right shoulder strain x 2
	08	31	Torn Meniscus - left knee/surgery 9/08
Torres,Andres	09	59	Strained left hamstring x 2
Tracy,Chad	07	57	Strained right knee; ribcage
	08	56	Recovery from microsurgery right knee
	09	31	Strained oblique
Treanor,Matt	06	15	Left shoulder
	08	28	Strained left hip
	09	166	Torn labrum - right hip
Tulowitzki,Troy	08	67	Torn tendon right quad; Cut left hand
Upton,B.J.	07	34	Strained left quad
	09	8	Recovery from labrum surgery - rt shoulder
Upton,Justin	08	55	Strained left oblique muscle
	09	20	Strained right oblique
Uribe,Juan	08	15	Strained left hamstring
Utley,Chase	07	31	Fractured right hand
Van Every,Jonathan	09	18	Sprained right ankle
Varitek,Jason	06	33	Cartilage damage, left knee
Victorino,Shane	07	22	Strained right calf
	08	16	Strained right calf
Vizquel,Omar	08	40	Surgery left knee
Votto,Joey	09	24	Stress-related issue
Ward,Daryle	07	40	Strained right calf; Left hip
	08	41	Herniated disc - lumbar spine
Weeks,Rickie	06	69	Right wrist surgery
	07	19	Tendinitis right wrist
	08	15	Sprained left knee
	09	140	Torn sheath left wrist.
Wells,Vernon	07	10	Left shoulder surgery (labrum & cyst)
	08	59	Fractured left wrist; Strained left hamstring
Werth,Jayson	05	65	Fractured left wrist; bursitis
	06	182	Left wrist surgery
	07	33	Sprained last wrist
	08	15	Strained left oblique
Wigginton,Ty	06	33	Broken bone in left hand
	08	26	Fractured thumb left hand
Willingham,Josh	05	95	Stress fracture, left forearm
	06	15	Strained ligament - left hand
	08	57	Back spasms
Willits,Reggie	08	17	Concussion
Wilson,Jack	08	51	Strained left calf
	09	17	Sprained left index finger
Wise,DeWayne	08	15	Strained left adductor
	09	61	Separated right shoulder; strained A/C joint
Wright,David	09	15	Concussion
Youkilis,Kevin	09	15	Strained left oblique
Young,Delmon	09	10	Recovery from elbow (right) surgery
Young,Dmitri	06	80	Strained right quad x 2
	08	116	Diabetes; strained back; strained left hip
	09	183	Strained back and hip
Zaun,Gregg	05	15	Concussion
	06	5	Muscle pull, right calf
	07	44	Fractured right thumb
	08	19	Strained right elbow
Zimmerman,Ryan	08	57	Torn labrum - left shoulder
Zobrist,Ben	07	43	Strained left oblique muscle

PITCHERS	Yr	Days	Injury
Aardsma,David	08	40	Strained right groin
Accardo,Jeremy	08	143	Tightness right forearm
Acosta,Manny	08	49	Strained right hamstring
Adams,Mike	09	90	Labrum surgery - rt shoulder; str shoulder
Affeldt,Jeremy	05	67	Left groin strain x 2
Albaladejo,Jonathan	08	143	Sprained UCL right elbow
Albers,Matt	08	96	Torn labrum - pitching shoulder
Alvarez,Mario	08	25	Stiffness - right elbow
Arias,Alberto	09	42	Strained right hamstring
Ascanio,Jose	09	54	Tendinitis - right shoulder
Ayala,Luis	06	182	Right elbow surgery
	07	80	Tommy John surgery 3/2006
Backe,Brandon	05	40	Left intercostal strain
	06	143	Right elbow sprain; elbow surgery
	07	153	Tommy John surgery 9/2006
	09	52	Intercoastal strain - left ribcage

PITCHERS	Yr	Days	Injury
Badenhop, Burke	08	100	Tendinitis right shoulder
	09	30	Strained right trapezius muscle
Baek, Cha Seung	06	7	Right triceps tendinitis
	07	92	Inflammation right shoulder
	09	183	Strained right forearm
Baez, Danys	06	40	Appendectomy
	07	27	Tendinitis pitching forearm
	08	184	Tommy John surgery 9/2007
Baker, Scott	08	32	Strained right groin
	09	10	Stiffness - right shoulder
Bale, John	07	103	Strained left biceps and shoulder
	08	139	Tightness left shoulder & dead arm feeling
	09	49	Recovery from thyroid surgery
Bannister, Brian	06	120	Strained right hamstring
Bastardo, Antonio	09	69	Strained right shoulder
Bautista, Denny	05	144	Right shoulder tendinitis
	06	24	Sore right pectoral muscle
	08	33	Tendinitis right shoulder
Beckett, Josh	05	32	Strained left oblique; finger
	07	15	Avulsion of skin - right index finger
	08	32	Back spasms; Sore pitching elbow
Bedard, Erik	05	57	Strained left MCL
	07	22	Strained right oblique
	08	102	Torn labrum surgery 10/08; Sore hip
	09	100	Inflamed left shoulder x 2
Beimel, Joe	09	15	Strained left hip flexor
Belisario, Ronald	09	33	Strained right elbow
Bell, Rob	05	56	Personal reasons
Bennett, Jeff	08	22	Subluxation of right shoulder
	09	102	Fractured left hand
Benoit, Joaquin	05	46	Sore right shoulder; Right elbow tendinitis
	08	34	Soreness - right shoulder
	09	183	Recovery from R/C surgery - right shoulder
Benson, Kris	05	31	Strained right pectoral
	06	17	Right elbow tendinitis
	07	183	Torn rotator cuff
	09	21	Tendinitis - right elbow
Bergesen, Brad	09	66	Contusion - left leg
Bergmann, Jason	07	72	Tight left hamstring; sore elbow
Betancourt, Rafael	05	18	Right shoulder inflammation
	06	26	Right upper back strain
	09	38	Strained right groin
Bierd, Randor	08	80	Rotator cuff impingement right shoulder
Birkins, Kurt	08	17	Neuritis pitching elbow
Bonderman, Jeremy	07	15	Blister right middle finger
	08	115	Thoracic outlet syndrome
	09	148	Recovery from thoracic outlet syndrome x 2
Bonser, Boof	09	185	Surgery - torn rotator cuff right shoulder
Bootcheck, Chris	06	19	Strained left hamstring
	08	45	Strained left oblique; Strained right forearm
Bradford, Chad	05	100	Lower back surgery
	09	114	Recovery from strained back; elbow surgery
Bradon, Dallas	09	65	Infection - left foot
Brocail, Doug	06	113	Coronary angioplasty; hamstring
	07	16	Strained left gluteus muscle
	09	128	Strained rt shoulder x 2; strained left hamstring
Brown, Andrew	08	90	Soreness - right shoulder
Bruney, Brian	08	97	Lisfranc injury right foot
	09	54	Strained right elbow x 2
Buchholz, Clay	08	18	Broken fingernail right hand
Buchholz, Taylor	09	183	Sprained UCL - right elbow
Burgos, Ambriorix	08	184	Tommy John surgery
Burnett, A.J.	06	73	Right elbow soreness x 2
	07	59	Sore pitching shoulder x 2
Burton, Jared	07	57	Lower back spasms; Left hamstring
	08	45	Strained right lat muscle
	09	16	Fatigue right shoulder
Bush, Dave	09	106	Fatigue right arm
Byrdak, Tim	06	102	Bone spurs in left elbow
	07	26	Strained flexor tendon - pitching arm
Cabrera, Daniel	05	20	Lower back strain
	06	21	Tightness in right shoulder
	08	16	Sprained pitching elbow
Cabrera, Fernando	06	16	Bruised right heel
	08	88	Recovery from surgery on right elbow

FIVE-YEAR INJURY LOG

PITCHERS	Yr	Days	Injury
Calero, Kiko	05	27	Right elbow tendinitis
	07	17	Inflammation right shoulder
	08	66	Torn rotator cuff right shoulder
	09	21	Inflammation right shoulder
Cameron, Kevin	08	82	Sprained right elbow
Campillo, Jorge	09	163	Tendinitis - right shoulder x 2
Capps, Matt	08	54	Bursitis - pitching shoulder
Capuano, Chris	07	22	Strained left groin
	08	184	Tommy John surgery 5/08
Carlyle, Buddy	08	17	Strained neck muscle
	09	73	Strained upper back
Carmona, Fausto	08	63	Strained left hip
Carpenter, Chris	06	15	Right shoulder bursitis
	07	182	Bone chips right elbow
	08	184	TJS recovery; Compressed nerve right arm
	09	35	Strained left ribcage muscle
Casilla, Santiago	08	33	Sore right elbow
	09	15	Sprained lateral collateral ligament right knee
Chamberlain, Joba	08	26	Tendinitis - right rotator cuff
Chen, Bruce	09	17	Torn left oblique muscle
Chico, Matt	08	130	Tommy John Surgery - left elbow
	09	94	Recovery from TJ Surgery
Choate, Randy	08	102	Fractured finger left hand
Chulk, Vinnie	07	35	Blood clot - right hand
	08	16	Tendinitis right shoulder
Colome, Jesus	05	67	Right shoulder inflammation x 2
	07	56	Soft tissue infection
	09	18	Strained right forearm
Colon, Bartolo	06	130	Inflammation & right R/C tear
	07	67	Sore pitching elbow; R/C
	08	82	Strained oblique
	09	99	Inflamed right knee; right elbow
Condrey, Clay	09	83	Strained left oblique x 2
Contreras, Jose	06	16	Pinched nerve in right hip
	08	74	Ruptured Achilles; Strained right elbow
Cook, Aaron	05	117	Pulmonary embolism
	07	46	Strained right oblique
	09	34	Strained right shoulder
Corcoran, Roy	09	44	Strained neck
Corcoran, Tim	07	60	Strained pitching elbow
Cordero, Chad	08	166	Torn labrum/ biceps tendon - right shoulder
Corey, Brian	08	17	Strained left hamstring
Cormier, Lance	06	15	Strained left oblique
	07	84	Tired pitching arm; triceps
Corpas, Manuel	09	102	Bone spurs & surgery - right elbow
Correia, Kevin	08	48	Strained left intercostals
Crain, Jesse	07	138	Torn R/C and Labrum
	09	16	Inflamed right shoulder
Cruz, Juan	06	29	Sore right shoulder
	07	18	Strained muscle - right shoulder
	08	27	Strained left oblique
	09	48	Strained right shoulder
Cueto, Johnny	09	15	Inflammation right shoulder
Daley, Matt	09	18	Sprained left foot
Davidson, David	09	135	Strained left shoulder
Davies, Kyle	06	108	Strained right groin
Davis, Doug	08	23	Thyroid surgery
Day, Dewon	07	20	Strained lower back
De La Rosa, Jorge	06	45	Blisters on left hand
	07	41	Strained pitching elbow
Dempster, Ryan	07	27	Strained left oblique muscle
	09	25	Fractured right big toe
Devine, Joey	08	67	Inflammation - right elbow setback
	09	183	Sprained right elbow
DiFelice, Mark	09	21	Strained right shoulder
Dinardo, Lenny	06	101	Neck strain
Donnelly, Brendan	07	112	Strained pitching forearm
	09	16	Strained right calf
Dotel, Octavio	05	137	Right elbow surgery
	06	135	Recovery from right elbow surgery
	07	94	Strained left oblique; shoulder
Downs, Scott	09	43	Bruised left toe; sprained left toe
Duchscherer, Justin	06	47	Right elbow tendinitis
	07	139	Strained right hip
	08	62	Strained right hip; Strained rt biceps tendon
	09	183	Recovery from surgery on right elbow

FIVE-YEAR INJURY LOG

PITCHERS	Yr	Days	Injury
Duke, Zach	05	23	Sprained left ankle
	07	75	Tightness in pitching elbow
Dumatrait, Phil	08	95	Sore pitching shoulder/ surgery 8/08
	09	138	Inflammation left shoulder
Durbin, Chad	09	19	Strained lat muscle
Eaton, Adam	05	46	Strained right middle finger x 2
	06	113	Right finger surgery
	07	16	Strained pitching shoulder
Embree, Alan	06	15	Strained left groin
	09	86	Fractured right tibia
Ennis, John	09	35	Recovery from elbow surgery
Escobar, Kelvim	05	89	Right elbow strain x 3
	06	15	Right elbow irritation
	07	15	Irritation right shoulder
	08	184	Torn labrum - right Shoulder
	09	182	Recovery from labrum surgery
Estes, Shawn	05	65	Stress fracture, left navicular bone
	06	179	Left elbow surgery
	07	183	Tommy John surgery 6/2006
	08	95	Fractured left thumb
Eyre, Scott	06	16	Strained right hamstring
	08	66	Bone spur left elbow; Strained left groin
	09	23	Strained left calf
Eyre, Willie	09	64	Tightness right groin
Feierabend, Ryan	09	183	Recovery from elbow surgery
Figaro, Alfredo	09	72	Sprained right wrist
Flores, Randy	05	15	Avulsed callus pad on left foot
	08	22	Tendinitis left ankle
Fogg, Josh	07	15	Strained left groin
	08	55	Strained right groin; Lower back spasms
Fox, Chad	09	148	Inflammation - right elbow
Francis, Jeff	08	38	Inflammation - pitching shoulder
	09	183	Recovery from labrum surgery - left shoulder
Francisco, Frank	05	181	Right elbow surgery
	06	77	Recovery from right elbow surgery
	09	53	Tendinitis right shoulder x 2; pneumonia
Fuentes, Brian	07	41	Strained left LAT muscle
Fultz, Aaron	07	35	Strained rib cage muscle
Gabbard, Kason	08	110	Surgery bone spur - left elbow 7/08
Gagne, Eric	05	151	Right elbow sprain & surgery
	06	174	Back surgery & elbow surgery
	07	27	Strained right hip, back.elbow
	08	40	Tendinitis right Shoulder
Gallagher, Sean	08	20	Fatigue - right shoulder
Gallardo, Yovani	08	165	Two knee surgeries
Garcia, Anderson	08	59	Inflammation right Shoulder
Garcia, Freddy	07	127	Tendinitis right biceps; R/C; labrum
Garcia, Harvey	08	184	Tendinitis - right shoulder
Garcia, Jaime	09	137	Sore left elbow
Gardner, Lee	08	165	Inflammation pitching elbow
Garza, Matt	08	16	Inflamed radial nerve in right arm
Gaudin, Chad	08	14	Left hip surgery (labrum)
Geary, Geoff	05	15	Right eye contusion
	08	18	Strained right groin
	09	37	Tendinitis right biceps tendon
Giese, Dan	08	17	Inflammation - pitching shoulder
	09	142	Ulnaritis right elbow
Glavine, Tom	08	125	Sore pitching forearm
	09	184	Rehab from surgery
Glover, Gary	08	34	Strained left calf; right shoulder
Gonzalez, Miguel	09	183	Rehab from right elbow surgery
Gonzalez, Mike	05	54	Sprained MCL - left knee
	06	38	Left arm fatigue
	07	138	Torn UCL
	08	80	Tommy John surgery 6/2008
Gordon, Tom	06	21	Strained right shoulder
	07	74	Inflamed R/C right shoulder
	08	85	Inflammation - right elbow
	09	121	Strained left hamstring, Sore right elbow
Gorzelanny, Tom	06	29	Left elbow soreness
	08	19	Irritated left middle finger
Grabow, John	07	23	Inflamed pitching elbow
Green, Sean	06	50	Back spasms; strained side
Gregerson, Luke	09	28	Strained right shoulder
Greinke, Zack	06	79	Personal reasons

FIVE-YEAR INJURY LOG

PITCHERS	Yr	Days	Injury
Grilli, Jason	09	20	Inflammation-right elbow
Guardado, Eddie	06	43	Left elbow surgery
	07	128	Tommy John surgery 9/2006
	08	20	Sore pitching shoulder
	09	17	Inflammation - left knee
Guerrier, Matt	06	53	Fractured right thumb
Guevara, Carlos	08	62	Strained right Groin
Guthrie, Jeremy	08	21	Impingement - right rotator cuff
Guzman, Angel	07	121	Strained right elbow
	08	155	Tommy John surgery 9/2008
	09	15	Strained right triceps
Halladay, Roy	05	86	Fractured left tibia
	07	20	Appendectomy
	09	15	Right groin strain
Hamels, Cole	06	18	Left shoulder strain
	07	32	Strained pitching elbow
Hampson, Justin	08	64	Tendinitis left shoulder
Hampton, Mike	08	118	Strained left pectoral muscle
	09	69	Torn left R/C; strained left groin
Hansen, Craig	09	163	Neck Spasms
Harang, Aaron	08	28	Strained pitching forearm
	09	45	Appendectomy
Harden, Rich	05	38	Strained right oblique
	06	146	Sprain right elbow; back strain
	07	151	Strained pitching shoulder x 2
	08	37	Strained right subscapularis muscle
	09	26	Strained lower back
Harrison, Matt	09	125	Inflamed left elbow; shoulder
Hawkins, LaTroy	05	24	Right ulnar neuritis
	07	31	Inflammation in pitching elbow
	09	16	Shingles
Hendrickson, Mark	05	16	Left shoulder stiffness
	06	18	Left shoulder tightness
Henn, Sean	08	31	Inflammation left shoulder
Hensley, Clay	07	34	Strained groin; Labrum surgery
	08	68	Strained right shoulder
Herges, Matt	08	15	Lower back stiffness
Hernandez, Felix	07	26	Strained flexor muscle - right forearm
	08	16	Sprained left ankle
Hill, Rich	08	30	Lower back soreness
	09	110	Inflamed right shoulder; left elbow
Hill, Shawn	06	95	Right elbow soreness
	07	94	Strained left (non-throwing) shoulder
	08	117	Right elbow (spurs) surgery 9/08; Forearm
	09	162	Inflammation - right elbow
Hirsh, Jason	07	84	Fractured right fibula; ankle
	08	74	Strained right Shoulder
Hochevar, Luke	08	41	Ribcage contusion
Hoey, James	08	184	Biceps tendinitis/shoulder surgery
Hoffman, Trevor	09	21	Strained right oblique
Hudson, Tim	05	32	Strained left oblique
	08	65	Torn ulnar collateral ligament - right elbow
	09	150	Recovery from Tommy John surgery
Hughes, Philip	07	94	Strained left hamstring
	08	90	Fractured rib
Hurley, Eric	08	91	Strained left hamstring; sore right shoulder
	09	183	Torn rotator cuff - right shoulder
Isringhausen, Jason	05	16	Strained right abdominal muscle
	08	73	Torn flexor tendon; Lacerated right hand
	09	155	Torn UCL right elbow; surgery
James, Chuck	06	32	Strained right hamstring
	07	15	Sore pitching shoulder
	08	10	Torn rotator cuff
Janssen, Casey	08	184	Torn labrum - right shoulder surgery
	09	66	Sore right shoulder x 2
Jenks, Bobby	08	18	Bursitis - left scapula area
Jennings, Jason	05	74	Fractured right finger
	07	91	Torn flexor tendon; elbow
	08	152	Irritated ulnar nerve - right elbow
Jepsen, Kevin	09	15	Lower back spasms
Jimenez, Cesar	07	183	Stress Fx pitching elbow
	09	183	Tendinitis left biceps tendon
Jiminez, Kelvin	08	17	Bruised right hand
Johnson, Jim	08	29	Impingement - right shoulder
Johnson, Josh	07	166	Tight pitching elbow; nueritis
	08	102	Tommy John surgery

PITCHERS	Yr	Days	Injury
Johnson, Randy	07	134	Lower back pain x 3
	08	15	Recovery from back surgery
	09	72	Torn rotator cuff
Johnson, Tyler	07	48	Tendinitis - left triceps
	08	184	Left rotator cuff shoulder surgery
Jurrjens, Jair	07	16	Sore pitching shoulder
Karstens, Jeff	07	104	Fractured right fibula; elbow
	08	50	Strained right groin
	09	22	Strained lower back
Kazmir, Scott	06	55	Left shoulder sorenes x 2
	08	35	Strained Left elbow
	09	37	Strained right quadriceps
Kelley, Shawn	09	58	Strained left oblique
Kennedy, Ian	08	26	Strained right lat, bursitis, pitching shoulder
Kensing, Logan	05	130	Sore right elbow
	06	56	Right wrist flexor strain
	07	129	Tommy John surgery 8/2006
Kinney, Josh	07	184	Tommy John surgery 3/2007
	08	156	2 setbacks from TJ Surgery
Kuo, Hong-Chih	07	126	Irritation - left elbow x 2
	09	85	Sore left elbow
Kuroda, Hiroki	08	19	Tendinitis - right shoulder
	09	72	Strained left oblique; concussion
Lackey, John	08	44	Grade 2 strain, right triceps
	09	41	Inflammation - right elbow
Laffey, Aaron	09	46	Strained right oblique
League, Brandon	07	135	Strained lat; strained oblique
Lee, Cliff	07	32	Strained upper abdominal muscle
Lerew, Andrew	07	134	Ulnar nerve neuritis
	08	117	Tommy John surgery 7/2008
Leroux, Chris	09	22	Inflamed right shoulder
Lester, Jon	06	39	Lymphoma
	07	71	Recovery from lymphoma
Lewis, Scott	09	128	Strained left elbow
Lidge, Brad	07	23	Stained left oblique
	08	6	Surgery (cartilage damage) right knee
	09	19	Sprained right knee
Lieber, Jon	06	38	Strained left groin
	07	110	Ruptured tendon left foot; oblique
	08	73	Strained right foot; Sprained right foot
Lilly, Ted	05	49	Left biceps tendinitis x 2
	09	27	Inflamed left shoulder; surgery left knee
Lincoln, Mike	09	114	Herniated disc in neck
Lindstrom, Matt	09	37	Strained right elbow
Linebrink, Scott	08	40	Inflamed subscapularis muscle
Liriano, Francisco	06	34	Sore left elbow and forearm
	07	183	Torn UCL - pitching elbow and surgery
	09	22	Left arm fatigue
Litsch, Jesse	09	174	Strained right forearm
Livingston, Bobby	07	40	Torn labrum - pitching shoulder
	08	109	Recovery from shoulder surgery
Lohse, Kyle	09	54	Strained right forearm; left groin
Looper, Braden	07	16	Strained pitching shoulder
Lopez, Rodrigo	07	106	Torn flexor tendon-pitching arm x 2
Loux, Shane	08	16	Oral surgery
	09	56	Tendinitis right shoulder
Lowe, Mark	06	43	Right elbow tendinitis
	07	148	Sore right elbow; surgery
Lowry, Noah	06	31	Right oblique strain
	08	184	Left forearm surgery
	09	183	Strained left shoulder
Lugo, Ruddy	06	23	Mid-back strain
Lyon, Brandon	05	92	Right elbow tendinitis
MacDougal, Mike	06	101	Right shoulder strain
	07	28	Inflamed pitching shoulder
Madson, Ryan	07	81	Strained pitching shoulder; oblique
Mahay, Ron	05	16	Groin strain
	07	34	Strained ribcage muscle
	08	11	Plantar fasciitis - left foot
Maine, John	06	40	Inflammation in right middle finger
	08	46	Strained R/C, bone spur right shoulder
	09	98	Weakness right shoulder
Marcum, Shaun	08	33	Strained pitching elbow
	09	183	Recovery from Tommy John surgery 9/08
Marmol, Carlos	06	16	Right shoulder fatigue

FIVE-YEAR INJURY LOG

PITCHERS	Yr	Days	Injury
Marshall, Sean	06	40	Strained left oblique muscle
Marte, Damaso	05	17	Inflamed left trapezius
	09	117	Tendinitis left shoulder
Martinez, Carlos	06	147	Right elbow strain; surgery
	07	183	Tommy John surgery 7/2006
Martinez, Joseph	09	117	Concussion; skull fractures
Martinez, Pedro	06	60	Right hip inflammation; calf
	07	156	Rotator cuff surgery
	08	61	Strained left hamstring
	09	28	Strained right shoulder
Masset, Nick	09	15	Strained left oblique
Mateo, Julio	06	56	Broken left hand; shoulder
Mathieson, Scott	06	29	Right elbow surgery
	07	183	Tommy John surgery 9/2006
	08	184	Setbacks from TJ Surgery
Mathis, Doug	08	84	Inflammation pitching shoulder
Matsuzaka, Daisuke	08	24	Strained rotator cuff - right shoulder
	09	124	Weak and strained right shoulder
Mazzaro, Vin	09	27	Tendinitis right shoulder
McCarthy, Brandon	07	53	Stress fx - right shoulder blade; blister
	08	146	Inflammation right Forearm/setback 4/08
	09	88	Stress fracture right scapula
McClung, Seth	09	56	Sprained right elbow
McGowan, Dustin	08	83	Frayed labrum, surgery 7/08
	09	183	Recovery from labrum surgery - rt shoulder
Meche, Gil	05	27	Right knee patellar tendinitis
	09	32	Back spasms
Meek, Evan	09	54	Strained left oblique
Mendoza, Luis	08	59	Inflammation right shoulder, Blister right hand
Mickolio, Kam	09	28	Inflammation right shoulder
Miller, Andrew	07	20	Strained left hamstring
	08	49	Tendinitis in right patellar tendon
	09	25	Strained right oblique
Miller, Justin	08	19	Inflammation - right elbow
	09	22	Inflammation right elbow
Millwood, Kevin	05	21	Strained right groin
	07	50	Strained left hamstring x 2
	08	40	Strained right groin x 2
Milton, Eric	09	120	Strained lower back; back surgery
Miner, Zach	07	23	Tendinitis pitching elbow
Mitre, Sergio	06	88	Right shoulder inflammation
	07	17	Torn callus on pitching hand
	08	184	Strained right Forearm
Moehler, Brian	06	28	Sprained right ankle
	09	19	Sprained right knee
Morales, Franklin	09	51	Strained left shoulder
Morrow, Brandon	09	15	Tendinitis right triceps
Morton, Charlie	09	7	Strained left oblique
Moseley, Dustin	08	22	Forearm stiffness pitching arm
	09	170	Irritation - right elbow
Mota, Guillermo	05	26	Right elbow inflammation
	09	15	Ingrown toenail
Moylan, Peter	08	171	Soreness right Elbow, TJS 5/08
Mulder, Mark	06	99	Left shoulder soreness; surgery
	07	184	Recovery from shoulder surgery
	08	171	Recovery from shoulder surgery
Murray, A.J.	08	118	Strained rotator cuff - left shoulder
Myers, Brett	07	64	Soreness in pitching shoulder
	09	98	Torn and frayed labrum - right hip
Nelson, Joe	07	183	Shoulder surgery
Neshek, Pat	08	145	Partially torn UCL - right elbow
	09	185	Recovery from Tommy John surgery
Niese, Jonathon	09	60	Torn right hamstring tendon
Nieve, Fernando	09	77	Torn right quadriceps
Nippert, Dustin	08	38	Blister - right foot
	09	93	Back spasms; inflammation in back
Nolasco, Ricky	07	119	Inflamed right elbow x 2
Nunez, Leo	07	183	Hairline Fx - right wrist
	08	54	Strained right lat muscle
O'Connor, Mike	07	78	Elbow surgery 11/06
Ohman, Will	09	130	Inflammation left shoulder
Oliver, Darren	09	11	Strained left triceps
Olsen, Scott	09	129	Tendinitis & torn labrum right shoulder
Osoria, Franquelis	08	16	Bursitis - right ankle

FIVE-YEAR INJURY LOG

PITCHERS	Yr	Days	Injury
Oswalt, Roy	06	15	Strained middle back
	08	16	Strained left abductor muscle
	09	19	Lower back pain
Outman, Josh	09	107	Sprained left elbow
Owens, Henry	07	132	Inflamed pitching shoulder x 2
	08	184	Surgery to repair torn R/C right Shoulder
Owings, Micah	07	15	Strained right hamstring
	09	24	Tightness - right shoulder
Padilla, Vicente	05	15	Right triceps tendinitis
	07	54	Strained right triceps
	08	30	Strained left hamstring; Strained neck
	09	16	Strained deltoid muscle - right shoulder
Park, Chan Ho	06	49	Abdominal pain; intestinal bleeding
Paronto, Chad	07	16	Strained right groin
Parra, Manny	07	21	Displaced chip fracture - left thumb
Patton, David	09	59	Strained right groin
Patton, Troy	08	184	Torn labrum
Paulino, Felipe	08	184	Pinched nerve in upper pitching arm
	09	19	Strained right groin
Pavano, Carl	05	97	Right shoulder tendinitis
	06	182	Back strain, bone chips in right elbow
	07	174	Torn ulnar collateral ligament
	08	145	Tommy John surgery 8/2007
Peavy, Jake	08	28	Strained right elbow
	09	101	Strained tendon - right ankle
Penny, Brad	05	19	Nerve irritation - right arm
	08	95	Inflammation right shoulder
Percival, Troy	05	113	Torn forearm muscle x 2
	06	182	Partial tear, right flexor pronator
	08	52	Strained left hamstring x 2; Sore right knee
	09	136	Tendinitis - right shoulder
Perdomo, Luis	09	18	Strained left knee
Perez, Odalis	05	88	Left shoulder soreness; oblique
	07	43	Strained left knee
	08	15	Tendinitis - left shoulder
Perez, Oliver	05	68	Fractured left big toe
	07	18	Lower back stiffness
	09	105	Tendinitis right kneecap x 2
Perkins, Glen	07	112	Strained teres major muscle
	09	52	Inflammation left shoulder; elbow
Petit, Yusmeiro	09	56	Strained right shoulder
Pettitte, Andy	08	6	Backs spasms
Pichardo, Kelvin	09	99	Strained right shoulder
Pineiro, Joel	05	11	Sore right shoulder
	07	15	Sprained right ankle
	08	36	Sore right shoulder; Sore right groin
Pinto, Renyel	07	42	Strained left shoulder
	08	15	Strained left hamstring
	09	27	Tendinitis left elbow
Ponson, Sidney	09	49	Strained right elbow
Proctor, Scott	08	71	Tendinitis pitching elbow
	09	183	Sore right elbow
Putz, J.J.	08	57	Costochondritis; Hyperextended right elbow
	09	122	Bone chips - right elbow
Qualls, Chad	09	35	Dislocated kneecap - left leg
Ramirez, Horacio	06	105	Sprained finger; left hamstring strain
	07	51	Tendinitis pitching shoulder
Ramirez, Ramon S.	07	48	Inflammation right elbow x 2
Rapada, Clay	08	18	Biceps tendinitis left arm
Rasner, Darrell	06	83	Right shoulder tendinitis
	07	11	Fractured right index finger
Rauch, Jon	05	103	Torn right labrum
Ray, Chris	07	72	Bone spur pitching elbow
	08	184	Tommy John surgery 8/2007
	09	25	Biceps tendinitis - right arm
Ray, Robert	09	136	Sore right shoulder
Redding, Tim	05	44	Strained right shoulder
	09	43	Fatigued - right shoulder
Reyes, Anthony	08	19	Strained pitching elbow
	09	135	Inflammation - right elbow
Reyes, Dennys	07	64	Inflamed elbow; shoulder
Reyes, Jo-Jo	09	56	Strained left hamstring
Reynolds, Greg	09	34	Sore right shoulder
Rheinecker, John	07	65	Back spasms
	08	184	Thoracic outlet syndrome surgery

FIVE-YEAR INJURY LOG

PITCHERS	Yr	Days	Injury
Richmond, Scott	09	28	Tendinitis right shoulder
Rincon, Juan	09	25	Stiffness -right elbow
Riske, David	06	47	Lower back strain
	08	35	Hyperextended right elbow
	09	178	Tightness right elbow
Robertson, Connor	07	132	Fractured right thumb
Robertson, Nate	07	20	Tired pitching arm
	09	77	Strained lower back; left elbow
Rodney, Fernando	05	66	Right shoulder inflammation
	07	56	Tendinitis right shoulder; biceps
	08	78	Tendinitis right shoulder
Rodriguez, Francisco	05	17	Strained right forearm
Rodriguez, Wandy	08	38	Strained left groin
Romero, J.C.	09	70	Strained left forearm
Romero, Ricky	09	22	Strained left oblique
Romo, Sergio	09	54	Sprained right elbow
Rosario, Francisco	07	107	Strained pitching shoulder
	08	184	Strained pitching shoulder
Rowland-Smith, Ryan	09	69	Tendinitis - left triceps
Ryan, B.J.	07	169	Strained pitching elbow
	08	14	Tommy John surgery
	09	22	Sore left shoulder
Sabathia, C.C.	05	13	Strained right oblique muscle
	06	30	Strained right oblique muscle
Sadler, Billy	09	24	Scapular dyskinesis - Right shoulder
Saito, Takashi	08	31	Sprained pitching elbow
Sampson, Chris	07	29	Sprained ulnar collateral ligament
	09	15	Muscle Spasms right shoulder
Sanchez, Anibal	08	123	Labrum surgery - right Shoulder
	09	104	Sprained right shoulder x 2
Sanchez, Duaner	06	64	Separated right shoulder
	07	184	Shoulder surg, Fx bone right shoulder
	08	16	Rehab of right shoulder surgery
Sanchez, Humberto	07	183	Tommy John surgery
	08	162	Recovery from TJS
Sanchez, Jonathan	07	23	Strained rib cage muscle
	08	20	Strained left shoulder
Santana, Ervin	09	60	Sprained MCL - right elbow; inflamed triceps
Santana, Johan	09	45	Bone spurs-left elbow - out for the year
Santos, Victor	06	25	Right rotator cuff strain
Sarfate, Dennis	08	20	Fractured clavicle
	09	121	Numbness fingers right hand
Saunders, Joe	09	18	Tightness - left shoulder
Scherzer, Max	09	9	Sore right shoulder
Schlichting, Travis	09	35	Back Injury
Schmidt, Jason	05	16	Strained right shoulder
	07	157	R/C surgery; bursitis
	08	184	Torn right biceps tendon
	09	166	Recovery labrum surgery right shoulder
Schoeneweis, Scott	09	28	Depression
Seanez, Rudy	05	35	Right shoulder strain
	08	15	Strained pitching shoulder
Seay, Bobby	05	49	Strained left pectoral muscle
Sheets, Ben	05	74	Torn back muscle; virus
	06	96	Right shoulder strain; tendinitis
	07	45	Sprained index finger right hand
Sherrill, George	08	26	Inflammation left shoulder
Shields, Scot	08	6	Strained right Shoulder
	09	131	Tendinitis right patella tendon
Shouse, Brian	06	16	Strained right calf
	09	63	Strained left elbow
Silva, Carlos	05	15	Torn meniscus in right knee
	08	15	Tendinitis right shoulder
	09	131	Strained rotator cuff right shoulder
Silva, Walter	09	37	Strained right forearm
Simon, Alfredo	09	173	Soreness right elbow
Sisco, Andrew	08	185	Recovery from Tommy John surgery
Slaten, Doug	08	25	Strained right knee
Slowey, Kevin	08	25	Strained biceps muscle right arm
	09	95	Strained right wrist
Smith, Greg	09	34	Strained lower back
Smith, Joe	09	66	Sprained left knee; sore right R/C
Smoltz, John	07	15	Inflamed pitching shoulder
	08	161	Torn labrum; Inflammed Trap; Right biceps
	09	81	Recovery from labrum surgery - right shoulder

FIVE-YEAR INJURY LOG

PITCHERS	Yr	Days	Injury
Snell, Ian	08	15	Strained pitching elbow
Soria, Joakim	07	15	Inflammation right shoulder
	09	25	Strained rotator cuff right shoulder
Soriano, Rafael	05	154	Recovery from right elbow surgery
	06	15	Right shoulder fatigue
	08	154	Inflammation right elbow x 2
Sosa, Henry	09	61	Torn muscle-right shoulder
Sosa, Jorge	07	14	Strained left hamstring
Speier, Justin	06	32	Right forearm tightness
	07	74	Intestinal virus
Speier, Ryan	08	22	Bruised rotator cuff right shoulder
	09	91	Strained left hamstring
Springer, Russ	08	16	Irritated ulnar nerve right elbow
Stauffer, Tim	08	184	Torn Labrum/surgery 5/08
Street, Huston	06	20	Strained right groin
	07	71	Irritated pitching elbow
Stults, Eric	09	31	Sprained left thumb
Suppan, Jeff	08	15	Irritation right elbow
	09	28	Strained left oblique
Tallet, Brian	08	19	Fractured toe - right foot
Tazawa, Junichi	09	14	Strained left groin
Tejeda, Robinson	09	30	Tendinitis right rotator cuff
Thompson, Brad	08	57	Inflamed pitching elbow
Threets, Erick	08	44	Intercostal strain -right side
Tomko, Brett	06	33	Strained left oblique
	08	49	Strained right elbow
Uehara, Koji	09	121	Tendinitis right elbow; strained left hamstring
Valdez, Merkin	07	183	Tommy John surgery
	08	138	Strained right elbow
Valverde, Jose	05	28	Right biceps tendinitis
	09	47	Strained right calf
VandenHurk, Rick	09	60	Sore right elbow
Vargas, Claudio	05	37	Right elbow sprain
	07	15	Lower back spasms
	09	88	Tendinitis - right elbow
Vargas, Jason	07	9	Bone spur right elbow
	08	184	Left hip surgery (labrum) 3/08
Veal, Donnie	09	75	Strained right groin; sprained index finger
Veras, Jose	07	136	Inflammation right arm
Villone, Ron	07	14	Strained lower back
Vizcaino, Luis	08	64	Strained right shoulder
Volquez, Edinson	09	140	Inflamed nerve right elbow; back spasms
Waddell, Jason	09	26	Non-baseball related medical issue
Wade, Cory	08	19	Inflammation right shoulder
	09	40	Strained & bursitis - right shoulder
Waechter, Doug	08	19	Strained rotator cuff - right shoulder
	09	161	Strained right elbow; shoulder
Wagner, Billy	08	58	Sprained left forearm
	09	137	Tommy John surgery 9/08
Wainwright, Adam	08	75	Sprained middle finger - right hand
Wakefield, Tim	06	57	Stress fracture in rib cage
	08	18	Soreness - pitching shoulder
	09	48	Lower back strain
Walker, Jaime	08	32	Inflammation pitching elbow

FIVE-YEAR INJURY LOG

PITCHERS	Yr	Days	Injury
Walker, Tyler	05	18	Right shoulder inflammation
	06	111	Right elbow surgery
	07	183	Tommy John surgery
Wang, Chien-Ming	05	59	Right shoulder inflammation
	07	23	Strained right hamstring
	08	106	Lisfranc sprain, torn tendon - right foot
	09	125	Strained right shoulder; weak hip muscles
Washburn, Jarrod	05	18	Left forearm strain
Weathers, David	08	15	Ulnar neuritis pitching elbow
Weaver, Jeff	07	29	Inflammation in pitching shoulder
Weaver, Jered	07	16	Tendinitis right biceps
Webb, Brandon	09	176	Bursitis - right shoulder
Wellemeyer, Todd	07	81	Sore pitching elbow
	09	29	Inflammation-right elbow
Wells, Kip	06	127	Sprained right foot; blood clot
	08	83	Blood clot right hand
	09	16	Strained right adductor muscle
Westbrook, Jake	07	52	Strained left internal oblique muscle
	08	162	Tommy John surgery 06/08
	09	183	Recovery from TJ Surgery
White, Sean	09	20	Tendinitis right shoulder
Willis, Dontrelle	08	38	Hyperextended right Knee
	09	152	Anxiety disorder
Wilson, C.J.	06	11	Right hamstring strain
	08	53	Bone spurs - left elbow, surgery 8/08
Wise, Matt	05	23	Strained left intercostal
	06	49	Right elbow surgery
	08	167	Bruise right forearm; weak right shoulder
Wolf, Randy	05	113	Left elbow surgery
	06	118	Recovery from left elbow surgery
	07	89	Soreness -pitching shoulder
Wolfe, Brian	08	48	Strained triceps right Arm
Wood, Kerry	05	108	Strained right shoulder; surgery
	06	162	Post surgical; R/C tear
	07	124	Shoulder stiffness
	08	22	Blister on pitching hand
Worrell, Mark	09	183	Tommy John surgery 3/09
Wright, Jamey	07	66	Inflamed right shoulder
Wright, Wesley	09	20	Strained left shoulder
Yates, Tyler	05	182	Torn rotator cuff
	09	142	Inflammation right elbow
Young, Chris	07	15	Strained left oblique
	08	89	Strained right forearm; nasal fractures
	09	112	Inflammation right shoulder
Young, Terrell	09	38	Inflammation - right shoulder
Zagurski, Mike	07	43	Pulled left hamstring
	08	184	Tommy John surgery 4/08
	09	183	Recovery from TJ Surgery
Zambrano, Carlos	08	15	Strained right shoulder
	09	42	Strained left hamstring; strained back
Zimmermann, Jordan	09	78	Right elbow soreness
Zumaya, Joel	07	107	Ruptured tendon right middle finger
	08	130	Recovery from surgery on right shoulder
	09	96	Sore right shoulder x 2

V.
PROSPECTS

Top Prospects for 2010

by Jeremy Deloney

Tim Alderson (RHP, PIT) offers intelligence and command, though his velocity is a tick below average. At 6'6", he throws on a downhill plane and has some projection, but a fringe-average changeup may limit his effectiveness. Between High-A and Double-A, he went 10-3 with a 3.93 ERA, 2.0 bb/9 and 5.5 K/9.

Brandon Allen (1B, ARI) was traded from the White Sox in early July and promoted to the Majors in August. The 23 year-old slugger hit only .202 with 4 HR with Arizona after a .298/.372/.506 line between Double-A and Triple-A. He has legitimate power to all fields, but his BA could lag as he strikes out a lot and struggles against lefties.

Yonder Alonso (1B, CIN) broke his hand in June and missed two months of development. Nevertheless, he's a pure hitter with an abundance of bat speed and keen plate discipline. He signed late in '08 and '09 was his first pro season – he hit .292/.384/.464 with 9 HR.

Pedro Alvarez (3B, PIT) was a first round selection in '08 and struggled at the onset of the '09 season in High-A. He was later promoted to Double-A where he hit .333 with 13 HR. Between the two levels, he hit .288/.378/.535 with 32 doubles and 27 HR. Making contact was an issue and the lack of quickness may signal a move to 1B.

J.P. Arencibia (C, TOR) had a disappointing '09 campaign in Triple-A where he hit .236/.284/.444 with 32 doubles and 21 HR. He may have earned a return trip to Triple-A to begin '10, but his power should get him to the Majors. His aggressive approach needs to be tweaked and he needs some defensive enhancements to play full-time in Toronto.

Jake Arrieta (RHP, BAL) is expected to join a terrific cast of young pitchers in Baltimore in the near future. Armed with four average to above-average pitches, the 24 year-old keeps hitters off balance by mixing his offerings effectively. He'll run his fastball into the 93-95 mph range, but his command needs to be sharper. He was 11-11 with a 3.40 ERA and 8.8 K/9 between Double-A and Triple-A.

Michael Bowden (RHP, BOS) hasn't been successful in short stints with the Red Sox, but the 23 year-old still has a bright future. He has a repeatable, deceptive delivery that allows him to have plus command. He may never become an ace, but he has a good, moving fastball and a curveball that can get swings and misses.

Reid Brignac (SS, TAM) could win the starting shortstop job if Jason Bartlett departs. The 24 year-old left-handed hitter hit .283/.327/.417 with 8 HR in Triple-A. He's wiry strong with excellent athleticism. His power output has decreased in each of the past three seasons, but he offers above-average offensive skills and improving defense.

Madison Bumgarner (LHP, SF) was been as good as any minor league pitcher in each of the past two seasons. Between '08 and '09, the 20 year-old is 27-5 with a 1.65 ERA (from Low-A to Double-A). He also struck out 10 in 10 big league innings. He has plus velocity (88-95 mph) and solid command of a three pitch mix.

Carlos Carrasco (RHP, CLE) struggled upon making his big league debut. In five starts, the 23 year-old was 0-4 with a 8.87 ERA. Regardless, he has the skills and pitch mix to become a #2-3 starter. He can dominate at times with an 88-94 mph fastball and solid-average curve and changeup. He was 11-10 with a 4.64 ERA and 8.5 Dom in the minors in '09.

Jhoulys Chacin (RHP, COL) is an extreme groundball pitcher due to solid sinking and cutting action on his low 90's fastball. He isn't overpowering, but his quick arm produces outstanding movement to all of his offerings. He may never become a high strikeout pitcher in the Majors, but he'll be difficult to make hard contact against.

Tyler Colvin (OF, CHC) was a late-season call-up after hitting .286/.332/.480 with 15 HR between High-A and Double-A. The 24 year-old left-handed hitter could battle for a starting job in '10. He is a fundamental hitter with a quick bat and enough strength to project to slightly above average pop. He can also play all outfield positions.

Aaron Cunningham (OF, OAK) hasn't hit in a few stints with Oakland. Still only 23, the right-handed hitter batted .302/.372/.479 with 11 HR and 11 SB in Triple-A in '09. He has moderate power potential and BA ability because of his bat speed, but he has to make better contact.

Wade Davis (RHP, TAM) was outstanding in a late-season trial with the Rays. He posted a 3.72 ERA and 8.9 K/9 in six starts and may have cemented a spot on the Opening Day roster. The 24 year-old has cleaned up his delivery and could use some more polish, but his four pitch mix gives him significant upside.

Ian Desmond (SS, WAS) broke out in '09 after several disappointing seasons. The 24 year-old hit .330/.401/.477 with 7 HR and 21 SB between Double-A and Triple-A and hit .280 with 4 HR with the Nationals. Those numbers greatly exceeded his career stats, but he's spectacular with the glove and could win the starting SS position in '10.

Scott Elbert (LHP, LA) was the Dodgers' minor league pitcher of the year after going 4-4 with a 3.84 ERA as a starter in Double-A and Triple-A. He was primarily a situational reliever in the Majors. He'll likely contend for a #4-5 rotation spot as he's able to miss bats due to his pitch movement and easy low 90's velocity.

Alcides Escobar (SS, MIL) is among the top defensive shortstops in baseball. Add speed to the equation and the 23 year-old is an intriguing player. He was promoted to Milwaukee when J.J. Hardy was sent to Triple-A and he hit .304 in 125 AB. He doesn't project to much power, but his legs and glove should make him a steady performer.

Neftali Feliz (RHP, TEX) showed serious heat in a short relief role for the Rangers at the end of '09. His future most likely is as a starter, but Texas converted him to a reliever in late June and he thrived. The 21 year-old had a 1.74 ERA, 2.3 bb/9 and 11.3 K/9 in the Rangers pen and his mid-to-high 90's fastball and stellar changeup were dominating.

Tyler Flowers (C, CHW) is tall and strong and projects as an offensive-minded backstop with the power and patience to become a run producer in the middle of a lineup. He can hit both lefties and righties and has a discerning eye at the plate that allows him to hit for BA. If he can improve his defense, he could become an All-Star.

Todd Frazier (INF, CIN) may have finally found a position. The Reds used the 24 year-old at 2B late in the season and he's currently working there in the off-season. He possesses well above average bat speed and good power and should hit for BA and HR. He hit .293/.353/.483 with 45 doubles and 16 HR at Double-A and Triple-A.

Jason Heyward (OF, ATL) could very well be the top prospect in baseball after hitting .323/.408/.555 with 17 HR and a 1.00 Eye between High-A, Double-A and Triple-A. He projects as an All-Star RF with no evident weakness offensively or defensively. The 20 year-old left-handed hitter makes easy, hard contact and knows the strike zone well.

Austin Jackson (OF, NYY) hit .300/.354/.405 with 4 HR and 24 SB in Triple-A, but may be used as a trading chip in the off-season. The 23 year-old saw his power output decline and his strikeout totals increase, but his plus athleticism and bat speed should eventually lead to more power.

Jeremy Hellickson (RHP, TAM) dominated in '09, going 9-2 with a 2.45 ERA, 10.4 K/9, and .178 oppBA between Double-A and Triple-A. He has exquisite command and control to go along with a plus 88-94 mph fastball and swing-and-miss curveball. He's short, but the 22 year-old hasn't experienced any stamina issues.

Desmond Jennings (OF, TAM) is among the most exciting prospects in baseball. The 23 year-old has projectable power and tremendous speed, making him an electric leadoff hitter. He established career-highs in HR and SB by hitting .318/.401/.487 with 31 doubles, 11 HR, and 52 SB. He also walked as many times as he fanned (57).

Mat Gamel (3B, MIL) has been a relative disappointment in the Majors. However, his ability to hit lefties and righties still gives him good upside. The 24 year-old left-handed hitter batted .278 with 11 HR in Triple-A and .242 with 5 HR in the Majors. He needs to shorten his stroke and make better contact in addition to improving his footwork at 3B.

Chris Heisey (OF, CIN) was a major surprise in '09. He batted .314/.378/.523 with 35 doubles, 22 HR and 21 SB between Double-A and Triple-A. Some still see him as a 4th outfielder, but he makes easy contact and easily eclipsed his previous career high in HR. He can play any OF position.

Jaime Garcia (LHP, STL) should contend for a starting spot with the Cardinals in '10, even after elbow surgery in September '08 wiped out the majority of '09. He posted a 2.87 ERA, 3.4 bb/9 and 9.8 K/9 in 37 innings between Rookie ball, High-A and Triple-A. He notches both groundballs and strikeouts with a solid fastball and plus curveball.

Daniel Hudson (RHP, CHW) will be given an opportunity to secure an Opening Day roster slot after an '09 campaign that saw him pitch on every level of the ladder. He was 14-5 with a 2.32 ERA, 2.1 bb/9 and 10.1 K/9 in the minors before pitching 18 innings with the Sox. He offers a nice blend of pitches, including a solid 87-93 mph fastball and slider.

Fernando Martinez (OF, NYM) underwent knee surgery in mid-July and never returned. He made his Major League debut with the Mets and hit only .176 with 1 HR in 91 AB. At Triple-A, the 21 year-old hit .290/.337/.540. He's never hit double-digits in HR or SB, but he could evolve into a power-speed impact-type player.

Brian Matusz (LHP, BAL) is tall and athletic with an above-average repertoire of pitches. The '09 season was his first as a professional and ended the year in the Majors. He went 5-2 with a 4.63 ERA and 7.7 K/9 with the Orioles after posting a 1.91 ERA and 9.6 K/9 in the minors. He can register strikeouts with three pitches and his command continues to improve.

Logan Morrison (1B, FLA) missed approximately two months after a wrist fracture. His power, particularly against left-handed pitching, hasn't yet emerged, but his mature hitting approach helped him hit for a solid BA with line drive power. He hit .277/.408/.439 with a 1.33 Eye between High-A and Double-A.

Jonathan Niese (LHP, NYM) was on a roll when he tore a hamstring tendon in early August. A groundball pitcher, the 23 year-old sets up his pitches well and is able to add and subtract from his sinker through a repeatable delivery. He was 1-1 with a 4.21 ERA with the Mets after going 5-6 with a 3.82 ERA and 7.8 K/9 in Triple-A.

Jarrod Parker (RHP, ARI) has an electric fastball that generates easy mid-90s velocity along with a slider with which he can get strikeouts. Unfortunately, the 21 year-old was shut down due to elbow soreness and surgery hasn't been ruled out. He is currently rehabbing, and if fortunate, could see time in the Majors in '10.

Aaron Poreda (LHP, SD) was a deadline acquisition from the White Sox and was used in the pen in the Majors. As a starter in Double-A and Triple-A, the 23 year-old was 5-7 with a 3.92 ERA, 6.4 bb/9 and 9.1 K/9. He has an outstanding fastball that can reach the upper 90s, but the lack of a consistent secondary pitch may relegate him to the bullpen.

Buster Posey (C, SF) is the top catching prospect in baseball. He hit .325/.416/.531 with 31 doubles and 18 HR in High-A and Triple-A before a late-season promotion to the Majors. The 23 year-old has no apparent weakness and could evolve into one of the game's best all-around players.

Max Ramirez (C, TEX) was hindered by wrist issues throughout the season and performed terribly as a result. He hit .234/.323/.336 with 5 HR in Triple-A, but the 25 year-old is still a career .300/.399/.490 hitter. He's not gifted with the glove, but if he rebounds with the bat, he could become a valuable contributor for the Rangers.

Wilkin Ramirez (OF, DET) received a small taste of the big leagues after a solid all-around season in Triple-A. He has excellent bat speed and good power to go along with his above-average speed. If anybody could be a 20-20 player in the Tigers system, this 24 year-old is the guy.

Josh Reddick (OF, BOS) is lean and athletic with a fluid, level stroke that results in a moderately-high BA and average, line-drive power. He had 59 AB with the Red Sox in '09 and hit only .169 with 2 HR. After smashing 23 HR in '08, the 23 year-old left-handed hitter batted .245/.317/.446 with 13 HR between Double-A and Triple-A in '09.

Michael Saunders (OF, SEA) showed glimpses of success in 122 AB with the Mariners in '09. He didn't show much punch in the Majors and failed to make consistent contact, but his fluid bat gives him moderate power to all fields. He also has the speed to steal bases and play effective defense.

Jordan Schafer (OF, ATL) had a disappointing stint in the Majors, hitting .204 with 2 HR. His time in the minors wasn't positive either as he batted .229 with 2 HR in 35 AB. The 23 year-old had wrist surgery in August, but should be ready for Spring Training. The left-handed hitter has good upside with the bat and is above average defensively.

Scott Sizemore (2B, DET) is likely to get first crack at the 2B job if Placido Polanco leaves via free agency as expected. The 25 year-old easily eclipsed previous career highs in both HR (17) and SB (21) while hitting .308/.389/.500 with 39 doubles between Double-A and Triple-A. He has fine instincts to match his offensive production.

Justin Smoak (1B, TEX) has one of the best approaches of all minor league prospects. He understands the strike zone innately and knows which pitches he can drive. He hit .290/.410/.443 with 21 doubles and 12 HR between Double-A and Triple-A. The switch-hitter projects as a high BA batter with excellent power and above-average defense.

Drew Storen (RHP, WAS) could potentially play a pivotal role in the Nationals bullpen in '10. The 10th overall pick in the '09 draft pitched 37 innings in his pro debut between Low-A, High-A and Double-A, posting a 1.95 ERA, 2.0 bb/9, 11.9 K/9 and .162 oppBA. He has a nice 90-94 mph fastball, low 80's slider and an average changeup.

Stephen Strasburg (RHP, WAS) is among the most hyped prospects in recent memory. He's tall, athletic and physically imposing. With a dominating fastball that sits between 94-99 mph and a nasty slider, he can register strikeouts and induce weak contact. Not only does he have great stuff, but he has fine control and good command.

Jose Tabata (OF, PIT) has yet to produce double-digit HR totals in a season, but his body is still developing and he's learning his swing. The 21 year-old has the bat speed and leverage to hit for power, but struggles with breaking balls and an overly aggressive approach. He hit .293/.357/.406 with 5 HR and 11 SB between Double-A and Triple-A.

Michael Taylor (OF, PHI) ranks among the strongest position prospects in the minors. The 24 year-old feasted on minor league pitching by hitting .320/.395/.549 with 28 doubles, 20 HR and 21 SB in Double-A and Triple-A. He drastically improved his plate discipline in '09 and he could become a legitimate middle-of-the-order run producer.

Junichi Tazawa (RHP, BOS) signed with the Red Sox in December '08 and showcased his mature approach to pitching. He was 9-7 with a 2.55 ERA and 7.7 K/9 between Double-A and Triple-A. He also pitched 25 innings with Boston and posted a 7.46 ERA. He has good command and control and can mix his pitches effectively.

Josh Thole (C, NYM) doesn't hit many HR and doesn't project to do so, but he has impeccable on-base skills and the ability to flirt with .300 consistently. He hit .328/.395/.422 with 29 doubles and 1 HR in Double-A before a promotion to New York where he hit .321 in 53 AB. His catching skills aren't yet up to snuff, but he has the work ethic to improve.

Brett Wallace (3B, OAK) was acquired from St. Louis in late July and continued to hit upon his acquisition. The 23 year-old batted .293/.367/.455 with 26 doubles and 20 HR in Double-A and Triple-A. He's strong and muscular and should be a consistent offensive performer in the big leagues. The question remains as to where he plays defensively, and he could end up as a DH.

Travis Wood (LHP, CIN) was quite a revelation for Reds farmhands in '09. He went 13-5 with a 1.77 ERA, 2.8 bb/9, 7.3 K/9 and .204 oppBA in Double-A and Triple-A. He's not a dominator, but he has excellent command and keeps hitters off-guard with an outstanding changeup. His curveball showed significant improvement as well.

Top Ranked 2010 Prospects

1. Jason Heyward (OF, ATL)
2. Desmond Jennings (OF, TAM)
3. Brian Matusz (LHP, BAL)
4. Madison Bumgarner (LHP, SF)
5. Wade Davis (RHP, TAM)
6. Alcides Escobar (SS, MIL)
7. Neftali Feliz (RHP, TEX)
8. Buster Posey (C, SF)
9. Scott Sizemore (2B, DET)
10. Daniel Hudson (RHP, CHW)
11. Reid Brignac (INF, TAM)
12. Tyler Flowers (C, CHW)
13. Drew Storen (RHP, WAS)
14. Aaron Poreda (LHP, SD)
15. Stephen Strasburg (RHP, WAS)
16. Justin Smoak (1B, TEX)
17. Brett Wallace (3B, OAK)
18. Ian Desmond (SS, WAS)
19. Carlos Carrasco (RHP, CLE)
20. Jake Arrieta (RHP, BAL)
21. Junichi Tazawa (RHP, BOS)
22. Jeremy Hellickson (RHP, TAM)
23. Mat Gamel (3B, MIL)
24. Michael Saunders (OF, SEA)
25. Brandon Allen (1B, ARI)
26. Michael Bowden (RHP, BOS)
27. Aaron Cunningham (OF, OAK)
28. Jaime Garcia (LHP, STL)
29. Jordan Schafer (OF, ATL)
30. Tyler Colvin (OF, CHC)
31. Josh Reddick (OF, BOS)
32. Fernando Martinez (OF, NYM)
33. Tim Alderson (RHP, PIT)
34. Austin Jackson (OF, NYY)
35. J.P. Arencibia (C, TOR)
36. Logan Morrison (1B, FLA)
37. Michael Taylor (OF, PHI)
38. Jhoulys Chacin (RHP, COL)
39. Scott Elbert (LHP, LAD)
40. Pedro Alvarez (3B, PIT)
41. Wilkin Ramirez (OF, DET)
42. Jonathan Niese (LHP, NYM)
43. Todd Frazier (INF, CIN)
44. Chris Heisey (OF, CIN)
45. Max Ramirez (C, TEX)
46. Josh Thole (C, NYM)
47. Yonder Alonso (1B, CIN)
48. Jose Tabata (OF, PIT)
49. Travis Wood (LHP, CIN)
50. Jarrod Parker (RHP, ARI)

Top Japanese Prospects

by Tom Mulhall

Shinnosuke Abe (C, Yomiuri Giants) is a 29-year-old catcher with 30 HR power, solid BA and league-leading OPS. This Gold Glover was already the highest paid catcher in Japan and is now eligible for domestic free agency. He's one year away from international free agency but has never expressed any desire to play in the ML.

Possible ETA: 2011.

Norichika Aoki (OF, Yakult Swallows) is a speedy outfielder and Gold Glove winner who shines in international play. No power, but five successive seasons of .300+ BA. Aoki wants to be posted and his team did successfully post Iwamura. We've been calling him a "mini-Ichiro" for years and there's no reason to change now. He should be a free agent after the 2011 season which means his team could post him after the 2010 season.

Probable ETA: 2011.

Yu Darvish (SP, Nippon Ham Fighters) is just 23 but it seems like we've been talking about him forever. Normally, he would be years away from being posted, but nothing about Darvish is normal. The hugely talented pitcher had a league best 1.73 ERA in 2009. However, he has pitched a lot of innings in his young career which could lead to arm troubles. He suffered from back pain and shoulder fatigue late this season and did not pitch in the League Series. But a pitcher like this only comes around once in a long while.

Possible ETA: 2012 unless a MLB club makes an obscene offer his team can't refuse.

Kyuji Fujikawa (Closer, Hanshin Tigers) had another great season pitching in a relatively big stadium. The transition to MLB may not be as difficult for this pitcher who desperately wants to make the jump. He has the talent to succeed in the MLB but probably will have to wait for free agency. His team says they do not intend to even review the latest in a long line of his requests to be posted.

Probable ETA: 2012 but possibly in 2011 if his team owner wakes up and smells the saki.

Hirokazu Ibata (SS, Chunichi Dragons) believes he is the best SS in Japan, which could mean he wants to try MLB now that he's an international free agent. He's tops defensively with good speed, solid BA and decent eye. Ibata has trouble getting along with his front office and perhaps that was the reason he was left off the 2009 WBC roster. He could be the rare Japanese player who fits in better in the U.S.

Possible ETA: 2010.

Ryota Igarashi (MR, Tokyo Yakult Swallows) is now eligible for international free agency and could be a very capable middle reliever. Regardless, he can hit 98 mph and has more than a 9.0 K/9 lifetime. As with most fireballers, control is an issue. A reasonable long shot for cheap saves, with the emphasis on "long."

Probable ETA: 2010.

Hirotoshi Ishii (MR/Closer, Yakult Swallows) injured his shoulder in 2006 and hasn't played in their majors since. Now not likely to come to MLB anytime soon and is a significant injury risk.

Possible ETA: 2012.

Hisashi Iwakuma (SP, Tohoku Rakuten Golden Eagles) is nearing free agency. He had an amazing 2008 season (2.18 ERA) and a solid 2009 after coming off an astounding performance in the WBC. Put him on your radar.

Possible ETA: 2011, but 2012 more likely.

Tatsuhiko Kinjoh (3B/OF, Yokohama BayStars) has consistently maintained a good OBP with moderate power. The switch-hitter has been mentioned as a possibility for the Majors but is probably no more than a utility player.

Possible ETA: 2010.

Chang Yong Lim (Closer, Yakult Swallows) is a Korean playing in the Japanese leagues. His team exercised his 2010 option but then he will be a free agent. He's talked about playing in MLB and in the right situation he could be an adequate closer. He has a sidearm delivery with a mid-90's fastball complemented with decent off pitches. He's hit 100 mph on the radar gun, so take a chance.

Probable ETA: 2011.

Shuichi Murata (3B, Yokohama Bay Stars) has an improving but still-average batting average with very good power. At 5'9", he may be too small to make the power transition to MLB, but he held his own in the WBC.

Possible ETA: 2012.

Kazumi Saito (SP, Fukuoka Softbank Hawks) had consistent sub 3.00 ERA's and was once considered to be better than Dice-K. Surgery to repair a damaged rotator cuff in his pitching shoulder in 2008 makes him a very risky selection. Saito did not pitch in their majors in 2009.

Possible ETA: 2011, but more likely 2012.

Yuki Saito (SP, Waseda University) is another phenomenal young arm, nearly the same level as Darvish. According to a Mets scout, he could be "the next Pedro Martinez." He did not enter their professional draft after high school, opting to attend college instead, where he has dominated. At a minimum, he wants to keep his options open about MLB.

Probable ETA: MLB minors in 2011.

Toshiya Sugiuchi (SP, Fukuoka Softbank Hawks) is getting close to free agency but his team does not post early. Four straight solid seasons (three with a sub 2.70 ERA) were capped in 2009 when he was in the top four in his league in ERA, strikeouts, WHIP and wins. The lefty former MVP and Sawamura Award winner could be a very capable MLB pitcher.

Possible ETA: 2011, but 2012 more likely.

Hitoshi Tamura (OF, Fukuoka Softbank Hawks) just achieved full free agency and has expressed a desire to try the Majors. He's often injured due to his all-out style of play. Tamura had some moderate power but is now 32. Still, he could make a decent fourth or fifth outfielder.

Possible ETA: 2010.

Avoid even if in MLB:

Shota Ichinoseki (Pitcher), Hidetaka Kawagoe (Pitcher), Koji Mitsui (Pitcher), Toshihisa Nishi (Infielder), Saburo Ohmura (OF), Naoyuki Shimizu (Pitcher)

Major League Equivalents

In his 1985 *Baseball Abstract*, Bill James introduced the concept of major league equivalencies. His assertion was that, with the proper adjustments, a minor leaguer's statistics could be converted to an equivalent major league level performance with a great deal of accuracy.

Because of wide variations in the level of play among different minor leagues, it is difficult to get a true reading on a player's potential. For instance, a .300 batting average achieved in the high-offense Pacific Coast League is not nearly as much of an accomplishment as a similar level in the Eastern League. MLEs normalize these types of variances, for all statistical categories.

The actual MLEs are not projections. They represent how a player's previous performance might look at the major league level. However, the MLE stat line can be used in forecasting future performance in just the same way as a major league stat line would.

The model we use contains a few variations to James' version and updates all of the minor league and ballpark factors. In addition, we designed a module to convert pitching statistics, which is something James did not originally do.

Do MLEs really work?

Used correctly, MLEs are excellent indicators of potential. But, just like we cannot take traditional major league statistics at face value, the same goes for MLEs. The underlying measures of base skill — batting eye ratios, pitching command ratios, etc. — are far more accurate in evaluating future talent than raw home runs, batting averages or ERAs.

The charts we present here also provide the unique perspective of looking at two years' worth of data. These are only short-term trends, for sure. But even here we can find small indications of players improving their skills, or struggling, as they rise through more difficult levels of competition. Since players — especially those with any modicum of talent — are promoted rapidly through major league systems, a two-year scan is often all we get to spot any trends. Five-year trends do appear in the *Minor League Baseball Analyst*.

Here are some things to look for as you scan these charts:
Target players who...
- spent a full year in AA and then a full year in AAA
- had consistent playing time from one year to the next
- improved their base skills as they were promoted

Raise the warning flag for players who...
- were stuck at the same level both years, or regressed
- displayed marked changes in playing time from one year to the next
- showed large drops in BPIs from one year to the next

Players are listed on the charts if they spent at least part of 2008 or 2009 in Triple-A or Double-A and had at least 100 AB or 30 IP within those two levels. Each is listed with the organization with which they finished the season.

Only statistics accumulated in Triple-A and Double-A are included (players who split a season are indicated as a/a); Major League and Single-A (and lower) stats are excluded.

Each player's actual AB and IP totals are used as the base for the conversion. However, it is more useful to compare performances using common levels, so rely on the ratios and sabermetric gauges. Complete explanations of these formulas appear in the Glossary.

Batters who had a BPV of at least 50, and pitchers who had a BPV of at least 90, and are less than 26 years of age (the "unofficial" break point between prospect and suspect) are indicated with an "a" after their age. This should provide a pool of the best rising prospects. Obvious prospects like Billy Butler and Adam Lind were tagged as "a" in 2008. However, there were also lesser players tagged in last year's book who ended up getting significant playing time in 2009. Among them were Michael Brantley, Dexter Fowler, Nolan Reimold, Daniel Bard, Neftali Feliz, Shawn Kelley, Vince Mazzaro, James McDonald, Kris Medlen, Clayton Richard, David Robertson, Max Scherzer and Chris Tillman .

Also keep an eye on players more than 26, but less than 30, with similarly high BPVs. These are your "Bull Durham" prospects, indicated with a "b" after their age. Keep these players on your end-game or reserve list radar as there could be hidden short-term value here. Among the players tagged as "b" is last year's book were Nelson Cruz, Ryan Raburn and Ben Zobrist.

Major League Equivalent Statistics

BATTERS

BATTER	Yr	B	Age	Pos	Lev	Org	ab	r	h	d	t	hr	rbi	bb	k	sb	cs	ba	ob	slg	ops	bb%	ct%	eye	px	sx	rc/g	bpv
Abercrombie,Reg	08	R	28	8	aa	HOU	289	25	60	11	1	8	24	6	81	11	10	207	224	332	556	2%	72%	0.08	77	97	2.11	-15
	09	R	28	8	aa	HOU	517	43	109	22	4	8	35	19	141	18	11	211	240	313	553	4%	73%	0.14	67	111	2.36	-12
Abreu,Michel	08	R	30	3	aa	NYM	425	46	94	19	0	10	48	28	58	1	0	221	268	338	606	6%	86%	0.47	77	43	3.12	34
	09	R	31	3	aa	NYM	171	12	29	6	0	3	13	9	36	0	0	169	212	249	461	5%	79%	0.26	54	23	1.71	-23
Abreu,Miguel	09	R	25	4	aa	BAL	489	53	135	29	1	4	43	12	53	24	8	277	293	363	657	2%	89%	0.22	66	105	3.79	47
Abreu,Tony	09	B	25 a	4	aa	LA	307	38	90	19	2	10	44	12	46	3	3	294	319	463	782	4%	85%	0.25	109	77	5.28	60
Adams,Russ	08	L	28	84	aaa	TOR	429	51	94	17	2	13	51	41	99	9	2	219	288	359	647	9%	77%	0.42	86	93	3.65	24
	09	L	29	4	a/a	SD	207	22	43	10	2	1	15	14	34	2	2	208	257	287	544	6%	84%	0.41	58	92	2.45	23
Adduci,James	09	L	24	8	aa	CHC	467	51	126	19	3	4	41	47	69	29	13	269	336	347	684	9%	85%	0.68	55	108	4.22	37
Affronti,Michael	08	R	25	4	aa	OAK	128	10	31	10	0	1	12	0	19	0	0	240	240	338	578	0%	85%	0.00	78	3	2.72	7
	09	R	26	4	aa	OAK	189	14	36	5	0	2	14	8	19	1	3	189	224	244	467	4%	90%	0.44	37	43	1.67	13
Albernaz,Craig	09	R	27	2	a/a	TAM	133	13	19	4	2	0	8	12	30	1	0	145	216	201	416	8%	77%	0.39	37	118	1.47	-8
Aldridge,Cory	08	L	29	0	aa	KC	167	17	36	5	1	7	30	19	36	2	3	216	296	381	677	10%	78%	0.52	96	60	3.66	30
	09	L	30	8	aa	KC	354	32	87	17	3	14	48	16	78	0	1	245	278	430	708	4%	78%	0.21	112	49	4.10	27
Alfonzo,Eliezer	08	R	30	2	aa	SF	196	19	52	14	1	5	30	7	49	1	0	268	292	426	718	3%	75%	0.14	107	58	4.45	12
	09	R	31	2	aa	SD	204	19	45	8	0	9	25	5	52	1	0	221	240	383	623	2%	75%	0.10	98	38	3.08	-5
Allen,Brandon	08	L	23 a	3	aa	CHW	153	27	41	6	1	15	29	18	37	3	1	268	345	614	959	11%	76%	0.49	192	91	7.67	107
	09	L	24 a	3	a/a	ARI	447	57	120	23	4	16	55	37	62	5	2	267	324	441	764	8%	86%	0.60	107	92	5.18	75
Almonte,Erick	08	R	31	640	aaa	DET	395	36	78	20	1	7	36	40	68	3	2	198	272	306	577	9%	83%	0.59	74	53	2.84	27
	09	R	32	3	aaa	MIL	247	20	54	9	0	2	21	20	52	3	0	220	277	275	553	7%	79%	0.38	41	51	2.73	-19
Alonso,Yonder	09	L	22 a	3	aa	CIN	105	10	29	10	0	2	12	12	13	1	0	276	350	429	779	10%	88%	0.92	114	36	5.72	75
Alvarez,Pedro	09	L	23 a	5	aa	PIT	222	35	68	18	0	10	33	27	47	1	0	306	382	523	904	11%	79%	0.57	141	43	7.80	65
Ambres,Chip	08	R	29 b	8	aa	SD	412	62	88	20	4	15	58	41	92	6	3	214	285	393	678	9%	78%	0.45	109	124	3.84	55
	09	R	30	8	a/a	NYM	465	40	94	22	1	9	43	34	85	3	6	202	255	307	562	7%	82%	0.40	71	45	2.51	13
Anderson,Brian	09	R	28	8	aaa	BOS	123	14	25	5	1	5	12	8	41	0	3	205	254	373	627	6%	67%	0.20	102	79	2.84	-14
Anderson,Bryan	08	L	22	2	aa	STL	315	31	86	16	1	3	33	28	45	2	0	273	332	359	692	8%	86%	0.63	63	57	4.50	30
	09	L	23	2	aa	STL	163	17	35	6	2	3	9	8	32	1	0	215	251	331	583	5%	80%	0.25	72	103	2.84	21
Anderson,Drew M	08	L	26	4	a/a	CIN	238	25	52	13	1	4	20	18	34	4	0	217	272	328	600	7%	86%	0.52	77	85	3.15	46
	09	L	27	4	aa	TAM	255	24	48	14	4	1	13	18	41	2	0	188	242	281	524	7%	84%	0.45	66	114	2.31	38
Anderson,Drew T	08	L	27	8	aaa	CIN	404	40	95	23	5	6	52	15	91	3	6	234	262	361	623	4%	77%	0.17	85	94	3.01	15
	09	L	28	8	a/a	MIL	406	41	93	20	2	7	41	35	77	6	6	230	291	340	632	8%	81%	0.46	75	72	3.34	23
Anderson,Lars	08	L	21 a	3	aa	BOS	133	22	40	14	0	4	24	23	34	1	0	304	407	501	908	15%	75%	0.69	141	46	8.21	57
	09	L	22	3	aa	BOS	447	42	102	26	0	7	43	54	92	2	0	228	311	334	645	11%	79%	0.58	76	42	3.78	15
Anson,Kyle	09	B	26	2	aa	NYY	163	20	33	8	0	2	21	32	35	1	0	203	335	288	622	16%	79%	0.93	62	42	3.66	12
Antonelli,Matt	08	R	24	4	aa	SD	451	51	82	16	3	5	32	62	79	5	5	183	281	263	544	12%	83%	0.79	53	81	2.54	23
	09	R	24	4	aa	SD	189	19	30	9	1	3	16	20	26	1	1	157	239	259	498	10%	86%	0.77	69	70	2.04	42
Apodaca,Juan	09	R	23	2	aa	BOS	216	22	50	13	0	4	24	17	46	1	0	231	286	345	631	7%	79%	0.36	80	43	3.49	8
Ardoin,Danny	09	R	35	2	aa	LA	104	8	21	5	1	0	8	3	20	0	1	204	230	270	499	3%	81%	0.17	51	71	1.96	-7
Arencibia,JP	08	R	23	2	aa	TOR	262	26	68	13	0	13	35	5	46	0	0	260	273	458	731	2%	82%	0.11	121	17	4.36	37
	09	R	24	2	aaa	TOR	466	49	94	28	1	17	55	19	91	0	1	202	233	374	607	4%	81%	0.21	111	44	2.83	34
Arias,Joaquin	08	R	24 a	64	aa	TEX	432	44	110	13	7	6	36	14	43	17	6	256	280	358	637	3%	90%	0.34	62	145	3.47	62
	09	R	25	6	aa	TEX	504	48	115	13	3	4	39	15	41	19	3	228	250	287	537	3%	92%	0.36	40	118	2.52	42
Armstrong,Cole	08	L	25	2	a/a	CHW	356	33	82	25	0	8	40	13	53	0	1	230	257	364	622	4%	85%	0.25	96	30	3.14	35
	09	L	26	2	aaa	CHW	246	23	54	11	0	9	27	10	50	0	0	221	251	378	629	4%	80%	0.20	98	22	3.20	13
Arnal,Cristo	09	R	24	4	a/a	CLE	258	34	65	9	0	0	14	23	20	15	7	253	314	287	601	8%	92%	1.16	30	96	3.26	40
Ashley,Nevin	09	R	25	2	aa	TAM	118	8	22	6	1	1	13	16	31	0	0	183	281	271	551	12%	74%	0.52	62	50	2.68	-14
Aubrey,Michael	08	L	26	30	a/a	CLE	388	36	94	25	1	7	44	21	52	0	0	242	281	368	649	5%	87%	0.41	88	32	3.61	39
	09	L	27 b	3	aaa	BAL	376	34	94	24	1	7	43	16	37	2	2	249	280	376	656	4%	90%	0.44	89	50	3.62	57
Avila,Alex	09	L	23 a	2	aa	DET	329	43	79	21	1	10	46	43	62	2	1	240	328	401	729	12%	81%	0.69	106	60	4.77	53
Baez,Edgardo	08	R	23	8	aa	WAS	167	17	34	8	1	1	10	12	41	4	4	205	258	282	539	7%	76%	0.29	56	95	2.29	-9
	09	R	24	8	aa	WAS	323	36	75	12	3	8	24	24	72	5	11	232	285	360	645	7%	78%	0.33	79	91	3.13	17
Bailey,Jeff	08	R	30 b	38	aaa	BOS	418	64	102	27	2	16	54	45	86	3	2	245	318	434	752	10%	79%	0.52	121	79	4.92	59
	09	R	31	8	aaa	BOS	229	29	52	7	0	8	23	30	58	2	0	226	315	356	672	11%	75%	0.52	78	49	4.10	1
Baisley,Jeff	08	R	26 a	5	aa	OAK	299	33	72	21	1	6	32	23	34	0	1	242	295	374	669	7%	89%	0.66	93	43	3.86	58
	09	R	27	5	aa	OAK	355	29	68	17	1	6	26	17	63	1	0	192	230	290	520	5%	82%	0.28	68	53	2.21	10
Bankston,Wes	08	R	25	30	aa	OAK	375	41	86	16	1	13	54	15	54	0	2	230	261	387	647	4%	86%	0.28	96	42	3.34	42
	09	R	26	5	aaa	CIN	457	46	107	23	2	16	60	24	81	2	1	234	273	397	670	5%	82%	0.30	101	59	3.72	40
Barden,Brian	08	R	28	6	aa	STL	411	42	92	16	3	5	25	27	61	2	4	223	271	315	587	6%	85%	0.44	61	68	2.86	24
	09	R	28	3	aa	STL	187	18	39	9	0	3	19	7	39	1	1	207	236	296	532	4%	79%	0.18	64	51	2.28	-7
Barfield,Josh	08	R	26	4	a/a	CLE	303	25	66	16	1	4	20	13	60	8	5	217	250	313	563	4%	80%	0.22	69	83	2.53	12
	09	R	27	4	aaa	CLE	305	20	64	13	0	2	27	6	43	4	3	211	227	271	499	2%	86%	0.15	47	55	1.98	3
Barker,Kevin	08	L	33	3	aaa	CIN	399	50	82	17	0	16	53	38	94	0	1	205	274	369	643	9%	76%	0.41	100	34	3.42	16
	09	L	34	3	aaa	CIN	354	43	81	18	2	19	50	40	81	1	1	228	306	447	753	10%	77%	0.49	131	52	4.78	51
Barney,Darwin	09	R	24	6	aa	CHC	464	46	124	23	1	3	41	29	58	8	2	268	312	340	652	6%	87%	0.51	55	75	3.90	30
Barnwell,Chris	08	R	30	6	aa	FLA	330	35	71	15	1	4	30	30	50	11	3	214	279	305	584	8%	85%	0.60	64	95	3.03	38
	09	R	31	8	aa	PIT	270	17	41	10	0	2	10	11	56	2	4	151	184	208	392	4%	79%	0.20	43	49	1.11	-24
Barton,Brian	09	R	27	8	a/a	ATL	397	39	84	14	3	5	37	40	109	15	7	211	282	302	584	9%	73%	0.36	59	108	2.92	-10
Barton,Daric	09	L	24 a	3	aa	OAK	253	34	53	17	1	6	34	32	31	1	0	209	297	353	650	11%	88%	1.01	99	64	3.70	73
Bates,Aaron	08	R	25	30	aa	BOS	457	47	113	30	1	8	53	38	95	0	0	248	306	368	674	8%	79%	0.41	86	33	4.04	13
	09	R	26	3	a/a	BOS	478	59	119	25	0	9	49	34	101	1	0	250	299	362	661	7%	79%	0.33	77	47	3.88	7
Baxter,Michael	08	L	24 a	80	aa	SD	324	34	75	15	3	6	40	32	38	2	2	233	303	351	653	9%	88%	0.86	76	76	3.72	57
	09	L	25	8	aa	SD	505	60	131	32	4	7	61	48	84	11	9	259	323	376	699	9%	83%	0.57	83	93	4.26	47
Beckham,Gordon	09	R	23 a	6	a/a	CHW	175	25	52	21	0	4	22	13	23	2	0	297	345	482	826	7%	87%	0.54	139	63	6.33	92
Bell,Bubba	08	L	26	8	aa	BOS	312	38	76	15	2	9	37	29	53	2	1	245	308	392	700	8%	83%	0.54	93	71	4.30	46
	09	L	27	8	a/a	BOS	451	51	99	22	2	5	32	49	86	8	3	220	296	308	604	10%	81%	0.57	63	88	3.26	22
Bell,Joshua	09	B	23 a	5	aa	BAL	448	65	133	34	1	22	76	59	93	3	5	297	379	525	903	12%	79%	0.63	145	46	7.40	72
Bellhorn,Mark	08	B	34	3	aa	LA	207	23	37	11	1	5	20	26	45	1	0	181	271	316	587	11%	78%	0.57	89	62	2.95	27
	09	B	35	3	aa	COL	196	21	43	10	2	8	24	22	46	0	0	217	296	403	700	10%	77%	0.48	114	57	4.17	37
Bellorin,Edwin	08	R	27	2	aa	COL	335	18	81	22	2	4	43	10	32	1	1	242	264	352	615	3%	91%	0.32	80	44	3.16	48
	09	R	28	2	aa	COL	202	11	48	9	1	1	21	6	16	0	2	236	259	303	562	3%	92%	0.41	50	35	2.57	28

BATTER	Yr	B	Age	Pos	Lev	Org	ab	r	h	d	t	hr	rbi	bb	k	sb	cs	ba	ob	slg	ops	bb%	ct%	eye	px	sx	rc/g	bpv
Benjamin,Casey	08	L	28	6	aa	TEX	309	32	61	4	3	7	22	29	65	2	1	197	266	293	559	9%	79%	0.45	53	82	2.67	2
	09	L	29	8	aa	TEX	299	32	54	9	3	3	22	38	66	2	0	181	273	265	538	11%	78%	0.57	53	88	2.56	5
Bernier,Doug	08	B	28	6	aa	COL	337	36	68	8	3	6	26	40	60	1	2	201	285	295	580	11%	82%	0.66	56	67	2.91	17
	09	B	29	6	aaa	NYY	227	27	34	8	1	0	16	28	78	1	0	148	240	189	429	11%	66%	0.35	34	78	1.60	-63
Berry,Quintin	09	L	25	8	aa	PHI	516	70	120	15	1	5	22	49	102	38	15	233	299	294	593	9%	80%	0.48	42	116	3.11	9
Bertram,Michael	09	L	26 a	3	aa	DET	123	17	30	6	2	7	24	10	27	0	0	245	303	481	785	8%	78%	0.39	137	94	5.15	69
Betemit,Wilson	09	B	28	5	aaa	CHW	261	30	54	16	0	10	40	17	73	2	0	207	256	383	638	6%	72%	0.23	114	57	3.32	10
Bianchi,Jeffrey	09	R	23	6	aa	KC	270	33	78	17	1	4	33	15	44	8	5	289	326	404	730	5%	84%	0.34	82	88	4.68	39
Bixler,Brian	08	R	26	6	aa	PIT	321	36	80	8	4	6	29	22	98	19	8	249	296	348	645	6%	70%	0.22	58	146	3.58	-17
	09	R	27	6	aa	PIT	403	54	93	20	5	6	33	26	111	10	3	231	277	352	628	6%	72%	0.23	79	145	3.39	11
Blanco,Andres	08	B	24	6	aa	CHC	298	22	72	8	1	1	27	11	25	7	4	242	268	283	551	3%	92%	0.42	31	73	2.57	22
	09	B	25 a	6	aa	CHC	230	24	62	15	1	6	24	13	26	5	1	270	309	417	726	5%	89%	0.52	99	78	4.69	72
Blanco,Gregor	09	L	26	8	aaa	ATL	333	42	65	8	1	2	24	39	63	8	3	195	280	240	520	11%	81%	0.63	31	92	2.41	0
Blanks,Kyle	08	R	22	3	aa	SD	492	65	141	19	4	16	92	43	82	4	5	287	344	439	783	8%	83%	0.52	92	77	5.49	48
	09	R	23	3	aa	SD	233	27	55	7	1	9	30	31	54	0	0	236	326	387	713	12%	77%	0.58	88	38	4.59	15
Boggs,Brandon	09	B	27	8	aa	TEX	332	34	75	13	2	6	35	44	88	6	2	224	316	333	648	12%	73%	0.50	69	85	3.83	0
Bogusevic,Brian	08	L	25 a	8	aa	HOU	124	15	38	9	1	2	14	12	20	6	1	310	368	441	810	9%	84%	0.58	92	106	6.46	61
	09	L	26	8	aa	HOU	520	49	117	22	2	5	39	39	98	16	4	224	278	300	578	7%	81%	0.39	54	97	2.96	13
Bolivar,Luis	08	R	28	564	a/a	CIN	370	41	81	16	2	8	34	20	80	15	5	219	259	338	597	5%	78%	0.25	77	117	2.97	22
	09	R	29	4	aaa	CIN	353	45	67	13	3	4	24	12	68	21	5	189	217	279	496	3%	81%	0.18	59	165	2.00	28
Bond,Brock	09	B	24	4	aa	SF	450	79	136	20	4	1	28	56	61	11	16	303	380	371	751	11%	86%	0.91	50	98	5.02	39
Boone,James	08	B	26	8	aa	PIT	329	29	63	11	1	8	33	31	97	2	3	191	261	300	561	9%	71%	0.32	68	52	2.59	-28
	09	B	27	8	aa	PIT	123	8	18	5	0	1	7	5	25	2	0	150	180	209	390	4%	80%	0.18	45	67	1.23	-16
Borbon,Julio	08	L	23 a	8	aa	TEX	255	31	78	11	2	4	17	11	25	13	13	306	335	412	746	4%	90%	0.44	69	106	4.40	58
	09	L	24 a	8	aa	TEX	407	57	114	11	6	2	28	26	34	20	8	279	323	349	672	6%	92%	0.79	44	146	4.11	60
Borchard,Joe	08	B	30	8	aaa	ATL	117	12	25	4	1	3	9	9	29	3	2	213	272	331	603	7%	75%	0.33	73	94	2.99	4
	09	B	31	8	a/a	SF	346	36	61	16	3	9	37	16	85	0	1	177	214	319	533	4%	76%	0.19	90	75	2.16	7
Boscan,Jean	08	R	29	2	aa	ATL	255	18	48	11	0	2	21	25	45	0	0	186	258	248	507	9%	82%	0.54	47	20	2.21	-8
	09	R	30	2	a/a	ATL	294	19	60	13	0	0	24	27	60	1	1	205	271	249	520	8%	79%	0.44	39	30	2.35	-24
Bourgeois,Jason	08	R	27 b	8	aaa	CHW	510	67	125	19	3	8	39	28	62	24	11	245	284	343	627	5%	88%	0.45	63	120	3.30	51
	09	R	28 b	8	aaa	MIL	424	44	107	14	4	2	30	17	37	26	7	253	282	316	598	4%	91%	0.47	44	132	3.17	50
Bourjos,Peter	09	R	22 a	8	aa	LAA	437	65	117	16	10	5	46	43	68	29	13	268	333	384	718	9%	84%	0.63	70	188	4.56	70
Bourquin,Ron	09	L	24	3	aa	DET	127	12	26	5	2	4	15	12	35	0	2	204	275	363	638	9%	72%	0.35	94	96	3.19	12
Bowers,Jason	08	R	31	5	aa	PIT	368	35	75	20	1	4	31	20	62	10	3	203	245	298	543	5%	83%	0.33	69	96	2.47	29
	09	R	32	6	aa	TAM	330	31	61	8	5	3	21	26	66	5	2	185	246	263	508	7%	80%	0.40	46	130	2.18	13
Bowker,John	09	L	26 b	8	aa	SF	366	66	108	20	3	16	67	60	60	8	6	294	393	493	886	14%	84%	1.00	122	95	7.29	91
Bowman,Shawn	08	R	24	5	aa	NYM	113	10	25	6	0	2	8	2	30	3	1	217	230	321	551	2%	74%	0.07	73	75	2.42	-19
	09	R	25	5	aa	NYM	347	33	86	21	2	7	35	20	85	0	0	249	290	379	669	5%	75%	0.24	89	46	3.88	-1
Boyer,Brad	09	L	26 a	5	aa	SF	367	40	96	21	8	2	34	24	63	9	6	261	306	379	685	6%	83%	0.37	78	162	4.03	57
Bozied,Tagg	08	R	29 b	38	aa	FLA	425	62	101	22	2	18	58	38	79	5	2	237	299	425	724	8%	81%	0.48	116	87	4.46	63
	09	R	30	8	aa	PIT	215	22	48	14	1	3	13	14	56	3	2	225	274	344	618	6%	74%	0.26	84	75	3.19	-1
Brantley,Michael	08	L	21 a	83	aa	MIL	420	65	119	15	1	3	32	42	22	22	10	284	349	346	696	9%	95%	1.95	45	102	4.51	66
	09	L	22 a	8	aaa	CLE	457	66	110	19	1	5	30	51	40	38	6	241	317	319	636	10%	91%	1.28	56	125	3.95	69
Brignac,Reid	08	L	23	6	aaa	TAM	352	36	78	23	2	7	36	21	78	4	2	222	265	358	623	6%	78%	0.27	94	86	3.21	25
	09	L	24	6	aaa	TAM	415	44	106	25	2	7	38	24	62	4	6	255	295	375	670	5%	85%	0.38	84	67	3.74	40
Britton,Phillip	09	R	25	2	aa	ATL	126	8	25	9	0	0	11	6	23	1	3	198	233	267	500	4%	82%	0.25	61	45	1.85	0
Broadway,Larry	08	L	28	3	aaa	WAS	429	43	92	24	2	6	42	43	101	3	8	214	286	323	609	9%	76%	0.43	77	56	3.00	4
	09	L	29	0	aa	PIT	206	15	39	9	0	5	19	11	58	0	4	188	231	308	538	5%	72%	0.20	77	26	2.07	-30
Brown,Andrew	08	R	24	3	aa	STL	247	27	51	12	0	9	29	22	65	1	0	206	271	358	629	8%	74%	0.34	95	42	3.33	3
	09	R	25	3	aa	STL	263	30	61	9	1	8	31	23	39	1	0	232	293	372	665	8%	85%	0.57	85	55	3.85	42
Brown,Corey	09	L	24 a	8	aa	OAK	250	33	55	17	2	6	31	20	50	4	3	220	276	372	649	7%	80%	0.39	102	105	3.42	50
Brown,Dee	08	L	31	08	aa	LAA	485	50	100	26	0	8	53	43	64	7	2	207	272	308	580	8%	87%	0.68	72	70	2.91	45
	09	L	31	8	aa	LA	396	57	89	27	0	14	58	43	66	7	3	225	300	404	704	10%	83%	0.65	117	76	4.24	71
Brown,Dominic	09	L	22	8	aa	PHI	147	17	37	8	2	3	17	11	31	7	1	252	304	395	698	7%	79%	0.35	92	143	4.41	48
Brown,Dusty	08	R	26	2	aaa	BOS	297	30	75	14	1	8	42	30	73	0	0	251	320	387	708	9%	75%	0.42	87	32	4.51	2
	09	R	27	2	aaa	BOS	295	20	73	14	0	2	21	33	79	0	0	247	323	314	638	10%	73%	0.42	53	12	3.76	-39
Brown,Emil	09	R	35	8	aa	NYM	271	25	52	15	0	4	24	17	53	2	5	191	239	295	534	6%	80%	0.32	74	48	2.14	9
Brown,Jordan	08	L	25	30	aaa	CLE	420	47	108	28	2	6	46	33	67	3	4	256	310	373	682	7%	84%	0.49	84	64	4.04	39
	09	L	26 a	8	aaa	CLE	417	51	120	30	1	11	52	24	57	2	5	289	328	446	774	6%	86%	0.43	108	47	5.19	58
Brown,Matt	08	R	26 b	350	aa	LAA	400	59	109	29	3	16	52	25	73	3	2	271	314	476	790	6%	82%	0.34	132	87	5.34	72
	09	R	27	3	aa	LAA	388	46	81	24	0	10	56	35	90	5	5	209	274	348	622	8%	77%	0.39	95	60	3.16	20
Buchanan,Brian	08	R	35	0	aa	KC	232	26	43	9	1	5	25	11	53	1	1	183	220	297	517	5%	77%	0.21	73	77	2.10	1
	09	R	36	0	aa	KC	122	7	22	6	0	4	17	5	16	1	0	181	214	334	548	4%	86%	0.31	97	26	2.33	42
Buck,Travis	08	L	25	8	aa	OAK	169	21	41	7	1	1	12	18	26	3	1	244	318	312	630	10%	85%	0.70	49	86	3.66	25
	09	L	26	8	aa	OAK	232	25	50	10	2	3	20	16	33	2	1	215	265	312	577	6%	86%	0.48	65	89	2.82	37
Budde,Ryan	08	R	29	2	aa	LAA	173	11	28	7	1	2	16	7	45	3	0	159	191	239	430	4%	74%	0.15	55	86	1.49	-25
	09	R	30	2	aa	LAA	273	25	51	14	1	5	24	23	76	1	1	187	250	299	549	8%	72%	0.30	76	54	2.49	-18
Burke,Chris	09	R	30	6	a/a	ATL	312	34	69	16	1	3	27	22	59	11	3	221	273	303	576	7%	81%	0.38	62	103	2.92	19
Butera,Andrew	08	R	25	2	aa	MIN	302	30	55	15	1	5	30	26	51	0	1	184	249	286	535	8%	83%	0.52	71	47	2.37	21
	09	R	26	2	aaa	MIN	298	18	52	14	1	2	19	17	47	0	1	176	219	247	466	5%	84%	0.35	53	37	1.74	4
Bynum,Freddie	08	L	29	5	a/a	BAL	150	14	31	4	3	1	13	16	39	6	2	205	281	282	563	10%	74%	0.41	45	152	2.83	0
	09	L	30	6	a/a	WAS	232	22	46	8	1	3	12	8	50	8	3	196	222	271	493	3%	78%	0.15	50	107	1.92	-6
Bynum,Seth	08	R	28	64	aa	WAS	273	36	56	13	1	10	35	20	81	1	4	204	258	366	624	7%	70%	0.24	100	67	3.00	-3
	09	R	29	4	a/a	WAS	480	46	105	20	2	15	54	25	135	5	3	218	256	361	618	5%	72%	0.18	89	74	3.09	-8
Byrne,Bryan	08	L	24	3	aa	ARI	416	52	115	25	0	8	44	56	59	2	3	277	362	392	755	12%	86%	0.94	82	36	5.34	45
	09	L	25	3	aa	ARI	374	40	79	21	1	2	40	54	63	1	2	211	310	287	597	13%	83%	0.85	59	45	3.19	21
Cabrera,Jolbert	08	R	36	8	aaa	CIN	215	18	48	13	3	3	20	9	38	3	3	221	254	352	606	4%	82%	0.25	87	104	2.85	41
	09	R	37	3	aaa	BAL	294	23	63	14	1	6	39	9	62	7	2	214	238	330	568	3%	79%	0.15	77	84	2.62	10
Cabrera,Willie	09	R	23	8	aa	ATL	371	39	94	18	2	7	47	30	49	3	8	254	310	367	677	8%	87%	0.62	75	58	3.79	42
Cain,Lorenzo	08	R	22	8	a/a	MIL	167	16	38	8	3	3	15	18	38	5	2	228	303	365	668	10%	77%	0.47	86	139	3.88	41
	09	R	23	8	aa	MIL	145	14	27	5	0	3	12	9	31	2	3	189	236	284	520	6%	79%	0.29	61	59	2.04	-4

Major League Equivalent Statistics

BATTER	Yr	B	Age	Pos	Lev	Org	ab	r	h	d	t	hr	rbi	bb	k	sb	cs	ba	ob	slg	ops	bb%	ct%	eye	px	sx	rc/g	bpv
Cairo,Miguel	09	R	35	6	aaa	PHI	296	32	67	9	1	4	24	11	41	6	1	227	255	307	562	4%	86%	0.27	53	94	2.71	24
Calderone,Adam	09	L	26	8	a/a	TOR	401	45	84	21	5	10	40	22	76	7	5	209	249	361	610	5%	81%	0.29	96	121	2.90	50
Caligiuri,Jay	09	R	29	3	aa	LAA	174	12	28	4	0	3	15	18	30	1	0	158	237	227	465	9%	83%	0.60	45	35	1.85	-2
Camacaro,Armando	09	R	30	2	aa	CLE	135	12	24	4	0	1	9	6	20	1	1	176	211	227	438	4%	85%	0.30	38	58	1.52	-1
Camp,Matt	08	L	24	68	aa	CHC	482	51	107	10	3	2	27	36	46	17	10	221	275	265	539	7%	90%	0.77	29	105	2.47	32
	09	L	25	8	aa	CHC	395	41	98	15	1	2	39	21	44	15	5	247	285	305	590	5%	89%	0.47	43	97	3.09	32
Campbell,Eric	09	R	24	5	aa	ATL	369	25	81	15	1	4	34	33	54	1	3	219	282	297	579	8%	85%	0.60	55	32	2.85	13
Campbell,Scott	08	L	24	4	aa	TOR	417	55	110	19	2	8	36	49	55	2	7	265	342	375	717	11%	87%	0.89	73	53	4.54	45
	09	L	25	5	a/a	TOR	278	38	62	11	2	3	20	34	32	3	0	224	308	307	615	11%	88%	1.04	56	93	3.49	50
Cancel,Robinson	09	R	33	2	aa	NYM	258	17	48	9	1	2	11	13	27	5	3	184	223	247	470	5%	90%	0.47	45	74	1.75	28
Canham,Mitchell	09	L	25	2	aa	SD	407	37	86	15	2	4	41	36	59	4	5	212	276	288	563	8%	85%	0.60	52	65	2.66	21
Canizares,Barbaro	08	R	29	30	aaa	ATL	504	42	122	23	0	10	50	33	68	1	0	243	289	346	634	6%	86%	0.48	70	31	3.53	25
	09	R	30	3	aaa	ATL	506	40	117	24	1	9	57	38	66	2	2	231	285	333	618	7%	87%	0.57	70	37	3.29	31
Cannizaro,Andy	08	R	30	4	aaa	CLE	255	25	55	10	0	3	22	20	28	1	0	216	272	297	569	7%	89%	0.71	57	43	2.82	31
	09	R	31	6	aaa	CHW	237	14	47	10	0	1	18	16	32	0	1	197	248	251	500	6%	87%	0.51	44	21	2.08	2
Canzler,Russell	09	R	23	3	aa	CHC	233	23	55	14	0	6	29	25	37	2	6	236	311	370	681	10%	84%	0.69	91	35	3.75	42
Cardenas,Adrian	09	L	22 a	4	aa	OAK	508	59	130	35	2	3	59	40	51	6	8	256	311	352	663	7%	90%	0.78	74	69	3.77	56
Carlin,Luke	09	B	29	2	aa	ARI	237	33	64	15	0	5	26	34	50	4	4	271	363	401	764	13%	79%	0.69	90	52	5.28	31
Carp,Mike	08	L	22 a	380	aa	NYM	478	57	129	27	1	14	61	67	74	1	2	270	360	418	778	12%	85%	0.91	97	35	5.64	53
	09	L	23	3	aa	SEA	413	58	101	23	1	13	56	53	95	0	1	244	330	396	726	11%	77%	0.56	98	42	4.74	24
Carrera,Ezequiel	09	L	22	8	aa	SEA	329	61	103	11	3	2	34	55	59	24	15	313	411	383	794	14%	82%	0.93	47	126	6.02	34
Carroll,Brett	09	R	27	8	aa	FLA	103	13	20	3	1	4	10	6	23	0	1	197	244	348	592	6%	78%	0.28	87	89	2.69	21
Carson,Matt	08	R	27 b	8	a/a	NYY	417	59	102	14	6	14	53	24	86	9	4	244	286	406	691	6%	79%	0.28	94	147	4.00	50
	09	R	28 b	8	aa	OAK	440	44	85	22	2	15	50	25	75	10	4	194	237	354	591	5%	83%	0.33	100	93	2.70	53
Carte,Daniel	08	R	24	8	aa	COL	422	36	99	13	0	8	40	15	79	3	10	234	261	321	582	4%	81%	0.19	56	38	2.58	-10
	09	R	25	8	aa	COL	252	18	48	8	1	4	22	13	55	2	1	190	230	276	506	5%	78%	0.24	56	60	2.09	-13
Carter,Chris	08	L	26	80	aaa	BOS	470	51	122	25	1	17	63	31	75	0	0	260	306	423	729	6%	84%	0.42	103	29	4.65	42
	09	L	27	8	aaa	BOS	428	44	117	27	0	13	54	38	67	1	0	273	332	425	757	8%	84%	0.57	101	31	5.23	46
Carter,Vernon	09	R	23 a	3	aa	OAK	544	86	152	37	1	20	86	63	95	10	8	279	354	461	816	10%	83%	0.66	119	73	5.93	70
Casilla,Alexi	09	B	25	4	aaa	MIN	156	17	46	3	3	2	14	8	21	8	7	295	332	386	717	5%	86%	0.40	51	139	4.23	40
Castillo,Javier	08	R	25	5	a/a	CHW	489	61	124	24	6	8	64	43	102	4	2	254	314	371	685	8%	79%	0.42	77	104	4.21	27
	09	R	26	5	a/a	NYM	442	31	90	21	2	6	31	23	83	1	2	204	243	298	541	5%	81%	0.28	65	47	2.38	3
Castillo,Welington	08	R	21	2	aa	CHC	203	19	54	10	0	3	19	11	40	0	0	264	302	358	660	5%	80%	0.28	67	23	3.89	-5
	09	R	22	2	aa	CHC	319	23	69	15	0	10	32	12	62	1	0	216	245	357	602	4%	81%	0.19	90	30	2.94	13
Castillo,Wilkin	08	B	24	25	a/a	CIN	428	32	91	16	1	5	36	19	49	4	4	213	247	289	536	4%	89%	0.39	53	55	2.33	24
	09	B	25	2	aaa	CIN	122	9	24	5	1	2	6	1	18	3	1	193	199	293	492	1%	85%	0.05	65	43	1.83	9
Casto,Kory	08	L	27	8	aaa	WAS	130	15	33	5	0	5	20	15	26	1	2	255	331	396	727	10%	80%	0.56	86	36	4.58	22
	09	L	28	5	aaa	WAS	447	44	101	19	1	6	45	34	79	3	4	226	281	314	595	7%	82%	0.43	61	52	3.00	10
Castro,Jason	09	L	22	2	aa	HOU	239	29	62	10	1	2	22	19	27	2	1	259	314	335	649	7%	89%	0.70	54	70	3.82	36
Castro,Jose	09	B	23	4	aa	CIN	333	25	83	12	1	1	25	10	26	2	5	249	271	300	571	3%	92%	0.38	39	47	2.66	22
Castro,Ofilio	08	R	25	5	a/a	WAS	418	40	96	24	1	3	36	24	37	0	2	229	270	310	581	5%	91%	0.63	62	40	2.85	39
	09	R	26	4	aa	WAS	301	26	78	14	1	3	30	31	48	0	4	260	329	339	669	9%	84%	0.65	57	28	3.95	12
Castro,Ramon	09	R	30	5	aa	SF	130	15	29	7	0	2	9	9	24	0	1	225	273	318	591	6%	81%	0.35	67	43	2.91	6
Castro,Starlin	09	R	19 a	6	aa	CHC	111	9	32	6	2	0	13	8	10	5	0	284	334	378	713	7%	91%	0.88	67	138	5.03	77
Caufield,Charles	09	R	26	8	aa	MIL	302	26	63	11	1	3	28	16	52	2	2	210	249	280	529	5%	83%	0.30	49	59	2.31	0
Cervelli,Francisco	09	R	24	2	a/a	NYY	127	14	28	6	0	3	13	9	26	0	2	224	274	340	614	6%	80%	0.35	77	39	2.99	8
Cervenak,Mike	08	R	32	053	aaa	PHI	456	48	113	24	1	9	48	9	67	3	3	248	263	360	623	2%	85%	0.14	77	63	3.17	28
	09	R	33	5	aaa	PHI	462	49	111	29	1	8	56	20	47	1	1	241	273	357	630	4%	90%	0.43	83	50	3.36	51
Chang,Ray	09	R	26 b	4	aa	PIT	127	17	31	13	0	2	15	11	14	1	2	246	307	391	698	8%	89%	0.78	112	56	4.06	80
Chapman,Stephen	09	L	24	8	aa	CIN	135	13	26	4	1	5	14	5	40	3	4	196	224	348	573	4%	71%	0.12	88	102	2.22	-8
Chaves,Brandon	08	B	29	6	aa	CLE	247	19	39	2	2	2	12	23	49	9	3	157	229	198	428	9%	80%	0.48	23	104	1.55	-10
	09	B	30	6	a/a	TAM	357	31	59	9	1	2	25	43	68	6	9	164	253	210	463	11%	81%	0.62	33	65	1.71	-8
Chavez,Angel	08	R	27	564	aa	LA	463	49	108	25	0	7	49	21	50	4	4	233	266	334	600	4%	89%	0.41	72	56	2.98	42
	09	R	28	5	aaa	BOS	442	35	103	25	0	4	33	16	52	3	2	233	259	313	572	3%	88%	0.30	62	47	2.75	25
Chavez,Ozzie	08	B	25	64	a/a	MIL	271	17	51	5	2	3	24	14	45	4	2	187	227	250	477	5%	84%	0.32	38	78	1.86	0
	09	B	26	6	aa	PHI	363	29	79	15	0	1	26	22	52	6	1	218	263	266	529	6%	86%	0.42	40	65	2.45	7
Chen,Yung	08	R	25	45	aa	SEA	249	28	52	9	0	2	19	17	30	7	2	208	258	268	526	6%	88%	0.57	45	86	2.40	29
	09	R	26	4	aa	OAK	160	17	38	6	0	1	12	11	21	4	0	236	285	293	578	6%	87%	0.53	45	72	3.07	21
Christian,Justin	08	R	28 b	8	aaa	NYY	268	38	68	14	1	5	35	15	35	18	4	253	292	371	663	5%	87%	0.42	80	127	3.94	62
	09	R	29	8	aaa	BAL	356	42	79	15	3	3	20	15	52	21	3	222	255	300	554	4%	85%	0.30	54	146	2.74	39
Christy,Jeffrey	08	R	24	2	a/a	MIN	164	19	30	9	0	0	7	20	36	0	1	181	271	234	505	11%	78%	0.55	47	44	2.19	-14
	09	R	25	2	a/a	MIN	138	8	22	2	0	0	9	10	29	0	0	157	215	170	386	7%	79%	0.36	12	23	1.24	-51
Cintron,Alex	09	B	31	4	a/a	SEA	131	7	28	3	1	2	9	2	20	2	0	214	224	292	516	1%	85%	0.09	49	68	2.20	3
Ciofrone,Peter	08	L	25	58	aa	SD	437	64	110	17	3	13	52	37	69	2	0	252	310	394	703	8%	84%	0.53	87	84	4.41	49
	09	L	26	5	aa	SD	284	22	40	5	1	4	19	24	52	0	1	142	208	205	413	8%	82%	0.45	38	45	1.38	-12
Cipriano,William	09	R	25	4	aa	TAM	147	15	27	6	1	2	12	14	33	0	0	183	256	274	530	9%	77%	0.43	61	60	2.39	-4
Ciriaco,Pedro	09	R	24	6	aa	ARI	469	46	129	15	3	4	44	14	58	32	11	276	296	345	641	3%	88%	0.24	46	121	3.63	31
Clark,Douglas	08	R	27	2	aa	KC	106	8	18	3	1	4	12	4	18	1	1	170	197	314	511	3%	83%	0.20	83	82	1.88	32
	09	R	28 b	2	aa	KC	199	25	50	12	0	5	22	12	24	1	2	252	296	394	689	6%	88%	0.52	96	47	3.99	57
Clark,Howie	08	L	35	84	aaa	MIN	338	36	76	14	4	4	34	17	31	2	1	224	261	327	588	5%	91%	0.56	66	99	2.90	58
	09	L	36	4	aaa	TOR	387	43	90	19	1	4	32	22	25	2	2	233	274	318	593	5%	94%	0.89	62	58	3.00	54
Clement,Jeff	08	L	25 a	2	aa	SEA	172	31	49	15	0	10	33	28	27	0	0	284	385	552	937	14%	85%	1.06	170	29	8.16	113
	09	L	26	0	aa	PIT	470	62	109	31	2	15	69	40	93	2	1	231	292	399	691	8%	80%	0.43	111	68	4.07	48
Clevenger,Steven	09	L	23	2	aa	CHC	307	27	81	16	3	1	30	21	35	3	3	265	311	345	656	6%	89%	0.59	59	79	3.80	40
Clevlen,Brent	08	R	25	8	aaa	DET	476	60	117	20	6	17	66	44	142	6	2	246	310	422	732	8%	70%	0.31	104	120	4.66	19
	09	R	26	8	aaa	DET	479	52	113	23	4	13	54	35	129	8	1	235	287	381	668	7%	73%	0.27	91	109	3.88	14
Clifford,Pete	09	L	26	8	aa	ARI	280	21	59	11	0	4	25	18	41	4	2	212	259	292	551	6%	85%	0.43	56	51	2.56	15
Closser,JD	08	B	29	2	a/a	SD	207	14	34	6	0	4	17	20	42	0	1	166	240	247	487	9%	80%	0.48	53	21	1.95	-13
	09	B	30	2	aa	LA	321	28	69	16	0	3	32	32	65	3	3	214	285	289	575	9%	80%	0.49	57	48	2.86	-1
Coats,Buck	08	L	26	8	aaa	TOR	447	56	113	21	5	6	37	29	92	12	6	253	299	364	664	6%	79%	0.32	73	122	3.78	27
	09	L	27 b	8	aaa	TOR	500	56	120	27	3	5	38	32	57	17	8	239	284	331	616	6%	89%	0.56	66	106	3.23	54

Major League Equivalent Statistics

BATTER	Yr	B	Age	Pos	Lev	Org	ab	r	h	d	t	hr	rbi	bb	k	sb	cs	ba	ob	slg	ops	bb%	ct%	eye	px	sx	rc/g	bpv
Colina,Alvin	08	R	27	2	aaa	CIN	227	18	49	6	1	6	40	13	60	2	1	215	257	336	593	5%	74%	0.22	73	59	2.91	-17
	09	R	28	2	aaa	ATL	225	23	48	10	0	6	32	19	52	1	1	212	273	340	613	8%	77%	0.36	82	41	3.16	3
Colina,Javier	08	R	30	5	a/a	CHW	181	18	42	7	1	5	17	9	30	2	0	233	268	366	633	5%	83%	0.28	82	71	3.41	31
	09	R	31	3	aa	CHW	315	31	65	12	1	5	31	16	59	2	3	205	244	297	541	5%	81%	0.27	61	61	2.35	4
Collins,Michael	08	R	24 a	3	aa	LAA	250	36	59	16	1	4	30	12	32	7	7	234	271	353	624	5%	87%	0.39	85	107	3.00	60
	09	R	25	2	aa	SD	161	10	29	7	0	2	15	21	30	0	0	181	274	257	531	11%	81%	0.69	54	12	2.48	-2
Colonel,Christian	08	R	27 b	853	aa	COL	429	48	109	28	1	8	43	22	48	5	6	255	292	382	673	5%	89%	0.46	89	63	3.77	57
	09	R	28	5	aa	COL	391	41	93	14	2	5	51	29	50	2	3	237	289	325	614	7%	87%	0.58	58	59	3.24	29
Colvin,Tyler	08	L	23 a	8	aa	CHC	540	51	121	25	8	11	60	32	81	5	5	223	267	358	625	6%	85%	0.40	84	106	3.17	52
	09	L	24 a	8	aa	CHC	307	41	83	12	5	12	40	12	52	4	1	269	297	463	760	4%	83%	0.24	113	130	4.91	71
Concepcion,Ambiorix	08	R	27	8	aa	NYM	456	43	90	18	2	9	42	14	100	18	6	198	221	307	528	3%	78%	0.14	71	117	2.18	12
	09	R	28	8	a/a	BAL	459	42	101	23	2	9	51	28	91	14	6	220	264	337	602	6%	80%	0.31	79	92	2.97	25
Conger,Hank	09	B	22	2	aa	LAA	459	56	130	20	2	9	63	48	59	3	2	284	352	396	748	10%	87%	0.82	74	61	5.26	46
Conrad,Brooks	08	B	29	4	aa	OAK	465	58	84	23	3	18	62	31	105	3	1	182	233	356	588	6%	78%	0.29	107	93	2.70	38
	09	B	30	4	aaa	ATL	398	47	83	20	0	9	46	39	107	9	1	210	280	324	604	9%	73%	0.36	77	86	3.23	0
Constanza,Jose	08	B	25	8	aa	CLE	338	37	82	10	4	0	28	24	40	20	7	242	293	295	588	7%	88%	0.60	37	137	3.10	38
	09	B	26	8	aa	CLE	486	83	120	13	5	0	39	66	66	41	14	246	337	292	628	12%	86%	1.00	32	150	3.77	42
Contreras,Anthony	09	L	26	4	aa	SD	221	14	43	8	2	1	21	9	26	2	2	196	228	259	488	4%	88%	0.37	44	76	1.90	22
Contreras,Ivan	09	B	23	8	aa	LAA	142	14	35	4	1	0	8	9	27	4	3	246	291	289	580	6%	81%	0.33	31	95	2.86	-9
Cook,David	08	R	27	8	a/a	CHW	436	61	106	22	2	18	45	77	110	12	7	244	358	425	783	15%	75%	0.70	111	81	5.50	45
	09	R	28 b	8	a/a	CHW	447	70	97	19	1	23	67	52	94	7	7	217	298	417	715	10%	79%	0.55	119	76	4.13	57
Coon,Bradley	08	L	26	8	aa	LAA	337	58	89	8	1	3	24	38	47	13	10	265	339	321	660	10%	86%	0.80	38	99	3.84	26
	09	L	27	8	aa	LAA	442	65	107	14	2	3	30	50	72	19	8	241	318	300	618	10%	84%	0.69	41	110	3.48	23
Cooper,Craig	08	R	24	8	aa	SD	408	38	98	20	2	6	46	35	81	4	3	240	301	341	642	8%	80%	0.44	69	66	3.60	14
	09	R	25	3	aa	SD	503	54	129	28	1	8	74	57	76	7	6	256	331	361	692	10%	85%	0.74	74	58	4.30	39
Cooper,David	09	L	23	3	aa	TOR	473	60	119	32	0	10	63	57	93	0	0	252	332	383	715	11%	80%	0.61	93	28	4.68	27
Cooper,James	08	L	25	8	aa	NYY	168	12	36	5	1	0	15	19	28	3	3	211	292	251	544	10%	83%	0.68	30	66	2.54	0
	09	L	26	8	aa	NYY	258	39	56	11	2	1	28	20	28	3	2	219	274	288	562	7%	89%	0.71	51	105	2.71	45
Copeland,Ben	08	L	25 a	8	aa	SF	457	60	113	19	10	4	39	41	66	21	8	248	310	357	667	8%	86%	0.63	69	173	3.96	68
	09	L	26	8	aa	SF	342	38	85	17	3	6	29	20	54	12	7	247	288	363	651	5%	84%	0.36	77	113	3.54	45
Corley,William	08	R	25	80	aa	PIT	500	49	119	24	2	9	41	20	94	4	10	238	268	346	613	4%	81%	0.22	73	60	2.93	11
	09	R	26	8	aa	COL	285	24	56	13	2	6	22	14	59	2	5	198	236	317	552	5%	79%	0.24	77	72	2.28	13
Corona,Reegie	08	B	22	46	aa	NYY	457	70	121	26	2	3	37	47	73	24	4	265	334	351	686	9%	84%	0.65	65	124	4.54	46
	09	B	23 a	4	a/a	NYY	467	66	115	27	1	6	38	62	67	15	4	246	335	347	681	12%	86%	0.93	73	95	4.36	55
Coronado,Jose	08	B	22	6	aa	NYM	507	47	119	22	0	1	33	48	66	8	3	235	301	284	585	9%	87%	0.73	41	63	3.10	19
	09	B	23	4	aa	NYM	446	32	94	16	1	1	33	30	72	10	5	211	261	257	518	6%	84%	0.42	36	73	2.29	1
Corporan,Carlos	08	B	25	2	a/a	MIL	200	16	41	12	1	5	20	12	32	2	2	206	250	346	595	5%	84%	0.36	92	65	2.79	42
	09	B	26	2	aaa	MIL	179	7	29	8	1	1	13	7	37	0	1	163	192	231	424	4%	79%	0.18	50	40	1.36	-22
Corsaletti,Jeffrey	08	L	26 a	8	a/a	BOS	446	64	113	32	4	10	49	55	80	7	2	253	334	411	745	11%	82%	0.68	107	104	5.05	69
	09	L	27	8	a/a	PIT	317	26	58	13	2	2	18	39	36	6	5	183	272	252	524	11%	89%	1.08	50	75	2.33	41
Cortez,Fernando	08	L	27	6	aaa	CHW	355	22	77	10	1	4	28	13	32	8	5	218	245	281	526	3%	91%	0.39	43	67	2.23	27
	09	L	28	0	aa	TAM	442	33	89	9	4	4	37	28	58	11	4	201	249	271	520	6%	87%	0.49	42	104	2.26	26
Costanzo,Michael	08	L	25	530	aaa	BAL	483	44	107	24	1	9	50	41	136	2	2	222	283	333	616	8%	72%	0.30	75	46	3.26	-21
	09	L	26	5	a/a	BAL	272	29	49	14	2	3	32	34	78	0	2	179	271	274	545	11%	71%	0.43	67	64	2.50	-18
Coughlin,Sean	09	L	24 a	3	aa	ARI	161	19	45	8	0	6	16	29	16	0	0	280	389	435	825	15%	90%	1.84	98	15	6.65	76
Cousins,Scott	09	L	25 a	8	aa	FLA	482	51	114	29	10	10	62	37	104	23	10	237	292	396	688	7%	78%	0.36	101	171	3.93	62
Cozart,Zachary	09	R	24	6	aa	CIN	463	59	108	26	1	10	48	52	78	8	2	232	310	355	664	10%	83%	0.66	83	81	3.96	46
Crabbe,Callix	08	B	26	48	aaa	MIL	204	24	44	8	2	1	13	30	35	7	6	217	317	286	603	13%	83%	0.86	48	102	3.14	28
	09	B	27	4	aa	SEA	356	38	63	12	3	3	27	44	48	6	7	176	267	248	515	11%	87%	0.92	49	88	2.16	36
Craig,Allen	08	R	24	5	aa	STL	506	64	130	25	0	15	65	36	70	2	1	256	306	397	703	7%	86%	0.52	91	49	4.34	47
	09	R	25	8	aa	STL	472	58	126	22	1	18	62	27	78	2	0	267	307	430	737	5%	84%	0.35	101	57	4.77	45
Craig,Matthew	08	B	27 b	3	aa	CHC	223	30	56	13	0	7	24	32	38	2	0	250	343	404	747	12%	83%	0.83	100	49	5.19	54
	09	B	28	3	aa	CHC	372	36	84	20	1	9	34	25	70	1	0	225	273	355	628	6%	81%	0.35	87	48	3.35	23
Crawford,Brandon	09	L	23	6	aa	SF	392	33	95	25	2	3	27	17	85	10	8	242	274	339	613	4%	78%	0.20	73	88	3.03	8
Creek,Greg	08	L	26	35	aa	ATL	351	37	78	17	5	5	41	32	66	0	3	223	288	335	624	8%	81%	0.49	74	81	3.28	26
	09	L	27	3	aa	ATL	321	22	64	12	1	4	34	21	67	3	3	199	248	275	522	6%	79%	0.31	52	53	2.23	-12
Crowe,Trevor	08	B	25 a	8	a/a	CLE	344	61	93	26	2	8	36	38	70	15	8	271	344	424	768	10%	80%	0.55	106	120	5.23	62
	09	B	26	8	aaa	CLE	185	21	47	9	1	2	15	24	28	11	8	254	341	346	687	12%	85%	0.88	65	96	4.07	46
Crozier,Eric	09	L	31	3	aa	BAL	217	27	40	6	3	9	29	30	76	1	2	184	282	364	647	12%	65%	0.39	101	101	3.43	-3
Cruz,Arnoldi	09	R	23	2	aa	STL	405	33	75	22	1	7	36	26	65	1	0	186	236	295	531	6%	84%	0.41	75	50	2.32	25
Cruz,Lee	08	R	25 a	80	aa	CHW	197	22	49	11	1	10	24	10	38	0	3	248	286	472	758	5%	81%	0.27	136	47	4.40	57
	09	R	26	0	aa	CHW	227	23	50	15	0	6	29	10	49	0	1	219	252	357	609	4%	78%	0.21	95	37	2.97	11
Cruz,Luis	08	R	25 a	6	aa	PIT	495	50	126	33	1	7	51	18	43	4	8	254	281	365	645	4%	91%	0.43	81	54	3.36	56
	09	R	26	6	aa	PIT	229	22	50	13	0	2	18	5	22	2	3	218	233	300	533	2%	90%	0.21	64	61	2.20	36
Cumberland,Shaun	08	L	24	8	a/a	CIN	436	57	108	18	4	8	31	36	84	14	7	247	305	359	664	8%	81%	0.43	72	120	3.83	34
	09	L	25	8	aa	CIN	295	24	60	14	1	3	24	22	63	9	7	204	258	287	545	7%	79%	0.34	60	84	2.39	4
Cunningham,Aaron	08	R	22 a	8	aa	OAK	423	67	121	21	4	12	51	38	80	12	6	286	345	440	785	8%	81%	0.48	96	119	5.55	56
	09	R	23 a	8	aa	OAK	334	45	83	21	1	8	35	24	54	8	5	249	299	387	686	7%	84%	0.43	93	90	3.97	52
Curtis,Colin	08	L	24	8	aa	NYY	495	64	119	19	2	10	67	50	84	6	3	240	309	344	654	9%	83%	0.60	67	79	3.81	30
	09	L	25	8	a/a	NYY	464	53	107	22	3	7	44	40	83	8	2	230	291	333	624	8%	82%	0.48	70	98	3.45	31
Daniel,Mike	08	L	24	8	aa	WAS	485	47	102	11	1	10	43	44	105	14	12	210	276	295	571	8%	78%	0.42	52	74	2.63	-4
	09	L	25	8	a/a	WAS	423	43	94	15	6	6	37	29	79	10	5	222	272	324	597	6%	81%	0.37	64	128	3.01	30
Danielson,Sean	08	B	26	8	a/a	BOS	346	34	79	13	3	1	17	25	83	19	5	229	280	290	570	7%	76%	0.30	44	130	2.94	-6
	09	B	27	8	aaa	BOS	154	16	34	6	1	1	17	19	36	8	3	222	307	292	599	11%	77%	0.53	50	105	3.28	3
Danks,Jordan	09	L	23	8	aa	CHW	284	43	63	11	1	6	17	32	65	6	3	221	300	328	628	10%	77%	0.50	69	94	3.46	14
Davis,Blake	08	L	25	6	aa	BAL	457	48	114	19	5	4	44	22	70	7	8	250	285	338	623	5%	85%	0.32	59	100	3.20	28
	09	L	26	6	aaa	BAL	180	18	34	4	1	1	12	11	37	3	2	188	236	235	471	6%	79%	0.30	31	90	1.82	-17
Davis,Bradley	08	R	26	2	aa	FLA	249	24	42	13	1	5	22	28	53	0	2	170	254	287	541	10%	79%	0.53	79	46	2.38	14
	09	R	27	2	aa	FLA	315	29	59	22	0	7	38	26	73	1	0	187	248	327	575	8%	77%	0.35	98	42	2.73	16
Davis,Chris	08	L	23 a	3	aa	TEX	297	53	90	19	1	19	57	20	57	5	1	303	347	566	913	6%	81%	0.35	159	91	7.41	92
	09	L	24	5	aa	TEX	165	22	49	11	1	5	25	21	33	0	1	297	375	463	838	11%	80%	0.63	109	51	6.59	48

BATTER	Yr	B	Age	Pos	Lev	Org	ab	r	h	d	t	hr	rbi	bb	k	sb	cs	ba	ob	slg	ops	bb%	ct%	eye	px	sx	rc/g	bpv
Davis,Isaac	09	L	23	3	aa	NYM	207	24	57	13	0	10	35	21	49	0	0	275	342	483	825	9%	76%	0.43	130	16	6.13	35
Davis,Leonard	08	L	25	8	a/a	WAS	221	23	53	12	2	8	31	9	46	2	1	239	268	417	685	4%	79%	0.19	111	88	3.79	42
	09	L	26	8	a/a	WAS	440	42	105	18	5	13	46	30	99	11	2	239	288	391	679	6%	78%	0.30	92	119	3.99	34
Dawkins,Gookie	08	R	29	56	a/a	KC	402	31	77	21	1	7	28	22	105	4	4	193	234	300	533	5%	74%	0.21	74	61	2.22	-15
	09	R	30	6	a/a	FLA	381	29	71	15	1	3	19	21	98	6	5	185	228	257	485	5%	74%	0.22	51	71	1.85	-28
De Aza,Alejandro	09	L	25 a	8	aa	FLA	267	38	71	19	5	7	28	24	53	9	6	264	324	444	767	8%	80%	0.44	116	154	4.97	77
De La Cruz,Chris	08	B	26	4	a/a	FLA	170	13	32	6	0	2	15	18	25	0	4	189	269	254	523	10%	85%	0.74	45	25	2.16	7
	09	B	27	6	aa	FLA	308	36	70	13	3	2	18	31	52	4	1	228	298	304	602	9%	83%	0.59	53	98	3.26	24
De Leon,Santo	08	R	25 a	5	aa	DET	169	19	39	10	1	5	19	6	21	1	1	233	258	386	644	3%	88%	0.28	99	76	3.32	61
	09	R	26	5	aa	DET	297	25	68	15	2	6	31	8	57	1	1	228	249	348	597	3%	81%	0.15	80	65	2.89	14
DeCaster,Yurendell	08	R	29	5	a/a	WAS	366	39	72	18	1	9	45	26	101	4	5	197	250	322	572	7%	72%	0.26	82	71	2.56	-9
	09	R	30	5	aaa	NYY	186	19	46	10	0	4	17	10	31	3	0	250	289	375	664	5%	83%	0.33	85	58	3.89	30
Deeds,Douglas	08	L	27	83	aa	CHC	416	50	109	32	2	9	41	30	88	5	1	262	311	411	722	7%	79%	0.34	104	86	4.64	40
	09	L	28	8	aa	CHC	349	41	81	26	2	8	28	16	77	4	3	232	265	383	649	4%	78%	0.20	104	88	3.40	32
DeJesus,Antonio	09	L	24	8	aa	STL	179	21	35	5	1	1	15	20	30	3	2	197	276	252	528	10%	83%	0.66	38	86	2.41	12
Delaney,Jason	08	R	26	3	aa	PIT	465	49	118	25	3	6	41	68	93	6	4	253	348	356	703	13%	80%	0.73	72	72	4.60	27
	09	R	27	3	aa	PIT	438	38	99	22	3	5	50	42	79	1	5	227	295	321	616	9%	82%	0.53	66	49	3.23	15
DeLome,Collin	09	L	24	8	aa	HOU	467	59	103	16	7	16	45	27	112	11	10	220	264	384	648	6%	76%	0.24	95	141	3.19	35
Denker,Travis	08	R	23	4	aa	SF	296	40	70	23	1	6	31	38	62	3	1	235	323	377	700	11%	79%	0.61	101	73	4.42	44
	09	R	24	4	a/a	BOS	404	38	93	28	1	5	39	42	80	3	3	230	303	340	643	9%	80%	0.53	81	52	3.61	22
Denorfia,Chris	08	R	28	8	aa	OAK	189	23	44	11	1	1	13	8	26	4	4	233	264	312	576	4%	86%	0.30	61	94	2.59	32
	09	R	29	8	aa	OAK	432	40	84	13	3	5	31	20	43	9	7	195	230	273	503	4%	90%	0.46	50	97	1.98	40
Denove,Chris	08	R	26	2	aa	CIN	164	8	33	10	0	0	10	14	24	1	2	201	264	264	528	8%	85%	0.58	56	27	2.30	11
	09	R	27	2	a/a	CIN	219	17	52	15	0	4	23	16	35	0	2	239	290	357	647	7%	84%	0.45	85	22	3.52	27
Derba,Nicholas	09	R	24	2	aa	STL	108	7	12	4	0	1	5	15	26	0	1	107	218	169	387	12%	76%	0.59	45	28	1.22	-25
Descalso,Daniel	09	L	23 a	4	aa	STL	438	55	115	26	3	7	54	37	48	2	1	263	320	384	704	8%	89%	0.77	83	75	4.47	63
Desmond,Ian	08	R	23	6	aa	WAS	323	32	69	13	0	9	34	24	64	10	10	212	266	334	600	7%	80%	0.37	77	69	2.73	18
	09	R	24	6	a/a	WAS	348	46	104	22	2	6	27	31	64	18	6	298	355	422	777	8%	82%	0.48	87	111	5.69	48
Dewitt,Blake	08	L	23 a	4	aa	LA	111	13	29	4	1	3	14	8	12	1	0	265	313	397	711	7%	89%	0.64	80	78	4.57	59
	09	L	24 a	4	aa	LA	352	53	78	18	5	6	38	40	41	2	2	221	301	349	650	10%	88%	0.99	83	109	3.67	76
Diaz,Argenis	08	R	22	6	aa	BOS	139	16	38	9	1	1	19	8	24	0	1	276	316	378	694	5%	83%	0.34	76	66	4.24	25
	09	R	23	6	aa	PIT	423	29	96	14	1	0	26	23	69	7	6	227	267	265	532	5%	84%	0.33	31	62	2.36	-9
Diaz,Jonathan	09	B	24	6	a/a	TOR	262	30	44	9	0	1	14	38	41	3	5	169	275	213	487	13%	84%	0.95	35	55	1.99	10
Diaz,Robinzon	08	R	25	2	a/a	PIT	145	6	33	7	1	1	13	4	9	1	3	227	246	305	551	3%	94%	0.44	56	48	2.30	43
	09	R	26	2	aa	PIT	149	14	33	4	0	2	11	6	11	0	1	222	255	284	539	4%	93%	0.59	41	37	2.39	25
Diaz,Victor	08	R	27	08	aa	SEA	485	52	112	33	0	18	80	48	158	6	4	231	300	414	714	9%	68%	0.30	119	54	4.30	1
	09	R	28	0	aaa	BAL	109	10	22	5	0	1	7	6	36	1	0	198	242	264	506	5%	67%	0.18	49	53	2.18	-62
Dickerson,Joe	09	L	23 a	8	aa	KC	126	12	27	7	1	0	10	14	14	4	1	214	293	286	579	10%	89%	1.00	56	98	3.04	52
Dillon,Joe	08	R	33	5	aaa	MIL	171	23	33	6	1	3	15	20	28	1	2	194	277	298	575	10%	83%	0.69	66	74	2.76	31
	09	R	34	3	aaa	TAM	123	14	23	4	0	2	9	10	18	3	0	187	249	263	511	8%	86%	0.58	52	75	2.30	24
Dinkelman,Brian	08	L	25 a	4	aa	MIN	198	21	42	12	2	2	17	8	22	2	2	213	243	325	568	4%	89%	0.35	79	101	2.54	59
	09	L	26	4	aa	MIN	459	53	118	34	2	7	55	44	71	4	7	258	323	383	706	9%	84%	0.62	91	60	4.31	48
Dirks,Andy	09	L	24	8	aa	DET	361	37	82	13	1	5	36	29	50	9	6	228	286	309	596	8%	86%	0.59	55	78	3.01	29
Dlugach,Brent	09	R	27	6	aaa	DET	466	48	119	31	4	7	49	32	129	4	3	255	303	385	688	6%	72%	0.25	91	85	4.11	2
Donachie,Adam	08	R	25	2	aa	KC	264	25	51	8	0	4	24	31	61	1	1	193	277	265	542	10%	77%	0.50	48	38	2.56	-20
	09	R	26	2	aa	BAL	276	24	55	17	0	6	31	40	81	0	3	198	300	320	620	13%	71%	0.50	86	17	3.27	-16
Donald,Jason	08	R	24	6	aa	PHI	362	40	94	16	2	12	38	33	68	8	2	260	321	411	732	8%	81%	0.48	94	87	4.82	45
	09	R	25	6	aaa	CLE	243	27	49	14	1	2	13	14	56	6	0	201	245	290	535	5%	77%	0.25	67	109	2.48	6
Donaldson,Josh	09	R	24 a	2	aa	OAK	455	48	101	31	1	6	66	57	66	5	3	222	308	334	642	11%	85%	0.86	83	62	3.66	51
Donovan,Todd	08	R	30	8	aa	OAK	307	35	62	10	1	1	17	27	54	24	6	202	267	249	516	8%	82%	0.50	36	123	2.43	14
	09	R	31	8	aa	TOR	353	47	73	13	3	3	20	60	89	31	8	207	323	284	607	15%	75%	0.67	52	146	3.56	15
Doolittle,Sean	08	L	22	3	aa	OAK	201	19	44	13	0	3	23	13	39	1	1	219	266	328	595	6%	81%	0.33	80	45	2.95	14
	09	L	23 a	8	aa	OAK	105	12	23	4	1	3	10	11	16	0	1	219	293	362	655	9%	85%	0.69	86	72	3.57	51
Dopirak,Brian	09	R	26	3	a/a	TOR	546	61	151	38	2	23	81	38	112	1	3	277	324	477	801	6%	80%	0.34	128	40	5.54	47
Dorn,Daniel	08	L	24 a	83	aa	CIN	336	47	81	18	1	17	44	31	68	1	0	240	304	454	758	8%	80%	0.45	130	57	4.89	59
	09	L	25	8	aaa	CIN	357	36	86	19	1	13	38	24	71	2	1	242	291	411	702	6%	80%	0.34	106	50	4.17	35
Dorta,Melvin	08	R	27 b	45	aa	PIT	403	35	100	16	4	6	35	24	40	15	16	249	291	347	638	6%	90%	0.59	64	98	3.13	53
	09	R	28	5	a/a	BAL	431	44	103	18	1	4	30	30	52	10	10	238	287	309	596	6%	88%	0.57	52	73	2.93	30
Dowdy,Brett	08	R	27	64	aa	SD	479	66	112	20	3	9	40	30	83	10	6	234	280	346	626	6%	83%	0.37	72	108	3.30	35
	09	R	28	4	aa	SD	329	22	59	12	0	2	14	13	46	5	4	178	208	230	438	4%	86%	0.28	40	60	1.49	4
Downs,Matthew	09	R	26 a	4	aa	SF	424	56	112	31	3	10	61	21	53	7	2	264	298	423	722	5%	87%	0.39	108	103	4.49	79
Drennen,John	09	L	23	8	aa	CLE	325	40	82	22	3	7	36	20	56	0	2	253	296	401	697	6%	83%	0.35	99	72	4.10	45
Duarte,Jose	08	R	24	8	aa	KC	528	58	123	20	2	8	39	43	77	24	9	232	290	321	611	8%	86%	0.56	59	103	3.26	37
	09	R	25	8	aa	KC	381	42	80	13	3	3	33	40	59	14	12	209	285	282	567	10%	84%	0.68	50	106	2.60	30
Dubois,Jason	08	R	30	83	a/a	CHC	330	45	71	13	0	20	47	25	84	3	2	214	269	433	702	7%	75%	0.30	127	57	3.88	34
	09	R	30	8	aa	NYM	377	33	77	18	1	11	43	26	106	2	1	205	256	345	600	6%	72%	0.24	89	50	2.96	-11
Duda,Lucas	09	L	24	3	aa	NYM	395	38	96	25	1	7	42	49	76	2	2	243	327	365	691	11%	81%	0.65	86	44	4.31	30
Duncan,Eric	08	L	24	503	aaa	NYY	437	41	93	21	1	10	52	31	103	5	4	213	266	332	598	7%	76%	0.30	78	63	2.94	3
	09	L	25	5	aaa	NYY	323	32	60	11	1	4	22	14	68	1	0	187	222	262	483	4%	79%	0.21	50	67	1.91	-13
Duncan,Shelley	08	R	29	8	aaa	NYY	205	29	40	11	0	9	34	30	57	4	1	193	296	386	682	13%	72%	0.53	120	72	4.00	34
	09	R	30 b	8	aaa	NYY	452	69	103	25	1	26	81	52	103	2	0	228	307	459	766	10%	77%	0.50	139	61	4.98	60
Duran,German	09	R	25	4	aa	HOU	131	6	15	1	1	1	7	6	22	1	1	115	151	158	309	4%	83%	0.25	24	72	0.71	-17
Durango,Luis	09	B	23	8	aa	SD	456	62	107	7	1	0	20	64	60	34	21	234	328	254	582	12%	87%	1.06	15	102	2.99	17
Durham,Miles	09	R	27	3	aa	PIT	240	24	56	15	1	4	26	15	49	6	2	234	278	349	627	6%	80%	0.30	81	91	3.38	24
Dyson,Jarrod	09	L	25	8	aa	KC	248	28	55	7	3	0	10	21	44	27	7	220	280	269	549	8%	82%	0.47	34	163	2.81	23
Einertson,Mitch	08	R	23	8	aa	HOU	382	38	86	22	1	9	46	19	67	4	4	225	262	359	620	5%	82%	0.28	90	66	3.08	33
	09	R	23	8	aa	HOU	288	27	65	12	0	6	25	18	40	2	1	225	269	327	596	6%	86%	0.44	68	48	3.02	27
Eldred,Brad	08	R	28	3	aaa	CHW	427	48	88	18	1	31	77	22	141	3	3	206	245	468	713	5%	67%	0.16	150	52	3.69	15
	09	R	29	3	aaa	WAS	353	40	75	21	0	12	44	22	93	4	4	212	259	373	632	6%	74%	0.24	105	61	3.12	10
Eldridge,Rashad	08	B	27	8	aa	TAM	435	53	104	16	5	4	42	49	80	18	11	239	316	321	637	10%	82%	0.61	54	123	3.54	29
	09	B	28	8	a/a	TAM	469	51	113	21	2	3	42	49	81	20	10	240	311	309	620	9%	83%	0.60	51	96	3.41	21

Major League Equivalent Statistics

BATTER	Yr	B	Age	Pos	Lev	Org	ab	r	h	d	t	hr	rbi	bb	k	sb	cs	ba	ob	slg	ops	bb%	ct%	eye	px	sx	rc/g	bpv
Ellis,A.J.	08	R	28	2	aa	LA	274	32	70	14	2	3	42	38	41	0	2	256	346	348	695	12%	85%	0.92	65	50	4.45	33
	09	R	28	2	aa	LA	283	36	71	11	1	0	29	50	45	2	2	252	365	295	660	15%	84%	1.10	36	54	4.19	13
Ellison,Jason	08	R	31	8	aa	TEX	477	43	86	16	3	2	30	41	69	9	10	180	245	235	480	8%	85%	0.59	40	85	1.82	17
	09	R	31	8	aaa	PHI	449	39	92	16	0	4	27	31	86	11	3	204	255	269	524	6%	81%	0.36	46	77	2.36	-2
Emaus,Bradley	09	R	23 a	4	aa	TOR	505	63	123	27	2	10	63	56	71	10	3	243	318	363	681	10%	86%	0.78	82	88	4.20	57
Engel,Reid	09	L	22	8	aa	BOS	214	23	49	17	0	2	18	20	54	4	0	229	295	336	631	9%	75%	0.37	85	71	3.61	7
Escobar,Alcides	08	R	22	6	aa	MIL	547	77	160	23	3	7	61	26	67	28	10	292	324	384	708	5%	88%	0.39	62	121	4.55	48
	09	R	23 a	6	aaa	MIL	430	61	114	22	4	3	27	27	54	33	12	265	309	356	664	6%	87%	0.50	64	148	3.89	59
Espino,Damaso	08	B	25	2	aa	CLE	138	8	29	3	0	0	9	13	17	0	0	211	280	232	511	9%	88%	0.77	18	15	2.32	-11
	09	B	26	2	a/a	CLE	247	20	51	12	1	2	18	13	16	0	1	205	244	283	527	5%	93%	0.79	58	45	2.28	45
Espinosa,David	09	B	28	4	aa	SEA	193	23	34	5	1	2	23	22	41	7	3	177	260	242	503	10%	79%	0.53	43	107	2.19	4
Esposito,Brian	08	R	30	2	aa	COL	247	16	39	2	1	3	15	5	36	3	1	157	174	212	386	2%	85%	0.14	31	75	1.15	-5
	09	R	31	2	aa	HOU	260	15	48	7	1	3	25	6	38	0	0	183	201	255	456	2%	86%	0.16	46	32	1.64	-5
Evans,Nick	08	R	23 a	38	aa	NYM	296	44	83	17	5	11	45	22	54	2	1	280	330	483	813	7%	82%	0.41	123	124	5.84	79
	09	R	24	8	aa	NYM	342	33	68	19	2	10	30	26	63	2	0	198	255	350	605	7%	82%	0.42	98	73	3.02	42
Evans,Terry	08	R	27	8	aa	LAA	174	24	40	11	0	3	17	16	54	5	6	227	291	338	629	8%	69%	0.29	81	78	3.12	-19
	09	R	28	8	aa	LAA	537	85	133	30	4	20	74	32	144	23	5	248	290	427	717	6%	73%	0.22	112	144	4.39	38
Everidge,Tommy	08	R	25	30	aa	OAK	531	65	120	28	0	15	84	39	103	0	0	227	280	365	645	7%	81%	0.38	91	33	3.55	21
	09	R	26 b	3	aa	OAK	430	55	113	27	1	13	64	35	53	0	1	263	319	419	738	8%	88%	0.66	103	39	4.81	62
Eymann,Eric	08	R	25	56	aa	CIN	445	46	114	27	2	7	53	18	53	4	5	257	286	371	657	4%	88%	0.34	81	67	3.60	47
	09	R	26	4	a/a	CIN	312	25	58	14	1	2	23	21	52	1	3	187	237	256	493	6%	83%	0.40	52	51	1.95	5
Falu,Irving	08	B	25	864	aa	KC	362	46	97	10	2	4	34	31	28	9	9	267	325	338	663	8%	92%	1.12	46	85	3.78	50
	09	B	26 b	4	aa	KC	465	46	105	17	3	1	29	39	28	8	6	226	285	281	566	8%	94%	1.37	42	85	2.77	52
Fasano,Sal	09	R	38	2	aa	COL	212	16	40	9	0	3	14	7	58	2	0	188	214	281	494	3%	73%	0.12	64	54	1.97	-33
Feliciano,Jesus	08	L	29	8	aa	NYM	509	52	122	16	3	2	40	30	56	9	14	240	282	292	575	6%	89%	0.54	38	76	2.63	23
	09	L	30	8	aa	NYM	495	39	116	23	1	1	29	18	42	9	5	234	260	288	549	3%	91%	0.42	45	73	2.53	33
Felmy,Robert	09	L	25	8	aa	SF	388	39	86	17	3	5	41	23	56	8	8	223	266	317	583	5%	85%	0.40	64	94	2.71	34
Fields,Matthew	09	R	24	3	aa	TAM	284	34	62	12	1	5	28	16	81	1	0	220	262	321	583	5%	71%	0.20	68	70	2.89	-26
Figueroa,Danny	09	R	27	8	aa	BAL	238	40	69	9	2	2	22	36	54	10	4	290	383	367	750	13%	77%	0.66	53	116	5.57	14
Figueroa,Francisco	09	R	27 b	0	aa	BAL	226	29	63	17	4	0	26	27	39	12	3	277	353	383	736	11%	83%	0.68	79	152	5.23	63
Figueroa,Luis	08	B	35	645	aa	CHC	370	38	84	14	1	2	30	21	28	1	2	227	269	285	554	5%	92%	0.75	44	52	2.62	33
	09	B	36	4	aa	LAA	116	7	23	6	1	1	12	3	8	0	1	198	221	286	506	3%	93%	0.41	63	55	1.97	46
Fiorentino,Jeff	08	L	25	8	a/a	BAL	250	23	57	10	1	2	23	31	50	7	3	229	314	301	615	11%	80%	0.62	52	76	3.44	8
	09	L	26 b	8	a/a	BAL	388	63	104	24	4	12	59	43	65	13	6	268	341	441	782	10%	83%	0.66	111	123	5.47	80
Fixler,Jonathon	09	R	23 a	2	aa	HOU	115	11	19	4	1	7	18	8	21	0	2	162	215	392	607	6%	81%	0.37	130	67	2.44	65
Florence,Branden	09	R	31	8	aa	LAA	166	17	41	8	0	1	10	8	25	1	2	246	279	307	586	4%	85%	0.31	49	48	2.89	5
Florentino,Jhon	09	R	26	5	aa	HOU	399	30	86	13	4	4	30	21	60	5	1	214	254	293	547	5%	85%	0.35	51	93	2.55	21
Flores,Joshua	09	R	24	8	aa	HOU	163	19	33	9	1	1	8	11	27	7	2	204	254	289	542	6%	84%	0.41	63	120	2.51	35
Flowers,Tyler	09	R	24	2	a/a	CHW	353	59	97	25	1	15	49	60	99	3	0	275	380	478	857	14%	72%	0.60	131	70	7.02	45
Folli,Mike	09	B	24 a	5	aa	STL	235	18	42	10	3	3	17	13	29	5	1	180	224	282	506	5%	88%	0.46	66	116	2.09	51
Ford,Shelby	08	B	24 a	4	aa	PIT	319	36	84	23	7	3	27	17	43	17	6	264	301	406	706	5%	87%	0.39	96	176	4.27	88
	09	B	25	4	aa	PIT	401	36	70	15	1	5	35	19	63	8	1	175	212	254	466	5%	84%	0.31	55	97	1.79	22
Forsythe,Logan	09	R	23	5	aa	SD	244	30	58	7	2	2	25	33	53	4	0	238	329	307	636	12%	78%	0.62	45	100	3.86	5
Fortenberry,Seth	09	L	26	8	aa	NYY	125	11	17	6	2	0	7	13	42	5	1	140	220	213	434	9%	66%	0.30	52	158	1.63	-26
Fox,Adam	08	R	27	54	aa	TEX	384	36	72	12	2	7	33	27	73	6	0	187	240	285	525	6%	81%	0.37	61	93	2.34	16
	09	R	28	4	aa	TEX	364	36	80	11	2	14	38	18	77	5	3	220	257	378	635	5%	79%	0.23	92	80	3.23	25
Fox,Jake	08	R	26 b	38	aa	CHC	505	65	120	33	1	23	74	33	89	5	2	237	284	443	726	6%	82%	0.37	130	71	4.33	69
	09	R	27 b	3	aa	CHC	164	33	58	13	2	14	41	16	30	2	1	351	410	713	1123	9%	82%	0.54	214	101	11.74	148
Francisco,Juan	09	L	22 a	5	a/a	CIN	529	69	146	29	2	26	79	21	99	5	2	276	304	486	789	4%	81%	0.21	128	76	5.27	60
Frandsen,Kevin	09	R	27 b	6	aa	SF	427	53	106	16	2	9	43	18	32	3	4	249	279	358	637	4%	92%	0.56	70	71	3.39	57
Frazier,Jeffrey	08	R	26	08	a/a	DET	458	41	114	17	1	5	42	24	47	1	1	249	286	321	608	5%	90%	0.51	51	42	3.24	25
	09	R	27	8	a/a	DET	486	50	127	29	1	10	52	21	58	1	3	261	291	385	676	4%	88%	0.36	86	40	3.89	43
Frazier,Todd	09	R	24 a	8	a/a	CIN	514	57	137	41	1	16	64	41	69	8	9	267	321	442	764	7%	87%	0.59	120	59	4.89	76
Freeman,Freddie	09	L	20	3	aa	ATL	149	14	36	7	0	2	23	10	17	0	0	242	291	332	623	6%	88%	0.59	64	25	3.42	27
Freese,David	08	R	25	5	aa	STL	464	62	117	24	2	18	68	29	91	4	2	251	295	427	723	6%	80%	0.32	110	78	4.43	46
	09	R	26	5	aa	STL	216	27	53	13	0	7	30	17	45	1	0	247	303	409	712	7%	79%	0.39	106	45	4.44	32
Frey,Christopher	08	L	25	8	aa	COL	421	34	103	21	4	2	28	15	38	8	5	246	272	326	598	3%	91%	0.39	58	96	3.00	48
	09	L	26	8	aa	COL	320	34	75	8	4	4	23	17	45	11	1	233	271	316	587	5%	86%	0.37	51	136	3.08	38
Frey,Evan	09	L	23	8	aa	ARI	506	51	126	21	6	1	42	48	64	25	16	250	315	320	634	9%	87%	0.75	49	122	3.47	45
Friday,Brian	09	R	24	6	aa	PIT	407	39	97	21	2	5	37	39	56	6	6	238	305	335	640	9%	86%	0.70	68	69	3.52	39
Frostad,Emerson	08	L	26	253	aa	TEX	342	38	74	22	2	6	31	26	67	3	4	217	273	341	614	7%	80%	0.39	86	76	3.08	30
	09	L	27	2	aa	TEX	252	24	51	12	2	3	21	34	42	0	1	201	296	296	592	12%	83%	0.80	65	54	3.08	27
Fuld,Sam	08	L	27	8	aa	CHC	402	41	86	17	2	5	37	40	45	7	11	215	287	300	587	9%	89%	0.91	58	72	2.76	44
	09	L	28 b	8	aa	CHC	328	48	78	14	6	2	25	29	23	17	5	239	300	338	638	8%	93%	1.23	64	172	3.62	93
Furmaniak,J.J.	09	R	30	4	aaa	PHI	378	26	68	15	1	4	35	16	73	3	3	180	213	259	472	4%	81%	0.22	55	57	1.74	-6
Gaetti,Joe	08	R	27	8	aa	MIN	289	41	67	15	2	13	40	23	87	2	0	232	289	430	719	7%	70%	0.26	120	91	4.36	20
	09	R	28	8	aa	TAM	156	12	23	5	1	4	14	20	57	0	1	144	241	254	494	11%	64%	0.35	66	53	2.00	-52
Gall,John	08	R	31	8	aa	FLA	359	35	86	23	0	9	54	23	53	6	4	239	285	374	659	6%	85%	0.43	93	58	3.61	47
	09	R	31	3	aa	HOU	398	22	73	14	0	6	29	26	61	3	4	184	234	265	499	6%	85%	0.43	55	30	1.97	6
Gamel,Mat	08	L	23	5	a/a	MIL	529	76	148	31	4	16	76	46	101	5	9	280	337	443	780	8%	81%	0.46	105	80	5.24	50
	09	L	24	5	aaa	MIL	273	32	64	15	1	9	36	31	76	1	0	236	313	394	707	10%	72%	0.40	102	55	4.44	9
Garcia,Emmanuel	08	L	23	4	aa	NYM	367	43	80	11	1	3	34	29	69	14	10	218	275	278	553	7%	81%	0.42	42	96	2.51	4
	09	L	24	8	aa	NYM	491	52	103	14	2	3	31	31	93	15	12	210	257	263	520	6%	81%	0.34	38	97	2.17	-3
Garcia,Sergio	09	R	29	5	aa	LA	211	23	38	9	0	1	10	17	35	1	1	179	241	236	478	8%	83%	0.49	46	57	1.91	5
Garcia,Travis	09	R	27	6	aa	SEA	151	15	32	7	1	3	18	6	41	1	1	215	246	328	574	4%	73%	0.15	75	80	2.65	-15
Garciaparra,Michael	08	R	26	3	aa	MIL	103	9	29	4	1	2	15	3	22	2	1	283	302	392	694	3%	78%	0.13	69	90	4.21	2
	09	R	26	6	a/a	MIL	189	6	34	5	0	1	9	17	39	0	0	180	250	219	469	8%	79%	0.45	29	2	1.89	-40
Gardenhire,Toby	08	B	26	536	aa	MIN	284	23	61	4	1	1	17	20	49	2	1	214	266	243	509	7%	83%	0.41	19	58	2.25	-21
	09	B	27	4	aa	MIN	200	17	44	7	0	0	15	11	37	2	1	221	260	257	517	5%	82%	0.29	32	53	2.29	-20
Garner,Cole	09	R	25 a	8	aa	COL	396	52	104	23	3	13	51	18	63	11	6	262	294	436	731	4%	84%	0.29	110	110	4.39	69
Gartrell,Maurice	08	R	25	80	aa	CHW	409	47	95	20	1	14	45	40	99	6	1	232	301	392	693	9%	76%	0.41	100	74	4.21	25
	09	R	26	8	a/a	CHW	474	72	118	26	3	22	74	45	121	5	2	248	313	452	765	9%	74%	0.37	125	93	5.03	45

Major League Equivalent Statistics

BATTER	Yr	B	Age	Pos	Lev	Org	ab	r	h	d	t	hr	rbi	bb	k	sb	cs	ba	ob	slg	ops	bb%	ct%	eye	px	sx	rc/g	bpv
Gathright,Joey	09	L	28	8	aaa	BOS	332	43	98	11	2	0	18	24	45	21	7	294	341	339	681	7%	86%	0.52	35	116	4.41	24
Gentry,Craig	08	R	25	8	aa	TEX	360	36	82	15	0	3	25	19	58	12	10	227	266	293	559	5%	84%	0.33	50	78	2.48	11
	09	R	26 a	8	aa	TEX	512	77	134	19	6	7	40	38	56	38	7	263	313	360	673	7%	89%	0.67	62	159	4.27	69
German,Esteban	09	R	32	5	aa	TEX	389	44	97	12	3	3	41	45	61	25	9	249	327	317	644	10%	84%	0.74	45	123	3.85	33
Gilbert,Archie	09	R	26	8	aa	OAK	449	55	98	13	3	2	27	40	40	19	17	217	282	270	552	8%	91%	1.01	37	108	2.42	45
Giles,Thomas	09	L	26	8	aa	LA	179	23	38	9	0	9	24	26	57	0	1	211	310	416	726	13%	68%	0.46	125	27	4.45	9
Gillespie,Cole	08	R	24 a	8	aa	MIL	462	55	109	33	2	11	60	59	88	12	1	237	323	384	707	11%	81%	0.67	102	98	4.61	60
	09	R	25 a	8	a/a	ARI	374	43	86	16	8	9	38	41	66	9	6	229	306	387	693	10%	82%	0.63	95	147	4.06	71
Gimenez,Chris	08	R	26	2	a/a	CLE	372	59	100	22	1	8	39	67	93	2	2	268	379	392	771	15%	75%	0.72	85	56	5.72	18
	09	R	27	2	aaa	CLE	136	15	27	6	0	5	11	12	36	0	0	196	261	345	606	8%	74%	0.33	94	28	3.05	-4
Gimenez,Hector	08	B	26	2	aaa	TAM	146	8	27	6	2	2	12	6	33	0	0	183	217	290	507	4%	78%	0.20	70	68	2.04	-3
	09	B	27	5	aa	PIT	301	24	70	16	1	6	29	14	49	2	2	232	266	345	611	4%	84%	0.28	77	51	3.09	23
Ginter,Keith	08	R	32	54	aaa	BOS	444	35	89	20	0	4	38	39	88	3	1	201	266	274	539	8%	80%	0.44	54	50	2.53	-3
	09	R	33	4	aaa	CHW	363	27	76	17	1	5	26	31	76	2	2	208	270	302	572	8%	79%	0.40	65	44	2.78	-1
Godwin,Adam	08	R	26	8	aa	LA	417	43	91	14	2	2	27	39	59	24	6	219	286	275	561	9%	86%	0.67	41	114	2.89	30
	09	R	27	8	aa	LA	248	24	52	10	1	1	17	14	49	10	7	211	253	271	524	5%	80%	0.28	45	100	2.15	0
Goedert,Jared	09	R	24	5	aa	CLE	313	30	63	20	1	4	33	31	46	1	0	202	274	310	583	9%	85%	0.67	79	53	2.95	40
Golson,Greg	08	R	23	8	aa	PHI	426	46	104	16	2	11	43	25	100	16	6	244	285	366	651	5%	77%	0.25	76	103	3.60	11
	09	R	24	8	aa	TEX	457	36	104	15	7	2	32	23	98	15	5	227	264	302	566	5%	79%	0.24	49	139	2.75	7
Gomes,Jonny	08	R	28	8	aaa	TAM	107	14	22	9	0	2	11	9	30	0	1	202	264	336	600	8%	72%	0.30	100	55	2.90	2
	09	R	29 b	8	aaa	CIN	131	13	31	8	1	8	20	9	35	3	1	235	283	490	774	6%	73%	0.25	153	81	4.74	54
Gonzalez,Andy	08	R	27	4	aaa	CLE	289	31	61	12	0	6	30	34	73	2	2	210	293	309	602	11%	75%	0.47	66	44	3.16	-11
	09	R	28	6	aa	FLA	352	36	76	10	0	6	34	40	82	6	2	215	294	297	591	10%	77%	0.48	53	64	3.13	-10
Gonzalez,Angel	09	L	24	5	aa	PIT	172	14	29	6	1	1	11	11	30	2	1	171	220	234	453	6%	83%	0.36	44	81	1.68	5
Gonzalez,Carlos	08	L	23	8	aa	OAK	173	18	42	8	1	3	22	12	26	1	1	243	292	353	644	6%	85%	0.46	73	66	3.58	33
	09	L	24 a	8	aa	COL	192	34	61	11	6	9	48	18	26	5	3	316	374	572	946	8%	87%	0.69	148	191	8.00	141
Gonzalez,Edwar	08	R	26	80	aa	NYY	396	52	106	27	0	13	60	18	76	8	5	268	300	437	737	4%	81%	0.24	112	73	4.53	46
	09	R	27	8	aa	NYY	413	41	86	23	1	4	33	27	98	6	3	207	255	294	549	6%	76%	0.27	65	82	2.53	-4
Gonzalez,Juan	08	R	27	46	aa	LA	360	33	77	18	0	11	43	43	75	2	1	215	299	358	657	11%	79%	0.58	93	35	3.76	25
	09	R	28	4	aa	LA	231	18	43	10	0	0	17	36	58	3	0	187	297	230	526	13%	75%	0.62	38	49	2.57	-26
Gorecki,Reid	08	R	28	8	a/a	ATL	253	41	63	7	0	7	33	25	47	13	5	249	317	363	680	9%	82%	0.54	69	97	4.07	31
	09	R	29	8	aaa	ATL	371	42	84	21	4	6	36	26	70	11	7	228	277	353	631	6%	81%	0.36	84	117	3.23	42
Gorneault,Nick	08	R	29	8	aa	HOU	370	38	71	13	1	13	36	29	85	5	8	191	250	335	585	7%	77%	0.34	87	64	2.57	14
	09	R	30	8	aa	TOR	415	42	72	20	2	9	46	29	135	9	4	174	228	293	521	7%	67%	0.21	79	100	2.14	-22
Gosewisch,James	09	R	26	2	a/a	PHI	260	17	52	17	0	1	17	12	43	0	1	198	233	272	506	4%	83%	0.28	62	27	2.07	1
Gotay,Ruben	09	B	27 b	5	aa	ARI	371	50	89	27	2	9	44	80	60	2	4	241	375	397	772	18%	84%	1.34	106	51	5.54	74
Gradoville,Chris	09	R	25	2	aa	TEX	181	10	35	5	0	1	11	3	27	0	0	192	205	234	438	2%	85%	0.11	31	22	1.54	-22
Graffanino,Tony	09	R	37	4	aaa	CLE	261	27	53	19	0	4	28	13	45	2	0	202	239	322	562	5%	83%	0.29	89	63	2.59	32
Green,Andy	08	R	31	4	a/a	NYM	440	55	91	20	3	9	33	48	76	5	4	207	284	321	605	10%	83%	0.62	74	85	3.10	37
	09	R	32	5	aa	NYM	174	16	33	5	1	3	14	13	31	2	0	191	246	274	519	7%	82%	0.42	53	75	2.30	10
Green,Taylor	09	L	23	5	aa	MIL	306	28	71	14	0	4	35	29	32	0	1	232	299	317	616	9%	90%	0.91	61	24	3.34	33
Greene,Tyler	08	R	25	6	aa	STL	485	58	100	18	3	10	36	24	109	15	7	205	244	318	561	5%	78%	0.23	71	122	2.53	15
	09	R	26	6	aa	STL	340	51	80	8	3	10	30	28	72	22	4	235	293	365	658	8%	79%	0.38	75	148	3.91	37
Griffin,John-Ford	08	L	29	8	aa	LA	319	40	77	15	2	11	47	26	57	1	1	243	301	400	701	8%	82%	0.46	98	63	4.23	43
	09	L	30	8	aa	CHC	340	28	73	24	2	4	29	26	88	3	2	215	270	334	604	7%	74%	0.29	87	74	3.08	4
Griffin,Michael	08	R	25	584	a/a	CIN	452	34	105	28	3	4	30	15	73	9	9	233	258	333	590	3%	84%	0.20	74	85	2.71	28
	09	R	26	8	a/a	CIN	304	22	59	12	1	3	17	10	41	3	4	195	221	269	490	3%	86%	0.25	53	62	1.85	15
Gutierrez,Chris	08	R	25	64	a/a	TOR	282	35	61	15	3	2	29	36	63	0	4	218	305	313	619	11%	78%	0.57	68	75	3.25	13
	09	R	26	5	aa	LAA	182	24	43	8	1	1	11	24	45	0	1	238	325	310	635	11%	75%	0.53	54	59	3.65	-13
Guyer,Brandon	09	R	24	8	aa	CHC	189	18	32	12	1	1	12	8	30	6	6	171	204	259	463	4%	84%	0.26	68	115	1.48	36
Guzman,Freddy	08	B	28 b	80	a/a	DET	518	74	115	14	12	4	43	38	49	51	12	222	275	316	591	7%	91%	0.77	55	213	3.13	86
	09	B	29	8	a/a	NYY	350	37	66	8	3	2	14	21	59	38	8	189	235	241	476	6%	83%	0.36	34	161	2.04	22
Guzman,Jesus	08	R	24 a	54	aa	OAK	400	46	116	20	1	12	63	28	53	4	5	290	337	432	769	7%	87%	0.52	91	53	5.23	51
	09	R	25	3	aa	SF	452	62	128	24	4	12	58	30	76	0	2	283	328	435	762	6%	83%	0.40	97	65	5.17	45
Guzman,Joel	08	R	24	5	aaa	TAM	436	42	94	20	0	17	59	16	88	1	2	216	243	375	618	3%	80%	0.18	99	36	2.98	18
	09	R	25	5	a/a	WAS	418	47	101	24	1	10	50	31	73	1	1	241	293	372	665	7%	83%	0.42	88	49	3.82	31
Gwynn,Tony	08	L	26	8	aaa	MIL	375	33	82	7	2	2	18	21	47	14	6	218	260	263	523	5%	88%	0.45	29	99	2.31	16
	09	L	27 b	8	aaa	MIL	152	25	39	6	1	1	6	16	18	11	1	254	324	327	651	9%	88%	0.85	52	136	4.23	55
Haad,Yamid	08	R	31	2	aaa	CLE	108	7	14	3	0	1	5	7	31	0	0	134	185	181	366	6%	72%	0.22	33	27	1.08	-65
	09	R	32	2	aa	SD	255	17	46	9	0	3	18	10	58	1	2	180	212	257	468	4%	77%	0.18	53	37	1.70	-27
Haerther,Cody	08	L	25	8	aa	STL	332	28	71	18	0	3	23	25	53	2	5	212	268	292	560	7%	84%	0.48	61	39	2.55	12
	09	L	26	8	aa	TOR	132	11	26	6	1	1	11	12	23	0	1	195	262	272	534	8%	83%	0.52	54	59	2.37	10
Hall,James	08	L	24	8	aa	TAM	189	22	39	12	1	4	15	16	53	1	1	208	271	340	612	8%	72%	0.31	90	74	3.12	0
	09	L	25	8	aa	TAM	299	37	58	12	3	6	27	39	84	4	3	195	287	311	598	11%	72%	0.46	74	103	3.06	2
Hall,Michael	08	L	23	8	aa	BOS	263	38	56	17	1	10	27	29	82	3	1	212	292	395	687	10%	69%	0.36	117	85	3.99	17
	09	L	24	8	a/a	CLE	253	23	44	6	2	3	21	37	69	4	2	175	281	247	528	13%	73%	0.54	44	87	2.46	-19
Hall,Noah	08	R	31	08	a/a	SEA	175	13	34	9	0	1	16	20	20	3	3	194	275	262	538	10%	89%	0.98	55	45	2.38	34
	09	R	32	0	aa	NYY	200	24	40	6	2	3	27	17	25	4	2	200	262	285	547	8%	88%	0.69	54	109	2.55	44
Hallberg,Marcus	09	R	24	4	aa	ARI	455	42	109	22	1	2	34	32	36	12	4	239	290	304	593	7%	92%	0.91	51	82	3.13	49
Halman,Gregory	08	R	21	8	aa	SEA	236	35	59	13	1	8	24	14	57	7	7	248	291	415	706	6%	76%	0.25	106	104	3.82	32
	09	R	22	8	aa	SEA	457	57	87	16	1	22	64	27	172	8	8	190	236	374	610	6%	62%	0.16	107	88	2.69	-25
Hamilton,Mark	08	L	24	3	aa	STL	245	20	49	10	0	6	22	26	53	0	0	200	276	310	586	10%	78%	0.49	71	16	2.97	-4
	09	L	25	3	aa	STL	293	36	74	18	0	9	35	30	65	0	1	253	323	411	734	9%	78%	0.46	104	28	4.76	23
Hammock,Robby	08	R	31	2	aa	ARI	217	21	43	5	2	4	20	14	45	1	0	196	243	294	537	6%	79%	0.30	58	79	2.41	2
	09	R	32	2	aaa	BAL	278	22	47	13	0	3	20	19	65	2	1	168	221	251	471	6%	77%	0.29	60	51	1.80	-16
Hankerd,Kevin	08	R	24	8	aa	ARI	436	29	100	16	3	5	43	18	55	2	7	229	259	312	572	4%	87%	0.32	55	52	2.57	19
	09	R	25	8	aa	ARI	440	46	107	32	1	6	54	34	67	1	6	242	296	358	654	7%	85%	0.50	86	40	3.56	36
Harman,Brad	08	R	23	46	aa	PHI	443	36	82	15	1	14	41	31	103	2	1	185	238	318	557	7%	77%	0.30	81	48	2.50	1
	09	R	24	4	aa	PHI	422	37	75	21	2	5	33	30	100	0	2	179	234	272	506	7%	76%	0.30	65	52	2.06	-12
Harper,Brett	08	L	27 b	03	aa	SF	352	39	93	28	0	14	48	10	54	0	1	263	284	465	749	3%	85%	0.18	133	29	4.58	61
	09	L	28 b	3	a/a	LA	390	33	89	19	1	14	49	18	45	0	0	228	263	390	653	5%	88%	0.41	102	23	3.50	53

Major League Equivalent Statistics

BATTERS

BATTER	Yr	B	Age	Pos	Lev	Org	ab	r	h	d	t	hr	rbi	bb	k	sb	cs	ba	ob	slg	ops	bb%	ct%	eye	px	sx	rc/g	bpv
Harvey,Ryan	08	R	24	8	aa	CHC	111	6	20	6	0	2	11	5	31	1	1	182	216	285	501	4%	72%	0.15	73	37	1.92	-33
	09	R	25 a	8	aa	COL	345	34	76	19	2	20	63	23	82	2	0	221	269	458	726	6%	76%	0.28	142	62	4.20	51
Hatcher,David	09	R	25 a	2	aa	FLA	156	24	31	9	3	7	23	12	42	1	0	197	256	418	675	7%	73%	0.30	132	154	3.60	62
Hayes,Brett	08	R	25	2	aa	FLA	297	32	65	10	1	9	28	12	60	2	6	220	249	346	595	4%	80%	0.19	77	63	2.64	8
	09	R	26	2	aa	FLA	321	23	67	13	0	3	31	17	65	2	0	208	248	275	523	5%	80%	0.26	50	45	2.33	-15
Head,Jerad	09	R	27	8	aa	CLE	327	41	80	20	3	5	40	20	73	5	2	245	289	366	655	6%	78%	0.28	84	108	3.70	24
Head,Stephen	08	L	25	38	aa	CLE	404	43	105	22	1	11	42	21	71	1	1	259	296	397	693	5%	82%	0.30	91	47	4.15	29
	09	L	26	8	aaa	CLE	280	22	58	14	0	5	24	14	30	1	2	208	246	309	555	5%	89%	0.47	71	35	2.48	36
Heether,Adam	08	R	27	65	aaa	MIL	390	50	85	26	1	8	36	48	77	7	1	217	303	351	654	11%	80%	0.62	93	87	3.84	46
	09	R	28	5	a/a	MIL	419	49	100	26	1	14	52	47	88	4	1	238	315	402	717	10%	79%	0.53	107	61	4.55	42
Heisey,Chris	09	R	25 a	8	a/a	CIN	516	75	146	32	2	21	63	40	69	17	3	283	335	474	809	7%	87%	0.59	121	105	5.96	91
Henley,Paul	09	L	24 a	8	aa	STL	423	47	107	27	2	10	48	31	51	7	5	252	303	393	695	7%	88%	0.60	95	78	4.12	67
Henry,Sean	08	R	23 a	8	aa	CIN	396	50	99	20	3	10	47	32	59	12	9	250	307	389	695	8%	85%	0.55	89	103	4.02	59
	09	R	24 a	8	aa	CIN	420	54	102	20	1	11	31	34	58	18	10	242	298	370	669	7%	86%	0.58	83	97	3.75	57
Hernandez,Diory	08	R	25	465	a/a	ATL	536	43	135	23	3	6	49	21	72	7	10	253	281	339	619	4%	87%	0.29	59	66	3.12	23
	09	R	25	6	aaa	ATL	204	14	55	14	1	1	25	17	31	7	7	272	328	364	692	8%	85%	0.55	72	70	4.02	36
Hernandez,Gorkys	09	R	22	8	aa	PIT	556	65	144	24	3	2	41	31	103	17	18	259	298	324	622	5%	81%	0.30	49	96	3.12	6
Hernandez,Luis	08	B	24	6	aaa	BAL	205	14	33	6	0	0	9	7	23	2	2	159	186	187	373	3%	89%	0.29	25	63	1.06	2
	09	B	25	6	aa	KC	198	18	52	9	0	1	20	12	14	1	4	261	304	323	627	6%	93%	0.88	49	36	3.29	36
Herrera,Jonathan	08	B	24	64	aa	COL	226	28	62	6	0	2	22	14	20	11	3	273	315	325	640	6%	91%	0.67	36	91	3.81	34
	09	B	25	6	aa	COL	381	50	92	10	4	2	26	38	41	12	6	242	311	302	614	9%	89%	0.95	39	119	3.39	45
Hessman,Mike	08	R	31	5	aaa	DET	399	60	83	15	3	24	52	43	134	3	3	209	286	443	729	10%	66%	0.32	134	98	4.26	24
	09	R	32	5	aaa	DET	466	44	81	24	3	18	59	48	174	3	1	173	251	350	601	9%	63%	0.28	109	74	2.92	-19
Hester,John	08	R	25	2	aa	ARI	306	30	73	24	2	9	39	13	67	3	2	240	271	421	692	4%	78%	0.20	121	78	3.85	43
	09	R	26 b	2	aa	ARI	329	47	96	29	5	7	51	17	57	10	3	291	327	473	799	5%	83%	0.31	124	145	5.69	86
Heyward,Jason	09	L	20 a	8	a/a	ATL	173	32	59	12	3	6	29	28	18	5	1	339	431	554	985	14%	89%	1.51	134	137	9.95	135
Hicks,Brandon	09	R	24	6	aa	ATL	464	56	99	22	3	9	42	47	127	15	1	213	286	329	615	9%	73%	0.37	76	124	3.42	9
Hill,Steven	09	R	25	2	aa	STL	464	47	109	22	1	13	48	27	84	1	2	236	278	374	652	5%	82%	0.32	89	42	3.55	24
Hodges,Wes	08	R	24	5	aa	CLE	504	60	130	27	2	15	83	46	99	3	1	257	319	410	729	8%	80%	0.47	98	64	4.74	38
	09	R	25	5	aaa	CLE	332	25	75	21	0	4	29	15	56	7	6	227	260	323	583	4%	83%	0.27	73	59	2.71	19
Hoffmann,Jaime	08	R	24	8	aa	LA	478	49	113	17	2	8	54	43	61	22	11	237	300	329	630	8%	87%	0.70	60	96	3.43	44
	09	R	25 a	8	aa	LA	358	55	88	20	3	8	52	45	52	12	12	247	331	389	720	11%	85%	0.87	92	107	4.28	72
Hoffpauir,Jarrett	08	R	25	4	aa	STL	410	36	92	25	1	3	34	36	36	2	5	225	287	312	599	8%	91%	0.99	67	43	3.02	50
	09	R	26 b	4	aa	STL	358	39	84	17	2	9	39	26	23	3	1	234	285	370	655	7%	94%	1.13	88	71	3.69	81
Holcomb,Darin	09	R	24 a	5	aa	COL	479	54	121	25	1	12	42	43	40	2	1	252	313	381	694	8%	92%	1.08	85	50	4.30	68
Hollimon,Michael	08	B	26	4	aaa	DET	331	43	58	13	4	11	26	35	96	6	3	175	254	336	590	10%	71%	0.37	96	129	2.81	21
	09	B	27	5	aa	DET	104	11	18	3	2	3	15	13	31	0	1	173	262	312	574	11%	70%	0.41	78	116	2.67	2
Holm,Steve	09	R	30	2	aa	SF	198	17	39	10	0	4	12	11	40	0	0	195	238	313	551	5%	80%	0.28	80	26	2.47	4
Holt,John	08	L	26	4	a/a	ATL	472	51	111	15	6	2	40	42	80	23	13	235	298	303	601	8%	83%	0.53	45	130	3.07	26
	09	L	27	4	aaa	ATL	266	34	63	10	2	0	23	21	47	11	5	235	292	287	579	7%	82%	0.45	40	120	2.96	14
Hoover,Paul	08	R	32	2	aa	FLA	175	19	33	6	0	4	14	10	46	1	1	189	234	296	530	6%	74%	0.22	68	54	2.25	-21
	09	R	33	2	aaa	PHI	245	19	48	13	1	1	20	20	67	1	2	198	259	267	527	8%	73%	0.30	54	51	2.32	-33
Hopf,Mike	09	L	27	2	aa	MIL	192	14	40	11	0	3	17	16	35	1	0	206	266	307	573	8%	82%	0.45	73	34	2.82	13
Hopper,Norris	09	R	31	8	aaa	WAS	409	36	91	11	2	0	26	26	25	17	8	222	268	258	526	6%	94%	1.03	28	98	2.37	41
Horton,Joshua	09	L	24	6	aa	OAK	510	58	110	18	4	3	45	46	47	7	4	215	280	282	563	8%	91%	0.98	46	95	2.75	47
Horwitz,Brian	08	R	26	8	aa	SF	264	34	64	10	1	6	24	25	38	1	1	242	309	353	661	9%	85%	0.66	71	59	3.88	36
	09	R	27	8	aa	SF	210	22	52	9	2	3	21	19	34	0	1	250	313	350	663	8%	84%	0.57	67	63	3.91	27
House,J.R.	08	R	29	32	aa	HOU	454	41	106	18	0	12	40	34	45	1	3	235	288	357	645	7%	90%	0.76	78	25	3.53	46
	09	R	30	2	aa	KC	505	40	100	21	0	6	36	22	50	0	0	198	232	274	506	4%	90%	0.45	55	26	2.10	23
Howard,Kevin	08	L	27 b	4	aa	SEA	247	25	54	13	0	8	33	28	32	1	5	219	298	368	666	10%	87%	0.87	96	29	3.59	56
	09	L	28 b	5	a/a	TOR	433	51	110	25	1	11	45	36	51	4	3	254	311	388	700	8%	88%	0.71	90	59	4.29	60
Howell,Jeffery	09	R	26	2	aa	KC	195	16	42	9	1	3	17	12	29	0	2	217	262	316	578	6%	85%	0.41	68	45	2.71	21
Hu,Chin-Lung	08	R	25	6	aa	LA	156	16	39	5	2	1	12	6	17	2	0	252	279	326	605	4%	89%	0.35	48	106	3.25	36
	09	R	26	6	aa	LA	496	53	125	18	3	5	42	21	52	11	6	252	282	328	610	4%	89%	0.40	52	97	3.19	38
Hubbard,Marshall	08	L	26 b	3	aa	SEA	309	40	74	20	2	8	40	44	60	2	5	238	333	396	729	13%	81%	0.74	105	64	4.59	52
	09	L	27	3	aa	SEA	447	59	100	24	1	11	56	60	116	2	3	223	316	354	670	12%	74%	0.52	87	52	3.96	8
Huber,Justin	08	R	26	3	aa	SD	199	13	39	9	0	2	21	14	50	0	1	194	246	268	515	6%	75%	0.28	55	23	2.18	-34
	09	R	27	0	aaa	MIN	440	47	97	19	2	15	59	38	82	3	3	221	283	376	659	8%	81%	0.46	95	59	3.61	37
Hudson,Robert	08	R	25	46	aa	CHW	320	24	71	16	0	1	24	16	53	8	6	220	257	279	536	5%	83%	0.30	49	68	2.35	5
	09	R	26	6	aa	CHW	315	32	67	6	1	3	23	12	36	12	3	213	242	263	505	4%	89%	0.33	32	108	2.19	21
Huffman,Chad	08	R	23	8	aa	SD	437	57	106	25	1	7	49	56	77	1	1	242	328	350	678	11%	82%	0.73	76	50	4.20	30
	09	R	24	8	aa	SD	469	50	102	23	1	14	53	44	101	6	6	217	284	362	647	9%	78%	0.44	93	60	3.44	25
Huffman,Royce	08	R	32	305	aaa	CHW	370	34	77	20	0	9	32	31	94	3	3	207	267	331	598	8%	75%	0.33	84	47	2.94	-3
	09	R	33	3	aa	TEX	440	36	100	23	0	5	37	39	81	3	0	228	291	315	606	8%	82%	0.48	64	50	3.29	11
Hughes,John	08	L	25	3	aa	TAM	395	44	89	23	1	11	40	36	99	2	1	226	290	374	664	8%	75%	0.36	97	56	3.78	13
	09	L	26	3	a/a	BAL	512	63	129	30	2	25	69	38	170	3	0	252	303	464	767	7%	67%	0.22	131	69	5.01	9
Hughes,Luke	08	R	24	5	a/a	MIN	391	57	105	19	3	13	49	27	92	5	1	268	315	435	749	6%	77%	0.29	103	103	4.97	35
	09	R	25	5	a/a	MIN	335	34	73	21	4	9	53	29	72	3	1	219	281	387	669	8%	78%	0.40	108	98	3.76	47
Hulett,Tug	08	L	26 a	64	aa	SEA	336	55	84	19	3	10	37	39	67	8	6	249	328	414	742	11%	80%	0.59	105	110	4.74	60
	09	L	27 b	4	aa	KC	374	45	92	25	3	7	39	43	65	6	2	246	324	386	710	10%	83%	0.66	96	95	4.57	58
Hunter,Cedric	09	L	22	8	aa	SD	541	58	121	16	4	1	43	20	36	10	4	224	252	274	526	4%	93%	0.57	36	109	2.34	44
Inglett,Joe	09	L	31	4	aaa	TOR	161	19	43	11	1	2	16	10	16	3	3	269	313	380	693	6%	90%	0.62	82	78	4.12	62
Iorg,Cale	09	R	24	6	aa	DET	491	45	95	14	2	9	33	25	126	11	8	194	233	284	516	5%	74%	0.20	57	90	2.08	-19
Iribarren,Hernan	08	L	24	84	aaa	MIL	361	35	83	14	2	0	22	22	51	14	10	229	273	279	552	6%	86%	0.43	40	102	2.50	19
	09	L	25	4	aaa	MIL	379	35	99	16	3	2	40	23	55	9	8	260	302	332	634	6%	85%	0.41	52	90	3.43	23
Jackson,Anthony	09	B	25	8	aa	COL	422	47	82	9	3	4	26	33	48	21	6	194	252	256	508	7%	89%	0.69	39	128	2.25	41
Jackson,Austin	08	R	22	8	aa	NYY	520	73	143	31	3	9	67	53	107	18	6	276	342	400	742	9%	79%	0.49	86	110	5.11	39
	09	R	23	8	aaa	NYY	504	64	144	22	6	4	62	38	117	23	4	286	336	377	713	7%	77%	0.32	61	145	4.87	16
Jaso,John	08	L	25 a	2	a/a	TAM	392	51	90	17	2	9	52	56	41	2	1	230	327	355	682	13%	89%	1.36	80	63	4.24	67
	09	L	26	2	aaa	TAM	331	34	75	12	2	4	24	38	47	1	0	225	304	306	610	10%	86%	0.81	54	59	3.37	27
Jay,Jonathan	08	L	24 a	8	aa	STL	430	51	116	18	3	9	44	34	44	8	10	269	323	385	708	7%	90%	0.78	74	80	4.24	59
	09	L	25	8	aa	STL	505	55	119	19	1	7	40	26	51	15	10	236	273	317	591	5%	90%	0.51	56	88	2.88	42

Major League Equivalent Statistics

BATTER	Yr	B	Age	Pos	Lev	Org	ab	r	h	d	t	hr	rbi	bb	k	sb	cs	ba	ob	slg	ops	bb%	ct%	eye	px	sx	rc/g	bpv
Jenkins,Andrew	08	R	25	38	aa	FLA	347	29	75	13	1	6	41	16	62	2	3	217	251	309	560	4%	82%	0.26	61	52	2.54	4
	09	R	26	3	aa	FLA	269	24	61	18	0	2	16	12	47	4	0	226	259	315	573	4%	83%	0.26	71	68	2.84	18
Jennings,Desmond	09	R	23 a	8	a/a	TAM	497	83	147	29	8	10	56	61	61	47	8	296	373	447	819	11%	88%	1.00	97	175	6.70	105
Jeroloman,Brian	08	L	23	2	a/a	TOR	301	29	70	16	0	6	30	47	58	0	0	231	335	342	677	14%	81%	0.81	76	17	4.25	18
	09	L	24	2	aa	TOR	364	30	74	15	1	6	30	58	126	1	0	203	312	298	610	14%	65%	0.46	64	41	3.40	-46
Jimenez,Jorge	08	L	24	5	aa	BOS	211	18	51	12	1	2	17	6	24	1	1	241	261	337	598	3%	89%	0.24	70	61	2.97	36
	09	L	25	5	aa	BOS	498	50	131	24	2	9	70	41	61	3	2	262	319	374	693	8%	88%	0.68	74	55	4.32	45
Johnson,Brent	08	R	26 b	8	aa	SEA	349	34	72	17	2	5	30	30	37	6	7	206	269	306	575	8%	89%	0.82	69	76	2.63	54
	09	R	27	8	aa	SEA	227	24	41	11	0	3	14	28	31	10	7	178	268	262	530	11%	86%	0.90	61	82	2.27	42
Johnson,Chris	08	R	24	5	aa	HOU	431	38	108	21	1	10	48	18	69	4	0	249	280	370	650	4%	84%	0.27	80	65	3.67	30
	09	R	25	5	aa	HOU	384	36	92	17	4	11	31	15	73	2	1	240	269	388	657	4%	81%	0.21	91	83	3.57	32
Johnson,Elliot	08	B	25	46	aaa	TAM	387	39	86	22	4	7	39	26	91	12	3	223	272	352	624	6%	77%	0.29	86	126	3.32	28
	09	B	26	4	aaa	TAM	233	25	53	8	1	9	29	14	52	6	2	226	270	387	657	6%	78%	0.27	95	87	3.56	26
Johnson,Joshua	09	B	24	5	aa	KC	132	20	23	3	0	0	7	23	18	2	2	171	292	193	485	15%	86%	1.23	20	69	2.07	12
Johnson,Michael	08	B	27	2	aa	LAA	480	50	103	18	1	17	70	14	79	5	6	215	237	360	597	3%	83%	0.17	89	66	2.69	32
	09	B	28	8	aa	LAA	248	27	45	14	2	4	23	20	43	3	4	181	242	298	540	7%	83%	0.46	80	93	2.27	39
Johnston,Seth	08	R	26	5	aa	SD	460	54	93	20	0	12	53	32	87	3	2	202	254	325	579	6%	81%	0.37	79	59	2.76	20
	09	R	27	5	aa	SD	405	31	76	11	1	8	44	25	89	4	5	189	235	282	517	6%	78%	0.28	58	54	2.11	-12
Jones,Brandon	08	L	25	8	aaa	ATL	346	36	79	21	1	7	42	38	68	8	7	228	305	352	657	10%	80%	0.57	87	70	3.63	34
	09	L	26	8	aaa	ATL	384	39	92	24	1	6	45	40	69	5	3	240	312	353	665	10%	82%	0.58	81	63	3.92	33
Jones,Daryl	08	L	21 a	8	aa	STL	124	15	31	5	1	4	11	17	23	5	1	253	343	407	751	12%	82%	0.75	94	101	5.27	58
	09	L	22	8	aa	STL	294	39	72	12	2	2	23	26	50	6	5	245	306	320	626	8%	83%	0.52	53	98	3.39	22
Jones,Garrett	08	L	27	38	aaa	MIN	527	62	119	27	2	16	69	36	96	7	2	225	275	376	651	6%	82%	0.38	96	87	3.57	45
	09	L	28 b	8	aa	PIT	277	33	69	16	0	8	36	12	42	11	4	248	280	391	671	4%	85%	0.29	95	88	3.71	52
Jones,Mitch	08	R	31	8	aa	LA	200	26	42	11	1	11	31	14	53	3	0	208	262	438	699	7%	74%	0.27	138	85	3.90	46
	09	R	32	8	aa	LA	387	52	89	20	2	26	75	30	107	7	3	231	286	496	782	7%	72%	0.28	156	89	4.83	57
Jones,Travis	09	R	24	4	aa	ATL	366	36	84	21	1	4	36	46	89	21	9	230	316	324	640	11%	76%	0.52	69	93	3.66	10
Joyce,Matt	08	L	24 a	8	aaa	DET	200	29	47	12	2	11	34	20	53	2	3	235	305	470	776	9%	73%	0.38	141	97	4.80	56
	09	L	25 a	8	aaa	TAM	417	60	99	30	2	13	55	56	93	11	6	237	328	413	740	12%	78%	0.61	117	95	4.79	59
Joynt,Brian	09	R	25	8	aa	SD	233	21	44	6	1	4	24	12	58	3	0	190	231	272	503	5%	75%	0.21	51	83	2.12	-22
Justis,Shane	08	R	26	54	aa	LA	338	35	74	14	1	2	27	31	43	8	9	220	285	284	569	8%	87%	0.73	48	75	2.63	29
	09	R	27	4	aa	MIL	473	53	109	24	3	4	38	28	61	7	6	230	272	315	587	6%	87%	0.45	62	93	2.88	39
Kaaihue,Kala	08	R	24	3	aa	ATL	376	51	91	21	1	11	49	72	101	0	5	242	363	388	752	16%	73%	0.71	95	31	5.11	12
	09	R	24	3	aa	ATL	191	14	27	6	1	4	13	32	61	1	1	141	263	241	504	14%	68%	0.52	62	54	2.19	-32
Ka'aihue,Kila	08	L	25 a	30	aa	KC	401	76	113	15	0	29	84	88	58	3	2	282	412	536	948	18%	85%	1.51	145	44	8.60	109
	09	L	25 a	3	aa	KC	441	61	95	25	1	12	42	77	68	0	1	215	332	360	692	15%	85%	1.13	96	38	4.34	58
Kainer,Carson	09	R	25	8	aa	CIN	148	9	32	6	0	1	10	7	29	1	1	214	248	272	521	4%	80%	0.23	44	35	2.24	-22
Kalish,Ryan	09	L	21 a	8	aa	BOS	391	54	103	21	3	10	47	36	70	12	3	263	326	411	737	9%	82%	0.52	95	115	4.93	58
Kata,Matt	08	B	31	84	aa	PIT	396	37	77	15	3	5	33	16	65	14	6	195	227	290	517	4%	84%	0.25	62	126	2.10	32
	09	B	32	4	aa	HOU	227	14	46	8	1	2	14	8	24	5	0	202	228	266	494	3%	90%	0.33	45	83	2.09	28
Katin,Brendan	08	R	26	8	aaa	MIL	321	34	71	19	2	14	52	9	93	5	2	223	245	425	669	3%	71%	0.10	125	96	3.42	21
	09	R	27	8	aaa	MIL	459	49	91	28	4	17	67	27	147	2	0	198	242	389	631	5%	68%	0.18	119	92	3.13	8
Kazmar,Sean	08	R	24	6	aa	SD	382	43	84	16	2	2	32	31	63	6	5	221	279	289	568	7%	84%	0.49	50	86	2.74	17
	09	R	25	6	aa	SD	366	30	68	11	0	4	35	28	53	6	2	185	243	247	490	7%	85%	0.53	43	65	2.04	12
Kelly,Don	08	L	29 b	465	aa	ARI	436	46	101	20	4	6	41	25	41	2	1	232	273	341	614	5%	91%	0.60	72	85	3.22	58
	09	L	30 b	8	aaa	DET	372	44	101	16	4	4	31	33	51	21	3	270	329	372	702	8%	86%	0.64	67	138	4.70	58
Kennelly,Timothy	09	R	23 a	2	aa	PHI	117	11	27	5	1	2	14	10	13	1	1	231	291	342	633	8%	89%	0.77	72	73	3.43	53
Kervin,Bryan	09	L	25	5	aa	TOR	143	10	21	2	1	1	11	6	40	0	3	148	181	195	375	4%	72%	0.15	28	74	0.97	-56
Khoury,Ryan	08	R	25	54	aa	BOS	299	35	77	20	1	3	31	34	54	3	3	257	332	360	692	10%	82%	0.62	77	61	4.31	30
	09	R	26	4	aa	BOS	368	48	75	24	1	2	25	50	89	3	1	204	299	291	590	12%	76%	0.56	69	73	3.13	6
Kiger,Mark	08	R	28	6	aa	SEA	376	35	65	10	1	2	28	54	95	2	6	173	276	218	494	12%	75%	0.56	32	44	2.04	-36
	09	R	29	3	aa	NYM	150	13	26	3	0	1	8	26	45	3	5	172	294	212	506	15%	70%	0.57	29	49	2.10	-52
Kindel,Jeff	08	L	25	3	aa	COL	506	40	123	21	1	8	49	36	67	3	3	243	293	333	626	7%	87%	0.53	61	42	3.41	24
	09	L	26	3	aa	COL	463	47	106	23	2	5	49	51	73	6	6	229	305	316	620	10%	84%	0.69	63	66	3.35	29
Kirkland,Kody	08	R	25	5	a/a	DET	376	37	76	11	5	8	37	32	99	8	2	203	265	318	582	8%	74%	0.32	69	126	2.90	5
	09	R	26	5	a/a	ATL	302	30	54	13	2	3	17	19	73	4	6	180	229	262	491	6%	76%	0.27	57	92	1.84	-9
Klosterman,Ryan	08	R	26	6	aa	TOR	318	35	60	11	2	5	29	33	68	8	6	188	265	278	542	9%	78%	0.48	58	97	2.40	11
	09	R	27	6	aa	FLA	359	45	75	17	2	6	30	32	89	10	3	208	274	318	592	8%	75%	0.36	74	111	3.03	12
Koshansky,Joe	08	L	26	3	aa	COL	457	60	113	29	3	21	80	40	116	1	0	248	308	463	771	8%	75%	0.34	134	68	5.07	44
	09	L	27	3	aaa	MIL	455	51	78	17	2	17	57	48	151	5	5	172	251	330	581	9%	67%	0.32	95	76	2.67	-13
Kozma,Peter	09	R	21	6	aa	STL	407	40	77	13	2	4	29	33	65	3	2	189	250	261	511	8%	84%	0.51	48	76	2.19	14
Kratz,Erik	08	R	28	2	a/a	TOR	247	26	49	13	1	13	33	16	59	3	0	200	248	420	668	6%	76%	0.27	133	72	3.49	47
	09	R	29	2	aa	PIT	319	32	69	25	0	7	31	22	66	5	0	216	265	359	624	6%	79%	0.32	103	73	3.32	36
Kroeger,Josh	08	L	26 b	8	aa	CHC	430	52	109	33	2	11	49	30	71	8	4	255	304	417	721	7%	84%	0.43	112	88	4.46	65
	09	L	27	8	aaa	CHW	501	49	114	23	0	16	46	30	87	19	7	228	271	370	641	6%	83%	0.34	90	81	3.39	40
Kroski,Chris	09	L	27	2	aa	CIN	104	12	17	5	1	2	10	13	27	0	1	164	255	286	540	11%	74%	0.47	80	82	2.37	10
Krum,Austin	09	L	24	8	aa	NYY	290	41	64	14	3	2	23	34	67	11	2	220	302	308	610	11%	77%	0.51	61	139	3.43	21
Krynzel,Dave	09	L	28	8	a/a	BAL	394	35	90	11	3	7	32	27	113	16	5	228	278	324	602	6%	71%	0.24	59	111	3.13	-20
Kulbacki,Kellen	09	L	24	8	aa	SD	134	9	23	4	1	0	9	7	19	2	1	168	209	212	421	5%	86%	0.35	32	86	1.43	6
Kunkel,Jeff	09	B	27	2	aa	DET	142	11	26	5	0	3	12	10	29	0	1	181	236	272	508	7%	79%	0.34	59	29	2.06	-12
Lahair,Bryan	08	L	26	3	aa	SEA	316	30	69	22	1	8	40	36	80	1	1	217	297	372	668	10%	75%	0.45	105	44	3.84	18
	09	L	27	8	aa	SEA	457	59	111	24	1	21	70	39	120	0	6	244	303	439	741	8%	74%	0.32	120	34	4.46	19
Lalli,Blake	09	L	26	3	aa	CHC	373	39	101	22	0	5	40	25	48	0	2	271	317	368	684	6%	87%	0.52	71	26	4.18	28
Lamb,Mike	09	L	34	5	aa	NYM	440	30	87	22	1	3	37	14	33	0	0	197	223	274	497	3%	93%	0.44	58	31	2.00	34
Lambo,Andrew	09	L	21	8	aa	LA	492	61	115	35	1	10	53	34	84	3	3	234	284	372	656	7%	83%	0.41	97	64	3.61	44
Lane,Jason	08	R	32	8	aaa	BOS	400	46	75	21	2	12	43	41	81	3	3	187	262	338	600	9%	80%	0.50	97	70	2.93	38
	09	R	33	8	aaa	TOR	411	41	78	31	3	9	30	37	65	3	2	190	256	341	598	8%	84%	0.56	105	76	2.91	62
Langerhans,Ryan	08	L	29	8	aaa	WAS	213	30	53	13	2	2	24	29	57	9	3	248	338	351	689	12%	73%	0.51	75	121	4.45	16
	09	L	30	8	aaa	WAS	205	25	46	13	0	6	29	22	49	5	6	222	299	373	672	10%	76%	0.46	101	65	3.57	27
LaPorta,Matt	08	R	24 a	8	aa	CLE	362	54	92	23	1	19	65	44	69	2	1	254	335	476	812	11%	81%	0.64	137	59	5.80	74
	09	R	25 a	3	aaa	CLE	338	50	87	20	1	13	47	35	50	1	4	258	327	443	770	9%	85%	0.69	117	51	5.06	70

Major League Equivalent Statistics

BATTER	Yr	B	Age	Pos	Lev	Org	ab	r	h	d	t	hr	rbi	bb	k	sb	cs	ba	ob	slg	ops	bb%	ct%	eye	px	sx	rc/g	bpv
Larish,Jeff	08	L	26	3	aaa	DET	384	39	82	17	2	16	51	40	95	0	1	213	288	392	680	10%	75%	0.43	108	41	3.87	21
	09	L	27	3	aaa	DET	211	31	49	11	0	5	21	34	53	2	2	231	338	349	687	14%	75%	0.64	80	52	4.28	9
LaTorre,Tyler	09	L	26	2	aa	SF	181	22	41	8	1	1	19	23	33	1	2	229	316	300	616	11%	82%	0.71	53	65	3.36	14
Lehmann,Daniel	09	R	24	2	aa	MIN	168	10	28	8	0	0	9	10	17	0	1	166	211	211	422	5%	90%	0.58	40	30	1.41	15
Lemon,Marcus	09	L	21	4	aa	TEX	451	46	108	18	4	1	33	34	57	6	5	240	293	305	598	7%	87%	0.60	47	92	3.10	30
Leon,Carlos	09	B	30	6	a/a	PHI	215	20	37	5	1	2	11	20	34	3	2	170	239	225	465	8%	84%	0.57	37	74	1.80	7
Leon,Maxwell	08	B	24	6	a/a	DET	296	31	76	6	3	0	23	37	60	13	8	256	340	295	635	11%	80%	0.62	26	110	3.69	-3
	09	B	25	8	a/a	DET	265	32	56	9	3	7	30	21	46	5	3	213	270	344	614	7%	83%	0.45	79	113	3.10	45
Leone,Justin	08	R	32	85	aa	SF	358	48	71	18	1	11	48	48	98	12	6	197	293	344	637	12%	73%	0.50	94	92	3.43	20
	09	R	33	5	a/a	TEX	210	14	29	10	0	3	22	19	68	3	0	138	208	235	443	8%	68%	0.27	68	54	1.63	-41
Lerud,Steven	08	L	24	2	aa	PIT	146	15	31	7	0	3	16	12	37	1	0	215	273	322	596	7%	75%	0.32	73	46	3.08	-12
	09	L	25	2	aa	PIT	304	25	64	15	0	3	20	29	44	2	1	212	280	291	570	9%	86%	0.66	59	42	2.84	22
Lillibridge,Brent	08	R	25	6	aaa	ATL	355	37	67	15	5	3	31	26	82	19	8	188	244	281	525	7%	77%	0.32	62	158	2.25	20
	09	R	26	6	aaa	CHW	246	29	53	7	2	3	20	25	57	14	1	217	289	295	584	9%	77%	0.44	50	132	3.24	8
Limonta,Johan	08	L	25	38	aa	SEA	360	39	89	27	3	8	45	30	80	2	2	248	306	402	708	8%	78%	0.38	106	76	4.33	37
	09	L	26	8	aa	SEA	438	47	109	27	5	5	43	46	76	6	6	250	321	363	685	10%	83%	0.60	79	94	4.09	43
Linden,Todd	08	B	28	8	a/a	CLE	402	51	96	23	1	13	50	55	130	4	2	239	330	398	728	12%	68%	0.42	103	61	4.75	-2
	09	B	29	8	aaa	NYY	237	35	61	14	3	6	34	22	67	4	0	258	319	414	733	8%	72%	0.32	100	128	4.90	24
Lindsey,John	08	R	32	30	aa	LA	481	58	116	28	1	19	68	45	80	0	0	240	305	419	724	9%	83%	0.56	113	32	4.54	53
	09	R	33	3	aa	FLA	443	40	87	18	1	14	62	30	124	1	2	196	246	332	578	6%	72%	0.24	85	41	2.68	-17
Lis,Erik	08	L	25	083	aa	MIN	405	39	96	32	2	9	41	21	84	1	1	237	275	389	664	5%	79%	0.25	106	58	3.67	31
	09	L	26	0	aa	MIN	459	55	113	26	1	13	58	36	98	1	1	246	300	393	693	7%	79%	0.36	97	49	4.17	23
Lisson,Mario	08	R	24	56	aa	KC	476	47	97	23	2	11	54	28	91	26	7	204	248	327	574	6%	81%	0.31	81	120	2.73	37
	09	R	25	6	aa	KC	475	39	92	25	0	9	44	24	95	8	8	194	233	307	540	5%	80%	0.26	78	64	2.23	14
Loadenthal,Carl	08	L	27	8	a/a	ATL	306	26	67	5	0	1	12	21	66	17	8	219	270	244	513	6%	78%	0.32	18	85	2.25	-32
	09	L	28	8	aa	NYM	188	18	35	5	1	1	13	23	30	7	8	187	274	235	508	11%	84%	0.75	33	88	2.00	12
Lobaton,Jose	08	B	24	2	aa	SD	294	29	65	17	0	7	37	32	69	1	1	220	297	347	644	10%	76%	0.47	86	35	3.61	7
	09	B	25	2	aa	TAM	217	24	48	12	0	6	16	22	52	0	0	221	293	354	647	9%	76%	0.42	88	26	3.65	3
Locke,Andrew	09	R	27	8	aa	HOU	503	58	140	26	2	15	77	33	72	2	2	278	323	424	747	6%	86%	0.46	94	53	4.97	48
Lopez,Jesus	09	R	22	6	aa	SD	259	22	50	11	1	1	18	18	29	2	0	193	245	255	500	6%	89%	0.62	47	70	2.15	29
Lopez,Pedro	08	R	24	64	aaa	TOR	339	34	73	12	1	2	24	28	63	4	1	215	275	272	547	8%	82%	0.45	41	73	2.64	-2
	09	R	25	4	aa	PIT	332	31	77	8	1	2	23	16	34	1	6	232	267	277	545	5%	90%	0.47	31	47	2.38	9
Lough,David	09	L	24 a	8	aa	KC	236	32	70	13	1	7	25	10	23	10	5	295	323	444	767	4%	90%	0.42	96	101	5.07	78
Lowrance,Marvin	08	L	24	8	aa	WAS	154	21	36	12	0	6	18	15	33	1	0	237	306	424	730	9%	78%	0.46	124	51	4.63	48
	09	L	25	8	aa	WAS	361	40	77	20	2	12	39	35	83	1	2	214	283	380	663	9%	77%	0.42	105	59	3.64	30
Lubanski,Chris	08	L	24	8	aa	KC	393	43	88	21	6	12	45	32	109	4	1	224	283	396	680	8%	72%	0.30	106	127	3.90	29
	09	L	24	8	aa	KC	132	15	26	7	1	1	12	13	21	5	1	196	271	284	554	9%	84%	0.65	63	114	2.73	42
Lucas,Edward	08	R	26	5	aa	KC	317	36	76	9	3	3	24	29	55	11	8	241	305	313	619	8%	83%	0.53	47	107	3.25	19
	09	R	27	5	aa	KC	363	44	86	20	1	6	42	40	67	13	4	236	311	347	658	10%	82%	0.59	77	93	3.91	38
Lucroy,Jonathan	09	R	23 a	2	aa	MIL	419	49	99	28	1	8	53	67	57	1	1	236	341	365	706	14%	86%	1.17	91	42	4.60	60
Lucy,Donny	09	R	27	2	a/a	CHW	222	16	41	7	0	2	10	10	60	2	2	182	217	239	457	4%	73%	0.17	41	51	1.65	-49
Luna,Hector	08	R	29	5	aaa	TOR	429	54	101	21	1	10	34	23	80	5	2	236	275	357	632	5%	81%	0.29	80	82	3.39	27
	09	R	30 b	5	aa	LA	313	44	87	15	3	13	46	22	55	3	2	278	324	464	788	6%	83%	0.39	112	87	5.43	61
Machado,Andy	08	B	28	5	aa	NYM	252	23	45	12	1	4	21	32	56	3	0	179	270	275	545	11%	78%	0.57	66	70	2.62	10
	09	B	29	6	aa	CHC	153	12	22	5	1	0	6	20	43	7	1	144	244	190	434	12%	72%	0.47	36	110	1.75	-26
Macias,Drew	08	L	26	8	aa	SD	504	74	119	22	3	8	53	66	78	14	7	237	325	341	666	12%	85%	0.85	69	103	4.01	50
	09	L	27	8	aa	SD	297	31	53	14	0	4	20	29	51	4	4	180	252	263	515	9%	83%	0.56	60	62	2.17	18
Macri,Matt	08	R	26	64	aaa	MIN	313	27	66	20	3	8	37	19	79	2	2	212	257	373	631	6%	75%	0.24	106	79	3.17	21
	09	R	27	3	aaa	MIN	365	44	67	21	2	8	32	25	82	4	5	182	235	316	551	6%	77%	0.31	89	90	2.30	23
Maddox,Marc	08	R	25	4	aa	KC	453	55	115	29	0	3	24	39	64	12	12	253	313	336	649	8%	86%	0.62	67	71	3.54	36
	09	R	26	4	aa	KC	149	15	20	6	0	3	12	15	18	3	2	136	214	228	442	9%	88%	0.80	61	73	1.55	42
Mahar,Kevin	09	R	28	8	aa	PHI	407	43	104	15	1	10	40	18	77	5	3	255	287	368	655	4%	81%	0.24	71	69	3.69	12
Majewski,Dustin	08	L	27	8	aa	TEX	430	50	98	26	3	7	50	57	70	5	6	228	318	352	670	12%	84%	0.81	85	71	3.87	50
	09	L	28	8	aa	TEX	340	33	72	17	2	2	24	35	42	2	3	212	286	287	573	9%	88%	0.84	56	61	2.84	35
Majewski,Val	08	L	27 b	8	aa	HOU	160	18	37	8	1	5	16	13	20	1	4	231	287	394	681	7%	88%	0.63	102	64	3.57	67
	09	L	28	8	aa	LAA	131	14	26	4	1	3	14	11	22	4	1	195	259	296	555	8%	84%	0.53	61	100	2.64	31
Malec,Chris	08	B	26	53	aa	NYY	405	57	104	24	2	5	45	58	59	0	2	257	350	359	709	13%	86%	0.99	74	48	4.67	43
	09	B	27	3	a/a	NYY	492	43	116	21	1	8	59	41	78	1	1	236	295	331	626	8%	84%	0.53	64	37	3.46	17
Malo,Jonathan	08	R	25	45	aa	NYM	276	39	61	12	1	3	24	23	47	9	3	221	280	303	583	8%	83%	0.48	58	111	2.99	29
	09	R	26	4	aa	NYM	366	31	67	8	2	1	24	27	55	8	4	182	239	221	460	7%	85%	0.49	27	91	1.77	4
Mangini,Matthew	08	L	23	5	aa	SEA	237	18	42	4	0	2	20	10	55	0	1	177	211	219	430	4%	77%	0.18	28	36	1.47	-50
	09	L	24	5	aa	SEA	422	42	103	17	3	10	59	34	89	9	2	244	301	367	668	8%	79%	0.39	77	97	3.96	24
Manzella,Thomas	08	R	25	6	aa	HOU	452	32	95	21	4	3	35	24	60	3	9	210	249	291	540	5%	87%	0.39	58	66	2.22	25
	09	R	26	6	aa	HOU	530	48	124	26	4	6	40	29	85	8	4	234	273	333	607	5%	84%	0.34	68	91	3.13	30
Marrero,Christian	09	L	23 a	3	aa	CHW	229	25	64	14	1	11	34	16	45	1	1	278	324	488	812	6%	80%	0.35	130	48	5.72	55
Marson,Lou	08	R	22	2	aa	PHI	322	41	89	16	0	4	34	50	53	2	4	276	374	363	737	13%	84%	0.94	63	36	5.12	24
	09	R	23	2	aaa	CLE	314	33	77	16	1	2	26	33	50	3	1	247	319	321	640	10%	84%	0.67	57	64	3.77	22
Marte,Andy	09	R	26 a	5	aaa	CLE	300	38	84	21	1	14	52	18	45	2	0	279	319	495	814	6%	85%	0.40	137	60	5.80	81
Martin,Dustin	08	L	25	8	aa	MIN	510	55	128	30	6	8	58	37	114	18	12	250	302	376	678	7%	78%	0.33	85	123	3.80	32
	09	L	25	8	aaa	MIN	422	47	91	14	4	4	42	29	85	21	8	216	267	294	561	6%	80%	0.34	51	133	2.65	15
Martinez,Fernando	08	L	20	8	aa	NYM	352	43	96	19	3	6	39	24	58	5	2	271	318	397	715	6%	83%	0.42	83	100	4.58	45
	09	L	21 a	8	aa	NYM	176	20	46	14	1	6	24	9	26	2	1	263	300	462	763	5%	85%	0.35	132	75	4.88	81
Martinez,Gabriel	08	L	25	038	aa	TAM	511	54	118	24	0	16	72	39	95	0	0	232	286	373	659	7%	81%	0.41	91	24	3.73	22
	09	L	26	3	aa	LA	260	25	65	13	0	7	35	24	70	0	2	251	314	386	700	8%	73%	0.34	88	20	4.25	-12
Martinez,Michael	09	B	27	4	aa	WAS	188	18	36	6	2	1	6	16	33	0	3	191	256	259	514	8%	82%	0.49	46	75	2.11	6
Martinez-Esteve,E	08	R	25	80	aa	SF	396	35	103	13	0	5	35	44	34	2	1	261	335	330	665	10%	91%	1.30	48	34	4.14	36
	09	R	26 b	8	aa	SF	436	47	109	29	3	6	52	38	58	2	3	251	311	367	678	8%	87%	0.65	83	63	4.03	51
Mastroianni,Darin	09	R	24	8	aa	TOR	247	36	62	10	2	1	23	36	47	36	8	253	349	319	668	13%	81%	0.78	47	150	4.55	35
Mateo,Henry	09	B	33	4	aaa	TAM	307	31	66	14	3	3	17	28	66	9	5	216	282	302	583	8%	79%	0.43	59	108	2.90	13
Mather,Joe	08	R	26 b	8	aa	STL	211	33	51	11	1	11	30	23	30	6	2	240	315	458	772	10%	86%	0.76	131	95	5.08	97
	09	R	27	8	aa	STL	194	14	28	7	1	3	17	10	32	5	4	144	185	232	417	5%	83%	0.31	58	92	1.26	20

Major League Equivalent Statistics

BATTER	Yr	B	Age	Pos	Lev	Org	ab	r	h	d	t	hr	rbi	bb	k	sb	cs	ba	ob	slg	ops	bb%	ct%	eye	px	sx	rc/g	bpv
Mathews,Aaron	08	R	26	8	aa	TOR	297	35	74	11	2	5	38	17	43	2	4	248	290	344	633	6%	85%	0.40	62	73	3.36	26
	09	R	27	8	aaa	TOR	518	45	112	17	4	5	52	25	43	3	2	215	252	294	545	5%	92%	0.58	52	73	2.48	41
Matranga,Dave	08	R	32	45	aa	KC	201	24	43	7	3	4	23	16	52	2	3	216	274	338	612	7%	74%	0.31	74	110	3.05	6
	09	R	33	5	aa	FLA	232	26	49	10	2	5	21	37	71	3	1	213	320	337	657	14%	70%	0.52	79	84	3.91	-4
Maxwell,Justin	08	R	25 a	8	aa	WAS	146	27	28	5	2	5	21	23	23	10	5	191	301	348	649	14%	84%	1.01	92	160	3.50	88
	09	R	26	8	aaa	WAS	384	55	81	8	4	10	34	43	120	28	8	211	290	333	623	10%	69%	0.36	70	157	3.40	0
May,Lucas	08	R	24	2	aa	LA	392	41	78	24	1	11	41	25	94	5	1	200	249	348	596	6%	76%	0.27	98	81	2.90	21
	09	R	25	2	aa	LA	235	26	63	15	1	5	26	26	54	2	1	270	342	404	747	10%	77%	0.48	93	60	5.14	22
Mayberry,John	08	R	25 a	8	aa	TEX	519	48	118	33	5	15	53	25	84	8	4	228	263	398	661	5%	84%	0.30	110	98	3.50	63
	09	R	26	8	aaa	PHI	316	36	71	18	1	11	35	26	86	5	2	223	283	393	675	8%	73%	0.31	108	76	3.81	17
Maybin,Cameron	08	R	22	8	aa	FLA	390	61	99	14	7	11	41	54	109	18	8	254	344	412	756	12%	72%	0.49	92	170	5.11	39
	09	R	22 a	8	aa	FLA	298	39	89	17	7	3	34	35	54	7	2	299	372	433	805	11%	82%	0.65	87	160	6.28	68
Mayora,Daniel	09	R	24	4	aa	COL	441	48	114	21	1	6	38	31	65	16	9	259	307	350	658	7%	85%	0.48	65	87	3.76	34
Mayorson,Manuel	08	R	26 a	6	aa	FLA	424	42	113	30	1	2	39	27	20	17	17	266	310	355	665	6%	95%	1.35	72	80	3.53	76
	09	R	27	4	a/a	TOR	399	36	82	12	2	1	20	14	27	11	5	205	232	251	483	3%	93%	0.51	34	103	1.92	40
Maysonet,Edwin	08	R	27	64	aa	HOU	406	40	87	18	1	5	23	30	58	3	4	215	270	299	569	7%	86%	0.53	60	57	2.71	24
	09	R	28	4	aa	HOU	187	14	34	9	0	1	10	18	33	2	0	183	255	245	500	9%	82%	0.54	50	50	2.19	3
Maza,Luis	08	R	28	48	aa	LA	238	36	71	9	3	2	20	23	28	1	2	299	361	381	742	9%	88%	0.81	54	87	5.20	41
	09	R	29	4	aa	LA	327	40	77	15	2	3	33	13	42	0	1	234	263	321	584	4%	87%	0.31	61	66	2.86	27
Mc Fall,Brian	08	R	25	8	aa	KC	348	35	76	15	2	14	51	32	89	6	7	218	283	397	680	8%	75%	0.36	108	73	3.63	25
	09	R	26	3	aa	KC	204	22	43	12	0	5	27	14	46	2	1	212	263	341	604	6%	78%	0.31	89	56	3.03	13
McAnulty,Paul	08	L	28 b	8	aa	SD	181	26	49	11	1	9	39	27	39	0	0	269	363	487	851	13%	79%	0.69	134	44	6.67	62
	09	L	29	3	a/a	COL	381	26	69	18	1	10	36	33	76	0	1	180	245	310	554	8%	80%	0.43	84	26	2.50	13
McBride,Matt	09	R	24 a	8	aa	CLE	361	42	81	27	0	11	55	16	41	1	1	223	257	386	643	4%	89%	0.40	111	51	3.32	70
McBryde,Mike	09	R	25	8	aa	SF	376	58	100	21	3	4	36	15	56	18	12	266	294	368	662	4%	85%	0.27	72	135	3.52	48
McConnell,Chris	09	R	24	6	aa	KC	169	20	33	7	1	0	9	11	31	5	6	197	245	249	495	6%	82%	0.35	41	109	1.82	7
McCoy,Mike	08	R	28	4	a/a	COL	292	35	72	11	2	4	27	21	33	8	5	247	296	333	629	7%	89%	0.62	57	99	3.42	45
	09	R	28 b	6	aa	COL	462	74	118	23	4	2	38	57	61	29	6	255	337	331	669	11%	87%	0.93	56	138	4.34	57
McCutchen,Andrew	08	R	22 a	8	aa	PIT	512	66	138	26	2	7	44	59	73	30	21	270	345	371	716	10%	86%	0.80	70	98	4.39	51
	09	R	23 a	8	aa	PIT	201	34	56	10	5	3	17	14	19	8	2	279	326	423	748	7%	91%	0.74	89	189	5.09	105
McDonald,Darnell	08	R	30	8	aaa	MIN	369	38	78	20	3	8	41	25	83	14	3	212	262	343	605	6%	78%	0.30	86	121	3.11	30
	09	R	31	8	aaa	CIN	280	31	70	18	4	8	29	12	58	6	3	249	280	425	705	4%	79%	0.21	112	135	4.06	58
Melillo,Kevin	08	L	26	45	a/a	TOR	372	33	83	17	3	12	41	36	87	3	1	223	291	381	672	9%	77%	0.41	98	73	3.87	26
	09	L	27	3	aa	MIL	385	44	77	18	2	7	39	47	64	3	3	201	288	313	601	11%	83%	0.73	74	68	3.10	37
Mercado,Orlando	08	R	24	2	aa	ARI	194	19	41	6	0	2	19	33	23	0	2	212	328	273	600	15%	88%	1.42	42	22	3.24	23
	09	R	25	2	aa	ARI	283	26	76	15	1	2	34	35	23	0	0	268	348	349	697	11%	92%	1.51	62	30	4.62	49
Mercedes,Victor	08	B	29	4	aa	CHW	416	45	92	23	2	11	46	13	79	9	9	221	245	366	611	3%	81%	0.16	95	92	2.72	35
	09	B	30	4	aa	LA	128	4	14	3	1	0	6	6	25	3	3	113	152	153	305	4%	81%	0.24	29	85	0.66	-17
Merchan,Jesus	08	R	28	6	aa	ARI	436	39	128	20	5	4	55	14	40	2	2	293	316	384	700	3%	91%	0.36	62	73	4.41	43
	09	R	28	4	a/a	CLE	141	14	35	5	1	0	9	8	20	1	0	250	290	300	589	5%	85%	0.39	39	71	3.12	7
Mertins,Kurt	09	R	23	4	aa	KC	495	49	122	23	6	1	44	32	83	9	12	245	292	321	612	6%	83%	0.39	54	103	3.06	22
Metcalf,Travis	08	R	26	5	aa	TEX	265	26	55	12	1	4	27	13	49	0	1	208	245	302	547	5%	82%	0.26	65	51	2.44	4
	09	R	27	5	aa	TEX	440	35	77	15	2	8	40	28	87	3	1	176	225	274	499	6%	80%	0.32	63	67	2.02	6
Meyer,Drew	08	L	27	458	aa	TEX	284	30	58	8	4	2	17	25	39	7	2	203	268	276	543	8%	86%	0.65	46	126	2.59	38
	09	L	28	4	aa	HOU	443	48	100	23	1	4	34	33	66	2	0	226	281	306	587	7%	85%	0.51	60	61	3.03	23
Milledge,Lastings	09	R	24	8	a/a	PIT	139	14	36	11	0	0	9	9	22	8	3	256	299	332	631	6%	84%	0.39	67	89	3.51	31
Miller,Jai	08	R	24	8	aa	FLA	434	54	102	20	4	15	45	45	120	16	7	235	307	400	707	9%	72%	0.37	100	121	4.25	27
	09	R	25	8	aa	FLA	343	47	88	22	2	12	44	34	103	5	3	257	324	442	766	9%	70%	0.33	118	88	5.10	21
Miller,Matthew	08	R	26 a	8	aa	COL	531	67	154	30	0	8	72	39	44	4	3	290	339	389	729	7%	92%	0.91	72	52	4.92	56
	09	R	27 b	8	aa	COL	523	63	145	34	6	7	75	38	66	3	1	278	327	410	736	7%	87%	0.57	90	98	4.94	66
Mills,Beau	09	L	23	3	aa	CLE	516	53	128	31	1	12	74	29	90	1	2	249	289	382	671	5%	83%	0.33	91	42	3.84	28
Milner,Kenneth	09	R	25	8	a/a	PHI	265	22	53	10	1	3	22	19	69	3	8	199	252	277	528	7%	74%	0.27	54	60	2.04	-28
Miranda,Juan	08	L	25	30	aaa	NYY	356	34	90	19	0	10	44	45	76	2	1	253	337	393	731	11%	79%	0.60	92	32	4.89	23
	09	L	26	3	aaa	NYY	438	64	112	27	1	17	72	48	104	1	0	256	329	441	771	10%	76%	0.46	118	54	5.32	37
Mitchell,Lee	08	R	26	5	aa	FLA	324	28	63	19	2	5	40	52	84	3	3	196	306	310	616	14%	74%	0.62	80	62	3.33	8
	09	R	27	5	aa	FLA	431	41	83	21	3	9	49	58	160	1	0	192	287	315	603	12%	63%	0.36	80	66	3.18	-39
Mitchell,Russell	08	R	24	53	aa	LA	485	50	111	20	2	13	58	35	80	6	5	228	281	356	636	7%	84%	0.44	80	70	3.37	35
	09	R	25	3	aa	LA	456	52	96	26	2	11	52	31	78	3	1	211	260	345	606	6%	83%	0.39	90	77	3.05	41
Moeller,Chad	09	R	35	2	aaa	BAL	118	5	20	5	0	0	8	3	22	0	1	166	189	209	398	3%	81%	0.15	38	29	1.19	-29
Molina,Felix	08	L	25	46	a/a	MIN	302	23	62	15	2	2	27	15	48	4	8	205	243	286	529	5%	84%	0.31	59	73	2.05	17
	09	L	26	4	aa	HOU	209	19	40	6	1	4	17	15	28	2	2	194	247	286	533	7%	86%	0.52	58	68	2.31	28
Molina,Gustavo	08	R	27	2	aa	NYM	228	17	39	6	0	6	21	12	51	0	0	169	211	266	477	5%	78%	0.23	59	21	1.81	-24
	09	R	28	2	aaa	WAS	211	14	36	13	0	2	18	5	23	0	1	171	188	256	444	2%	89%	0.19	66	39	1.47	27
Montero,Jesus	09	R	20 a	2	aa	NYY	167	19	55	11	0	9	34	14	19	0	0	327	378	560	937	8%	89%	0.72	143	10	8.31	89
Montz,Luke	08	R	25	2	a/a	WAS	388	38	86	19	1	11	55	33	73	1	2	223	284	363	647	8%	81%	0.45	90	41	3.52	26
	09	R	26	2	a/a	WAS	320	27	50	13	0	7	29	38	64	1	4	155	244	265	509	11%	80%	0.59	71	30	2.07	9
Monzon,Erick	08	R	27	6	aa	SEA	148	12	25	3	1	2	6	12	41	4	0	168	230	236	466	7%	72%	0.29	41	98	1.90	-32
	09	R	28	4	aa	SEA	164	11	31	4	0	4	12	11	49	4	3	187	237	274	511	6%	70%	0.22	53	52	2.06	-47
Mooney,Michael	08	R	25	8	aa	SF	138	12	24	7	0	6	18	3	32	3	2	170	187	341	527	2%	77%	0.09	105	78	1.87	21
	09	R	26	8	aa	SF	340	33	75	15	5	5	38	17	72	9	6	219	255	330	586	5%	79%	0.23	71	132	2.70	23
Moore,Adam	08	R	24	2	aa	SEA	428	47	118	31	1	11	56	34	70	0	1	276	329	426	755	7%	84%	0.48	104	33	5.12	44
	09	R	25	2	aa	SEA	435	46	108	21	0	9	47	37	72	1	1	249	307	361	668	8%	83%	0.51	76	35	3.96	22
Moore,Scott	08	L	25	5	aaa	BAL	287	33	61	17	1	6	36	18	56	3	0	214	261	341	602	6%	80%	0.32	87	82	3.07	30
	09	L	26 a	5	aaa	BAL	123	16	28	7	0	7	18	7	20	1	0	229	268	443	712	5%	84%	0.33	130	54	4.10	67
Morales,Jose	08	B	26	2	aaa	MIN	197	14	52	6	1	3	12	6	27	0	1	262	283	344	627	3%	86%	0.21	52	39	3.36	7
	09	B	27	2	aaa	MIN	211	24	60	11	1	2	21	21	26	1	3	283	349	371	719	9%	88%	0.81	64	52	4.70	37
Moreland,Mitchell	09	L	24 a	8	aa	TEX	301	40	86	17	3	7	46	18	36	1	1	287	328	431	758	6%	88%	0.50	94	81	5.18	64
Moresi,Nicholas	09	R	25	8	aa	HOU	183	15	32	9	1	6	16	6	42	1	0	173	198	325	524	3%	77%	0.14	95	72	2.06	15
Morrison,Logan	09	L	22 a	3	aa	FLA	278	42	72	17	2	7	41	58	43	8	4	259	387	410	797	17%	85%	1.35	99	93	6.07	82
Morse,Mike	09	R	28	5	a/a	WAS	425	47	116	23	2	13	68	28	73	2	1	273	318	424	741	6%	83%	0.38	97	57	4.89	40
Moses,Matthew	08	L	24	8	aa	MIN	387	34	78	19	2	2	28	27	61	6	5	203	255	276	531	7%	84%	0.45	55	81	2.32	20
	09	L	25	8	aa	MIN	255	29	50	9	1	6	36	14	49	4	5	196	239	305	544	5%	81%	0.29	68	85	2.24	16

Major League Equivalent Statistics

BATTER	Yr	B	Age	Pos	Lev	Org	ab	r	h	d	t	hr	rbi	bb	k	sb	cs	ba	ob	slg	ops	bb%	ct%	eye	px	sx	rc/g	bpv
Mota,Jonathan	09	R	22	6	aa	CHC	320	27	71	15	1	2	19	29	51	2	7	222	287	294	580	8%	84%	0.57	54	46	2.72	12
Mount,Ryan	09	L	23	4	aa	LAA	305	31	72	16	0	3	27	18	58	5	8	235	276	315	591	5%	81%	0.30	60	59	2.75	3
Munson,Eric	09	L	32	2	aa	OAK	351	31	66	16	1	8	43	33	59	0	1	189	259	305	564	9%	83%	0.56	77	35	2.65	24
Murillo,Agustin	09	R	27	5	aa	ARI	233	28	55	14	1	2	24	23	30	3	1	236	305	328	634	9%	87%	0.78	70	75	3.61	47
Murphy,Steven	08	L	24 a	8	aa	TEX	508	62	115	31	7	15	64	27	100	12	5	227	266	404	670	5%	80%	0.27	112	140	3.60	65
	09	L	25	8	aa	TEX	359	42	64	16	3	9	39	22	80	3	2	178	225	317	542	6%	78%	0.27	87	104	2.28	25
Murphy,Tommy	08	B	29	8	a/a	FLA	453	53	101	18	3	3	23	34	91	27	11	222	276	296	572	7%	80%	0.37	52	126	2.78	15
	09	B	30	8	aa	KC	272	23	48	11	1	2	9	21	55	11	6	175	235	241	475	7%	80%	0.38	48	98	1.82	3
Murton,Matt	08	R	27 b	8	aa	OAK	321	32	73	19	2	1	20	29	32	5	4	227	291	306	596	8%	90%	0.89	61	77	3.07	51
	09	R	28 b	8	aa	COL	373	54	104	23	1	10	59	29	44	9	2	277	329	425	754	7%	88%	0.65	99	92	5.21	75
Myrow,Brian	08	L	32	3	aa	SD	328	44	77	16	1	9	43	59	78	0	1	233	350	365	715	15%	76%	0.76	86	38	4.74	18
	09	L	33	8	a/a	PIT	365	43	88	19	1	10	43	44	66	3	2	240	322	380	702	11%	82%	0.67	91	54	4.39	40
Nanita,Ricardo	08	L	27	8	aa	CHW	412	42	101	19	1	9	42	32	57	12	9	245	298	360	659	7%	86%	0.56	76	74	3.60	45
	09	L	28 b	8	aa	WAS	126	14	31	9	1	4	15	7	18	1	2	244	284	412	696	5%	86%	0.39	111	76	3.87	67
Natale,Jeff	08	R	26 b	3	a/a	BOS	111	12	26	4	1	3	11	13	11	2	1	232	312	356	668	10%	90%	1.18	75	80	3.95	68
	09	R	27	4	aaa	BOS	170	21	45	10	1	3	17	28	28	0	1	265	368	381	750	14%	84%	1.00	81	46	5.31	43
Nava,Daniel	09	B	27 b	8	aa	BOS	118	19	39	10	1	3	17	19	11	0	0	327	422	499	921	14%	91%	1.78	119	55	8.67	105
Navarro,Oswaldo	08	R	24	6	aa	SEA	357	36	80	18	1	1	24	25	64	2	4	223	274	288	562	7%	82%	0.39	52	58	2.64	3
	09	R	25	6	aa	SEA	349	31	79	12	1	1	21	36	76	7	3	226	299	272	571	9%	78%	0.48	36	72	2.94	-16
Navarro,Yamaico	09	R	22	6	aa	BOS	135	13	24	7	1	2	9	12	23	4	1	180	247	292	539	8%	83%	0.53	76	106	2.45	44
Negron,Miguel	08	L	26	8	aa	CHW	479	61	124	15	3	6	48	54	59	21	16	259	335	342	677	10%	88%	0.92	53	98	3.97	45
	09	L	27	8	aaa	CHW	384	33	90	13	2	4	32	22	63	12	13	234	275	305	580	5%	84%	0.34	48	83	2.61	10
Negrych,James	09	L	25 a	4	aa	PIT	323	40	78	16	1	2	24	35	30	7	1	241	314	315	629	10%	91%	1.14	57	88	3.69	56
Nelson,Brad	08	L	26 a	3	aaa	MIL	475	56	111	30	1	13	56	55	66	9	9	234	314	384	698	10%	86%	0.84	101	66	4.07	68
	09	L	27	0	aa	SEA	275	29	57	7	1	12	37	26	58	0	0	207	275	371	647	9%	79%	0.45	94	34	3.50	21
Nelson,Chris	08	R	23	6	aa	COL	283	26	59	16	1	2	29	25	47	4	1	208	271	291	562	8%	83%	0.52	63	76	2.75	25
	09	R	24 a	6	aa	COL	107	16	27	5	2	4	13	10	17	4	2	251	313	440	752	8%	84%	0.58	111	152	4.75	91
Nelson,Kevin	09	R	28	2	a/a	PHI	170	16	35	7	1	7	20	17	34	0	1	207	278	383	661	9%	80%	0.49	105	42	3.57	37
Newhan,David	08	L	35	84	aa	HOU	198	25	45	10	1	6	23	9	29	5	3	228	259	378	637	4%	85%	0.29	96	101	3.23	58
	09	L	36	4	aaa	PHI	356	31	77	17	2	5	35	24	74	3	2	217	266	318	584	6%	79%	0.32	69	66	2.87	6
Nivar,Ramon	09	R	30 b	4	aa	LA	171	22	40	13	2	3	15	3	20	10	6	231	247	372	619	2%	88%	0.17	99	156	2.75	86
Nowak,Chris	08	R	26 a	5	a/a	TAM	515	68	129	31	3	12	63	49	81	5	7	250	315	392	707	9%	84%	0.60	95	73	4.28	54
	09	R	27	5	a/a	TAM	437	40	99	20	2	5	49	33	90	6	2	227	282	314	595	7%	79%	0.37	61	81	3.11	7
Nowicki,Joseph	09	L	27	8	aa	BAL	184	18	37	7	0	6	23	12	54	2	2	200	249	330	579	6%	70%	0.22	82	53	2.65	-23
Nunez,Abraham	08	B	33	54	aa	NYM	323	28	51	4	0	3	20	39	53	6	1	158	249	195	444	11%	84%	0.74	24	69	1.75	-2
	09	B	34	6	aa	ARI	253	20	51	7	2	2	23	35	38	3	3	202	298	262	560	12%	85%	0.93	40	63	2.77	18
Nunez,Eduardo	09	R	22	6	aa	NYY	497	68	156	25	1	9	54	21	61	19	7	314	342	423	764	4%	88%	0.34	74	96	5.42	49
Ochoa,Ivan	08	R	26	64	aa	SF	292	45	82	10	3	5	26	28	57	17	11	280	343	383	727	9%	80%	0.49	65	130	4.54	32
	09	R	27 b	6	aaa	BOS	128	23	28	4	2	2	7	18	23	8	0	216	314	316	630	13%	82%	0.81	60	170	3.96	55
Oeltjen,Trent	08	L	26 a	8	aa	ARI	442	60	127	25	9	5	48	20	59	12	8	287	318	419	737	4%	87%	0.34	86	161	4.68	75
	09	L	27 b	8	aa	ARI	442	60	120	26	13	8	49	24	88	17	8	271	308	443	751	5%	80%	0.27	106	209	4.72	80
Olmedo,Ray	08	B	27	6	aaa	WAS	353	29	73	13	2	3	24	14	38	8	12	207	238	275	513	4%	89%	0.38	48	83	1.89	30
	09	B	28	5	aaa	TAM	412	31	84	11	2	4	36	16	73	6	7	203	232	269	502	4%	82%	0.22	43	73	1.94	-5
Ori,Mark	09	L	26	3	aa	HOU	423	38	92	24	0	1	32	29	73	0	1	218	268	280	548	6%	83%	0.40	53	30	2.58	-3
Orr,Pete	08	L	29 b	4	aaa	WAS	284	34	60	13	7	2	24	15	56	14	4	212	251	324	575	5%	80%	0.26	71	205	2.72	52
	09	L	30	5	aaa	WAS	412	37	79	10	3	6	37	20	75	13	8	192	228	276	505	5%	82%	0.26	52	115	1.98	14
Ortiz,Wilberto	08	R	24	6	aa	LAA	254	22	61	11	0	2	20	13	33	3	1	239	276	305	580	5%	87%	0.39	50	54	2.94	16
	09	R	25	5	aa	LAA	435	37	103	14	1	0	36	30	44	8	9	236	285	274	559	6%	90%	0.68	31	63	2.61	18
Ortiz,Yancarlos	09	B	25	6	aa	MIN	327	26	63	6	2	0	22	30	66	2	3	193	261	221	482	8%	80%	0.46	20	64	1.96	-26
Ortmeier,Dan	09	B	28	3	aa	COL	431	43	106	14	4	5	53	36	81	8	5	245	303	331	634	8%	81%	0.45	55	92	3.51	14
Osuna,Renny	09	R	24	6	aa	TEX	252	28	54	6	1	0	14	17	28	0	5	213	264	244	508	6%	89%	0.61	24	55	2.04	6
Otness,John	08	R	27	2	aa	BOS	251	25	56	14	1	1	24	19	28	0	3	222	277	294	571	7%	89%	0.68	56	47	2.71	31
	09	R	28	2	a/a	BOS	118	9	26	9	0	1	12	11	18	0	0	224	292	321	613	9%	85%	0.63	78	17	3.32	25
Owens,Jerry	08	L	28	8	aaa	CHW	351	31	81	9	0	1	17	31	54	23	13	231	292	264	557	8%	84%	0.56	27	85	2.64	3
	09	L	29	8	a/a	SEA	397	55	99	8	5	2	28	34	51	17	9	250	310	310	620	8%	87%	0.67	36	139	3.40	37
Ozuna,Pablo	09	R	35	4	aaa	PHI	187	18	43	12	1	0	11	7	25	6	2	232	259	305	563	4%	87%	0.28	60	102	2.71	35
Pacheco,Jonel	08	R	26	8	aa	PIT	416	52	104	16	0	9	41	33	76	9	4	250	305	354	659	7%	82%	0.44	68	74	3.85	20
	09	R	27	8	aa	PIT	447	46	106	24	1	10	47	21	83	11	13	237	271	362	633	5%	82%	0.26	84	76	3.04	27
Padilla,Jorge	08	R	29	8	a/a	WAS	388	45	94	12	1	3	28	30	50	10	11	242	296	304	600	7%	87%	0.60	43	77	2.95	22
	09	R	30	8	aaa	WAS	311	43	91	14	2	3	15	18	32	10	10	292	331	374	705	5%	90%	0.56	59	96	4.20	48
Padron,Raul	09	L	25	2	aa	OAK	152	10	32	8	0	1	13	8	24	0	0	210	252	278	530	5%	84%	0.35	53	20	2.38	-3
Pagnozzi,Matt	08	R	26	2	aa	STL	221	18	42	9	0	2	15	13	38	2	1	191	237	259	496	6%	83%	0.34	51	53	2.04	0
	09	R	27	2	aa	STL	253	15	45	6	0	4	23	18	64	0	1	178	234	244	478	7%	75%	0.29	42	18	1.87	-47
Paniagua,Salvador	08	R	25	2	aa	NYM	113	13	24	6	0	6	15	3	33	1	0	208	227	408	635	2%	71%	0.09	121	60	3.06	5
	09	R	26	2	aa	NYM	143	6	25	6	0	2	11	10	47	0	0	174	228	251	479	7%	67%	0.22	54	4	1.90	-71
Parejo,Freddy	08	R	24	8	aa	MIL	334	30	78	10	2	2	25	7	49	10	5	235	250	293	544	2%	85%	0.14	40	103	2.42	11
	09	R	25	8	a/a	MIL	300	24	60	12	1	2	20	13	49	2	4	198	233	266	498	4%	84%	0.27	50	60	1.94	3
Parker,Logan	09	L	25	3	aa	CIN	392	29	75	16	3	6	39	43	88	4	7	192	272	290	562	10%	77%	0.49	65	66	2.57	3
Parra,Gerardo	08	L	21 a	8	aa	ARI	265	30	71	13	6	4	28	20	28	14	10	267	319	408	727	7%	90%	0.73	88	164	4.27	94
	09	L	22 a	8	aa	ARI	108	19	37	3	1	3	10	19	11	6	5	343	441	472	913	15%	90%	1.73	76	102	7.96	83
Parraz,Jordan	09	R	25 a	8	aa	KC	273	32	84	22	2	5	36	26	31	3	12	309	369	457	826	9%	89%	0.83	105	62	5.61	76
Pascucci,Val	08	R	30	83	a/a	NYM	478	54	102	20	0	19	63	68	128	3	2	214	312	374	686	12%	73%	0.53	98	39	4.13	10
	09	R	31	3	aa	SD	436	43	77	17	1	12	53	45	118	2	0	175	253	300	553	9%	73%	0.38	78	55	2.57	-8
Patchett,Gary	08	R	30	46	aa	LAA	318	21	60	9	1	3	25	20	79	2	3	187	236	246	482	6%	75%	0.26	41	49	1.88	-38
	09	R	31	6	aa	LAA	313	30	62	8	1	3	20	15	64	0	7	198	236	253	488	5%	80%	0.24	37	48	1.77	-26
Patterson,Corey	09	L	30	8	aaa	MIL	387	37	85	21	3	9	42	15	87	15	9	220	249	354	603	4%	78%	0.18	88	115	2.79	25
Patterson,Eric	08	L	26 a	4	aa	OAK	312	38	83	21	3	7	35	15	57	14	2	265	299	413	712	5%	82%	0.26	99	135	4.53	57
	09	L	26 b	4	aa	OAK	466	62	111	23	6	7	39	35	63	29	7	239	292	363	655	7%	86%	0.55	80	163	3.78	75
Paul,Xavier	08	L	24	8	aa	LA	443	65	123	25	3	8	53	35	82	14	8	277	330	398	728	7%	82%	0.43	82	109	4.69	42
	09	L	25 a	8	aa	LA	116	11	34	9	1	2	13	9	21	7	2	290	339	430	769	7%	82%	0.41	99	106	5.45	55
Paulk,Michael	09	L	25	8	aa	COL	413	49	105	17	2	7	47	48	57	6	7	255	332	353	685	10%	86%	0.83	65	67	4.16	39

Major League Equivalent Statistics

BATTERS

BATTER	Yr	B	Age	Pos	Lev	Org	ab	r	h	d	t	hr	rbi	bb	k	sb	cs	ba	ob	slg	ops	bb%	ct%	eye	px	sx	rc/g	bpv
Pavkovich,Adam	08	R	27	8	aa	LAA	450	59	106	22	3	16	63	29	99	6	3	235	282	401	683	6%	78%	0.30	103	99	3.89	38
	09	R	28	8	aa	LAA	397	36	82	18	1	5	36	23	68	6	2	206	249	290	539	5%	83%	0.33	60	80	2.45	16
Pearce,Steve	08	R	25	83	aa	PIT	386	39	86	24	1	9	49	25	68	9	4	224	272	365	637	6%	82%	0.37	96	84	3.37	46
	09	R	26 b	3	aa	PIT	273	29	65	17	1	9	41	25	40	2	7	239	303	408	710	8%	85%	0.62	109	47	3.91	61
Pena,Ramiro	08	B	23	6	aa	NYY	443	53	111	19	5	2	42	37	84	8	6	250	308	327	636	8%	81%	0.45	54	110	3.54	18
	09	B	24	6	aaa	NYY	156	16	33	9	0	2	9	16	27	5	1	209	284	302	586	9%	83%	0.60	68	75	3.07	28
Pena,Wily Mo	09	R	28	3	aa	NYM	145	9	32	4	0	4	15	4	26	0	0	217	236	317	553	2%	82%	0.14	60	12	2.49	-12
Pennington,Cliff	08	B	24	64	aa	OAK	440	66	102	13	3	1	25	68	53	23	7	231	334	281	616	13%	88%	1.28	36	121	3.65	46
	09	B	25 a	6	aa	OAK	360	33	75	18	2	2	27	31	40	19	5	209	272	285	556	8%	89%	0.77	57	112	2.75	52
Perez,Antonio	09	R	30	6	a/a	ATL	138	15	22	4	1	2	7	9	27	3	2	162	216	243	459	6%	81%	0.35	52	108	1.66	12
Perez,Eduardo	09	B	25	3	aa	LA	292	37	71	19	1	9	38	24	69	0	2	241	300	409	709	8%	76%	0.35	110	47	4.22	25
Perez,Kenny	08	B	27 b	5	aa	COL	133	15	37	11	1	1	13	10	12	1	0	277	328	392	720	7%	91%	0.81	88	71	4.80	71
	09	B	28	3	aa	COL	315	26	78	18	2	3	36	23	37	2	1	249	301	343	643	7%	88%	0.64	69	60	3.68	42
Perez,Miguel	08	R	25	2	aa	PIT	171	11	42	4	0	2	18	8	29	1	1	247	279	302	581	4%	83%	0.26	36	31	2.92	-18
	09	R	26	2	aa	PIT	106	12	23	5	0	2	10	7	26	0	1	213	259	310	569	6%	76%	0.26	67	47	2.62	-15
Perez,Yohannis	09	R	27	6	aa	MIL	248	19	53	12	0	3	14	16	35	1	1	215	262	297	558	6%	86%	0.45	60	36	2.63	17
Perry,Jason	08	L	28	8	a/a	ATL	365	53	78	17	1	17	48	36	105	4	0	215	285	403	688	9%	71%	0.35	114	87	4.02	22
	09	L	29	8	aa	TAM	103	13	17	4	0	4	12	17	34	1	0	167	286	334	620	14%	67%	0.51	102	45	3.34	-5
Petersen,Bryan	09	L	23	8	aa	FLA	431	55	118	14	6	6	42	45	63	11	13	273	342	373	715	9%	85%	0.71	61	112	4.38	45
Petersen,Joshua	08	R	25	8	aa	NYM	241	20	57	11	1	2	24	13	51	3	3	238	277	316	593	5%	79%	0.26	57	64	2.95	-8
	09	R	26	8	aa	NYM	282	23	68	12	1	3	24	22	37	2	2	241	297	320	616	7%	87%	0.60	56	50	3.32	23
Peterson,Brock	08	R	25	3	a/a	MIN	461	55	101	29	2	12	59	35	108	1	1	219	273	364	638	7%	77%	0.32	98	63	3.40	19
	09	R	26	3	aaa	MIN	316	39	82	16	2	8	35	26	72	0	0	259	316	393	708	8%	77%	0.36	87	54	4.50	11
Peterson,Shane	09	L	22	8	aa	OAK	228	19	54	12	1	3	18	13	30	4	0	235	276	337	613	5%	87%	0.44	72	79	3.32	42
Petit,Gregorio	08	R	24	6	aa	OAK	308	29	71	12	2	1	26	17	45	2	6	229	269	290	558	5%	85%	0.37	44	69	2.48	10
	09	R	25	6	aa	OAK	357	32	70	14	0	3	22	18	60	0	3	196	235	261	496	5%	83%	0.30	48	34	1.96	-7
Pettit,Christopher	08	R	24	8	aa	LAA	222	22	48	12	1	5	21	12	34	4	2	216	258	342	600	5%	85%	0.36	83	82	2.94	42
	09	R	25 a	8	aa	LAA	371	60	108	28	2	7	51	25	59	15	2	291	337	431	767	6%	84%	0.43	99	125	5.57	69
Phillips,Andy	08	R	32	3	aaa	CIN	146	19	36	7	1	4	15	14	19	2	0	245	309	390	699	9%	87%	0.72	91	78	4.38	64
	09	R	32	3	a/a	CHW	217	20	52	7	1	5	22	14	32	1	1	239	284	349	632	6%	85%	0.43	68	49	3.43	24
Phillips,Kyle	08	L	25	3	aa	TOR	268	26	72	14	0	7	27	20	36	0	2	269	320	398	717	7%	86%	0.55	86	21	4.51	37
	09	L	25	5	a/a	TOR	317	30	78	11	0	8	24	25	57	0	0	246	302	353	655	7%	82%	0.44	68	20	3.82	5
Phillips,Paul	08	R	31	2	aaa	CHW	253	16	54	12	0	2	13	13	33	0	0	212	249	279	528	5%	87%	0.39	52	18	2.36	7
	09	R	32	2	aa	COL	123	8	27	5	2	1	10	3	16	0	0	221	237	311	548	2%	87%	0.15	60	70	2.45	21
Pilittere,Peter	08	R	27	2	aa	NYY	364	40	89	13	1	3	42	17	34	0	1	245	280	308	588	5%	91%	0.52	45	47	3.00	24
	09	R	28	2	a/a	NYY	182	11	34	8	0	1	14	8	17	0	0	188	223	247	470	4%	91%	0.49	47	20	1.81	18
Pill,Brett	09	R	25 a	3	aa	SF	527	58	138	35	1	14	90	30	66	5	3	262	302	412	714	5%	87%	0.46	101	61	4.40	62
Pina,Manuel	09	R	22	2	aa	TEX	321	29	76	16	1	7	34	15	48	1	0	237	271	358	629	4%	85%	0.31	81	51	3.37	31
Pinckney,Brandon	08	R	26	46	aa	CLE	322	33	76	13	1	5	29	11	47	2	1	237	262	326	588	3%	85%	0.24	60	65	2.92	18
	09	R	27	5	a/a	BAL	295	26	76	11	1	2	23	5	42	0	3	256	270	317	587	2%	86%	0.13	45	42	2.84	-3
Place,Jason	09	R	21	8	aa	BOS	141	18	36	7	0	3	14	14	43	1	2	258	326	372	698	9%	70%	0.33	78	47	4.24	-24
Plouffe,Trevor	08	R	22	654	a/a	MIN	477	55	112	31	5	7	50	24	78	4	3	235	271	365	636	5%	84%	0.31	90	103	3.35	49
	09	R	23	6	aaa	MIN	430	45	100	21	4	8	51	27	61	3	7	232	279	353	632	6%	86%	0.45	79	79	3.20	44
Pope,Van	08	R	25	5	aa	ATL	350	37	79	18	1	3	39	28	47	7	6	225	282	307	589	7%	87%	0.59	61	77	2.90	35
	09	R	26	5	aaa	ATL	322	30	55	12	0	3	22	26	55	2	1	169	232	234	466	8%	83%	0.48	47	56	1.81	3
Portes,Juan	09	R	24 a	8	aa	MIN	327	39	88	20	2	5	35	28	42	6	3	270	328	387	715	8%	87%	0.68	82	86	4.62	58
Posey,Buster	09	R	22 a	2	aa	SF	131	18	39	8	1	4	19	15	20	0	1	298	370	466	836	10%	85%	0.75	108	60	6.46	66
Powell,Pedro	09	R	25	8	aa	TAM	179	13	36	3	2	0	10	8	40	14	6	200	232	236	468	4%	77%	0.19	23	143	1.78	-19
Price,Jared	08	R	27	2	a/a	CHW	183	12	26	3	0	6	6	14	70	0	0	141	201	246	447	7%	62%	0.20	60	14	1.59	-84
	09	R	28	2	aa	CHW	173	14	32	6	0	5	14	5	59	1	0	182	203	297	499	3%	66%	0.08	73	50	1.93	-56
Pridie,Jason	08	L	25	8	aaa	MIN	559	66	128	18	11	9	48	23	140	20	9	229	259	351	610	4%	75%	0.16	72	183	2.98	22
	09	L	26	8	aaa	MIN	513	55	117	20	4	7	43	15	79	20	8	227	249	319	568	3%	85%	0.19	60	127	2.64	33
Putnam,Danny	08	L	26	8	aa	OAK	326	40	71	15	1	10	45	34	72	2	2	217	291	361	653	9%	78%	0.47	91	59	3.62	23
	09	L	27	8	aa	SD	435	44	86	18	1	11	56	35	89	5	5	199	258	319	577	7%	80%	0.39	77	67	2.71	17
Quintana,Al	09	R	27	5	a/a	TOR	318	26	61	15	1	4	27	15	66	0	0	191	227	278	504	4%	79%	0.22	61	40	2.07	-11
Quiroz,Guillermo	09	R	28	2	aa	SEA	205	16	41	9	1	5	25	9	37	0	0	202	236	320	556	4%	82%	0.25	77	39	2.50	12
Raburn,John	08	B	30	846	aa	TAM	353	29	64	5	3	0	23	22	45	10	5	180	227	214	442	6%	87%	0.47	22	117	1.60	14
	09	B	31	6	a/a	MIL	235	24	47	4	1	2	13	30	29	4	4	199	289	246	535	11%	87%	1.01	30	69	2.45	19
Rahl,Christopher	08	R	25	8	aa	ARI	421	38	83	23	2	5	20	22	97	14	12	196	236	294	530	5%	77%	0.23	70	103	2.07	7
	09	R	26	8	aa	ARI	435	56	110	21	8	5	38	27	88	16	8	253	297	372	669	6%	80%	0.31	76	170	3.81	44
Raines Jr.,Tim	08	B	29 b	8	aa	ARI	502	70	130	25	11	14	57	20	91	21	8	259	287	435	722	4%	82%	0.22	106	192	4.28	80
	09	B	30	8	aa	KC	273	24	49	9	1	4	19	12	46	10	0	181	215	268	483	4%	83%	0.26	57	112	2.00	23
Ramirez,Max	08	R	24 a	20	aa	TEX	280	41	84	16	2	16	43	30	55	2	2	301	369	539	908	10%	80%	0.55	142	70	7.49	78
	09	R	25	2	aa	TEX	274	23	56	12	0	4	34	27	73	1	0	203	274	287	562	9%	73%	0.37	59	36	2.76	-29
Ramirez,Wilkin	08	R	23	8	a/a	DET	469	62	121	22	6	15	59	36	117	22	14	258	311	426	737	7%	75%	0.31	102	143	4.40	41
	09	R	24	8	aaa	DET	434	61	104	17	5	15	45	35	127	29	11	239	297	402	698	8%	71%	0.28	96	159	4.07	25
Ramirez,Yordany	08	R	24	8	aa	HOU	432	36	83	18	2	9	37	8	51	13	11	191	205	302	507	2%	88%	0.15	72	102	1.79	47
	09	R	25	8	aa	HOU	457	29	97	19	1	8	34	8	53	10	9	212	225	313	537	2%	88%	0.14	67	68	2.12	33
Ramos,Wilson	09	R	22	2	aa	MIN	205	28	60	15	0	3	26	5	21	0	0	293	310	410	719	2%	90%	0.24	87	41	4.64	48
Randel,Kevin	09	L	28	4	aa	FLA	352	42	72	18	2	9	38	50	98	4	1	205	304	340	644	12%	72%	0.51	87	79	3.69	10
Rapoport,James	08	L	23	8	aa	STL	183	19	38	4	2	1	14	6	28	9	1	209	233	268	501	3%	85%	0.21	37	145	2.20	21
	09	L	24	8	aa	STL	458	52	98	13	4	3	43	54	57	9	8	214	296	279	575	11%	87%	0.94	43	94	2.85	36
Raynor,John	08	R	25	8	aa	FLA	452	84	123	26	5	11	40	53	114	38	12	272	348	421	769	10%	75%	0.47	96	164	5.40	49
	09	R	26	8	aa	FLA	447	52	101	22	2	5	30	37	120	16	8	225	284	313	597	8%	73%	0.30	63	104	3.02	-9
Recker,Anthony	08	R	25	2	aa	OAK	430	41	96	24	3	8	46	31	109	1	2	223	275	345	621	7%	75%	0.29	83	64	3.23	0
	09	R	26	2	aa	OAK	329	28	68	12	1	9	37	24	78	1	0	207	261	333	593	7%	76%	0.31	78	45	2.96	-4
Reddick,Josh	08	L	22 a	8	aa	BOS	117	18	23	4	1	4	20	10	20	2	1	199	262	354	616	8%	83%	0.51	92	117	3.08	59
	09	L	23 a	8	a/a	BOS	327	44	79	20	4	11	32	33	66	5	6	242	311	428	739	9%	80%	0.50	117	110	4.47	66
Redman,Prentice	08	R	29 b	8	aa	SEA	455	68	102	23	1	17	53	45	70	6	9	225	294	393	687	9%	85%	0.64	105	71	3.75	64
	09	R	30	8	aa	SEA	414	64	96	28	2	15	50	26	86	5	2	232	278	419	697	6%	79%	0.31	121	101	4.00	58
Reimold,Nolan	08	R	25 a	8	aa	BAL	507	73	128	26	2	22	70	53	71	6	3	252	322	441	764	9%	86%	0.75	116	77	5.09	81
	09	R	26 a	8	aaa	BAL	109	18	39	9	0	8	24	15	23	6	1	362	440	681	1121	12%	79%	0.64	196	67	12.68	118

Major League Equivalent Statistics

BATTER	Yr	B	Age	Pos	Lev	Org	ab	r	h	d	t	hr	rbi	bb	k	sb	cs	ba	ob	slg	ops	bb%	ct%	eye	px	sx	rc/g	bpv
Repko,Jason	08	R	28	8	aa	LA	459	64	104	21	4	9	36	38	99	14	6	225	284	345	630	8%	78%	0.38	77	125	3.37	30
	09	R	29	8	aa	LA	393	53	87	16	2	12	35	22	83	18	7	222	263	365	628	5%	79%	0.27	88	123	3.17	36
Restovich,Mike	09	R	31	8	aaa	CHW	489	65	115	28	2	19	48	46	126	0	1	235	300	414	714	9%	74%	0.36	113	48	4.35	21
Retherford,Chris	09	R	24 a	4	aa	CHW	478	60	126	40	2	10	64	26	64	3	3	263	301	416	717	5%	87%	0.41	109	69	4.39	67
Reyes,Argenis	08	B	26	4	aa	NYM	311	32	73	9	1	0	17	24	42	10	6	234	288	269	558	7%	86%	0.56	29	87	2.67	11
	09	B	27	4	aa	NYM	379	32	86	16	2	2	23	22	40	7	4	228	271	294	564	6%	89%	0.55	48	83	2.72	34
Reynolds,Kyle	08	L	25	53	aa	CHC	357	28	72	19	1	8	34	21	78	2	4	203	246	332	578	5%	78%	0.27	86	47	2.61	9
	09	L	26	3	aa	CHC	107	8	14	5	0	2	5	5	28	1	1	129	165	224	388	4%	74%	0.16	65	68	1.09	-23
Rhinehart,William	08	L	24	3	aa	WAS	219	18	43	13	0	5	23	21	40	0	0	197	266	322	588	9%	82%	0.52	86	17	2.93	21
	09	L	25	3	aa	WAS	414	36	89	22	1	10	49	27	97	6	1	216	263	343	607	6%	77%	0.28	85	73	3.11	11
Rhymes,William	08	L	26	4	a/a	DET	541	62	141	18	7	2	47	36	59	13	7	261	306	328	635	6%	89%	0.61	45	120	3.59	43
	09	L	26	4	aaa	DET	404	40	91	15	5	3	34	29	54	17	8	225	278	305	583	7%	87%	0.54	53	125	2.87	42
Richar,Danny	08	L	25	4	aaa	CIN	362	39	81	19	2	9	41	24	62	10	6	223	271	364	634	6%	83%	0.38	91	97	3.26	48
	09	L	26 b	4	aaa	CIN	169	16	42	9	1	4	13	8	16	2	3	250	285	381	666	5%	90%	0.51	87	66	3.59	62
Richard,Chris	08	L	34	3	aaa	TAM	467	58	105	25	3	19	62	39	126	3	0	224	284	408	692	8%	73%	0.31	114	86	4.04	26
	09	L	35	3	aaa	TAM	365	42	75	17	0	18	56	39	86	2	1	205	282	398	680	10%	76%	0.46	117	41	3.83	33
Richardson,Kevin	08	R	28	2	aa	TEX	187	17	37	8	1	4	15	12	47	0	0	198	247	320	567	6%	75%	0.26	78	45	2.65	-9
	09	R	29	2	aa	TEX	255	23	43	8	1	9	25	13	100	0	0	169	209	317	526	5%	61%	0.13	87	46	2.11	-62
Rivas,Luis	09	R	30	4	aa	CHC	191	16	36	12	1	1	11	14	19	3	0	187	244	271	516	7%	90%	0.77	66	79	2.28	53
Rivera,Luis	09	R	26	4	aa	NYM	136	14	36	5	0	0	8	6	13	0	0	263	292	297	589	4%	91%	0.44	31	33	3.11	7
Rivera,Rene	08	R	25	23	aa	LA	252	19	53	10	0	8	23	17	46	0	1	209	259	339	598	6%	82%	0.37	83	18	2.92	13
	09	R	26	2	aa	NYM	239	17	45	11	0	6	22	9	58	0	0	189	219	316	534	4%	76%	0.16	83	17	2.24	-16
Rivero,Carlos	09	R	21	6	aa	CLE	480	46	111	23	1	6	54	48	67	1	0	231	302	322	624	9%	86%	0.72	64	45	3.50	29
Robbins,Whitney	09	L	25	3	aa	MIN	425	45	105	21	2	7	42	36	71	0	3	246	304	352	657	8%	83%	0.50	72	43	3.74	22
Roberson,Chris	08	B	29	8	aaa	BAL	437	38	95	10	1	4	41	28	60	15	17	218	265	276	540	6%	86%	0.46	38	74	2.19	11
	09	B	30	8	aa	ARI	425	52	91	23	7	5	42	25	56	21	8	214	257	336	593	5%	87%	0.44	81	169	2.87	75
Roberson,Ryan	08	R	25	3	a/a	DET	465	59	112	18	1	19	67	26	106	6	5	241	281	404	686	5%	77%	0.25	98	71	3.83	21
	09	R	26	3	aaa	DET	295	22	58	17	0	6	29	19	84	1	3	196	246	309	555	6%	72%	0.23	79	31	2.43	-27
Roberts,Brandon	09	L	25	8	aa	MIN	397	56	102	16	2	2	32	24	56	18	8	256	299	322	620	6%	86%	0.43	48	119	3.39	31
Robinson,Chris	08	R	24	2	aa	CHC	159	10	29	5	0	1	13	9	31	0	1	181	223	229	453	5%	80%	0.28	36	27	1.64	-29
	09	R	25	2	aa	CHC	310	29	89	20	2	2	39	10	41	8	3	288	311	382	693	3%	87%	0.25	71	91	4.31	39
Robinson,Shane	08	R	24	8	aa	STL	385	43	101	18	3	4	32	17	46	12	10	262	293	354	647	4%	88%	0.36	63	104	3.42	44
	09	R	25 a	8	aa	STL	345	35	68	15	2	4	30	21	33	12	4	198	244	287	530	6%	90%	0.63	62	113	2.35	58
Robnett,Richie	08	L	25	8	aa	OAK	293	29	57	18	0	3	20	27	66	2	0	196	264	286	550	9%	77%	0.41	69	55	2.62	1
	09	L	26	8	a/a	NYY	255	25	52	11	3	4	18	18	63	6	3	202	256	310	566	7%	75%	0.29	70	121	2.65	9
Rodriguez,Concep'n	09	R	23	8	aa	ATL	395	38	96	18	1	3	28	26	65	8	10	243	291	315	606	6%	83%	0.41	53	68	2.99	11
Rodriguez,Guilder	08	B	25	4	aa	MIL	175	22	35	2	0	0	4	15	21	8	2	199	262	209	472	8%	88%	0.71	10	101	2.04	7
	09	B	26	6	aa	TEX	277	26	63	4	3	1	16	19	36	7	6	226	276	269	545	7%	87%	0.54	26	102	2.45	15
Rodriguez,Guillermo	09	R	31	2	a/a	BAL	298	23	60	16	1	4	25	11	56	5	0	203	231	305	536	4%	81%	0.20	73	83	2.39	16
Rodriguez,John	08	L	31	8	a/a	NYM	211	23	44	7	1	7	22	19	52	0	1	209	274	346	620	8%	75%	0.36	82	49	3.20	0
	09	L	32	8	aaa	NYY	322	37	69	14	1	12	48	30	94	0	2	214	280	375	655	8%	71%	0.32	99	42	3.54	-6
Rodriguez,Joshua	08	R	24	64	aa	CLE	532	66	115	21	6	6	43	69	112	11	7	216	305	309	615	11%	79%	0.61	61	114	3.32	24
	09	R	25	4	aa	CLE	105	15	29	4	0	0	11	21	29	2	3	274	396	311	707	17%	72%	0.72	32	51	4.71	-35
Rodriguez,Sean	08	R	23 a	4	aa	LAA	248	57	69	18	1	17	43	25	39	3	1	277	342	557	899	9%	84%	0.63	170	102	6.98	124
	09	R	24 a	4	a/a	TAM	385	75	102	16	5	26	84	48	115	8	2	264	346	534	879	11%	70%	0.42	153	144	6.78	71
Rogers,Eddie	08	R	30	64	a/a	WAS	324	26	63	9	0	3	16	9	48	10	10	194	215	254	469	3%	85%	0.18	42	78	1.56	5
	09	R	31	6	aa	ARI	254	31	58	15	0	3	30	10	40	7	3	228	257	328	585	4%	84%	0.26	74	93	2.84	34
Rohlinger,Ryan	08	R	25 a	5	aa	SF	159	23	41	11	1	5	16	10	18	1	1	260	305	432	737	6%	89%	0.57	114	78	4.63	83
	09	R	26 a	5	aa	SF	474	61	117	34	2	12	64	34	82	4	2	246	296	403	699	7%	83%	0.41	107	77	4.18	55
Rojas,Carlos	08	R	25	4	aa	BAL	441	61	97	12	1	2	32	41	66	1	3	220	287	263	550	9%	85%	0.63	32	59	2.63	3
	09	R	26	6	a/a	BAL	297	24	47	6	1	0	12	19	39	2	4	158	208	184	392	6%	87%	0.48	20	66	1.19	-4
Romak,Jamie	08	R	23	3	aa	PIT	120	13	23	6	0	6	20	14	28	0	0	188	271	384	655	10%	77%	0.50	119	19	3.52	32
	09	R	24	3	aa	PIT	211	10	33	12	0	4	20	14	53	1	0	158	209	269	479	6%	75%	0.26	78	27	1.83	-16
Romero,Alex	08	L	25 a	8	aa	ARI	173	23	51	8	2	3	15	9	17	3	3	293	330	413	743	5%	90%	0.55	78	100	4.83	65
	09	L	26 b	8	aa	ARI	279	31	86	18	3	2	36	25	23	6	5	307	363	412	776	8%	92%	1.09	77	89	5.57	74
Romero,Niuman	09	B	25	6	a/a	CLE	367	38	78	12	1	1	29	29	42	11	6	212	269	259	528	7%	89%	0.69	36	89	2.38	27
Roof,Shawn	08	R	24	6	aa	DET	124	12	24	3	0	0	6	9	18	1	0	194	246	217	463	7%	86%	0.49	21	54	1.86	-9
	09	R	25	4	aa	DET	184	16	41	2	2	1	12	9	33	3	2	225	262	271	533	5%	82%	0.29	26	97	2.40	-10
Rooney,Sean	09	B	23	2	aa	WAS	110	11	24	5	1	0	5	5	22	0	0	214	247	276	524	4%	80%	0.22	47	73	2.31	-11
Rosales,Adam	08	R	25 a	56	aaa	CIN	432	54	106	25	4	9	44	17	71	6	1	246	274	387	662	4%	84%	0.24	93	113	3.71	52
	09	R	26 b	5	aaa	CIN	109	21	33	7	1	5	16	10	14	3	0	304	363	515	878	8%	87%	0.72	133	113	7.34	107
Rosario,Jovanny	09	B	24	8	aa	LA	142	13	33	1	1	1	8	1	20	4	1	230	235	270	505	1%	86%	0.05	22	43	2.15	-22
Rose,Mike	09	B	33	2	aa	LA	105	5	16	0	1	2	4	8	35	1	0	154	211	219	430	7%	66%	0.22	32	69	1.54	-72
Rottino,Vinny	08	R	29	2	aaa	MIL	431	40	85	24	2	5	37	22	65	6	4	198	237	298	535	5%	85%	0.34	71	83	2.28	34
	09	R	29	3	aa	LA	414	46	83	14	0	3	40	46	55	10	2	201	282	260	542	10%	87%	0.85	42	83	2.67	28
Rowlett,Casey	08	R	26	84	aa	STL	216	25	44	7	2	4	21	16	35	6	8	205	259	305	564	7%	84%	0.46	62	109	2.35	33
	09	R	27	4	aa	STL	148	11	26	3	0	1	9	9	20	2	1	174	222	211	434	6%	87%	0.47	26	55	1.55	-2
Ruggiano,Justin	08	R	26	8	aaa	TAM	257	38	67	15	2	8	40	17	71	16	4	261	306	430	736	6%	73%	0.23	107	140	4.74	32
	09	R	27	8	aaa	TAM	471	56	98	23	1	12	57	41	144	18	4	208	272	334	607	8%	69%	0.29	82	105	3.19	-7
Ruiz,Randy	08	R	31	03	aaa	MIN	416	42	102	26	2	11	48	15	119	1	2	245	272	394	666	4%	71%	0.13	99	55	3.65	-9
	09	R	32	3	aaa	TOR	462	52	111	33	2	17	68	30	92	0	0	241	287	431	717	6%	80%	0.32	124	40	4.31	46
Rundgren,Rex	08	R	28	6	aa	LA	108	8	16	1	0	1	5	3	14	1	0	150	171	183	354	2%	87%	0.19	20	63	0.99	-11
	09	R	29	4	aa	COL	341	22	67	12	2	1	18	13	45	2	1	196	226	250	476	4%	87%	0.29	41	63	1.86	8
Russo,Kevin	08	R	24	45	aa	NYY	267	42	76	15	2	2	31	20	42	8	3	284	334	378	712	7%	84%	0.48	68	115	4.69	43
	09	R	25	4	aaa	NYY	353	45	103	16	1	5	27	38	55	11	7	293	361	383	744	10%	84%	0.68	63	80	5.17	33
Ryal,Rusty	08	R	26	45	aa	ARI	460	52	113	20	4	14	53	29	83	3	4	245	290	396	687	6%	82%	0.35	93	77	3.93	39
	09	R	27 b	4	aa	ARI	404	50	104	29	6	15	53	26	82	4	3	257	302	467	769	6%	80%	0.32	133	112	4.91	73
Ryan,Dusty	08	R	24	2	a/a	DET	369	45	84	20	3	12	49	35	100	2	1	229	295	401	696	9%	73%	0.35	108	84	4.12	22
	09	R	25	2	aaa	DET	202	21	46	7	1	8	29	24	60	2	0	228	311	396	707	11%	71%	0.41	98	62	4.44	3
Ryan,Mike	08	L	31	8	aa	FLA	109	11	27	5	2	6	20	5	27	1	0	250	283	491	774	4%	75%	0.19	140	106	4.88	55
	09	L	32	8	aa	FLA	367	46	87	20	0	10	49	37	71	2	1	236	307	375	682	9%	81%	0.53	92	48	4.10	32

Major League Equivalent Statistics

BATTER	Yr	B	Age	Pos	Lev	Org	ab	r	h	d	t	hr	rbi	bb	k	sb	cs	ba	ob	slg	ops	bb%	ct%	eye	px	sx	rc/g	bpv
Saccomanno,Mark	08	R	28	53	aa	HOU	528	55	121	25	1	18	55	23	82	3	4	228	260	383	644	4%	85%	0.28	97	51	3.31	41
	09	R	29	3	aa	HOU	493	44	104	18	3	10	44	22	79	3	0	211	245	324	570	4%	84%	0.28	71	86	2.69	29
Sadler,Ray	08	R	28	8	aa	HOU	452	48	94	21	4	18	51	20	92	4	4	208	242	387	630	4%	80%	0.22	109	87	3.02	42
	09	R	29	8	a/a	HOU	381	30	59	10	1	10	37	22	95	3	5	156	201	269	469	5%	75%	0.23	68	61	1.61	-15
Salazar,Jeff	09	L	29	8	aa	PIT	315	32	68	6	2	7	28	21	51	11	0	215	264	313	577	6%	84%	0.41	57	113	3.00	29
Salazar,Oscar	08	R	30	30	aaa	BAL	443	53	108	31	2	10	61	31	54	6	2	244	293	391	684	6%	88%	0.57	102	84	4.04	73
	09	R	31	3	aaa	BAL	199	24	61	14	1	9	34	10	28	0	3	308	341	513	854	5%	86%	0.36	130	42	6.26	72
Salome,Angel	08	R	22 a	2	aa	MIL	367	53	117	27	1	11	66	28	47	2	2	319	367	488	855	7%	87%	0.60	114	56	6.86	73
	09	R	23	2	aaa	MIL	283	25	71	13	1	5	34	19	46	0	0	249	296	353	649	6%	84%	0.41	70	33	3.72	15
Sammons,Clint	08	R	25	2	aaa	ATL	278	19	56	15	0	1	18	17	54	6	2	203	249	267	516	6%	80%	0.31	53	64	2.26	-3
	09	R	26	2	aaa	ATL	299	26	53	10	0	6	29	16	57	6	0	178	219	277	496	5%	81%	0.28	63	77	2.04	10
Sanchez,Angel	08	R	25	6	aa	KC	372	33	82	13	2	2	29	30	53	4	7	220	278	280	559	7%	86%	0.57	44	64	2.57	14
	09	R	26	6	aaa	TOR	449	46	111	25	3	5	41	27	58	1	2	248	290	346	636	6%	87%	0.46	70	60	3.50	36
Sanchez,Gaby	08	R	25 a	35	aa	FLA	478	55	127	37	1	13	72	57	66	13	8	265	344	429	773	11%	86%	0.87	112	70	5.28	79
	09	R	26 b	3	aa	FLA	318	45	78	10	0	13	46	35	45	4	0	246	321	399	720	10%	86%	0.78	91	65	4.70	58
Sanchez,Luis	09	B	22	6	aa	TOR	262	22	49	12	1	1	23	27	68	1	0	187	263	252	515	9%	74%	0.40	50	58	2.32	-26
Sanchez,Yunesky	08	B	24	6	aa	ARI	494	50	133	17	3	0	18	19	34	7	14	270	297	317	614	4%	93%	0.56	36	71	3.02	32
	09	B	25	4	aa	ARI	199	22	48	7	2	2	14	11	22	3	4	241	282	321	603	5%	89%	0.50	52	93	2.97	38
Sandoval,Danny	08	B	30	64	aaa	TOR	465	42	107	17	0	7	38	22	71	7	3	229	265	311	575	5%	85%	0.32	56	63	2.79	14
	09	B	30	6	aa	COL	201	15	43	4	0	1	10	9	15	3	2	211	243	245	489	4%	92%	0.56	25	55	1.98	16
Sandoval,Freddy	08	B	26 b	534	aa	LAA	525	72	150	40	1	11	69	37	67	5	3	286	332	429	762	7%	87%	0.55	102	67	5.25	66
	09	B	27 b	5	aa	LAA	277	38	71	14	3	5	38	21	39	10	3	257	308	377	685	7%	86%	0.53	80	127	4.20	62
Santana,Carlos	09	B	23 a	2	aa	CLE	429	81	115	28	1	21	87	84	80	2	2	267	388	482	870	16%	81%	1.06	135	56	7.11	85
Santangelo,Louis	08	R	26	2	aa	HOU	388	26	74	8	0	8	31	21	81	1	1	191	232	279	511	5%	79%	0.26	53	29	2.12	-20
	09	R	27	2	aa	HOU	269	17	46	15	1	4	18	15	66	0	0	171	214	274	488	5%	75%	0.22	73	33	1.89	-18
Sardinha,Dane	08	R	30	2	aaa	DET	183	14	28	7	0	4	13	6	56	1	0	155	182	263	445	3%	70%	0.11	70	50	1.51	-43
	09	R	30	2	aaa	DET	118	8	17	6	0	3	12	9	34	0	0	144	202	259	461	7%	71%	0.25	78	18	1.67	-32
Saunders,Michael	08	L	22	8	aa	SEA	343	47	85	20	2	9	38	33	82	11	9	247	314	398	712	9%	76%	0.41	98	103	4.17	33
	09	L	23 a	8	aa	SEA	248	52	71	14	1	11	29	23	46	5	3	286	347	484	831	8%	81%	0.50	122	103	6.12	74
Scales,Bobby	08	B	31	4	aa	CHC	387	61	94	16	1	10	38	38	84	4	5	244	312	369	681	9%	78%	0.46	80	74	3.98	20
	09	B	32	5	aa	CHC	306	30	67	13	1	4	28	33	62	6	8	219	296	308	604	10%	80%	0.53	61	64	3.00	8
Schoop,Sharlon	09	R	22	5	aa	SF	320	31	72	15	0	2	31	17	54	5	6	225	264	291	555	5%	83%	0.31	51	62	2.47	4
Scott Jr.,Lorenzo	08	L	27	8	aa	FLA	265	39	65	8	3	6	23	36	83	23	13	246	336	361	697	12%	69%	0.43	69	147	4.12	0
	09	L	28	8	aa	FLA	400	51	88	11	4	7	36	50	129	16	13	221	308	320	627	11%	68%	0.39	60	121	3.28	-20
Scram,Deik	08	L	25	8	aa	DET	482	52	103	20	3	10	52	43	100	11	4	213	278	327	604	8%	79%	0.43	73	99	3.14	24
	09	L	26 a	8	aa	DET	441	58	96	20	6	16	55	49	104	7	2	217	296	396	692	10%	76%	0.47	107	126	4.09	51
Sedbrook,Colt	09	R	24	4	aa	STL	174	16	35	4	0	2	12	17	24	6	2	199	271	254	525	9%	86%	0.72	37	72	2.43	16
Sellers,Justin	08	R	23	64	aa	OAK	439	55	96	13	5	4	35	36	56	8	7	219	278	298	576	8%	87%	0.64	50	115	2.77	41
	09	R	24	6	aa	LA	393	37	98	25	1	2	27	43	64	9	9	249	324	332	655	10%	84%	0.67	65	65	3.72	28
Sellers,Neil	08	R	27	5	aa	PHI	483	43	109	25	1	15	53	30	66	2	6	225	271	371	642	6%	86%	0.46	94	37	3.28	45
	09	R	27 b	5	aa	PHI	518	53	136	27	1	14	64	35	66	4	5	262	309	401	711	6%	87%	0.54	91	45	4.31	50
Shelby III,John	09	R	24 a	8	aa	CHW	428	54	92	28	2	10	41	42	70	25	10	215	286	357	642	9%	84%	0.61	96	119	3.46	68
Shelton,Chris	08	R	28	3	aa	TEX	256	26	70	18	2	8	35	21	48	0	0	272	327	447	774	8%	81%	0.44	115	46	5.36	48
	09	R	29	5	aa	SEA	405	55	101	24	1	11	65	46	95	0	2	248	326	395	721	10%	76%	0.49	97	40	4.61	18
Shoffit,Sean	09	L	24	8	aa	TOR	100	10	17	3	3	0	10	15	42	4	5	173	283	259	542	13%	58%	0.37	51	223	2.24	-30
Shorey,Mark	08	L	24	8	aa	STL	388	37	99	24	1	8	50	22	89	1	0	255	295	381	676	5%	77%	0.25	88	48	4.01	6
	09	L	25	8	aa	STL	258	15	62	10	0	4	20	12	40	2	2	240	275	324	599	5%	84%	0.30	58	31	3.03	4
Singleton,Steven	09	L	24	6	aa	MIN	158	12	41	10	2	1	15	6	22	1	1	261	287	365	652	4%	86%	0.26	74	84	3.63	38
Sizemore,Scott	09	R	25 a	4	a/a	DET	520	73	143	35	4	14	55	53	83	17	4	275	342	439	781	9%	84%	0.63	108	116	5.64	78
Skelton,James	09	L	24	2	aa	ARI	214	27	36	8	2	0	13	43	33	7	3	169	309	224	533	17%	85%	1.32	41	110	2.63	40
Slayden,Jeremy	08	L	26	8	aa	PHI	483	50	117	28	1	14	55	36	87	1	6	242	294	389	683	7%	82%	0.41	96	33	3.81	31
	09	L	27	8	a/a	PHI	257	25	55	13	0	11	32	23	58	0	1	214	277	389	666	8%	78%	0.39	108	22	3.64	21
Smith,Coby	08	R	28	8	aa	LAA	329	32	66	12	1	2	18	26	49	11	5	201	260	259	519	7%	85%	0.54	44	90	2.28	20
	09	R	29	8	aa	LAA	464	53	98	15	2	6	36	28	58	32	12	211	255	291	546	6%	87%	0.47	53	126	2.47	43
Smith,Corey	08	R	26	530	aa	LAA	518	46	116	28	1	19	63	24	95	12	7	224	258	393	651	4%	82%	0.25	106	72	3.28	45
	09	R	27	3	aa	KC	550	48	112	26	1	14	64	28	111	8	8	203	241	332	574	5%	80%	0.25	84	64	2.52	17
Smith,Jason	08	L	31	546	aa	KC	423	38	86	18	4	14	45	17	125	3	1	203	234	362	595	4%	71%	0.14	96	98	2.78	-2
	09	L	32	4	aa	HOU	262	20	38	4	1	4	18	9	75	7	2	146	173	217	390	3%	71%	0.11	42	107	1.18	-41
Smith,Kevin	09	L	26	3	aa	NYY	158	17	36	7	1	2	13	9	46	0	1	226	270	315	585	6%	71%	0.21	61	67	2.85	-34
Smith,Marquez	09	R	25	5	aa	CHC	411	45	104	32	1	9	39	27	75	3	0	252	298	397	695	6%	82%	0.36	103	66	4.25	43
Smith,Timothy	09	L	23 a	8	aa	TEX	139	18	38	8	0	3	25	11	17	7	1	275	327	395	722	7%	88%	0.62	83	86	4.92	58
Smoak,Justin	09	B	23	3	aa	TEX	380	45	99	20	0	9	43	61	66	0	0	261	363	384	747	14%	83%	0.92	83	20	5.33	33
Snider,Travis	08	L	21	80	a/a	TOR	426	65	113	26	0	19	74	47	115	2	1	266	339	457	796	10%	73%	0.41	121	50	5.70	26
	09	L	22 a	8	aaa	TOR	175	24	54	12	1	11	30	21	37	2	4	306	381	577	958	11%	79%	0.58	165	61	7.87	90
Snyder,Brad	08	L	26	8	aaa	CLE	411	45	87	25	3	10	52	24	127	6	3	213	256	360	616	5%	69%	0.19	98	106	3.08	-1
	09	L	27	8	aa	CHC	237	30	56	14	2	12	33	15	66	7	5	235	282	456	738	6%	72%	0.23	134	112	4.19	44
Snyder,Brandon	09	R	23	3	a/a	BAL	463	57	130	35	2	13	84	47	100	3	2	281	347	449	796	9%	78%	0.47	114	63	5.79	44
Snyder,Justin	09	L	23	4	aa	NYY	262	24	48	9	0	3	27	27	48	1	2	183	261	251	511	9%	82%	0.57	47	38	2.20	-3
Sogard,Eric	09	L	23 a	4	aa	SD	458	63	112	20	2	4	40	46	42	8	7	244	313	321	634	9%	91%	1.10	55	84	3.53	53
Solano,Donovan	08	R	21	6	aa	STL	106	9	25	4	0	1	9	4	17	2	1	233	262	301	563	4%	84%	0.25	49	60	2.67	5
	09	R	22	6	aa	STL	415	38	92	12	1	1	23	24	50	3	0	221	264	263	527	6%	88%	0.49	32	69	2.44	11
Solano,Jhonatan	09	R	24	2	a/a	WAS	276	20	57	15	0	2	24	10	35	2	1	205	232	282	514	3%	87%	0.27	60	50	2.15	20
Sosa,Ricardo	09	R	25	5	aa	ARI	443	48	103	24	0	10	55	30	69	3	1	233	282	356	639	6%	84%	0.44	83	54	3.51	35
Spann,Charles	08	R	25	5	a/a	KC	256	21	49	7	0	3	25	13	56	1	1	191	232	251	483	5%	78%	0.24	41	44	1.91	-30
	09	R	26	5	aa	HOU	192	13	33	6	0	1	8	10	38	0	0	171	214	215	429	5%	80%	0.27	34	26	1.51	-33
Spearman,Jemel	08	R	28	8	a/a	WAS	141	12	28	5	1	2	14	11	24	6	0	198	255	287	542	7%	83%	0.44	59	108	2.68	27
	09	R	29	4	aa	WAS	161	14	36	7	1	3	18	11	30	4	3	224	272	328	600	6%	82%	0.36	69	86	2.97	22
Spears,Nathaniel	08	L	23 a	4	aa	CHC	402	57	105	22	3	6	39	45	58	5	6	261	335	373	708	10%	86%	0.78	77	85	4.45	51
	09	L	24	5	aa	CHC	368	39	83	18	3	2	30	28	39	5	6	224	279	305	584	7%	90%	0.72	59	87	2.83	47
Spencer,Matthew	09	L	24	8	aa	OAK	371	43	90	25	2	6	45	19	54	1	4	243	279	367	646	5%	85%	0.34	88	64	3.41	43
Spidale,Michael	08	R	27 b	8	a/a	PHI	359	40	81	12	2	6	28	17	37	16	1	226	260	323	583	4%	90%	0.45	62	125	3.02	56
	09	R	28	8	a/a	PHI	353	41	86	12	3	3	26	12	39	13	7	245	269	316	585	3%	89%	0.30	48	119	2.81	38

Major League Equivalent Statistics

BATTER	Yr	B	Age	Pos	Lev	Org	ab	r	h	d	t	hr	rbi	bb	k	sb	cs	ba	ob	slg	ops	bb%	ct%	eye	px	sx	rc/g	bpv
Spring,Matthew	08	R	24	2	aa	TAM	246	23	53	14	1	7	25	18	58	1	1	215	268	363	630	7%	76%	0.30	96	54	3.27	14
	09	R	25	2	aa	TAM	224	20	39	12	0	7	29	19	71	0	0	176	241	317	558	8%	68%	0.27	92	23	2.53	-28
St. Pierre,Maxim	08	R	28	2	a/a	DET	306	23	55	10	0	5	33	14	39	0	1	181	217	265	482	4%	87%	0.36	55	29	1.84	13
	09	R	29	2	a/a	DET	207	18	40	9	0	6	18	9	26	0	0	191	226	324	551	4%	88%	0.37	85	25	2.40	37
Stansberry,Craig	08	R	27	6	aa	SD	273	34	54	10	2	6	21	35	54	4	6	199	290	310	600	11%	80%	0.64	70	83	2.91	26
	09	R	28	5	aa	SD	427	38	87	18	3	5	30	32	68	6	5	204	261	291	551	7%	84%	0.48	59	84	2.52	25
Stanton,Michael	09	R	20	8	aa	FLA	299	45	67	15	2	14	49	30	88	1	1	225	296	425	721	9%	71%	0.35	120	85	4.35	25
Statia,Hainley	08	B	23 a	6	aa	LAA	223	22	50	11	2	1	17	12	14	7	5	224	264	305	569	5%	94%	0.86	59	109	2.60	67
	09	B	24 a	6	aa	LAA	381	42	85	21	1	1	38	30	33	13	3	224	281	291	572	7%	91%	0.93	54	100	2.93	56
Stavinoha,Nick	08	R	26 b	8	aa	STL	427	50	117	18	2	11	54	15	42	2	1	274	298	403	701	3%	90%	0.35	82	64	4.29	54
	09	R	27	3	aa	STL	259	28	58	14	1	7	40	18	41	2	0	222	273	365	638	6%	84%	0.44	92	66	3.46	45
Stavisky,Brian	08	L	28	80	aa	LAA	314	42	79	15	0	11	38	36	59	9	3	252	329	409	738	10%	81%	0.61	99	74	4.92	48
	09	L	29	3	aa	PHI	394	39	87	25	1	9	47	42	81	2	2	220	296	354	649	10%	79%	0.52	92	46	3.64	26
Stern,Adam	08	L	29	8	aaa	BAL	122	11	21	4	1	1	6	4	20	4	2	173	196	238	434	3%	83%	0.17	43	127	1.46	13
	09	L	30	8	a/a	MIL	488	53	107	16	3	3	28	34	62	22	11	219	269	282	551	6%	87%	0.54	44	118	2.53	35
Stewart,Caleb	08	R	26 b	8	aa	NYM	471	52	105	29	3	10	52	42	76	6	2	223	287	359	646	8%	84%	0.56	92	90	3.60	55
	09	R	27	8	aa	NYM	204	23	36	11	0	2	12	23	56	2	2	176	261	256	517	10%	73%	0.42	61	59	2.25	-20
Stewart,Chris	08	R	27	2	aaa	NYY	272	27	65	16	0	2	19	22	37	2	1	240	297	318	615	8%	86%	0.60	61	48	3.37	26
	09	R	28	2	aaa	NYY	232	28	56	10	0	1	15	21	30	1	1	241	303	295	598	8%	87%	0.69	44	48	3.20	16
Still,Jonathan	09	R	25	0	aa	BOS	507	42	110	43	1	12	72	36	125	2	0	218	269	381	650	7%	75%	0.28	115	49	3.51	23
Stocker,Mel	08	L	28	8	aaa	MIL	145	16	30	5	0	0	4	9	19	12	1	206	252	243	495	6%	87%	0.46	32	119	2.37	22
	09	L	29	8	aa	SEA	305	32	56	13	3	2	17	28	52	27	6	183	251	259	510	8%	83%	0.53	54	151	2.33	38
Strait,William	08	R	25	8	aa	CIN	226	24	48	14	2	4	14	10	46	4	4	212	247	341	588	4%	80%	0.23	88	104	2.64	32
	09	R	26	8	aa	TAM	431	63	98	24	2	5	50	33	95	16	5	228	283	324	608	7%	78%	0.35	69	122	3.24	21
Strieby,Ryan	09	R	24 a	3	aa	DET	294	52	79	15	1	15	47	45	68	2	0	268	365	483	848	13%	77%	0.67	130	69	6.70	61
Stubbs,Drew	08	R	24	8	a/a	CIN	167	20	44	11	1	2	14	13	34	5	1	264	319	374	693	7%	79%	0.39	79	98	4.42	27
	09	R	25	8	aaa	CIN	411	47	98	22	1	3	32	43	94	37	9	238	311	318	628	10%	77%	0.46	60	118	3.73	14
Suarez,Ignacio	08	R	27	6	aa	BOS	442	41	90	23	0	4	36	30	78	11	5	204	254	279	533	6%	82%	0.38	58	77	2.36	14
	09	R	28	6	a/a	BOS	254	29	39	9	0	2	17	28	76	7	2	152	237	208	445	10%	70%	0.37	41	92	1.73	-37
Suarez,RCesar	09	R	26 b	5	aa	TAM	246	24	47	15	1	4	19	13	28	5	4	191	231	303	534	5%	89%	0.46	79	88	2.19	56
Sulentic,Matthew	09	L	22	8	aa	OAK	413	44	101	18	3	5	38	26	72	16	11	245	290	340	630	6%	82%	0.36	64	109	3.25	28
Sullivan,Cory	08	L	29	8	aa	COL	381	43	95	25	2	4	29	19	50	8	8	248	284	357	640	5%	87%	0.38	79	87	3.32	49
	09	L	30	8	aa	NYM	286	26	62	12	0	2	16	20	28	2	2	217	269	276	545	7%	90%	0.72	46	45	2.54	26
Suomi,Richard	08	L	28	2	a/a	PHI	192	14	37	11	1	4	16	8	22	0	0	193	224	312	536	4%	89%	0.37	81	39	2.29	41
	09	L	29	2	aa	KC	195	18	38	8	1	5	18	11	26	0	4	194	235	325	560	5%	87%	0.40	82	54	2.29	40
Sutil,Wladimir	08	R	24	6	aa	HOU	316	32	69	11	0	0	18	12	24	16	5	217	245	251	496	4%	92%	0.48	30	104	2.11	34
	09	R	25	6	aa	HOU	472	57	108	18	0	1	27	33	34	14	15	230	280	275	554	6%	93%	0.95	37	80	2.44	40
Sutton,Drew	09	B	26	4	a/a	CIN	172	26	38	11	1	5	17	22	38	1	2	219	308	374	683	11%	78%	0.58	103	76	3.95	41
Sutton,Nathanael	08	L	26	4	aa	LAA	453	45	106	11	4	6	34	21	62	15	10	234	268	311	578	4%	86%	0.34	48	108	2.71	27
	09	L	27	8	aa	LAA	455	54	115	22	4	2	41	45	66	20	8	253	320	328	649	9%	86%	0.69	55	116	3.82	41
Tabata,Jose	08	R	20	8	aa	PIT	383	50	101	15	1	5	44	30	55	16	2	264	317	350	666	7%	86%	0.54	59	108	4.20	38
	09	R	21 a	8	aa	PIT	362	43	99	21	1	4	29	24	34	9	9	273	319	371	690	6%	91%	0.72	72	77	4.03	58
Taguchi,So	09	R	40	8	aa	CHC	258	26	51	7	1	3	20	23	33	3	4	198	263	270	533	8%	87%	0.70	47	64	2.31	24
Tatum,Craig	08	R	26	2	a/a	CIN	332	24	69	16	1	7	45	20	63	1	1	207	251	320	571	6%	81%	0.31	76	41	2.68	11
	09	R	27	2	aaa	CIN	213	17	43	10	0	3	17	14	51	0	0	203	251	289	541	6%	76%	0.27	62	24	2.46	-25
Taylor,Michael	09	R	24 a	8	a/a	PHI	428	61	124	25	3	19	70	39	61	18	6	291	350	495	845	8%	86%	0.64	126	110	6.43	95
Thole,Joshua	09	L	23 a	2	aa	NYM	384	39	111	26	1	1	37	36	28	6	5	289	350	370	720	9%	93%	1.29	66	61	4.79	61
Thomas,Anthony	09	R	23	4	aa	CHC	427	55	98	23	1	10	34	41	94	11	15	230	297	356	653	9%	78%	0.44	84	78	3.32	22
Thomas,Clete	08	L	25	8	aaa	DET	291	36	62	15	2	7	36	31	75	23	12	214	289	350	639	10%	74%	0.41	88	130	3.23	28
	09	L	26	8	aaa	DET	175	23	45	15	1	1	14	22	46	15	3	258	339	371	710	11%	74%	0.47	89	127	4.89	29
Thompson,Rich	08	L	29	8	a/a	PHI	362	29	74	14	3	3	29	27	70	17	2	204	259	290	549	7%	81%	0.38	57	131	2.71	23
	09	L	30	8	aaa	PHI	445	50	93	17	3	3	26	27	74	19	4	208	254	279	533	6%	83%	0.37	49	134	2.47	27
Thorman,Scott	08	L	27	3	aaa	ATL	387	37	82	18	1	15	44	15	77	6	1	212	240	378	618	4%	80%	0.19	103	77	3.04	35
	09	L	28	8	aa	KC	399	35	94	14	1	14	48	17	63	5	4	235	266	377	643	4%	84%	0.27	86	60	3.35	34
Tiffee,Terry	08	B	29 b	538	aa	LA	392	51	114	31	2	7	48	20	42	1	2	292	326	432	758	5%	89%	0.47	101	58	5.14	67
	09	B	30	5	aaa	PHI	246	13	52	9	0	4	25	7	25	0	1	211	232	301	533	3%	90%	0.28	60	15	2.26	20
Timmons,Wes	08	R	29 b	5	aaa	ATL	239	28	47	14	0	2	19	34	24	9	0	198	297	277	574	12%	90%	1.37	62	90	3.13	62
	09	R	30	3	aaa	ATL	322	44	71	15	1	1	22	45	36	9	5	222	317	282	600	12%	89%	1.24	48	89	3.25	47
Timpner,Clay	08	L	25	8	aa	SF	436	54	94	17	2	2	39	27	55	10	7	216	262	276	538	6%	87%	0.49	45	102	2.40	30
	09	L	26	8	aa	SF	392	37	85	18	3	5	34	26	47	5	6	216	264	312	576	6%	88%	0.55	66	79	2.66	43
Tolbert,Matt	09	B	27 b	4	aaa	MIN	236	27	56	9	5	2	17	10	31	5	5	236	267	336	603	4%	87%	0.32	62	147	2.91	51
Tolleson,Steven	08	R	25	64	aa	MIN	343	43	88	25	1	7	40	34	68	10	7	257	324	395	718	9%	80%	0.50	97	83	4.45	43
	09	R	26	4	a/a	MIN	503	64	116	24	2	6	33	40	68	10	8	230	287	318	605	7%	86%	0.59	62	89	3.07	39
Tomlin,James	08	R	26 b	8	aa	LA	383	43	98	26	1	2	26	28	42	10	6	257	307	343	650	7%	89%	0.65	69	83	3.68	51
	09	R	27	8	aa	LA	387	42	100	19	2	2	26	43	73	9	10	258	333	330	663	10%	81%	0.59	55	76	3.82	13
Toregas,Wyatt	08	R	26	2	a/a	CLE	317	32	72	15	0	12	52	28	51	2	1	228	291	391	683	8%	84%	0.55	102	39	3.97	47
	09	R	27	2	aaa	CLE	208	17	49	8	0	6	22	13	39	0	1	234	279	354	633	6%	81%	0.33	76	20	3.37	5
Torrealba,Steve	08	R	31	0	aa	BAL	120	12	26	6	0	6	20	9	21	1	0	220	276	418	694	7%	82%	0.44	121	35	3.98	53
	09	R	32	2	a/a	BAL	151	9	31	8	0	4	20	25	31	0	0	203	315	338	652	14%	80%	0.81	88	3	3.82	21
Torres,Eider	08	B	26	4	aaa	BAL	473	55	124	17	4	1	37	30	52	23	12	262	306	320	626	6%	89%	0.58	42	117	3.40	38
	09	B	27	6	aaa	CHW	359	30	74	10	1	1	24	20	62	11	7	205	247	246	493	5%	83%	0.33	31	86	1.97	-6
Torres,Tim	09	B	26	6	aa	FLA	224	21	44	8	2	1	23	21	57	7	1	197	265	260	525	8%	74%	0.36	44	114	2.47	-15
Tosoni,Rene	09	L	23	8	aa	MIN	425	56	104	24	3	12	63	37	91	7	9	244	305	397	702	8%	79%	0.41	98	90	4.02	38
Towles,J.R.	08	R	25 a	2	aa	HOU	168	20	42	7	1	6	20	10	25	3	4	251	292	406	698	5%	85%	0.38	94	81	3.84	52
	09	R	26 a	2	aa	HOU	145	17	33	10	1	3	16	16	22	2	0	227	304	370	673	10%	85%	0.72	99	82	4.06	64
Tracy,Andy	08	L	35	3	aaa	PHI	430	52	100	27	0	19	63	47	100	3	0	233	308	427	735	10%	77%	0.47	123	54	4.71	44
	09	L	36	3	aaa	PHI	453	55	92	18	1	21	70	53	112	5	1	203	286	387	672	10%	75%	0.47	109	70	3.83	32
Tracy,Chad	09	R	24 a	3	aa	TEX	535	55	131	29	1	21	84	36	89	4	2	244	292	420	712	6%	83%	0.41	110	53	4.28	53
Trumbo,Mark	08	R	23 a	3	aa	LAA	123	11	31	7	1	5	21	6	24	1	2	252	287	447	734	5%	80%	0.25	120	69	4.20	50
	09	R	24	3	aa	LAA	533	48	145	34	2	13	78	32	91	5	3	272	314	416	729	6%	83%	0.36	97	59	4.68	41
Tucker,Jonathan	08	R	25 a	546	aa	BAL	418	60	99	22	3	6	39	40	56	7	8	236	303	342	645	9%	87%	0.72	73	94	3.51	52
	09	R	26 b	8	a/a	BAL	453	66	109	22	4	1	35	47	59	29	11	240	311	311	622	9%	87%	0.80	53	138	3.49	53

Major League Equivalent Statistics

BATTERS

BATTER	Yr	B	Age	Pos	Lev	Org	ab	r	h	d	t	hr	rbi	bb	k	sb	cs	ba	ob	slg	ops	bb%	ct%	eye	px	sx	rc/g	bpv
Tuiasosopo,Matt	08	R	22	5	aa	SEA	437	71	109	29	1	10	60	40	90	3	0	249	312	389	701	8%	79%	0.44	96	83	4.42	38
	09	R	23	5	aa	SEA	226	37	53	14	0	10	30	32	80	3	1	234	330	425	755	13%	65%	0.41	121	65	5.07	2
Tupman,Matt	08	L	29	2	aa	KC	288	27	55	9	1	3	26	17	41	0	1	189	234	254	488	5%	86%	0.41	44	50	1.95	6
	09	L	30	2	aa	ARI	195	11	40	5	1	1	19	9	20	0	0	207	244	256	500	5%	90%	0.48	34	32	2.11	8
Turner,Justin	08	R	24	4	aa	CIN	280	34	72	13	1	7	31	25	43	2	1	256	318	382	699	8%	85%	0.59	81	63	4.38	41
	09	R	25 a	4	aaa	BAL	387	48	107	25	0	2	37	29	34	8	4	275	326	355	680	7%	91%	0.84	65	72	4.22	54
Valaika,Chris	08	R	23	6	aa	CIN	379	44	100	17	1	10	38	22	59	5	5	264	303	390	694	5%	84%	0.36	81	66	4.08	35
	09	R	24	6	aaa	CIN	366	26	77	18	1	6	30	13	69	1	0	210	238	312	550	4%	81%	0.20	71	46	2.48	4
Valdez,Alexander	09	B	25	5	aa	OAK	275	30	61	12	3	3	32	23	32	3	4	222	281	318	599	8%	88%	0.71	64	92	2.98	50
Valencia,Daniel	08	R	24	5	aa	MIN	266	33	66	16	2	8	26	13	64	2	1	249	285	411	697	5%	76%	0.21	105	88	4.08	27
	09	R	25 a	5	a/a	MIN	487	65	120	34	3	10	57	31	73	0	4	247	292	392	684	6%	85%	0.42	99	59	3.90	51
Valido,Robert	08	R	23	6	a/a	CHW	407	31	78	9	4	3	25	18	82	16	11	193	226	255	481	4%	80%	0.22	39	120	1.76	-3
	09	R	24	6	aa	BAL	334	35	70	10	4	3	23	13	44	7	3	210	240	287	528	4%	87%	0.31	49	124	2.28	34
Vallejo,Jose	08	B	22	4	aa	TEX	259	27	69	14	2	2	24	12	35	12	1	266	299	359	658	4%	86%	0.34	67	123	4.03	47
	09	B	23	4	aa	HOU	412	35	88	12	4	2	28	20	72	8	4	214	250	276	526	5%	82%	0.27	41	107	2.30	6
Van Ostrand,James	09	R	25	3	aa	HOU	367	32	86	15	1	12	51	31	55	0	0	236	295	382	677	8%	85%	0.56	90	24	3.98	36
Vazquez,Jorge	09	R	28	3	aa	NYY	225	26	65	14	1	12	49	7	49	0	0	288	310	512	822	3%	78%	0.15	137	37	5.78	42
Vechionacci,Marcos	09	B	23	5	aa	NYY	422	42	85	17	1	10	41	33	112	0	0	202	260	316	576	7%	73%	0.30	73	38	2.80	-20
Velazquez,Gil	08	R	29	6	aaa	BOS	350	40	75	17	3	7	34	16	68	3	3	214	248	337	585	4%	81%	0.23	80	93	2.72	25
	09	R	30	6	aaa	BOS	290	22	51	14	0	3	15	16	55	3	1	175	219	249	468	5%	81%	0.30	56	58	1.79	-1
Velez,Eugenio	08	B	26 b	8	aa	SF	171	20	46	10	3	4	12	14	30	11	9	269	324	425	749	7%	82%	0.45	100	148	4.27	70
	09	B	27 b	8	aa	SF	182	23	46	12	3	2	21	10	24	13	9	252	291	376	667	5%	87%	0.41	85	159	3.32	75
Venable,Will	08	L	26	8	aa	SD	442	56	106	21	3	10	47	35	100	6	3	240	296	370	666	7%	77%	0.35	83	94	3.83	21
	09	L	27	8	aa	SD	200	25	40	7	2	8	22	15	42	1	0	202	257	382	639	7%	79%	0.35	105	91	3.31	42
Vento,Mike	09	R	31	8	aaa	WAS	159	17	31	9	1	3	13	3	28	2	2	198	210	326	537	2%	82%	0.09	85	98	2.11	32
Viciedo,Dayan	09	R	21	5	aa	CHW	504	65	135	19	0	12	70	22	76	4	2	268	298	378	676	4%	85%	0.29	71	63	4.01	25
Wabick,David	09	L	25	8	aa	NYM	426	31	104	26	1	3	41	15	68	4	4	245	271	331	602	3%	84%	0.22	67	53	3.02	14
Wagner,Mark	08	R	24	2	aa	BOS	342	35	67	19	0	7	37	29	65	0	0	196	259	312	570	8%	81%	0.45	80	29	2.74	15
	09	R	25 a	2	a/a	BOS	307	28	76	33	0	5	37	33	51	1	0	248	321	401	722	10%	83%	0.64	119	33	4.68	60
Wald,Jake	08	R	28	6	aa	SF	365	45	76	20	3	4	31	33	102	6	1	207	273	306	579	8%	72%	0.33	70	116	2.94	-3
	09	R	29	6	aa	SF	252	27	48	7	3	4	28	23	68	3	2	192	259	283	542	8%	73%	0.34	56	106	2.47	-13
Walker,Neil	08	B	23	5	aa	PIT	505	59	113	25	5	13	69	24	89	9	7	223	258	367	625	4%	82%	0.26	91	113	3.06	47
	09	B	24 a	5	aa	PIT	356	30	83	29	1	11	55	20	50	4	2	232	273	407	680	5%	86%	0.40	120	59	3.78	70
Wallace,Brett	09	L	23	5	aa	OAK	532	55	129	22	0	14	46	33	84	1	3	243	288	361	649	6%	84%	0.40	76	31	3.58	21
Watkins,Tommy	08	R	28	8	aaa	MIN	233	24	40	7	2	1	13	18	31	4	4	174	232	230	462	7%	87%	0.57	39	97	1.67	24
	09	R	29	8	aaa	MIN	129	13	25	5	0	0	8	8	21	2	3	193	239	233	472	6%	84%	0.37	35	67	1.74	-3
Watson,Brandon	08	L	27	8	aaa	PHI	518	61	134	18	1	5	32	20	52	9	9	259	286	328	615	4%	90%	0.38	48	75	3.15	30
	09	L	28 b	8	aa	ARI	463	54	111	14	5	5	37	23	26	14	10	239	274	319	593	5%	94%	0.88	51	115	2.87	65
Weber,Jonathan	08	L	31	8	aaa	TAM	389	41	78	18	3	9	36	28	98	8	6	201	255	332	587	7%	75%	0.29	84	98	2.72	11
	09	L	32	8	aaa	TAM	451	48	106	36	0	10	52	43	102	3	7	236	301	383	684	9%	77%	0.42	105	37	3.86	24
Weeks,Jemile	09	B	23	4	aa	OAK	105	7	21	4	0	1	9	7	11	3	0	200	250	267	517	6%	90%	0.64	48	61	2.38	30
Weglarz,Nick	09	L	22 a	8	aa	CLE	339	64	73	16	1	14	60	73	71	2	3	215	353	393	747	18%	79%	1.02	109	64	5.02	60
Wells,Casper	08	R	24 a	8	aa	DET	270	46	68	16	5	13	40	24	51	6	4	250	311	486	797	8%	81%	0.46	141	157	5.16	102
	09	R	25	8	aa	DET	311	41	71	15	3	12	33	34	86	7	9	228	304	417	720	10%	72%	0.39	114	105	4.05	33
Whitesell,Josh	08	L	26	3	aa	ARI	475	67	137	32	0	22	86	60	121	1	2	289	368	496	864	11%	75%	0.50	132	30	6.89	37
	09	L	27	3	aa	ARI	225	26	57	13	1	6	44	31	43	1	1	252	342	400	742	12%	81%	0.71	96	50	5.01	41
Whiteside,Eli	08	R	29	2	a/a	SF	175	11	31	5	0	2	16	9	28	2	0	176	215	236	452	5%	84%	0.31	42	48	1.70	-5
	09	R	30	2	aa	SF	116	12	22	6	1	4	18	6	40	0	0	193	233	371	603	5%	66%	0.15	110	68	2.82	-16
Whitney,Matthew	08	R	25	30	aa	CLE	463	49	110	27	1	9	50	52	88	0	0	238	315	357	672	10%	81%	0.59	82	31	4.07	22
	09	R	26	3	a/a	WAS	280	39	66	16	1	7	31	36	59	2	1	235	322	369	691	11%	79%	0.61	90	68	4.29	33
Whittleman,John	09	L	23	5	aa	TEX	438	49	89	26	1	8	46	65	90	3	2	203	306	322	628	13%	79%	0.72	83	56	3.50	29
Wieters,Matt	08	B	22 a	2	aa	BAL	208	36	71	13	1	11	45	34	24	1	0	341	434	572	1006	14%	88%	1.42	141	57	10.37	114
	09	B	23 a	2	aaa	BAL	141	23	40	8	1	5	27	18	27	0	0	285	364	459	823	11%	81%	0.66	109	60	6.39	54
Williams,Jackson	09	R	23	2	aa	SF	300	28	62	20	0	2	21	29	52	1	6	206	277	291	567	9%	83%	0.56	68	36	2.58	16
Willits,Reggie	09	B	28	8	aa	LAA	234	32	51	9	1	1	21	26	44	9	4	218	297	275	572	10%	81%	0.60	42	104	2.94	12
Wilson,Bobby	09	R	26	2	aa	LAA	354	31	84	17	1	6	46	17	54	0	0	236	272	346	618	5%	85%	0.32	74	33	3.26	19
Wilson,Josh	08	R	28	64	a/a	BOS	405	32	90	23	1	5	32	22	63	10	5	222	262	318	579	5%	84%	0.34	70	77	2.76	29
	09	R	28	6	aa	SEA	103	11	21	4	1	2	11	7	15	2	1	205	256	316	572	6%	86%	0.48	72	100	2.70	45
Wilson,Michael	08	B	25	8	aa	SEA	407	58	93	23	1	20	65	49	109	7	0	229	311	434	746	11%	73%	0.45	126	86	4.88	44
	09	B	26	8	aa	SEA	235	28	39	6	1	8	24	25	83	5	0	164	244	301	546	10%	65%	0.30	79	99	2.53	-27
Wimberly,Corey	08	B	25	46	aa	COL	388	45	98	14	1	0	18	28	31	40	19	252	302	294	597	7%	92%	0.89	35	118	3.01	47
	09	B	26	6	aa	OAK	297	39	70	8	2	0	20	17	23	15	9	234	275	275	551	5%	92%	0.72	31	123	2.49	43
Winfree,David	08	R	23	8	aa	MIN	453	48	100	25	2	15	72	32	78	2	3	221	273	381	653	7%	83%	0.42	102	58	3.47	46
	09	R	24	8	aaa	MIN	422	39	100	28	2	11	51	22	80	0	2	237	275	387	661	5%	81%	0.28	101	43	3.59	30
Wipke,Flint	09	R	27	2	aa	LAA	185	21	37	8	0	4	18	19	59	3	2	199	275	303	578	9%	68%	0.33	70	62	2.83	-31
Witter,Adam	08	L	26	2	aa	SF	400	47	82	16	2	15	64	53	94	0	6	204	297	367	664	12%	77%	0.56	98	42	3.59	22
	09	L	27	0	aa	SF	243	18	40	7	1	6	27	17	53	0	0	167	223	273	495	7%	78%	0.33	65	37	1.98	-9
Wood,Brandon	08	R	24 a	6	aa	LAA	395	69	105	20	1	25	70	37	90	5	6	265	329	506	835	9%	77%	0.41	142	74	5.76	64
	09	R	25 a	5	aa	LAA	386	57	103	27	3	18	62	31	74	1	1	266	320	492	813	7%	81%	0.42	141	75	5.66	76
Woodward,Chris	08	R	32	64	aaa	MIL	297	20	60	13	1	2	26	18	40	2	1	200	246	266	512	6%	87%	0.45	49	51	2.20	14
	09	R	33	6	a/a	BOS	205	20	48	12	1	1	12	19	39	3	1	232	296	311	607	8%	81%	0.48	61	76	3.32	15
Worth,Danny	08	R	23 a	6	a/a	DET	297	35	67	16	3	4	26	25	47	6	0	224	286	337	622	8%	84%	0.54	76	119	3.47	51
	09	R	24	4	a/a	DET	436	35	91	19	3	0	24	31	97	6	7	209	262	265	527	7%	78%	0.32	44	81	2.28	-14
Wright,Ty	09	R	25	8	aa	CHC	442	55	115	21	1	8	47	28	54	4	5	261	304	365	669	6%	88%	0.51	71	62	3.86	40
Yarbrough,Brandon	08	L	24	20	aa	STL	306	30	63	12	5	2	28	34	78	2	1	205	285	295	580	10%	75%	0.44	58	116	2.95	2
	09	L	25	2	aa	STL	119	11	29	6	1	1	9	16	33	0	1	242	333	331	664	12%	72%	0.49	62	59	3.98	-18
Yepez,Marcos	08	B	27	4	aa	WAS	167	16	34	7	2	1	22	17	33	6	5	204	276	286	562	9%	80%	0.51	57	113	2.56	22
	09	B	28	5	aaa	WAS	102	7	22	5	0	0	8	8	21	3	2	212	270	256	526	7%	79%	0.38	39	58	2.33	-18
Young Jr.,Eric	08	B	23 a	4	aa	COL	403	52	103	21	3	2	24	42	53	32	20	255	326	336	661	9%	87%	0.79	59	125	3.66	53
	09	B	24 a	4	aa	COL	472	93	129	19	8	6	34	43	64	45	15	273	334	382	716	8%	87%	0.68	69	191	4.65	78
Young,Matt	08	L	26 b	8	aa	ATL	491	56	119	13	7	2	38	52	55	23	13	242	314	309	623	9%	89%	0.93	42	137	3.40	51
	09	L	27 b	8	a/a	ATL	486	70	118	19	6	4	29	80	62	35	17	242	349	331	681	14%	87%	1.29	59	142	4.21	69
Zawadzki,Lance	09	B	24	6	aa	SD	346	46	82	14	4	4	34	35	66	11	1	236	305	333	638	9%	81%	0.53	64	136	3.77	36

Major League Equivalent Statistics

PITCHER	Yr	Age	Th		Lev	Org	w	l	g	sv	ip	h	er	hr	bb	k	era	whip	bf/g	oob	ctl	dom	cmd	hr/9	h%	s%	bpv
							Actual				Major League Equivalents																
Abreu,Erick	09	26	R		a/a	HOU	5	2	33	0	75	99	44	13	28	48	5.33	1.69	10.5	311	3.3	5.7	1.7	1.6	34%	73%	15
Abreu,Winston	09	33	R		aaa	TAM	3	1	37	15	51	27	15	5	17	65	2.60	0.87	5.2	155	3.0	11.4	3.8	0.9	22%	76%	145
Accardo,Jeremy	09	28	R		aaa	TOR	2	1	27	13	30	36	12	1	8	22	3.47	1.47	4.9	290	2.5	6.6	2.6	0.3	36%	76%	81
Additon,Nicholas	09	22	L		aa	STL	2	3	8	0	48	39	18	5	19	22	3.38	1.21	24.8	218	3.6	4.1	1.2	0.9	23%	75%	32
Adkins,James	08	23	L		aa	LA	1	3	8	0	38	46	22	5	28	23	5.21	1.95	23.1	293	6.6	5.4	0.8	1.2	33%	75%	11
	09	24	L		aa	LA	6	10	27	0	138	169	86	9	77	70	5.57	1.78	24.1	295	5.0	4.5	0.9	0.6	33%	68%	24
Alaniz,Adrian	08	25	R		aa	WAS	0	5	13	0	66	67	31	8	29	37	4.16	1.47	22.3	259	4.0	5.0	1.3	1.1	28%	75%	26
	09	26	R		aa	WAS	3	4	24	1	64	92	51	12	38	41	7.18	2.03	13.2	330	5.3	5.8	1.1	1.7	36%	67%	-5
Albaladejo,Jonathan	09	27	R	b	aaa	NYY	3	0	27	11	36	31	10	5	3	21	2.58	0.95	5.2	227	0.8	5.3	6.9	1.3	24%	82%	148
Albano,Marco	09	26	R		aa	LAA	6	6	30	0	88	101	55	13	44	64	5.64	1.64	13.4	282	4.5	6.5	1.5	1.3	32%	68%	29
Alderson,Tim	09	21	R		aa	PIT	9	2	20	0	111	123	53	9	24	56	4.32	1.32	23.6	275	1.9	4.5	2.3	0.7	31%	68%	55
Alfonzo,Edgar	08	24	L		aa	NYM	2	2	28	0	38	49	22	7	14	27	5.13	1.68	6.2	308	3.4	6.4	1.9	1.7	35%	75%	20
	09	25	L		aa	NYM	4	5	49	0	70	89	36	3	31	35	4.59	1.71	6.6	304	3.9	4.5	1.2	0.4	35%	72%	33
Alvarado,Giancarlo	08	31	R		aa	LAA	7	5	26	0	130	200	106	20	90	79	7.31	2.23	25.8	345	6.2	5.5	0.9	1.4	38%	68%	-4
	09	32	R		aaa	LA	13	10	27	0	152	154	63	17	52	118	3.74	1.35	24.1	257	3.1	7.0	2.3	1.0	31%	75%	63
Ambriz,Hector	08	24	R		aa	ARI	5	13	27	0	152	194	114	29	49	100	6.72	1.60	25.5	304	2.9	5.9	2.0	1.7	33%	61%	20
	09	25	R		a/a	ARI	12	11	28	0	156	213	103	16	45	113	5.94	1.65	25.5	318	2.6	6.5	2.5	0.9	38%	64%	56
Anderson,Jason	08	29	R		a/a	PHI	3	3	47	2	64	111	48	7	32	34	6.68	2.23	7.0	372	4.5	4.7	1.1	1.0	41%	70%	0
	09	30	R		a/a	PHI	3	3	51	8	70	80	41	11	29	32	5.29	1.55	6.2	281	3.7	4.1	1.1	1.4	29%	69%	4
Anton,Michael	09	25	L		aa	LAA	3	8	20	0	81	104	63	7	47	51	7.00	1.87	19.4	305	5.3	5.7	1.1	0.8	35%	61%	26
Antonini,Michael	08	23	L		aa	NYM	1	3	8	0	45	49	23	10	16	27	4.52	1.46	24.7	273	3.3	5.4	1.6	2.1	28%	78%	6
	09	24	L		a/a	NYM	7	6	27	0	122	178	95	11	38	79	6.99	1.77	21.2	333	2.8	5.8	2.1	0.8	39%	59%	41
Aquino,Greg	09	32	R		aaa	CLE	1	2	30	16	31	31	14	3	16	23	3.95	1.48	4.6	251	4.6	6.6	1.4	0.9	30%	76%	47
Arguello,Douglas	09	25	L		aa	HOU	3	4	14	0	75	80	32	4	26	46	3.79	1.42	23.2	268	3.2	5.5	1.7	0.5	31%	73%	56
Arias,Wilkin	09	29	L		aa	NYY	5	4	48	0	61	83	44	6	30	45	6.43	1.84	6.1	316	4.4	6.6	1.5	0.9	37%	65%	35
Armas Jr.,Tony	08	30	R		aa	NYM	5	7	17	0	102	136	49	13	27	53	4.28	1.59	27.1	313	2.4	4.7	2.0	1.1	34%	76%	28
	09	31	R		a/a	ATL	1	2	14	0	64	89	40	10	27	32	5.62	1.80	21.6	322	3.7	4.4	1.2	1.4	35%	72%	0
Arnesen,Erik	09	26	R		aa	WAS	8	6	22	0	123	179	82	14	30	71	6.01	1.70	25.8	332	2.2	5.2	2.4	1.1	37%	65%	38
Arrieta,Jacob	09	24	R		a/a	BAL	11	11	28	0	150	177	82	19	59	124	4.91	1.57	24.1	288	3.5	7.4	2.1	1.1	35%	71%	52
Ascanio,Jose	08	23	R		aa	CHC	2	1	40	11	54	61	36	11	24	49	5.99	1.56	6.1	278	3.9	8.1	2.0	1.9	32%	66%	34
	09	24	R	a	aaa	PIT	2	5	13	0	58	60	24	2	18	46	3.72	1.34	19.0	262	2.8	7.1	2.6	0.3	33%	71%	90
Atencio,Greg	08	27	R		aa	KC	4	4	36	4	79	98	51	5	43	62	5.76	1.78	10.3	297	4.9	7.1	1.4	0.5	37%	66%	52
	09	28	R		a/a	CIN	5	9	39	2	54	88	60	5	26	44	9.98	2.11	7.0	358	4.3	7.4	1.7	0.8	44%	49%	40
Atilano,Luis	09	24	R		a/a	WAS	9	8	23	0	125	188	75	16	29	55	5.41	1.73	25.3	339	2.1	4.0	1.9	1.2	36%	71%	16
Atkins,Mitch	08	23	R		aa	CHC	17	7	28	0	164	176	85	28	52	110	4.64	1.39	25.3	269	2.8	6.0	2.1	1.5	30%	72%	36
	09	24	R		aaa	CHC	8	12	27	0	146	188	131	32	54	109	8.07	1.66	24.8	306	3.3	6.7	2.0	2.0	34%	53%	17
Augenstein,Bryan	09	23	R	a	a/a	ARI	7	5	17	0	81	78	31	2	14	57	3.44	1.13	19.4	248	1.6	6.3	4.1	0.2	31%	68%	122
Austen,David	08	27	R		aa	LAA	3	4	20	0	70	128	66	11	16	28	8.52	2.05	17.4	385	2.0	3.6	1.8	1.4	41%	58%	-4
	09	28	R		aaa	LAA	2	5	10	0	42	68	39	4	13	16	8.26	1.91	20.4	355	2.8	3.4	1.2	0.9	38%	55%	2
Avery,James	08	24	R		aa	CIN	7	8	24	0	130	177	86	19	46	77	5.97	1.71	25.1	317	3.2	5.3	1.7	1.3	35%	67%	19
	09	25	R		aa	CIN	2	3	10	0	56	71	30	4	22	25	4.82	1.67	25.7	303	3.6	4.1	1.1	0.7	33%	71%	21
Avery,Matt	08	25	R		aa	CHC	4	2	32	1	66	81	41	12	39	40	5.59	1.81	9.8	296	5.3	5.4	1.0	1.7	32%	73%	0
	09	26	R		aa	WAS	1	1	28	1	47	75	37	8	31	26	7.01	2.24	8.7	352	5.9	5.0	0.8	1.5	38%	71%	-14
Axford,John	09	27	R		a/a	MIL	5	0	26	1	40	37	20	3	24	38	4.48	1.52	6.9	238	5.5	8.5	1.5	0.7	31%	71%	68
Backe,Brandon	09	32	R		a/a	HOU	3	1	6	0	36	39	11	0	11	16	2.78	1.39	25.9	270	2.8	4.1	1.5	0.0	31%	78%	56
Baez,Federico	09	28	R		a/a	CIN	6	3	43	0	58	93	38	9	25	36	5.84	2.03	6.7	354	3.8	5.5	1.4	1.5	40%	74%	4
Bailey,Homer	08	22	R		aaa	CIN	4	7	19	0	111	130	69	12	45	88	5.55	1.57	26.2	285	3.6	7.1	2.0	1.0	34%	65%	52
	09	23	R		aaa	CIN	8	5	14	0	89	103	35	14	28	72	3.53	1.47	28.0	283	2.8	7.3	2.6	1.4	33%	82%	54
Baker,Brian	09	27	R		aa	TAM	5	6	31	0	121	172	91	14	48	78	6.75	1.82	18.5	328	3.6	5.8	1.6	1.0	38%	63%	28
Baldwin,Andrew	08	26	R		aa	SEA	10	5	30	0	147	216	97	14	47	70	5.91	1.78	23.1	334	2.9	4.3	1.5	0.9	37%	67%	19
	09	27	R		aaa	SEA	6	11	31	0	151	179	82	20	39	88	4.89	1.44	21.3	288	2.3	5.3	2.3	1.2	32%	69%	41
Balester,Collin	08	22	R		aaa	WAS	9	3	15	0	78	82	36	11	21	57	4.17	1.32	22.1	264	2.4	6.5	2.7	1.3	30%	73%	59
	09	23	R		aaa	WAS	7	10	20	0	107	150	67	5	37	61	5.63	1.75	25.0	324	3.1	5.1	1.6	0.4	38%	66%	43
Ballard,Michael	08	25	L		aa	TEX	11	6	25	0	134	197	85	8	41	77	5.72	1.77	25.2	334	2.8	5.2	1.9	0.6	38%	67%	42
	09	26	L		aa	TEX	8	8	28	0	151	200	88	21	33	79	5.26	1.54	24.1	312	1.9	4.7	2.4	1.3	34%	68%	34
Banks,Josh	08	26	R		a/a	SD	1	3	12	0	47	69	37	3	14	26	7.02	1.77	18.4	334	2.8	5.0	1.8	0.6	38%	58%	37
	09	27	R		aaa	SD	7	7	26	0	125	135	54	5	37	78	3.87	1.37	20.6	270	2.7	5.6	2.1	0.4	32%	71%	68
Bannister,John	09	26	R		a/a	KC	4	3	46	1	62	78	51	7	35	34	7.31	1.81	6.4	300	5.0	4.9	1.0	1.1	33%	59%	13
Banwart,Travis	09	24	R		a/a	OAK	10	6	28	0	145	184	85	11	40	68	5.28	1.54	23.1	303	2.5	4.2	1.7	0.7	34%	65%	35
Barnes,Scott	09	22	L		aa	CLE	2	2	6	0	31	42	27	8	15	26	7.79	1.83	24.7	316	4.3	7.5	1.7	2.3	35%	61%	4
Barnette,Anthony	08	25	R		aa	ARI	11	7	27	0	153	179	91	23	44	112	5.32	1.46	24.8	286	2.6	6.6	2.5	1.4	33%	66%	50
	09	26	R		aaa	ARI	14	8	29	0	164	196	109	24	56	106	5.98	1.53	25.2	290	3.0	5.8	1.9	1.3	32%	63%	32
Baron,Casey	09	25	L		aa	MIL	4	6	37	1	48	55	16	4	16	40	2.96	1.47	5.7	281	3.0	7.5	2.5	0.8	35%	83%	73
Barone,Daniel	08	25	R		aa	FLA	4	6	16	0	81	114	57	11	23	48	6.28	1.70	23.4	326	2.6	5.3	2.0	1.2	36%	64%	28
	09	26	R		a/a	OAK	2	8	17	0	68	111	57	12	16	26	7.48	1.86	19.2	358	2.1	3.4	1.7	1.6	37%	61%	-9
Bascom,Timothy	09	25	R		aa	BAL	3	7	15	0	81	111	62	6	33	47	6.88	1.76	25.4	318	3.6	5.2	1.4	0.7	36%	59%	31
Bastardo,Alberto	09	26	L		a/a	LA	6	3	14	0	73	85	40	6	32	49	4.92	1.60	23.6	285	3.9	6.1	1.6	0.8	33%	70%	44
Bastardo,Antonio	08	23	L		aa	PHI	1	5	14	0	67	62	31	15	37	50	4.15	1.48	21.0	240	5.0	6.8	1.4	2.1	25%	81%	14
	09	24	L	a	a/a	PHI	3	2	13	3	49	39	12	2	10	44	2.27	1.01	14.8	215	1.9	8.0	4.2	0.4	28%	78%	138
Bateman,Joe	08	28	R		a/a	MIL	3	1	49	8	77	79	24	5	26	59	2.75	1.36	6.7	259	3.0	6.8	2.3	0.5	32%	81%	75
	09	29	R		aaa	TAM	6	2	44	4	62	55	29	0	40	51	4.13	1.52	6.3	232	5.7	7.4	1.3	0.0	31%	70%	80
Batista,Kendy	09	28	R		aa	LA	5	1	24	1	58	59	21	3	31	40	3.30	1.55	10.8	258	4.8	6.2	1.3	0.4	31%	79%	56
Baugh,Kenneth	08	30	R		aa	FLA	3	1	15	0	36	65	36	8	27	17	8.95	2.54	13.2	382	6.6	4.1	0.6	2.0	40%	67%	-43
	09	31	R		aa	HOU	4	4	12	0	65	85	53	8	37	25	7.38	1.89	26.0	310	5.2	3.4	0.7	1.1	33%	60%	-6
Baumgardner,Thomas	09	26	L		aa	COL	2	2	53	2	57	84	26	1	24	30	4.16	1.89	5.2	334	3.8	4.8	1.3	0.2	39%	76%	38
Bautista,Denny	09	29	R		aaa	PIT	2	3	36	1	48	67	34	2	35	44	6.39	2.13	6.7	324	6.6	8.2	1.2	0.4	41%	68%	53
Bayliss,Jonah	08	28	R		a/a	TOR	3	5	54	5	72	111	54	12	31	38	6.75	1.96	6.5	344	3.8	4.8	1.3	1.5	37%	67%	-3
	09	29	R		aaa	TOR	7	2	38	5	50	46	25	5	26	37	4.55	1.45	5.8	240	4.7	6.7	1.4	1.0	28%	70%	47
Bazardo,Yorman	08	24	R		aaa	DET	4	13	25	0	130	202	117	20	43	66	8.10	1.88	25.0	347	3.0	4.6	1.5	1.4	38%	57%	4
	09	25	R		aaa	HOU	9	6	23	0	135	140	60	18	33	68	3.97	1.29	24.7	263	2.2	4.6	2.0	1.2	28%	73%	36

Major League Equivalent Statistics

						Actual				Major League Equivalents																
PITCHER	Yr	Age Th		Lev	Org	w	l	g	sv	ip	h	er	hr	bb	k	era	whip	bf/g	oob	ctl	dom	cmd	hr/9	h%	s%	bpv
Beam,T.J.	08	28 R		aa	PIT	2	1	30	5	43	53	24	3	18	27	4.95	1.62	6.5	294	3.6	5.7	1.6	0.5	35%	69%	47
	09	29 R		aaa	TOR	8	4	39		119	160	84	12	32	69	6.31	1.61	13.9	316	2.4	5.2	2.2	0.9	36%	60%	41
Beato,Pedro	09	23 R		aa	BAL	1	3	6	0	32	42	24	9	7	15	6.75	1.53	23.7	310	2.0	4.2	2.1	2.5	30%	63%	-13
Beavan,Blake	09	21 R		aa	TEX	4	4	15	0	89	123	47	5	12	30	4.71	1.52	26.4	321	1.2	3.1	2.5	0.5	35%	68%	47
Belisle,Matt	08	28 R		a/a	CIN	6	1	27	4	47	67	28	1	13	22	5.41	1.70	8.0	328	2.5	4.2	1.7	0.2	37%	66%	44
	09	29 R		aaa	COL	1	1	33	9	58	68	23	2	14	36	3.57	1.42	7.6	287	2.2	5.6	2.5	0.3	34%	74%	75
Bell,Trevor	09	23 R		a/a	LAA	7	7	22	0	140	136	49	6	34	75	3.15	1.21	26.3	250	2.2	4.8	2.2	0.4	29%	74%	69
Benacka,Michael	09	27 R	b	a/a	OAK	3	1	55	4	79	70	26	0	38	67	3.01	1.37	6.2	233	4.3	7.6	1.8	0.0	31%	76%	91
Benson,Kris	08	34 R		aaa	PHI	1	4	11	0	60	105	51	11	16	27	7.57	2.01	27.0	375	2.4	4.0	1.7	1.6	40%	64%	-8
	09	35 R		a/a	TEX	4	6	12	0	73	108	60	8	28	41	7.38	1.85	29.1	335	3.4	5.1	1.5	1.0	38%	59%	21
Berg,Justin	08	24 R		aa	CHC	4	9	32	0	118	139	80	14	62	48	6.09	1.70	17.1	287	4.7	3.6	0.8	1.0	30%	65%	4
	09	25 R		aaa	CHC	6	2	37	0	55	47	18	2	30	30	2.96	1.41	6.5	228	4.9	4.8	1.0	0.3	27%	79%	49
Berger,Eric	09	23 L		aa	CLE	3	1	6	0	33	39	13	1	18	29	3.63	1.71	25.6	288	4.8	7.9	1.7	0.3	37%	78%	71
Berken,Jason	08	25 R		aa	BAL	12	4	26	0	145	171	75	12	39	104	4.63	1.44	24.4	287	2.4	6.4	2.7	0.7	34%	68%	70
	09	26 R		aa	BAL	3	1	7	0	33	31	12	3	14	19	3.14	1.33	20.2	239	3.7	5.2	1.4	0.9	27%	79%	41
Bierd,Randor	09	26 R		aaa	BOS	3	1	25	0	61	89	48	9	23	48	7.14	1.84	11.6	333	3.4	7.0	2.0	1.3	39%	62%	33
Birkins,Kurt	08	28 L		aaa	TAM	2	3	36	0	40	69	42	4	30	23	9.39	2.46	6.0	370	6.7	5.2	0.8	1.0	42%	60%	0
	09	29 L		a/a	COL	3	3	27	0	76	109	45	12	33	43	5.34	1.86	13.5	328	3.9	5.0	1.3	1.4	36%	75%	3
Blackley,Travis	08	26 L		aaa	PHI	5	10	28	0	123	158	96	20	63	73	7.02	1.79	20.7	305	4.6	5.4	1.2	1.5	33%	62%	6
	09	27 L		aaa	ARI	4	7	38	3	111	143	63	11	34	86	5.09	1.60	13.2	306	2.8	7.0	2.5	0.9	37%	69%	61
Bleich,Jeremy	09	22 L		aa	NYY	3	6	13	0	65	104	68	8	37	51	9.42	2.17	25.4	354	5.1	7.1	1.4	1.1	42%	55%	22
Blevins,Jerry	08	25 L	a	aa	OAK	2	2	28	10	32	37	11	3	6	28	3.12	1.32	4.9	281	1.6	7.8	5.0	0.9	35%	80%	123
	09	26 L		aaa	OAK	5	3	45	2	63	72	30	5	16	51	4.26	1.41	6.1	281	2.4	7.3	3.1	0.7	35%	70%	86
Bloom,Kyle	08	26 L		aa	PIT	5	8	28	0	109	132	71	10	61	70	5.86	1.77	18.3	293	5.0	5.8	1.1	0.8	34%	67%	30
	09	27 L		aa	PIT	6	9	22	0	104	118	63	3	62	51	5.47	1.73	22.0	280	5.4	4.4	0.8	0.3	32%	66%	34
Boggs,Mitchell	08	25 R		aa	STL	9	3	21	0	125	121	55	11	44	66	3.94	1.32	25.3	249	3.2	4.7	1.5	0.8	28%	71%	42
	09	26 R		aaa	STL	6	4	14	0	76	100	46	8	30	50	5.50	1.71	25.2	310	3.6	5.9	1.6	1.0	36%	69%	34
Bonderman,Jeremy	09	27 R		aaa	DET	1	4	14	1	34	49	22	5	7	21	5.73	1.67	11.1	333	1.9	5.6	3.0	1.4	37%	68%	44
Bonilla,Henry	08	30 R		aa	LAA	5	2	51	3	71	116	69	16	46	39	8.68	2.27	7.2	358	5.8	4.9	0.8	2.0	38%	64%	-29
	09	31 R		aaa	LA	3	11	41	3	77	100	56	7	29	49	6.50	1.68	8.7	307	3.4	5.8	1.7	0.9	35%	60%	38
Bonine,Eddie	08	27 R		a/a	DET	12	5	18	0	110	143	67	11	22	54	5.45	1.49	27.0	307	1.8	4.4	2.5	0.9	34%	64%	44
	09	28 R		aaa	DET	4	5	17	0	102	144	70	12	17	41	6.17	1.58	27.0	326	1.5	3.6	2.4	1.0	35%	61%	30
Boone,Randy	09	25 R		a/a	TOR	9	10	27	0	137	171	85	8	51	80	5.60	1.61	23.0	299	3.3	5.2	1.6	0.6	35%	64%	43
Bootcheck,Chris	09	31 R		aaa	PIT	3	2	40	20	42	50	21	1	8	41	4.50	1.37	4.5	289	1.7	8.8	5.3	0.2	39%	65%	155
Bostick II,Adam	08	26 L		aa	NYM	2	2	11	0	44	60	39	7	21	23	7.92	1.84	19.1	317	4.3	4.8	1.1	1.4	35%	57%	3
	09	27 L		a/a	NYM	3	3	39	3	56	61	24	7	24	50	3.93	1.53	6.4	272	3.9	8.0	2.0	1.1	33%	77%	59
Bowden,Michael	08	22 R	a	a/a	BOS	9	7	26	0	144	129	52	10	29	111	3.25	1.10	22.3	235	1.8	6.9	3.8	0.6	29%	72%	111
	09	23 R		aaa	BOS	4	6	24	0	126	137	68	14	52	76	4.85	1.50	23.2	271	3.7	5.4	1.5	1.0	31%	69%	34
Bowers,Cedrick	08	31 L		aa	COL	6	1	35	1	65	79	43	7	56	44	5.93	2.07	9.3	293	7.7	6.1	0.8	1.0	34%	72%	20
	09	32 L		aaa	PHI	4	3	48	5	60	46	17	1	48	54	2.52	1.57	5.6	209	7.2	8.1	1.1	0.2	28%	83%	81
Boyd,Leon	09	26 R		aa	TOR	1	5	36	6	52	75	52	3	56	29	8.92	2.51	7.9	329	9.7	5.0	0.5	0.6	38%	62%	12
Bramhall,Bobby	09	24 L		aa	MIL	6	7	31	0	97	124	71	9	52	79	6.54	1.81	14.8	305	4.8	7.3	1.5	0.9	37%	63%	44
Bray,Stephen	08	28 R		a/a	MIL	2	8	46	1	75	99	56	17	32	57	6.76	1.75	7.6	311	3.9	6.8	1.8	2.1	34%	66%	8
	09	29 R		aa	SEA	7	8	26	0	144	188	76	16	45	64	4.76	1.61	25.1	308	2.8	4.0	1.4	1.0	33%	72%	17
Bright,Adam	08	24 L		aa	COL	3	8	47	0	49	65	28	4	13	30	5.22	1.59	4.7	313	2.3	5.6	2.4	0.8	36%	67%	53
	09	25 L		aa	COL	1	2	36	1	37	46	26	4	24	23	6.18	1.88	5.0	295	5.9	5.7	1.0	1.1	34%	68%	18
Broadway,Lance	08	25 R		aaa	CHW	11	7	24	0	145	199	99	33	45	89	6.14	1.69	27.8	320	2.8	5.5	2.0	2.1	34%	69%	3
	09	26 R		aaa	NYM	5	9	19	0	100	145	92	9	41	47	8.24	1.86	25.2	332	3.7	4.2	1.1	0.8	37%	53%	12
Brooks,Richard	09	25 R	a	aa	CHW	3	1	25	1	37	32	17	3	6	28	4.05	1.02	5.8	230	1.4	6.8	5.0	0.8	27%	61%	131
Broshuis,Garrett	08	27 R		aa	SF	13	9	28	0	157	239	95	18	40	73	5.47	1.78	26.3	343	2.3	4.2	1.8	1.1	37%	70%	18
	09	28 R		a/a	SF	6	5	13	0	65	109	39	7	23	27	5.41	2.03	24.8	365	3.2	3.7	1.2	1.0	40%	74%	0
Brown,Brooks	08	23 R		aa	ARI	6	15	26	0	144	186	90	10	69	97	5.60	1.77	26.0	306	4.3	6.1	1.4	0.6	36%	68%	40
	09	24 R		a/a	DET	8	13	26	0	149	184	89	12	65	50	5.35	1.67	26.3	297	3.9	3.0	0.8	0.7	32%	68%	8
Brown,Eric	08	25 R		aa	NYM	6	9	30	0	123	169	85	16	29	66	6.24	1.62	18.6	321	2.2	4.8	2.2	1.2	35%	62%	32
	09	26 R		aa	NYM	7	14	32	0	117	174	92	14	38	61	7.09	1.81	17.3	338	2.9	4.7	1.6	1.1	37%	61%	16
Browning,Barret	08	24 L		aa	LAA	1	1	27	1	31	36	26	2	14	28	7.43	1.62	5.2	284	4.2	8.1	1.9	0.6	36%	51%	70
	09	25 L		aa	LAA	3	10	48	0	90	115	58	9	48	58	5.78	1.81	8.9	303	4.8	5.8	1.2	0.3	36%	66%	45
Brownlie,Robert	08	28 R		a/a	WAS	9	7	30	0	150	201	96	29	54	72	5.78	1.70	23.1	315	3.2	4.3	1.3	1.8	33%	70%	-7
	09	29 R		aaa	ATL	5	2	14	0	56	75	34	8	19	37	5.46	1.66	18.4	313	3.0	6.0	2.0	1.2	36%	69%	33
Brummett,Tyson	08	24 R		aa	PHI	2	9	14	0	80	119	74	12	46	38	8.28	2.06	28.5	337	5.2	4.3	0.8	1.3	36%	60%	-9
	09	25 R		a/a	PHI	3	10	27	2	102	153	80	17	29	59	7.05	1.78	17.8	339	2.6	5.2	2.0	1.5	37%	62%	16
Buchholz,Clay	08	24 R	a	a/a	BOS	5	2	11	0	58	52	20	3	19	50	3.03	1.20	21.8	233	2.9	7.8	2.7	0.5	30%	75%	98
	09	25 R		aaa	BOS	7	2	17	0	99	88	40	9	33	76	3.67	1.22	24.1	233	3.0	6.9	2.3	0.8	28%	72%	73
Buck,Dallas	09	25 R		aa	CIN	2	3	8	0	37	61	27	1	20	21	6.64	2.18	23.7	360	4.9	5.1	1.0	0.3	42%	67%	28
Buckner,Billy	08	25 R		aaa	ARI	5	10	21	0	116	179	92	13	48	55	7.15	1.95	26.9	345	3.7	4.3	1.1	1.0	38%	63%	5
	09	26 R		aaa	ARI	9	3	18	0	103	98	40	5	41	82	3.51	1.35	24.4	246	3.6	7.2	2.0	0.5	31%	74%	78
Bueno,Francisley	08	28 L		aa	ATL	2	6	19	0	84	120	62	8	31	48	6.65	1.79	20.8	328	3.3	5.2	1.6	0.9	37%	62%	27
	09	29 L		aaa	ATL	4	1	33	1	54	57	24	1	23	27	3.93	1.47	7.2	265	3.7	4.5	1.2	0.2	31%	71%	49
Buente,Jay	09	26 R		a/a	FLA	5	2	51	2	83	96	38	8	50	65	4.10	1.75	7.6	283	5.4	7.0	1.3	0.8	34%	78%	43
Bullington,Bryan	08	28 R		a/a	CLE	5	9	25	1	128	215	113	20	47	81	7.94	2.05	25.4	365	3.3	5.7	1.7	1.4	41%	62%	10
	09	29 R	b	aaa	TOR	3	1	28	3	38	49	18	2	8	34	4.15	1.50	6.0	308	1.8	8.0	4.4	0.5	39%	72%	118
Bumgarner,Madison	09	20 L		aa	SF	9	1	20	0	107	90	28	6	29	62	2.32	1.10	21.5	223	2.4	5.2	2.2	0.5	26%	81%	73
Bump,Nate	08	32 R		aa	SF	4	3	17	0	58	65	25	2	26	20	3.83	1.56	15.3	276	4.0	3.2	0.8	0.4	30%	75%	24
	09	33 R		aaa	DET	7	1	10	0	68	73	25	4	11	27	3.34	1.22	28.2	268	1.4	3.5	2.5	0.6	29%	73%	59
Burnett,Alex	09	22 R	a	aa	MIN	1	2	40	9	55	42	17	2	19	43	2.78	1.11	5.5	207	3.1	7.0	2.3	0.3	26%	75%	93
Burns,Mike	08	30 R		aa	CHC	8	12	37	2	133	236	110	29	34	60	7.44	2.03	17.8	378	2.3	4.1	1.8	1.9	40%	66%	-17
	09	31 R		aaa	MIL	8	3	14	0	92	103	32	9	17	55	3.08	1.30	27.8	277	1.6	5.4	3.3	0.9	31%	80%	73
Burres,Brian	09	29 L		aaa	TOR	6	7	19	0	107	139	65	12	31	68	5.42	1.58	25.4	307	2.6	5.7	2.2	1.0	35%	67%	44

Major League Equivalent Statistics

							Actual				Major League Equivalents																
PITCHER	Yr	Age	Th		Lev	Org	w	l	g	sv	ip	h	er	hr	bb	k	era	whip	bf/g	oob	ctl	dom	cmd	hr/9	h%	s%	bpv
Burton,TJ	08	25	R		aa	CLE	2	2	29	0	30	53	18	1	17	18	5.33	2.33	5.4	378	5.0	5.4	1.1	0.3	44%	76%	24
	09	26	R		a/a	HOU	0	4	37	12	49	77	36	13	16	20	6.50	1.87	6.4	348	2.8	3.6	1.3	2.4	35%	72%	-39
Buschmann,Matt	08	25	R		aa	SD	10	6	27	0	148	157	57	13	61	96	3.46	1.47	24.1	266	3.7	5.8	1.6	0.8	31%	78%	47
	09	26	R		a/a	SD	5	11	35	0	140	181	96	15	44	67	6.16	1.61	18.1	307	2.8	4.3	1.5	0.9	34%	62%	22
Bush,Paul	09	30	R		a/a	NYY	3	3	12	0	37	33	21	4	24	30	5.17	1.52	13.7	231	5.8	7.2	1.2	0.9	28%	67%	51
Butler,Joshua	09	25	R		a/a	MIL	3	2	11	0	56	60	23	4	14	43	3.65	1.33	21.6	268	2.3	6.9	3.0	0.7	33%	74%	85
Butto,Francisco	09	29	R		a/a	PHI	2	1	24	2	33	57	18	2	26	21	4.97	2.51	7.5	372	7.0	5.8	0.8	0.7	43%	80%	13
Butts,Brett	09	23	R		aa	ATL	7	3	53	5	73	77	28	6	39	58	3.43	1.59	6.2	266	4.8	7.2	1.5	0.8	32%	80%	53
Buzachero,Edward	08	27	R		a/a	CLE	3	4	45	11	71	94	37	9	29	44	4.66	1.73	7.3	312	3.6	5.6	1.5	1.2	35%	76%	24
	09	28	R		a/a	TOR	5	4	49	10	72	64	28	9	18	41	3.52	1.13	6.0	232	2.2	5.1	2.3	1.2	25%	74%	53
Cabrera,Fernando	09	28	R		aaa	BOS	0	3	43	22	52	55	17	4	25	42	2.90	1.53	5.4	264	4.4	7.2	1.7	0.7	32%	83%	58
Capellan,Jose	08	28	R		aa	KC	4	1	9	0	53	66	37	6	23	22	6.33	1.68	27.1	299	3.9	3.8	1.0	1.0	32%	62%	8
	09	29	R		aaa	HOU	2	10	30	0	98	165	102	15	54	60	9.38	2.23	16.8	365	4.9	5.5	1.1	1.4	41%	57%	-3
Caridad,Esmailin	08	25	R		aa	CHC	7	3	14	0	82	78	35	17	22	41	3.80	1.22	24.3	245	2.4	4.5	1.8	1.8	24%	78%	16
	09	26	R		aaa	CHC	5	10	25	0	131	162	76	21	48	96	5.20	1.60	23.7	297	3.3	6.6	2.0	1.5	34%	71%	33
Carmona,Fausto	09	26	R		a/a	CLE	2	3	6	0	40	44	19	7	6	28	4.26	1.26	27.9	275	1.4	6.2	4.4	1.7	30%	73%	79
Carpenter,Christopher	09	24	R		aa	CHC	0	3	7	0	32	36	23	0	12	20	6.38	1.51	20.3	279	3.5	5.7	1.6	0.0	34%	53%	68
Carpenter,Drew	09	24	R		aaa	PHI	11	6	25	0	156	188	73	23	48	102	4.21	1.51	27.7	292	2.8	5.9	2.1	1.3	33%	77%	37
Carrasco,Carlos	08	22	R		a/a	PHI	9	9	26	0	151	154	70	16	55	138	4.14	1.39	25.0	259	3.3	8.2	2.5	1.0	32%	72%	76
	09	23	R	a	aaa	CLE	11	10	26	0	157	160	91	17	43	141	5.24	1.29	25.4	259	2.5	8.1	3.3	1.0	32%	60%	91
Carrillo,Cesar	09	25	R		a/a	SD	8	7	25	0	150	168	82	11	47	68	4.92	1.44	26.2	278	2.8	4.1	1.4	0.6	31%	65%	35
Carrillo,Marco	09	23	R		aa	CHC	4	1	31	0	51	60	31	8	31	39	5.46	1.78	7.7	287	5.5	6.9	1.3	1.4	33%	72%	23
Cashner,Andrew	09	23	R		aa	CHC	3	4	12	0	58	55	29	0	30	34	4.47	1.46	21.2	244	4.6	5.3	1.1	0.0	30%	66%	62
Cassel,Jack	08	28	R		aa	HOU	9	5	19	0	107	149	56	13	35	50	4.73	1.72	26.1	322	2.9	4.2	1.4	1.1	35%	74%	14
	09	29	R		aaa	CLE	5	7	15	0	90	135	75	13	42	42	7.46	1.96	29.3	339	4.2	4.2	1.0	1.3	36%	62%	-6
Cassel,Justin	08	24	R		aa	CHW	10	4	28	0	165	218	81	11	63	88	4.42	1.70	27.2	311	3.4	4.8	1.4	0.6	35%	74%	34
	09	25	R		a/a	CHW	7	11	27	0	126	184	93	19	53	67	6.61	1.88	22.4	333	3.8	4.7	1.3	1.4	36%	66%	3
Cassevah,Robert	09	24	R		aa	LAA	3	7	57	4	73	80	43	2	40	36	5.31	1.64	5.9	272	4.9	4.4	0.9	0.3	31%	65%	38
Castillo,Alberto	09	34	L		aaa	BAL	2	3	50	13	52	63	23	3	18	43	4.01	1.56	4.7	294	3.1	7.4	2.4	0.5	37%	74%	74
Castillo,Jesus	08	24	R		aa	LA	7	4	23	0	114	142	48	8	36	66	3.82	1.56	22.2	299	2.8	5.2	1.8	0.7	34%	76%	45
	09	25	R		aa	LA	7	9	29	0	150	191	97	12	66	71	5.80	1.71	24.0	304	3.9	4.3	1.1	0.7	34%	65%	21
Castro,Fabio	08	24	L		a/a	PHI	8	4	30	0	120	138	74	19	52	89	5.55	1.58	18.0	282	3.9	6.7	1.7	1.4	32%	68%	32
	09	25	L		a/a	TOR	9	6	29	0	164	192	91	8	72	88	4.98	1.61	25.6	286	4.0	4.8	1.2	0.5	33%	68%	39
Cecil,Brett	08	22	L		a/a	TOR	8	5	24	0	108	109	45	6	41	98	3.75	1.39	19.4	257	3.4	8.2	2.4	0.5	33%	73%	88
	09	23	L		aaa	TOR	1	5	9	0	49	57	33	2	19	28	6.06	1.55	24.3	285	3.5	5.1	1.5	0.4	33%	58%	49
Cedeno,Xavier	08	22	L		aa	COL	7	7	19	0	102	138	53	11	33	44	4.67	1.67	24.7	316	2.9	3.9	1.3	1.0	34%	74%	14
	09	23	L		aa	COL	3	2	28	0	47	56	33	8	22	20	6.32	1.65	7.7	289	4.1	3.9	0.9	1.6	30%	64%	-7
Chacin,Gustavo	09	29	L		a/a	PHI	9	4	20	0	115	154	59	14	53	48	4.60	1.80	27.2	314	4.1	3.7	0.9	1.1	34%	77%	0
Chacin,Jhoulys	09	22	R		a/a	COL	9	8	22	0	117	105	47	13	42	86	3.58	1.25	22.2	234	3.2	6.6	2.1	1.0	27%	75%	60
Chacon,Shawn	09	32	R		aaa	OAK	8	4	14	0	73	87	58	13	40	43	7.14	1.74	24.3	291	4.9	5.3	1.1	1.6	31%	61%	4
Chapman,Chance	09	26	R		aa	PHI	7	1	38	1	52	54	21	4	20	37	3.64	1.43	6.0	263	3.4	6.4	1.8	0.8	31%	76%	56
Chen,Bruce	09	32	L		aaa	KC	4	2	14	0	82	71	42	9	24	58	4.62	1.16	23.9	228	2.7	6.4	2.4	1.0	26%	62%	67
Chen,Hung-Wen	09	24	R		aa	CHC	8	11	27	0	142	201	94	16	35	81	5.94	1.66	24.1	326	2.2	5.2	2.3	1.0	37%	65%	38
Cherry,Rocky	08	29	R		a/a	BAL	0	1	30	0	39	50	17	4	13	29	3.93	1.62	5.9	305	3.1	6.6	2.1	0.8	36%	78%	53
	09	30	R		aaa	SD	3	2	44	0	70	93	33	3	46	38	4.28	1.98	7.8	313	5.8	4.9	0.8	0.4	36%	78%	26
Chiavacci,Ron	08	31	R		a/a	HOU	6	12	25	0	131	204	109	29	52	85	7.47	1.96	25.6	348	3.6	5.8	1.6	2.0	38%	65%	-5
	09	32	R		aaa	DET	1	5	20	2	46	73	38	7	26	28	7.40	2.15	11.7	350	5.1	5.4	1.0	1.4	39%	67%	-4
Chick,Travis	08	24	R		aa	SEA	7	5	32	0	129	132	62	11	62	94	4.33	1.50	17.8	259	4.3	6.6	1.5	0.7	31%	72%	52
	09	25	R		aa	LA	8	7	23	0	113	139	71	16	53	78	5.66	1.70	22.7	296	4.2	6.2	1.5	1.2	34%	69%	27
Chico,Matt	09	26	L		aa	WAS	2	4	12	0	50	75	37	2	33	27	6.61	2.16	21.2	338	6.0	4.8	0.8	0.4	39%	67%	21
Childers,Jason	08	34	R		aaa	CHW	4	2	50	17	59	42	11	3	15	51	1.61	0.96	4.6	196	2.2	7.8	3.5	0.5	25%	86%	121
	09	35	R		aaa	TAM	9	6	55	5	79	101	51	12	25	52	5.76	1.60	6.5	305	2.9	6.0	2.1	1.3	34%	66%	34
Choi,Hyang-Nam	09	39	R		aaa	LA	9	2	33	0	57	57	16	6	21	65	2.48	1.36	7.4	254	3.3	10.2	3.1	1.0	34%	87%	100
Christensen,Daniel	08	25	L		aa	DET	7	10	27	0	158	204	89	19	60	77	5.06	1.67	26.9	307	3.4	4.4	1.3	1.1	33%	71%	15
	09	26	L		aa	SEA	1	6	24	0	75	110	49	6	39	36	5.92	1.99	15.4	334	4.7	4.3	0.9	0.7	37%	70%	12
Cisco,Michael	09	22	R		aa	PHI	2	4	7	0	39	50	24	5	9	17	5.52	1.51	24.7	305	2.1	3.9	1.9	1.2	33%	65%	23
Claggett,Anthony	08	24	R		aa	NYY	4	2	29	9	58	67	20	1	34	44	3.09	1.74	9.3	284	5.2	6.8	1.3	0.2	36%	81%	61
	09	25	R		aaa	NYY	7	7	39	4	82	96	39	8	34	37	4.32	1.59	9.5	286	3.8	4.0	1.1	0.9	31%	74%	18
Clark,Zachary	08	25	R		a/a	BAL	5	4	14	0	78	96	44	8	19	29	5.09	1.47	24.5	296	2.2	3.4	1.6	1.0	31%	66%	20
	09	26	R		a/a	BAL	2	1	15	0	31	54	27	1	12	14	7.72	2.14	10.5	375	3.5	4.2	1.2	0.3	42%	61%	20
Clippard,Tyler	08	24	R		aaa	WAS	6	13	27	0	143	140	81	13	63	105	5.10	1.42	23.0	251	4.0	6.6	1.7	0.8	30%	64%	55
	09	25	R	a	aaa	WAS	4	1	24	1	39	23	5	2	15	36	1.15	0.97	6.3	168	3.5	8.3	2.4	0.5	22%	92%	108
Cochran,Thomas	09	27	L		a/a	CIN	5	6	20	1	102	132	54	13	52	63	4.76	1.80	24.1	307	4.6	5.5	1.2	1.1	35%	76%	19
Cody,Chris	09	26	L		a/a	MIL	13	9	27	0	152	176	80	20	42	92	4.73	1.43	24.5	284	2.5	5.5	2.2	1.2	32%	70%	41
Cofield,Kyle	09	23	R		aa	ATL	10	5	26	0	140	145	80	11	94	77	5.14	1.70	24.9	262	6.0	4.9	0.8	0.7	30%	70%	28
Coleman,Casey	09	22	R		aa	CHC	14	6	27	0	149	167	78	10	61	72	4.71	1.53	24.6	277	3.7	4.3	1.2	0.6	31%	69%	32
Collazo,Willie	08	29	L		aa	NYM	4	9	37	2	135	188	89	23	43	49	5.91	1.70	16.9	322	2.8	3.2	1.1	1.5	33%	68%	-11
	09	30	L		aaa	FLA	9	5	34	0	126	149	63	14	38	61	4.47	1.49	16.4	289	2.7	4.4	1.6	1.0	31%	72%	26
Concepcion,Alexander	09	25	R		a/a	PHI	2	3	38	3	95	102	44	13	13	45	4.18	1.21	10.3	269	1.2	4.2	3.5	1.2	29%	69%	65
Contreras,Jose	09	38	R		aaa	CHW	3	1	5	0	33	24	15	3	18	23	4.01	1.27	27.8	200	4.9	6.2	1.3	0.9	23%	70%	53
Corcoran,Tim	08	30	R		aa	FLA	4	2	16	0	55	97	46	6	24	34	7.45	2.20	17.7	376	4.0	5.5	1.4	0.9	43%	65%	14
	09	32	R		a/a	HOU	6	7	34	1	99	133	74	11	48	61	6.76	1.83	13.8	315	4.3	5.6	1.3	1.0	36%	63%	22
Corey,Bryan	09	36	R		aaa	TEX	7	9	31	0	116	185	95	15	25	64	7.34	1.81	17.7	353	2.0	4.9	2.5	1.1	39%	59%	33
Cortes,Daniel	08	22	R		aa	KC	10	4	23	0	116	121	63	14	54	96	4.88	1.51	22.4	263	4.2	7.4	1.8	1.1	32%	70%	52
	09	23	R		aa	SEA	7	11	26	0	135	147	79	8	91	101	5.27	1.76	24.3	272	6.1	6.7	1.1	0.5	33%	69%	48
Cotter,Aaron	09	26	R		aa	SEA	0	1	17	1	34	58	37	8	12	11	9.68	2.05	10.0	367	3.2	2.9	0.9	2.1	37%	54%	-44
Coultas,Ryan	09	27	R		aa	NYM	4	3	11	0	64	78	27	2	22	24	3.72	1.56	26.1	295	3.0	3.4	1.1	0.3	33%	75%	29
Cox,J.B.	08	24	R		a/a	NYY	5	4	33	1	42	41	28	4	21	17	5.94	1.47	5.6	251	4.4	3.7	0.8	0.9	27%	59%	19
	09	25	R		aa	BOS	1	5	45	12	56	84	26	2	31	29	4.10	2.06	6.2	340	5.0	4.6	0.9	0.4	39%	79%	23

Major League Equivalent Statistics

							Actual				Major League Equivalents																
PITCHER	Yr	Age	Th		Lev	Org	w	l	g	sv	ip	h	er	hr	bb	k	era	whip	bf/g	oob	ctl	dom	cmd	hr/9	h%	s%	bpv
Cramer,Bob	09	30	L		a/a	OAK	4	5	18	0	57	91	32	1	22	37	5.01	1.99	15.5	355	3.5	5.8	1.7	0.2	42%	73%	49
Cromer,Jason	08	28	L		aa	TAM	5	3	29	0	75	123	46	6	29	39	5.49	2.02	12.8	359	3.5	4.7	1.3	0.7	40%	73%	18
	09	29	L		a/a	TAM	11	6	28	0	153	218	75	11	54	66	4.43	1.78	25.7	327	3.2	3.9	1.2	0.6	36%	75%	20
Crotta,Michael	09	25	R		aa	PIT	7	8	27	0	143	224	98	8	34	73	6.15	1.81	25.1	349	2.2	4.6	2.1	0.5	40%	64%	42
Cruz,Rafael	09	32	R		a/a	ATL	1	3	30	13	31	42	17	3	11	20	4.82	1.71	4.8	317	3.2	5.7	1.8	1.0	36%	73%	34
Culp,Nathanial	09	25	L		aa	SD	8	9	28	0	158	200	83	13	31	53	4.74	1.46	24.7	302	1.8	3.0	1.7	0.8	32%	68%	26
Daigle,Casey	08	28	R		aaa	MIN	1	5	44	1	69	74	38	9	37	50	4.94	1.60	7.1	268	4.8	6.6	1.4	1.2	31%	72%	32
	09	29	R		aaa	HOU	4	3	49	5	55	75	24	4	28	43	3.86	1.87	5.4	318	4.6	7.0	1.5	0.7	39%	80%	44
Davidson,Daniel	08	28	L		aa	LAA	1	0	24	0	53	58	24	5	18	33	4.08	1.43	9.6	271	3.1	5.6	1.8	0.8	31%	73%	49
	09	29	L		aaa	LAA	2	3	45	0	50	76	46	12	24	36	8.31	2.00	5.5	343	4.2	6.5	1.5	2.1	38%	61%	-6
Davies,Kyle	08	25	R		aa	KC	6	2	11	0	57	61	19	4	23	30	2.97	1.48	22.9	268	3.7	4.7	1.3	0.7	30%	82%	35
	09	26	R		aaa	KC	4	2	8	0	46	57	14	3	14	38	2.82	1.54	25.7	296	2.8	7.4	2.6	0.6	37%	83%	77
Davis,Jason	08	28	R		aa	PIT	6	9	21	0	116	164	89	5	59	46	6.88	1.92	26.7	326	4.6	3.5	0.8	0.4	36%	61%	16
	09	29	R		aaa	PIT	0	8	35	0	62	89	55	2	37	19	7.96	2.04	8.8	329	5.4	2.8	0.5	0.3	36%	58%	7
Davis,Wade	08	23	R		a/a	TAM	13	8	28	0	160	159	71	13	65	117	3.99	1.40	24.7	254	3.7	6.6	1.8	0.7	30%	73%	60
	09	24	R		aaa	TAM	10	8	28	0	158	160	74	16	61	123	4.21	1.40	24.4	257	3.5	7.0	2.0	0.9	31%	72%	61
Day,Dewon	08	28	R		a/a	CHW	1	9	35	0	71	113	74	9	41	45	9.38	2.17	10.3	352	5.2	5.7	1.1	1.2	40%	55%	6
	09	29	R		a/a	OAK	3	1	38	1	49	84	45	5	33	30	8.29	2.39	6.8	370	6.0	5.6	0.9	0.9	42%	64%	7
De La Cruz,Eulogio	09	26	R		aaa	SD	2	6	48	9	69	56	25	2	43	50	3.29	1.43	6.3	216	5.7	6.6	1.2	0.3	27%	76%	68
De La Cruz,Julio	09	29	R		aa	NYM	0	4	30	4	40	65	33	3	31	25	7.50	2.40	7.1	359	6.9	5.6	0.8	0.6	42%	67%	16
De La Rossa,Wilkins	09	25	L		aa	NYY	4	5	16	0	82	87	47	16	46	63	5.19	1.63	23.4	267	5.1	6.9	1.4	1.7	30%	73%	19
De La Torre,Jose	09	24	R	a	aa	NYM	3	2	18	2	30	26	11	1	17	31	3.15	1.43	7.3	230	5.0	9.4	1.9	0.3	32%	78%	95
De La Vara,Gilbert	08	24	L		aa	KC	3	0	21	2	32	28	14	0	16	17	3.82	1.37	6.6	232	4.4	4.8	1.1	0.0	28%	69%	60
	09	25	L		aa	KC	6	2	38	2	71	107	54	6	35	36	6.80	2.00	9.2	341	4.4	4.6	1.0	0.8	38%	65%	12
Deduno,Samuel	09	26	R		a/a	COL	12	5	25	0	138	123	54	3	78	100	3.55	1.46	24.2	234	5.1	6.5	1.3	0.2	29%	74%	68
Degerman,Eddie	09	26	R		aa	STL	2	2	26	0	30	36	31	2	43	17	9.28	2.60	6.4	288	12.7	5.2	0.4	0.7	33%	62%	16
DeHoyos,Gabe	08	28	R		aa	SD	6	4	60	4	83	96	34	3	41	75	3.65	1.65	6.3	284	4.5	8.1	1.8	0.3	37%	77%	77
	09	30	R		a/a	SD	1	4	28	0	41	48	10	1	21	25	2.13	1.66	6.7	283	4.5	5.4	1.2	0.3	34%	87%	48
Del Rosario,Enerio	09	24	R		a/a	CIN	1	0	19	5	30	32	5	1	6	17	1.54	1.27	6.6	267	1.8	5.2	2.8	0.3	31%	89%	83
Delaney,Robert	08	24	R	a	aa	MIN	2	1	24	5	34	23	5	2	7	29	1.39	0.90	5.4	189	1.9	7.8	4.0	0.6	24%	89%	131
	09	25	R		a/a	MIN	8	4	62	7	83	91	41	6	22	61	4.44	1.35	5.7	271	2.4	6.6	2.8	0.7	33%	67%	77
Delgado,Jesus	08	24	R		aa	FLA	5	2	48	1	68	74	44	4	39	50	5.85	1.66	6.5	271	5.2	6.7	1.3	0.6	33%	63%	51
	09	26	R		aaa	SEA	3	3	33	0	56	75	42	5	28	35	6.82	1.84	8.1	314	4.5	5.6	1.2	0.8	36%	62%	27
DeMark,Mike	09	26	R		a/a	SD	2	3	60	1	64	66	24	2	39	45	3.44	1.63	4.9	260	5.5	6.3	1.2	0.3	32%	78%	56
Demel,Samuel	09	24	R		a/a	OAK	2	5	55	14	61	52	15	2	26	50	2.21	1.27	4.7	225	3.8	7.4	1.9	0.3	29%	83%	86
Denham,Dan	08	26	R		aa	LAA	9	10	25	0	146	198	96	18	63	77	5.89	1.79	27.5	317	3.9	4.8	1.2	1.1	35%	68%	13
	09	27	R		aaa	LAA	9	9	29	0	128	166	77	14	58	50	5.43	1.75	20.6	307	4.1	3.5	0.9	1.0	33%	70%	3
DePaula,Julio	08	26	R		aaa	MIN	3	5	51	2	77	97	58	11	42	52	6.72	1.81	7.1	301	5.0	6.1	1.2	1.3	34%	64%	19
	09	27	R		aaa	TAM	2	3	48	1	79	97	43	7	41	49	4.93	1.75	7.7	296	4.7	5.5	1.2	0.8	34%	72%	29
DeSalvo,Matt	08	28	R		aaa	ATL	2	11	34	0	92	120	65	8	60	73	6.30	1.96	13.2	309	5.9	7.2	1.2	0.7	38%	67%	40
	09	29	R		aaa	FLA	1	6	22	4	74	87	56	7	52	39	6.82	1.87	16.1	287	6.3	4.8	0.8	0.8	32%	63%	18
Dessens,Elmer	09	39	R		aaa	NYM	3	2	27	11	35	33	13	2	9	24	3.25	1.20	5.3	242	2.4	6.1	2.5	0.5	29%	74%	80
Detwiler,Ross	09	24	L		a/a	WAS	4	5	16	0	76	99	34	5	30	60	4.02	1.69	22.0	308	3.5	7.1	2.0	0.6	38%	77%	60
DeVries,Cole	09	25	R		aa	MIN	7	14	26	0	137	196	95	17	49	70	6.21	1.79	24.8	328	3.2	4.6	1.4	1.1	36%	66%	14
Deza,Fredy	09	27	R		a/a	BAL	8	8	36	1	92	118	66	22	47	43	6.41	1.79	12.0	305	4.6	4.2	0.9	2.2	31%	70%	-26
Diamond,Scott	09	23	L		aa	ATL	5	10	23	0	131	187	69	6	58	95	4.75	1.87	27.3	328	4.0	6.5	1.6	0.4	40%	74%	50
Diamond,Thomas	08	26	R		aa	TEX	3	3	12	0	53	67	47	3	39	36	7.89	1.98	21.7	300	6.6	6.1	0.9	0.6	36%	58%	34
	09	27	R		a/a	TEX	2	3	38	1	55	71	37	6	50	45	5.98	2.19	7.4	306	8.2	7.3	0.9	0.9	37%	73%	30
Diaz,Amalio	08	22	R		aa	LAA	3	4	10	0	57	70	34	5	27	33	5.36	1.70	26.4	296	4.3	5.2	1.2	0.8	34%	68%	29
	09	23	R		aa	LAA	3	7	36	0	113	140	62	11	35	68	4.92	1.55	14.0	298	2.8	5.4	1.9	0.9	34%	69%	41
Diaz,Jose	09	26	R		aa	TEX	3	1	36	10	39	38	21	2	26	29	4.85	1.62	4.9	248	5.9	6.6	1.1	0.5	30%	69%	53
Dickey,R.A.	08	34	R		aa	SEA	2	5	7	0	49	75	25	2	9	23	4.52	1.72	32.6	344	1.7	4.2	2.4	0.4	39%	73%	50
	09	35	R		aaa	MIN	2	1	5	0	33	46	23	1	9	14	6.30	1.69	30.5	324	2.6	3.9	1.5	0.3	36%	60%	36
Dickson,Brandon	09	25	R		aa	STL	8	10	28	0	147	181	71	12	48	92	4.31	1.56	23.5	296	3.0	5.6	1.9	0.7	34%	73%	48
Dillard,Tim	08	25	R		aaa	MIL	6	1	37	2	63	62	15	5	27	50	2.16	1.41	7.4	251	3.9	7.1	1.8	0.7	31%	88%	64
	09	26	R		aaa	MIL	11	7	24	0	147	184	86	11	54	57	5.23	1.61	27.8	299	3.3	3.5	1.1	0.7	32%	67%	18
DiNardo,Lenny	08	29	L		aa	OAK	6	5	15	0	71	152	73	8	19	32	9.28	2.40	25.2	423	2.4	4.0	1.7	1.0	46%	60%	-1
	09	30	L		aaa	KC	10	5	29	2	151	181	80	7	42	101	4.76	1.48	22.9	291	2.5	6.0	2.4	0.4	35%	66%	71
Dobies,Andrew	09	27	L		aa	BOS	2	3	27	0	39	44	24	1	15	30	5.57	1.50	6.4	277	3.4	6.8	2.0	0.3	35%	60%	74
Dolsi,Freddy	09	27	R		aaa	DET	4	3	39	10	51	60	30	2	20	26	5.26	1.55	5.9	286	3.4	4.6	1.3	0.4	33%	64%	43
Doubront,Felix	09	22	L		aa	BOS	8	6	26	0	121	140	58	8	52	87	4.31	1.59	21.0	284	3.9	6.5	1.7	0.6	34%	73%	54
Downs,Brodie	08	29	R		aa	SEA	5	2	36	2	94	144	64	8	59	41	6.12	2.15	13.3	344	5.6	3.9	0.7	0.8	38%	71%	2
	09	30	R		a/a	SEA	5	2	31	0	55	100	65	6	50	27	10.60	2.72	10.0	383	8.2	4.4	0.5	1.0	42%	59%	-14
Drabek,Kyle	09	22	R		aa	PHI	8	2	15	0	96	105	47	11	31	64	4.40	1.42	27.8	272	2.9	6.0	2.1	1.0	31%	71%	49
Drucker,Scot	09	27	R		aaa	DET	8	3	29	0	113	145	83	17	41	63	6.62	1.65	17.8	306	3.3	5.0	1.5	1.3	33%	61%	16
Dubee,Michael	09	24	R		aa	PIT	3	0	26	1	34	45	13	5	9	22	3.55	1.61	5.9	314	2.5	5.9	2.4	1.4	35%	83%	37
Duckworth,Brandon	08	33	R		aa	KC	5	11	27	1	134	182	107	29	56	77	7.18	1.78	23.4	318	3.8	5.2	1.4	2.0	34%	63%	-8
	09	34	R		aaa	KC	3	6	20	0	105	129	83	14	39	56	7.13	1.60	23.8	297	3.3	4.8	1.4	1.2	33%	55%	19
Duensing,Brian	08	26	L		aaa	MIN	5	11	25	0	138	170	78	16	35	62	5.07	1.48	24.3	296	2.3	4.1	1.8	1.1	32%	67%	26
	09	27	L		aaa	MIN	4	6	13	0	75	101	46	2	20	35	5.56	1.61	26.1	315	2.3	4.2	1.8	0.2	36%	63%	47
Duff,Grant	09	27	R		aa	NYY	4	2	21	1	36	43	21	1	20	28	5.16	1.72	8.0	287	4.9	6.9	1.4	0.3	36%	68%	60
Dumesnil,Bryan	09	26	L		aa	TOR	1	7	41	2	52	67	39	5	40	43	6.74	2.05	6.3	304	6.9	7.4	1.1	0.8	37%	66%	37
Dunn,Michael	09	24	L		a/a	NYY	4	3	38	2	73	73	39	5	51	82	4.82	1.69	8.9	255	6.2	10.2	1.6	0.6	35%	71%	80
Durbin,J.D.	08	27	R		a/a	PHI	5	14	34	0	130	192	110	21	66	68	7.62	1.98	18.7	336	4.5	4.7	1.0	1.5	36%	62%	-6
	09	28	R		a/a	LA	2	9	30	3	101	118	60	8	59	53	5.32	1.75	15.8	286	5.2	4.7	0.9	0.7	32%	69%	24
Durden,Brandon	09	25	L		aa	COL	7	4	17	0	101	124	56	11	26	29	4.95	1.48	26.2	297	2.3	2.6	1.1	1.0	31%	68%	5
Eaton,Adam	09	32	R		aaa	COL	4	3	14	0	79	92	32	4	15	40	3.59	1.34	24.1	284	1.7	4.5	2.7	0.5	32%	73%	68
Edell,Ryan	08	25	L		aa	CLE	7	8	26	0	144	189	86	18	24	79	5.34	1.48	24.4	310	1.5	4.9	3.2	1.1	34%	65%	57
	09	26	L		a/a	CLE	4	7	32	0	136	193	78	19	39	104	5.15	1.71	19.7	327	2.6	6.9	2.7	1.3	38%	72%	50

PITCHER	Yr	Age	Th		Lev	Org	Actual				Major League Equivalents																
							w	l	g	sv	ip	h	er	hr	bb	k	era	whip	bf/g	oob	ctl	dom	cmd	hr/9	h%	s%	bpv
Edlefsen,Steven	09	24	R		a/a	SF	7	0	28	2	41	37	14	3	24	26	3.16	1.48	6.5	236	5.2	5.7	1.1	0.7	27%	80%	45
Egbert,Jack	08	25	R		a/a	CHW	4	12	25	0	133	174	95	22	46	103	6.40	1.65	24.4	309	3.1	6.9	2.2	1.5	36%	63%	37
	09	26	R		aaa	CHW	6	11	30	1	108	166	87	20	36	68	7.20	1.87	17.3	344	3.0	5.6	1.9	1.6	38%	63%	11
Ekstrom,Mike	08	25	R		aa	SD	11	8	41	1	108	166	67	14	38	77	5.56	1.88	12.7	344	3.1	6.5	2.0	1.2	40%	72%	32
	09	26	R		aaa	SD	4	2	42	0	62	48	13	2	16	36	1.94	1.05	5.9	211	2.4	5.2	2.2	0.3	25%	82%	81
Elbert,Scott	08	23	L	a	aa	LA	4	1	25	0	41	25	12	2	20	41	2.71	1.08	6.6	171	4.3	8.9	2.1	0.5	23%	76%	104
	09	24	L	a	a/a	LA	4	4	20	0	96	105	46	7	45	108	4.35	1.57	21.5	273	4.3	10.1	2.4	0.7	38%	73%	91
Ellis,Jonathan	08	26	R		aa	SD	10	7	60	1	77	97	36	5	38	53	4.16	1.74	6.0	300	4.4	6.2	1.4	0.5	36%	76%	45
	09	27	R		aaa	SD	7	3	51	1	72	82	37	8	34	46	4.61	1.61	6.4	281	4.2	5.7	1.4	1.1	32%	74%	30
Ellis,Joshua	09	25	R	a	a/a	ARI	7	3	40	1	61	67	32	2	20	56	4.66	1.43	6.6	274	3.0	8.3	2.8	0.3	36%	65%	99
Ellison,Derrick	09	31	L		a/a	NYM	3	2	28	2	45	40	22	6	20	32	4.44	1.33	6.8	233	4.0	6.3	1.6	1.1	27%	69%	46
Ely,John	09	23	R		aa	CHW	14	2	27	0	156	172	67	12	54	107	3.86	1.45	25.2	274	3.1	6.2	2.0	0.7	32%	74%	57
Englebrook,Evan	08	26	R		aa	HOU	2	2	34	4	55	66	29	3	26	24	4.69	1.67	7.4	289	4.3	4.0	0.9	0.6	32%	71%	23
	09	27	R		a/a	HOU	3	1	30	9	36	43	23	3	14	18	5.75	1.56	5.4	288	3.4	4.6	1.3	0.9	32%	63%	27
English,Jesse	09	25	L		aa	SF	7	7	26	0	100	128	67	10	63	55	5.99	1.91	18.6	304	5.7	4.9	0.9	0.9	34%	69%	15
Enright,Barry	09	24	R		aa	ARI	10	9	27	0	156	208	93	22	38	88	5.35	1.58	26.0	314	2.2	5.1	2.3	1.2	35%	68%	34
Erbe,Brandon	09	22	R		aa	BAL	5	3	14	0	73	56	29	8	37	52	3.58	1.27	21.9	208	4.6	6.4	1.4	1.0	24%	75%	52
Escalona,Edgmer	09	23	R		aa	COL	1	2	31	4	36	40	13	6	11	26	3.33	1.42	5.1	276	2.8	6.5	2.3	1.5	31%	84%	41
Escalona,Sergio	09	25	L		a/a	PHI	2	3	47	14	60	63	27	6	23	43	4.10	1.44	5.6	265	3.5	6.4	1.8	0.9	31%	74%	51
Espineli,Geno	08	26	L		aa	SF	1	1	38	1	61	75	26	2	13	36	3.90	1.43	7.0	296	1.9	5.3	2.8	0.3	35%	72%	77
	09	27	L		aaa	SF	3	4	52	19	59	77	25	2	13	26	3.85	1.51	5.0	308	1.9	3.9	2.0	0.3	35%	73%	50
Estanga,Edgar	09	24	L		aa	TOR	3	4	44	2	63	80	46	5	37	52	6.61	1.85	6.8	303	5.3	7.5	1.4	0.8	37%	63%	46
Estes,Shawn	08	36	L		aa	SD	5	2	8	0	44	58	24	4	12	21	4.79	1.57	24.8	309	2.4	4.3	1.8	0.7	34%	70%	36
	09	37	L		aaa	LA	3	4	13	0	73	81	27	3	27	34	3.37	1.48	24.8	275	3.4	4.2	1.2	0.4	31%	77%	40
Estrada,Jesse	08	25	R		aa	CHC	7	3	39	1	75	99	51	12	24	50	6.05	1.64	8.8	311	2.9	6.0	2.1	1.4	35%	65%	31
	09	26	R		a/a	WAS	1	2	21	1	41	69	47	12	12	16	10.37	1.97	9.6	367	2.5	3.5	1.4	2.5	37%	48%	-44
Estrada,Marco	08	25	R		a/a	WAS	9	6	25	0	139	152	53	7	53	95	3.40	1.47	24.4	272	3.4	6.1	1.8	0.5	33%	77%	61
	09	26	R		aaa	WAS	9	5	27	0	136	160	71	11	34	82	4.70	1.42	21.9	287	2.2	5.5	2.4	0.7	33%	67%	59
Etherton,Seth	09	33	R		aaa	ARI	11	8	28	0	160	208	97	28	37	99	5.44	1.53	25.5	308	2.1	5.6	2.7	1.6	34%	68%	35
Evans,Cody	08	25	R		aa	ARI	5	8	33	0	74	100	52	13	31	35	6.34	1.77	10.5	316	3.8	4.3	1.1	1.6	33%	67%	-8
	09	26	R		aa	ARI	5	11	28	0	136	216	122	36	54	42	8.05	1.98	23.9	352	3.6	2.8	0.8	2.4	35%	63%	-53
Eveland,Dana	09	26	L		aaa	OAK	8	6	21	0	124	144	74	11	46	78	5.35	1.54	26.3	285	3.4	5.7	1.7	0.8	33%	65%	43
Everts,Clinton	09	25	R		a/a	WAS	5	1	31	4	40	43	13	1	22	34	2.84	1.63	5.9	270	5.0	7.7	1.5	0.2	35%	82%	73
Eyre,Willie	09	31	R		aaa	TEX	0	0	19	2	34	29	11	1	14	21	2.78	1.27	7.5	228	3.6	5.5	1.5	0.3	27%	78%	66
Faris,Stephen	08	24	R		aa	SD	8	5	26	0	138	165	68	8	41	83	4.46	1.50	23.4	291	2.7	5.4	2.0	0.5	34%	70%	55
	09	25	R		aa	SD	4	11	38	0	115	156	66	8	41	49	5.13	1.71	14.0	317	3.2	3.8	1.2	0.6	35%	69%	21
Farquhar,Daniel	09	23	R		aa	TOR	1	4	37	15	45	38	17	1	34	44	3.38	1.59	5.5	224	6.8	8.8	1.3	0.2	31%	77%	84
Feierabend,Ryan	08	23			aa	SEA	7	1	13	0	75	72	20	5	15	42	2.35	1.17	23.6	248	1.9	5.0	2.7	0.6	28%	83%	74
Felix,Francisco	08	25	R		aa	LA	0	1	15	1	31	39	24	6	12	24	7.10	1.65	9.4	301	3.5	7.1	2.0	1.6	35%	59%	31
	09	26	R		a/a	LA	4	2	43	3	76	87	32	4	30	62	3.81	1.53	7.9	280	3.5	7.3	2.1	0.5	35%	75%	71
Feliz,Neftali	08	20	R	a	aa	TEX	4	3	10	0	45	35	16	1	21	42	3.23	1.25	18.8	211	4.2	8.4	2.0	0.2	29%	72%	99
	09	21	R	a	aaa	TEX	4	6	25	0	77	75	35	2	28	72	4.14	1.33	13.1	249	3.3	8.3	2.5	0.2	33%	67%	102
Fernandez,Jason	08	24	R		aa	OAK	1	4	9	0	40	56	28	3	19	27	6.23	1.85	21.3	322	4.2	6.1	1.5	0.7	38%	65%	37
	09	25	R		aa	OAK	8	8	30	0	125	161	71	12	49	60	5.08	1.68	19.2	306	3.6	4.3	1.2	0.8	34%	70%	20
Field,Nate	08	33	R		aa	NYM	1	3	50	13	50	55	35	11	33	41	6.35	1.76	4.7	275	5.9	7.3	1.2	1.9	31%	68%	13
	09	34	R		aaa	FLA	5	4	49	9	55	49	23	7	23	53	3.78	1.32	4.8	235	3.8	8.7	2.3	1.2	29%	76%	72
Fields,Joshua	09	24	R		aa	SEA	2	2	31	1	33	39	31	2	24	30	8.30	1.91	5.2	287	6.6	8.3	1.3	0.6	37%	53%	56
Fien,Casey	08	25	R		a/a	DET	5	3	52	13	60	60	23	7	15	50	3.39	1.25	4.8	254	2.3	7.5	3.3	1.1	31%	77%	86
	09	26	R	b	aaa	DET	2	1	42	14	58	63	30	6	15	54	4.64	1.35	5.9	271	2.4	8.4	3.5	1.0	34%	67%	96
Figaro,Alfredo	09	25	R		aa	DET	6	3	16	0	80	86	43	10	24	53	4.88	1.38	21.5	268	2.8	6.0	2.2	1.1	30%	67%	49
Figueroa,Nelson	08	34	R		aa	NYM	4	7	20	0	113	159	76	18	38	71	6.08	1.74	26.4	325	3.0	5.7	1.9	1.4	36%	67%	22
	09	35	R		aaa	NYM	7	5	17	0	112	113	38	6	26	79	3.05	1.24	27.4	256	2.1	6.3	3.0	0.5	31%	76%	89
Fister,Douglas	08	25	R		aa	SEA	6	14	31	0	134	179	96	13	48	88	6.43	1.70	20.0	314	3.2	5.9	1.8	0.8	36%	61%	41
	09	26	R	a	a/a	SEA	7	4	24	0	112	155	54	11	13	71	4.31	1.49	20.6	321	1.0	5.7	5.6	0.8	37%	72%	118
Flande,Yohan	09	24	L		aa	PHI	4	4	13	0	70	95	44	6	22	41	5.68	1.66	24.7	316	2.8	5.2	1.9	0.8	36%	65%	39
Flores,Randy	09	34	L		aaa	COL	0	2	38	0	31	42	17	2	11	27	4.86	1.69	3.8	316	3.0	7.7	2.5	0.6	39%	71%	73
Fogg,Josh	09	33	R		aaa	COL	3	1	8	0	40	49	29	8	16	13	6.62	1.63	22.8	297	3.5	3.0	0.8	1.9	29%	63%	-26
Foppert,Jesse	08	28	R		aa	SF	2	1	24	1	41	66	55	11	54	19	12.04	2.92	10.0	356	11.8	4.2	0.4	2.5	36%	60%	-57
	09	29	R		aa	SF	0	3	10	0	33	61	39	5	36	14	10.55	2.95	19.4	389	9.8	3.9	0.4	1.5	42%	64%	-35
Fossum,Casey	08	31	L		aaa	DET	3	0	11	0	46	27	13	4	20	38	2.61	1.01	16.5	166	3.9	7.4	1.9	0.9	19%	79%	80
	09	32	L		aaa	CHC	9	7	25	0	129	138	65	19	47	102	4.55	1.44	22.5	268	3.3	7.1	2.1	1.3	31%	72%	49
Fox,Matthew	09	27	R		aa	MIN	9	9	28	0	151	189	84	14	66	85	5.00	1.68	24.8	299	3.9	5.1	1.3	0.8	34%	71%	28
French,Luke	08	23	L		aa	DET	9	11	27	0	170	220	87	16	58	76	4.58	1.63	28.7	307	3.1	4.0	1.3	0.9	33%	73%	19
	09	24	L		aaa	DET	4	4	13	0	81	85	36	7	20	62	3.99	1.29	26.3	264	2.2	6.9	3.1	0.8	32%	70%	85
Frieri,Ernesto	09	24	R		aa	SD	10	9	27	0	140	138	60	12	63	97	3.85	1.44	22.6	252	4.1	6.2	1.5	0.7	30%	74%	52
Frontz,Neal	09	26	R		aa	TAM	2	0	43	1	64	86	54	8	32	36	7.63	1.83	7.1	313	4.5	5.0	1.1	1.1	35%	58%	13
Furnish,Thomas	09	25	L		aa	STL	2	2	19	0	42	64	48	5	39	24	10.35	2.45	11.9	343	8.3	5.1	0.6	1.1	38%	56%	-4
Gabino,Armando	08	25	R		aa	MIN	6	5	49	3	81	104	37	7	36	45	4.07	1.73	7.7	306	3.9	5.0	1.3	0.7	35%	78%	28
	09	26	R		aaa	MIN	6	4	38	1	98	93	38	7	25	51	3.50	1.20	10.6	245	2.3	4.7	2.1	0.7	28%	72%	58
Gamble,Jerome	08	29	R		a/a	ATL	3	10	31	0	98	127	81	12	46	56	7.45	1.76	14.8	307	4.2	5.2	1.2	1.1	34%	57%	18
	09	30	R		a/a	ATL	3	4	35	3	61	82	39	10	46	43	5.74	2.09	8.8	314	6.8	6.4	0.9	1.4	36%	75%	7
Garate,Victor	09	25	L		aa	LA	0	1	47	4	53	46	16	1	27	45	2.64	1.36	4.8	227	4.5	7.6	1.7	0.2	30%	80%	85
Garcia,Angel	09	26	R		aa	OAK	2	0	21	1	38	43	19	1	24	24	4.46	1.78	8.5	280	5.8	5.7	1.0	0.3	34%	73%	46
Garcia,Geivy	09	27	R		aa	SF	2	3	34	1	70	84	57	5	58	42	7.27	2.03	10.2	292	7.4	5.3	0.7	0.6	34%	62%	25
Garcia,Ramon	09	25	L		aa	DET	4	4	35	2	92	159	81	14	22	36	7.92	1.97	12.9	371	2.2	3.5	1.6	1.3	39%	60%	-4
Garr,Brennan	08	25	R		aa	TEX	2	1	32	7	44	51	22	2	26	44	4.52	1.75	6.4	282	5.4	8.9	1.7	0.4	38%	73%	74
	09	26	R		aa	TEX	3	3	32	2	50	61	32	3	28	32	5.78	1.77	7.4	294	5.0	5.8	1.2	0.6	35%	66%	38
Gaub,John	09	24	L	a	a/a	CHC	4	2	52	5	60	43	20	5	36	66	2.94	1.32	4.9	198	5.4	9.9	1.8	0.8	27%	81%	90
Geary,Geoff	09	33	R		aaa	HOU	1	3	26	2	40	64	28	5	12	21	6.39	1.89	7.4	355	2.6	4.7	1.8	1.2	39%	67%	15

Major League Equivalent Statistics

							Actual				Major League Equivalents																
PITCHER	Yr	Age	Th		Lev	Org	w	l	g	sv	ip	h	er	hr	bb	k	era	whip	bf/g	oob	ctl	dom	cmd	hr/9	h%	s%	bpv
Gee,Dillon	09	23	R		aaa	NYM	1	3	9	0	48	56	28	6	17	37	5.24	1.52	23.7	285	3.2	6.9	2.2	1.1	34%	67%	52
Geer,Josh	08	25	R		aa	SD	8	9	28	0	166	226	102	22	50	82	5.54	1.66	27.2	317	2.7	4.4	1.6	1.2	34%	68%	16
	09	26	R		aaa	SD	2	5	9	0	52	66	28	4	14	17	4.80	1.54	25.9	302	2.5	3.0	1.2	0.7	32%	69%	17
George,Chris	08	29	L		a/a	TOR	1	6	49	1	67	118	67	7	43	41	8.98	2.40	7.3	376	5.7	5.5	1.0	1.0	43%	61%	3
	09	30	L		aaa	BAL	2	1	17	0	49	64	26	7	10	22	4.67	1.51	12.8	310	1.8	4.0	2.2	1.2	33%	72%	26
George,Jonathan	08	24	R		aa	COL	0	2	25	0	40	55	32	11	7	15	7.07	1.54	7.2	318	1.6	3.4	2.1	2.4	31%	59%	-16
	09	25	R		aa	COL	4	2	32	0	47	74	47	13	22	23	8.90	2.05	7.3	351	4.2	4.5	1.1	2.5	36%	60%	-43
Geronimo,Ramon	09	26	R		aa	CIN	4	3	50	5	64	89	52	9	49	36	7.25	2.15	6.5	321	6.9	5.0	0.7	1.3	35%	67%	-3
Gervacio,Samuel	08	24	R		aa	HOU	3	5	50	5	73	81	34	8	28	80	4.19	1.49	6.5	276	3.4	9.8	2.9	1.0	37%	74%	88
	09	25	R		aaa	HOU	2	2	39	0	52	50	34	6	22	50	5.87	1.38	5.7	247	3.8	8.6	2.3	1.0	31%	58%	74
Gil,Jerry	09	27	R		aa	CIN	3	4	24	0	49	72	70	14	60	22	12.81	2.70	11.5	335	11.0	4.0	0.4	2.7	33%	53%	-60
Ginter,Matt	08	31	R		aaa	CLE	6	6	18	0	100	147	74	13	38	52	6.70	1.84	26.5	334	3.4	4.7	1.4	1.2	37%	64%	9
	09	32	R		aaa	MIL	3	3	38	2	75	98	38	7	25	46	4.54	1.64	9.0	308	3.0	5.5	1.8	0.9	35%	74%	38
Gleason,Sean	09	24	R		aa	BAL	3	5	10	0	51	97	54	6	25	17	9.46	2.39	27.1	394	4.4	3.0	0.7	1.1	42%	59%	-25
Glen,William	08	31	R		aa	FLA	9	5	25	0	96	101	44	9	59	57	4.15	1.67	17.6	266	5.5	5.3	1.0	0.8	30%	76%	30
	09	32	R		a/a	FLA	3	10	24	0	104	146	73	12	58	57	6.35	1.96	21.1	324	5.0	4.9	1.0	1.1	36%	68%	9
Godfrey,Graham	09	25	R		aa	OAK	11	8	28	0	159	174	67	8	49	85	3.77	1.40	24.6	273	2.8	4.8	1.7	0.4	31%	73%	52
Gomes,Brandon	09	25	R	a	aa	SD	4	1	65	3	72	62	23	3	30	77	2.92	1.28	4.7	228	3.8	9.7	2.6	0.4	32%	78%	109
Gomez,Jeanmar	09	22	R		aa	CLE	10	4	22	0	123	140	63	13	43	99	4.61	1.49	24.7	280	3.1	7.2	2.3	1.0	34%	71%	62
Gomez,Mariano	08	26	L		aaa	MIN	5	2	54	1	65	78	24	3	23	36	3.28	1.55	5.4	292	3.1	5.0	1.6	0.4	34%	79%	47
	09	27	L		aaa	ATL	8	4	47	8	72	61	20	3	31	30	2.50	1.27	6.4	225	3.8	3.8	1.0	0.4	25%	81%	42
Gonzalez,Edgar	09	27	R		aaa	OAK	3	2	7	0	39	54	26	4	14	22	5.92	1.74	26.1	319	3.3	5.1	1.5	0.9	36%	66%	26
Gonzalez,Enrique	08	26	R		aa	SD	7	5	35	0	99	132	62	10	57	61	5.64	1.91	13.7	314	5.2	5.5	1.1	0.9	36%	71%	20
	09	27	R		aaa	BOS	8	11	26	0	139	217	128	26	61	82	8.32	2.00	26.3	348	4.0	5.3	1.3	1.7	38%	59%	-6
Gonzalez,Gio	08	23	L		aa	OAK	8	7	23	0	123	116	63	11	56	106	4.60	1.40	23.1	245	4.1	7.7	1.9	0.8	30%	68%	67
	09	24	L		aaa	OAK	4	1	12	0	61	45	18	5	31	61	2.66	1.25	21.2	202	4.6	9.0	2.0	0.7	26%	82%	88
Gonzalez,Marco	08	24	R		aa	STL	7	0	47	2	57	54	26	4	21	29	4.14	1.31	5.1	243	3.3	4.5	1.4	0.7	27%	69%	42
	09	25	R		a/a	STL	0	5	49	0	67	89	43	5	32	20	5.79	1.80	6.5	313	4.2	2.7	0.6	0.7	33%	67%	0
Gonzalez,Reidier	09	24	R		aa	TOR	4	6	17	0	93	104	43	5	29	56	4.19	1.43	23.8	277	2.8	5.4	1.9	0.5	32%	70%	58
Gordon,Brian	08	30	R		aa	TEX	6	5	34	3	95	151	60	23	27	42	5.68	1.88	13.4	353	2.6	4.0	1.5	2.2	36%	76%	-24
	09	31	R		aaa	TEX	7	3	43	2	77	89	41	6	22	42	4.79	1.45	7.8	284	2.6	4.9	1.9	0.7	32%	67%	45
Gorgen,Scott	09	23	R		aa	STL	4	5	11	0	55	56	34	7	33	40	5.55	1.62	22.7	258	5.4	6.5	1.2	1.1	30%	67%	34
Gorzelanny,Tom	08	26	L	b	aa	PIT	3	1	7	0	35	37	11	1	5	24	2.96	1.18	20.5	265	1.2	6.3	5.3	0.3	32%	74%	142
	09	27	L		aaa	PIT	4	3	15	0	87	87	31	3	31	67	3.16	1.36	24.8	256	3.2	6.9	2.2	0.3	32%	76%	81
Gosling,Mike	08	28	L		aaa	TOR	5	6	58	7	68	101	41	4	26	49	5.39	1.86	5.6	337	3.4	6.5	1.9	0.6	40%	70%	50
	09	29	L		aaa	CLE	7	4	29	1	67	97	46	8	26	60	6.19	1.83	11.0	330	3.5	8.1	2.3	1.0	41%	67%	54
Graham,Andrew	09	25	R		aa	COL	4	4	33	0	84	90	59	11	33	56	6.30	1.47	11.2	268	3.6	6.0	1.7	1.2	30%	57%	37
Graham,Connor	09	24	R		aa	CLE	1	3	8	0	38	49	29	4	28	34	6.82	2.03	23.6	308	6.6	8.0	1.2	1.0	38%	66%	38
Gray,Jeff	08	27	R		aa	OAK	2	7	54	4	67	105	40	9	23	37	5.39	1.90	6.0	348	3.1	5.0	1.6	1.2	39%	74%	13
	09	28	R	b	aaa	OAK	2	2	37	16	41	34	7	2	5	18	1.62	0.95	4.3	220	1.2	4.0	3.4	0.5	24%	86%	93
Green,Nicholas	08	24	R		aa	LAA	8	8	28	0	159	222	119	33	45	92	6.73	1.68	26.1	324	2.6	5.2	2.0	1.8	35%	63%	9
	09	25	R		a/a	MIL	3	10	20	0	108	154	83	17	21	63	6.92	1.61	24.5	327	1.8	5.2	3.0	1.4	36%	58%	41
Griffin,Daniel	09	25	R		aa	SF	8	7	46	0	73	111	62	7	26	67	7.67	1.87	7.6	343	3.2	8.2	2.6	0.8	43%	57%	66
Guerra,Deolis	09	21	R		aa	MIN	6	3	12	0	62	68	42	4	17	42	6.06	1.36	22.2	271	2.5	6.1	2.5	0.6	32%	53%	72
Guevara,Carlos	09	28	R		a/a	SD	0	0	32	0	40	40	11	2	18	25	2.57	1.46	5.5	255	4.1	5.6	1.4	0.5	30%	84%	51
Gulin,Lindsay	08	32	L		aaa	MIL	7	7	26	0	137	126	61	17	76	104	4.01	1.47	23.2	240	5.0	6.8	1.4	1.1	28%	76%	43
	09	33	L		aaa	MIL	7	10	27	0	139	147	87	9	81	85	5.65	1.64	23.5	266	5.2	5.5	1.0	0.6	31%	64%	38
Gunderson,Kevin	08	24	L		aa	ATL	2	2	36	3	43	54	28	2	15	18	5.92	1.58	5.4	299	3.1	3.8	1.2	0.4	33%	60%	30
	09	25	L		a/a	ATL	1	3	46	2	52	59	23	3	25	33	4.01	1.62	5.1	280	4.4	5.8	1.3	0.5	33%	75%	45
Gustafson,Timothy	09	25	R		aa	ATL	2	3	20	1	61	72	36	4	36	41	5.26	1.75	14.3	286	5.3	6.0	1.1	0.6	34%	69%	39
Gutierrez,Carlos	09	23	R		aa	MIN	1	3	22	0	52	73	45	6	26	25	7.84	1.90	11.4	325	4.5	4.4	1.0	1.1	36%	58%	5
Hacker,Eric	08	26	R		aa	NYY	7	4	17	0	91	112	43	4	33	63	4.28	1.60	24.2	297	3.3	6.2	1.9	0.4	36%	72%	60
	09	27	R		a/a	PIT	6	7	27	0	147	212	96	10	60	77	5.84	1.85	26.0	331	3.7	4.7	1.3	0.6	37%	67%	25
Haeger,Charlie	08	25	R		aaa	CHW	10	13	28	0	178	200	116	18	80	103	5.87	1.57	28.6	278	4.0	5.2	1.3	0.9	31%	63%	30
	09	26	R		aaa	LA	11	6	22	0	144	145	60	15	58	89	3.73	1.41	28.4	257	3.6	5.6	1.5	1.0	29%	76%	41
Halama,John	08	37	L		aaa	CLE	8	6	16	0	107	156	78	17	21	35	6.54	1.65	30.6	332	1.8	3.0	1.7	1.4	34%	62%	-1
	09	38	L		aaa	ATL	4	7	16	0	90	109	56	8	35	46	5.57	1.60	25.5	294	3.5	4.6	1.3	0.8	33%	65%	26
Hamilton,Clayton	08	26	R		aa	TEX	1	3	20	1	35	43	26	6	14	12	6.80	1.61	7.9	294	3.5	3.1	0.9	1.5	30%	59%	-11
	09	27	R		aa	TEX	1	4	40	5	70	105	51	7	24	34	6.48	1.83	8.3	338	3.1	4.4	1.4	0.9	37%	64%	17
Hamman,Corey	08	28	L		aa	PIT	9	9	28	0	133	209	94	15	54	52	6.34	1.97	23.3	349	3.6	3.5	1.0	1.0	37%	68%	-4
	09	30	L		a/a	PIT	1	5	55	1	59	90	56	4	27	36	8.53	1.98	5.3	343	4.1	5.5	1.3	0.6	40%	54%	31
Hammond,Steven	08	26	L		a/a	SF	12	11	28	0	155	199	99	18	57	101	5.74	1.65	25.3	305	3.3	5.8	1.8	1.0	35%	66%	35
	09	27	L		aaa	SF	11	12	29	0	157	193	107	24	67	75	6.15	1.66	24.8	296	3.9	4.3	1.1	1.4	31%	65%	3
Hamulack,Tim	09	33	L		aaa	KC	4	3	41	1	64	100	48	8	23	45	6.79	1.92	7.6	348	3.2	6.3	1.9	1.2	40%	65%	28
Hand,Donovan	08	22	R		aa	MIL	3	4	16	0	81	110	51	11	26	37	5.66	1.68	23.3	317	2.9	4.1	1.4	1.2	34%	68%	9
	09	24	R		aa	MIL	8	5	27	1	98	119	47	13	22	46	4.35	1.43	15.8	293	2.0	4.2	2.1	1.2	31%	73%	29
Hankins,Derek	08	25	R		aa	PIT	2	11	24	0	119	174	83	17	29	68	6.30	1.71	23.0	334	2.2	5.1	2.3	1.3	37%	64%	30
	09	26	R		aa	PIT	3	4	19	1	71	90	47	7	28	48	5.97	1.65	17.1	302	3.5	6.1	1.7	0.9	35%	64%	41
Hanson,Thomas	08	22	R	a	aa	ATL	8	4	18	0	98	78	38	9	41	99	3.49	1.21	22.5	214	3.8	9.1	2.4	0.8	28%	74%	93
	09	23	R	a	aaa	ATL	3	3	11	0	66	45	13	5	17	79	1.77	0.94	23.2	189	2.3	10.8	4.6	0.7	27%	86%	159
Hardy,Rowdy	08	26	L		aa	KC	6	11	28	0	155	254	122	17	34	69	7.09	1.86	26.5	360	2.0	4.0	2.0	1.0	39%	61%	20
	09	27	L		aa	KC	4	4	11	0	60	76	30	6	22	30	4.48	1.63	24.8	302	3.3	4.4	1.4	0.9	33%	74%	24
Harrell,Lucas	08	23	R		aa	CHW	3	3	11	0	54	70	30	4	21	29	4.96	1.67	22.6	307	3.4	4.8	1.4	0.7	35%	70%	32
	09	24	R		aa	CHW	12	4	25	0	146	169	74	10	75	80	4.58	1.67	26.8	284	4.6	4.9	1.1	0.6	32%	73%	31
Hart,Kevin	08	26	R		aa	CHC	4	2	27	5	60	49	23	3	24	50	3.49	1.22	9.2	218	3.7	7.5	2.1	0.5	28%	71%	85
	09	27	R		aaa	CHC	3	3	22	3	52	46	23	6	22	48	3.92	1.31	10.0	234	3.7	8.2	2.2	1.1	29%	73%	72
Hartsock,Aaron	09	26	R		a/a	KC	3	1	29	8	52	56	23	5	18	25	4.01	1.42	7.8	269	3.1	4.3	1.4	0.9	29%	74%	29
Hawksworth,Blake	08	26	R		aa	STL	5	7	18	0	88	133	72	12	39	64	7.37	1.95	23.9	341	4.0	6.5	1.6	1.2	40%	63%	23
	09	27	R		aaa	STL	5	4	12	0	73	69	34	3	20	48	4.19	1.21	25.2	245	2.4	5.9	2.4	0.4	29%	64%	81

Major League Equivalent Statistics

						Actual				Major League Equivalents																
PITCHER	Yr	Age Th		Lev	Org	w	l	g	sv	ip	h	er	hr	bb	k	era	whip	bf/g	oob	ctl	dom	cmd	hr/9	h%	s%	bpv
Hayes,Chris	08	26 R		aa	KC	5	2	40	12	65	64	17	4	14	31	2.30	1.21	6.7	253	2.0	4.2	2.1	0.6	28%	84%	56
	09	27 R		a/a	KC	4	6	44	6	85	127	39	3	13	32	4.11	1.64	8.8	337	1.4	3.4	2.4	0.4	37%	74%	49
Hayhurst,Dirk	08	28 R		aa	SD	2	3	46	2	84	110	46	7	34	70	4.91	1.71	8.4	309	3.6	7.5	2.1	0.8	38%	72%	58
	09	29 R		aaa	TOR	4	6	25	0	57	81	28	6	13	38	4.40	1.64	10.4	326	2.0	6.0	3.0	1.0	38%	75%	57
Hearne,Trey	09	26 R		a/a	STL	14	4	28	0	154	164	61	11	50	76	3.57	1.39	23.7	268	2.9	4.4	1.5	0.6	30%	75%	40
Heath,Deunte	08	23 R		aa	ATL	4	5	13	0	66	88	48	5	33	39	6.60	1.82	24.1	312	4.5	5.3	1.2	0.7	36%	63%	28
	09	24 R		a/a	ATL	2	6	32	1	98	128	73	7	54	76	6.71	1.85	14.6	308	4.9	6.9	1.4	0.7	37%	62%	45
Hellickson,Jeremy	08	22 R		aa	TAM	4	4	13	0	75	93	38	16	15	68	4.55	1.44	25.2	298	1.8	8.1	4.5	1.9	35%	76%	82
	09	23 R	a	a/a	TAM	9	2	20	0	114	84	39	9	30	116	3.08	1.00	22.3	201	2.4	9.2	3.9	0.7	27%	71%	130
Henn,Sean	09	28 L		aaa	MIN	1	1	28	6	38	44	13	3	17	34	3.04	1.60	6.2	283	4.1	8.1	2.0	0.8	36%	83%	66
Hensley,Clay	08	29 R		aa	SD	1	1	16	0	48	67	31	8	21	22	5.75	1.83	14.3	322	4.0	4.1	1.0	1.5	34%	72%	-9
	09	30 R		aaa	FLA	9	4	25	0	124	142	60	10	51	71	4.35	1.56	22.2	282	3.7	5.2	1.4	0.7	32%	73%	37
Hernandez,Carlos	09	30 L		aaa	TAM	7	6	21	0	112	126	55	10	47	65	4.42	1.55	23.8	279	3.8	5.2	1.4	0.8	32%	72%	35
	09	23 L		a/a	OAK	6	1	10	0	42	60	20	2	15	22	4.28	1.78	19.8	328	3.2	4.7	1.5	0.4	37%	75%	36
Hernandez,David	08	23 R		aa	BAL	10	4	27	0	141	133	54	12	71	141	3.42	1.45	22.8	244	4.5	9.0	2.0	0.8	32%	78%	78
	09	24 R	a	a/a	BAL	3	2	12	0	61	57	33	7	21	68	4.86	1.27	21.3	241	3.0	10.0	3.3	1.1	32%	63%	104
Hernandez,Fernando	08	24 R		aa	CHW	6	5	41	0	58	77	43	3	32	40	6.70	1.87	6.8	312	4.9	6.2	1.3	0.5	37%	62%	42
	09	25 R		a/a	CHW	3	4	57	20	69	57	19	3	28	59	2.46	1.23	5.0	220	3.7	7.7	2.1	0.4	28%	81%	88
Hernandez,Gabriel	08	22 R		aa	SEA	6	9	23	0	120	169	91	20	46	84	6.83	1.79	24.6	325	3.5	6.3	1.8	1.5	37%	64%	21
	09	23 R		aaa	SEA	10	9	26	0	146	165	86	14	47	88	5.30	1.45	24.6	279	2.9	5.4	1.9	0.9	32%	64%	45
Herndon,Kenneth	09	24 R		aa	LAA	5	6	50	11	65	87	31	11	15	28	4.22	1.57	5.8	315	2.0	3.8	1.9	1.5	33%	78%	10
Herrera,Yoslan	08	27 R		aa	PIT	7	9	22	0	121	169	69	13	45	52	5.10	1.76	25.8	323	3.3	3.9	1.2	1.0	35%	72%	9
	09	28 R		a/a	PIT	12	2	27	0	113	146	54	7	45	51	4.31	1.69	19.3	306	3.6	4.1	1.1	0.6	34%	74%	25
Herrmann,Frank	08	24 R		a/a	CLE	11	8	25	0	144	187	84	12	45	86	5.21	1.61	26.1	307	2.8	5.4	1.9	0.8	35%	68%	43
	09	25 R		a/a	CLE	4	4	49	2	106	135	46	8	20	53	3.93	1.46	9.5	303	1.7	4.5	2.7	0.7	34%	74%	56
Herron,Tyler	08	22 R		aa	STL	5	5	15	0	81	109	51	8	27	50	5.66	1.68	24.9	315	3.0	5.5	1.9	0.9	36%	66%	38
	09	23 R		aa	PIT	2	6	17	0	71	90	42	3	36	45	5.34	1.77	19.6	301	4.6	5.6	1.2	0.4	36%	68%	43
Heuser,James	09	26 L		aa	OAK	0	2	32	1	37	46	27	3	31	29	6.47	2.07	5.8	296	7.5	7.0	0.9	0.8	36%	68%	33
Hill,Jeremy	09	32 R		a/a	LAA	3	4	57	20	61	87	43	8	31	44	6.38	1.93	5.2	327	4.6	6.5	1.4	1.1	38%	68%	24
Hill,Josh	08	26 R		aa	PIT	4	11	22	0	111	153	78	14	53	49	6.30	1.86	24.1	321	4.3	3.9	0.9	1.2	34%	67%	-2
	09	27 R		aa	PIT	0	1	22	0	34	53	28	5	11	15	7.26	1.88	7.5	346	3.0	3.9	1.3	1.2	37%	62%	0
Hill,Nicholas	09	25 L	a	aa	SEA	5	6	36	2	95	101	42	5	27	86	3.98	1.35	11.3	267	2.6	8.1	3.1	0.5	34%	70%	101
Hinckley,Mike	08	26 L		a/a	WAS	5	5	43	1	90	126	53	6	58	55	5.32	2.03	10.4	323	5.8	5.5	1.0	0.6	38%	73%	27
	09	27 L		aaa	TEX	1	1	33	0	49	66	25	5	25	27	4.62	1.86	7.1	316	4.6	4.9	1.1	1.0	35%	77%	14
Hinshaw,Alex	09	27 L	b	aaa	SF	1	2	46	1	52	45	24	3	30	60	4.10	1.44	4.9	230	5.2	10.4	2.0	0.5	33%	71%	98
Hinton,Robert	08	24 R		aa	MIL	3	4	30	3	53	57	37	8	32	49	6.23	1.66	8.1	268	5.3	8.4	1.6	1.4	32%	64%	42
	09	25 R		a/a	MIL	0	6	53	12	75	83	44	6	40	65	5.31	1.64	6.5	275	4.8	7.8	1.6	0.8	34%	68%	58
Hirsh,Jason	08	27 R		aa	COL	4	4	18	0	99	145	83	20	54	38	7.52	2.01	27.1	334	4.9	3.5	0.7	1.8	34%	65%	-29
	09	28 R		aaa	NYY	10	7	26	0	128	198	115	22	46	65	8.07	1.91	23.8	346	3.3	4.5	1.4	1.6	37%	58%	-4
Hochevar,Luke	09	26 R		aaa	KC	5	1	8	0	48	49	10	2	12	31	1.93	1.29	25.3	261	2.3	5.8	2.5	0.4	31%	86%	79
Hoey,Jim	09	27 R		aa	BAL	2	6	36	0	48	70	41	7	39	34	7.76	2.27	6.9	333	7.3	6.4	0.9	1.3	38%	66%	6
Holland,Gregory	09	24 R		a/a	KC	4	3	35	10	54	66	28	4	23	44	4.66	1.65	7.1	295	3.8	7.3	1.9	0.7	36%	72%	60
Holliman,Mark	08	25 R		aa	CHC	4	5	31	0	108	148	70	18	72	71	5.82	2.03	17.3	319	6.0	5.9	1.0	1.5	36%	74%	3
	09	26 R		aa	MIL	7	10	26	0	137	193	95	24	67	70	6.26	1.89	25.4	325	4.4	4.6	1.1	1.6	35%	70%	-8
Holt,Bradley	09	23 R		aa	NYM	3	6	11	0	58	65	45	9	23	38	7.04	1.51	23.4	277	3.5	5.9	1.7	1.4	31%	54%	27
Houser Jr.,James	08	24 L		aa	TAM	3	3	20	0	94	79	35	9	40	65	3.35	1.27	19.7	224	3.8	6.2	1.6	0.9	26%	77%	55
	09	25 L		aaa	TAM	4	5	18	0	82	96	58	11	51	39	6.37	1.79	21.5	286	5.6	4.3	0.8	1.2	31%	65%	3
Houston,Ryan	08	29 R		aa	HOU	1	3	39	1	45	76	52	12	31	23	10.38	2.37	6.1	366	6.1	4.6	0.8	2.4	38%	58%	-46
	09	30 R		aaa	MIL	5	4	40	7	49	58	24	3	27	34	4.47	1.72	5.7	287	4.9	6.3	1.3	0.6	34%	74%	44
Huber,Jon	08	27 R		aa	SEA	4	3	52	6	70	125	67	8	25	42	8.66	2.15	6.8	380	3.2	5.3	1.6	1.1	43%	58%	13
	09	28 R	b	aaa	ATL	4	0	27	1	42	54	26	3	8	34	5.52	1.46	6.8	304	1.6	7.4	4.6	0.7	37%	61%	114
Hudgins,John	09	28 R		a/a	SD	1	3	39	2	54	51	32	4	39	34	5.29	1.66	6.3	243	6.5	5.7	0.9	0.6	28%	67%	41
Hudson,Daniel	09	23 R	a	a/a	CHW	9	0	14	0	80	71	24	3	20	77	2.70	1.14	23.2	233	2.2	8.7	3.9	0.3	31%	76%	131
Hudspeth,Casey	08	24 R		aa	HOU	4	5	10	0	55	63	36	4	27	29	5.86	1.65	25.1	282	4.5	4.8	1.1	0.7	32%	63%	29
	09	25 R		aa	HOU	4	6	14	0	73	111	61	14	37	23	7.51	2.02	25.8	342	4.5	2.8	0.6	1.8	34%	65%	-37
Huff,David	08	24 L	a	a/a	CLE	11	5	27	0	146	137	55	15	32	123	3.37	1.16	22.1	243	2.0	7.6	3.9	1.0	30%	74%	104
	09	25 L		aaa	CLE	5	1	7	0	39	39	22	5	16	29	5.12	1.42	24.2	257	3.7	6.6	1.8	1.2	30%	66%	46
Hughes,Dustin	08	26 L		aa	KC	8	4	32	3	108	152	71	14	47	61	5.94	1.84	16.1	325	3.9	5.1	1.3	1.1	36%	69%	13
	09	27 L		aaa	KC	3	3	34	1	87	98	46	7	43	64	4.79	1.62	11.6	278	4.5	6.6	1.5	0.8	33%	71%	47
Hughes,William	08	23 R		aa	PIT	2	2	6	0	31	42	22	4	16	15	6.29	1.90	24.9	318	4.8	4.2	0.9	1.2	34%	68%	-1
	09	24 R		aa	PIT	1	6	17	3	46	65	24	1	16	29	4.73	1.76	12.7	327	3.1	5.6	1.8	0.2	39%	71%	55
Hull,Eric	08	29 R		aaa	BOS	2	3	40	0	54	83	34	2	23	51	5.71	1.94	6.6	343	3.7	8.5	2.3	0.4	44%	69%	74
	09	30 R		a/a	SEA	7	4	45	1	76	112	74	11	50	51	8.81	2.13	8.5	336	5.9	6.0	1.0	1.3	38%	58%	6
Humber,Philip	08	26 R		aaa	MIN	10	8	31	0	136	165	82	21	51	86	5.41	1.58	19.8	293	3.3	5.7	1.7	1.4	33%	69%	24
	09	27 R		aaa	MIN	7	9	23	0	119	156	86	15	46	69	6.46	1.70	23.9	309	3.5	5.2	1.5	1.2	34%	62%	21
Hunter,Tommy	08	22 R		aa	TEX	8	4	16	0	105	118	44	12	25	48	3.77	1.36	28.1	278	2.1	4.1	1.9	1.0	30%	76%	34
	09	23 R		a/a	TEX	4	2	13	0	71	97	42	7	21	44	5.32	1.66	25.0	319	2.7	5.6	2.1	0.9	37%	68%	42
Hunton,Jonathan	09	27 R		aa	OAK	4	4	40	4	54	53	22	2	13	34	3.64	1.21	5.6	251	2.1	5.7	2.7	0.4	30%	69%	84
Hyatt,Jared	08	24 R		aa	TEX	5	3	11	0	60	59	25	3	18	42	3.78	1.28	22.9	251	2.7	6.3	2.3	0.5	30%	70%	77
	09	25 R		a/a	TEX	2	6	12	0	47	74	49	11	20	19	9.47	1.99	19.2	349	3.8	3.6	1.0	2.0	36%	53%	-34
Hynick,Brandon	08	24 R		aa	COL	10	7	27	0	172	207	98	30	29	81	5.12	1.37	27.4	292	1.5	4.2	2.8	1.6	30%	67%	34
	09	25 R		aaa	CHW	11	9	27	0	162	192	92	24	53	83	5.11	1.51	26.6	289	2.9	4.6	1.6	1.3	31%	69%	18
Igawa,Kei	08	29 L		aaa	NYY	14	6	26	0	156	182	85	21	51	89	4.88	1.49	26.5	286	2.9	5.1	1.8	1.2	32%	70%	30
	09	30 L		aaa	NYY	10	8	26	0	145	223	102	30	48	81	6.34	1.87	26.7	345	3.0	5.0	1.7	1.9	37%	70%	-4
Inman,William	08	22 R		aa	SD	9	8	28	0	135	129	58	9	72	120	3.86	1.49	21.3	246	4.8	8.0	1.7	0.6	31%	74%	71
	09	23 R		a/a	SD	7	9	27	0	150	163	83	17	44	86	4.98	1.38	23.9	271	2.6	5.2	2.0	1.0	30%	65%	42
Jackson,Randy	09	22 R		a/a	CHC	6	5	17	0	88	87	42	10	42	72	4.28	1.46	22.7	252	4.3	7.4	1.7	1.0	30%	73%	56
Jackson,Steven	08	27 R		a/a	NYY	4	3	49	6	79	96	54	6	37	68	6.19	1.67	7.4	292	4.2	7.8	1.9	0.6	37%	61%	63
	09	28 R		aaa	PIT	1	0	19	1	32	46	20	2	8	20	5.61	1.71	7.8	331	2.4	5.6	2.4	0.6	39%	66%	54

Major League Equivalent Statistics

							Actual				Major League Equivalents																
PITCHER	**Yr**	**Age**	**Th**		**Lev**	**Org**	**w**	**l**	**g**	**sv**	**ip**	**h**	**er**	**hr**	**bb**	**k**	**era**	**whip**	**bf/g**	**oob**	**ctl**	**dom**	**cmd**	**hr/9**	**h%**	**s%**	**bpv**
Jackson,Zach	08	25	L		aaa	CLE	4	6	30	0	84	128	84	16	25	48	8.98	1.83	13.3	343	2.7	5.1	1.9	1.7	37%	51%	4
	09	26	L		aaa	CLE	4	8	30	0	99	148	81	14	34	59	7.39	1.84	15.7	339	3.1	5.4	1.7	1.3	38%	60%	17
James,Brad	08	24	R		aa	HOU	6	6	18	0	93	119	49	9	35	36	4.79	1.65	23.6	305	3.4	3.5	1.0	0.9	33%	72%	9
	09	25	R		aa	HOU	2	10	23	0	107	152	97	11	67	43	8.12	2.04	23.1	327	5.6	3.6	0.6	0.9	35%	59%	-3
Jensen,Brett	09	26	R		aa	DET	5	5	43	12	53	61	26	10	20	45	4.32	1.52	5.5	282	3.4	7.6	2.3	1.7	33%	78%	41
Jimenez,Kelvin	08	28	R		aa	STL	1	6	46	12	52	71	22	4	13	20	3.75	1.62	5.1	318	2.3	3.4	1.5	0.6	35%	78%	25
	09	29	R		aaa	CHW	6	3	40	1	78	126	52	17	23	45	5.95	1.90	9.4	356	2.6	5.1	2.0	2.0	38%	74%	-3
Joaquin,Waldis	09	23	R	a	a/a	SF	5	5	44	2	64	45	18	0	28	48	2.53	1.14	5.9	194	3.9	6.8	1.7	0.0	25%	75%	93
Johnson,Alan	08	25	R		aa	COL	4	14	28	0	175	264	127	22	54	71	6.51	1.82	29.7	341	2.8	3.7	1.3	1.1	36%	65%	2
	09	26	R		aaa	COL	10	6	26	0	143	187	99	24	48	62	6.23	1.64	25.1	309	3.0	3.9	1.3	1.5	32%	64%	-1
Johnson,Blake	08	23	R		aa	KC	10	9	26	0	143	204	102	23	39	74	6.42	1.70	25.4	328	2.5	4.6	1.9	1.4	36%	64%	14
	09	24	R		aa	KC	8	8	24	0	122	174	75	12	40	51	5.51	1.75	23.7	328	3.0	3.8	1.3	0.9	36%	69%	13
Johnson,David	08	26	R		aa	MIL	5	3	40	3	62	68	29	6	31	57	4.16	1.59	7.0	272	4.5	8.2	1.8	0.8	34%	75%	63
	09	27	R		aaa	MIL	3	1	47	5	55	72	27	3	21	36	4.46	1.68	5.4	308	3.4	5.9	1.7	0.5	36%	73%	49
Johnson,Jason	08	35	R		aa	LA	11	5	20	0	113	165	64	19	35	73	5.06	1.77	26.5	333	2.8	5.8	2.1	1.5	37%	75%	22
	09	36	R		a/a	NYY	2	4	9	0	46	94	58	10	23	17	11.28	2.55	28.0	412	4.6	3.3	0.7	2.0	43%	56%	-51
Johnson,Jeremy	08	26	R		aaa	DET	5	3	23	1	81	118	56	10	29	50	6.17	1.80	16.7	331	3.2	5.6	1.7	1.1	38%	67%	25
	09	27	R		aaa	HOU	5	8	21	2	95	117	47	5	29	47	4.49	1.54	20.2	296	2.8	4.4	1.6	0.5	34%	70%	40
Johnson,Kristofer	08	24	L		aa	BOS	8	9	27	0	136	173	69	5	57	89	4.57	1.69	23.2	304	3.7	5.9	1.6	0.3	36%	72%	53
	09	25	L		a/a	BOS	3	16	25	0	113	195	119	11	54	64	9.47	2.20	23.1	371	4.3	5.1	1.2	0.8	42%	54%	11
Johnson,Steven	09	22	R		aa	BAL	4	3	9	0	48	41	21	6	21	44	3.92	1.29	22.5	226	3.9	8.2	2.1	1.1	28%	73%	70
Johnston,Andrew	09	26	R		aa	COL	2	4	56	31	53	82	31	4	21	29	5.26	1.94	4.6	346	3.6	4.9	1.4	0.8	39%	73%	21
Jones,Beau	09	23	L		aa	TEX	3	4	36	2	54	69	34	2	32	48	5.66	1.87	7.2	304	5.3	7.9	1.5	0.3	39%	68%	63
Jones,Hunter	09	26	L		aaa	BOS	4	3	36	2	53	59	39	9	26	34	6.69	1.60	6.7	275	4.5	5.7	1.3	1.5	30%	60%	15
Jones,Jason	08	26	R		a/a	NYY	13	8	27	0	160	192	81	15	56	81	4.56	1.55	26.5	291	3.1	4.5	1.4	0.8	32%	71%	30
	09	27	R		aaa	MIN	5	11	31	0	134	199	103	20	40	58	6.91	1.78	20.4	337	2.7	3.9	1.4	1.3	36%	62%	2
Jones,Justin	08	24	L		aa	WAS	2	5	12	0	55	72	37	3	25	35	6.02	1.76	21.5	308	4.1	5.7	1.4	0.5	36%	64%	42
	09	25	L		aa	WAS	4	13	36	1	115	164	91	14	54	73	7.12	1.90	15.4	328	4.3	5.7	1.3	1.1	37%	63%	18
Jones,Mike	08	25	R		aa	MIL	1	6	18	0	57	66	48	12	50	26	7.52	2.02	15.7	282	7.9	4.1	0.5	1.9	28%	66%	-23
	09	26	R		a/a	MIL	4	7	17	0	89	131	63	12	36	51	6.40	1.87	25.1	335	3.6	5.2	1.4	1.2	37%	67%	12
Judy,Josh	09	24	R	a	aa	CLE	4	3	36	11	49	43	24	2	20	55	4.35	1.28	5.7	232	3.6	10.1	2.8	0.4	33%	64%	117
Jukich,Benjamin	08	26	L		a/a	CIN	11	5	27	0	161	211	87	11	61	105	4.88	1.68	27.5	309	3.4	5.8	1.7	0.6	36%	71%	47
	09	27	L		aaa	CIN	9	6	29	0	123	156	77	23	44	88	5.62	1.63	19.3	303	3.2	6.5	2.0	1.7	34%	70%	24
Julianel,Ben	08	29	L		aa	MIN	3	2	56	26	68	93	28	4	41	48	3.70	1.98	6.0	319	5.5	6.3	1.2	0.5	38%	82%	38
	09	30	L		aaa	COL	4	1	33	1	39	56	32	6	17	28	7.44	1.85	5.6	328	3.8	6.4	1.7	1.3	38%	60%	25
Kendrick,Kyle	09	25	R		aaa	PHI	9	7	24	0	143	157	67	11	36	51	4.20	1.35	25.4	273	2.3	3.2	1.4	0.7	29%	69%	29
Kennard,Jeff	08	27	R		aa	LAA	4	4	47	0	63	111	64	13	39	32	9.11	2.37	7.1	376	5.5	4.5	0.8	1.9	40%	63%	-33
	09	28	R		aaa	CIN	3	1	40	2	54	57	24	5	24	39	3.94	1.49	6.0	265	3.9	6.5	1.7	0.9	31%	76%	49
Kensing,Logan	09	27	R	b	aaa	WAS	2	1	31	17	33	35	15	2	6	29	4.01	1.24	4.4	264	1.7	7.7	4.5	0.6	33%	68%	126
Keppel,Bobby	08	26	R		aa	FLA	9	11	28	0	159	267	140	31	69	68	7.93	2.11	28.6	365	3.9	3.8	1.0	1.8	38%	64%	-27
	09	27	R		aaa	MIN	3	3	23	1	55	60	18	1	14	22	2.92	1.33	10.2	271	2.2	3.6	1.6	0.2	31%	77%	51
Kibler,Jonathan	09	23	L		aa	DET	6	9	27	0	161	198	92	16	68	72	5.12	1.65	27.3	296	3.8	4.0	1.1	0.9	32%	70%	14
Kiely,Tim	09	24	R		aa	LAA	4	3	15	0	94	131	71	18	19	38	6.74	1.59	28.3	322	1.8	3.6	2.0	1.7	33%	60%	3
Kiker,Kasey	09	22	L		aa	TEX	7	7	25	0	126	124	65	10	67	104	4.64	1.52	22.4	252	4.8	7.4	1.6	0.7	31%	70%	60
Kilby,Brad	08	26	L		aa	OAK	7	2	51	2	70	60	31	9	26	50	4.00	1.22	5.7	227	3.3	6.5	2.0	1.1	26%	71%	56
	09	27	L	b	aaa	OAK	4	2	45	2	63	44	16	5	23	64	2.35	1.06	5.6	194	3.2	9.1	2.8	0.7	26%	82%	108
Kinney,Josh	09	31	R		aaa	STL	3	3	38	1	44	52	23	7	21	41	4.76	1.66	5.3	289	4.3	8.3	1.9	1.4	35%	75%	46
Kinney,Matt	09	33	R		aaa	SF	8	14	30	0	157	199	102	29	42	109	5.85	1.53	23.3	302	2.4	6.3	2.6	1.7	34%	66%	36
Kintzler,Brandon	09	25	R		aa	MIL	1	2	9	0	35	51	23	6	10	26	5.97	1.74	18.2	332	2.6	6.7	2.6	1.4	38%	68%	41
Kirkman,Michael	09	23	L		aa	TEX	5	7	18	0	96	109	57	10	44	53	5.30	1.60	24.1	280	4.1	5.0	1.2	1.0	31%	68%	25
Kite,Josh	09	28	L		aa	DET	2	4	23	0	35	54	23	7	22	20	5.85	2.16	7.8	345	5.5	5.1	0.9	1.8	37%	77%	-20
Klinker,Matthew	09	25	R		a/a	CIN	5	4	11	0	65	61	27	8	28	59	3.78	1.37	25.4	243	3.9	8.1	2.1	1.2	30%	77%	64
Kluber,Corey	09	24	R		aa	SD	2	4	9	0	45	48	24	4	34	29	4.74	1.83	23.8	269	6.8	5.8	0.9	0.8	31%	75%	29
Knight,Brandon	08	33	R		aa	NYM	5	1	12	1	43	36	15	6	14	41	3.19	1.17	14.7	225	2.9	8.5	2.9	1.2	27%	79%	85
	09	34	R		aaa	NYM	4	9	20	3	89	125	68	13	32	67	6.92	1.76	20.8	325	3.2	6.7	2.1	1.3	38%	61%	36
Kniginyzky,Matthew	09	27	R		aa	KC	5	10	26	0	134	210	113	25	64	50	7.60	2.04	25.6	349	4.3	3.3	0.8	1.7	36%	65%	-29
Knox,Brad	08	26	R		aa	OAK	7	5	29	0	146	207	105	20	46	70	6.44	1.73	23.4	327	2.8	4.3	1.5	1.2	35%	64%	11
	09	27	R		aaa	LAA	9	8	28	0	152	200	98	22	49	56	5.79	1.64	24.8	310	2.9	3.3	1.1	1.3	32%	67%	-3
Kontos,George	08	23	R		aa	NYY	6	11	27	0	151	169	89	20	63	123	5.28	1.53	24.9	277	3.7	7.3	2.0	1.2	33%	67%	50
	09	24	R		a/a	NYY	4	5	13	0	71	79	36	8	33	52	4.57	1.58	24.6	277	4.2	6.6	1.6	1.0	32%	73%	41
Koplove,Mike	08	32	R		aa	LA	2	1	41	9	54	55	28	6	21	36	4.69	1.41	5.7	259	3.5	5.9	1.7	1.0	30%	68%	45
	09	33	R		aaa	SEA	5	4	55	11	72	63	19	4	28	59	2.37	1.27	5.5	231	3.5	7.4	2.1	0.5	29%	83%	81
Korecky,Bobby	08	29	R		aaa	MIN	6	5	53	26	74	81	31	3	24	53	3.74	1.42	6.1	273	2.9	6.4	2.2	0.4	33%	73%	73
	09	30	R		aaa	ARI	2	1	27	13	30	30	8	1	3	20	2.33	1.11	4.5	255	1.0	5.9	5.9	0.3	31%	79%	154
Koronka,John	08	28	L		aa	COL	5	3	13	0	67	120	50	8	40	20	6.70	2.38	27.4	379	5.4	2.7	0.5	1.0	40%	72%	-24
	09	29	L		aaa	FLA	4	10	30	0	128	191	84	18	48	64	5.86	1.87	20.5	338	3.4	4.5	1.3	1.2	37%	70%	5
Kown,Andrew	08	26	R		a/a	WAS	8	9	22	0	113	167	83	17	41	42	6.64	1.84	24.4	336	3.3	3.4	1.0	1.3	35%	65%	-10
	09	27	R		a/a	WAS	8	3	27	1	82	107	51	6	24	32	5.54	1.60	13.7	308	2.6	3.5	1.3	0.6	34%	64%	24
Kroenke,Zachary	08	24	L		a/a	NYY	7	0	41	1	53	43	24	5	30	44	4.01	1.38	5.6	218	5.1	7.4	1.5	0.9	26%	73%	60
	09	26	L		aaa	NYY	7	1	36	4	72	67	22	5	32	47	2.77	1.37	8.6	241	4.0	5.8	1.4	0.6	28%	82%	53
Kulik,Ryan	09	24	L		aa	STL	6	10	24	0	125	173	84	15	40	46	6.01	1.71	24.1	322	2.9	3.3	1.1	1.1	34%	66%	1
Kunz,Eddie	08	23	R		aa	NYM	1	5	50	27	54	54	23	1	26	41	3.83	1.48	4.8	255	4.3	6.8	1.6	0.2	32%	72%	73
	09	24	R		aaa	NYM	4	5	40	1	61	64	44	9	32	33	6.49	1.57	6.9	264	4.7	4.9	1.0	1.3	28%	60%	13
Lahey,Tim	08	27	R		aaa	MIN	5	5	48	8	63	79	45	7	24	42	6.48	1.64	6.0	301	3.4	6.0	1.8	1.0	35%	60%	36
	09	28	R		aaa	MIN	2	3	41	1	56	82	44	6	22	34	7.08	1.85	6.5	333	3.5	5.5	1.5	1.0	38%	61%	23
Lambert,Casey	09	24	L		a/a	CHC	7	6	31	0	96	129	59	10	34	45	5.53	1.70	14.3	315	3.2	4.2	1.3	0.9	35%	68%	17
Lambert,Chris	08	26	R		aaa	DET	12	8	26	0	149	165	71	7	46	108	4.27	1.42	24.9	274	2.8	6.5	2.3	0.4	34%	69%	75
	09	27	R		aaa	BAL	7	9	24	0	138	174	84	15	36	93	5.44	1.52	25.6	302	2.4	6.1	2.6	1.0	35%	65%	55
Lansford,Jared	09	23	R		a/a	OAK	1	3	44	12	56	59	23	4	28	26	3.68	1.55	5.7	264	4.5	4.2	0.9	0.6	29%	77%	27

PITCHER	Yr	Age	Th		Lev	Org	Actual w	l	g	sv	Major League Equivalents ip	h	er	hr	bb	k	era	whip	bf/g	oob	ctl	dom	cmd	hr/9	h%	s%	bpv
Large,Terry	08	25	R		aa	BOS	0	2	22	1	33	47	30	3	26	29	8.13	2.18	7.7	325	6.9	7.8	1.1	0.9	40%	61%	33
	09	26	R		a/a	BOS	6	4	56	9	72	94	46	2	42	34	5.69	1.90	6.2	310	5.3	4.3	0.8	0.3	35%	68%	27
Larrison,Preston	08	28	R		aaa	CLE	3	4	48	1	60	76	33	5	24	34	4.89	1.66	5.7	302	3.6	5.1	1.4	0.8	34%	71%	31
	09	29	R		aaa	WAS	0	1	26	0	31	55	22	1	22	12	6.22	2.45	6.4	377	6.2	3.5	0.6	0.3	42%	73%	3
Latos,Mat	09	22	R	a	aa	SD	5	1	9	0	47	33	10	0	9	40	1.91	0.89	19.9	194	1.7	7.7	4.4	0.0	26%	76%	156
Laughter,Andrew	08	24	R		aa	TEX	2	3	30	9	45	45	28	3	21	30	5.57	1.47	6.6	257	4.1	6.0	1.5	0.6	30%	61%	52
	09	25	R		aa	TEX	3	2	28	0	41	62	28	2	19	14	6.24	1.98	7.2	342	4.2	3.1	0.8	0.5	37%	67%	7
Lawrence,Brian	08	32	R		aaa	ATL	6	6	16	0	86	136	67	4	20	45	7.05	1.81	25.4	351	2.1	4.7	2.2	0.4	40%	58%	47
	09	33	R		aaa	FLA	7	4	14	0	83	114	55	9	20	42	5.94	1.61	26.9	319	2.2	4.5	2.1	1.0	35%	64%	31
Lawson,Donald	08	23	R		aa	BOS	1	1	6	0	31	33	18	1	18	15	5.09	1.63	23.5	267	5.1	4.2	0.8	0.3	30%	67%	35
	09	24	R		aa	BOS	3	12	23	0	115	154	103	12	60	47	8.07	1.86	23.9	314	4.7	3.6	0.8	0.9	34%	55%	3
Layne,Tom	09	25	L		aa	ARI	0	3	6	0	31	34	23	0	20	20	6.72	1.73	24.0	271	5.8	5.8	1.0	0.0	33%	57%	56
Leach,Brent	08	26	L		aa	LA	2	2	40	12	59	53	23	2	38	40	3.55	1.54	6.6	236	5.8	6.0	1.0	0.3	29%	76%	56
	09	27	L		a/a	LA	2	1	27	2	31	36	19	3	27	30	5.45	1.99	5.7	281	7.7	8.6	1.1	1.0	36%	74%	45
Leblanc,Wade	08	24	L		aa	SD	11	9	26	0	138	156	95	20	44	113	6.17	1.45	23.2	279	2.9	7.4	2.6	1.3	33%	58%	58
	09	25	L		aaa	SD	4	9	24	0	121	117	56	13	30	81	4.13	1.22	20.9	249	2.3	6.0	2.7	1.0	29%	68%	68
Lecure,Samuel	08	24	R		aa	CIN	9	7	27	0	155	172	72	15	60	106	4.15	1.49	25.4	275	3.5	6.2	1.8	0.9	32%	74%	49
	09	25	R		aaa	CIN	10	8	25	0	143	172	94	23	46	109	5.91	1.52	25.4	291	2.9	6.8	2.3	1.5	34%	64%	43
Ledezma,Wil	09	29	L		a/a	TOR	1	3	26	1	35	65	21	1	22	28	5.41	2.47	7.3	386	5.7	7.2	1.3	0.3	47%	77%	38
Lehr,Justin	08	31	R		aaa	CIN	6	2	16	1	64	62	19	6	12	34	2.66	1.15	16.3	249	1.6	4.8	3.0	0.9	28%	81%	69
	09	32	R		aaa	CIN	13	3	20	0	117	125	59	12	28	50	4.53	1.31	24.8	268	2.2	3.9	1.8	0.9	29%	67%	35
Lentz,Richard	09	25	R		aa	BOS	1	0	29	0	36	43	39	2	37	37	9.72	2.22	6.4	292	9.2	9.2	1.0	0.6	39%	53%	56
Leon,Alex	09	21	R		aa	OAK	2	3	33	1	74	73	28	3	24	54	3.40	1.31	9.5	252	2.9	6.6	2.3	0.4	31%	73%	80
Lerew,Anthony	08	26	R		aaa	ATL	1	4	9	0	37	49	21	5	20	19	5.16	1.88	19.7	314	4.9	4.6	0.9	1.2	34%	75%	2
	09	27	R		aa	KC	10	6	27	0	152	210	91	16	59	77	5.38	1.77	26.4	322	3.5	4.6	1.3	1.0	36%	70%	17
Leroux,Chris	09	26	R		aa	FLA	5	3	46	2	60	77	26	0	20	45	3.83	1.61	5.9	304	3.0	6.8	2.3	0.0	38%	74%	82
Lewis Jr.,Rommie	08	26	L		aa	BAL	1	6	38	0	66	107	36	6	29	48	4.86	2.06	8.6	357	3.9	6.5	1.7	0.8	42%	77%	34
	09	27	L		a/a	TOR	4	7	45	1	66	76	29	5	37	49	3.92	1.71	6.8	282	5.0	6.6	1.3	0.6	34%	78%	47
Lincoln,Brad	09	24	R		a/a	PIT	7	7	25	0	136	157	62	11	27	86	4.09	1.35	23.2	283	1.8	5.7	3.2	0.7	33%	71%	78
Lindblom,Joshua	09	22	R		a/a	LA	6	5	34	1	96	97	45	7	26	73	4.21	1.28	11.9	257	2.4	6.8	2.8	0.7	31%	67%	84
Link,Jon	08	25	R		aa	CHW	5	4	56	35	56	61	27	4	29	56	4.38	1.61	4.5	271	4.7	9.0	1.9	0.7	36%	73%	74
	09	26	R		aaa	CHW	1	2	48	13	56	68	35	7	29	57	5.67	1.73	5.4	292	4.7	9.2	2.0	1.1	38%	69%	59
Littleton,Wes	08	26	R		aa	TEX	7	1	44	6	58	70	33	3	28	44	5.16	1.68	6.1	292	4.3	6.7	1.6	0.5	36%	68%	54
	09	27	R		a/a	MIL	0	5	35	0	45	70	44	5	45	30	8.70	2.54	7.1	347	8.9	6.1	0.7	0.9	40%	65%	9
Livingston,Bobby	08	26	L		aaa	CIN	4	4	9	0	56	74	39	8	18	30	6.30	1.64	28.4	312	2.8	4.8	1.7	1.3	34%	63%	18
	09	27	L		a/a	PIT	9	7	27	0	156	229	97	9	39	53	5.57	1.72	26.8	334	2.3	3.1	1.4	0.5	36%	66%	19
Liz,Radhames	08	25	R		aaa	BAL	3	7	15	0	87	88	41	7	30	73	4.28	1.36	24.8	257	3.1	7.6	2.4	0.7	32%	69%	78
	09	26	R		aaa	BAL	4	4	25	0	92	141	67	4	30	58	6.51	1.86	17.6	344	2.9	5.6	1.9	0.4	40%	63%	47
Lo,Chia-Jen	09	24	R		aa	HOU	0	2	30	2	39	33	11	1	20	33	2.62	1.35	5.5	225	4.5	7.6	1.7	0.2	29%	80%	84
Lofgren,Charles	08	23	L		aa	CLE	2	6	28	0	85	109	72	10	54	64	7.61	1.91	14.7	305	5.7	6.8	1.2	1.1	36%	59%	28
	09	24	L		a/a	CLE	9	11	25	0	141	137	81	18	50	84	5.17	1.33	23.9	250	3.2	5.4	1.7	1.1	28%	63%	38
Logan,Boone	09	25	L		aaa	ATL	4	2	29	2	35	29	15	2	17	34	3.87	1.32	5.1	222	4.4	8.6	2.0	0.5	29%	70%	88
Long,Matthew	09	26	R		a/a	CHW	6	3	22	0	65	76	33	1	22	39	4.51	1.50	13.1	285	3.1	5.4	1.8	0.1	34%	67%	63
Lopez,Arturo	09	27	L		aaa	NYM	0	2	35	0	61	76	35	1	28	36	5.16	1.70	8.1	300	4.1	5.3	1.3	0.2	36%	67%	49
Lopez,Javier	09	32	L		aaa	BOS	1	1	38	0	39	47	23	3	15	19	5.32	1.58	4.6	293	3.4	4.4	1.3	0.7	33%	66%	28
Lopez,Rodrigo	09	34	R		aaa	PHI	7	5	18	0	100	149	63	12	15	57	5.68	1.64	25.4	338	1.3	5.1	3.9	1.0	38%	66%	68
Lopez,Wilton	08	25	R		aa	SD	0	2	28	0	39	51	27	2	12	19	6.14	1.62	6.3	309	2.8	4.4	1.5	0.5	35%	60%	36
	09	26	R		aa	HOU	4	5	29	0	110	166	72	9	15	52	5.92	1.64	17.3	340	1.2	4.3	3.5	0.8	38%	63%	63
Luebke,Cory	09	25	L		aa	SD	3	2	9	0	41	42	18	2	15	27	3.92	1.38	19.7	260	3.2	5.8	1.8	0.5	31%	71%	62
Lugo,Jose	09	26	L		a/a	MIN	4	2	59	4	67	74	38	2	39	52	5.09	1.68	5.2	274	5.2	7.0	1.3	0.3	34%	68%	62
Lugo,Ruddy	08	28	R		aa	NYM	7	12	24	0	134	193	116	23	63	73	7.80	1.90	26.9	330	4.2	4.9	1.2	1.5	36%	60%	-2
	09	29	R		aaa	DET	13	9	25	0	141	195	93	19	64	64	5.95	1.83	26.8	321	4.1	4.1	1.0	1.2	34%	69%	1
Lujan,John	08	24	R		aa	CHW	3	2	50	4	76	81	41	9	43	43	4.86	1.63	6.9	268	5.1	5.1	1.0	1.1	29%	72%	19
	09	25	R		aa	CHW	3	5	37	1	58	68	42	1	32	41	6.53	1.72	7.3	285	5.0	6.3	1.3	0.2	35%	58%	57
Lumsden,Tyler	08	25	L		aa	KC	3	13	28	1	107	180	122	18	68	35	10.27	2.31	20.0	365	5.7	2.9	0.5	1.5	38%	55%	-34
	09	26	L		a/a	HOU	2	4	30	0	62	90	43	10	41	19	6.29	2.11	10.4	332	6.0	2.7	0.5	1.5	34%	72%	-29
Lyman,Jeff	09	23	R		a/a	ATL	5	9	38	0	98	94	45	3	55	78	4.13	1.52	11.5	247	5.1	7.2	1.4	0.3	31%	71%	70
Lynn,Michael	09	22	R		a/a	STL	11	4	23	0	133	133	47	5	50	92	3.18	1.38	24.8	255	3.4	6.2	1.8	0.3	31%	76%	70
MacDonald,Mike	08	27	R		a/a	TOR	1	7	39	5	104	149	63	17	29	51	5.48	1.71	12.3	329	2.5	4.4	1.8	1.4	35%	71%	10
	09	28	R		aaa	LAA	8	13	30	0	147	203	116	14	58	64	7.09	1.78	23.0	321	3.5	3.9	1.1	0.8	35%	59%	12
Machi,Jean	08	26	R		aa	TOR	2	6	21	1	69	92	47	4	46	38	6.07	1.99	16.2	313	5.9	4.9	0.8	0.6	36%	68%	22
	09	27	R		a/a	PIT	3	4	41	12	51	46	16	3	20	28	2.73	1.28	5.2	234	3.5	4.9	1.4	0.6	27%	80%	49
Maclane,Evan	08	26	L		aa	ARI	7	8	30	0	152	242	121	30	34	67	7.17	1.82	24.0	353	2.0	3.9	1.9	1.8	37%	63%	-5
	09	27	L		aaa	STL	8	11	27	0	165	221	87	23	23	80	4.72	1.47	26.9	314	1.2	4.3	3.5	1.2	34%	71%	55
Maday,Daryl	09	24	R		aa	SF	6	6	25	0	135	184	85	11	46	54	5.68	1.71	25.0	318	3.1	3.6	1.2	0.7	35%	66%	17
Madrigal,Warner	08	25	R		aa	TEX	1	0	31	14	36	36	15	3	16	35	3.68	1.43	5.1	254	3.9	8.8	2.2	0.8	33%	76%	80
	09	26	R		aaa	TEX	2	2	42	17	49	51	18	6	12	41	3.34	1.28	4.9	261	2.2	7.5	3.3	1.1	31%	79%	84
Maekawa,Katsuhiko	09	31	L		aaa	STL	1	2	18	0	39	54	26	4	32	28	6.07	2.19	11.1	320	7.3	6.4	0.9	1.0	38%	73%	18
Maestri,Alessandro	09	24	R		aa	CHC	4	2	54	3	85	87	47	11	58	59	5.01	1.71	7.3	260	6.1	6.2	1.0	1.1	30%	73%	28
Magee,Brandon	08	25	R		aa	TOR	7	13	28	0	163	229	111	19	74	50	6.13	1.86	27.8	325	4.1	2.8	0.7	1.0	34%	68%	-10
	09	26	R		aa	TOR	4	5	12	0	52	78	48	5	28	17	8.34	2.03	21.5	339	4.8	2.9	0.6	0.8	36%	57%	-7
Mahon,Reid	08	25	R		aa	ARI	0	2	52	24	65	88	40	11	27	41	5.54	1.76	5.9	316	3.7	5.6	1.5	1.5	35%	72%	11
	09	26	R		a/a	ARI	6	4	37	5	50	74	33	2	18	28	5.98	1.84	6.5	337	3.2	5.0	1.6	0.4	39%	65%	39
Maine,Scott	09	25	L		aa	ARI	4	5	48	7	62	79	24	2	22	52	3.44	1.63	5.9	305	3.1	7.6	2.4	0.3	39%	78%	81
Majewski,Gary	09	30	R		aaa	PHI	0	5	51	5	62	93	38	5	27	33	5.57	1.94	5.9	340	4.0	4.7	1.2	0.8	38%	71%	17
Mallett,Justin	08	27	R		a/a	CIN	6	3	30	0	108	128	71	16	44	60	5.93	1.59	16.3	288	3.7	5.0	1.4	1.3	31%	65%	17
	09	28	R		a/a	CIN	0	2	7	0	33	46	18	1	8	19	5.00	1.63	21.5	322	2.2	5.2	2.4	0.3	38%	67%	62
Maloney,Matt	08	25	L		aaa	CIN	11	5	25	0	140	164	89	23	40	115	5.72	1.46	24.5	286	2.6	7.4	2.9	1.5	33%	64%	58
	09	26	L		a/a	CIN	9	9	23	0	150	182	68	17	28	109	4.11	1.40	28.2	294	1.7	6.6	3.8	1.0	35%	73%	86

Major League Equivalent Statistics

							Actual				Major League Equivalents																
PITCHER	Yr	Age	Th		Lev	Org	w	l	g	sv	ip	h	er	hr	bb	k	era	whip	bf/g	oob	ctl	dom	cmd	hr/9	h%	s%	bpv
Mandel,Jeff	09	24	R		aa	WAS	4	2	8	0	52	60	24	6	13	29	4.19	1.40	28.1	283	2.2	4.9	2.3	1.1	31%	73%	43
Mann,Brandon	09	25	L		aa	TAM	7	9	27	1	125	176	89	8	56	57	6.39	1.85	22.1	324	4.0	4.1	1.0	0.6	36%	64%	19
Manning,Charlie	09	31	L		aaa	STL	1	2	44	1	48	58	27	2	22	33	5.00	1.67	5.0	292	4.2	6.2	1.5	0.4	35%	69%	53
Manship,Jeff	08	24	R		aa	MIN	3	6	14	0	76	104	45	8	26	49	5.36	1.70	25.2	319	3.0	5.8	1.9	1.0	37%	69%	37
	09	25	R		a/a	MIN	10	6	21	0	126	146	66	3	38	60	4.71	1.46	26.3	285	2.7	4.3	1.6	0.2	33%	65%	50
Manuel,Robert	08	25	R	a	a/a	CIN	5	3	48	3	79	58	15	2	16	76	1.68	0.93	6.3	201	1.8	8.7	4.8	0.2	28%	82%	161
	09	26	R		aaa	SEA	4	5	51	14	65	54	22	5	16	43	2.99	1.08	5.1	220	2.3	5.9	2.6	0.7	26%	75%	79
Marek,Stephen	08	25	R		aa	ATL	3	8	44	4	60	63	31	3	29	53	4.65	1.53	6.1	265	4.3	7.9	1.8	0.5	34%	69%	73
	09	26	R		a/a	ATL	3	4	44	2	45	60	41	3	41	28	8.22	2.25	5.3	313	8.2	5.6	0.7	0.7	36%	61%	20
Mariotti,John	09	25	R		aa	BAL	2	9	18	0	82	123	57	7	50	23	6.21	2.11	22.9	340	5.5	2.5	0.5	0.7	36%	70%	-11
Marquez,Jeffrey	08	24	R		a/a	NYY	7	8	17	0	96	130	65	15	34	37	6.09	1.71	26.1	317	3.2	3.5	1.1	1.4	33%	67%	-8
	09	25	R		aaa	CHW	2	8	11	0	45	89	70	17	23	24	13.88	2.48	22.2	402	4.6	4.7	1.0	3.4	41%	45%	-78
Marshall,Jay	08	26	L		aa	OAK	4	6	57	3	70	92	33	4	27	32	4.28	1.70	5.7	311	3.4	4.2	1.2	0.6	35%	75%	26
	09	27	L		aaa	OAK	5	3	50	7	50	59	20	2	14	25	3.51	1.46	4.4	286	2.6	4.5	1.7	0.4	33%	75%	51
Marte,Jose	08	25	R		aa	ARI	4	2	36	7	49	66	34	9	27	29	6.31	1.88	6.5	314	4.9	5.3	1.1	1.6	34%	69%	-2
	09	26	R		aaa	ARI	4	1	47	2	71	73	38	3	31	53	4.82	1.46	6.6	260	3.9	6.7	1.7	0.4	32%	65%	68
Marte,Luis	08	22	R		aa	DET	4	4	10	0	57	62	35	8	24	28	5.53	1.51	25.2	271	3.8	4.4	1.2	1.3	29%	65%	14
	09	23	R		aa	DET	5	8	19	0	105	125	59	21	28	70	5.03	1.45	24.2	289	2.4	6.0	2.5	1.8	31%	71%	33
Marte,Victor	09	29	R		a/a	KC	3	5	39	8	64	67	22	1	28	40	3.14	1.49	7.2	264	4.0	5.6	1.4	0.2	32%	78%	61
Martin,Adrian	09	25	R		a/a	TOR	4	2	34	2	93	120	55	15	29	61	5.29	1.61	12.4	306	2.8	5.9	2.1	1.4	34%	70%	30
Martin,J.D.	08	26	R		a/a	CLE	12	3	35	0	89	99	33	8	23	67	3.29	1.37	10.9	275	2.3	6.7	2.9	0.8	33%	79%	75
	09	27	R	b	aaa	WAS	8	3	16	0	88	90	34	4	10	52	3.48	1.14	22.3	259	1.1	5.4	5.1	0.4	30%	69%	129
Martinez,Carlos	08	26	R		aa	FLA	4	4	45	3	53	62	33	9	24	42	5.66	1.63	5.4	286	4.1	7.1	1.7	1.6	33%	69%	30
	09	26	R		aa	WAS	7	6	28	2	79	107	52	8	29	33	5.93	1.71	13.1	316	3.3	3.8	1.2	0.9	34%	65%	12
Martinez,Cristhian	09	28	R		aa	FLA	9	3	17	0	104	135	52	10	29	46	4.48	1.58	27.5	308	2.5	4.0	1.6	0.8	34%	73%	26
Martinez,Joe	08	26	R		aa	SF	10	10	27	0	148	170	58	7	41	86	3.51	1.43	23.8	282	2.5	5.2	2.1	0.4	33%	75%	61
	09	27	R		aaa	SF	0	2	7	0	35	42	20	1	7	18	5.04	1.41	21.7	293	1.9	4.7	2.6	0.3	34%	62%	71
Martis,Shairon	08	22	R		a/a	WAS	5	6	21	0	116	116	47	6	40	87	3.62	1.35	23.6	255	3.1	6.8	2.2	0.4	31%	73%	77
	09	23	R		aaa	WAS	4	4	13	0	74	100	49	10	17	37	5.90	1.58	25.7	316	2.1	4.5	2.1	1.2	34%	64%	29
Mason,Chris	08	24	R		aaa	TAM	3	10	33	0	108	161	87	20	40	78	7.24	1.86	15.7	338	3.3	6.5	2.0	1.7	38%	63%	17
	09	25	R		a/a	NYM	5	7	32	0	90	137	69	7	36	49	6.93	1.91	13.6	342	3.6	4.9	1.4	0.7	39%	62%	23
Mata,Frank	08	25	R		aa	MIN	1	1	23	1	30	42	29	7	19	17	8.84	2.04	6.5	325	5.7	5.1	0.9	2.2	34%	59%	-27
	09	26	R		aa	MIN	2	5	53	3	78	106	44	3	39	44	5.12	1.85	7.0	316	4.5	5.1	1.1	0.4	37%	71%	35
Mateo,Juan	08	26	R		aa	PIT	8	1	38	5	76	90	43	9	24	49	5.12	1.50	8.9	288	2.9	5.7	2.0	1.1	33%	67%	42
	09	27	R		a/a	PIT	7	7	49	4	72	88	39	4	17	34	4.85	1.45	6.4	294	2.1	4.3	2.1	0.6	33%	66%	48
Mateo,Marcos	09	26	R		aa	CHC	3	6	34	0	97	127	62	12	51	54	5.77	1.83	13.6	309	4.7	5.0	1.1	1.1	34%	70%	11
Mathes,JR	08	27	L		aa	CHC	9	5	27	0	140	198	86	20	37	54	5.53	1.67	23.8	326	2.4	3.5	1.5	1.3	34%	69%	4
	09	28	L		aaa	CHC	12	8	26	0	129	181	67	14	16	42	4.70	1.52	22.1	324	1.1	2.9	2.6	1.0	34%	71%	35
Mathis,Doug	08	25	R		aa	TEX	5	1	10	0	53	62	26	9	14	28	4.32	1.44	23.2	286	2.4	4.7	1.9	1.5	30%	75%	22
	09	26	R		aaa	TEX	4	2	11	0	57	78	25	4	16	32	3.91	1.66	23.8	320	2.6	5.1	1.9	0.7	37%	77%	43
Matos,Osiris	08	24	R	a	aa	SF	1	0	32	9	46	37	6	0	14	40	1.23	1.10	5.8	215	2.7	7.8	2.9	0.0	29%	88%	120
	09	25	R		aaa	SF	3	3	45	2	54	60	21	6	12	41	3.53	1.33	5.1	274	2.0	6.8	3.3	1.0	32%	77%	81
Matusz,Brian	09	23	L	a	aa	BAL	7	0	8	0	46	40	12	3	12	39	2.34	1.13	23.3	229	2.3	7.6	3.3	0.6	29%	82%	106
Maxwell,Blake	09	25	R		aa	BOS	7	8	32	0	111	172	94	11	37	46	7.64	1.88	16.7	347	3.0	3.7	1.3	0.9	38%	58%	7
Mazone,Brian	08	32	L		aaa	PHI	9	12	28	0	164	218	102	28	40	93	5.60	1.57	26.3	312	2.2	5.1	2.3	1.6	34%	68%	25
	09	33	L		aaa	PHI	2	7	24	0	70	106	47	6	18	37	6.09	1.77	13.7	342	2.3	4.8	2.1	0.8	38%	65%	34
Mazzaro,Vince	08	22	R	a	aa	OAK	15	6	28	0	171	174	54	5	40	112	2.84	1.25	25.5	258	2.1	5.9	2.8	0.3	31%	77%	90
	09	23	R	a	aaa	OAK	2	2	10	0	56	45	16	2	15	38	2.56	1.07	22.4	215	2.4	6.1	2.5	0.3	26%	76%	92
Mc Keller,Ryan	08	25	R		aa	HOU	4	6	45	1	70	103	52	11	38	55	6.70	2.01	7.7	335	4.9	7.0	1.5	1.4	39%	68%	18
	09	26	R		a/a	HOU	3	6	45	0	81	110	57	9	28	60	6.29	1.70	8.3	317	3.1	6.7	2.2	1.0	38%	63%	48
McAllister,Zachary	09	22	R		aa	NYY	7	5	22	0	121	121	43	5	36	82	3.20	1.30	23.2	255	2.7	6.1	2.3	0.4	31%	75%	77
McBeth,Marcus	08	28	R		aaa	BOS	2	1	28	2	31	32	26	8	17	25	7.44	1.59	5.0	261	5.0	7.2	1.5	2.2	28%	56%	12
	09	29	R		aaa	BOS	2	3	44	3	67	62	34	7	36	52	4.58	1.46	6.7	239	4.9	7.0	1.4	0.9	29%	70%	52
McCardell,Michael	09	25	R		aa	MIN	5	2	9	0	48	55	28	4	17	31	5.32	1.49	23.6	280	3.2	5.9	1.9	0.8	33%	64%	50
McClendon,Michael	09	25	R		aa	MIL	4	3	41	3	84	102	38	4	21	49	4.05	1.46	9.0	293	2.3	5.3	2.3	0.5	34%	72%	64
McCrory,Bob	08	26	R		aaa	BAL	2	3	35	5	45	47	24	1	24	30	4.74	1.58	5.8	265	4.7	6.0	1.3	0.2	32%	68%	58
	09	27	R		aaa	BAL	0	3	50	5	62	84	39	8	26	34	5.64	1.78	5.8	317	3.8	4.9	1.3	1.2	35%	70%	12
McCulloch,Kyle	08	24	R		aa	CHW	8	11	28	0	156	235	113	13	65	74	6.53	1.92	27.0	340	3.7	4.2	1.1	0.8	38%	65%	13
	09	25	R		aa	CHW	9	9	28	1	149	233	106	12	35	53	6.42	1.79	25.1	348	2.1	3.2	1.5	0.7	38%	63%	16
McCutchen,Daniel	08	26	R		a/a	PIT	11	12	28	0	171	210	92	30	39	113	4.85	1.45	26.7	296	2.0	6.0	2.9	1.6	33%	72%	45
	09	27	R		aaa	PIT	13	6	24	0	142	173	68	11	29	86	4.33	1.42	25.7	294	1.9	5.5	2.9	0.7	34%	70%	71
McDonald,James	08	24	R		aa	LA	7	4	27	0	141	131	59	16	55	124	3.75	1.32	22.1	241	3.5	7.9	2.3	1.1	30%	75%	70
	09	25	R	a	aaa	LA	1	0	6	0	30	22	11	2	14	36	3.32	1.21	20.7	202	4.2	10.7	2.5	0.6	29%	74%	113
McLeary,Marty	09	35	R		a/a	TOR	7	4	14	0	79	92	38	9	34	43	4.29	1.60	25.6	285	3.9	4.9	1.3	1.0	32%	75%	23
McLemore,Mark	09	29	L		aaa	HOU	5	10	18	0	92	123	67	9	38	38	6.55	1.75	23.9	314	3.8	3.7	1.0	0.9	34%	62%	10
McNab,Tim	08	28	R		aa	NYM	3	3	50	0	73	105	66	14	31	27	8.17	1.87	7.0	330	3.9	3.4	0.9	1.7	34%	57%	-23
	09	29	R		a/a	NYM	5	4	44	4	69	115	43	10	23	22	5.57	2.00	7.7	363	3.0	2.9	1.0	1.3	38%	74%	-18
McNiven,Brooks	08	27	R		aa	SF	2	4	26	0	75	98	51	6	25	21	6.06	1.63	13.2	308	3.0	2.5	0.8	0.7	32%	62%	4
	09	28	R		aa	SF	1	4	16	0	57	109	49	5	18	14	7.67	2.21	18.3	394	2.8	2.1	0.8	0.8	41%	64%	-18
Medina,Ruben	09	23	R		aa	CIN	2	4	51	0	70	72	41	8	52	45	5.29	1.76	6.4	260	6.6	5.7	0.9	1.1	29%	71%	24
Medlen,Kris	08	23	R	a	aa	ATL	7	8	36	1	120	139	56	8	28	102	4.17	1.39	14.4	284	2.1	7.6	3.7	0.6	36%	70%	102
	09	24	R	a	aaa	ATL	5	0	8	0	37	23	6	0	10	39	1.45	0.89	17.7	175	2.4	9.4	3.9	0.0	26%	82%	159
Medlock,Calvin	08	26	R		aaa	TAM	3	3	41	0	63	76	37	7	32	35	5.34	1.72	7.1	292	4.6	5.0	1.1	1.0	32%	70%	19
	09	27	R		a/a	TAM	4	2	47	13	82	89	41	16	18	63	4.51	1.30	7.4	271	2.0	6.9	3.5	1.7	30%	72%	66
Mejia,Jenrry	09	20	R		aa	NYM	0	5	10	0	44	46	23	2	21	43	4.66	1.51	19.5	262	4.3	8.8	2.1	0.4	35%	68%	87
Melancon,Mark	08	24	R	a	a/a	NYY	7	1	31	3	69	52	21	5	17	58	2.73	1.00	8.7	205	2.2	7.5	3.4	0.7	26%	75%	111
	09	25	R	a	aaa	NYY	4	0	32	3	53	45	23	4	12	46	3.91	1.08	6.6	225	2.0	7.8	3.8	0.7	28%	64%	117
Meloan,Jon	08	24	R		a/a	CLE	5	11	33	0	119	160	87	9	75	96	6.54	1.97	17.7	315	5.7	7.3	1.3	0.7	39%	66%	41
	09	25	R		aaa	OAK	0	0	44	0	68	74	35	8	27	51	4.68	1.49	6.8	271	3.6	6.8	1.9	1.1	32%	71%	49

Major League Equivalent Statistics

						Actual				Major League Equivalents																
PITCHER	Yr	Age Th		Lev	Org	w	l	g	sv	ip	h	er	hr	bb	k	era	whip	bf/g	oob	ctl	dom	cmd	hr/9	h%	s%	bpv
Mendez,Adalberto	09	28 R		aa	FLA	2	4	27	0	36	41	22	2	20	24	5.42	1.71	6.2	280	5.1	6.0	1.2	0.6	33%	67%	42
Mendoza,Luis	08	25 R		aa	TEX	2	3	9	0	36	51	25	1	11	16	6.30	1.69	18.5	324	2.6	4.0	1.5	0.3	37%	60%	39
	09	26 R		aaa	TEX	6	7	25	0	111	156	74	5	53	66	5.97	1.87	21.3	324	4.3	5.4	1.3	0.4	38%	66%	37
Mendoza,Thomas	09	22 R		a/a	LAA	9	8	24	0	150	166	64	13	41	80	3.84	1.38	26.9	275	2.5	4.8	2.0	0.8	31%	74%	46
Merritt,Roy	09	24 L		aa	NYM	4	5	56	14	62	78	27	8	25	47	3.96	1.66	5.1	300	3.7	6.7	1.8	1.2	35%	80%	38
Messenger,Randy	08	27 R		aa	SEA	9	4	41	4	63	87	37	7	28	34	5.32	1.81	7.3	320	3.9	4.8	1.2	1.0	36%	72%	15
	09	28 R		aaa	SEA	0	2	52	25	56	73	19	4	15	33	3.10	1.57	4.9	308	2.4	5.4	2.2	0.7	36%	82%	52
Meszaros,Daniel	09	24 R		aa	HOU	3	3	37	1	61	72	26	7	17	39	3.87	1.44	7.2	286	2.5	5.7	2.3	1.1	32%	77%	48
Meyers,Bradley	09	24 R	a	aa	WAS	5	1	9	0	48	51	17	2	12	35	3.16	1.29	22.5	265	2.2	6.6	3.0	0.4	33%	75%	93
Mickolio,Kam	08	24 R		a/a	BAL	3	1	45	3	58	61	30	2	31	53	4.63	1.58	5.8	264	4.8	8.3	1.7	0.3	35%	69%	78
	09	25 R		aaa	BAL	3	3	35	0	43	39	23	6	16	44	4.84	1.29	5.2	238	3.4	9.1	2.7	1.3	30%	65%	81
Middleton,Kyle	08	28 R		aa	HOU	1	2	17	4	39	51	29	6	10	17	6.62	1.57	10.3	310	2.3	3.9	1.7	1.4	32%	59%	8
	09	29 R		aa	OAK	5	2	9	0	60	64	24	4	15	24	3.59	1.31	28.2	267	2.2	3.6	1.6	0.6	29%	73%	40
Miller,Jim	08	26 R		a/a	BAL	3	6	56	10	80	78	38	7	29	76	4.25	1.33	6.1	250	3.3	8.5	2.6	0.8	32%	69%	89
	09	27 R		aaa	BAL	4	4	54	17	64	82	27	4	20	47	3.84	1.59	5.4	305	2.8	6.5	2.3	0.6	37%	76%	64
Miller,Ryne	09	24 R		aa	BOS	2	2	14	1	39	35	16	2	14	31	3.63	1.24	11.6	233	3.1	7.2	2.3	0.5	29%	70%	85
Mills,Adam	08	24 R	a	aa	BOS	0	5	11	0	63	79	35	2	8	31	5.01	1.39	24.7	301	1.2	4.4	3.8	0.3	35%	61%	92
	09	25 R		a/a	BOS	12	7	26	0	141	203	93	14	32	75	5.92	1.67	24.9	330	2.0	4.8	2.3	0.9	37%	64%	39
Mills,Brad	08	24 L		aa	TOR	3	2	6	0	32	28	5	2	12	26	1.44	1.25	22.4	228	3.5	7.3	2.1	0.6	29%	92%	80
	09	25 L		aaa	TOR	2	8	14	0	84	89	40	6	34	62	4.28	1.46	26.3	266	3.6	6.6	1.8	0.6	32%	71%	61
Milton,Eric	09	34 L		aaa	LA	3	2	7	0	35	32	12	3	6	23	2.98	1.08	20.0	236	1.6	5.9	3.6	0.8	27%	76%	94
Misch,Pat	08	27 L		aa	SF	6	5	20	0	87	142	80	18	33	39	8.23	2.01	21.4	359	3.4	4.0	1.2	1.9	38%	61%	-23
	09	28 L		aaa	NYM	4	2	18	1	52	65	25	2	9	27	4.27	1.40	12.5	298	1.5	4.7	3.1	0.4	34%	68%	78
Mitchell,Andy	08	30 R		aaa	BAL	12	8	32	0	138	171	87	16	61	56	5.65	1.68	19.9	298	4.0	3.6	0.9	1.0	32%	67%	6
	09	31 R		aaa	BAL	11	5	37	0	113	161	95	19	56	47	7.54	1.92	14.8	328	4.4	3.7	0.8	1.5	34%	62%	-16
Mitre,Sergio	09	29 R	b	aaa	NYY	3	1	7	0	45	53	18	4	5	28	3.66	1.29	27.1	286	1.1	5.6	5.2	0.9	33%	74%	114
Mobley,Chris	08	25 R		aa	FLA	5	3	58	28	62	79	40	4	22	59	5.80	1.63	4.9	303	3.2	8.6	2.7	0.6	39%	63%	83
	09	26 R		a/a	FLA	3	3	44	3	61	99	39	6	26	37	5.72	2.03	6.9	356	3.8	5.4	1.4	0.8	41%	72%	22
Mock,Garrett	08	25 R	a	aaa	WAS	6	3	19	0	104	108	38	8	24	79	3.32	1.27	23.0	262	2.1	6.8	3.3	0.7	32%	76%	91
	09	26 R	b	aaa	WAS	5	1	13	2	51	43	20	2	13	40	3.46	1.11	15.8	225	2.4	7.0	3.0	0.4	28%	68%	103
Molleken,Dustin	09	25 R		aa	PIT	1	1	18	1	37	46	24	6	17	20	5.95	1.68	9.5	297	4.1	4.8	1.2	1.4	32%	67%	9
Montano,Luis	09	25 R		aa	CIN	0	6	7	0	39	67	41	7	19	15	9.45	2.21	28.6	371	4.4	3.5	0.8	1.7	39%	57%	-32
Morales,Franklin	08	23 L		aa	COL	10	5	21	0	110	119	75	15	74	71	6.13	1.75	24.5	270	6.0	5.8	1.0	1.2	30%	66%	19
	09	24 L		aaa	COL	2	2	8	0	41	42	17	4	17	31	3.72	1.44	22.4	259	3.7	6.8	1.8	0.9	31%	76%	56
Moreno,Edwin	08	28 R		aa	SD	5	8	60	26	71	73	43	10	40	45	5.39	1.58	5.3	259	5.1	5.7	1.1	1.3	29%	68%	23
	09	29 R		aaa	SD	3	3	39	10	45	54	24	7	22	32	4.82	1.68	5.3	290	4.4	6.4	1.4	1.3	33%	75%	26
Morillo,Juan	08	25 R		aa	COL	1	0	52	0	59	61	41	3	54	45	6.24	1.94	5.5	261	8.2	6.8	0.8	0.5	32%	66%	47
	09	26 R		aaa	MIN	6	6	46	5	67	64	34	1	52	70	4.61	1.72	6.8	245	6.9	9.4	1.4	0.1	35%	71%	87
Morlan,Eduardo	08	23 R		aa	TAM	4	2	30	1	47	49	22	5	15	39	4.21	1.36	6.7	263	2.9	7.5	2.6	1.0	32%	71%	73
	09	24 R		aa	TAM	7	5	48	4	70	81	41	10	32	53	5.30	1.62	6.6	285	4.1	6.9	1.7	1.3	33%	70%	34
Morrow,Brandon	08	24 R		aa	SEA	1	2	12	0	30	23	16	2	18	29	4.71	1.36	10.8	208	5.3	8.8	1.6	0.6	27%	65%	82
	09	25 R		aaa	SEA	5	3	10	0	55	53	22	2	22	36	3.64	1.36	23.5	246	3.6	5.8	1.6	0.3	30%	72%	64
Morse,Ryan	09	26 L		aa	TAM	4	6	20	0	74	108	60	9	46	30	7.26	2.08	18.5	333	5.6	3.7	0.7	1.1	36%	65%	-9
Mortensen,Clayton	08	23 R		aa	STL	8	10	26	0	139	162	86	16	61	87	5.53	1.60	24.2	285	3.9	5.6	1.4	1.1	32%	67%	30
	09	25 R		aaa	OAK	9	8	23	0	137	154	72	12	43	86	4.73	1.44	26.0	278	2.8	5.6	2.0	0.8	32%	68%	52
Morton,Charlie	08	25 R	a	aaa	ATL	5	2	13	0	79	58	22	0	27	63	2.51	1.08	24.3	201	3.1	7.2	2.3	0.0	27%	74%	107
	09	26 R	a	aaa	PIT	7	2	11	0	71	64	21	3	16	50	2.68	1.12	26.2	234	2.0	6.4	3.1	0.4	29%	76%	101
Moscoso,Guillermo	08	25 R	a	aa	DET	3	1	6	0	34	27	14	4	7	42	3.60	1.02	22.4	215	1.9	11.0	5.7	1.1	30%	69%	164
	09	26 R		a/a	TEX	8	5	21	0	112	119	52	4	32	79	4.14	1.34	22.8	267	2.5	6.3	2.5	0.3	33%	68%	82
Mosebach,Robert	08	24 R		aa	LAA	9	12	29	0	177	251	115	6	72	72	5.83	1.82	28.9	326	3.6	3.7	1.0	0.3	36%	66%	23
	09	25 R		a/a	LAA	4	2	52	13	66	54	14	1	27	37	1.86	1.22	5.3	217	3.7	5.0	1.4	0.1	26%	84%	66
Moskos,Daniel	09	23 L		aa	PIT	11	10	27	0	149	184	74	11	57	62	4.48	1.61	25.0	297	3.4	3.7	1.1	0.7	32%	73%	21
Moss,Damian	08	32 L		aaa	ATL	5	9	41	0	96	126	54	8	66	71	5.03	2.00	11.5	310	6.2	6.7	1.1	0.8	37%	75%	32
	09	33 L		aaa	COL	8	3	59	0	76	98	32	5	43	47	3.73	1.85	6.2	306	5.1	5.5	1.1	0.6	36%	81%	31
Motte,Jason	08	26	b	aa	STL	4	3	63	9	66	79	30	6	28	82	4.06	1.61	4.8	291	3.8	11.1	3.0	0.8	41%	76%	102
Muecke,Josh	08	27 L		aa	HOU	8	13	29	0	165	205	106	26	69	79	5.76	1.66	26.1	298	3.8	4.3	1.1	1.4	32%	68%	2
	09	28 L		aaa	HOU	7	11	29	0	136	181	96	19	73	69	6.34	1.87	22.4	313	4.8	4.6	1.0	1.3	34%	67%	2
Mullins,Ryan	08	25 L		aa	MIN	9	9	30	0	148	200	87	19	63	77	5.31	1.78	23.2	316	3.8	4.7	1.2	1.2	35%	72%	11
	09	26 L		aa	MIN	11	11	28	0	145	223	88	14	41	97	5.45	1.82	24.6	345	2.6	6.0	2.4	0.9	40%	71%	45
Mulvey,Kevin	08	23 R		aaa	MIN	7	9	27	0	148	171	72	16	49	99	4.38	1.49	24.2	284	3.0	6.0	2.0	1.0	33%	73%	48
	09	24 R		aaa	MIN	5	8	24	0	149	172	76	12	54	93	4.59	1.52	27.5	283	3.3	5.6	1.7	0.7	33%	70%	46
Munoz,Luis	08	27 R		aa	SEA	5	9	27	0	129	198	110	22	67	61	7.69	2.05	23.8	344	4.6	4.2	0.9	1.5	37%	64%	-15
	09	28 R		a/a	SEA	8	10	27	0	140	178	89	20	68	82	5.69	1.76	24.3	304	4.4	5.3	1.2	1.3	34%	70%	13
Munter,Scott	08	29 R		a/a	SF	3	1	46	0	57	91	28	6	18	21	4.44	1.89	6.0	352	2.8	3.3	1.2	0.9	38%	78%	2
	09	30 R		aaa	COL	4	6	46	1	55	66	35	3	27	27	5.74	1.70	5.5	291	4.5	4.5	1.0	0.5	33%	65%	28
Murphy,Bill	08	27 L		aaa	TOR	8	10	32	2	142	197	119	20	97	120	7.54	2.07	22.1	322	6.1	7.6	1.2	1.3	39%	64%	24
	09	28 L		aaa	TOR	0	6	45	0	53	81	51	5	37	41	8.57	2.21	6.1	342	6.2	6.9	1.1	0.9	41%	60%	24
Murray,A.J.	08	27 L		aa	OAK	2	2	9	0	45	62	24	3	15	27	4.83	1.71	23.2	321	3.0	5.4	1.8	0.7	37%	72%	40
	09	28 L		a/a	TEX	4	2	41	1	59	82	28	1	26	30	4.19	1.83	6.9	321	4.0	4.5	1.1	0.2	37%	75%	36
Musgrave,Mike	09	26 R		a/a	SF	3	0	25	0	32	42	24	1	25	20	6.77	2.09	6.5	309	7.1	5.6	0.8	0.3	37%	65%	34
Muyco,Jake	09	25 R		aa	CHC	3	3	34	1	43	73	29	11	20	19	6.05	2.17	6.4	369	4.2	4.0	0.9	2.3	38%	78%	-45
Narron,Sam	08	27 L		a/a	MIL	15	5	28	0	172	226	100	25	59	62	5.23	1.66	28.1	311	3.1	3.2	1.1	1.3	32%	71%	-5
	09	28 L		a/a	MIL	2	7	20	0	88	151	67	8	26	38	6.86	2.01	21.7	369	2.6	3.9	1.5	0.8	40%	65%	10
Narveson,Chris	08	27 L		aaa	MIL	6	13	28	0	136	156	91	24	58	110	6.00	1.57	21.8	282	3.8	7.3	1.9	1.6	33%	65%	35
	09	28 L	b	aaa	MIL	4	4	26	5	75	68	37	3	27	67	4.42	1.28	12.1	238	3.3	8.0	2.4	0.4	31%	64%	95
Nestor,Scott	08	24 R		aa	FLA	1	1	55	0	61	63	62	9	54	56	9.13	1.91	5.4	261	7.9	8.2	1.0	1.4	32%	51%	32
	09	25 R		a/a	PIT	2	3	38	10	47	46	43	8	44	42	8.25	1.92	6.0	252	8.4	8.0	0.9	1.6	29%	58%	24
Newby,Joey	09	28 R		a/a	SEA	1	1	31	0	49	56	18	1	40	29	3.37	1.97	7.7	282	7.4	5.3	0.7	0.2	33%	82%	39
Newby,Kyler	09	25 R		aa	ARI	2	3	42	4	65	83	40	14	25	40	5.53	1.67	7.1	304	3.5	5.5	1.6	1.9	33%	72%	4

Major League Equivalent Statistics

PITCHERS

							Actual				Major League Equivalents																
PITCHER	Yr	Age	Th		Lev	Org	w	l	g	sv	ip	h	er	hr	bb	k	era	whip	bf/g	oob	ctl	dom	cmd	hr/9	h%	s%	bpv
Ni,Fu-Te	09	27	L		aaa	DET	3	0	24	0	34	38	13	5	9	26	3.53	1.39	6.1	276	2.4	6.9	2.8	1.4	32%	80%	60
Nickerson,Jonah	09	25	R		aa	DET	8	12	28	0	165	262	125	27	45	61	6.83	1.86	28.2	352	2.5	3.3	1.3	1.5	37%	65%	-12
Nicoll,Chris	08	25	R	a	aa	KC	4	1	19	3	43	54	20	2	8	46	4.17	1.44	9.9	299	1.8	9.5	5.4	0.4	40%	70%	153
	09	26	R		a/a	KC	9	2	39	1	88	108	56	8	36	64	5.69	1.64	10.3	296	3.7	6.5	1.8	0.9	35%	65%	46
Niese,Jonathon	08	22	L		aa	NYM	11	8	29	0	164	171	67	9	56	124	3.68	1.38	24.3	263	3.1	6.8	2.2	0.5	32%	73%	75
	09	23	L		aaa	NYM	5	6	16	0	94	107	50	8	25	76	4.74	1.40	25.4	280	2.4	7.2	3.1	0.7	34%	66%	85
Niesen,Eric	09	24	L		aa	NYM	4	7	16	0	83	85	49	6	41	71	5.36	1.52	23.0	260	4.5	7.7	1.7	0.7	33%	64%	65
Nieve,Fernando	08	26	R		aa	HOU	2	5	36	6	72	106	54	15	29	47	6.74	1.87	9.6	334	3.6	5.9	1.6	1.9	37%	67%	2
	09	27	R		a/a	NYM	3	1	9	0	42	44	28	3	18	32	5.88	1.47	20.6	262	3.9	6.9	1.8	0.7	32%	59%	59
Norrick,Floyd	09	26	L		a/a	STL	3	1	58	5	65	68	39	7	50	66	5.37	1.81	5.3	263	6.9	9.1	1.3	0.9	34%	71%	57
Norris,Bud	08	24	R		aa	HOU	3	8	19	0	80	97	38	8	30	70	4.29	1.59	19.0	293	3.4	7.9	2.3	0.9	36%	75%	65
	09	25	R		aaa	HOU	4	9	19	0	120	120	43	7	54	97	3.23	1.45	27.6	255	4.1	7.3	1.8	0.5	32%	78%	70
Nova,Ivan	09	23	R		a/a	NYY	6	8	24	0	139	168	80	9	63	77	5.18	1.66	26.5	293	4.1	5.0	1.2	0.6	34%	68%	35
Novoa,Yunior	08	24	L		aa	WAS	2	1	32	0	51	40	15	2	23	40	2.59	1.23	6.6	211	4.1	7.0	1.7	0.4	27%	79%	80
	09	25	L		a/a	WAS	2	2	38	2	49	65	28	5	23	33	5.22	1.80	6.1	313	4.3	6.1	1.4	1.0	36%	72%	30
Nunez,Jhonny	09	24	R		a/a	CHW	5	0	42	4	70	69	27	8	27	70	3.46	1.37	7.2	252	3.5	9.0	2.6	1.0	32%	78%	82
Nunez,Vladimir	08	34	R		aaa	ATL	3	1	37	3	57	65	28	1	29	50	4.48	1.66	7.1	281	4.6	7.9	1.7	0.2	37%	71%	77
	09	35	R		aaa	ATL	3	2	45	5	83	82	25	7	39	67	2.74	1.46	8.1	253	4.2	7.2	1.7	0.8	31%	84%	60
O'Connor,Mike	08	28	L		aaa	WAS	5	3	16	0	99	96	28	10	17	55	2.54	1.14	25.2	248	1.6	5.0	3.2	0.9	28%	82%	76
	09	29	L		a/a	KC	3	10	26	0	90	162	83	12	29	46	8.27	2.12	17.5	381	2.9	4.6	1.6	1.2	42%	61%	3
Ohka,Tomo	08	33	R		aaa	CHW	5	11	28	0	135	182	86	34	38	95	5.75	1.63	22.0	316	2.5	6.3	2.5	2.2	34%	72%	15
	09	34	R		aaa	CLE	3	3	9	0	52	63	25	6	9	23	4.36	1.39	25.0	293	1.6	3.9	2.4	1.1	31%	71%	38
Olenberger,Kasey	08	31	R		aa	LAA	4	6	36	0	116	191	106	26	74	49	8.20	2.29	16.8	361	5.8	3.8	0.7	2.0	37%	67%	-40
	09	32	R		aa	FLA	7	1	52	3	65	66	12	1	24	49	1.62	1.37	5.4	257	3.2	6.8	2.1	0.2	32%	88%	84
Oliveros,Rayner	09	24	R		a/a	TAM	6	3	22	1	79	80	38	7	23	54	4.33	1.30	15.2	258	2.6	6.2	2.4	0.8	30%	68%	66
Olson,Garrett	08	25	L	a	aaa	BAL	1	2	7	0	36	40	14	1	15	34	3.49	1.52	22.9	275	3.7	8.5	2.3	0.2	37%	76%	91
	09	26	L		aaa	SEA	2	3	9	0	47	41	27	2	23	33	5.12	1.36	22.4	231	4.3	6.3	1.5	0.4	28%	60%	65
Omogrosso,Brian	08	24	R		aa	CHW	2	3	17	1	39	41	23	3	27	22	5.34	1.75	10.7	265	6.3	5.0	0.8	0.7	30%	69%	27
	09	25	R		a/a	CHW	7	2	17	0	78	100	62	8	47	59	7.15	1.88	22.1	305	5.5	6.8	1.2	1.0	36%	61%	32
Ondrusek,Logan	09	25	R		a/a	CIN	2	1	43	19	52	45	13	1	15	30	2.32	1.17	5.0	230	2.7	5.2	1.9	0.2	28%	79%	76
Orta,Enrique	09	25	R		aa	SEA	3	2	24	3	41	35	12	1	20	35	2.53	1.33	7.3	224	4.4	7.7	1.8	0.2	29%	80%	86
Ortegano,Jose	09	22	L		aa	ATL	5	2	8	0	47	55	20	2	16	37	3.81	1.50	26.1	285	3.1	7.1	2.3	0.4	36%	74%	77
Ortiz,Ramon	09	36	R		aaa	SF	5	6	35	0	129	137	47	9	33	92	3.30	1.31	15.6	266	2.3	6.4	2.8	0.7	32%	76%	80
Ortiz,Russ	09	35	R		aaa	COL	2	2	6	0	31	36	16	3	17	17	4.58	1.70	23.9	283	4.9	5.0	1.0	0.9	32%	74%	22
Orvella,Chad	09	29	R		a/a	KC	1	2	27	0	43	60	35	7	13	21	7.38	1.70	7.4	322	2.8	4.5	1.6	1.5	34%	57%	5
Ostlund,Ian	08	30	L	b	aaa	DET	3	0	44	0	69	78	25	7	18	62	3.29	1.38	6.8	279	2.3	8.0	3.5	0.9	35%	79%	96
	09	31	L		aaa	STL	2	0	23	0	52	72	40	7	18	35	6.91	1.72	10.5	320	3.1	6.1	2.0	1.3	36%	60%	31
O'Sullivan,Sean	09	22	R		a/a	LAA	7	6	17	0	87	107	62	10	19	52	6.40	1.44	22.4	296	2.0	5.4	2.7	1.0	33%	55%	55
Osuna,Edgar	09	22	L		aa	ATL	4	4	13	0	77	89	43	8	22	43	5.02	1.44	25.9	283	2.6	5.0	2.0	0.9	32%	66%	41
Otero,Daniel	09	25	R		aa	SF	0	3	39	19	39	49	6	0	11	26	1.46	1.54	4.5	303	2.4	5.9	2.4	0.0	37%	89%	81
Ottavino,Adam	08	23	R		aa	STL	3	7	24	0	115	143	72	14	48	82	5.63	1.66	22.0	298	3.8	6.4	1.7	1.1	35%	67%	37
	09	24	R		aaa	STL	7	12	27	0	144	156	86	11	77	103	5.38	1.62	24.2	271	4.8	6.4	1.3	0.7	32%	66%	47
Ouellette,Ryan	09	24	R		aa	BAL	4	6	37	5	49	67	28	3	23	22	5.21	1.84	6.3	320	4.2	4.0	0.9	0.6	36%	71%	18
Overholt,Patrick	08	25	R		aa	PHI	3	8	49	10	78	86	58	12	49	59	6.67	1.74	7.4	275	5.7	6.8	1.2	1.3	32%	63%	26
	09	26	R		a/a	PHI	1	1	49	0	66	79	41	13	46	39	5.59	1.90	6.5	290	6.3	5.3	0.8	1.7	31%	75%	-5
Owen,Dylan	09	23	R		aa	NYM	4	10	23	0	123	170	91	13	53	72	6.64	1.81	25.3	321	3.8	5.3	1.4	1.0	36%	63%	21
Palazzolo,Steve	08	27	R		aa	SF	5	6	29	1	50	54	37	1	45	32	6.59	1.97	8.5	269	8.0	5.8	0.7	0.2	33%	64%	45
	09	28	R		aaa	SF	3	3	44	1	68	82	40	6	24	41	5.29	1.56	6.9	293	3.2	5.4	1.7	0.8	33%	66%	39
Papelbon,Jeremy	09	26	L		a/a	CHC	6	6	33	0	108	161	61	12	32	61	5.08	1.79	15.4	338	2.7	5.1	1.9	1.0	38%	73%	27
Parcell,Garrett	09	25	R	a	aa	FLA	0	0	23	1	36	21	1	0	18	34	0.28	1.07	6.3	166	4.4	8.5	1.9	0.0	24%	97%	113
Parise,Peter	09	25	R		a/a	STL	5	2	57	8	77	73	34	6	24	50	3.97	1.26	5.6	245	2.8	5.9	2.1	0.7	29%	69%	64
Parker,Blake	09	24	R		a/a	CHC	2	3	55	25	63	53	25	4	38	64	3.53	1.44	5.0	222	5.4	9.1	1.7	0.6	30%	76%	83
Parker,Jarrod	09	21	R		aa	ARI	4	6	16	0	78	92	41	3	32	68	4.72	1.60	22.1	288	3.7	7.9	2.1	0.3	37%	69%	79
Parker,Kyle	09	25	R		aa	SEA	5	5	25	0	116	132	59	11	59	63	4.57	1.64	21.2	279	4.6	4.9	1.1	0.8	31%	73%	26
Paronto,Chad	08	33	R		aa	HOU	0	2	35	3	52	75	21	2	15	42	3.65	1.74	6.9	331	2.6	7.2	2.7	0.4	41%	79%	77
	09	34	R		aaa	HOU	2	1	44	24	51	41	11	1	15	32	1.85	1.09	4.7	215	2.6	5.7	2.2	0.2	26%	83%	86
Parr,James	08	23	R		a/a	ATL	13	7	28	0	150	154	70	13	51	109	4.19	1.36	23.0	260	3.1	6.5	2.1	0.8	31%	70%	64
	09	24	R		aaa	ATL	1	1	7	0	30	38	21	5	5	18	6.30	1.43	18.7	303	1.5	5.4	3.6	1.5	33%	58%	57
Paterson,Joe	09	23	L	a	aa	SF	5	6	55	10	69	57	20	3	25	57	2.55	1.18	5.1	220	3.2	7.5	2.3	0.4	28%	79%	92
Patterson,Scott	08	29	R		aaa	NYY	2	1	42	5	47	60	29	10	14	41	5.46	1.59	5.1	305	2.7	7.8	2.9	1.9	35%	71%	44
	09	30	R		aaa	OAK	3	4	58	1	63	73	33	4	44	56	4.75	1.86	5.2	284	6.3	7.9	1.3	0.6	36%	75%	53
Patton,Troy	09	24	L		a/a	BAL	7	5	20	0	108	143	68	24	34	59	5.67	1.64	24.6	312	2.8	4.9	1.7	2.0	33%	71%	-1
Pauley,David	08	25	R		aaa	BOS	14	4	25	0	147	173	74	10	41	87	4.51	1.46	25.7	287	2.5	5.3	2.1	0.6	33%	69%	55
	09	26	R		aaa	BAL	9	12	27	0	152	214	104	22	47	87	6.16	1.72	26.1	326	2.8	5.2	1.8	1.3	36%	66%	21
Paulino,Felipe	09	26	R		aaa	HOU	2	1	7	0	34	36	15	1	25	24	4.07	1.78	23.0	265	6.5	6.4	1.0	0.3	33%	76%	53
Pendleton,Lance	09	26	R		aa	NYY	1	3	8	0	44	56	36	6	18	32	7.27	1.69	25.4	304	3.8	6.6	1.8	1.2	35%	57%	35
Penn,Hayden	08	24	R		aaa	BAL	6	7	21	0	99	124	63	16	33	57	5.72	1.58	21.3	300	3.0	5.2	1.7	1.5	33%	67%	19
	09	25	R		aaa	FLA	2	4	14	0	70	78	35	9	26	55	4.55	1.49	22.0	276	3.4	7.1	2.1	1.2	33%	72%	52
Peralta,Joel	09	34	R		aaa	COL	6	0	31	4	36	35	12	3	11	26	2.88	1.25	4.9	247	2.6	6.4	2.4	0.8	29%	80%	71
Perez,Juan	09	31	L		aaa	ATL	2	4	47	1	57	47	27	7	38	49	4.32	1.50	5.4	222	6.0	7.8	1.3	1.2	26%	74%	50
Perez,Luis	09	25	L		aa	TOR	9	11	28	0	162	188	95	16	80	92	5.26	1.66	26.5	285	4.4	5.1	1.2	0.9	32%	69%	27
Perez,Oneli	08	25	R		a/a	NYY	2	3	38	2	60	87	56	14	34	61	8.34	2.01	7.8	332	5.0	9.1	1.8	2.0	40%	61%	20
	09	26	R		aaa	STL	4	3	18	0	67	75	25	7	22	51	3.32	1.45	16.3	278	2.9	6.9	2.4	1.0	33%	80%	62
Perez,Sergio	09	25	R		aa	HOU	11	11	27	0	142	189	84	16	61	59	5.33	1.76	24.6	313	3.9	3.7	1.0	1.0	34%	71%	5
Perkins,Vince	09	28	R		a/a	CHC	7	2	53	5	86	108	42	2	71	49	4.43	2.08	8.1	301	7.4	5.2	0.7	0.2	35%	77%	33
Perrault,Josh	08	26	R		a/a	WAS	4	2	49	1	70	90	41	10	21	49	5.27	1.58	6.5	305	2.7	6.2	2.3	1.3	35%	69%	41
	09	27	R		a/a	BAL	1	4	59	18	72	82	28	11	22	54	3.45	1.44	5.3	280	2.7	6.7	2.5	1.4	32%	83%	48
Pestano,Vinnie	09	25	R		aa	CLE	2	3	34	24	34	38	16	2	15	27	4.16	1.54	4.5	275	3.9	7.0	1.8	0.6	34%	73%	63
Peterson,Matthew	09	28	R		aa	FLA	4	4	56	37	58	70	37	4	35	40	5.79	1.80	4.9	292	5.4	6.2	1.1	0.6	35%	67%	41

							Actual				Major League Equivalents																
PITCHER	Yr	Age	Th		Lev	Org	w	l	g	sv	ip	h	er	hr	bb	k	era	whip	bf/g	oob	ctl	dom	cmd	hr/9	h%	s%	bpv
Pettyjohn,Adam	08	31	L		aaa	CIN	15	6	28	0	174	227	115	26	46	79	5.93	1.57	27.9	309	2.4	4.1	1.7	1.4	33%	64%	13
	09	32	L		aaa	NYM	4	11	27	0	105	160	65	13	34	48	5.58	1.84	18.6	342	2.9	4.1	1.4	1.1	37%	71%	8
Phillips,Heath	08	27	L		aaa	TAM	4	5	44	0	77	103	48	7	34	51	5.65	1.78	8.2	314	4.0	6.0	1.5	0.8	37%	68%	35
	09	28	L		aaa	KC	8	7	27	0	149	217	112	14	52	93	6.73	1.80	26.1	332	3.1	5.6	1.8	0.8	38%	62%	35
Phillips,Paul	09	26	R		a/a	TAM	3	3	31	7	44	33	14	1	19	34	2.79	1.17	5.8	202	3.9	7.0	1.8	0.2	26%	75%	88
Phillips,Zachary	09	23	L		aa	TEX	0	0	20	2	33	32	7	1	20	24	1.96	1.55	7.4	248	5.3	6.6	1.2	0.3	31%	88%	62
Pinango,Miguel	08	26	R		aa	LA	5	9	27	0	136	202	98	24	42	76	6.47	1.80	23.8	337	2.8	5.0	1.8	1.6	37%	67%	7
	09	27	R		aaa	LA	2	5	11	0	53	79	47	8	18	26	8.02	1.82	22.9	338	3.0	4.4	1.5	1.4	36%	56%	3
Pino,Johan	08	25	R		aa	MIN	7	7	26	0	109	136	67	17	40	59	5.56	1.61	19.0	299	3.3	4.9	1.5	1.4	32%	68%	14
	09	26	R	a	a/a	CLE	9	3	42	0	127	135	53	11	32	105	3.73	1.31	12.8	267	2.2	7.5	3.3	0.7	33%	73%	94
Plummer,Jarod	08	25	R		aa	KC	4	1	29	3	58	71	37	14	16	54	5.72	1.49	8.8	294	2.5	8.4	3.4	2.1	34%	68%	55
	09	26	R		aa	BOS	8	7	23	0	112	144	72	7	57	71	5.80	1.79	23.0	306	4.5	5.7	1.3	0.5	36%	66%	38
Polanco,Celson	09	25	R		aa	TOR	1	2	19	0	32	42	23	4	20	26	6.52	1.93	8.2	310	5.6	7.3	1.3	1.2	37%	67%	27
Pollok,Dwayne	08	28	R		aa	LA	10	5	40	4	105	160	75	14	24	47	6.40	1.75	12.3	343	2.1	4.1	2.0	1.2	37%	65%	15
	09	29	R		aaa	LA	3	4	36	0	76	103	56	13	24	44	6.61	1.67	9.7	317	2.8	5.2	1.8	1.5	35%	62%	16
Ponson,Sidney	09	33	R		aaa	KC	2	1	6	0	33	42	11	2	5	16	2.87	1.44	24.0	304	1.4	4.4	3.1	0.6	34%	81%	68
Pope,Ryan	09	23	R		aa	NYY	5	12	26	0	141	198	109	9	38	88	6.97	1.67	24.9	325	2.4	5.6	2.3	0.6	38%	56%	55
Poreda,Aaron	08	22	L		aa	CHW	3	4	15	0	87	98	39	7	23	64	4.03	1.39	25.0	278	2.4	6.6	2.8	0.7	33%	72%	76
	09	23	L		a/a	SD	5	7	20	0	107	88	49	3	73	93	4.12	1.50	23.7	220	6.1	7.8	1.3	0.3	29%	71%	77
Poveda,Omar	09	22	R		a/a	TEX	11	6	23	0	137	160	81	13	54	66	5.32	1.56	26.7	286	3.5	4.3	1.2	0.9	31%	66%	24
Powell,Jeremy	09	33	R		aaa	PIT	4	7	34	2	98	136	52	9	26	48	4.73	1.65	13.2	321	2.4	4.4	1.8	0.9	36%	72%	30
Price,David	08	23	L		a/a	TAM	8	1	13	0	75	71	24	7	25	62	2.88	1.28	24.2	245	3.0	7.4	2.5	0.8	30%	81%	78
	09	24	L		aaa	TAM	1	4	8	0	34	32	18	6	18	31	4.75	1.47	18.7	243	4.8	8.2	1.7	1.6	29%	73%	44
Province,Christopher	09	25	R		aa	BOS	2	4	43	1	79	89	32	3	34	46	3.59	1.56	8.2	279	3.8	5.2	1.4	0.4	33%	76%	48
Pucetas,Kevin	09	25	R		aaa	SF	10	6	28	0	159	181	91	13	45	82	5.15	1.42	24.7	280	2.5	4.6	1.8	0.7	31%	63%	43
Purcey,David	08	26	L		aaa	TOR	8	6	19	0	117	121	48	11	38	96	3.73	1.36	26.3	261	2.9	7.4	2.5	0.9	32%	75%	74
	09	28	L		aaa	TOR	9	6	24	0	139	148	77	7	80	89	4.97	1.64	26.4	268	5.2	5.8	1.1	0.5	32%	69%	45
Putnam,Zach	09	22	R	a	aa	CLE	4	2	33	2	56	71	35	2	19	52	5.60	1.60	7.7	302	3.0	8.3	2.7	0.3	39%	63%	92
Rainville,Jay	08	23	R		aa	MIN	9	9	24	0	123	160	92	22	45	68	6.73	1.67	23.5	308	3.3	5.0	1.5	1.6	33%	62%	7
	09	24	R		aa	MIN	3	3	19	0	69	108	55	6	26	31	7.12	1.95	17.7	349	3.4	4.1	1.2	0.8	38%	62%	10
Rainwater,Josh	08	24	R		aa	DET	10	7	24	0	132	152	68	7	61	67	4.64	1.61	24.9	282	4.1	4.6	1.1	0.5	32%	70%	34
	09	25	R		a/a	DET	3	4	39	5	71	80	40	5	26	45	5.09	1.49	8.0	279	3.3	5.6	1.7	0.7	33%	65%	50
Ramirez,Edwar	09	29	R	b	aaa	NYY	1	5	29	4	51	52	27	4	18	49	4.74	1.37	7.5	257	3.2	8.7	2.7	0.8	33%	66%	90
Ramirez,Elizardo	08	26	R		aa	TEX	10	7	27	0	160	237	100	29	36	66	5.63	1.70	27.4	336	2.0	3.7	1.8	1.6	35%	71%	0
	09	27	R		aaa	TEX	9	11	28	0	142	201	98	21	39	62	6.21	1.69	23.4	327	2.5	3.9	1.6	1.3	35%	65%	7
Ramirez,Horacio	09	30	L		aaa	WAS	3	7	16	0	85	142	70	12	26	27	7.45	1.98	26.0	364	2.8	2.9	1.0	1.3	38%	63%	-17
Ramirez,Ramon	08	26	R		a/a	CIN	6	8	30	1	145	147	77	19	63	113	4.76	1.45	21.1	257	3.9	7.0	1.8	1.2	30%	70%	48
	09	27	R		aaa	CIN	6	7	31	0	127	153	78	19	55	66	5.52	1.63	18.7	291	3.9	4.6	1.2	1.3	31%	69%	9
Ramos,Cesar	08	24	L		aa	SD	9	11	28	0	149	209	101	17	60	86	6.10	1.81	25.2	325	3.6	5.2	1.4	1.0	36%	67%	20
	09	25	L		aaa	SD	5	6	15	0	76	91	36	6	30	39	4.29	1.59	22.9	290	3.6	4.6	1.3	0.7	32%	74%	30
Randolph,Stephen	08	34	L		a/a	PHI	3	1	46	6	62	47	21	4	47	73	3.06	1.51	6.0	205	6.8	10.6	1.6	0.6	29%	81%	91
	09	35	L		aaa	KC	5	3	21	0	50	52	44	7	40	45	7.94	1.83	11.3	261	7.2	8.0	1.1	1.3	31%	56%	35
Rapada,Clay	08	28	L	b	aaa	DET	0	1	28	2	35	38	12	2	15	38	2.98	1.50	5.5	270	3.8	9.8	2.6	0.5	37%	81%	97
	09	29	L		aaa	DET	4	2	42	5	45	65	19	1	18	37	3.85	1.83	5.1	328	3.6	7.4	2.0	0.2	41%	78%	70
Ray,Ken	09	35	R		aaa	CLE	2	10	20	0	90	151	85	14	35	59	8.53	2.06	22.4	364	3.5	5.9	1.7	1.4	41%	58%	12
Ray,Ronnie	08	24	R		aa	SF	6	4	46	1	72	98	34	3	25	38	4.20	1.71	7.3	317	3.1	4.7	1.5	0.4	36%	75%	40
	09	25	R		aaa	SF	1	5	43	0	65	93	43	7	18	39	6.00	1.71	7.0	328	2.5	5.3	2.1	1.0	37%	65%	37
Reckling,Trevor	09	20	L		aa	LAA	8	7	23	0	135	133	55	4	72	93	3.68	1.52	26.1	253	4.8	6.2	1.3	0.3	31%	75%	61
Redmond,Todd	08	23	R		aa	ATL	13	5	28	0	166	189	77	18	34	113	4.19	1.34	25.3	280	1.8	6.1	3.3	0.9	32%	71%	77
	09	24	R		aaa	ATL	9	6	27	0	145	171	84	22	47	93	5.21	1.50	23.8	288	2.9	5.8	2.0	1.4	32%	68%	33
Register,Steven	08	25	R		aa	COL	5	3	56	16	59	70	28	4	19	40	4.24	1.51	4.7	289	2.9	6.0	2.1	0.7	34%	72%	57
	09	26	R		aaa	PHI	2	5	50	13	57	79	32	9	23	34	5.04	1.79	5.4	323	3.6	5.4	1.5	1.5	36%	76%	10
Reid,Ryan	08	23	R		aa	TAM	5	4	31	4	46	47	29	1	32	45	5.64	1.72	6.9	261	6.2	8.7	1.4	0.2	35%	64%	78
	09	24	R		aa	TAM	0	1	42	1	58	81	37	4	31	42	5.71	1.92	6.7	323	4.7	6.5	1.4	0.7	39%	70%	38
Reineke,Chad	08	27	R		aa	SD	5	10	23	0	129	161	79	21	47	84	5.52	1.61	25.4	299	3.3	5.9	1.8	1.4	33%	69%	25
	09	28	R		aaa	OAK	9	4	30	2	125	152	75	17	49	74	5.38	1.61	18.9	293	3.6	5.3	1.5	1.2	33%	69%	23
Reinhard,Greg	08	25	R		aa	CHC	5	4	45	4	85	90	48	10	46	67	5.05	1.59	8.5	266	4.8	7.0	1.5	1.1	32%	70%	43
	09	26	R		aaa	CHC	2	4	42	0	73	89	55	10	36	74	6.74	1.71	8.0	294	4.4	9.1	2.0	1.3	37%	61%	56
Rembisz,Brian	09	24	R		aa	LAA	2	3	40	0	59	71	39	11	20	28	5.93	1.53	6.6	290	3.0	4.2	1.4	1.6	30%	64%	3
Reyes,Jo-Jo	08	24	L		aaa	ATL	1	1	8	0	39	35	12	2	16	33	2.77	1.31	20.6	235	3.7	7.6	2.1	0.5	30%	80%	83
	09	25	L		aaa	ATL	4	2	15	0	66	77	25	6	24	28	3.41	1.53	19.6	285	3.3	3.8	1.2	0.8	31%	80%	21
Reynoso,Ryne	09	25	R		a/a	ATL	7	10	26	0	153	160	80	14	65	76	4.73	1.47	25.8	263	3.8	4.5	1.2	0.8	29%	69%	28
Rhoades,Chad	08	26	R		aa	BOS	5	3	41	2	61	90	48	7	31	50	7.04	1.98	7.3	335	4.6	7.4	1.6	1.0	41%	64%	37
	09	27	R		aa	BOS	6	2	56	2	82	97	53	5	41	62	5.80	1.68	6.7	287	4.5	6.8	1.5	0.5	35%	64%	54
Richardson,Dustin	08	25	L		aa	BOS	7	10	22	0	106	131	96	18	53	92	8.12	1.72	22.4	296	4.5	7.8	1.8	1.5	35%	53%	34
	09	26	L	a	a/a	BOS	2	2	45	4	74	65	32	3	46	79	3.84	1.51	7.3	232	5.6	9.6	1.7	0.4	32%	74%	90
Ring,Royce	09	29	L		aaa	STL	5	2	51	4	47	53	19	4	15	31	3.70	1.44	4.0	277	2.9	5.9	2.0	0.8	32%	76%	53
Rivera,Mumba	08	28	R		aa	SEA	5	3	41	11	51	64	33	5	29	39	5.73	1.82	5.9	300	5.1	6.9	1.3	0.8	36%	68%	39
	09	29	R		aa	SEA	6	6	42	1	64	85	49	6	58	45	6.86	2.23	7.8	313	8.1	6.3	0.8	0.9	37%	69%	20
Rivera,Saul	09	32	R		aaa	WAS	2	5	30	2	45	69	24	1	26	27	4.82	2.12	7.6	345	5.2	5.3	1.0	0.2	40%	76%	33
Robertson,Connor	08	27	R		aa	ARI	7	4	47	1	71	99	63	11	36	53	7.92	1.90	7.3	322	4.6	6.7	1.5	1.4	37%	58%	21
	09	28	R		a/a	NYM	2	4	47	11	59	74	39	7	22	41	5.92	1.64	5.7	301	3.4	6.2	1.8	1.1	35%	64%	38
Rodriguez,Aneury	09	22	R		aa	TAM	9	11	27	0	142	144	92	20	62	98	5.83	1.45	23.0	258	3.9	6.2	1.6	1.3	29%	61%	36
Rodriguez,Derek	08	25	R		a/a	CHW	5	2	49	2	79	68	41	11	36	74	4.67	1.32	6.8	229	4.1	8.4	2.1	1.2	28%	67%	67
	09	26	R		a/a	CHW	2	3	43	4	64	78	33	4	29	41	4.69	1.67	6.8	294	4.1	5.7	1.4	0.6	34%	72%	41
Rodriguez,Fernando	09	25	R		a/a	LAA	4	2	49	4	79	76	45	5	45	62	5.15	1.53	7.2	247	5.2	7.0	1.4	0.6	30%	65%	58
Rodriguez,Francisco	08	26	R		aa	LAA	5	5	50	2	75	96	42	10	36	54	5.06	1.75	7.0	303	4.3	6.5	1.5	1.2	35%	73%	29
	09	27	R		aaa	LAA	5	4	44	0	77	74	37	7	38	49	4.33	1.46	7.7	248	4.5	5.7	1.3	0.8	28%	72%	41

Major League Equivalent Statistics

PITCHER	Yr	Age	Th		Lev	Org	w	l	g	sv	ip	h	er	hr	bb	k	era	whip	bf/g	oob	ctl	dom	cmd	hr/9	h%	s%	bpv
							Actual				Major League Equivalents																
Rodriguez,Henry	08	22	R		aa	OAK	2	7	14	0	41	54	36	1	39	37	7.90	2.27	15.2	311	8.6	8.1	0.9	0.2	40%	62%	55
	09	23	R	a	aaa	OAK	2	1	37	4	43	39	29	4	32	64	5.95	1.65	5.3	236	6.7	13.3	2.0	0.8	38%	63%	106
Rodriguez,Jesus	08	23	R		aa	LA	5	5	13	0	67	80	44	15	32	38	5.95	1.68	23.7	291	4.3	5.1	1.2	2.1	30%	70%	-10
	09	24	R		aa	LA	6	5	46	1	80	103	39	12	22	35	4.38	1.56	7.8	306	2.5	3.9	1.6	1.3	32%	76%	12
Rodriguez,Kenny	09	25	R		aa	TOR	4	5	13	0	68	84	51	8	39	43	6.69	1.81	24.7	298	5.2	5.7	1.1	1.1	34%	63%	19
Rodriguez,Rafael	08	24	R		aa	LAA	4	4	51	11	67	79	26	5	18	46	3.52	1.44	5.7	287	2.4	6.1	2.5	0.7	34%	77%	67
	09	25	R		aaa	LAA	1	0	22	3	34	29	7	3	9	19	1.87	1.13	6.3	228	2.4	5.0	2.1	0.8	25%	89%	59
Rodriguez,Ryan	09	25	L		aa	BAL	1	2	26	1	44	83	59	7	28	21	12.05	2.53	9.2	393	5.7	4.2	0.7	1.4	43%	50%	-24
Roe,Chaz	08	22	R		aa	COL	5	4	16	0	105	108	56	16	31	60	4.80	1.32	27.9	260	2.7	5.1	1.9	1.4	28%	67%	33
	09	23	R		aa	COL	7	3	20	0	117	128	55	9	43	63	4.20	1.46	25.6	272	3.3	4.9	1.5	0.7	31%	72%	39
Roemer,Wesley	09	23	R		aa	ARI	9	9	22	0	134	161	86	18	44	83	5.74	1.53	27.1	291	3.0	5.6	1.9	1.2	33%	64%	35
Rogers,Esmil	09	24	R		a/a	COL	11	7	27	0	155	190	93	13	52	106	5.39	1.56	25.7	295	3.0	6.1	2.1	0.8	35%	65%	52
Rohrbaugh,Robert	08	25	L		aa	SEA	7	5	19	1	96	126	66	8	31	65	6.22	1.63	23.0	311	2.9	6.1	2.1	0.8	36%	61%	50
	09	26	L		aa	SEA	3	3	9	0	47	60	24	6	14	34	4.66	1.58	23.6	303	2.8	6.5	2.4	1.1	36%	73%	51
Rollins,Lewis	09	24	R		a/a	TAM	9	11	31	0	140	186	79	12	39	75	5.10	1.61	20.4	312	2.5	4.8	1.9	0.8	35%	68%	38
Romero,Davis	08	26	L		aaa	TOR	5	9	25	0	106	130	60	14	32	72	5.05	1.53	18.9	296	2.7	6.1	2.2	1.2	34%	69%	44
	09	27	L		a/a	TOR	3	6	28	1	95	158	83	21	42	55	7.89	2.10	17.1	362	4.0	5.2	1.3	2.0	39%	65%	-19
Romero,Felix	08	28	R		a/a	BAL	8	3	45	1	85	95	44	11	28	78	4.60	1.45	8.3	277	3.0	8.3	2.8	1.1	34%	71%	74
	09	29	R	b	aaa	SF	5	5	50	4	73	87	40	3	15	54	4.86	1.40	6.3	289	1.9	6.6	3.5	0.4	35%	63%	98
Rondon,Hector	09	22	R	a	a/a	CLE	11	10	27	0	146	158	66	11	29	130	4.05	1.28	22.7	270	1.8	8.0	4.6	0.7	34%	69%	124
Roquet,Rocky	08	26	R		aa	CHC	4	2	39	3	48	49	24	3	30	41	4.56	1.64	5.6	258	5.6	7.7	1.4	0.6	33%	72%	60
	09	27	R		aa	OAK	1	3	43	1	58	93	39	3	25	34	6.04	2.03	6.7	354	3.9	5.2	1.3	0.5	41%	69%	28
Rosa,Carlos	08	24	R	a	aa	KC	8	5	19	0	95	100	39	5	20	72	3.68	1.26	20.9	265	1.9	6.8	3.6	0.5	33%	71%	104
	09	25	R		aaa	KC	2	8	43	7	71	82	46	7	32	69	5.89	1.61	7.5	283	4.1	8.8	2.1	0.9	36%	63%	69
Ross,Tyson	09	22	R		aa	OAK	5	4	9	0	50	41	21	3	17	27	3.78	1.16	22.7	219	3.1	4.9	1.6	0.5	25%	67%	57
Rowland-Smith,R	09	27	L		aaa	SEA	5	3	10	0	56	66	28	5	10	33	4.47	1.36	24.0	287	1.7	5.3	3.2	0.8	33%	68%	72
Ruckle,Jacob	09	23	R		aa	NYM	2	4	17	1	50	67	45	10	16	31	8.16	1.67	13.5	315	3.0	5.6	1.9	1.9	34%	52%	9
Ruhlman,Jayson	09	25	L		a/a	CHC	2	1	59	4	61	79	42	7	31	37	6.19	1.79	4.9	306	4.5	5.4	1.2	1.1	35%	66%	19
Rundles,Rich	08	27	L		aaa	CLE	5	4	55	4	52	51	24	4	27	50	4.17	1.49	4.2	249	4.7	8.7	1.8	0.7	32%	73%	74
	09	28	L		aaa	CLE	2	2	45	1	41	66	28	3	18	31	6.11	2.04	4.5	353	4.0	6.7	1.7	0.7	42%	69%	39
Rupe,Josh	09	27	R		aaa	TEX	5	7	24	1	89	144	91	6	45	51	9.15	2.13	18.7	357	4.6	5.2	1.1	0.6	41%	54%	19
Rusch,Matt	08	25	R		a/a	DET	4	1	48	1	73	97	47	13	21	52	5.83	1.61	6.9	312	2.6	6.4	2.5	1.6	35%	67%	37
	09	26	R		aaa	DET	2	4	38	1	74	110	55	11	25	40	6.65	1.83	9.2	338	3.0	4.8	1.6	1.4	37%	65%	9
Russell,Adam	08	25	R		aaa	CHW	3	2	25	0	37	33	16	4	20	25	3.92	1.44	6.5	235	4.9	6.0	1.2	1.0	27%	76%	40
	09	27	R		aaa	SD	2	2	43	9	68	56	30	5	25	49	3.95	1.18	6.5	219	3.3	6.4	2.0	0.7	26%	67%	70
Russell,James	08	23	L		aa	CHC	4	8	18	0	86	122	68	20	25	53	7.11	1.71	22.1	327	2.6	5.5	2.1	2.1	35%	62%	5
	09	24	L		a/a	CHC	5	6	37	0	102	135	58	14	29	62	5.11	1.60	12.5	311	2.6	5.5	2.1	1.2	35%	71%	33
Ryan,Patrick	08	25	R		aa	MIL	5	5	39	6	64	76	22	3	32	31	3.12	1.68	7.6	288	4.5	4.3	0.9	0.5	32%	82%	29
	09	26	R		aa	SEA	2	5	16	0	50	85	52	9	25	27	9.29	2.20	16.0	368	4.5	4.8	1.1	1.7	40%	58%	-17
Rzepczynski,Marc	09	24	L	a	a/a	TOR	9	5	16	0	88	102	32	1	43	87	3.27	1.65	25.1	284	4.4	8.9	2.0	0.1	39%	79%	91
Saarloos,Kirk	08	29	R		aa	OAK	9	4	22	0	140	212	92	21	43	51	5.91	1.82	30.2	341	2.7	3.3	1.2	1.4	36%	70%	-10
	09	30	R		aaa	CLE	3	10	15	0	86	140	71	17	39	43	7.42	2.08	28.7	357	4.1	4.5	1.1	1.7	38%	66%	-18
Sadler,Billy	08	27	R		aa	SF	1	0	22	1	33	27	6	0	25	29	1.64	1.57	6.7	216	6.9	7.9	1.1	0.0	29%	88%	84
	09	28	R		aaa	HOU	5	3	16	0	63	90	47	5	34	46	6.75	1.98	19.3	329	4.9	6.5	1.3	0.8	39%	65%	33
Sadowski,Ryan	08	26	R		aa	SF	9	4	40	0	91	143	68	8	48	60	6.69	2.09	11.4	349	4.8	5.9	1.2	0.8	41%	67%	23
	09	27	R		aaa	SF	6	3	18	0	89	93	54	13	41	59	5.42	1.50	21.9	263	4.1	5.9	1.4	1.3	29%	66%	30
Salamida,Christopher	09	25	L		aa	HOU	1	2	22	0	30	51	31	6	11	14	9.33	2.07	6.8	368	3.3	4.3	1.3	1.7	39%	55%	-16
Salas,Noel	08	23	R	a	aa	STL	7	3	60	25	74	72	33	11	15	83	4.01	1.18	5.1	250	1.9	10.1	5.4	1.4	33%	72%	138
	09	24	R		a/a	STL	4	2	34	0	38	36	18	4	11	26	4.14	1.24	4.7	245	2.7	6.2	2.3	1.0	28%	69%	62
Salmon,Brad	08	29	R		aa	KC	8	7	47	3	101	155	84	15	66	63	7.46	2.19	11.0	344	5.9	5.6	1.0	1.3	39%	67%	0
	09	30	R		aaa	LAA	8	4	33	1	108	134	64	11	60	66	5.30	1.80	15.5	298	5.0	5.5	1.1	0.9	34%	71%	24
Samardzija,Jeff	08	24	R		aa	CHC	7	6	22	0	113	116	63	12	60	70	5.00	1.56	23.0	261	4.8	5.6	1.2	1.0	29%	69%	31
	09	25	R		aaa	CHC	6	6	18	0	89	113	53	15	28	61	5.36	1.58	22.3	303	2.8	6.2	2.2	1.5	34%	70%	32
Samuel,Francisco	09	23	R		aa	STL	3	4	52	22	47	39	32	2	42	51	6.10	1.72	4.2	221	8.0	9.7	1.2	0.4	31%	62%	83
Sanchez,Eduardo	09	21	R	a	aa	STL	2	0	41	10	50	32	15	4	17	50	2.74	0.99	4.8	182	3.1	9.1	2.9	0.7	24%	75%	114
Sanchez,Jose	08	24	R		aa	NYM	13	7	29	0	152	189	80	12	45	97	4.73	1.54	23.4	299	2.7	5.7	2.1	0.7	35%	69%	54
	09	25	R		a/a	NYM	1	7	13	0	63	100	57	7	28	35	8.11	2.04	24.1	352	4.1	5.0	1.2	1.1	39%	59%	9
Sanchez,Romulo	08	24	R		aa	PIT	5	1	33	4	54	61	27	5	20	26	4.54	1.50	7.3	278	3.3	4.3	1.3	0.9	30%	71%	26
	09	25	R		aaa	NYY	6	5	29	0	77	95	48	5	42	67	5.67	1.78	12.5	297	5.0	7.9	1.6	0.6	38%	67%	58
Sandoval,Juan	08	28	R		aa	MIL	2	6	45	20	48	54	24	6	33	27	4.52	1.81	5.0	279	6.1	5.1	0.8	1.1	31%	78%	14
	09	29	R		a/a	MIL	4	3	49	2	58	80	46	2	34	38	7.10	1.96	5.8	320	5.3	5.9	1.1	0.4	38%	61%	39
Sanit,Amauri	09	30	R		a/a	NYY	1	5	40	10	45	60	30	5	20	22	6.08	1.76	5.3	312	3.9	4.4	1.1	1.0	34%	66%	14
Santeliz,Clevelan	09	23	R		aa	CHW	4	0	40	10	56	53	8	3	38	45	1.32	1.62	6.4	243	6.1	7.2	1.2	0.5	30%	94%	59
Santos,Jarrett	08	27	R		aa	FLA	5	2	33	0	65	95	42	6	20	25	5.84	1.78	9.3	334	2.8	3.4	1.2	0.8	36%	67%	9
	09	28	R		aa	FLA	8	8	40	0	117	175	69	9	21	43	5.34	1.68	13.5	339	1.6	3.3	2.0	0.7	37%	68%	27
Santos,Reid	08	26	L		a/a	CLE	4	3	45	2	77	112	61	10	26	55	7.13	1.79	8.1	333	3.0	6.4	2.1	1.2	39%	60%	37
	09	27	L		aaa	MIN	2	6	25	0	97	156	62	11	36	51	5.75	1.97	19.0	354	3.3	4.8	1.4	1.0	39%	72%	13
Sartor,Matthew	09	25	R		aa	LA	4	6	49	11	71	82	46	9	32	61	5.76	1.61	6.6	283	4.1	7.7	1.9	1.1	34%	65%	51
Satterwhite,Cody	09	23	R		aa	DET	4	6	34	12	49	53	23	6	26	44	4.22	1.61	6.5	270	4.8	8.1	1.7	1.1	33%	77%	52
Savery,Joseph	09	24	L		a/a	PHI	16	6	28	0	151	176	91	16	78	81	5.42	1.68	24.8	285	4.6	4.8	1.0	1.0	32%	68%	20
Scherer,Matthew	08	26	R		aa	STL	2	3	45	1	59	67	30	6	18	29	4.57	1.43	5.7	279	2.7	4.4	1.6	0.8	31%	69%	34
	09	27	R		aaa	STL	3	4	52	1	73	90	34	8	18	42	4.18	1.46	6.2	296	2.2	5.1	2.4	1.0	33%	74%	46
Schlitter,Brian	09	24	R		aa	CHC	1	7	59	22	61	75	39	10	26	43	5.76	1.65	4.7	296	3.8	6.3	1.7	1.5	33%	68%	23
Schmidt,Jason	09	37	R		aaa	LA	2	0	6	0	32	39	16	3	7	21	4.43	1.44	23.3	294	2.1	5.9	2.8	0.9	34%	71%	64
Schmidt,Joshua	09	27	R		aa	NYY	8	4	46	0	83	80	24	3	47	71	2.61	1.53	8.1	249	5.1	7.7	1.5	0.4	32%	83%	72
Schroder,Chris	08	30	R		aaa	WAS	5	4	43	8	45	58	24	3	21	41	4.88	1.75	4.9	305	4.2	8.3	2.0	0.7	39%	72%	65
	09	31	R		aaa	OAK	3	1	45	3	56	41	16	4	35	37	2.53	1.35	5.3	200	5.6	5.9	1.1	0.7	23%	84%	53
Scribner,Evan	09	24	R	a	aa	SD	8	4	58	21	70	66	25	3	20	64	3.24	1.23	5.0	245	2.6	8.2	3.2	0.4	32%	73%	110

Major League Equivalent Statistics

							Actual				Major League Equivalents																
PITCHER	Yr	Age	Th		Lev	Org	w	l	g	sv	ip	h	er	hr	bb	k	era	whip	bf/g	oob	ctl	dom	cmd	hr/9	h%	s%	bpv
Seddon,Chris	08	25	L		aa	FLA	10	9	28	0	152	200	104	25	76	109	6.17	1.81	25.7	311	4.5	6.5	1.4	1.5	35%	68%	17
	09	26	L		aaa	SEA	9	8	25	0	131	152	69	15	54	70	4.74	1.56	23.5	283	3.7	4.8	1.3	1.1	31%	72%	23
Segovia,Zack	08	25	R		aa	WAS	4	2	12	0	42	67	39	6	20	19	8.29	2.05	17.5	351	4.3	4.0	0.9	1.2	38%	59%	-7
	09	27	R		a/a	WAS	3	5	51	6	72	99	38	3	30	51	4.72	1.79	6.7	320	3.7	6.4	1.7	0.4	39%	73%	53
Sencion,Carlos	08	24	L		aa	ATL	6	4	25	0	76	85	47	6	44	53	5.61	1.69	14.0	276	5.2	6.3	1.2	0.7	33%	66%	41
	09	25	L		aa	KC	3	1	25	1	46	68	38	5	29	36	7.40	2.12	9.3	337	5.8	7.0	1.2	1.0	40%	65%	25
Sharpe,Steven	08	27	R		aa	OAK	1	0	19	1	31	55	34	2	16	11	9.79	2.29	8.5	380	4.5	3.1	0.7	0.7	41%	54%	-9
	09	28	R		a/a	OAK	11	1	36	1	54	65	36	4	26	26	6.08	1.68	6.9	291	4.3	4.3	1.0	0.6	33%	62%	25
Shell,Steven	08	26	R	a	aaa	WAS	3	2	22	1	58	54	19	4	13	45	2.97	1.15	10.7	240	2.0	6.9	3.4	0.6	29%	76%	101
	09	27	R		a/a	SEA	6	3	22	1	61	79	40	11	23	35	5.90	1.68	12.7	307	3.4	5.2	1.5	1.6	33%	68%	7
Shirek,Charles	09	24	R		aa	CHW	6	4	15	0	90	120	46	11	19	27	4.63	1.53	26.7	313	1.9	2.7	1.5	1.1	32%	72%	6
Silva,Walter	09	33	R		aaa	SD	7	5	23	0	81	111	61	9	27	46	6.78	1.70	16.3	318	3.0	5.1	1.7	1.1	36%	60%	25
Simmons,James	08	22	R	a	aa	OAK	9	6	25	0	136	159	55	10	28	103	3.64	1.38	23.4	286	1.9	6.8	3.7	0.7	35%	75%	96
	09	23	R		aaa	OAK	7	7	23	0	119	149	81	7	42	69	6.12	1.60	23.4	300	3.2	5.2	1.6	0.5	35%	60%	45
Simons,Zachary	09	23	R		a/a	DET	4	2	42	4	69	63	27	5	25	54	3.52	1.27	6.9	238	3.3	7.0	2.2	0.7	29%	73%	75
Sinkbeil,Brett	08	24	R		aa	FLA	5	9	26	0	143	198	95	12	55	58	5.97	1.77	25.8	321	3.4	3.7	1.1	0.8	35%	66%	12
	09	25	R		aaa	FLA	2	8	47	0	83	116	62	9	45	47	6.72	1.94	8.6	324	4.9	5.1	1.0	1.0	36%	65%	13
Slama,Anthony	09	26	R	a	a/a	MIN	4	4	62	29	81	68	31	5	42	87	3.39	1.36	5.6	224	4.7	9.7	2.1	0.6	31%	76%	94
Slaten,Doug	09	30	L		aaa	ARI	3	2	39	9	43	47	16	3	14	32	3.43	1.42	4.8	273	3.0	6.6	2.2	0.7	33%	77%	67
Slocum,Brian	08	28	R		aaa	CLE	3	7	30	1	85	103	63	15	47	68	6.68	1.77	13.3	293	5.0	7.2	1.4	1.6	34%	64%	23
	09	29	R		aaa	PIT	1	3	19	2	32	37	18	1	19	21	5.14	1.75	7.9	281	5.4	6.0	1.1	0.3	34%	69%	49
Smit,Alexander	09	24	L		a/a	CIN	4	3	21	0	71	67	33	13	46	61	4.14	1.60	15.3	245	5.9	7.7	1.3	1.6	28%	80%	32
Smith,Carlton	09	24	R		aa	CLE	6	2	37	3	79	85	33	6	26	35	3.75	1.39	9.2	268	2.9	4.0	1.4	0.7	29%	74%	33
Smith,Chris	08	28	R		aaa	BOS	1	5	37	15	59	66	27	6	12	42	4.17	1.32	6.8	278	1.8	6.4	3.6	1.0	32%	71%	85
	09	29	R	b	aaa	MIL	2	0	28	17	42	37	8	3	6	42	1.61	1.02	5.9	229	1.4	8.9	6.5	0.7	30%	89%	178
Smith,Greg	09	26	L		a/a	COL	1	3	9	0	37	55	38	9	12	16	9.17	1.78	19.4	335	2.8	3.9	1.4	2.3	34%	50%	-28
Smith,Jordan	08	23	R		aa	CIN	2	6	11	0	55	80	38	7	17	37	6.22	1.76	23.4	333	2.8	6.1	2.2	1.1	38%	66%	36
	09	24	R		aa	CIN	5	3	13	0	73	94	37	5	23	33	4.57	1.59	25.4	305	2.8	4.1	1.5	0.6	34%	71%	30
Smith,Sean	08	25	R		a/a	COL	6	8	22	0	114	127	78	18	54	72	6.17	1.58	23.4	276	4.2	5.7	1.3	1.4	30%	63%	21
	09	26	R		a/a	TOR	4	3	32	7	99	101	39	7	46	72	3.54	1.48	13.6	259	4.1	6.5	1.6	0.6	31%	77%	57
Snell,Ian	09	28	R	b	aaa	PIT	2	2	6	0	37	34	5	0	13	37	1.28	1.25	25.8	237	3.1	9.0	2.9	0.0	33%	89%	123
Snyder,Benjamin	08	23	L		aa	SF	1	6	13	0	61	93	54	9	24	36	7.88	1.90	22.7	342	3.5	5.3	1.5	1.4	38%	59%	9
	09	24	L		aa	SF	4	4	34	1	97	101	41	4	40	70	3.81	1.45	12.5	263	3.7	6.5	1.8	0.4	32%	73%	67
Snyder,Kyle	08	31	R		aaa	BOS	1	4	14	1	37	42	29	5	13	25	7.13	1.47	11.7	279	3.1	6.0	2.0	1.3	31%	51%	38
	09	32	R		aaa	NYM	3	8	33	1	104	143	66	15	35	62	5.73	1.71	14.6	320	3.0	5.3	1.8	1.3	36%	68%	22
Sonnanstine,Andy	09	27	R		aaa	TAM	5	3	9	0	57	80	35	5	9	31	5.52	1.57	28.5	325	1.5	4.9	3.3	0.8	37%	65%	65
Sosa,Henry	09	24	R		aa	SF	6	0	14	0	72	75	25	4	26	36	3.15	1.40	22.3	262	3.3	4.5	1.4	0.5	30%	78%	43
Sosa,Jorge	08	31	R		aa	SEA	2	2	27	4	36	44	21	6	25	27	5.28	1.89	6.4	292	6.2	6.8	1.1	1.5	34%	75%	16
	09	32	R		aaa	WAS	1	2	20	3	48	49	20	3	14	44	3.74	1.31	10.2	260	2.6	8.2	3.2	0.6	33%	72%	101
Souza,Justin	09	24	R		aa	OAK	6	8	25	0	98	111	53	4	25	62	4.83	1.39	16.9	280	2.3	5.7	2.5	0.4	33%	63%	75
Sowers,Jeremy	08	25	L		aaa	CLE	4	3	10	0	60	68	19	5	18	38	2.87	1.43	26.2	278	2.7	5.6	2.1	0.8	32%	83%	54
	09	26	L		aaa	CLE	2	2	6	0	37	42	14	2	9	23	3.50	1.39	26.6	281	2.3	5.6	2.5	0.5	33%	75%	70
Speier,Ryan	09	30	R		a/a	COL	2	2	33	0	33	63	25	4	19	18	6.78	2.45	5.4	392	5.1	4.8	0.9	1.0	44%	73%	-6
Speigner,Levale	08	28	R		a/a	WAS	4	0	35	0	59	55	15	4	14	29	2.33	1.17	6.9	243	2.1	4.4	2.0	0.5	27%	82%	60
	09	29	R		a/a	FLA	6	6	58	1	84	105	34	6	26	37	3.65	1.55	6.5	299	2.7	3.9	1.4	0.7	33%	77%	30
Spradlin,Jack	09	25	L		a/a	WAS	4	3	47	4	74	88	44	3	28	48	5.38	1.58	7.1	290	3.5	5.8	1.7	0.4	35%	64%	55
Stammen,Craig	08	25	R		a/a	WAS	4	5	15	0	81	92	45	3	26	53	5.03	1.45	23.6	279	2.9	5.9	2.1	0.3	34%	63%	68
	09	26	R		aaa	WAS	4	2	7	0	40	38	10	4	8	12	2.27	1.16	23.3	247	1.8	2.7	1.5	0.9	25%	86%	25
Stange,Daniel	09	24	R		aa	ARI	0	4	39	10	51	80	39	5	15	38	6.89	1.87	6.3	350	2.7	6.6	2.4	0.9	41%	63%	49
Stanley,Patrick	09	27	R		a/a	DET	7	4	16	0	87	106	60	18	38	45	6.20	1.65	24.9	293	3.9	4.6	1.2	1.8	30%	66%	-6
Stark,Denny	08	34	R		aa	SEA	6	3	23	1	63	89	35	5	29	34	5.04	1.89	13.2	327	4.2	4.9	1.2	0.7	37%	73%	23
	09	35	R		aaa	SEA	2	2	38	1	51	61	36	5	36	37	6.30	1.90	6.5	290	6.3	6.5	1.0	0.9	34%	67%	30
Starner,Nathan	09	25	L		aa	TOR	1	2	33	2	61	90	46	8	50	30	6.70	2.29	9.7	335	7.4	4.4	0.6	1.1	37%	71%	-8
Stauffer,Tim	09	27	R		a/a	SD	3	1	16	1	42	36	11	2	9	21	2.46	1.07	10.5	225	2.0	4.5	2.3	0.5	25%	78%	70
Stephens,Jason	09	25	R		a/a	NYY	2	2	16	0	52	61	28	7	21	24	4.92	1.58	14.6	287	3.6	4.1	1.1	1.3	30%	72%	8
Stevens,Jeff	08	25	R	a	a/a	CLE	5	4	36	6	58	47	28	6	31	68	4.40	1.34	6.9	218	4.7	10.6	2.2	1.0	30%	69%	93
	09	26	R	b	aaa	CHC	1	3	42	1	57	41	16	1	27	50	2.60	1.19	5.6	198	4.2	7.9	1.9	0.2	27%	77%	98
Stewart,Zachary	09	23	R		a/a	TOR	3	0	27	2	62	66	14	2	25	53	2.03	1.46	10.1	267	3.6	7.7	2.1	0.3	34%	87%	84
Stidfole,Sean	08	25	R		a/a	TOR	2	4	50	4	69	73	37	6	39	45	4.83	1.63	6.3	266	5.1	5.8	1.1	0.8	31%	71%	36
	09	26	R		a/a	TOR	3	1	55	0	65	86	35	8	25	39	4.81	1.72	5.5	313	3.5	5.4	1.5	1.2	35%	74%	22
Stiller,Erik	08	24	R		aa	CLE	6	5	35	0	56	58	35	6	23	47	5.56	1.44	7.0	261	3.7	7.5	2.0	1.0	32%	62%	59
	09	25	R		aa	CLE	8	3	41	0	69	74	37	2	36	56	4.77	1.59	7.6	269	4.6	7.3	1.6	0.3	34%	68%	69
Stone,Bradley	09	25	R		a/a	FLA	6	3	34	0	96	101	36	4	25	46	3.35	1.31	12.0	265	2.4	4.3	1.8	0.4	30%	74%	54
Stoner,Tobi	08	24	R		aa	NYM	4	6	15	0	79	92	45	7	29	49	5.17	1.53	23.4	285	3.3	5.6	1.7	0.8	33%	66%	43
	09	25	R		a/a	NYM	9	9	23	0	144	139	69	15	48	79	4.31	1.30	26.5	248	3.0	4.9	1.6	1.0	27%	69%	40
Strickland,Scott	08	32	R		aaa	NYY	4	0	52	12	66	62	35	9	29	57	4.73	1.39	5.5	243	4.0	7.8	1.9	1.3	29%	69%	55
	09	33	R		aaa	LA	2	1	50	32	48	44	17	5	23	48	3.15	1.40	4.2	239	4.3	9.1	2.1	1.0	31%	81%	76
Strop,Pedro	09	24	R		a/a	TEX	6	6	47	5	64	73	46	4	35	51	6.52	1.69	6.3	281	4.9	7.2	1.5	0.6	35%	59%	55
Stults,Eric	08	29	L		aa	LA	7	7	20	0	117	163	70	19	44	74	5.38	1.76	27.4	322	3.4	5.7	1.7	1.4	36%	73%	17
	09	30	L		aaa	LA	5	4	12	0	64	99	42	5	25	33	5.87	1.94	25.9	346	3.6	4.6	1.3	0.8	39%	69%	17
Stutes,Michael	09	23	R		aa	PHI	8	8	27	0	145	172	86	19	60	89	5.30	1.60	24.3	289	3.7	5.5	1.5	1.2	32%	69%	27
Sues,Jeff	08	25	R		aa	PIT	3	1	24	1	43	46	24	3	22	41	5.12	1.58	8.1	266	4.7	8.7	1.9	0.7	35%	67%	72
	09	26	R		aa	PIT	2	6	48	2	90	99	61	9	48	64	6.10	1.63	8.5	273	4.8	6.4	1.3	0.9	32%	62%	40
Swaggerty,Ben	09	27	L		aa	KC	4	1	26	1	43	71	29	4	23	40	6.02	2.18	8.5	360	4.8	8.3	1.7	0.8	45%	72%	47
Swarzak,Anthony	08	23	R		a/a	MIN	8	8	27	0	146	187	85	16	52	84	5.23	1.63	24.7	305	3.2	5.2	1.6	1.0	34%	69%	29
	09	24	R		aaa	MIN	4	5	13	0	79	89	34	4	21	37	3.86	1.39	26.3	278	2.4	4.2	1.8	0.5	31%	72%	48
Swindle,R.J.	08	25	L	a	a/a	PHI	3	1	38	1	53	48	12	1	8	54	1.97	1.07	5.6	238	1.4	9.2	6.4	0.2	33%	81%	192
	09	26	L		aaa	CLE	4	1	37	2	50	45	9	3	16	41	1.67	1.23	5.6	237	3.0	7.3	2.5	0.6	30%	89%	87

Major League Equivalent Statistics

PITCHERS

							Actual				Major League Equivalents																
PITCHER	Yr	Age	Th		Lev	Org	w	l	g	sv	ip	h	er	hr	bb	k	era	whip	bf/g	oob	ctl	dom	cmd	hr/9	h%	s%	bpv
Switzer,Jon	08	29	L		aaa	BOS	5	1	52	3	75	109	52	14	21	51	6.18	1.72	6.7	331	2.5	6.1	2.4	1.7	37%	68%	25
	09	30	L		aaa	NYM	1	3	41	4	52	60	28	6	27	39	4.81	1.67	5.8	283	4.6	6.7	1.5	1.0	34%	73%	40
Tabor,Lee	08	24	L		aa	CIN	1	1	37	1	42	64	31	4	23	28	6.60	2.05	5.7	342	4.8	6.0	1.2	0.9	40%	68%	22
	09	25	L		a/a	CIN	3	2	18	0	52	60	24	5	15	25	4.10	1.45	12.6	283	2.7	4.4	1.6	0.9	31%	74%	32
Takahashi,Ken	09	41	L		aaa	NYM	1	3	18	0	56	68	20	2	25	31	3.20	1.67	14.3	294	4.0	5.0	1.2	0.3	34%	80%	42
Talbot,Mitch	08	25	R	a	aaa	TAM	13	9	28	0	161	184	80	9	35	122	4.47	1.36	24.6	281	2.0	6.8	3.5	0.5	35%	66%	98
	09	26	R		aaa	TAM	4	4	10	0	54	79	34	3	19	34	5.66	1.81	25.6	334	3.1	5.6	1.8	0.5	39%	67%	45
Tanaka,Ryohei	09	27	R		aa	BAL	4	4	21	3	75	108	44	10	31	38	5.24	1.85	17.1	330	3.7	4.6	1.2	1.2	36%	74%	5
Taubenheim,Ty	08	26	R		aa	PIT	4	9	19	0	98	131	84	14	43	50	7.76	1.78	24.2	314	4.0	4.5	1.1	1.3	34%	56%	4
	09	27	R		aaa	PIT	7	9	26	0	106	126	53	8	36	50	4.46	1.53	18.1	289	3.1	4.3	1.4	0.7	32%	71%	31
Taylor,Graham	09	25	L		aa	FLA	8	7	23	0	126	149	72	11	64	58	5.15	1.69	25.3	288	4.6	4.1	0.9	0.8	32%	70%	17
Tazawa,Junichi	09	23	R		a/a	BOS	9	7	20	0	109	107	44	9	28	81	3.63	1.24	22.7	251	2.3	6.7	2.9	0.7	30%	72%	83
Teaford,Everett	09	25	L		aa	KC	3	7	16	0	81	107	59	13	36	33	6.54	1.76	23.7	311	4.0	3.7	0.9	1.5	32%	65%	-10
Tejera,Michael	08	32	L		aaa	BOS	3	6	34	2	77	94	59	14	35	38	6.87	1.66	10.4	294	4.0	4.4	1.1	1.6	31%	61%	-2
	09	33	L		a/a	CLE	2	2	12	0	40	69	40	3	21	19	9.00	2.25	17.2	371	4.8	4.3	0.9	0.8	41%	58%	3
Texeira,Kanekoa	09	24	R		aa	NYY	9	6	41	2	101	114	46	9	48	73	4.13	1.61	11.2	279	4.3	6.5	1.5	0.8	33%	76%	45
Thall,Chad	09	24	L		aa	BAL	2	2	53	1	60	64	28	5	32	44	4.26	1.59	5.1	268	4.7	6.5	1.4	0.8	32%	74%	46
Thayer,Dale	08	28	R		aaa	TAM	3	1	52	9	68	85	25	2	25	63	3.34	1.62	5.9	300	3.3	8.3	2.5	0.3	39%	79%	88
	09	29	R		aaa	TAM	2	5	51	17	63	73	22	3	16	36	3.07	1.41	5.4	284	2.3	5.2	2.2	0.5	33%	79%	63
Thomas,Justin	08	25	L		aa	SEA	9	8	32	1	135	152	76	14	71	108	5.05	1.64	19.3	277	4.7	7.2	1.5	0.9	34%	70%	48
	09	26	L		aaa	SEA	2	4	53	6	60	71	31	5	39	48	4.69	1.83	5.4	287	5.9	7.1	1.2	0.8	35%	75%	43
Thompson,Aaron	08	22	L		aa	FLA	2	5	16	0	81	124	59	9	42	49	6.54	2.04	25.2	343	4.7	5.4	1.2	1.0	39%	68%	13
	09	23	L		aa	WAS	5	12	26	0	146	184	86	12	55	88	5.29	1.63	25.6	301	3.4	5.4	1.6	0.7	35%	67%	39
Thompson,Rich	09	25	R	a	aaa	LAA	3	1	29	0	43	44	16	6	10	43	3.37	1.27	6.2	261	2.1	8.9	4.2	1.3	33%	79%	107
Threets,Erick	08	27	L		aa	SF	4	5	37	0	66	71	37	6	41	34	5.01	1.70	8.3	270	5.6	4.6	0.8	0.8	30%	71%	23
	09	28	L		aaa	LA	3	0	33	1	41	32	7	1	16	24	1.61	1.15	5.1	208	3.5	5.2	1.5	0.2	25%	86%	69
Tillman,Chris	08	20	R	a	aa	BAL	11	4	28	0	135	126	56	11	60	141	3.74	1.37	20.7	242	4.0	9.4	2.3	0.8	32%	74%	89
	09	22	R	a	aaa	BAL	8	6	18	0	96	94	36	6	25	91	3.40	1.23	22.2	250	2.3	8.5	3.7	0.6	33%	73%	117
Todd,Jesse	08	22	R		aa	STL	5	6	21	0	125	106	47	14	32	86	3.38	1.10	24.0	225	2.3	6.2	2.7	1.0	26%	73%	73
	09	24	R	a	aaa	CLE	4	2	44	25	53	45	14	3	13	60	2.38	1.09	4.8	225	2.2	10.2	4.6	0.5	32%	80%	153
Tomlin,Joshua	09	25	R		aa	CLE	14	9	26	0	145	199	99	28	32	102	6.14	1.59	25.2	320	2.0	6.3	3.2	1.7	36%	65%	44
Torra,Matthew	09	25	R		aa	ARI	10	13	28	0	180	252	108	34	31	92	5.39	1.57	28.9	324	1.6	4.6	3.0	1.7	34%	71%	28
Torres,Alexander	09	22	L		aa	TAM	3	3	7	0	34	35	14	1	23	28	3.68	1.70	22.6	260	6.1	7.4	1.2	0.3	33%	77%	65
Torres,Carlos	08	26	R		a/a	CHW	9	5	29	0	121	138	64	8	44	95	4.78	1.51	18.5	281	3.3	7.1	2.1	0.6	34%	68%	68
	09	27	R		aaa	CHW	10	4	23	1	128	121	48	6	62	112	3.41	1.43	24.2	244	4.3	7.8	1.8	0.4	31%	76%	78
Towers,Josh	08	32	R		aa	COL	6	7	31	0	116	201	107	15	31	58	8.30	2.00	18.4	372	2.4	4.5	1.9	1.2	41%	58%	12
	09	33	R		aaa	NYY	7	6	20	0	103	122	51	18	27	45	4.41	1.45	22.5	289	2.4	3.9	1.6	1.6	30%	75%	8
Traber,Billy	08	29	L		aaa	NYY	2	1	40	4	47	59	25	4	14	31	4.82	1.56	5.3	301	2.7	5.9	2.2	0.8	35%	70%	51
	09	30	L		aaa	BOS	7	8	38	0	84	127	57	11	30	26	6.06	1.86	10.6	340	3.2	2.8	0.9	1.2	35%	69%	-14
Trinidad,Polin	08	24	L		aa	HOU	6	5	18	0	107	118	45	13	21	62	3.81	1.29	25.0	273	1.7	5.2	3.0	1.1	30%	74%	61
	09	25	L		a/a	HOU	13	10	26	1	170	203	85	29	36	94	4.48	1.41	28.3	290	1.9	5.0	2.6	1.5	31%	74%	36
Ungs,Nick	08	29	R		a/a	MIL	6	4	15	0	79	104	51	13	24	38	5.82	1.62	24.0	310	2.8	4.3	1.5	1.5	33%	67%	6
	09	30	R		aa	FLA	10	3	18	0	106	131	47	11	43	54	3.96	1.63	26.8	297	3.6	4.6	1.3	0.9	33%	78%	23
Urquidez,Jason	08	26	R		aa	ARI	3	1	18	0	32	38	23	5	16	29	6.43	1.68	8.2	287	4.5	8.0	1.8	1.3	35%	63%	45
	09	27	R		a/a	ARI	5	1	50	2	67	70	40	3	26	42	5.39	1.44	5.9	263	3.5	5.6	1.6	0.5	31%	60%	55
Valdez,Cesar	09	25	R		aaa	ARI	7	6	19	0	96	108	52	16	26	53	4.88	1.40	21.8	278	2.4	5.0	2.0	1.5	30%	69%	27
Valdez,Jose	09	27	R		a/a	NYY	3	2	43	10	57	74	34	6	39	46	5.42	1.98	6.5	308	6.1	7.2	1.2	0.9	37%	73%	35
Valdez,Luis	08	24	R		aa	ATL	4	3	55	28	65	57	24	3	38	64	3.35	1.46	5.2	230	5.2	8.8	1.7	0.4	31%	77%	84
	09	25	R	a	aaa	ATL	5	4	58	27	71	75	31	4	19	65	3.96	1.32	5.2	265	2.4	8.3	3.4	0.5	34%	70%	108
Valdez,Rolando	09	24	R		a/a	SD	1	1	18	0	33	43	21	4	15	25	5.71	1.75	8.6	308	4.1	6.8	1.7	1.1	36%	69%	37
Valiquette,Philippe	09	23	L		aa	CIN	1	1	27	3	32	29	13	3	21	24	3.63	1.55	5.3	236	5.9	6.7	1.1	0.8	28%	79%	47
Van Benschoten,J	08	28	R		aa	PIT	7	4	22	0	80	101	55	4	40	42	6.18	1.76	17.1	302	4.5	4.7	1.0	0.4	35%	63%	32
	09	30	R		aaa	CHW	2	8	22	0	78	130	84	14	35	54	9.64	2.11	17.8	363	4.1	6.2	1.5	1.6	41%	54%	2
Van Hekken,Andy	08	29	L		aa	HOU	6	3	11	0	67	115	33	8	12	36	4.46	1.88	29.4	369	1.6	4.8	3.0	1.1	41%	79%	41
	09	30	L		a/a	HOU	8	6	33	0	123	191	79	11	33	52	5.76	1.82	17.7	347	2.4	3.8	1.6	0.8	38%	68%	17
VanAllen,Cory	08	24	L		aa	WAS	3	3	10	0	47	69	28	3	10	29	5.32	1.69	21.7	334	2.0	5.6	2.8	0.6	39%	68%	63
	09	25	L		aa	WAS	3	5	31	0	94	147	75	16	34	57	7.16	1.93	14.7	349	3.2	5.5	1.7	1.5	39%	64%	8
VandenHurk,Rick	08	23	R		aa	FLA	5	4	14	0	73	71	40	11	32	68	4.96	1.41	22.6	250	3.9	8.4	2.1	1.4	30%	69%	58
	09	24	R	a	aaa	FLA	5	2	11	0	59	47	21	3	16	46	3.19	1.06	21.4	214	2.4	7.0	2.9	0.5	27%	70%	101
Vaquedano,Jose	08	27	R		a/a	BOS	8	1	43	1	62	80	32	6	34	30	4.67	1.85	6.9	308	5.0	4.4	0.9	0.8	34%	76%	14
	09	28	R		aaa	BOS	4	2	43	3	64	72	45	9	48	27	6.33	1.88	7.2	278	6.8	3.8	0.6	1.2	29%	67%	-2
Vargas,Jason	09	27	L		aaa	SEA	4	3	9	0	51	52	19	3	15	40	3.26	1.31	24.1	256	2.7	7.0	2.6	0.5	32%	76%	83
Varvaro,Anthony	09	25	R	a	aa	SEA	4	3	36	8	54	36	22	1	49	54	3.68	1.58	6.8	185	8.2	9.0	1.1	0.2	26%	75%	90
Vasquez,Carlos	09	27	L		a/a	FLA	1	1	27	0	31	40	31	4	30	30	9.00	2.25	6.0	306	8.7	8.6	1.0	1.3	38%	59%	28
Vasquez,Virgil	08	26	R		aaa	DET	12	12	27	0	159	210	105	30	37	98	5.95	1.56	26.4	312	2.1	5.5	2.6	1.7	34%	65%	31
	09	27	R		aaa	PIT	7	4	19	0	107	138	59	15	16	57	4.95	1.43	24.6	306	1.3	4.8	3.6	1.2	33%	68%	61
Vaughan,Beau	08	27	R		a/a	BOS	3	2	46	17	58	63	22	3	28	51	3.39	1.57	5.7	272	4.3	8.0	1.9	0.5	35%	79%	71
	09	28	R		a/a	TEX	7	2	46	8	62	80	39	5	27	42	5.64	1.73	6.3	306	3.9	6.0	1.5	0.7	36%	67%	42
Vazquez,Camilo	08	25	L		a/a	CIN	3	4	10	0	40	65	34	15	20	27	7.56	2.13	20.2	358	4.5	6.0	1.3	3.3	37%	73%	-52
	09	26	L		a/a	CIN	5	4	39	0	93	144	79	10	52	67	7.63	2.11	12.0	347	5.1	6.4	1.3	1.0	41%	63%	22
Venters,Jonathan	09	25	L		a/a	ATL	8	11	29	0	156	195	99	10	82	83	5.70	1.78	25.3	299	4.8	4.8	1.0	0.6	34%	67%	27
Viola,Pedro	08	25	L		aa	CIN	4	7	52	2	82	109	52	8	39	66	5.72	1.80	7.5	312	4.3	7.2	1.7	0.9	38%	68%	46
	09	26	L		aaa	CIN	2	2	54	8	49	59	40	10	36	49	7.37	1.93	4.4	291	6.6	8.9	1.3	1.9	35%	65%	22
Voss,Jay	09	22	L		aa	FLA	3	0	30	1	36	30	15	2	16	33	3.74	1.27	5.0	222	4.0	8.2	2.1	0.5	29%	70%	88
Waddell,Jason	08	27	L		aa	SF	0	3	44	2	64	66	36	7	43	49	5.08	1.71	6.7	262	6.1	6.9	1.1	1.0	31%	72%	37
	09	28	L		a/a	DET	1	3	37	2	42	51	22	1	14	25	4.79	1.54	5.1	292	3.0	5.3	1.7	0.3	35%	67%	57
Wagner,Neil	09	26	R		aa	CLE	1	3	46	2	61	64	30	4	38	57	4.43	1.68	6.1	266	5.6	8.4	1.5	0.7	34%	74%	64
Wahpepah,Joshua	09	25	R		aa	MIL	1	2	33	0	66	88	49	2	50	43	6.67	2.09	10.0	313	6.8	5.9	0.9	0.3	37%	66%	37
Walden,Jordan	09	22	R		aa	LAA	1	5	13	0	60	86	46	4	30	48	6.90	1.93	22.4	329	4.5	7.2	1.6	0.6	40%	63%	48

Major League Equivalent Statistics

PITCHERS

PITCHER	Yr	Age	Th		Lev	Org	Actual											Major League Equivalents									
							w	l	g	sv	ip	h	er	hr	bb	k	era	whip	bf/g	oob	ctl	dom	cmd	hr/9	h%	s%	bpv
Waldrop,Steven	09	24	R		aa	MIN	2	3	31	0	55	60	11	2	19	24	1.85	1.42	7.7	271	3.0	4.0	1.3	0.3	31%	88%	42
Walters,P.J.	08	24	R		aa	STL	10	6	29	0	158	175	88	20	66	129	4.99	1.53	24.2	275	3.8	7.3	2.0	1.1	33%	69%	52
	09	25	R		aaa	STL	8	10	21	0	121	141	69	6	41	98	5.13	1.50	25.5	285	3.0	7.3	2.4	0.4	36%	64%	78
Ward,Zach	08	25	R		aa	MIN	5	6	46	1	93	113	48	4	55	63	4.69	1.80	9.5	293	5.3	6.1	1.1	0.4	35%	73%	45
	09	26	R		aa	CIN	4	6	32	0	46	80	68	4	52	23	13.26	2.87	8.3	373	10.2	4.6	0.4	0.9	42%	50%	-9
Warden,Jim	08	29	R		a/a	WAS	4	7	57	9	77	93	37	1	38	40	4.27	1.69	6.2	292	4.4	4.7	1.1	0.1	34%	73%	43
	09	30	R		a/a	NYM	2	1	32	3	46	53	16	4	23	33	3.17	1.62	6.6	280	4.4	6.4	1.5	0.7	33%	82%	46
Wassermann,Ehren	08	28	R	b	aaa	CHW	3	0	32	7	39	36	7	1	14	35	1.70	1.27	5.1	239	3.2	8.1	2.6	0.2	32%	87%	102
	09	29	R		aaa	CHW	7	3	43	1	63	95	39	4	20	47	5.51	1.82	7.0	339	2.9	6.6	2.3	0.6	41%	69%	56
Waters,Chris	08	28	L		a/a	BAL	8	6	24	0	122	156	89	16	58	70	6.60	1.76	23.8	305	4.3	5.1	1.2	1.2	34%	63%	14
	09	29	L		aaa	BAL	9	7	29	0	114	153	86	19	53	54	6.76	1.80	18.6	314	4.2	4.2	1.0	1.5	33%	64%	-5
Watson,Sean	08	23	R		aa	CIN	1	2	31	3	35	31	21	1	29	38	5.30	1.71	5.2	232	7.4	9.7	1.3	0.3	33%	67%	86
	09	24	R		a/a	CIN	4	5	50	8	71	71	45	9	49	56	5.75	1.70	6.6	255	6.3	7.1	1.1	1.2	30%	68%	35
Weatherby III,Charles	09	31	R		aa	HOU	1	5	19	0	36	56	28	5	19	15	6.96	2.06	9.5	346	4.6	3.7	0.8	1.3	37%	67%	-15
Webb,Ryan	08	23	R		aa	OAK	9	8	25	0	130	175	78	11	39	80	5.40	1.65	23.7	316	2.7	5.5	2.1	0.8	36%	67%	45
	09	24	R		aaa	SD	7	1	35	2	49	64	24	3	16	35	4.39	1.63	6.4	308	2.9	6.4	2.2	0.5	37%	73%	61
Weber,Thad	09	25	R		aa	DET	7	3	13	0	75	99	46	9	20	34	5.46	1.58	26.0	311	2.4	4.1	1.7	1.1	34%	67%	21
Weinhardt,Robbie	09	24	R		aa	DET	0	1	20	2	31	33	10	0	16	26	2.98	1.59	7.0	266	4.8	7.6	1.6	0.0	35%	79%	81
Weiser,Keith	08	24	L		aa	COL	1	2	5	0	35	43	17	2	5	10	4.32	1.38	30.1	297	1.4	2.7	2.0	0.5	32%	68%	37
	09	25	L		aa	COL	9	15	27	0	156	256	130	32	31	74	7.49	1.84	27.5	359	1.8	4.3	2.4	1.9	38%	62%	3
Welch,David	08	25	L		aa	MIL	11	4	26	0	147	177	79	27	57	77	4.82	1.59	25.5	291	3.5	4.7	1.4	1.6	31%	75%	5
	09	26	L		aa	MIL	8	8	24	0	118	176	71	15	37	53	5.43	1.80	23.2	338	2.8	4.0	1.4	1.1	36%	72%	8
Wells,Jared	08	27	R		aa	SEA	1	5	52	20	60	79	54	8	41	44	8.08	2.00	5.7	311	6.2	6.5	1.1	1.2	36%	59%	18
	09	28	R		a/a	SEA	2	0	30	1	38	46	25	6	30	25	5.97	1.99	6.2	292	7.1	6.0	0.8	1.4	33%	72%	9
West,Sean	09	23	L		aa	FLA	7	3	12	0	64	81	44	13	31	57	6.23	1.76	24.9	304	4.3	8.0	1.9	1.9	36%	69%	25
Whelan,Kevin	09	26	R	a	a/a	NYY	4	0	44	3	67	58	29	1	46	69	3.95	1.55	6.8	228	6.2	9.3	1.5	0.1	32%	72%	92
Whisler,Wesley	08	26	L		aaa	CHW	12	10	27	0	156	209	87	17	46	62	5.01	1.64	26.3	315	2.7	3.6	1.3	1.0	34%	71%	12
	09	27	L		aaa	CHW	10	12	26	0	152	209	98	14	62	66	5.79	1.78	27.5	320	3.7	3.9	1.1	0.9	35%	67%	11
Wilhite,Matt	08	27	R		aa	LAA	7	0	47	0	63	102	48	11	19	42	6.88	1.93	6.5	358	2.8	6.0	2.2	1.5	40%	66%	19
	09	28	R		aaa	COL	0	4	38	10	48	68	44	9	12	25	8.23	1.65	5.8	325	2.2	4.7	2.1	1.6	35%	50%	15
Wilkie,Josh	09	25	R	a	a/a	WAS	7	5	51	5	71	84	28	2	18	53	3.59	1.43	6.1	288	2.3	6.7	3.0	0.3	36%	74%	92
Williams,Dave	09	31	L		a/a	WAS	1	4	40	3	52	103	50	10	24	33	8.65	2.43	7.0	403	4.1	5.7	1.4	1.7	45%	66%	-14
Williams,Jerome	09	28	R		aaa	OAK	5	6	27	0	101	132	71	15	39	42	6.27	1.69	17.3	308	3.5	3.7	1.1	1.3	32%	64%	-1
Williams,Randy	09	34	L		aaa	CHW	3	0	33	1	36	40	20	4	13	33	4.97	1.45	4.8	275	3.1	8.3	2.6	1.0	34%	67%	74
Willis,Dontrelle	09	28	L		a/a	DET	2	2	6	0	30	33	22	2	23	16	6.53	1.87	24.0	275	6.9	4.7	0.7	0.7	31%	64%	22
Winters,Kyle	09	22	R		aa	FLA	1	2	7	0	35	50	25	1	14	23	6.43	1.83	23.7	329	3.6	5.9	1.6	0.3	39%	62%	52
Wise,Brendan	08	23	R		aa	DET	2	1	30	3	43	47	18	4	13	18	3.75	1.39	6.2	271	2.7	3.8	1.4	0.8	29%	75%	27
	09	24	R		aa	DET	4	1	21	0	41	63	25	2	12	13	5.43	1.84	9.3	344	2.7	2.8	1.0	0.5	37%	69%	11
Wlodarczyk,Michael	09	27	L		a/a	TAM	1	4	48	5	67	93	54	2	30	38	7.31	1.84	6.6	323	4.0	5.1	1.3	0.3	38%	57%	38
Wolf,Ross	08	26	R		aa	FLA	5	2	38	1	39	58	22	4	18	16	5.13	1.94	5.0	337	4.1	3.7	0.9	1.0	36%	75%	-2
	09	27	R		aaa	BAL	4	2	47	1	82	89	52	7	36	58	5.66	1.53	7.8	272	3.9	6.4	1.6	0.8	32%	63%	48
Wolfe,Brian	08	28	R		aaa	TOR	2	3	17	1	36	49	20	3	12	23	4.97	1.69	9.8	319	2.9	5.7	2.0	0.8	37%	71%	43
	09	29	R		aaa	TOR	2	3	34	3	46	68	29	3	13	21	5.67	1.75	6.3	335	2.5	4.2	1.7	0.6	37%	67%	29
Wood,Blake	08	23	R		aa	KC	5	7	18	0	86	116	67	8	33	65	7.00	1.73	22.3	316	3.4	6.8	2.0	0.9	38%	58%	48
	09	24	R		aa	KC	2	8	17	0	78	107	62	8	26	41	7.15	1.71	21.3	320	3.0	4.7	1.6	1.0	36%	57%	23
Wood,Timothy	09	27	R		aaa	FLA	1	2	31	0	39	47	15	1	18	33	3.55	1.66	5.8	293	4.0	7.6	1.9	0.2	37%	77%	74
Wood,Travis	08	22	L		aa	CIN	4	9	17	0	80	101	73	11	47	50	8.21	1.85	22.4	302	5.3	5.6	1.1	1.2	34%	55%	14
	09	23	L		a/a	CIN	13	5	27	0	167	143	43	8	55	119	2.31	1.18	25.4	227	3.0	6.4	2.2	0.4	28%	82%	81
Woods,Jake	08	27	L		aa	SEA	6	1	32	1	64	84	39	8	34	41	5.42	1.84	9.5	311	4.7	5.7	1.2	1.2	35%	73%	17
	09	28	L		aaa	PHI	5	2	42	2	80	102	42	10	32	42	4.71	1.68	8.8	304	3.6	4.7	1.3	1.1	33%	74%	17
Woody,Abraham	08	26	R		aa	ARI	2	7	45	3	70	98	49	4	40	41	6.27	1.96	5.4	323	5.1	5.2	1.0	0.6	37%	67%	26
	09	27	R		a/a	ARI	1	3	43	0	65	106	66	11	38	21	9.08	2.21	7.7	357	5.2	2.9	0.5	1.5	37%	59%	-34
Wordekemper,Eric	08	25	R		aa	NYY	3	2	33	6	50	80	34	9	31	35	6.19	2.22	7.8	354	5.6	6.3	1.1	1.6	40%	75%	-2
	09	26	R		a/a	NYY	3	2	38	2	58	68	34	8	18	34	5.33	1.47	6.7	285	2.7	5.3	1.9	1.2	32%	66%	34
Worley,Vance	09	22	R		aa	PHI	7	12	27	0	153	186	109	21	49	85	6.41	1.53	25.3	294	2.9	5.0	1.7	1.2	32%	59%	26
Wright,Chase	08	26	L		a/a	NYY	10	3	22	0	131	140	58	8	47	57	3.97	1.43	25.9	268	3.2	3.9	1.2	0.6	30%	72%	33
	09	27	L		aaa	MIL	9	7	26	0	131	172	76	15	52	50	5.23	1.71	23.3	310	3.5	3.5	1.0	1.1	33%	71%	2
Wright,Matt	08	27	R		aa	KC	4	10	27	0	148	229	133	37	68	69	8.11	2.00	27.0	346	4.1	4.2	1.0	2.2	36%	63%	-35
	09	28	R		aaa	KC	1	5	9	0	40	58	40	3	16	25	9.00	1.84	21.2	331	3.6	5.6	1.6	0.7	38%	48%	34
Wright,Steven	08	24	R		aa	CLE	4	3	14	0	75	98	47	17	19	49	5.68	1.56	24.0	309	2.3	5.9	2.6	2.0	33%	69%	23
	09	25	R	a	a/a	CLE	10	0	38	2	87	94	32	1	22	59	3.27	1.33	9.7	269	2.3	6.1	2.7	0.1	33%	73%	90
Yabuta,Yasuhiko	08	35	R		aa	KC	4	3	20	3	40	64	36	4	19	26	8.19	2.05	10.0	352	4.2	5.5	1.3	0.8	40%	58%	22
	09	36	R		aaa	KC	2	1	26	0	45	48	24	6	18	45	4.82	1.47	7.6	268	3.6	8.9	2.5	1.3	34%	70%	69
Yourkin,Matt	08	27	L		aa	FLA	2	5	35	0	47	80	45	6	33	32	8.52	2.38	7.1	366	6.2	6.0	1.0	1.2	42%	64%	4
	09	28	L		aa	SF	6	2	50	0	63	76	28	6	33	50	3.92	1.72	5.9	293	4.6	7.1	1.5	0.9	35%	79%	44
Zagurski,Mike	09	27	L		aa	PHI	3	4	45	8	53	55	29	9	31	46	4.88	1.63	5.4	263	5.3	7.8	1.5	1.6	31%	75%	34
Zaleski,Matthew	09	28	R		a/a	CHW	6	3	23	1	90	122	32	9	29	45	3.21	1.67	18.0	316	2.9	4.5	1.6	0.9	35%	84%	24
Zinicola,Zechry	08	24	R		a/a	WAS	6	5	39	6	53	70	37	5	28	29	6.27	1.85	6.5	311	4.7	4.9	1.0	0.8	35%	66%	19
	09	25	R		a/a	WAS	1	2	43	5	54	81	43	2	20	40	7.22	1.87	6.0	341	3.3	6.6	2.0	0.3	41%	58%	59
Zink,Charlie	08	29	R		aaa	BOS	14	6	28	0	174	185	78	15	54	83	4.03	1.37	26.7	266	2.8	4.3	1.5	0.8	29%	72%	36
	09	30	R		aaa	BOS	6	15	27	0	135	192	144	14	113	37	9.62	2.26	25.9	328	7.5	2.5	0.3	1.0	34%	55%	-18

VI.
RATINGS,
RANKINGS,
CHEAT
SHEETS

Ratings, Rankings, Cheat Sheets

Here is what you will find in this section:

Skills Rankings

We start by looking at some important component skills. For batters, we've ranked the top players in terms of pure power, speed, and batting average skill, breaking each down in a number of different ways to provide more insight. For pitchers, we rank some of the key base skills, differentiating between starters and relievers, and provide a few interesting cuts that might uncover some late round sleepers.

These are clearly not exhaustive lists of sorts and filters. If there is another cut you'd like to see, drop me a note and I'll consider it for next year's book. Also note that the database at BaseballHQ.com allows you to construct your own custom sorts and filters. Finally, remember that these are just tools. Some players will appear on multiple lists — even mutually exclusive lists — so you have to assess what makes most sense and make decisions for your specific application.

POWER

Top PX, 400+ AB: Top power skills from among projected full-time players.

Top PX, -300 AB: Top power skills from among projected part-time players. Possible end-game options are here.

Position Scarcity: A quick scan to see which positions have deeper power options than others.

Top PX, Ct% over 85%: Top power skills from among the top contact hitters. Best pure power options here.

Top PX, Ct% under 75%: Top power skills from among the worst contact hitters. These are free-swingers who might be prone to streakiness or lower batting averages.

Top PX, FB% over 40%: Top power skills from among the most extreme fly ball hitters. Most likely to convert their power into home runs.

Top PX, FB% under 35%: Top power skills from among those with lesser fly ball tendencies. There may be more downside to their home run potential.

SPEED

Top SX, 400+ AB: Top speed skills from among projected full-time players.

Top SX, -300 AB: Top speed skills from among projected part-time players. Possible end-game options here.

Position Scarcity: A quick scan to see which positions have deeper speed options than others.

Top SX, OB% over .350: Top speed skills from among those who get on base most often. Best opportunities for stolen bases here.

Top SX, OB% under .310: Top speed skills from among those who have trouble getting on base. These names may bear watching if they can improve their on base ability.

Top SX, SBO% over 20%: Top speed skills from among those who get the green light most often. Most likely to convert their speed into stolen bases.

Top SX, SBO% under 15%: Top speed skills from among those who are currently not getting the green light. There may be sleeper SB's here if given more opportunities to run.

BATTING AVERAGE

Top Ct%, 400+ AB: Top contact skills from among projected full-time players. Contact does not always convert to higher BAs, but is still strongly correlated.

Top Ct%, -300 AB: Top contact skills from among projected part-time players. Possible end-gamers here.

Low Ct%, 400+ AB: The poorest contact skills from among projected full-time players. Potential BA killers.

Top Ct%, bb% over 10%: Top contact skills from among the most patient hitters. Best batting average upside here.

Top Ct%, bb% under 6%: Top contact skills from among the least patient hitters. These are free-swingers who might be prone to streakiness or lower batting averages.

Top Ct%, GB% over 50%: Top contact skills from among the most extreme ground ball hitters. A ground ball has a higher chance of becoming a hit than a non-HR fly ball so there may be some batting average upside here.

Top Ct%, GB% under 40%: Top contact skills from among those with lesser ground ball tendencies. These players are making contact but hitting more fly balls, which tend to convert to hits at a lower rate than GB.

PITCHING SKILLS

Top Command: Leaders in projected K/BB rates.

Top Control: Leaders in fewest projected walks allowed.

Top Dominance: Leaders in projected strikeout rate.

Top Ground Ball Rate: GB pitchers tend to have lower ERA's (and higher WHIP) than fly ball pitchers.

Top Fly Ball Rate: FB pitchers tend to have higher ERA's (and lower WHIP) than ground ball pitchers.

High GB, Low Dom: GB pitchers tend to have lower K rates, but these are the most extreme examples.

High GB, High Dom: The best at dominating hitters and keeping the ball down. These are the pitchers who keep runners off the bases and batted balls in the park, a skills combination that is the most valuable a pitcher can own.

Lowest xERA: Leaders in projected skills-based ERA.

Top BPV: Two lists of top skilled pitchers here. For starters, those projected to be rotation regulars (180+ IP) and fringe starters with skill (-150 IP). For relievers, those projected to be frontline closers (10+ saves) and high-skilled bullpen fillers (9- saves).

Random Variance—Rebounds and Corrections

These charts list players with +4/5 and –4/5 Rand Var scores. The scores identify players who, in 2009, posted outlying levels of gauges that are prone to regression; these are the players who should regress in 2010. The +4/5 scores are players we expect to rebound; –4/5 scores are players due for a negative correction. Within each break, players are listed in alphabetical order. A full description appears in the Glossary. (More corrections than rebounds? Just the Gravity Principle at work. More pitchers than batters? Variability among pitchers is higher. Makes sense, right?)

Risk Management

Lists include players who've accumulated the most days on the disabled list over the past five years (Grade "F" in Health) and whose performance was the most consistent over the past three years. Also listed are the most reliable batters and pitchers overall, with a focus on positional and skills reliability. As a reminder, reliability in this context is not tied to skill level; it is a gauge of which players manage to accumulate playing time and post consistent output from year to year, whether that output is good or bad.

Position Scarcity Chart

There has been much discussion about position scarcity, its importance and how to leverage it in your draft. This chart provides a visual representation of the depth of talent for the top 45 players at each position and shows you why, in a snake draft league, it might make sense to draft a Joe Mauer before you draft a Jacoby Ellsbury.

Portfolio3 Plan

Players are sorted and ranked based on how they fit into the three draft tiers of the Portfolio3 Plan. A full description of how this plan works appears in the Gaming section.

Mayberry Method

Players are grouped based on how they score out in the Mayberry Method. A full description of how this plan works appears in the Introduction. One set of rankings focuses on raw skills only; the second set includes our early estimates of playing time.

Rotisserie Auction Draft

This list is presented with both AL and NL players, mostly because we don't know who is going to end up on what team yet. The values are representative of standard 75%-plus depth leagues. However, remember that these values are for player-to-player comparative purposes only, and allow us to provide rankings. You should not use these as actual in-draft bid values (see the Consumer Advisory earlier in the book for a full explanation).

The free projections update in March will provide better estimates of playing time, and as such, better information for drafting purposes. The custom draft guides on Baseball HQ are available to those who wish to produce accurate valuations for their particular league configuration. But in the interim, you can still use this information to plan out the core of your draft. For those who subscribe to Baseball HQ, full projections begin appearing online in December.

Rotisserie Snake Draft

This ranking takes the previous auction list, re-sets it into rounds and adjusts the rankings based on position scarcity. Given the growing popularity of 15-team mixed leagues, like the National Fantasy Baseball Championship, we've set this list up for that type of format.

In the first eight rounds, your target players should be those that are shaded (though your first round pick may depend upon your seed). These are the position scarcity picks. Also pay attention to the bolded players; these are categorical scarcity picks (primarily steals and saves).

If you reach a point where there are still undrafted players from earlier rounds, you can judiciously target those. To build the best foundation, you should come out of the first 10 rounds with all your middle infielders, all your corner infielders, one outfielder, at least one catcher and two pitchers (at least one closer).

The reason we target scarce positions first is that there will be plenty of solid outfielders and starting pitchers later on. The Position Scarcity Chart shows you why. The 20th best catcher on the list is Ramon Hernandez; the 20th best starting pitcher is Chris Carpenter. Which one would you rather have on your team?

IMPORTANT CAVEAT ABOUT THESE LISTS

The auction and snake draft rankings do not represent average draft positions (ADP) or average auction values (AAV). They represent where each player's true value may lie. It is the variance between this true value and the ADP/AAV market values — or better, the value that your league-mates place on each player — where you will find your potential for profit or loss.

That means *you cannot take these lists right into your draft with you.* You have to compare these rankings with your ADPs and AAVs, and build your draft list from there. In other words, if we project Matt Kemp as a first round pick but you know the other owners (or your ADP's) see him as a third-rounder, you can probably wait to pick him up in round 2. If you are in an auction league with owners who overvalue saves and Mariano Rivera (projected at $21) gets bid past $25, you will take a loss should you decide to chase the bidding.

Simulation League Draft

Using Runs Above Replacement creates a more real-world ranking of player value, which serves simulation gamers well. Batters and pitchers are integrated, and value break-points are delineated.

BATTER SKILLS RANKINGS - POWER

TOP PX, 400+ AB

NAME	POS	PX
Pena,Carlos	3	199
Reynolds,Mark	53	193
Howard,Ryan	3	192
Dunn,Adam	379	186
Fielder,Prince	3	174
Stewart,Ian	54	173
Pujols,Albert	3	168
Cruz,Nelson	9	165
Youkilis,Kevin	35	164
Gomes,Jonny	79	163
Bay,Jason	7	163
Davis,Chris	3	162
Longoria,Evan	5	160
Votto,Joey	3	160
Braun,Ryan	7	160
Ortiz,David	0	158
Teixeira,Mark	3	158
Ramirez,Manny	7	157
Hawpe,Brad	9	157
Swisher,Nick	93	156
Uggla,Dan	4	155
Werth,Jayson	9	155
Upton,Justin	9	154
Berkman,Lance	3	154
Cust,Jack	9	154
Lind,Adam	7	152
Rodriguez,Alex	5	151
Gonzalez,Adrian	3	150
Bruce,Jay	9	150
Delgado,Carlos	3	149
Zimmerman,Ryan	5	149
LaRoche,Adam	3	149
Holliday,Matt	7	148
Willingham,Josh	79	147
Cameron,Mike	8	147
Lee,Derrek	3	146
Young,Chris	8	146
Ross,Cody	89	146

TOP PX, -300 AB

NAME	POS	PX
Ross,David	2	156
Rodriguez,Sean	4	150
Nix,Laynce	7	146
Giambi,Jason	30	146
Hinske,Eric	9	145
Joyce,Matt	9	132
Flowers,Tyler	2	130
Teagarden,Taylor	2	129
Chavez,Eric	5	127
Allen,Brandon	3	127
Ransom,Cody	5	126
Snyder,Chris	2	125
Francisco,Ben	7	123
Hoffpauir,Micah	39	123
Torres,Andres	87	122
Avila,Alex	2	122
Balentien,Wladimir	7	122
Michaels,Jason	7	122
Kapler,Gabe	9	115
Anderson,Brian	8	115
Kottaras,George	2	114
Castro,Ramon	2	114
Gamel,Mat	5	113
Stairs,Matt	9	113
Ramirez,Wilkin	7	113

POSITIONAL SCARCITY

NAME	POS	PX
Thome,Jim	DH	171
Ortiz,David	2	158
Jones,Andruw	3	153
Giambi,Jason	4	146
Ruiz,Randy	5	142
Jacobs,Mike	6	138
Shoppach,Kelly	CA	163
Iannetta,Chris	2	162
Napoli,Mike	3	160
Ross,David	4	156
Olivo,Miguel	5	142
Posada,Jorge	6	139
Soto,Geovany	7	139
McCann,Brian	8	137
Pena,Carlos	1B	199
Reynolds,Mark	2	193
Howard,Ryan	3	192
Branyan,Russell	4	191
Dunn,Adam	5	186
Fielder,Prince	6	174
Pujols,Albert	7	168
Youkilis,Kevin	8	164
Davis,Chris	9	162
Votto,Joey	10	160
Stewart,Ian	2B	173
Uggla,Dan	2	155
Rodriguez,Sean	3	150
Utley,Chase	4	140
Zobrist,Ben	5	127
Kinsler,Ian	6	120
Uribe,Juan	7	117
Kendrick,Howie	8	113
Reynolds,Mark	3B	193
Stewart,Ian	2	173
Youkilis,Kevin	3	164
Longoria,Evan	4	160
Rodriguez,Alex	5	151
Zimmerman,Ryan	6	149
Fox,Jake	7	148
Wood,Brandon	8	135
Beckham,Gordon	9	133
Ramirez,Aramis	10	130
Ramirez,Hanley	SS	130
Tulowitzki,Troy	2	126
Lowrie,Jed	3	119
Uribe,Juan	4	117
Rollins,Jimmy	5	115
Drew,Stephen	6	114
Peralta,Jhonny	7	105
Hardy,J.J.	8	103
Dunn,Adam	OF	186
Cruz,Nelson	2	165
Gomes,Jonny	3	163
Bay,Jason	4	163
Braun,Ryan	5	160
Ramirez,Manny	6	157
Hawpe,Brad	7	157
Swisher,Nick	8	156
Werth,Jayson	9	155
Upton,Justin	10	154
Cust,Jack	11	154
Lind,Adam	12	152
Thames,Marcus	13	151
Bruce,Jay	14	150
Fox,Jake	15	148
Holliday,Matt	16	148

TOP PX, Ct% over 85%

NAME	Ct%	PX
Pujols,Albert	89	168
Ramirez,Aramis	86	130
Sandoval,Pablo	87	122
Butler,Billy	85	121
Kinsler,Ian	86	120
Murphy,Daniel	87	115
Rollins,Jimmy	89	115
Matsui,Hideki	85	114
Ruiz,Carlos	88	114
Hill,Aaron	85	112
Guerrero,Vladimir	86	112
Lee,Carlos	90	110
Lopez,Jose	89	110
Lowell,Mike	86	109
Byrnes,Eric	87	107
Prado,Martin	88	107
Salazar,Oscar	86	106
Phillips,Brandon	85	105
Pedroia,Dustin	93	105
Mauer,Joe	89	104
Crede,Joe	85	103
Cano,Robinson	89	102
Molina,Bengie	88	102
Rivera,Juan	88	101
Rolen,Scott	85	100
Helton,Todd	86	100
Martinez,Victor	87	100
Ordonez,Magglio	87	100
Pena,Brayan	91	99
Gerut,Jody	86	99
Coghlan,Chris	86	98
Wells,Vernon	87	98
Blanco,Andres	89	96
Jackson,Conor	87	95
Abreu,Tony	86	93
Anderson,Garret	86	91
Sanchez,Gaby	87	91
Victorino,Shane	88	91

TOP PX, Ct% under 75%

NAME	Ct%	PX
Pena,Carlos	67	199
Reynolds,Mark	63	193
Howard,Ryan	68	192
Branyan,Russell	64	191
Dunn,Adam	68	186
Stewart,Ian	72	173
Thome,Jim	68	171
Cruz,Nelson	75	165
Gomes,Jonny	70	163
Shoppach,Kelly	64	163
Bay,Jason	72	163
Iannetta,Chris	75	162
Davis,Chris	73	162
Napoli,Mike	71	160
Hawpe,Brad	72	157
Ross,David	70	156
Swisher,Nick	74	156
Uggla,Dan	73	155
Werth,Jayson	71	155
Upton,Justin	72	154
Cust,Jack	62	154
Jones,Andruw	72	153
Thames,Marcus	72	151
Rodriguez,Sean	74	150
Cameron,Mike	71	147

TOP PX, FB% over 40%

NAME	FB%	PX
Pena,Carlos	51	199
Reynolds,Mark	47	193
Branyan,Russell	52	191
Dunn,Adam	47	186
Fielder,Prince	42	174
Stewart,Ian	44	173
Pujols,Albert	42	168
Cruz,Nelson	45	165
Youkilis,Kevin	44	164
Gomes,Jonny	50	163
Bay,Jason	47	163
Iannetta,Chris	47	162
Davis,Chris	42	162
Longoria,Evan	42	160
Napoli,Mike	47	160
Ortiz,David	48	158
Teixeira,Mark	41	158
Ramirez,Manny	40	157
Ross,David	47	156
Swisher,Nick	45	156
Uggla,Dan	47	155
Werth,Jayson	41	155
Jones,Andruw	46	153
Thames,Marcus	49	151
Bruce,Jay	44	150
Rodriguez,Sean	49	150
Zimmerman,Ryan	41	149
LaRoche,Adam	43	149
Fox,Jake	48	148
Willingham,Josh	42	147
Cameron,Mike	47	147
Lee,Derrek	41	146
Nix,Laynce	41	146
Giambi,Jason	52	146
Young,Chris	50	146
Ross,Cody	45	146
Hinske,Eric	44	145
Soriano,Alfonso	49	142

TOP PX, FB% under 35%

NAME	FB%	PX
Pence,Hunter	33	128
Sandoval,Pablo	35	122
Butler,Billy	35	121
Overbay,Lyle	34	120
Bradley,Milton	35	114
Schierholtz,Nate	34	114
Kendrick,Howie	27	113
Tatis,Fernando	34	113
Jones,Adam	30	111
Fukudome,Kosuke	30	108
Diaz,Matt	28	105
Peralta,Jhonny	33	105
Phillips,Brandon	34	105
Mauer,Joe	29	104
Church,Ryan	33	104
Spilborghs,Ryan	31	103
Cano,Robinson	33	102
Abreu,Bobby	32	102
Lewis,Fred	26	101
Maybin,Cameron	27	101
Young,Michael	31	101
Ordonez,Magglio	33	100
Posey,Buster	31	100
Young,Delmon	32	99
Pena,Brayan	27	99

BATTER SKILLS RANKINGS - SPEED

TOP SX, 400+ AB

NAME	POS	SX
Bourn,Michael	8	172
Cabrera,Everth	6	170
Crawford,Carl	7	164
Davis,Rajai	8	158
Ellsbury,Jacoby	8	157
Rollins,Jimmy	6	154
Victorino,Shane	8	152
Reyes,Jose	6	151
Fowler,Dexter	8	150
Weeks,Rickie	4	146
Morgan,Nyjer	78	144
Gomez,Carlos	8	144
Andrus,Elvis	6	141
Granderson,Curtis	8	137
Kemp,Matt	8	136
Span,Denard	879	133
McCutchen,Andrew	8	132
Maybin,Cameron	8	132
Bartlett,Jason	6	131
Kinsler,Ian	4	129
Utley,Chase	4	129
Sizemore,Grady	8	129
Upton,Justin	9	129
Podsednik,Scott	78	128
Gonzalez,Carlos	78	128
Aybar,Erick	6	128
Braun,Ryan	7	128
Figgins,Chone	5	126
Dickerson,Chris	789	124
Johnson,Kelly	4	124
McLouth,Nate	8	123
Borbon,Julio	0	123
Matsui,Kaz	4	122
Roberts,Brian	4	122
Hart,Corey	9	119
Getz,Chris	4	118
Young,Chris	8	117
Upton,B.J.	8	117

TOP SX, -300 AB

NAME	POS	SX
Perez,Fernando	8	147
Oeltjen,Trent	7	147
Torres,Andres	87	147
Young Jr.,Eric	4	146
Bonifacio,Emilio	5	143
Wise,Dewayne	89	138
Pagan,Angel	87	138
Ramirez,Wilkin	7	136
Anderson,Josh	798	136
Lewis,Fred	7	134
Maxwell,Justin	8	131
Patterson,Eric	7	131
Greene,Tyler	6	128
Ryan,Brendan	6	128
Tolbert,Matt	45	125
Harris,Willie	87	125
Gwynn,Tony	8	118
Byrnes,Eric	7	115
Sullivan,Cory	7	115
Crowe,Trevor	78	113
McDonald,Darnell	7	113
Fuld,Sam	78	112
Rodriguez,Sean	4	111
Ransom,Cody	5	110
Lillibridge,Brent	4	108

POSITIONAL SCARCITY

NAME	POS	SX
Borbon,Julio	DH	123
Guillen,Carlos	2	84
Guerrero,Vladimir	3	73
Jones,Andruw	4	64
Blalock,Hank	5	63
Pena,Brayan	6	57
Olivo,Miguel	CA	94
Laird,Gerald	2	79
Martin,Russell	3	74
Kendall,Jason	4	73
Hundley,Nick	5	71
Mauer,Joe	6	71
Napoli,Mike	7	69
Towles,J.R.	8	68
Reynolds,Mark	1B	103
Cuddyer,Michael	2	102
Allen,Brandon	3	89
Jones,Garrett	4	89
Tatis,Fernando	5	80
Howard,Ryan	6	79
Crosby,Bobby	7	78
Berkman,Lance	8	78
Ishikawa,Travis	9	78
Loney,James	10	75
Weeks,Rickie	2B	146
Young Jr.,Eric	2	146
Velez,Eugenio	3	145
Kinsler,Ian	4	129
Utley,Chase	5	129
Tolbert,Matt	6	125
Johnson,Kelly	7	124
Matsui,Kaz	8	122
Bonifacio,Emilio	3B	143
Figgins,Chone	2	126
Tolbert,Matt	3	125
Ransom,Cody	4	110
Wright,David	5	106
Stewart,Ian	6	103
Reynolds,Mark	7	103
Pena,Ramiro	8	99
Counsell,Craig	9	99
Teahen,Mark	10	95
Cabrera,Everth	SS	170
Rollins,Jimmy	2	154
Reyes,Jose	3	151
Andrus,Elvis	4	141
Bartlett,Jason	5	131
Greene,Tyler	6	128
Aybar,Erick	7	128
Ryan,Brendan	8	128
Gardner,Brett	OF	173
Bourn,Michael	2	172
Crawford,Carl	3	164
Davis,Rajai	4	158
Ellsbury,Jacoby	5	157
Victorino,Shane	6	152
Fowler,Dexter	7	150
Perez,Fernando	8	147
Oeltjen,Trent	9	147
Torres,Andres	10	147
Velez,Eugenio	11	145
Morgan,Nyjer	12	144
Gomez,Carlos	13	144
Crisp,Coco	14	141
Pierre,Juan	15	141
Wise,Dewayne	16	138

TOP SX, OB% over .350

NAME	OB%	SX
Fowler,Dexter	369	150
Crisp,Coco	352	141
Span,Denard	359	133
Maybin,Cameron	354	132
Utley,Chase	360	129
Sizemore,Grady	359	129
Upton,Justin	354	129
Braun,Ryan	352	128
Figgins,Chone	376	126
Roberts,Brian	358	122
Choo,Shin-Soo	365	115
Ramirez,Hanley	383	112
Castillo,Luis	375	110
Zobrist,Ben	372	109
Abreu,Bobby	378	109
Damon,Johnny	365	107
Furcal,Rafael	357	106
Wright,David	382	106
Suzuki,Ichiro	357	106
Tulowitzki,Troy	360	106
Coghlan,Chris	362	103
Beltran,Carlos	383	101
Bay,Jason	371	99
Smith,Seth	355	99
Werth,Jayson	361	98
Jeter,Derek	366	96
Holliday,Matt	378	95
Pedroia,Dustin	362	94
DeJesus,David	351	90
Longoria,Evan	358	89
Gordon,Alex	353	89
Fukudome,Kosuke	372	89
Jackson,Conor	355	88
Rodriguez,Alex	393	86
Dukes,Elijah	351	84
Howard,Ryan	358	79
Scutaro,Marco	357	79
Berkman,Lance	404	78

TOP SX, OB% under .310

NAME	OB%	SX
Oeltjen,Trent	283	147
Torres,Andres	310	147
Velez,Eugenio	305	145
Gomez,Carlos	296	144
Bonifacio,Emilio	307	143
Wise,Dewayne	257	138
Taveras,Willy	283	138
Ramirez,Wilkin	291	136
Anderson,Josh	280	136
Patterson,Eric	309	131
Greene,Tyler	276	128
Tolbert,Matt	309	125
Byrnes,Eric	296	115
Sullivan,Cory	298	115
Saunders,Michael	308	114
McDonald,Darnell	289	113
Ransom,Cody	292	110
Guzman,Cristian	308	109
Lillibridge,Brent	291	108
Reddick,Josh	287	103
Izturis,Cesar	297	102
Burriss,Emmanuel	301	102
Barmes,Clint	288	100
Venable,Will	299	100
Pena,Ramiro	302	99

TOP SX, SBO% over 20%

NAME	SBO	SX
Gardner,Brett	39%	173
Bourn,Michael	37%	172
Cabrera,Everth	30%	170
Crawford,Carl	43%	164
Davis,Rajai	48%	158
Ellsbury,Jacoby	40%	157
Rollins,Jimmy	28%	154
Victorino,Shane	23%	152
Reyes,Jose	27%	151
Fowler,Dexter	27%	150
Perez,Fernando	40%	147
Oeltjen,Trent	30%	147
Torres,Andres	21%	147
Young Jr.,Eric	43%	146
Velez,Eugenio	40%	145
Morgan,Nyjer	35%	144
Gomez,Carlos	34%	144
Bonifacio,Emilio	24%	143
Crisp,Coco	23%	141
Andrus,Elvis	34%	141
Pierre,Juan	35%	141
Wise,Dewayne	37%	138
Taveras,Willy	31%	138
Ramirez,Wilkin	35%	136
Kemp,Matt	25%	136
Anderson,Josh	38%	136
Span,Denard	21%	133
McCutchen,Andre	28%	132
Bartlett,Jason	21%	131
Maxwell,Justin	33%	131
Patterson,Eric	28%	131
Kinsler,Ian	22%	129
Podsednik,Scott	32%	128
Greene,Tyler	25%	128
Aybar,Erick	20%	128
Escobar,Alcides	27%	126
Figgins,Chone	25%	126
Dickerson,Chris	21%	124

TOP SX, SBO% under 15%

NAME	SBO	SX
Granderson,Curtis	14%	137
Maybin,Cameron	14%	132
Utley,Chase	12%	129
Gonzalez,Carlos	15%	128
Johnson,Kelly	10%	124
Drew,Stephen	5%	116
Choo,Shin-Soo	14%	115
Iwamura,Akinori	9%	114
Izturis,Maicer	15%	114
Jones,Adam	13%	112
Winn,Randy	12%	111
Rodriguez,Sean	9%	111
Castillo,Luis	13%	110
Ransom,Cody	8%	110
Zobrist,Ben	12%	109
Guzman,Cristian	7%	109
Lugo,Julio	10%	107
Damon,Johnny	10%	107
Furcal,Rafael	11%	106
Tulowitzki,Troy	13%	106
Spilborghs,Ryan	12%	105
Stewart,Ian	10%	103
Johnson,Reed	11%	103
Reddick,Josh	13%	103
Reynolds,Mark	15%	103

BATTER SKILLS RANKINGS - BATTING AVERAGE

TOP Ct%, 400+ AB

NAME	Ct%	BA
Polanco,Placido	93	294
Pedroia,Dustin	93	298
Callaspo,Alberto	92	292
Izturis,Cesar	92	258
Molina,Yadier	92	289
Eckstein,David	91	257
Betancourt,Yuniesk	91	262
Tejada,Miguel	91	290
Lee,Carlos	90	303
Rollins,Jimmy	89	278
Cabrera,Orlando	89	276
Pujols,Albert	89	326
Kendall,Jason	89	248
Brantley,Michael	89	267
Suzuki,Ichiro	89	317
Borbon,Julio	89	278
Cano,Robinson	89	308
Castillo,Luis	89	289
Lopez,Jose	89	284
Mauer,Joe	89	332
Rivera,Juan	88	273
Wilson,Jack	88	254
Molina,Bengie	88	263
Ramirez,Alexei	88	281
Aybar,Erick	88	288
Victorino,Shane	88	289
Pierzynski,A.J.	88	277
Reyes,Jose	88	285
Prado,Martin	88	301
Suzuki,Kurt	88	268
Ruiz,Carlos	88	261
Sandoval,Pablo	87	308
Schumaker,Skip	87	286
Ellsbury,Jacoby	87	292
Theriot,Ryan	87	280
Cabrera,Melky	87	272
Martinez,Victor	87	295
Feliz,Pedro	87	257

TOP Ct%, -300 AB

NAME	Ct%	BA
Diaz,Robinson	94	270
Thole,Josh	93	271
Frandsen,Kevin	92	260
Keppinger,Jeff	92	267
Pena,Brayan	91	285
Fuld,Sam	91	238
Rodriguez,Luis	91	225
Cora,Alex	90	254
Kotchman,Casey	90	275
Kotsay,Mark	90	267
Blanco,Andres	89	253
Loretta,Mark	89	252
Ojeda,Augie	89	239
Sweeney,Mike	89	274
Chavez,Endy	89	272
Valdez,Wilson	88	226
Catalanotto,Frank	88	281
Burriss,Emmanuel	88	252
Gload,Ross	88	269
Romero,Alex	88	265
Aubrey,Michael	88	245
Miles,Aaron	88	239
Redmond,Mike	88	257
Hernandez,Michel	87	215
Garciaparra,Nomar	87	268

LOW Ct%, 400+ AB

NAME	Ct%	BA
Cust,Jack	62	235
Reynolds,Mark	63	248
Pena,Carlos	67	249
Dunn,Adam	68	257
Howard,Ryan	68	268
Gomes,Jonny	70	236
Cameron,Mike	71	249
Inge,Brandon	71	224
Werth,Jayson	71	262
Hawpe,Brad	72	280
Bay,Jason	72	272
Upton,Justin	72	277
Stewart,Ian	72	246
Dickerson,Chris	72	255
Davis,Chris	73	264
Snider,Travis	73	267
Uggla,Dan	73	250
Burrell,Pat	73	250
Jacobs,Mike	73	246
Young,Chris	73	237
Upton,B.J.	74	260
Weeks,Rickie	74	264
Blanks,Kyle	74	252
Headley,Chase	74	267
Swisher,Nick	74	251
Cruz,Nelson	75	274
LaRoche,Adam	75	275
Hermida,Jeremy	75	264
Saunders,Michael	76	252
Maybin,Cameron	76	278
Choo,Shin-Soo	76	287
Ludwick,Ryan	76	267
Wood,Brandon	76	251
Venable,Will	76	242
Longoria,Evan	76	288
Teahen,Mark	76	264
Willingham,Josh	76	270
Soriano,Alfonso	77	266
Rowand,Aaron	77	254
Blake,Casey	77	275
Soto,Geovany	77	268
Bruce,Jay	77	269
Peralta,Jhonny	77	264
Scott,Luke	77	256
Gordon,Alex	77	260
Kemp,Matt	77	299
Youkilis,Kevin	77	301
Ross,Cody	77	269
Fielder,Prince	77	289
Hafner,Travis	78	269
Drew,J.D.	78	274
Granderson,Curtis	78	265
Wright,David	78	295
Baker,John	78	265
Gomez,Carlos	78	243
Bourn,Michael	78	267
DeRosa,Mark	78	265
Hamilton,Josh	78	284
Dukes,Elijah	78	257
Rodriguez,Alex	78	295
Cabrera,Everth	78	266
Gutierrez,Franklin	78	267
Delgado,Carlos	78	278
Encarnacion,Edwin	78	257
Ramirez,Manny	78	301
Fowler,Dexter	78	282

TOP Ct%, bb% over 10%

NAME	bb%	Ct%
Fuld,Sam	10	91
Rodriguez,Luis	11	91
Pujols,Albert	16	89
Ojeda,Augie	10	89
Castillo,Luis	12	89
Mauer,Joe	13	89
Giles,Brian	13	88
Ruiz,Carlos	12	88
Martinez,Victor	10	87
Sanchez,Gaby	11	87
Scutaro,Marco	12	87
Jackson,Conor	11	87
Hanigan,Ryan	11	87
Schneider,Brian	10	86
Helton,Todd	16	86
Pennington,Cliff	10	86
Counsell,Craig	11	85
Crisp,Coco	11	85
Matsui,Hideki	12	85
Martin,Russell	12	85
Barton,Daric	13	85
Beltran,Carlos	13	84
Morneau,Justin	11	84
LaRoche,Andy	11	84
Damon,Johnny	11	84
Span,Denard	10	83
Sheffield,Gary	12	83
Jones,Chipper	16	83
Roberts,Brian	11	83
Smith,Seth	10	83
Konerko,Paul	11	83
Zaun,Gregg	12	83
Ethier,Andre	10	82
Posey,Buster	10	82
Guillen,Carlos	11	82
Ramirez,Hanley	10	82
Marson,Lou	12	82
Figgins,Chone	13	82

TOP Ct%, bb% under 6%

NAME	bb%	Ct%
Pierre,Juan	6	94
Diaz,Robinzon	3	94
Polanco,Placido	6	93
Frandsen,Kevin	5	92
Izturis,Cesar	5	92
Betancourt,Yuniesk	4	91
Tejada,Miguel	4	91
Blanco,Andres	5	89
Suzuki,Ichiro	6	89
Borbon,Julio	6	89
Cano,Robinson	5	89
Lopez,Jose	4	89
Rivera,Juan	6	88
Wilson,Jack	6	88
Molina,Bengie	3	88
Aybar,Erick	5	88
Pierzynski,A.J.	4	88
Aubrey,Michael	5	88
Miles,Aaron	5	88
Redmond,Mike	6	88
Feliz,Pedro	6	87
Escobar,Alcides	5	87
Guzman,Cristian	4	87
McDonald,John	4	86
Aviles,Mike	4	86

TOP Ct%, GB% over 50%

NAME	GB%	Ct%
Pierre,Juan	53	94
Diaz,Robinzon	56	94
Thole,Josh	51	93
Frandsen,Kevin	52	92
Keppinger,Jeff	52	92
Pena,Brayan	51	91
Kotchman,Casey	53	90
Blanco,Andres	51	89
Suzuki,Ichiro	56	89
Borbon,Julio	54	89
Chavez,Endy	56	89
Castillo,Luis	62	89
Valdez,Wilson	62	88
Catalanotto,Frank	51	88
Burriss,Emmanue	60	88
Romero,Alex	52	88
Miles,Aaron	53	88
Redmond,Mike	52	88
Schumaker,Skip	59	87
Ellsbury,Jacoby	51	87
Theriot,Ryan	52	87
Hernandez,Michel	57	87
Escobar,Alcides	52	87
Escobar,Yunel	53	87
Guzman,Cristian	54	87
Furcal,Rafael	51	87
Schneider,Brian	54	86
Ryan,Brendan	51	86
Casilla,Alexi	51	86
Young Jr.,Eric	59	86
Anderson,Josh	60	85
Jeter,Derek	57	85
Parra,Gerardo	52	85
Morgan,Nyjer	55	85
Andrus,Elvis	55	85
Martinez,Fernand	52	84
Podsednik,Scott	52	84
Crawford,Carl	51	84

TOP Ct%, GB% under 40%

NAME	GB%	Ct%
Lee,Carlos	36	90
Loretta,Mark	40	89
Pujols,Albert	40	89
Sweeney,Mike	39	89
Molina,Bengie	32	88
Aubrey,Michael	34	88
Garciaparra,Noma	37	87
Vizquel,Omar	38	87
Scutaro,Marco	39	87
Jackson,Conor	39	87
Byrnes,Eric	37	87
Lowell,Mike	36	86
Hairston,Jerry	34	86
Kinsler,Ian	32	86
Helton,Todd	39	86
Ramirez,Aramis	34	86
Hill,Aaron	39	85
Rolen,Scott	37	85
Infante,Omar	33	85
Crede,Joe	31	85
Stavinoha,Nick	29	85
Ellis,Mark	38	85
McCann,Brian	38	85
Barton,Daric	33	85
Quentin,Carlos	39	84

PITCHER SKILLS RANKINGS - Starting Pitchers

Top Command (k/bb)

NAME	Cmd
Halladay,Roy	5.1
Slowey,Kevin	5.0
Haren,Dan	4.9
Vazquez,Javie	4.4
Nolasco,Ricky	4.3
Hamels,Cole	4.0
Beckett,Josh	4.0
Greinke,Zack	3.9
Baker,Scott	3.9
Anderson,Bret	3.7
Verlander,Just	3.7
Sabathia,CC	3.6
Shields,James	3.5
Lee,Cliff	3.5
Martinez,Pedr	3.5
Carpenter,Chr	3.4
Rodriguez,Wa	3.4
Lilly,Ted	3.3
Lincecum,Tim	3.3
Lester,Jon	3.3
Santana,Joha	3.3
Harang,Aaron	3.3
Kuroda,Hiroki	3.1
Pavano,Carl	3.1
Wainwright,Ac	3.1
Hammel,Jaso	3.0
Lackey,John	3.0
Oswalt,Roy	2.9
Smoltz,John	2.9
Hernandez,Fe	2.9
Peavy,Jake	2.9

Top Control (bb/9)

NAME	Ctl
Slowey,Kevin	1.4
Halladay,Roy	1.4
Blackburn,Nicl	1.7
Haren,Dan	1.7
Pineiro,Joel	1.9
Pavano,Carl	1.9
Lee,Cliff	1.9
Baker,Scott	2.0
Hamels,Cole	2.0
Shields,James	2.0
Buehrle,Mark	2.0
Kuroda,Hiroki	2.0
Carpenter,Chr	2.0
Vazquez,Javie	2.1
Nolasco,Ricky	2.1
Beckett,Josh	2.1
Sonnanstine,A	2.2
Martinez,Pedr	2.2
Duke,Zach	2.2
McCutchen,Da	2.2
Oswalt,Roy	2.2
Hammel,Jaso	2.3
Cook,Aaron	2.3
Sabathia,CC	2.3
Anderson,Bret	2.3
Greinke,Zack	2.3
Lilly,Ted	2.3
Stammen,Crai	2.4
Bergesen,Bra	2.4
Lackey,John	2.4
Mitre,Sergio	2.4

Top Dominance (k/9)

NAME	Dom
Harden,Rich	10.6
Lincecum,Tim	10.3
Bedard,Erik	9.9
Sanchez,Jonathan	9.7
Scherzer,Max	9.7
Gallardo,Yovani	9.5
Chamberlain,Joba	9.4
Verlander,Justin	9.3
Kershaw,Clayton	9.3
Vazquez,Javier	9.1
Nolasco,Ricky	9.0
Peavy,Jake	9.0
Gonzalez,Gio	9.0
Lester,Jon	9.0
de la Rosa,Jorge	9.0
Greinke,Zack	9.0
Hanson,Tommy	9.0
Rzepczynski,Marc	8.8
Burnett,A.J.	8.6
Haren,Dan	8.6
Anderson,Brett	8.5
Beckett,Josh	8.5
Perez,Oliver	8.5
Jimenez,Ubaldo	8.5
Rodriguez,Wandy	8.5
Billingsley,Chad	8.4
Matsuzaka,Daisuke	8.3
Morrow,Brandon	8.3
Hernandez,Felix	8.3
Garza,Matt	8.2
Sabathia,CC	8.1

Top Ground Ball Rate

NAME	GB
Hudson,Tim	61
Webb,Brandon	60
Lowe,Derek	60
Carmona,Fausto	59
Bumgarner,Madiso	58
Cook,Aaron	57
Mitre,Sergio	57
Wang,Chien-Ming	57
Carpenter,Chris	56
Hernandez,Felix	55
Pineiro,Joel	54
Romero,Ricky	54
Porcello,Rick	54
Masterson,Justin	54
Maholm,Paul	53
Jimenez,Ubaldo	53
Lannan,John	53
Halladay,Roy	52
Marquis,Jason	52
Rzepczynski,Marc	51
Anderson,Brett	51
Buchholz,Clay	51
Laffey,Aaron	50
Kuroda,Hiroki	50
Pelfrey,Mike	50
Volstad,Chris	50
Morton,Charlie	50
Parra,Manny	49
Wainwright,Adam	49
Duke,Zach	49
Mock,Garrett	49

Top Fly Ball Rate

NAME	FB
Feliz,Neftali	57
Hernandez,David	54
Young,Chris	53
VandenHurk,Rick	50
Perez,Oliver	50
Weaver,Jered	49
Petit,Yusmeiro	49
Lilly,Ted	48
Matusz,Brian	48
Wakefield,Tim	47
Purcey,David	47
LeBlanc,Wade	47
Slowey,Kevin	47
Richmond,Scott	46
Kazmir,Scott	46
Baker,Scott	46
Morrow,Brandon	46
Tillman,Chris	45
Gallagher,Sean	45
Braden,Dallas	44
Harden,Rich	44
Cain,Matt	43
Owings,Micah	43
Santana,Johan	43
Rowland-Smith,R.	43
Happ,J.A.	43
Matsuzaka,Daisuke	43
Washburn,Jarrod	43
Guthrie,Jeremy	43
Norris,Bud	43
Maine,John	43

High GB, Low Dom

NAME	GB	Dom
Lowe,Derek	60	5.5
Bumgarner,M	58	5.4
Cook,Aaron	57	4.0
Wang,Chien-M	57	5.2
Pineiro,Joel	54	4.8
Porcello,Rick	54	4.7
Lannan,John	53	4.5
Marquis,J	52	4.9
Laffey,Aaron	50	4.7
Duke,Zach	49	4.6
Cahill,Trevor	48	5.0
Bergesen,B	47	4.9
Suppan,Jeff	47	4.6
Saunders,Joe	47	5.0
Looper,B	47	4.7
Stammen,C	46	4.1
Buehrle,Mark	46	5.0
Miner,Zach	46	5.4
Garland,Jon	46	4.7
Silva,Carlos	46	3.9
Moehler,Brian	45	5.1
Blackburn,N	45	4.3
Hendrickson,N	45	5.4
Perkins,Glen	44	4.8
Stauffer,Tim	43	5.4
Hernandez,L	41	4.5
McCutchen,D	40	5.4
Sowers,J	39	4.4
Guthrie,J	38	5.3
Hunter,T	37	4.8
Washburn,J	37	5.0

High GB, High Dom

NAME	GB	Dom
Hudson,Tim	61	5.8
Webb,B	60	6.8
Carmona,F	59	5.9
Carpenter,C	56	6.9
Hernandez,F	55	8.3
Romero,Ricky	54	6.9
Masterson,J	54	7.7
Maholm,Paul	53	5.8
Jimenez,U	53	8.5
Halladay,Roy	52	7.4
Rzepczynski	51	8.8
Anderson,B	51	8.5
Buchholz,C	51	7.6
Kuroda,Hiroki	50	6.3
Pelfrey,Mike	50	5.7
Volstad,Chris	50	5.7
Morton,Charlie	50	6.2
Parra,Manny	49	7.6
Wainwright,A	49	7.7
Mock,Garrett	49	7.0
Buckner,Billy	49	6.7
Hochevar,L	49	6.7
Richard,C	48	6.4
Dempster,R	48	7.9
Lincecum,Tim	48	10.3
Feldman,S	48	5.8
Wells,Randy	48	5.9
Oswalt,Roy	48	6.6
Johnson,Josh	48	7.9
Niese,J	47	6.3
Contreras,J	47	6.5

Lowest xERA

NAME	xERA
Lincecum,Tim	2.88
Carpenter,Chris	3.05
Halladay,Roy	3.06
Hernandez,Felix	3.17
Haren,Dan	3.18
Vazquez,Javier	3.24
Anderson,Brett	3.25
Webb,Brandon	3.26
Beckett,Josh	3.27
Lester,Jon	3.31
Jimenez,Ubaldo	3.33
Sabathia,CC	3.40
Nolasco,Ricky	3.42
Hudson,Tim	3.42
Wainwright,Adam	3.43
Verlander,Justin	3.45
Bedard,Erik	3.46
Rodriguez,Wandy	3.47
Greinke,Zack	3.47
Scherzer,Max	3.48
Chamberlain,Joba	3.50
Peavy,Jake	3.52
Harden,Rich	3.52
Rzepczynski,Marc	3.52
Johnson,Josh	3.53
Dempster,Ryan	3.54
Hamels,Cole	3.54
Lowe,Derek	3.57
Kuroda,Hiroki	3.57
Hanson,Tommy	3.62
Buchholz,Clay	3.66

Top BPV, 180+ IP

NAME	BPV
Haren,Dan	129
Lincecum,Tim	127
Vazquez,Javier	127
Halladay,Roy	125
Nolasco,Ricky	122
Anderson,Brett	121
Beckett,Josh	119
Verlander,Justin	116
Greinke,Zack	116
Lester,Jon	112
Hamels,Cole	109
Sabathia,CC	107
Rodriguez,Wandy	106
Hernandez,Felix	105
Carpenter,Chris	104
Scherzer,Max	100
Wainwright,Adam	99
Baker,Scott	95
Santana,Johan	95
Shields,James	94
Hanson,Tommy	93
Harang,Aaron	92
Johnson,Josh	91
Lee,Cliff	90
Lilly,Ted	87
Dempster,Ryan	87
Gallardo,Yovani	86
Lackey,John	86
Webb,Brandon	85
Garza,Matt	85
Hammel,Jason	84

Top BPV, -150 IP

NAME	BPV
Bedard,Erik	95
Harden,Rich	92
Martinez,Pedro	90
Smoltz,John	86
Marcum,Shaun	74
Rzepczynski,Marc	73
Hochevar,Luke	71
Sheets,Ben	71
Bush,David	71
Mitre,Sergio	71
VandenHurk,Rick	67
Garcia,Freddy	65
Gonzalez,Gio	65
Mock,Garrett	61
Niese,Jonathon	61
Feliz,Neftali	61
Cecil,Brett	60
Bumgarner,Madiso	59
McCutchen,Daniel	56
Petit,Yusmeiro	55
Norris,Bud	54
LeBlanc,Wade	53
Kawakami,Kenshin	53
Bailey,Homer	52
Mazzaro,Vince	51
Buckner,Billy	48
Gorzelanny,Tom	48
Hendrickson,Mark	45
Penny,Brad	45
Carmona,Fausto	45
McCarthy,Brandon	44

PITCHER SKILLS RANKINGS - Relief Pitchers

Top Command (k/bb)

NAME	Cmd
Street,Huston	5.2
Soria,Joakim	4.7
Qualls,Chad	4.4
Rivera,Marian	4.2
Papelbon,Jona	4.1
Mujica,Edwar	4.0
Kelley,Shawn	4.0
Madson,Ryan	4.0
Thornton,Matt	3.9
Capps,Matt	3.9
Soriano,Rafae	3.9
Broxton,Jonat	3.8
Hughes,Phil	3.8
Wagner,Billy	3.7
Uehara,Koji	3.7
Romo,Sergio	3.6
Walker,Tyler	3.4
Bell,Heath	3.4
Francisco,Frai	3.4
Valverde,Jose	3.3
Frasor,Jason	3.3
Nathan,Joe	3.3
Corpas,Manny	3.2
Betancourt,Ra	3.1
Hoffman,Trev	3.1
Todd,Jess	3.1
League,Brand	3.1
Thatcher,Joe	3.1
Wheeler,Dan	3.0
Perez,Chris	3.0
Medlen,Kris	3.0

Top Control (bb/9)

NAME	Ctl
Qualls,Chad	1.8
Mujica,Edward	1.9
Capps,Matt	1.9
Uehara,Koji	1.9
Street,Huston	1.9
Kelley,Shawn	2.0
Rivera,Mariano	2.1
Corpas,Manny	2.1
Mathis,Doug	2.1
Guerrier,Matt	2.1
Walker,Tyler	2.2
Madson,Ryan	2.2
Aceves,Alfredo	2.2
Martin,J.D.	2.3
Soria,Joakim	2.3
Wheeler,Dan	2.3
Sampson,Chris	2.3
Geer,Josh	2.3
Fister,Doug	2.3
Burns,Mike	2.4
Hoffman,Trevor	2.5
Rauch,Jon	2.5
Papelbon,Jonathan	2.5
Hughes,Phil	2.5
Pena,Tony	2.5
Coffey,Todd	2.5
Albaladejo,Jonathan	2.5
Hawkins,LaTroy	2.5
Ayala,Luis	2.5
Swarzak,Anthony	2.5
Kendrick,Kyle	2.6

Top Dominance (k/9)

NAME	Dom
Broxton,Jonathan	12.1
Wagner,Billy	11.9
Robertson,David	11.8
Bard,Daniel	11.4
Soria,Joakim	11.0
Marmol,Carlos	10.9
Gonzalez,Mike	10.6
Dotel,Octavio	10.6
Soriano,Rafael	10.6
Balfour,Grant	10.6
Sipp,Tony	10.6
Perez,Chris	10.6
Francisco,Frank	10.4
Nathan,Joe	10.3
Wuertz,Mike	10.3
Schlereth,Daniel	10.3
Papelbon,Jonathan	10.2
Thornton,Matt	10.2
Valverde,Jose	10.2
Wood,Kerry	10.2
Lidge,Brad	10.1
Street,Huston	10.1
Romo,Sergio	10.1
Bell,Heath	9.9
Rodriguez,Francisc	9.9
Kuo,Hong-Chih	9.9
Gregerson,Luke	9.8
Howell,J.P.	9.7
Motte,Jason	9.6
Bulger,Jason	9.5
Aardsma,David	9.5

Top Ground Ball Rate

NAME	GB
Meredith,Cla	65
Green,Sean	64
Moylan,Peter	64
Ziegler,Brad	62
MacDougal,Mike	60
Arias,Alberto	60
Downs,Scott	60
League,Brandon	59
Bass,Brian	59
Smith,Joe	59
Reyes,Dennys	59
Wright,Jamey	59
Shouse,Brian	59
Romero,J.C.	58
Choate,Randy	58
Gervacio,Sammy	57
Jepsen,Kevin	57
Condrey,Clay	57
Troncoso,Ramon	57
Schlereth,Daniel	57
Qualls,Chad	56
Badenhop,Burke	56
Camp,Shawn	55
Affeldt,Jeremy	55
Sampson,Chris	55
Feliciano,Pedro	55
Boyer,Blaine	54
Dolsi,Freddy	54
Hawksworth,Blake	54
Baez,Danys	54
Johnson,Jim	54

Top Fly Ball Rate

NAME	FB
Clippard,Tyler	58
Percival,Troy	58
DiFelice,Mark	57
Springer,Russ	57
Ni,Fu-Te	55
Romo,Sergio	55
Daley,Matt	55
Wheeler,Dan	53
Uehara,Koji	53
Betancourt,Rafael	52
Kelley,Shawn	52
Marmol,Carlos	51
Zavada,Clay	51
Mijares,Jose	51
Sipp,Tony	50
Sanches,Brian	50
Soriano,Rafael	50
Cruz,Juan	50
Smith,Chris	50
Hudson,Daniel	49
Okajima,Hideki	49
Hoffman,Trevor	49
Howry,Bob	49
Calero,Kiko	49
Bruney,Brian	49
Stetter,Mitch	48
Dotel,Octavio	48
Tejeda,Robinson	48
French,Luke	48
Sherrill,George	48
Narveson,Chris	47

High GB, Low Dom

NAME	GB	Dom
Bass,Brian	59	5.3
Shouse,Brian	59	5.3
Condrey,Clay	57	5.0
Sampson,C	55	4.7
Boyer,Blaine	54	5.2
Dolsi,Freddy	54	4.7
Hawksworth	54	5.4
Baez,Danys	54	5.3
Janssen,Case	53	5.0
Cormier,L	53	4.3
Palmer,Matt	52	5.0
Thompson,B	51	4.3
Keppel,Bobby	50	4.6
White,Sean	48	4.0
Jakubauskas	47	4.8
Loux,Shane	47	3.1
Kendrick,Kyle	47	3.9
Dickey,R.A.	47	5.0

High GB, High Dom

NAME	GB	Dom
Green,Sean	64	6.7
Moylan,Peter	64	7.3
Ziegler,Brad	62	6.3
MacDougal,M	60	6.6
Arias,Alberto	60	6.1
Downs,Scott	60	7.8
League,B	59	8.1
Smith,Joe	59	7.7
Reyes,D	59	7.2
Wright,Jamey	59	6.2
Romero,J.C.	58	6.8
Choate,R	58	6.2
Gervacio,S	57	9.5
Jepsen,Kevin	57	8.0
Troncoso,R	57	6.5
Schlereth,D	57	10.3
Qualls,Chad	56	7.8
Badenhop,B	56	7.2
Camp,Shawn	55	7.0
Affeldt,J	55	7.9
Feliciano,P	55	9.1
Johnson,Jim	54	6.3
Boggs,M	54	6.0
Belisario,R	54	7.0
Rivera,Saul	53	5.7
Coffey,Todd	53	6.9
Rivera,M	53	8.7
Albaladejo,J	53	6.0
Perdomo,L	53	8.5
Wilson,C.J.	52	9.2
Masset,Nick	52	7.7

Lowest xERA

NAME	xERA
Broxton,Jonathan	2.40
Rivera,Mariano	2.84
Soria,Joakim	2.85
Qualls,Chad	2.87
Thornton,Matt	2.89
League,Brandon	2.91
Wagner,Billy	2.92
Gervacio,Sammy	2.94
Bell,Heath	2.96
Street,Huston	2.99
Feliciano,Pedro	3.03
Bard,Daniel	3.03
Madson,Ryan	3.09
Smith,Joe	3.10
Downs,Scott	3.15
Nathan,Joe	3.17
Robertson,David	3.18
Moylan,Peter	3.19
Gregerson,Luke	3.21
Wuertz,Mike	3.21
Kuo,Hong-Chih	3.24
Wilson,C.J.	3.28
Papelbon,Jonathan	3.29
Ziegler,Brad	3.30
Howell,J.P.	3.34
Jepsen,Kevin	3.37
Thatcher,Joe	3.37
Wilson,Brian	3.39
Hughes,Phil	3.40
Medlen,Kris	3.41
Valverde,Jose	3.41

Top BPV, 10+ Saves

NAME	BPV
Broxton,Jonathan	161
Soria,Joakim	155
Street,Huston	146
Wagner,Billy	143
Thornton,Matt	139
Rivera,Mariano	131
Papelbon,Jonathan	129
Qualls,Chad	127
Bell,Heath	126
Soriano,Rafael	125
Madson,Ryan	123
Nathan,Joe	121
Valverde,Jose	116
Francisco,Frank	114
Perez,Chris	108
Frasor,Jason	106
Wilson,Brian	101
Bailey,Andrew	96
Gonzalez,Mike	95
Capps,Matt	95
Howell,J.P.	94
Downs,Scott	91
Wood,Kerry	89
Wilson,C.J.	89
Jenks,Bobby	87
Hoffman,Trevor	86
Lidge,Brad	76
Gregg,Kevin	76
Lindstrom,Matt	74
Fuentes,Brian	72
Gutierrez,Juan	71

Top BPV, 9- Saves

NAME	BPV
Romo,Sergio	116
Bard,Daniel	116
Hughes,Phil	115
Gervacio,Sammy	114
Robertson,David	113
Feliciano,Pedro	113
League,Brandon	112
Kuo,Hong-Chih	112
Wuertz,Mike	112
Gregerson,Luke	110
Thatcher,Joe	109
Kelley,Shawn	100
Medlen,Kris	98
Farnsworth,Kyle	98
Mujica,Edward	98
Adams,Mike	97
Smith,Joe	97
Walker,Tyler	93
Corpas,Manny	93
Betancourt,Rafael	93
Miller,Trever	92
Motte,Jason	92
Neshek,Pat	89
Coffey,Todd	88
Jepsen,Kevin	86
Sipp,Tony	86
O'Day,Darren	86
Balfour,Grant	85
Masset,Nick	85
Todd,Jess	83
Pena,Tony	82

RANDOM VARIANCE — Rebounds and Corrections

REBOUNDS

BATTERS

BATTERS	Pos	+
Aviles,Mike	6	+5
Bruce,Jay	9	+5
Bruntlett,Eric	4	+5
Buck,Travis	9	+5
Byrnes,Eric	7	+5
Castro,Ramon	2	+5
Crisp,Coco	8	+5
Erstad,Darin	7	+5
Giles,Brian	9	+5
Gimenez,Chris	7	+5
Glaus,Troy	5	+5
Greene,Khalil	6	+5
Jackson,Conor	7	+5
Johnson,Kelly	4	+5
Lowrie,Jed	6	+5
Macias,Drew	7	+5
Martinez,Fernando	7	+5
Miles,Aaron	4	+5
Soto,Geovany	2	+5
Valdez,Wilson	6	+5
Atkins,Garrett	53	+4
Bard,Josh	2	+4
Carroll,Brett	9	+4
Duncan,Chris	7	+4
Giambi,Jason	30	+4
Griffey Jr.,Ken	0	+4
Iannetta,Chris	2	+4
Jones,Andruw	0	+4
Jones,Chipper	5	+4
Navarro,Dioner	2	+4
Pena,Carlos	3	+4
Quentin,Carlos	7	+4
Rollins,Jimmy	6	+4
Shoppach,Kelly	2	+4
Stairs,Matt	9	+4
Sullivan,Cory	7	+4
Varitek,Jason	2	+4

PITCHERS

PITCHERS	+
Arredondo,Jose	+5
Bonderman,Jeremy	+5
Bush,David	+5
Capps,Matt	+5
Carrasco,Carlos	+5
Casilla,Santiago	+5
Corpas,Manny	+5
Farnsworth,Kyle	+5
Harrison,Matt	+5
Holland,Derek	+5
Janssen,Casey	+5
Jepsen,Kevin	+5
Johnson,Randy	+5
League,Brandon	+5
Lidge,Brad	+5
Lindstrom,Matt	+5
Litsch,Jesse	+5
Matsuzaka,Daisuke	+5
Mitre,Sergio	+5
Myers,Brett	+5
Nolasco,Ricky	+5
O'Sullivan,Sean	+5
Paulino,Felipe	+5
Perdomo,Luis	+5
Perez,Rafael	+5
Ray,Chris	+5
Schoeneweis,Scott	+5
Shouse,Brian	+5
Silva,Carlos	+5
Smoltz,John	+5
Sonnanstine,Andy	+5
Wang,Chien-Ming	+5
Webb,Brandon	+5
Bass,Brian	+4
Buckner,Billy	+4
Carmona,Fausto	+4
Elbert,Scott	+4
Eveland,Dana	+4
Linebrink,Scott	+4
Olsen,Scott	+4
Parra,Manny	+4
Pavano,Carl	+4
Ponson,Sidney	+4
Samardzija,Jeff	+4
Wright,Wesley	+4
Zimmermann,Jordan	+4

CORRECTIONS

BATTERS

BATTERS	Pos	-
Ausmus,Brad	2	-5
Aybar,Erick	6	-5
Bartlett,Jason	6	-5
Castro,Juan	64	-5
Choo,Shin-Soo	97	-5
Davis,Rajai	8	-5
Desmond,Ian	6	-5
Diaz,Matt	97	-5
Dickerson,Chris	789	-5
Flores,Jesus	2	-5
Hill,Koyie	2	-5
Infante,Omar	4	-5
Ishikawa,Travis	3	-5
Johnson,Nick	3	-5
Mauer,Joe	2	-5
Morgan,Nyjer	78	-5
Nieves,Wil	2	-5
Perez,Fernando	8	-5
Ramirez,Hanley	6	-5
Ryan,Brendan	6	-5
Salazar,Oscar	7	-5
Santiago,Ramon	64	-5
Span,Denard	879	-5
Suzuki,Ichiro	9	-5
Torrealba,Yorvit	2	-5
Torres,Andres	87	-5
Wright,David	5	-5
Abreu,Tony	4	-4
Baker,Jeff	45	-4
Beltran,Carlos	8	-4
Bourn,Michael	8	-4
Carroll,Jamey	45	-4
Figgins,Chone	5	-4
Garciaparra,Nomar	0	-4
Helms,Wes	5	-4
Helton,Todd	3	-4
Jeter,Derek	6	-4
LaRue,Jason	2	-4
Lopez,Felipe	4	-4
McGehee,Casey	54	-4
Montero,Miguel	2	-4
Morales,Kendry	3	-4
Pagan,Angel	87	-4
Ramirez,Aramis	5	-4
Reimold,Nolan	7	-4
Roberts,Ryan	4	-4
Ross,David	2	-4
Upton,Justin	9	-4
Uribe,Juan	564	-4
Vizquel,Omar	65	-4
Votto,Joey	3	-4
Wieters,Matt	2	-4
Youkilis,Kevin	35	-4
Young,Delwyn	49	-4
Zobrist,Ben	49	-4

PITCHERS

PITCHERS	-
Aardsma,David	-5
Accardo,Jeremy	-5
Adams,Mike	-5
Affeldt,Jeremy	-5
Bailey,Andrew	-5
Belisario,Ronald	-5
Breslow,Craig	-5
Bumgarner,Madison	-5
Byrdak,Tim	-5
Cain,Matt	-5
Calero,Kiko	-5
Clippard,Tyler	-5
Cordero,Francisco	-5
Dessens,Elmer	-5
Eyre,Scott	-5
Franklin,Ryan	-5
Frasor,Jason	-5
Gonzalez,Mike	-5
Greinke,Zack	-5
Guerrier,Matt	-5
Guzman,Angel	-5
Happ,J.A.	-5
Hawkins,LaTroy	-5
Hoffman,Trevor	-5
Howry,Bob	-5
Jurrjens,Jair	-5
Lyon,Brandon	-5
Marmol,Carlos	-5
Masset,Nick	-5
Mijares,Jose	-5
Miller,Justin	-5
Miller,Trever	-5
Mota,Guillermo	-5
Nathan,Joe	-5
Ni,Fu-Te	-5
O'Day,Darren	-5
Papelbon,Jonathan	-5
Pinto,Renyel	-5
Ramirez,Ramon	-5
Rhodes,Arthur	-5
Rivera,Mariano	-5
Romero,J.C.	-5
Saito,Takashi	-5
Sanches,Brian	-5
Sherrill,George	-5
Smith,Chris	-5
Soria,Joakim	-5
Tejeda,Robinson	-5
Troncoso,Ramon	-5
Valverde,Jose	-5
Vargas,Claudio	-5
Wagner,Billy	-5
Walker,Tyler	-5
Westbrook,Jake	-5
White,Sean	-5
Bergmann,Jason	-4
Burnett,Sean	-4
Carpenter,Chris	-4
Gallagher,Sean	-4
Grabow,John	-4
Hanson,Tommy	-4
Hudson,Daniel	-4
Kennedy,Ian	-4
Kershaw,Clayton	-4
Latos,Mat	-4
Medders,Brandon	-4
Moylan,Peter	-4
Rosales,Leo	-4
Wheeler,Dan	-4

RISK MANAGEMENT

GRADE "F" in HEALTH

Pitchers	Pitchers
Adams,Mike	Stults,Eric
Ayala,Luis	Uehara,Koji
Baez,Danys	Valdez,Merkin
Bedard,Erik	Vargas,Jason
Bonderman,Jeremy	Volquez,Edinson
Bruney,Brian	Wagner,Billy
Carpenter,Chris	Wang,Chien-Ming
Chen,Bruce	Webb,Brandon
Colon,Bartolo	Wells,Kip
Devine,Joey	Westbrook,Jake
Dotel,Octavio	Willis,Dontrelle
Duchscherer,Justin	Wood,Kerry
Escobar,Kelvim	Young,Chris
Francisco,Frank	Zumaya,Joel
Francis,Jeff	
Gallardo,Yovani	**Batters**
Gonzalez,Mike	Abreu,Tony
Guardado,Eddie	Aviles,Mike
Hampton,Mike	Baldelli,Rocco
Harden,Rich	Blalock,Hank
Harrison,Matt	Byrnes,Eric
Hill,Rich	Chavez,Endy
Hudson,Tim	Chavez,Eric
Hughes,Phil	Crede,Joe
Janssen,Casey	Crisp,Coco
Johnson,Josh	Delgado,Carlos
Johnson,Randy	Doumit,Ryan
Karstens,Jeff	Everett,Adam
Kuo,Hong-Chih	Flores,Jesus
Lewis,Scott	Frandsen,Kevin
Liriano,Francisco	Freel,Ryan
Litsch,Jesse	Furcal,Rafael
Maine,John	Garciaparra,Nomar
Marcum,Shaun	Gerut,Jody
Martinez,Pedro	Giles,Brian
Matsuzaka,Daisuke	Glaus,Troy
McCarthy,Brandon	Gonzalez,Alex
McGowan,Dustin	Greene,Khalil
Mitre,Sergio	Guzman,Cristian
Moylan,Peter	Infante,Omar
Myers,Brett	Iwamura,Akinori
Neshek,Pat	Jackson,Conor
Nippert,Dustin	Johnson,Nick
Olsen,Scott	Johnson,Reed
Ortiz,Russ	Kearns,Austin
Paulino,Felipe	Kotsay,Mark
Pavano,Carl	Nady,Xavier
Peavy,Jake	Pagan,Angel
Percival,Troy	Perez,Fernando
Perez,Oliver	Posada,Jorge
Putz,J.J.	Reyes,Jose
Ray,Chris	Sweeney,Mike
Rhodes,Arthur	Weeks,Rickie
Rodney,Fernando	
Ryan,B.J.	
Sanchez,Anibal	
Sheets,Ben	
Shields,Scot	
Silva,Carlos	
Smoltz,John	
Soriano,Rafael	
Stauffer,Tim	

Highest Reliability Grades - Health / Experience / Consistency (Min. Grade = BBB)

CA	POS	Rel
Martin,Russell	2	AAB
Kendall,Jason	2	ABA
Molina,Yadier	2	ABA
Pierzynski,A.J.	2	ABA
Rodriguez,Ivan	2	ABA
Suzuki,Kurt	2	ABA
Molina,Bengie	2	ABB

1B/DH	POS	Rel
LaRoche,Adam	3	AAA
Loney,James	3	AAA
Morneau,Justin	3	AAA
Teixeira,Mark	3	AAA
Dunn,Adam	379	AAB
Gonzalez,Adrian	3	AAB
Konerko,Paul	3	AAB
Pujols,Albert	3	AAB
Youkilis,Kevin	35	AAB
Cabrera,Miguel	3	AAB
Garko,Ryan	3	ABA
Jacobs,Mike	0	ABB
Cantu,Jorge	35	ABB
Millar,Kevin	30	ABB
Griffey Jr.,Ken	0	BBB
Thome,Jim	0	BBB
Overbay,Lyle	3	BBB

2B	POS	Rel
Pedroia,Dustin	4	AAA
Phillips,Brandon	4	AAA
Roberts,Brian	4	AAA
Utley,Chase	4	AAA
Lopez,Jose	4	AAB
Polanco,Placido	4	AAB
Schumaker,Skip	47	ABA
Hudson,Orlando	4	BBA
Castillo,Luis	4	BBB

3B	POS	Rel
Kouzmanoff,Kevin	5	AAA
Teahen,Mark	59	AAA
Peralta,Jhonny	56	AAB
Wright,David	5	AAB
Inge,Brandon	5	ABA
Longoria,Evan	5	ABA
Blake,Casey	5	BAA
Feliz,Pedro	5	BAA
Rodriguez,Alex	5	BAB
Zimmerman,Ryan	5	BAB

SS	POS	Rel
Cabrera,Orlando	6	AAA
Ramirez,Hanley	6	AAA
Rollins,Jimmy	6	AAB
Theriot,Ryan	6	AAB
Betancourt,Yuniesk	6	ABA
Escobar,Yunel	6	ABA
Cabrera,Asdrubal	64	ABB
Harris,Brendan	65	ABB
Scutaro,Marco	6	ABB
Tejada,Miguel	6	BAB

OF	POS	Rel
Abreu,Bobby	9	AAA
Victorino,Shane	8	AAA
Young,Chris	8	AAA
Young,Delmon	7	AAA
Damon,Johnny	7	AAB
DeJesus,David	7	AAB
Dye,Jermaine	9	AAB
Ellsbury,Jacoby	8	AAB
Ethier,Andre	9	AAB
Granderson,Curtis	8	AAB
Hawpe,Brad	9	AAB
Holliday,Matt	7	AAB
Kemp,Matt	8	AAB
Pence,Hunter	9	AAB
Suzuki,Ichiro	9	AAB
Winn,Randy	978	AAB
Bautista,Jose	795	ABB
Matthews Jr.,Gary	89	ABB
Pierre,Juan	7	ABB
Scott,Luke	7	ABB
Cameron,Mike	8	BAA
Ibanez,Raul	7	BAA
Lee,Carlos	7	BAB
Rowand,Aaron	8	BAB
Sizemore,Grady	8	BAB
Werth,Jayson	9	BBA
Willingham,Josh	79	BBA
Anderson,Garret	7	BBB
Byrd,Marlon	87	BBB
Drew,J.D.	9	BBB
Hart,Corey	9	BBB
Kubel,Jason	97	BBB
McLouth,Nate	8	BBB

RP		Rel
Gaudin,Chad		AAA
Gregg,Kevin		AAA
Moyer,Jamie		AAA
Nathan,Joe		AAA
Rivera,Mariano		AAA
Rodriguez,Francisc		AAA
Cordero,Francisco		AAB
Papelbon,Jonathan		AAB
Broxton,Jonathan		ABA
Jenks,Bobby		ABA
Wilson,Brian		ABA
Batista,Miguel		ABB
Bell,Heath		ABB
Byrd,Paul		ABB
Franklin,Ryan		ABB
Kendrick,Kyle		ABB
Ni,Fu-Te		ABB
Sherrill,George		ABB
Villanueva,Carlos		ABB
Capps,Matt		BBA
Soria,Joakim		BBA
Hoffman,Trevor		BBB
Lidge,Brad		BBB
Redding,Tim		BBB
Street,Huston		BBB

SP	Rel
Arroyo,Bronson	AAA
Billingsley,Chad	AAA
Blackburn,Nick	AAA
Buehrle,Mark	AAA
Cain,Matt	AAA
Davis,Doug	AAA
Floyd,Gavin	AAA
Garland,Jon	AAA
Garza,Matt	AAA
Greinke,Zack	AAA
Hamels,Cole	AAA
Haren,Dan	AAA
Hernandez,Felix	AAA
Hernandez,Livan	AAA
Jackson,Edwin	AAA
Lincecum,Tim	AAA
Lowe,Derek	AAA
Maholm,Paul	AAA
Marquis,Jason	AAA
Pelfrey,Mike	AAA
Saunders,Joe	AAA
Shields,James	AAA
Washburn,Jarrod	AAA
Weaver,Jered	AAA
Blanton,Joe	AAB
Danks,John	AAB
Guthrie,Jeremy	AAB
Jimenez,Ubaldo	AAB
Jurrjens,Jair	AAB
Lannan,John	AAB
Looper,Braden	AAB
Pettitte,Andy	AAB
Sabathia,CC	AAB
Snell,Ian	AAB
Vazquez,Javier	AAB
Verlander,Justin	AAB
Zito,Barry	AAB
Cueto,Johnny	ABA
Hammel,Jason	ABA
Hendrickson,Mark	ABA
Sonnanstine,Andy	ABA
Gorzelanny,Tom	ABB
Baker,Scott	BAA
Beckett,Josh	BAA
Dempster,Ryan	BAA
Duke,Zach	BAA
Halladay,Roy	BAA
Lilly,Ted	BAA
Meche,Gil	BAA
Oswalt,Roy	BAA
Pineiro,Joel	BAA
Rodriguez,Wandy	BAA
Santana,Johan	BAA
Suppan,Jeff	BAA
Zambrano,Carlos	BAA
Bannister,Brian	BBA
Moehler,Brian	BBA
Sanchez,Jonathan	BBA
Carmona,Fausto	BBB
Correia,Kevin	BBB
de la Rosa,Jorge	BBB
Owings,Micah	BBB

RISK MANAGEMENT

GRADE "A" in CONSISTENCY

Pitchers (min 120 IP)	Pitchers (min 120 IP)
Anderson,Brett	Sonnanstine,Andy
Arroyo,Bronson	Stammen,Craig
Bailey,Homer	Suppan,Jeff
Baker,Scott	Tillman,Chris
Bannister,Brian	Volstad,Chris
Beckett,Josh	Wakefield,Tim
Bergesen,Brad	Washburn,Jarrod
Billingsley,Chad	Weaver,Jered
Blackburn,Nick	Wolf,Randy
Braden,Dallas	Zambrano,Carlos
Buehrle,Mark	**Batters (min 400 AB)**
Bush,David	Abreu,Bobby
Cain,Matt	Beltran,Carlos
Cook,Aaron	Betancourt,Yuniesky
Cueto,Johnny	Blake,Casey
Davies,Kyle	Blanks,Kyle
Davis,Doug	Borbon,Julio
Davis,Wade	Cabrera,Orlando
Dempster,Ryan	Cameron,Mike
Duke,Zach	Eckstein,David
Feldman,Scott	Ellis,Mark
Floyd,Gavin	Escobar,Yunel
Francis,Jeff	Feliz,Pedro
Garland,Jon	Fowler,Dexter
Garza,Matt	Getz,Chris
Gonzalez,Gio	Gomez,Carlos
Greinke,Zack	Hairston,Scott
Halladay,Roy	Hernandez,Ramon
Hamels,Cole	Hudson,Orlando
Hammel,Jason	Ibanez,Raul
Hanson,Tommy	Inge,Brandon
Harang,Aaron	Iwamura,Akinori
Harden,Rich	Izturis,Cesar
Haren,Dan	Janish,Paul
Hernandez,Felix	Kendall,Jason
Hernandez,Livan	Kendrick,Howie
Hochevar,Luke	Kouzmanoff,Kevin
Hudson,Tim	LaRoche,Adam
Hunter,Tommy	Loney,James
Jackson,Edwin	Longoria,Evan
Lackey,John	Maybin,Cameron
Lilly,Ted	Molina,Yadier
Lincecum,Tim	Morneau,Justin
Liriano,Francisco	Murphy,David
Lohse,Kyle	Parra,Gerardo
Lowe,Derek	Pedroia,Dustin
Maholm,Paul	Pennington,Cliff
Maine,John	Phillips,Brandon
Marcum,Shaun	Pierzynski,A.J.
Marquis,Jason	Ramirez,Aramis
Meche,Gil	Ramirez,Hanley
Millwood,Kevin	Roberts,Brian
Moehler,Brian	Saunders,Michael
Myers,Brett	Schumaker,Skip
Olsen,Scott	Stewart,Ian
Oswalt,Roy	Suzuki,Kurt
Padilla,Vicente	Sweeney,Ryan
Paulino,Felipe	Teahen,Mark
Peavy,Jake	Teixeira,Mark
Pelfrey,Mike	Upton,Justin
Pineiro,Joel	Utley,Chase
Rodriguez,Wandy	Victorino,Shane
Rowland-Smith,Ryan	Werth,Jayson
Sanchez,Jonathan	Willingham,Josh
Santana,Johan	Wood,Brandon
Saunders,Joe	Young,Chris
Shields,James	Young,Delmon

TOP COMBINATION OF SKILLS AND RELIABILITY
Maximum of one "C" in Reliability Grade

BATTING POWER

PX over 120	PX	Rel
Pena,Carlos	199	BAC
Reynolds,Mark	193	AAC
Howard,Ryan	192	AAC
Dunn,Adam	186	AAB
Stewart,Ian	173	ACA
Thome,Jim	171	BBB
Pujols,Albert	168	AAB
Youkilis,Kevin	164	AAB
Bay,Jason	163	AAC
Longoria,Evan	160	ABA
Votto,Joey	160	ABC
Braun,Ryan	160	AAC
Teixeira,Mark	158	AAA
Ramirez,Manny	157	ABC
Hawpe,Brad	157	AAB
Uggla,Dan	155	AAC
Werth,Jayson	155	BBA
Berkman,Lance	154	BAC
Cust,Jack	154	ABC
Lind,Adam	152	ABC
Rodriguez,Alex	151	BAB
Gonzalez,Adrian	150	AAB
Zimmerman,Ryan	149	BAB
LaRoche,Adam	149	AAA
Holliday,Matt	148	AAB
Willingham,Josh	147	BBA
Cameron,Mike	147	BAA
Lee,Derrek	146	BAC
Young,Chris	146	AAA
Ethier,Andre	146	AAB
Drew,J.D.	145	BBB
Olivo,Miguel	142	ACB
Ruiz,Randy	142	ACB
Cabrera,Miguel	141	AAB
Utley,Chase	140	AAA
Morneau,Justin	140	AAA
Jacobs,Mike	138	ABB
McCann,Brian	137	ABC
Scott,Luke	137	ABB
Wood,Brandon	135	ACA
Ibanez,Raul	134	BAA
Kemp,Matt	134	AAB
Kubel,Jason	131	BBB
Dye,Jermaine	131	AAB
Hunter,Torii	130	CAB
Ramirez,Aramis	130	CBA
Ramirez,Hanley	130	AAA
Sizemore,Grady	130	BAB
Pence,Hunter	128	AAB
Murphy,David	128	BCA
Hall,Bill	127	ACB
Granderson,Curtis	127	AAB
Wright,David	126	AAB
Francisco,Ben	123	ACB
Griffey Jr.,Ken	123	BBB
Butler,Billy	121	ABC
Konerko,Paul	121	AAB
Blake,Casey	120	BAA

RUNNER SPEED

SX over 100	SX	Rel
Crawford,Carl	164	BAC
Ellsbury,Jacoby	157	AAB
Rollins,Jimmy	154	AAB
Victorino,Shane	152	AAA
Morgan,Nyjer	144	BCB
Gomez,Carlos	144	BCA
Bonifacio,Emilio	143	ACA
Pierre,Juan	141	ABB
Taveras,Willy	138	BCC
Granderson,Curtis	137	AAB
Kemp,Matt	136	AAB
Lewis,Fred	134	ACB
McCutchen,Andrew	132	ACB
Bartlett,Jason	131	BBC
Patterson,Eric	131	ACB
Utley,Chase	129	AAA
Sizemore,Grady	129	BAB
Braun,Ryan	128	AAC
Harris,Willie	125	ACA
McLouth,Nate	123	BBB
Roberts,Brian	122	AAA
Casilla,Alexi	120	ACB
Hart,Corey	119	BBB
Young,Chris	117	AAA
Drew,Stephen	116	AAC
Rios,Alex	115	AAC
Phillips,Brandon	115	AAA
Jones,Adam	112	BBC
Ramirez,Hanley	112	AAA
Winn,Randy	111	AAB
Castillo,Luis	110	BBB
Abreu,Bobby	109	AAA
Theriot,Ryan	109	AAB
Pennington,Cliff	109	ACA
Cabrera,Asdrubal	108	ABB
Damon,Johnny	107	AAB
Wright,David	106	AAB
Suzuki,Ichiro	106	AAB
Stewart,Ian	103	ACA
Reynolds,Mark	103	AAC
Hudson,Orlando	102	BBA
Gutierrez,Franklin	100	ABC

OVERALL PITCHING SKILL

BPV over 75	BPV	Rel
Broxton,Jonathan	161	ABA
Soria,Joakim	155	BBA
Street,Huston	146	BBB
Thornton,Matt	139	ACB
Rivera,Mariano	131	AAA
Haren,Dan	129	AAA
Papelbon,Jonathan	129	AAB
Lincecum,Tim	127	AAA
Qualls,Chad	127	BCA
Vazquez,Javier	127	AAB
Bell,Heath	126	ABB
Halladay,Roy	125	BAA
Madson,Ryan	123	BCA
Anderson,Brett	121	ACA
Nathan,Joe	121	AAA
Beckett,Josh	119	BAA
Verlander,Justin	116	AAB
Greinke,Zack	116	AAA
Valverde,Jose	116	CAA
Feliciano,Pedro	113	ACB
Wuertz,Mike	112	ACB
Hamels,Cole	109	AAA
Sabathia,CC	107	AAB
Rodriguez,Wandy	106	BAA
Hernandez,Felix	105	AAA
Wilson,Brian	101	ABA
Wainwright,Adam	99	CAB
Chamberlain,Joba	96	ACB
Baker,Scott	95	BAA
Santana,Johan	95	BAA
Capps,Matt	95	BBA
Shields,James	94	AAA
Howell,J.P.	94	ACA
Corpas,Manny	93	ACA
Harang,Aaron	92	CAA
Downs,Scott	91	BCA
Lee,Cliff	90	BAC
Wilson,C.J.	89	BBC
Lilly,Ted	87	BAA
Dempster,Ryan	87	BAA
Jenks,Bobby	87	ABA
Hoffman,Trevor	86	BBB
Lackey,John	86	CAA
Garza,Matt	85	AAA
Hammel,Jason	84	ABA
Jimenez,Ubaldo	84	AAB
Oswalt,Roy	84	BAA
Pena,Tony	82	ACA
Sanchez,Jonathan	81	BBA
Linebrink,Scott	77	BCB
Cueto,Johnny	76	ABA
Lidge,Brad	76	BBB
Gregg,Kevin	76	AAA
Billingsley,Chad	76	AAA
de la Rosa,Jorge	75	BBB

POSITION SCARCITY CHART

30	$30+ players	29	$20-29 players
15	$15-19 players	10	$10-14 players

FIRST BASE	SECOND BASE	THIRD BASE	SHORTSTOP	CATCHERS	OUTFIELDERS	STARTERS	RELIEVERS
Pujols,Albert	Utley,Chase	Rodriguez,Alex	Ramirez,Hanley	Mauer,Joe	Kemp,Matt	Lincecum,Tim	Broxton,Jonathan
Fielder,Prince	Phillips,Brandon	Wright,David	Rollins,Jimmy	McCann,Brian	Crawford,Carl	Halladay,Roy	Street,Huston
Cabrera,Miguel	Pedroia,Dustin	Longoria,Evan	Reyes,Jose	Martinez,Victor	Braun,Ryan	Sabathia,CC	Nathan,Joe
Teixeira,Mark	Roberts,Brian	Zimmerman,Ryan	Tulowitzki,Troy	Wieters,Matt	Ellsbury,Jacoby	Hernandez,Felix	Soria,Joakim
Howard,Ryan	Kinsler,Ian	Ramirez,Aramis	Jeter,Derek	Soto,Geovany	Holliday,Matt	Verlander,Justin	Valverde,Jose
Votto,Joey	Cano,Robinson	Reynolds,Mark	Drew,Stephen	Montero,Miguel	Werth,Jayson	Haren,Dan	Rivera,Mariano
Berkman,Lance	Kendrick,Howie	Sandoval,Pablo	Escobar,Yunel	Martin,Russell	Bay,Jason	Greinke,Zack	Papelbon,Jon
Youkilis,Kevin	Zobrist,Ben	Young,Michael	Bartlett,Jason	Napoli,Mike	Cruz,Nelson	Lester,Jon	Bell,Heath
Lee,Derrek	Lopez,Jose	Figgins,Chone	Andrus,Elvis	Molina,Bengie	Upton,Justin	Beckett,Josh	Qualls,Chad
Gonzalez,Adrian	Uggla,Dan	Beckham,Gordon	Ramirez,Alexei	Suzuki,Kurt	Sizemore,Grady	Wainwright,Adam	Francisco,Frank
Morneau,Justin	Hill,Aaron	Lowell,Mike	Tejada,Miguel	Iannetta,Chris	Victorino,Shane	Rodriguez,Wandy	Bailey,Andrew
Morales,Kendry	Weeks,Rickie	Jones,Chipper	Cabrera,Asdrubal	Doumit,Ryan	Lee,Carlos	Hamels,Cole	Wilson,Brian
Dunn,Adam	Stewart,Ian	Blake,Casey	Cabrera,Everth	Molina,Yadier	Ethier,Andre	Vazquez,Javier	Soriano,Rafael
Pena,Carlos	Prado,Martin	Kouzmanoff,Kevin	Aybar,Erick	Ruiz,Carlos	Abreu,Bobby	Lee,Cliff	Wood,Kerry
Cuddyer,Michael	Castillo,Luis	Gordon,Alex	Furcal,Rafael	Posada,Jorge	Bourn,Michael	Jimenez,Ubaldo	Frasor,Jason
Butler,Billy	Johnson,Kelly	Headley,Chase	Theriot,Ryan	Pierzynski,A.J.	Lind,Adam	Hanson,Tommy	Rodriguez,F
Helton,Todd	Getz,Chris	DeRosa,Mark	Cabrera,Orlando	Olivo,Miguel	McCutchen,A	Baker,Scott	Hoffman,Trevor
Delgado,Carlos	Polanco,Placido	Beltre,Adrian	Scutaro,Marco	Baker,John	Ramirez,Manny	Anderson,Brett	Howell,J.P.
Loney,James	Callaspo,Alberto	Encarnacion,Edwin	Peralta,Jhonny	Shoppach,Kelly	Choo,Shin-Soo	Nolasco,Ricky	Cordero,Francisco
LaRoche,Adam	Matsui,Kaz	Wood,Brandon	Escobar,Alcides	Hernandez,R	Beltran,Carlos	Carpenter,Chris	Wagner,Billy
Cantu,Jorge	Hudson,Orlando	LaRoche,Andy	Guzman,Cristian	Flores,Jesus	Hunter,Torii	Lilly,Ted	Aardsma,David
Jones,Garrett	Barmes,Clint	Rolen,Scott	Desmond,Ian	Pena,Brayan	Suzuki,Ichiro	Garza,Matt	Gonzalez,Mike
Konerko,Paul	Lopez,Felipe	Fox,Jake	Hardy,J.J.	Barajas,Rod	Markakis,Nick	Shields,James	Capps,Matt
Davis,Chris	Valbuena,Luis	Teahen,Mark	Renteria,Edgar	Hundley,Nick	McLouth,Nate	Santana,Johan	Fuentes,Brian
Swisher,Nick	Iwamura,Akinori	Glaus,Troy	Uribe,Juan	Posey,Buster	Granderson,C	Weaver,Jered	Jenks,Bobby
Murphy,Daniel	Izturis,Maicer	Atkins,Garrett	Bloomquist,Willie	Rodriguez,Ivan	Pence,Hunter	Peavy,Jake	Thornton,Matt
Huff,Aubrey	McGehee,Casey	Feliz,Pedro	Hairston,Jerry	Saltalamacchia,J	Damon,Johnny	Billingsley,Chad	Lidge,Brad
Wigginton,Ty	Ellis,Mark	Mora,Melvin	Lowrie,Jed	Buck,John	Hart,Corey	Floyd,Gavin	Gregg,Kevin
Johnson,Nick	Sanchez,Freddy	Inge,Brandon	Gonzalez,Alex	Avila,Alex	Span,Denard	Niemann,Jeff	Wilson,C.J.
Blalock,Hank	Velez,Eugenio	Freese,David	Pennington,Cliff	Laird,Gerald	Ibanez,Raul	Lackey,John	Franklin,Ryan
Overbay,Lyle	Roberts,Ryan	Bautista,Jose	Izturis,Cesar	Kendall,Jason	Upton,B.J.	Cain,Matt	Madson,Ryan
Branyan,Russell	Kennedy,Adam	Crede,Joe	Betancourt,Y	Torrealba,Yorvit	Davis,Rajai	Dempster,Ryan	Robertson,David
Barton,Daric	Schumaker,Skip	Gamel,Mat	Ryan,Brendan	Navarro,Dioner	Fowler,Dexter	Kershaw,Clayton	Rodney,Fernando
Garko,Ryan	Belliard,Ronnie	Bonifacio,Emilio	Aviles,Mike	Paulino,Ronny	Coghlan,Chris	Slowey,Kevin	Marmol,Carlos
Giambi,Jason	Lugo,Julio	Hall,Bill	Wilson,Jack	Thole,Josh	Wells,Vernon	Jurrjens,Jair	Hughes,Phil
Tatis,Fernando	Infante,Omar	Blum,Geoff	Cedeno,Ronny	Zaun,Gregg	Hamilton,Josh	Burnett,A.J.	Masterson,Justin
Tracy,Chad	Casilla,Alexi	Dobbs,Greg	Harris,Brendan	Towles,J.R.	Reimold,Nolan	Webb,Brandon	Correia,Kevin
Kotchman,Casey	Aybar,Willy	Fields,Josh	Santiago,Ramon	Teagarden,T	Ludwick,Ryan	Chamberlain,J	Romo,Sergio
Sanchez,Gaby	Fontenot,Mike	Johnson,Chris	Greene,Khalil	Ross,David	Bruce,Jay	Johnson,Josh	Aceves,Alfredo
Marte,Andy	Punto,Nick	DeWitt,Blake	Counsell,Craig	Ramirez,Max	Ross,Cody	Harang,Aaron	Wuertz,Mike
Ishikawa,Travis	Rodriguez,Sean	Chavez,Eric	Janish,Paul	Johnson,Rob	Gonzalez,Carlos	Price,David	Perez,Chris
Hoffpauir,Micah	Burriss,Emmanuel	Rosales,Adam	Everett,Adam	Snyder,Chris	Soriano,Alfonso	Gallardo,Yovani	Bard,Daniel
Pearce,Steven	Eckstein,David	Loretta,Mark	Cora,Alex	Flowers,Tyler	Kubel,Jason	Liriano,Francisco	Downs,Scott
Kotsay,Mark	Baker,Jeff	Helms,Wes	Brignac,Reid	Hanigan,Ryan	Hawpe,Brad	Buchholz,Clay	Johnson,Jim
Allen,Brandon	Nix,Jayson	Ransom,Cody	Greene,Tyler	Mathis,Jeff	Jones,Adam	Harden,Rich	Gregerson,Luke

PORTFOLIO3 PLAN

TIER 1

High Skill, Low Risk

BATTERS	Age	Bats	Pos	REL	Ct%	PX	SX	R$
				BBB	**80**	**100**	**100**	
Pujols,Albert	30	R	3	AAB	89	168	73	$37
Ramirez,Hanley	26	R	6	AAA	82	130	112	$33
Ellsbury,Jacoby	26	L	8	AAB	87	68	157	$30
Utley,Chase	31	L	4	AAA	82	140	129	$29
Holliday,Matt	30	R	7	AAB	82	148	95	$29
Rollins,Jimmy	31	B	6	AAB	89	115	154	$29
Cabrera,Miguel	26	R	3	AAB	81	141	54	$29
Teixeira,Mark	29	B	3	AAA	81	158	58	$29
Zimmerman,Ryan	25	R	5	BAB	82	149	72	$27
Phillips,Brandon	28	R	4	AAA	85	105	115	$26
Victorino,Shane	29	B	8	AAA	88	91	152	$25
Lee,Carlos	33	R	7	BAB	90	110	57	$25
Ethier,Andre	27	L	9	AAB	82	146	76	$25
Abreu,Bobby	36	L	9	AAA	80	102	109	$25
Pedroia,Dustin	26	R	4	AAA	93	105	94	$25
Morneau,Justin	28	L	3	AAA	84	140	43	$24
Roberts,Brian	32	B	4	AAA	83	110	122	$23
Suzuki,Ichiro	36	L	9	AAB	89	50	106	$22
McLouth,Nate	28	L	8	BBB	81	109	123	$22
Pence,Hunter	26	R	9	AAB	81	128	94	$21
Damon,Johnny	36	L	7	AAB	84	106	107	$21
Hart,Corey	28	R	9	BBB	80	115	119	$21
Ibanez,Raul	37	L	7	BAA	80	134	60	$21
Lopez,Jose	26	R	4	AAB	89	110	50	$21
Cantu,Jorge	28	R	35	ABB	84	105	49	$19
Cabrera,Asdrubal	24	B	64	ABB	82	87	108	$18
Byrd,Marlon	32	R	87	BBB	82	112	90	$17
Konerko,Paul	34	R	3	AAB	83	121	46	$17
Theriot,Ryan	30	R	6	AAB	87	46	109	$17
Kouzmanoff,Kevin	28	R	5	AAA	80	117	53	$16
Castillo,Luis	34	B	4	BBB	89	33	110	$15
Pierre,Juan	32	L	7	ABB	94	36	141	$14
Hudson,Orlando	32	B	4	BBA	83	92	102	$14
Molina,Bengie	35	R	2	ABB	88	102	32	$14
Winn,Randy	35	B	978	AAB	84	78	111	$11
Griffey Jr.,Ken	40	L	0	BBB	80	123	21	$7

TIER 2

Low Risk, ++ PT

BATTERS	Age	Bats	Pos	REL	Ct%	PX	SX	R$
				BBB	**80**	**100**	**100**	**<$20**
*Kemp,Matt	26	R	8	AAB	77	134	136	$34
*Rodriguez,Alex	35	R	5	BAB	78	151	86	$30
*Wright,David	27	R	5	AAB	78	126	106	$28
*Longoria,Evan	25	R	5	ABA	76	160	89	$28
*Werth,Jayson	31	R	9	BBA	71	155	98	$27
*Youkilis,Kevin	31	R	35	AAB	77	164	71	$26
*Sizemore,Grady	28	L	8	BAB	79	130	129	$26
*Gonzalez,Adrian	28	L	3	AAB	79	150	44	$24
*Granderson,Curtis	29	L	8	AAB	78	127	137	$21
Escobar,Yunel	27	R	6	ABA	87	77	77	$19
Loney,James	26	L	3	AAA	87	87	75	$19
LaRoche,Adam	30	L	3	AAA	75	149	48	$19
Hawpe,Brad	31	L	9	AAB	72	157	58	$19
Tejada,Miguel	36	R	6	BAB	91	83	79	$18
Young,Delmon	25	R	7	AAA	80	99	82	$18
DeJesus,David	30	L	7	AAB	85	85	90	$17
Willingham,Josh	31	R	79	BBA	76	147	76	$17
Drew,J.D.	34	L	9	BBB	78	145	75	$17
Blake,Casey	37	R	5	BAA	77	120	82	$16
Cameron,Mike	37	R	8	BAA	71	147	83	$15
Young,Chris	27	R	8	AAA	73	146	117	$15
Polanco,Placido	35	R	4	AAB	93	63	87	$15
Cabrera,Orlando	35	R	6	AAA	89	66	92	$14
Martin,Russell	27	R	2	AAB	85	71	74	$14
Scutaro,Marco	34	R	6	ABB	87	68	79	$14
Suzuki,Kurt	27	R	2	ABA	88	79	63	$14
Peralta,Jhonny	28	R	56	AAB	77	105	53	$13
Scott,Luke	32	L	7	ABB	77	137	48	$12
Molina,Yadier	28	R	2	ABA	92	57	48	$12
Anderson,Garret	38	L	7	BBB	86	91	60	$12
Jacobs,Mike	29	L	0	ABB	73	138	39	$12
Overbay,Lyle	33	L	3	BBB	79	120	40	$12
Pierzynski,A.J.	33	L	2	ABA	88	73	44	$11
Rowand,Aaron	33	R	8	BAB	77	102	57	$11
Feliz,Pedro	35	R	5	BAA	87	76	46	$10
Schumaker,Skip	30	L	47	ABA	87	64	78	$10
Inge,Brandon	33	R	5	ABA	71	111	73	$10
Betancourt,Y	28	R	6	ABA	91	68	80	$8

TIER 1

High Skill, Low Risk

PITCHERS	Age	Thrw	REL	BPV	R$
			BBB	**75**	
Lincecum,Tim	25	R	AAA	127	$32
Halladay,Roy	32	R	BAA	125	$31
Sabathia,CC	29	L	AAB	107	$30
Hernandez,Felix	23	R	AAA	105	$29
Verlander,Justin	27	R	AAB	116	$29
Haren,Dan	29	R	AAA	129	$29
Greinke,Zack	26	R	AAA	116	$28
Beckett,Josh	29	R	BAA	119	$27
Rodriguez,Wandy	31	L	BAA	106	$25
Hamels,Cole	26	L	AAA	109	$24
Vazquez,Javier	33	R	AAB	127	$24
Jimenez,Ubaldo	26	R	AAB	84	$24
Nathan,Joe	35	R	AAA	121	$23
Baker,Scott	28	R	BAA	95	$23
Lilly,Ted	34	L	BAA	87	$22
Rivera,Mariano	40	R	AAA	131	$21
Garza,Matt	26	R	AAA	85	$21
Papelbon,Jonathan	29	R	AAB	129	$21
Shields,James	28	R	AAA	94	$21
Santana,Johan	31	L	BAA	95	$21
Billingsley,Chad	25	R	AAA	76	$20
Dempster,Ryan	32	R	BAA	87	$19
Oswalt,Roy	32	R	BAA	84	$17
Gregg,Kevin	31	R	AAA	76	$12

TIER 2

Mod Skill, Low Risk

PITCHERS	Age	Thrw	REL	BPV	R$
			BBB	**50**	**<$20**
*Weaver,Jered	28	R	AAA	70	$21
*Floyd,Gavin	27	R	AAA	74	$20
Cain,Matt	26	R	AAA	73	$19
Jurrjens,Jair	24	R	AAB	59	$19
Rodriguez,F	28	R	AAA	69	$18
Buehrle,Mark	31	L	AAA	60	$17
Cordero,Francisco	35	R	AAB	64	$17
Danks,John	25	L	AAB	61	$16
Pettitte,Andy	38	L	AAB	57	$14
Blanton,Joe	29	R	AAB	64	$14
Lowe,Derek	37	R	AAA	64	$14
Meche,Gil	32	R	BAA	62	$14
Arroyo,Bronson	33	R	AAA	55	$13
Pineiro,Joel	32	R	BAA	68	$12
Zambrano,Carlos	29	R	BAA	54	$12
Blackburn,Nick	28	R	AAA	54	$11
Sonnanstine,Andy	27	R	ABA	63	$11
Correia,Kevin	30	R	BBB	56	$11
Maholm,Paul	28	L	AAA	63	$11
Sherrill,George	33	L	ABB	71	$9
Duke,Zach	27	L	BAA	51	$7
Gaudin,Chad	27	R	AAA	50	$6
Villanueva,Carlos	26	R	ABB	72	$5
Ni,Fu-Te	27	L	ABB	51	$4

* Tier 2 players should be less than $20.
  If you are going to spend $20 or more
  here, be aware of the added risk.

PORTFOLIO3 PLAN

TIER 3

High Skill, High Risk	Filters:			n/a	80	100	100	<$10
BATTERS	Age	Bats	Pos	REL	Ct%	PX	SX	R$
Reimold,Nolan	26	R	7	ADC	81	124	81	$19
Hill,Aaron	28	R	4	DBC	85	112	61	$19
Guerrero,Vladimir	35	R	0	CBC	86	112	73	$19
Andrus,Elvis	21	R	6	ADB	85	55	141	$18
Beckham,Gordon	23	R	5	AFF	84	133	80	$18
Quentin,Carlos	27	R	7	CCF	84	129	70	$18
Aybar,Erick	26	B	6	BCC	88	60	128	$18
Furcal,Rafael	32	B	6	FBF	87	74	106	$18
Prado,Martin	26	R	453	BDB	88	107	71	$18
Wieters,Matt	23	B	2	AFF	82	107	46	$17
Borbon,Julio	24	L	0	AFA	89	52	123	$16
Matsui,Hideki	35	L	0	DBB	85	114	40	$16
Jones,Chipper	37	B	5	CAD	83	115	75	$16
Rivera,Juan	31	R	7	DDC	88	101	34	$15
Brantley,Michael	22	L	8	ADB	89	42	111	$15
Smith,Seth	27	L	7	ADB	83	121	99	$15
Johnson,Kelly	28	L	4	DBB	81	113	124	$15
Getz,Chris	26	L	4	BDA	87	56	118	$15
Matsui,Kaz	34	B	4	DBC	83	76	122	$14
Montero,Miguel	26	L	2	ADB	80	124	46	$14
Parra,Gerardo	22	L	78	AFA	85	75	105	$14
Barmes,Clint	31	R	4	BBD	81	108	100	$14
Valbuena,Luis	24	L	46	ADB	82	103	82	$14
Huff,Aubrey	33	L	30	AAF	84	108	47	$14
Izturis,Maicer	29	B	46	DCB	90	72	114	$13
Podsednik,Scott	34	L	78	CDB	84	66	128	$13
Gardner,Brett	26	L	8	BDA	81	51	173	$13
Schierholtz,Nate	26	L	9	ADC	83	114	102	$13
Rolen,Scott	35	R	5	DBB	85	100	80	$13
LaPorta,Matt	25	R	7	AFF	83	119	57	$13
Escobar,Alcides	23	R	6	ADB	87	49	126	$13
Guzman,Cristian	32	B	6	FCC	87	69	109	$13
Doumit,Ryan	29	B	2	FDB	81	115	67	$13
Fox,Jake	27	R	57	AFF	80	148	62	$12
Guillen,Carlos	34	B	70	DBB	82	101	84	$12
Ruiz,Carlos	31	R	2	ACD	88	114	51	$12
Velez,Eugenio	27	B	74	ADB	84	76	145	$11
Crisp,Coco	30	B	8	FCA	85	82	141	$11
Roberts,Ryan	29	R	4	AFB	81	86	101	$11
Spilborghs,Ryan	30	R	79	BDD	80	103	105	$10
Belliard,Ronnie	34	R	4	BCC	81	109	70	$10
Bloomquist,Willie	32	R	968	BDA	83	39	123	$10
Lugo,Julio	34	R	46	DCB	83	71	107	$10
Byrnes,Eric	34	R	7	FCC	87	107	115	$9
Taveras,Willy	28	R	8	BCC	86	29	138	$9
Pagan,Angel	28	B	87	FFC	83	95	138	$9
Barajas,Rod	34	R	2	ADB	82	105	31	$9
Lowrie,Jed	25	B	6	DDD	80	119	59	$8
Nady,Xavier	31	R	9	FCC	80	112	58	$8
Punto,Nick	32	B	46	CCC	81	53	113	$8
Izturis,Cesar	30	B	6	DCA	92	39	102	$8
Tatis,Fernando	35	R	357	ADB	82	113	80	$7
Burriss,Emmanuel	25	B	4	BFC	88	30	102	$7
Crowe,Trevor	26	B	78	ADD	83	71	113	$7
Ryan,Brendan	28	R	6	BDB	86	57	128	$7
Kapler,Gabe	34	R	9	AFA	82	115	82	$7
Crede,Joe	31	R	5	FDD	85	103	40	$6
Young Jr.,Eric	24	B	4	AFA	86	62	146	$6
Gwynn,Tony	27	L	8	ADD	86	39	118	$6
Marte,Andy	26	R	3	ADD	82	104	52	$6
Hoffpauir,Micah	30	L	39	AFF	83	123	74	$6
Pearce,Steven	26	R	3	ACC	81	112	70	$5
Towles,J.R.	26	R	2	AFD	80	101	68	$5
Tolbert,Matt	27	B	45	CFB	84	63	125	$5
Johnson,Reed	33	R	8	FDC	81	89	103	$4
Anderson,Josh	27	L	798	ACC	85	39	136	$4
Salazar,Oscar	31	R	7	ADD	86	106	63	$3
Evans,Nick	24	R	7	AFF	80	112	85	$3
Reddick,Josh	23	L	7	AFC	80	108	103	$3
Sullivan,Cory	30	L	7	ADA	85	59	115	$3
Wise,Dewayne	32	L	89	CFD	80	99	138	$3
Clement,Jeff	26	L	0	ADB	81	107	37	$3
Oeltjen,Trent	27	L	7	ADC	82	87	147	$3
Fuld,Sam	28	L	78	AFC	91	67	112	$1

High Skill, High Risk	Filters:		n/a	75	<$10
PITCHERS	Age	Thrw	REL	BPV	R$
Wilson,Brian	28	R	ABA	101	$19
Slowey,Kevin	25	R	DBB	99	$19
Soriano,Rafael	30	R	FCC	125	$19
Wood,Kerry	32	R	FCC	89	$19
Webb,Brandon	30	R	FAC	85	$19
Frasor,Jason	32	R	ACC	106	$18
Johnson,Josh	26	R	FCC	91	$18
Gallardo,Yovani	24	R	FCB	86	$18
Hoffman,Trevor	42	R	BBB	86	$18
Liriano,Francisco	26	L	FCA	76	$18
Sanchez,Jonathan	27	L	BBA	81	$18
Harden,Rich	28	R	FBA	92	$17
Scherzer,Max	25	R	ACC	100	$17
Wagner,Billy	38	L	FCA	143	$16
de la Rosa,Jorge	29	L	BBB	75	$16
Kuroda,Hiroki	35	R	DAB	87	$16
Cueto,Johnny	24	R	ABA	76	$16
Gonzalez,Mike	31	L	FDB	95	$15
Capps,Matt	26	R	BBA	95	$15
Jenks,Bobby	29	R	ABA	87	$15
Myers,Brett	29	R	FBA	81	$14
Pavano,Carl	34	R	FCB	78	$13
Lidge,Brad	33	R	BBB	76	$13
Hammel,Jason	27	R	ABA	84	$13
Bedard,Erik	31	L	FBC	95	$12
McDonald,James	25	R	ADA	78	$12
Lewis,Scott	26	L	FDB	79	$12
Martinez,Pedro	38	R	FCB	90	$12
Robertson,David	24	R	AFA	113	$12
Hughes,Phil	23	R	FDB	115	$12
Medlen,Kris	24	R	ADC	98	$12
Romo,Sergio	27	R	BDA	116	$11
Perez,Chris	24	R	ADB	108	$10
Bard,Daniel	24	R	AFA	116	$10
Smoltz,John	42	R	FCB	86	$10
Gregerson,Luke	25	R	ADB	110	$10
Dotel,Octavio	36	R	FCB	80	$10
Jepsen,Kevin	25	R	AFA	86	$9
League,Brandon	27	R	CDC	112	$9
Elbert,Scott	24	L	CDD	78	$9
Kelley,Shawn	25	R	BFB	100	$9
Betancourt,Rafael	34	R	CCB	93	$9
Carrasco,Carlos	23	R	ADC	89	$8
O'Day,Darren	27	R	BDC	86	$8
Uehara,Koji	35	R	FCD	81	$7
Masset,Nick	27	R	ADC	85	$7
Smith,Joe	26	R	CDA	97	$7
Walker,Tyler	33	R	DDB	93	$7
Thatcher,Joe	28	L	AFF	109	$7
Adams,Mike	31	R	FFB	97	$6
Kuo,Hong-Chih	28	L	FDC	112	$6
Balfour,Grant	32	R	DDC	85	$6
Badenhop,Burke	27	R	DDC	76	$6
Farnsworth,Kyle	33	R	ADB	98	$6
Coffey,Todd	29	R	ADF	88	$6
Neshek,Pat	29	R	FDA	89	$6
Motte,Jason	27	R	ADC	92	$6
Gervacio,Sammy	25	R	AFD	114	$5
Todd,Jess	23	R	ADA	83	$5
Miller,Trever	36	L	ADB	92	$5
Sipp,Tony	26	L	DFC	86	$5
Mujica,Edward	25	R	ADB	98	$5
Sanches,Brian	31	R	AFF	76	$4
Camp,Shawn	34	R	ADB	79	$4
Perdomo,Luis	25	R	ADA	75	$4
Maloney,Matt	26	L	ADC	81	$3
Zimmermann,Jordan	23	R	CDA	97	$1

ROTISSERIE AUCTION DRAFT — Top 560 players ranked for 75% depth leagues

NAME	POS	5x5	NAME	POS	5x5	NAME	POS	5x5	NAME	POS	5x5
Pujols,Albert	3	$37	Roberts,Brian	4	$23	Soriano,Rafael	P	$19	Gordon,Alex	5	$16
Kemp,Matt	8	$34	Kinsler,Ian	4	$23	Soriano,Alfonso	7	$19	Soto,Geovany	2	$16
Crawford,Carl	7	$34	Jeter,Derek	6	$23	Burnett,A.J.	P	$19	Cueto,Johnny	P	$16
Ramirez,Hanley	6	$33	Hunter,Torii	8	$23	Weeks,Rickie	4	$19	Murphy,David	7	$16
Lincecum,Tim	P	$32	Anderson,Brett	P	$22	Kubel,Jason	97	$19	Wolf,Randy	P	$16
Braun,Ryan	7	$32	Nolasco,Ricky	P	$22	Hawpe,Brad	9	$19	Rasmus,Colby	8	$16
Halladay,Roy	P	$31	Suzuki,Ichiro	9	$22	Wood,Kerry	P	$19	Headley,Chase	75	$16
Fielder,Prince	3	$30	Valverde,Jose	P	$22	Guerrero,Vladimir	0	$19	DeRosa,Mark	57	$16
Sabathia,CC	P	$30	Cano,Robinson	4	$22	Cantu,Jorge	35	$19	Cameron,Mike	8	$15
Rodriguez,Alex	5	$30	Markakis,Nick	9	$22	Webb,Brandon	P	$19	Gonzalez,Mike	P	$15
Ellsbury,Jacoby	8	$30	Carpenter,Chris	P	$22	Jones,Adam	8	$19	Castillo,Luis	4	$15
Utley,Chase	4	$29	Lilly,Ted	P	$22	Andrus,Elvis	6	$18	Bradley,Milton	9	$15
Holliday,Matt	7	$29	McLouth,Nate	8	$22	Frasor,Jason	P	$18	Swisher,Nick	93	$15
Rollins,Jimmy	6	$29	Rivera,Mariano	P	$21	Ramirez,Alexei	6	$18	Rivera,Juan	7	$15
Hernandez,Felix	P	$29	Garza,Matt	P	$21	Chamberlain,Joba	P	$18	Capps,Matt	P	$15
Verlander,Justin	P	$29	Kendrick,Howie	4	$21	Tejada,Miguel	6	$18	Fuentes,Brian	P	$15
Haren,Dan	P	$29	McCann,Brian	2	$21	Cabrera,Asdrubal	64	$18	Brantley,Michael	8	$15
Cabrera,Miguel	3	$29	Papelbon,Jonathan	P	$21	Johnson,Josh	P	$18	Smith,Seth	7	$15
Teixeira,Mark	3	$29	Bell,Heath	P	$21	Harang,Aaron	P	$18	Beltre,Adrian	5	$15
Greinke,Zack	P	$28	Young,Michael	5	$21	Young,Delmon	7	$18	Tillman,Chris	P	$15
Wright,David	5	$28	Shields,James	P	$21	Price,David	P	$18	Jenks,Bobby	P	$15
Longoria,Evan	5	$28	Figgins,Chone	5	$21	Beckham,Gordon	5	$18	Young,Chris	8	$15
Lester,Jon	P	$28	Granderson,Curtis	8	$21	Quentin,Carlos	7	$18	Johnson,Kelly	4	$15
Howard,Ryan	3	$28	Pence,Hunter	9	$21	Rodriguez,Francisco	P	$18	Hudson,Tim	P	$15
Votto,Joey	3	$28	Pena,Carlos	3	$21	Jones,Garrett	93	$18	Santana,Ervin	P	$15
Bailey,Andrew	P	$28	Damon,Johnny	7	$21	Gallardo,Yovani	P	$18	Murphy,Daniel	37	$15
Zimmerman,Ryan	5	$27	Hart,Corey	9	$21	Cabrera,Everth	6	$18	Jackson,Edwin	P	$15
Werth,Jayson	9	$27	Santana,Johan	P	$21	Aybar,Erick	6	$18	Dukes,Elijah	98	$15
Beckett,Josh	P	$27	Span,Denard	879	$21	Furcal,Rafael	6	$18	Getz,Chris	4	$15
Phillips,Brandon	4	$26	Weaver,Jered	P	$21	Stewart,Ian	54	$18	Polanco,Placido	4	$15
Bay,Jason	7	$26	Zobrist,Ben	49	$21	Hoffman,Trevor	P	$18	Blanks,Kyle	9	$15
Berkman,Lance	3	$26	Ibanez,Raul	7	$21	Howell,J.P.	P	$18	Callaspo,Alberto	4	$14
Cruz,Nelson	9	$26	Qualls,Chad	P	$21	Prado,Martin	453	$18	Matsui,Kaz	4	$14
Ramirez,Aramis	5	$26	Lopez,Jose	4	$21	Liriano,Francisco	P	$18	Cabrera,Orlando	6	$14
Upton,Justin	9	$26	Upton,B.J.	8	$20	Rios,Alex	98	$18	Montero,Miguel	2	$14
Youkilis,Kevin	35	$26	Uggla,Dan	4	$20	Buchholz,Clay	P	$18	Pierre,Juan	7	$14
Sizemore,Grady	8	$26	Cuddyer,Michael	93	$20	Sanchez,Jonathan	P	$18	Myers,Brett	P	$14
Victorino,Shane	8	$25	Davis,Rajai	8	$20	Jackson,Conor	7	$18	Pettitte,Andy	P	$14
Mauer,Joe	2	$25	Butler,Billy	3	$20	Harden,Rich	P	$17	Encarnacion,Edwin	5	$14
Lee,Carlos	7	$25	Peavy,Jake	P	$20	Oswalt,Roy	P	$17	Porcello,Rick	P	$14
Ethier,Andre	9	$25	Billingsley,Chad	P	$20	Morgan,Nyjer	78	$17	Martin,Russell	2	$14
Lee,Derrek	3	$25	Helton,Todd	3	$20	DeJesus,David	7	$17	Parra,Gerardo	78	$14
Reynolds,Mark	53	$25	Floyd,Gavin	P	$20	Scherzer,Max	P	$17	Hudson,Orlando	4	$14
Sandoval,Pablo	53	$25	Niemann,Jeff	P	$20	Buehrle,Mark	P	$17	Scutaro,Marco	6	$14
Abreu,Bobby	9	$25	Fowler,Dexter	8	$20	Ortiz,David	0	$17	Blanton,Joe	P	$14
Wainwright,Adam	P	$25	Francisco,Frank	P	$20	Dye,Jermaine	9	$17	Barmes,Clint	4	$14
Rodriguez,Wandy	P	$25	Coghlan,Chris	7	$20	Lowell,Mike	5	$17	Feldman,Scott	P	$14
Reyes,Jose	6	$25	Delgado,Carlos	3	$20	Byrd,Marlon	87	$17	Gomes,Jonny	79	$14
Pedroia,Dustin	4	$25	Thornton,Matt	P	$20	Cordero,Francisco	P	$17	Lowe,Derek	P	$14
Broxton,Jonathan	P	$25	Drew,Stephen	6	$19	Willingham,Josh	79	$17	Napoli,Mike	2	$14
Bourn,Michael	8	$24	Wells,Vernon	8	$19	Konerko,Paul	3	$17	Lopez,Felipe	4	$14
Lind,Adam	7	$24	Lackey,John	P	$19	Wieters,Matt	2	$17	Meche,Gil	P	$14
Hamels,Cole	P	$24	Martinez,Victor	23	$19	Kazmir,Scott	P	$17	Matsuzaka,Daisuke	P	$14
Gonzalez,Adrian	3	$24	Escobar,Yunel	6	$19	Drew,J.D.	9	$17	Matusz,Brian	P	$14
Vazquez,Javier	P	$24	Bartlett,Jason	6	$19	Gutierrez,Franklin	8	$17	Valbuena,Luis	46	$14
McCutchen,Andrew	8	$24	Wilson,Brian	P	$19	Davis,Chris	3	$17	Dickerson,Chris	789	$14
Ramirez,Manny	7	$24	Hamilton,Josh	89	$19	Theriot,Ryan	6	$17	Raburn,Ryan	7	$14
Lee,Cliff	P	$24	Loney,James	3	$19	Wagner,Billy	P	$16	Wood,Brandon	5	$14
Morneau,Justin	3	$24	Cain,Matt	P	$19	Borbon,Julio	0	$16	Maybin,Cameron	8	$14
Street,Huston	P	$24	Reimold,Nolan	7	$19	Matsui,Hideki	0	$16	Molina,Bengie	2	$14
Jimenez,Ubaldo	P	$24	Ludwick,Ryan	9	$19	Jones,Chipper	5	$16	Huff,Aubrey	30	$14
Hanson,Tommy	P	$23	Dempster,Ryan	P	$19	Diaz,Matt	97	$16	Iwamura,Akinori	4	$14
Choo,Shin-Soo	97	$23	Kershaw,Clayton	P	$19	de la Rosa,Jorge	P	$16	Suzuki,Kurt	2	$14
Morales,Kendry	3	$23	Bruce,Jay	9	$19	Aardsma,David	P	$16	Izturis,Maicer	46	$13
Nathan,Joe	P	$23	Hill,Aaron	4	$19	Kuroda,Hiroki	P	$16	Peralta,Jhonny	56	$13
Dunn,Adam	379	$23	Ross,Cody	89	$19	Snider,Travis	79	$16	Gutierrez,Juan	P	$13
Tulowitzki,Troy	6	$23	Gonzalez,Carlos	78	$19	Danks,John	P	$16	LaRoche,Andy	5	$13
Beltran,Carlos	8	$23	Slowey,Kevin	P	$19	Davis,Wade	P	$16	Pavano,Carl	P	$13
Soria,Joakim	P	$23	Jurrjens,Jair	P	$19	Blake,Casey	5	$16	Lidge,Brad	P	$13
Baker,Scott	P	$23	LaRoche,Adam	3	$19	Kouzmanoff,Kevin	5	$16	Hafner,Travis	0	$13

ROTISSERIE AUCTION DRAFT   Top 560 players ranked for 75% depth leagues

NAME	POS	5x5	NAME	POS	5x5	NAME	POS	5x5	NAME	POS	5x5
Podsednik,Scott	78	$13	Winn,Randy	978	$11	Carmona,Fausto	P	$9	Ray,Chris	P	$7
Hammel,Jason	P	$13	Correia,Kevin	P	$11	Moylan,Peter	P	$9	Clippard,Tyler	P	$7
Iannetta,Chris	2	$13	Velez,Eugenio	74	$11	Bannister,Brian	P	$9	Lewis,Fred	7	$7
Francoeur,Jeff	9	$13	Maholm,Paul	P	$11	Young,Chris	P	$9	Saltalamacchia,Ja	2	$7
Milledge,Lastings	7	$13	VandenHurk,Rick	P	$11	Jones,Andruw	0	$9	LeBlanc,Wade	P	$7
Gardner,Brett	8	$13	Crisp,Coco	8	$11	Thames,Marcus	7	$9	Uehara,Koji	P	$7
Schierholtz,Nate	9	$13	Gerut,Jody	89	$11	Elbert,Scott	P	$9	Nix,Laynce	7	$7
Sweeney,Ryan	98	$13	Roberts,Ryan	4	$11	Hairston,Jerry	567	$9	Tatis,Fernando	357	$7
Rolen,Scott	5	$13	Mazzaro,Vince	P	$11	Taveras,Willy	8	$9	Perez,Fernando	8	$7
McGehee,Casey	54	$13	Glaus,Troy	5	$11	Sherrill,George	P	$9	Lyon,Brandon	P	$7
Marcum,Shaun	P	$13	Atkins,Garrett	53	$11	Hochevar,Luke	P	$9	Duke,Zach	P	$7
Arroyo,Bronson	P	$13	Romo,Sergio	P	$11	Hunter,Tommy	P	$9	Davies,Kyle	P	$7
LaPorta,Matt	7	$13	Branyan,Russell	3	$11	Ankiel,Rick	897	$9	Masset,Nick	P	$7
Escobar,Alcides	6	$13	Kennedy,Adam	54	$11	Church,Ryan	98	$9	Duchscherer,Justi	P	$7
Guzman,Cristian	6	$13	Venable,Will	9	$11	Pagan,Angel	87	$9	Latos,Mat	P	$7
Burrell,Pat	0	$13	Cook,Aaron	P	$11	Freese,David	5	$9	Devine,Joey	P	$7
Thome,Jim	0	$13	Huff,David	P	$11	Volstad,Chris	P	$9	Mock,Garrett	P	$7
Saunders,Joe	P	$13	Renteria,Edgar	6	$11	Infante,Omar	4	$9	Cecil,Brett	P	$7
Doumit,Ryan	2	$13	Cahill,Trevor	P	$11	Kelley,Shawn	P	$9	Burriss,Emmanue	4	$7
Hairston,Scott	78	$13	Rowand,Aaron	8	$11	Casilla,Alexi	4	$9	Wheeler,Dan	P	$7
Ellis,Mark	4	$13	Aceves,Alfredo	P	$11	Ohlendorf,Ross	P	$9	McCarthy,Brando	P	$7
Fukudome,Kosuke	89	$13	Wuertz,Mike	P	$11	Nunez,Leo	P	$9	Smith,Joe	P	$7
Sanchez,Freddy	4	$13	Wells,Randy	P	$11	Morton,Charlie	P	$9	Eckstein,David	4	$7
Gonzalez,Gio	P	$13	Saunders,Michael	7	$11	Betancourt,Rafael	P	$9	Matthews Jr.,Gary	89	$7
Bergesen,Brad	P	$13	Sheets,Ben	P	$10	Pena,Brayan	20	$9	Walker,Tyler	P	$7
Braden,Dallas	P	$12	Feliz,Pedro	5	$10	Lannan,John	P	$9	Crowe,Trevor	78	$7
Cabrera,Melky	897	$12	Olivo,Miguel	2	$10	Davis,Doug	P	$9	Penny,Brad	P	$7
Bedard,Erik	P	$12	Baker,John	2	$10	Bush,David	P	$9	Guerrier,Matt	P	$7
McDonald,James	P	$12	Uribe,Juan	564	$10	Bautista,Jose	795	$9	Sanchez,Anibal	P	$7
Scott,Luke	7	$12	Pie,Felix	78	$10	Barajas,Rod	2	$9	Ryan,Brendan	6	$7
Molina,Yadier	2	$12	Mora,Melvin	5	$10	Guillen,Jose	9	$8	Thatcher,Joe	P	$7
Gomez,Carlos	8	$12	Garland,Jon	P	$10	Looper,Braden	P	$8	Buck,John	2	$7
Lewis,Scott	P	$12	Schumaker,Skip	47	$10	Niese,Jonathon	P	$8	Marshall,Sean	P	$7
Fox,Jake	57	$12	Perez,Chris	P	$10	Lowrie,Jed	6	$8	Carlson,Jesse	P	$7
Wigginton,Ty	350	$12	Bard,Daniel	P	$10	Aybar,Willy	340	$8	Tracy,Chad	3	$7
Happ,J.A.	P	$12	Romero,Ricky	P	$10	Nady,Xavier	9	$8	Nippert,Dustin	P	$7
Pineiro,Joel	P	$12	Spilborghs,Ryan	79	$10	Fontenot,Mike	45	$8	Kotchman,Casey	3	$7
Feliz,Neftali	P	$12	Belliard,Ronnie	4	$10	Lindstrom,Matt	P	$8	Baker,Jeff	45	$7
Gregg,Kevin	P	$12	Ruiz,Randy	0	$10	Maine,John	P	$8	Kapler,Gabe	9	$7
Anderson,Garret	7	$12	Inge,Brandon	5	$10	Parra,Manny	P	$8	Aviles,Mike	6	$6
Desmond,Ian	6	$12	Morrow,Brandon	P	$10	Corpas,Manny	P	$8	Pena,Tony	P	$6
Johnson,Nick	3	$12	Shoppach,Kelly	2	$10	Bumgarner,Madiso	P	$8	Tejeda,Robinson	P	$6
Wilson,C.J.	P	$12	Pelfrey,Mike	P	$10	Gonzalez,Alex	6	$8	Crede,Joe	5	$6
Franklin,Ryan	P	$12	Downs,Scott	P	$10	Pennington,Cliff	6	$8	Adams,Mike	P	$6
Jacobs,Mike	0	$12	Rzepczynski,Marc	P	$10	Punto,Nick	46	$8	Sanchez,Gaby	3	$6
Zambrano,Carlos	P	$12	Smoltz,John	P	$10	Carrasco,Carlos	P	$8	Heilman,Aaron	P	$6
Guillen,Carlos	70	$12	Hernandez,Ramon	23	$10	Sheffield,Gary	7	$8	Gaudin,Chad	P	$6
Madson,Ryan	P	$12	Lohse,Kyle	P	$10	Garko,Ryan	3	$8	Nix,Jayson	4	$6
Hermida,Jeremy	97	$12	Barton,Daric	3	$10	Hanrahan,Joel	P	$8	Young,Delwyn	49	$6
Blalock,Hank	30	$12	Washburn,Jarrod	P	$10	Bailey,Homer	P	$8	Gamel,Mat	5	$6
Cust,Jack	9	$12	Gorzelanny,Tom	P	$10	Harris,Willie	87	$8	Ramirez,Ramon	P	$6
Ruiz,Carlos	2	$12	Johnson,Jim	P	$10	O'Day,Darren	P	$8	Feliciano,Pedro	P	$6
Posada,Jorge	2	$12	Marquis,Jason	P	$10	Hundley,Nick	2	$8	Herrera,Daniel	P	$6
Martinez,Pedro	P	$12	Zito,Barry	P	$10	Ziegler,Brad	P	$8	Breslow,Craig	P	$6
Overbay,Lyle	3	$12	Bloomquist,Willie	968	$10	Izturis,Cesar	6	$8	Young Jr.,Eric	4	$6
Ordonez,Magglio	90	$12	Padilla,Vicente	P	$10	Giles,Brian	9	$8	Avila,Alex	2	$6
Robertson,David	P	$12	Stubbs,Drew	8	$10	Posey,Buster	2	$8	Laird,Gerald	2	$6
Richard,Clayton	P	$12	Gregerson,Luke	P	$10	Rodriguez,Sean	4	$8	Hinske,Eric	9	$6
Rodney,Fernando	P	$12	Flores,Jesus	2	$10	Betancourt,Yuniesk	6	$8	Bonifacio,Emilio	5	$6
Marmol,Carlos	P	$12	Paulino,Felipe	P	$10	Mickolio,Kam	P	$8	Wilson,Jack	6	$6
Hughes,Phil	P	$12	Lugo,Julio	46	$10	Bulger,Jason	P	$8	Francisco,Ben	7	$6
Masterson,Justin	P	$12	Dotel,Octavio	P	$10	Martin,J.D.	P	$8	Gwynn,Tony	8	$6
Medlen,Kris	P	$12	Rowland-Smith,Ry	P	$10	Garcia,Freddy	P	$8	Gallagher,Sean	P	$6
Holland,Derek	P	$11	Guthrie,Jeremy	P	$10	West,Sean	P	$7	Kuo,Hong-Chih	P	$6
Pierzynski,A.J.	2	$11	Jepsen,Kevin	P	$9	Kennedy,Ian	P	$7	Okajima,Hideki	P	$6
Blackburn,Nick	P	$11	League,Brandon	P	$9	Griffey Jr.,Ken	0	$7	Hernandez,David	P	$6
Sonnanstine,Andy	P	$11	Byrnes,Eric	7	$9	Giambi,Jason	30	$7	Coke,Phil	P	$6
Teahen,Mark	59	$11	Martinez,Fernando	7	$9	Rodriguez,Ivan	2	$7	Kendall,Jason	2	$6
Hardy,J.J.	6	$11	Kawakami,Kenshin	P	$9	McCutchen,Daniel	P	$7	Balfour,Grant	P	$6
Millwood,Kevin	P	$11	Norris,Bud	P	$9	Hawkins,LaTroy	P	$7	Mitre,Sergio	P	$6

ROTISSERIE SNAKE DRAFT   15 TEAM MIXED LEAGUE

#	NAME	POS	#	NAME	POS	#	NAME	POS	#	NAME	POS
1	Pujols,Albert	3	5	Hunter,Torii	8	9	Ross,Cody	89	13	Webb,Brandon	P
	Ramirez,Hanley	6		Abreu,Bobby	9		Gonzalez,Carlos	78		Napoli,Mike	2
	Braun,Ryan	7		Zobrist,Ben	49		Papelbon,Jonathan	P		Frasor,Jason	P
	Utley,Chase	4		Roberts,Brian	4		Bell,Heath	P		Chamberlain,Joba	P
	Kemp,Matt	8		Suzuki,Ichiro	9		Prado,Martin	453		Castillo,Luis	4
	Mauer,Joe	2		Wainwright,Adam	P		Shields,James	P		Johnson,Josh	P
	Crawford,Carl	7		Kinsler,Ian	4		Figgins,Chone	5		Harang,Aaron	P
	Fielder,Prince	3		Rodriguez,Wandy	P		LaRoche,Adam	3		Price,David	P
	Rodriguez,Alex	5		Lopez,Jose	4		Soriano,Alfonso	7		Molina,Bengie	2
	Holliday,Matt	7		Broxton,Jonathan	P		Soto,Geovany	2		Suzuki,Kurt	2
	Lincecum,Tim	P		Bourn,Michael	8		Kubel,Jason	97		Matsui,Hideki	0
	Cabrera,Miguel	3		Hamels,Cole	P		Bartlett,Jason	6		Jones,Chipper	5
	Teixeira,Mark	3		Uggla,Dan	4		Santana,Johan	P		Rodriguez,Francisco	P
	Wright,David	5		Markakis,Nick	9		Hawpe,Brad	9		Diaz,Matt	97
	Phillips, Brandon	4		Vazquez,Javier	P		Span,Denard	879		Gallardo,Yovani	P
2	Rollins,Jimmy	6	6	McCutchen,Andrew	8	10	Weaver,Jered	P	14	Snider,Travis	79
	Longoria,Evan	5		McLouth,Nate	8		Guerrero,Vladimir	0		Johnson,Kelly	4
	Halladay,Roy	P		Lee,Cliff	P		Cantu,Jorge	35		Hoffman,Trevor	P
	Howard,Ryan	3		Street,Huston	P		Jones,Adam	8		Howell,J.P.	P
	Votto,Joey	3		Young,Michael	5		Qualls,Chad	P		Blake,Casey	5
	Zimmerman,Ryan	5		Granderson,Curtis	8		Young,Delmon	7		Kouzmanoff,Kevin	5
	Werth,Jayson	9		Jimenez,Ubaldo	P		Upton,B.J.	8		Gordon,Alex	5
	Sabathia,CC	P		Hanson,Tommy	P		Beckham,Gordon	5		Liriano,Francisco	P
	Ellsbury,Jacoby	8		Pence,Hunter	9		Theriot,Ryan	6		Buchholz,Clay	P
	Pedroia,Dustin	4		Drew,Stephen	6		Quentin,Carlos	7		Sanchez,Jonathan	P
	Bay,Jason	7		Pena,Carlos	3		Jones,Garrett	93		Iannetta,Chris	2
	Hernandez,Felix	P		Damon,Johnny	7		Davis,Rajai	8		Murphy,David	7
	Verlander,Justin	P		Escobar,Yunel	6		Andrus,Elvis	6		Rasmus,Colby	8
	Berkman,Lance	3		Nathan,Joe	P		Peavy,Jake	P		Polanco,Placido	4
	Cruz,Nelson	9		Hart,Corey	9		Billingsley,Chad	P		Harden,Rich	P
3	Haren,Dan	P	7	Hill,Aaron	4	11	Floyd,Gavin	P	15	Headley,Chase	75
	Ramirez,Aramis	5		Soria,Joakim	P		Niemann,Jeff	P		Oswalt,Roy	P
	Upton,Justin	9		Baker,Scott	P		Fowler,Dexter	8		Callaspo,Alberto	4
	Youkilis,Kevin	35		Ibanez,Raul	7		Francisco,Frank	P		Matsui,Kaz	4
	Greinke,Zack	P		Weeks,Rickie	4		Rios,Alex	98		Morgan,Nyjer	78
	McCann,Brian	2		Anderson,Brett	P		Thornton,Matt	P		Cabrera,Orlando	6
	Tulowitzki,Troy	6		Wieters,Matt	2		Jackson,Conor	7		DeRosa,Mark	57
	Lester,Jon	P		Nolasco,Ricky	P		Lackey,John	P		Cameron,Mike	8
	Lee,Carlos	7		Cuddyer,Michael	93		Wilson,Brian	P		Scherzer,Max	P
	Ethier,Andre	9		Butler,Billy	3		Cain,Matt	P		Buehrle,Mark	P
	Lee,Derrek	3		Valverde,Jose	P		Cabrera,Everth	6		Hudson,Orlando	4
	Reynolds,Mark	53		Ramirez,Alexei	6		Dempster,Ryan	P		Scutaro,Marco	6
	Bailey,Andrew	P		Tejada,Miguel	6		Kershaw,Clayton	P		Cordero,Francisco	P
	Sandoval,Pablo	53		Cabrera,Asdrubal	64		DeJesus,David	7		Bradley,Milton	9
	Jeter,Derek	6		Helton,Todd	3		Montero,Miguel	2		Doumit,Ryan	2
4	Lind,Adam	7	8	Coghlan,Chris	7	12	Slowey,Kevin	P	16	Swisher,Nick	93
	Gonzalez,Adrian	3		Delgado,Carlos	3		Jurrjens,Jair	P		Barmes,Clint	4
	Beckett,Josh	P		Carpenter,Chris	P		Soriano,Rafael	P		Rivera,Juan	7
	Reyes,Jose	6		Lilly,Ted	P		Ortiz,David	0		Kazmir,Scott	P
	Ramirez,Manny	7		Wells,Vernon	8		Burnett,A.J.	P		Smith,Seth	7
	Morneau,Justin	3		Hamilton,Josh	89		Dye,Jermaine	9		Beltre,Adrian	5
	Cano,Robinson	4		Loney,James	3		Lowell,Mike	5		Lopez,Felipe	4
	Choo,Shin-Soo	97		Reimold,Nolan	7		Martin,Russell	2		Young,Chris	8
	Morales,Kendry	3		Aybar,Erick	6		Byrd,Marlon	87		Molina,Yadier	2
	Martinez,Victor	23		Ludwick,Ryan	9		Willingham,Josh	79		Valbuena,Luis	46
	Dunn,Adam	379		Rivera,Mariano	P		Konerko,Paul	3		Murphy,Daniel	37
	Beltran,Carlos	8		Furcal,Rafael	6		Wood,Kerry	P		Wagner,Billy	P
	Kendrick,Howie	4		Bruce,Jay	9		Drew,J.D.	9		Dukes,Elijah	98
	Sizemore,Grady	8		Stewart,Ian	54		Gutierrez,Franklin	8		Iwamura,Akinori	4
	Victorino,Shane	8		Garza,Matt	P		Davis,Chris	3		Borbon,Julio	0

ROTISSERIE SNAKE DRAFT   15 TEAM MIXED LEAGUE

#	NAME	POS	#	NAME	POS	#	NAME	POS	#	NAME	POS
17	Izturis,Maicer	46	21	Meche,Gil	P	25	Richard,Clayton	P	29	Washburn,Jarrod	P
	Blanks,Kyle	9		Matsuzaka,Daisuke	P		Rodney,Fernando	P		Gorzelanny,Tom	P
	de la Rosa,Jorge	P		Matusz,Brian	P		Saunders,Michael	7		Johnson,Jim	P
	Aardsma,David	P		Fox,Jake	57		Marmol,Carlos	P		Marquis,Jason	P
	Kuroda,Hiroki	P		Wigginton,Ty	350		Bloomquist,Willie	968		Zito,Barry	P
	Danks,John	P		Hardy,J.J.	6		Hughes,Phil	P		Rodriguez,Ivan	2
	Davis,Wade	P		Anderson,Garret	7		Masterson,Justin	P		Punto,Nick	46
	Encarnacion,Edwin	5		Johnson,Nick	3		Feliz,Pedro	5		Ankiel,Rick	897
	Ruiz,Carlos	2		Jacobs,Mike	0		Medlen,Kris	P		Church,Ryan	98
	Cueto,Johnny	P		Velez,Eugenio	74		Lugo,Julio	46		Pagan,Angel	87
	Posada,Jorge	2		Guillen,Carlos	70		Pie,Felix	78		Freese,David	5
	Wolf,Randy	P		Gutierrez,Juan	P		Mora,Melvin	5		Padilla,Vicente	P
	Getz,Chris	4		Shoppach,Kelly	2		Holland,Derek	P		Saltalamacchia,Jarr	2
	Parra,Gerardo	78		Pavano,Carl	P		Blackburn,Nick	P		Gregerson,Luke	P
	Gomes,Jonny	79		Roberts,Ryan	4		Sonnanstine,Andy	P		Paulino,Felipe	P
18	McGehee,Casey	54	22	Lidge,Brad	P	26	Spilborghs,Ryan	79	30	Dotel,Octavio	P
	Gonzalez,Mike	P		Hermida,Jeremy	97		Pena,Brayan	20		Rowland-Smith,Ryal	P
	Escobar,Alcides	6		Podsednik,Scott	78		Barajas,Rod	2		Guthrie,Jeremy	P
	Guzman,Cristian	6		Hernandez,Ramon	23		Ruiz,Randy	0		Jepsen,Kevin	P
	Dickerson,Chris	789		Blalock,Hank	30		Millwood,Kevin	P		League,Brandon	P
	Pierzynski,A.J.	2		Cust,Jack	9		Correia,Kevin	P		Bautista,Jose	795
	Raburn,Ryan	7		Hammel,Jason	P		Inge,Brandon	5		Guillen,Jose	9
	Capps,Matt	P		Kennedy,Adam	54		Maholm,Paul	P		Kawakami,Kenshin	P
	Fuentes,Brian	P		Overbay,Lyle	3		VandenHurk,Rick	P		Izturis,Cesar	6
	Ellis,Mark	4		Ordonez,Magglio	90		Mazzaro,Vince	P		Norris,Bud	P
	Brantley,Michael	8		Gardner,Brett	8		Barton,Daric	3		Nady,Xavier	9
	Wood,Brandon	5		Marcum,Shaun	P		Romo,Sergio	P		Carmona,Fausto	P
	Sanchez,Freddy	4		Arroyo,Bronson	P		Hairston,Jerry	567		Rodriguez,Sean	4
	Maybin,Cameron	8		Renteria,Edgar	6		Cook,Aaron	P		Moylan,Peter	P
	Huff,Aubrey	30		Flores,Jesus	2		Stubbs,Drew	8		Bannister,Brian	P
19	Tillman,Chris	P	23	Saunders,Joe	P	27	Huff,David	P			
	Jenks,Bobby	P		Teahen,Mark	59		Cahill,Trevor	P			
	Peralta,Jhonny	56		Gonzalez,Gio	P		Aceves,Alfredo	P			
	LaRoche,Andy	5		Winn,Randy	978		Wuertz,Mike	P			
	Hudson,Tim	P		Bergesen,Brad	P		Wells,Randy	P			
	Santana,Ervin	P		Braden,Dallas	P		Hundley,Nick	2			
	Hafner,Travis	0		Bedard,Erik	P		Byrnes,Eric	7			
	Jackson,Edwin	P		McDonald,James	P		Sheets,Ben	P			
	Desmond,Ian	6		Uribe,Juan	564		Infante,Omar	4			
	Francoeur,Jeff	9		Schumaker,Skip	47		Martinez,Fernando	7			
	Milledge,Lastings	7		Crisp,Coco	8		Casilla,Alexi	4			
	Schierholtz,Nate	9		Gerut,Jody	89		Garland,Jon	P			
	Sweeney,Ryan	98		Gomez,Carlos	8		Perez,Chris	P			
	Pierre,Juan	7		Lewis,Scott	P		Bard,Daniel	P			
	Myers,Brett	P		Happ,J.A.	P		Romero,Ricky	P			
20	Rolen,Scott	5	24	Pineiro,Joel	P	28	Posey,Buster	2			
	Pettitte,Andy	P		Feliz,Neftali	P		Jones,Andruw	0			
	LaPorta,Matt	7		Belliard,Ronnie	4		Thames,Marcus	7			
	Porcello,Rick	P		Glaus,Troy	5		Lowrie,Jed	6			
	Burrell,Pat	0		Atkins,Garrett	53		Aybar,Willy	340			
	Thome,Jim	0		Gregg,Kevin	P		Taveras,Willy	8			
	Blanton,Joe	P		Branyan,Russell	3		Fontenot,Mike	45			
	Hairston,Scott	78		Wilson,C.J.	P		Morrow,Brandon	P			
	Feldman,Scott	P		Franklin,Ryan	P		Pelfrey,Mike	P			
	Lowe,Derek	P		Venable,Will	9		Downs,Scott	P			
	Fukudome,Kosuke	89		Zambrano,Carlos	P		Rzepczynski,Marc	P			
	Olivo,Miguel	2		Madson,Ryan	P		Gonzalez,Alex	6			
	Baker,John	2		Rowand,Aaron	8		Smoltz,John	P			
	Cabrera,Melky	897		Martinez,Pedro	P		Lohse,Kyle	P			
	Scott,Luke	7		Robertson,David	P		Pennington,Cliff	6			

MAYBERRY METHOD — TOP 250 BATTERS — Pure Skills Ratings

POWER (PX)	
0-49	0
50-79	1
80-99	2
100-119	3
120-159	4
160+	5

SPEED (SX)	
0-49	0
50-79	1
80-99	2
100-119	3
120-139	4
140+	5

Expected BA	
.000 - .239	0
.240 - .254	1
.255 - .269	2
.270 - .284	3
.285 - .299	4
.300+	5

These rankings represent each player's base skill level, regardless of playing time. All players within a section are similar commodities from a skills perspective. Asterisked players (*) are potential sleepers, those with good skill whose ranking could rise with more playing time or better role.

BATTERS	P	S	B	REL
Braun,Ryan	5	4	4	AAC
Rollins,Jimmy	3	5	4	AAB
Utley,Chase	4	4	3	AAA
Pujols,Albert	5	1	5	AAB
Kemp,Matt	4	4	3	AAB
Votto,Joey	5	1	5	ABC
*Gonzalez,Carlos	4	4	3	ADF
Crawford,Carl	2	5	4	BAC
Kinsler,Ian	4	4	3	CAC
Teixeira,Mark	4	1	5	AAA
Victorino,Shane	2	5	3	AAA
Ramirez,Hanley	4	3	3	AAA
Pedroia,Dustin	3	2	5	AAA
Roberts,Brian	3	4	3	AAA
Wright,David	4	3	3	AAB
Granderson,Curtis	4	4	2	AAB
Youkilis,Kevin	5	1	4	AAB
Holliday,Matt	4	2	4	AAB
Fielder,Prince	5	1	4	AAD
Longoria,Evan	5	2	3	ABA
*Stewart,Ian	5	3	2	ACA
McCutchen,Andrew	3	4	3	ACB
Cruz,Nelson	5	2	3	ACC
*Schierholtz,Nate	3	3	4	ADC
Sandoval,Pablo	4	1	5	ADC
*Fowler,Dexter	3	5	2	AFA
Beckham,Gordon	4	2	4	AFF
Sizemore,Grady	4	4	2	BAB
Rodriguez,Alex	4	2	4	BAB
Tulowitzki,Troy	4	3	3	BAD
Upton,Justin	4	4	2	CCA
Zobrist,Ben	4	3	3	CCD
*Beltran,Carlos	3	3	4	DAA
Cuddyer,Michael	4	3	3	DBC
*Kendrick,Howie	3	3	4	DDA
Reyes,Jose	2	5	3	FAB
Abreu,Bobby	3	3	3	AAA
Phillips,Brandon	3	3	3	AAA
Ellsbury,Jacoby	1	5	3	AAB
Damon,Johnny	3	3	3	AAB
Ethier,Andre	4	1	4	AAB
Pence,Hunter	4	2	3	AAB
Cabrera,Miguel	4	1	4	AAB
Reynolds,Mark	5	3	1	AAC
Bay,Jason	5	2	2	AAC
Howard,Ryan	5	1	3	AAC
*Pierre,Juan	0	5	4	ABB
McCann,Brian	4	1	4	ABC
Lind,Adam	4	1	4	ABC
*Lewis,Fred	3	4	2	ACB
*Maybin,Cameron	3	4	2	ADA
Andrus,Elvis	1	5	3	ADB
*Smith,Seth	4	2	3	ADB
Reimold,Nolan	4	2	3	ADC
*Davis,Chris	5	1	3	ADC
Coghlan,Chris	2	3	4	ADD
*Raburn,Ryan	4	3	2	ADF
*Young Jr.,Eric	1	5	3	AFA
Zimmerman,Ryan	4	1	4	BAB
Berkman,Lance	4	1	4	BAC
Lee,Derrek	4	1	4	BAC
Mauer,Joe	3	1	5	BAC
Jones,Adam	3	3	3	BBC
*Murphy,David	4	2	3	BCA
Choo,Shin-Soo	4	3	2	BCF
*Spilborghs,Ryan	3	3	3	BDD
Hunter,Torii	4	2	3	CAB
Ramirez,Aramis	4	1	4	CBA
Hamilton,Josh	4	2	3	CCC
*Torres,Andres	4	5	0	CFC
*Johnson,Kelly	3	4	2	DBB
*Diaz,Matt	3	3	3	DDF
*Crisp,Coco	2	5	2	FCA

BATTERS	P	S	B	REL
Young,Chris	4	3	1	AAA
Morneau,Justin	4	0	4	AAA
Gonzalez,Adrian	4	0	4	AAB
Dye,Jermaine	4	1	3	AAB
Lopez,Jose	3	1	4	AAB
Rios,Alex	3	3	2	AAC
Young,Michael	3	1	4	AAC
Drew,Stephen	3	3	2	AAC
Cano,Robinson	3	1	4	AAD
Cabrera,Asdrubal	2	3	3	ABB
Butler,Billy	4	0	4	ABC
Ramirez,Manny	4	0	4	ABC
Wood,Brandon	4	2	2	ACA
Murphy,Daniel	3	1	4	ACB
Ruiz,Carlos	3	1	4	ACD
Jones,Garrett	4	2	2	ACD
*Hinske,Eric	4	2	2	ADB
*Tatis,Fernando	3	2	3	ADB
*Velez,Eugenio	1	5	2	ADB
Valbuena,Luis	3	2	3	ADB
*Oeltjen,Trent	2	5	1	ADC
Pie,Felix	3	3	2	ADC
*Rodriguez,Sean	4	3	1	ADC
Davis,Rajai	1	5	2	ADD
*Iannetta,Chris	5	1	2	ADF
Gomes,Jonny	5	2	1	ADF
*Kapler,Gabe	3	2	3	AFA
*Pena,Brayan	2	1	5	AFA
Borbon,Julio	1	4	3	AFA
*Fuld,Sam	1	3	4	AFC
*Fox,Jake	4	1	3	AFF
*Allen,Brandon	4	2	2	AFF
Ibanez,Raul	4	1	3	BAA
Blake,Casey	4	2	2	BAA
Lee,Carlos	3	1	4	BAB
Pena,Carlos	5	1	2	BAC
Werth,Jayson	4	2	2	BBA
Willingham,Josh	4	1	3	BBA
Hudson,Orlando	2	3	3	BBA
Byrd,Marlon	3	2	3	BBB
Kubel,Jason	4	1	3	BBB
McLouth,Nate	3	4	1	BBB
Hart,Corey	3	3	2	BBB
Drew,J.D.	4	1	3	BBB
Fukudome,Kosuke	3	2	3	BBC
Bartlett,Jason	2	4	2	BBC
Ross,Cody	4	1	3	BCD
Prado,Martin	3	1	4	BDB
*Napoli,Mike	5	1	2	BDF
Guerrero,Vladimir	3	1	4	CBC
Quentin,Carlos	4	1	3	CCF
Bruce,Jay	4	2	2	CDC
*Blanco,Andres	2	2	4	CFD
Cabrera,Everth	1	5	2	CFF
Gordon,Alex	4	2	2	DBB
Soriano,Alfonso	4	2	2	DBC
*Byrnes,Eric	3	3	2	FCC
Weeks,Rickie	3	5	0	FCC
Blalock,Hank	4	1	3	FDC
*Pagan,Angel	2	4	2	FFC

BATTERS	P	S	B	REL
LaRoche,Adam	4	0	3	AAA
DeJesus,David	2	2	3	AAB
Dunn,Adam	5	0	2	AAB
Konerko,Paul	4	0	3	AAB
Suzuki,Ichiro	1	3	3	AAB
Hawpe,Brad	4	1	2	AAB
Markakis,Nick	3	1	3	AAC
Jeter,Derek	1	2	4	AAC
Upton,B.J.	3	3	1	AAD
*Harris,Willie	2	4	1	ACA
*Olivo,Miguel	4	2	1	ACB
*Francisco,Ben	4	1	2	ACB
*Patterson,Eric	2	4	1	ACB
Morales,Kendry	4	0	3	ACC
Span,Denard	1	4	2	ACC
*Ankiel,Rick	4	2	1	ACD
*Catalanotto,Frank	2	2	3	ADA
Montero,Miguel	4	0	3	ADB
*Joyce,Matt	4	2	1	ADB
*McDonald,Darnell	3	3	1	ADC
Michaels,Jason	4	2	1	ADC
*Fontenot,Mike	3	2	2	ADF
*Ramirez,Wilkin	3	4	0	AFC
LaPorta,Matt	3	1	3	AFF
*Evans,Nick	3	2	2	AFF
*Hoffpauir,Micah	4	1	2	AFF
Cameron,Mike	4	2	1	BAA
Tejada,Miguel	2	1	4	BAB
*Ordonez,Magglio	3	0	4	BAC
Ortiz,David	4	0	3	BAD
*Thome,Jim	5	0	2	BBB
Overbay,Lyle	4	0	3	BBB
Barmes,Clint	3	3	1	BBD
Callaspo,Alberto	2	1	4	BCB
Morgan,Nyjer	0	5	2	BCB
Aybar,Erick	1	4	2	BCC
Bourn,Michael	1	5	1	BCF
Dickerson,Chris	2	4	1	BDB
*Ryan,Brendan	1	4	2	BDB
*Nix,Laynce	4	1	2	BFB
Helton,Todd	3	0	4	CAD
Jones,Chipper	3	1	3	CAD
Lowell,Mike	3	1	3	CBB
*Branyan,Russell	5	1	1	CDB
Podsednik,Scott	1	4	2	CDB
*Ransom,Cody	4	3	0	CDC
*Tolbert,Matt	1	4	2	CFB
*Baker,Jeff	3	2	2	CFC
*Wise,Dewayne	2	4	1	CFD
Rolen,Scott	3	2	2	DBB
Guillen,Carlos	3	2	2	DBB
Hill,Aaron	3	1	3	DBC
Matsui,Kaz	1	4	2	DBC
Hairston,Scott	4	2	1	DCA
*Izturis,Maicer	1	3	3	DCB
Delgado,Carlos	4	0	3	FBB
Furcal,Rafael	1	3	3	FBF
Guzman,Cristian	1	3	3	FCC
*Nady,Xavier	3	1	3	FCC
*Posada,Jorge	4	0	3	FCD
*Doumit,Ryan	3	1	3	FDB
*Johnson,Reed	2	3	2	FDC
*Abreu,Tony	2	2	3	FFA
*Gerut,Jody	2	2	3	FFD

BATTERS	P	S	B	REL
Kouzmanoff,Kevin	3	1	2	AAA
Teahen,Mark	2	2	2	AAA
Loney,James	2	1	3	AAA
Young,Delmon	2	2	2	AAA
Peralta,Jhonny	3	1	2	AAB
Winn,Randy	1	3	2	AAB
Polanco,Placido	1	2	3	AAB
Uggla,Dan	4	1	1	AAC
Swisher,Nick	4	0	2	AAD
Schumaker,Skip	1	1	4	ABA
Scott,Luke	4	0	2	ABB
Cabrera,Melky	1	2	3	ABC
Gutierrez,Franklin	2	3	1	ABC
Ludwick,Ryan	4	1	1	ABF
*Bonifacio,Emilio	0	5	1	ACA
Uribe,Juan	3	1	2	ACB
Ruiz,Randy	4	1	1	ACB
Headley,Chase	3	2	1	ACC
*Pearce,Steven	3	1	2	ACC
*Anderson,Josh	0	4	2	ACC
*Sullivan,Cory	1	3	2	ADA
Brantley,Michael	0	3	3	ADB
Snider,Travis	4	1	1	ADB
*Balentien,Wladimir	4	1	1	ADB
*Crowe,Trevor	1	3	2	ADD
Salazar,Oscar	3	1	2	ADD
*Maxwell,Justin	2	4	0	AFA
Parra,Gerardo	1	3	2	AFA
*Nix,Jayson	3	2	1	AFB
*Greene,Tyler	2	4	0	AFB
*Reddick,Josh	3	3	0	AFC
*Sutton,Drew	3	2	1	AFC
Sanchez,Freddy	2	1	3	BAC
Wells,Vernon	2	2	2	BAC
DeRosa,Mark	3	1	2	BAC
Figgins,Chone	1	4	1	BAD
Castillo,Luis	0	3	3	BBB
Griffey Jr.,Ken	4	0	2	BBB
Barton,Daric	3	1	2	BBC
Gomez,Carlos	1	5	0	BCA
Belliard,Ronnie	3	1	2	BCC
Gardner,Brett	1	5	0	BDA
Getz,Chris	1	3	2	BDA
Buck,John	4	1	1	BDB
*Gload,Ross	2	1	3	BDB
Beltre,Adrian	2	2	2	CAB
Ellis,Mark	2	2	2	CBA
Martinez,Victor	3	0	3	CBD
Church,Ryan	3	1	2	CCB
Jones,Andruw	4	1	1	CCF
Dukes,Elijah	3	2	1	CDD
Hairston,Jerry	2	2	2	CDF
Matsui,Hideki	3	0	3	DBB
Soto,Geovany	4	0	2	DCD
Bradley,Milton	3	1	2	DCF
Hafner,Travis	4	0	2	DCF
Rivera,Juan	3	0	3	DDC
Jackson,Conor	2	2	2	FCD
Perez,Fernando	1	5	0	FDD
*Baldelli,Rocco	3	2	1	FFD
*Chavez,Eric	4	0	2	FFF

MAYBERRY METHOD   TOP 235 PITCHERS   Pure Skills Ratings

Expected ERA	
0.00 - 3.19	5
3.20 - 3.59	4
3.60 - 3.99	3
4.00 - 4.39	2
4.40 - 4.79	1
4.80+	0

Dominance (K/9)	
0.0 - 4.9	0
5.0 - 5.9	1
6.0 - 6.9	2
7.0 - 7.9	3
8.0 - 8.9	4
9.0+	5

Saves potential	
0	No hope for saves; starting pitchers
1	Speculative closer
2	Frontline or shared closer in a pen with alternatives
3	Frontline closer in a firm bullpen role

PITCHERS	E	K	S	REL
Lincecum,Tim	5	5	0	AAA
Nathan,Joe	5	5	3	AAA
Broxton,Jonathan	5	5	3	ABA
Bell,Heath	5	5	3	ABB
*Thornton,Matt	5	5	2	ACB
*Feliciano,Pedro	5	5	0	ACB
*Robertson,David	5	5	1	AFA
*Bard,Daniel	5	5	0	AFA
*Gervacio,Sammy	5	5	0	AFD
Soria,Joakim	5	5	3	BBA
Street,Huston	5	5	3	BBB
Wagner,Billy	5	5	2	FCA
Hernandez,Felix	5	4	0	AAA
Haren,Dan	5	4	0	AAA
Rivera,Mariano	5	4	3	AAA
*Madson,Ryan	5	4	1	BCA
*League,Brandon	5	4	0	CDC
Greinke,Zack	4	5	0	AAA
Papelbon,Jonathan	4	5	3	AAB
Verlander,Justin	4	5	0	AAB
Vazquez,Javier	4	5	0	AAB
Wilson,Brian	4	5	3	ABA
Howell,J.P.	4	5	2	ACA
*Wuertz,Mike	4	5	0	ACB
Chamberlain,Joba	4	5	0	ACB
Scherzer,Max	4	5	0	ACC
*Farnsworth,Kyle	4	5	0	ADB
*Perez,Chris	4	5	1	ADB
*Gregerson,Luke	4	5	1	ADB
*Schlereth,Daniel	4	5	0	AFF
*Thatcher,Joe	4	5	0	AFF
Halladay,Roy	5	3	0	BAA
Wilson,C.J.	4	5	1	BBC
*Downs,Scott	5	3	1	BCA
Qualls,Chad	5	3	3	BCA
Valverde,Jose	4	5	3	CAA
Lester,Jon	4	5	0	CAC
Nolasco,Ricky	4	5	0	CBC
*Smith,Joe	5	3	0	CDA
Peavy,Jake	4	5	0	FAA
Harden,Rich	4	5	0	FBA
*Bedard,Erik	4	5	0	FBC
Francisco,Frank	4	5	3	FCC
Soriano,Rafael	4	5	2	FCC
Gonzalez,Mike	4	5	2	FDB
*Hughes,Phil	4	5	0	FDB
*Moylan,Peter	5	3	1	FDB
*Kuo,Hong-Chih	4	5	0	FDC
Hamels,Cole	4	4	0	AAA
Sabathia,CC	4	4	0	AAB
Jimenez,Ubaldo	4	4	0	AAB
Anderson,Brett	4	4	0	ACA
*Frasor,Jason	4	4	2	ACC
*Perdomo,Luis	4	4	0	ADA
*Medlen,Kris	4	4	0	ADC
Bailey,Andrew	4	4	3	ADD
*Jepsen,Kevin	4	4	1	AFA
*Rzepczynski,Marc	4	4	0	AFF
Rodriguez,Wandy	4	4	0	BAA
Beckett,Josh	4	4	0	BAA
*Zimmermann,Jordan	4	4	0	CDA
Carpenter,Chris	5	2	0	FCC
*Adams,Mike	4	4	0	FFB

PITCHERS	E	K	S	REL
*Gregg,Kevin	3	5	1	AAA
Rodriguez,Francisco	3	5	3	AAA
Jenks,Bobby	4	3	2	ABA
*Affeldt,Jeremy	4	3	0	ACB
*Hanrahan,Joel	3	5	1	ACC
Kershaw,Clayton	3	5	0	ACC
Gonzalez,Gio	3	5	0	ADA
Hanson,Tommy	3	5	0	ADA
*Miller,Trever	3	5	0	ADB
*Camp,Shawn	4	3	0	ADB
*Masset,Nick	4	3	0	ADC
*Motte,Jason	3	5	0	ADC
*Carrasco,Carlos	4	3	0	ADC
*Bulger,Jason	3	5	0	ADD
Dempster,Ryan	4	3	0	BAA
Sanchez,Jonathan	3	5	0	BBA
Lidge,Brad	3	5	2	BBB
de la Rosa,Jorge	3	5	0	BBB
*Romo,Sergio	3	5	0	BDA
Wainwright,Adam	4	3	0	CAB
*Betancourt,Rafael	3	5	0	CCB
*Badenhop,Burke	4	3	0	DDC
*Balfour,Grant	3	5	0	DDC
*Sipp,Tony	3	5	0	DFC
Gallardo,Yovani	3	5	0	FCB
*Dotel,Octavio	3	5	1	FCB
Johnson,Josh	4	3	0	FCC
Wood,Kerry	3	5	2	FCC
*Neshek,Pat	3	5	0	FDA
Garza,Matt	3	4	0	AAA
Billingsley,Chad	3	4	0	AAA
Cordero,Francisco	3	4	2	AAB
*Green,Sean	4	2	0	ACA
*Heilman,Aaron	3	4	0	ACA
*Corpas,Manny	4	2	1	ACA
*Ziegler,Brad	4	2	0	ADA
*Arredondo,Jose	3	4	0	ADA
McDonald,James	3	4	0	ADA
*Todd,Jess	3	4	0	ADA
*Coffey,Todd	4	2	0	ADF
*Mickolio,Kam	3	4	1	AFB
Santana,Johan	3	4	0	BAA
*Linebrink,Scott	3	4	0	BCB
Harang,Aaron	3	4	0	CAA
Burnett,A.J.	3	4	0	CAB
*Elbert,Scott	3	4	0	CDD
Kuroda,Hiroki	4	2	0	DAB
Webb,Brandon	4	2	0	FAC
Liriano,Francisco	3	4	0	FCA
*Shields,Scot	3	4	0	FDD

PITCHERS	E	K	S	REL
Lowe,Derek	4	1	0	AAA
Shields,James	3	3	0	AAA
Floyd,Gavin	3	3	0	AAA
Cueto,Johnny	3	3	0	ABA
*Villanueva,Carlos	3	3	0	ABB
*Grilli,Jason	2	5	0	ACA
*Pena,Tony	3	3	0	ACA
Parra,Manny	3	3	0	ACB
Buchholz,Clay	3	3	0	ACB
Marmol,Carlos	2	5	2	ACB
Meredith,Cla	4	1	0	ACB
Masterson,Justin	3	3	0	ACB
*Marshall,Sean	3	3	0	ADA
*Wright,Wesley	2	5	0	ADB
*Perez,Rafael	3	3	0	ADD
*Mock,Garrett	3	3	0	ADF
Lilly,Ted	3	3	0	BAA
Baker,Scott	3	3	0	BAA
Capps,Matt	3	3	2	BBA
Hoffman,Trevor	3	3	3	BBB
*Lindstrom,Matt	3	3	1	BCA
Aardsma,David	2	5	2	BCB
*Park,Chan Ho	3	3	0	BCF
*O'Day,Darren	3	3	0	BDC
*Meek,Evan	3	3	0	BDC
*Reyes,Dennys	3	3	0	BDC
*Calero,Kiko	2	5	0	BDF
*Belisario,Ronald	3	3	0	BDF
Lackey,John	3	3	0	CAA
Shouse,Brian	4	1	0	CDA
*McClellan,Kyle	3	3	0	CDB
*Walker,Tyler	3	3	0	DDB
Myers,Brett	3	3	0	FBA
Hudson,Tim	4	1	0	FBA
*Martinez,Pedro	3	3	0	FCB
*Smoltz,John	3	3	0	FCB
*Zumaya,Joel	2	5	0	FDB
Jurrjens,Jair	3	2	0	AAB
Hammel,Jason	3	2	0	ABA
Sherrill,George	2	4	1	ABB
Romero,Ricky	3	2	0	ACC
Johnson,Jim	3	2	1	ACC
Byrdak,Tim	2	4	0	ADA
Lewis,Jensen	2	4	0	ADA
Herrera,Daniel	3	2	0	ADB
Troncoso,Ramon	3	2	0	ADB
Veras,Jose	2	4	0	ADC
Mijares,Jose	2	4	0	ADD
Fisher,Carlos	2	4	0	ADD
Gutierrez,Juan	2	4	2	ADF
O'Flaherty,Eric	3	2	0	ADF
Albaladejo,Jonathan	3	2	0	AFB
Choate,Randy	3	2	0	AFD
Perry,Ryan	2	4	1	AFF
Sanches,Brian	2	4	0	AFF
Oswalt,Roy	3	2	0	BAA
Lee,Cliff	3	2	0	BAC
Fuentes,Brian	2	4	2	BBC
Hochevar,Luke	3	2	0	BCA
Hawkins,LaTroy	3	2	1	BCA
Arias,Alberto	3	2	0	BFB
Kelley,Shawn	2	4	0	BFB
Kazmir,Scott	2	4	0	CAB
Lowe,Mark	2	4	0	CDD
Matsuzaka,Daisuke	2	4	0	FAB
Rodney,Fernando	2	4	2	FCA
Putz,J.J.	2	4	0	FCC
Devine,Joey	2	4	0	FDA
Ray,Chris	2	4	1	FDC

PITCHERS	E	K	S	REL
Gaudin,Chad	2	3	0	AAA
Cain,Matt	2	3	0	AAA
Weaver,Jered	2	3	0	AAA
Maholm,Paul	3	1	0	AAA
Danks,John	2	3	0	AAB
Bailey,Homer	2	3	0	ACA
Grabow,John	2	3	0	ACA
Rauch,Jon	2	3	0	ACB
Tallet,Brian	2	3	0	ACB
Okajima,Hideki	2	3	0	ACB
Tillman,Chris	2	3	0	ADA
Davis,Wade	2	3	0	ADA
Seay,Bobby	2	3	0	ADA
Poreda,Aaron	2	3	0	ADA
Coke,Phil	2	3	0	ADB
Cecil,Brett	2	3	0	ADB
Guzman,Angel	2	3	0	ADB
Mujica,Edward	2	3	0	ADB
Kennedy,Ian	2	3	0	ADB
Parnell,Bobby	2	3	0	ADB
Price,David	2	3	0	ADB
Norris,Bud	2	3	0	ADC
Meyer,Dan	2	3	0	ADC
Delcarmen,Manny	2	3	0	ADC
Carlson,Jesse	2	3	0	ADD
Holland,Derek	2	3	0	ADF
Mathis,Doug	3	1	0	AFF
Bumgarner,Madison	3	1	0	AFF
Zambrano,Carlos	2	3	0	BAA
Meche,Gil	2	3	0	BAA
Carmona,Fausto	3	1	0	BBB
Casilla,Santiago	2	3	0	BDA
Bale,John	2	3	0	BDC
Tejeda,Robinson	1	5	0	BDC
Wolf,Randy	2	3	0	CAA
Santana,Ervin	2	3	0	CAC
Miller,Andrew	2	3	0	CCA
Burton,Jared	2	3	0	CDB
VandenHurk,Rick	2	3	0	CDB
Slowey,Kevin	2	3	0	DBB
Nunez,Leo	2	3	1	DCB
Accardo,Jeremy	2	3	0	DCC
Condrey,Clay	3	1	0	DDA
Marcum,Shaun	2	3	0	FBA
Volquez,Edinson	2	3	0	FBA
Johnson,Randy	2	3	0	FBA
Mitre,Sergio	3	1	0	FCA
McGowan,Dustin	2	3	0	FCB
Rhodes,Arthur	2	3	0	FDA
Paulino,Felipe	2	3	0	FDA
Nippert,Dustin	2	3	0	FDB
Sanchez,Anibal	2	3	0	FDC
Valdez,Merkin	2	3	0	FDC

MAYBERRY METHOD TOP 250 BATTERS Full Scores & Rankings

This chart contains full Mayberry Method scores for the top batters, which includes AB in the formula. Scores can be easily recalculated if AB projections change:

MM Score = (PX score + SX score + xBA score + AB score) x AB score

BATTERS	P	S	B	A	REL	M
Braun,Ryan	5	4	4	5	AAC	90
Rollins,Jimmy	3	5	4	5	AAB	85
Utley,Chase	4	4	3	5	AAA	80
Kemp,Matt	4	4	3	5	AAB	80
Pujols,Albert	5	1	5	5	AAB	80
Votto,Joey	5	1	5	5	ABC	80
Gonzalez,Carlos	4	4	3	5	ADF	80
Crawford,Carl	2	5	4	5	BAC	80
Kinsler,Ian	4	4	3	5	CAC	80
Teixeira,Mark	4	1	5	5	AAA	75
Roberts,Brian	3	4	3	5	AAA	75
Pedroia,Dustin	3	2	5	5	AAA	75
Ramirez,Hanley	4	3	3	5	AAA	75
Victorino,Shane	2	5	3	5	AAA	75
Wright,David	4	3	3	5	AAB	75
Holliday,Matt	4	2	4	5	AAB	75
Granderson,C	4	4	2	5	AAB	75
Youkilis,Kevin	5	1	4	5	AAB	75
Fielder,Prince	5	1	4	5	AAD	75
Longoria,Evan	5	2	3	5	ABA	75
McCutchen,A	3	4	3	5	ACB	75
Cruz,Nelson	5	2	3	5	ACC	75
Sandoval,Pablo	4	1	5	5	ADC	75
Beckham,G	4	2	4	5	AFF	75
Rodriguez,Alex	4	2	4	5	BAB	75
Sizemore,Grady	4	4	2	5	BAB	75
Tulowitzki,Troy	4	3	3	5	BAD	75
Upton,Justin	4	4	2	5	CCA	75
Zobrist,Ben	4	3	3	5	CCD	75
Cuddyer,Michael	4	3	3	5	DBC	75
Reyes,Jose	2	5	3	5	FAB	75
Abreu,Bobby	3	3	3	5	AAA	70
Phillips,Brandon	3	3	3	5	AAA	70
Cabrera,Miguel	4	1	4	5	AAB	70
Ellsbury,Jacoby	1	5	3	5	AAB	70
Ethier,Andre	4	1	4	5	AAB	70
Damon,Johnny	3	3	3	5	AAB	70
Pence,Hunter	4	2	3	5	AAB	70
Howard,Ryan	5	1	3	5	AAC	70
Bay,Jason	5	2	2	5	AAC	70
Reynolds,Mark	5	3	1	5	AAC	70
Lind,Adam	4	1	4	5	ABC	70
McCann,Brian	4	1	4	5	ABC	70
Andrus,Elvis	1	5	3	5	ADB	70
Reimold,Nolan	4	2	3	5	ADC	70
Coghlan,Chris	2	3	4	5	ADD	70
Zimmerman,R	4	1	4	5	BAB	70
Lee,Derrek	4	1	4	5	BAC	70
Mauer,Joe	3	1	5	5	BAC	70
Berkman,Lance	4	1	4	5	BAC	70
Jones,Adam	3	3	3	5	BBC	70
Choo,Shin-Soo	4	3	2	5	BCF	70
Hunter,Torii	4	2	3	5	CAB	70
Ramirez,Aramis	4	1	4	5	CBA	70

AT BATS	
0-99	0
100-199	1
200-299	2
300-399	3
400-499	4
500+	5

BATTERS	P	S	B	A	REL	M
Young,Chris	4	3	1	5	AAA	65
Morneau,Justin	4	0	4	5	AAA	65
Dye,Jermaine	4	1	3	5	AAB	65
Gonzalez,Adrian	4	0	4	5	AAB	65
Lopez,Jose	3	1	4	5	AAB	65
Drew,Stephen	3	3	2	5	AAC	65
Young,Michael	3	1	4	5	AAC	65
Rios,Alex	3	3	2	5	AAC	65
Cano,Robinson	3	1	4	5	AAD	65
Cabrera,A	2	3	3	5	ABB	65
Butler,Billy	4	0	4	5	ABC	65
Jones,Garrett	4	2	2	5	ACD	65
Valbuena,Luis	3	2	3	5	ADB	65
Ibanez,Raul	4	1	3	5	BAA	65
Lee,Carlos	3	1	4	5	BAB	65
Hudson,Orlando	2	3	3	5	BBA	65
Werth,Jayson	4	2	2	5	BBA	65
McLouth,Nate	3	4	1	5	BBB	65
Byrd,Marlon	3	2	3	5	BBB	65
Hart,Corey	3	3	2	5	BBB	65
Kubel,Jason	4	1	3	5	BBB	65
Bartlett,Jason	2	4	2	5	BBC	65
Ross,Cody	4	1	3	5	BCD	65
Prado,Martin	3	1	4	5	BDB	65
Cabrera,Everth	1	5	2	5	CFF	65
Soriano,Alfonso	4	2	2	5	DBC	65
LaRoche,Adam	4	0	3	5	AAA	60
Konerko,Paul	4	0	3	5	AAB	60
Dunn,Adam	5	0	2	5	AAB	60
Suzuki,Ichiro	1	3	3	5	AAB	60
DeJesus,David	2	2	3	5	AAB	60
Markakis,Nick	3	1	3	5	AAC	60
Jeter,Derek	1	2	4	5	AAC	60
Upton,B.J.	3	3	1	5	AAD	60
Span,Denard	1	4	2	5	ACC	60
Morales,Kendry	4	0	3	5	ACC	60
Tejada,Miguel	2	1	4	5	BAB	60
Ortiz,David	4	0	3	5	BAD	60
Barmes,Clint	3	3	1	5	BBD	60
Morgan,Nyjer	0	5	2	5	BCB	60
Callaspo,Alberto	2	1	4	5	BCB	60
Aybar,Erick	1	4	2	5	BCC	60
Bourn,Michael	1	5	1	5	BCF	60
Helton,Todd	3	0	4	5	CAD	60
Hill,Aaron	3	1	3	5	DBC	60
Furcal,Rafael	1	3	3	5	FBF	60
Guzman,Cristian	1	3	3	5	FCC	60
Stewart,Ian	5	3	2	4	ACA	56
Schierholtz,Nate	3	3	4	4	ADC	56
Fowler,Dexter	3	5	2	4	AFA	56
Beltran,Carlos	3	3	4	4	DAA	56
Kendrick,Howie	3	3	4	4	DDA	56
Young,Delmon	2	2	2	5	AAA	55
Kouzmanoff,K	3	1	2	5	AAA	55
Loney,James	2	1	3	5	AAA	55
Polanco,Placido	1	2	3	5	AAB	55
Peralta,Jhonny	3	1	2	5	AAB	55
Uggla,Dan	4	1	1	5	AAC	55
Gutierrez,F	2	3	1	5	ABC	55
Ludwick,Ryan	4	1	1	5	ABF	55
Headley,Chase	3	2	1	5	ACC	55
Snider,Travis	4	1	1	5	ADB	55
Parra,Gerardo	1	3	2	5	AFA	55
Wells,Vernon	2	2	2	5	BAC	55
Sanchez,F	2	1	3	5	BAC	55
Figgins,Chone	1	4	1	5	BAD	55
Beltre,Adrian	2	2	2	5	CAB	55
Martinez,Victor	3	0	3	5	CBD	55
Jackson,Conor	2	2	2	5	FCD	55

BATTERS	P	S	B	A	REL	M
Maybin,Cameron	3	4	2	4	ADA	52
Davis,Chris	5	1	3	4	ADC	52
Murphy,David	4	2	3	4	BCA	52
Hamilton,Josh	4	2	3	4	CCC	52
Johnson,Kelly	3	4	2	4	DBB	52
Cabrera,Orlando	1	2	2	5	AAA	50
Theriot,Ryan	0	3	2	5	AAB	50
Escobar,Yunel	1	1	3	5	ABA	50
Cantu,Jorge	3	0	2	5	ABB	50
LaRoche,Andy	2	1	2	5	ACD	50
Rasmus,Colby	2	2	1	5	ADC	50
Wieters,Matt	3	0	2	5	AFF	50
Iwamura,Akinori	1	3	1	5	FBA	50
Ramirez,Manny	4	0	4	4	ABC	48
Wood,Brandon	4	2	2	4	ACA	48
Murphy,Daniel	3	1	4	4	ACB	48
Ruiz,Carlos	3	1	4	4	ACD	48
Davis,Rajai	1	5	2	4	ADD	48
Gomes,Jonny	5	2	1	4	ADF	48
Borbon,Julio	1	4	3	4	AFA	48
Blake,Casey	4	2	2	4	BAA	48
Pena,Carlos	5	1	2	4	BAC	48
Willingham,J	4	1	3	4	BBA	48
Drew,J.D.	4	1	3	4	BBB	48
Fukudome,K	3	2	3	4	BBC	48
Guerrero,V	3	1	4	4	CBC	48
Quentin,Carlos	4	1	3	4	CCF	48
Bruce,Jay	4	2	2	4	CDC	48
Gordon,Alex	4	2	2	4	DBB	48
Weeks,Rickie	3	5	0	4	FCC	48
Blalock,Hank	4	1	3	4	FDC	48
Lopez,Felipe	1	1	2	5	AAC	45
Inge,Brandon	3	1	0	5	ABA	45
Suzuki,Kurt	1	1	2	5	ABA	45
Scutaro,Marco	1	1	2	5	ABB	45
Ramirez,Alexei	1	1	2	5	ABD	45
Hawpe,Brad	4	1	2	4	AAB	44
Montero,Miguel	4	0	3	4	ADB	44
LaPorta,Matt	3	1	3	4	AFF	44
Cameron,Mike	4	2	1	4	BAA	44
Overbay,Lyle	4	0	3	4	BBB	44
Dickerson,Chris	2	4	1	4	BDB	44
Jones,Chipper	3	1	3	4	CAD	44
Lowell,Mike	3	1	3	4	CBB	44
Podsednik,S	1	4	2	4	CDB	44
Rolen,Scott	3	2	2	4	DBB	44
Guillen,Carlos	3	2	2	4	DBB	44
Matsui,Kaz	1	4	2	4	DBC	44
Hairston,Scott	4	2	1	4	DCA	44
Delgado,Carlos	4	0	3	4	FBB	44
Teahen,Mark	2	2	2	4	AAA	40
Winn,Randy	1	3	2	4	AAB	40
Swisher,Nick	4	0	2	4	AAD	40
Pierzynski,A.J.	1	0	2	5	ABA	40
Schumaker,Skip	1	1	4	4	ABA	40
Scott,Luke	4	0	2	4	ABB	40
Cabrera,Melky	1	2	3	4	ABC	40
Brantley,Michael	0	3	3	4	ADB	40
DeRosa,Mark	3	1	2	4	BAC	40
Castillo,Luis	0	3	3	4	BBB	40
Gomez,Carlos	1	5	0	4	BCA	40
Getz,Chris	1	3	2	4	BDA	40
Ellis,Mark	2	2	2	4	CBA	40
Dukes,Elijah	3	2	1	4	CDD	40
Matsui,Hideki	3	0	3	4	DBB	40
Soto,Geovany	4	0	2	4	DCD	40
Hafner,Travis	4	0	2	4	DCF	40
Rivera,Juan	3	0	3	4	DDC	40

BATTERS	P	S	B	A	REL	M
Atkins,Garrett	2	1	2	4	AAC	36
Francoeur,Jeff	2	1	2	4	AAC	36
Huff,Aubrey	3	0	2	4	AAF	36
Betancourt,Y	1	2	2	4	ABA	36
Jacobs,Mike	4	0	1	4	ABB	36
Pierre,Juan	0	5	4	3	ABB	36
Molina,Bengie	3	0	2	4	ABB	36
Venable,Will	2	3	0	4	ACB	36
Smith,Seth	4	2	3	3	ADB	36
Raburn,Ryan	4	3	2	3	ADF	36
Saunders,M	2	3	0	4	AFA	36
Roberts,Ryan	2	3	0	4	AFB	36
Desmond,Ian	2	2	1	4	AFF	36
Rowand,Aaron	3	1	1	4	BAB	36
Hardy,J.J.	3	0	2	4	BAC	36
Burrell,Pat	4	0	1	4	BAD	36
Anderson,Garret	2	1	2	4	BBB	36
Hermida,Jeremy	3	1	1	4	BBC	36
Wigginton,Ty	3	0	2	4	BBC	36
Renteria,Edgar	1	2	2	4	BBC	36
Sweeney,Ryan	1	1	3	4	BCA	36
Kennedy,Adam	1	2	2	4	BCB	36
Spilborghs,Ryan	3	3	3	3	BDD	36
Blanks,Kyle	4	1	0	4	BFA	36
Izturis,Cesar	0	3	2	4	DCA	36
Encarnacion,E	3	1	1	4	DCB	36
Diaz,Matt	3	3	3	3	DDF	36
Crisp,Coco	2	5	2	3	FCA	36
Aviles,Mike	1	2	2	4	FDF	36
Velez,Eugenio	1	5	2	3	ADB	33
Pie,Felix	3	3	2	3	ADC	33
Iannetta,Chris	5	1	2	3	ADF	33
Fox,Jake	4	1	3	3	AFF	33
Napoli,Mike	5	1	2	3	BDF	33
Byrnes,Eric	3	3	2	3	FCC	33
Martin,Russ	1	1	2	4	AAB	32
Cust,Jack	4	0	0	4	ABC	32
Pennington,C	1	3	0	4	ACA	32
Milledge,L	1	2	1	4	ACB	32
Baker,John	2	0	2	4	ADC	32
McGehee,Casey	2	0	2	4	ADC	32
Mora,Melvin	1	1	2	4	BBC	32
Eckstein,David	1	1	2	4	CBA	32
Guillen,Jose	2	1	1	4	DBB	32
Hernandez,R	2	0	2	4	DCA	32
Olivo,Miguel	4	2	1	3	ACB	30
Ankiel,Rick	4	2	1	3	ACD	30
Fontenot,Mike	3	2	2	3	ADF	30
Ordonez,Magglio	3	0	4	3	BAC	30
Thome,Jim	5	0	2	3	BBB	30
Branyan,Russell	5	1	1	3	CDB	30
Izturis,Maicer	1	3	3	3	DCB	30
Posada,Jorge	4	0	3	3	FCD	30
Doumit,Ryan	3	1	3	3	FDB	30
Gerut,Jody	2	2	3	3	FFD	30
Molina,Yadier	1	0	2	4	ABA	28
Feliz,Pedro	1	0	2	4	BAA	28
Wilson,Jack	1	1	1	4	CCB	28
Ruiz,Randy	4	1	1	3	ACB	27
Uribe,Juan	3	1	2	3	ACB	27
Griffey Jr.,Ken	4	0	2	3	BBB	27
Barton,Daric	3	1	2	3	BBC	27
Belliard,Ronnie	3	1	2	3	BCC	27
Gardner,Brett	1	5	0	3	BDA	27
Buck,John	4	1	1	3	BDB	27
Church,Ryan	3	1	2	3	CCB	27
Jones,Andruw	4	1	1	3	CCF	27
Hairston,Jerry	2	2	2	3	CDF	27
Bradley,Milton	3	1	2	3	DCF	27

MAYBERRY METHOD TOP 235 PITCHERS Full Scores & Rankings

This chart contains full Mayberry Method scores for the top pitchers, which includes IP in the formula. Scores can be easily recalculated if IP and/or Sv projections change:

$$\text{MM Score} = ((\text{xERA score} \times 2) + \text{K/9 score} + \text{Sv score} + \text{IP score}) \times (\text{IP score} + \text{Sv score})$$

PITCHERS	E	K	S	I	REL	M
Lincecum,Tim	5	5	0	5	AAA	100
Haren,Dan	5	4	0	5	AAA	95
Hernandez,Felix	5	4	0	5	AAA	95
Greinke,Zack	4	5	0	5	AAA	90
Verlander,Justin	4	5	0	5	AAB	90
Vazquez,Javier	4	5	0	5	AAB	90
Scherzer,Max	4	5	0	5	ACC	90
Halladay,Roy	5	3	0	5	BAA	90
Lester,Jon	4	5	0	5	CAC	90
Nolasco,Ricky	4	5	0	5	CBC	90
Hamels,Cole	4	4	0	5	AAA	85
Jimenez,Ubaldo	4	4	0	5	AAB	85
Sabathia,CC	4	4	0	5	AAB	85
Anderson,Brett	4	4	0	5	ACA	85
Rodriguez,W	4	4	0	5	BAA	85
Beckett,Josh	4	4	0	5	BAA	85
Carpenter,Chris	5	2	0	5	FCC	85
Kershaw,Clayton	3	5	0	5	ACC	80
Hanson,Tommy	3	5	0	5	ADA	80
Dempster,Ryan	4	3	0	5	BAA	80
Sanchez,J	3	5	0	5	BBA	80
de la Rosa,J	3	5	0	5	BBB	80
Wainwright,A	4	3	0	5	CAB	80
Gallardo,Yovani	3	5	0	5	FCB	80
Johnson,Josh	4	3	0	5	FCC	80
Nathan,Joe	5	5	3	1	AAA	76
Broxton,J	5	5	3	1	ABA	76
Street,Huston	5	5	3	1	BBB	76
Billingsley,Chad	3	4	0	5	AAA	75
Garza,Matt	3	4	0	5	AAA	75
Santana,Johan	3	4	0	5	BAA	75
Harang,Aaron	3	4	0	5	CAA	75
Burnett,A.J.	3	4	0	5	CAB	75
Webb,Brandon	4	2	0	5	FAC	75
Rivera,Mariano	5	4	3	1	AAA	72
Floyd,Gavin	3	3	0	5	AAA	70
Lowe,Derek	4	1	0	5	AAA	70
Shields,James	3	3	0	5	AAA	70
Cueto,Johnny	3	3	0	5	ABA	70
Buchholz,Clay	3	3	0	5	ACB	70
Lilly,Ted	3	3	0	5	BAA	70
Baker,Scott	3	3	0	5	BAA	70
Lackey,John	3	3	0	5	CAA	70
Hudson,Tim	4	1	0	5	FBA	70
Wilson,Brian	4	5	3	1	ABA	68
Chamberlain,J	4	5	0	4	ACB	68
Qualls,Chad	5	3	3	1	BCA	68
Valverde,Jose	4	5	3	1	CAA	68
Peavy,Jake	4	5	0	4	FAA	68
Jurrjens,Jair	3	2	0	5	AAB	65
Hammel,Jason	3	2	0	5	ABA	65
Romero,Ricky	3	2	0	5	ACC	65
Oswalt,Roy	3	2	0	5	BAA	65
Lee,Cliff	3	2	0	5	BAC	65
Bailey,Andrew	4	4	3	1	ADD	64
Rodriguez,F	3	5	3	1	AAA	60
Maholm,Paul	3	1	0	5	AAA	60
Weaver,Jered	2	3	0	5	AAA	60
Cain,Matt	2	3	0	5	AAA	60
Danks,John	2	3	0	5	AAB	60
Price,David	2	3	0	5	ADB	60
Meche,Gil	2	3	0	5	BAA	60
Wolf,Randy	2	3	0	5	CAA	60
Paulino,Felipe	2	3	0	5	FDA	60
Kuroda,Hiroki	4	2	0	4	DAB	56
Liriano,Francisco	3	4	0	4	FCA	56
Arroyo,Bronson	2	2	0	5	AAA	55
Blanton,Joe	2	2	0	5	AAB	55
Pettitte,Andy	2	2	0	5	AAB	55
Niemann,Jeff	2	2	0	5	ACD	55
Pineiro,Joel	3	0	0	5	BAA	55
Correia,Kevin	2	2	0	5	BBB	55
Cook,Aaron	3	0	0	5	DAA	55
Pavano,Carl	2	2	0	5	FCB	55
Bell,Heath	5	5	3	0	ABB	54
Thornton,Matt	5	5	2	1	ACB	54
Soria,Joakim	5	5	3	0	BBA	54
Masterson,Justin	3	3	0	4	ACB	52
Parra,Manny	3	3	0	4	ACB	52
Myers,Brett	3	3	0	4	FBA	52
Pelfrey,Mike	2	1	0	5	AAA	50
Buehrle,Mark	2	1	0	5	AAA	50
Feldman,Scott	2	1	0	5	ACA	50
Papelbon,Jon	4	5	3	0	AAB	48
Howell,J.P.	4	5	2	1	ACA	48
Kazmir,Scott	2	4	0	4	CAB	48
Matsuzaka,D	2	4	0	4	FAB	48
Harden,Rich	4	5	0	3	FBA	48
Soriano,Rafael	4	5	2	1	FCC	48
Francisco,Frank	4	5	3	0	FCC	48
Gonzalez,Mike	4	5	2	1	FDB	48
Davis,Doug	1	2	0	5	AAA	45
Jackson,Edwin	1	2	0	5	AAA	45
Marquis,Jason	2	0	0	5	AAA	45
Lannan,John	2	0	0	5	AAB	45
Zito,Barry	1	2	0	5	AAB	45
Frasor,Jason	4	4	2	1	ACC	45
Medlen,Kris	4	4	0	3	ADC	45
Porcello,Rick	2	0	0	5	ADF	45
Davis,Wade	2	3	0	4	ADA	44
Tillman,Chris	2	3	0	4	ADA	44
Holland,Derek	2	3	0	4	ADF	44
Zambrano,C	2	3	0	4	BAA	44
Santana,Ervin	2	3	0	4	CAC	44
Slowey,Kevin	2	3	0	4	DBB	44
Gonzalez,Gio	3	5	0	3	ADA	42
Wood,Kerry	3	5	2	1	FCC	42
Saunders,Joe	1	1	0	5	AAA	40
Braden,Dallas	1	1	0	5	ACA	40
Richard,Clayton	2	2	0	4	ACB	40
Millwood,Kevin	1	1	0	5	CAA	40
Padilla,Vicente	2	2	0	4	CAA	40
Cordero,F	3	4	2	1	AAB	39
McDonald,J	3	4	0	3	ADA	39
Sonnanstine,A	2	1	0	4	ABA	36
Volstad,Chris	2	1	0	4	ACA	36
Happ,J.A.	1	3	0	4	ACB	36
Marmol,Carlos	2	5	2	1	ACB	36
Wells,Randy	2	1	0	4	ADD	36
Mock,Garrett	3	3	0	3	ADF	36
Matusz,Brian	1	3	0	4	AFF	36
Capps,Matt	3	3	2	1	BBA	36
Hoffman,Trevor	3	3	3	0	BBB	36
Aardsma,David	2	5	2	1	BCB	36
Lohse,Kyle	2	1	0	4	CAA	36
Garland,Jon	1	0	0	5	AAA	35
Blackburn,Nick	1	0	0	5	AAA	35
Looper,Braden	1	0	0	5	AAB	35
Snell,Ian	0	2	0	5	AAB	35
Robertson,D	5	5	1	1	AFA	34
Wagner,Billy	5	5	2	0	FCA	34
Gutierrez,Juan	2	4	2	1	ADF	33
Hochevar,Luke	3	2	0	3	BCA	33
Rodney,F	2	4	2	1	FCA	33
Ohlendorf,Ross	1	2	0	4	ACD	32
Huff,David	1	2	0	4	ADC	32
Duke,Zach	2	0	0	4	BAA	32
Bergesen,Brad	2	0	0	4	CDA	32
Guthrie,Jeremy	0	1	0	5	AAB	30
Bailey,Homer	2	3	0	3	ACA	30
Gregerson,Luke	4	5	1	1	ADB	30
Norris,Bud	2	3	0	3	ADC	30
Bumgarner,M	3	1	0	3	AFF	30
Carmona,Fausto	3	1	0	3	BBB	30
Wilson,C.J.	4	5	1	1	BBC	30
Downs,Scott	5	3	1	1	BCA	30
VandenHurk,R	2	3	0	3	CDB	30
Marcum,Shaun	2	3	0	3	FBA	30
Bedard,Erik	4	5	0	2	FBC	30
Moylan,Peter	5	3	1	1	FDB	30
Sanchez,Anibal	2	3	0	3	FDC	30
Cahill,Trevor	1	1	0	4	ACF	28
Jepsen,Kevin	4	4	1	1	AFA	28
Rzepczynski,M	4	4	0	2	AFF	28
Bannister,Brian	1	1	0	4	BBA	28
Rowland-Smith,R	1	1	0	4	CDA	28
Buckner,Billy	2	2	0	3	ACF	27
Morton,Charlie	2	2	0	3	ADB	27
Morrow,Brandon	1	4	0	3	ADB	27
Kawakami,K	2	2	0	3	CAB	27
Bush,David	2	2	0	3	DAA	27
Gregg,Kevin	3	5	1	1	AAA	26
Jenks,Bobby	4	3	2	0	ABA	26
Hanrahan,Joel	3	5	1	1	ACC	26
Lidge,Brad	3	5	2	0	BBB	26
Dotel,Octavio	3	5	1	1	FCB	26
Corpas,Manny	4	2	1	1	ACA	24
Stammen,Craig	1	0	0	4	ADA	24
West,Sean	1	3	0	3	ADF	24
Mickolio,Kam	3	4	1	1	AFB	24
Feliz,Neftali	1	3	0	3	AFC	24
Davies,Kyle	0	2	0	4	BCA	24
Petit,Yusmeiro	1	3	0	3	BCB	24
Elbert,Scott	3	4	0	2	CDD	24
Young,Chris	1	3	0	3	FBB	24
Marshall,Sean	3	3	0	2	ADA	22
Lindstrom,Matt	3	3	1	1	BCA	22
Martinez,Pedro	3	3	0	2	FCB	22
Smoltz,John	3	3	0	2	FCB	22
Franklin,Ryan	1	2	2	1	ABB	21
Gorzelanny,Tom	1	2	0	3	ABB	21
Galarraga,A	1	2	0	3	ABD	21
Mazzaro,Vince	1	2	0	3	ADC	21
Detwiler,Ross	1	2	0	3	ADF	21
Olsen,Scott	1	2	0	3	FAA	21
Perez,Oliver	0	4	0	3	FAB	21
Maine,John	1	2	0	3	FBA	21
Washburn,J	0	1	0	4	AAA	20
Sherrill,George	2	4	1	1	ABB	20
Johnson,Jim	3	2	1	1	ACC	20
Fuentes,Brian	2	4	2	0	BBC	20
Hawkins,LaTroy	3	2	1	1	BCA	20
Ray,Chris	2	4	1	1	FDC	20
Gaudin,Chad	2	3	0	2	AAA	18
Cecil,Brett	2	3	0	2	ADB	18
McCutchen,D	1	1	0	3	ADD	18
Moehler,Brian	1	1	0	3	BBA	18
Nunez,Leo	2	3	1	1	DCB	18
Francis,Jeff	1	1	0	3	FBA	18
Mitre,Sergio	3	1	0	2	FCA	18
Stauffer,Tim	1	1	0	3	FDF	18
Aceves,Alfredo	2	2	0	2	ACA	16
Hunter,Tommy	0	0	0	4	ADA	16
Clippard,Tyler	1	4	1	1	ADC	16
Bard,Daniel	5	5	0	1	AFA	16
Contreras,Jose	2	2	0	2	CBA	16
Garcia,Freddy	2	2	0	2	CDA	16
Niese,Jonathon	2	2	0	2	CDA	16
Sheets,Ben	2	2	0	2	FBA	16
Madson,Ryan	5	4	1	0	BCA	15
Laffey,Aaron	1	0	0	3	BCC	15
League,Brandon	5	4	0	1	CDC	15
Silva,Carlos	1	0	0	3	FBB	15
Hendrickson,M	2	1	0	2	ABA	14
Wuertz,Mike	4	5	0	1	ACB	14
Perez,Chris	4	5	1	0	ADB	14
Latos,Mat	1	3	0	2	AFF	14
Penny,Brad	2	1	0	2	CAB	14
Smith,Joe	5	3	0	1	CDA	14
Wang,Chien-M	2	1	0	2	FBA	14
Hughes,Phil	4	5	0	1	FDB	14
Carrasco,Carlos	4	3	0	1	ADC	12
Masset,Nick	4	3	0	1	ADC	12
LeBlanc,Wade	1	2	0	2	ADC	12
Bulger,Jason	3	5	0	1	ADD	12
Romo,Sergio	3	5	0	1	BDA	12
Betancourt,R	3	5	0	1	CCB	12
Wakefield,Tim	0	1	0	3	DAA	12
Badenhop,B	4	3	0	1	DDC	12
McCarthy,B	1	2	0	2	FCA	12
Lewis,Scott	1	2	0	2	FDB	12
Green,Sean	4	2	0	1	ACA	11
Heilman,Aaron	3	4	0	1	ACA	11
Ziegler,Brad	4	2	0	1	ADA	11
Coffey,Todd	4	2	0	1	ADF	11

INNINGS	
0-69	0
70-99	1
100-129	2
130-159	3
160-189	4
190+	5

SIMULATION LEAGUE DRAFT   TOP 500

NAME	POS	RAR	NAME	POS	RAR	NAME	POS	RAR	NAME	POS	RAR
Mauer,Joe	2	41.0	Votto,Joey	3	17.0	Soria,Joakim	P	11.3	Branyan,Russell	3	7.6
Pujols,Albert	3	38.3	Ramirez,Aramis	5	16.5	Sandoval,Pablo	53	11.3	Valverde,Jose	P	7.6
Lincecum,Tim	P	38.0	Johnson,Josh	P	16.5	Santana,Johan	P	11.3	Soriano,Rafael	P	7.6
Rodriguez,Alex	5	37.5	Hanson,Tommy	P	16.1	Robertson,David	P	11.2	Pettitte,Andy	P	7.6
Halladay,Roy	P	36.8	Rollins,Jimmy	6	16.1	Carmona,Fausto	P	11.2	Pavano,Carl	P	7.6
Hernandez,Felix	P	35.2	Morneau,Justin	3	16.1	Ortiz,David	0	11.2	Doumit,Ryan	2	7.4
Ramirez,Hanley	6	35.2	Fowler,Dexter	8	16.0	Cust,Jack	9	11.1	Pena,Brayan	20	7.4
Bay,Jason	7	31.0	Roberts,Brian	4	16.0	Cano,Robinson	4	11.0	Smoltz,John	P	7.3
Longoria,Evan	5	30.9	Jeter,Derek	6	15.9	Wuertz,Mike	P	10.9	Scutaro,Marco	6	7.3
Beckett,Josh	P	30.3	Lowe,Derek	P	15.7	Hammel,Jason	P	10.8	Price,David	P	7.3
Teixeira,Mark	3	30.0	Prado,Martin	453	15.4	Smith,Joe	P	10.5	Cook,Aaron	P	7.2
Haren,Dan	P	29.9	Lackey,John	P	15.4	Wilson,C.J.	P	10.3	Ramirez,Alexei	6	7.2
Ramirez,Manny	7	29.9	Jones,Chipper	5	15.3	Gonzalez,Adrian	3	10.3	Scott,Luke	7	7.1
Lester,Jon	P	29.3	Ruiz,Carlos	2	15.3	Ross,Cody	89	10.3	Francisco,Frank	P	7.1
Utley,Chase	4	28.2	Granderson,Curtis	8	15.3	Lowell,Mike	5	10.3	Jurrjens,Jair	P	7.0
Sabathia,CC	P	27.8	Drew,Stephen	6	15.2	Street,Huston	P	10.3	Cueto,Johnny	P	6.9
Youkilis,Kevin	35	27.8	Howard,Ryan	3	15.2	Nathan,Joe	P	10.2	Meche,Gil	P	6.9
Anderson,Brett	P	27.4	Cruz,Nelson	9	15.1	Ziegler,Brad	P	10.1	Pence,Hunter	9	6.9
Carpenter,Chris	P	27.4	Hunter,Torii	8	15.1	Kendrick,Howie	4	10.0	Raburn,Ryan	7	6.9
Verlander,Justin	P	27.2	Broxton,Jonathan	P	15.0	Harang,Aaron	P	10.0	Lilly,Ted	P	6.9
Pena,Carlos	3	26.9	Masterson,Justin	P	14.6	Gonzalez,Gio	P	9.9	Hill,Aaron	4	6.8
Holliday,Matt	7	26.8	Kuroda,Hiroki	P	14.4	Lowrie,Jed	6	9.9	Rodriguez,Sean	4	6.8
Greinke,Zack	P	25.9	Shoppach,Kelly	2	14.4	Lee,Derrek	3	9.8	Feldman,Scott	P	6.8
McCann,Brian	2	25.9	Garza,Matt	P	14.4	Johnson,Kelly	4	9.7	Kuo,Hong-Chih	P	6.7
Vazquez,Javier	P	25.7	Montero,Miguel	2	14.3	Pineiro,Joel	P	9.7	Posey,Buster	2	6.7
Hawpe,Brad	9	25.7	Billingsley,Chad	P	14.1	Maholm,Paul	P	9.6	Badenhop,Burke	P	6.7
Cabrera,Miguel	3	24.5	Swisher,Nick	93	14.1	Willingham,Josh	79	9.6	Masset,Nick	P	6.7
Zobrist,Ben	49	24.3	Oswalt,Roy	P	14.0	Moylan,Peter	P	9.6	Byrd,Marlon	87	6.6
Jimenez,Ubaldo	P	24.2	Beckham,Gordon	5	13.9	Gregerson,Luke	P	9.4	Markakis,Nick	9	6.6
Martinez,Victor	23	24.0	Bradley,Milton	9	13.9	Gervacio,Sammy	P	9.4	Porcello,Rick	P	6.5
Webb,Brandon	P	23.4	Gallardo,Yovani	P	13.6	Helton,Todd	3	9.4	Wood,Kerry	P	6.5
Tulowitzki,Troy	6	23.3	League,Brandon	P	13.6	Crawford,Carl	7	9.4	Perez,Chris	P	6.5
Kemp,Matt	8	23.3	Young,Michael	5	13.5	Bell,Heath	P	9.3	Camp,Shawn	P	6.5
Upton,Justin	9	23.3	Lee,Cliff	P	13.4	Mitre,Sergio	P	9.3	Corpas,Manny	P	6.4
Ethier,Andre	9	23.2	Kershaw,Clayton	P	13.3	Snider,Travis	79	9.2	Meredith,Cla	P	6.4
Werth,Jayson	9	23.1	Harden,Rich	P	13.2	Hughes,Phil	P	9.2	Flowers,Tyler	2	6.4
Beltran,Carlos	8	22.9	Rzepczynski,Marc	P	13.0	Bailey,Andrew	P	9.2	McLouth,Nate	8	6.4
Sizemore,Grady	8	22.8	Sanchez,Jonathan	P	13.0	Callaspo,Alberto	4	9.1	Thatcher,Joe	P	6.4
Iannetta,Chris	2	22.8	Qualls,Chad	P	13.0	Quentin,Carlos	7	9.0	Green,Sean	P	6.4
Wainwright,Adam	P	22.5	Myers,Brett	P	12.9	Frasor,Jason	P	9.0	Jenks,Bobby	P	6.3
Fielder,Prince	3	22.4	Floyd,Gavin	P	12.9	Abreu,Bobby	9	9.0	Gonzalez,Mike	P	6.3
Lind,Adam	7	22.0	Medlen,Kris	P	12.9	Wagner,Billy	P	8.9	Dukes,Elijah	98	6.1
Soto,Geovany	2	21.7	Thome,Jim	0	12.9	Howell,J.P.	P	8.8	Coffey,Todd	P	6.1
Uggla,Dan	4	21.4	Rivera,Mariano	P	12.8	Bartlett,Jason	6	8.8	Ross,David	2	6.1
Pedroia,Dustin	4	21.3	Escobar,Yunel	6	12.7	Matsui,Hideki	0	8.7	Farnsworth,Kyle	P	6.0
Nolasco,Ricky	P	21.2	Damon,Johnny	7	12.7	Jepsen,Kevin	P	8.6	Ibanez,Raul	7	5.9
Rodriguez,Wandy	P	20.9	Davis,Chris	3	12.6	McDonald,James	P	8.6	Hafner,Travis	0	5.8
Napoli,Mike	2	20.2	McCutchen,Andrew	8	12.6	Furcal,Rafael	6	8.6	Young,Chris	8	5.8
Chamberlain,Joba	P	20.2	de la Rosa,Jorge	P	12.6	Phillips,Brandon	4	8.6	Richard,Clayton	P	5.8
Drew,J.D.	9	20.1	Thornton,Matt	P	12.5	Carrasco,Carlos	P	8.6	Molina,Yadier	2	5.7
Dunn,Adam	379	19.9	Reyes,Jose	6	12.4	Stewart,Ian	54	8.5	Davis,Wade	P	5.6
Wieters,Matt	2	19.6	Baker,Scott	P	12.4	Madson,Ryan	P	8.4	Parra,Manny	P	5.5
Hamels,Cole	P	19.4	Bedard,Erik	P	12.2	Kubel,Jason	97	8.4	Morales,Kendry	3	5.5
Berkman,Lance	3	19.1	Romero,Ricky	P	12.1	Cabrera,Asdrubal	64	8.4	Marcum,Shaun	P	5.5
Scherzer,Max	P	18.9	Reimold,Nolan	7	12.0	Slowey,Kevin	P	8.3	Marshall,Sean	P	5.5
Hudson,Tim	P	18.8	Kinsler,Ian	4	11.9	Papelbon,Jonathan	P	8.2	Buehrle,Mark	P	5.5
Braun,Ryan	7	18.8	Fukudome,Kosuke	89	11.8	Hochevar,Luke	P	8.1	Lee,Carlos	7	5.4
Posada,Jorge	2	18.5	Bruce,Jay	9	11.8	Maybin,Cameron	8	8.1	Cain,Matt	P	5.4
Reynolds,Mark	53	18.4	Choo,Shin-Soo	97	11.8	Elbert,Scott	P	8.1	Butler,Billy	3	5.4
Wright,David	5	18.1	Cameron,Mike	8	11.7	Weeks,Rickie	4	8.0	Adams,Mike	P	5.4
Dempster,Ryan	P	17.8	Hamilton,Josh	89	11.6	Feliciano,Pedro	P	8.0	Romo,Sergio	P	5.4
Peavy,Jake	P	17.8	Liriano,Francisco	P	11.5	Hudson,Orlando	4	8.0	Murphy,David	7	5.3
Zimmerman,Ryan	5	17.5	Downs,Scott	P	11.5	Niemann,Jeff	P	7.9	Holland,Derek	P	5.3
Buchholz,Clay	P	17.4	Bard,Daniel	P	11.4	Wilson,Brian	P	7.9	Shouse,Brian	P	5.3
Shields,James	P	17.3	Victorino,Shane	8	11.4	Martin,Russell	2	7.8	Danks,John	P	5.3
Burnett,A.J.	P	17.2	Gordon,Alex	5	11.3	Bumgarner,Madiso	P	7.7	Overbay,Lyle	3	5.3

SIMULATION LEAGUE DRAFT   TOP 500

NAME	POS	RAR	NAME	POS	RAR	NAME	POS	RAR	NAME	POS	RAR
Martinez,Pedro	P	5.2	Herrera,Daniel	P	3.2	Morton,Charlie	P	1.6	Dolsi,Freddy	P	0.2
O'Day,Darren	P	5.2	Sipp,Tony	P	3.2	Burnett,Sean	P	1.5	Uehara,Koji	P	0.2
Affeldt,Jeremy	P	5.2	Johnson,Nick	3	3.1	Hart,Corey	9	1.5	Mulvey,Kevin	P	0.2
Pena,Tony	P	5.2	Arredondo,Jose	P	3.1	Upton,B.J.	8	1.5	Zumaya,Joel	P	0.2
Perdomo,Luis	P	5.0	O'Flaherty,Eric	P	3.1	Bass,Brian	P	1.4	Rhodes,Arthur	P	0.2
Flores,Jesus	2	5.0	Encarnacion,Edwin	5	3.1	Saltalamacchia,Jar	2	1.4	Stairs,Matt	9	0.2
Johnson,Jim	P	4.9	Ludwick,Ryan	9	3.1	Delgado,Carlos	3	1.4	Crain,Jesse	P	0.1
Burrell,Pat	0	4.9	Hanrahan,Joel	P	3.1	Hernandez,Ramon	23	1.4	Lewis,Scott	P	0.1
Meek,Evan	P	4.8	Duchscherer,Justin	P	3.0	Glaus,Troy	5	1.3	Giles,Brian	9	-0.1
Zambrano,Carlos	P	4.8	Wang,Chien-Ming	P	3.0	Lewis,Jensen	P	1.3	Hawksworth,Blake	P	-0.1
Avila,Alex	2	4.8	Neshek,Pat	P	3.0	Delcarmen,Manny	P	1.3	Blackburn,Nick	P	-0.1
Schlereth,Daniel	P	4.8	Linebrink,Scott	P	3.0	Chavez,Eric	5	1.2	Litsch,Jesse	P	-0.1
Mickolio,Kam	P	4.7	Kelley,Shawn	P	2.9	Wells,Randy	P	1.2	Mazzaro,Vince	P	-0.1
Figgins,Chone	5	4.6	Arias,Alberto	P	2.9	Paulino,Felipe	P	1.2	Fulchino,Jeff	P	-0.2
DeJesus,David	7	4.6	Paulino,Ronny	2	2.9	Powell,Landon	2	1.2	Varitek,Jason	2	-0.2
Bulger,Jason	P	4.6	Blanks,Kyle	9	2.8	Ellsbury,Jacoby	8	1.2	Hanigan,Ryan	2	-0.2
Dotel,Octavio	P	4.5	Perry,Ryan	P	2.8	Hardy,J.J.	6	1.2	Valdez,Merkin	P	-0.2
Hawkins,LaTroy	P	4.5	Sheets,Ben	P	2.8	Jones,Andruw	0	1.2	Boyer,Blaine	P	-0.2
Tillman,Chris	P	4.5	Rolen,Scott	5	2.8	Iwamura,Akinori	4	1.2	Bannister,Brian	P	-0.2
Guillen,Carlos	70	4.4	Harris,Willie	87	2.7	Guzman,Angel	P	1.1	Tavarez,Julian	P	-0.2
Smith,Seth	7	4.4	Villanueva,Carlos	P	2.7	DeRosa,Mark	57	1.1	Francisco,Ben	7	-0.2
Zaun,Gregg	2	4.4	Sampson,Chris	P	2.7	Suzuki,Kurt	2	1.1	Lugo,Julio	46	-0.2
Heilman,Aaron	P	4.4	Sherrill,George	P	2.7	Seay,Bobby	P	1.1	Castro,Ramon	2	-0.2
Balfour,Grant	P	4.3	Pelfrey,Mike	P	2.7	Bale,John	P	1.1	Wheeler,Dan	P	-0.2
Cuddyer,Michael	93	4.3	Carlson,Jesse	P	2.7	Kottaras,George	2	1.1	Ramirez,Ramon	P	-0.3
Santana,Ervin	P	4.3	Fuentes,Brian	P	2.6	Wood,Brandon	5	1.0	Counsell,Craig	456	-0.3
Mock,Garrett	P	4.2	Oliver,Darren	P	2.6	Torres,Andres	87	1.0	Miller,Andrew	P	-0.3
Kazmir,Scott	P	4.2	Diaz,Matt	97	2.6	Bergesen,Brad	P	1.0	Tejada,Miguel	6	-0.3
Blake,Casey	5	4.2	Buck,John	2	2.6	Fox,Jake	57	1.0	Bowden,Michael	P	-0.3
Baker,John	2	4.2	Ray,Chris	P	2.5	Rauch,Jon	P	1.0	Cormier,Lance	P	-0.4
Carrasco,D.J.	P	4.1	Span,Denard	879	2.5	Jones,Garrett	93	1.0	Hampton,Mike	P	-0.4
Choate,Randy	P	4.0	Weaver,Jered	P	2.5	Bailey,Homer	P	1.0	Bonderman,Jerem	P	-0.4
Troncoso,Ramon	P	3.9	Baez,Danys	P	2.4	Schneider,Brian	2	0.9	Volquez,Edinson	P	-0.4
Ordonez,Magglio	90	3.9	Devine,Joey	P	2.4	Catalanotto,Frank	9	0.9	Ayala,Luis	P	-0.4
Albaladejo,Jonatha	P	3.8	Lyon,Brandon	P	2.4	Sonnanstine,Andy	P	0.9	Penny,Brad	P	-0.5
Perez,Rafael	P	3.8	Lopez,Felipe	4	2.3	Mijares,Jose	P	0.9	Kawakami,Kenshi	P	-0.5
Belliard,Ronnie	4	3.7	Mujica,Edward	P	2.3	Herges,Matt	P	0.9	Romero,J.C.	P	-0.5
Wright,Jamey	P	3.7	Kennedy,Ian	P	2.3	Correia,Kevin	P	0.9	Percival,Troy	P	-0.5
Blanton,Joe	P	3.7	Gutierrez,Juan	P	2.3	Marmol,Carlos	P	0.9	Contreras,Jose	P	-0.5
Cordero,Francisco	P	3.7	Condrey,Clay	P	2.2	Valbuena,Luis	46	0.8	Schierholtz,Nate	9	-0.5
Gregg,Kevin	P	3.6	Thames,Marcus	7	2.2	Jones,Adam	8	0.8	Schumaker,Skip	47	-0.5
Lidge,Brad	P	3.6	Konerko,Paul	3	2.2	Putz,J.J.	P	0.8	Breslow,Craig	P	-0.5
Snyder,Chris	2	3.6	Belisario,Ronald	P	2.2	Poreda,Aaron	P	0.8	Meyer,Dan	P	-0.5
Todd,Jess	P	3.6	Castillo,Luis	4	2.1	Escobar,Kelvim	P	0.8	Nunez,Leo	P	-0.5
Rodney,Fernando	P	3.6	Gaudin,Chad	P	2.0	Burton,Jared	P	0.8	Harrison,Matt	P	-0.5
Reyes,Dennys	P	3.6	Hoffman,Trevor	P	2.0	Wells,Vernon	8	0.7	Abreu,Tony	4	-0.6
Capps,Matt	P	3.5	LaPorta,Matt	7	1.9	Volstad,Chris	P	0.7	Albers,Matt	P	-0.6
Lopez,Jose	4	3.5	Johnson,Randy	P	1.9	Olivo,Miguel	2	0.7	Thole,Josh	2	-0.6
Walker,Tyler	P	3.5	Garcia,Freddy	P	1.9	Gerut,Jody	89	0.7	Outman,Josh	P	-0.6
Rodriguez,Francisc	P	3.5	Cecil,Brett	P	1.9	Casilla,Santiago	P	0.7	Thompson,Brad	P	-0.6
Niese,Jonathon	P	3.5	Guerrero,Vladimir	0	1.9	Duke,Zach	P	0.6	Lohse,Kyle	P	-0.6
Shields,Scot	P	3.4	Nippert,Dustin	P	1.9	Boggs,Mitchell	P	0.6	Rivera,Saul	P	-0.6
Lindstrom,Matt	P	3.4	Matsuzaka,Daisuke	P	1.8	Bush,David	P	0.6	Molina,Bengie	2	-0.6
Mathis,Doug	P	3.4	Aardsma,David	P	1.8	Fisher,Carlos	P	0.6	Saito,Takashi	P	-0.6
Wolf,Randy	P	3.4	Aceves,Alfredo	P	1.8	Okajima,Hideki	P	0.6	Roberts,Ryan	4	-0.6
Motte,Jason	P	3.3	Baker,Jeff	45	1.8	Tallet,Brian	P	0.5	Byrdak,Tim	P	-0.7
McClellan,Kyle	P	3.3	Fontenot,Mike	45	1.8	Hendrickson,Mark	P	0.5	Ramirez,Max	2	-0.7
Guerrier,Matt	P	3.3	McGowan,Dustin	P	1.8	Giambi,Jason	30	0.5	Acosta,Manny	P	-0.7
Crisp,Coco	8	3.3	Padilla,Vicente	P	1.7	Grilli,Jason	P	0.5	Burke,Greg	P	-0.7
LaRoche,Adam	3	3.3	Accardo,Jeremy	P	1.7	MacDougal,Mike	P	0.5	VandenHurk,Rick	P	-0.7
Izturis,Maicer	46	3.2	Janssen,Casey	P	1.6	Sanches,Brian	P	0.4	Teagarden,Taylor	2	-0.7
Westbrook,Jake	P	3.2	Buckner,Billy	P	1.6	Hermida,Jeremy	97	0.4	Keppel,Bobby	P	-0.7
Lowe,Mark	P	3.2	Park,Chan Ho	P	1.6	Veras,Jose	P	0.4	Calero,Kiko	P	-0.8
Betancourt,Rafael	P	3.2	Zimmermann,Jorda	P	1.6	Wright,Wesley	P	0.3	Dessens,Elmer	P	-0.9
Coghlan,Chris	7	3.2	Dye,Jermaine	9	1.6	Hinske,Eric	9	0.3	Morales,Jose	2	-0.9
Miller,Trever	P	3.2	Coke,Phil	P	1.6	Eveland,Dana	P	0.3	Blanco,Andres	4	-0.9

VII.
SABERMETRIC TOOLS

One Glossary
Abbreviations and Beginner Concepts

Avg   Batting average (see also BA)

BA   Batting average (see also Avg)

BABIP   Batting average on balls-in-play (see Hit rate)

Base Performance Indicator (BPI): A statistical formula that measures an isolated aspect of a player's situation-independent raw skill or a gauge that helps capture the effects that random chance has on skill. Although there are many such formulas, there are only a few that we are referring to when the term is used in this book. For batters, the skills BPIs are linear weighted power index (PX), speed score index (SX), walk rate (bb%), contact rate (ct%), batting eye (Eye), ground ball/line drive/fly ball ratios (G/L/F), home run to fly ball rate (hr/f) and expected batting average (xBA). Random chance is measured with hit rate on balls in play (h%). For pitchers, our BPIs are control (bb/9), dominance (k/9), command (k/bb), opposition on base avg (OOB), ground/line/fly ratios (G/L/F) and expected ERA (xERA). Random chance is measured with hit rate (H%), strand rate (S%) and home run to fly ball ratio (hr/f).

Batting Average (BA, or Avg): A grand old nugget that has long outgrown its usefulness. We revere .300 hitting superstars and scoff at .250 hitters, yet the difference between the two is 1 hit every 20 ABs. This 1 hit every five games is not nearly the wide variance that exists in our perceptions of what it means to be a .300 or .250 hitter. BA is a poor evaluator of performance in that it neglects the offensive value of the base on balls and assumes that all hits are created equal.

bb%   Walk rate (hitters)

bb/9   Opposition walks per 9 IP

BF/G   Batters faced per game

BIP   Balls-in-play

BPI   Base performance indicator

BPV   Base performance value

Ceiling: The highest professional level at which a player maintains acceptable BPIs. Also, the peak performance level that a player will likely reach, given his BPIs.

Cmd   Command ratio

Ct%   Contact rate

Ctl   Control rate

DIS%   PQS disaster rate

Dom   Dominance rate

DOM%   PQS domination rate

Eye   Batting eye

Fanalytics: The scientific approach to fantasy baseball analysis. A contraction of "fantasy" and "analytics," fanalytic gaming might be considered a mode of play that requires a more strategic and quantitative approach to player analysis and game decisions.

FB%   Fly ball percentage

G/L/F: Ground balls, line drives, and fly balls as percentages of total balls in play (hits *and* outs)

GB%   Ground ball percentage

Gopheritis (also, Acute Gopheritis and Chronic Gopheritis): The dreaded malady in which a pitcher is unable to keep the ball in the ballpark. Pitchers with gopheritis have a fly ball rate of at least 40%. More severe cases have a FB% over 45%.

H%   Hits allowed per balls in play (pitchers)

h%   Fair hits per balls in play (batters)

hr/9   Opposition home runs per 9 IP

hr/f   Home runs hit (batters), or allowed (pitchers), per fly ball

IP/G   Innings pitched per game appearance

k/9   Dominance rate (opposition strikeouts per 9 IP)

LD%   Line drive percentage

Leading Indicator: A statistical formula that can be used to project potential future performance.

LW   Linear weights

LWPwr   Linear weighted power

Major League Equivalency (*Bill James*): A formula that converts a player's minor or foreign league statistics into a comparable performance in the major leagues. These are not projections, but conversions of current performance. Contains adjustments for the level of play in individual leagues and teams. Works best with Triple-A stats, not quite as well with Double-A stats, and hardly at all with the lower levels. Foreign conversions are still a work in process. James' original formula only addressed batting. Our research has devised conversion formulas for pitchers, however, their best use comes when looking at BPI's, not traditional stats.

Mendoza Line: Named for Mario Mendoza, it represents the benchmark for batting futility. Usually refers to a .200 batting average, but can also be used for low levels of other statistical categories. Note that Mendoza's lifetime batting average was actually a much more robust .215.

MLE   Major league equivalency

Noise: Irrelevant or meaningless pieces of information that can distort the results of an analysis. In news, this is opinion or rumor that can invalidate valuable information. In forecasting, these are unimportant elements of statistical data that can artificially inflate or depress a set of numbers.

OB   On base average (batters)

OBA   Opposition batting average (pitchers)

OOB   Opposition on base average (pitchers)

Opposition Strikeouts per Game: See Dominance rate.

Opposition Walks per Game: See Control rate.

OPS   On base plus slugging average

PQR   Pure Quality Relief

PQS   Pure Quality Starts

Pw   Linear weighted power

PX	Linear weighted power index

QC | Quality/Consistency Score

R$ | Rotisserie value

RAR | Runs above replacement

RC | Runs created

RC/G | Runs created per game

REff% | Relief efficiency percentage

Rotisserie Value (R$): The dollar value placed on a player's performance in a Rotisserie league, and designed to measure the impact that player has on the standings. These values are highly variable depending upon a variety of factors:

- the salary cap limit
- the number of teams in the league
- each team's roster size
- the impact of any protected players
- each team's positional demands at the time of bidding
- the statistical category demands at the time of bidding
- external factors, e.g. media inflation or deflation of value

In other words, **a $30 player is only a $30 player if someone in your draft pays $30 for him.**

There are a variety of methods to calculate value, most involving a delineation of a least valuable performance level (given league size and structure), and then assigning a certain dollar amount for incremental improvement from that base. The method we use is a variation of the Standings Gain Points method described in the book, *How to Value Players for Rotisserie Baseball,* by Art McGee. (2nd edition available now)

Since we currently have no idea who is going to close games for the Orioles, or whether Jason Heyward is going to break camp with Atlanta, all the projected values are slightly inflated. They are roughly based on a 12-team AL and 13-team NL league. We've attempted to take some contingencies into account, but the values will not total to anywhere near $3120, so don't bother adding them up and save your irate e-mails.

A $25 player in this book might actually be worth $21. Or $28. This level of precision is irrelevant in a process that is going to be driven by market forces anyway. *So, don't obsess over it.*

How do other writers publish perfect Rotisserie values over the winter? Do they make arbitrary decisions as to where free agents are going to sign and who is going to land jobs in the spring? I'm not about to make those massive leaps of faith. Bottom line... Some things you can predict, to other things you have to react. As roles become more defined over the winter, our online updates will provide better approximations of playing time, and projected Roto values that add up to $3120.

S% | Strand rate

Save: There are six events that need to occur in order for a pitcher to post a single save...

1. The starting pitcher and middle relievers must pitch well.
2. The offense must score enough runs.
3. It must be a reasonably close game.
4. The manager must put the pitcher in for a save opportunity.
5. The pitcher must pitch well and hold the lead.
6. The manager must let him finish the game.

Of these six events, only one is within the control of the relief pitcher. As such, projecting saves for a reliever has little to do with skill and a lot to do with opportunity. However, pitchers with excellent skills sets may create opportunity for themselves.

SBO | Stolen base opportunity per cent

Situation Independent: Describing performance that is separate from the context of team, ballpark, or other outside variables. Home runs, as they are unaffected by the performance of a batter's team, are often considered a situation independent stat (they are, however, affected by park dimensions). Strikeouts and Walks are better examples.

Conversely, RBI's are situation dependent because individual performance varies greatly by the performance of other batters on the team (you can't drive in runs if there is nobody on base). Similarly, pitching wins are as much a measure of the success of a pitcher as they are a measure of the success of the offense and defense performing behind that pitcher, and are therefore a poor measure of pitching performance alone.

Situation independent gauges are important for us to be able to separate a player's contribution to his team and isolate his performance so that we may judge it on its own merits.

Slg | Slugging average

Soft Stats (also, Soft Skills): Batting eyes less than 0.50. Command ratios less than 2.0. Strikeout rates less than 5.0. Etc.

Soft-tosser: A pitcher with a strikeout rate of 5.5 or less.

Spd | Speed score

Strikeouts per Game: See Opposition strikeouts per game.

Surface Stats: Traditional statistical gauges that the mainstream uses to measure performance. Stats like batting average, wins, and ERA only touch the surface of a player's skill. Component skills analysis digs beneath the surface to reveal true skill.

Sv% | Saves conversion rate

SX | Speed Score Index

Vulture: A pitcher, typically a middle reliever, who accumulates an unusually high number of wins by preying on other pitchers' misfortunes. More accurately, this is a pitcher typically brought into a game after a starting pitcher has put his team behind, and then pitches well enough and long enough to allow his offense to take the lead, thereby "vulturing" a win from the starter.

Walks per Game: See Opposition walks per game.

Wasted talent: A player with a high level skill that is negated by a deficiency in another skill. For instance, base path speed can be negated by poor on base ability. Pitchers with strong arms can be wasted because home plate is an elusive concept to them.

WHIP | Walks plus Hits divided by Innings Pitched

Wins: There are five events that need to occur in order for a pitcher to post a single win...

1. He must pitch well, allowing few runs.
2. The offense must score enough runs.
3. The defense must successfully field all batted balls.
4. The bullpen must hold the lead.
5. The manager must leave the pitcher in for 5 innings, and not remove him if the team is still behind.

Of these five events, only one is within the control of the pitcher. As such, projecting wins can be an exercise in futility.

xBA | Expected batting average

xERA | Expected ERA

The Other Glossary
Sabermetrics, Fanalytics and Advanced Concepts

Balls-in-play (BIP)

Batting: *(AB – K)*   *Pitching*: *((IP x 2.82)) + H – K*

The total number of batted balls that are hit fair, both hits and outs. An analysis of how these balls are hit – on the ground, in the air, hits, outs, etc. – can provide analytical insight, from player skill levels to the impact of luck on statistical output.

Base Performance Value (BPV): A single value that describes a player's overall raw skill level. This is more useful than traditional statistical gauges to track player performance trends and project future statistical output. The BPV formula combines and weights several BPIs.

Batting BPV: ((Walk rate - 5) x 2) + ((Contact rate - 75) x 4) +
(Power Index - 80) x 0.8) + ((Speed Index - 80) x 0.3)

This **NEW** formula combines the individual raw skills of batting eye, contact rate, power and speed. **BENCHMARKS:** The best hitters will have a BPV of 50 or greater.

Pitching BPV1: (Dominance Rate x 6) + (Command Ratio x 21) - (Expected Opp. HR Rate x 30) - ((Opp. Batting Average - .275) x 200)

Pitching BPV2: ((Dominance Rate - 5.0) x 18) + (4.0 - Walk Rate) x 27)) + (Ground ball rate - 40%)

The BPV2 formula combines the individual raw skills of power, control and the ability to keep the ball down in the zone, all characteristics that are unaffected by most external factors. In tandem with a pitcher's strand rate, it provides a more complete picture of the elements that contribute to ERA, and therefore serves as an accurate tool to project likely changes in ERA. **BENCHMARKS:** A BPV of 50 is the minimum level required for long-term success. The elite of the bullpen aces will have BPV's in excess of 100 and it is rare for these stoppers to enjoy long term success with consistent levels under 75.

Note: BPV2 is used in the player boxes for years when G/L/F data is available. Other years use the BPV1 formula.

Batters faced per game *(Craig Wright)*

((IP x 2.82) + H + BB) / G

A measure of pitcher usage and one of the leading indicators for potential pitcher burnout. (See Usage Warning Flags in the Forecaster's Toolbox.)

Batting average on balls in play *(Voros McCracken)*

Batting BABIP: (H—HR) / (AB – HR - K)

Pitching BABIP: (H—HR) / ((IP x 2.82) + H - K - HR)

Also called Hit rate (H%). The percent of balls hit into the field of play that fall for hits. See Forecaster's Toolbox for a complete discussion. **BENCHMARK:** The league average H% is 30%, which is also the level that individual pitching performances will regress to on a year to year basis. Any +/- variance of 3% or more can affect a pitcher's ERA. Batters tend to regress to their own historical three-year mean level.

Batting eye (Eye)

(Walks / Strikeouts)

A measure of a player's strike zone judgment. **BENCHMARKS:** The best hitters have eye ratios more than 1.00 (indicating more walks than strikeouts) and are the most likely to be among a league's .300 hitters. Ratios less than 0.50 represent batters who likely also have lower BA's. (See Forecaster's Toolbox for more.)

Command ratio (Cmd)

(Strikeouts / Walks)

A measure of a pitcher's ability to get the ball over the plate. There is no more fundamental a skill than this, and so it is used as a leading indicator to project future rises and falls in other gauges, such as ERA. **BENCHMARKS:** Baseball's best pitchers will have ratios in excess of 3.0. Pitchers with ratios less than 1.0 — indicating that they walk more batters than they strike out — have virtually no potential for long term success. If you make no other changes in your approach to drafting a pitching staff, limiting your focus to only pitchers with a command ratio of 2.0 or better will substantially improve your odds of success. (See the Forecaster's Toolbox for more command ratio research.)

Contact rate (ct%)

((AB - K) / AB)

Measures a batter's ability to get wood on the ball and hit it into the field of play. **BENCHMARKS:** Those batters with the best contact skill will have levels of 90% or better. The hackers of society will have levels of 75% or less.

Control rate (bb/9), or Opposition walks per game

BB Allowed x 9 / IP

Measures how many walks a pitcher allows per game equivalent. **BENCHMARK:** The best pitchers will have bb/9 levels of 3.0 or less.

Dominance rate (k/9), or Opposition Strikeouts per Game

(K Allowed x 9 / IP)

Measures how many strikeouts a pitcher allows per game equivalent. **BENCHMARK:** The best pitchers will have k/9 levels of 5.6 or higher.

ERA variance: The variance between a pitcher's ERA and his xERA, which is a measure of over or underachievement. A positive variance indicates the potential for a pitcher's ERA to rise. A negative variance indicates the potential for ERA improvement. (See Expected ERA) **BENCHMARK:** Discount variances that are less than 0.50. Any variance more than 1.00 (one run per game) is regarded as a indicator of future change.

Expected batting average *(John Burnson)*

$xCT\% * [xH1\% + xH2\%]$
where
$xH1\% = GB\% \; x \; [0.0004 \; PX + 0.062 \; ln(SX)]$
$+ LD\% \; x \; [0.93 - 0.086 \; ln(SX)]$
$+ FB\% \; x \; 0.12$
and
$xH2\% = FB\% \; x \; [0.0013 \; PX - 0.0002 \; SX - 0.057]$
$+ GB\% \; x \; [0.0006 \; PX]$

A hitter's batting average as calculated by multiplying the percentage of balls put in play (contact rate) by the chance that a ball in play falls for a hit. The likelihood that a ball in play falls for a hit is a product of the speed of the ball and distance it is hit (PX), the speed of the batter (SX), and distribution of ground balls, fly balls, and line drives. We further split it out by non-homerun hit rate (xH1%) and homerun hit rate (xH2%). **BENCHMARKS:** In general, xBA should approximate batting average fairly closely. Those hitters who have large variances between the two gauges are candidates for further analysis.

Expected earned run average (*Gill and Reeve*)

(.575 x H [per 9 IP]) + (.94 x HR [per 9 IP]) + (.28 x BB [per 9 IP]) - (.01 x K [per 9 IP]) - Normalizing Factor

"xERA represents the expected ERA of the pitcher based on a normal distribution of his statistics. It is not influenced by situation-dependent factors." xERA erases the inequity between starters' and relievers' ERA's, eliminating the effect that a pitcher's success or failure has on another pitcher's ERA.

Similar to other gauges, the accuracy of this formula changes with the level of competition from one season to the next. The normalizing factor allows us to better approximate a pitcher's actual ERA. This value is usually somewhere around 2.77 and varies by league and year.

BENCHMARKS: xERA should approximate a pitcher's ERA fairly closely. Those pitchers who have large variances between the two gauges are candidates for further analysis.

Projected xERA or projected ERA? Projected xERA is more accurate for looking ahead on a purely skills basis. Projected ERA includes situation-*dependent* events — bullpen support, park factors, etc. — which are reflected better by ERA. The optimal approach is to use *both* gauges as a range of the expectation for the coming year.

Expected earned run average2 (*John Burnson*)

(xER x 9)/IP, where xER is defined as

xER% *x (FB/10) + (1-***xS%***) x [(0.3 x BIP - (FB/10)) + BB]*

where

xER% = 0.96 - (0.0284 x (GB/FB))

and

xS% = (64.5 + (K/9 x 1.2) - (BB/9 x (BB/9 + 1)) / 20
+ ((0.0012 x (GB^2)) - (0.001 x GB%) - 2.4)

Note: xERA2 is used in the player boxes for years when G/L/F data is available. Other years use the Gill and Reeve formula.

Expected home run rate (xHR/9): *See Home runs to fly ball rate*

Ground ball, fly ball, line drive percentages (G/F/L): The percentage of all Balls-in-Play that are hit on the ground, in the air and as line drives. For batters, increased fly ball tendency may foretell a rise in power skills; increased line drive tendency may foretell an improvement in batting average. For a pitcher, the ability to keep the ball on the ground can contribute to his statistical output exceeding his demonstrated skill level .

*BIP Type	Total%	Out%
Ground ball	45%	72%
Line drive	20%	28%
Fly ball	35%	85%
TOTAL	100%	69%

* Data only includes fieldable balls and is net of home runs.

Hit rate (H% and h%): *See Batting average on balls in play*

Home runs to fly ball rate

HR / FB

Also, expected home run rate = (FB x 0.10) x 9 / IP

The percent of fly balls that are hit for HRs. BENCHMARK: The league average level is 10%, which is also the level that individual pitching performances will regress to on a year to year basis. Batters tend to regress to their own historical three-year mean level.

Linear weights (*Pete Palmer*)

((Singles x .46) + (Doubles x .8) + (Triples x 1.02) + (Home runs x 1.4) + (Walks x .33) + (Stolen Bases x .3) - (Caught Stealing x .6) - ((At bats - Hits) x Normalizing Factor)

(Also referred to as Batting Runs.) Formula whose premise is that all events in baseball are linear, that is, the output (runs) is directly proportional to the input (offensive events). Each of these offensive events is then weighted according to its relative value in producing runs. Positive events — hits, walks, stolen bases — have positive values. Negative events — outs, caught stealing — have negative values.

The normalizing factor, representing the value of an out, is an offset to the level of offense in a given year. It changes every season, growing larger in high offense years and smaller in low offense years. The value is about .26 and varies by league.

LW is no longer included in the player forecast boxes, but the LW concept is used with the linear weighted power gauge.

Linear weighted power (LWPwr)

((Doubles x .8) + (Triples x .8) + (HR x 1.4)) / (At bats- K) x 100

A variation of the linear weights formula that considers only events that are measures of a batter's pure power. BENCHMARKS: Baseball's top sluggers typically top the 17 mark. Weak hitters will have a LWPwr level of less than 10.

Linear weighted power index (PX)

(Batter's LWPwr / League LWPwr) x 100

LWPwr is presented in this book in its normalized form to get a better read on a batter's accomplishment in each year. For instance, a 30-HR season today is not nearly as much of an accomplishment as 30 HRs hit in a lower offense year like 1995. BENCHMARKS: A level of 100 equals league average power skills. Any player with a value more than 100 has above average power skills, and those more than 150 are the Slugging Elite.

On base average (OB)

(H + BB) / (AB + BB)

Addressing one of the two deficiencies in BA, OB gives value to those events that get batters on base, but are not hits. An OB of .350 can be read as "this batter gets on base 35% of the time." When a run is scored, there is no distinction made as to how that runner reached base. So, two thirds of the time — about how often a batter comes to the plate with the bases empty — a walk really is as good as a hit.

Note that the "official" version of this formula includes hit batsmen. We do not include it here because our focus is on purely skills-based gauges; research has shown that HBP is not a measure of batting skill but a measure of pitching deficiency. BENCHMARKS: We all know what a .300 hitter is, but what represents "good" for OB? That comparable level would likely be .400, with .275 representing the comparable level of futility.

On base plus slugging average (OPS): A simple sum of the two gauges, it is considered one of the better evaluators of overall performance. OPS combines the two basic elements of offensive production — the ability to get on base (OB) and the ability to advance baserunners (Slg). BENCHMARKS: The game's top batters will have OPS levels more than .900. The worst batters will have levels less than .600.

Opposition batting average (OBA)

(Hits Allowed / ((IP x 2.82) + Hits Allowed))

A close approximation of the batting average achieved by opposing batters against a particular pitcher. **BENCHMARKS:** The converse of the benchmark for batters, the best pitchers will have levels less than .250; the worst pitchers levels more than .300.

Opposition home runs per game (hr/9)

(HR Allowed x 9 / IP)

Measures how many home runs a pitcher allows per game equivalent. **BENCHMARK:** The best pitchers will have hr/9 levels of less than 1.0.

Opposition on base average (OOB)

(Hits Allowed + BB) / ((IP x 2.82) + H + BB)

A close approximation of the on base average achieved by opposing batters against a particular pitcher. **BENCHMARK:** The best pitchers will have levels less than .300; the worst pitchers levels more than .375.

Power/contact rating: *(BB + K) / IP*

Measures the level by which a pitcher allows balls to be put into play and helps tie a pitcher's success to his team's level of defensive ability. In general, extreme power pitchers can be successful even with poor defensive teams. Power pitchers tend to have greater longevity in the game. Contact pitchers with poor defenses behind them are high risks to have poor W-L records and ERA. **BENCHMARKS:** A level of 1.13 or greater describes the pure throwers. A level of .93 or less describes the high contact pitcher. Tip... if you have to draft a pitcher from a poor defensive team, going with power over contact will usually net you more wins in the long run.

PQS disaster rate *(Gene McCaffrey):* The percentage of a starting pitcher's outings that rate as a PQS-0 or PQS-1. See the Pitching Consistency Chart section for more information on DIS%.

PQS domination rate *(Gene McCaffrey):* The percentage of a starting pitcher's outings that rate as a PQS-4 or PQS-5. See the Pitching Consistency Chart for more information on DOM%.

Pure Quality Starts: PQS is a method of evaluating individual starting pitcher performances. The old Quality Start method — minimum 6 IP, maximum 3 earned runs — is simplistic and does not measure any real skill. Bill James' "game score" methodology is better, but is not feasible for quick calculation.

In PQS, we give a starting pitcher credit for exhibiting certain skills in each of his starts. Then by tracking his "PQS Score" over time, we can follow his progress. A starter earns one point for each of the following criteria...

1. The pitcher must go a minimum of 6 innings. This measures stamina. If he goes less than 5 innings, he automatically gets a total PQS score of zero, no matter what other stats he produces.

2. He must allow no more than an equal number of hits to the number of innings pitched. This measures hit prevention.

3. His number of strikeouts must be no fewer than two less than his innings pitched. This measures dominance.

4. He must strike out at least twice as many batters as he walks. This measures command.

5. He must allow no more than one home run. This measures his ability to keep the ball in the park.

A perfect PQS score would be 5. Any pitcher who averages 3 or more over the course of the season is probably performing admirably. The nice thing about PQS is it allows you to approach each start as more than an all-or-nothing event.

Note the absence of earned runs. No matter how many runs a pitcher allows, if he scores high on the PQS scale, he has hurled a good game in terms of his base skills. The number of runs allowed — a function of not only the pitcher's ability but that of his bullpen and defense — will tend to even out over time.

Pure Quality Relief *(Patrick Davitt):* A similar system for evaluating relief pitchers. The scoring system:

1. Two points for the first out, and one point for each subsequent out, to a maximum of four points.

2. One point for having at least one strikeout for every four full outs (one K for 1-4 outs, two Ks for 5-8 outs, three Ks for 9 outs).

3. One point for zero baserunners, minus one point for each baserunner, though allowing the pitcher one unpenalized baserunner for each three full outs (one baserunner for 3-5 outs, two for 6-8 outs, three for nine outs)

4. Minus one point for each earned run, though allowing one ER for 8– or 9-out appearances.

5. An automatic PQR-0 for allowing a home run.

Quality/Consistency Score (QC)

(PQS DOM% - (2 x PQS DIS%)) x 2)

Using the PQS system and DOM/DIS percentages, this score measures both the quality of performance as well as week-to-week (for batters) or start-to-start (for pitchers) consistency. For batters, a week with a BPV level of 50 qualifies as a DOM week; BPV's less than 0 are DIS weeks.

Random Variance (Rand Var): A gauge that measures the probability that a player's performance in the subsequent year will exceed or fall short of the immediate past year's numbers. Expressed on a scale of –5 to +5, this only measures variables for which outliers tend to regress. Positive scores indicate rebounds; negative scores indicate corrections. The further the score is from zero, the higher the likelihood of a performance swing. The variables tracked for batters and pitchers:

Batting: Outlying levels for h%, hr/f and xBA.

Pitching: Outlying levels for H%, S%, hr/f and xERA.

Reliever efficiency per cent (REff%)

(Wins + Saves + Holds) / (Wins + Losses + SaveOpps + Holds)

This is a measure of how often a reliever contributes positively to the outcome of a game. A record of consistent, positive impact on game outcomes breeds managerial confidence, and that confidence could pave the way to save opportunities. For those pitchers suddenly thrust into a closer's role, this formula helps gauge their potential to succeed based on past successes in similar roles. **BENCHMARK:** Minimum of 80%.

Runs above replacement (RAR): An estimate of the number of runs a player contributes above a "replacement level" player. "Replacement" is defined as the level of performance at which another player can easily be found at little or no cost to a team. What constitutes replacement level is a topic that is hotly debated. There are a variety of formulas and rules of thumb used to determine this level for each position (replacement level for a shortstop will be very different from replacement level for an outfielder). Our estimates appear below.

One of the major values of RAR for fantasy applications is that it can be used to assemble an integrated ranking of batters and pitchers for drafting purposes.

Batters create runs; pitchers save runs. But are batters and pitchers who have comparable RAR levels truly equal in value? Pitchers might be considered to have higher value. Saving an additional run is more important than producing an additional run. A pitcher who throws a shutout is guaranteed to win that game, whereas no matter how many runs a batter produces, his team can still lose given poor pitching support.

To calculate RAR for batters:

Start with a batter's runs created per game (RC/G).

Subtract his position's replacement level RC/G.

Multiply by number of games played: (AB - H + CS) / 25.5.

Replacement levels used in this book, for 2009:

POS	AL	NL
C	4.27	4.26
1B	5.71	6.51
2B	4.93	4.53
3B	4.68	5.14
SS	4.45	4.66
LF	5.01	5.56
CF	4.64	4.73
RF	5.33	4.88
DH	5.17	

To calculate RAR for pitchers:

Start with the replacement level league ERA.

Subtract the pitcher's ERA. (To calculate *projected* RAR, use the pitcher's xERA.)

Multiply by number of games played, calculated as plate appearances (IP x 4.34) divided by 38.

Multiply the resulting RAR level by 1.08 to account for the variance between earned runs and total runs.

RAR can also be used to calculate rough projected team won-loss records. *(Roger Miller)* Total the RAR levels for all the players on a team, divide by 10 and add to 53 wins.

Runs created *(Bill James)*

(H + BB - CS) x (Total bases + (.55 x SB)) / (AB + BB)

A formula that converts all offensive events into a total of runs scored. As calculated for individual teams, the result approximates a club's actual run total with great accuracy.

Runs created per game *(Bill James)*

Runs Created / ((AB - H + CS) / 25.5)

RC expressed on a per-game basis might be considered the hypothetical ERA compiled against a particular batter. Another way to look at it... a batter with a RC/G of 7.00 would be expected to score 7 runs per game if he were cloned nine times and faced an average pitcher in every at bat. However, cloning batters is not a practice we recommend.

BENCHMARKS: Few players surpass the level of a 10.00 RC/G in any given season, but any level more than 7.50 can still be considered very good. At the bottom are levels less than 3.00.

Runs created per game2 *(Neil Bonner)*

(SS x 37.96) + (ct% x 10.38) + (bb% x 14.81) – 13.04

where SS, or "swing speed" is defined as

((1B x 0.5) + (2B x 0.8) + (3B x 1.1) + (HR x 1.2)) / (AB - K)

This is the version that is currently used in this book.

Saves conversion rate *(Sv%)*

Saves / Save Opportunities

The percentage of save opportunities that are successfully converted. **BENCHMARK:** We look for a minimum 80% for long-term success.

Slugging average *(Slg)*

(Singles + (2 x Doubles) + (3 x Triples) + (4 x HR)) / AB

A measure of the total number of bases accumulated (or the minimum number of runners' bases advanced) per at bat. It is a misnomer; it is not a true measure of a batter's slugging ability because it includes singles. Slg also assumes that each type of hit has proportionately increasing value (i.e. a double is twice as valuable as a single, etc.) which is not true. For instance, with the bases loaded, a HR always scores four runs, a triple always

scores three, but a double could score two or three and a single could score one, or two, or even three.

BENCHMARKS: The top batters will have levels more than .500. The bottom batters will have levels less than .300.

Speed score *(Bill James):* A measure of the various elements that comprise a runner's speed skills. Although this formula (a variation of James' original version) may be used as a leading indicator for stolen base output, SB attempts are controlled by managerial strategy which makes Spd somewhat less valuable.

The speed scores in this book are calculated as the mean value of the following four elements...

1. Stolen base efficiency = *(((SB + 3)/(SB + CS + 7)) - .4) x 20*
2. Stolen base freq. = *Square root of ((SB + CS)/(Singles + BB)) / .07*
3. Triples rating = *(3B / (AB - HR - K))* and the result assigned a value based on the following chart:

< 0.001	0
0.001	1
0.0023	2
0.0039	3
0.0058	4
0.008	5
0.0105	6
0.013	7
0.0158	8
0.0189	9
.0223+	10

4. Runs scored as a percentage of times on base = *(((R - HR) / (H + BB - HR)) - .1) / .04*

Speed score index *(SX)*

(Batter's Spd / League Spd) x 100

Normalized speed scores are presented in this book to get a better read on a runner's accomplishment in context. A level of 100 equals league average speed skill. Values more than 100 indicate above average skill, more than 200 represent the Fleet of Feet Elite.

Stolen base opportunity per cent *(SBO)*

(SB + CS) / (BB + Singles)

A rough approximation of how often a base-runner attempts a stolen base. Provides a comparative measure for players on a given team and, as a team measure, the propensity of a manager to give a "green light" to his runners.

Strand rate *(S%)*

(H + BB - ER) / (H + BB - HR)

Measures the percentage of allowed runners a pitcher strands (earned runs only), which incorporates both individual pitcher skill and bullpen effectiveness. **BENCHMARKS:** The most adept at stranding runners will have S% levels more than 75%. Once a pitcher's S% starts dropping down less than 65%, he's going to have problems with his ERA. Those pitchers with strand rates more than 80% will have artificially low ERAs, which will be prone to relapse. (See the Forecaster's Toolbox for more research.)

Walks plus hits divided by innings pitched (WHIP): Decreed as a base Rotisserie category. **BENCHMARKS:** Usually, a WHIP of less than 1.20 is considered top level and more than 1.50 is indicative of poor performance. Levels less than 1.00 — allowing fewer runners than IP — represent extraordinary performance and are rarely maintained over time.

Walk rate *(bb%)*

(BB / (AB + BB))

A measure of a batter's plate patience. **BENCHMARKS:** The best batters will have levels more than 10%. Those with poor plate patience will have levels of 5% or less.

2010 CHEATER'S BOOKMARK

	BATTING STATISTICS		BAD	'09 LG AVG		BEST
Abbrv	**Term**	**Formula / Descr.**	**UNDER**	**AL**	**NL**	**OVER**
Avg	Batting Average	h/ab	250	267	266	300
xBA	Expected Batting Average	*See glossary*		268	258	
OB	On Base Average	(h+bb)/(ab+bb)	300	332	336	375
Slg	Slugging Average	total bases/ab	350	427	423	500
OPS	On Base plus Slugging	OB+Slg	650	760	759	875
bb%	Walk Rate	bb/(ab+bb)	5%	9%	10%	10%
ct%	Contact Rate	(ab-k) / ab	75%	80%	80%	85%
Eye	Batting Eye	bb/k	0.50	0.50	0.53	1.00
PX	Power Index	Normalized power skills	80	100	100	120
SX	Speed Index	Normalized speed skills	80	100	100	120
SBO	Stolen Base Opportunity %	(sb+cs)/(singles+bb)		10%	9%	
G/F	Groundball/Flyball Ratio	gb / fb		1.1	1.2	
G	Ground Ball Per Cent	gb / balls in play		43%	44%	
L	Line Drive Per Cent	ld / balls in play		19%	19%	
F	Fly Ball Per Cent	fb / balls in play		39%	37%	
RC/G	Runs Created per Game	*See glossary*	3.00	4.92	4.91	7.50
RAR	Runs Above Replacement	*See glossary*	-0.0			+25.0

	PITCHING STATISTICS		BAD	'09 LG AVG		BEST
Abbrv	**Term**	**Formula / Descr.**	**OVER**	**AL**	**NL**	**UNDER**
ERA	Earned Run Average	er*9/ip	5.00	4.45	4.19	4.00
xERA	Expected ERA	*See glossary*		4.44	4.28	
WHIP	Baserunners per Inning	(h+bb)/ip	1.50	1.40	1.38	1.25
BF/G	Batters Faced per Game	((ip*2.82)+h+bb)/g	28.0			
PC	Pitch Counts per Start		120	96	95	
OBA	Opposition Batting Avg	Opp. h/ab	290	266	259	250
OOB	Opposition On Base Avg	Opp. (h+bb)/(ab+bb)	350	334	332	300
BABIP	BatAvg on balls in play	(h-hr)/((ip*2.82)+h-k-hr)		305	302	
Ctl	Control Rate	bb*9/ip		3.4	3.5	3.0
hr/9	Homerun Rate	hr*9/ip		1.1	1.0	1.0
hr/f	Homerun per Fly ball	hr/fb		10%	10%	10%
S%	Strand Rate	(h+bb-er)/(h+bb-hr)		71%	72%	
DIS%	PQS Disaster Rate	% GS that are PQS 0/1		26%	23%	20%

			BAD	'09 LG AVG		BEST
			UNDER	**AL**	**NL**	**OVER**
RAR	Runs Above Replacement	*See glossary*	-0.0			+25.0
Dom	Dominance Rate	k*9/ip		6.9	7.0	6.5
Cmd	Command Ratio	k/bb		2.0	2.0	2.2
G/F	Groundball/Flyball Ratio	gb / fb		1.10	1.19	
BPV	Base Performance Value	*See glossary*	50	49	49	75
DOM%	PQS Dominance Rate	% GS that are PQS 4/5		39%	43%	50%
Sv%	Saves Conversion Rate	(saves / save opps)		67%	67%	80%
REff%	Relief Effectiveness Rate	*See glossary*		66%	65%	80%

NOTES

2010 MINOR LEAGUE BASEBALL ANALYST

By Rob Gordon and Jeremy Deloney

Available January 2010

The **Minor League Baseball Analyst** is the first book to integrate sabermetrics and scouting. For baseball analysts and those who play in fantasy leagues with farm systems, the *Analyst* is the perfect complement to the *Baseball Forecaster* and is designed exactly for your needs:

* *Stats and Sabermetrics...* Over three dozen categories for 1000 minor leaguers, including batter skills ratings, pitch repertoires and more
* *Performance Trends...* spanning each player's last five minor league stops, complete with leading indicators
* *Scouting reports...* for all players, including expected major league debuts, potential major league roles and more
* *Major League Equivalents...* Five year scans for every player
* *Mega-Lists...* The Top 100 of 2010, retrospective looks at the Top 100's of 2005-2009, organizational Top 15's, top prospects by position, power and speed prospects, and more
* *Strategy essays...* on drafting and managing your fantasy team's farm system
* *Player Potential Ratings...* Baseball HQ's exclusive system that evaluates each player's upside potential and chances of achieving that potential.

The *Analyst* was founded by Deric McKamey, a Bill James disciple and graduate of Major League Baseball's scout school. Deric is now a scout for the St. Louis Cardinals.

BOOKS

Art McGee's
HOW TO VALUE PLAYERS FOR ROTISSERIE® BASEBALL

Learn how to calculate the best player values for your draft or auction! Art McGee applies concepts from economics, finance, and statistics to develop a pricing method that far surpasses any other published. His method is highly sophisticated, yet McGee explains it in terms that any fantasy baseball owner can understand and apply.

In the 2nd Edition...
* Discover the power of Standings Gain Points (SGP)
* Learn how to adjust values for position scarcity, injury risk and future potential
* Set up your own pricing spreadsheet, as simple or sophisticated as you want
* Make better decisions on trades, free agents, and long-term contracts
* Apply these methods even if your league uses non-standard categories or has a non-standard number of teams
* PLUS... 10 additional essays to expand your knowledge base.

CONSUMER ADVISORY

AN IMPORTANT MESSAGE FOR FANTASY LEAGUERS
REGARDING PROPER USAGE OF THE *BASEBALL FORECASTER*

This document is provided in compliance with authorities to outline the prospective risks and hazards possible in the event that the *Baseball Forecaster* is used incorrectly. Please be aware of these potentially dangerous situations and avoid them. Ron Shandler assumes no risk related to any financial loss or stress-induced illnesses caused by ignoring the items as described below.

1. The statistical projections in this book are intended as general guidelines, not as gospel. It is highly dangerous to use the projected statistics alone, and then live and die by them. That's like going to a ballgame, being given a choice of any seat in the park, and deliberately choosing the last row in the right field corner with an obstructed view. The projections are there, you can look at them, but there are so many better places to sit.

We have to publish those numbers, but they are stagnant, inert pieces of data. This book focuses on a *live forecasting process* that provides the tools so that you can understand the leading indicators and draw your own conclusions. If you at least attempt your own analyses of the data, and enhance them with the player commentaries, you can paint more robust, colorful pictures of the future.

In other words...

If you bought this book purely for the projected statistics and do not intend to spend at least some time learning about the process, then you might as well just buy an $8 magazine.

2. The player commentaries in this book are written by humans, just like you. These commentaries provide an overall evaluation of performance and likely future direction, but 40-word capsules cannot capture everything. Your greatest value will be to use these as a springboard to your own analysis of the data. Odds are, if you take the time, you'll find hidden indicators that we might have missed. *Forecaster* veterans say that this self-guided excursion is the best part of owning the book.

3. This book does not attempt to tackle playing time. Rather than making arbitrary decisions about how roles will shake out, the focus is on performance. The playing time projections presented here are merely to help you better evaluate each player's talent. Our online pre-season projections update provides more current AB/IP expectations based on how roles are being assigned.

4. The dollar values in this book are intended solely for player-to-player comparisons. They are not driven by a finite pool of playing time – which is required for valuation systems to work properly – so they cannot be used for bid values to be used in your own draft.

There are two reasons for this:

a. The finite pool of players that will generate the finite pool of playing time will not be determined until much closer to Opening Day. And, if we are to be brutally honest, there is really no such thing as a finite pool of players.

b. Your particular league's construction will drive the values; a $10 player in a 10-team mixed league will not be the same as a $10 player in a 13-team NL-only league.

Note that book dollar values also cannot be compared to those published at BaseballHQ.com as the online values *are* generated by a more finite player pool.

5. Do not pass judgment on the effectiveness of this book based on the performance of a few individual players. The test, rather, is on the collective predictive value of the book's methods. Are players with better base skills more likely to produce good results than bad ones? Years of research suggest that the answer is "yes." Does that mean that every high skilled player will do well? No. But many more of them will perform well than will the average low-skilled player. You should always side with the better percentage plays, but recognize that there are factors we cannot predict. Good decisions that beget bad outcomes do not invalidate the methods.

6. If your copy of this book is not marked up and dog-eared by Draft Day, you probably did not get as much value out of it as you might have.

7. This book is not intended to provide absorbency for spills of more than 6.5 ounces

8. This book is not intended to provide stabilizing weight for more than 15 sheets of 20 lb. paper in winds of more than 45 mph.

9. The pages of this book are not recommended for avian waste collection. In independent laboratory studies, 87% of migratory water fowl refused to excrete on interior pages, even when coaxed.

10. This book, when rolled into a cylindrical shape, is not intended to be used as a weapon for any purpose, including but not limited to insect extermination, canine training or to influence bidding behavior at a fantasy draft.

NOTES

NOTES